THE KITAB AL-LUMA'
FI 'L-TAṢAWWUF

OF

ABŪ NAṢR 'ABDALLAH B. 'ALI AL-SARRĀJ AL-ṬŪSĪ

EDITED FOR THE FIRST TIME, WITH CRITICAL NOTES,
ABSTRACT OF CONTENTS, GLOSSARY, AND INDICES

BY

REYNOLD ALLEYNE NICHOLSON,

M.A.. Litt. D., Hon. LL.D. (Aberdeen),

Lecturer on Persian in the University of Cambridge,
Formerly Fellow of Trinity College.

LEYDEN: E. J. BRILL, IMPRIMERIE ORIENTALE.
LONDON: LUZAC & Co., 46 GREAT RUSSELL STREET.
1914.

"*E. J. W. GIBB MEMORIAL*" *SERIES.*

PUBLISHED.

1. *The* Bábar-náma, *reproduced in facsimile from a MS. belonging to the late Sir Sálár Jang of Haydarábád, and edited with Preface and Indexes, by Mrs. Beveridge, 1905. (Out of print.)*

2. *An abridged translation of Ibn Isfandiyár's* History of Ṭabaristán, *by Edward G. Browne, 1905. Price 8s.*

3. *Al-Khazrají's* History of the Rasúlí Dynasty of Yaman, *with introduction by the late Sir J. Redhouse, now edited by E. G. Browne, R. A. Nicholson, and A. Rogers. Vols. I, II (Translation), 1906, 07. Price 7s. each. Vol. III (Annotations), 1908. Price 5s. Vol. IV (first half of Text), 1913. Price 8s. Vol. V, (second half of Text), in the Press. Text edited by Shaykh Muḥammad 'Asal.*

4. Umayyads and ᶜAbbásids: *being the Fourth Part of Jurjí Zaydán's* History of Islamic Civilisation, *translated by Professor D. S. Margoliouth, D. Litt., 1907. Price 5s.*

5. *The Travels of* Ibn Jubayr, *the late Dr. William Wright's edition of the Arabic text, revised by Professor M. J. de Goeje, 1907. Price 6s.*

6. *Yáqút's Dictionary of Learned Men, entitled* Irshád al-aríb ilá maᶜrifat al-adíb: *edited by Professor D. S. Margoliouth, D. Litt. Vols. I, II, 1907, 09. Price 8s. each. Vol. III, part 1, 1910. Price 5s. Vol. V, 1911. Price 10s. Vol. VI, 1913. Price 10s.*

7. *The* Tajáribu 'l-Umam *of Ibn Miskawayh: reproduced in facsimile from MSS. 3116—3121 of Áyá Sofia, with Prefaces and Summaries by il Principe di Teano. Vol. I, to A.H. 37, 1909; Vol. V, A.H. 284—326, 1913. Price 7s. Each. (Further volumes in preparation).*

8. *The* Marzubán-náma *of Saᶜdu'd-Dín-i-Waráwíní, edited by Mirzá Muḥammad of Qazwín, 1909. Price 8s.*

9. *Textes persans relatifs à la* secte des Houroûfîs *publiés, traduits, et annotés par Clément Huart, suivis d'une étude sur la religion des Houroûfîs par "Feylesouf Rizá", 1909. Price 8s.*

10. *The* Muᶜjam fí Maᶜáyíri Ashᶜári 'l-ᶜAjam *of Shams-i Qays, edited from the British Museum MS. (Or. 2814) by Edward G. Browne and Mirzá Muḥammad of Qazwín, 1909. Price 8s.*

11. *The* Chahár Maqála *of Niḍhámí-i Arúḍí-i Samarqandí, edited, with notes in Persian, by Mirzá Muḥammad of Qazwín, 1910. Price 8s.*

12. Introduction à l'Histoire des Mongols *de Faḍl Allah Rashid ed-Din, par E. Blochet, 1910. Price 8s.*

13. *The* Díwán *of Hassán b. Thábit, edited by Hartwig Hirschfeld, Ph. D., 1910. Price 5s.*

14. *The* Ta'ríkh-i-Guzída *of Ḥamdu'lláh Mustawfí of Qazwín. Part I, containing the Reproduction in facsimile of an old MS., with Introduction by Edward G. Browne, 1910. Price 15s. Part II, containing abridged Translation and Indices, 1913. Price 10s.*

15. *The* Earliest History of the Bábís, *composed before 1852 by Hájjí Mirzá Jání of Káshán, edited from the Paris MSS. by Edward G. Browne, 1911. Price 8s.*

16. *The* Ta'ríkh-i Jahán-gushá *of 'Alá'u'd-Dín ʿAṭá Malik-i Juwayní, edited from seven MSS. by Mírzá Muḥammad of Qazwín. Vol. I, 1912. Price 8s. (Vols. II and III in preparation).*

17. *A translation of the* Kashfu'l-Maḥjúb *of ʿAlí b. ʿUthmán al-Jullábí al-Hujwírí, the oldest Persian manual of Ṣúfism, by R. A. Nicholson, 1911. Price 8s.*

18. Tarikh-i moubarek-i Ghazani, *histoire des Mongols de la* Djami el-Tévarikh *de Fadl Allah Rashid ed-Din, éditée par E. Blochet. Vol. II, contenant l'histoire des successeurs de Tchinkkiz Khaghan, 1911. Prix 12s. (Vol. III, contenant l'histoire des Mongols de Perse, sous presse; pour paraître ensuite, Vol. I, contenant l'histoire des tribus turkes et de Tchinkkiz Khaghan.)*

19. *The* Governors and Judges of Egypt, *or* Kitâb el 'Umarâ' (el Wulâh) wa Kitâb el-Qudâh *of El Kindí, with an Appendix derived mostly from* Rafʿ el Iṣr *by Ibn Ḥajar, edited by Rhuvon Guest, 1912. Price 12s.*

20. *The* Kitāb al-Ansāb *of al-Samʿāní. Reproduced in facsimile from the MS. in the British Museum (Add. 23,355), with an Introduction by Professor D. S. Margoliouth, D. Litt., 1912. Price £1.*

21. *The* Dīwāns *of* ʿAbīd ibn al-Abraṣ *and* ʿĀmir ibn aṭ-Ṭufail, *edited, with a translation and notes, by Sir Charles Lyall, 1913. Price 12s.*

22. *The* Kitáb al-Lumaʿ *fi l'-Taṣawwuf of Abú Naṣr al-Sarráj, edited from two MSS., with critical notes and Abstract of Contents, by R. A. Nicholson, 1914. Price 12s.*

IN PREPARATION.

An abridged translation of the Ihyá'u 'l-Mulúk, *a Persian History of Sístán by Sháh Ḥusayn, from the British Museum MS. (Or. 2779), by A. G. Ellis.*

The geographical part of the Nuzhatu 'l-Qulúb *of Ḥamdulláh Mustawfí of Qazwín, with a translation, by G. le Strange. (In the Press.)*

The Futúhu Miṣr wa 'l-Maghrib wa 'l-Andalus *of Ibn ʿAbdi'l-Ḥakam (d. A.H. 257), edited and translated by Professor C. C. Torrey.*

The Qábús-náma, *edited in the original Persian, with a translation, by E. Edwards.*

The Díwáns *of aṭ-Ṭufayl b. ʿAwf and aṭ-Tirimmáḥ b. Ḥakím, edited and translated by F. Krenkow. (In the Press).*

The Persian text of the Fárs Námah *of Ibnu 'l-Balkhí, edited from the British Museum MS. (Or. 5983), by G. le Strange.*

Extracts relating to Southern Arabia, *from the Dictionary entitled* Shamsu 'l-ʿUlúm, *of Nashwán al-Ḥimyarí, edited, with critical notes, by ʿAẓímu 'd-Din Ahmad, Ph. D. (In the Press).*

Contributions to the History *and* Geography of Mesopotamia, *being portions of the* Ta'ríkh Mayyáfárikín *of Ibn al-Azrak al-Fáriki, B. M. MS. Or. 5803, and of al-Aʿlák al-Khaṭíra of ʿIzz ad-Dín Ibn Shaddád al-Ḥalabí, Bodleian MS. Marsh 333, edited by W. Sarasin, Ph. D.*

The Ráḥatu 's-Ṣudúr wa Áyatu 's-Surúr, *a history of the Seljúqs, by Najmu 'd-Dín Abú Bakr Muhammad ar-Ráwandí, edited from the unique Paris MS. (Suppl. persan, 1314) by Edward G. Browne.*

(Translations of the three Inscriptions
on the Cover.)

1. Arabic.

"These are our works which prove
what we have done;
Look, therefore, at our works
when we are gone."

2. Turkish.

"His genius cast its shadow o'er the world,
And in brief time he much achieved and
wrought:
The Age's Sun was he, and ageing suns
Cast lengthy shadows, though their time be
short."

(Kemál Páshá-zádé.)

3. Persian.

"When we are dead, seek for our
resting-place
Not in the earth, but in the
hearts of men."

(Jalálu 'd-Dín Rúmí.)

"E. J. W. GIBB MEMORIAL"
SERIES.

VOL. XXII.

(All communications respecting this volume should be addressed to R. A. Nicholson, 12 Harvey Road, Cambridge, who is the Trustee specially responsible for its production).

TABLE OF CONTENTS.

ENGLISH PORTION.

ARABIC PORTION.

INTRODUCTION.

This volume marks a further step in the tedious but indispensable task, on which I have long been engaged, of
providing materials for a history of Ṣúfism, and more especially for the study of its development in the oldest period,
beginning with the second and ending with the fourth
century of Islam (approximately 700—1000 A. D.). A list
of the titles known to us of mystical books written during
these three hundred years would occupy several pages, but
the books themselves have mostly perished, although the
surviving remnant includes some important works on various
branches of Ṣúfistic theory and practice by leaders of the
movement, for example, Ḥárith al-Muḥásibí, Ḥusayn b. Manṣúr
al-Ḥalláj, Muḥammad b. ꜤAlí al-Tirmidhí, and others whom
I need not mention now. M. Louis Massignon, by his recent
edition of the *Kitáb al-Ṭawásín* of Ḥalláj, has shown what
valuable results might be expected from a critical examination of the early literature. It is certain that a series of
such monographs would form the best possible foundation
for a general survey, but in the meanwhile we have mainly
to rely on more or less systematic and comprehensive treatises dealing with the lives, legends, and doctrines of the
ancient Ṣúfís. I am preparing and hope, as soon as may be,
to publish a work on this subject derived, to a large extent,
from the following sources:

1. The *Kitáb al-LumaꜤ* by Abú Naṣr al-Sarráj († 378 A. H.).
2. The *Kitáb al-TaꜤarruf li-madhhab ahl al-Taṣawwuf* by
   Abú Bakr al-Kalábádhí († 380 or 390 A. H.).

3. The *Qút al-Qulúb* by Abú Ṭálib al-Makkí († 386 A. H.).
4. The *Ṭabaqát al-Ṣúfiyya* by Abú ʿAbd al-Raḥmán al-Sulamí († 412 A. H.).
5. The *Ḥilyat al-Awliyá* by Abú Nuʿaym al-Iṣbahání († 430 A. H.).
6. The *Risálat al-Qushayriyya* by Abu 'l-Qásim al-Qushayrí († 465 A. H.).
7. The *Kashf al-Maḥjúb* by ʿAlí b. ʿUthmán al-Hujwírí († *circa* 470 A. H.).
8. The *Tadhkirat al-Awliyá* by Faríduddín ʿAṭṭár († *circa* 620 A. H.).

Nos. 1, 3, 6, 7, 8 of the above list are now accessible in European or Oriental editions, and Nº. 7 also in an English translation. Nos. 2, 4 and 5 are still unedited and therefore comparatively useless for purposes of reference. May I suggest that some of our younger scholars should turn their attention to the manuscript copies of these texts in London, Leyden, Vienna, Constantinople and elsewhere?

Little material exists for the biography of Sarráj. The authors of the oldest Ṣúfí Lives pass him over in silence.[1] The first separate notice of him that is known to me occurs in the Supplement to the *Tadhkirat al-Awliyá* (II, 182), from which the article in Jámí's *Nafaḥát al-Uns* (Nº. 353) is chiefly compiled. Shorter notices are given by Abu 'l-Maḥásin (*Nujúm*, ed. by Popper, II, part 2, Nº. 1, p. 42), Dhahabí, *Ta'ríkh al-Islám* (British Museum, Or. 48, 156a), Abu 'l-Faláḥ ʿAbd al-Ḥayy al-ʿAkarí (*Shadharát al-Dhahab*, MS. in my possession, I, 185a),[2] and Dárá Shikúh,

---

1) Abú ʿAbd al-Raḥmán al-Sulamí, who does not notice Sarráj in his *Ṭabaqát al-Ṣúfiyya* (British Museum, Add. 18520), appears to have supplied the omission in his *Ta'ríkh al-Ṣúfiyya*. See the extract from Dhahabí cited below.

2) See *JRAS* for 1899, p. 911, and for 1906, p. 797. The article on Sarráj copies Dhahabí and concludes with a short quotation from Sakháwí:

Safínat al-Awliyá (Ethé, Catalogue of Persian manuscripts in the Library of the India office, col. 301, N°. 271). Since the passage in the *Ta'ríkh al-Islám* has not been published before, I will transcribe it.

عبد الله بن علّى بن محمّد بن يحيى ابو نصر السرّاج الطوسى الصوفى مصنّف كتاب اللمع فى التصوف سمع جعفرًا الخُلْدى وابا بكر محمّد بن داود الدُقّى واحمد بن محمّد السايح روى عنـه ابو سعيد محمّد بن علّى النقّاش وعبد الرحمن بن محمّد السرّاج وغيرهم قال السُلمى كان ابو نصر من اولاد الزهّاد وكان المنظور اليه فى ناحيته فى الفتوّة ولسان القوم مع الاستظهار بعلم الشريعـة هو فقيه مشايخهم اليوم، ومات فى رجب ومات ابوه ساجدًا

The few facts contained in this notice may be summarised as follows.

Abú Naṣr ʿAbdallah b. ʿAlí b. Muḥammad b. Yaḥyá al-Sarráj, the author of the *Kitáb al-Lumaʿ* was a native of Ṭús. His teachers were Jaʿfar al-Khuldí, Abú Bakr Muḥammad b. Dáwúd al-Duqqí, and Aḥmad b. Muḥammad al-Sáʾiḥ. [1]) The family to which he belonged was noted for asceticism. Abú Naṣr was a zealous Sunní, but although he based himself on knowledge of the religious law, [2]) he was learned in mystical theology and was regarded by the Ṣúfís as an authoritative exponent of their doctrines. Amongst his countrymen

---

وقال السخاوى كان على طريقة السنّة قال خرجت مع ابى عبد الله الروذبارى لنلقى انبليا الراهب بصور فتقدّمنا الى ديره وقلنا له ما الذى حبسك ههنا فقال استرقّ حلاوة قول الناس لى يا راهب

1) No person of this name is mentioned in the *Lumaʿ*. It seems to me certain that السايح is a mistake for السالى, in which case the reference will be to Abu 'l-Ḥasan Aḥmad b. Muḥammad b. Sálim. See under Ibn Sálim in the List of Authorities.

2) الاستظهار بعلم الشريعة is literally "to use the knowledge of the religious law as a support or guard."

he was celebrated for his nobility of soul. [1]) He died in
the month of Rajab, 378 A. H. = October—November,
988 A. D. [2])

From the Persian biographies we learn that Sarráj was
surnamed "the Peacock of the Poor" (*tá'ús al-fuqará*). The
statement that he had seen Sarí al-Saqatí (*ob.* 253) and Sahl
b. ʿAbdallah al-Tustarí (*ob.* 283) is manifestly false, nor does
the *Kitáb al-Lumaʿ* bear out the assertion that he was a
pupil of Abú Muḥammad al-Murtaʿish of Naysábúr (*ob.* 328).
It may be that, as the *Nafaḥát* says, he composed many
works on Ṣúfism in addition to the *Lumaʿ*, but if so, every
trace of them has vanished. The following anecdote, which
first occurs in the *Kashf al-Maḥjúb* of Hujwírí, [3]) is related
by both the Persian biographers. "Abú Naṣr al-Sarráj came
to Baghdád in the month of Ramaḍán and was given a
private chamber in the Shúníziyya mosque and was appointed
to preside over the dervishes until the Feast. During the
nightly prayers of Ramaḍán (*taráwíḥ*) he recited the whole
Koran five times. Every night a servant brought a loaf of
bread to his room. On the day of the Feast, when Sarráj
departed, the servant found all the thirty loaves untouched."
Another story describes how, in the course of a theosophical
discussion, he was seized with ecstasy, and threw himself in

---

1) *Futuwwat* (altruism), the quality which was displayed by Iblís when he
chose to incur damnation rather than deny the Unity of God by worshipping
Adam. Cf. Massignon, *al-Hallāj*, in *Revue de l'histoire des religions*, 1911. The
meaning of the word is discussed by Thorning in his *Beiträge zur Kenntniss
des islamischen Vereinswesens* Türkische Bibliothek, vol. 16, pp. 184—221,
and by R. Hartmann, *Das Ṣûfîtum nach al-Ḳuschairî*, p. 44 foll.

2) According to the *Nujúm*, his death took place at Naysabúr while he
was engaged in prayer (cf. the final words of Dhahabí's notice); but the *Nafaḥát*
states that he was buried at Ṭús. Before his death he said, "Every one whose
bier is carried past my tomb will be forgiven." Consequently the people of
Ṭús used to bring their dead to his tomb and halt beside it for a time and
then move on.

3) P. 323 of my translation.

the attitude of prayer upon a blazing fire, which had no power to burn his face. [1])

He must have travelled extensively. The *Kitáb al-Luma*ᶜ records his meetings and conversations with Ṣúfís in many parts of the Muḥammadan empire, *e. g.*, Baṣra, Baghdád, Damascus, Ramla, Antioch, Tyre, Aṭrábulus, Raḥbat Málik b. Ṭawq, Cairo, Dimyáṭ, Bisṭám, Tustar, and Tabríz. Probably the duties of a spiritual director were not congenial to him. It is interesting, however, to observe that the only one of his pupils who attained to eminence, Abu 'l-Faḍl b. al-Ḥasan of Sarakhs, afterwards became the Sheykh of the famous Persian mystic, Abú Saᶜíd b. Abi 'l-Khayr. [2])

Sarráj explains (p. ٤, l. ١٨ foll.) that he wrote the *Kitáb al-Luma*ᶜ at the request of a friend, whose name he does not mention. His purpose in writing it was to set forth the true principles of Ṣúfism and to show by argument that they agree with, and are confirmed by, the doctrines of the Koran and the Apostolic Traditions; that they involve imitation of the Prophet and his Companions as well as conformity with the religious practice of pious Moslems. The work, therefore, is avowedly apologetic and controversial in character. Its contents are fully detailed in the Abstract, but a brief analysis will not be out of place here.

---

1) *Tadh. al-Awliyá*, II, 183, 3; *Nafaḥát*, 320, 2.
2) *Nafaḥát*, 320, 18.

The *Kitáb al-Luma*ᶜ can hardly be called an original work
in the sense that it deals with the author's theories and
speculations on the subject of Ṣúfism. In the main he con-
fines himself to recording and interpreting the spoken or
written words of his predecessors, and he rebukes contemporary writers for the ostentatious discussions in which they
indulged. From the historical point of view, his reserve is
welcome. It throws into sharp relief the invaluable collection
of documents which he has brought together and arranged,
documents that are in many instances nowhere else to be
found, illustrating the early development of Islamic mysticism and enabling us to study its language, ideas, and
methods during the critical time of adolescence. Considering
the variety of topics which the author has managed to in-
clude in a comparatively short treatise, we can easily forgive
him for having often suppressed the *isnáds* and abbreviated
the text of traditions and anecdotes; but if he had allowed
himself a freer hand in exposition, his book would be even
more instructive than it is. There are many passages which
only a Ṣúfí could explain adequately.

Its compendious style, the wide range of its subject-matter,
and the writer's close adherence to his authorities do not
permit such a systematic and exhaustive analysis of mystical
doctrines as we find, for example, in the *Qút al-qulúb* of Abú
Ṭálib al-Makkí. The nineteen chapters on 'states' (*aḥwál*) and
'stations' (*maqámát*) occupy a little over thirty pages in the present edition — about half the space which Abú Ṭálib devotes to
the single *maqám* of 'trust in God' (*tawakkul*). Here as well
as in other sections of his work Sarráj adopts an artificial
scheme of classification by triads, which is characteristic of
this kind of Ṣúfí literature. On the whole, however, it may
be claimed for him that his readers will obtain a clear notion,
uncomplicated by elaborate details, of what is most important for them to understand. Without attempting a complete

review, I would mention as especially novel or noteworthy the chapters on Ṣúfistic interpretation *(istinbáṭ)* of the Koran and the Ḥadíth; those on audition and ecstasy, which embody excerpts from the lost *Kitáb al-wajd* of Abú Saʿíd b. al-Aʿrábí and have been utilised by Ghazzálí in the *Iḥyá*; the seventy pages on 'manners', treating of the ritual and social aspects of Ṣúfism; the interesting selection of poems and epistles; the large vocabulary of technical terms; the specimens of *shaṭḥiyyát* with explanations partly derived from Junayd's commentary on the ecstatic sayings that were attributed to Abú Yazíd al-Bisṭámí; and the final chapters on errors of mystical doctrine. I have already published the text and translation of certain passages relating to the conception of *faná* in an article entitled "The Goal of Muḥammadan Mysticism" (*J. R. A. S.* for 1913, p. 55 foll.)

As regards the word 'Ṣúfí', it is remarkable that Sarráj favours (not on linguistic grounds, however) the now accepted derivation from *ṣúf*. He tells us that, according to some, 'Ṣúfí' was a modern designation invented by the people of Baghdád. This statement, though he naturally rejects it, does in all probability give a true account of the origin of the name.

Notwithstanding that Sarráj takes for granted the reality of the higher mystical experiences and is eager to justify the apparent blasphemies uttered by many Ṣúfís at such moments, he constantly appeals to the Koran and the Apostolic Traditions as the supreme arbiters which every Ṣúfí must recognise. If we admit his principles of interpretation, we cannot deny his orthodoxy. *Faná* itself, as defined by him, means nothing more than realisation of the Divine Unity (*tawḥíd*) and is in logical harmony with Islamic monotheism. Whether this view indicates that the *faná* theory, as Professor Margoliouth has contended, [1] was simply evolved

---

1) *The Early Development of Mohammedanism*, p. 199.

from *tawḥíd*, or whether it represents the result of impregnation of the monotheistic idea by foreign influences, is a difficult question. We cannot yet decide with certainty, but the evidence, so far as it goes, seems to me to render the latter hypothesis more probable. [1] Sarráj denounces *ḥulúl* and other heretical forms of the *faná* doctrine. While disapproving of excessive asceticism, he enjoins the strictest obedience to the sacred law. The Ṣúfí (he says) differs from the ordinary Moslem only in laying greater stress upon the inward religious life of which the formal acts of worship are an outward expression.

Sarráj was closely associated with Ibn Sálim (Abu 'l-Ḥasan Aḥmad b. Muḥammad) [2] of Baṣra, who, "though extremely orthodox in some respects, was opposed to certain fundamental articles of the Sunna". [3] This Ibn Sálim was the son of Abú ᶜAbdallah b. Sálim; and their followers, a group of theologians known as the Sálimís, occupied an advanced position on the left wing of the mystical movement, as appears from the fact that they sympathised with Halláj and defended his orthodoxy. [4] From the account of their tenets given by ᶜAbd-al-Qádir al-Jílání in his *Ghunya* [5] we might assert with confidence that Sarráj cannot have been a member of the school. None of the heresies there enumerated occurs in the *Lumaᶜ*, and on the last page of his book Sarráj declares that the spirit dies like the body, a state-

---

1) Cf. my *Mystics of Islam*, p. 16 foll.

2) See under Ibn Sálim in the List of Authorities.

3) *Shadharát al-Dhahab*, I, 172a (citation from the ᶜ*Ibar* of Dhahabí). Possibly these words refer to Ibn Sálim the Elder. Muḥammadan writers frequently fail to distinguish between the father and the son.

4) Concerning the Sálimís and their doctrines see Goldziher, *Die dogmatische Partei der Sälimijja*, *ZDMG*. vol. 61, p. 73 foll.; Amedroz in *JRAS*. for 1912, p. 573 foll.; and Massignon, *Kitáb al-Ṭawásín*, Index under Sálimíyah.

5) Goldziher, *loc. cit.* p. 77.

ment which is at variance with the Sálimí belief in its im-
mortality. [1]) On the other hand, it would be absurd to suppose that each individual Sálimí embraced all the heresies
in ʿAbd al-Qádir's list. That Ibn Sálim himself did so is
most unlikely in view of the respect shown to him by
Sarráj and the friendly intercourse that was maintained between them. Moreover, Sarráj on several occasions quotes
sayings and verses by Halláj, whom he seems to have regarded as a profound Unitarian (cf. 303, 20 foll.). But though
he agreed with the Sálimís on this point, I doubt whether
any trace of their peculiar doctrines can be discovered in
the *Lumaᶜ*. A follower of Ibn Sálim would scarcely have
twitted his leader with excusing in Sahl b. ʿAbdallah (the
Sheykh of Abú ʿAbdallah b. Sálim) what he condemned in
Abú Yazíd al-Bistámí, nor would he have described Sahl
as "the Imám of Ibn Sálim and the most excellent of
mankind *in his opinion*" (394, 12 foll.). It is a striking circumstance that two of the three oldest surviving Arabic
treatises on Súfism were directly influenced by Ibn Sálim.
In the *Lumaᶜ* his personality stands out conspicuously amongst
the author's contemporaries, and the *Qút al-qulúb* is the work
of his pupil, Abú Tálib al-Makkí, whom the Sálimís justly
claim as one of themselves.

Sarráj obtained his materials partly from books and partly
from oral tradition, but the information which he gives us
concerning his sources is by no means complete.

The following books are cited:

1. A History of Mecca (اخبار مكة), possibly the work of
Azraqí (22, 12).
2. The *Kitáb al-musháhadat* by ʿAmr b. ʿUthmán al-Makkí
(69, 12 and 117, 8).

---

1) Cf. Massignon, *Kitáb al-Tawásin*, p. 136, n. 2.

3. The *Kitáb al-Sunan* by Abú Dáwúd al-Sijistání (139, 13).

4. A work on the rules of prayer (*adab al-ṣalát*) by Abú Saʿíd al-Kharráz (153, 7).

5. A book of which the title is not mentioned, by Abú Turáb al-Nakhshabí (205, 19).

6. The *Kitáb al-munáját* by Junayd (259, 2).

7. The *Kitáb al-wajd* by Abú Saʿíd b. al-Aʿrábí (308, 5; 310, 1; 314, 17).

8. The *Kitáb maʿrifat al-maʿrifat* by Ibráhím al-Khawwáṣ (362, 14).

9. A commentary by Junayd on the ecstatic expressions (*shaṭḥiyyát*) attributed to Abú Yazíd al-Bisṭámí (381, 2; 382, 5, etc.).

The persons cited as authorities at first hand are forty in number, all being Ṣúfís with a single exception — the celebrated philologist Ibn Khálawayh. Most of them are unknown, but the list includes several mystics of eminence, e. g. Duqqí, Abu ʾl-Ḥasan al-Ḥuṣrí, Jaʿfar al-Khuldí, Abú ʿAmr b. Nujayd, Abú ʿAbdallah al-Rúdhabárí, Abu ʾl-Ḥasan b. Sálim, and Abu ʾl-Ḥusayn al-Sírawání. The names of the forty in alphabetical order, together with some biographical details and references, are printed below, and those most frequently cited are marked with an asterisk.

LIST OF AUTHORITIES.

Abbreviations: [1]

A = *Ansáb* of Samᶜání (Gibb Memorial Series, vol. XX).

H = *Ḥilyat al-Awliyá* of Abú Nuᶜaym al-Iṣbahání, Leyden MS. 311*b* and 311*a* Warn.

K = *Kashf al-Maḥjúb* of Hujwírí, my translation (Gibb Memorial Series, vol. XVII).

N = *Nafaḥát al-Uns* of Jámí, ed. by Nassau Lees (Calcutta, 1859). The figures cited refer to the numbered biographies, not to the pages.

Q = Qushayrí's *Risála* (Cairo, 1318 A. H.).

Sh = Shaᶜrání's *Ṭabaqát al-Kubrá* (Cairo, 1299 A. H.).

TA = *Tadhkirat al-Awliyá* of Faríduddín ᶜAṭṭár, ed. by me in *Persian Historical Texts*, vols. III and V (1905—1907).

TS = *Ṭabaqát al-Ṣúfiyya* of Abú ᶜAbd al-Raḥmán al-Sulamí, British Museum, Add. 18520.

Y = Yáqút, *Muᶜjam al-Buldán*, ed. by Wüstenfeld (1866—1873).

ᶜ*A k k í*, Abu 'l-Ṭayyib Aḥmad b. Muqátil al-Baghdádí.

A 397*a* penult. قال ابو نصر السرّاج صاحب اللمع ثنا ابو الطيّب العكّى بعكّا

This quotation does not occur in the *Lumaᶜ*, but Samᶜání may have found it in another work by Sarráj.

---

1) In referring to MSS. I have used the italicised letters *a* and *b* to denote the two pages which face each other when the MS. lies open before the reader, *a* being on his right hand and *b* on his left. According to the method commonly adopted *a* and *b* denote the front and back of the same leaf. Therefore the figures of the references given below are always one page ahead of the ordinary reckoning. For example, 200*a* = 199*b* and 200*b* = 200*a*.

ᶜAkkí reports a description of Shiblí's behaviour on his
deathbed, derived from his famulus, Bundár al-Dínawarí,
whom ᶜAkkí met on the same day in the house of
Jaᶜfar al-Khuldí (104, 6); part of a letter written to
Jaᶜfar al-Khuldí by Abu 'l-Khayr al-Tínátí (236, 13);
an account derived from Jaᶜfar al-Khuldí of the way in
which Abu 'l-Ḥusayn b. Zírí, a pupil of Junayd, expressed
his approval or disapproval of *samá*ᶜ (272, 13); an ecstasy
of Shiblí which he witnessed (282, 17).

The author relates that ᶜAkkí showed him a list that
he had compiled of persons who recovered their lost
property by means of a prayer which Jaᶜfar al-Khuldí
used for that purpose (317, 6).

ᶜAlawi, Ḥamza b. ᶜAbdallah. N. 64.

A pupil of Abu 'l-Khayr al-Tínátí (*ob.* 349 A. H.).
Speaking from personal experience, he vouches for his
master's telepathic powers (317, 8).

ᶜAlawi, Yaḥyá b. al-Riḍá.

He related at Baghdád, and copied for the author with
his own hand, an anecdote of the Ṣúfí Abú Ḥulmán (289, 7).

ᶜAṣá'idi, Ṭalḥat al-Baṣrí.

He related at Baṣra an anecdote of Sahl b. ᶜAbdallah
al-Tustarí which he derived from one of Sahl's disciples
(330, 8). The name of the disciple is defectively written
in the MSS. and cannot be ascertained.

Bániyási, Muḥammad b. Maᶜbad.

He relates a story of al-Kurdí al-Ṣúfí (203, 5).

Baṣri, Aḥmad b. Muḥammad.

Possibly identical with Abu 'l-Ḥasan Aḥmad b. Muḥammad b. Sálim of Baṣra (see under *Ibn Sálim*). [1]) He
reports a saying of al-Jalájilí al-Baṣrí (143, 14).

---

1) The author uses the name Abu 'l-Ḥasan Muḥammad b. Aḥmad (which is
a mistake for Aḥmad b. Muḥammad) in reference to Ibn Sálim (292, 11).

Baṣrí, Abu 'l-Ḥusayn.

He may, perhaps, be Abu 'l-Ḥasan al-Ḥuṣrí of Baṣra (see under *Ḥuṣrí*). He reports, as eye-witness, a miracle that was granted to a negro *faqír*, at ʿAbbádán (316, 8).

Baṣrí, Ṭalḥat al-ʿAṣáʾidí. See *ʿAṣáʾidí*.

Bayrútí, Abú Bakr, Aḥmad b. Ibráhím al-Muʾaddib.

He recited to the author at Cairo some verses by Ibráhím al-Khawwáṣ (250, 1).

Bisṭámí, Ṭayfúr b. ʿÍsá.

He reports two sayings of the celebrated Abú Yazíd al-Bisṭámí on the authority of Músá b. ʿÍsá al-Bisṭámí (known as ʿUmayy), who heard them from his father. He describes the poverty in which Abú Yazíd died (188, 12).

Ibn Dillawayh,[1]) Aḥmad.

He reports a saying of Abú ʿImrán al-Ṭabaristání (171, 13).

Dínawarí, Abú ʿAbdallah al-Khayyáṭ.

His *waṣiyyat* to the author (265, 11).

Dínawarí, ʿÍsá al-Qaṣṣár.

He was the famulus of Shiblí (148, 7). He reports a saying of Ruwaym (189, 8). A saying by him on hunger (202, 14). He witnessed the removal of Ḥalláj from prison to the place of execution (24th of Dhu 'l-Qaʿda, 309 A. H.) and reports the last words which he uttered before his death (303, 20).

Dínawarí, Muḥammad b. Dáwúd. See *Duqqí*.

Dínawarí, Abú Saʿíd.

The author was present in his *majlis* at Aṭrábulus and gives the text of a prayer which he heard him pronounce on that occasion (260, 4).

---

1) For the name Dillawayh (Dillúya) or Dallawayh see Nöldeke, *Persische Studien*, S. B. W. A. 1888, vol. 116, part I, p. 403. Zakariyyá b. Dillawayh of Naysábúr (*ob.* 294 A. H.) is noticed in N. 77, where the text has ديلويه.

*Duqqí, Abú Bakr Muḥammad b. Dáwúd al-Dínawarí. TS.
103b. Q. 33. N. 229. Sh. I, 158. A. 228a, 24.

Originally of Dínawar, he resided for some time at
Baghdád and finally settled at Damascus, where he died
in 359 or 360 A. H. He was a pupil of Abú Bakr al-
Zaqqáq the Elder (see the List of Ṣúfís given below)
and Abú ʿAbdallah b. al-Jallá (Q. 24. Sh. I, 116. N.
112). That Duqqí, to whom there are eighteen references in the *Lumaʿ*, was a trustworthy reporter may be
judged from the fact that he made a special journey
from Syria to the Ḥijáz in order to hear from the lips
of Abú Bakr al-Kattání the true version of an anecdote
concerning the latter (178, 18). He relates sayings and
anecdotes of Jarírí, Abú Bakr al-Farghání, [1]) Abú Bakr
al-Kattání, Ibn al-Jallá, Abú Bakr al-Zaqqáq, Abu ʾl-
Ḥusayn al-Darráj, and verses of Abú ʿAlí al-Rúdhabárí.
He also describes the hunger which he endured at Mecca
(170, 6) and tells the story of the slave whose sweet
voice was the death of his master's camels (270, 3). [2])
The author mentions, several times, that he received
information from Duqqí at Damascus.

Farrá, Muḥammad b. Aḥmad b. Ḥamdún. TS. 117b. N.
231. Sh. I, 166 (where القراد is a mistake for الفرّاء).

His *kunya* is Abú Bakr. N. gives his name as Aḥmad
b. Ḥamdún, which is incorrect. He was an eminent
Ṣúfí of Naysábúr and died in 370 A. H. He reports a
saying of ʿAbd al-Raḥmán al-Fárisí (40, 5).

Ḥimṣí, Qays b. ʿUmar.

He relates an anecdote of Abu ʾl-Qásim b. Marwán al-
Naháwandí (288, 16).

---

1) Generally known as Abú Bakr al-Wásiṭí (Q. 29. K. 154. TA. II, 265.
Sh. I. 132. N. 212).

2) See K. 399, where the same story is told on the authority of Ibráhím
al-Khawwáṣ.

Ḥuṣrí, Abu 'l-Ḥasan. TS. 114*a.* Q. 35. K. 160. TA. II, 288. N. 290. Sh. I, 164.

Died 371 A. H. A native of Baṣra but resided at Baghdád. He was a pupil of Shiblí, two of whose sayings he reports (396, 8; 398, 6). Sarráj quotes six sayings by Ḥuṣrí, including a definition of 'Ṣúfí' (28, 2) and a summary of the principles of Ṣúfism (218, 1).

Ibn Jábán, Abú ʿAbdallah Aḥmad.

He relates an anecdote of Shiblí, whose house he visited (395, 18).

Ibn Khálawayh, Abú ʿAbdallah al-Ḥusayn.

The well-known grammarian (Brockelmann, I, 125). He died in 370 A. H. He reports from Ibn al-Anbárí (Brockelmann, I, 119) fourteen verses of Kaʿb b. Zuhayr's ode beginning with the words *Bánat Suʿád* (275, 8). [1]

Khayyáṭ, Abú Ḥafṣ ʿUmar.

He reports Abú Bakr b. al-Muʿallim, who related to him at Antioch how, after sixty years, he was called upon to pronounce the Moslem profession of faith (207, 21).

*Khuldí, Jaʿfar b. Muḥammad b. Nuṣayr. Q. 33. K. 156. TA. II, 283. N. 278. Sh. I, 156. A. 205*b,* 13.

A native of Baghdád, pupil of Junayd and Ibráhím al-Khawwáṣ. He died in 348 A. H.

He reports Junayd and through him Sarí al-Saqaṭí (seven references). A story of his own pilgrimage to Mecca (168, 13). A manuscript in his handwriting is mentioned as the authority for an anecdote of Junayd (204, 5) and for an extract from a letter written by a certain Sheykh (237, 14). The author's use of the words فيا قرأت عليه (251, 2; 306, 5; 434, 10) shows that in these cases he obtained from Jaʿfar al-Khuldí a personal assurance that the tradition was accurate.

---

1) The word بانثاد (275, 9) is an obvious misprint for باسناد

Malaṭi, ʿUmar.

He reports to the author at Antioch the reply which
he received from a certain Sheykh whom he had asked
to pray for him (261, 17).

Muhallab, Abú Muḥammad b. Aḥmad b. Marzúq al-Miṣrí.

He associated with Abú Bakr b. Ṭáhir al-Abharí, who
died *circa* 330 A. H. (N. p. 207, l. 4 foll.). He relates
that Abú Muḥammad al-Murtaʿish of Naysábúr on his
deathbed (*ob.* 328 A. H.) enjoined him to pay the debts
wich he (Murtaʿish) had contracted (266, 2).

Ibn Nujayd, Abú ʿAmr Ismáʿíl. TS. 105a. Q. 34. TA. II,
262. N. 281. Sh. I, 159.

Died in 366 A. H. He was the maternal grandfather
of Abú ʿAbd al-Raḥmán al-Sulamí and the pupil of
Abú ʿUthmán al-Ḥírí of Naysábur. He reports three
sayings of Abú ʿUthmán al-Ḥírí. [1]

Rázi, Abú ʿAbdallah Ḥusayn b. Aḥmad.

He reports (316, 12) a story told by Abú Sulaymán al-
Khawwáṣ, a Maghribí, who died at Damascus and was
contemporary with Abu 'l-Khayr al-Tínátí (*ob.* 349 A.H.).
See N. 286, where the same story is related.

Rázi, Ḥusayn b. ʿAbdallah.

He reports (215, 20) a saying of Abú Bakr ʿAbdallah
b. Ṭáhir al-Abharí who died *circa* 330 A. H.

Rúdhabári, Abú ʿAbdallah Aḥmad b. ʿAṭá. TS. 115b. Q.
35. N. 328. Sh. I, 164.

He lived at Ṣúr and died there in 369 A. H. He was a
nephew (son of the sister) of Abú ʿAlí al-Rúdhabári
(*ob.* 322 A. H.). He tells an anecdote of his uncle (185,
14) and recites some verses by him (249, 10). He relates

---

1) In the *Lumaʿ* his name is given as Saʿíd b. ʿUthmán al-Ḥírí (al-Rází),
but according to all other authorities it is Saʿíd b. Ismáʿíl. He was originally
a native of Rayy.

that one night his prayer for forgiveness was answered
by a heavenly voice (316, 17). The author states that
Abú ʿAbdallah al-Rúdhabári [1]) wrote an impromptu
letter in his presence at Ramla, begging the owner of
a slave-girl, who was famed for her singing, to permit
the author and his companions to hear her performance
(234, 6).

*Ibn Sálim, Abu 'l-Ḥasan Aḥmad b. Muḥammad. Dhahabí,
Ta'ríkh al-Islám (British Museum, Or. 48, 71a) cited in
Notes on some Ṣúfí Lives by H. F. Amedroz in *JRAS*
for 1912, p. 573, note 2. *Shadharát al-Dhahab*, I, 172a.
He is the son of Abú ʿAbdallah Muḥammad b. Sálim [2])
of Baṣra (TS. 95b. H. II, 321b. N. 124. Sh. I, 154), who
was a pupil of Sahl b. ʿAbdallah al-Tustarí and founder
of a school of mystical theologians known after him as
the Sálimís *(al-Sálimiyya)*. [3]) Ibn Sálim *Senior* died in
297 A. H. [4]) He is often confused with his son, the
subject of the present notice, who died *circa* 360 A. H.
Thus the author of the *Lumaʿ* records (177, 21) a statement by Ibn Sálim *Junior* that he associated with Sahl
b. ʿAbdallah for a period of sixty years. Evidently this
refers to his father and, as it happens, the mistake is
corrected in a later passage (292, 11). Again, it must
have been Ibn Sálim *Senior* who had the conversation
with Sahl which is reported by Ibn Sálim *Junior* as a
personal experience (293, 2).

---

1) The text has Abú ʿAlí al-Rúdhabári, but the reading of B is correct.

2) Muḥammad b. Aḥmad b. Sálim, according to Abú ʿAbd al-Raḥmán al-
Sulamí, Abú Nuʿaym al-Iṣbahání and Samʿání.

3) See p. X above.

4) The passage cited by Dhahabí from the *Ḥilyat al-Awliyá* of Abú Nuʿaym
(*ob.* 430 A. H.) makes the latter say that he was born before the death of
Ibn Sálim the Elder, which is absurd. The correct reading of the text after
the words وحافظ كلامه (*JRAS*, 1912, p. 574, l. 7 of the Arabic text) is:
سلك مسلك اسٔتاده سهل وأبنُهُ أبو الحسن ادركتُهُ وله اصحاب ينسبون اليه (H. II, 321b).

Abu 'l-Ḥasan b. Sálim is cited as authority for several anecdotes and sayings of Sahl b. ʿAbdallah, and in about half of these instances it is expressly mentioned that his information was .obtained from his father. If he and Aḥmad b. Muḥammad al-Baṣrí (143, 14) are the same person, he also reports a saying of al-Jalájilí of Baṣra, concerning whom nothing is known.

Sarráj was intimately acquainted with Ibn Sálim. He was present in his *majlis* at Baṣra (195, 18; 390, 12; 394, 8); he reports conversations with him (319, 2; 326, 17, 390, 12) and a considerable number of his sayings (116, 9; 152, 13; 202, 9; 219, 2; 223, 3; 315, 12—316, 2; 417, 17).

Ṣayrafí, Abu 'l-Ḥasan ʿAlí b. Muḥammad.

Apparently identical with Abu 'l-Ḥasan ʿAlí b. Bundár b. al-Ḥusayn al-Ṣayrafí of Naysábúr, who associated with Ruwaym and died in 359 A.H. (Q 34, N. 118, Sh. I, 165). He reports a saying of Ruwaym (288, 13).

Shimsháṭí, Abú Ḥafṣ ʿUmar.

He recited some verses by Ibráhím al-Khawwáṣ to the author at Ramla (250, 8).

Shírází, Abu 'l-Ṭayyib.

He reports a saying of one of his Sheykhs (342, 17).

Sírawání, Abu 'l-Ḥusayn. N. 336.

There are two Ṣúfís of this name: Abu 'l-Ḥusayn ʿAlí b. Muḥammad al-Sírawání, a native of Sírawán in the Maghrib, who resided at Dimyáṭ (N. 283), and his pupil Abu 'l-Ḥusayn ʿAlí b. Jaʿfar b. Dáwúd al-Sírawání al-Ṣaghír, who associated with Ibráhím al-Khawwáṣ in Egypt and afterwards settled at Mecca, where he died. Jámí says, on the authority of the *Ta'ríkh al-Ṣúfiyya* of al-Sulamí, that al-Sírawání al-Ṣaghír lived to the age of a hundred and twenty-four. He is the person cited in the *Lumaʿ*, for he is described as the *ṣáḥib* of al-Khawwáṣ.

He met Ṣarráj at Dimyáṭ and related to him a saying
of Junayd (285, 18).

Ibn Sunayd, Aḥmad b. Muḥammad.

Qáḍí of Dínawar. He reports an anecdote of Ruwaym
(163, 12).

Ṣúrí, Abú ʿAlí b. Abí Khálid.

He recited to the author at Ṣúr some verses written by
him to Abú ʿAlí al-Rúdhabárí and by the latter in reply
to him (234, 14).

Ṭallí,[1] Aḥmad b. Muḥammad.

He reported to the author at Antioch from his father,
from Bishr (or ʿÍsá), a saying of Isḥáq b. Ibráhím al-
Mawṣilí concerning the expert singer (271, 3).

Ṭarasúsí, Aḥmad.

He is probably Abú Bakr ʿAlí b. Aḥmad al-Ṭarasúsí
al-Ḥaramí, who associated with Ibráhím b. Shaybán al-
Qarmísíní (*ob.* 337 A.H.) and died in 364 A.H. at Mecca
(N. 233). He reports from Ibráhím b. Shaybán a story
told by Ibráhím al-Khawwáṣ (170, 14).

Ṭúsí, Abú Bakr Aḥmad b. Jaʿfar.

He reports a saying of Naṣr b. al-Ḥammámí (48, 15)
and relates to the author at Damascus an anecdote of
Abú Yaʿqúb al-Nahrajúrí, who died in 330 A.H. (203, 13).

*Ibn ʿUlwán, Abú ʿAmr ʿAbd al-Wáḥid.

Fourteen references. He reports sayings and anecdotes
of Junayd, whom he had met (116, 20), and a story of
Abu ʾl-Ḥusayn al-Núrí (193, 20). The author mentions
twice that Ibn ʿUlwán communicated information to
him at Raḥbat Málik b. Ṭawq.

*Wajíhí, Abú Bakr Aḥmad b. ʿAlí.

Twenty-four references. He is called (293, 17) Aḥmad
b. ʿAlí al-Karají (or al-Karkhí), generally known as Wa-

---

1) Variant Ṭalḥí.

jíhí. He reports Abú ʿAlí al-Rúdhabárí (eleven references), Jarírí, Abú Bakr al-Zaqqáq, Ibn Mamlúla al-ʿAṭṭár
al-Dínawarí, Abú Jaʿfar al-Ṣaydalání, Jaʿfar al-Ṭayálisí
al-Rází, and Muḥammad b. Yúsuf al-Banná. He relates
anecdotes of Bunán al-Ḥammál, Ḥasan al-Qazzáz, and
Mimshádh al-Dínawarí, and recites verses by Núrí.

Zanjání, Abú ʿAmr.

He recited to the author at Tabríz some verses by
Shiblí (251, 12).

About two hundred names of Ṣúfís are mentioned in the
Kitáb al-Lumaʿ. Many of these are familiar and will be
found in almost any Arabic or Persian 'Lives of the Saints'.
On the other hand, a great proportion of them either do
not occur in the published works of reference, or are recorded only in one or two of such works, or are not mentioned,
to my knowledge, except in the *Lumaʿ*. In the hope that
further information may be forthcoming, I append the names
of those more or less obscure mystics, accompanied by a few
notes which I have made while endeavouring to identify
them. Names included in the List of Authorities are omitted
from the following list, which is also arranged alphabetically.

LIST OF ṢŪFĪS.

1. ʿAbdallah b. al-Ḥusayn (248, 15). 4th century.
2. ʿAbd al-Raḥmán b. Aḥmad (325, 3). A ṣáḥib of Sahl b. ʿAbdallah of Tustar.
3. Abharí, Abú Bakr ʿAbdallah b. Ṭáhir. Died 330 A. H. TS. 90b. Q. 32. H. II, 315a, N. 223, Sh. I, 149.
4. Anmáṭí, Abú ʿUmar (329, 20).
5. ʿAṭṭár al-Dínawarí = Ibn Mamlúla.
6. ʿAṭṭár, Abú Ḥátim (180, 17). Contemporary with Abú Turáb al-Nakhshabí (ob. 245 A. H.). Abú Saʿíd al-Kharráz and Junayd were his pupils. N. 35.
7. ʿAṭúfí, Abu ʾl-Ḥasan (205, 11). Contemporary with Abú ʿAlí al-Rúdhabárí (ob. 322 A. H.).
8. Awlásí, Abu ʾl-Ḥárith. His name is Fayḍ b. al-Khaḍir. He was a pupil of Ibráhím b. Saʿd al-ʿAlawí (ob. circa 260 A. H.). N. 16.
9. Abu ʾl-Azhar (325, 7). Contemporary with Abú Bakr al-Kattání (ob. 322 A. H.).
10. Banná, Muḥammad b. Yúsuf (325, 19). Author of many excellent works on Ṣúfism. He travelled with Abú Turáb al-Nakhshabí (ob. 245 A. H.) and was the Sheykh of ʿAlí b. Sahl al-Iṣbahání (ob. 307 A. H.). N. 103. H. II, 328a.
11. Baráthí, Abú Shuʿayb (200, 3). He is described as one of the ancient Sheykhs of Baghdád. Junayd said that Abú Shuʿayb was the first who dwelt at Baráthá (a quarter of Baghdád) in a kúkh, or hut made of

rushes, and devoted himself to asceticism. His wife, Jawhara, died in 170 A. H. (*Nujúm*, ed. by Juynboll, I, 460). H. II, 304*b*, gives the same anecdote which is related here.

12. Bárizí, Abú Bakr (207, 6; 264, 4).

13. Basrí, Ahmad b. al-Husayn (248, 15). Contemporary with Junayd.

14. Bunán al-Hammál al-Misrí. Died 316 A. H. Q. 28. N. 184. Sh. I, 130.

15. Ibn Bunán al-Misrí (193, 18; 209, 20). A pupil of Abú Saʿíd al-Kharráz (*ob*. 277 or 286 A. H.). Notices of him under the name of Abu 'l-Husayn b. Bunán [1]) occur in TS. 90*a*, H. II, 317*b*, Q. 32, and N. 271.

16. Bundár b. al-Husayn. A pupil of Shiblí. He was a native of Shíráz but resided at Arraján, [2]) where he died in 353 A. H. H. II, 323*a*. Q. 34. Sh. I, 161. N. 280.

17. Busrí, Abú ʿUbayd. A pupil of Abú Turáb al-Nakhshabí (*ob*. 245 A. H.) Q. 26. A. 81*b*, 5. N. 114. Y. I, 621, 8. Sh. I, 118.

18. Dámaghání, al-Hasan [3]) b. ʿAlí b. Hayawayh. [4])

19. Darráj, Abú Jaʿfar (194, 19).

20. Darráj, Abú 'l-Husayn, of Baghdád. N. 207. Famulus of Ibráhím al-Khawwás. He had a brother, Bukayr al-Darráj, who was also a Súfí (N. 208). Abu 'l-Husayn al-Darraj died in 320 A. H.

---

1) نَبَان in N. is a mistake for بُنَان.

2) الرجالى, the reading of B at 278, 7, is a mistake for الارجانى.

3) Qushayrí has al-Husayn. See 41, 9, note 8.

4) Examples of the name Hayawayh, which appears to be the correct reading here, are found in my MS. of the *Shadharát al-Dhahab* (see *JRAS*. for 1899, p. 911, and for 1906, p. 797) I, 177*a*, 24, Abu 'l-Hasan Muhammad b. ʿAbdallah b. Zakariyyá b. Hayawayh al-Naysábúrí al-Misrí al-Qádí (*ob*. 367 A.H.); I, 183*a*, 17, Abú Bakr Muhammad b. Hayawayh al-Karkhí, the grammarian (*ob*. 373 A. H); and I, 188*a*, 10, Abú ʿAmr b. Hayawayh al-Khazzáz of Baghdád, the traditionist (*ob*. 382 A. H.).

21. Dínawarí, Abú Bakr al-Kisá'í = Kisá'í.

22. Dínawarí, Bakrán (210, 14). Contemporary with Shiblí.

23. Dínawárí, Bundár (104, 7). Famulus of Shiblí.

24. Dínawarí, Ḥasan al-Qazzáz = Qazzáz.

25. Ibn al-Farají = Abú Jaᶜfar Muḥammad b. Yaᶜqúb al-Farají. A *ṣáhib* of Ḥarith al-Muḥásibí (*ob.* 243 A.H.). Author of the *Kitáb al-waraᶜ*, the *Kitáb ṣifat al-muridín* and other works on Ṣúfism. H. II, 293*b*.

26. Farghání, Abú Bakr Muḥammad b. Músá (228, 10) = Abú Bakr al-Wásiṭí (*ob. circa* 320 A. H.). Q. 29. K. 154. TA II, 265. N. 212. Sh. I, 132.

27. Fárisí, ᶜAbd al-Raḥmán (40, 6). Contemporary with Muḥammad b. Aḥmad b. Ḥamdún al-Farrá (*ob.* 370 A.H.).

28. Fárisí, Abu 'l-Ḥusayn ᶜAlí b. Hind al-Qurashí (230, 2). He associated with Junayd and ᶜAmr b. ᶜUthmán al-Makkí, but himself belonged to a younger generation. TS 92*a*. N. 272. Sh. I, 150.

29. Fatḥ al-Mawṣilí. Died in 220 A. H. N. 25. Sh. I, 105.

30. Fatḥ b. Shakhraf al-Marwazí (228, 6). Died in 273 A.H. N. 26.

31. Ibn al-Fuwaṭí (286, 1) [1]. Contemporary with Abu 'l-Ḥusayn al-Darráj (*ob.* 320 A. H.).

32. Ghassání, Kulthúm (142, 13).

33. Ḥaddád, Abú Jaᶜfar (332, 5). There are two Ṣúfís of this name: (1) Abú Jaᶜfar al-Ḥaddád al-Kabír of Baghdád, who was contemporary with Junayd (*ob.* 298 A. H.) and Ruwaym (*ob.* 303 A. H.); and (2) Abú Jaᶜfar b. Bukayr al-Ḥaddád al-Ṣaghír al-Miṣrí, a pupil of Abú Jaᶜfar al-Ḥaddád the elder. At first sight it would seem that the former is referred to here, since he is described as having had a conversation with Abú Turáb, whom we should naturally

---

1) Fuwaṭí (not Qúṭí or Ghúṭí) seems to be the correct form of the *nisba*. Cf. N. p. 216, l. 2 and *JRAS.* for 1901, p. 708.

identify with Abú Turáb al-Nakhshabí (*ob.* 245 A.H.), but in N. p. 190, l. 1 foll. the same story is told of Abú Ja'far al-Ḥaddád the younger, and it is expressly stated on the authority of 'Abdallah Anṣárí that the Abú Turáb in question is not Abú Turáb al-Nakhshabí [1]). N. 201.

34. Abu 'l-Ḥadíd (256, 13). Contemporary with Abú 'Abdallah al-Qurashí.

35. Ibn Ḥamawayh, Abú Bakr Aḥmad (197, 12). A *ṣáḥib* of Ṣubayḥí (*q. v.*)

36. Ibn al-Ḥammámí, Naṣr (48, 17). Contemporary with Abú Bakr Aḥmad b. Ja'far al-Ṭúsí. See List of Authorities under Ṭúsí.

37. Harawí, Abú Muḥammad (209, 12). Contemporary with Shiblí.

38. Ḥasan, Sheykh (178, 4). He consorted for seventy years with Abú 'Abdallah al-Maghribí (*ob.* 299 A. H.).

39. Haykalí, Abú 'Abdallah. Contemporary with Abú 'Abdallah al-Qurashí.

40. Abú Ḥulmán al-Ṣúfí (289, 8). A Persian, who resided at Damascus and gave his name to the sect of the Ḥulmánís, who are reckoned among the Ḥulúlis. Cf. *al-Farq bayna 'l-firaq*, p. 245, l. 3 foll., and K. 260.

41. Ḥuṣrí, Abú 'Abdallah, of Baṣra. A pupil of Fatḥ al-Mawṣilí (*ob.* 220 A. H.). N. 116.

42. Iṣbahání, Sahl b. 'Alí b. Sahl. (48, 7). Apparently the son of 'Alí b. Sahl al-Iṣbahání (*ob.* 307 A. H.).

43. Iṣṭakhrí, Abú 'Imrán (211, 6). Contemporary with Abú Turáb al-Nakhshabí (*ob.* 245 A. H.).

44. Iṣṭakhrí, Yaḥyá (211, 8). Contemporary with Ibn 'Aṭá of Baghdád (*ob.* 309 A. H.).

---

1) On the other hand it is said in H. II, 310*b* that Abú Ja'far al-Ḥaddád

صحب ابا تراب واكابر العبّاد.

45. Jabala, Sheykh (287, 5). A Maghribí, contemporary with Abú ᶜAbdallah Aḥmad b. Yaḥyá al-Jallá (ob. 306 AH.).

46. Jaᶜfar al-Mubarqaᶜ (287, 11; 332, 11). Probably identical with Jaᶜfar ibn al-Mubarqaᶜ (N. 117), who was contemporary with Abú ᶜAbdallah al-Ḥuṣrí (q. v).

47. Jalájilí, al-Baṣrí (143, 15) [1]. Contemporary with Aḥmad b. Muḥammad al-Baṣrí = Ibn Sálim (see List of Authorities).

48. Ibn al-Karanbí, Abú Jaᶜfar, of Baghdád [2]. Teacher of Junayd and pupil of Abú ᶜAbdallah b. Abí Jaᶜfar al-Baráthí (H. II, 304b). H. II, 275b. N. 72.

49. Ibn al-Kátib, Abú ᶜAlí (206, 7). Q. 32. Sh. I, 148. N. 249.

50. Khawwáṣ, Abú Sulaymán. N. 286. See under Rází, Abú ᶜAbdallah Ḥusayn b. Aḥmad in the List of Authorities.

51. Kisá'í, Abú Bakr al-Dínawarí. A ṣaḥib of Junayd, whom he predeceased. N. 135.

52. Ibn al-Kurríní. See Ibn al-Karanbí.

53. Magházilí, Abú ᶜAlí (281, 19). Contemporary with Shiblí.

54. Magházilí, Isḥáq (195, 14). Contemporary with Bishr b. al-Ḥárith al-Ḥáfí (ob. 227 A. H.).

55. Magházilí, Abú Muḥammad (209, 9). Contemporary with Jaᶜfar al-Khuldí (ob. 348 A. H.). Cited in TA II 46,20 and 84, 6.

56. Makkí, Abu 'l-Ḥasan of Baṣra (165, 22). One of the author's contemporaries. Ibn Sálim refused to salute

---

1) This passage is cited by Qushayrí, 152, 11 foll.

2) Karanbí (cabbage-seller) is probably the correct form of the *nisba*, which appears in the MSS. of the *Lumaᶜ* as كرىنى and in the present edition as كُرّىنى. The reading كرىبى (*Iḥya*, Búláq, 1289 A. H. IV, 345, 26) is certainly false. According to H. and N. the name of this Ṣúfí is Ábú Jaᶜfar al-Karanbí but he is called Ibn al-Karanbí (N. p. 93, l. 2) in a story of him which also occurs in the *Lumaᶜ*, 337, 16 foll. Cf. the Introduction to *al-Hidāya 'ilā farā'iḍ al-qulúb*, ed. by Dr. A. S. Yahuda, p. 108.

him, on the ground that he had made himself celebrated by his fasting.

57. Ibn Mamlúla al-ʿAṭṭár al-Dínawarí (201, 14). According
to H. II, 327a, Muhammad b. Maʿrúf al-ʿAṭṭár, generally known as Mammúla, was the Imám of the
congregational mosque. He heard Traditions from
Yahyá b. Saʿíd al-Qaṭṭán (ob. 198 A. H.) and Yazíd
b. Hárún (ob. 206 A. H.). The Mosque of Mammúla
b. Maʿrúf is named after him.

58. Marandí, Husayn b. Jibríl (238, 1).

59. Márastání, Ibráhím. His full name is Abú Isháq Ibráhím b. Ahmad al-Márastání. He was a friend of Junayd. H. II, 308a, where the text is given of a letter
written to him by Junayd.

60. Marwazí, ʿAbdallah (178, 20). Contemporary with Abú
ʿAlí al-Ribáṭí (q. v.).

61. Ibn Masrúq, Abu 'l-ʿAbbás Ahmad b. Muhammad al-
Ṭúsí. Died at Baghdád in 298 or 299 A. H. Q. 27.
K. 146. N. 83. TA I, 115.

62. Ibn Masrúq, Muhammad al-Baghdádí (297, 5). Contemporary with Junayd (K. 415). Probably the same as
N°. 61.

63. Mimshádh al-Dínawarí. Died in 299 A. H. N. 88. TA
II, 157. Sh. I, 135.

64. Ibn al-Miṣrí, Husayn (198, 16). Contemporary with Junayd.

65. Ibn al-Muʿallim, Abú Bakr (208, 1). See the List of
Authorities under Khayyáṭ.

66. Muhammad b. Ahmad, Abu 'l-Hasan (292, 11) = Ahmad
b. Muhammad Abu 'l-Hasan = Ibn Sálim. See the
List of Authorities.

67. Muhammad b. Ismáʿíl (189, 9). Contemporary with Abú
Bakr al-Kattání (ob. 322 A. H.).

68. Muhammad b. Yaʿqúb (287, 11) = Ibn al-Farají.

69. Munádí, Abu 'l-Qásim, of Naysábúr. Contemporary with Abu l'-Ḥasan al-Búshanjí of Naysábúr (*ob.* 347 or 348 A. H.). Q. 125, 4 from foot and 126, 3.

70. Muqrí, Abú ʿAbdallah al-Rází (149, 16) = Abú ʿAbdallah b. al-Muqrí (191, 22). His full name is Abú ʿAbdallah Muḥammad b. Aḥmad b. Muḥammad al-Muqrí. He died in 366 A. H. TS 118*a*. N. 332. Sh. i, 166.

71. Abu 'l-Musayyib (207, 11). Contemporary with Abu 'l-Ḥusayn al-Darráj (*ob.* 320 A. H.).

72. Mushtúlí, Abú ʿAlí (158, 21). His full name is Abú ʿAlí Ḥasan b. ʿAlí b. Músá al-Mushtúlí. He was a pupil of Abú ʿAlí b. al-Katib and Abú Yaʿqúb al-Súsí. He died in 340 A. H. N. 250.

73. Ibn al-Muwaffaq, ʿAlí, of Baghdád (290, 18). He met Dhu 'l-Nún al-Miṣrí (*ob.* 245 A. H.). He performed more than fifty pilgrimages to Mecca. H. II, 301*a*. N. 108.

74. Ibn al-Muwallad = Raqqí.

75. Muzayyin, Abu 'l-Ḥasan. Died in 328 A. H. Q. 32. N. 188.

76. Muzayyin al-Kabír = Abu 'l Ḥasan al-Muzayyin. See A 528*a*, 3 from foot and foll. According to ʿAbdallah Anṣárí (N. p. 180, l. 18 foll.) there were two Ṣúfís named Abu 'l-Ḥasan al-Muzayyin. The elder, known as Muzayyin al-Kabír, was a native of Baghdád and was buried there. The younger, known as Muzayyin al-Ṣaghír, was also a native of Baghdád, but was buried at Mecca. Samʿání, on the other hand, says that Abu 'l-Ḥasan al-Muzayyin al-Kabír was buried at Mecca.

77. Muzayyin, Abú ʿUthmán (307, 20).

78. Naháwandí, Abu 'l-Qásim b. Marwán (288, 16). A *ṣáḥib* of Abú Saʿíd al-Kharráz (*ob.* 277 or 286 A. H.).

79. Naṣíbí, Abú ʿAbdallah (190, 1).

80. Nassáj, Abú Muḥammad (399, 1). 4th century.

81. Nawribátí, Abú ʿAlí (183, 7). Perhaps the same as Abú ʿAlí al-Ribátí (*q. v.*).

82. Nibájí, Abú ʿAbdallah (222, 12). His full name is Abú ʿAbdallah Saʿíd b. Yazíd al-Nibájí. He was contemporary with Dhu 'l-Nún (*ob.* 245 A. H.) and was one of the teachers of Aḥmad b. Abi 'l-Ḥawárí of Damascus (*ob.* 230 or 246 A. H.), who related anecdotes of him. H. II, 181*b*. A. 553*a*, 6. N. 86.

83. Qalánisí, Abú ʿAbdallah Aḥmad. He is said to have been the teacher of Junayd (175, 20), but this statement, which has been added by a corrector, is probably untrue. The answer given by him (176, 3) is ascribed in H. and in the *Kitáb al-Lumaʿ* itself (217, 16) to Abú Aḥmad al-Qalánisí. H. II, 256*a* and N. 111, merely relate how he saved his life by keeping a vow which he had made that he would never eat elephant's flesh.

84. Qalánisí, Abú Aḥmad Muṣʿab. He originally belonged to Merv but resided in Baghdád. Abú Saʿíd b. al-Aʿrábí associated with him. He died in 290 A. H. at Mecca. H. II, 299*b*. N. 109.

85. Qannád, Abu 'l-Ḥasan ʿAlí b. ʿAbd al-Raḥím. He related sayings of Ḥusayn b. Manṣúr al-Halláj (*ob.* 309 A.H.). A. 462*b*, 13.

86. Qarawí, Abú Jaʿfar (216, 5). One of the MSS. has Farwí.

87. Qarmísíní, al-Muẓaffar (191, 8). He was a *ṣáḥib* of ʿAbdallah b. Muḥammad al-Kharráz, who died before 320 A. H. Al-Muẓaffar died at Ramla (N. p. 113, l. 18). TS. 91*a*. Q. 32. N. 270. Sh. I, 150.

88. Qaṣṣáb, Abú Jaʿfar (205, 15). He resided at Ramla and was contemporary with Abú Saʿíd al-Kharráz (*ob.* 277 or 286 A. H.).

89. Qaṣṣáb, Muḥammad b. ʿAlí (24, 20). Teacher of Junayd.

90. Qaṣṣár, Muḥammad b. ʿAlí (199, 10). Probably these two names refer to the same person.

91. Qazzáz, Ḥasan al-Dínawarí. Contemporary with Mimshádh al-Dínawarí (*ob.* 299 A. H.).

92. Qurashí, Abú ʿAbdallah. His full name is Abú ʿAbdallah Muḥammad b. Saʿíd al-Qurashí. H. II, 310*a*, where a passage is quoted from a book by him entitled *Sharḥ al-tawḥíd.*

93. Raqqí, Ibráhím b. al-Muwallad. TS. and N. call him Abú Isḥáq Ibráhím b. Aḥmad b. al-Muwallad. He died in 342 A. H. TS. 94*b*. H. II, 317*b*. N. 265. Sh. I, 153.

94. Ibn Razʿán (?), Abu ʾl-Ḥasan (297, 13).

95. Ribáṭí, ʿAbdallah (328, 16). Contemporary with Abú Ḥafṣ al-Ḥaddád of Naysábúr (*ob.* 271 A. H.).

96. Ribáṭí, Abú ʿAlí (178, 20). A *ṣáḥib* of ʿAbdallah al-Marwazí. Perhaps identical with Ibráhím al-Ribáṭí of Herát (N. 18), who was a pupil of Ibráhím Sitanbah (N. 17), the contemporary of Abú Yazíd al-Bisṭámí (*ob.* 261 A. H.).

97. Ibn Rufayʿ al-Dimashqí (197, 20). Contemporary with Abú ʿAlí al-Rúdhabárí (*ob.* 322 A. H.).

98. Ṣáʾigh, Ibráhím (205, 2). He associated with Abú Aḥmad al-Qalánisí (*ob.* 290 A. H.).

99. Ṣáʾigh, Yúsuf (197, 16). Abú Bakr al-Zaqqáq (*q. v.*) met him in Egypt.

100. Samarqandí, Muḥammad b. al-Faḍl = Muḥammad b. al-Faḍl al-Balkhí (*ob.* 319 A. H.). Q. 24. K. 140. TA. II, 87. N. 119. Sh. I, 117.

101. Ṣaydalání, Abú Jaʿfar, of Baghdád. He was contemporary with Junayd and was one of the teachers of Abú Saʿíd b. al-Aʿrábí. He died in Egypt. N. 197.

102. Sijzí, Abú ʿAbdallah (191, 22). He associated with Abú Ḥafṣ al-Ḥaddád (*ob.* 271 A. H.). TS. 57*b*. H. II,

313*b*. N. 115. Sh. I, 132 (where الثبخرى is a mistake for السبزى).

103. Sindí, Abú ʿAlí. Abú Yazíd al-Bisṭámí (*ob.* 261 A. H.) learned from him the theory of *faná*. N. 43.

104. Ṣubayḥí, Abú ʿAbdallah, of Baṣra. He was a great ascetic and is said to have lived for thirty years in a cellar. H. gives his name as Abú ʿAbdallah al-Ḥusayn b. ʿAbdallah b. Bakr. Abú Nuʿaym al-Iṣbahání (*ob.* 430 A. H.). says that his father was a *ṣáḥib* of Ṣubayḥí, before the latter left Baṣra and settled at Sús. TS. 75*b*. H. II. 315*a*. N. 190. Sh. I, 136 (where الصنبى is a mistake for الصبيبى).

105. Sulamí, Aḥmad b. Muḥammad (185, 23). Contemporary with Abú ʿAbdallah al-Ḥuṣrí (*q. v.*).

106. Sulamí, Ismáʿíl (332, 13). Contemporary with Abú Bakr al-Zaqqáq (*q. v.*).

107. Súsí, Abú Yaʿqúb. He resided chiefly at Baṣra and Ubulla. He was the teacher of Abú Yaʿqúb al-Nahrajúrí (*ob.* 330 A. H.). N. 139.

108. Ṭabaristání, Abú ʿImrán (171, 15; 190, 16).

109. Ṭayálisí, Jaʿfar al-Rází. The *nisba* Ṭayálisí is conjectural. See notes at 288, 10; 336, 13; and 359, 6.

110. Ṭúsí, Abu ʾl-ʿAbbás Aḥmad b. Muḥammad == Ibn Masrúq al-Ṭúsí.

111. Ṭúsí, Muḥammad b. Manṣúr of Baghdád (183, 4). He was the teacher of Ibn Masrúq al-Ṭúsí, Abú Saʿíd al-Kharráz, and Junayd. N. 53.

112. ʿUkbarí, Abu ʾl-Faraj (252, 10). Contemporary with Shiblí.

113. ʿUmar b. Baḥr (260, 9). Contemporary with Shiblí.

114. Urmawí, al-Kurdí al-Ṣúfí. Perhaps identical with Abu ʾl-Ḥusayn al-Urmawí (N. 295), who was contemporary with Abú ʿAbdallah al-Rúdhabárí (*ob.* 369 A. H.).

115. Ibn Yazdániyár, Abú Bakr al-Ḥusayn b. ʿAlí, of Urmiya. He followed a 'path' of his own in Ṣúfism and came into conflict with Shiblí and other Sheykhs of ʿIráq whose doctrines he opposed. It is greatly to be regretted that the chapter which Sarráj devotes to him in the *Kitáb al-Lumaʿ* is wanting in both MSS. See p. ٢.v. TS. 94*a*. Q. 32. N. 219. Sh. I, 151.

116. Záhirábádhí, Abú Bakr (41, 10).

117. Zajjájí, Aḥmad b. Yúsuf (177, 3).

118. Zaqqáq, Abú Bakr. His full name is Abú Bakr Aḥmad b. Naṣr al-Zaqqáq al-Kabír al-Miṣrí. He was a contemporary of Junayd. Amongst his pupils were Abú Bakr al-Zaqqáq al-Ṣaghír of Baghdád and Abú Bakr al-Duqqí. Q. 25. N. 213. Sh. I, 117 (where الدقاق is a mistake for الرقاق).

119. Ibn Zírí (194, 2) = Abu 'l-Ḥusayn b. Zírí (272, 14). A *ṣáḥib* of Junayd.

120. Zurayq, Sheykh (287, 6). A Maghribí, contemporary with Abú ʿAbdallah b. al-Jallá (*ob*. 306 A. H.).

Until five years ago the *Kitáb al-Luma^c fi 'l-Taṣawwuf* (Ḥájjí Khálífa, ed. Fluegel, V 331, N°. 11178) was known only by its title. Since then two copies have come to light, one of which belongs to Mr. A. G. Ellis, while the other has recently been acquired by the British Museum (Or. 7710). Owing to the kindness of Mr. Ellis, the former MS. has remained in my hands from the date whom I began to prepare this edition until the last proof-sheets were corrected. The conditions under which the British Museum codex is accessible are not attractive to any one living at a distance from London, and I have to thank Dr. Barnett, Head of the Oriental Department, for the readiness with which he granted my request that he would allow me to have the MS. photographed. The photographs made by Mr. R. B. Fleming are so excellent that whatever inaccuracies may be found in the critical notes are probably due to me.

In the following description of these two MSS. I shall call Mr. Ellis's manuscript **A** and the British Museum manuscript **B**. They are similarly designated in the critical notes.

A contains 197 folios. The text of the *Kitáb al-Luma^c* (ff. 1*a*—193*b*) is preceded by a title-page, bearing the inscription كتاب اللمع للسرّاج فى التصوّف as well as a number of memoranda (mostly illegible) by different hands. Following the title-page is a full table of contents, beginning باب البيان باب فى ذكر من غلط فى الروح نمّت and ending عن علم التصوّف الفهرسة بحمد الله وعونه وبمنه وإلحمد لله ربّ العالمين وصلّى الله على سيّدنا محمّد وآله وسلم. The text is written with great distinctness, each page containing twenty-one lines, but diacritical points are left out frequently, and vowel-marks almost invariably.

A is dated the 10th of Rabí^c II, 683 A. H. = June 26th, 1284 A. D. The name of the copyist, Aḥmad b. Muḥammad al-Záhirí, occurs at the end of three of the four *samáᶜs* (**A** ff. 193*b*—196*a*) which he transcribed from a MS. dated the 7th of Shaᶜbán, 566 A. H. = April 15th, 1171 A. D. This MS. is the original (الاصل) of which **A** is a copy.

A is superior to **B** in all respects but that of age. There can be few manuscripts of the 13th century that are so well preserved. The ink seems to have lost scarcely anything of its firm and glossy blackness, and nearly every word is as clear as if it had been written yesterday. The margins have been curtailed by the binder's knife and honeycombed here and there by worms, so that a small portion of the numerous marginal notes has disappeared. These notes afford evidence of careful collation not only with the *aṣl*, to which I have referred above, but also with other MSS. of the work [1]). In some cases the scribe has copied *samáᶜs* (ff. 21*b*, 43*a*, 63*b*, 85*b*, 109*a*, 128*b*, 147*b*, 163*b*, 177*b*, 183*a*); on f. 139*b* he has supplied several words that were omitted in the *aṣl*. Most of the annotations, however, have been made by later hands; they are plentiful in the first half of the text but then become sparse. Unfortunately **A** has a lacuna (179*a*, last line) which probably covers between ten and fifteen folios, and **B** does not fill the gap. Five chapters have been wholly lost:

(1) Concerning the accusation of infidelity brought against Abu 'l-Ḥusayn al-Núrí in the presence of the Caliph.

(2) Concerning Abú Ḥamza al-Ṣúfí [2]).

(3) Concerning a number of Sheykhs who were charged with infidelity and persecuted.

(4) Concerning Abú Bakr ᶜAlí b. al-Ḥusayn (*read* al-Ḥusayn b. ᶜAlí) b. Yazdáníyár.

---

1) This is attested by such phrases as بلغ مقابلة , بلغ مقابلة وقرآءة, بلغ مقابلة وقرآ ءة . فقيل بأصله فصحّ ان شاء الله تعالى and بأصل معتمد.

2) Probably Abú Ḥamza Muḥammad b. Ibráhím al-Baghdádí (*ob.* 289 A.H.).

(5) Concerning Muḥammad b. Músá al-Farghání and some of his sayings.

The beginning of a sixth chapter, in explanation of the sayings of Wásiṭí [1]), has also disappeared.

B (British Museum, Or. 7710) is dated Jumádá II, 548 A. H. = August—September 1153 A. D. The text, though worm-eaten in many places, is written clearly and remains, on the whole, in a tolerable state of preservation. **B** contains 243 folios. After the *Bismillah* there is an incomplete table of contents (2a—b). The text begins in the middle of a sentence (3a, l. 1) and concludes (242b, l. 4 foll.) with a passage on love (maḥabbat), which is now for the most part illegible and which does not occur in **A**. This passage, however, covers less than a page. The omissions in **B** are very serious; as compared with **A**, it is defective to the extent of over a third of the text. Its arrangement is chaotic. The correct order is given in the second column of the following table, which also shows what portions of the text are missing.

A	**B**
A, fol. 1a, ll. 2—10.	B, om.
A, fol. 1a, ll. 10—16.	B, fol. 3a, ll. 1—11.
A, fol. 1a, l. 17—fol. 5b, l. 7.	B, om.
A, fol. 5b, l. 7—fol. 6a, l. 9.	B, fol. 3b, l. 1—fol. 4a, last line.
A, fol. 6a, l. 9—fol. 10b, l. 1.	B, om.
A, fol. 10b, l. 1—fol. 16b, l. 1.	B, fol. 4b, l. 1—fol. 15a, last line.
A, fol. 16b, l. 1—fol. 17a, l. 3.	B, om.
A, fol. 17a, l. 4—fol. 32a, l. 7.	B, fol. 15b, l. 1—fol. 43a, last line.
A, fol. 32a, l. 7—fol. 41b, l. 15.	B, fol. 69b, l. 1—fol. 87b, l. 7.
A, fol. 41b, l. 15—fol. 62a, last line.	B, om.
A, fol. 62b, l. 1—fol. 63b, penult.	B, fol. 87b, l. 8—fol. 90a, last line.
A, fol. 63b, last line—fol. 68b, l. 10.	B, fol. 43b, l. 1—fol. 52a, last line.
A, fol. 68b, l. 10—fol. 69a, l. 12.	B, fol. 68b, l. 1—fol. 69a, last line.
A, fol. 69a, l. 12—fol. 95b, l. 8.	B, om.
A, fol. 95b, l. 8—fol. 105b, l. 12.	B, fol. 90b, l. 1—fol. 109b, l. 1.
A, fol. 105b, l. 12—fol. 108b, l. 2.	B, fol. 232a, l. 6—fol. 238a, last line.

---

1) Abú Bakr al-Wásiṭí, the same person as Muḥammad b. Músá al-Farghání mentioned in the preceding chapter. See List of Ṣúfís under Farghání.

A, fol. 108*b*, l. 2—fol. 109*a*, l. 16.   B, fol. 239*b*, l. 1—fol. 241*a*, last line.

A, fol. 109*a*, l. 16—fol. 109*b*, l. 12.   B, fol. 238*b*, l. 1—fol. 239*a*, last line.

A, fol. 109*b*, l. 13—fol. 112*b*, l. 8.   B, fol. 62*b*, l. 1—fol. 68*a*, last line.

A, fol. 112*b*, l. 9—fol. 113*b*, l. 4.   B, fol. 54*b*, l. 1—fol. 56*a*, last line.

A, fol. 113*b*, l. 5—fol. 114*a*, l. 7.   B, fol. 241*b*, l. 1—fol. 242*a*, last line.

A, fol. 114*a*, l. 8—fol. 115*b*, l. 4.   B, fol. 52*b*, l. 1—fol. 54*a*, last line.

A, fol. 115*b*, l. 5—fol. 119*a*, l. 19.   B, fol. 56*b*, l. 1—fol. 62*a*, last line.

A, fol. 119*a*, penult.—fol. 147*b*, l. 2.   B, fol. 131*a*, last line—fol. 191*a*, l. 4.

A, fol. 147*b*, l. 2—fol. 153*a*, l. 18.   B, fol. 109*b*, l. 2—fol. 122*a*, l. 10.

A, fol. 153*a*, l. 18—fol. 172*a*, l. 8.   B, fol. 191*a*, l. 4—fol. 230*a*, last line.

A, fol. 172*a*, l. 8—fol. 172*b*, l. 10.   B, om.

A, fol. 172*b*, l. 10—fol. 173*a*, last line.   B, fol. 230*b*, l. 1—fol. 232*a*, l. 6.

A, fol. 173*a*, last line—fol. 178*a*, l. 2.   B, fol. 122*a*, l. 10—fol. 131*a*, penult.

A, fol. 178*a*, l. 3—fol. 193*b*, l. 4.   B, om.

A, om.   B, fol. 242*b*, ll. 4—17.

As regards the provenance of the present text of the *Kitáb al-Lumaᶜ*, in the opening lines of **A** (p. ١, ll. ١.—١ in this edition) it is stated that the text was put together by an anonymous editor from written materials which were communicated to him by several persons residing in Baghdád and Damascus, all of whom derived their information from Abu 'l-Waqt ᶜAbd al-Awwal b. ᶜÍsá al-Sijzí; and that Abu 'l-Waqt obtained his text in 465 A. H. from Aḥmad b. Abí Naṣr al-Kúfání, who in turn received it from Abú Muḥammad al-Ḥasan b. Muḥammad al-Khabúshání, presumably a pupil of the author.

This *isnád* will not bear examination. According to the *Shadharát al-Dhahab*, Abu 'l-Waqt died in 553 A. H. at the age of ninety-five, [1]) so that he was only seven years

_____

1) Under 553 A. H. the *Shadharát* gives the following account of Abu 'l-Waqt:

وفيها توفّى مسند الدنيا ابو الوقت عبد الاوّل بن عيسى السجزى ثمّ الهروى المالينى

الصوفى الزاهد سمع الصحيح ومسند الدارى وعَيْد ابن حميد (157 ,Brockelmann i)

من جمال الاسلام الداودى (.467 A. H .*ob*) فى سنة خمس وستّين واربعاية وسمع من

ابى عاصم الفُضَيْلى (.471 A. H .*ob*) ومحمّد بن ابى مسعود وطايفة وصحب شيخ الاسلام

الانصارى وخدمه وعُمّر الى هذا الوقت وقدم بغداد فازدحم الخلق عليه وكان خيّرًا

متواضعا متودّدا حسن السمت متين الديانة محبّا للرواية توفّى فى سادس ذى القعدة

ببغداد وله خمس وتسعون سنة قاله فى العِبر وقال ابن شهبة فى تاريخ الاسلام حمله ابوه

old at the time when Kúfání is alleged to have transmitted
the text to him. [1]) Moreover, Kúfání died at Herát in 464
A. H. [2]) Then, as regards the persons (four men and one
woman) whom the anonymous editor mentions by name as
his immediate authorities, we learn from the *Ṭabaqát al-
Ḥanábila* of Ibn Rajab that Abu 'l-Qásim ᶜAlí, the son of
Abu 'l-Faraj ᶜAbd al-Raḥmán Ibn al-Jawzí, died in 630
A.H. at the age of eighty [3]). He was therefore born in 550
A. H., three years before the death of Abu 'l-Waqt, and
could not possibly have received information from him. A
further anachronism is involved in the appearance of a
great-grandson of the Caliph Mutawakkil as one of the five
reporters of the text. Mutawakkil died in 247 A. H., and
even if we allow 50 years for each generation we only
reach 400 A. H.

At the end of **A** (ff. 193*b*, 16 — 196*a*, 8) the copyist,
Aḥmad b. Muḥammad al-Ẓáhirí, has transcribed four *samáᶜs*,
which he found in his original.

The first of these was copied in an abridged form by
Ibn Yaḥyá [4]) in 566 A. H. It gives the names of seven per-

من هراة الى بوسنج فسمع صحيح البخارى وغيره من جمال الاسلام الداودى عزم على
الحج وهيّأ ما يحتاج اليه فاصبح ميّتا وكان آخر كلمة قالها يا ليت قوى يعلمون بما غفر
لى ربى وجعلنى من المكرمين ودُفن بالشونيزيّة وعُمّر حتى أَلْحَقَّ الاصاغر بالاكابر انتهى

1) The *Shadharát*, it will be noticed, makes the almost equally incredible
statement that in the same year (465 A. H.) Abu 'l-Waqt attended lectures
on the *Ṣaḥíḥ* of Bukhárí and other books of Traditions.

2) Yáqút, ed. by Wüstenfeld, IV 321, 14 foll. The *Lumaᶜ* gives Abú Naṣr
as his *kunya*, but Yáqút reads Abú Bakr; which is confirmed by the *samáᶜs*
written on the margin of A. For Abu 'l-Waqt al-Baḥrí (l. 16) read Abu
'l-Waqt al-Sijzí.

3) I owe these details to Mr. A. G. Ellis, who possesses a MS. of the
Ṭabaqát al-Ḥanábila. He adds that in the life of Ibn al-Jawzí (*ob*. 597 A.H.)
it is stated that his eldest son, ᶜAbd al-ᶜAzíz, received instruction from Abu
'l-Waqt and Muḥammad b. Náṣir al-Silafí (*ob*. 550 A. H.). This is quite possible, since ᶜAbd al-ᶜAziz died in 554 A. H. during his father's lifetime.

4) Abu 'l-Maᶜálí Aḥmad b. Yaḥyá b. Hibatallah al-Bayyiᶜ. He seems to
have been the owner of the original MS. from which A was copied. See below.

sons, including Abu 'l-Waqt al-Sijzí, who heard a portion of the *Kitáb al-Lumaᶜ* in 465 A. H. The name of the person from whom they heard it is not mentioned. [1]

The second was copied by ᶜAbd al-ᶜAzíz b. Maḥmúd b. al-Akhḍar [2] at an unspecified date. It gives the names of twenty-five persons (headed by Abu 'l-Maᶜálí Aḥmad b. Yaḥyá b. Hibatallah) who heard the whole of the *Kitáb al-Lumaᶜ* in a series of sessions which were completed on the 12th of Rabíᶜ II, 553 A. H. The names of two persons are added who attended every session except one. The text which these twenty-seven persons heard was read to them by Sheykh Abu 'l-Fatḥ Yúsuf b. Muḥammad b. Muqallad al-Dimashqí on the authority of Abu 'l-Waqt al-Sijzí, from Kúfání, from Khabúshání.

The third *samáᶜ* contains the names of a hundred and forty persons to whom the entire text, as derived from Abu 'l-Waqt, was read by Abu 'l-Faḍl b. Sháfiᶜ during a number of sessions, the last of which took place on the 9th of Shaᶜbán, 553 A. H. Many of these names are illegible. Among them occurs the name of ᶜAbd al-Razzáq, the fifth son of ᶜAbd al-Qádir al-Jílí. ᶜAbd al-Qádir died in 561 A. H. ᶜAbd al-Razzáq (born 528 A. H.; died 623 A. H.) was twenty-five years of age when he heard the *Kitáb · al-Lumaᶜ* on this occasion.

The fourth *samáᶜ* enumerates thirty-one persons, including two women, who heard Abu 'l-Waqt's text of the whole volume. At the head of the list stands the well-known author of the *Ádáb al-murídin*, Abu 'l-Najíb ᶜAbd al-Qáhir b. ᶜAbd-

---

[1] The same *samáᶜ* is given more fully in various places on the margin of A (see p. XXXV *supra*), each record covering a certain portion of the text. These marginal *samáᶜs* name Abú Bakr al-Kúfání as the authority for the text and Abú Ḥafṣ ᶜUmar al-Faráwí as the reader.

[2] MS. ﺍﻻﺧﺼﺮ, The penultimate letter is clearly *ṣád*, not *mím*.

dallah al-Suhrawardí (*ob.* 563 A. H.), with his sons ᶜAbd al-Raḥím and ᶜAbd al-Laṭíf. The reader was Yúsuf b. Muḥammad b. Muqallad al-Dimashqí (already mentioned in the second *samáᶜ*), and the last meeting was held on the 11th of Rajab, 553 A. H. The *samáᶜ* ends with the following words:

نقله احمد بن محمّد الظاهرى فى يوم الاربعآء عاشر ربيع الآخر من سنة
ثلث وثمانين وستّمابة كما شاهده على نسخة ابى المعالى احمد بن يحيى البيّع
بخطّه وصحّ

It seems to me likely that the *isnád* is a fiction based upon the *samáᶜs*. The date 465 A. H. occurs in the first *samáᶜ*; those written in the margin of **A** record that Kúfání's text of the *Lumaᶜ* was read to Abu 'l-Waqt in that year; and in the second *samáᶜ* it is asserted that Kúfání derived his text from Khabúshání. For reasons indicated above, I do not see how we can accept the statement that Abu 'l-Waqt received the text from Kúfání himself or that he heard it from any one as early as 465 A. H.; but he may have received it at a later date from one of Kúfání's pupils. The list given in the *isnád* of five persons who are said to have transmitted Abu 'l-Waqt's text to the anonymous editor is discredited on chronological grounds and also lacks external authority. None of those five names appears in the *samáᶜs*.

Had the authenticity of the text been doubtful, I should have felt myself obliged to print the *samáᶜs* in full, since they might have helped us to settle the question one way or the other. But there is nothing in the book, as it stands, to support or justify such a suspicion, and the evidence from outside is equally convincing. Qushayrí in his *Risála* (437 A. H.) cites many passages from the *Lumaᶜ* which agree with our text. Hujwírí, writing twenty or thirty years later, made free use of the work, and he quotes verbatim a passage on *adab*, which occurs in the present edition, p. ١٤٢, l. ١٩,

foll. [1]) The *Kitáb al-Luma*ᶜ is one of the sources of Ghazzálí's
Iḥyá. [2]) M. Louis Massignon has called my attention to a
passage in the *Ṭabaqát al-Sháfiᶜiyyat al-Kubrá* of Subkí
(Cairo, 1324 A. H., part V, p. 123, ll. 13—19), where Sarráj
is cited by Abu 'l-Qásim al-Ráfiᶜí as impugning the genuineness
of the Ḥadíth, "Lo, a veil is drawn over my heart and I
ask pardon of God a hundred times every day." This refers
to *Luma*ᶜ, p. ٣٧٣, l. ١٥, foll. (under الغين). [3]) Another passage
of the *Luma*ᶜ (p. ٣٠٣, l. ٢., foll.) was cited in the lost *Ta'-
ríkh al-Ṣúfiyya* of Sulamí (*ob.* 412 A. H.), whence it was
extracted by Khaṭíb and published by him in the *History
of Baghdád* [4]).

The description of the two MSS. which has been given
above will sufficiently explain my decision to make **A** the
basis of the present edition, notwithstanding its relative inferiority in age. Although, as a rule, the textual differences
are unimportant, I have recorded almost every variation,
however trivial, so that the reader practically has both texts
before him. The readings of **A** have been followed throughout
except in a comparatively small number of instances which
will be found in the foot-notes.

---

1) See *Kashf al-Maḥjúb*, Lucknow ed., 265, 8 foll. = my translation, p.
341. The same passage is cited by Qushayrí, 153, 5 foll. and in Persian by
ᶜAṭṭár, *Tadhkirat al-Awliyá*, II, 183, 15—21, and Jámí, *Nafaḥát al-Uns*,
320, 7—14.

2) Sarráj is cited by name in the *Iḥyá* (Búláq, 1289 A.H.), II, 278, 6. The
passage following, which has been translated by Prof. D. B. Macdonald in
JRAS for 1901, p. 745, is an abridgment of *Luma*ᶜ, p. ٢٨١, l. ١., foll.
Two quotations from Abú Saᶜíd b. al-Aᶜrábí (*Luma*ᶜ, p. ٣٠٢, ll. ١.——١ and p.
٣١., ll. ١١—٣) occur in the *Iḥyá*, II, 269, 17—29 = *JRAS ibid.*, p. 720. The
extent of Ghazzálí's debt to Sarráj may be estimated by comparing the chapters in the *Luma*ᶜ that treat of music and ecstasy with the corresponding
portion of the *Iḥyá*.

3) According to Ráfiᶜí the Tradition in question was described by Sarráj as
حديث منكر, but the words used in the *Luma*ᶜ are خبر ضعيف.

4) See Massignon, *Quatre textes inédits, relatifs à la biographie a'al-Ḥosayn
ibn Manṣour al-Ḥallāj*, p. 25*, Nᵒ. 23.

The omission of words or passages in one of the MSS. is always noted, but I have not thought it necessary to record every occasion when words which occur in **B** have been supplied in **A** by a later hand.

As regards spelling, the printed text does not retain all the peculiarities of the MSS., *e. g.* such forms as معانى for اغنا ,تدعو for ندعو ,اغنى ,معانٍ for أَغْنَى. *Hamza* very rarely appears in the MSS., but I have generally restored it. Where it has been added over a medial *yá*, the dots under that letter are allowed to stand: thus, ملائكة (the MSS. write ملايكة). I must admit that my practice in this respect is not entirely consistent, for sometimes the MS. spelling has been left unaltered, as سُئِلَ = سيل. *Yá* is often substituted for *alif hamzatum* in the final radical of the verb. *e. g.* اوى = أَوْمَأَ, أَبْطَأَ = ابطى, and consequently we meet with many incorrect forms, *e. g.* تبريه = تَبَرُّوهُ, التجوا = إِلْتَجَأُوا, اطفوها = أَطْفَأُوها, تهنيه = تَهْنِئَهُ. In such cases the MS. readings have been retained.

One can only conjecture how far the author shares with his copyists responsibility for the numerous grammatical mistakes and irregularities which are found in the MSS. As he says (p. ١٢٢ l. ١٩ foll.), the *adab* of the Ṣúfís is not philological but theosophical; and though we may acquit him of gross blunders, it is more than likely that his knowledge of Arabic grammar was imperfect, and that in writing the language he did not observe all the niceties appropriate to a high standard of literary composition. The most common errors and solecisms may be classified as follows: Use of the accusative instead of the nominative (ين — instead of ون—), and of the nominative instead of the accusative (especially after إِنَّ); omission of the *ʿáʾid*, with or without a preposition, after ما and الذى (19, 8; 95, 19; 154, 6, 16; 198, 2;

282, 4; 313, 4; 406, 5, *etc.*); use of the plural verb when it precedes a plural subject (17, 1; 18, 2; 158, 22; 165, 9; further examples in the foot-notes); use of the Imperfect in the apodosis of conditional sentences (116, 19; 165, 18 *et passim*); use of the Indicative instead of the Subjunctive; omission of ف after أما. With regard to these irregularities and others of the same kind, I have acted on the principle that while an editor is bound to correct flagrant faults of syntax, it is no part of his business to improve the author's style.

But the chief difficulties of the *Kitáb al-Lumaᶜ* are not essentially linguistic; they arise from the subtlety and abstruseness of the ideas which mystical writers have to express. In their effort to express such ideas the Ṣúfís often employ language that no grammarian can make intelligible, though it undoubtedly suggests a meaning to the initiated: it may be comprehended as a whole, but will not bear logical analysis. A text of this character is peculiarly liable to corruption and almost beyond the reach of emendation. The critic is disarmed when the notions presented to him are so obscure and elusive that he cannot draw any sharp line between sense and nonsense, or convince himself that one reading is superior to another.

For a large portion of the book we have to depend on a single MS., and there are many passages which the author cannot have written exactly as they now stand. The mystical verses are sometimes unmetrical as well as corrupt. I have done my best to alleviate the difficulties of the text, without altering it except in a few places where the remedy seemed to be fairly obvious. That it requires further correction is evident, but in editing a work of this description for the first time, conjectural emendation is only justified when it can claim a high degree of probability.

The Abstract of Contents will, I believe, be found useful both by those who wish to refer to the original and by those who do not read Arabic but are interested in the study of Muḥammadan mysticism. It should be pointed out that the English Index (pp. 122—130) supplies references to the principal subjects discussed by Sarráj and also to the Arabic technical terms which he explains in the course of his work.

In the Glossary I have collected a number of words and forms which illustrate the author's somewhat unclassical style. Many of them occur in Dozy, but his examples of their usage are generally drawn from writers belonging to a much later period. The fact that Ṣúfism was largely a popular movement in close touch with the poorer and uneducated Moslems could not fail to lower its literary standards and vulgarise its vocabulary; but this is not entirely to be deplored. Unlike the philologists and lexicographers, the Ṣúfí authors availed themselves freely of the living and growing language of their time, and helped to overcome the academic influences which, if unchecked, would have raised a barrier against the extension and diffusion of Muḥammadan culture amongst those who needed it most.

The book has been printed with the accurate and finished workmanship that Orientalists have learned to expect from Messrs Brill, and though the list of Corrigenda and Addenda is a long one, there are few serious errors. For these I am responsible, but I hope they will be excused as misfortunes which befall the most careful proof-reader in moments of preoccupation or fatigue. It only remains to express once more my gratitude to Mr. A. G. Ellis for having placed at my disposal, without any restriction whatever, the manuscript that forms the basis of the present edition and is the unique authority for a large portion of the original text.

REYNOLD A. NICHOLSON.

ADDENDA ET CORRIGENDA.

Page	Line	
۴	۱۰	*For* وحلّاعا *read* وحلاعا.
٦	۱۹	*For* وجَيلهُ مِن جَيلهُ *read* وجَيلهُ مِن جَيلهُ.
۱۴	۱۰	*For* وأَمَارَاتِها *read* وأَمارَاتِها.
۱۴	۱۲	*Dele* the hamza *in* والنتبرئَ.
۱۸	۳	*For* واجب *read* واجبة.
۲۳	۱۲	(note ۱.) *For* يشار *read* بشار.
۲۵	٦	الجَوِيرى. Anṣárí in his commentary on the *Risála* of Qushayrí (I, 172, 1) says: الجَوِيرى بضم للجيم نسبة الى جَرِيرُ بن عبّاد مِن بنى بكر بن وائل. On the other hand, Faríduddín ʿAṭṭár (*Tadhkirat al-Awliyá*, II, 132, 3) rhymes جَوِيرى with بَصيرى, and though he is often at fault in historical matters, it seems to me that he is a more trustworthy authority than Anṣárí as regards the correct pronunciation of the *nisba*.
۲۸	۸	*For* الموحّد *read* الموحِّد.
۲۹	۸	*For* قدرته *read* قدرتِه.
۳۳	۱	*For* الانيّة *read* الأنّيّة.
۳۵	۳	*For* جبريل *read* جبريلاً.
۳۵	۱۹	*For* المعرفة *read* المعوفة.
۳۹	۱۹	*For* ظاعرٌ *read* ظاعرٌ. This saying in a somewhat different form is attributed by Qushayrí (12, 8) to Sarí al-Saqaṭí.

Page	Line	
٤٠	١٤	*For* يذلّ *read* يذلّ.
٤٨	19	يعرّض. The correct reading is probably يعارض. See Glossary.
٤٩	v	*For* صدقةُ *read* صدقةٌ.
٥٠	٢	*Dele* ا *after* لله.
٥٠	١٥	The accusative كذّابين, instead of the nominative, is contrary to rule, (Wright II, 85), but the author may have written it so.
٤٢	٩	*For* أرجأ *read* أرجى.
٤٨	١v	*For* العَبَر *read* العَبَر.
٤٩	v	„ „ „ „
٤٩	١٥	*For* والخصور *read* والخُصور.
٥٠	٩	*For* الخبَر *read* الخَبَر. Cf. Freytag, *Arabum Proverbia*, II, 421.
٧٤	٣	*For* ربةُ *read* ربّةً.
٩٩	٩	*For* شىء *read* شيئًا.
٩٨	١٣	*For* التّبيهان *read* التّيهان.
١١٤	٤	*For* وأمر *read* وأُمِر.
١١٤	١v	*For* جعل *read* جُعل (as in A).
١١٨	١٠	*For* جاحيفة *read* حاحيفة.
١٢١	٥	أصحاب has dropped out before رسول الله.
١٢٩	١v	*For* نُحبّ *read* نَحبّ.
١٢v	١٣	*For* آثَرَ *read* آثَر.
١٣٣	١٥	*Read* جماعة من اهل الصفّة.
١٣٣	19	*For* ترتفع (so A, but the points over the initial ت have been added by a later hand) *read* يرتفع.
١٣٥	٢	*For* الخبَر *read* الخَبَر.

Page	Line	
١٤٩	١	*For* ابن الكَرّبِىى *read* ابن الكَرَنْبِى. The same correction must be made on p. ١٨٢, l. ١., p. ١٨٨, l. ١٤, p. ١٩٨, l. ٨, p. ٢١., l. ٧, and p. ٣٣٧, l. ١٧. See the Introduction, p. XXVII n. 2.
١٤٩	٣	(note ٣). *For* تحاربوه *read* تحاربوه.
١٥٣	١٩	*For* فالاذبُ *read* فالاذبُ.
١٩٥	٤	*For* يَقْتَحُ *read* يَقْتَحُ.
١٩٨	٢٢	*Perhaps* لو اَظْفرتَنى الطَّرْفَ.
١٨٠	٧	*For* مُكجابك *read* مكانك.
١٨٤	١٢	*For* الكِسائى *read* الكتانى.
١٨٧	٦	I have little doubt that we should read من غير تذاهب and omit the words الى ذلك ولا تساكر. Cf. p. ٢٩١, l. ١, where read التساكر والتذاهب.
١٨٨	١٩	*For* اللَّبَد *read* اللَّبَد.
١٩٠	١٨	*Read* عِلمٍ يسوسه وورعٍ يحاجزه ووجدٍ يحمله وخُلق يصونه.
١٩٧	٢٠	*For* رَفِيع *read* رفِيع.
٢٠٤	١٥	*For* جُلوسًا *read* جُلوس.
٢٠٩	١٣	*For* غداة *read* الغداة.
٢٢١	١	*Perhaps* تملَّقتِ *instead of* تعلَّقتِ,
٢٢٢	٢	*Possibly* لَحظات *instead of* لدغات.
٢٢٢	٨	*Possibly* ملاحظات *instead of* ملادغات.
٢٢٤	٩	*Read* يَسْتَنوعَبُ حالُهُ.
٢٢٤	٢٠	A f. 102a should be printed opposite this line.
٢٢٥	٣	*For* لاشتغالها *read* لاشتمالها.
٢٣٢	٧	*Read* شَىءٌ *for* شَىّ.
٢٣٣	٤	*For* موقوفًا *read* موقوف.
٢٣٤	٨	*For* ابا عبد الله الروذبارى *read with* B ابا علىّ الروذبارى.

٢٣٥   ٤   *For* نَجَعْتَ *read* نَجَّعْتَ.

٢٣٥   ١٣   *For* انسك *read* آنَسَك.

٢٤٢   ٢   *For* حقيقة *read* حقيقةِ.

٢٤٢   ١٤   The *saj‘* suggests إِكْنَاتِها in the sense of "metaphorical description" or "symbolism".

٢٤٣   ١٧   For the construction بصالح العبيد *see* Wright, II, 218 CD.

٢٤٤   ٥   *Read* مُلَوَّحًا *for* تَلَوُّحِ.

٢٤٥   ٤   *Perhaps* مِن ذلك. Cf. p. ٢٤٩, l. ٩.

٢٤٨   ٥   The following verses occur thrice (pp. 22*, 33*, and 53*) in Massignon's *Quatre textes inédits, relatifs à la biographie d'al-Ḥosayn ibn Mansour al-Ḥalláj*, where they are attributed to Ḥalláj himself. QT. gives eight verses, and the order is different from that in the *Luma‘*. The variants that seem to me worth noting are these:

٢٤٨, ٩ سحائب الوحى فيها.

٢٤٨, ٨ اودى وتذكارِه.

٢٤٨, ٩ أَسْمَاعُ *for* اقوال.

٢٤٨, ١٠ من مكمد الكظم, but in the third version مِن ممكن (*sic*) لكظم.

٢٤٨   ٩   *Read* فيها *with* B.

٢٤٨   ١٢—١٣   In the *Kashkúl* (Búláq, 1288 A. H.), p. 118, l. 26, these verses are attributed to Ḥalláj.

٢٥٤   ٥   The metre of this verse requires لأَنَّ ذا تَعَاجِيبُ whereas in the remaining verses the rhyme-letter must be pronounced with the *i‘ráb*. Moreover, the rhymes are highly irregular, although the MSS. present an appearance of uniformity, which has been obtained at the expense of grammar.

Page   Line

٢٥٤   ٥   *For* يَجْتَمِعَنْ = يَجْتَمِعَا *read* يَجْتَمِعَا.

٢٥٤   ٢٠.—١٩   These verses are cited by Qushayrí (95, 4 foll.). together with the opening verse:

$$\text{أَعَابُكَ أَنْ أَبْدَى إِلَيْكَ الَّذِى أَخْفَى } * \text{ وَسِرَّى يُبْدِى مَا يَقُولُ لَهُ طَرْفِى}$$

See the supercommentary by Muṣṭafá al-ʿArúsí on Za-kariyyá al-Anṣárí's *Sharḥ al-Risálat al-Qushayriyya*, III, 62, 2 foll.

٢٥٤   ١٩   *Read* بِالْفَهْمِ مِنْكَ عَنِ الْكَشْفِ.

٢٥٤   ٢٠   *Read* تَلَطَّفْتَ فِى أَمْرِى فَأَبْدَأْتَ شَاهِدِى. Qushayrí has فَأَبْدَيْتِ.

٢٩٢   ٢١   *For* بزيد *read* يزيد.

٢٩٣   ١١   It is unnecessary to alter the reading of the MSS. لاجِى = لاجِّى, but cf. the Introduction, p. XLII.

٢٩٩   ٢   *For* الْمُهَلَّب *read* الْمُهَلَّب.

٣٠٥   ٩   *For* بانشاد *read* بإسناد.

٢٧٩   ١٣   (note ١٤). *For* Aghání, IV 21 foll. *read* Aghání, IV 39, 21 foll.

٢٧٨   ٥   *For* مُطَّرَح *read* (probably) مُطَّرِدٌ.

٢٨٧   ١   *For* تُرَاكَ *read* يَرَاكَ. Cf. ٢١., ٤

٢٨٨   ١.   (note ٨). *Dele* the reference to the *Ansáb*. The person noticed there, Abú ʿAbdallah Muḥammad al-Ṭayálisí al-Rází, cannot be identified with this Ṣúfí, whose name is Jaʿfar (cf. ٣٥٩, ٥).

٢٩١   ١   *For* انتساكر *read* انتساكن.

٢٩٣   ١١   *For* محمّد بن احمد *read* احمد بن محمّد = Abu 'l-Ḥasan Aḥmad b. Muḥammad b. Sálim.

٣٠٧   ٦   *For* فيد *read* فيها.

٣٢٥   ١٥   *For* تضىء *read* تضىء.

٣٣٣   ٢   *For* الجارنة *read* الجارية.

٣٣٣   ٧   *For* وانتساكر *read* وانتساكن.

Page	Line	
۳۳۳	۱۲	*For* والنَّقْس *read* والنَّفْس.
۳۵۸	۹	It seems probable that أَنْمَسَ and the following verbs should be read as Imperatives. In this case أَخْفِ must be substituted for أَخْفَى and اقْطَعْ for قطع.
۳۹۰	۱۷	*For* الاشياۤءَ *read* الاشياۤء. Cf. ۳۹۹, ۸
۳۷۱	۴	*For* نعطَفُ *read* نعطِفُ.
۳۹۲	۱۲	*For* وجَّهْتُ *read* وجَّهتُ.
۳۹۴	۱۷	*For* تفضّلونى *read* تفضّلونى.
۴۰۳	۱	*Perhaps* محدثانِ بلا حدّ.
۴۰۳	۹	Grammar requires واحدة.
۴۰۵	۲۳	*Read* والحال نازلة الخ.
۴۰۹	۱۱	*Read* فان ملأنا كذى ففى النار وان ملأنا كذى ففى النار (Cf. ۲۹۹, ۱۰).
۴۱۰	۸	*Cf.* الطايفات الذين غلطوا. Cf. الفرقة الذين غلطوا (۴۱۱, ۱۵).
۴۱۱	۷	*Read* الطبقات الثلث.
۴۱۳	۸	*Read* حجاب للفقير.
۴۱۴	۱۲	*Perhaps* المتمسّكين may stand. Cf. التمسّك بالاشدّ من المتمسّكين الطاعات (۱۳۹, ۹).
۴۲۳	۹	*Read* عيسى *for* موسى.

ABSTRACT OF CONTENTS.

78	9	For *laqá* read *liqá*.

KITÁB AL-LUMA'

ABSTRACT OF CONTENTS.

1 The anonymous editor mentions the names of several persons (four residing in Baghdád and one in Damascus) through
whom the text of the *Kitáb al-Luma*ᶜ was transmitted to
him. All of them derive it from the same authority, namely,
Abu 'l-Waqt ᶜAbd al-Awwal b. ᶜÍsá b. Shuᶜayb b. Isḥáq al-
Sijzí al-Ṣúfí al-Harawí al-Málíní, who received it in 465 A. H.
from his teacher Abú Naṣr [1]) al-Kúfání, to whom it was
communicated by Abú Muḥammad al-Khabúshání. Doxology.
Praise to God, who has endowed the elect among His servants with various degrees of knowledge and understanding
of Himself. The whole of knowledge is comprised in three
sources, (*a*) the Koran, (*b*) the Traditions of the Prophet,
2 (*c*) that which is revealed to the Saints. Blessings on the
Prophet and his family. Preface. The author describes the
nature of the present work. It is a treatise on the principles
and sciences of Ṣúfism, including an account of the traditions and poems of the Ṣúfís, their questions and answers,
their 'stations' and 'states', their peculiar symbolism and
technical terms. The author has indicated the salient features
of each topic to the best of his power. He writes as an
orthodox Moslem and begs his readers to study the work
in a spirit of pious devotion and friendliness towards the

---

1) This should be Abú Bakr.

a

Ṣúfís, who, though few in number, are highly esteemed and
honoured by God. Some knowledge of the principles, aims,
and method of genuine Ṣúfís is necessary in this age, in
order that they may be distinguished from the impostors
3 who appropriate their name and dress. Description of the
genuine Ṣúfís, whose hearts God has vivified by gnosis and
whose bodies He has adorned with worship, so that they
have renounced all things for His sake. Many of the author's
contemporaries were only theoretically acquainted with Ṣúfism,
yet they composed pretentious books on the subject. This
contrasts unfavourably with the behaviour of the eminent
Ṣúfís of old who did not discourse upon mystical questions
until they had undergone austerities and had mortified their
passions and had endeavoured to cut every tie that hindered
them from attaining to God, and who combined theory with
4 perfection of practice. The author states that he has often suppressed the *isnáds* and abridged the text of the traditions
and anecdotes in this volume. He has recorded the answers
and sayings of the ancient Ṣúfís inasmuch as these enable
him to do without the ostentatious discussions in which contemporary writers indulge. God is the enemy of any one
who embellishes or clothes in different language a mystical
thought belonging to the ancients and attributes it to himself for the purpose of winning fame or popularity.

CHAPTER I: "Explanation of the science of Ṣúfism and
the doctrine of the Ṣúfís and their position in regard to
the *ʿulamá*."

The author was asked, by some one who pointed out
that many diverse opinions were held concerning Ṣúfism,
5 to explain the principles of its doctrine and to show by
argument how it is connected with the Koran and the Apostolic
Traditions. He replies by quoting Kor. 3, 16, where the most
excellent of the believers and those of the highest rank in
religion are described as "the possessors of knowledge"

(*ulu 'l-ᶜilm*). Similarly, Muḥammad said that the savants (*ᶜulamá*) are the heirs of the prophets. The author divides these *ᶜulamá* into three classes: the Traditionists (*aṣḥáb al-ḥadíth*), the Jurists (*fuqahá*), and the Ṣúfís. Corresponding to these three classes there are three kinds of religious knowledge: knowledge of the Koran, knowledge of the Sunna,

6 and knowledge of the realities of Faith. The last is identical with *iḥsán* (well-doing), which, according to the definition imparted to the Prophet by Gabriel, consists in "worshipping God as though thou sawest Him, for if thou seest Him not, yet He sees thee." Knowledge is joined with action, and action with sincerity (*ikhláṣ*), and sincerity is this, that a man should seek God alone (*wajh Allah*) with his knowledge and his actions. The three classes mentioned above differ in their theory and practice and spiritual rank, each possessing characteristics peculiar to itself, as the author

7 now proceeds to explain.

CHAPTER II: "Description of the classes of Traditionists, their system of transmission, their critical sifting of the Ḥadíth, and their special knowledge of it."

The Traditionists attached themselves to the external form of the Ḥadíth, and regarding this as the foundation of religion they travelled to all parts of the world and sought out the relaters of Traditions, from whom they handed down stories about the Prophet and his Companions. They took pains to verify all the information that they received, to discover whether the relaters were trustworthy or not, to arrange the materials which they had collected, and to distinguish the genuine Traditions from those which were of doubtful

8 authority. In this critical investigation some achieved greater success than others and gained such a reputation for learning that their testimony as to what the Prophet said and did and commanded and forbade was universally accepted. The Prophet prayed that God would make radiant the face of

any man who heard an Apostolic Tradition and transmitted
it: hence all Traditionists, it is said, have shining faces.

CHAPTER III: "Account of the classes of Jurists and the
various sciences with which they are specially endowed."

9 It is the function of the Jurists to study, interpret, and codify
the Ḥadíth — a task in which they are guided by the Koran, the Sunna, the consensus of public opinion, and analogy.

10 CHAPTER IV: "Account of the Ṣúfís, their theory and
practice, and the excellent qualities by which they are characterised."

The Ṣúfís agree with the Traditionists and Jurists in their
beliefs and accept their sciences and consult them in difficult matters of religious law. Should there be a difference
of opinion, the Ṣúfís always adopt the principle of following
the strictest and most perfect course; they venerate the
commandments of God and do not seek to evade them.
Such is their practice in regard to the formal sciences handled
by the Traditionists and Jurists, but having left these behind
they rise to heights of mystical devotion and ethical self-
11 culture which are exclusively their own.

CHAPTER V: "Account of the moral culture and spiritual
feelings of the Ṣúfís, and of the sciences in which the other
ᶜulamá have no share."

The first point of distinction is that the Ṣúfís renounce
what does not concern them, i. e. everything that hinders
them from attaining the object of their quest, which is God
only. In the next place, they possess many moral, ascetic,
and mystical qualities. Enumeration of these (pp. 11—13).

13 CHAPTER VI: "How the Ṣúfís are distinguished from the
ᶜulamá in other respects."

The Ṣúfís are specially distinguished by their practical
application of certain verses of the Koran and Traditions
which inculcate noble qualities and lofty feelings and excellent actions such as formed part of the Prophet's nature

and character. The *ʿulamá* and the jurists acknowledge the truth of these verses and Traditions without studying them closely and drawing forth their inmost meaning, but the Ṣúfís realise the qualities and feelings referred to, *e. g.*, 14 repentance, abstinence, patience, fear, hope, etc., so that each of these 'states' is represented by a special class of persons who attain to diverse degrees therein. Again, the Ṣúfís are distinguished by self-knowledge, for they examine themselves in order to detect any trace of hypocrisy and secret lust and latent polytheism, that they may escape from those evils and take refuge with God. Finally, they have derived from the Koran and the Traditions mystical sciences which it is hard for the jurists and *ʿulamá* to under-15 stand. Examples are given. The Ṣúfís are distinguished from the rest of the *ʿulamá* by grappling with these recondite questions and solving them and speaking about them with the certainty that comes of immediate experience. The whole of Ṣúfism is to be found in the Koran and the Traditions of the Prophet, a fact which is not denied by the *ʿulamá* when they investigate it. Those who deny it are the formalists who recognise in the Koran and the Traditions only the external ordinances and whatever will serve them in controversy with opponents. The author laments that in his time this formal theology, inasmuch as it offered a ready means of obtaining power and worldly success, was far more popular than Ṣúfism, which involves bitterness and anguish and self-mortification.

16   CHAPTER VII: "Refutation of those who maintain that the Ṣúfís are ignorant, and that the Koran and the Traditions supply no evidence in favour of Ṣúfism."

The Koran mentions numerous classes of men and women endowed with particular qualities, *e. g.* "the sincere", "the patient", "those who trust in God", "the friends of God", etc.

In the Traditions, too, we find examples not only of

special classes but also of individuals who are described as peculiarly holy, such as ʿUmar b. al-Khaṭṭáb, al-Bará, Wábiṣa, Uways al-Qaraní, and Ṭalq b. Ḥabíb. The circumstance that these men, though included among the Faithful, are set apart 17 by special designations, indicates their distinction from the mass of believers. Moreover, the prophets, who occupy a more exalted position before God than the persons above-mentioned, are allowed by the greatest religious authorities to have been like common men in respect of eating and sleeping and the ordinary events of life. The distinction enjoyed by the prophets and by these holy persons was the result of their intimate communion with God and their exceeding faith in His Word; but the prophets are distin-guished from the rest by inspiration (waḥy), the apostolic office, and evidences of prophecy.

CHAPTER VIII: "Account of the objection raised by the Ṣúfís against those who claim the title of jurist or divine (faqíh), together with an argument showing what is meant by 'understanding in religion' (al-fiqh fi 'l-dín)."

Tradition: "when God wishes to confer a blessing on any one, He gives him understanding in religion." Definition of faqíh by Ḥasan of Baṣra. Religion is a term comprehending all the commandments, both outward and inward, and the endeavour to understand the mystical 'states' and 'stations' mentioned above is no less profitable than the endeavour to become expert in legal knowledge. The latter is seldom required and can be obtained from a lawyer whenever the 18 occasion for it arises, but knowledge of the 'states' and 'stations' in which the Ṣúfís strive to become proficient is obligatory upon all believers at all times. The lore deduced (from the Koran and the Traditions) by the Ṣúfís must be more abundant than the legal deductions drawn by the divines from the same source, because the mystical science is infinite, whereas all other sciences are finite.

CHAPTER IX: "The permissibility of a special endowment
19 in the religious sciences, and the exclusive possession of
every science by its representatives. Confutation of those
who arbitrarily refuse to recognise a particular science instead of referring the question to the experts in that science."

Some ʿulamá deny that there is any special endowment in
the science of religion. The Prophet, however, said, "If ye
knew what I know, ye would laugh little and weep much."
Now, if this knowledge had been part of the knowledge which
he was commanded to proclaim to mankind, he would have
proclaimed it; and if it had been allowable for his Companions to ask him about it, they would have asked him.
Ḥudhayfa, one of the Companions, had a special knowledge
of the names of the Hypocrites, and ʿAlí b. Abí Ṭálib
declared that he learned from the Prophet seventy catego-
ries of knowledge which the Prophet did not impart to any
one else. The truth is that the science of religion is divided
20 amongst the Traditionists, the Jurists, and the Ṣúfís, and
each of these three classes is independent of the others. No
traditionist will consult a jurist upon any difficulty connected
with the science of Tradition, nor will a jurist bring legal
problems to a traditionist. By the same rule, any one who
desires to be instructed in the mysteries of Ṣúfism must
seek information from those who have thoroughly mastered
the subject. Let none vituperate a class of men of whose science
and feelings and aims he knows nothing.

CHAPTER X: "Why the Ṣúfís are so called and why the
name is derived from their fashion of dress."

The author explains that the name Ṣúfí is not connected
with any science or spiritual condition, because the Ṣúfí is not
characterised by one particular science or quality but, on the
contrary, by all sciences and all praiseworthy qualities. He is
continually advancing from one state to another, and his pre-
21 dominant characteristics vary from time to time, so that he

cannot be designated by a name derived from them. The appellation Ṣúfí is derived from the garments of wool (ṣúf) which used to be worn by the prophets and saints: it is a general term connoting all that is praiseworthy. Similarly the disciples of Jesus were named al-Ḥawáriyyún on account of their white robes.

CHAPTER XI: "Confutation of those who say that they never heard mention of the Ṣúfís in ancient times and that the name is modern."

If it be argued that there were no Ṣúfís amongst the 22 Prophet's Companions, the reason is, that it was impossible to apply the name Ṣúfí to men who were known by the title of Companion, which is of all titles the highest and most honourable. The statement that 'Ṣúfí' is a name of recent origin invented by the people of Baghdád is absurd: the name was current in the time of Ḥasan of Baṣra and Sufyán al-Thawrí, and according to a tale related in the *History of Mecca* on the authority of Muḥammad b. Isḥáq and others it existed before the promulgation of Islam.

23   CHAPTER XII: "Demonstration of the reality of the esoteric science."

Some formalists recognise only the science of the external religious law comprised in the Koran and the Sunna, and declare that the esoteric science, *i. e.* Ṣúfism, is without meaning. In fact, however, the science of the religious law has an internal as well as an external aspect and inculcates inward as well as outward actions. The outward actions are bodily, such as hunger, fasting, almsgiving and the like, while the inward actions, or the actions of the heart, are faith, sincerity, knowledge of God, etc. 'The esoteric science' 24 signifies 'the science of the actions of the interior which depend on the interior organ, namely, the heart (al-qalb)', and is identical with Ṣúfism. The inward aspect of religion is the necessary complement of the outward aspect, and *vice versâ*. Both aspects are inherent in the Koran, in the Traditions of the Prophet, and in Islam itself.

CHAPTER XIII: "The nature and quality of Ṣúfism."

25   Definitions of Ṣúfism by Muḥammad b. ʿAlí al-Qaṣṣáb, Junayd, Ruwaym, Sumnún, Abú Muḥammad al-Jarírí [1]), ʿAmr b. ʿUthmán al-Makkí, and ʿAlí b. ʿAbd al-Raḥím al-Qannád.

CHAPTER XIV: "Description of the Ṣúfís and who they are."

Sayings of ʿAbd al-Wáḥid b. Zayd, Dhu 'l-Nún al-Miṣrí, 26 Junayd, Abu 'l-Ḥusayn al-Núrí. The people of Syria call the Ṣúfís 'poor men' (*fuqará*). Meaning of 'Ṣúfí' explained by Abú ʿAbdallah al-Jallá. It is said that the original form of the word was *Ṣafawí*. According to Abu 'l-Ḥasan al-Qannád 'Ṣúfí' is derived from *ṣafá* (purity). Anonymous definitions of 'Ṣúfí'. The author's explanation of what is really implied by the name 'Ṣúfí'.

27   Qannád says that it refers to the dress in which the Ṣúfís resemble each other outwardly, though they are very different spiritually. Shiblí's answer to the question why the Ṣúfís were so named. It has been said that they are a remnant of the *Ahl al-ṣuffa*. Ibráhím b. Muwallad al-Raqqí gave more then a hundred definitions of Ṣúfism. Verses by ʿAlí b. ʿAbd al-Raḥím al-Qannád on the decay of Ṣúfism. Three definitions by an anonymous Shaykh referring to three 28 points of view from which Ṣúfism may be regarded. Definitions given by Ḥuṣrí to the author. Saying of the Caliph Abú Bakr.

CHAPTER XV: "On unification (*tawḥíd*)."

Definitions of unification, according to the sense which the Moslems generally attach to it, by Dhu 'l-Nún and Junayd.

Definitions of the term, according to the sense which the 29 Ṣúfís attach to it, by Junayd. The author's comment on the saying of Junayd that "man should return from his last state to his first state and be as he was before he existed". Saying

---

1) Or Jurayrí. See note on p. ۲٥, l. ۹ in List of Addenda et Corrigenda.

30 of Shiblí to the effect that the unity of God is utterly in-
expressible and indefinable, with a brief explanation by the
author. Explanation of three answers of Yúsuf b. al-Ḥusayn
31 al-Rází concerning unification. The author then calls attention to another class of definitions, namely, those uttered in
the language of ecstasy, and says that he will explain them
as far as is possible, lest any of his readers should be misled.
One must be a mystic in order to understand mystical symbolism. Ruwaym's saying, that unification is the effacement
of human nature, signifies the transformation of the nature
32 of the lower soul (nafs). Explanation of several anonymous
sayings on tawḥíd and waḥdániyyat, and of a saying by
33 Shiblí. Another anonymous definition of tawḥíd. Description
of the first stage of tawḥíd and the first sign of tawḥíd by
Abú Saʿíd al-Kharráz, together with the author's commentary.
34 Saying of Shiblí: "egoism impairs unification". Another
saying of Shiblí to the same effect, with the author's explanation. Distinction made by Shiblí between the 'unification
of humanity' (tawḥíd al-bashariyyat) and the 'unification of
Divinity' (tawḥíd al-iláhiyyat). The author's explanation of
this saying. Two contradictory sayings of Shiblí: on one
occasion he said that whoever is acquainted with an atom
of the science of unification cannot bear the weight of a
gnat; but on another occasion he said that such a person
sustains the whole heaven and earth on a single eyelash.
Meaning of the latter saying. It is related that Gabriel covers
35 the East and the West with two of his six hundred wings.
Other traditions respecting the size of Gabriel and the dimen-
sions of the heavenly kingdom (malakút). Saying of Aḥmad
b. ʿAṭá al-Baghdádí: "the reality of unification consists in forgetting unification, etc." The author explains what this means.

CHAPTER XVI: "Concerning what has been said on the
subject of gnosis (maʿrifat) and the characteristics of the
gnostic (ʿárif)."

Two sources of gnosis according to Abú Saʿíd al-Kharráz.
Description of the gnostic by Abú Turáb al-Nakhshabí. Two
kinds of gnosis, *maʿrifat al-ḥaqq* and *maʿrifat al-ḥaqíqat*,
36 distinguished by Aḥmad b. ʿAṭá. The author's explanation
of part of this saying: God is really unknowable; hence it
has been said that none knows Him save Himself, and the
Caliph Abú Bakr said, "Praise to God who hath given His
creatures no way of attaining to the knowledge of Him except
through their inability to know Him." Three sayings of
Shiblí on gnosis. Abú Yazíd al-Bisṭámí said, describing the
gnostic, that the colour of water is the colour of the vessel
37 which contains it. The author explains the meaning of this
metaphor. Saying of Junayd. Anonymous definition of gnosis.
Saying of Junayd: what gnostics desire of God. Muḥammad
b. al-Faḍl of Samarcand asserted that gnostics desire nothing
and that they have no personal volition, but when some
one asked him what gnostics desire of God he answered,
"Steadfastness"(*istiqámat*)[1]). Description of the gnostic by Yaḥyá
b. Muʿádh al-Rází. Reply of Abu 'l-Ḥusayn al-Núrí to one
38 who asked him why the intellect is unable to apprehend
God. Explanation of this saying by the author. Saying of
Aḥmad b. ʿAṭá (which is sometimes wrongly attributed to
Abú Bakr al-Wásiṭí): "What is deemed evil is evil only
through His occultation, and what is deemed good is good
only through His manifestation, etc." The author quotes a
similar saying of Abú Sulaymán al-Dárání and says that Ibn
39 ʿAṭá's words bear the same meaning as the Tradition in
which it is related that the Prophet went forth with a scroll
in his right hand and another scroll in his left hand, and
that he said, "Here are written the names of the people of
Paradise, and here are written the names of the people of

---

1) Cf. Flügel, *Taʿrífát*, p. 19, l. 18, where *istiqámat* is defined as "not
preferring anything to God." The term is explained by Qushayrí, 111, 27 fol.

Hell." A saying of Abú Bakr al-Wásiṭí concerning gnostics, with the author's explanation thereof.

CHAPTER XVII: "Description of the gnostic and what has been said about him."

Three sayings of Yaḥyá b. Muʿádh al-Rází. Three signs of the gnostic enumerated by Dhu 'l-Nún al-Miṣrí. Anonymous 40 sayings: no one who describes gnosis is a true gnostic; if the gnostic turns from God towards mankind without His permission, God will abandon him; none can know God unless his heart is filled with awe. Perfect gnosis defined by ʿAbd al-Raḥmán al-Fárisí. The author's explanation of this definition.

CHAPTER XVIII: "Concerning the means by which God is known. The difference between the believer and the gnostic." Abu 'l-Ḥusayn al-Núrí said that God is known only through Himself, and that the intellect cannot know Him. On being asked what is the first duty imposed by God on His servants, he replied, "To know Him." Anonymous definition of gnosis. 41 Gnosis is originally a divine gift. Distinction between the believer and the gnostic. The former sees by the light of God, the latter through God Himself. Three kinds of gnosis: gnosis of acknowledgment, gnosis of reality, gnosis of contemplation. Definition of gnosis by Abú Bakr al-Záhirábádhí.

BOOK OF THE STATES AND STATIONS.

CHAPTER XIX: "Concerning the stations (*al-maqámát*) and their realities."

Definition of the term *maqám*.

42 Explanation by Abú Bakr al-Wásiṭí of the Tradition, "The spirits are hosts arrayed (*junúd mujannada*)." Examples of the qualities to which the term 'station' is applied.

CHAPTER XX: "Concerning the meaning of 'states' (*al-aḥwál*)."

Definition of the term *aḥwál* by the author.

Definition by Junayd. Anonymous description of the 'state' (*ḥál*) as 'secret recollection' (*al-dhikr al-khafí*). It is not gained, like the 'stations', by means of ascetic practices and works of devotion. Examples of 'states'. The author's explanation of a saying by Abú Sulaymán al-Dárání: "the body obtains relief when man's dealings with God pass over to the heart."

43 Sayings of Muḥammad b. Wásiʿ, Málik b. Dínár, and Junayd.
CHAPTER XXI: "On the station of repentance (*tawbat*)."
Definitions of repentance by Abú Yaʿqúb al-Súsí, Sahl b. ʿAbdallah al-Tustarí ("that you should not forget your sins"), and Junayd ("forgetting your sins"). The author points out that the definitions of al-Súsí and Sahl b. ʿAbdallah refer to the repentance of disciples and seekers, whereas that of Junayd refers to the repentance of spiritual adepts. It was in the latter sense that Ruwaym defined repentance as "repenting of repentance."

44 So Dhu 'l-Nún said that common men repent of sin but the elect repent of forgetting God. The expressions used by gnostics and ecstatics in regard to repentance are illustrated by the definition of Abu 'l-Ḥusayn al-Núrí: "that you should repent of everything except God." Dhu 'l-Nún alludes to the above distinction in his saying, "The sins of the saints (*al-muqarrabín*) are the good deeds of the pious (*al-abrár*)." Another similar saying: "The hypocrisy of gnostics is the sincerity of disciples." Explanation of the different spiritual degrees.

CHAPTER XXII: "On the station of abstinence (*waraʿ*)."
Three classes of those who practise abstinence.
The first class abstain from what is 'dubious', *i.e.* neither plainly lawful nor plainly unlawful. Saying of Ibn Sírín.

45 The second class abstain from whatever their consciences bid them avoid. Definition of abstinence by Abú Saʿíd al-Kharráz. Ḥárith al-Muḥásibí never ate anything 'dubious':

a vein in his finger throbbed when he attempted to take such food. Story of Bishr al-Ḥáfí. Definition of 'lawful' by Sahl b. ʿAbdallah al-Tustarí and the author's comment. Traditions justifying the appeal to conscience. The third class, namely, the gnostics and ecstatics, share the view of Abú Sulaymán al-Dárání, that whatever diverts the attention from God is 46 abominable. Similar sayings by Sahl b. ʿAbdallah and Shiblí.

CHAPTER XXIII: "On the station of renunciation (zuhd)."

Renunciation is the basis of spiritual progress, because every sin originates in love of this world, and every act of goodness and obedience springs from renunciation. The name of 'ascetic' (záhid) is equivalent to a hundred names of praise. Renunciation has reference only to what is lawful, since the avoidance of unlawful and dubious things is obligatory. Three classes of ascetics (zuhhád). The first class are the novices whose hands are empty of possessions and whose hearts are empty of that which is not in their hands. Sayings of Junayd and Sarí al-Saqatí. The second class are the adepts in renunciation (al-mutaḥaqqiqún fi 'l-zuhd), to whom Ru-47 waym's definition of zuhd as the renunciation of all selfish interests is applicable. There is a selfish interest in renouncing the world, inasmuch as the ascetic gains joy and praise and reputation, but the real ascetic banishes all these interests from his heart. The third class are those who recognise the utter vanity of this world and hold it so cheap that they scorn to look at it: hence they regard even renunciation of it as an act of turning away from God. Sayings of Shiblí and Yaḥyá b. Muʿádh al-Rází.

CHAPER XXIV: "On the station of poverty (faqr) and the characteristics of the poor."

Verse of the Koran describing the poor. Poverty is a great ornament to the believer (Tradition). Saying in praise 48 of poverty by Ibráhím al-Khawwáṣ. Three classes of poor men (fuqará). The first class are those who possess nothing

and do not seek outwardly or inwardly anything from anyone,
and if anything is offered to them they will not accept it.
Saying of Sahl b. ʿAlí b. Sahl al-Iṣbahání. The reality of
poverty explained by Abú ʿAbdallah b. al-Jallá. The question
why faqírs refuse to accept food when they need it answered
by Abú ʿAlí al-Rúdhabárí and Abú Bakr al-Zaqqáq. Answer
given by Naṣr b. al-Ḥammámí to the question why the
Ṣúfís prefer poverty to everything else. The second class
possess nothing and do not beg either directly or indirectly,
but if anything is offered to them they accept it. Saying of
Junayd: the sign of the true faqír. Definition of the true
faqír by Sahl b. ʿAbdallah al-Tustarí.

49   Real poverty defined by Abú ʿAbdallah b. al-Jallá. Characteristics of the true faqír according to Ibráhím al-Khawwáṣ.
The third class do not possess anything, but when they are
in want they beg of a brother Ṣúfí and expiate the act of
begging by their sincerity. ¹). Sayings of Jarírí and Ruwaym.

    CHAPTER XXV: "On the station of patience (ṣabr)."

    Sayings of Junayd and Ibráhím al-Khawwáṣ. Dialogue
50 between Shiblí and a man who asked him, "What is the
hardest kind of patience?" The mutaṣabbir, the ṣábir, and the
ṣabbár defined by Ibn Sálim. These definitions are illustrated
by a saying of al-Qannád and stories of Dhu 'l-Nún and
Shiblí. Verses which Shiblí used to quote.

51   Tradition as to the effect of one moan uttered by Zakariyyá,
when the saw was laid on his neck.

    CHAPTER XXVI: "On the station of trust in God (tawakkul)."

    Passages in the Koran showing that trust in God is con-
nected with faith. Other passages referring to the trust of
the 'elect of the elect' (khuṣúṣ al-khuṣúṣ). Three kinds of trust
52 in God. The first is the trust of the faithful (al-muʾminún).

---

1) Read صلبه instead of صلقه (cf. p. ۱۹۲ l. ۲ foll.). 'Sincerity' (ṣidq)
involves the entire absence of self-interest and self-regard.

Definitions of this by Abú Turáb al-Nakhshabí, Dhu 'l-Nún,
Abú Bakr al-Zaqqáq, Ruwaym, and Sahl b. ʿAbdallah al-
Tustarí. The second kind is the trust of the elect (*ahl
al-khuṣúṣ*). Definitions by Ibn ʿAṭá, Abú Yaʿqúb al-Nahrajúrí,
Abú Bakr al-Wásiṭí, and Sahl b. ʿAbdallah al-Tustarí. The third
kind is the trust of the elect of the elect (*khuṣúṣ al-khuṣúṣ*).
Definitions by Shiblí, an anonymous Ṣúfí, Ibn al-Jallá, Junayd,
53 Abú Sulaymán al-Dárání, and another anonymous mystic.

CHAPTER XXVII: "On the station of satisfaction (*riḍá*)
and the characteristics of the satisfied."

According to the Koran (9, 73), God's satisfaction with man
precedes man's satisfaction with God. Definitions of *riḍá*
by the author, Junayd, al-Qannád, Dhu 'l-Nún, and Ibn ʿAṭá.
54 Saying of Abú Bakr al-Wásiṭí. Three classes of the satisfied: (1) those who strive to preserve equanimity towards
God in all circumstances (2) those who pay no regard to
their own satisfaction but consider only the fact that God is
satisfied with them (3) those who realise that the question
whether they are satisfied with God and God with them
depends absolutely on the eternal providence of God. Saying
of Abú Sulaymán al-Dárání in this sense. *Riḍá* is the last
of the 'stations' and is followed by the mystical 'states', of
which the first is observation (*murágabat*).

CHAPTER XXVIII: "On the observation of mystical states
and the characteristics of such observers."

55 The observer is he who knows that God is acquainted
with his most secret thoughts: consequently he keeps watch
over the evil thoughts that hinder him from thinking of
God. Sayings of Abú Sulaymán al-Dárání, Ibráhím al-Ajurrí,
and Ḥasan b. ʿAlí al-Dámaghání. Three types of *murágabat*.
The first is that of beginners and is described in the saying
of Ḥasan b. ʿAlí al-Dámaghání. The second is described in
a saying of Ibn ʿAṭá. The third is peculiar to those who observe
God and ask Him to keep their minds always fixed upon Him.

56   Saying of Ibn ʿAṭá.

CHAPTER XXIX: "On the state of nearness to God (*qurb*)."
Koranic texts declaring that God is near. The state of
nearness belongs to one who contemplates God's nearness
to him, and seeks to draw near to God by means of obedience
to His commands, and concentrates his thoughts by constant
recollection of God. Such persons form three classes. The
first class are those who seek to draw near to God by
various acts of devotion. The second class are those who
realise God's nearness to such an extent that they resemble
ʿAmir b. ʿAbd al-Qays who said, "I never looked at anything without regarding God as nearer to it than I was."
57 Verses describing the inward feeling of nearness produced by
ecstasy. Saying of Junayd: God is near to man in proportion
as man feels himself near to God. An anonymous saying to
the same effect. The third and highest class are those whose
nearness to God causes them to be unconscious of nearness.
Sayings of Abu 'l-Ḥusayn al-Núrí and Abú Yaʿqúb al-Súsí.

CHAPTER XXX: "On the state of love (*maḥabbat*)."

It appears from several passages in the Koran that God
58 loves man and that God's love of man precedes man's
love of God. The author describes the man who loves God.
Three forms of love. The first is the love of the vulgar
(*al-ʿámmat*), which results from God's kindness towards them,
according to the Tradition that men naturally love their
benefactors. Descriptions of this form of love by Sumnún,
Sahl b. ʿAbdallah al-Tustarí, Ḥusayn b. ʿAlí [1], and an anonymous authority on Ṣúfism. The second form of love, which
is the love of the sincere (*al-ṣádiqún*), is produced by regarding
the majesty, omnipotence, and omniscience of God. Descript-
59 ions of it by Abu 'l-Ḥusayn al-Núrí, Ibráhím al-Khawwáṣ,
and Abú Saʿíd al-Kharráz. The third form of love, *i.e.* the

---

1 Ḥusayn (Ḥasan) b. ʿAlí al-Dámaghání is probably meant.

love of saints and gnostics (*al-ṣiddíqún wa 'l-ᶜárifún*) results from their knowledge of the eternal and causeless Divine love: hence they love God without any cause for loving Him. Descriptions of this exalted love by Dhu 'l-Nún, Abú Yaᶜqúb al-Súsí, and Junayd. Tradition: God becomes the eye, ear, and hand of any one whom He loves.

60 CHAPTER XXXI: "On the state of fear (*khawf*)."

Nearness to God (*qurb*) may produce either love or fear. Three kinds of fear mentioned in the Koran. While the vulgar (*al-ᶜámmat*) fear the vengeance of God, the middle class (*al-awsáṭ*) fear separation from God and the occurrence of anything that might impair their gnosis. Sayings on the latter kind of fear by Shiblí, an anonymous gnostic in reply to Abú Saᶜíd al-Kharráz, Ibn Khubayq, and al-Qannád. The

61 third class are the elect (*ahl al-khuṣúṣ*). Their fear is described by Sahl b. ᶜAbdallah al-Tustarí, Ibn al-Jallá, and al-Wásiṭí.

CHAPTER XXXII: "On hope (*rajá*)."

62 Tradition: if the believer's hope and fear were weighed, they would balance each other. Some one whose name is not given said that fear and hope are the two wings of (devotional) work, without which it will not fly. Saying of Abú Bakr al-Warráq. Three kinds of hope: hope in God, hope in the abundance of God's mercy, and hope in God's recompense (*thawáb*). Description of one who possesses the second and third kinds of hope. Sayings by Dhu 'l-Nún and an anonymous Ṣúfí. He whose hope is in God desires nothing of God except God Himself. Sayings of Shiblí and a woman who met Dhu 'l-Nún in a desert.

SECTION: on the meaning of hope and fear.

The language used by spiritual adepts concerning hope and fear is illustrated by a saying of Ibn ᶜAṭá.

63 Another saying in the same style by Abú Bakr al-Wásiṭí. Anonymous saying, that love is not perfect without fear, nor fear without hope, nor hope without fear.

CHAPTER XXXIII: "On the state of longing (*shawq*)."

Tradition on the longing for Paradise. The Prophet prayed, that he might be filled with longing to meet God, and he 64 also said that those who long for Paradise hasten to do good works. Another Tradition giving the names of three persons whom Paradise longed for. Description of the mystic who feels longing. Two anonymous definitions of *shawq*. Saying of Jarírí on the pleasure and pain of longing. Description by Abú Saʿíd al-Kharráz of those who feel longing. Three classes of such. The first class long for the blessings which God has promised to His friends, the second class long for Him whom they love, and the third class, contemplating God as present with them, not absent, say that longing is felt only in the absence of the desired object; hence they lose consciousness of the longing which characterises them in the eyes of their brethren.

CHAPTER XXXIV: "On the state of joy or intimacy (*uns*)."

The author's definition of *uns*: reliance on God and seeking help from Him; he adds that no further explanation is pos- 65 sible. Letter written by Muṭarraf b. ʿAbdallah to ʿUmar b. ʿAbd al-ʿAzíz. Anonymous saying to the effect that those who enjoy *uns* with God feel no fear of aught except Him. Description of one who is in the state of *uns*. Three classes of 'intimates'. The first class are intimate with the recollection (*dhikr*) of God and with obedience to Him. Saying of Sahl b. ʿAbdallah al-Tustarí. The second class are intimate with God and shrink from all thoughts that distract them from Him. Sayings of Dhu 'l-Nún and Junayd.

66 Ibráhím al-Márastání defined *uns* as the heart's joy in the Beloved. The third class are they whose feelings of awe in the presence of God cause them to become unconscious of being 'intimate'. Saying of an anonymous gnostic, the answer written by Dhu 'l-Nún to a man who had said in a letter to him, "May God grant thee the joy

of being near to Him!", and a definition of *uns* by Shiblí.
CHAPTER XXXV: "On the state of tranquillity (*iṭma'nínat*)."
Saying of Sahl b. ʿAbdallah al-Tustarí.

67 Explanation of the text, 'Those whose hearts are at rest
in the recollection of God' (Kor. 13, 28), by Ḥasan b. ʿAlí
al-Dámaghání. Shiblí's interpretation of a saying of Abú
Sulaymán al-Dárání. Characteristics of the tranquil man.
Three kinds of tranquillity. The first belongs to the vulgar
who find peace in thinking of God; the second to the elect
who resign themselves to the Divine decree and are patient
in tribulation, but at the same time are conscious of their
devotional acts; the third to the elect of the elect who reve
rently acknowledge that their hearts cannot rest with God
68 inasmuch as He is infinite and unique: therefore they advance
in their ardent search and fall into the unimaginable Sea.

CHAPTER XXXVI: "On the state of contemplation (*musháhadat*)."

Mystical interpretation of Kor. 85, 3 by Abú Bakr al-Wásiṭí.
Sayings on contemplation by Abú Saʿíd al-Kharráz and ʿAmr
b. ʿUthmán al-Makkí. Saying of the Prophet: "worship God as
though thou sawest Him." Explanation of *shahíd* (Kor. 5, 306).

69 Three more sayings by ʿAmr al-Makkí. Three kinds of
contemplation indicated respectively by Abú Bakr al-Wásiṭí,
Abú Saʿíd al-Kharráz, and ʿAmr al-Makkí in his *Kitáb al-
musháhadat*.

70 CHAPTER XXXVII: "On the state of certainty (*yaqín*)."

Three forms of *yaqín* are mentioned in the Koran: *ʿilm
al-yaqín, ʿayn al-yaqín,* and *ḥaqq al-yaqín*. Tradition: "ask
God for certainty in this world and the next." The Prophet
also said that if Jesus had possessed more *yaqín* he would
have walked in the air. Saying of ʿAmir b. ʿAbd Qays: "if
the veil were lifted my certainty would not be increased."
Saying of Abú Yaʿqúb al-Nahrajúrí. The author says that
yaqín is revelation (*mukáshafat*), which is of three kinds:

(*a*) ocular vision on the Day of Resurrection (*b*) revelation to the heart by real faith (*c*) revelation of the Divine Power by means of miracles. Three classes of those who possess *yaqín*. The *yaqín* of the first class is described by an anonymous Ṣúfí, Junayd, Abú Yaʿqúb (al-Nahrajúrí), and Ruwaym.

71 The *yaqín* of the second class is described by Ibn ʿAṭá, Abú Yaʿqúb al-Nahrajúrí, and Abu 'l-Ḥusayn al-Núrí; that of the third class by ʿAmr b. ʿUthmán al-Makkí and Abú Yaʿqúb al-Nahrajúrí. *Yaqín* is the beginning and end of all the 'states': its extreme point is a profound and real belief in the Unseen. Saying of al-Wásiṭí.

72 THE BOOK OF THE PURE IN UNDERSTANDING AND OBEDIENCE TO THE BOOK OF GOD.

CHAPTER XXXIII: "On conformity to the Book of God." Tradition of the Prophet on this subject. Saying of ʿAbdallah b. Masʿúd. The Koran is a guide to those who fear God and believe in the Unseen (Kor. 2, 1).

73 Verses of the Koran from which the Ṣúfís infer that a hidden meaning lies beneath every word of the Holy Book, and that this meaning can be found only by means of deep thought and attentive study.

74 Such thought and study demand a sound heart (*qalb salím*), *i. e.*, a heart in which there is nothing but God. Saying of Sahl b. ʿAbdallah al-Tustarí to the effect that the hidden meanings of the Koran are inexhaustible, because it is the Word of God, who is infinite: it cannot be understood by human minds, except in so far as God reveals its meanings to those whom He loves.

CHAPTER XXXIX: "On the particular application of the term *call* (daʿwat), and the nature of *election* (iṣṭifá)."

Sahl b. ʿAbdallah said in reference to Kor. 10, 26, that *call* is general and *guidance* (hidáyat) special. Many are called but few chosen.

75 It appears from two passages of the Koran (22,74 and 35, 29) that the elect are (a) the Prophets (b) certain of the Faithful. The Prophets are distinguished by sinlessness, the revelation of God's Word to them, and the apostolic office; the other believers by their pure devotion, self-mortification, and cleaving to spiritual realities. All the Faithful are commanded to hasten to good works.

76 Verses of the Koran specifying different kinds of good works.

77 CHAPTER XL: "On the diversity of those who hear the Divine admonition and their various degrees in respect of receiving it."

Some hear the Divine command but are hindered from fulfilling it by worldliness and sensuality. Verses of the Koran referring to such persons.

78 Others hear the Divine command and comply with it and repent and become active in good works and devote themselves sincerely to the pursuit of moral and spiritual excellence. Verses of the Koran referring to persons of this sort. The meaning of *laghw* (Kor. 23, 3) explained by ʿAmr b. ʿUthmán al-Makkí. A third class are the savants (*ʿulamá*) who fear God (Kor. 35, 25). Among these, again, are a special class, whom the (Koran 3, 5) describes as "well grounded in knowledge."

79 Explanation by Abú Bakr al-Wásiṭí of the characteristics of those who are "well grounded in knowledge". The words of al-Wásiṭí are elucidated by a saying of Abú Saʿíd al-Kharráz. "To follow what is best in God's Word" (Kor. 39,19) refers to the wonderful things which are revealed to the hearts of mystics who hear the Koran with understanding.

80 CHAPTER XLI: "How the hidden meaning of the Koran is elicited by listening with studious attention when it is read aloud."

According to Abú Saʿíd al-Kharráz, there are three ways of listening attentively to the recitation of the Koran: (1) when you listen as though the Prophet were reading it to you (2) when you listen as though you heard Gabriel reading it to the Prophet (3) when you listen as though you heard God reading it. In the last case, understanding is produced — you being absent from wordly concerns and from your 'self' — by power of contemplation and purity of recollection (*dhikr*) and concentration of thought.

81 This explanation is drawn from a verse of the Koran (2, 2) referring to belief in the Unseen. Saying of Abú Saʿíd b. al-Aʿrábí. Definition of the Unseen by Abú Saʿíd al-Kharráz: "that which God causes men's hearts to behold of conviction as to His attributes, whether described by Himself or conveyed by Tradition. Since the ultimate apprehension of the divine attributes, no less than of the divine essence, is impossible to man, mystical theologians are agreed that 'the Unseen' (*al-ghayb*) includes all the manifold experiences of theosophists, ecstatics, gnostics, and Unitarians."

82 CHAPTER XLII: "Description of the way in which the Koran is understand by mystics."

Mystical interpretation of Kor. 5, 39; 23, 57—59. The words *khashyat* and *ishfáq* distinguished and defined.

83 According to the mystic sense of Kor. 7, 158, there is no limit to the increase of faith, and all mystical experience, from beginning to end, is the fruit of real and infinite faith. Again, from Kor. 23, 61, it appears that those who fear God and believe in Him are free from polytheism (*shirk*). This *shirk*, as mystics interpret it, consists in having regard to one's acts of devotion and in seeking recompense for them; it is a thing insidious and hard to detect, and the only means of discovering and removing it is *ikhlás*, that is to say, a purely disinterested belief in God alone. Sayings on *ikhlás* by Sahl b. ʿAbdallah al-Tustarí.

84 The Koran (23, 62) mentions those whose hearts are terror-stricken by the thought that they shall at last return to God, notwithstanding their piety and zeal in doing good

works. Mystics interpret this terror (*wajal*) as being due to
the inscrutable fact that God, in His eternal foreknowledge,
has doomed them either to happiness or to misery hereafter.
They cannot know what their fate shall be, hence they turn
to God with supplication and utter poverty of spirit. The
words of the Koran quoted above do not refer to evil-doers,
as is proved by the Prophet's answer to a question which
ᶜA'isha asked him.

CHAPTER XLIII: "Account of the *sábiqún* and the *muqarrabún* and the *abrár* according to the method of mystical
interpretation."

The author cites a number of passages in the Koran in
85-86 which these classes of persons are mentioned, and using the
method called *instinbáṭ* (that is, drawing out the hidden
sense), he shows that the *muqarrabún* are superior to the
sábiqún and the *abrár*.

CHAPTER XLIV: "How the duty of exerting one's self
to the utmost (*tashdíd*) is set forth in the Koran."

The Koran says (64, 16) "Fear God with all your might".
This obligation in its real nature is such that, even if men
should perform all the works of the angels and prophets and
saints, that which they had done would be less than that
which they had left undone. The angels themselves say,
"Glory to Thee, O Lord! We have not worshipped Thee
as Thou oughtest to be worshipped."

87 The true meaning of "Fear God with all your might".
If you performed a prayer of a thousand *rakᶜas* and were
able to perform one *rakᶜa* more, but postponed it to another
time, you would have failed to pray 'with all your might'.
Similarly in the case of recollection (*dhikr*) or almsgiving.
A passage of the Koran (4, 68) implies that any inward
reluctance to accept the decision of the Prophet, even were
it a sentence of death against one's self, constitutes a depar.
ture from the Faith.

88   CHAPTER XLV: "Concerning what is said on the subject
of the mystical sense of the Words (in the Koran) and the
Divine Names."

It is said that whatever lies within the range of knowledge
and understanding is derived from two phrases at the beginning of the Koran, *viz.*, '*Bismillah*' (in the name of God)
and *al-ḥamd lillah* (the praise to God), because the faculties
of knowledge and understanding are not self-subsistent but
are *through* God and *to* God. When Shiblí was asked to
explain the mystical sense of the *B* in *Bismillah*, he replied
that spirits, bodies, and actions subsist in God, not in themselves. In answer to the question, "What is that in which
the hearts of gnostics put their trust?" Abu 'l-ᶜAbbás b.
ᶜAṭá said, "In the first letter of God's Book, *i. e.*, the *B* in
Bismillah al-Raḥmán al-Raḥím; for it signifies that through
God all things appear and pass away and through His manifestation are fair, and through His occultation are foul;
because His name *Allah* expresses His awfulness and majesty,
and His name *al-Raḥmán* expresses His love and affection,
and His name *al-Raḥím* expresses His help and assistance."
The author explains that good things are called good only
because God accepts them, and that evil things are called
evil only because God rejects them. Abú Bakr al-Wásiṭí
89 said that every divine Name (attribute) can be used as a
means of forming one's character except the names *Allah*
and *al-Raḥmán* which, like the attribute of Lordship (*ṣama-
diyyat*), are beyond human comprehension. It has been said
that the Greatest Name of God is Allah (الله) because when
the initial *alif* is removed, there remains *llh* (= *lillah*, to
Allah), and when you remove the first *lám*, there remains
lh (= *lahu*, to Him), and when you remove the second
lám, there remains *h*, in which all mysteries are contained,
inasmuch as *h* means *huwa* (He). Thus the name Allah is
unlike all the other names of God, which become meaning-

less when a single letter is taken away from them. Sahl b. ʿAbdallah al-Tustarí said that *alif* is the first and chief of the letters, because it signifies Allah who united (*allafa bayn*) all things and is Himself separated from all things. Abú Saʿíd al-Kharráz said that when a man is concentrated on God, he reads the Koran with real understanding, which is greater in proportion to his love of God and his feeling of nearness to Him. Saying of Abú Sulaymán al-Dáraní: rapture, not reflection, is necessary for understanding the Koran. Saying of Wuhayb b. al-Ward on the emotional effects produced by reading and study of the Koran.

90   CHAPTER XLVI: "Description of the right and wrong methods of mystical interpretation (*istinbáṭ*)."

A sound interpretation must be based on the following principles: (*a*) that the interpreter shall not change the order of the words in the Koran (*b*) that he shall not overpass the limits suitable to one who is a faithful and obedient servant of God (*c*) that he shall not pervert the form or meaning of the sacred text. Examples of such perversion (Kor. 21, 83; 93, 6; 18, 110). The sound method of interpretation is illustrated by Abú Bakr al-Kattání's explanation of *bi-qalb^{in} salím^{in}* (Kor. 26, 89).

91   The author elucidates the meaning of a phrase occurring in al-Kattání's explanation, *viz.*, "he passes away from God through God" (*faniya ʿani 'llah billah*). Further examples of sound interpretation: (1) Sháh al-Kirmání on Kor. 26, 78—80; (2) Abú Bakr al-Wásiṭí on Kor. 13, 28; (3) Shiblí on Kor. 24, 30; (4) Shiblí on Kor. 50, 36.

92   Another kind of interpretation is indirect and allusive (*ishárat*). Specimens of this are given: two from Abu 'l-ʿAbbás b. ʿAṭá, and others from Abú Yazíd al-Bisṭámí, Junayd, Abú ʿAlí al-Rúdhabárí, and Abú Bakr al-Zaqqáq. Abú Yazíd al-Bisṭámí, when some one questioned him concerning gnosis, replied by quoting Kor. 27, 34: "Lo, when kings enter a

city they spoil it and abase the mighty men of its people",
meaning to say that when gnosis enters the heart it con-
sumes and casts out everything besides. The author declares
that such interpretations are sound, though he adds that
God knows best.

93   THE BOOK OF IMITATION OF THE
APOSTLE OF GOD.

CHAPTER XLVII: "Description of the Pure (Ṣúfís) in
respect of their understanding (the Koran) and their conformity and obedience to the Prophet."

The Prophet was sent to all mankind (Kor. 7, 157), that
he might teach them "the Book and the Wisdom" (Kor·
62, 2), *i. e.*, the Koran and the Sunna. God has commanded
all mankind to obey him (Kor. 24, 53), and has promised
94 that those who obey him will be rightly guided, while the
disobedient will suffer a grievous punishment. The love of
God towards the Faithful depends on their following the
Prophet (Kor. 3, 29). He is held up as a pattern to true
believers (Kor. 33, 21), who must accept as binding every
Tradition that has come down to them from him on trustworthy authority. Those who act in conformity with the
Koran but do not follow the Sunna are really at variance
with the Koran. Imitation of the Prophet in his character
and actions, in doing what he commands and in not doing
what he forbids, is incumbent on his followers, save in
95 certain cases which the Koran or the Traditions expressly
mention as exceptions to the general rule. Whereas theologians and lawyers have codified the religious and legal
ordinances of the Prophet and are the recognised defenders,
propagandists, and exponents of the religious law, the elect
among them (namely, the Ṣúfís) have laid upon themselves
the duty of imitating his moral and spiritual character. The
Prophet's character, as ʿA'isha said, is the Koran, *i. e.*, con-

formity with the Koran: he describes himself as having been
sent "with a noble disposition" (*bi-makárim al-akhláq*).

96 CHAPTER XLVIII: "What is related concerning the character and actions and feelings with which God endowed
the Apostle."

Traditions regarding the excellence of the Prophet's conduct, his knowledge and fear of God, his humility, his
asceticism, his trust in God.

97 He would not allow food to be kept for the next day's
meal. He never found fault with his food. Signs of his
humility. How he prayed for lowliness. Description of his
manners and appearance by Abú Saʿíd al-Khudrí.

98 Saying of ʿAʾisha about his liberality. It was said of him
that he gave like one who had no fear of being poor.

He always behaved with the utmost humility and meekness.
Stories illustrating his frugality and dislike of ostentation.

99 He said that he loved equally those on whom he bestowed
and those from whom he withheld his bounty. His praise
of the *faqírs* of Medina. He said that the poor Moslems
shall enter Paradise five hundred years before the rich.
Religious men suffer tribulation, the prophets most of all.
Sayings and anecdotes showing his unworldliness. The nobility
of his character.

100 List of the virtues which he possessed. He was habitually
sorrowful and thoughtful. In order that he might render due
thanks to God, he stood in prayer until his feet became
swollen. He did not revenge himself upon his enemies but
returned good for evil. His kindness to widows and orphans.
His clemency described by Anas b. Málik, and exemplified
by his treatment of the Quraysh when he conquered Mecca.

101 CHAPTER XLIX: "On the Apostolic Traditions relating
to the indulgences and alleviations which God has granted
to the Moslem community."

Under this head the author enumerates various articles

of luxury owned by the Prophet and quotes the words which he addressed to his Companions, "Eat your fill". Had such indulgences not been granted by God, His creatures would have been undone, for He calls them not to money-making and industry and commerce (which are only per-mitted as a concession to human weakness), but to obey and worship Him and trust in Him and entirely devote themselves to Him.

102 In this respect the prophets are not as other men. Whereas the majority of mankind betake themselves to indulgences on account of the weakness of their faith and their propen-sity to pleasure, and consequently are sometimes led into sin, the prophets have within them a God-given strength that raises them above self-interest. Moslems comply with the Koran and obey the Prophet in different ways. Three classes may be distinguished: (1) those who avail themselves of indulgences; (2) those who base their conduct on know-ledge of the religious law; (3) those whose knowledge of the law does not extend beyond what is indispensable, but who set their minds on spiritual states and good works and noble dispositions, and strive after perfection and truth and such real faith as Ḥáritha attained. It is said that the whole

103 theory of mysticism is founded upon four Traditions, viz., those of Gabriel, ʿAbdallah b. ʿAbbás, Wábiṣa, and Nuʿmán b. Bashír. The author adds a fifth, namely, the saying of the Prophet, "No Moslem shall do harm to another with or without provocation."

CHAPTER L: "On what is recorded of the leading Ṣúfís in regard to their following the Apostle of God".

Saying of Junayd: "Ṣúfism is intimately connected with the Apostolic Traditions". Saying of Abú ʿUthmán al-Ḥírí. Story of Abú Yazíd al-Bisṭámí: how be turned his back without cere-mony on a celebrated ascetic who spat on the floor of a mosque.

104 Another story of Abú Yazíd: from respect for the Prophet

he would not ask God to relieve him of the pains of hunger
and lust, and God rewarded him by making him utterly in-
sensible to the charms of women. Anecdote of Shiblí: when
he was dying and unable to speak he seized the hand of
his servant, who was washing him, and passed it through
his beard in order that the ablution might be performed
in the manner prescribed by the Prophet. Abú ʿAlí al-Rúdhabárí mentioned the names of his teachers in four subjects:
Ṣúfism, theology, grammar, and the Apostolic Traditions.
Dhu 'l-Nún said: "I know God through God Himself and I
know all besides God through the Apostle of God". Sahl b.
ʿAbdallah al-Tustarí declared that no ecstasy is real unless
it is attested by the Koran and the Sunna. Saying of Abú
Sulaymán al-Dáraní to the same effect.

105   THE BOOK OF MYSTICAL INTERPRETATIONS
(al-mustanbaṭát).

CHAPTER LI: "On the method by which the Ṣúfís elicit
the true meanings of the Koran and the Traditions, etc."
Definition of *mustanbaṭát*. They are derived by men of
profound spiritual intelligence who, alike in theory and
practice, conform to the Koran and obey the Prophet. When
such men act upon that which they know, God endows
them with the knowledge of that which they did not know
before, a knowledge peculiar to themselves, and removes
from their hearts the rust produced by sin and passion and
worldliness. Then they utter on their tongues the myste-
rious lore which flows into their hearts from the Unseen.
106 The key to this knowledge is attentive study of the Koran
(Kor. 4, 84). Its possessors constitute an elect class among
the ʿulamá (Kor. 4, 85). Only those who are thoroughly
grounded in the rudiments of religious knowledge can reach
the higher knowledge that belongs to mystics, as is shown

by the Prophet's reply to a man who sought instruction in the latter. The Moslem lawyers and divines have their own *mustanbaṭát*, which they use for controversial purposes; and so have the scholastic theologians. All these interpretations are good in the opinion of the people who make them, but the interpretations of the Ṣúfís are still more excellent.

107 CHAPTER LII: "On the nature of the difference in the interpretations of mystics concerning the meanings of their sciences and states."

The Ṣúfís differ in their interpretations just as the formalists do, but whereas the differences of the latter lead to error, differences in mystical science do not produce this result. It has been said that difference of opinion amongst the authorities on exoteric science is an act of divine mercy, because he who holds the right view refutes and exposes the error of his adversary. So, too, the difference of opinion amongst mystics is an act of divine mercy, because each one speaks according to his predominant state and feeling: hence mystics of every sort — whether novices or adepts, whether engaged in works of devotion or in spiritual meditation — can derive profit from their words. This statement is illustrated by the varying definitions of the true *faqír*

108 *(al-faqír al-ṣádiq)* given by Dhu 'l-Nún, Abú ʿAbdallah al-Maghribí, Abu 'l-Ḥárith al-Awlásí, Yúsuf b. al-Ḥusayn, Ḥusayn b. Manṣúr (al-Ḥalláj), Núrí, Sumnún, Abú Ḥafṣ al-Naysábúrí, Junayd, and Murtaʿish. All these definitions are different in accordance with the different states and feelings of their authors, yet all are good; and every single definition is suitable and instructive to mystics of a certain class.

109 CHAPTER LIII: "On the Ṣúfistic interpretations of the Koran concerning the peculiar excellence of the Prophet and his superiority to other prophets."

110 Interpretations of Kor. 12, 108 and 7, 28.

Interpretation of Kor. 41, 53, confirmed by a line of La-

bíd which the Prophet described as "the truest word that
the Arabs have spoken". The Prophet's superiority to Moses
is shown by a comparison of Kor. 20, 26—27, and Kor. 94, 1
foll.; his superiority to Abraham by a comparison of Kor.
26, 87 and Kor. 66, 8. Moreover, while God calls Muḥammad to regard Himself (Kor. 25, 47). He bids all His other
creatures consider His kingdom and glory and the wonders
of His creation.

111   Again, love is more intimate than friendship, for love
effaces from the heart all that is not itself: therefore Muḥammad, the Beloved *(Ḥabíb)* of God, is superior to Abraham, who was His Friend *(Khalíl)*. Furthermore, it appears from several passages in the Koran that whereas the
sins of other prophets are mentioned before the fact that
God forgave them, in Muḥammad's case the forgiveness is
mentioned before the sin, *i. e.*, his sins were forgiven before
they were committed. Muḥammad wrought not only the
same miracles as the former prophets did, but also many
others which God vouchsafed to him alone. God bestowed
on him no special attribute such as He bestowed on each
of the former prophets (*e. g.*, on Abraham friendship, on Job
patience): He attached nothing to Muḥammad except Himself, and He said, "Thou didst not throw when thou threw-
est, but God threw" (Kor. 8, 17).

112   Mystical interpretation of Koran 18, 17 by Shiblí. As regards the meaning of the words describing Muḥammad's
Ascension, "He transported His servant by night" (Kor. 17, 1),
it has been said that if, as his opponents alleged, the Prophet had ascended to heaven in the spirit only, God would
not have applied to him the name of 'servant', which ne-
cessarily includes the spirit and the body together. "The
great favour that God conferred on the Prophet" (Kor. 4, 113)
consisted in his being chosen by God, for the prophetic and
apostolic offices are not conferred as a reward for merit:

otherwise Muḥammad would not have been judged superior to the rest of the prophets, who lived longer and performed a larger amount of good works. God demands patience from His creatures on the ground of the recompense which they shall receive hereafter, but He bade Muḥammad be patient inasmuch as he was in God's eye (Kor. 52, 48). That is to say, God honoured him too much to require him to do anything that entailed recompense. His position is one of unique distinction.

113 CHAPTER LIV: "On the Ṣūfistic interpretations of Apostolic Traditions relating to the peculiar distinction of the Prophet and his superiority to other prophets".

Mystical interpretation of the Tradition, "I take refuge from Thine anger in Thy good pleasure, and from Thy chastisement in Thy forgiveness, and from Thee in Thyself: I cannot praise Thee: Thou art even as Thou dost praise Thyself".

114 Meaning of the Traditions, "If ye knew what I knew, ye would laugh little and weep much, etc.," and "I am not as one of you; I am with my Lord, who gives me food and drink." The Prophet implored God to tend him as a child and never leave him to himself for a single moment. Saying of Abú Bakr al-Wásiṭí. Explanation of the words which were uttered by the Prophet on his deathbed, "O my grief!"

115 The Prophet said, "I am the chief of the children of Adam, but I make no boast of it." Explanation of this saying by Abú Muḥammad al-Jaríri. The point of the Prophet's words concerning Zaynab, the wife of Zayd, explained by Junayd. Explanation by Junayd of the Traditions, "I ask pardon of God and turn towards Him a hundred times daily," and "May God have mercy upon my brother Jesus! Had his faith been greater, he would have walked in the air." Comment by Ḥuṣrí on the Tradition, "Sometimes I am with God in a state which I do not share with anything other than God."

c

116   CHAPTER LV: "On the meanings derived by the Ṣúfís from certain Apostolic Traditions."

Explanation by Aḥmad b. Muḥammad b. Sálim of the Tradition, "A man's best food is that which his hand hath earned".

Explanation by Shiblí of the Tradition, "My daily bread is set under the shadow of my sword."

117   Explanation by Junayd of the Tradition, "If ye had trust in God as ye ought, He would feed you even as He feeds the birds, etc." Explanation by ʿAmr b. ʿUthmán al-Makkí of the words addressed by the Prophet to ʿAbdallah b. ʿUmar, "Worship God as though thou sawest Him, for if thou seest Him not, yet He sees thee". Explanation by Abú Bakr al-Wásiṭí of the Tradition, "The friend (walí) of God is created with a disposition to generosity and good-nature." Explanation by Shiblí of

118 the Tradition, "When the lower soul (nafs) is assured of her sustenance, she becomes quiet." Explanation by Junayd of the Tradition, "Thy love for anything makes thee blind and deaf." Explanation by Shiblí of the Tradition, "When ye see the afflicted, ask God to make you free from tribulation." Explanation by Shiblí of the Tradition, "A heart ruled by the present world is debarred from feeling the sweetness of the world to come." Explanation by Muḥammad b. Músá al-Farghání of the Prophet's advice to Abú Juḥayfa, "Question the savants and be on terms of sincere friendship with the sages and associate with the great (mystics)." Explanations by Sahl b. ʿAbdallah al-Tustarí of the Traditions, "The true believer is he who is made glad by his good actions and grieved by his evil actions", and "Accursed is the world and accursed all that is therein except the recollection (dhikr) of God."

The author declares that the principle of Ṣúfistic divination (istinbáṭ) is founded on the Tradition that the Prophet

119 asked a number of his Companions, amongst whom was

ʿAbdallah b. ʿUmar, "What tree resembles Man?" ʿAbdallah divined that the Prophet was referring to the date-palm, but since he was the youngest man present, he felt ashamed to answer. This proves that mystical divination does not depend on age or experience but on knowledge of the Unseen which is communicated by God.

BOOK OF THE COMPANIONS.

CHAPTER LVI: "Concerning the Companions of the Prophet and their good qualities."

120   Explanation of the Prophet's saying, "My Companions are like the stars: whomsoever of them ye take as your pattern, ye will be rightly guided." Their authority as regards matters of practice is well-known. The Prophet recognised the pre-eminence of particular Companions in certain details of external conduct. His description of their spiritual characteristics under four heads. Muḥammad b. ʿAlí al-Kattání enumerates the different religious and moral qualities which
121   prevailed in the first four generations of Islam.

CHAPTER LVII: "Account of Abú Bakr the Veracious and how he was distinguished from the other Companions of the Prophet by states which the Ṣúfís imitate and model themselves upon."

A saying of Abú Bakr showing the intensity of his fear as well as the greatness of his hope. His words to the Moslems immediately after the death of the Prophet. Definition of the term *rabbání*. Abú Bakr al-Wásiṭí said that Abú Bakr was the first Moslem who spoke mystically, alluding
122   to the fact that, when he abandoned all his possessions and the Prophet asked him what he had left behind for his family, he replied, "Allah and His Apostle". This is a sublime allegory for Unitarians. His being firmly grounded in unification (*tawḥíd*) is also indicated by his speech to the people after the Prophet's death. When the Prophet implored

God to help the Moslems on the field of Badr, Abú Bakr calmed him, saying, "God will fulfil unto thee His promise." Such was the reality of his faith in God. The author explains the reason why the Prophet showed agitation and Abú Bakr equanimity, although the Prophet was more perfect than Abú Bakr. Moreover, Abú Bakr was endowed in a peculiar

123 degree with inspiration (*ilhám*) and insight (*firásat*). Three occasions on which he displayed these qualities. Bakr b. ʿAbdallah al-Muzaní said that Abú Bakr surpassed the Companions of the Prophet, not in the amount of his fasts and prayers, but in something that was within his heart. It is said that this thing was the love of God.

124 Other sayings of Abú Bakr. Three verses of the Koran by which his mind was occupied. Lines by Abu 'l-ʿAtáhiya attributed to him. Junayd declared that the loftiest saying on unification is that of Abú Bakr, "Glory be to Him who hath given His creatures no means of knowing Him save their inability to know Him."

125 CHAPTER LVIII: "Account of ʿUmar b. al-Khattáb."

ʿUmar was described by the Prophet as an inspired man (*muhaddath*). Evidence of his inspiration afforded by the story of his crying out, "O Sáriya! the hill, the hill." Anecdotes and sayings of ʿUmar.

126 Characteristics in respect of which ʿUmar is taken as a pattern by the Súfís. Discussion of his attitude towards quietists (*mutawakkilún*). Four things which, according to him, constitute devotion (*ʿibádat*).

127 CHAPTER LIX: "Account of ʿUthmán."

He was specially distinguished by the quality of firmness (*tamkín*), which is one of the highest spiritual degrees. Although he was brought into contact with the things of this world, he really dwelt apart from them, as the true gnostic does: he used his wealth to benefit others, not for his own pleasure. Therefore he liked spending money better

than amassing it. Instances of his generosity. Definition by
Sahl b. ʿAbdallah al-Tustarí of the person who is justified
in departing from the rule of poverty. Sahl b. ʿAbdallah
said that sometimes a man who possesses great wealth is
128 more ascetic than any of his contemporaries, *e. g.*, ʿUmar b.
ʿAbd al-ʿAzíz. Hence those who exalt wealth above poverty
are mistaken, for wealth does not consist in abundance of
wordly goods, nor poverty in the lack of such: it is true
wealth to have God, and true poverty to need God. Anecdotes illustrating the asceticism of ʿUthmán. His steadfastness
appeared in his behaviour on the day when he was murdered.
129 Saying of Junayd concerning firmness (*tamkín*). Four things
in which ʿUthmán found spiritual good comprised.

CHAPTER LX: "Account of ʿAlí b. Abí Ṭálib."

Junayd said that if ʿAlí had been less occupied with war
he would have imparted to the Moslems much of the esoteric
knowledge that was bestowed upon him. This esoteric knowledge was possessed by Khaḍir (Kor. 18, 64), hence the
erroneous doctrine that saintship is superior to prophecy.
130 Characteristics of ʿAlí which are imitated by the Ṣúfís. His
definition of the nature of God. The mystery of Creation.
Sayings on faith. His analysis of 'states' (*aḥwál*) and 'stations'
(*maqámát*): if it be genuine, he was the first who discoursed
on the subject. His answer to the question, "Who is safest
from faults?" On one occasion ʿAlí pointed to his breast
and exclaimed, "Here is a secret knowledge, if I could but
find any one worthy to receive it!"

131 ʿAlí was distinguished from the rest of the Companions
by his power of elucidating mystical ideas such as unification and gnosis. Exposition (*bayán*) is a great gift. Saying
on friendship. His asceticism: when ʿAlí was murdered, his
son Ḥasan announced that the whole of the worldly wealth
which he had left behind was a sum of 400 dirhems. At the
hour of prayer he used to tremble and turn pale for fear

that he might fail in the trust committed to him (Kor. 33, 72).

132 Comparison of the passions (*nafs*) to a flock of sheep which as soon as they are collected on one side break away on the other. Statement of the characteristics in respect of which each one of the four Orthodox Caliphs is an example to the Ṣúfís. Saying of ʿAlí concerning four things wherein spiritual good entirely consists.

CHAPTER LXI: "Description of the People of the Bench (*Ahl al-Ṣuffa*)."

133 Passages of the Koran in which they are mentioned. God rebuked the Prophet for treating one of their number scornfully. Marks of respect shown towards them by the Prophet. Their ascetic dress and food.

134 The Prophet approved of their quietism and did not command them to work or trade.

CHAPTER LXII: "Account of the other Companions from this point of view."

The author illustrates the asceticism and quietism of the Companions of the Prophet by relating anecdotes and sayings of the following: Ṭalḥa b. ʿUbaydallah, Muʿádh b. Jabal, ʿImrán b. Ḥuṣayn, Salmán al-Fárisí,

135 Abu 'l-Dardá, Abú Dharr, Abú ʿUbayda b. al-Jarráḥ,

136 ʿAbdallah b. Masʿúd, Bará b. Málik, ʿAbdallah b. al-ʿAbbás, Kaʿb al-Aḥbár,

137 Ḥáritha, Abú Hurayra, Anas b. Málik, ʿAbdallah b. ʿUmar, Ḥudhayfa b. al-Yamán,

138 ʿAbdallah b. Jaḥsh, Ṣafwán b. Muḥriz al-Máziní, Abú Farwa, Abú Bakra, ʿAbdallah b. Rawáḥa, Tamím al-Dárí, ʿAdí b. Ḥátim, Abú Ráfiʿ the Prophet's client,

139 Muḥammad b. Kaʿb, Zurára b. Awfá, Ḥanẓala al-Kátib, al-Lajláj (Abú Kuthayyir), Abú Juḥayfa, Ḥakím b. Ḥizám,

140 Usáma, Bilál, Ṣuhayb, ʿAbdallah b. Rabíʿa, Muṣʿab b. ʿUmar, ʿAbd al-Raḥmán b. ʿAwf, Saʿd b. al-Rabíʿ.

141 BOOK OF THE MANNERS *(ádáb)* PRACTISED BY
THOSE WHO SEEK TO BECOME ṢÚFÍS

CHAPTER LXIII: "Concerning Manners."

142 The Prophet said, "No sire ever begot a son more excellent than Good Manners", and he also said, "God disci-
plined me and made my manners good." Answer given by
Muḥammad b. Sírín to one who asked him what manners
bring a man nearest to God and most advance him in God's
sight. Answer given by Ḥasan b. Abi 'l-Ḥasan al-Baṣrí to the
question, "What manners are most useful in this world and bring
one nearest to God in the next world?" Sayings of Saʿíd b.
al-Musayyib and Kulthúm al-Ghassání. Ibn al-Mubárak said,
"We have more need of a little manners than of much
knowledge." Another saying of Ibn al-Mubárak.

The author divides men, as regards their manners, into
three classes: the worldly, the religious, and the elect
among the religious. The manners of the worldly consist,
for the most part, in such polite accomplishments as elegant
143 speech, learning, poetry and rhetoric. The manners of the
religious are mostly a discipline of soul and body: they
keep the commandments, refrain from lusts, and devote
themselves to piety and good works. Sayings of Sahl b.
ʿAbdallah and others on this topic. The manners of the
elect among the religious (*i. e.*, the Ṣúfís) consist mainly in
purity of heart, spiritual meditation, faithful observance of
that which they have promised to perform, concentration on
their mystical 'states', etc. Saying of al-Jalájílí al-Baṣrí.
Definition of *adab* by Abu 'l-ʿAbbás b. ʿAtá.

144 The Ṣúfís are distinguished from other people and recognised amongst themselves by their manners, which enter into
every detail of their practical lives.

CHAPTER LXIV: "Concerning their manners in ablution
and purification."

The first thing requisite is to know what is obligatory, what is recommended, and what is most excellent in itself. Ordinary men should be excused if they take advantage of the indulgences and remissions which are granted to them, 145 but there is no excuse for Ṣúfís who fall below the highest standard of outward purity and cleanliness. The author mentions the exemplary practice of some Ṣúfís whom he had seen. It belongs to the manners of the Ṣúfís that they should always be in a state of purity both at home and abroad, so as to avoid the risk of dying unclean. Saying of Ḥuṣrí explained by the author. Anecdote of Abú ᶜAbdallah al-Rúdhabárí. Saying concerning the endeavour of Satan to get something for himself out of every human action.

146   Story of Ibn al-Kurríní (al-Karanbí) the teacher of Junayd. Why Sahl b. ᶜAbdallah urged his disciples to drink plenty of water and pour as little as possible on the ground. Description of the rule of purity observed by Abú ᶜAmr al-Zajjájí during his thirty years' residence at Mecca. How Ibráhím al-Khawwáṣ preferred to suffer from thirst rather than neglect his ablutions in the desert. Various practices 147 adopted or rejected by Ṣúfís for the sake of purification. Account of the manner in which Ibráhím al-Khawwáṣ used to journey from Mecca to Kúfa. Certain eminent Ṣúfís disliked entering public baths, and when obliged to do so, took 148 strict precautions that decency should be observed. Practices connected with ablution and cleanliness. The most punctilious attention to these rules does not constitute *waswasat*, 149 which the author defines as a misplaced zeal for superfluities that causes neglect of what is obligatory. The right course in such matters depends on circumstances, *e. g.* the quantity of water available. Stories of Ṣúfís who persevered in ablution though it was hurtful to them.

150   Stories of Ibráhím b. Adham and Ibráhím al-Khawwáṣ.

CHAPTER LXV: "Concerning their manners in prayer".

The knowledge necessary for the due performance of
151 prayer. Ṣúfís should make themselves ready for prayer
before the hour arrives. Consequently they need some knowledge of astronomy and geography.

152　Sahl b. ʿAbdallah used to say that it was a sign of the
sincere mystic to have an attendant Jinní who impelled
him to pray at the proper time, and awakened him if he
were asleep. Some Ṣúfís engaged in devotional exercises by
day and night, and through force of habit never failed to
perform them at the appointed time. Description of the initial
rites of prayer. Sayings of Junayd and Ibn Sálim on the
importance of intention (*niyyat*). Answer given by Abú Saʿíd
al-Kharráz to the question, "How should one enter upon
prayer?" Anonymous sayings describing the reverence that
153 should be felt by one who begins to perform the service of
prayer. At this time there must be no thought of anything
except God. Quotation from a book on the manners of
154 prayer by Abú Saʿíd al-Kharráz, with explanations by Sarráj.

The holy meditation and concentration of mind which
prayer demands should commence before the prayer itself
and remain after it, so that the worshipper when he begins
to pray only proceeds, as it were, from one prayer to another, and when he has ceased to pray, nevertheless continues
in the mental attitude of prayer.

155　Saying of the Prophet on this subject. Awe of God causes
some to blush or grow pale when they begin to pray. Story
of a man whose concentration in prayer was such that he
could not count the number of genuflexions which he performed: accordingly he used to make one of his friends sit
beside him and count for him. Sahl b. ʿAbdallah was too
weak to rise from his place, but when the hour of prayer
arrived his strength was restored and he stood erect throughout
the service. Anecdote of a man who, though he was alone
in the desert, performed his devotions with the same punc-

tilious ceremony as at home. Account of a hermit who used to perform a prayer of two *rakᶜas* whenever he ate or drank or put on a garment, or entered or quitted the mosque, or felt joy or sorrow or anger.

156   Story of Abú ᶜAbdallah b. Jábán. The Ṣúfís dislike to act as Imám (leader in prayer), to pray in the first row in the mosque, and to make their prayers too long. Even if one of them knew the whole Koran by heart, he would prefer as Imám someone who could only recite the *Fátiḥa* and another chapter, because the Imám, as the Prophet said, is responsible (for the correctness of the prayer).

The reason why the Ṣúfís dislike to pray in the first row and to make long prayers. Junayd, notwithstanding his great age, refused to forgo his prayers, by means of which (he said) he had attained to God in the beginning of his religious life. Four qualities which belong to prayer.

157   CHAPTER LXVI: "Concerning their manners in almsgiving."

It is not obligatory on the Ṣúfís either to pay the legal tithes (*zakát*) or to give the voluntary alms (*ṣadaqa*), because God has removed from them the worldly wealth that would make it incumbent on them to give such alms. Saying of Muṭarraf b. ᶜAbdallah b. al-Shikhkhír. God has bestowed a greater favour on the Ṣúfís by taking wealth away from them than He would have bestowed by endowing them with much wealth. Verse of a poet who boasts that, in con-
158 sequence of his generosity, he is too poor to be liable for the payment of tithes. Reply given by Shiblí to Ibráhím b. Shaybán, who asked him what amount of tithes was payable on five camels. Some Ṣúfís neither ask for alms nor accept them when offered. Their motive in acting thus. Anecdote of Muḥammad b. Manṣúr. Story of a Ṣúfí who expended 1000 dínárs every year upon his poor brethren. Munificence of Abú ᶜAlí al-Mushtúlí towards the Ṣúfís. Story of an eminent
159 Ṣúfí and a rich man. Extract from a letter written by a

celebrated Imám to a poor Ṣúfí. It is not proper that Ṣúfís should refuse to accept alms that have been freely offered by strangers. Tradition of the Prophet on this subject. Such alms are a gift from God and may either be used to purchase food or handed to any one whom the recipient knows to be more deserving than himself. Anecdote of Abú Bakr al-Farghání. Anonymous saying on the principle that should be followed in giving and receiving alms. The true criterion of the Ṣúfí who gives or takes or refuses alms for God's sake alone is that he feels no difference whether alms are given to him or withheld from him. Another class of Ṣúfís
160 choose to receive alms rather than presents, arguing that when they receive alms they only receive what is due to the poor from the rich, and that the refusal to take alms is a sort of pride and shows a dislike of poverty. Story of Abú Muḥammad al-Murtaʿish. The Prophet said that it is not allowable to give alms to the rich. Those who hold that the Ṣúfís ought not to accept alms base their objection upon this Tradition, for the Ṣúfís, though poor from a worldly point of view, are spiritually rich. Saying of ʿAlí b. Sahl al-Iṣbahání. Another interpretation of the Tradition quoted above. Derivation of the word *faqr* (poverty).
161 Although it is said that alms are filth, the poor may accept them without loss of dignity. If a man has no worldly wealth and is unable to give alms of that sort, let him give alms of kind words and deeds. Bishr b. al-Ḥárith urged the Traditionists to pay a tithe on the Traditions which they wrote down and committed to memory, *i. e.*, to practise five out of every two hundred Traditions. Four things necessary for those who pay tithes. The rich who pay tithes to the poor are only restoring what really belongs to the latter.

CHAPTER LXVII: "Concerning their manners in fasting."
Explanation of the Tradition that God said, "Fasting is Mine and I give recompense for it." Other Traditions on

fasting. The author defines the qualities which constitute good manners in fasting. Description of the fasting of Sahl b. ʿAbdallah al-Tustarí.

163 How Abú ʿUbayd al-Busrí fasted during Ramaḍán. Voluntary fasts. Some eminent Ṣúfís used to fast continually, whether they were staying at home or travelling: their object was to protect themselves from the Devil and lust and passion. Story of Ruwaym and a girl of whom he begged a drink of water. Other Ṣúfís adopt the fast of David, i. e., they fast every second day. The author explains why the Prophet declared this method of fasting to be the best.

164 Saying of Sahl b. ʿAbdallah. Anecdote of Abú ʿAbdallah Aḥmad b. Jábán, who fasted continually for more than fifty years. Some dislike continual fasting on the ground that the lower 'self' (*nafs*) is gratified by every habitual act, even though it be an act of devotion. Story of Ibráhím b. Adham, showing the importance of 'lawful' food. The state of the dervishes who are entirely detached from this world and depend on God for their daily bread is more excellent than the state of those who, when they break their fast, partake as usual of the food prepared for them. The dervishes of the former class have their own manners in fasting. For example, none of them will fast without having obtained permission from his companions, who need not wait for him 165 to complete his fast, unless he is an invalid or a spiritual director. Anecdote of Junayd. It is said, "When you see a Ṣúfí fasting voluntarily, hold him in suspicion, for he must have got with him something of this world." Rules of fasting applicable to a company of dervishes amongst whom there is a novice or a Sheykh. Story of a Sheykh who fasted for the sake of one of his disciples. The author relates that Abu 166 'l-Ḥasan al-Makkí, whom he saw at Baṣra, became celebrated for his fasting, and that Ibn Sálim banished him from his

presence on that account. Anecdote of a Ṣúfí of Wásiṭ.
Saying of Shiblí.

CHAPTER LXVIII: "Concerning their manners in making
the Pilgrimage."

The first rule is that they should make every possible
effort to perform the Pilgrimage once at least during their lives.
67   Want of provisions and means of conveyance does not
relieve them from this duty, since it is a rule of the Ṣúfís
to fulfil the utmost obligations laid upon them by the religious law. Ṣúfís who make the Pilgrimage may be divided
into three classes. The first class are those who perform
only one Pilgrimage, and for the rest of their lives are
content with mystical experiences. Sahl b. ʿAbdallah and
other eminent Ṣúfís followed this rule. The second class are
those who cut themselves free from all worldly ties and set
out to make the Pilgrimage, penniless and unprovisioned;
they journey alone through pathless deserts, trusting in none
but God, and never tire of going as pilgrims to His holy
168 temple. Anecdotes illustrating the manners of Ṣúfís who
belong to this class. Ḥasan al-Qazzáz al-Dínawarí made
twelve pilgrimages with bare feet and uncovered head. Stories
of Abú Turáb al-Nakhshabí, Abú ʿAbdallah al-Maghribí, Jaʿfar
al-Khuldí, and Ibráhím al-Khawwáṣ.
169   Another story of Ibráhím al-Khawwáṣ, who quitted Mecca
with the resolution not to touch food until he should
arrive at Qádisiyya. The third class are those who by their
own choice become residents at Mecca or in the neighbour-
hood, either on account of the sanctity of the place or from
ascetic motives. Their manners are illustrated by anecdotes
of Abú ʿAbdallah b. al-Jallá,
170   Abú Bakr al-Kattání, Abú ʿAmr al-Zajjájí, and al-Duqqí.
It is said that anyone who can endure hunger at Mecca
for a day and a night can endure it for three days in the
rest of the world. There used to be a saying that residence

at Mecca alters the disposition and reveals the inmost nature, and that only true mystics can live there uncorrupted. Story of a dervish who refused some money which Ibráhím al-Khawwáṣ offered to him. Tho reasons why Ṣúfís willingly
171 undergo hardships in travelling to Mecca. Story of some dervishes who found fault with one of their number for circumambulating the Kaᶜba in the daytime, because they fancied that he did so in the hope of receiving alms. Another rule of the Ṣúfís is this, that when they have vowed to make the Pilgrimage they keep their word even though it should cost them their lives. Story of Aḥmad b. Dillawayh. Also, while crossing the desert, they perform the obligatory acts of devotion, so far as they can, no less punctiliously than at home. They do not travel by regular stages or complete the journey within a fixed time, but set out when God causes them to set out and halt when God causes them to halt. Every rite connected with the Pilgrimage should be accompanied by the spiritual action or feeling appropriate to it.
172-3 Exemplifying this principle in detail, the author describes the allegorical meaning of the various ceremonies, such as the *iḥrám*, the *talbiyat*, the kissing of the Black Stone, the standing at ᶜArafát, the casting of the pebbles at Miná, and indicates the right way of performing them. Story, related by Ibráhím al-Khawwáṣ, of a Sheykh who taught the doctrine of trust in God but proved false to it in practice. Anecdote of al-Zaqqáq: though starving, he would not accept food from some soldiers whom he met in the Desert of the Israelites.
174 Another story of al-Zaqqáq: how he lost the sight of one eye.

CHAPTER LXIX: "Concerning the manners of dervishes in their mutual intercourse, and the principles which they observe at home and abroad".

Two sayings of Junayd. Sayings of the above-mentioned

Abú Bakr al-Zaqqáq and Abú ᶜAbdallah b. al-Jallá. Three
rules of conduct for dervishes stated by Sahl b. ᶜAbdallah
175 and by an anonymous Ṣúfí. Three things necessary for the
dervish, according to Sahl b. ᶜAbdallah. Saying of Junayd.
Twelve qualities of thc dervish enumerated by Ibráhím al-
Khawwáṣ. Anonymous sayings on poverty. It is a breach of
manners for a dervish to say anything that suggests egoism.
Anecdotes of Ibráhím b. Shaybán, Abú ᶜAbdallah Aḥmad
al-Qalánisí, and Ibráhím b. al-Muwallad al-Raqqí.

176   Three fundamental principles of Ṣúfism according to al-
Qalánisí and another whose name is not mentioned. Anonymous saying on the false dervish. Saying of Ibráhím al-
Khawwáṣ: the dervish must not regard secondary causes
(asbáb). Saying of Junayd: how to treat dervishes.

CHAPTER LXX: "Concerning their manners in companionship."

Saying of Ibráhím b. Shaybán: "We were not used to
associate with anyone who said, 'My shoe' or 'My bucket'.
Sayings of Sahl b. ᶜAbdallah and Dhu 'l-Nún al-Miṣrí to
the effect that God is the best companion for the Ṣúfí.

177   Sayings by Dhu 'l-Nún and Aḥmad b. Yúsuf al-Zajjájí.
Disagreement condemned. Abú Saᶜíd al-Kharráz said that
he consorted with the Ṣúfís for fifty years and never quar-
relled with them, because he always sided with them against
himself. Junayd said that he preferred a good-natured liber-
tine to an ill-natured pietist. Story of Abú Ḥafṣ. How Abú
Yazíd and Abú ᶜAlí al-Sindí instructed one another. Story
of Abú Ḥafṣ and Abú ᶜUthmán (al-Ḥírí). Answer given by
Sahl b. ᶜAbdallah to his pupil, Ibn Sálim, who complained
that Sahl had never pointed out to him any of the *Abdál*.

178   Story told by Ibráhím b. Shaybán of his companionship
with Abú ᶜAbdallah al-Maghribí. Sahl b. ᶜAbdallah would
not take as his companion anyone who was afraid of wild
beasts. Dhu 'l-Nún's answer to the question, "With whom

shall I associate?" Three conditions imposed by Ibráhím b. Adham on those who desired his company. How Abú Bakr al-Kattání overcame the dislike which he felt towards one of his friends. The duty of a true companion exemplified by ʿAbdallah al-Marwazí while travelling with Abú ʿAlí al-Ribátí.

179   Three classes of men whose society, according to Sahl b. ʿAbdallah, should be avoided.

CHAPTER LXXI: "Concerning their manners in discussing mystical topics".

Sayings of Abú Muḥammad al-Jarírí, Abú Yazíd al-Bistámí, Junayd, Abu Jaʿfar b. al-Farají, and Abú Ḥafṣ.

Story of Abú ʿAbdallah b. al-Jallá who refused to speak on the subject of trust in God (tawakkul) until he had given away four small coins which he possessed.

180   Anecdote of Abú ʿAbdallah al-Ḥuṣrí and Ibn Yazdániyár. Saying of Ibráhím al-Khawwáṣ on the qualifications necessary for those who discuss the theory of mysticism. Abú Saʿíd al-Kharráz rebuked a man for using symbols (ishárat) in reference to God. Junayd said that he did not know any theory and practice more excellent than the theory and practice of Ṣúfism. Abú ʿAlí al-Rúdhabárí declared that the knowledge of the mystic cannot be expressed in plain words. Anecdote of Abú Saʿíd al-Kharráz and Abú Ḥátim al-ʿAṭṭár. Saying of Junayd.

181   Shiblí told those who were listening to his discourse that the angels would like to be in their place. When Sarí al-Saqaṭí heard that Junayd gathered round him an audience of Ṣúfís in the mosque, he said, "Alas, you have become a resort for idle folk". How Sarí asked Junayd to explain the meaning of thanksgiving (shukr). Sahl b. ʿAbdallah would not speak in public so long as Dhu 'l-Nún was alive. Sayings of Abú Sulaymán al-Dárání and Abú Bakr al-Zaqqáq on the value of oral instruction in Ṣúfism. Why al-

Jallá, the father of Abú ʿAbdallah b. al-Jallá, was so named.

182   Saying of Ḥárith al-Muḥásibí. How Junayd used to answer those who questioned him on matters which lay beyond their spiritual capacity. Abú ʿAmr al-Zajjájí said that it is better to commit a gross breach of etiquette than to interrupt a Sheykh in his discourse. Saying of Ibn al-Kurríní (al-Karanbí) to Junayd. Sayings of Shiblí and Sarí al-Saqaṭí.

CHAPTER LXXII: "Concerning their manners at mealtime and in their gatherings and entertainments".

Three occasions, enumerated by Junayd, when the divine mercy descends upon Ṣúfís.

183   Muḥammad b. Manṣúr al-Ṭúsí said to his guest, "Stay three nights with us, and if you stay longer it will be a gift of alms from you to us." Saying of Sarí al-Saqaṭí on the difficulty of obtaining 'lawful' food. Saying of Abú ʿAlí al-Nawribáṭí on the way to treat dervishes, theologians, and ascetics when they enter a house. Story of Abú Ḥamza and Sarí al-Saqaṭí. Sayings of Abú ʿAlí al-Rúdhabárí in praise of dervishes who meet together. Eating after a meal condemned by Jaʿfar al-Khuldí. Another saying of Jaʿfar on gluttony. Two sayings of Shiblí.

184   How one should behave when eating with friends, men of the world, and dervishes. The author's account of the manners which it is proper for the Ṣúfí faqírs to observe in eating. A Sheykh who had eaten no food for ten days was reproached by his host because he ate with two fingers instead of three. Saying of Ibráhím b. Shaybán. Abú Bakr al-Kattání would not eat any food that was not offered spontaneously. Saying of Junayd. How Abú Turáb al-Nakhshabí was punished for refusing an offer of food. Saying of Junayd on the importance of purity as regards food, clothing, and dwelling-place. Sarí al-Saqaṭí said that the Ṣúfís eat like sick men and sleep like men who are in danger of being drowned. Saying of Abú ʿAbdallah al-Ḥuṣrí. Anecdote of

Faṭḥ al-Mawṣilí, describing the manner in which he was entertained by Bishr al-Ḥáfí.

185   Maʿrúf al-Karkhí accepted every invitation, saying that he was only a guest in the world and had no home except the house that he was bidden to enter. Description by Abú Bakr al-Kattání of a gathering of three hundred Ṣúfís at Mecca: instead of talking about religion they acted towards each other with good-nature and kindness and unselfishness. Saying of Abú Sulaymán al-Dárání: eating deadens the heart. Ruwaym said that during twenty years he never thought of food until it was set before him. Story of Abú ʿAlí al-Rúdhabárí. Anecdote related by Abú ʿAbdallah al-Rúdhabárí of a man who entertained a party of guests and lighted a thousand lamps; on being charged with extravagance, he successfully challenged his accuser to extinguish any lamp that had not been lighted for God's sake. Anecdote of Aḥmad b. Muḥammad al-Sulamí.

186   CHAPTER LXXIII: "Concerning their manners at the time of audition (samáʿ) and ecstasy."

Junayd mentioned three things necessary in audition, and if these were absent, he disapproved of it. Saying of Ḥárith al-Muḥásibí. Story of Dhu 'l-Nún's ecstasy on hearing some erotic verses recited. When Ibráhím al-Márastání was asked about dancing and rending the garments in audition, he quoted the word of God that was revealed to Moses, "Rend thy heart and do not rend thy garments." The author says that this subject will be fully set forth in a subsequent chapter.

187   Junayd said that excess of ecstasy combined with deficiency of religious knowledge is harmful. Explanation of this saying by the author. Ecstasy, provided that it is involuntary, is not improper for dervishes who are entirely detached from worldly interests. No one, however, should seek to produce ecstasy in himself by joining a number of

persons already enraptured and by participating in their audition. This, if it become a habit, is most destructive to spiritual illumination. So long as the heart is polluted with worldliness, audition is idle and vain.

CHAPTER LXXIV: "Concerning their manners in dress." Three sayings of Abú Sulaymán al-Dárání. Reply given by a young Ṣúfí to Bishr b. al-Hárith (al-Háfí), who had expressed the opinion that Ṣúfís should not wear patched frocks (*muraqqaʿát*).

188 Story related by al-Jarírí of a dervish who wore the same garment both in summer and winter because of a vision which he had seen. Saying of Abú Hafṣ al-Haddád. Abú Yazíd's criticism of Yaḥyá b. Muʿádh al-Rází. Abú Yazíd left nothing behind him except the shirt which he was wearing at the time of his death. Description of the patched frock belonging to Ibn al-Kurríní (al-Karanbí). The fine clothes worn by Abú Hafṣ al-Naysábúrí. The author mentions the general rules observed by dervishes in regard to dress.

189 CHAPTER LXXV: "Concerning their manners in travelling." Counsel given by Abú ʿAlí al-Rúdhabárí to a man who was setting out on a journey. Ruwaym's advice to the traveller. Muḥammad b. Ismáʿíl describes a journey on which he was accompanied by Abú Bakr al-Zaqqáq and Abú Bakr al-Kattání. Saying of Abu 'l-Ḥasan al-Muzayyin. Ibráhím al-Khawwáṣ would not allow al-Muzayyin the Elder to kill a scorpion that was crawling on his thigh. What Shiblí said to his disciples who suffered hardships in travelling.

190 Three rules observed by Abú ʿAbdallah al-Naṣíbí during thirty years of travel. The author enumerates the various reasons for which Ṣúfís travel; he says that they perform their religious duties just as carefully as when they are at home, and if a party of dervishes are travelling together, they show the utmost consideration to their weaker brethren.

Other Ṣúfís follow a stricter rule, which is illustrated by sayings of Ibráhím al-Khawwás and Abú ʿImrán al-Ṭabaristání. According to Abú Yaʿqúb al-Súsí there are four qualities that are indispensable to the traveller: religious knowledge, piety, enthusiasm, and good-nature. Abú Bakr al-Kattání said that the Ṣúfís refuse to associate with any one of their number who journeys to Yemen more than once. Derivation of *safar* (travel).

191   CHAPTER LXXVI: "Concerning their manners in sacrificing prestige (honour, influence, popularity), and in begging, and in acting for the sake of their friends."

The author quotes a saying related by the pupils of Abú ʿAbdallah al-Ṣubayḥí to the effect that it behoves the dervish to sacrifice the prestige that accrues to him in consequence of his having resigned all worldly goods; but he is not entirely 'poor' until he has made a further sacrifice, namely, the sacrifice of 'self'. Story of al-Muẓaffar al-Qarmísíní and another Ṣúfí who made themselves so despised that no one would give them anything. Ibráhím b. Shaybán's praise of al-Muẓaffar al-Qarmísíní. Anecdote of a Ṣúfí who abased himself by begging, which he disliked intensely. Story of a novice whose devotion and austerities had gained for him a great reputation: he was told by a certain Sheykh that he must go from door to door and beg his bread and eat nothing else, but he found himself unable to obey; and when he was reduced to beggary in his old age, he regarded this as a punishment for having disobeyed the Sheykh.

192   Story of an eminent Ṣúfí who never broke his fast except with pieces of bread that he had begged. Anecdote of Mimshádh al-Dínawarí. How Bunán al-Ḥammál learned that he was a parasite. Story of a novice who begged food for his companions and partook of it with them: on this account he was blamed by some Sheykhs who said that he had really begged for himself. The author explains the true principles

of begging. Anecdote of a Sheykh who refrained from begging for fear that he might endanger the spiritual welfare of a fellow-Moslem, in accordance with the tradition that he who repulses a sincere beggar will not prosper.

193   CHAPTER LXXVII: "Concerning their manners when they receive a gift of worldly goods".

Story of a dervish who lost his faith and his spiritual feeling (*ḥál*) in consequence of receiving a gift. Another story of a dervish who, for the same reason, was deprived of the tribulation which mystics hold dear. Abú Turáb al-Nakhshabí said that any one upon whom much bounty was bestowed ought to weep for himself. How Bunán al-Ḥammál refused a thousand dinars.

Story of Ibn Bunán: four hundred dirhems were brought to him while he was asleep, but he was warned in a dream not to take more than he needed. Story of Abu 'l-Ḥusayn al-Núrí: he dropped three hundred dinars, one by one, into the Tigris. Anecdote of Ibn Zírí, a pupil of Junayd, who 194 came into possession of some money and left his companions. Abú Aḥmad al-Qalánisí would not let his pupils visit one of their number who had travelled and returned with money. How Abú Ḥafṣ al-Ḥaddád spent a thousand dinars on the dervishes of Ramla. Story of Shiblí, who bestowed on dervishes nearly all the money that was given him to buy food for his starving children. Story of a Ṣúfí Sheykh who saved four dirhems in order that he might return them to God on the Day of Judgment and say, "These are all the worldly goods Thou hast given me."

195   Shiblí received a sum of money from the vizier of al-Muʿtadid to distribute amongst the Ṣúfís of Baghdád; when every one had taken as much he wanted, Shiblí said, "The more ye have taken, the farther are ye from God, and the more ye have rejected, the nearer are ye to God."

Chapter LXXVIII: "Concerning the manners of those who earn their livelihood."

Sahl b. ʿAbdallah said that while it is an offence against the Sunna to condemn work, it is an offence against the Faith to condemn trust in God. Saying of Junayd. How Isḥáq al-Magházilí rebuked Bishr b. al-Ḥárith for earning his livelihood by spinning thread. The reply of Ibn Sálim to one who asked him whether it is the duty of Moslems to earn their livelihood or to trust in God.

196 Two sayings of ʿAbdallah b. al-Mubárak in justification of earning. Abú Saʿíd al-Kharráz once passed a whole night mending the shoes of the dervishes with whom he was travelling. Saying of Abú Ḥafṣ (al-Ḥaddád). Story of a negro at Damascus who was a follower of the Ṣúfís. Anecdote of Abu ʾl-Qásim al-Munádí. Sayings of Ibráhím al-Khawwáṣ, and Ibráhím b. Adham. General rules to be observed by Ṣúfís who work.

197 Abú Ḥafṣ al-Ḥaddád earned a dinar every day and bestowed it upon the Ṣúfís. Saying of Shiblí to a cobbler. Dhu ʾl-Nún said that the true gnostic does not attempt to gain a livelihood.

Chapter LXXIX: "Concerning their manners in taking and giving and in showing courtesy to the poor."

A short way to Paradise described by Sarí al-Saqaṭí. Saying of Junayd: none has the right to take money unless he prefers spending to receiving. Saying of Abú Bakr Aḥmad b. Ḥamawayh: money should be accepted or rejected for God's sake, not from any other motive. Story of al-Zaqqáq and Yúsuf al-Ṣáʾigh. Anecdote showing the tact and delicacy with which Ibn Rufayʿ of Damascus bestowed a gift of money upon Abú ʿAlí al-Rúdhabárí.

198 Sayings of Abú Bakr al-Zaqqáq and Abú Muḥammad al-Murtaʿish. How Junayd induced Ibn al-Kurríní (al-Karanbí) to accept some money from him. Whenever Abu ʾl-Qásim

al-Munádí saw smoke issuing from a neighbour's house, he used to send and ask for food. Story of Junayd and Ḥusayn b. al-Miṣrí. Answer given by Yúsuf b. al-Ḥusayn to the question whether one is justified in bestowing all one's property upon a brother in God.

199 CHAPTER LXXX: "Concerning the manners of those who are married and those who have children."

Story of the marriage of Abú Aḥmad al-Qalánisí. How Muḥammad b. ʿAlí al-Qaṣṣár trained his little daughter to trust in God. Story of Bunán al-Ḥammál and his son. Ibráhím b. Adham said that a man who marries embarks on a ship, and that he suffers shipwreck when a child is born to him.

200 Saying of Bishr b. al-Ḥárith. Story of a woman who offered herself in marriage to Abú Shuʿayb al-Baráthí and refused to enter his hut until he removed a piece of matting. The author says that a married Ṣúfí must not commit his wife and children to the care of God but must provide for their needs unless they are in the same spiritual state as he is. Ṣúfís ought to wed poor women and not take advantage of rich women who desire to marry them. One day when Fatḥ al-Mawṣilí kissed his son he heard a heavenly voice saying, "O Fatḥ, art not thou ashamed to love another besides Me?" The author points out that although the Prophet used to kiss his children and clasp them to his bosom, his spiritual rank and endowments were unique; and that God is jealous of the Ṣúfís when they turn their thoughts towards any one except Himself.

201 CHAPTER LXXXI: "Concerning their manners in sitting alone or with others."

Sitting in mosques condemned by Sarí al-Saqaṭí. His definition of generosity (*muruwwat*). Saying of a Ṣúfí Sheykh: "the prayer-mat of the dervish ought to be on his buttocks." Stories of Abú Yazíd and Ibráhím b. Adham which indicate that it is a breach of manners to stretch out one's feet or

to cross one's legs. Story of Ibráhím al-Khawwáṣ and a
dervish who had an excellent way of sitting. Saying of
Yaḥyá b. Muᶜádh (al-Rází) on sitting with the unspiritual.
Anecdote of Ibn Mamlúla al-ᶜAṭṭár al-Dínawarí. Anonymous
saying: a man's friends show his character. Ḥasan al-Qazzáz,
who often sat awake during the night, said that Ṣúfism is
founded on three things: hunger, silence, and sleeplessness.
Junayd preferred sitting with Ṣúfís to prayer.

202   CHAPTER LXXXII: "Concerning their manners in hunger".
Two sayings of Yaḥyá b. Muᶜádh on hunger. Sahl b.
ᶜAbdallah used to be strong when he abstained from eating
and weak when he ate. Saying of Sahl b. ᶜAbdallah. Abú
Sulaymán (al-Dárání) said that hunger is one of God's trea-
sures which He bestows upon those whom He loves dearly.
A saying of Sahl b. 'Abdallah on hunger repeated to the
author by Ibn Sálim. Saying of ᶜÍsá al-Qaṣṣár. Why a Ṣúfí
Sheykh said, "Thou art a liar", to a man who said, "I am
hungry". Another Sheykh's rebuke to a Ṣúfí who came to
visit him after having eaten no food for five days.

203   CHAPTER LXXXIII: "Concerning their manners in sickness."
Anecdote of Mimshádh al-Dínawarí. It is related of al-
Kurdí that part of his body was infested by worms, and
when a worm fell to the ground he would put it back in
its place. Story of Dhu 'l-Nún and a sick disciple to whom
he paid a visit. Advice which Sahl b. ᶜAbdallah used to
give to his disciples when they were ill. How Abú Yaᶜqúb
al-Nahrajúrí refused to let himself be cured of a disease in
his stomach by means of cautery. Saying of al-Thawrí to a
disciple who made excuses for delay in visiting him. Sahl
b. ᶜAbdallah know a remedy for piles but would not use it.

204   When Bishr al-Ḥáfí described his symptoms to the phys-
ician, he was asked whether he was not complaining (of
God): his reply. Saying of Dhu 'l-Nún quoted by Junayd
when he was suffering from a severe illness.

it was better for people like himself to perform their devotions in the sight of one another.

wild beasts. Description of the death of Yaḥyá al-Isṭakhrí. Junayd's remark when he was told that Abú Saʿíd al-Kharráz fell into an ecstasy before he died.

CHAPTER LXXXIX: "Concerning the differences of doctrine shown in their answers to questions on mystical subjects".

212   *Question concerning* concentration *(jamʿ) and* dispersion *(tafriqat)*.

The author's definition of these terms. Their meaning explained by Abú Bakr ʿAbdallah b. Ṭáhir al-Abharí. Verses by Junayd. Saying attributed to Núrí.

213   Anonymous doctrines on the subject. Sayings of Junayd and Abú Bakr al-Wásiṭí.

Question concerning passing-away *(faná) and* continuance *(baqá)*.

Two sayings of Abú Yaʿqúb al-Nahrajúrí: the true theory of *faná* and *baqá* requires that Man's normal relation to God — the relation of a slave to his master — should be maintained. The author says that *faná* and *baqá* are the attributes of those who declare God to be One, and who ascend in their unification to a particular degree, which is not reached by ordinary Moslems. He explains the original meaning and application of the terms. Two sayings of Sumnún.

214   Sayings of Abú Saʿíd al-Kharráz, Junayd, Ibn ʿAṭá, and Shiblí. Saying attributed to Ruwaym. The author enumerates five stages of *faná*.

215   *Question concerning* the realities *(al-ḥaqáʾiq)*.

Description by Sarí al-Saqaṭí of those who seek the realities. Sayings of Junayd, Abú Turáb (al-Nakhshabí) and Ruwaym. Three kinds of reality *(ḥaqíqat)* distinguished by Abú Jaʿfar al-Ṣaydalání. Anecdote of Abú Bakr al-Zaqqáq: "every reality that contradicts the religious law is an infidelity". Ruwaym's answer to the question, "When does a man realise the meaning of servantship *(ʿubúdiyyat)*"? Another saying of Ruwaym. A saying of Junayd. Definition by al-Muzayyin al-Kabír of the nature of God as conceived by the Ṣúfís.

216   Saying of ᶜAbdallah b. Ṭáhir al-Abharí, in which he iden-tifies reality with positive religion (ᶜilm). Distinction made by Shiblí between ᶜilm, ḥaqíqat, and ḥaqq. The reality of 'humanity' (insániyyat) explained by Abú Jaᶜfar al-Qarawí. Anonymous definition of the reality of 'union' (wuṣúl). Reality described by Junayd as that which removes every obstacle in the mystic's way. Saying of Abú Bakr al-Wásiṭí.

Question concerning veracity *(ṣidq).*

Saying of Junayd. Definition of veracity given by Abú Saᶜíd al-Kharráz to two angels whom he saw in a dream. A detailed definition by Yúsuf b. al-Ḥusayn.

217   Sayings of an anonymous sage, Dhu 'l-Nún, Ḥarith (al-Muḥásibí), Junayd, Abú Yaᶜqúb, and another whose name is not mentioned.

Question concerning the fundamental principles *(uṣúl) of Ṣúfism.*

Five qualities enumerated by Junayd. Two principles men-tioned by Abú ᶜUthmán (al-Ḥírí). Saying of Junayd on the importance of taking care not to fail in fundamental prin-ciples. Three principles of the Ṣúfís, according to Abú Aḥmad al-Qalánisí. Seven principles of Ṣúfism enumerated by Sahl b. ᶜAbdallah.

218   List of six principles, according to Ḥuṣrí, and another list of seven principles, according to an anonymous dervish.

Question concerning sincerity *(ikhláṣ).*

Definitions by Junayd, Ibn ᶜAṭá, Ḥárith al-Muḥásibí, Dhu 'l-Nún, and Abú Yaᶜqúb al-Súsí. Two sayings of Sahl b. ᶜAbdallah. Definitions by Junayd and an anonymous Sheykh. Three signs of the sincere man. Definition of sincerity attrib-uted to Abu 'l-Ḥusayn al-Núrí.

219   *Question concerning* recollection *(dhikr).*

Ibn Sálim distinguished three kinds of recollection: (a) with

the tongue, (b) with the heart, (c) recollection which he
defined as "being filled with love and shame because of
nearness to God". Ibn ʿAṭá said that recollection causes the
human nature *(bashariyyat)* to disappear. Two sayings of
Sahl b. ʿAbdallah. Three verses of the Koran in which the
Moslems are commanded to recollect God. There are different kinds of recollection, corresponding to the different
language used in these verses. Saying of an anonymous
Sheykh. Verbal recollection (repetition of the formulas "There
in no god but Allah" and "Glory be to Allah!" or recitation
of the Koran) and spiritual recollection (concentration of the
heart upon God and His attributes).

220　　Recollection assumes various forms in accordance with the
predominant 'state' or 'station' of each mystic. Shiblí said
that real recollection is the forgetting of recollection, *i. e.*,
forgetfulness of everything except God.

Question concerning spiritual wealth *(ghiná)*.

Junayd said that spiritual poverty and wealth are complementary, and that neither is perfect without the other. The
signs of spiritual wealth described by Yúsuf b. al-Ḥusayn.
Saying of ʿAmr b. ʿUthmán al-Makkí on the spiritual wealth
which consists in being independent of spiritual wealth.

221　Saying of Junayd.

Question concerning poverty *(faqr)*.

Junayd said that poverty is a sea of tribulation but that
all its tribulation is glorious. Description by Junayd of the
true *faqír* who enters Paradise five hundred years before
the rich. Ibn al-Jallá said that poverty must be accompanied
by piety *(waraʿ)*. Sayings of Junayd and al-Muzayyin.

Question concerning the spirit *(rúḥ) and the doctrines of
the Ṣúfís on the subject.*

222　　Two sayings of Shiblí. Abú Bakr al-Wásiṭí distinguished
two spirits, *viz.*, the vital spirit and the spirit whereby the
heart is illumined. Other sayings of al-Wásiṭí. Abú ʿAbdallah

al-Nibájí said that there are two spirits in the gnostic who
has attained to union with God. Distinction between the
human spirit (*al-rúḥ al-bashariyya*) and the eternal spirit (*al-
rúḥ al-qadíma*) in man. Traditions illustrating this doctrine.
223   The author declares it to be false. Ibn Sálim asserted
that the spirit and the body together produce good or evil,
and that both are liable to reward or punishment. Those
who believe in metempsychosis and the eternity of the
spirit go far astray from the truth.

Question concerning symbolic allusion (*ishárat*).

The meaning of *ishárat*. Sayings of Shiblí and Abú Yazíd
al-Bisṭámí to the effect that God cannot be indicated by
means of symbols. How a man rebuked Junayd for raising
his eye to heaven. ʿAmr b. ʿUthmán al-Makkí said that the
symbolism of the Ṣúfís is polytheism (*shirk*). Junayd said
to a certain man, "How long will you give indications to
God? Let God give indications to you."
224   Abú Yazíd (al-Bisṭámí) condemned both theological and
mystical symbolism. Zaqqáq said that *ishárat* is proper for
novices, but the adept finds God by abandoning *ishárat*.
Saying of Shiblí on nearness to God. Saying of Yaḥyá b.
Muʿádh on the different kinds of symbolism used by different
classes of religious men. Ṣúfism described by Abú ʿAlí al-
Rúdhabárí as an *ishárat*. The use of *ishárat* disapproved by
Abú Yaʿqúb al-Súsí.

Diverse questions. Question concerning elegance (*ẓarf*).

Definition of the term by Junayd.

Question concerning generosity (*muruwwat*).

Definition by Aḥmad b. ʿAṭá.

Question concerning the reason why the Ṣúfís are so called.
225   Sayings by Ibn ʿAṭá (who connects 'Súfí' with *ṣafá*), Núrí,
Shiblí, and an anonymous mystic.

Question concerning the daily bread (*rizq*).

Sayings of Yaḥyá b. Muʿádh and another whose name is

not mentioned. Various opinions as to the cause of *rizq*. How Abú Yazíd (al-Bistámí) rebuked a theologian who questioned him about the source of *rizq*.

Question. Junayd's answer to a question concerning the disappearance of the name of 'servant' and the subsistence of the power of God, (as happens in *faná*).

Question. Junayd was asked, "When is a man indifferent
226 to praise and blame?" His answer.

Question. Answer given by Ibn ʿAṭá when he was asked, "What is the means of obtaining security of mind (*salámat al-ṣadr*)?"

Question. "What is the explanation of the grief which a man feels without knowing its cause?" Answer by Abú ʿUthmán (al-Ḥírí).

Question concerning sagacity (*firásat*).

Comment by Yúsuf b. al-Ḥusayn on the Tradition, "Beware of the sagacity of the true believer, for he sees by the light of God."

Question concerning the imagination (*wahm*).

Definition of *wahm* by Ibráhím al-Khawwáṣ.

227 *Question.* Explanations by Abú Yazíd al-Bistámí and other mystics of the words *sábiq*, *muqtaṣid*, and *ẓálim* in Kor. 35, 29.

Question concerning wishing (*tamanní*).

Ruwaym said that the disciple may hope, but that he should not wish. The reason of this distinction.

Question concerning the secret of the soul (*sirr al-nafs*).

Sahl b. ʿAbdallah said that the secret of the soul was never revealed in any created being except in Pharaoh when he said, "I am your supreme Lord."

228 *Question.* Human and divine jealousy (*ghayrat*) distinguished by Shiblí.

Question. Fatḥ b. Shakhraf asked Isráfíl, the teacher of Dhu 'l-Nún, whether secret thoughts (*asrár*) are punished before actual sins. The answer given by Isráfíl.

Question. Three different 'states' of the heart described by Abú Bakr al-Wásiṭí.

Question. Three kinds of tribulation (*balá*) described by Jarírí.

Question concerning the difference between the lower and higher degrees of love (*ḥubb* and *wudd*).

229   *Question concerning* weeping (*buká*).

Saying of Abú Saʿíd al-Kharráz. Eighteen causes of weeping.

Question concerning the term *sháhid*.

Definitions by Junayd and the author.

230   *Question concerning* the sincere practice of devotion.

Abu 'l-Ḥusayn ʿAlí b. Hind al-Qurashí, when questioned on this subject by the Sheykhs of Mecca, replied that sincerity in devotion depends on the knowledge of four things, *viz.*, God, self, death, and retribution after death.

Question as to the nature of the generous man (*karím*).

Definitions of the generous man by Ḥárith (al-Muḥásibí) and Junayd.

Question concerning generosity (*karámat*).

Two anonymous definitions.

Question concerning reflection (*fikr*).

Definitions of *fikr* and *tafakkur* by Ḥárith al-Muḥásibí and others. Distinction between *fikr* and *tafakkur*.

231   *Question concerning* induction (*iʿtibár*).

Definitions by Ḥárith al-Muḥásibí and others.

Question as to the nature of intention (*niyyat*).

Definitions by Junayd and others.

Question as to the nature of right (*ṣawáb*).

Definitions by Junayd and another.

Question. Junayd's explanation of what is meant by compassion towards the creatures (*shafaqat ʿala 'l-khalq*).

Question concerning fear of God (*taqiyyat*).

Five definitions of the word.

Question concerning the ground of the soul (*sirr*).

Definitions. Saying of Ḥusayn b. Manṣúr al-Ḥalláj.

232 Two sayings of Yúsuf b. al-Ḥusayn. Verses concerning the *sirr* by Núrí and others.

The author remarks that the questions discussed by the Ṣúfís are too numerous to mention. Saying of ʿAmr b. ʿUthmán al-Makkí: "One half of knowledge is question, and the other half is answer."

CHAPTER XC: "Concerning the letters sent by Ṣúfís to one another".

233 Words written by Mimsháḏh al-Dínawarí on the back of a letter which Junayd wrote to him. Letter from Abú Saʿíd al-Kharráz to Aḥmad b. ʿAṭá. Part of a letter addressed by ʿAmr b. ʿUthmán al-Makkí to the Ṣúfís of Baghdád, together with the observations made upon it by Junayd, Shiblí, and Jarírí. Part of a letter sent by Shiblí to Junayd.

234 Junayd's reply. The author relates how he and other Ṣúfís asked Abú ʿAbdallah [1]) al-Rúdhabárí to write a letter to a certain Háshimite at Ramla, begging him to permit them to hear a singing-girl who was famous for the beauty of her voice. Copy of the letter which al-Rúdhabárí wrote *impromptu* on this occasion. Verses inserted by Abú ʿAlí b. Abí Khálid al-Ṣúrí in a letter which he wrote to Abú ʿAlí al-Rúdhabárí.

235 Verses written by Abú ʿAlí al-Rúdhabárí in reply to the above. Answer sent by Dhu 'l-Nún to a sick man who had asked him to invoke God on his behalf. Another letter written by Dhu 'l-Nún. Letter written by Sarí al-Saqaṭí to Junayd containing some verses which he heard a camel-driver chanting in the desert.

236 Letter written to (Abú ʿAbdallah) al-Rúdhabárí by one of his friends. Part of a letter from Abú ʿAbdallah al-Rúdhabárí to a friend. Letter written by an eminent Ṣúfí to a certain Sheykh. Extract from a letter addressed by Abu 'l-Khayr

---

1) This is the correct reading.

e

al-Tínátí to Ja°far al-Khuldí. Letter written by a certain
sage in answer to Yúsuf b. al-Husayn, who had complained
of being a prey to worldly feelings and dispositions.

237   Letter written by one sage to another who had asked
him by what means he might gain salvation. Part of a letter
written by Aḥmad b. °Aṭá to Abú Sa°íd al-Kharráz, and
the latter's reply. Letter of a lover to his beloved. Quotation
from a letter written by a certain Sheykh.

238   Part of a letter written to Ḥusayn b. Jibríl al-Marandí
by one of his pupils, relating how he became friendly with
a gazelle and shared his food with it. Letter sent by Sháh
al-Kirmání to Abú Ḥafṣ (al-Ḥaddád) and the latter's reply.
Letter written by Sarí al-Saqaṭí to a friend. Part of a letter
from Junayd to °Alí b. Sahl al-Iṣbahání.

239   The author says that it is impossible for him to quote
the long epistles which celebrated Ṣúfís have written to one
another, such as the epistle of Núrí to Junayd on the subject of tribulation (*balá*), etc., but that he will give the text
of one short epistle written by Junayd to Abú Bakr al-
Kisá'í al-Dínawarí.

240   Continuation of the epistle of Junayd to Abú Bakr al-Kisá'í.

241   Conclusion of the same.
CHAPTER XCI: "Concerning the introductions (*ṣudúr*) of
books and epistles".

241-3   Five introductions by Junayd.

243   Specimens by Abú °Alí al-Rúdhabárí and Abú Sa°íd b. al-
A°rábí.

244   Two more specimens by Ibn al-A°rábí, and one by Abú
Sa°íd al-Kharráz.

245   Another by al-Kharráz and a third which the author attributes to him. An introduction by al-Kurdí of Urmiya.
Another by Abú Bakr al-Duqqí.

246   Another by the same hand. Two anonymous specimens.
CHAPTER XCII: "Concerning their mystical poems".

him utter at Aṭrábulus. A prayer of Shiblí. Prayers of
Yaḥyá b. Muᶜádh (al-Rází).

261   A number of prayers by the same. Answer given by a
certain Shaykh to ᶜUmar al-Malaṭí who had begged him to
invoke God on his behalf. How Ibráhím b. Adham refused
to pray for his fellow-passengers when they were overtaken
by a storm at sea.

262   Anonymous saying on the effect of sincerity in prayer.
Prayer of Sarí al-Saqaṭí. Prayer of Sarí in answer to the
request of Abú Ḥamza. A prayer which Ibráhím al-Márastání
learned from al-Khaḍir, whom he saw in a dream. A prayer
which Abú ᶜUbayd al-Busrí learned from ᶜÁ'isha who appeared to him while he was asleep. Prayer of a Sheykh
whose name is not mentioned. Answer given to the author
by a certain Sheykh whom he questioned concerning the
real purpose of prayer.

A prayer of Junayd.

263   CHAPTER XCIV: "Concerning their precepts (waṣáyá) to
one another."

Precepts by Ruwaym and Yúsuf b. al-Ḥusayn (al-Rází).

264   Precepts by Sarí al-Saqaṭí, Abú Bakr al-Bárizí, Abu 'l-ᶜAbbás
b. ᶜAṭá, Junayd, and Abú Saᶜíd al-Kharráz.

265   Precepts by Dhu 'l-Nún, Junayd, Abú ᶜAbdallah al-Khayyáṭ
al-Dínawarí, and Abú Bakr al-Warráq. Dhu 'l-Nún's reason for
refusing to give a precept to a man who had asked him for one.

266   Story of Abú Muḥammad al-Murtaᶜish: when dying, he
gave instructions that his debts should be paid; and the sale
of the clothes on his corpse produced eighteen dirhams,
exactly the amount of his debts. A precept of Ibráhím b.
Shaybán. Precept by an anonymous Sheykh.

Precepts by Abú Bakr al-Wásiṭí, by an unnamed Ṣúfí, by
a man whom Dhu 'l-Nún met on Mount Muqaṭṭam, and by
Dhu 'l-Nún himself.

267   Precept by Junayd.

THE BOOK OF AUDITION (samá°).

CHAPTER XCV: "Concerning the beauty of the voice, and audition, and the difference of those who practise it."

The Prophet said that all the prophets before him had fine voices.

268 Further Traditions showing that the Prophet held a sweet voice in high esteem and that he liked to hear the Koran read with a musical intonation. The author's explanation of the Tradition, "Beautify the Koran by your voices."

269 Sayings on this subject by Dhu 'l-Nún, Yahyá b. Mu°ádh al-Rází, an anonymous Sheykh, Hárith al-Muhásibí, and Bundár b. al-Husayn. The subtle influence of sweet sounds is illustrated by the fact that they lull sick children to sleep and restore the health of persons suffering from melancholia. Moreover, the camel-driver's chant has a marvellous effect upon camels worn out by fatigue.

270 Story, related to the author by al-Duqqí, of a negro slave whose master had thrown him into chains because the sweetness of his voice excited the heavily laden camels to rush along with such speed that all of them, except one, died on arriving at the end of their journey. [1]

271 Definition of the expert singer by Isháq b. Ibráhím al-Mawsilí.

CHAPTER XCVI: "Concerning audition and the various opinions of the Súfís as to its nature."

Definition by Dhu 'l-Nún. Saying of Abú Sulaymán al-Dárání on the recitation of poetry with a musical accompaniment. Definitions by Abú Ya°qúb al-Nahrajúrí and an anonymous mystic. Description of samá° by Abu 'l-Husayn al-Darráj.

[1] The same story is told by Hujwírí, on the authority of Ibráhím al-Khawwás. See my translation of the *Kashf al-Mahjúb* p. 399.

272   Sayings of Shiblí, Junayd, and an unnamed Ṣúfí. Junayd said that audition is one of the three occasions on which the mercy of God descends upon dervishes. Audition condemned by Abú ʿAlí al-Rúdhabárí. Abu 'l-Ḥusayn al-Núrí defined the Ṣúfí as one who practises audition. Abu 'l-Ḥusayn b. Zírí used to stay and listen to music (*samáʿ*) if he approved of it; otherwise he would take up his shoes and go. Al-Ḥuṣrí wished for a *samáʿ* that should never cease, and should be more desired the more it was enjoyed.

273   CHAPTER XCVII: "Concerning the audition of the vulgar (*al-ʿámmat*) and its permissibility when they listen to sweet sounds which inspire them with hope or fear and impel them to seek the afterworld".

Saying of Bundár b. al-Ḥusayn on the pleasure and lawfulness of audition when it is not connected with any evil purpose. Quotations from the Koran showing that audition is lawful. The five senses enable us to distinguish things from their opposites, and the ear can distinguish sweet sounds from harsh.

274   Sweet sounds form part of the pleasures of Paradise which are enumerated in the Koran. Audition is not like winedrinking: the latter is forbidden in this world, but the former is permitted. The Prophet allowed two singing-girls to play the tambourine in his house.

275   Verses recited by Abú Bakr, Bilál, and ʿÁ'isha. Many of the Prophet's Companions recited poetry. Fourteen verses are quoted from the famous poem, *Bánat Suʿádu*, which Kaʿb b. Zuhayr recited in the presence of the Prophet.

276   The Prophet said, "Wisdom is sometimes to be found in poetry". Since poetry may be recited, there is no objection to reciting it with musical notes and melodies and with an agreeable intonation. Various divines and lawyers have pronounced in favour of audition, *e. g.*, Málik b. Anas. Story of Málik and a man whom he rebuked for singing badly.

It is well-known that Málik[1]) and the people of Medina did not dislike audition.

277   Sháfi'í was of the same opinion. Ibn Jurayj departed from Yemen and settled at Mecca in consequence of hearing two verses of poetry. He declared that audition is neither a good nor an evil act, but resembles an idle word (*laghw*) for which a man will not be punished hereafter (Kor. 2, 225). The author sums up the discussion by stating that audition is lawful, if it has no corrupt end in view and if it does not involve the use of certain musical instruments forbidden by the Prophet.

CHAPTER XCVIII: "Concerning the audition of the elect and their various degrees therein."

Description by Abú 'Uthmán Sa'íd b. 'Uthmán al-Rází of three kinds of audition: (1) that of novices and beginners; (2) that of more advanced mystics (*ṣiddíqín*); and (3) that of gnostics (*'árifín*).

278   Three classes of auditors described by Abú Ya'qúb al-Nahrajúrí. Three kinds of audition defined by Bundár b. al-Ḥusayn: some hear with their natures (*ṭab'*), some with their spiritual feelings (*ḥál*), and some through God (*ḥaqq*). The author's explanation of this saying.

279   The author's explanation continued. Three classes of auditors distinguished by an anonymous Ṣúfí: (1) the followers of realities (*abná al-ḥaqá'iq*); (2) those who depend on their spiritual feelings; (3) the poor (*fuqará*) who are entirely detached from worldly things.

280   CHAPTER XCIX: "Concerning the different classes of auditors".

Those who prefer to listen the Koran.

---

1) The contrary opinion is attributed to Málik and the Medina school by Ghazálí (*Iḥyá*, Búláq, 1289 A. H., II, 247, 17), but cf. Goldziher, *Muhamm. Studien*, II, 79, note 2.

Verses of the Koran and Traditions of the Prophet which
prove that listening to the Koran is allowable.

281   Further Traditions on this subject. The Koran condemns
those who listen only with their ears and praises those who
listen with attentive minds. Examples of the emotion produced by listening to the Koran. In some cases the listeners
die. Answer given by Shiblí to Abú ʿAlí al-Magházilí who
complained that the effect produced by listening to the
Koran was not permanent.

282   Abú Sulaymán al-Dárání said that he sometimes spent
five nights in pondering over a single verse of the Koran
and that unless he had ceased to think about it he would
never have continued his reading.

Junayd saw a man who had swooned on hearing a verse
of the Koran. He recommended that the same verse should
be read to him again; whereupon the man recovered his
senses. A certain Ṣúfí repeated several times the verse,
"Every soul shall taste death" (Kor. 3, 182). He heard a
voice from heaven saying, "How long wilt thou repeat this
verse which has already killed four of the Jinn?" Abu
'l-Ṭayyib Aḥmad b. Muqátil al-ʿAkkí describes the terror
and anguish of Shiblí on hearing a verse of the Koran.

283   Those who lack the spiritual emotion which accords with
the hearing of the Koran and is excited thereby are like
beasts: they hear but do not understand.

CHAPTER C: "Concerning those who prefer listening to
odes and verses of poetry".

Traditions of the Prophet in praise of poetry. The con-
siderations which lead some Ṣúfís to listen to poetry rather
than to the Koran are stated by the author as follows. The
Koran is the Word of God, i. e. an eternal attribute of God,
which men cannot bear when it appears, because it is uncreated. If God were to reveal it to their hearts as it really
284 is, their hearts would crack. It is, however, a matter of

common knowledge that a man may read the whole Koran many times over without being touched with emotion, whereas if the reading is accompanied by a sweet voice and plaintive intonation he feels emotion and delight in hearing it. These feelings, then, are not caused by the Koran, but by sweet sounds and melodies which accord with human temperaments. The harmonies of poetry are similar in their nature and their effects and easily blend with music. Since a certain homogeneity exists between them and the spirit of man, their influence is much less powerful and dangerous than that of God's Word. Those who prefer listening to poetry are animated by reverence for the Koran.

285   "It is more fitting", they say, "that so long as we retain our human nature we should take delight in poetry instead of making the Koran a means of indulging ourselves". Some theologians have regarded with dislike the practice of trilling the Koran, but if this is done, the reason is that men shrink from hearing and reciting the Koran because it is a reality (*haqq*), and they intone it musically in order that the people may be drawn to listen when it is read.

CHAPTER CI: "Concerning the audition of novices and beginners".

Story of a young man, a pupil of Junayd, who used to shriek whenever he heard any *dhikr*. Junayd threatened to dismiss him if he did so again, and after that time he used to put such restraint on himself that a drop of water trickled from every hair of his body, until one day he uttered a loud cry and expired. A saying of Junayd related by Abu 'l-Husayn al-Sírawání.

286   Story related by al-Darráj of a youth who died on hearing a slave-girl sing two verses of poetry [1]). Another story of the same kind related by Abú ʿAlí al-Rúdhabárí.

---

1) This story occurs in my translation of Hujwírí's *Kashf al-Maḥjúb*, p. 408 *seq.*

287 Abú ʿAbdallah b. al-Jallá mentions two marvellous things which he saw in the Maghrib: (1) a Ṣúfí begging for alms; (2) a Sheykh named Jabala, one of whose disciples had died on hearing a passage of the Koran, came to the reader on the next day and asked him to a recite part of the Koran. While he was reciting, Jabala gave a shriek which caused him (the reader) to fall dead on the spot. Anecdote of Jaʿfar al-Mubarqaʿ. The author states the conditions under which it is proper for novices to practise samáʿ.

288 If the beginner is ignorant of these conditions, he must learn them from a Sheykh, lest he should be seduced and corrupted.

CHAPTER CII: "Concerning the audition of the Ṣúfí Sheykhs."

Isráfíl, the teacher of Dhu 'l-Nún, asked al-Ṭayálisí al-Rází whether he could recite any poetry. On receiving a negative answer, Isráfíl said to him, "Thou hast no heart." Ruwaym described the state of the Ṣúfí Sheykhs during audition as resembling that of a flock of sheep attacked by wolves. Abu 'l-Qásim b. Marwán al-Naháwandí, who had taken no part in the samáʿ for many years, attended a

289 meeting where some poetry was recited. The audience fell into ecstasy. When they became quiet again, Abu 'l-Qásim questioned them concerning the mystical meaning which they attached to the verse, and finally gave his own interpretation. Story of Abú Ḥulmán, who swooned on hearing the street-cry of a herb-seller. The author points out that the influence of samáʿ depends on the spiritual state of the hearer. Thus, the same words may be regarded as true by one mystic and as false by another. Story of ʿUtba al-

290 Ghulám. Anecdote of Dhu 'l-Nún al-Miṣrí, who was overcome by ecstasy on hearing some verses recited, but rebuked a man who followed his example. Some Sheykhs possess insight into the spiritual state of those below them; in that case, they should not permit them to claim a higher state

than that which really belongs to them. Account of Núrí's ecstasy a few days before his death. The ecstasy of ꜥAlí b. al-Muwaffaq.

291 Description of a visit which Abu 'l-Ḥusayn al-Darráj paid to Yúsuf b. al-Ḥusayn at Rayy. The latter burst into tears on hearing two verses which al-Darráj recited, though he had previously read aloud to himself a large portion of the Koran without any such sign of emotion.

292 A verse that used to throw Shiblí into ecstasy. Another verse that had the like effect on al-Duqqí.

CHAPTER CIII: "Concerning the characteristics of the perfect adepts in audition."

During sixty years Sahl b. ꜥAbdallah never changed countenance when he heard the *dhikr* or the Koran or anything else; it was only the weakness of old age that at last caused him to show emotion. Another similar anecdote of Sahl b.

293 ꜥAbdallah. The answer given by Sahl to Ibn Sálim who asked what it is that makes a man spiritually strong and enables him to retain his composure. Saying of the Caliph Abú Bakr. Sahl b. ꜥAbdallah said that his state during prayer was the same as his state before he began to pray. Explanation of this saying by the author. Sahl was the same after audition as he had been before it, *i.e.*, his ecstasy continued without interruption. Story of Mimshádh al-Dínawarí, who said that all the musical instruments in the world could not divert his thoughts from God.

294 The author observes that when Ṣúfís attain to perfection their senses are purified to such an extent that they take no pleasure in music and singing. Verse of the Koran quoted by Junayd in reply to one who noticed how quiet and unmoved he was during the *samá*ꜥ. Various reasons which induce spiritual adepts to attend musical concerts.

295 CHAPTER CIV: "On listening to *dhikr* and sermons and moral sayings."

The profound impression made upon Abú Bakr al-Zaqqáq by a saying of Junayd. Answer given by Junayd to the question, "When does a man regard praise and blame with equal indifference?" Saying on Wisdom (*ḥikmat*) by Yaḥyá b. Muᶜádh. It is said that when words come from the heart they penetrate to the heart, but when they proceed from the tongue they do not pass beyond the ears. Many further examples might be given of the ecstasy and enthusiasm caused by listening to *dhikr* or moral exhortations. Saying of Abú ᶜUthmán (al-Ḥírí). Influences from the unseen world, whether they be audible or visible, produce a powerful effect upon the heart when they are in harmony with it, *i.e.*, when the heart is pure; otherwise, their effect is weak.

296 The adepts, however, are not affected in this way, although sometimes their spiritual life is renewed and replenished by hearing words of wisdom. The object of the Ṣúfís in audition is not solely the delight of listening to sweet voices and melodies, but rather the inward feeling of something homogeneous with the ecstasy already existent in their hearts, since their ecstasy is strengthened by feeling it.

CHAPTER CV: "Further observations concerning audition."

The influence of *samáᶜ* depends on, and corresponds with, the spiritual state of the hearer. Hence the Ṣúfís, when they listen to poetry, do not think of the poet's meaning, nor when the Koran is read aloud are they distressed by the negligence of the reader whilst they themselves are alert.

297 If speaker and hearer are one in feeling and intention, the ecstasy will be stronger; but the Ṣúfís are safe from any evil consequences so long as the divine providence encompasses them. Stories illustrating this. Muḥammad b. Masrúq of Baghdád was singing a verse in praise of wine when he heard some one say in the same metre and rhyme: "In Hell there is a water that leaves no entrails in the belly of him whose throat shall swallow it." This was the cause

of his conversion to Ṣúfism. Abu 'l-Ḥasan b. Razʿán(?) heard a mandoline-player singing some erotic verses, but a friend with whom he was walking improvised a mystical variation of them. Here, says the author, we have a proof that verses of which the intention is bad may be interpreted in a sense that accords with the inward feelings of the hearer.

298   Shiblí's answer to a man who asked him to explain the meaning of "God is the best of deceivers" (Kor. 3, 47).

CHAPTER CVI: "Concerning those who dislike the *samáʿ* and dislike to be present in places where the Koran is recited with a musical intonation, or where odes are chanted and the hearers fall into an artificial ecstasy and begin to dance."

Different reasons for such dislike: (1) *samáʿ* is condemned by some great religious authorities; (2) *samáʿ* is very danger-ous for novices and penitents: it may lead them to break 299 their vows and indulge in sensual pleasures; (3) listening to quatrains (*rubáʿiyyát*) is the mark of two classes of men, either the frivolous and dissolute or the adepts in mysticism who have mortified their passions and are entirely devoted to God. Accordingly, some Ṣúfís reject *samáʿ* on the ground that they are not yet fit for it. They think it better to occupy themselves with performing their religious duties and with avoiding forbidden things. Saying of Abú ʿAlí al-Rúdhabárí on the dangers of *samáʿ*. Saying of Sarí al-Saqaṭí on the recitation of odes. (4) *samáʿ* is apt to lead astray the vulgar who misunderstand the purpose of the Ṣúfís in listening to music; (5) *samáʿ* may bring a man into bad company.

300   (6) Some abstain from *samáʿ* on account of the Tradition that a good Moslem leaves alone what does not concern him; (7) some advanced gnostics are so fully occupied with *inward* communion that they have no room for the *out-ward* experience of audition.

BOOK OF ECSTASY *(wajd)*.

CHAPTER CVII: "Concerning the different opinions of the Ṣúfís as to the nature of ecstasy."

Definition of *wajd* by ʿAmr b. ʿUthmán al-Makkí.

301   The meaning of *wajd* explained by Junayd. It has been said that *wajd* is a revelation from God. In some cases it produces symptoms of violent emotion, while in others the subject remains calm. One of the ancient Ṣúfís distinguished two kinds of ectasy: *wajdu mulk* and *wajdu laqá*. Explanation of these terms by another mystic. Abu 'l-Ḥasan al-Ḥuṣrí enumerated four classes of men, the last class being "ecstatics who have passed away from themselves." Sahl b. ʿAbdallah said that if an ecstasy is not attested by the Koran and the Traditions, it is worthless.

302   Three quotations from Abú Saʿíd Ibn al-Aʿrábí on the nature of ecstasy.

CHAPTER CVIII: "On the characteristics of ecstatic persons."

The Koran and the Traditions show that fear and trembling and shrieking and moaning and weeping and swooning are among the characteristics of such persons. Ecstasy may be either genuine *(wajd)* or artificial *(tawájud)*. The author divides those whose ecstasy is genuine *(al-wájidún)* into three classes:

303   (1) those whose ecstasy is disturbed at times by the intrusion of sensual influences; (2) those whose ecstasy is interrupted only by the delight which they take in audition; (3) those whose ecstasy is perpetual and who, in consequence of their ecstasy, have utterly passed away from themselves.

Also, there are three classes of those whose ecstasy is artificial *(al-mutawájidún)*.

(1) those who take pains to induce ecstasy and imitate others, and those who are frivolous and despicable; (2) ascetics and mystics who endeavour to excite lofty states

(of ecstasy). Although it might become them better not to do this, such ecstasy is approved in them since they have renounced worldly things, and their ecstasy is the result of the joy which they feel in austerities and asceticism. They are justified by the Tradition, "Weep, and if ye weep not, then try to weep!" (3) mystics of the weaker type who, being unable to control their movements or to hide their inward feelings, fall into artificial ecstasy as a means of throwing off a burden which they find intolerable. The last words of Ḥusayn b. Manṣúr (al-Ḥalláj).

304   The criterion of 'sound' and 'unsound' ecstasy according to Abú Yaʿqúb al-Nahrajúrí.

CHAPTER CIX: "Concerning the artificial ecstasy (tawájud) of the Sheykhs who are sincere."

305   Two anecdotes of Shiblí. Story of Núrí.

He threw a whole company into ecstasy by his recitation of some erotic verses. Abú Saʿíd al-Kharráz was frequently overcome by ecstasy when he meditated on death.

The reason of this explained by Junayd. Explanation by an unnamed Sheykh of the difference between wujúd and tawájud. Those who dislike ecstasy, because of seeing some defect in the person whose ecstasy is induced by artificial means, follow the authority of Abú ʿUthmán al-Ḥírí.

306   He said to a man whom he saw in an ecstasy of this kind, "If you are sincere, you have divulged His secret, and if you are not sincere, you are guilty of polytheism." The author suggests what Abú ʿUthmán may have meant by these words.

CHAPTER CX: "Concerning the mighty power and transporting influence of ecstasy."

Sarí al-Saqaṭí expressed his conviction that if a man who had fallen into a deep fit of ecstasy were struck on the face with a sword, he would not feel the blow. According to Junayd, such a person is more perfect than one who devotes

himself to the religious law; but on another occasion he said
that abundance of positive religion is more perfect than abundance of ecstasy. A saying of Junayd to the effect that the
state of quiet in ecstasy is superior to the transport which
precedes it, and that the ecstatic transport is superior to the
state of quiet which precedes it. Explanation by the author.

307   The ecstasies of Sahl b. ʿAbdallah described by Ibn Sálim.
Junayd's criticism of Shiblí. A story, related by Junayd, of
Sarí al-Saqatí who said that his love of God had shrivelled
the skin on his arm; then he swooned, and his face became
so radiant that none of those present could bear to behold
it. Description by ʿAmr b. ʿUthmán al-Makkí of the ecstasy
which fills the soul and increases its knowledge of the divine
omnipotence and makes it unconscious of all sensible objects.

308 Verse recited by Abú ʿUthmán al-Muzayyin.

CHAPTER CXI: "Concerning the question which is the more
perfect, one who is quiet in ecstasy or one who is agitated".

This question is discussed by Abú Saʿíd Ibn al-Aʿrábí in
his book on ecstasy. He declares that in some cases the
proper and perfect condition is quiet, while in others it is
agitation.

309   The quiet ecstatics are preferred on account of the superior firmness of their minds, the agitated on account of the
superior strength of their ecstasies. Quiet would be more
perfect, if we presupposed two equal minds; but no two
minds or men or ecstasies are just on the same level, and
therefore it is useless to assert that quiet is superior or
inferior to agitation. The superiority or inferiority of either
depends on the particular nature and circumstances of the
ecstatic state.

310   CHAPTER CXII: "A compendious summary of the subject
from the *Book of Ecstasy* composed by Abú Saʿíd Ibn al-
Aʿrábí."

Various feelings and spiritual states by which ecstasy may

be produced. Definition and description of ecstasy. It comes in a moment and is gone in a moment. God shows His wisdom and His lovingkindness towards His friends by causing ecstasy to be so transient.

311 Were it otherwise, they would lose their wits. A further description of ecstasy. Some ecstatics are able to give a partial account of their experience, and this serves them as an argument against sceptics; else they would not divulge it. Remarks on the difficulty of distinguishing true ecstasy from the similar phenomena which sometimes result from sensuous impressions.

312 Description of the ecstasy of quietists who keep the path of Moslem theology, and of those mystics who diverge from it. The latter imperil their salvation by leaving this high-way. Ibn al-Aʿrábí says that the foregoing observations refer to the outward sciences of ecstasy which can be explained in ordinary or symbolic language; the rest is indescribable, since it consists of immediate experience of the Unseen, self-evident to those who have enjoyed it, but incapable of demonstration.

313 The essence of ecstasy and of other mystical states is incommunicable, and is better described by silence than by speech.

314 Those who are fit to receive such knowledge do not ask questions, inasmuch as they feel no doubt.

Ecstatic states are a gift from God and cannot be acquired by human effort, though some of them are the fruit of good works. Any one who begs God to grant him an increase (of ecstasy) has thereby strengthened the capital that renders increase necessary, and any one who neglects this duty runs the risk of being deprived of the capital which he has.

f

315 BOOK ESTABLISHING THE REALITY OF DIVINE
SIGNS AND MIRACLES.

CHAPTER CXIII: "Concerning the meanings of divine signs
(*áyát*) and miracles (*karámát*), with some mention of persons
who were thus gifted."

Saying of Sahl b. ʿAbdallah on *áyát*, *muʿjizát*, and *karámát*.
Sahl said that the gift of miracles would be granted to any
one who sincerely renounced the world for forty days; if
no miracles were wrought, his renunciation must have been
incomplete. Saying of Junayd on those who dispute about
miracles but cannot perform them. Saying of Sahl on one
who renounces the world for forty days. Four principles of
Faith, according to Ibn Sálim. One of these is faith in the
power (*qudrat*) of God, *i. e.*, belief in miracles.

316 Sahl said to one of his companions, "Do not consort with
me any more, if you are afraid of wild beasts." The author
relates that he visited Sahl's house at Tustar and went into
a room called 'the Wild Beasts' Room' where Sahl used to
receive and feed the wild beasts. Story of a negro at
ʿAbbádán who turned earth into gold. Story of a donkey
which spoke to Abú Sulaymán al-Khawwás when he was
beating its head. Aḥmad b. ʿAṭá al-Rúdhabárí tells how his
prayer for forgiveness was answered by a heavenly voice.

317 How Jaʿfar al-Khuldí recovered a gem which had fallen
into the Tigris by means of a 'prayer for lost property.'
Text of the prayer. Abu 'l-Ṭayyib al-ʿAkkí showed the
author a long list compiled by him of persons who, in the
course of a short time, had used this prayer with success.
How Abu 'l-Khayr al-Tínátí read the thoughts of Ḥamza
b. ʿAbdallah al-ʿAlawí. The author declares that all these
men were famous for veracity and piety, and that their
evidence is above suspicion.

318   CHAPTER CXIV: "Concerning the arguments of theologians who deny the reality of miracles, and the arguments
in favour of miracles wrought by the saints, and the distinction
between the saints and the prophets in this matter."

Some theologians hold that the gift of miracles is bestowed
on the prophets exclusively, and assert that its attribution
to others involves their equality with the prophets. The
object of this doctrine is to confirm the prophetic miracles,
but it is mistaken, because there are several points in which
the two classes of miracles differ from each other: (1) the
prophets reveal their miracles and use them as a means of
convincing the people, whereas the saints ought to conceal
theirs; (2) the prophets employ miracles as an argument
against unbelievers, but the saints employ them as an argument against themselves for the purpose of strengthening
their own faith.

319   Saying of Ibn Sálim illustrating the use of miracles as an
aid to faith. Story of the advice given by Sahl b. ʿAbdallah
to Isḥáq b. Aḥmad who came to him in great anxiety lest
he should be deprived of his daily bread. The lower soul
(*nafs*) is satisfied with nothing less than ocular evidence.

320   (3) While the prophets are perfected and encouraged in
proportion as a greater quantity of miracles is bestowed
upon them, the saints in the same circumstances become
more dismayed and fearful, because they dread that God
may be secretly deceiving them and that the miracles which
He bestows upon them may lead to loss of spiritual rank.

CHAPTER CXV: "Concerning the evidences for the reality
of miracles wrought by the saints, and the unsoundness of
the doctrine that miracles are wrought by none except the
prophets."

It appears from the Koran and the Traditions that many
persons who were not prophets had the gift of miracles,
e. g., Mary, the mother of Jesus, the Christian anchorite

Jurayj, and the three men who took shelter in the cave (as is related in the *Ḥadīth al-ghár*).

321   Further Traditions concerning persons endowed with miraculous powers: ʿUmar b. al-Khaṭṭáb, ʿAlí, Fáṭima, Usayd b. Ḥuḍayr, ʿAṭṭáb b. Bashír, Abu 'l-Dardá, Salmán al-Fárisí, al-ʿAlá b. al-Haḍramí, ʿAbdallah b. ʿUmar, al-Bará b. Málik,
322 ʿĀmir b. ʿAbd al-Qays, Ḥasan al-Baṣrí, Uways al-Qaraní and others. These miracles are related and attested by the
323 greatest religious authorities, whose evidence on this subject is no less worthy of credit than their evidence, which is universally accepted, on matters of law and religion. All miracles that have been manifested since the time of the Prophet and all that shall be manifested until the Resurrection are granted by God as a mark of honour to Muḥammad. Some Moslems, however, consider miracles a temptation, and dread the loss of spiritual rank, and do not reckon amongst the elect those who desire them and are satisfied with them.

324   CHAPTER CXVI: "On the various positions occupied by the elect in regard to miracles, together with an account of those who dislike the miraculous grace manifested to them and fear lest it lead them into temptation."

Sahl b. ʿAbdallah said that the greatest miracle is the substitution of a good quality for a bad one. Abú Yazíd al-Bisṭámí declared that when he paid no attention to the miracles which God offered to bestow on him, he received the gnosis. Other sayings of Abú Yazíd. Junayd said that the hearts of the elect are veiled from God by regarding His favours, by taking delight in His gifts, and by relying on miracles.

325   Warning given by Sahl b. ʿAbdallah to a man who boasted of a miracle which took place when he performed his ablutions. How Abú Ḥamza opened a door. Núrí found the banks of the Tigris joined together in order that he might cross

the river, but he swore that he would not cross except in a boat. Story of Abú Yazíd al-Bisṭámí and his teacher, Abú ʿAlí al-Sindí. Story of Abú Turáb al-Nakhshabí and a youth who was in his company.

not open his hand until he came to Khayr and confessed what he had done.

CHAPTER CXVIII: "Concerning the states of the elect which are not regarded as miraculous, although they are essentially more perfect and subtle than miracles".

Sahl b. ʿAbdallah used to fast for seventy days, and when he ate he became weak, whereas he became strong when he abstained from food. Saying of Abu 'l-Ḥárith al-Awlásí. How Abú ʿUbayd al-Busrí fasted during the month of Ramaḍán. Saying of Abú Bakr al-Kattání.

331   The meaning of security (*amn*) explained to Abú Ḥamza by a man of Khurásán. How Junayd tested one of his disciples who was able to read men's thoughts.

Story of Ḥárith al-Muḥásibí, who could not swallow any food that was not legally pure.

332   Story of Abú Jaʿfar al-Ḥaddád and Abú Turáb al-Nakhshabí. Three persons endowed with extraordinary powers whom Ḥuṣrí had seen. Why Jaʿfar al-Mubarqaʿ did not make any vow to God during a period of thirty·years. Story of Ismáʿíl al-Sulamí who fell from the top of a mountain and broke his leg.

333   BOOK OF THE EXPLANATION OF OBSCURITIES.

CHAPTER CXIX: "Concerning the interpretation of the difficult words which are used in the speech of the Ṣúfís."
List of Ṣúfistic technical terms.

334   Continuation of the above list.
CHAPTER CXX: "On the explanation of these words".
(1) *al-ḥaqq bi 'l-ḥaqq li 'l-ḥaqq*. *Al-ḥaqq* signifies Allah.
Sayings of Abú Saʿíd al-Kharráz and Abú ʿAlí al-Sindí.

335   (2) *al-ḥál*. Definitions by the author and Junayd.
(3) *al-maqám*. Definition by the author.
(4) *al-makán*. The author defines the term and illustrates his definition by quoting an anonymous verse.

(5) *al-musháhadat.* This term is nearly equivalent to *al-mukáshafat.* Definition by ʿAmr b. ʿUthmán al-Makkí.

(6) *al-lawá'iḥ.* Definition by the author. Saying of Junayd.

336 (7) *al-lawámiʿ.* Almost synonymous with the preceding. Derivation of the term. Saying of ʿAmr b. ʿUthmán al-Makkí.

(8) *al-ḥaqq.* Allah, according to Kor. 24, 25.

(9) *al-ḥuqúq.* These are 'states', 'stations', mystic sciences, etc. As al-Ṭayálisí al-Rází said, *ḥuqúq* are opposed to *ḥuẓúẓ*, which are associated with the lower self (*nafs*).

(10) *al-taḥqíq.* The author's definition. Saying of Dhu 'l-Nún.

(11) *al-taḥaqquq.* This term is related to *al-taḥqíq* as *al-taʿallum* (learning) is related to *al-taʿlím* (teaching).

(12) *al-ḥaqíqat* and its plural *al-ḥaqá'iq.* Definition. The
337 answer given by Ḥáritha to the Prophet's question, "What is the *ḥaqíqat* of thy faith?" Saying of Junayd.

(13) *al-khuṣúṣ.* Definition of *ahl al-khuṣúṣ.*

(14) *khuṣúṣ al-khuṣúṣ.* Definition. Both classes, *khuṣúṣ* and *khuṣúṣ al-khuṣúṣ*, are referred to in Kor. 35, 29. A Saying of Junayd to Shiblí.

(15) *al-ishárat.* Definition. Abú ʿAlí al-Rúdhabárí said that the science of Ṣúfism is an *ishárat.*

(16) *al-ímá'.* Definition. Anecdote of Junayd and Ibn al-Kurríní (al-Karanbí). According to Shiblí, *ímá'* in reference to God is idolatry.

338 Two verses by an anonymous poet.

(17) *al-ramz.* Definition. Verse by al-Qannád. It has been said by a Ṣúfí, whose name is not mentioned, that those who wish to understand the symbolic utterances of eminent mystics should study the letters and epistles which they have written to one another, not their books.

(18) *al-ṣafá.* Definition. Sayings of Jarírí and Ibn ʿAṭá.

Definitions of *ṣafá* and *ṣafá al-ṣafá* by al-Kattání.

(19) *ṣafá al-ṣafá*. Definition. Three verses explaining the term.

(20) *al-zawá'id*. Definition. Saying of ʿAmr b. ʿUthmán al-Makkí.

339 (21) *al-fawá'id*. Definition. Saying of Abú Sulaymán al-Dárání.

(22) *al-sháhid*. Definition. Verse (by Labíd). Another meaning of *al-sháhid*. Definition of the term by Junayd.

(23) *al-mashhúd*. Definition. Abú Bakr al-Wásiṭí said that *al-sháhid* is God, and *al-mashhúd* the created world.

(24) *al-mawjúd* and *al-mafqúd*. Definitions. Saying of Dhu 'l-Nún.

(25) *al-maʿdúm*. Definition. Distinction between *al-maʿdúm* and *al-mafqúd*. A certain gnostic said that the universe is an existence bounded on either side by non-existence (*ʿadam*).

(26) *al-jamʿ*. A term denoting God without the created world.

(27) *al-tafriqat*. This term denotes the created world.

340   The two preceding terms are complementary to each other. Unification (*tawḥíd*) consists in combining them. Verse on this subject.

(28) *al-ghaybat*. Definition.

(29) *al-ghashyat*. Definition.

(30) *al-ḥuḍúr*. Definition. Verses by al-Núrí and another mystic.

(31) *al-ṣaḥw* and *al-sukr*. These terms are nearly synonymous with *al-ḥuḍúr* and *al-ghaybat*. Verses by a Ṣúfí whose name is not mentioned. Explanation of the difference between *al-sukr* and *al-ghashyat*.

341   The difference between *al-ḥuḍúr* and *al-ṣaḥw*.

(32) *ṣafw al-wajd*. Definition. A verse illustrating it.

(33) *al-hujúm* and *al-ghalabát*. The former is the action

of one who is under the influence of the latter. Definition.

(34) *al-faná* and *al-baqá*. These terms have been mentioned in a previous chapter. Definitions.

(35) *al-mubtadi'*. Definition.

(36) *al-muríd*. Definition.

342 (37) *al-murád*. Definition. This term denotes the gnostic in whom no will of his own is left.

(38) *al-wajd*. Definition.

(39) *al-tawájud* and *al-tasákur*. Definitions.

(40) *al-waqt*. Definition. Saying of Junayd.

(41) *al-bádí*. Definition. Saying of Ibráhím al-Khawwás.

(42) *al-wárid*. Definition. The difference between *al-wárid* and *al-bádí*. Saying of Dhu 'l-Nún.

(43) *al-khátir*. Definition.

(44) *al-wáqiᶜ*. Definition. Saying of a certain Sheykh which the author heard from Abu 'l-Ṭayyib al-Shírázi. Explanation of the words *maᶜa awwali khátirika* which were used by Junayd in speaking to Khayr al-Nassáj.

343 The thought that occurs first (*awwalu 'l-khátir*) is said to be the true one. Other meanings of *al-khátir*.

(45) *al-qádih*. This term is nearly synonymous with *al-khátir* but there is a difference in respect of its application. Derivation and primary meaning of *al-qádih*. Saying of a mystic whose name is not recorded.

(46) *al-ᶜárid*. Definition and scope of the term. It is always used in a bad sense. An illustrative verse. [1])

(47) *al-qabd* and *al-bast*. These terms denote two lofty states peculiar to gnostics. The author explains what is involved in each state. Junayd identifies *al-qabd* with fear and *al-bast* with hope.

344 Verses describing the gnostic in the state of *al-qabd*

---

1) By Abú ᶜAbdallah al-Qurashí. See p. ٢٥٥, l. ١٢.

and in the state of *al-basṭ*. The author explains that three classes of gnostics are distinguished in these verses. He adds that *al-ghaybat* and *al-ḥuḍúr* and *al-ṣaḥw* and *al-sukr* and *al-wajd* and *al-hujúm* and *al-ghalabát* and *al-faná* and *al-baqá* are mystical states belonging to hearts which are filled with a profound recollection (*dhikr*) and veneration of God.

(48) *al-ma'khúdh* and *al-mustalab*. These terms are synonymous although the former denotes a more complete state. The persons to whom they refer are described in two Traditions of the Prophet and in a saying of Ḥasan (al-Baṣrí) concerning Mujáhid.

345   A verse in which both terms are used.

(49) *al-dahshat*. Definition. Story of a mystic who swooned after having asked God to grant him spiritual rest, and who excused himself by pleading that he was distraught by Divine Love. Verse on the *dahshat* caused by love. A saying of Shiblí.

(50) *al-ḥayrat*. Definition. Saying of al-Wásiṭí.

(51) *al-taḥayyur*. Definition. A certain Ṣúfí said that *al-taḥayyur* is the first stage of gnosis (*maʿrifat*), and *al-ḥayrat* the last. Verse on *al-taḥayyur*.

(52) *al-ṭawálíʿ*. Definition.

346   Verses by Ḥusayn b. Manṣúr al-Ḥalláj.

(53) *al-ṭawáriq*. Definition. An unnamed mystic said that he would not let *ṭawáriq* enter his heart until he had submitted them to (the test of conformity with) the Koran and the Sunna. The primary meaning of *al-ṭawáriq*. A Tradition of the Prophet in which the word occurs.

(54) *al-kashf*. Definition. Saying of Abú Muḥammad al-Jarírí. Saying of Shiblí.

(55) *al-shaṭḥ*. Definition. A saying of Abú Ḥamza which a man of Khurásán described as *shaṭḥ*. Meaning of the expression *shaṭḥ al-lisán*. Junayd wrote a commentary

on the *shaṭaḥát* of Abú Yazíd al-Bisṭámí, and he would not have done so if, in his opinion, Abú Yazíd was to be condemned for indulging in *shaṭḥ*.

Two verses by al-Qannád.

347 (56) *al-ṣawl*. Definition. The practice denoted by this term is a blameworthy one. Saying of Abú ᶜAlí al-Rúdhabárí. Reasons why *ṣawl* should be avoided. The term is also used in reference to advanced mystics who *yaṣúlúna billáh*, and the Prophet said in his prayer, "O God, by Thee I spring to the assault" (*bika aṣúlu*). A similar expression quoted from the writings of Ibráhím al-Khawwáṣ. An anonymous verse.

(57) *al-dhaháb*. Identical in meaning with *al-ghaybat* but more complete. Definition. Junayd, in his commentary on the ecstatic sayings of Abú Yazíd al-Bisṭámí, explains the words *laysa bi-laysa* as being equivalent to *al-dhaháb ᶜan al-dhaháb*. Other mystical terms used in the same sense are *faná* and *faqd*.

(58) *al-nafas*. Definitions by the author and by an unnamed Ṣúfí. A synonym is *al-tanaffus*.

348 Verses by Dhu 'l-Nún. Here *al-nafas* is Divine, but it is also employed in reference to mankind. Saying of Junayd. An anonymous verse.

(59) *al-ḥiss*. Definition. Saying of ᶜAmr b. ᶜUthmán al-Makkí concerning those who assert that they feel no sensation (*ḥiss*) in ecstasy.

(60) *tawḥíd al-ᶜámmat*. Definition.

(61) *tawḥíd al-kháṣṣat*. This term has been mentioned in the chapter on Unification. Definition. Explanation of the term by Shiblí.

(62) *al-tafríd*. Definition. A certain Ṣúfí said that there are many *muwaḥḥidún* but few *mufarridún*. Ḥusayn b. Manṣúr al-Ḥalláj, when he was about to be killed, said, *ḥasb al-wájid ifrád al-wáḥid*.

(63) *al-tajríd*. Definition by the author.

349   Definition by an unnamed Sheykh. The terms *al-tajríd*, *al-tafríd*, and *al-tawḥíd* coincide in their meanings but are distinguished from each other in various ways by mystics. Anonymous verse on *al-tajríd*.

(64) *al-hamm al-mufarrad* and *al-sirr al-mujarrad*. These terms mean the same thing. Definition. A saying of Ibráhím al-Ájurrí addressed to Junayd. A saying of Shiblí.

(65) *al-muḥádathat*. A term describing the state of adepts. Saying of Abú Bakr al-Wásiṭí. The Prophet said that among the Moslems there are *muḥaddathún* and that ᶜUmar was one of them. Sahl b. ᶜAbdallah declared that God created His creatures in order that He might converse with them in secret (*yusárrahum*) and they with Him.

(66) *al-munáját*. Definition. An example of Junayd's *munáját*.

350 (67) *al-musámarat*. Definition by the author. Verse by al-Rúdhabárí. Definition by an unnamed Sheykh.

(68) *ru'yat al-qulúb*. Definition. A saying of ᶜAlí affirming spiritual vision of God in this world. A Tradition of the Prophet.

(69) *al-ism*. Definition. Two sayings of Shiblí. Verse cited by Abu 'l-Ḥusayn al-Núrí. Two more sayings of Shiblí.

(70) *al-rasm*. Definition.

351   Saying of Junayd concerning one who has no *rasm*. The *rusúm* of a man are the knowledge and actions which are attributed to him. An anonymous verse.

(71) *al-wasm*. Definition. Saying of Aḥmad b. ᶜAṭá.

(72) *al-rúḥ (al-rawḥ)* and *al-tarawwuḥ*. Definition. Two sayings of Yaḥyá b. Muᶜádh al-Rází. A saying of Sufyán.

(73) *al-naᶜt*. Definition. The terms *al-naᶜt* and *al-waṣf* may be synonymous, but the former is a detailed description, while the latter is a summary description.

(74) *al-ṣifat*. Definition.

(75) *al-dhát*. Definition. Relation of the *ism* and *naʿt* and *ṣifat* to the *dhát*.

352   Saying of Abú Bakr al-Wásiṭí. Two verses (by Abú ʿAbdallah al-Qurashí) [1]).

(76) *al-ḥijáb*. Definition. Saying of Sarí al-Saqaṭí. The author's explanation of a saying of Muḥammad b. ʿAlí al-Kattání.

(77) *al-daʿwá*. Definition. Saying of Sahl b. ʿAbdallah. Verse on the pretence (*daʿwá*) of love [2]). The author explains a saying of Abú ʿAmr al-Zajjájí.

(78) *al-ikhtiyár*. Definition.

353   Saying of Yaḥyá b. Muʿádh.

(79) *al-ikhtibár*. Definition. Explanation of the Prophet's saying *ukhbur taqlah*.

(80) *al-balá*. Definition. Saying of Abú Muḥammad al-Jarírí. A Tradition of the Prophet. Verses on the subject of *al-balá*.

(81) *al-lisán*. Definition. The use of the term exemplified in a letter written by Núrí to Junayd.

354   Shiblí's explanation of the difference between *lisán al-ʿilm, lisán al-ḥaqíqat*, and *lisán al-ḥaqq*.

(82) *al-sirr*. Definitions by the author and another Ṣúfí. The meaning of *sirr al-khalq* and *sirr al-ḥaqq*. The meaning of *sirr al-sirr*. A saying of Sahl b. ʿAbdallah. Two verses. [3])

(83) *al-ʿaqd*. Definition. Saying of a sage (*ḥakím*) on gnosis. The reason why Muḥammad b. Yaʿqúb al-Farají refrained from making an *ʿaqd* with God. Distinction between verbal promises and spiritual vows.

355 (84) *al-hamm*. Definition. Saying of Abú Saʿíd al-Kharráz. Saying of an unnamed mystic.

---

1) See p. ٢٥٩, l. ١١

2) Cf. p. ٢٥١, l. ٤

3) Cf. p. ٣٤٣, l. ٩

(85) *al-laḥẓ*. Definition. Verses by al-Rúdhabárí.

(86) *al-maḥw*. Definition. *Al-maḥw* distinguished from *al-ṭams*. A saying of Núrí, with explanation by the author.

(87) *al-maḥq*. Almost synonymous with *al-maḥw*. Saying of Shiblí in reply to a man who asked, "Is not He with thee and art not thou with Him?"

356   Verse of an anonymous poet.

(88) *al-athar*. Definition. Saying of an unnamed mystic.

Anonymous verse. A verse inscribed on the palace of a certain king. A saying of Ibráhím al-Khawwáṣ on the *tawḥid* of the Ṣúfís. Verse.

(89) *al-kawn*. Definition.

(90) *al-bawn*. Meaning of the term. Explanation of a saying of Junayd in which the terms *al-kawn* and *al-bawn* are used. Verses on the same topic.

(91) *al-waṣl*. Meaning of the term. Saying of Yaḥyá b. Muʿádh.

357   Saying of Shiblí. Anonymous saying and verse.

(92) *al-faṣl*. Definition. Anonymous sayings and verse.

(93) *al-aṣl*. Definition. Meaning of *al-uṣúl*.

(94) *al-farʿ*. Definition. The relation of the *furúʿ* to the *aṣl*. Saying of ʿAmr b. ʿUthmán al-Makkí. Saying of a certain theologian.

(95) *al-ṭams*. Definition. Quotation from a letter written by Junayd to Abú Bakr al-Kisáʾí.

358   Quotation from the Koran. Saying of ʿAmr b. ʿUthmán al-Makkí.

(96) *al-rams* and *al-dams*. Meaning of these terms. Extract from a letter written by Junayd to Yaḥyá b. Muʿádh, with explanation by Sarráj. Saying of Sahl b. ʿAbdallah.

(97) *al-qaṣm*. Meaning of the term. Saying of Abú Bakr al-Zaqqáq. Saying of al-Wásiṭí.

(98) *al-sabab*. Definition. Saying of Aḥmad b. ʿAṭá.

359   Verses by Abú ʿAlí al-Rúdhabárí.

(99) *al-nisbat*. Definition. Saying of Jaʿfar al-Ṭayálisí al-Rází. Definition of *al-gharíb* by al-Qannád. Saying of Núrí. *Al-nisbat* is equivalent to *al-iʿtiráf*. Saying of ʿAmr b. ʿUthmán al-Makkí.

(100) *fulán ṣáḥib qalb*. Meaning of the expression. Junayd used to apply it to the people of Khurásán.

(101) *rabb ḥál*. Definition.

(102) *ṣáḥib maqám*. Definition. Junayd said that true gnosis cannot be attained until one has traversed the *aḥwál* and *maqámát*. Saying of an anonymous Sheykh concerning Shiblí.

(103) *fulán bilá nafs*.

360   Meaning of the expression. Description of such a person by Abú Saʿíd al-Kharráz.

(104) *fulán ṣáḥib ishárat*. Meaning of the expression. Verse by al-Rúdhabárí.

(105) *ana bilá ana* and *naḥnu bilá naḥnu*. Meaning of these expressions. Explanation of Kor. 16, 55 by Abú Saʿíd al-Kharráz.

(106) *ana anta wa-anta ana*. The meaning of these words is explained in a saying of Shiblí which describes the love of Majnún and how he used to say, "I am Laylá." A story of two lovers, related by Shiblí.

361   A story of Shiblí and a youth. Three citations of verse [1].

(107) *huwa bilá huwa*. Meaning of this expression. A saying of Junayd on *tawḥíd*.

362 (108) *qaṭʿ al-ʿaláʾiq*. Definition of *ʿaláʾiq*. A saying of Abú Saʿíd al-Kharráz.

(109) *bádí bilá bádí*. Meaning of the expressions *bádí* and *bilá bádí*. Quotation from the *Kitáb maʿrifat al-maʿrifat* by Ibráhím al-Khawwáṣ.

---

1) The verses beginning انا من اهوى (l. 11) are commonly attributed to al-Ḥallaj. Cf. Massignon, *Kitáb al-Ṭawásín*, p. 134.

(110) *al-taḥallī*. Definition. A Tradition of the Prophet on the subject of faith.

363   Anonymous verse.

(111) *al-tajallī*. Definition. A saying of Núrí. Mystical interpretation of Kor. 64, 9 by al-Wásiṭí. Another saying of Núrí [1]).

Anonymous verse.

(112) *al-takhallī*. Definition. Saying of Junayd. Explanation by the author. Saying of Yúsuf b. al-Ḥusayn.

Anonymous verse.

(113) *al-ʿillat*. Definition. A saying of Shiblí. The author's explanation of a saying of Dhu 'l-Nún.

364   Anonymous verse.

(114) *al-azal*. This term is equivalent to *al-qidam*. The terms *azal* and *azaliyyat* are applied to God only. Saying of an ancient Ṣúfí, which some condemned on the ground that it involves the eternity of things (*qidam al-ashyá*).

(115) *al-abad* and *al-abadiyyat*. These are attributes of God. Distinction between *azaliyyat* and *abadiyyat*. Definition of *al-abad* by al-Wásiṭí. Definition of *al-wasm* and *al-rasm* by al-Wásiṭí. Saying by an unnamed mystic. Sayings of Shiblí and ʿAmr b. ʿUthmán al-Makkí.

(116) *waqtī musarmad*. Meaning of this expression.

365   A verse by Shiblí.

(117) *baḥrī bilá sháṭi*. This expression has almost the same meaning as *waqtī musarmad*. It was uśed by Shiblí in concluding one of his discourses. Explanation by the author. Anonymous saying and verse.

(118) *naḥnu musayyarún*. Meaning of this expression. Saying of Yaḥyá b. Muʿádh concerning the ascetic (*záhid*) and the gnostic (*ʿárif*), with explanation by Sarráj.

---

1) Cf. p. ٣٨, l. ٨ foll.

366   Two verses by Shiblí.

(119) *al-talwín*. Definition. According to some mystics, *al-talwín* is a mark of *al-ḥaqíqat*, while others hold the contrary doctrine. The latter refer to *talwín al-ṣifát*, whereas the former refer to *talwín al-qulúb*. Verse on *talwín al-ṣifát*. Saying of al-Wásiṭí.

Anonymous verses describing the *musayyarún*.

(120) *badhl al-muhaj*. Meaning of this expression. Saying of Ibráhím al-Khawwáṣ.

367   Anonymous verse. Meaning of *al-muhaj*.

(121) *al-talaf*. Equivalent in meaning to *al-ḥatf*. Story of the Ṣúfí Abú Ḥamza (al-Khurásání) and verses by him [1]. Saying of al-Jarírí.

(122) *al-laja'*. Definition. Saying of al-Wásiṭí. Mystical interpretation of Kor. 17, 82.

(123) *al-inziʿáj*. Definition. Saying of Junayd. Answer given by a certain Sheykh (Ibráhím al-Khawwáṣ, in the author's opinion) to one who found fault with his disciples for asserting that they received their food from God.

368 (124) *jadhb al-arwáḥ*. The meaning of this and similar expressions, such as *sumuww al-qulúb* and *musháhadat al-asrár*, etc. Sayings of Abú Saʿíd al-Kharráz and al-Wásiṭí.

(125) *al-waṭar*. Definition. Anonymous saying and verse. Two verses by Dhu 'l-Nún. How a certain sage answered the question, "What place does one love best as a home?"

369 (126) *al-waṭan*. Definition. Saying of Junayd. Verses by Núrí. Explanation of a saying of Abú Sulaymán al-Dárání on the superiority of *al-ímán* to *al-yaqín*.

(126) *al-shurúd*. Definition. Sayings of Abú Saʿíd b. al-Aʿrábí and Abú Bakr al-Wásiṭí.

---

1) Cf. p. ٣٥٢, l. ١٣ foll.

g

(127) *al-quṣúd*. Definition. Sayings of Ibn ᶜAṭá and al-Wásiṭí.
370   Explanation of the latter.

(128) *al-iṣṭináᶜ*. Definition. According to some, *al-iṣṭináᶜ* is a degree that belongs to none of the prophets except Moses, while others maintain that it is shared by all the prophets. Saying of Abú Saᶜíd al-Kharráz. Anonymous explanation of *al-iṣṭináᶜ*.

(129) *al-iṣṭifá*. Definition. Saying of al-Wásiṭí.

(130) *al-maskh*. Meaning of the term.

(131) *al-laṭífat*. The author says that the meaning of this term is too subtle to be expressed. Saying of Abú Saᶜíd b. al-Aᶜrábí.

371   Verse by Abú Ḥamza al-Ṣúfí (al-Khurásání).

(132) *al-imtiḥán*. Definition. Saying of a certain youth addressed to Khayr al-Nassáj, who relates it. Three kinds of *imtiḥán*.

(133) *al-ḥadath*. Definition. An anonymous saying.

(134) *al-kulliyyat*. Definition. Two anonymous sayings and a verse.

(135) *al-talbís*. Definition. Explanation of a saying of al-Wásiṭí. Saying of Junayd.

372   Verse by al-Qannád.

(136) *al-shirb*. Definition. Saying of Dhu 'l-Nún. Two anonymous verses.

(137) *al-dhawq*. Definition. Saying of Dhu 'l-Nún. Anonymous verse.

(138) *al-ᶜayn*. Definition. Saying of al-Wásiṭí.

     Junayd said that the anecdotes related of Abú Yazíd al-Bisṭámí show that he attained to the *ᶜayn al-jamᶜ*, which is one of the names of *al-tawḥíd*. Verse by Núrí.

(139) *al-iṣṭilám*. Definition. Anonymous saying.

373   Two verses by an unnamed author.

(140) *al-ḥurriyyat*. Definition. A saying of Bishr (b. al-

Ḥárith al-Ḥáfí) to Sarí (al-Saqaṭí). Junayd said that *al-ḥurriyyat* is the last station of the gnostic. An anonymous saying.

(141) *al-rayn.* Definition. A certain theologian includes *al-rayn* among four kinds of spiritual veils. The reason why the father of Ibn al-Jallá was called al-Jallá.

(142) *al-ghayn.* The term occurs in a Tradition of weak authority, according to which the Prophet said *yughánu ᶜalá qalbí.* This *ghayn* is compared by some to the momentary dimness of a mirror when it is breathed upon. Others deny that the Prophet's heart could be subject to any such creaturely invasion.

374   No one is entitled, the author says, to describe the state of the Prophet's heart either directly or symbolically. Verses on *ighánat* by Abú ᶜAlí al-Rúdhabárí.

The author professes to have explained the foregoing technical terms according to what God revealed to him of their meaning at the time. Desire for brevity has compelled him to leave much unsaid.

(143) *al-wasá'iṭ.* Definition. Three kinds of *wasá'iṭ* distinguished by a certain Sheykh. Saying of Abú ᶜAlí al-Rúdhabárí.

375 BOOK OF THE INTERPRETATION OF ECSTATIC
EXPRESSIONS (*shaṭḥiyyát*) AND SAYINGS
WHICH APPEAR TO BE DETESTABLE ALTHOUGH
THEIR INNER MEANING IS TRUE
AND RIGHT.

CHAPTER CXXI: "Concerning the signification of *al-shaṭḥ*, with a refutation of those who condemn it."

Definition and derivation of the term. Four anonymous verses, in the first of which *mishṭáḥ* denotes "a barn where flour is stored". Explanation of the word *mishṭáḥ.* The meaning of *al-shaṭḥ* as applied to ecstasy. It is wrong to censure expressions of this sort instead of trying to remove the ground of offence by consulting those who understand them.

376 Just as a river in flood overflows its banks (*shaṭaḥa 'l-mā' fi 'l-nahr*), so the Ṣūfī, when his ecstasy grows strong, cannot contain himself and finds relief in strange and obscure utterances, technically known as *shaṭḥ*, which express his real mystical experience and truly describe what God has revealed to his inmost self. Mystical experiences differ in degree, though not in kind, and the language in which they are shadowed forth must not be judged by ordinary standards. In such matters no one but an eminent theosophist

377 has the right to criticise. The uninitiated will adopt the safe course if they abstain from faultfinding and ask themselves whether they may not be mistaken in regard to those whom they blame.

CHAPTER CXXII: "Concerning the sciences in general, and the difficulty which the mystical sciences present to theologians, and the proof that these sciences are true."

Knowledge *(ʿilm)* is not bounded by the intellect. Let any one who doubts this consider the story of Moses and al-Khaḍir (Kor. 18, 64 foll.), and the Tradition of the Prophet, "If ye knew what I know, etc.", which shows that the Prophet

378 was endowed with a knowledge peculiar to himself. Three kinds of knowledge possessed by the Prophet. Hence no one ought to suppose that he comprehends all the sciences, and consequently he ought not to charge the elect with being infidels or freethinkers when he has never experienced their states. The sciences of the religious law *(al-sharīʿat)* fall into four divisions: Tradition, Jurisprudence, Scholasticism, and Mysticism. The last-named is the highest and most noble. Description of it.

379 Questions connected with any one of these four sciences are decided by the experts in that science, but whereas the possessors of the other three sciences can have only a limited knowledge of mysticism, the mystics may possess all those

other sciences of which mysticism is the crown and goal: hence the former often deny the sciences of mysticism, but the latter do not deny any brauch of the science of religion. Whoever has acquired a profound knowledge of one branch of religious science is recognised as the supreme authority in his department.

380 Similarly, a person who unites in himself all the four divisions of religious science, is the perfect Imám, the Quṭb, the Proof of God in this world, to whom ʿAlí b. Abí Ṭálib refers in a saying addressed to Kumayl b. Ziyád.

To return to *al-shaṭḥ*. It is characteristic of those who have reached the end of self-will (which is the beginning of the state of perfection) and are advancing towards the goal but have not yet attained it. In the adept who has finished his mystical journey *al-shaṭḥ* is very seldom found.

CHAPTER CXXIII: "Concerning some ecstatic expressions related of Abú Yazíd al-Bisṭámí and explained in part by Junayd."

The author says that since Junayd has explained a small portion of the *shaṭaḥát* of Abú Yazíd, it is impossible for himself to neglect that explanation and put forward one of his own. He quotes some remarks of Junayd upon the reason why so many different stories are told of Abú Yazíd, upon
381 the difficulty of understanding his sayings, and upon the character of his mystical experience and attainments. The author observes that although the sayings of Abú Yazíd which he is about to mention are not recorded in books *(muṣannafát)*, their meaning is much debated and commonly misinterpreted.

CHAPTER CXXIV: "Concerning an anecdote related of Abú Yazíd al-Bisṭámí."

The author says that he does not know whether Abú Yazíd really spoke the following words which many people attribute to him:

382   "Once He raised me up and caused me to stand before Him and said to me, 'O Abú Yazíd, My creatures desire to behold thee'. I answered, 'Adorn me with Thy Unity and clothe me in Thy I-ness and raise me to Thy Oneness, so that when Thy creatures behold me they may say that they behold Thee, and that only Thou mayst be there, not I'."

Junayd's explanation of this saying. The author points out that Junayd has not explained it in such a way as to meet the objections of hostile critics. Accordingly, he proceeds to interpret it himself. The words, "He caused me to stand before Him", signify spiritual presence, and the words, "He said to me and I said to Him", allude to inward communion and recollection *(dhikr)* when God is contemplated by the heart.

383   When a mystic feels and realises the nearness of God, every thought that enters his heart seems, as it were, to be the voice of God speaking to him. Anonymous verses on this subject. The remainder of Abú Yazíd's saying refers to the ultimate degree of unification and passing-away (*faná*) in the Oneness that is anterior to creation. All this is derived from the Apostolic Tradition that God said, "My servant ceases not to draw nigh unto Me by works of devotion until I love him; and when I love him, I am the eye by which he sees and the ear by which he hears, etc."

384   The poet uses similar language where he says, in describing his love for a mortal,

"I am he whom I love and he whom I love is I." [1]

If human love can produce words like these, what feelings must not Divine Love inspire! A certain sage said, "Lovers do not reach the height of true love until one says to the other, 'O thou who art I!'"

CHAPTER CXXV: "Concerning the explanation of another story told of Abú Yazíd."

---

[1] The two verses quoted here are usually ascribed to Ḥalláj.

It is related that he said, "As soon as I attained to His Unity, I became a bird with a body of Oneness and wings of Everlastingness; and I continued flying in the air of Quality for ten years, until I reached an atmosphere a million times as large; and I flew on, until I found myself in the field of Eternity, and I saw there the tree of Oneness." Then, after describing its soil ands roots and branches and foliage and fruit, he said, "I looked, and I knew that all this was a cheat."

385 Junayd's explanation of this saying. The author defends the phrases "I became a bird" and "I continued flying" by quoting instances in which *ṭára* is used metaphorically.

386 He shows that in applying the attributes of Oneness and Everlastingness to himself Abú Yazíd follows the familiar practice of ecstatic lovers, like Majnún, who could think of nothing but Laylá, so that on being asked his name he answered, "Laylá". Verses by Majnún and an anonymous poet.

387 The words "I knew that all this was a cheat" signify that those who regard phenomena are deceived. If Abú Yazíd had been far advanced in theosophy, he would not have thought of such things as birds, bodies, atmospheres, etc.

A hemistich by Labíd, which the Prophet described as the truest word ever spoken by an Arab.

CHAPTER CXXVI: "On the interpretation of a saying attributed to Abú Yazíd."

Text of the saying.

388 Explanation by Junayd. The subject of this saying is *faná* and *faná ʿan al-faná*.

389 Remarks by the author on the difficulty of understanding topics of this kind without a profound knowledge of mystical theology, and on the uninterrupted progression of mystical experience from lower to higher states. The latter point is illustrated by the interpretation which ʿAbdallah b. ʿAbbás gave of a passage in the Koran (41, 10).

390   Explanation by a certain gnostic of the tradition, which occurs in some unnamed book, that God threatened to burn Hell with His greatest fires if it disobeyed His command. The author's explanation of what Abú Yazíd meant by the words *laysa bi-laysa fí laysa*.

    CHAPTER CXXVII: "Concerning the interpretation of certain expressions attributed to Abú Yazíd, on account of which Ibn Sálim declared him to be an infidel, together with the author's report of a discussion of this question which took place between Ibn Sálim and himself at Baṣra."

    How Ibn Sálim denounced Abú Yazíd for having said, "Glory to me!" (*subḥáni*).

391   The author's controversy with Ibn Sálim. He contends that if the whole saying of Abú Yazíd had been recorded, it would be clear that he used the phrase *subḥáni* in reference to God. The author adds that when he visited Bisṭám and asked some descendants of Abú Yazíd about this story, they asserted that they had no knowledge of it. Other sayings of Abú Yazíd which, according to Ibn Sálim, could only have been uttered by an infidel. The author's further apology on behalf of Abú Yazíd.

392   His explanation of Abú Yazíd's saying, "I pitched my tent opposite the Throne of God". His explanation of Abú Yazíd's saying, when he passed a cemetery of the Jews, "They are forgiven" (*maᶜdhúrún*).

393   His explanation of Abú Yazíd's saying, when he passed a cemetery of the Moslems, "They are duped" (*maghrúrún*). The Prophet said that salvation does not depend on works, but on the divine mercy. Theologians have no right to criticise the obscure sayings of mystics who keep the religious law. Such words of profound wisdom are commonly misunderstood and misreported.

394   Junayd said that in his youth he used to associate with Ṣúfís and that although he did not understand what they

said, he bore no prejudice against them in his mind. The author relates that some time after the controversy mentioned above, he heard Ibn Sálim quote in public two sayings of Sahl b. ʿAbdallah; whereupon he remarked to one of Ibn Sálim's pupils that Ibn Sálim would have condemned Sahl b. ʿAbdallah and Abú Yazíd with the same severity, if he had not been so favourably disposed towards the former. The sayings of Sahl are equally open to criticism, and if a satisfactory explanation can be found in the one case, why not in the other?

395   Unless Moses had been divinely guided, he must have exacted the due penalty from al-Khaḍir when he slew the youth (Kor. 18, 73). Anecdotes showing the piety of Abú Yazíd.

CHAPTER CXXVIII: "Concerning some sayings of Shiblí and their explanation".

396   Shiblí said to a number of his friends who were taking leave of him, "Go: I am with you wherever you may be; you are under my care and in my keeping." The author explains that Shiblí meant to say, "God is with you", but al that time he was regarding himself as non-existent, and he spoke as one who contemplates the nearness (*qurb*) of God. Nevertheless, on another occasion Shiblí referred to the vileness of the Jews and Christians and said that he was viler then they. These two sayings do not contradict each other but are the expression of different states. Yaḥyá b. Muʿádh al-Rází said that the gnostic is proud when he thinks of God, and humble when he thinks of himself. Similarly, the Prophet once said, "I am the chief of mankind", and he also described himself as the son of a woman who used to eat *qadíd* [1]).

397   Another anecdote of Shiblí. He said that his flesh (*nafs*)

---

1) Meat cut into strips and dried in the sun.

felt a craving for bread, though his spirit (*sirr*) would have been consumed with fire if it had turned aside, even for a moment, from contemplation of God. A saying of Shiblí concerning Abú Yazíd al-Bisṭámí, with explanation by Sarráj. Shiblí, according to a certain Sheykh, discoursed exclusively on 'states' and 'stations', not on unification (*tawḥíd*).

398   CHAPTER CXXIX: "On the meaning of an anecdote which is related of Shiblí".

He is reported to have said, "God ordered the earth to swallow me if, for one or two months past, there were any room in me for thought of Gabriel and Michael"; and he said to Ḥuṣrí, "If the thought of Gabriel and Michael occurs to your mind, you are a polytheist." Inasmuch as the Prophet acknowledged the superiority of Gabriel, these sayings have given offence, but they would not give offence if instead of being presented in an abridged form they were related with their whole context and circumstances.

399   The complete version of the anecdote to which the former saying belongs, as related by Abú Muḥammad al-Nassáj.

400   CHAPTER CXXX: "Concerning various actions of Shiblí which were regarded with disapproval."

He used to burn costly clothes, ambergris, sugar, etc., although wastefulness is forbidden by the Prophet. Once he sold an estate for a large sum of money, which he immediately distributed amongst the people, without reserving anything for his own family. Here he is justified by the authority of Abú Bakr. Money is not wasted unless it is spent for a sinful purpose.

401   As regards his burning of valuable goods, he did this because they distracted his thoughts from God. Solomon acted on the same principle when he slaughtered three hundred Arab mares which had engaged his attention so deeply that he neglected to perform the evening prayer (Kor. 38, 29—32). The Prophet cursed the Jews for a like

reason. The author explains why the sun was turned back for Solomon, but not for the Prophet.

402   Mystics believe that whatever takes their thoughts away from God is their enemy, and they endeavour to escape from it by every means in their power. Traditions of the Prophet on this subject.

CHAPTER CXXXI: "Concerning the explanation of a saying uttered by Shiblí which is hard for theologians to understand, and of various conversations between him and Junayd."

Shiblí said, "I go towards the infinite, but I see only the finite, and I go on the right hand and the left hand towards the infinite, but I see only the finite; then I return and I see all this in a single hair of my little finger."

403   The author's explanation of this saying. Another saying of Shiblí, with the author's interpretation. Verses composed or recited by Shiblí.

404   He also said, "I studied the Traditions and jurisprudence (al-fiqh) for thirty years until the dawn shone forth. Then I went to all my teachers and told them that I desired knowledge (fiqh) of God, but none of them answered me." Explanation of this by the author. A question addressed by Shiblí to Junayd, and the latter's reply, with explanation by the author. A remark by Junayd concerning Shiblí. Another saying of Junayd to Shiblí. Report of a conversation between Shiblí and Junayd. Sayings of Shiblí on the subject of waqt.

405   Further ecstatic expressions of Shiblí in prose and verse, with explanations by the author. Such expressions are the product of a temporary state. If that state were permanent, all religious, moral, and social laws would be annulled.

406   A Tradition of the Prophet bearing on this question. Shiblí said that if he thought that Hell would burn a single hair of him, he would be guilty of polytheism. The author explains Shiblí's meaning and declares that he agrees with

it. Another saying of Shiblí, to the effect that Hell consists in separation from God. Two more sayings by him, the latter of which is supported by a Tradition of the Prophet.

407   CHAPTER CXXXII: "Concerning the explanation of the sayings of al-Wásiṭí" [1]).

A passage referring to ʿÁ'isha. When her innocence was revealed (Kor. 24, 11 foll.), she praised God, not the Prophet. Explanation of the saying of al-Wásiṭí, "Bless them (the prophets) in thy prayers but do not attach any value to it in thy heart." He means, "Do not think much of the blessings which thou bestowest upon them" or "do not let reverence for them have any place in thy heart in comparison with the veneration of God".

408   This refers to the mystical doctrine of unity *(tawḥíd)*. The reverence due to the prophets, and the superiority of Muḥammad to all other prophets, has been discussed above [2]). Sayings of Abú Yazíd al-Bisṭámí on the pre-eminence of Muḥammad. The Ṣúfís believe that God granted to him whatever he asked. His prayer for light.

409   Every peculiar excellence with which a Moslem is endowed belongs to the Prophet. Criticism of the saints is the result of habitual turning away from God.

CHAPTER CXXXIII: "Concerning the errors of those who call themselves Ṣúfís and the source and nature of their errors."

Saying of Abú ʿAlí al-Rúdhabárí. The author enumerates three principles which are the basis of all true Ṣúfism: (1) avoidance of things forbidden, (2) performance of religious duties, (3) renunciation of this world, so far as it is possible to the believer.

410   The Prophet mentioned four things which are *in* this

---

1) Between Chapters 131 and 132 there were originally five chapters which do not occur in either of the MSS. See note on p. ٤٠٧. The beginning of this chapter is also lost.

2) See Chapters 53 and 54.

world, but not *of* it: a piece of bread, a garment, a house, and a wife. Worldliness in other respects is an absolute barrier between God and man.

CHAPTER CXXXIV: "Concerning the different classes of those who err and the variety of errors into which they fall."

Three classes of the erring: (1) those who err in the fundamentals *(uṣúl)*; (2) those who err in the derivatives *(furúᶜ)*, *i. e.* in manners, morals, spiritual feelings, etc. Their error is caused by ignorance of the fundamentals, by selfishness, and by want of a director who should set them on the right way. Description of them.

411 (3) those whose error is a slip or a lapse rather than a serious fault, so that it can easily be repaired. Verse on affectation *(taḥallí)*. The Prophet's definition of faith.

CHAPTER CXXXV: "Concerning those who err in the derivatives, which does not lead them into heresy; and in the first place, concerning those who err as regards poverty and wealth."

Some Ṣúfís declare that wealth is superior to poverty, using the word 'wealth' in a spiritual sense. Others, however, have argued that worldly wealth is a praiseworthy state, and this is an error.

412 It is wrong to suppose that the *faqír* who lacks patience and does not acquiesce in the divine will is not superior to the man who is rich in worldly goods — for the soul hates poverty and loves riches; but the *faqír* who bears poverty with patience shall receive a recompense without end. Poverty is essentially praiseworthy, though it may be accompanied by some defect that incurs blame. Wealth, on the contrary, is essentially blameworthy and can only be praised in virtue of some good quality, *e. g.* pious works, that accompanies it, but not for itself. Some mystics hold that poverty and wealth are two states which must be transcended.

413 This is an advanced doctrine. It does not, as some have

maintained, imply that there is no spiritual difference between poverty and wealth. Those who pretend that there is no difference are proved to be in error by the fact that they dislike poverty but do not dislike wealth. True poverty consists, not merely in indigence, but also in patience and resignation and in having no regard to one's poverty and in taking no credit to one's self on account of it.

CHAPTER CXXXVI: "Concerning those who err in respect of luxury or frugality and asceticism, and those who err in respect of gaining the means of livelihood or of neglecting to do so."

Only a prophet or a saint has the right to live in abundance, because they know when God permits them to spend and when He permits them to refrain from spending. Until a man regards much and little as equal, he relies upon the 414 worldly goods which he possesses. If his heart is not empty of desire to obtain a worldly good that he lacks and of desire to keep the worldly goods that he has, then he is a worldling; and any one who imagines himself to be an exception to this rule is in error. Others, again, devote themselves to austerities and find fault with those who are less strict; but as luxury is unsound, so too is extreme asceticism when it is habitual and ostentatious and is not specially adopted for the purpose of self-discipline. Others of the religious insist on earning their daily bread and hold that no food is legally pure unless it is earned, but this is an error, since the Prophet and all mankind are commanded to trust in God and to feel assured that He will give them their appointed portion. To seek the means of livelihood is an indulgence granted to those who are too weak to trust in God absolutely. Conditions to be observed by those who seek the means of livelihood.

415 Others sit still and wait eagerly for some one who will attend to their wants, and they believe that this is the right

spiritual state. But they are mistaken. Any one who abstains from seeking a livelihood ought to be inspired by strong faith and patience; otherwise, he is commanded to seek a livelihood. The latter course is permissible, but the former is more excellent.

CHAPTER CXXXVIII: "Concerning the different classes of those who become remiss in their quest and err in respect of mortification and betake themselves to self-indulgence."

There are some who submit to austerities in the hope of gaining a reputation for sanctity and of being endowed with miraculous powers; and when they fail in their object, they discard asceticism and hold it in contempt, and this they call 'languor' (*futúr*).

416   'Languor', however, is only a temporary intermission which refreshes the hearts of mystics, whereas the conduct of the persons referred to here is properly described as laziness and negligence. Saying of Abú ᶜAlí al-Rúdhabárí. Others travel and boast of the number of Sheykhs whom they have met and deem themselves in a privileged position. They are wrong, for the purpose of travel is moral improvement. Others spend money and bestow gifts and cultivate liberality, but this is not Ṣúfism. The Ṣúfís regard worldly goods as an obstacle which prevents them from attaining to God, and their object in giving is the removal of that obstacle, not the desire to appear generous. Others indulge themselves unrestrainedly and claim that their spiritual state (*waqt*) justifies them in their license.

417   Such a belief is erroneous and leads to perdition.

CHAPTER CXXXVIII: "Concerning those who err in respect of abstaining from food, retirement from the world, solitude, etc."

Some aspirants and novices, supposing that hunger is the most effectual method of self-mortification, have abstained from food and drink during long periods of time, without having consulted a spiritual director. They are wrong, since the novice cannot dispense with the guidance of a teacher, and it is a mistake to think that the wickedness of human nature can be eradicated by means of hunger. Sayings of Ibn Sálim and Sahl b. ʿAbdallah. The author says that he has seen a number of persons who, on account of ill-regulated abstinence from food, were unable to perform their religious duties.

418 Others retire from the world and dwell in caves, fancying that solitude will deliver them from their passions and cause them to share in the mystical experiences of the saints, but the fact is that hunger and solitude, if self-imposed and not the result of an overpowering spiritual influence, are positively harmful. The author recalls instances known to him of young men who reduced themselves to such a state of weakness that they had to be nursed for several days before they could perform the obligatory prayers. Others castrate themselves in the hope of escaping from the lust of the flesh. This is useless and even injurious, inasmuch as lust arises from within and is incurable by any external remedy. Others imagine that they show sincere trust in God (*tawakkul*) when they roam through deserts and wildernesses without provision for the journey, but real *tawakkul* demands previous self-discipline and mortification.

419 Another erroneous belief is that Ṣúfism consists in wearing garments of wool and patched frocks and in carrying leathern water-buckets, etc. Such imitation avails nothing. Others vainly suppose that they can become Ṣúfís by learning mystical allegories and anecdotes and technical expressions, or by fasting, praying, and weeping, although they have already provided themselves with food and money. All Ṣúfís renounce worldly things in the initial stages of their spiritual progress and enjoin their disciples to do the same. If any of them acted otherwise, it was for the sake of his

family or brethren. According to others, Ṣúfism is music and dancing and ecstasy and the art of composing mystical ghazels. This is a mistake, because music and ecstasy are impure when the heart is polluted with worldliness and when the soul is accustomed to vanity.

420   CHAPTER CXXXIX: "Concerning those who err in the fundamentals and are thereby led into heresy; and in the first place, concerning those who err in respect of freedom and service."

Some ancient Ṣúfís held that in spiritual intercourse with God one should not be like a free man, who expects recompense for his work, but like a slave, who performs his master's bidding without expectation of wages or reward, and receives whatever his master may bestow upon him as a bounty, not as a right. A certain eminent Ṣúfí has written a book on this topic. There are heretics, however, who assert that as the free man is higher than the slave in ordinary life, so the relation of service (ʿubúdiyyat) to God only continues until union with God is attained; one who is united with God has become free and is no longer bound to service. They fail to recognise that no one can be a true servant (of God) unless his heart is free from everything except God. The name of 'servant' (ʿabd) is the best of all the names which God has given to the Faithful.

421   Passages from the Koran and the Traditions in support of this statement. Had it been possible for any creature to gain a higher dignity than that of service to God, Muḥammad would have gained it.

CHAPTER CXL: "Concerning those ʿIráqís who err in respect of sincerity (ikhláṣ)."

The heretics of ʿIráq declare that no one is perfectly sincere who regards created beings or seeks to please them by any action, whether good or bad. Now, certain mystics have held the doctrine that true sincerity involves the complete

h

absence of regard for created beings and phenomenal objects
and, in short, for everything but God. The heretics in question have taken over this doctrine in the hope that by
following it mechanically and deliberately, instead of letting
it develop in themselves as the gradual result of spiritual
experience, they would attain to perfect sincerity. Therefore
it has produced in them recklessness and want of manners
and antinomianism.

422 Sincerity must be sought by shunning evil, by devotion
to pious works, and by cultivating morality and spiritual
feelings. These pretenders are like a man who cannot distinguish a precious jewel from a glass bead.

CHAPTER CXLI: "Concerning those who err in respect of
prophecy and saintship."

Some assert that saintship is superior to prophecy, an
error which is caused by their arbitrary speculations on the
story of Moses and al-Khaḍir (Kor. 18, 64 foll.).

423 God confers peculiar gifts and endowments in accordance
with His inscrutable will. Examples of prophets and other
persons who were thus distinguished. The miracles of the
saints are granted to them in virtue of their obedience to
the prophet of their time. How, then, can the follower be
pronounced superior to the leader? As regards the argument
that the saints receive inspiration directly from God, whereas
the prophets receive it through an intermediary, the truth
is that the inspiration of the prophets is continuous, while
the inspiration of the saints is only occasional.

424 Al-Khaḍir could not have borne a single atom of the
illumination which Moses enjoyed. Saintship is illumined by
the splendour of prophecy, but it never equals prophecy,
much less surpasses it.

CHAPTER CXLII: "Refutation of those who err in respect
of permission and prohibition."

Those who err in this matter hold that all things were

originally permitted, and that prohibition refers only to excessive license. They justify their conduct by the example of the communism which prevailed amongst certain ancient Ṣúfís, who helped themselves to their brethren's food and money and gave extraordinary pleasure to the owner by doing so. Anecdote of Fatḥ al-Mawṣilí.

425   A story of Ḥasan of Baṣra and a saying of Ibráhím b. Shaybán. These heretics ignorantly suppose that the abovementioned Ṣúfís allowed themselves to transgress the religious law: consequently they go astray and follow their lusts and do not abstain from what is forbidden. Why should they not believe that all things were originally prohibited and that their use was only permitted as an indulgence? — although, in fact, lawfulness and unlawfulness depend on the ordinance of Allah. That which He has forbidden is like a preserved piece of ground: whoever roams around it is in danger of trespassing, and the proprietor does not permit any one to take possession of it without establishing his claim. The case of purity and impurity is different, since, according to lawyers and some theologians, a thing is presumed to be pure until the contrary has been proved. The cause of the distinction is that purity and impurity fall within the category of worship (ʿibádát), while permission and prohibition refer to property (amlák).

426   CHAPTER CXLIII: "Concerning the doctrines of the Incarnationists (al-Ḥulúliyya)."

The author is careful to state that he is not acquainted with any of this sect and has derived his information from other sources.

Some of the Ḥulúlís assert that God implants in certain chosen bodies the attributes of divinity and that He removes from them the attributes of humanity. This doctrine, if it is really professed by any one as a revelation of the divine Unity, is false. That which is contained in a thing must be homogeneous with that thing, but God is separate from all things, and all things are separate from Him in their qualities. God manifests in phenomena only the signs of His working and the evidences of His omnipotence. The Ḥulúlís have erred because they make no distinction between the power which is an attribute of the Almighty and the evidences which demonstrate His power. Various Ḥulúlí doctrines. The author says that whoever holds any of these opinions is an infidel. The bodies chosen by God are the bodies of saints and prophets. God's attributes are beyond description, and there is nothing like unto Him.

427 The Ḥulúlís confuse divine attributes with human. God does not dwell in men's hearts, but creaturely attributes dwell there, such as faith, and belief in the unity of God, and gnosis.

CHAPTER CXLIV: "Concerning those who err in respect of the passing-away of human nature *(faná al-bashariyyat)*."

This is a perversion of the mystical doctrine of *faná*. It is based on the notion that when the body is starved and weakened its human nature will disappear and that in this way a man may be invested with divine attributes. But human nature is inseparable from man, although its qualities are transmuted in the radiance of Reality. Human nature must be distinguished from the qualities of human nature. Definition of *faná* as the term is understood by true mystics. *Faná* does not involve the destruction of the 'self' *(nafs)* or the absence of change *(talwín)*, inasmuch as change and corruption are inherent in human nature.

428 CHAPTER CXLV: "Concerning those who err in respect of spiritual vision *(al-ru'yat bi 'l-qulúb)*."

The author says he has heard that some Syrian mystics claim to have spiritual vision of God in this world, resembling the ocular vision of Him which they shall enjoy hereafter. He adds that he has never seen any of them himself, nor received information that any man among them, whose mystical attainments could be regarded seriously, had been seen by others; but he formerly perused a letter written to the people of Damascus by Abú Saʿíd al-Kharráz, which refers to these persons and mentions a doctrine closely akin to theirs. The vision of true mystics is contemplation (*musháhadat*), which is the result of real faith (*yaqín*), as in the case of Háritha. Some Baṣrites, followers of al-Ṣubayḥí, went astray in this matter. Exalted by their austerities, they fell a prey to Iblís who appeared to them, seated on a throne and robed in light. Some of them were undeceived and brought back to the truth by their teachers. Story of a pupil of Sahl b. ʿAbdallah.

429   Anecdote of some disciples of ʿAbd al-Wáhid b. Zayd. They imagined that every night they were transported to Paradise. On one occasion ʿAbd al-Wáhid accompanied them, and at daybreak they found themselves on a dunghill. The mystic must know that all lights (*anwár*) seen by the eye in this world are created and bear no likeness to God. Yet the vision of faith is real, as the Apostolic Traditions and the sayings of holy men attest. The Prophet's vision (Kor. 53, 11) was peculiar to himself and is not granted to any one else.

CHAPTER CXLVI: "Concerning those who err in respect of purity."

Some pretend that their purity is complete and perpetual, 430 and hold that a man may become purged of all defilements and defects, in the sense that he is separated from them. This is an error. No man is at all times free from all impurity, *e. g.* thought of phenomenal objects, sin, vice and human frailties. One must turn to God and continuously pray to be forgiven in accordance with the practice of Muhammad, who used to ask pardon of God a hundred times daily.

CHAPTER CXLVII: "Concerning those who err in respect of illumination (*al-anwár*)."

There are some who assert that their hearts are illuminated by divine light — the light of gnosis and unification and majesty — and this light they declare to be uncreated. They commit a grave error, since all the lights that can be perceived and known are created, whereas the light of God does not admit of description or definition and cannot be comprehended by human knowledge.

431   The correct meaning of 'the light in the heart' is knowledge, derived from God, of the criterion *(furqán)*, which the commentators on Kor. 8, 23 interpret as "a light put in the heart in order that thereby truth may be distinguished from falsehood."

CHAPTER CXLVIII: "Concerning those who err in respect of essential union (*ᶜayn al-jamᶜ*)."

They refuse to attribute their actions to themselves, and they justify their refusal by the plea that the unity of God must be maintained. This doctrine leaves them outside the pale of Islam and leads them to neglect the laws of religion, inasmuch as they say that they act under divine compulsion and are thefore clear of blame. Their error is caused by inability to distinguish what is fundamental from what is derivative, so that they connect with union (*jamᶜ*) that which belongs to separation (*tafriqat*). Sahl b. ᶜAbdallah was asked what he thought of a man who said, "I am like a gate: I do not move until I am moved." Sahl replied, "This is either the speech of a saint (*ṣiddíq*) or the speech of a freethinker (*zindíq*)." He meant that the saint regards all things as sub-

432 sisting through God and proceeding from God, but at the same time recognises the obligations of religion and morality, while the freethinker only holds this doctrine in order that he may commit as many sins as be pleases without incurring blame.

CHAPTER CXLIX: "Concerning those who err in respect of intimacy (*uns*) and unrestraint (*basṭ*) and abandonment of fear."

Some imagine that they are very near to God and stand
in a close relation to Him, and when they believe this, they
are ashamed to observe the same rules of discipline and
keep the same laws as before. Hence they lose all restraint
and become familiar with actions from which they would
formerly have shrunk in horror; and they fancy that this
is nearness (*qurb*) to God. But they are much mistaken. Rules
of discipline and 'states' and 'stations' are the robes of
honour which God bestows on His servants; if they are
sincere in their quest, they merit an increase of bounty, but
if they disobey His commands, they are stripped of these
robes of good works and driven from the door. They may
still deem themselves to be favourites, but in truth they
have been rejected: the nearer to God they seem in imagination, the farther from Him are they in fact. Saying of
Dhu 'l-Nún.

433 Saying of an anonymous sage.

CHAPTER CL: "Concerning those who err in respect of
the doctrine of passing-away from their qualities (*al-faná
'an al-awṣáf*)."

Some mystics of Baghdád have held the erroneous doctrine
that in passing-away from their own qualities they enter into
the qualities of God. This involves the doctrine of incarna-
tion (*ḥulúl*) or the Christian doctrine concerning Christ. The
belief in question is said to be derived from one of the
ancient Ṣúfís. Its true meaning is that when a man passes
away from his own will, which is given to him by God, he
enters into the will of God, so that he no longer regards
himself but becomes entirely devoted to God. The doctrine
in this form is strictly Unitarian. Those who give it a false
interpretation suppose that God is identical with His qualities,
and are guilty of infidelity, inasmuch as God does not become immanent in men's hearts. What becomes immanent
in the heart is faith in God, and belief in His unity, and

reverence for His name; and this applies to the vulgar as well as to the elect, although the former, being in bondage to their passions, are hindered from attaining to the divine realities.

434   CHAPTER CLI: "Concerning those who err in respect of the doctrine of loss of sensation."

This doctrine is held by some mystics of ʿIráq. They assert that in ecstasy they lose their senses, so that they perceive nothing and transcend the qualities which belong to objects of sensible perception. But this is wrong, since loss of sensation cannot be known except by means of sensation; and sensation is inseparable from human nature: it may be obliterated in ecstasy, just as the light of the stars is rendered invisible by the sun, but it cannot be altogether lost. Under the influence of ecstasy a man may cease to be *conscious* of sensation; as Sarí al-Saqatí said, a person in this state will not feel the blow of a sword on his face.

CHAPTER CLII: "Concerning those who err in respect of the spirit (*al-rúḥ*)."

There are many theories as to the nature of the spirit, but all who speculate on this subject go astray from the truth, because God has declared that it is beyond human comprehension.

435   According to some, the spirit is part of the essential light of God: others say that it belongs to the life of God. Some hold that all spirits are created, while others regard the spirits of the vulgar as created, but the spirits of the elect as uncreated. Some think that the spirit is eternal and immortal, and does not suffer punishment hereafter; some believe in the transmigration of spirits; some give one spirit to an infidel, three to a Moslem, and five to prophets and saints; some hold that the spirit is created of light; some define it as a spiritual essence created of the heavenly kingdom (*al-malakút*), whither it returns when purified; some suppose there are two spirits, one divine, the other human.

All these manifestly erroneous doctrines are the result of forbidden speculation (Kor. 17, 87). In the author's opinion, orthodox Ṣúfís believe that all spirits are created; that there is no connexion or relationship between God and them except in so far as they belong to His kingdom and are subject to His absolute sway; that they do not pass from one body to another; that they die, like the body, and experience the pleasures and pains of the body, and are raised at the Resurrection in the same body from which they went forth.

INDEX OF SUBJECTS, TECHNICAL TERMS, ETC., WHICH OCCUR IN THE ABSTRACT OF CONTENTS.

GLOSSARY.

ا

ابد . أوابِدُ, "wilds, wildernesses" (240, 2).

أحد . أَحَدٌ = مِن أَحَدٍ in an affirmative sentence (195, 14).

أخذ . *With* ب *of person and* إلى, "to take *any one* to a place" (178, 16). *With acc. and* مع, "to take *a person* with one" (192, 9 ; 429, 6).

اخر . II أَخَّرَ الآخَرَ (37, 18).

آخِرِيّة (37, 19 ; 364, 11).

اخو . III وَاخَى (140, 10 ; 165, 16 ; 198, 20).

ادى . II "to sing." *Verbal noun* تَأْدِينٌ (276, 16).

إذا . Apparently used as an interrogative particle (225, 18).

ازب . الميزاب (168, 12) is the water-spout of the Kaʿba.

اسو . III آسَى = وَاسَى (133, 18).

اصل . أَصْلٌ, *feminine* (217, 17), but perhaps أُصُولٌ should be read.

امر . أَمَّارَةٌ, "an evil impulse". معرفة النفس وأماراتها وخواطرها (77, 12) ; أَمَّارَاتِ الهوى والشهوات (14, 10).

إن لو . (157, 13). Cf. Wright, II, 376.

أَنَّ . Synonymous with أَنِّيَّة (255, 11 ; 386, 15, 16). *See* Massignon, *Kitáb al-Ṭawásín*, p. 162.

أَنِّيَّة, "essence" (32, 10).

أَنْبَجَانِيَّة (98, 22). Dozy.

أنف . X مُسْتَأْنِف, "a beginner, a novice in Ṣúfism" (142, 18).

اول . II أَوَّلَ الأَوَّلَ (37, 18).

أَوَّلِيَّة (37, 19; 364, 4, 10).

اى . أَيْش أَيْشَ (18, 6; 50, 14; 60, 19, etc.). أَيْشَ مَا (188, 20; 190, 15).

أَيُّمَا, *interrogative* (308, 5; 329, 17).

إِيَّا, after prepositions. بِأَيَّاكَ (34, 5); الى إِيَّاهُ (405, 17).

ب

بَاتْخَت, "good fortune" (188, 12).

بدأ . IV *with* إِلَى, "to manifest" = أَبْدَى (254, 17).

بدل . البُدَلَاء, a class of the saints (177, 23).

بَذْبَخْت . The Persian words يَا بَذْبَخْت, "O unfortunate one!" occur in the reply made to Abú Ḥamza by a native of Khurásán (331, 4).

بذل . مَبْذُول, "common, profane" (10, 18).

برأ . V تَبَرَّى *for* تَبَرَّأَ. Cf. 14, 12; 87, 1; 386, 5.

بطأ . IV أَبْطَى *in verse* (251, 18).

بطل . *With* عَنْ, "to neglect, to abandon the observance of *religious laws*" (406, 2).

بطن . البِطَانِيَّة (168, 14) is mentioned as the name of a place where pilgrims were surrounded by an Arab brigand-chief (Ibn al-Athír, IX. 129, 16). It belonged to the territory of the Banú Asad and lay on the road from Baghdád and Kúfa to Mecca. Cf. *Bibl. Geogr. Arab.*, VII, pp. 175 and 311.

ت

تَخَارِيز (146, 3 = 188, 15), "pieces of cloth inserted in a garment for the purpose of widening it". Persian تَبْرِيز and تَوْرِيز.

See the Lexica under دخرص and Jawálíqí's *al-Muʿarrab* (ed. by Sachau), p. ٢٦, l. ٣. I have not found any other example of the word written with ز in Arabic. The usual forms are دخرص, دخرصة and دخريص, pl. دخاريص, and تخريص, pl. تخاريص.

تفل. تفلة, "a drop of spittle" (79, 6; 240, 5).

تهم. تهمة, "a foul smell". Shibli said, "What think you of a science in comparison with which theology stinks?" (182, 13). The words فيه تهمة in this passage differ in meaning from the same phrase as cited in the Lexica.

ث

ثنى. مثنى *opposed to* فرد (340, 4).

ج

جرأ. VIII اجترى (409, 14).

جزى. V "to be satisfied". بالقناعة والتجزّى (237, 3).

جلس. جلس جالسا (211, 10).

جلوس, *plural of* جالس (204, 15).

متجلس. متجلس قام متجلسا (150, 4; 211, 4), where متجلس = دفعة واحدة للبراز. *See* Dozy.

جمع. X مستجمع الهمّ, "concentrating my thoughts" (168, 19). مستجمعين *in the same sense* (297, 1).

مجمع, "a box or chest". المجمع is enumerated among the possessions of the Prophet (101, 9).

جوب. IV إجابة = مجاب (224, 15 = 180, 7), but the reading is doubtful.

ح

حدد . حادّ, of ecstasy, "violent" (306, 7 ; 434, 9, 11).

حدق . IV الْعُيونُ الْمُحَدِقة (27, 16). Does this mean "the eyes that are fixed intently"? *Cf.* Dozy *under* حدق II and IV.

حذف . *With* ب, "to throw" (193, 22).

حذن . حُذْنُ = حُجْزَةُ الازار, "the end of the *izár* or the part of the *izár* where it is tied or folded round the waist" (136, 18). Freytag renders حُذْن by "conclave domus", an error caused by his having mistaken حُجْزَة for حُجْرَة. See *Lisán* XVI, 264, 17 foll.

حرز . VIII مُحْتَرِز, of *language*, "guarded", "safe from criticism" (398, 16).

حرن . *With* عن, "to refuse obstinately to do anything". Used of the *nafs* of a Ṣúfí who shrank from making an ablution in water that was intensely cold (146, 4).

حسن . IV "to be able". Followed by أنْ and the Imperfect (131, 4 ; 156, 5 ; 166, 10 ; 291, 14). Followed by the Imperfect without أنْ (50, 19 ; 288, 12).

حصر . لحصرني فيه أنْ أمشي (181, 18), "I should have had a desire for his sake to walk....." *See* Dozy under حصر.

محاضر = "objects of sense" (388, 6).

حظظ . الحظوظ, "the desires and interests of the lower soul (*nafs*)". Whatever appertains to the *nafs* is حَظّ. The term حظوظ is opposed to حقوق. See especially 47, 1 foll. and 336, 12 foll.; also 15, 17 (حظوظ البشرية); 18, 7 ; 39, 6 ; 77, 11 ; 102, 9 ; 164, 8, 10 ; 413, 17 ; 414, 3.

حلو . حَلْوٌ = حَلْوَآءُ or حَلاوَةٌ, "sweetmeat" (101, 12).

حَلاوِى, "confectioner" (185, 16).

حمل . حُمْلانٌ, in ecstasy, "the state of quiet succeeding rapture" (306, 15). حَمَلٌ in used in the same sense (306, 18).

مَحْمُولٌ, of an ecstatic person, "one who has passed into the state of quiet" (306, 17; 307, 1).

مَحْمَلٌ, verbal noun (284, 16).

حنن . حَنِينٌ with عن, verbal noun from حَنَّ عَنْهُ, "he turned away from him" (229, 4).

حيث . II حَيَّثَ التَّحَيُّثَ (37, 17).

خ

خبأ . X "to hide" (139, 17).

خبط . V "to be agitated in ecstasy" (278, 6; 292, 4).

خربندج . Persian خَرِبنْدَ, "a man in charge of an ass".

خرز . خَارِيز. See under ث.

خرف . VIII "to be disordered in mind, to dote" (410, 21), if the reading is sound.

خرق . خِرْقَةٌ. Muẓaffar al-Qarmísíní (191, 12) and Abú Ḥafṣ al-Ḥaddád (194, 11) wore two khirqas at once. See Dozy under خِرْقَةٌ.

خُرَيْقَةٌ, "a rag" (188, 23).

خسف . خَسَفٌ (329, 21) "a hole (in the roof of a mosque)".

خشخش . خَشْخَاشَةٌ (325, 5), something given to a crying child to amuse it, a rattle (?). Cf. شَخْشِيخَةٌ (Dozy).

خصص . الخُصُوصُ, "the elect, the Ṣúfís who have enjoyed mystical experiences" (46, 4; 52, 16; 67, 12 et passim).

خُصوصُ الخُصوص, "the Ṣūfīs of the highest grade" (46, 5; 52, 17; 67, 16 etc.). *See under* عمم.

خاصّةٌ, "intimacy". اولياءُ الله تعالى وأهلُ خاصّته (400, 1).

خلج. VIII *noun of place.* الغامر المُخْتَلَج *of the ocean of Deity* (240, 5).

خلس. VIII "to draw in *the breath*" (248, 18; 271, 6).

خلص. V "to save, to rescue" (240, 15). See Glossary to Ṭabarí.

خلط. خَلِيطٌ *with* لِ, "mingled with" (256, 11).

خلف. خِلافى, "controversial" (106, 14).

خلق. خُلَيِّقٌ, *diminutive of* خَلَقٌ, "a worn-out garment" (249, 2).

خنس. خَنِسٌ, "withdrawn or concealed *from the mind*" (233, 15; 344, 8).

خوص. خَوْضٌ, "discussion" (394, 9).

د

دأب. دائِبًا, "habitually, ordinarily" (391, 5).

دخل. مَدْخولٌ, *of love,* "corrupt, spurious" (208, 19).

درع. V *with* بِ, "to wrap one's self in *a garment*" (38, 14).

دعو. X "to induce *ecstasy voluntarily or by means of music, etc.* (187, 5; 277, 19; 303, 9; 336, 16; 342, 6).

دمس. IV (358, 6) = رمس IV, *q. v.* VII اندماس, *used mystically* (358, 7). مُنْدَمِسٌ, "obscure", "occult" (240, 2).

دَيماس, *explained as* = مَقْبَرةٌ (358, 5).

دور. The Ṣūfīs do not travel لِلدَّوَرانِ, "for the purpose of making a tour" (190, 4).

دوست . The Persian words يا دوست, "O friend!" were used by
Sahl b. ʿAbdallah of Tustar in speaking to the father
of Ibn Sálim (326, 18).

دوم . دَيْمومِيّة (33, 11; 243, 3; 384, 14).

ن

ذكر . ذِكْر pl. أَذْكَار (14, 17; 42, 7; 54, 15; 296, 10; 335, 3).

ذهب . With على or عَنْ, "to escape the notice of *any one*"
(128, 10; 423, 3; 426, 8).

IV with ب, "to transport *the mind*" (344, 17).

VI "to affect the state known as ذَهَاب (*see the definition*, 347, 13) or to induce it by artificial means"
(187, 6; 291, 1, where the correct reading is عــن
الانتساكر والتذاهب).

ذوق . II "to let *any one* taste" (372, 10).

ر

رأس . رَأْسًا بِرَأْسٍ (266, 5). When dying, Murtaʿish desired Abú
Muḥammad al-Muhallab al-Miṣrí to pay his debts, which
amounted to eighteen dirhems. After his funeral, the
clothes which he wore were valued at eighteen dirhems
and were sold for that sum, فَخَرَجَ رَأْسًا بِرَأْسٍ, *i. e.* the
amount of money obtained by selling his clothes tallied
exactly with the amount of his debts.

The phrase bears another meaning in the sentence
لَيْتَنَا خَلَّصْنَا منه رَأْسًا بِرَأْسٍ (272, 11), "Would that we
were rid of it (the *samáʿ*) on even terms", *i. e.* with
neither loss nor gain. *See* Dozy.

رأى . IV أَوْرَى (252, 19 *in verse;* 317, 6; 404, 9). *See* Dozy
under ورى IV.

ربب · الرُّبّانيّون opposed to الحيوانيّون (368, 9).

ربع · رُباعيّات, "quatrains" (299, 3).

رجو · أرجَى with لِ, "giving more hope to any one" (62, 9, where the MSS. have ارجا and the text, wrongly, ارجأ).

رسم · V with بِ, to be characterised by anything (6, 17; 7, 1, etc.).

رسو · III مُراساة, "adjustment of rival claims", opposed to موأساة (425, 6).

رعن · The meaning of رُعونات النفّس is explained by the author as تدبيرها ودعواها ونظرها الى طاعاتها (61, 13).

رفق · VIII with مِن, "to seek profit for one's self from any one" (200, 14).

رمس · IV used mystically in reference to الفناء فى التّوحيد (358, 7; 385, 5). VIII in the same sense (358, 7; 388, 11). مَرْمَس (358, 7). Cf. دمس.

روح · أروَح with على, "most refreshing to the heart" (217, 2).

ز

زفن · الشّيخ الزّقّان, "the dancing Sheykh" (290, 19).

زلف · أزلَف with لِ, elative of زلف IV (142, 6).

زمن · سَرْمَديّة opposed to زَمانيّة (29, 12).

زنر · The words لشَدَدْتُ الزَّنانير (397, 8), "I should have bound the girdles", appear to mean, "I should have caused my hearers to depart from the true doctrine of unification tawhíd". The زنّار is the badge of dualism.

س

ساجر . يُسَاجَرُ‎ (329, 11) = يُوقَدُ فى الـنـار‎ according to the commentator on Qushayrí, 194, 11.

سرر . III سِوارُ‎, "secret converse", *feminine* (344, 8).

سرمد . مُسَرْمَكٌ‎ (364, 19). سَرْمَدِيّةٌ‎ (29, 12).

سعتر . سَعْتَر بَرّى‎, "wild marjoram" (289, 9). In the street-cry
يا سعترا برّى‎ the redundant *alif* is probably correct,
though Kalábádhí in his *Kitáb al-Ta‘arruf* has يا سعتر برّى‎
(Massignon, *Notes sur le dialecte Arabe de Bagdad* [*Bul-
letin de l'Institut français d'archéologie orientale*, vol. XI],
p. 11, n. 1).

سكر . VI التّسَاكُر‎ defined (342, 5). *See also under* ذهب‎ VI.

سكن . III *with* إلَى‎, "to rely upon *anything*" (347, 8; 413, 4, 10).
VI *with* إلى‎, "to affect reliance upon *anything*" (187, 6),
but see List of Addenda et Corrigenda. Instead of
النساكر‎ (291, 1) *read* النساكن‎.
مِسْكين‎ is used as a Persian adjective in the words
مِسْكِين يَكْيى‎. "Poor Yaḥyá!" (188, 12).

سمح . III *passive, with* لِ‎ *of person and* ب‎, "to be pardoned
for *a mistake*" (7, 16).

سمر . سمارِيّة‎ (317, 2), "a kind of boat". See Dozy.

سوء . IV *verb of surprise* (404, 20).

سوغ . II *with acc. of person*, "to permit" (177, 13).

سوى . سِيَةٌ‎, "just measure, due proportion" (417, 22).

سيب . II "to let go, to leave unharmed" (327, 3).

ش

شتت . V تَشَتُّتٌ, "inattentiveness" *opposed to* اِسْتِجْماعٌ (297, 1).

شَتَّانَ بَيْنَ (44, 11; 412, 19).

شدد . II التَّشْدِيدُ, "the command that religious obligations should be rigorously and perfectly fulfilled" (86, 13; 87, 6, *etc.*).

شرف . V *with* إِلَى, "to expect impatiently" (415, 6); *with* على, "to be acquainted with *anything*" = أَشْرَفَ على (404, 9).

X اِسْتِشْرافٌ, "eager expectation" (159, 7).

شَرْفَآءُ = شَرَفٌ (47, 18). See Lane under شَرِيفٌ.

شرى . شِرًى, "price" (131, 11).

شُشْتَكَةٌ . (317, 3), "a handkerchief used as a purse". Persian شُشْتَهْ.

The Arabicised form شُشْتَجَهْ occurs in the *Burhán-i Qáṭiᶜ* (Vullers, Lex. Pers. II, 426).

شطط . شَطَطٌ, "something unjust or tyrannical" (254, 5); "transgression" (410, 20).

شطح . شَطَحَ *in a non-mystical sense* (375, 6; 376, 3); *in a mystical sense, with* بِ (385, 12). *See* Dozy.

شَطْحٌ, *mystical term* (346, 11; 375, 5, *etc.*); pl. شَطَحاتٌ (346, 17; 380, 12); شَطَحِيّاتٌ (374, 11; 380, 5).

شَطَحِى, *adjective:* كلمات شطحيّات (380, 10).

مِشْطاحٌ, "a barn where meal is sifted and stored" (375, 6—14). This word is unknown to the lexicographers.

شعشع . II (284, 20; 345, 18; 346, 1). The last instance occurs in a verse by Ḥalláj and alludes to his نُور شَعْشَعانِى. *Cf.* Massignon, *Kitáb al-Ṭawásín*, p. 138, n. 3.

شمل . VIII *with* عن, "to be concealed from" (225, 3), but probably the correct reading is لاشتغالها.

شنع . V *with* على, *of a saying*, "to be unseemly or abominable in the opinion of *any one*" (398, 17).

شوشقة, "an ingot of gold or silver" (326, 11 foll.). Persian شوشه.

ص

صحب, *with* مع (177, 2).

صحف . V *with* على, *of a saying*, "to be altered to the detriment of *any one*, to be perverted in such a way as to excite suspicion against *its author*" (393, 14).

صدق . V "to beg for alms" (197, 3 ; 210, 15).

صديقية (72, 2 ; 424, 6). *Cf.* Dozy under صديقية, which is incorrectly vocalised.

صرر . IV مصر على المعصية (43, 6) = مصر.

صفح . The phrase أبدى له صفاحته (generally used in a bad sense = كاشفه بالعداوة) means, I think, *with* ل *of person* and ب, "to reveal *anything* to *any one*", in a passage (426, 7), which may be rendered: "If any one really professed this doctrine and supposed that his teaching was revealed to him by Unification (*tawhíd*), he is in error".

صفع . صفعان, "parasite" (192, 7). *See* Dozy.

صفو . صوافٍ, "crown-lands" (169, 18).

صلم . VIII "to bewilder, to distract" (296, 19); *mystical term,* "to transport, to deprive of consciousness" (228, 12 ; 372, 19 foll.). *Cf.* my translation of the *Kashf al-Mahjúb*, p. 390.

صمد . صمدية (162, 6).

صوغ . مصوغ, *of sounds*, "composed into a melody" (285, 8).

ض

ضيع . ذَهَبَ ذَهَابًا or قَنِىَ قَنَآء = ضَاعَ ضَيَاعًا used *mystically* (387, 14 foll.; 389, 11, 12).

تَضْيِيع , *mystical term* (*ibid.*).

ط

طبق . VI *of the eyelids*, "to become closed" (251, 1). VII *with* على, "to cover" (240, 3).

مُطَبَّقَة , "a garment worn by Ṣúfís" (27, 13; 38, 15, where it is joined with مُرَقَّعَة). Not in the Lexica.

طرق . طَارِق , *mystical term* (294, 3). *See under* طَوَارِق (346, 3).

طرى . طَرَا عَلَيْهِمْ = طَرَى عَلَيْهِمْ (303, 3).

طعن . طَعْنَة , "a tumour caused by plague" (135, 17).

مَطْعَن , "occasion of censure" (385, 13; 394, 20).

طفأ . IV أَطْفَى (185, 21; 406, 16).

طلع . V *with* الى, "to look forward to, to desire" (108, 5).

طَالِع . In the phrase الطَّالِع الْمُتَحَدَّث (349, 13) the meaning of the former word is uncertain. Read, perhaps, الْمُطَالِع.

طلق . بِوَجْهٍ طَلْقٍ, "with a cheerful countenance" (161, 9).

طمأن . طُمَأْنِينَة (52, 1; 66, 10 foll.; 412, 5, 8) = اطْمَأْنِينَة (14, 2).

طمس . طَمَس, *mystical term*, 228, 14; 357, 20 foll.

انْطَمَاس, *in a mystical sense* (388, 11).

طمع . طَمَع, "object of desire" (98, 2; 147, 18; 158, 17).

طُنْبُرَانِيَة, "a female player on the *ṭunbúr*" (298, 6).

طوى . مَطْوِيُّ الذَّرَى (344, 6), "reserved *or* morose in disposition".

طيب . III مُطَايَبَة (303, 12) appears to signify "cheerfulness, gaiety".

طِيبَة, purity *of heart* (279, 20).

مُطَيَّب, *of salt,* "mixed with أَبْزَار, seasoned" (328, 9).

ظ

ظلم . IV "to make dark" (411, 6).

مَظْلِمَة . دِرْهَم مَظْلِمَة, "a dirhem wrongfully obtained" (210, 15).

ظهر . VI *with* ب, ظُهُور = تَظَاهَر (225, 6).

ظهر . فِي ظَهْرِ الغَيْبِ, "in absence" (265, 13). *See* Lane *under* ظَهْر.

ع

عبد . X *passive, with* ب, "to have anything imposed upon one *by God* as an act of service" (116, 11; 195, 19; 318, 11, 13).

عجم . X *with* عن, "to become effaced" = فَنِيَ (214, 5).

عدد . VIII اِعْتَدَّى, "keep the *'iddat*" (139, 19), *used as a formula of divorce.*

عدو . X "to seek alms" (171, 7).

عرض . III "to present one's self to, occur to" (30, 15, 17; 71, 17; 83, 11); *of a dervish,* "to put one's self in the way of any one, to approach *any one in the hope of receiving alms* (48, 21; 175, 1; 184, 13).

مُعَارَضَات, "objections *to an argument*" (9, 11); "doubts", "evil suggestions" (71, 2). Cf. Anṣārī's commentary on Qushayrī, II 150, 25 and the definition of عَارِض (343, 8 foll.).

عرف . "to know *God*, to be *or* become a gnostic" (353, 3); V "to seek to know *God*" (353, 2).

مَعَارِفُ الْحَقّ, "the acquaintances of God" = الْعَارِفُونَ, "the gnostics" (344, 3).

عزز . VI تَعَازَزَ عِزُّ, in a verse recited by Shiblī (405, 5).

عزم . عَزِيمَة, "an obligatory religious ordinance", *opposed to* رُخْصَة (144, 15).

عسف . VIII *of the mind,* "to wander, to be distracted" (344, 6).

عطش . V *with* إِلَى, "to have a thirst for *mystical experiences*" (289, 3, 4).

عطل . V *with* عَنْ, "to cease from practising *rules of discipline*" (406, 2).

عظم . VI "to find *the vision of God or the like* too awful to be borne" (373, 2).

عقد . VIII "to form a thought in the mind" (331, 8 foll.).

عقل . عَقْل, "fortress" (265, 3). According to Lane, this meaning is of doubtful authority.

علم , *with acc. and* مِنْ, "to know (distinguish) one person from another" (159, 20).

مَعْلُوم, "a means of livelihood on which one can reckon" (326, 6; 419, 13, 15). Such مَعْلُومَات are inconsistent with real trust in God (*tawakkul*). Cf. Richard Hartmann, *Das Ṣûfîtum nach al-Kuschairî*, pp. 29 and 110.

عمم . اَلْعُمُوم, *opposed to* الْخُصُوص, "the Ṣúfís of the lowest grade, the novices who have not yet entered upon the mystical 'stations' and 'states'" (46, 4 ; 70, 16, etc.).

عمل . عَمِلَتْ عَلَيْهِ يَدُهُ, "his hand festered" (304, 10). The same phrase is used by Abulfeda, *Annales Muslemici*, vol. III, p. 420, l. 16 (*cf.* Freytag *under* عمل) in reference to an Amír who was wounded in the hand by an arrow and died of blood-poisoning. X *with acc. of person and* ب, *of God*, "to cause *any one* to be occupied with *actions of a certain kind*, to predestine *any one* to do good or evil" (26, 19, where به must be understood after عَزَّ وَجَلَّ ; 38, 18 ; 392, 17).

عمى . عَمًى, "blind" (255, 6).

غ

غرب . V "to become strange *or* extraordinary" (247, 10).

بَلَدٌ غَرِبَة, "a foreign country" (192, 21).

غرف . VIII مُغْتَرَف, "a source of inspiration" (381, 2).

غرق . II "to plunge *any one in ecstasy*" (381, 8).

غَرَق, a term denoting absorption in ecstasy (381, 9).

غزل . الْأَشْعَارُ الْغَزَلِيَّة, "erotic poems" (419, 21).

غسل . غَسِيل, "bleached" (187, 13). See Dozy.

غضى . II *with acc. and* عَلَى, "to conceal *any thing* from *any one*" (290, 21).

غمر . غَمْرَة, "senselessness caused by ecstasy" (311, 5).

غِمَار, *of a mystical saying*, "abysses, profundities" (181, 20).

k

غوث . X *with* إلَى, "to implore the help of *God*" (173, 12; 184, 16).

غور . غَوْر, *of mystical language*, "depth, profundity" (381, 1).

غيب . غَيْبوبَة, "absence" (387, 16, 17; 388, 16 foll.).

غين . IV and V *used in a mystical sense* (374, 4, 6). *Cf.* the definition of غَيْن (373, 16 (foll.).

ف

فتت . فَتِيت, "gruel" (183, 10).

فتح . عِلْمُ الْفُتُوحِ, "the science of mystical revelation" = Ṣúfism (18, 16).

فرد . I do not know the meaning of فرد in the phrase فرد كُمَّه وتَخاريزِه (146, 3; 188, 15).

الْفَرْدانِيَّة, "the Absolute Oneness of God" (348, 19).

فسخ . V "to become disordered in intellect, to lose one's wits" (285, 20).

فقد . V *with acc. and* بِ, "to provide *any one* with food" (415, 4). VIII *in the same sense* (415, 6).

فَقْد, *used mystically* = فَنآء (388, 10).

ق

قرأ . IV *with acc. of person and* سَلامًا, "to deliver a greeting to *any one* from (مِن) *any one*" (375, 11). *See* Dozy and the Glossary to Ṭabarí.

قرب . أقْرَب *with* إلَى, "bringing *any one* nearer to *God*" (142, 6).

قرح . IV "to fill *any one* with anguish" (266, 15), where the verb is parallel to, and apparently synonymous with, أَكْمَدَ.

قرظ . *Of a crude mystical saying*, "to adapt for use, to soften it in order that it might be communicated to others" 234, 4). The reading, however, is doubtful.

قشع . V *of clouds*, "to be cleared away" (343, 5).

قشف . V "to practise austerities", *used of material as opposed to spiritual asceticism* (5, 2; 56, 1; 413, 13; 414, 4).

قضى . V *of ecstasy*, "to come to an end, to pass away" (310, 15, 16).

أَقْضَى , *elative of* قَاصٍ (120, 12).

قطع , *with* ب *of person*, "to block any one's path, to prevent *any one* from going on his way" (62, 14). V "to be unable to continue one's journey" (189, 21; *cf.* Dozy under the seventh conjugation of قطع). VII "to be reduced to silence" (225, 18). X "to make one's self an obstacle to *any one*" (109, 11). The tenth conjugation does not seem to occur elsewhere except in the sense given by Dozy, which is inappropriate here.

قُطْعَة , "a piece of money, the fare paid to a boatman" (317, 3).

قعقع . II *of gates that are opened quickly*, "to rattle" (267, 5).

قلل . V "to eat little, to live frugally" (166, 9; 191, 17, etc.). X "to become capable *of doing anything*, to find one's strength restored" (329, 19).

لا أَقَلَّ مِنْ أَنْ أَرَاهُ , "the least I can do is to see him" (291, 6).

قول . قَوَّالٌ , "a professional chanter of poetry, which was gener-ally erotic in character and was recited for the purpose of throwing the hearers into ecstasy" (186, 11; 290, 1; 292, 5).

قوم . قَامَ signifies "to rise to one's feet under the influence of ecstasy" (186, 15, 16); قِيَامٌ is used in the same sense (187, 5).

القَوْمُ, "the Ṣúfís" (186, 16, etc.).

قِيَامٌ, "diarrhoea" (150, 1).

قَوَّامٌ, pl. of قَائِمٌ, "the attendants in a ḥammám" (147, 18).

قَيْمُومِيَّة, "subsistence" (243, 3).

ك

كبد . مُكَابَدَاتٌ, "acts of self-mortification" = مُجَاهَدَاتٌ (415, 14).

كثر . VI حُبّ التّكَاثُرِ, "love of amassing riches" (410, 3).

كثف . VI with عَلَى, "to throng round any one" (233, 16).

كدى . II "to beg" (191, 18 ; 199, 15).

كسر . كُسَيْرَة, "a small fragment or crumb of bread" (205, 16).

كسو . كُسٍ, pl. كَوَاسٍ, of limbs, "clothed with flesh" (251, 4 ; 352, 18).

كمن . مُكَمَّنَاتٌ, "the hidden vices of the soul, the secret feelings of the heart" (171, 4 ; 172, 22 ; 296, 16).

كنن . أَكْنَانٌ (242, 14) appears to signify "arcana, mysteries". The sajʿ, however, suggests that the true reading may be إِكْنَآء, "metaphorical description".

كنف . كَنْف, "a bag or satchel used by Ṣúfís for storing small articles" (194, 20 ; 266, 6). According to the Lisán (XI, 221, 10 foll.) the كَنْف is أداة يكون فيها الرّتَّفْلِيَاجة

الراعى ومتاعه وهو ايضًا وعآء طويل يكون فيه متاع النِّجَّار
وأسقاطهم. *Cf.* Jawáliqí under زنفليجة; and Vullers' Persian
Dictionary under زنبيله.

كنى . V تَكَنَّ seems to bear the same relation to مَنْشَأ as صفةٌ
to ذَاتٌ (355, 8).

كون . كائِن, *used as a noun*, "nature (?)", 241, 19; 363, 18.

     كائِنَةُ التَّغْيِير, "subject to change" (365, 1).

     كُلّ ما كان كائِنَةْ *in verse* (255, 13).

كيف . II كَيَّفَ الكَيْفَ (37, 17).

ل

لا . وَلا is equivalent to أَوْ (399, 17). Cf. 398, 5, where B reads
وَلا instead of أَوْ.

لبد . لَبْدٌ, "felt" *worn as a garment by* Súfís (188, 19). اللِّبَّد
in the text is a mistake.

لدغ . III مُلادَغاتْ (222, 8). Perhaps مُلاحَظاتْ should be read.
لَدْغَةٌ . لَدَغاتِ الحَقيقة (222, 2).

لذذ . II "to delight" (368, 7).

لسن . لِسان *feminine* (121, 18; 411, 9). In these passages لِسان
is equivalent to بَيان or عِبارَةٌ. Cf. also 44, 2; 62, 18;
and the definition, 353, 19 foll.

لطف . لَطيفةٌ, "a subtle or spiritual influence", such as resides
in music (269, 13; 284, 13).

لعق . IV "to cause *any one* to lick (taste) *anything*" (253, 6;
372, 10).

لقف . V *with* مِن, "to receive inspiration from *God*" (423, 22; 424, 1).

لقم . II "to give *any one* a mouthful of food" (184, 6). *Cf.* Dozy *under* لقم IV.

لقى . IV *with* إلَى, "to communicate *anything* to *any one*" (428, 16).

لمأ . IV *with* ب, of ecstasy, "to transport" (245, 14).

لمح . مَلامِح, "gleams, flashes" (239, 19).

لهف . مَلْهُوف, *with* إلَى, "taking refuge with, having the utmost need of *any one*" (235, 15).

لوح . II *with* ل of person and ب, "to indicate *or* signify anything to any one" (244, 7).

لوذ . لِياذَة *verbal noun* (100, 5; 173, 7).

لَيْسَ *used as a negative particle* (26, 8; 210, 11); *as a term equivalent to* كَلَّا (387, 13 foll.).

لَيْسِيَّة (387, 13; 390, 5).

م

ما *relative*, followed by feminine pronoun (2, 7; 11, 8; 123, 19; 257, 2); by feminine verb (320, 8, 9).

متع . مُتْعَة, "enjoyment" (64, 7).

محق . VIII = فَنِيَ (39, 5; 297, 11).

فان = مَحَقَ (396, 5).

مشمش, "apricots" (199, 16 foll.). *See* Dozy.

مضغ, *used figuratively in the sense of* "to read *the Koran* laboriously and without pleasure" (43, 3).

مكن . V اَلْمُتَمَكِّنونَ, "adepts in Ṣúfism" *opposed to* اهل البدايات والارادات (404, 16).

ملأ . فِى الْمَلَا, "in public", *opposed to* فِى الْخَلَآءِ, "in private" (262, 18).

مَلَا = مَلْآنٌ, "full" (194, 15). *See* Dozy.

منع . مَتْعَةٌ, "inaccessibility, secluding one's self *from society* (312, 1).

مهن . مَهْنَةُ الدُّنيا, "the ordinary materials of life" such as food, clothing, etc. (11, 12).

موت . II *with* عن, "to cause *any one to die (in a mystical sense)* to *anything*" (242, 4). IV *in the same sense* (244, 8).

ميز . V "to discern, to distinguish" (311, 19).

ن

نبط . X "to elicit by mystical interpretation the hidden meaning *of the Kŏran and the Traditions of the Prophet*" (4, 10; 6, 3; 9, 1; 14, 14; 81, 2, etc.).

ندب . VIII *with* لِ, "to comply with *a command*" (230, 9).

ندو . IV إِنْدَآءٌ, *of a sweet voice,* "melodiousness" (269, 17).

نزل . II "to draw a deduction" (306, 17); III "to come to close quarters with, to have actual experience of *anything*" (15, 2, 14; 20, 6; 75, 13; 77, 3; 179, 17; 358, 4; 369, 12; 379, 3; 404, 3; 422, 4).

مُنازَلاتٌ, "mystical experiences of a permanent kind" (3, 19; 78, 3; 378, 20). مُنـازَلـةٌ (345, 12), "a mystical 'state' that has become lasting". Cf. R. Hartmann, *Das Ṣúfitum nach al-Kuschairî,* p. 86, note 2, and p. 88.

نسف . VIII *in a mystical sense,* "to enravish *the heart*" (228, 12; 239, 18).

نشق . X *of spiritual delight* (217, 3).

نصص . اَلْحَرَامُ النَّصُّ, "that which is absolutely and unquestionably unlawful" (221, 14).

نصب . نَصَبَ, "to be intent, to concentrate one's faculties to the utmost *in prayer*" (153, 15). Cf. the Glossary to Ṭabarí.

نظر . نَظَرٌ, "*mystical* speculation, disputation" (239, 12, 13).

ناظِرٌ, pl. نُظَّارٌ, "one who speculates and disputes *on mystical subjects* (239, 12).

نعش . IV "to refresh, revive, exhilarate" (106, 3); VIII "to be refreshed with joy" (303, 4).

نفر . III *with* مِنْ, "to be averse to *anything*" (164, 10); VI *with* عَنْ, *in the same sense* (169, 11; 285, 7).

نفس . النَّفْسانِيّةُ, "the sensual nature" (368, 13).

نقض . VIII *of purity*, "to be destroyed" (341, 2). Cf. Dozy.

نكى . أَنْكَى, *elative, with* لِ, "making *grief* more poignant" (261, 16).

نوط . نِياطُ, *of those who are dumbfounded by fear of God*, تَقَطَّعَ نِياطُ قُلوبِهِمْ (84, 6).

نوق . V تَنَوُّقٌ, "elegance" (5, 2).

نوى . III مُناواةٌ *opp. to* مُوالاةٌ (2, 14).

ه

هتر . X *passive, with* بِ, "to be possessed by *the thought of God*" (398, 13). الواجِدِين والمُستهتَرِين (386, 7).

هجم . V *with* فِ, "to plunge into *sin*" (265, 7).

هفو . عَفْوَةٌ, "error, mistake, slip" (7, 16 ; 156, 11 ; 393, 13 ; 410, 20 ; 411, 3, where it is opposed to جَفْوَةٌ).

هنأ . V تَهَنَّى = تَهَنَّأَ, *with* بِ, "to rejoice in *contemplation of God*" (372, 3).

هو . هُوَ ذا or هُوَ ذَى, *used for the purpose of calling attention or for emphasis* (65, 18, 19 ; 117, 3 ; 153, 19 ; 159, 11 ; 171, 7 ; 177, 23 ; 183, 11 ; 325, 6 ; 404, 15, 21). The phrase must be translated in different ways according to the context. *Cf.* the Glossary to Ṭabarí under هو.

هُوِيَّةٌ, "essence or absolute nature *of God*" (81, 13 ; 255, 16).

هيج . هَاجَتْ عَيْنِى, "my eye became inflamed" (174, 3).

هَايِم, *contrasted with* هَايِم (349, 11).

قَيِّهات, *explained as meaning* التَّمْكِين (350, 1).

و

وحد . V تِيهُ التَّوَحُّد (356, 18).

وخى . *See* اخو.

ورخ . II = أَرَّخَ (7, 13).

ورى . IV *See* رَأَى.

وسط . وَسَطٌ, "a waist-belt or girdle", *in which money was carried* (194, 12).

وسع . سَعَةُ الْأَخْلَاق, "largeness of nature, generosity of disposition" (294, 18).

وسوس . II *with* فِى, "to regard with suspicion".

وَسْوَسَةٌ *in ritual religion* is defined by the author (149, 4 foll.). It denotes an excessive zeal for what is superfluous, (*faḍā'il*), leading to the neglect of what is obligatory (*farā'iḍ*). *Cf.* 145, 14; 148, 16.

وَسْوَاسٌ *in the same sense*, 149, 3; 154, 8; 156, 11. *Cf.* Dozy *under* وَسْوَاس.

وسى. *See* أسو.

وصل. VI تَوَاصُلٌ *opposed to* عَدَدٌ *and* تَفْرِقَةٌ (340, 4, 5).

وضأ. II وَضَّى (210, 16).

وطن. V *with* فِى, "to become settled and established in *a* mystical state or station" (369, 2).

وَطَنٌ, *feminine* (282, 2).

وعب. X "to bring to completion" (224, 6: *read* الَّذِى يَسْتَوْعِبُ حَالُهُ = "the adept in Ṣūfism" *as opposed to the novice;* 385, 9: الْغَايَةُ الْمُسْتَوْعِبَةُ, "the ultimate goal"); "to take entire possession of" (343, 3).

وفر. VI *with* عَلَى, *of benefits,* "to be bestowed abundantly upon *any one*" (193, 14).

وقع, "to make an impression on the mind" (342, 18) = وَقَعَ فِى الْقَلْبِ. *Cf.* Dozy.

وَقِيعَةٌ, *with* فِى, "detraction, censure" (2, 15; 20, 8; 376, 17; 393, 12).

وقى. وَاقِيَةٌ, "protection *given by God*" (240, 18).

ومأ. IV أَوْمَى (30, 6; 34, 2; 81, 16).

كتاب

اللُّمَع في التصوّف

تأليف

ابى نصر عبد الله بن علىّ السرّاج الطوسى

وقد اعتنى بنسخه وتصحيحه

رينولد الن نيكلسون

طبع فى مطبعة بريل فى مدينة ليدن
سنة ١٩١٤

فهرسة الابواب

بسم الله الرحمن الرحيم،

(١) كتب الينا ابو القسم على بن الامام ابى الفَرَج عبد الرحمن بن على ابن محمّد بن الجَوْزى وابو (٢)...... اسمعيل بن على بن (٣) باتكين الجَوْهرى وابو عبد الله محمّد بن عبد الواحد بن احمد بن المتوكّل على الله وابو (٤) الحَيّا عبد الله بن عمر بن على بن زيد بن (٥) اللَّيْثى وغيرهم من بغداد

٥ وكتبت الينا أُمّ النضل كريمة ابنة عبد الوهّاب بن على بن الخضر القُرَشيّة من دمشق كلّهم عن ابى الوَقْت عبد الاوّل بن عيسى بن شُعَيْب بن اسحق السّجزى الصوفى الهروى المالينى قال انا ابو نصر احمد بن ابى نصر الكوفانى قِرَاءَة عليه فى شهور سنة خمس وستّين واربعاية قال انا ابو محمّد الحسن بن محمّد الخَبُوشانى قِرَاءَة عليه قال انا ابو نصر عبد الله بن على

١٠ الطوسى السرّاج قال الحمد لله الذى خلق الخلق بقدرته (٦) ودلّهم على معرفته بآثار صنعته وشواهد ربوبيته واختار منهم صفوةً من عباده وخِيرَةً من خلقه خصّ منهم (٧) من شاءَ بما شاءَ (٨) كيف شاءَ وقسم لهم من العلم به والفهم عنه بما قسم وحكم لهم فى ذلك بما حكم وجعلهم فيا منح لهم من الهداية والتوفيق متفاوتين كتفاوتهم فى الاخلاق والارزاق والآجال والاعمال فلا علمٌ

١٥ معلوم ولا شىء مفهوم الاّ وذلك موجود فى كتاب الله عزّ وجلّ (٩) او مأثور

---

(١) This passage down to the words الذى خلق الخلق بقدرته (l. ١٠) is wanting in B.   (٢) Space left blank in A.   (٣) باتكين.   (٤) Perhaps الهيجاء should be read here, but الحيّا is distinctly written in the MS.   (٥) اللثى. (٦) The text of B begins here (f. 3a).   (٧) B اما.   (٨) A om. كيف شاءَ. (٩) وما ثور B.

عن رسول الله (١)صلم او فيا فُتِح على قلوب اولياَء (٢)الله ليهلك من هلك
(٣)عن بيّنة ويحيى من حى عن بيّنة وانّ الله لسميع عليم (٤)والصلاة على
المقدَّم المعظَّم (٥)[النبى] المُكرَّم من انبيائه شمس الاولياَء وقمر الاصفياَء محمّد
عبده ورسوله وعلى آله وسلَّم كثيرًا، امّا بعد فانّى قد استخرتُ الله تعالى
وجمعت ابوابًا فى معنى ما ذهب اليه اهل التصوّف ونكلّم مشايخهم المتقدمون
فى معانى علومهم وعُمْدَة أصولهم وأساس مذهبهم وأخبارهم وأشعارهم ومسايلهم
وأجوبتهم ومقاماتهم واحوالهم وما انفردوا بها من الاشارات اللطيفة والعبارات
A f. 1b النصيحة والالفاظ المشكلة الصحيحة على اصولهم وحقايقهم ومواجيدهم وفصولهم
وذكرتُ من كلّ فصل طَرَفًا ومن كلّ اصل طَرَفًا ونُتَفًا ومن كلّ باب لُمَعًا
على حسب ما سنح به الحالُ ومكّن منه الوقتُ وجاد به الحقُّ جلّ ذكره
مقتديًا بالأسوة والقُدْوة والبيان والحُجَّة فينظر الناظر فيه عند تيقّظ وتنبّه
وحضور قلب وفراغ نفس بحسن التوقّف والتفكّر والتأمّل والتدبّر بخلوص
النيّة وطهارة القلب وصحّة القصد متقرّبًا الى الله تعالى ذكره وشاكرًا له على
ما منحه من تسديده وتوفيقه وهدايته الى موالاة هذه العصابة ومناوأة من
بسط لسانه فيها بالوقيعة فيهم والإنكار عليهم وعلى سلفهم الماضين رحمة الله
ورضوانه عليهم اجمعين لانّهم العصابة القليلة عَدَدُها العظيمة عند الله قَدَرُها
وخَطَرُها وينبغى للعاقل فى عصرنا هذا ان يعرف شيئًا من اصول هذه العصابة
وقصودهم وطريقة (٦)اهل الصحّة والفضل منهم حتى يميّز بينهم وبين المتشبّهين
بهم والمتلبّسين بلبسهم والمنسبين باسمهم حتى لا يغلط ولا يأثم لانّ هذه العصابة

---

(١) صلى الله عليه وعلى آله وصحبه وسلّم and so always in A. B has صلى الله علم.
(٢) B الله تعالى. (٣) The words عن بينة ويحيى من حى are obliterated in B.
(٤) Here the text of B breaks off, the remainder of the page (f. 3a) having
been torn away. Several folios are missing here. Fol. 3b begins with the
words وشرح ذلك يطول غير انّى ابيّن من كلّ شىء طرفًا, which occur in A on
f. 5b, 1. 7 = p. ١١, l. ٢ in this edition. (٥) Suppl. in marg.
(٦) So in marg. Text: اهل الصدق والصحّة.

اعنى الصوفية هم أمناءُ الله جلّ وعزّ فى ارضه وخزَنَةُ اسراره وعلمه وصفوتُه
من خَلقه فهم عباده المُخْلصون واولياَءه المتّقون [١] واحبّاؤه الصادقون
الصالحون منهم الاخيار والسابقون والابرار والمقرّبون والبدلاَء والصدّيقون هم
الذين احيى الله بمعرفته قلوبهم [٢وزيّن] بخدمته جوارحهم وأبهج بذِكْره
٥ ألسنتهم وطهّر بمراقبته اسرارهم سبق لهم منه الحُسْنَى بحسن الرعاية ودوام
العناية فتوّجهم بتاج الوَلاية وألبسهم حُلَلَ الهداية وأقبل بقلوبهم عليه تعطُّفًا
وجمعهم بين يَديه نلطّفًا فاستغنوا به عمّا سواه وآثروه على [٤] ما دونه
وانقطعوا اليه وتوكّلوا عليه وعكفوا ببابه ورضوا بقضائه وصبروا على بَلائه
وفارقوا فيه الاوطان وهجروا له الاخوان وتركوا من أَجله الأنساب
A f. 2a [٣والأسباب] وقطعوا فيه العلائق وهربوا من الخلائق مستأنسين به
مستوحشين ممّا سواه [٥] ذٰلِكَ فَضْلُ ٱللَّهِ يُؤْتِيهِ مَنْ يَشَاءُ وَٱللَّهُ ذُو ٱلْفَضْلِ
ٱلْعَظِيمِ، [٦] فَمِنْهُمْ ظَالِمٌ لِنَفْسِهِ [٧] ٱلآيَة، [٨] قُلِ ٱلْحَمْدُ لِلَّهِ وَسَلَامٌ عَلَى عِبَادِهِ
ٱلَّذِينَ ٱصْطَفَى ٱلآيَة، واعلمْ ان فى زماننا هذا قد كثر الخائضون فى علوم
هذه الطائفة وقد كثر ايضًا المتشبهون بأهل التصوّف والمشيرون اليها
١٥ والمجيبون عنها وعن مسائلها وكلّ واحد منهم يضيف الى نفسه كتابًا قد
زخرفه وكلامًا [٢قد انّه وجوابًا قد] ألّفه وليس بمستحسَن منهم ذلك لانّ
الأوائل والمشايخ الذين تكلّموا فى هذه المسايل وإشاروا الى هذه الاشارات
ونطقوا بهذه الحِكَم انّما تكلّموا بعد قطع العلائق وإمانة النفوس بالمجاهدات
والرياضات والمنازلات والوجد والاحتراق والمبادرة [٩] والاشتياق الى قطع
٢٠ كلّ علاقة قطعتهم عن الله عزّ وجلّ طُرْفةَ عين وقاموا بشرط العلم ثم عملوا

---

(١) So in marg. Text: ونجباوه.   (٢) Suppl. in marg.   (٣) So above.

Text: لسانهم.   (٤) من in marg.   (٥) Kor. 57, 21.   (٦) Kor. 35, 29.

(٧) The words ومنهم مقتصد ومنهم سابق بالخيرات باذن الله are added in marg.

after لنفسه.   (٨) Kor. 27, 60.   (٩) والاشتياق.

به ثم تحقَّقوا فى العمل فجمعوا بين العلم والحقيقة والعمل، قال ابو نصر رحمه
الله وقد حذفتُ الاسانيد عن كثير ممّا ذكرت فى هذا الكتاب واقتصرت
على متون الاخبار والحكايات والآثار للاختصار فما أصَبتُ من ذلك فبعناية
الله عزّ وجلّ والحمدُ لله على ذلك وما اخطأتُ فى ذلك ووقع فيه شىء

٥ من الزيادة والنقصان فهو لازم لى وأنا استغفر الله من ذلك وإنّما ذكرتُ
فى كتابى هذا اجوبة هؤلاء المتقدّمين وألفاظهم لانّ لى غُنيةً عن تكلّفى
كتكلُّف المتأخّرين فى زماننا هذا اذا تكلّموا فى هذه المعانى بكلام او اجابوا
عنها بجواب او اضافوا ذلك الى انفسهم وهم (١) متعرّون عن حقايقهم واحوالهم
وكلّ (٢) من اخذ من كلام المتقدّمين الذين وصفناهم (٣) معنًى من معانيهم التى

١٠ هى احوالهم ووجدهم ومستنبطاتهم وحلاها من عند بجلية غير ذلك او كساها
عبارةً أُخرَى او اضافها الى نفسه حتى يشار اليه بذلك او (٤) يطلب بذلك
جاهًا عند العامّة او يريد ان يصرف بذلك وجوه الناس اليه لجرّ منفعةٍ
او لدفع مضرّةٍ فالله عزّ وجلّ خصمُهُ فى ذلك وهو حسيبه لانّه قد ترك
الامانة وعمل بالخيانة وهذه اعظم (٥) [وأكبر من] الخيانة التى فى اسباب

١٥ الدنيا (٦) وَأَللّٰهُ لَا يَهْدِى كَيْدَ ٱلْخَائِنِينَ وبالله التوفيق،

باب البيان عن علم التصوّف ومذهب الصوفية ومنزلتهم
من أولى العلم القايمين بالقسط،

قال الشيخ ابو نصر سألنى سايلٌ عن البيان عن علم التصوّف ومذهب
الصوفية وزعم انّ الناس اختلفوا فى ذلك فمنهم من يغلو فى تفضيله ورفعه
٢٠ فوق مرتبته ومنهم من يُخرجه عن حدّ المعقول والتفصيل ومنهم من يرى انّ

---

(١) So in marg. Text: متعديون.   (٢) So in marg. Text: ما.   (٣) مَعنًى
عن معانيهم (٤) Var. in marg. يَخذ.   (٥) Suppl. in marg.   (٦) Kor. 12, 52.
Kor. has وَإِنَّ ٱللّٰهَ الخ.

ذلك ضربٌ من اللهو واللعب وقلّة المبالاة بالجهل ومنهم من ينسب ذلك
الى التقوى والتقشّف ولبس الصوف والتكلّف فى تنوّق الكلام واللباس
وغير ذلك ومنهم من يُسرف فى الطعن وقُبْح المقال فيهم حتى ينسبهم الى
الزندقة والضلالة فسألنى ان اشرح له من ذلك ما صحّ عندى من أصول

٥ مذهبهم المؤيّد المنوط بمتابعة كتاب الله عزّ وجلّ والاقتداء برسول الله صلعم
والتخلّق بأخلاق الصحابة والتابعين والتأدّب بآداب عباد الله الصالحين وأقيّدَ
ذلك بالكتاب والاثر بالحُجّة ليحقّ الحقّ ويبطل الباطل ويُعْرَف الجدّ من
الهزل والصحيح من السقيم ويرتّب كلّ نوع منه فى (١) موضعه اذ كان ذلك
(٢) علمًا من علوم الدين، فأقولُ وباله التوفيق انّ الله تبارك وتعالى احكم

١٠ اساسَ الدين وأزال الشبهة عن قلوب المؤمنين بما امرهم به من الاعتصام
بكتابه والتمسّك بما وصل اليهم من خطابه اذ يقول جلّ جلاله (٣) وَاعْتَصِمُوا
بِحَبْلِ اللهِ جَمِيعًا وَلاَ تَفَرَّقُوا الاية وقال عزّ وجلّ (٤) وَتَعَاوَنُوا عَلَى ٱلْبِرِّ
وَٱلتَّقْوَى، ثم ذكر الله تعالى افضل المؤمنين عنده درجةً وأعلاهم فى الدين
رتبةً فذكرهم بعد ملائكته وشهد على شهادتهم له بالوحدانية بعد ما بدأ

١٥ بنفسه وثنّى ملائكته فقال عزّ وجلّ (٥) شَهِدَ ٱللهُ أَنَّهُ لاَ إِلهَ إِلاَّ هُوَ وَٱلْمَلاَئِكَةُ
وَأُولُوا ٱلْعِلْمِ قَائِمًا بِٱلْقِسْطِ، ورُوى عن النبى صلعم انّه قال العلماء وَرَثَةُ
الانبياء وعندى واله اعلم ان أولى العلم القايمين بالقسط الذين هم ورثة
الانبياء هم المعتصمون بكتاب الله تعالى المجتهدون فى متابعة رسول الله صلعم
المقتدون بالصحابة والتابعين السالكون سبيل اولياه المتّقين وعباده الصالحين

٢٠ هم ثلثة اصناف اصحاب الحديث والفقهاء والصوفية فهؤلاء الثلثة الاصناف
من أولى العلم القايمين بالقسط الذين هم ورثة الانبياء، وكذلك انواع العلوم
كثيرة فعلم الدين من ذلك (٦) ثلثة علوم علم القرآن وعلم السُّنن والبيان

---

(١) In marg. منزلته ومراتبه.   (٢) علم.   (٣) Kor. 3, 98. The remainder
of the verse is added in marg.   (٤) Kor. 5, 3. الآية has been supplied
above after ٱلتَّقْوَى.   (٥) Kor. 3, 16.   (٦) So in marg. Text: ثلث علم.

وعلم حقايق الايمان وهى العلوم المتداولة بين هؤلاَء الاصناف الثلثة وجملة
علوم الدين لا تخرج من ثلثِ آيةٍ من كتاب الله عزّ وجلّ او خبَر عن
رسول الله صلع او حِكْمة مستنبطة خطرت على قلب ولىّ من اولياَء الله
تعالى، وأَصْل ذلك حديث الايمان حيث سأل جبريل عليه السلم النبىّ
٥ صلع عن اصول ثلثٍ عن الاسلام والايمان والاحسان الظاهر والباطن
والحقيقة فالاسلام ظاهر والايمان ظاهر وباطن والاحسان حقيقة الظاهـر
والباطن وهو قول النبى صلع الاحسان ان تعبد الله كانّك تراه فان لم
تكن تراه فانّه يراك وصدّقه على ذلك جبريل، والعلم مقرون بالعمل والعمل
مقرون بالاخلاص والاخلاص ان يريد العبد بعلمه وعمله وَجْهَ الله تعالى
١٠ وهؤلاَء الثلثة الاصناف فى العلم والعمل متفاوتون وفى مقاصدهم ودرجاتهم
متفاضلون وقد ذكر الله تعالى تفاضلهم ودرجاتهم فقال عزّ وجلّ (١)وَٱلَّذِينَ
أُوتُوا ٱلْعِلْمَ دَرَجَاتٍ وقال (٢)وَلِكُلٍّ دَرَجَاتٌ مِمَّا عَمِلُوا وقال (٣)ٱنْظُرْ كَيْفَ
فَضَّلْنَا بَعْضَهُمْ عَلَى بَعْضٍ، وقال النبى صلع الناس أَكْفَاَء منساوون كأَسْنان
المشط لا فضل لأحد على أحد الاَّ بالعلم والتُّقَى فكلّ من اشكل عليه اصلٌ
١٥ من اصول الدين وفروعه وحقوقه وحقايقه وحدوده وأحكامه ظاهرًا وباطنًا
فلا بدّ له من الرجوع الى هؤلاَء الاصناف الثلثة اصحاب الحديث والنفهاَء
والصوفية وكلّ صنف من هؤلاَء (٤)مترسِّم بنوع من العلم والعمل والحقيقة
والحال ولكلّ صنف منهم فى معناه علم وعمل ومقام ومقال وفهم ومكان
وفقه وبيان عَلِمَهُ من عَلِمَهُ وجَهِلَهُ من جَهِلَهُ ولا يبلغ احد الى كمال يحوى
٢٠ جميع العلوم والاعمال والاحوال وكلّ واحد فمقامُه حيث اوقفه الله تعالى
ومحلُّهُ حيث حبسه الله عزّ وجلّ، وأنا ابيّن لك من ذلك ان شاَء الله
تعالى على حسب الطاقة أنّ كلّ صنف من هؤلاَء باىّ نوع من العلم

---

(١) Kor. 58, 12.   (٢) Kor. 46, 18.   (٣) Kor. 17, 22.   (٤) So in marg.

Text: منوسِّمين.

والعمل ترسّموا وباىّ حال تفاضلوا واىّهم أُعْلَى طبقةً بما لا يدفعـه عقلك
ويحيط به فهمك ان شآء الله تعالى،

باب فى نعت طبقات اصحاب الحديث ورَسْمِهِم فى النقل
ومعرفة الحديث وتخصيصهم بعلمه،

٥   قال الشيخ رحمه الله فاَمّا اصحاب الحديث فانّهم تعلّقوا بظاهر حديث
رسول الله صلعم وقالوا هذا اساس الدين لانّ الله تعالى يقول [1] ‹وَمَا آتَاكُمُ
الرَّسُولُ فَخُذُوهُ وَمَا نَهَاكُمْ عَنْهُ فَانْتَهُوا›، فلمّا خوطبوا بذلك جوّلوا البلاد
وطلبوا رُواة الحديث فلزموهم حتى نقلوا عنهم اخبار رسول الله صلعم وجمعوا
ما رُوى عن الصحابة والتابعين وضبطوا ما وصل اليهم من سِيَرِهِم وآثارهم
١٠ ومذاهبهم واختلافهم فى احكامهم واقوالهم وافعالهم واخلاقهم واحوالهم وصحّحوا
روايَاتِهم بسماع الأذن وحفْظ القلب والضبط من أُصول الثقات عن الثقات
العدول عن العدول فأتْقنوا ذلك وعرفوا اماكن الرُواة فى النقل والضبط
ودوّنوا اسمآءهم وكُناهم ومواليدهم ووفاتهم وورّخوا ذلك حتى عرفوا انّ كلّ
رجل من هؤُلاءِ كم من حديث رواه وعمّن [2] رواه وعمّن نُقل [3] اليه ومن
١٥ اخطأ منهم فى النقل ومن غلط منهم فى زيادة حرف او نقصان لفظة ومن
تعمّد منهم فى ذلك ومن سوّح له بغلطة او هفوة حتى عرفوا اسمآء المتَهَّمِين
منهم بالكذب على رسول الله صلعم وعرفوا من صحّ عنه الرواية ومن لا
يصحّ ومن انفرد منهم بحديث لا يرويه غيره او انفرد بلفظة [4] ليست عند
غيره فحفظوا انّ كلّ حديث من ذلك كم من نفس رواه وما العلّة فى
٢٠ [5] ناقله حتى جمعوا الابواب وبوّبوا السّنن وميّزوا ما يدخل فى الصحيح وما
يُختلف فى صحّته وما كان فى روايته رجل ضعيف ووقفوا على رواية المقلّين

(1) Kor. 59, 7.   (2) رواه ذلك.   (3) ذلك suppl. above after اليه.

(4) ليس suppl. above.   (5) كلّها suppl. above as variant of ناقله.

والمُكثرين وفهموا احاديث أيّة الامصار وطبقات الرُواة التابع من المتبوع
والكبير من الصغير وأحاط عِلمُهم بعلَل اختلاف الرواة وزياداتهم ونقصانهم
وأماكنهم فى رواية السُنَن والاَثار اذ كان ذلك اساس الدين وهم فى ذلك
متفاضلون حتى يستحقّ احدهم بزيادة علمه وإتقانه وحِنظـه قبولَ الشهادة
٥ على العلمآء فى العدل والتجريح والردّ والقبول وتكون شهادته مقبولةً على
رسول الله صلعم فيا قال وفعل وامر ونهى وندب وددعا، قال الله تعالى
(١) ﴿وَكَذَلِكَ جَعَلْنَاكُمْ أُمَّةً وَسَطًا﴾ اى عدلاً ﴿لِتَكُونُوا شُهَدَآءَ عَلَى ٱلنَّاسِ وَيَكُونَ
ٱلرَّسُولُ عَلَيْكُمْ شَهِيدًا﴾، يقال انّهم اصحاب الحديث يشهدون على رسول الله
صلعم وعلى الصحابة والتابعين فيا قالوا وفعلوا ﴿وَيَكُونُ ٱلرَّسُولُ عَلَيْكُمْ شَهِيدًا﴾
١٠ فيا شهدوا عليه من افعاله واقواله واحواله واخلاقه، قال النبى صلعم من
٨ f. 4b كذب علىّ متعمّدًا فَلْيَتَبَوَّأْ مقعَدَهُ من النار وقال النبى صلعم نضّر الله وجه
أمرئٍ سمع منّى حديثًا فبلّغه (٢) الحديث يقال انّه لا يكون واحد من اصحاب
الحديث الاّ وفى وجهه نضرة لموضع دعآء رسول الله صلعم، ولأصحاب
الحديث فى معانى علومهم ورسومهم مصنّفات وهم ائمّة مشهورون (٣) [كلّ منهم]
١٥ قد اجمع اهل عصره على امامته لفضل علمه وزيادة عقله وفهمـه ودينـه
وأمانته وشرح ذلك يطول وفيا ذكرتُ كفايةٌ لمن علم وبالله التوفيق،

باب ذكر طبقات الفقهآء وتخصيصهم بما ترسّموا به
من انواع العلوم،

قال الشيخ ابو نصر رحمه الله وامّا طبقات الفقهآء (٤) فانّهم فُضّلوا على
٢٠ اصحاب الحديث (٥) [بقبول علوم اصحاب الحديث] والاتّفاق معهم فى معانى

علومهم ورسومهم ثم خُصّوا بالفهم والاستنباط فى فقه الحديث والتعمّق بدقيق
النظر فى ترتيب الاحكام وحُدود الدين وأُصول الشرع فبيّنوا ذلك وميّزوا
الناسخ من المنسوخ والاصول من الفروع والخصوص من العموم بالكتاب
والسنّة والإجماع والقياس وبيّنوا للخلق فى احكام دينهم من القرآن والأثر ما

٥ نُسخ حُكْمه وبقى كتابته وما نُسخ كتابته وبقى حُكْمه وما كان لفْظه [١] عامًّا
المراد به خاصّ او كان لفظه [٢] خاصًّا المراد به عامّ او كان خطاب جماعةٍ
المراد به واحد او خطاب واحد المراد به جماعة وتكلّموا بالاحتجاجات
العقليّة على المخالفين واستدلّوا بالبراهين البيّنة على أهل الضلالة نصرةً
[٣] للدين وتمسّكوا بنصّ الكتاب او نصّ السنّة او [٤] قياس على النصّ او

١٠ إجماع الامّة وناظروا من خالفهم برسم النظر وجادلوا من جادلهم بأدب
الجدل وعارضوا خصمهم بالمُعارَضات واعترضوا عليهم [٥] برد الاعتراضات
وإطّراد العلَل فى المعلولات فوضعوا كل شيء فى مواضعه ورتّبوا كل [٦] حدّ
فى مراتبه وفرّقوا بين المقايسة والمشاكلة والمجانسة والمقارنة وميّزوا فى الاوامر
والنواهى ما كان منه حتمًا وما كان منه ندبًا وما كان منه ترغيبًا وترهيبًا

١٥ وما كان [٧] [منه] محثوثًا عليه ومدعوًّا اليه فبيّنوا المشكل وحلّوا العُقَد
وأوضحوا الطُرُق وأزالوا الشبهات وفرّعوا على الاصول وشرحوا المُجْمَل
وبسطوا المجموع وأخذوا حدود الدين بالاحتياط حتى لا يَتقلّد العالم عالمًا
ولا الجاهل جاهلًا ولا الخاصّ خاصًّا ولا العامّ عامًّا فى ظاهر الاحكام وحدود
الشريعة بهم يُحفَظُ على المسلمين حدودهم ، وقد ذكرهم الله تعالى فى كتابه

٢٠ فقال عزّ وجلّ [٨] ﴿فَلَوْلَا نَفَرَ مِنْ كُلِّ فِرْقَةٍ مِنْهُمْ طَآئِفَةٌ لِيَتَفَقَّهُوا فِى الدِّينِ
[٩] الآيَة، [٧] [وقال النبى صلّى الله عليه وسلّم من يُرِد الله به خيرًا يفقّهه فى
الدين]، وللفقهآء فى معانى علومهم ورسومهم ايضًا مصنّفات ولهم ابمّة مشهورون

(١) Text: عامّ.   (٢) Text: خاصّ.   (٣) الدين.   (٤) قياسًا.   (٥) In
marg. بضروب.   (٦) In marg. شى.   (٧) Suppl. in marg.   (٨) Kor. 9, 123.
(٩) Suppl. above.

قد اجمع اهل عصرهم على امامتهم لزيادة علهم (١) وفهمهم ودينهم وامانتهم
وشرح ذلك بطول والعاقل يستدلّ بالقليل على الكثير وباسه التوفيق ،

باب ذكر الصوفية وطبقاتهم وما ترسموا به من العلم والعمل وما خُصّوا به من الفضايل وحسن الشمايل ،

قال الشيخ ابو نصر رحمه اله ثم انّ طبقات الصوفية ايضًا اتّفقوا مع
الفقهآء واصحاب الحديث فى معتقدانهم (٢) وقبلوا علومهم ولم يخالفوهم فى معانيهم
ورسومهم اذ كان ذلك مجانبًا من البِدَع واتّباع الهوى ومنوطًا بالأسوة
والاقتداء وشاركوهم بالقبول والموافقة فى جميع علومهم (٣) [ولم يخالفوهم] ومن
لم يبلغ من الصوفية مراتب الفقهآء واصحاب الحديث فى الدراية والفهم ولم
يُحِطْ بما احاطوا به علمًا فانّهم راجعون اليهم فى الوقت الذى يُشكل عليهم
حكم من الاحكام الشرعيّة او حدّ من حدود الدين ، فاذا اجتمعوا فهم فى
جملتهم فيا اجتمعوا عليه فاذا اختلفوا فاستحباب الصوفية فى مذهبهم الأخذُ
بالأحسن والأولى والأتمّ احتياطًا للدين وتعظيمًا لما امر اله بـه عباده
واجتنابًا (٤) لما نهام اله عنه وليس من مذهبهم النزول على الرُخَص وطلب
التأويلات (٤) [والميل الى] الترفُّه (٥) والسَّعات وركوب الشبهات لانّ ذلك
تهاونٌ بالدين (٤) [وتخلّفٌ عن الاحتياط وانّما مذهبهم التمسّك بالأولى والاتمّ
فى امر الدين] ، فهذا الذى عرفنا من مذاهب الصوفية ورسومهم فى استعمال
العلوم الظاهرة المبذولة المتداولة بين طبقات الفقهآء واصحاب الحديث ، ثم
انهم (٤) [من] بعد ذلك ارتقوا الى درجات عالية وتعلّقوا بأحوال شريفة

---

(١) In marg. وفقههم .   (٢) So in marg. Text: وتحملهم .   (٣) Suppl. in
marg.   (٤) عمّا corr. above.   (٥) Text has والتَرَّعات , but the word
has been altered. The original reading appears to have been والسعات .

ومنازل رفيعة من انواع العبادات وحقايق الطاعات والاخلاق الجميلة
ولهم فى معانى ذلك (١)تخصيص ليس لغيرهم من العلماء والفقهاء واصحاب
الحديث (٢) وشرح ذلك يطول غير انّى ابيّن لك من كلّ شىء طرفًا حتى
تستدلّ بما اذكرُهُ على ما (٣)لا اذكره ان شآء الله تعالى،

٥ باب(٤) ذكر تخصيص الصوفية بالمعانى (٥)التى (٦)قد ترسّموا بها من
الآداب والاحوال (٧)والعلوم (٨)التى تفرّدوا بها من جملة العلماء،

قال (٩)الشيخ ابو نصر رحمه الله فاوّل شىء من (١٠)التخصيصات للصوفية
وما تفرّدوا بها عن جملة هؤلآء الذين ذكرتُهم من بعد ادآء الفرايض
واجتناب المحارم تَرْكُ ما لا يعنيهم وقطعُ كلّ علاقة تحول بينهم وبين مطلوبهم
١٠ ومقصودهم اذ ليس (١١)لهم مطلوب ولا مقصود غير الله (١٢)تعالى، (١٣)ثم لهم
آداب واحوال شتّى فمن ذلك القناعة بقليل الدنيا عن كثيرها والاكتفآء
بالقوت الذى لا بُدّ منه (١٤)والاختصار على ما لا بُدّ منه من مهنة الدنيا
من الملبوس (١٥)والمفروش والمأكول وغير ذلك واختيار الفقر على الغنا
(١٦)اختيارًا ومعانقة القلّة ومجانبة الكثرة وايثار الجوع على الشبع والقليل
١٥ على الكثير وترك العلوّ والترفّع وبذل الجاه والشفقة على الخلق والتواضع
(١٧)للصغير والكبير والايثار فى وقت الحاجة اليه وأن لا يبالى من أكلَ الدنيا
وحُسْن الظنّ بالله (١٨)والاخلاص فى المسابقة الى الطاعات والمسارعة الى

A f. 6a

---

(١) تخصيصا corr. in marg.   (٢) Here B resumes (fol. 3b, 1. 1).   (٣) B لم.

(٤) B om.   (٥) B om. التى قد ترسّموا بها.   (٦) Suppl. in marg. A.

(٧) B om.   (٨) B الذى.   (٩) B om.   (١٠) B تخصيصات الصوفية

(١١) هو B.   (١٢) B تبارك وتعالى.   (١٣) B ثم ان.   (١٤) B والاقتصار.

(١٥) B والمشروب,   (١٦) B om.   (١٧) B للكبير والصغير.   (١٨) A الخالصة,

but corr. in marg.

جميع الخيرات والتوجّه الى الله تعالى والانقطاع اليه (١)والعكوف على بلايه
والرضا عن (٢)قضايه والصبر على دوام المجاهدة ومخالفة الهوى ومجانبة حظوظ
النفس ومخالفتها اذ وصفها الله تعالى (٣)امّارَة بالسوء والنظر اليها (٤)بانّها
أَعْدَى عدوِّك التى بين جنبَيْك كما رُوى (٥)عن رسول الله صلعم،

فصل آخر،

ثم (٥)انّ من آدابهم وشمايلهم ايضًا مراعاة الاسرار ومراقبة المَلك الجبّار
(٦)ومداومة المحافظة على القلوب بنفى الخواطر المذمومة ومساكنة الافكار
(٧)الشاغلة التى لا يَعْلَمها غير (٨)الله عزّ وجلّ حتى يعبدوا الله تعالى بقلوب
حاضرة وهموم (٩)جامعة ونيّات (١٠)صادقة وقصود خالصة لانّ الله عزّ وجلّ
لا يقبل من عباده من اعمالهم الّا ما كان لوجهه خالصًا قال الله عزّ وجلّ
(١١)أَلَا لِلَّهِ الدِّينُ الْخَالِصُ،

(١٢)[فصل آخر]،

ومن آدابهم وشمايلهم وتخصيصهم ايضًا الاعتراض لسلوك سُبُل اوليايه
والنزول فى منازل اصفيايه ومباشرة حقيقة الحقوق ببذل الروح وتلف
النفس واختيار الموت على الحياة وإيثار الذلّ على العزّ وإستحباب الشدّة على
الرخاء طمعًا فى الوصول الى المراد وأن لا يريد الّا ما يريد وهذا فى اوّل
(١٤)بادٍ من بوادى الحقايق وحقيقة الحقوق أما ترى انّ النبى صلعم حيث

---

(١) B ودرام الاقبال عليه والعكوف على بابه والصبر على بلايه والرضا بمرّ قضايه والصبر.
(٢) القضاء A   but corr. in marg.   (٣) B امّارَة انّها.
(٤) B انّها.   (٥) B om.   (٦) A ودوام but corr. in marg.   على دوام المجاهدة الّخ.
(٧) A المشغلة but corr. in marg.   (٨) B الله تعالى.   (٩) A in marg.
فلمّا انسوا. Here B has a considerable lacuna extending to the words مجموعة
written above. صافية (١٠) الى الصحبة التى اجلّ الاحوال (A. fol. 10b, l. 1).
(١١) Kor. 39, 3.   (١٢) Suppl. in marg.   (١٤) بادى.

سأل حارثة (١)[فقال] لكلّ حقّ حقيقةٌ فما حقيقة ايمانك (٢)[بأىّ شىء اجابه]
فقال عزفت نفسى عن الدنيا فأسهرتُ ليلى وأظمأتُ نهارى وكأنّى انظر الى
عرش ربّى بارزًا وكأنّى انظر الى اهل الجنّة كيف يتزاورون والى اهل النار
فى النار كيف يتعاوون فقال له النبى صلعم عرفتَ فألزمْ او كما رُوى فى
٥ الحديث والله اعلم ،

باب فى تخصيص الصوفية من طبقات اهل العلم فى (٣)معانٍ أُخَرَ من العلم ،

قال الشيخ (١)[ابو نصر] رحمه الله والصوفية (٤)ايضًا تخصيص من
طبقات اهل العلم باستعمال آيات من كتاب الله تعالى (٥)متلوّة واخبار عن
١٠ رسول الله صلعم مرويّة ما نسختها آيةٌ وما رفع حُكمَها خبرٌ ولا أثّر بدعو
ذلك الى مكارم الاخلاق ويحثّ على معالى الاحوال وفضايل الاعمال وينبىء
عن مقامات عالية فى الدين ومنازل رفيعة خُصّ بذلك طايفة من المؤمنين
وتعلّق بذلك جماعة من الصحابة والتابعين وذلك آداب من آداب الرسول
صلعم وخُلُق من اخلاقه اذ يقول صلعم انّ الله أدّبنى فأحْسَنَ أدَبى واذ يقول
١٥ الله عزّ وجلّ (٦)وَإِنَّكَ لَعَلَى خُلُقٍ عَظِيمٍ ، وذلك موجود فى دواوين العلمآء
والفقهآء وليس لهم فى ذلك تنقّهٌ (٧)واستنباط كتنقّهم فى ساير العلوم وليس
لغير الصوفية من أولى العلم القايمين بالقسط فى ذلك نصيب غير الإقرار
به والايمان بانّه حقٌّ، وذلك مثل حقايق التوبة (٨)وصفاتها ودرجات التايبين
وحقايقهم ودقايق الورع واحوال الورعين وطبقات المتوكّلين ومقامات

(١) Suppl. in marg.   (٢) So in marg. Text: فأنبت اجابه erased.   (٣) معانى.
(٤) inserted before فيه.   (٥) مبية in marg.   (٦) Kor. 68, 4.
(٧) So in marg. Text: ومستنبطات.   (٨) So in marg. Text: ومقامها.

الراضين ودرجات الصابرين وكذلك فى باب الخشية والخشوع والمحبّة
والخوف والرجاء والشوق والمشاهدة (١) [والإنابة] والطمأنينة واليقين والقناعة
وهذه احوال أكثرُ من أن يُحْصَى عددها ولكلّ حال من ذلك اهل وطبقات
ولهم فى ذلك حقايق (١) [ومشاهدات واحوال ومراقبات واسرار واجتهادات
ومقامات ودرجات متباينات] وارادات متفاوتة وتفاضل فى قوّة الارادة
واعتراض الفترة وغلبات الوجد ولكلّ احد من ذلك حدٌّ ومقام وعلم
وبيان على مقدار ما قُسم له من الله عزّ وجلّ،

(١) [فصل]

وللصوفية ايضًا تخصيص فى معرفة الحرص والامل ودقايقها ومعرفة
النفس وأماراتها وخواطرها ودقايق الرياء والشهوة الخفيّة والشرك الخفيّ
وكيف الخلاص من ذلك وكيف وجه الانابة الى الله عزّ وجلّ وصدق
الالتجاء ودوام الافتقار والتسليم والتفويض والتبرّئ من الحول والقوّة،

فصل آخر

وللصوفية ايضا مستنبطات فى علوم مُشكلة على فهوم الفقهآء والعلمآء
لانّ ذلك لطايف مُوْدَعة فى اشارات لهم (٢) تخفى فى العبارة من دقّتها
ولطافتها وذلك فى معنى العوارض والعوايق والعلايق والحُجُب (٣) وخبايا
السرّ ومقامات الاخلاص واحوال المعارف وحقايق الأذكار ودرجات القرب
وتجريد التوحيد ومنازل التفريد وحقايق العبودية ومحو الكون بالازل
وتلاشى المُحْدَث اذا قورن بالقديم وفنآء رؤية الأعْواض وبقآء رؤية
المُعْطِى (١) [بفنآء رؤية العطآء] وعبور الاحوال والمقامات وجمع (١) [الاشخاص]
المتفرّقات وفنآء رؤية القصد ببقآء رؤية المقصود (١) [والإعراض عن رؤية
الأعْواض] وترك الاعتراض والهجوم على سلوك سُبُل منطمسة وعبور مفاوز

---

(١) Suppl. in marg.   (٢) So in marg. Text: تخفون.   (٣) خبايات.

مُهلِكة، فالصوفية مخصوصون من أُولى العلم القائمين بالقسط بحلّ هذه العُقَد والوقوف على المُشكِل من ذلك والمارسة لها بالمنازلة والمباشرة والهجوم عليها ببذل المُهَج [١] حتى [٢] يُخبِرون عن دَعها وذوقها ونقصانها وزيادتها ويطالبون من يدّعى حالاً منها بدلايلها ويتكلّمون فى صحيحها وسقيمها، وهذا أكثرُ من أن يتهيّأ لأحدٍ أن يذكر قليلَه اذ لا سبيل الى كثيره، وجميع ذلك موجود [٣] عِلمُهُ فى كتاب الله عزّ وجلّ وفى اخبار رسول الله صلعم مفهوم عند اهله ولا ينكره العلماء اذا استجنهوا عن ذلك وانّما انكر علم التصوّف جماعةٌ من المترسّمين بعلم الظاهر لانّهم لم يعرفوا من كتاب الله تعالى ولا من اخبار رسول الله صلعم الا ما كان فى الأحكام الظاهرة وما يصلح للاحتجاج على المخالفين، والناس فى زماننا هذا الى مثل ذلك أمْيَلُ لانّه أقْرَبُ الى طلب الرياسة واتّخاذ الجاه عند العامّة والوصول الى الدنيا وقلّ من تراه يشتغل بهذا العلم الذى ذكرْنا لانّ هـــذا علم الخصوص ممزوج بالمرارة والغصص وسماعه يُضعف الركبتَين ويُحزن القلب ويُدمع العين ويُصغر العظيم ويُعظم الصغير فكيف استعاله ومباشرته وذوقه ومنازلته وليس [٤] للنفس فى [٥] منازلته حظٌّ لانّه منوط بامانة النفوس وفقد الحسوس ومجانبة المراد فمن اجْل ذلك ترك العلماء هذا العلم واشتغلوا باستعمال علم يُخفّ عليهم المؤن ويحثّهم على التوسيع والرُخَص والتأويلات ويكون أقْرَبَ الى حُظوظ البشرية وأخفّ [٦] تحمّلاً على النفوس التى جُبِلت على متابعة الحظوظ والمنافرة عن الحقوق، والله تعالى [٧] اعلم،

---

(١) أنهم suppl. in marg. after حتى. (٢) Corr. to يُخبرون by later hand. (٣) Suppl. above. (٤) In marg. للنفوس. (٥) Text: منازلتها حظ لانها. (٦) So in marg. Text: يحمله. (٧) بالصواب added by later hand. منوطة.

باب الرّد على من زعم انّ الصوفية قومٌ جَهَلةٌ وليس
لعلم التصوّف دلالةٌ من الكتاب والأَثَر،

قال الشيخ [(١)][الامام ابو نصر] رحمه الله لا خلاف بين الايمّة أنّ الله
تبارك وتعالى ذكر فى كتابه الصادقين والصادقات والقانتين والقانتات
٥ والخاشعين والموقنين والمخلصين (٢) والمحسنين والخايفين والراجين والوجلين
والعابدين والسايحين والصابرين والراضين والمتوكلين والمخبتين والاولياَء
والمتقين والمصطفين [(١)][والمجتبين] والابرار والمقرّبين، وقد ذكر الله تعالى
المشاهدين فقال (٣)[أَوْ أَلْقَى السَّمْعَ] وَهُوَ شَهِيدٌ، وذكر (٤)الله المطمئنّين فقال
(٥)أَلاَ بِذِكْرِ اللهِ تَطْمَئِنُّ الْقُلُوبُ، وذكر الله تعالى السابقين والمقتصدين
١٠ والمسارعين الى الخيرات، وقال النبى صلعم إنّ من امّتى مكلّمون ومحدّثون
وإنّ عُمَرَ منهم، وقال النبى صلعم رُبُّ أَشْعَثَ أَغْبَرَ ذى طِمْرَيْن لو اقسم على
الله لأبرّه وإنّ البَرَاَء منهم، وقال لوابصة اسْتَفْتِ قَلْبَكَ ولم يقل لأحد غيره
ذلك، وقال النبى صلعم يدخل بشفاعة رجل من أُمّتى الجنّة مثلُ ربيعـة
ومُضر يقال له أُوَيْس القَرَنّى، وفى الحديث انّ فى أُمّتى من اذا قرأ (٦)أُربِتُ
٨ f. ٨a انه يخشى الله تعالى وإنّ طلق بن حبيب منهم، وقول النبى صلعم يدخل
من امّتى الجنّة سبعون الفًا بلا حسابـ قيل من هم يرسول الله قال هم
الذين لا يكتوون ولا يَسْتَرْقون وعلى ربّهم يتوكّلون، (٧)والآثار والاخبار فى
مثل هذا تكثر ولا خلاف انّ هؤلاَء كلّهم فى امّة محمّد صلعم ولو لم يكونوا
فى الامّة موجودين واشتغال كونهم فى كلّ وقت لم يذكرهم الله تعالى فى كتابه
٢٠ ولم يصنّهم رسول الله صلعم، ولمّا رأينا انّ اسم الايمان قد شمل جميع المؤمنين

---

(1) Suppl. in marg.   (٢) So in marg. Text: والمحبين.   (٣) Suppl. in
marg. Kor. 50, 36.   (٤) Suppl. above.   (٥) Kor. 13, 28.   (٦) In marg.
رايت.   (٧) In marg. والايات.

وأفردوا هؤلاء بأسماء مختصة من ذلك دلّ ذلك على تخصيصهم من عامّة
المؤمنين الذين شملهم اسم الايمان ولا يختلف احد من الايمة انّ الانبياء
عليهم السلم الذين هم أعلى درجة من هؤلاء (١) وأقرَبُ منزلة عند الله تعالى
منهم انّهم كانوا بشرًا يجرى عليهم ما يجرى على ساير البشر من الأكل والنوم
٥ والحوادث، وانّما وقع التخصيص للانبياء صلوات الله عليهم اجمعين ولساير
هؤلاء الذين ذكرتهم لسرّ بينهم وبين معبودهم ولزيادة يقينهم وايمانهم بما
خاطبهم الله تعالى (٢) به ونديهم اله الا الانبياء عليهم السلم فانّهم ينفردون
عن هؤلاء بتخصيص الوحى والرسالة ودلايل النبوّة فلا يجوز لأحدان يزاحمهم
فى ذلك والله (٣) اعلم ،

باب فى ذكر اعتراض الصوفية على المتفقهة وبيان الفقه
فى الدين ووجه ذلك بالُحجّة ،

قال الشيخ (٤) [ابو نصر] رحمه الله رُوى عن النبى صلعم انّه قال من
برد الله به خيرًا يُفقّهه فى الدين ، ويبلغنى عن الحسن البصرى رحمه الله انّه
قيل له فلان فقيه فقال الحسن وهل رأيتَ فقيهًا قطّ انّما الفقيه الزاهد فى
١٥ الدنيا الراغب فى الآخرة البصير بأمر دينه، وقول الله تعالى (٥) لِيَتَفَقَّهُوا فِى
الدِّين، فالدين اسم يشتمل على جميع الاحكام ظاهرًا وباطنًا وليس التفقه فى
احكام هذه الاحوال ومعانى (٢) هذه المقامات التى تقدّم ذِكرُها بأقلّ فايدةً من
التفقه فى احكام الطلاق والعتاق والظهار والقصاص والقسامة والحدود
لانّ (٦) تلك احكام ربّما لا تقع فى العمر حادثة تحتاج الى علم ذلك فاذا
٢٠ وقعت تلك الحادثة فمن سأل عنها (٧) قلّدَ فى ذلك وأخَذَ بقول بعض

A f. 8b

---

(١) Inserted below.   (٢) Suppl. above.   (٣) بالصواب added by later
hand.   (٤) Suppl. in marg.   (٥) Kor. 9, 123.   (٦) ذلك corr. above.
(٧) قيل.

النقهاَء فقد سقط عنه فرضُ ذلك الى أن تقع به حادثة أُخْرَى، وهـــذه الاحوال والمقامات والمجاهدات التى يتنقّهون فيها الصوفية ويتكلّمون فى حقايقها فالمؤمنون (١)مفتقرون الى ذلك ومعرفة ذلك واجب عليهم وليس لذلك وقت مخصوص دون وقت (٢)وذلك مثل الصدق والاخلاص والذكر ومجانبة الغفلة وغير ذلك ليس لها وقت معلوم بل يجب على العبد فى كلّ لحظة وخطرة ان يعلم (٣)ايش قصدُهُ وإرادته وخاطره فان كان حقًّا من الحقوق فواجبٌ عليه ان يلزمه وإن كان حظًّا من الحظوظ فواجبٌ عليه مجانبته، قال الله تعالى لنبيّه وصفيّه محمّد صلعم (٤)وَلَا تُطِعْ مَنْ أَغْفَلْنَا قَلْبَهُ عَنْ ذِكْرِنَا وَاتَّبَعَ هَوَاهُ وَكَانَ أَمْرُهُ فُرُطًا، فمن ترك حالًا من هذه الاحوال ما تركها الّا من غلبة الغفلة على قلبه، واعلم انّ مستنبطات الصوفيـــة فى معانى هذا العلوم ومعرفة دقايقها وحقايقها ينبغى ان تكون أكثر من مستنبطات النقهاَء فى معانى احكام الظاهر لانّ هذا العلم ليس له نهاية لانّه اشارات (٥)وبوادٍ وخواطر وعطايا وهبات يغرفها اهلها من بحر العطاَء وساير العلوم لها حدٌّ محدود وجميع العلوم يؤدّى الى علم التصوّف (٦)[وعلم التصوّف لا يؤدّى الّا الى نوع من علم التصوّف] وليس له نهاية لانّ المقصود ليس له غاية وهو علم النتوح يفتح الله تعالى على قلوب اولياَئه فى فهم كلامه ومستنبطات (٧)خطابه ما شاَء كيف شاَء، قال الله عزّ وجلّ (٨)قُلْ لَوْ كَانَ الْبَحْرُ مِدَادًا لِكَلِمَاتِ رَبِّى لَنَفَذَ الْبَحْرُ قَبْلَ أَنْ تَنْفَدَ كَلِمَاتُ رَبِّى وَلَوْ جِئْنَا بِمِثْلِهِ مَدَدًا، وقال (٩)لَئِنْ شَكَرْتُمْ لَأَزِيدَنَّكُمْ والزيادة من الله تعالى لا نهاية لهـا والشكر (٢)نعمة تستوجب شكرًا (٢)مستوجبًا لمزيدٍ لا نهاية له وبالله (١٠)التوفيق،

Ι ٨ f. 9a

---

(١) So in marg. Text: مندوبون .

(٢) Suppl. above.

(٣) In marg.

اى شى . (٤) Kor. 18, 27.

(٥) وبوادى .

(٦) Suppl. in marg.

(٧) So in marg. Text: احكامه .

(٨) Kor. 18, 109.

(٩) Kor. 14, 7.

(١٠) وبالله اعلم added.

باب ذكر جواز التخصيص فى علوم الدين وتخصيص كلّ علم
بأهله والردّ على من انكر علمًا برأيه ولم يدفع ذلك الى
اهله والى من يكون (١)ذلك من شأنه،

قال الشيخ رحمه الله انكرت جماعة من العلماء ان يكون فى علم الشريعة
٥ تخصيص، ولا خلاف بين (٢)[هذه] الامّة انّ الله تعالى امر رسوله صلعم بإبلاغ
ما أنزل عليه فقال (٣)يَا أَيُّهَا ٱلرَّسُولُ بَلِّغْ مَا أُنزِلَ إِلَيْكَ [مِن رَّبِّكَ] (٤)،
ورُوى عن النبى صلعم انّه قال لو تعلمون مـا أعْلَمُ لضحكتم قليلاً ولبكيتم
كثيرًا، فلو كان الذى علم ممّا لا يعلمون من العلوم التى امره (٥)بالإبلاغ
لأبْلَغَ ولو جاز لأصحابه ان يسألوه عن ذلك العلم لسألوه ولا خلاف بين
١٠ اهل العلم انّ فى اصحاب رسول الله صلعم من كان مخصوصًا بنوع من العلم
كما كان حُذَيْفة مخصوصًا بعلم اسماء المنافقين كان قد أسَرّه اليه رسول الله
صلعم حتى كان يسأله عُمَر رضى الله عنه (٦)فيقول هل انا منهم، ورُوى عن
على بن ابى طالب رضى الله عنه انّه قال علّمنى رسول الله صلعم سبعين بابًا
من العلم لم يعلّم ذلك احدًا غيرى، وقد ذكر هذا الباب بتمامه فى آخر
١٥ الكتاب والمراد من تكراره هاهنا انّ العلم (٧)المبثوث بين اصحاب الحديث
والفقهاء والصوفية هو علم الدين ولكلّ صنف من اهل العلم فى علمه دواوين
ومصنّفات (٢)[وكُتُب] وإقاويل ولكلّ (٨)صنف منهم ايمة مشهورون قد اجمع
اهل عصرهم على (٩)امامتهم لزيادة علمهم وفهمهم ولا خلاف انّ اصحاب الحديث
اذا اشكل عليهم علم من علوم الحديث وعِلَل الاخبار ومعرفة الرجال لا

---

(١) Suppl. above. (٢) Suppl. in marg. (٣) Kor. 5, 71. (٤) Suppl.
above. (٥) So in marg. Text: بالإبلاغ. (٦) So in marg. Text: فقال.
(٧) المبثوث. (٨) So in marg. Text: طبقة. (٩) امامتهم.

يرجعون فى ذلك الى الفقهاء كما ان الفقهاء لو اشكل عليهم مسئلة فى الخَلِّيَّة والبَرِيّة والدور والوصايا لا يرجعون فى ذلك الى اصحاب الحديث وكذلك من اشكل عليه علم من علوم هؤلاء الذين تكلّموا فى مواجيد القلوب ومواريث الاسرار ومعاملات القلوب و صنفوا (١)العلوم واستنبطوا فى ذلك باشارات لطيفة (٢)ومعانٍ جليلة فليس له أن يرجع فى ذلك الّا الى عالم ممّن يكون هذا شأنه ويكون ممّن قد مارس هذه الاحوال ونازلها واستبحث عن علومها (٣)ودقايقها فمن فعل غير ذلك فقد اخطأ وليس لأحد ان يبسط لسانه بالوقيعة فى قوم لا يعرف حالهم ولم يعلم علمهم (٤)ولم يقف على مقاصدهم ومراتبهم فيهلك ويظنّ انّه من الناصحين، اعاذنا الله تعالى وإيّاكم،

باب الكشف عن اسم الصوفية ولمَ سُمّوا بهذا الاسم ولمَ نسبوا الى (٥)[هذه] اللبسة،

قال الشيخ رحمه الله ان (٦)سأل سايلٌ فقال قد نسبتَ اصحاب الحديث الى الحديث ونسبتَ الفقهاء الى الفقه فلمَ قلتَ الصوفية (٧)ولم تنسبهم الى حال ولا الى علم ولم تضف اليهم حالًا كما اضفتَ الزهد الى الزهّاد والتوكّل الى المتوكّلين والصبر الى الصابرين فيقال له لأنّ الصوفية لم ينفردوا بنوع من العلم دون نوع ولم يترسّموا برسم من الاحوال والمقامات دون رسم وذلك لانّهم معدن جميع العلوم ومحل جميع الاحوال المحمودة والاخلاق الشريفة سالمًا ومستأنًا وهم مع الله تعالى فى الانتقال من حال الى حال مستجلبين للزيادة فلمّا كانوا فى الحقيقة كذلك لم يكونوا مستحقّين (٨)اسمًا دون اسم فلأجل ذلك ما اضفتُ اليهم حالًا دون حال ولا اضفتهم الى علم دون علم

---

(١) In marg. الخواطر, which appears to be a variant of العلوم. (٢) معانى.

(٣) In marg. وحقايقها. (٤) So in marg. Text: ولا. (٥) Suppl. in marg.

(٦) سائل. (٧) و suppl. below. (٨) باسم corr. by later hand.

لانّى لو اضفتُ اليهم فى كلّ وقت حالاً ما وجدتُ الأغلب عليهم من الاحوال والاخلاق والعلوم والاعمال وسيّرتهم بذلك لكان يلزم أن اسيّرهم فى كلّ وقت باسم آخر وكنت اضيف اليهم فى كلّ وقت حالاً دون حال على حسب ما يكون الاغلب عليهم، فلمّا لم يكن ذلك نسبتُهم الى ظاهر اللبسة لانّ لبسة الصوف دأب الانبياء عليهم السلم وشعار الاولياء والاصفياء ويكثر فى ذلك (١)الروايات والاخبار فلمّا اضفتهم الى ظاهر اللبسة كان ذلك اسمًا مُجملًا عامًّا مُخبرًا عن جميع العلوم والاعمال والاخلاق والاحوال الشريفة المحمودة، ألا ترى انّ الله تعالى ذكر طائفةً من خواصّ اصحاب عيسى عليه السلم فنسبهم الى ظاهر اللبسة فقال عزّ وجلّ (٢)وَإِذْ قَالَ الْحَوَارِيُّونَ (٣)[الآية] وكانوا قومًا يلبسون البياض فنسبهم الله تعالى الى ذلك ولم ينسبهم الى نوع من العلوم والاعمال والاحوال التى كانوا بها مترسّمين، فكذلك الصوفية عندى والله اعلم نُسبوا الى ظاهر (٤)اللباس ولم ينسبوا الى نوع من انواع العلوم والاحوال التى هم بها مترسّمون لانّ لبس الصوف كان دأب الانبياء عليهم السلم والصدّيقين وشعار (٥)[المساكين] المتنسكين،

باب الردّ على من قال لم نسمع (٥)بذكر الصوفية فى القديم وهو اسم مُحدَث،

ان سأل سايلٌ فقال لم (٦)نسمع بذكر الصوفية فى اصحاب رسول الله صلم ورضى الله عنهم اجمعين ولا فيمن كان بعدهم ولا نعرف الّا العبّاد والزهّاد والسيّاحين والفقراء وما قيل لأحد من اصحاب رسول الله صلم (٧)صوفٌ فنقول وبالله التوفيق الصحبة مع رسول الله صلم لها حرمة وتخصيص

من شَمَّهُ ذلك فلا يجوز ان يعلَّق عليه اسم على انه اشرفُ من الصحبـة
وذلك لشرف رسول الله صلعم وحرمته، ألا ترى انهم ايمّة الزهّاد والعبّاد
والمتوكّلين والفقراء والراضين والصابرين والمخبتين وغير ذلك ومـا نالوا
جميع ما نالوا الّا ببركة الصحبة مع رسول الله صلعم (١) فلمّا نُسبوا الى الصحبة A f.10b
التى هى اجلُّ الاحوال استحال ان ينتضلوا بنضيلة غير الصحبة التى هى اجلُّ ٥
الاحوال (٢) وبالله التوفيق، وامّا قول القايل انه اسم مُحْدَث أحْدَثه البغداديون
فمحال لانّ فى وقت الحسن البصرى (٣) رحمه الله كان يُعرف هذا (٤) الاسم
وكان الحسن قد ادرك جماعةً من اصحاب رسول الله صلعم (٥) ورضى عنهم وقد
رُوى عنه انه قال رأيتُ صوفيًّا فى الطواف فأعطيته شيئًا فلم (٦) يأخذه وقال
معى اربعة دوانيق فيكفينى ما معى، (٧) ورُوى عن سفيْن الثورى (٨) رحمه ١٠
الله (٩) انه قال لولا ابو هاشم الصوفى ما عرفت دقيق الرياء، وقد ذُكر فى
الكتاب الذى جُمع فيه اخبار مكّة عن محمد بن اسحق بن (١٠) يسار (١١) وعن
غيره يذكر فيه حديثًا ان قبل الاسلام قد (١٢) خلت مكّة فى وقت من
الاوقات حتى كان لا يطوف بالبيت احد وكان يجيء من بلد بعيد
(١٣) رجل صوفى فيطوف بالبيت (١٤) وينصرف، فان صحّ ذلك يدلّ على ان ١٥
قبل الاسلام (١٥) كان يعرف هذا الاسم وكان يُنسب اليه اهل الفضل
والصلاح، (١٦) والله اعلم،

---

(١) Here B resumes (fol. 4b, l. 1).   (٢) B والله اعلم وإما قوله اسم محدث.

(٣) B om.   (٤) B الحسن.   (٥) B om. رحمه الله.   احدثها البغداديون الخ.

(٦) B يأخذ.   (٧) B روى.   (٨) B om. رحمه الله.   ورضى عنهم.

(٩) Suppl. in marg. A.   (١٠) A يشار.   (١١) B عن.   (١٢) B خلا.

(١٣) A رجل معه رجل صوفى.   (١٤) B ثم ينصرف.   (١٥) B كان هذا الاسم يعرف.

(١٦) B om. والله اعلم.

باب اثبات علم الباطن والبيان عن صحّة ذلك بالحجّة،

‏‏(١)قال الشيخ رحمه الله انكرت (٢)طايفة من اهل الظاهــر وقالوا لا
نعرف الّا علم الشريعة الظاهرة التى جاَء (٣)بها الكتاب والسنّة (٤)وقالوا
لا معنى لقولكم علم الباطن وعلم التصوّف، (٥)فنقول وبالله التوفيق ان علم
الشريعة علم واحد (٦)وهو اسم واحد يجمع معنيَيْن الرواية (٧)والدراية فاذا
جمعتهما فهو علم الشريعة الداعية الى الاعمال الظاهرة والباطنة ولا يجوز ان
يجرّد القول فى العلم أنّه ظاهر او باطن لانّ العلم متى (٨)ما كان فى القلب
فهو باطن فيه الى ان (٩)يجرى ويظهر على اللسان (١٠)فاذا جرى على اللسان
فهو ظاهر غير انّا نقول انّ العلم (١١)ظاهر وباطن وهو علم الشريعة (١٢)الذى
بدلّ ويدعو الى الاعمال الظاهرة والباطنة (١٣)والاعمال الظاهرة كأعمال
الجوارح الظاهرة وهى العبادات والاحكام مثل الطهارة والصلاة والزكاة
والصوم والحجّ (١٤)والجهاد وغير ذلك فهذه العبادات، واما الاحكام فالحدود
والطلاق والعتاق والبيوع والفرايض (٨)والقصاص وغيرها فهذا كلّه على
الجوارح الظاهرة التى هى الاعضاَء (١٥)وهى الجوارح، واما (١٦)الاعمال الباطنة
فكأعمال القلوب وهى المقامات والاحوال مثل التصديق والايمان واليقين
والصدق والاخلاص والمعرفة والتوكّل والمحبّة والرضا والذكر والشكر والانابة
والخشية والتقوى والمراقبة والفكرة والاعتبار والخوف والرجاَء والصبر
والقناعة والتسليم والتفويض والقرب والشوق (١٧)والوجد والوجل والحزن

---

(١) B om. قال الشيخ رحمه الله.   (٢) B جماعة.   (٣) B به.   (٤) B om.

(٥) بفقال ان علم الشريعة علم واحد B.   (٦) وهذا B.   (٧) والهداية B.   قالوا

B ظاهرًا.   (١١) B واذا.   (١٠) B واذا.   (٩) بظاهر على اللسان B.   (٨) B om.

(١٢) الى تدلّ وتدعو B.   (١٣) فاعمال الظاهرة B.   (١٤) وغيرها B.

(١٥) وهى الجوارح B om.   (١٦) اعمال باطنه B.   (١٧) ولاجل والوجد B.

والندم والحياء والخجل والتعظيم والاجلال والهيبة ولكلّ [١]عمل من هذه
الاعمال الظاهرة والباطنة علمٌ وفقه وبيان [٢]وفهم وحقيقة ووجد [٣]ويدلّ
على صحّة كلّ [٤]عمل منها من الظاهر والباطن آيات من القران واخبار عن
الرسول صلعم علمه من علمه وجهله من جهله، فاذا قلنا علم الباطن اردنا
٥ بذلك علم اعمال الباطن التى هى على الجارحة الباطنة وهى القلب كما انّا
اذا قلنا علم الظاهر اشرنا الى علم الاعمال الظاهرة التى هى على [٥]الجوارح
الظاهرة وهى الاعضاء، وقد قال اله [٦]تعالى [٧]وَأَسْبَغَ عَلَيْكُمْ نِعَمَهُ ظَاهِرَةً
وَبَاطِنَةً [٨]فالنعمة الظاهرة ما انعم اله [٢]تعالى بها على الجوارح الظاهرة من
فعل الطاعات والنعمة الباطنة ما انعم اله [٢]تعالى بها على القلب من هذه
١٠ الحالات ولا يستغنى الظاهر عن الباطن ولا الباطن عن الظاهر، وقد قال
اله [٩]عزّ وجلّ [١٠]وَلَوْ رَدُّوهُ إِلَى ٱلرَّسُولِ وَإِلَى أُولِي ٱلأَمْرِ مِنْهُمْ لَعَلِمَهُ
ٱلَّذِينَ يَسْتَنْبِطُونَهُ مِنْهُمْ فالعلم المستنبط هو [١١]العلم الباطن وهو علم اهل
التصوّف لانّ لهم مستنبطات من القران والحديث وغير ذلك ونحن نذكر
ان شاء اله طرقًا من ذلك، [١٢]فالعلم ظاهر وباطن والقران ظاهر وباطن
١٥ وحديث رسول اله صلعم ظاهر وباطن والاسلام ظاهر وباطن ولأصحابنا فى
معنى ذلك استدلالات واحتجاجات من الكتاب والسنّة والعقل وشرحه
يطول ويخرج عن حدّ الاختصار الى حدّ الإكثار وفيا قلنا كفاية، وباله
التوفيق،

باب التصوّف ما هو [١٤]ونعته وماهيته،

٢٠   قال الشيخ رحمه اله فامّا التصوّف ونعته [٢]وماهيته فقد سُئل محمّد

(١) B علم.   (٢) B om.   (٣) B يدل.   (٤) A corrector has
written in marg. A واظنّه علم.   (٥) B الاعال.   (٦) B ذكره جل.
(٧) Kor. 31, 19.   (٨) B النعمة.   (٩) B تبارك وتعالى.   (١٠) Kor. 4, 85.
(١١) B علم.   (١٢) B والعلم.   (١٣) B proceeds: فاما التصوف الخ.

ابن على القصّاب وهو استاذ الجُنَيْد رحمه الله عن التصوّف ما [١]هو [٢]قال اخلاق [٣]كريمة ظهرت فى [٤]زمان كريم من رجل كريم مع قوم كرام، وسُئِل الجُنيد [٥]رحمه الله عن التصوّف فقال ان تكون مع الله تعالى بلا علاقة، وسُئِل رُوَيْم بن احمد [٥]رحمه الله عن التصوّف فقال استرسال النفس مع الله [٦]تعالى على ما يريد، وسُئِل سَمْنون [٦]رحمه الله عن التصوّف فقال ان لا [٧]تملك شيئًا ولا [٨]يَملكك شىء، وسُئِل ابو محمّد الجُرَيرى [٦]رحمه الله عن التصوّف فقال الدخول فى كلّ خُلق سنّى والخروج من كلّ خلق دنّى، وسُئِل عمرو بن عثمان المكّى [٦]رحمه الله عن التصوّف فقال ان يكون العبد فى كلّ وقت بما هو أوْلَى فى الوقت، وسُئِل على بن عبد [٩]الرحيم القنّاد [٦]رحمه الله عن التصوّف فقال نشر مقام واتّصال بدوام،

باب [١٠]صفة الصوفية ومن هم،

قال الشيخ رحمه الله وامّا صفة الصوفية ومن هم فقد قيل لعبد الواحد ابن زَيْد كما بلغنى وكان [١١]ممّن يصحب الحسن رحمه الله وكان من اجلّة اصحابه مَن الصوفيّة عندك فقال القايمون بعقولهم على [١٢]هومهم والعاكفون عليها بقلوبهم المعتصمون بسيّدهم من شرّ نفوسهم هم الصوفية، وسُئِل [١٣]ذو النون المصرى [٦]رحمه الله عن الصوفى فقال هو الذى لا يُتعبه طَلَب ولا يُزعِجه سَلَب، وقال ايضًا هم قوم آثروا الله [١٤]تعالى على كلّ شىء [١٥]فآثرهم [١٦]الله على كلّ شىء، وقيل لبعضهم من اصحبُ فقال أصحبِ الصوفيـة فانّ للقبيح عندهم وجوهًا من المعاذيـر وليس [١٧]للكثير عندهم مَوْقع

[١] B فى.   [٢] B فقال.   [٣] B كريم.   [٤] B app. نقاب.   [٥] B om. رحمه الله.   [٦] B om.   [٧] B أملك.   [٨] B يملكك.   [٩] B الرحمن.   [١٠] B proceeds: وإما صفة الصوفية ومن هم فقيل لعبد الواحد بن زيد الخ.   [١١] B.   [١٢] A ذا.   همهم A but corr. in marg.   [١٣] من اصحاب الحسن من اجلّة اصحابه.   [١٤] عز وجل B.   [١٥] وأثرهم A.   [١٦] الله عز وجل B.   [١٧] B app. الكبير.

^(١)فيرفعوك به فتُعجب نفسك، وسُئِل الجُنَيْد بن محمّد ^(٢)رحمه الله عن الصوفية من هم فقال أثرة الله ^(٣)فى خلقه يُخفيها اذا احبّ ويُظهرهـا اذا احبّ، وقيل لأبى الحسين احمد بن محمّد النورى ^(٣)رحمه الله من الصوفى فقال من سمع السماع وآثر ^(٤)بالاسباب، واهل الشأم يسمّون الصوفية فقرآء ويقولون قد سمّاهم الله ^(٢)تعالى ^(٢)فقرآء فقال ^(٥)لِلْفُقَرَآءِ ٱلْمُهَاجِرِينَ ٱلَّذِينَ أُخْرِجُوا ^(٦)مِنْ دِيَارِهِمْ الآية ^(٧)وقوله ^(٨)تعالى ^(٩)لِلْفُقَرَآءِ ٱلَّذِينَ أُحْصِرُوا فِى سَبِيلِ ٱللَّهِ الآية، وقيل لأبى عبد الله ^(١٠)احمد بن محمّد بن يحيى الجلّاء ^(٢)رحمه الله ما معنى الصوفى قال ليس نعرفه فى شرط العلم ولكن نعرف فقيرًا مجرّدًا من الاسباب كان مع الله ^(١١)عزّ وجلّ بلا مكان ولايمنعه الحقّ من علم كلّ مكان ^(١٢)سُمّى صوفيًّا، وقد قيل كان فى الاصل صَفوى فاستُثقِل ذلك فقيل صوفى، وسُئِل ابو الحسن القنّاد ^(٢)رحمه الله عن معنى ^(١٣)الصوفى فقال مأخوذ من الصفآء وهو القيام لله ^(٢)عزّ وجلّ فى ^(١٤)كلّ وقت بشرط الوفآء، وقال بعضهم ^(١٥)من اذا استقبله ^(١٦)حالان او ^(١٧)خُلقان حسنان فيكون مع الاحسن والاعلى، وسُئِل آخر عن معنى ^(١٨)الصوفى فقال معناه انّ العبد اذا تحقّق بالعبودية ^(١٨)وصافاه الحقّ حتى صفا من كدر البشرية ^(١٩)نازل ^(٢٠)منازل الحقيقة ^(٢١)وقارن احكام الشريعة فاذا فعل ذلك فهو صوفىٌّ لانّه قد صوفِيَ، ^(٢٢)قال الشيخ رحمه الله ^(٢٣)فاذا قيل لك الصوفية من هم فى الحقيقة صِفهم لنا فقُل هم العلمآء بالله وبأحكام الله العاملون بما علّمهم الله تعالى المتحقّقون بما استعملهم الله ^(٢)عزّ وجلّ الواجدون

---

^(١) B برفعوك.   ^(٢) B om.   ^(٣) A من but corr. in marg.   ^(٤) AB الاسباب.

^(٥) Kor. 59, 8.   ^(٦) B om. من ديارهم.   ^(٧) B omits this quotation.

^(٨) Suppl. above.   ^(٩) Kor. 2, 274.   ^(١٠) B om. احمد بن محمّد.   ^(١١) B om. عزّ وجلّ.

^(١٢) B فسمى.   ^(١٣) B صوفى.   ^(١٤) Instead of كلّ وقت.   ^(١٥) In A الصوفى has been written above.   B has كلفه and A in marg. خلقه.   ^(١٦) B حالين.   ^(١٧) B حالان.   ^(١٨) B صافا.   ^(١٩) B ونازل.

^(٢٠) B منازلات.   ^(٢١) B وقاده.   ^(٢٢) B om. قال الشيخ رحمه الله.   ^(٢٣) B واذا.

بما تحقّقوا [١] الفانون بما وجدوا لانّ كلّ واجد قد فنى بما وجد، وقال القنّاد
[٢] رحمه الله التصوّف اسم قد [٣] وقع على ظاهر اللبسة وهم متفاوتون فى
معانيهم واحوالهم، وسُئِل الشِّبلى [٢] رحمه الله لِمَ سُمّيت الصوفية بهذا الاسم
فقال [٤] إِبْقَايا بقيت عليهم من نفوسهم ولولا ذلك لما لاقت بهم الاسماء ولا
٥ تعلّقت [٢] بهم، وقد قيل [٢] ايضًا انّ [٥] الصوفية هم بقيّة من بقايا اهل الصُّفّة،
[٦] وامّا من قال [٢] انّه اسم واقع على ظاهر اللبسة فقد رُوى فى ذلك اخبار
فى ذكر من لبس الصوف واختار لبسه من الانبياء والصالحين وذكره بطول،
وقد اجاب [٧] عن التصوّف ما هو جماعة بأجوبة مختلفة منهم ابرهيم بن
المولّد الرقّى قد اجاب عنها بأكثر من مائة جواب [٨] وفيما ذكرنا كفاية،
١٠ وقد [٩] قال على بن عبد الرحيم القنّاد [٢] رحمه الله فى التصوّف واندراس
اهله [٢] شعرًا،

أَهْلُ التَّصَوُّفِ قَدْ مَضَوْا صَارَ التَّصَوُّفُ مَغْرَقَهْ

صَارَ التَّصَوُّفُ صَيْحَةً [١٠] وَتَوَاجُدًا وَمُطَابَقَهْ

مَضَتِ العُلُومُ فَلَا عُلُومٌ وَلَا قُلُوبٌ مُشْرِقَهْ

كَذَبَتْكَ نَفْسُكَ لَيْسَ ذَى سَنَنَ الطَّرِيقِ [١١] المُخْلَقَهْ

حَتَّى تَكُونَ بِعَيْنِ [١٢] مَنْ عَنْهُ العُيُونُ [١٢] المُحْدَقَهْ

تَجْرِى عَلَيْكَ صُرُوفُهُ وَهُمُومُ [١٤] سِرِّكَ [١٥] مُطْرِقَهْ،

ولبعض المشايخ فى التصوّف ثلثة اجوبة جواب بشرط العلم وهى تصفية
القلوب من الاكدار واستعمال الخُلُق مع الخليقة واتّباع الرسول فى الشريعة
٢٠ وجواب بلسان الحقيقة وهو [١٦] عدم الأملاك والخروج من رقّ [١٧] الصفات

---

[١] الفانون B.   [٣] B om.   [٣] وقعت B.   [٤] A in marg. لبقايا.

[٥] A has بقيّة من اهل الصفة هم but بقيّة الصوفية is suppl. in marg.   [٦] B فاما.

[٧] فى B.   [٨] A om. وفيما ذكرنا كفاية.   [٩] قال القناد B.   [١٠] وتواجد B.

[١١] المخلقه B.   [١٢] A in marg. ما.   [١٣] A in marg. محدقه.   [١٤] A in

marg. نفسك.   [١٥] A in marg. مشفقه.   [١٦] A in marg. عدم الامل الى

الابد.   [١٧] B app. تبعات.

والاستغناء بخالق السموات وجواب بلسان الحقّ اصفاهم بالصفاء عن صفائهم
وصفاءهم عن صفايهم فسُمُّوا صوفيةً، وقلتُ [٢] للحُصْرى [٣] رحمه الله من [A f.13a][١]
الصوفى عندك [٤] قال الذى لا تُقلّه الارض ولا تُظلّه السماء معنـاه انّـه
[٥] وان كان على [٦] الارض وثبت [٧] السماء فالله [٨] عزّ وجلّ الذى يقلّه
بالارض ويظلّه بالسماء [٨] لا السماء ولا الارض، [٩] وعن ابى بكر الصديّق   ٥
رضى الله عنه انّه كان يقول اىّ ارض تُقلّنى واىّ سماء يُظلّنى [١٠] اذا قلت
فى كتاب الله عزّ وجلّ برأيى ،

باب [١١] التوحيد وصفة الموحّد وحقيقته وكلامهم فى معنى ذلك،

[١٢] قال الشيخ رحمه الله بلغنى عن يوسف بن الحسين الرازى [٢] رحمه
الله انّه قال قام رجل بين يدى [١٣] ذى النون المصرى [٢] رحمه الله فقال   ١٠
خبّرنى عن التوحيد ما هو قال هو أن تعلم انّ قدرة الله [٢] تعالى فى الاشياء
بلا مزاج [١٤] وصُنْعه للاشياء بلا علاج وعلّة كلّ شىء صُنْعه ولا علّة لصُنْعه
وليس فى السموات العُلَى ولا فى الأرضين السُّفْلَى مدبّر غير الله [٢] تعالى
ومهما تصوّر فى [١٥] وهمك فالله [١٦] تعالى بخلاف ذلك [١٧] او قال غير
ذلك، وقال الجُنَيْد [٢] رحمه الله [١٨] وقد سُئل عن التوحيد فقال إفراد   ١٥
الموحَّد بتحقيق وحدانيته بكمال احديّته انّه الواحد الذى لم يلد ولم يولد بنفى
الاضداد والانداد والاشباه وما عُبد من دونه بلا تشبيه ولا تكييف ولا

---

[١] ‏B om. صفاءهم عن صفايهم.   [٢] ‏B الحُصْرى.   [٣] ‏B om.   [٤] ‏B فقال.

[٥] ‏B ان.   [٦] ‏B ظهر الارض.   [٧] ‏B ظلّ السماء.   [٨] ‏B om. لا السماء ولا.

[٩] ‏B الارض.   [١٠] ‏A اقول but corr. in marg.   [١١] ‏B فى.   وروى عن B.

[١٢] ‏B حكى عن يوسف بن الحسين الخ.   [١٣] ‏A ذا.   [١٤] ‏A وصنعته.

[١٥] ‏A adds شى after وهمك.   [١٦] ‏B عزّ وجلّ.   [١٧] ‏B om. وصنعه but orig.

[١٨] ‏B وسيل.   او قال غير ذلك.

نصوير ولا تمثيل الهًّا واحدًا صمدًا فردًا ليس كمثله شىء وهو السميع البصير،
وسُئِل جُنيْد (١) رحمه الله (٢) عن التوحيد مرّةً أُخرى فقال معنًى تضمحلّ فيه
الرسوم وتندرج فيه العلوم ويكون الله (٣) تعالى كما لم يزل، (٤) قال ابو نصر
رحمه الله فالجوابان الذان (٥) لذى النون والجنيد (١) رحمهما الله فى التوحيد
٥ ها ظاهران (٦) اجابا عن توحيد العامّ وهذا (٧) الجواب الذى (٨) ذكرنا اشار
الى (٩) توحيد الخاصّ، وقد (١٠) سُئِل (١١) الجنيد (١) رحمه الله عن توحيد
الخاصّ فقال أن يكون العبد شبحًا بين يدى (١٢) الله عزّ وجلّ تجرى عليه
نصاريف تدبيره فى مجارى احكام قدرته فى لُجَج بحار توحيده بالفناءَ عن
نفسه وعن دعوة الخلق له وعن استجابته (١٣) بحقايق وجود وحدانيته فى A f.136
١٠ حقيقة قُربه بذهاب (١٤) حسّه وحركته (١٥) لقيام الحقّ (١) له فيما اراد منه وهو
أن يرجع آخر العبد الى اوّله فيكون كما كان قبل ان يكون، وقال ايضًا
التوحيد هو الخروج من ضيق رسوم (١٦) الزمانية الى سعة (١٧) فناءَ السرمدية،
فان قال قايلٌ ما معنى قوله يرجع آخر العبد الى اوّله فيكون كما كان قبل
ان يكون فنقول بيان ذلك (١٨) فيما قال الله عزّ وجلّ (١٩) وَإِذْ أَخَذَ رَبُّكَ
١٥ مِنْ بَنِى آدَمَ (٢٠) مِنْ ظُهُورِهِمْ (٢١) ذُرِّيَّتَهُمْ (الآية، قال الجنيد (١) رحمه الله
فى (٢٢) معنى ذلك فمن كان وكيف كان قبل ان يكون وهل اجابت الاّ
الارواح (٢٣) الظاهرة باقامة القدرة (٢٤) وإنفاذ المشيّة فهو الآن فى الحقيقة كما

(١) B om.   (٢) B عزّ وجلّ.   (٣) B مرة أخرى عن التوحيد.   (٤) B proceeds:
والجوابان الذان الخ in الجواب.   (٥) A لذا.   (٦) B اجابة.   (٧) After الجواب
سيل B in marg. A.   (٨) B الاخر الذى للجنيد.   (٩) B التوحيد.   (١٠) B قد ذكرنا.
(١١) A جنيد.   (١٢) B الله تعالى.   (١٣) A لحقايق.   (١٤) B حملته.
(١٥) B بقيام.   (١٦) B الربانية and so A in marg.   (١٧) B فضا.   (١٨) B فى.
(١٩) Kor. 7, 171.   (٢٠) B om. من ظهورهم ذريتهم.   قوله تعالى
(٢١) A ذريّاتهم. The words وإشهدهم على انفسهم الست بربكم قالوا بلى are added in
marg. A.   (٢٢) B معناه.   (٢٣) A الظاهرة.   (٢٤) B وإنقياد.

كان قبل ان يكون، وهذا غاية حقيقة التوحيد للواحد ان يكون العبد كما
لم يكن ويبقى الله (١) تعالى كما لم يزل، (٢)قال رجل للشبلي (١) رحمه الله واسمه
دُلَف بن جَحْدَر (٣) يأبا بكر اخبرني عن توحيد مجرّد بلسان حقّ مفرّد فقال
ويحك من اجاب عن التوحيد بالعبارة فهو مُلْحِد ومن اشار اليه فهو ثَنَويّ
٥ (٤)ومن سكت عنه فهو جاهل ومن (٥) وهم انّه واصلٌ فليس له حاصلٌ ومن
اوى اليه فهو عابدُ وَثَنٍ ومن نطق فيه فهو غافل (٦) ومن (٧)ظنّ انّه قريب
فهو بعيد ومن تواجد فهو فاقد وكلّما ميّزتموه بأوهامكم وأدركتموه بعقولكم
فى أتمّ معانيكم فهو مصروف مردود اليكم مُحْدَث مصنوع مثلكم، وإن
اخذنا فى شرح ما قال الشبلى (١) رحمه الله كما يجب (٨) فيطول ذلك ولكن
١٠ على الايجاز والاختصار كأنّه يريد بما اجاب عن التوحيد إفراد القديم
(٩)عن المُحْدَث (١٠) وأن ليس للخلق طريق (١١) الّا الى ذكره و وصفه ونعته
على مقدار ما (١١)أبْدَى اليهم ورسم لهم، (١٢)قال الشيخ رحمه الله (١٣) و وجدت
(١٤)ليوسف بن الحسين فى التوحيد ثلثة اجوبة جواب منها فى توحيد العامّة
وهو الانفراد بالوحدانية بذهاب رؤية الاضداد والانداد والاشباه والاشكال
١٥ مع السكون الى معارضة الرغبة والرهبة بذهاب حقيقة التصديق (١٥) بقاءً
(١٦)الاقرار، والمعنى فى قوله بذهاب حقيقة التصديق لان (١٧) بقاءً حقيقة
التصديق لا يسكن الى معارضة الرغبة والرهبة، والجواب الثانى توحيد اهل
الحقايق (١)على الظاهر وهو الاقرار بالوحدانية بذهاب رؤية (١٨)الاسباب

A f.14a

---

(١) B om. (٢) B وقال. (٣) B om. يأبا بكر. (٤) B proceeds:

ومن أوى اليه الخ So Qushayrī, 161, 17. (٥) A أوهم. (٦) Here B proceeds:

ومن سكت عنه فهو جاهل ومن وهم انه واصل فليس له حاصل ومن ظن انه قريب الخ.

(٧) A رأى but ظن in marg. (٨) A يطول. (٩) B من.

(١٠) B om. أن. (١١) A أبدا. B بلام. (١٢) B om. قال الشيخ رحمه الله ووجدت.

(١٣) A يبقى. (١٤) B وليوسف. (١٥) A و added by a later hand.

(١٦) A الانفراد but corr. in marg. (١٧) A فيها erased: سوى written below.

(١٨) A الاضداد but corr. in marg. B app. لا دقى.

والاشباه (١)باقامة الامر والنهى فى الظاهر والباطن بازالة معارضة (٢)الرهبة
والرغبة ممّا سواه بقيام شواهد الحقّ مع قيام (٤)شواهد الدعوة والاستجابة،
فان قيل ما معنى قوله ازالة معارضة (٣)الرهبة والرغبة وهما حقّان (٤)فيقال
هما حقّان وهما فى موضعها كما هما ولكن قهَرَها سلطانُ الوحدانية كما قهر
سلطانُ ضوء الشمس ضوء الكواكب وهى فى مواضعها، والجواب الثالث
توحيد الخاصّة وهو ان يكون العبد بسرّه و وجدٍ وقلبه كأنّه قائم بين يدى
الله (٥)عزّ وجلّ تجرى عليه تصاريف تدبيره وتجرى عليه احكام (٦)قدرته
فى بحار توحيده بالفناء عن نفسه وذهاب حسّه (٧)بقيام الحقّ له فى مراده
(٨)منه فيكون كما كان قبل ان يكون يعنى فى جريان احكام الله عليه وإنفاذ
مشيّته فيه، وبيان ذلك كما قال ٩ الجُنيّد (١٠)رحمه الله فى قوله (٥)عزّ
وجلّ (١١)وَإِذْ أَخَذَ رَبُّكَ مِنْ بَنِي (١٢)آدَمَ الآية وقد ذكرناه، (١٣)قال الشيخ
رحمه الله ولم فى حقيقة التوحيد لسان آخر وهو لسان الواجدين وإشارتهم
فى ذلك تبعد عن الفهم ونحن نذكر من ذلك طرقًا كما يُمكن شرحه وهذا
العلم (١٤)أكثرُهُ اشارة لا تخفى على من يكون من اهله (١٥)فاذا صار الى
الشرح والعبارة يخفى ويذهب رَوْنقه (١٦)وإنّما دعانى الى شرحه لأنّى (١٧)وضعته
فى الكتاب والكتاب ربّما ينظر فيه من يفهم ومن لا يفهم (١٨)فيهلك وهو
مثل قول رُوَيْم بن احمد (١٩)بن يزيد البغدادى (١٠)رحمه الله حين سُيل
عن التوحيد فقال محوُ آثار البشرية وتجرّد الالوهية، وإنّما يريد بقوله محو
آثار البشرية ٢٠ تبديل اخلاق النفس لانّها تدّعى الربوبية بنظرها الى

---

(١) وإقامة B.   (٢) الرغبة والرهبة B.   (٣) A شاهد.   (٤) B فنقول.

(٥) تعالى B.   (٦) قضايه وقدره B.   (٧) A لقيام. In B the first letter is
obliterated. Qushayrí (161, 22) has بقيام.   (٨) A فيه corr. by a later hand.

(٩) A ظهورهم من.   (١٠) B om.   (١١) Kor. 7, 171.   (١٢) B adds جنيد.

(١٣) B om. قال الشيخ رحمه الله.   (١٤) B أكثر.   (١٥) B وإذا.   ذريتهم.

(١٦) B om. و.   (١٧) B وصفه.   (١٨) A adds in marg. فيها من لا يفهم.

(١٩) B om. بن يزيد.   (٢٠) A بتبديل.

افعالها كقول العبد أنا (١) وأنا لا يقول الاّ الله اذ الانيّة لله عزّ وجلّ (٢)
فهذا معنى محو (٤)آثار البشرية ومعنى قوله تجرّد الالوهية يعنى إفراد القديم
عن (٤)المُحْدَثات، (٥) وقال آخر التوحيد نسيان ما سوى التوحيد بالتوحيد
يعنى فيا يوجب حكْمُ الحقيقة، وقال الوحدانية بقاءَ الحقّ (٦) بناءَ كلّ ما
دونه يعنى فناءَ يوجب حكْمُ الحقيقة، (٧) وقيل الوحدانية بقاءَ الحقّ وفناءَ كلّ ٥
ما دونه (٨) يعنى فناءَ العبد عن ذكر نفسه وقلبه بدوام ذكر الله (٤)تعالى
وتعظيمه، وقال آخر ليس فى التوحيد (٩) خَلْقٌ وما وحّد الله غيرُالله والتوحيد
للحقّ والخلقُ (١٠) طُفَيْلٌ، (٤)قلنا وبيان ذلك وما اشار اليه هؤلاءِ والله اعلم A f.14b
فى قول الله (١١) تعالى (١٢) شَهِدَ ٱللّٰهُ أَنَّهُ لَا إِلٰهَ إِلَّا هُوَ وَٱلْمَلَائِكَةُ وَأُولُوا ٱلْعِلْمِ
قَائِمًا بِٱلْقِسْطِ لَا إِلٰهَ إِلَّا هُوَ ٱلْعَزِيزُ ٱلْحَكِيمُ فقد شهد لنفسه بالوحدانية قبل ١٠
الخلق فحقيقة التوحيد من حيث الحقّ ما شهد (١٣) الله لنفسه بالوحدانية قبل
الخلق ومن حيث الخلق فقد وحّدوه حقيقة (١٤) ووجدًا على مقدار ما قسم
لهم وأرادهم (١٥) بذلك وهو قوله تعالى وَٱلْمَلَائِكَةُ وَأُولُوا ٱلْعِلْمِ، وإمّا من
طريق الافرار فأهل القِبْلَة (١٦) متساوون فيها والمعوّلُ على ما فى (١٧)القلب
لا على ما فى اللسان، وقد قال الشبلى (٢) رحمه الله ما ثمّ روايجَ التوحيد ١٥
من تصوّر عنه التوحيد وشاهَدَ المعانى (١٨) وأثبت الاسامى وإضاف الصفات
وألزم النعوت ومن اثبت هذا كلّه ونفى (٢) هذا كلّه فهو موحّد حُكْمًا ورسمًا
لا حقيقة وَوَجْدًا، (١٩)قال الشيخ رحمه الله معناه والله اعلم انّه يُثبت الصفات

---

(١) A adds in marg. ‏فنقول انا انا‏. (٢) In A the words ‏وانا لا يقول‏
have been erased and ‏والقول انا لا يستحقّه‏ written in marg. (٣) B om.
(٤) ‏الحدث‏ B. (٥) The passage beginning ‏وقال آخر‏ and ending ‏بدوام ذكر‏
‏الله تعالى وتعظيمه‏ is wanting in the text of A but is suppl. in marg.
(٦) ‏وفيا‏ B. (٧) ‏وقال‏ B (٨) B ‏يعنى عن ذكر العبد وقلبه بدوام الخ‏.
(٩) A in marg. ‏حد‏. (١٠) ‏طفيل‏ B. (١١) ‏عزّ وجلّ‏ B. (١٢) Kor. 3, 16.
(١٣) ‏الله عزّ وجلّ‏ B. (١٤) A ‏وحُدُوا‏. (١٥) ‏بذلك الحقّ‏ B. (١٦) So A, but
‏متفاوتون‏ is written above. (١٧) B ‏القلوب‏. (١٨) Here B proceeds: ‏وألزم‏
‏النعوت ومن اثبت هذا كلّه الخ‏. (١٩) B proceeds: ‏معناه انه يُثبت الخ‏.

والنعوت على رسم مـا رسم له من ذلك ولا يُثبتها من حيث الادراك والاحاطة (۱) والتوهّم، وقال غيره من (۲) العارفين امّا التوحيد (۳) فهو الذى يُعمّى البصير ويحيّر العاقل ويُدهش الثابت، (٤) قلت لانّه من تحقّق بذلك (٥) وجد فى قلبه من عظمة الله (٦) تعالى وهيبته ما يُدهشه ويحيّر عقله الّا من يُثبته الله (٧) تعالى، وقال ابو سعيد احمد بن عيسى الخرّاز (٧) رحمه الله اوّل مقام لمن وَجَدَ علم التوحيد وتحقّق بذلك فناَء ذكر (٧) الاشياَء عن قلبه وانفراده بالله عزّ وجلّ، وقال ايضًا اوّل علامـة التوحيد خروج العبد عن كلّ شىء وردُّ جميع الاشياَء الى متولّيها حتى يكون المتولّى بالمتولّى ناظرًا الى الاشياَء قائمًا (٧) بها متمكّنًا فيها ثم يُخفيهم فى انفسهم من انفسهم ويُميت انفسهم فى انفسهم ويصطنعهم لنفسه فهذا اوّل دخول فى التوحيد

Af.15a من حيث ظهور التوحيد بالديمومية، (٦) قال وبيان ذلك (٧) والله اعلم فناَء ذكر الاشياَء عن قلبه وأن يغلب على قلبه ذكر الله (٧) تعالى فيذهب عن قلبه ذكر الاشياَء بذكر الله (٨) تعالى، ومعنى خروجه (٩) عن كلّ شىء يعنى لا يضيف الى نفسه واستطاعته شيئًا ويرى قوام الاشياَء بالله فى الحقيقة (۱۰) لا بهم، ومعنى قوله حتى يكون المتولّى بالمتولّى ناظرًا الى الاشياَء قائمًا (٦) بها يشير الى تولية الحقّ (٦) له وما يستولى عليه من حقايق التوحيد حتى يرى قوام الاشياَء بالله (۱۱) عزّ وجلّ لا بذواتها الّا ترى الى قول القايل ،

وفى كُلِّ شَىْءٍ لَهُ (۱۲) شَاهِدٌ * (۱۳) يَدُلُّ عَلَى أنّـهُ وَاحِدُ

وامّا قوله متمكّنًا فيها يريد بذلك انّ (۱٤) التلوين لا يجرى عليه فى نظره الى الاشياَء فانّ قوامها بالله عزّ وجلّ، ثم قال يُخفيهم فى انفسهم (۱٥) من

---

(۱) والتفهم B. (۲) A العراقيين but corr. in marg. (۳) B وهو. (٤) B.

ووجد A (٥). معناه لان من تحقق (٦) B om. (٧) B الاشيا ايضا.

(۸) B om. A adds in marg. فيفنيه. (۹) B من and so A in marg.

(۱۰) A om. these words but they are suppl. in marg. (۱۱) B تعالى.

(۱۲) A آية but corr. in marg. (۱۳) B دليل. (۱٤) B التكوين.

(۱٥) A om. من انفسهم.

3

انفسهم ويُبِيت انفسهم فى انفسهم يعنى لا يحسّون حسًّا ولا يلاحظون حركةً
من حركاتهم الظاهرة والباطنة يُوَى اليها فى الحقيقة الّا وهى منطمسة تحت
سلطان القدرة وإنفاذ المشيّة وإن اضيفت الى المضاف اليه، وقال الشبلى
(١) رحمه الله لرجل لا تدرى لِمَ لا يصحّ لك (٢) التوحيد قال لا قال لأنّك
٥ تطلبه بايّاك، وقال ايضًا لا يصحّ التوحيد الّا لمن كان جَحْدُهُ إثباتَهُ،
فسُيل عن الاثبات فقال إسقاط الياءات، معناه (١) والله اعلم انّ (٣) الموحّد
فى الحقيقة يجحد اثباته ايّاه يعنى اثبات نفسه فى جميع الاشياء بسرّه كقوله
بى ولى ومنّى (١) وإليّ وعليّ وبيّ وعنّى فيُسقط هذه الياءات ويجحدها بسرّه
وإن كانت جاريةً من حيث الرسم على لسانه، وقال الشبلى (١) رحمه الله
١٠ لرجل ايضًا (٤) تُوَحِّدُ توحيدَ البشرية او توحيد الالهية فقال بينهما فرق
فقال نَعَمْ توحيد البشرية خوف العقوبات وتوحيد (٥) الالوهية توحيد
التعظيم، (٦) قال الشيخ رحمه الله قلتُ انّ معناه انّ من صفة البشرية طلب
العوض ورؤية (٨) الفعل والطمع فى غير الله (١) عزّ وجلّ وليس من وحّد A f.156
الله (١) تعالى اجلالاً له كمن (٩) وحّه خوفًا من عقوبته وإن كان الخوف
١٥ من (١٠) عذاب الله (١) عزّ وجلّ (١١) حالةً شريفةً، وقال الشبلى (١) رحمه
الله من اطّلع على ذرّة من علم التوحيد (١٢) ضعف عن حمْل (١٣) بقّة لِثِقَل
ما حمل، وقال مرّةً أُخْرَى من اطّلع على ذرّة من علم التوحيد حمل
السموات والارض على شعرة من جفن عينَيْه، (١٤) قال معناه والله اعلم انّ
السموات والارض وجميع ما خلق الله (١٥) عزّ وجلّ يتصاغر فى عينه
٢٠ عند ما يشاهد بقلبه بأنوار التوحيد من عظمة الله (١٥) عزّ وجلّ، وقد
رُوى انّ لجبريل عليه السلم سِتّمِاية جناح (١٦) جناحان منها اذا نشرها غطّى

---

(١) B om.   (٢) B توحيد.   (٣) B التوحيد.   (٤) B توحيدك توحيد البشرية.
(٥) B الالهية.   (٦) B proceeds: الخ.   (٧) B الغرض.   ومعناه ان من صفة الخ.
(٨) B القصد.   (٩) B وحد اله.   (١٠) B عقوبة.   (١١) A om. but حال.
(١٢) B وقه.   (١٣) B app. منعت (تعب؟).   (١٤) B
written above.   (١٥) B تعالى.   (١٦) AB جناحين.
ومعناه.   (١٥) B

بهما المشرق والمغرب، وقد رُوى ايضًا فى الحديث عن (١)ابن عبّاس
(٢)رضى الله عنه انّ صورة جبريل (٢)عليه السلِم فى قايمة الكُرْسى مثل الزَّرَدة
فى الجوشن، ويقال انّ جبريلاً (٢)عليه السلم والعرش والكُرْسى كلَّ هذا
(٢)مع الملكوت الذى ظهر لأهل العلم بالله عزّ وجلّ (٣)فانّما هى كرَمْلة فيا
ه وراَء الملكوت (٤)بل اقلّ من ذلك، وقال ابو العبّاس (٢)احمد بن عطآء
(٢)البغدادى (٢)رحمه الله فى بعض كلامه (٥)علامة حقيقة التوحيد نسيان
التوحيد وصِدْقُ التوحيد أن يكون القايم (٦)به واحدًا، يريد بذلك ان
ينسى العبد روًية توحيده فى توحيده بروًية قيام الله (٢)عزّ وجلّ له بذلك
قبل خَلْقه لانّه لو لم يُرِدْهم بذلك ما ارادوه ولا وحّدوه، ولمشايخنا
١٠ فى التوحيد مصنّفات وقد قصدنا الى القليل (٢)المشكل من الفاظهم
(٧)ليستدرك (٨)به ما لم اذكره ان شآء الله،

باب ما قالوا فى المعرفة وصفة العارف وحقيقة ذلك (٩)ببيانها،

سُيل ابو (١٠)سعيد الخُرّاز (٢)رحمه الله عن المعرفة فقال المعرفة تأتى
(١١)من وجهيْن من عين الجود وبذل المجهود، وسُيل ابو تُراب النّخشبى
١٥ (٢)رحمه الله عن صفة العارف فقال هو الذى لا (١٢)يكدّره شىء ويصفو
به كلّ شىء، وقال (٢)احمد بن عطآء (٢)رحمه الله المعرفة معرفتان معرفة A f. 16a
حقّ ومعرفة حقيقة فمعرفة الحقّ (١٣)معرفة وحدانيته على ما ابرز للخلق من
الاساى والصفات ومعرفة الحقيقة (١٤)على أن لا سبيل اليها لامتناع الصمديّة

---

(١) B بن.   (٢) B om.   (٣) B ايضا.   (٤) B او.   (٥) A om.
but suppl. above.   (٦) B له.   (٧) A يستدلّ corr. to ليستدركوا.
(٨) A بذلك, after which على has been supplied by a later hand.
(٩) B وبيانها,   (١٠) B عبد الله.   (١١) B om. من وجهين.   (١٢) B يدرك.
(١٣) A om. from here to وتحقيق الربوبية but the passage in supplied in marg.
in two slightly different versions.   (١٤) B لان لا سبيل الخ.

وتحقيق الربوبيّة لقوله [١] عزّ وجلّ [٢] وَلاَ يُحِيطُونَ بِهِ عِلْمًا، [٢] قال ابو
نصر رحمه الله معنى قوله لا سبيل اليها يعنى الى المعرفة على الحقيقة لانّ
الله [٤] تعالى ابرز لخلقه [٥] من اسمآيه وصفاته ما علم انّهم [٦] يطيقونه ذلك
لانّ حقيقة معرفته لا [٧] يطيقها الخلق ولا ذرّة [٨] منها لانّ الكون [٩] بما
٥ فيها يتلاشى عند ذرّة من اوّل [١٠] بادٍ يبدو من بوادى سطوات عظمته
فمن يطيق معرفة من يكون هذا صفة من صفاته، فلذلك قال القايل ما
عَرَفَهُ غيرُهُ ولا [١١] احبّه سواه لانّ الصديّة ممتنعة عن الاحاطة والادراك
قال الله [١٢] عزّ وجلّ [١٢] وَلاَ يُحِيطُونَ [١٤] بِشَىْءٍ مِنْ عِلْمِهِ، وقد حُكى
[١٥] فى هذا المعنى عن ابى بكر الصدّيق رضى الله عنه انّه قال سبحان من
١٠ لم يجعل للخلق طريقًا الى معرفته الّا بالعجز عن معرفته، وسُيل الشِّبْلى متى
يكون العارف بمَشْهَد من الحقّ قال اذا بدا الشاهد وفنى الشواهد وذهب
الحواسّ واضمحلّ الإحساس، وسُيل ايضًا ما بدْءُ هذا الشأن وما انتهآؤه
قال بدوه معرفته وانتهآؤه توحيد، وقال من علامة المعرفة ان يرى نفسه
فى قبضة العزّة [١٦] ويجرى عليه نصاريف القدرة ومن علامة المعرفة المحبّة
١٥ [١٧] لانّه من عرفه احبّه، وبلغنى عن ابى يزيد [١٨] طَيْفور بن عيسى
البسطامى [١] رحمه الله انّه سُيل عن صفة العارف فقال لون المآء [١٩] لون
انآيه ان صببتَه فى انآء ابيض خلتُه ابيض وان صببته فى انآء اسود خلته
اسود وكذلك [٢٠] الاصفر والاحمر وغير ذلك يتداوله الاحوال وولّى الاحوال
وليّه، [٢١] قال الشيخ رحمه الله معناه [١] والله اعلم ان المآء على قدر ضفآيه

---

(١) B om.　　(٢) Kor. 20, 109.　　(٢) B om. ‏قال ابو نصر رحمه الله‎.

(٤) B ‏عز وجل‎.　　(٥) B ‏من صفاته واسمايه‎.　　(٦) A ‏يطيقون‎　　(٧) B

‏اجله‎.　　(٨) B ‏من ذلك‎.　　(٩) B ‏فما‎.　　(١٠) AB ‏بادى‎　　(١١) B ‏يطيق‎.

(١٢) B ‏جل ذكره‎.　　(١٤) Kor. 2, 256.　　(١٤) Instead of ‏بشىء من علمه‎ B

has ‏به علمًا‎.　　(١٥) B om. ‏فى هذا المعنى‎.　　(١٦) B ‏يجرى‎.　　(١٧) B ‏لان‎.

(١٨) B ‏واسمه طيفور‎.　　(١٩) B ‏فى انايه‎.　　(٢٠) A ‏سابر الالوان‎ but ‏الاصفر‎

‏والاحمر‎ in marg.　　(٢١) B om. ‏قال الشيخ رحمه الله‎.

(١) بصفة لون اناَّيه ولا يغيّره لون (٢) اناَّيه عن (٣) صفاَيه وحاله ويخال الناظر اليه ابيض (٤) او اسود وهو فى الاناَّء بمعنًى واحد وكذلك العارف وصفته مع الله (٥) عزّ وجلّ فيا يتداوله (٦) الاحوال يكون سرّه مع الله (٧) تعالى بمعنًى واحد، وسُئل الجُنَيْد (٥) رحمه الله عن معقول العارفين (٨) فقال ذهبوا عن وصف الواصفين، وسُئل بعضهم عن المعرفة فقــال مطالعة القلوب لافراده على لطايف تعريفه، وسُئل الجنيد رحمه الله فقيل له يأبا القسم ما حاجة العارفين (٩) [الى الله تعالى] قال حاجتهم اليه كلايته ورعايته لهم، وقال محمّد بن الفضل السمرقندى رحمه الله بل لا حاجة لهم ولا اختيار اذ بغير الحاجة والاختيار نالوا ما نالوا لانّ قيام العارفين بواجدهم و بقاؤهم بواجدهم وفناؤهم بواجدهم، وقيل لمحمّد بن الفضل رحمه الله حاجة العارفين الى ما ذى قال حاجتهم الى الخصلة التى كملت بهــا المحاسن كلّها وبفقدها قبحت (١٠) المقابح كلّها (١١) وهى الاستقامة، وسُئل يحيى بن مُعاذ رحمه الله عن صفة العارف فقال داخلٌ معهم باينٌ منهم، وسُئل مرّةً اخرى عن العارف فقال عبدٌ كان فبان، وقيل لابى الحسين النورى رحمه الله كيف لا تدركه العقول ولا يُعرف الّا بالعقول فقال كيف يدرك ذو أمَدٍ من لا أمَدَ له (١٢) ام كيف يدرك ذو عاهة من لا عاهة له ولا آفة له ام كيف يكون مكيّفًا من كيّف الكيّف ام كيف يكون محيّثًا من حيّث الحيّث فسمّاه حيثًا وكذلك أوّلَ الاوّل وأخّرَ الآخر فسمّاه اوّلاً وآخراً فلولا انّـه أوّلَ الاوّل وأخّرَ الآخر ما عُرف ما الاوّلية وما الآخرية، ثم قال وما الازلية فى الحقيقة الّا الابدية ليس بينهما حاجزٌ كما ان الاوّلية هى الآخرية والآخرية هى الاوّلية وكذلك الظاهرية والباطنية الّا انّه يُفقدك وقتًا ويُشهدك وقتًا لتجديد اللذّة

---

(١) B نصى.   (٢) B انا.   (٣) B صفاته.   (٤) B و.   (٥) B om.

(٦) من suppl. in marg. A before الاحوال. B وتعالى تبارك.   (٧) B تعالى.

(٨) Here B has a lacuna extending to كالادنى وإنما يقع عنده والاقصى (p. ٣٨, l. ٦).

(٩) Suppl. above.   (١٠) A المفاتح.   (١١) A وهى A.   (١٢) Suppl. in marg.

ورؤية العبودية لانّ من عرفه بالخلقة لم يعرفه بالمباشرة لانّ الخلقة على
معنى قوله كُنْ والمباشرة اظهار حُرْمة لا استهانة فيه، قلتُ معنى قوله مباشرة
يعنى مباشرة يقين ومشاهدة القلب بحقايق الايمان بالغيب، قال الشيخ رحمه Af.17a
الله والمعنى فيا اشار اليه والله اعلم انّ التوقيت والتغيير لا يجوز على الله
٥ تعالى فهو فيا كان فهو فيا يكون وهو فيا قال كهو فيا يقول والادنى عنه
كالاقصى والاقصى عنـه كالادنى وانّما يقع (١) التعارف للخلق من حيث
الخلق (٢) والتلوين فى القرب والبعد والسخط والرضا صفة للخلق وليس (٣) ذلك
من صفات الحقّ (٤) والله اعلم، وقال احمد بن عطاءً (٤) رحمه الله فى كلام
له فى معنى المعرفــة (٤) ايضًا عن ابى بكر الواسطى (٥) رحمه الله
١٠ والصحيح لابن عطاءً (٤) رحمه الله (٦) قال انّما قبحت المستقبحات (٧) باستتاره
وحسنت المستحسنات بتجلّيه (٨) فانّهما نعتان يجريان على (٩) الابد بما جرىا
فى الازل يُظهر الوسميَّن على المقبولين والمطرودين فقد بان شواهـد تجلّيه
على المقبولين (١٠) بضياًيها كما بان شواهد استتاره على المطرودين (١١) بظلمنها
فا ينفع بعد ذلك الالوان المصفرّة ولا (١٢) الأكام المقصّرة ولا (١٣) التدرّع
١٥ بالمطلقة والمرقّعة، (٤) قلتُ وهذا الذى قال ابن عطاءً (٤) رحمه الله معناه
(١٤) قريب من قول ابى سليمٰن عبد الرحمن بن احمد الدارانى (٤) رحمه الله
حيث يقول ليس اعمال الخلق بالذى يُسخطه ولا بالذى يُرضيه انّما رضى
عن قوم فاستعملهم بعل اهل الرضا وسخط على قوم فاستعملهم بعل اهل
السخط، ومعنى قول ابن عطاءً (٤) رحمه الله قبحت المستقبحات باستتاره
٢٠ يعنى (١٥) بإعراضه عنها (١٦) وحسنت المستحسنات بتجلّيه يعنى بإقباله عليها

(١) A in marg. (٢) B التكوين. (٣) A كذلك. (٤) B om.
(٥) B has أيضا instead of رحمه الله. (٦) B om. قال اغا. (٧) B استتار.
(٨) B وإنّا ها. (٩) B om. from الابد to الوسمين على. (١٠) B بصياها.
(١١) B om. A الدروع المطلقه. (١٢) B الأكهام المقصر. (١٣) B بظلمها.
(١٤) B قريبًا. (١٥) B اعراضه. (١٦) B om. from وحسنت to بإقباله عليها.

وقبوله لها ومعنى ذلك [١] كما جاء [٢] فى [٣] الحديث [٤] خرج رسول الله صلعم
وبيده كتابان كتاب بيمينه وكتاب بشماله فقال هذا كتاب اهل الجنّة
بأسمائهم واسماء آبائهم وهذا كتاب اهل النار بأسمائهم واسماء آبائهم
الحديث، وقال ابو بكر الواسطى [٤] رحمه الله لمّا تعرّف بنفسه الى خاصّته
امتحقت نفوسهم عن نفوسهم فلم يشهدوا وحشةً بشواهد الاوّل ممّا يبدو لهم
من شواهد الحظوظ وكذلك كلّ من أُعقِبَ بمعنًى، [٤] وهذا معناه [٤] والله
اعلم انّ من شاهد الاوّلية فيما عرف [٥] بما تعرّف اليه معبودُهُ لم يشهد
وحشةً مع معرفته بذلك فيما سواه ولا أُنسًا بهم،

Af.17b

باب فى صفة العارف وما [٦] قالوا فيه،

قال يحيى بن مُعاذ الرازى [٤] رحمه الله ما دام العبد يتعرّف فيقال لا
تَخْتَرْ شيئًا ولا تكن مع اختيارك حتى تَعْرِفَ فاذا عرف وصار عارفًا فيقال
له إن شئتَ اختر وان شئتَ لا تختر [٧] لانّك ان اختَرتَ فبأختيارنا اختَرتَ
وان تركتَ الاختيار فبأختيارنا تركتَ الاختيار فانّك بنا فى الاختيار وفى
ترك الاختيار، وقال يحيى [٨] بن معاذ رحمه الله الدنيا عروس ومن يطلبها
ماشطتها والزاهد فيها يسخّم وجهها وينتف شَعرها ويخرق ثوبها والعارف بالله
مشتغل بسيّه لا يلتفت اليها، وقال اذا ترك العارف ادبه عند [٩] معرفته
فقد هلك مع الهالكين، وقال [١٠] ذو النون [٤] رحمه الله علامة العارف ثلثة
لا [١١] يُطفئ نورُ معرفته نورَ ورعه ولا يعتقد باطنًا من العلم [٤] ما ينقض عليه
ظاهرًا من الحُكْم ولا يحمله كثرة نِعَم الله [٤] تعالى عليه وكرامته على هتك

١٠

١٥

(١) B om. كما جاء. (٢) B فى. (٣) الحديث رسول الله صلى الله عليه وسلم B. (٤) B om.

لما خرج وفى يده اليمنى كتاب وفى يده اليسرى كتاب فقال الخ. (٥) B لما.

بن معاذ. (٦) قالوه فى ذلك B. (٧) فانك B. (٨) B om. بن معاذ. (٥) B لما.

يطف. (١١) B يطف. (١٠) ذا B. (٩) معروفه B. رحمه الله

(١) أستار محارم الله (٢) تعالى، وقال بعضهم ليس بعارف من وصف المعرفة
عند ابناء الآخرة فكيف عند ابناء الدنيا، وقال إن النَّفثَ العارف الى
الخلق عن معروفه بغير إذنـه فهو مخذول بين خلقه، وقال كيف تعرفه
وليس فى قلبك سلطان هيبته وكيف تذكره وتحبّه وليس فى قلبك وجود
٥ ألطافه وأنت غافل عمّا ذكرك به قبل خلقه، سمعت محمّد بن احمد بن
حمدون (٢) النَّرَّاء يقول سمعت عبد الرحمن (٢) الفارسى وقد سُيِّل عن (٢) كمال
المعرفة فقال اذا اجتمعت المتفرّقات واستوت الاحوال والاماكن
وسقطت رؤية التمييز، (٥) وقال ابو نصر رحمه الله معنى ذلك ان يكون
وقت العبد وقتًا واحدًا بلا (٢) تغيير ويكون العبد فى جميع احواله بالله ٨ f.18a
١٠ ولله (٢) مأخوذًا عمّا سوى الله فعند ذلك يكون هذا (٢) حاله،

باب فى قول القائل بِمَ عرفتَ الله والفرق بين
(٨) المؤمن والعارف،

قيل لأبى الحسين النورى (٢) رحمه الله بِمَ عرفتَ الله (٢) تعالى (٩) فقال
بالله قيل فما بالُ العقل قال العقل عاجزٌ لا يدلّ الاّ على عاجز مثله لمّا
١٥ خلق الله العقل قال (٢) له من انا فسكت فكحله بنور الوحدانية فقال انت
الله فلم يكن للعقل أن يعرف الله الاّ بالله، وسُيِّل عن اوّل فرض افترض
الله (٢) تعالى على عباده ما هو (٩) فقال المعرفة لقوله (٢) تعالى (١٠) وَمَا خَلَقْتُ
الجِنَّ وَالإنْسَ إِلاّ لِيَعْبُدُونِ (٩) وقال (١١) ابن عبّاس (٢) رضى الله عنه
لِيَعْرِفُونِ، وسُيِّل بعضهم ما المعرفة (٩) فقال تحقيق (١٢) القلب بإثبات وحدانيته
٢٠ بكمال صفاته واسمآيه (١٢) فانّه المتنزّد بالعزّ والقدرة والسلطان والعظمة الحىّ

---

(١) A استنار.   (٢) B om.   (٢) B الفارسى يقول.   (٤) B وسقط.

(٥) B om. وقال ابو نصر رحمه الله.   (٢) B وماخوذ.   (٢) B حاله والله اعلم.

(٨) A المؤقن but corr. in marg.   (٩) B قال.   (١٠) Kor. 51, 56.   (١١) B بن.

(١٢) B للقلب.   (١٢) B والله.

الدايم الذى ليس كمثله شىء وهو السميع البصير بلا كيف ولا شبه ولا مثل
ينفى الاضداد والانداد والاسباب عن القلوب ، وقد قيل ايضًا ان اصل
المعرفة (١)موهبة والمعرفة نار والايمان نور والمعرفة وجدّ والايمان عطاءٌ،
والفرق بين المؤمن والعارف المؤمن ينظر بنور الله والعارف ينظر بالله

٥ (٢)عزّ وجلّ وللمؤمن قلب وليس للعارف قلب وقلب المؤمن مطمئنّ بالذكر
ولا يطمئنّ العارف بسواه ، والمعرفة على ثلثة اوجه معرفة إقرار ومعرفة
(٣)حقيقة ومعرفة (٤)مشاهدة وفى معرفة المشاهدة (٥)يندرج الفهم والعلم والعبارة
والكلام، والاشارات فى المعرفة (٦)ووصفها كثير وفى القليل (٧)كفاية وغُنْية
للمستدلّ والمسترشد وبالله التوفيق ، وعن (٨)الحسن بن على (٢)بن (٩)حيويه

١٠ (١٠)الدامغانى قال سُئل ابو بكر (١١)الزاهرابادى عن المعرفة فقال المعرفة اسم
Δ f.186 ومعناه (١٢)وجود تعظيم فى القلب يمنعك عن (١٣)التشبيه والتعطيل ،

كتاب الاحوال والمقامات ،

(٢)باب فى المقامات وحقايقها،

(١٤)قال الشيخ رحمه الله فان قيل ما معنى المقامات يقال (١٥)معناه مقام
١٥ العبد بين يدى الله (١٦)عزّ وجلّ فيما يقام فيه من العبادات والمجاهدات
والرياضات والانقطاع الى الله عزّ وجلّ، وقال الله (١٧)تعالى (١٨)ذَٰلِكَ لِمَنْ

---

(١) B يندرج فيها.   (٢) B om.   (٣) B الحقيقة.   (٤) B المشاهدة.   (٥) B وهبه (١)
.ووضعها Δ (٧) B غنية وكفاية.   (٨) Qushayrí, 4, 25, has الحسين.   (٩) Δ حيويه,
B حموه (١٠) B adds أنه رحمه أنه.   (١١) Δ الزاهد with الايادى suppl. in marg. B
الرودبارى. Qushayrí (4, 25) الزاهر أيادى and in marg. الزاهر ابادى, but the edition
containing the commentary of Zakariyyá Ansárí (Cairo, 1290 A. H.), I, 45, 11
marg. has الزامرابادى.   (١٢) ثبوت suppl. in A before وجود.   (١٣) B التعطيل
.معنى B (١٥)   .قال الشيخ رحمه الله B om.   والتشبيه ان شاء الله (١٤)
(١٦) B تبارك وتعالى.   (١٧) B تبرك وتعالى.   (١٨) Kor. 14, 17.

خَافَ مَقَامِى [١]وَخَافَ وَعِيدِ، وقال [٢]وَمَا مِنَّا إِلَّا لَهُ مَقَامٌ مَعْلُومٌ، [٣]وقال
سُئِل ابو بكر الواسطى [٤]رحمه الله عن قول النبى صلعم الارواح جنود
مجنّدة قال مجنّدة على قدر [٤]المقامات والمقامات مثل التوبة والورع والزهد
والفقر والصبر والرضا والتوكّل وغير ذلك،

[٥]باب فى معنى الاحوال،

قال الشيخ رحمه الله وامّا معنى الاحوال فهو ما يحلّ بالقلوب او تحلّ
به القلوب من صفاء [٦]الاذكار، وقد حُكى عن الجُنَيْد [٣]رحمه الله انه قال
[٣]الحال نازلة تنزل بالقلوب فلا [٧]تدوم، وقد قيل ايضًا انّ الحال هو
الذكر الخفىّ، وقد رُوى عن النبى صلعم [٨]انّه قال خيرُ الذكرِ الخفىُّ، وليس
الحال من طريق المجاهدات والعبادات والرياضات كالمقامات التى ذكرناها
وهى مثل المراقبة والقرب والمحبّة والخوف والرجاء والشوق والأنس والاطمأنينة
والمشاهدة واليقين وغير ذلك، وقد حُكى عن ابى سليمن الدارانى [٣]رحمه
الله انّه قال اذا صارت المعاملة الى القلوب استراحت الجوارح، وهذا الذى
قال ابو سليمن [٩]يحتمل معنيين احدها انّه اراد بذلك استراحت الجوارح
من المجاهدات والمكابدات من الاعمال اذا اشتغل بحفظ قلبه ومراعاة سره
من الخواطر المشغّلة والعوارض المذمومة التى تشغل قلبه عن ذكر الله A f.19a
تعالى ويحتمل ايضًا انّه اراد بذلك ان يتمكّن من المجاهدة والاعمال
[١٠]والعبادات وتصير وَطَنَهُ حتى يستلذّها بقلبه ويجد حلاوتها ويسقط

(١) B om. وخاف وعيد وقال.   (٢) Kor. 37, 164.   (٣) B om.   (٤) A adds
in marg. والفرق بين المقام والحال ان الحال ينزل بالقلوب فلا يدوم والمقام مقام الرجل.
وباطنه في حقائق الطاعات   (٥) B om. this heading and proceeds
ظاهره   (٦) الاذكار B.   (٧) A تدمع but corr. in marg.   وأما معنى الاحوال الخ
يحمل على معنيين   (٩) يحتمل معاني احدها A, but in marg.   انه قال.   (٨) B om.
احدها   (١٠) B والعبادة.

عنه النعب ووجود الالم الذى كان يجد ذلك قبل كما قال بعضهم [١] وأَظنّه
محمّد بن واسع [٢] رحمه الله [٢] قال كابدتُ الليلَ عشرين سنة [٣] فتنعَّمتُ
[٤] به عشرين سنة، وقال آخر وأَظنّه مُلك بن دينار [٢] رحمه الله مضغتُ
القرآن عشرين سنة ثم تنعَّمت [٥] بتلاوته عشرين سنة، وقال الجُنَيّد [٢] رحمه
٥ الله لا يُوصَل الى رعاية الحقوق الّا بحراسة القلوب ومن لم يكن له سِرٌّ فهو
مُصِرّ والمُصِرّ لا تصفو له حسنة، وأجوبة الشيوخ فى المقامات تكثر وكذلك
فى الاحوال وقد ذكرته على الاختصار [٢] والله الموفّق،

باب مقام التوبة،

قال ابو يعقوب يوسف بن [٦] حمدان السوسى رحمه الله اوّل مقام من
١٠ مقامات المنقطعين الى الله [٧] تعالى التوبة، وسُئل السوسى عن التوبة فقال
التوبة الرجوع من كلّ [٢] شىء ذمّه العلم الى ما مدحه العلم، وسُئل سهل
ابن عبد الله عن التوبة فقال أن لا تنسى ذنبك، وسُئل [٨] الجُنَيّد [٢] رحمه
الله عن التوبة [٩] فقال هى نسيان ذنبك، قال الشيخ رحمه الله فالذى اجاب
السوسى رحمه الله عن التوبة اجاب عن توبة المريدين [١٠] والمتعرّضين والطالبين
١٥ والقاصدين وهم الذين نارة لهم ونارة عليهم، والذى قال سهل [١١] بن عبد
الله ايضًا [١٢] فكذلك، وإمّا ما اجاب الجنيد [٢] رحمه الله عن التوبة ان
ينسى ذنبه اجاب عن توبة المحقّقين لا يذكرون ذنوبهم [١٣] لِما غلب على
قلوبهم من عظمة الله [٢] تعالى ودوام ذكره، وهو مثل ما سُئل رُوَيْم [١٤] بن
احمد رحمه الله عن التوبة فقال التوبة من التوبة، وكذلك سُئل [١٥] ذو

---

[١] أظنّه B.   [٢] B om.   [٣] تنعّمت B.   [٤] B بها.   [٥] بتلاوتها.

[٦] احمد B.   [٧] تبارك وتعالى B.   [٨] جنيد B.   [٩] B om. from

فقال   [١٠] والمعترّضين B.   [١١] B om. بن عبد الله.   [١٢] A كذلك

.عن التوبة to corr. by later hand.   [١٣] B لما.   [١٤] B om. بن

احمد رحمه الله.   [١٥] A ذا.

A f. 19b النون (١) رحمه الله عن التوبة فقال توبة العوامّ من الذنوب وتوبة (٢) الخواص
من الغفلة، (٣) فامّا لسان اهل المعرفة والواجدين وخصوص الخصوص فى
معنى التوبة فهو ما قاله (٤) ابو الحسين النورى (١) رحمه الله (٥) حين سُئل عن
التوبة (٦) فقال التوبة ان تتوب (٧) من كلّ شىء سوى الله (١) تعالى، وإلى
هذا اشار الذى اشار بقوله ذنوب المقرّبين حسنات الأبرار وهو (٨) ذو
(٩) النون والذى قال ايضًا ريآء العارفين إخلاص المُريدين لانّ الذى
كان يتقرّب به العارف الى الله (١) عزّ وجلّ فى وقت قصده وابتدآيه وتعرّضه
من القُربات والطاعات فلمّا تمكّن وتحقّق بذلك وشملته انوار الهداية وأتته
العناية وحوَّته الرعاية وشاهد ما شاهد بقلبه من عظمة سيّد والتفكّر فى صنع
صانعه وقديم إحسانه تاب عن الملاحظة والسكون والالتفات الى ما كان
من طاعاته وأعماله وقُرباته فى حين ارادته وبداياته فشتّان بين تايب وتايب
(١٠) فتايبٌ يتوب من (١١) الذنوب والسيّئات (١٠) وتايبٌ يتوب من الزلَل
والغفلات وتايبٌ يتوب من رؤية الحسنات والطاعات، والتوبة تقتضى الورع،

باب مقام الورع،

(١٢) قال الشيخ رحمه الله ومقام الورع مقام شريف، قال النبى صلعم
ملاكُ دينكم الورع، وأهل الورع على ثلث طبقات فمنهم من تورّع عن
الشبهات (١٣) التى اشتبهت عليه (١٤) وهى ما بين (١٥) الحرام البيّن والحلال
البيّن، وما لا يقع عليه اسم حلال مطلق ولا اسم حرام مطلق فيكون بين
ذلك فيتورّع (١٦) عنها، وهو كما قال (١٧) ابن سيرين (١) رحمه الله ليس شىء

---

(١) B om.   (٢) الخاص A.   (٣) وإما B.   (٤) B om. ابو الحسين.

(٥) حيث B.   (٦) فقال التوبة B om.   (٧) عن A.   (٨) ذا AB.

(٩) B adds المصرى.   (١٠) وتايبٌ B.   (١١) الذنب B.   (١٢) B om.

(١٣) B الحلال.   (١٤) وهو B.   (١٤) الذى اشتبه B.   (١٥) قال الشيخ رحمه الله B.

(١٦) عنها B.   (١٧) بن B.   والحرام البين.

اَهوَنُ علىَّ من الورع اذا راٰبنى شىء، تَركتُهُ، ومنهم من يتورّع عمّا [١] يقف
عنه قلبه ويجيك فى صدره عند تناولها وهذا لا يعرفه الّا اربابُ القلوب
[٢] والمتحقّقون وهو كما رُوى عن النبى صلعم انّه قال الإثم ما حاك فى صدرك،
وقال ابو سعيد الخرّاز [٣] رحمه الله الورع ان [٤] تبرّأ من مظالم الخلق من A f. 20a
مثاقيل الذرّ حتى لا يكون [٥] لأحدهم قِبَلَك مظلمة ولا دعوًى ولا طِلْبة،
[٦] وكما حُكى عن [٧] الحارث المحاسبى [٢] رحمه الله انّه كان لا يمدّ يه الى طعام
فيه شبهة، وقال جعفر الخُلْدى [٢] رحمه الله كان على طرف اصبعه [٨] الوُسْطَى
عِرْقٌ اذا مدّ يه الى طعام فيه شبهة ضرب عليه ذلك العِرقُ، وكما حُكى
عن بِشْر الحافى [٢] رحمه الله انّه [٨] حُمِل الى دعوة فوُضِع بين يديه طعام
فجَهد أن يمدّ يه اليه [٩] فلم تمتدّ ثم جهد فلم تمتدّ ثلث مرّات فقال رجل
ممّن كان يعرفه انّ يه لا تمتدّ الى طعام حرام او فيه شبهة [١٠] ما كان أغْنَى
صاحب هذه الدعوة أن يدعو هذا الرجل الى بيته، وتقوى هذا حكايةُ سهل
ابن عبد الله [١١] سمعتُ احمد بن محمّد بن سالم بالبصرة يقول سُيل سهل
ابن عبد الله عن الحلال فقال الحلال الذى لا يُعْصَى الله فيه، [١٢] قال
ابو نصر رحمه الله والذى لا يعصى الله فيه لا يتهيّاً لأحد الوقوف عليه
الّا باشارة القلب، فان [١٣] قال قايلٌ هل تَجِدُ لذلك اصلاً يَتعلّق به من
العلم [١٤] فيقال نَعَمْ قول النبى صلعم لوابصة اَسْتَفْتِ قَلْبَكَ وان أَفْتاك المُفْتون
والذى قال ايضًا الاثم ما حاك فى صدرك، اَلا ترى انّه قد ردّه الى مــا
يشير به عليه قلبه، وامّا الطبقة الثالثة فى الورع فهم العارفون والواجدون
وهو كما قال ابو سليمن الدارانى [٢] رحمه الله كلّ ما شغلك عن الله فهو
مشئوم [٢] عليك، وكما قال سهل بن عبد الله حين سُيل عن الحلال الصافى

فقال الحلال الذى لا يُعْصَى الله فيه والحلال الصافى الذى لا يُنْسَى الله
فيه، (١)فالورع فيا لا ينسى الله فيه هو الورع الذى سُئِل عنه الشِّبْلى (٢)رحمه
الله فقيل له (٣)يأبا بكر ما الورع فقال ان تتورَّع ان لا يتشتَّت قلبك عن
الله (٢)عزّ وجلّ طرفةَ عين، فالاوّل ورع العموم والثانى ورع الخصوص
والثالث ورع خصوص الخصوص، والورع يقتضى الزهد،

باب مقام الزهد، A. f. 20b

(٤)قال الشيخ رحمه الله والزهد مقام شريف وهو اساس الاحوال (٥)الرضيّة
والمراتب السنيّة وهو اوّل قدم القاصدين الى الله عزّ وجلّ والمنقطعين الى
الله والراضين عن الله والمتوكّلين على الله تعالى فمن لم يُحْكِم اساسه فى الزهد
لم يصحّ له شىء ممّا بعده لانّ حُبّ الدنيا رأس كلّ خطيّة والزهد فى الدنيا
رأس كلّ خير وطاعة ويقال انّ من (٦)سُمِّىَ (٧)باسم (٨)الزهد فى الدنيا
فقد سُمِّى بألف اسم (٩)محمود ومن سُمِّى باسم الرغبة فى الدنيا فقد سُمِّى
بألف اسم (١٠)مذموم، وهو ما اختار رسول الله صلعم لنفسه (١١)باختيار الله
له، والزهد فى الحلال الموجود وامّا الحرام والشبهة فتَرْكُهُ واجب، والزهّاد
على ثلث طبقات فمنهم (١٢)المبتدئون وهم الذين خلت ايديهم (١٣)من الاملاك
وخلت قلوبهم ممّا (١٤)خلت منه ايديهم (١٥)كما سُئِل الجُنَيْد (٢)رحمه الله عن
الزهد فقال تخلّى (١٦)الايدى من الاملاك وتخلّى القلوب من الطمع، وسُئِل
سرىّ السَّقَطى (٢)رحمه الله عن الزهد فقال ان يخلو قلبه ممّا خلت منه
يداه، وفرقة منهم متحقّقون (١٧)فى الزهد ووَصْفُهم ما اجاب رُوَيْم بن احمد

---

(١) B والورع.   (٢) B om.   (٣) يأبا بكر om. in A, but suppl. in marg.
(٤) قال الشيخ رحمه الله B om.   (٥) A المرضية.   (٦) B يسى.   (٧) باسم
suppl. in marg. A.   (٨) B الزاهد.   (٩) B محمودة.   (١٠) B مذمومة.
(١١) B باختياره واختيار الله له.   (١٢) B المبدين.   (١٣) A عن.   (١٤) A تخلت.
(١٥) B وسيل.   (١٦) B الابدان.   (١٧) A بالزهد but corr. in marg.

^(۱) رحمه الله حين سُئِل عن الزهد فقال نَرْكُ حظوظ ^(۲)النفس من جميع ما فى الدنيا، فهذا زهد المُتحقّقين لانّ فى الزهد فى الدنيا حظّ ^(۳)للنفس لِما فى الزهد من الراحة والثناَء والمحمدة وإتّخاذ الجاه عند الناس فمن زهد بقلبه فى هذه الحظوظ فهو متحقّق فى زهنه، والفرقة الثالثة علموا وتيقّنوا ان لو كانت الدنيا كلّها لهم ^(٤)ملكًا حلالاً ولا ^(٥)يحاسبون عليها فى الآخرة ولا ينقص ذلك ممّا لهم عند الله شيئًا ثم زهدوا فيها ^(٦)لله عزّ وجلّ ^(٧)لكان زُهْدُهم فى شىء منذ خلقها الله ^(۱)تعالى ما نظر اليها ولو كانت ^(۱)الدنيا تَزِنُ عند الله جناحَ بعوضة ما ^(۸)سقى الكافرَ منها شربةً ^(۹)من ماَء فعند ذلك زهدوا فى زهدهم وتابوا ^(۱۰)من زهدهم كما سُئِل الشِّبْلِى ^(۱)رحمه الله عن الزهد فقال الزهد غفلة لانّ الدنيا لا شىء والزهد فى لا شىء غفلة، وقال يحيى بن مُعاذ ^(۱)رحمه الله الدنيا كالعروس ومن يطلبها ماشطتها والزاهد فيها يسخّم وجهها وينتف شعرها ويخرق ثوبها والعارف مشتغل بالله لا يلتفت اليها، والزهد يقتضى معانقة الفقر وأختياره،

باب مقام الفقر ^(۱۱)وصفة الفقراَء،

١٥

^(۱۲)قال الشيخ رحمه الله والفقر مقام شريف وقد وصف الله ^(۱۳)تعالى الفقراَء وذكرهم فى كتابه ^(۱۴)فقال ^(۱۵)لِلْفُقَرَاَءِ ٱلَّذِينَ أُحْصِرُوا فِى سَبِيلِ ٱللَّهِ ^(۱)الآيَة، وقال صلعم الفقر أزيَنُ بالعبد المؤمن من العذار الجيّد على خدّ الفرس، وقال ابرهيم بن احمد الخوّاص ^(۱)رحمه الله الفقر رداَء الشَّرَف

---

^(۱) B om.　　　^(۲) B النفوس.　　^(۳) B النفوس.　　^(٤) B ملك حلال.

^(٥) A يحاسبوا altered to يحاسبون by a later hand.　　^(٦) B فالله.　　^(۷) B كان.

^(۸) B سقا.　　Instead of لزهدوا عن زهدهم A in marg. has لكان زهدهم.

^(۹) من suppl. in A.　　^(۱۰) B فى.　　^(۱۱) These words are suppl. in A.

^(۱۲) B om. قال الشيخ رحمه الله.　　^(۱۳) B عز رجل.　　^(۱۴) B فقال عز وجل.

^(۱۵) Kor. 2, 274.

ولباس المرسَلين وجِلْباب الصالحين وتاج المتّقين وزَيْن المؤمنين وغنيمة
العارفين ومُنْية المريدين وحصن المطيعين وسجن المذنبين ومكفِّر للسيّئات
ومُعظّم للحسنات (١) ورافع للدرجات ومبلغ الى الغايات ورضا الجبّار وكرامة
(٢) لأهل ولايته من الابرار والفقر هو شعار الصالحين ودأب المتّقين، والفقرآء
٥ على ثلث طبقات فمنهم من لا يملك شيئًا ولا يطلب بظاهره ولا بباطنه من
احد شيئًا ولا ينتظر (٣) من احد شيئًا وان أُعطى شيئًا لم (٤) يأخذ فهذا مقامه
مقام المقرّبين كما حُكى عن (٥) سهل بن على بن سهل الاصبهانى انّه كان يقول
حرامٌ على كلّ من يسمّى (٦) اصحابنا الفقرآء لانّهم أغْنَى خَلْق الله عزّ وجلّ،
وكما سُئل ابو عبد الله بن الجلّآء عن حقيقة الفقر فقال اضْرِبْ بكُفّيْك على
١٠ الحايط وقل ربّى الله، وكما قال ابو على الروذبارى سألنى ابو بكر (٧) الزقّاق
فقال يأبا على لِمَ (٨) ترك الفقرآء أخْذَ البُلْغة فى وقت الحاجة قال فقلت
لانّهم مستغنون بالمُعْطِى عن العطآء فقال نعم ولكن وقع لى شىء آخر
فقلت هات (٩) أفِدْنى ما وقع لك فقال لانّهم قوم لا ينفعهم الوجود اذ الله
فاقتُهم ولا تضرّهم الفاقة اذ الله وجودهم، وسمعت ابا بكر الوجيهى يقول
١٥ سمعت ابا على يقول هذا، وسمعت ابا بكر الطوسى (١٠) يقول كنت مدّةً
طويلةً أسأل عن معنى اختيار اصحابنا لهذا الفقر على ساير الاشيآء فلم يُجبنى
احد بجواب يُقنعنى حتى سألت نصر بن الحمّاى فقال لى لانّه اوّل منزلة
من منازل التوحيد فقنعت بذلك، ومنهم من لا يملك شيئًا ولا يسأل احدًا
(١١) ولا يطلب ولا يعرّض وان أُعطى شيئًا من غير (١٢) مسئلة اخذ، وقد
٢٠ حُكى عن الجُنَيْد (١٠) رحمه الله انّه قال علامة الفقير الصادق ان لا يسأل ولا
يعارض وان عورض سكت، وكما حُكى عن سهل بن عبد الله (١٠) رحمه الله

A f. 21 b

(١) ومرفع الدرجات B.   (٢) لاوليايه من الابرار B.   (٣) B om. من احد.

(٧) B app.   (٦) اصحابنا B.   (٥) B om. سهل بن.   (٤) B ياخذها.   شيئًا

(١١) B ولا.   (١٠) B om.   (٩) افتى بما وقع B.   (٨) تركوا B.   الدقاق

يعارض ولا بطلب.   (١٢) A in marg. طلب.

انّه سُئل عن الفقير الصادق فقال لا يسأل ولا يردّ ولا يحبس، وكما سُئل
(١)ابو عبد الله بن الجلاّء (٢)رحمه الله عن حقيقة الفقر فقال هو ان لا يكون
لك (٣)فاذا كان لك لا يكون لك (٤)ومن حيث لم يكن لك لم يكن لك،
وكما سُئل ابرهيم الخوّاص (٢)رحمه الله عن علامة الفقير الصادق فقال تَرْكُ
٥ (٥)الشكوى (٦)واخفاء اثر البلوى، وهذا قد قيل ان هذا مقامه مقام الصدّيقين،
ومنهم من لا يملك شيئًا واذا احتاج انبسط الى بعض اخوانه ممّن يعلم انّه
يفرح بانبساطه (٧)اليه فككفّارة مسئلته صدقةٌ، وهذا كما سُئل (٨)الجريرى
(٢)رحمه الله عن حقيقة الفقر فقال لا يطلب المعدوم حتى ينقد الموجود،
وكما سُئل رُوَيْم (٢)رحمه الله عن الفقر فقال عدم كلّ موجود ويكون دخوله
١٠ فى الاشياء لغيره لا له وهذا مقامه مقام (٩)الصدّيقين فى الفقر، والفقر يقتضى
(٢)مقام الصبر،

باب مقام الصبر،

(١٠)قال الشيخ رحمه الله والصبر مقام شريف وقد مدح الله (٢)تعالى
الصابرين وذكرهم فى كتابه فقال (١١)إِنَّمَا يُوَفَّى ٱلصَّابِرُونَ أَجْرَهُمْ بِغَيْرِ
١٥ (١٢)حِسَابٍ، وقد سُئل الجُنَيْد عن الصبر فقال حَمْلُ المؤن لله (١٣)تعالى
حتى تنقضى اوقات المكروه، وقال ابرهيم الخوّاص (٢)رحمه الله هرب اكثر	A f. 22a
الخلق من حَمْلِ اثقال الصبر (١٤)فالتجوا الى الطلب والاسباب واعتمدوا
عليها كانّها لهم ارباب، (١٥)قال ووقف رجل على الشبْلِى (٢)رحمه الله فقال

---

(١) B om. ابو عبد الله.	(٢) B om.	(٣) واذا B.	(٤) من B.

(٥) السكون B.	(٦) واختفنا B.	(٧) Suppl. in A. B اليهم.	(٨) الجريرى B.

(٩) الصادقين A but corr. in marg.	(١٠) B om. قال الشيخ رحمه الله.

(١١) Kor. 39, 13.	(١٢) B adds: وقد ذكرم الله عز وجل فى غير موضع من كتابه.

(١٣) عز وجل B.	(١٤) فالتجوا A corr. in marg. B والتجوا.	(١٥) وقال وقف B.

له اىّ صبر اشدّ على الصابرين فقال الصبر فى الله [١] تعالى فقال لا [٢] فقال
الصبر له[١] لا فقال الرجل [٣] فقال الصبر مع الله فقال لا قال فغضب
الشبلى [١] رحمه الله وقال وَيْحُك [٤] فأَيْشَ فقال الرجل الصبر عن الله [١] عزّ
وجلّ قال فصرخ الشبلى [١] رحمه الله صرخةً كاد ان يتلف روحه، وسألت
ابن سالم بالبصرة عن الصبر فقال على ثلثة أَوْجُه منصبّر وصابر وصبّار
فالمنصبّر [١] من صَبَرَ فى الله [١] تعالى مرّةً يصبر على المكاره ومرّةً يعجز، وهذا
كما سُئِل القتّاد [١] رحمه الله عن الصبر فقال ملازمة [٦] الواجب فى الإعراض
عن المنهىّ عنه والمواظبة على المأمور به، والصابر من يصبر فى الله وله ولا
يجزع [٧] ولا يتمكّن منه الجزع ويُتوقع منه الشكوى، كما حُكى عن [٨] ذى
النون [٩] رحمه الله انّه قال دخلت على مريض اعوده فبينا [١] كان يكلّمنى أن
انّةً فقلت له ليس بصادق فى حبّه من [١٠] لم يصبر على ضربه قال فقال
[١] بل ليس بصادق فى حبّه من لم يتلذّذ بضربه، وكما قال الشبلى [١] رحمه
الله لمّا أُدخِلَ المارستان وقُيّد فدخل عليه [١١] بعض اصدقآبه فقال لم
أَيْشَ انتم فقالوا نحن قوم نحبّك فأخذ يرميهم [١٢] بالآجرّ فهربوا فقال يـا
كذّابين تدّعون محبّتى ولم تصبروا على ضربى، وإمّا الصبّار [١٣] فذاك الذى
صبره فى الله وله وبالله فهذا لو وقع عليه جميع البلايا لا يعجز ولا يتغيّر من
جهة [١٤] الوجوب والحقيقة لا من جهة الرسم والخِلْقة، وكان يتمثّل [١٥] الشبلى
رحمه الله [١٦] بهنه الابيات اذا سُئِل عن الصبر،

عَبَرَاتٌ خَطَطْنَ فى الخَدّ سَطْرًا ٭ قَدْ [١٧] قَرَاها مَنْ لَيْسَ يُحَسِنُ يَقْرا

---

(١) B om.   (٢) قال فقال B.   (٣) B om.   (٤) هو الصبر
added in A by a later hand.   (٥) بن B.   (٦) الواحد B.   (٧) ولكن
B.   (٨) A ذا but corr. by a later hand.   (٩) المصرى B instead of تمكن
المصرى.   (١٠) لا B.   (١١) جماعة من A. in marg.   (١٢) بالاجر B رحمه الله
الشِبلى رحمه الله.   (١٣) فذلك B.   (١٤) الوجود B om.   (١٥) B om. ويضربهم
(١٦) بهذين البيتين AB. بهذه الابيات A in marg.   (١٧) قراهن B.

A f. 22b

(١)إِنَّ (٢)صَوْتَ الْمُحِبِّ مِنْ أَلَمِ الشَّوْ. قٍ (٣)وخَوْفِ الفِراقِ يُورِثُ (٤)ضُرًّا صابَرَ الصَّبْرَ فاسْتَغاثَ بِهِ الصَّبْرُ فصاحَ الْمُحِبُّ (٥)بالصَّبْرِ صَبْرا، وحجّة هذا (٦)فى العلم ما رُوِى فى الخبر ان زكريّا عليه السلم لمّا وُضِع على رأسه المنشار أنَّ واحدة فاوحى الله (٧)تعالى اليه ان صعدت (٨)منك الىّ انَّه اخرى لأقلبنَّ السموات (٩)والارضين بعضها على بعض، والصبر يقتضى التوكّل،

باب مقام التوكل،

(١٠)قال الشيخ رحمه الله والتوكّل مقام شريف وقد امر الله (١١)تعالى بالتوكّل وجعله مقرونًا بالايمان لقوله (٧)تعالى (١٢)وَعَلَى اللهِ فَتَوَكَّلُوا إِنْ كُنْتُمْ مُؤْمِنِينَ، وقال (١٣)وَعَلَى اللهِ فَلْيَتَوَكَّلِ الْمُتَوَكِّلُونَ، (١٤)وقال فى موضع آخر (١٥)وَعَلَى اللهِ فَلْيَتَوَكَّلِ الْمُؤْمِنُونَ، فخصَّ توكّل المتوكّلين من توكّل المؤمنين ثم ذكر توكّل خصوص الخصوص فقال (١٦)وَمَنْ يَتَوَكَّلْ عَلَى اللهِ فَهُوَ حَسْبُهُ، لم يردّهم الى شىء سواه كما قال لسيّد المرسلين وامام المتوكّلين (١٧)وَتَوَكَّلْ عَلَى الْحَيِّ الَّذِى لَا يَمُوتُ وَكَفَى بِهِ (١٨)وَتَوَكَّلْ عَلَى الْعَزِيزِ الرَّحِيمِ الَّذِى يَرَاكَ حِينَ تَقُومُ (٧)الآيَةَ، (١٩)فهم على ثلث طبقات فامّا توكّل المؤمنين فشرْطُهُ ما قال ابو تُراب النخشبى (٧)رحمه الله حين سُئِل عن التوكّل فقال التوكّلُ

---

(1) A corrector of A has indicated that this verse should follow the next one.   (٢) B موت and so A in marg.   (٣) A in marg. وحسن العزاء. (٤) In marg. This hemistich in B runs: وطول الاحزان والوجد يورث عذرا.   (٥) A للصبر but corr. in marg. A صبرا.   (٦) B من.   (٧) B om. (٨) B منك الى.   (٩) B والارض.   (١٠) B om. قال الشيخ رحمه الله.   (١١) B عز وجل.   (١٢) Kor. 5, 26.   (١٣) Kor. 14, 15.   (١٤) B om. from وقال to المؤمنون.   (١٥) Kor. 14, 14.   (١٦) Kor. 65, 3.   (١٧) Kor. 25, 60.   (١٨) Kor. 26, 217—218.   (١٩) B وهم and so corr. in A.

طَرحُ البدن فى العبودية وتعلّق القلب (١)بالربوبية والاطمأنينة الى الكفاية
(٢)فان أعطى شكر وان مُنع صبر (٣)راضيًا موافقًا (٤)للقدر، وكما سُئل (٥)ذو
النون (٦)رحمه الله عن التوكّل فقال (٧)التوكّل ترك تدبير النفس والانخلاع
من الحول والقوّة، وكما قال ابو بكر (٧)الزقّاق (٦)رحمه الله التوكّل ردّ
العيش الى يوم واحد وإسقاط همّ (٨)غد، وسُئل رُوَيم (٦)رحمه الله عن
التوكّل فقال الثقة بالوعد، وسُئل سهل بن عبد الله (٦)رحمه الله عن التوكل
فقال (٩)الاسترسال مع الله تعالى على ما يريد، وإمّا توكّل اهل الخصوص
فكما قال (١٠)ابو العبّاس بن عطآء (٦)رحمه الله من توكّل على الله لغير الله A f. 23a
لم يتوكّل على الله (١١)فى توكّله حتى يتوكّل على الله بالله (١٢)الله ويكون متوكّلًا
على الله فى توكّله لا لسبب آخر، (١٣)او كما قال ابو يعقوب النهرجورى
(٦)رحمه الله وقد سُئل عن التوكّل فقال موت (١٤)النفس عند ذهاب
حظوظها (١٥)من اسباب الدنيا والآخرة، وقد قال ايضًا ابو بكر (٦)الواسطى
اصل التوكّل (١٦)الفاقة والافتقار وأن لا يفارق التوكّل فى امانيه ولا يلتفت
(١٧)بسرّه الى توكّله لحظةً فى عمره، وسُئل سهل بن عبد الله (٦)رحمه الله
(٦)ايضًا عن التوكّل فقال التوكّل وجهٌ كلّه وليس له قفًا ولا يصحّ الّا لأهل
(١٨)المقابر، فهولآء اشاروا الى حقيقة توكّل المتوكّلين وهم الخصوص، وإمّا توكّل
خصوص الخصوص فعلى ما قال الشبلى (٦)رحمه الله حين سُئل عن التوكّل
فقال ان تكون لله كما لم تكن ويكون الله (١٩)تعالى لك كما لم يزل، وكما
قال بعضهم حقيقة التوكّل لا يقوم له احد من خَلْقه على الكمال لانّ الكمال

---

(١) A adds in marg. والانقطاع الى الله بالكلية.   (٢) B وأن.   (٣) AB
راضى موافق.   (٤) B القدرة.   (٥) A ذا.   (٦) B om.   (٧) B app.
الدقاق.   (٨) B الى غد.   (٩) B استرسال.   (١٠) B om. ابو العباس.
(١١) B om. فى توكّه.   (١٢) B عز وجل الله.   (١٣) B وكا.   (١٤) A النفوس.
(١٥) The passage beginning من اسباب الدنيا and ending فى امانيه in suppl. in
marg. A.   (١٦) A صدق الفاقة.   (١٧) B لسرة.   (١٨) A المقادير but
corr. by a later hand.   (١٩) B عز وجل.

بالكمال لا يكون الّا لله (١)جلّ جلاله ، وسُئِل ابو عبد الله بن الجلّاء عن
التوكّل فقال (٢)الايواءُ الى الله وحده ، وسُئِل الجُنَيْد (٣)رحمه الله عن التوكّل
فقال اعتماد القلب على الله (٤)تعالى فى جميع الاحوال ، وقد حُكِى عن ابى
سليمن الدارانى (٤)رحمه الله انه قال لأحمد بن ابى الحوارى (٤)رحمه الله
٥ يا احمد انّ طُرُق الآخرة كثيرة وشيخك عارفٌ بكثير منها الّا هذا التوكّل
المبارك فانّى ما شممت منه رائحةً (٤)وليس لى (٥)منه مشامّ الريح ، وقال بعضهم
من اراد ان يقوم (٦)بحقّ التوكّل فليحفِر لنفسه قبرًا ويدفنها فيه وينسى الدنيا
وأهلها لانّ حقيقة التوكّل لا يقوم له احد من الخلق على كماله ، والتوكّل
يقتضى الرضا ،

باب مقام الرضا وصفة اهله ،

(٧)قال الشيخ رحمه الله (٨)الرضا مقام شريف وقد ذكر الله (٩)عزّ وجلّ
الرضا فى كتابه فقال (١٠)رَضِىَ اللّٰهُ عَنْهُمْ وَرَضُوا عَنْهُ ، وقال (١١)وَرِضْوَانٌ
مِنَ اللّٰهِ أَكْبَرُ فذكر انّ رضا الله (٤)عزّ وجلّ عن عباده أكبرُ وأقدمُ من
رضاهم عنه ، والرضا باب الله الأعظمُ وجنّة (٣)الدنيا وهو ان يكون قلب
١٥ العبد ساكنًا تحت حُكْمِ الله (٤)عزّ وجلّ ، وسُئِل الجُنَيْد (٤)رحمه الله عن
الرضا فقال رفعُ الاختيار ، (١٢)وسُئِل (١٣)القنّاد رحمه الله عن الرضا
فقال (١٤)سكون القلب بمَرّ القضاءِ ، (١٥)وسُئِل ذو النون عن الرضا فقال
سرور القلب بمَرّ القضاءِ ، وقال (١٦)ابن عطاءٍ (٤)رحمه الله الرضا نظرُ

---

(١) وقال B. (٢) B om. (٣) B ان لا يكون الا الله وحده. (٤) عز وجل B.
(٥) منها B. (٦) لحق B. (٧) B om. قال الشيخ رحمه الله. (٨) ليس.
والرضا B. (٩) تعلى B. (١٠) Kor. 5, 119. (١١) Kor. 9, 73. A has
القناد النورى A. (١٢) B om. from وسيل to بمرّ القضاءِ. (١٣) رضوان.
written above. (١٤) سرور A but corr. in marg. (١٥) وسيل — بمرّ القضاءِ
is suppl. in marg. A. (١٦) بن B.

القلب الى قديم اختيار الله (٢)تعالى للعبد لانّه يعلم انّه (٢)اختار له الافضل
فيرضى به ويترك السخط، (٣) وقال ابو بكر الواسطى (١) رحمه الله اَسْتَعْمِل
الرضا جَهْدَك ولا تَدَع الرضا يستعملك فتكون محجوبًا بلذّته ورؤية حقيقته،
غير انّ اهل الرضا فى الرضا على ثلثة (٤)احوال فمنهم من عمل فى إسقاط
الجزع حتى يكون قلبه (٥)مستويًا لله (١)عزّ وجلّ فيا يجرى عليه من حُكُم
(٦)الله من المكاره والشدايد والراحات والمنع والعطآء، ومنهم من ذهب عن
رؤية (٧)رضايه عن الله (١)عزّ وجلّ برؤية رضا الله عنه لقوله (١)تعالى رَضِىَ
اللهُ عَنْهُم (٩)وَرَضُوا عَنْهُ (١٠)فلا يثبت لنفسه قدم فى الرضا (١١)وإن استوى
عنه الشدّة والرخآء، والمنع والعطآء، ومنهم من جاوز هذا وذهب عن رؤية
رضا الله عنه ورضاه عن الله لما سبق من الله (١)تعالى لخلّقه من الرضا كا
قال ابو سليمُن الدارانى (١) رحمه الله ليس اعمال الخلق بالذى (١٢) يُرضيه ولا
بالذى (١٣) يُسخطه ولكنّه رضى (١)عن قوم فاستعملهم بعمل اهل الرضا وسخط
(١) على قوم فاستعملهم بعمل اهل السخط، والرضا آخر المقامات ثم يقتضى من
بعد ذلك احوال ارباب القلوب ومطالعة الغيوب وتهذيب الاسرار لصفآء
(١٤) الأَذْكار وحقايق الاحوال، فاوّل حال من احوال ارباب القلوب
حال (١٥)المراقبة،

(١٦)باب مراقبة الاحوال وحقايقها وصفة اهلها،

(١٧)قال الشيخ رحمه الله (١٨)والمراقبة حال شريف قال الله تعالى

---

(١) B om.   (٢) B له اختياره.   (٣) Here B has the saying of القنّاد
given above: (with برور for) وسُئِل القنّاد عن الرضا فقال سكون القلب بِرور القصاء
النفس والمكاره A 8   (٤) B اوجه.   (٥) B يسنوى.   (٦) وقال B for قال بَرّ.
but النفس erased and تعا الله written in marg.   (٧) B رضاه.   (٨) Kor.
5, 119.   (٩) B om. ورضوا عنه.   (١٠) B ولا.   (١١) B فان.   (١٢) A ترضيه.
(١٣) B تسخطه.   (١٤) B الادكار.   (١٥) B المراقبة الاحوال وحقايقها.   (١٦) B باب
المراقبة.   (١٧) B om. قال الشيخ رحمه الله.   (١٨) B المراقبة.
حال المراقبة وصفة اهلها

Δ f. 24 a (١) وَكَانَ اللّٰهُ عَلَى كُلِّ شَىْءٍ رَقِيبًا، وقال (٢) عزّ وجلّ (٣) مَا يَلْفِظُ مِنْ قَوْلٍ إِلَّا لَدَيْهِ رَقِيبٌ عَتِيدٌ، وقال (٤) يَعْلَمُ سِرَّكُمْ وَتَجْوِيَكُمْ (٥) وَيَعْلَمُ مَا تُسِرُّونَ وَمَا تُعْلِنُونَ، ومثله فى القران كثير، وروى عن النبى صلعم انّه قال اُعْبُدِ اللّٰه كأنّك تراه فان (٦) لم تكن تراه فانّه يراك، (٧) والمراقبة لعبد قد علم وتيقّن انّ الله (٨) تعالى مطّلع على ما فى قلبه وضميره (٩) وعالم بذلك فهو يراقب الخواطر المذمومة المشغّلة للقلب عن ذكر (١٠) سيّده كما قال ابو سليمن الدارانى (٢) رحمه الله كيف يخفى عليه ما فى القلوب ولا يكون فى القلوب الّا ما يُلقى (١١) فيها افيخْفى عليه ما هو (١١) منه، (٢) وقال الجُنَيْد (٢) رحمه الله قال (٢) لى ابرهيم الآجرّى (٢) رحمه الله يا غلام لَأَنْ تَرُدَّ من همّك الى الله تعالى ذرّة خيرٌ لك ممّا طلعت عليه الشمس، وقال (١٢) الحسن بن على الدامغانى (٢) رحمه الله عليكم بحفظ السرائر (١٣) فانّه مطّلع على الضماير، وأهل المراقبة على ثلثة احوال فى مراقبتهم فامّا ما قال (١٤) الحسن بن (١٥) على فهذا حال الابتداء فى المراقبة، وامّا الحال الثانى فى المراقبة (١٦) فكما حُكى عن احمد بن عطاء (٢) رحمه الله انّه قال خَيْرُكُم من راقب الحقّ بالحقّ فى فناء ما دون الحقّ وتابع المصطفى (٢) صلعم فى افعاله واخلاقه وآدابه، وامّا (١٧) الحال الثالث فحال الكبراء من اهل المراقبة فانّهم يراقبون الله (٢) تعالى ويسألونه ان يرعاهم فيها لانّ (١٨) الله (٢) عزّ وجلّ قد خصّ نجباءه وخاصّته بأن لا يَكِلَهم فى جميع احوالهم الى نفوسهم ولا الى احد وهو الذى يتولّى امرهم فقال (٢) عزّ وجلّ (١٩) وَهُوَ يَتَوَلَّى الصَّالِحِينَ، وقال (٢٠) ابن عطاء (٢) رحمه

---

(١) Kor. 33, 52.   (٢) B om.   (٣) Kor. 50, 17.   (٤) Kor. 9, 79. Kor.
has سِرَّكُمْ وَنَجْوَاكُمْ.   (٥) Kor. 64, 4.   (٦) B om. لم تكن.   (٧) B وكأنّ
.والمراقبة   (٨) B تعالى وعلى.   (٩) B عالم.   (١٠) B سيّده.
(١١) B فيه.   (١٢) In A a later hand has supplied أبو before الحسن.
(١٣) B وانّه.   (١٤) أبو suppl. in A.   (١٥) B adds: بحفظ عليكم الدامغانى
.السرائر فانّه مطّلع على الضماير   (١٦) A كما.   (١٧) B حال.   (١٨) B تعالى.
(١٩) Kor. 7, 195،   (٢٠) B بن.

الله لبعض حكمآء خراسان ممّن قد ولع بالجهل وقارن التقشّف [1] أوَما
علمتَ انّ ما تقارن ببدنك [2] اقذار فى جنب ما تطالع بقلبك وما [3] تطالعه
بقلبك هبآء فى جنب ما تراقب فى سرّك [4] فراقبِ الله [5] تعالى فى سرّك
وعلانيتك [5] فانه [6] خير ممّا تقارن من عملك وعبادتك، والمراقبة تقتضى
ه حال القرب،

باب حال القُرْب،

[7] قال الشيخ رحمه الله قال الله [8] تعالى [9] وَإِذَا سَأَلَكَ عِبَادِى عَنِّى
فَإِنِّى [8] قَرِيبٌ، [10] وقال [11] وَنَحْنُ أَقْرَبُ إِلَيْهِ مِنْ حَبْلِ الْوَرِيدِ، وقال
[12] وَنَحْنُ أَقْرَبُ إِلَيْهِ مِنْكُمْ وَلَكِنْ لَا تُبْصِرُونَ، ثم قال فى صفة ملايكته
[13] أُولَئِكَ الَّذِينَ [ع] يَبْتَغُونَ إِلَى رَبِّهِمُ الْوَسِيلَةَ أَيُّهُمْ أَقْرَبُ، [14] الوسيلة
يعنى القرب، وقال وَنَحْنُ أَقْرَبُ إِلَيْهِ مِنْكُمْ وَلَكِنْ لَا تُبْصِرُونَ، فذكر الله تعالى
قُرْبَهم منه [15] ثم ذكر قربهم بمعنى توسّلهم الى الله تعالى بالقرب أَيُّهُمْ أَقْرَبُ،
وحال القرب لعبدٍ شاهد بقلبه قرب الله منه فتقرّب الى الله [5] تعالى بطاعته
وجمع همّه بين يدى الله [16] تعالى بدوام ذكره فى علانيته وسرّه، وهم على
ه١ ثلثة احوال فمنهم المتقرّبون اليه [17] بأنواع الطاعات لعلْمهم بعلم الله [5] تعالى
بهم وقُرْبه منهم وقدرته عليهم، ومنهم من تحقّق بذلك كما قال عامر بن عبد
[18] القيس [5] رحمه الله ما نظرتُ الى شىء الاّ [19] رأيتُ الله [5] تعالى [20] أقربَ
اليه منّى، وهو كما قال القايل،

---

[1] B اما.   [2] B امرارا.   [3] B تطالع.   [4] B فمراقبة.   [5] B om.

[6] B خيرا.   [7] B om. قال الشيخ رحمه الله.   [8] B تعلى ذكره.   [9] Kor.

2, 182.   [10] B om. from وقال to الوريد.   [11] Kor. 50, 15.   [12] Kor.

56, 84.   [13] Kor. 17, 59.   [14] B om. from الوسيلة to أيّهم أقرب.

[15] The words ثم ذكر قربهم are suppl. in marg. A.   [16] B عز وجل.

[17] B باحوال.   [18] B قيس.   [19] B ورايت.   [20] B أقرب منه.

In marg. A الىّ منّى is written over اليه منه.

وَتَحَقَّقْتُكَ فى (١)السِّرِّ (٢)فَنَاجَاكَ لِسَانى * (٣)فَاجْتَمَعْنَا لِمَعَانٍ وَافْتَرَقْنَا لِمَعَانٍ إِنْ يَكُنْ (٤)غَيَّبَكَ التَّعْظِيمُ عَنْ لَحْظِ عِيَانى * فَلَقَدْ صَيَّرَكَ الوَجْدُ مِنَ الأَحْشَاءِ دَانى، وقال الجُنَيْد (٥)رحمه الله واعلم انّه (٦)يقرب من قلوب عباده على حسب ما يرى من قرب قلوب عباده منه فانظُرْ (٧)ما ذا يقرب من قلبك، وقال ٥ آخَرُ انّ لله (٥)تعالى عبادًا قرّبهم (٨)الله عزّ وجلّ بما هو (٩)به قريب منهم (١٠)وكانوا قريبين منه بما هو (١١)به قريب اليهم، (١٢)وهذه الدرجة الثانية من حال القرب، فامّا حال الكُبَرَاءَ وأهل النهايات فهو على ما قال ابو الحسين النورى (٥)رحمه الله لرجل دخل عليه فقال من أَيْنَ أَنْتَ (١٣)قال من بغداد قال مَنْ صحِبتَ بها قال (١٤)ابا حمزة قال اذا رجعتَ الى بغداد ١٠ فقُلْ لأبى حمزة قُرْبُ القُرْب فى معنى ما نحن نشير اليه بُعْدُ البُعْد، وكا قال

ابو يعقوب السوسى (٥)رحمه الله ما دام العبد يكون بالقرب لم يكن قربٌ حتى يغيب عن القرب بالقرب فاذا ذهب عن رؤية القرب بالقرب (١٥)فذلك قربٌ يعنى عن رؤية (٥)قربه من الله (٥)عزّ وجلّ بقرب الله منه، (١٦)وحال القرب يقتضى (٥)حال المحبّة وحال الخوف،

باب حال المحبّة،

(١٧)قال الشيخ رحمه الله (١٨)فامّا حال المحبّة فقد ذكر الله (١٩)تعالى (٢٠)المحبّة فى مواضع من كتابه فقال (٢١)فَسَوْفَ (٢٢)يَأْتِى اللهُ بِقَوْمٍ يُحِبُّهُمْ

---

(١) B سرى. (٢) B فتخاطبك. (٣) B فاجتمعا لمعانى وافترقا لمعانى. (٤) B غيبرك.
(٥) B om. (٦) A تقرب. (٧) B بما ذا بقربك. (٨) B om عز الله.
وجل. (٩) A has اليه as a variant. (١٠) B فكانوا. (١١) AB om.
but suppl. in A. (١٢) B وهذا درجة الثانى. (١٣) B فقال. (١٤) B ابو.
(١٨) B واما. (١٧) B om قال الشيخ رحمه الله. (١٦) B وقال. (١٥) B فذاك.
(١٩) B تعلى ذكره. (٢٠) B المحبة فقال فى موضع من كتابه. (٢١) Kor. 5, 59.
(٢٢) B يات.

وَيُحِبُّونَهُ، وقال (١) قُلْ إِنْ كُنْتُمْ تُحِبُّونَ اللَّهَ فَاتَّبِعُونِى يُحْبِبْكُمُ اللَّهُ وقال فى

موضع آخر (٢) يُحِبُّونَهُمْ كَحُبِّ اللَّهِ وَالَّذِينَ آمَنُوا أَشَدُّ حُبًّا لِلَّهِ، (٣) فذكر فى

الآية الأولى محبّته قَبْلَ محبّتهم وفى (٤) الآية الثانية ذكر محبّتهم له ومحبّته لهم وفى

الآية الثالثة ذكر محبّتهم له، وحالُ المحبّة لعبدٍ نظر بعينه الى ما انعم الله

٥ (٥) به عليه ونظر بقلبه الى قُرْب الله تعالى منه وعنايته (٥) به وحفظه وكلايته

له (٦) فنظر بإيمانه وحقيقة يقينه الى ما سبق له من الله تعالى من العنايـة

والهداية وقديم حبّ الله له فأَحبَّ اللهَ (٧) عزّ وجلّ، وأهل المحبّة على ثلثة

احوال فالحال الاوّل من المحبّة محبّة العامّة يتولّد ذلك من احسان الله

(٤) تعالى اليهم وعطفه عليهم، وقد رُوى عن النبى صلعم انّه قال جُبِلَت

١٠ القلوب على حبّ من أَحْسَنَ اليها وبغض من اسآء اليها الحديث، وهذا

الحال من المحبّة شَرْطُها ما سُئِل سُمْنُون (٤) رحمه الله عن المحبّة فقال صفآء

الودّ مع دوام الذكر لأنّ من احبّ شيئًا أَكْثَرَ (٤) من ذكره، وكا سُئِل سَهْل

ابن عبد الله (٤) رحمه الله عن المحبّة فقال موافقة القلوب لله والتزام الموافقة

لله وإتّباع الرسول صلعم مع دوام الاستهتار بذكر الله (٤) تعالى ووجود حلاوة

١٥ المناجاة لله عزّ وجلّ، وسُئِل الحسين بن (٨) علىّ (٤) رضى الله عنه عن المحبّة

فقال بَذْلُ المجهود والحبيبُ يفعل ما يشآء، وكا سُئِل بعض المشايخ عن

المحبّة فقال استهتار القلوب بالثنآء على المحبوب (٤) وإيثار طاعته والموافقة له

كما قال القايل،

(١٠) لَوْ كَانَ حُبُّكَ صَادِقًا لَأَطَعْتَهُ ٭ إِنَّ المُحِبَّ لِمَنْ يُحِبُّ مُطِيعُ،

٢٠ والحال الثانى من المحبّة وهو يتولّد من نظر القلب الى غِنآء الله (١١) وجلاله

وعَظَمته وعلمه وقدرته وهو حبّ (١٢) الصادقين والمحقّقين وشَرْطُها ووَصْفُها

---

(١) Kor. 3, 29. B om. قُلْ.   (٢) Kor. 2, 160.   (٣) B وذكر.   (٤) B om.

(٥) A om.   (٦) B ونظر.   (٧) B جل وعلا.   (٨) الدامغانى added in marg. A.

(٩) لوكنت بور (توّر) حبّه. A in marg. لو كنت تذكر حبّه B (١٠)   إتباع B (٩).

(١١) B جل جلاله.   (١٢) A الصديقين but corr. in marg.

كما حُكى عن ابى الحسين النورى (١) رحمه الله انّه سُئل عن المحبّة فقال
هَتْكُ الأَستار وكَشْفُ الأَسرار، وسُئل (٢) ايضًا ابرهيم الخوّاص عن المحبّة
فقال مَحْوُ الارادات واحتراق جميع الصفات والحاجات، وقد سُئل ابو
سعيد (٣) الخرّاز رحمه الله عن المحبّة فقال طوبى لمن شرب كأسًا من محبّته
وذاق نعيمًا من مناجاة الجليل وقُرْبِه (٤) بما وجد من اللذّات بحبّة فمُلِئ قلبُه ٥
حبًّا وطار بالله (١) طربًا وهام اليه اشتياقًا فيا من وامقٍ أَسِفٍ بريّة كَلِفٍ
دَنِفٍ ليس له سَكَنٌ غيره ولا مألوفٌ سواه، وإمّا الحال الثالث من المحبّة
فهو محبّة الصدّيقين والعارفين تولّدت من نظرهم ومعرفتهم بقديم حبّ الله
تعالى بلا عِلّة فكذلك احبّوه بلا عِلّة، وصفة هذه المحبّة ما سُئل (٥) ذو
النون (١) المصرى فقيل له ما المحبّة (٦) الصافية التى لا (٧) كدرة فيها قال ١٠
حبّ الله الصافى الذى لا كدرة فيه سقوط المحبّة عن القلب والجوارح حتى
لا يكون فيها المحبّة وتكون الاشياء (٨) بالله ولله فذلك المحبّ (٩) لله، وقال
ابو يعقوب السوسى (١) رحمه الله لا تصحّ المحبّة حتى (١٠) يخرج من رؤية
المحبّة الى رؤية المحبوب (١١) بفناء علم المحبّة من حيث كان له المحبوب فى
الغيب ولم يكن هو بالمحبّة فاذا خرج المحبّ الى هذه النسبة كان (١٢) محبًّا ١٥
من غير محبّة، وسُئل الجنيد (١) رحمه الله عن المحبّة فقال دخولُ صفات
المحبوب على البدل من صفات المحبّ، فهذا على معنى قوله حتى أُحِبّه فاذا
أَحبَبْتُه كُنْتُ عَيْنَهُ الذى يُبصِر (١٣) به وسَمْعَهُ الذى يسمع به ويَدَهُ الذى A f. 26a
يبطش به،

---

(١) B om. ‎‎‎   (٢) In B follows ايضًا الخوّاص.   (٣) B om. الخرّاز رحمه الله.

(٤) B لما.   (٥) A ذا.   (٦) B الصافى الذى.   (٧) Altered in A to
كدورة.   (٨) B وبالله.   (٩) B لله عز وجل.   (١٠) المحبّ suppl. in
marg. A after يخرج.   (١١) B على المحبة (؟) تغبا.   (١٢) B محب.

(١٣) Altered in A to بها.

باب حال الخوف،

(١)قال الشيخ رحمه الله (٢)فاما (٢)حال الخوف فانّما ذكرنا الخوف
والمحبّة لأنّ حال القُرْب يقتضى حالَين فمنهم من يغلب على قلبه الخوف من
نظرِهِ الى قُرْب الله منه ومنهم من يغلب على قلبه المحبّة (٤)وذلك على حسب
ما قسم (٥)الله للقلوب من التصديق وحقيقة اليقين والخشية وذلك من
كشفِ الغُيوب فان شاهَدَ قلبُه فى قربه من سيّده عظمتَهُ وهيبته وقدرتـه
فيوّديه ذلك الى الخوف والحياء، والوجل وان شاهد قلبه فى (٦)قربه لُطْفَ
سيّده وقديم عطفه واحسانه (٥)له ومحبّته ادّاه (٥)ذلك الى المحبّة والشوق
والقلق والحَرَق والتبرّم بالبقَاء وذلك بعلمه ومشيئته (٧)وقدرته ذلك تقدير
العزيز العليم، والخوف على ثلثة اوجه وقد ذكر الله تعالى الخوف وقرنه
بالايمان بقوله (٨)فَلَا تَخَافُوهُمْ وَخَافُونِ إِنْ كُنتُم مُّؤْمِنِينَ فهذا خوف الأجِلّة،
وقوله (٩)وَلِمَنْ خَافَ مَقَامَ رَبِّهِ جَنَّتَانِ فهذا خوف الأوْساط، وقال (١٠)يَخَافُونَ
يَوْمًا تَتَقَلَّبُ فِيهِ الْقُلُوبُ وَالْأَبْصَارُ فهذا خوف العامّة، فمنهم من خاف من
سخطه وعقابه كما ذكر الله (٥)تعالى يَخَافُونَ يَوْمًا تَتَقَلَّبُ فِيهِ الْقُلُوب وَالْأَبْصَار
وهم العامّة فخوفهم اضطراب قلوبهم ممّا علموا من سطوة معبودهم، واما
الاوساط فخوفهم من القطيعة واعتراض الكدورة فى صفاء المعرفة، وسُيل
الشِبْلى (٥)رحمه الله عن الخوف فقال ان لا يسلُّمك الىك كما قال
ابو سعيد الخَرّاز (٥)رحمه الله فى (١١)كلام له قال شكوتُ الى بعض العارفين
الخوف فقال لى إنّى اشتهى ان أرى رجلاً بدرى أَيْشَ الخوف من الله ثم
قال انّ اكثر الخايفين خافوا على انفسهم من الله شفقةً منهم على انفسهم وعملاً

---

(١) B om. قال الشيخ رحمه الله.   (٢) B واما.   (٣) B om. حال الخوف فاننا.
(٤) B ذلك.   (٥) B om.   (٦) B قربه من سيده.   (٧) B وتقديره.
(٨) Kor. 3, 169.   (٩) Kor. 55, 46.   (١٠) Kor. 24, 37.   (١١) B كلامه
for كلام له.

فى خلاصها من أمره (١) عزَّ وجلَّ، وقال ابن خُبَيْق (١) رحمه الله الخايف
عندى أن يكون بحكُم الوقت فوقتٌ يخافه (٢)المخلوق ووقتٌ يأمنه، وقال
القنّاد (١) رحمه الله علامة الخوف ان لا يعلّل نفسَه بعَسَى وسَوْف، وقال

A f.26b

بعضهم علامة خوف الله (١) تعالى هيجان القلوب وشدّة الذعر من الترهيب،
وقال (٢)ابن خُبَيْق (١) رحمه الله الخايف عندى من (٤) يخاف من نفسه أكثرَ
ممّا يخاف من (٥)الشيطان، (٦) وامّا اهل الخصوص من الخايفين فخوفهم على
ما قال سهّل بن عبد الله (١) رحمه الله لو قسم (٧) ذرّة من خوف الخايفين
على اهل الارض لسَعِدوا بذلك اجمعين، فقيل له فكم يكون مع الخايفين
من هذا الخوف قال مثل الجبل، وقال (٢)ابن الجلّاء الخايف عنده
الذى لا يخاف غيرَ الله (١)تعالى، وقال الواسطى (١) رحمه الله الاكابر يخافون
القطع والاصاغر يخافون العقوبة وخوف الاكابر أقْطَعُ لأن ما دام (٨)للنفس
فى النفس من رعوناتها (١) بقيّةٌ (٩) فليس بمُحْسن وإن اتى بكلّ تفويض
وتسليم، (١٠) قال الشيخ رحمه الله معنى (١١) رعوناتها تدبيرها ودعواها ونظرها
الى طاعاتها، والرجاءُ مقرون بالخوف،

باب (١٢)الرجاء،

١٥

(١٠)قال الشيخ رحمه الله والرجاءُ حال شريف، قال الله (١٣) تعالى (١٤)لَقَدْ
كَانَ لَكُمْ فِى رَسُولِ اللَّهِ أُسْوَةٌ حَسَنَةٌ لِمَنْ كَانَ يَرْجُوا اللَّهَ وَٱلْيَوْمَ ٱلْآخِرَ،
وقال فى آية أخرى (١٥) يَرْجُونَ رَحْمَتَهُ وَيَخَافُونَ عَذَابَهُ، وقال فى آية أخرى
(١٦) فَمَنْ كَانَ يَرْجُوا لِقَاءَ رَبِّهِ فَلْيَعْمَلْ عَمَلاً (١٧)صَالِحًا قالوا فى التفسير ثواب

---

(١) B om.   (٢) AB المخاوف. A in marg. المخلوق.   (٣) B بن.   (٤) B om.
النفس B (٨)   ذرّة B (٧)   فاما B (٦)   السلطان B (٥)   يخاف من.
رعوناتها وليس B (١١)   قال الشيخ رحمه الله B om. (١٠)   وليس B (٩).
حال الرجا B (١٣)   جل ذكره B (١٤)   Kor. 33, 21. (١٤)   Kor. 17, 59. (١٥).
(١٦) Kor. 18, 110.   (١٧) B adds the remainder of the verse: ولا يشرك بعبادة ربّه أحدًا.

ربّه، وقال صلعم لو وُزِن خوف المؤمن (١) ورجاؤه لاعتدلا، وقال بعضهم
الخوف والرجآء (٢) جناحا (٣) العمل لا يطير الّا بهما، وقال ابو بكر الورّاق
الرجآء ترويح من الله (٤) تعالى لقلوب الخايفين (٤) ولولا ذلك لتلفتْ نفوسهم
وذهلتْ عقولهم، والرجآء على ثلثة اقسام رجآء فى الله ورجآء فى سعة رحمة
٥ الله ورجآء فى ثواب الله، (٥) فالرجآء فى ثواب الله وفى سعة (٦) رحمته لعبدٍ
مريد قد سمع من الله ذكر المِنَن فرجاه وعلم (٧) انّ الكرم والفضل والجود
من صفات الله فارتاح قلبه الى المرجوّ من كرمه وفضله كما حُكى عن (٨) ذى
النون المصرى (٩) رحمه الله انّه كان يدعو ويقول اللهمّ انّ سعة رحمتك
أَرْجأ لنا من أعمالنا عندنا واعتمادُنا على عفوك ارجأ (٩) عندنا من عقابك
١٠ لنا، وكما قال بعضهم آلهى أنت لطيف لمن قَصَدَك فى ارادته ورجاك (١٠) فى
ملمّانه فيا منتهَى آمال الراجين (١٠) أَرْجِنا راحةً عاجلةً تُوردُنا مَناهلِ مسرّتك
وتوؤدّينا الى قربك، والراجى فى الله تعالى هو عبد تحقّق (١١) فى الرجآء (١٢) فلا
يرجو من الله شيئًا سوى الله كما سُئِل الشّبْلى (٢) رحمه الله عن الرجآء فقال
الرجآء أن ترجوه أن لا يقطع بك دونه، وقال (١٣) ذو النون (٢) رحمه الله بينا
١٥ انا أَسِير فى بعض البوادى اذ لقيتْنى امرأة فقالت لى من (١٤) انت قلت
رجلٌ غريبٌ فقالت وهل (١٥) يُوجَدُ مع الله تعالى احزان (١٦) الغربة،

فصل فى معنى الخوف والرجآء،

(١٧) قال الشيخ رحمه الله وإمّا لسان اهل النهايات والمتحقّقين فى الخوف
والرجآء فالذى يقول احمد بن عطآء (٢) رحمه الله حين سُئِل عن الخوف

---

(١) B ورجاه.   (٢) B العلم.   (٣) B om.   (٤) B فلولا.   (٥) AB

(٦) رحمة الله B.   (٧) بان B.   (٨) ذا AB.   (٩) A لنا.   فالراجى

but عندنا written above.   (١٠) B للمّانه.   (١١) من B.   (١٢) B ولا.

انها A.   (١٣) A ذا.   (١٤) A ابن.   (١٥) B برجى.   (١٦) In marg. A

قال الشيخ رحمه الله.   (١٧) B om.   الغريب من يكون عنه غريبًا.

والرجاءَ فقال انّ الخَلْق (١)بالرجاءَ والخوف (٢) مُوَّذنون وما دام لم (٣)يَتَرَقَّ
العبد فى طُرقِهما ولم (٤)يترقَّ من بينهما لم يَصِل الى حقيقة حقّهـا ويكون
مرتَبطًا بما لا حاصل له فيهما عند الحقيقة ، قيل فما يعنى الخوف والرجاءَ
قال زمامان (٥)للنفس حتى لا تخرج الى رعوناتها من الإدلال والأمن والإياس
والقطع ، (٦)وقال ابو بكر الواسطى (٧)رحمه الله الخوف له ظُلَم يتغيَّر صاحبُ
تحته يطلب ابدًا المخرج منه فاذا جاءَ الرجاءَ بضياءَه خرج الى مواضع الراحة
(٨)فغلب عليه التمنَّى ولا (٩)ينفع حسن النهار الاّ (١٠)بظلمة الليل (١١)وفيهـا
صلاح الكون فكذلك القلب مرّةً فى ظُلَم الخوف اسيرٌ (١٢)فاذا طَرَق طوارق
الرجاءَ فهو امِيرٌ ، والمحبّة والخوف والرجاءَ (١٣)مقرون بعضها ببعض قال   A.f.27b
بعضهم كلّ محبّة لا خوف معها فهى مأُروفة وكلّ خوف لا رجاءَ معه فهو
مأُروف وكلّ رجاءَ لا خوف معه كذلك ، والرجاءَ والمحبّة يقتضيان (١٤)الشوق ،

(١٥)باب حال الشوق ،

قال الشيخ رحمه الله تعالى (١٦) وحال الشوق حال شريف ، رُوى عن
النبى صلعم انّه قال (١٧)ألا هل مشتاق الى الجنّة (١٨)هى وربِّ الكعبة رَيْحانةٌ
تهتزّ ونَهَر مُطّرد وزوجة (١٩)حسناءَ ، ورُوى (٢٠)عنه عليه السلم انّه كان يقول
فى دعاءَه (١٧)أسئَلُكَ (٧)لذّة النظر الى وجهك والشوق الى لقآيك ، (٢١)ولذّةُ
النظر الى وجه الله (٧)تعالى فى الآخرة والشوقُ الى لقائه فى الدنيا ، وقد

---

(١) B والرجا وبالخوف.   (٢) A موذنين B app. مودين.   (٣) B يترقا.

(٤) B يرق.   (٥) B للنفوس.   (٦) B قال.   (٧) B om.   (٨) B فنلت.

(٩) B يقع.   (١٠) B بظلم.   (١١) B وفيها.   (١٢) B واذا.   (١٣) A مقرونة.

(١٤) A adds وحال الشوق حال شريف but these words have been stroked out.

(١٥) B om. from باب to رحمه الله تعالى in marg. A.   (١٦) وحال الخ in marg. A.

(١٧) B الاهل مشتاقون.   (١٨) Suppl. in marg. B.   (١٩) A in marg.

(٢٠) B عن النبى صلى الله عليه وسلم.   (٢١) B فلذة.   ولم يتشرف النبى صلعم الى الجنّة.

رُوى ايضًا من اشتاق الى الجنّة (١)سارَعَ الى الخيرات، وقد رُوى ايضًا
(٢)اشتاقت الجنّة الى (٣)ثلثة الى علىّ وعمّار وسَلْمانَ رضى الله عنهم (٤)اجمعين،
والشوق (٤)هو لعبدٍ قد تبرّم ببقايه شوقًا الى لقآء محبوبه، وسُئِل بعضهم عن
الشوق فقال (٥)هيمان القلب عند ذكر المحبوب، وقال آخر الشوق نار الله
٥ (٤)تعالى أشعلها فى قلوب اوليآيه حتى يحرق بها ما فى قلوبهم من الخواطر
والارادات والعوارض والحاجات، وقال (٦)الجُريرى (٧)رحمه الله تعالى لولا
أنّ فى الشوق مُنعةً ما حُمِلَ (٨)الضرُّ، وقال ابو سعيد الخرّاز (٤)رحمه الله
مُلِئَتْ (٩)قلوبهم من المحبّة فطاروا باله (٤)عزّ وجلّ طربًا وهاموا اليه اشتياقًا
فيا لَهُمْ من (١٠)قَلِى مشتاقٍ أَسِفٍ بربّه كَلِفٍ دَنِفٍ ليس لهم سَكَنٌ غيره ولا
١٠ مألوفٌ سواه، وأهل الشوق فى الشوق على ثلثة احوال فمنهم من اشتاق الى
ما وعد الله (٤)تعالى لأوليآيه من الثواب والكرامة والفضل والرضوان ومنهم
من اشتاق الى محبوبه من شدّة محبّته وتبرّمه ببقايه شوقًا الى لقآيه ومنهم من
A f. 28a شاهد قُرْبَ سيّده (١١)أنّه حاضرٌ لا يغيب فتنعّم قلبه بذكره وقال انّما يشتاقُ
الى غايب وهو حاضرٌ لا يغيب فذهب بالشوق عن رؤية الشوق فهو مشتاق
بلا شوق (١٢)ودلايلُهُ تصِفُهُ عند اهله بالشوق وهو لا يصف نفسَهُ بالشوق،
١٥ والشوق يقتضى الأُنس،

باب حال الأُنس،

(١٣)قال الشيخ رحمه الله تعالى ومعنى الأُنس باله (٤)تعالى الاعتماد عليه
والسكون اليه (١٤)والاستعانة به ولا يتهيّأ أن يُعبَّر عنه بأكثر من هذا، وقد

(١) سارَع B. (٢) ثلك B. (٣) اشتاق B. (٤) B om. (٥) هيمان A
but هيمان written above. (٦) الحريرى B. (٧) B om. رحمه الله تعالى.
(٨) الصبر B. (٩) After قلوبهم B has a word which is partly obliterated:
ودلايل B (١٢) انّه. before is suppl. و In A ((١١)). قلوب B. (١٠) لمه(؟)
قال B om. (١٣) and a corrector has restored this reading in A. الشوق
(١٤) والاستغاثة B. الشيخ رحمه الله تعالى.

رُوى فى الخبر انّ مُطَرّف بن عبد الله بن الشِّخِّير (١) رحمه الله كتب الى
عمر بن عبد العزيز (١) رضى الله عنه ليكُنْ أُنْسُك بالله وانقطاعُك اليه فانّ
لله (١) تعالى (٢) عِبادًا استأنَسوا بالله فكانوا فى وحدتهم اشدّ استيناسًا من
الناس فى كثرتهم وأوْحَشُ ما بكون الناس آنَسُ ما يكونون وآنَسُ ما
٥ (٣) يكون الناس أوْحَشُ ما يكونون، ومُطَرّف بن عبد الله من كبار التابعين
وكذلك عمر بن عبد العزيز (١) رضى الله عنه من الائمّة الراشدين، وذُكر
عن بعض العارفين انّه قال انّ لله (١) عزّ وجلّ عِبادًا ارادهم بحقّ حقايق
الأُنْس به (٤) فأخَذهم به عن وجد طعم الخُوف (٥) ممّا سواه، والأُنس بالله
لعبدٍ قد كَملت طهارته وصفاً ذِكرِه واستوحش من كلّ ما يشغله عن الله
١٠ تعالى فعند ذلك آنَسَه الله (١) تعالى به، وأهل الأُنْس فى الأُنس على ثلثة
احوال فمنهم من أنس بالذِكر واستوحش من الغفلة وأنس بالطاعة واستوحش
من (٦) الذنب كما (٧) حُكى عن سهل بن عبد الله (١) رحمه الله انّه قال اوّل
الأُنس من العبد أن تأنس النفس والجوارح (٨) بالعقل ويأنس العقل والنفس
بعلم الشرع ويأنس العقل والنفس والجوارح (٩) بالعمل لله خالصًا فيأنس
١٥ العبد بالله اى يسكن اليه، والحال الثانى من الأُنس فهو لعبدٍ قد استانس
A f. 28b بالله واستوحش ممّا سواه من العوارض والخواطر المشتغلة كما (١٠) ذكر عن
ذى النون (١١) رحمه الله انّه قيل له (١) ما علامة الأُنس بالله قال اذا (١٢) رأيتَهُ
يؤنسك بخَلْقه (١٣) فانّه هو ذا يُوحشك من نفسه وإذا رأيتَهُ يوحشك من
خَلْقه فهو (١٣) ذا يؤنسك (١٥) بنفسه ، وسبيل الجُنيد (١) رحمه الله عن الأُنس

---

(١) B om. ما.   (٢) B عباد.   (٣) B يكون الناس for يكونون ما.   (٤) B ما.
أحد حذم was A of reading orig. The .اخذهم لما B (٥) which also appears
in A as a variant.   (٦) A المعصية but الذنب written above.   (٧) A ذكر
but حكى written above.   (٨) B om. from بالعقل to والجوارح.   (٩) AB بالعلم.
In A العمل is written above as a variant.   (١٠) B حكى.   (١١) B المصرى
رحمه الله for رحمه.   (١٢) A had orig. ان رايته but ان has been stroked out.
(١٣) B فهو ذى.   (١٤) B ذى.   (١٥) AB من نفسه.

بالله فقال ارتفاع الحُشمة مع وجود الهيبة ، وقال ابرهيم المارستانى [١] رحمه
الله وسُئِل عن الانس [٢] قال فرحُ القلب بالمحبوب ، والحال الثالث من
الانس هو الذهاب عن رؤية الانس بوجود الهيبة والقُربِ والتعظيم مع
الانس كما ذُكر عن بعض اهل المعرفة انّه قال انّ لله عِبادًا اوجَدَهم من
الهيبة له ما اخذهم به عن الانس بغيره ، وهذا كما ذُكر عن [٣] ذى النون
[١] رحمه الله ان رجلاً كتب اليه آنَسَك الله بقُربه فكتب اليه [٤] ذو النون
أوْحَشَك الله من قُربه [٥] فانّه اذا آنسك بقربه فهو قَدَرُك واذا اوحشك
من قربه فهو قَدَرُهُ [٦] معنى قوله اوحشك من قربه [١] يعنى بأَنْ يُوجدك
هيبةَ قربه ، وسُئِل الشبْلى رحمه الله عن الانس فقال وَحْشتُك منك ومن
نفسك ومن [٧] الكون ، والانس [٨] بالله يقتضى الاطمأنينة ،

باب حال الاطمأنينة ،

[٩] قال الشيخ رحمه الله وقد قال الله [١٠] تعالى [١١] يَا أَيَّتُهَا ٱلنَّفْسُ ٱلْمُطْمَئِنَّةُ
وفى التفسير المطمئنّة بالايمان ، وقال عزّ وجلّ [١٢] ٱلَّذِينَ آمَنُوا وَتَطْمَئِنُّ قُلُوبُهُم
بِذِكْرِ ٱللَّهِ أَلَا بِذِكْرِ ٱللَّهِ تَطْمَئِنُّ ٱلْقُلُوبُ ، وقال فى قصّة ابرهيم عليه السلم
[١٤] وَلَكِنْ لِيَطْمَئِنَّ قَلْبِي ، وقال سهل بن عبد الله [١] رحمه الله اذا سكن
قلب العبد الى مولاه واطمأنّ اليه قَوِيَتْ حال العبد فاذا قويت أَنِسَ بالعبد

A f.29a

---

[١] B om.   [٢] فقال B.   [٣] ذا AB.   [٤] ذا A.   [٥] فاذا B
انسك.   [٦] فمعنى B.   [٧] Here both A and B add the passage beginning من معرفة احسان الله ولطفه which and ending وسُئِل الحسن بن على الدامغانى
evidently belongs to the next chapter. It has been supplied in marg. A in
its proper place by a corrector (see the following page, l. ١ to l. ٥). Here
the corrector has written in marg. A بعد فى الباب موضعه مكمل.   [٨] B بالله
[٩] B om. قال الشيخ رحمه الله.   [١٠] B عز وجل.   عز وجل.
[١١] Kor. 89, 27.   [١٢] Kor. 13, 28.   [١٤] Kor. 2, 262.

كُلّ شىء، (١) وسُئل الحسن بن على الداsمغانى (٢) رحمه الله عن قوله (٢) عزّ
وجلّ (٢) اَلَّذِينَ آمَنُوا وَتَطْمَئِنُّ قُلُوبُهُمْ بِذِكْرِ اَللَّهِ الآية فقال ان القلوب
هشّت وبشّت وسكتت واستأنست ثمّ كُشف عنه، (٤) قال هشّت (٥) من معرفة
اجلال الله (٢) تعالى وعظمته وبشّت (٥) من معرفة (٢) رحمة الله وفضله وسكتت
(٥) من معرفة كفاية الله وصدقه واستأنست من معرفة (٧) احسان الله ولطفه،
قال وسُئل الشبلى (٢) رحمه الله عن معنى قول ابى سليمن الدارانى (٢) رحمه
الله النفس اذا احرزت قوتها اطمأنّت (٨) فقال اذا عرفت من يقوتها اطمأنّت،
والاطمأنينة حال رفيع (٩) وهى لعبدٍ رجح عقلُه وقوِيَ ايمانه ورسخ عِلمه وصفا
ذكرُه وثبتت حقيقته (٩) وهى على ثلثة ضروب فضربٌ منها للعامّة لأنّهم اذا
ذكروه اطمأنّوا الى ذكرهم له فَعَظُم منه الاجابة للدعوات باتّساع الرزق ودفع
الآفات، وهو ما قال الله عزّ وجلّ اَلنَّفْسُ اَلْمُطْمَئِنَّةُ يعنى بالايمان بأن لا
دافع ولا مانع الّا الله، (٢) قال والضرب الثانى للخصوص لأنّهم رضوا بقضابه
وصبروا (١٠) على بلآيه واخلصوا (١١) واتّقوا وسكنوا واطمأنّوا (١٢) الى قوله
(١٢) عزّ وجلّ (١٤) إِنَّ اَللَّهَ مَعَ اَلَّذِينَ اَتَّقَوْا وَاَلَّذِينَ هُمْ مُحْسِنُونَ (١٥) وَإِنَّ اَللَّهَ
مَعَ اَلصَّابِرِينَ، فاطمأنّوا وسكنوا الى (١٦) قوله (١٧) مَعَ فكانت اطمأنينتهم ممزوجة
برؤية طاعتهم، والضرب الثالث (١٨) للخصوص الخصوص علموا ان سرايرهم لا
تقدر أن تطمئنّ اليه ولا تسكن معه هيبةً وتعظيمًا لأنّه ليس له غاية تُدرَكُ

---

(١) This passage occurs in AB above (see note ٧ on p. ٦٦) and is also
written on the margin of A in this place. I give the text according to A.
(٢) B om. (٣) Kor. 13, 28. (٤) B فقال. (٥) A عن. (٦) A om.
٠ The marginal version in A has وسكتت من معرفة كفاية for من رحمة from
(٧) B app. اختيار. (٨) A om. from فقال to اطمأنت. (٩) B وهو.
(١٠) B om. على بلآيه. (١١) A واتقوا but وايقنوا written above. (١٢) B
واطمأنوا الى. (١٣) B om. from عز وجل to محسنون. (١٤) Kor. 16, 128.
(١٥) Kor. 2, 148. B ان. (١٦) B قوله عز وجل. (١٧) In marg. A مع
الصابرين. (١٨) B خصوص.

وليسَ كَمِثْلِهِ شَيْءٌ وَلَمْ يَكُنْ لَهُ كُفُوًا أَحَدٌ فمن كانت الاشياء فى سرّه كذلك
فإلى ما ذا يطمئنّ (١)او يسكن قلبُهُ ومن وقع فى عطش التمنّى فى طلب
الزيادة (٢)وقع فى البحر الذى لا تجرى فيه الاوهام، وهذا كلام قد اختصرتُهُ
من كلام الواسطى، والاطمأنينة تقتضى حال المشاهدة،

بابُ حال المشاهدة،

(٣)قال الشيخ رحمه الله وقد قال الله تعالى (٤)إِنَّ فِى ذَلِكَ لَذِكْرَى
لِمَنْ كَانَ لَهُ قَلْبٌ أَوْ أَلْقَى ٱلْسَّمْعَ وَهُوَ شَهِيدٌ يعنى (٥)حاضرُ القلب، وقال
ايضًا (٦)وَشَاهِدٍ وَمَشْهُودٍ، (٧)وقال ابو بكر الواسطى (١)رحمه الله فالشاهد
الربّ والمشهود الكَوْن (٨)أَعْدَمَهم ثم أُوْجَدَهم، وقال ابو سعيد الخرّاز (١)رحمه A f.29b
الله (٩)فمن شاهَدَ الله بقلبه (١٠)خنس عنه ما دونه وتلاشى كلّ شىء وغاب
عند (١١)وجود عظمة الله (١٢)تعالى (١٣)ولم يَبْقَ فى القلب الاّ الله عزّ وجلّ،
وقال عمرو بن عثمن المكّى (١)رحمه الله المشاهدة ما لاقت القلوبُ من
الغيب بالغيب (١٤)ولا يجعلها عِيانًا (١٥)ولا يجعلها وَجْدًا، وقال ايضًا المشاهدة
(١٦)وَصْلٌ بين رؤية القلوب (١٧)وبين رؤية العيان لانّ رؤية القلوب (١٨)عند
كشف اليقين فى (١٩)زيادة توهُّم، وهو قول النبى صلعم لعبد الله بن عمر
(١)رضى الله عنه اعْبُدِ اللهَ كأنّك تراه الحديث، وإمّا قوله عزّ وجلّ وَهُوَ
شَهِيدٌ (٢٠)فقالوا هو مشاهدة الاشياء بعَيْن (٢١)العَبَر ومعاينتها بأَعْيُن الفكر،

(١) B om.   (٢) B ووقع.   (٣) B om. قال الشيخ رحمه الله.   (٤) Kor.
50, 36.   (٥) A حاظر.   (٦) Kor. 85, 3.   (٧) B قال.   (٨) B adds شاهد.
فصل أوجدهم after B (٩)   (١٠) B حلس.   (١١) B وجوده.
(١٢) B عزّ وجلّ.   (١٣) B om. from ولم to عزّ وجلّ.   (١٤) B فلم.   (١٥) B ولم.
(١٦) B فصل.   (١٧) B om. بين.   (١٨) B عنه.   (١٩) B زيادة which
is written in A as a variant.   (٢٠) B فقال.   (٢١) B العبرة.

وقال عمرو المكّى [١] رحمه الله المشاهدة [٢] يعنى المحاضرة يعنى المداناة كما ذكر الله عزّ وجلّ [٣] وَسَلُمْ عَنِ الْقَرْيَةِ الَّتِى كَانَتْ حَاضِرَةَ الْبَحْرِ يعنى قريبة [٤] من البحر شاهدة البحر، وقال عمرو المكّى [١] رحمه الله المشاهدة زوايد اليقين سطعت بكواشف الحضور غير خارجة من تغطية القلب، وقال ايضًا المشاهدة

٥ حضور [٥] بمعنى قُرْب مقرون [٦] بعلم اليقين وحقايقها، وأهل المشاهدة على ثلثة احوال [٧] فالاوّل منها الأصاغر وهم المُريدون [٨] وهو ما قال ابو بكر الواسطى [١] رحمه الله يشاهدون الاشياء بعين [٩] العَبَر ويشاهدونها بأَعْيُن الفكر، والحال الثانى من المشاهدة [١٠] الأوساط وهو الذى اشار اليه ابو سعيد الخرّاز [١] رحمه الله حيث يقول الخلق فى قبضة [١١] الحقّ وفى ملّكه

١٠ فاذا وقعت المشاهدة فيما بين الله وبين العبد لا يبقى فى سرّه [١٢] ولا فى وهم غير الله [١٣] تعالى، والحال الثالث من المشاهدة ما اشار اليه عمرو بن عثمن المكّى [١] رحمه الله فى كتاب المشاهدة فقال انّ قلوب العارفين [١٤] شاهدت الله [١٥] مشاهدةً تثبيت فشاهدوه بكلّ شىء وشاهدوا كلّ [١٦] الكاينات به فكانت مشاهدتهم لَدَيْه ولم به فكانوا غايبين حاضرين وحاضرين غايبين

١٥ [١٧] على انفراد الحقّ فى الغيبة والحضور فشاهدوه ظاهرًا وباطنًا وباطنًا وظاهرًا وآخرًا أوّلاً وأوّلاً آخرًا كما قال عزّ وجلّ [١٩] هُوَ الْاَوَّلُ وَالْاَخِرُ وَالظَّاهِرُ وَالْبَاطِنُ وَهُوَ بِكُلِّ شَىْءٍ عَلِيمٌ، والمشاهدة حال رفيع وهى من لوايح زيادات حقايق اليقين، [٢٠] وتقتضى [٢١] حال اليقين،

(١) B om.   (٢) B om. from يعنى to وسلم.   (٣) Kor. 7, 163.   (٤) من B

فالاولى suppl.   (٥) معنى B.   (٦) بعلم A.   (٧) A om. المشاهد والبحر

in marg.   (٨) وهم كما B.   (٩) الغير A. The reading of B is doubtful.

(١٠) وهو الاوساط B.   (١١) الله B.   (١٢) ولا همه B.   (١٣) عزّ وجل B.

(١٤) شاهدوا B.   (١٥) مشاهدةً تثبت B app.   (١٦) A الكليات.   (١٧) B om.

(١٨) و has been suppl. in A.   (١٩) Kor. 57, 3.   بانفراد A in marg.

(٢٠) A adds in marg. حال المشاهدة.   (٢١) B حقايق.

باب حال اليقين،

(١)قال الشيخ رحمه الله وقد ذكر الله تعالى اليقين فى مواضع من كتابه
على ثلثة اوجه عِلْم اليقين وعَيّن اليقين وحَقّ اليقين، وقال النبى صلعم
سَلُوا الله (٢)تعالى العفو والعافية واليقين فى الدنيا والآخرة، وقال (٢)صلعم
رحم الله اخى عيسى (٢)عليه السلم لو ازداد يقينًا لمشى فى (٣)الهوآء، وقال
عامر بن عبد قَيْس (٢)رحمه الله لو كُشف الغطآء ما ازددتُ يقينًا يعنى عند
معاينتى لما آمنت به من الغيب، وهذا كلام غلبات ووَجْد وتحقيق، وقد
رُوى عن النبى صلعم انّه قال الخَلْق يُبْعَثون على ما يموتون عليه، ولا يكون
الخُبَر كالمعاينة فى جميع معانيها ويجوز ان يكون له وجه آخر وهو (٤)أن
يعنى ما ازددت عِلْمٍ يقين، وقال ابو يعقوب النَّهْرجورى (٢)رحمه الله اذا
استكمل العبد حقايق اليقين صار البلآء عنده نعمة والرخآء مصيبة، واليقين
هو المكاشفة والمكاشفة على ثلثة اوجه مكاشفة العِيان بالأبصار يوم القِيمة
ومكاشفة (٢)القلوب بحقايق الايمان بمباشرة اليقين بلا كَيْف ولا حَدّ (٥)والحالة
الثالثة مكاشفة الآيات بإظهار القدرة (٦)للأنبيآء عليهم السلم بالمُعْجِزات
ولغيرهم (٧)بالكرامات والإجابات، واليقين حال رفيع وأهل اليقين على ثلثة
(٨)احوال فالاوّل الاصاغر وهم المريدون (٩)والعموم وهو (١٠)كما قال بعضهم
اوّلُ مقام (١١)اليقين الثقةُ بما فى يد الله (٢)تعالى والإياس (١٢)ممّا فى ايدى
الناس، وهو ما قال الجُنَيْد (٢)رحمه الله حيث سُئل عن اليقين فقال اليقين
ارتفاع الشكّ، وقال ابو يعقوب اذا وجد العبدُ الرضا بما قسم الله له فقد
تكامل فيه اليقين، وسُئل رُوَيْم بن احمد (٢)رحمه الله عن اليقين فقال

(١) B om. قال الشيخ رحمه الله. (٢) B om. (٣) B الهوى. (٤) B انه.
(٥) A om. والحالة الثالثة but الثالث has been supplied by a later
hand. (٦) B والانبيا والمعجزات. (٧) B بالمكرمات. (٨) B اوجه. عنى به
(٩) B العوام. (١٠) B ما. (١١) B من اليقين. (١٢) A عمّا.

تحقيق القلب بالمعنى على ما هو به، والثانى الاوساط وهم الخُصوص وهو ما
سُئل (١)ابن عطاءَ عن اليقين فقال ما زالت فيه (٢)المعارضات على دوام
الاوقات، وكما قال ابو يعقوب (٣)النهرجورى (٤)رحمه الله العبد اذا تحقّق
باليقين (٤)ترحّل من يقين الى يقين حتى يصير اليقين له وَطَنًا، وسُئل ابو
الحسين النورى (٣)رحمه الله عن اليقين فقال اليقين المشاهدة، ومعنى المشاهدة
قد ذكرناه، والثالث الاكابر وهم خُصوص الخُصوص وهو ما قال عمرو بن
عثمٰن المكّى (٣)رحمه الله اليقين فى جملته (٣)تحقيق الإثبات لله عزّ وجلّ بكلّ
صفاته، وقال (٥)حدّ اليقين دوام انتصاب القلوب لله عزّ وجلّ بما أوْرَدَ
عليها اليقينُ من حركات ما لاقى به الإلهام، وقال ابو يعقوب لا يستحقّ
العبدُ اليقينَ حتى يقطع (٦)كلّ سبب بينه وبين الله (٣)تعالى من العرش الى
الثرى حتى (٧)يكون مرادَهُ اللهُ لا (٨)غير (٩)ويؤثر الله (٣)تعالى على كلّ شىء
سواه، وليس لزيادات اليقين نهاية كلّما (١٠)تفهّموا وتفقّهوا فى الدين ازدادوا
يقينًا على يقين، واليقين اصل جميع الاحوال (١١)واليه تنتهى جميع الاحوال
وهو (١٢)آخر الاحوال وباطن جميع الاحوال وجميع الاحوال ظاهر اليقين
ونهاية اليقين تحقيق التصديق بالغيب بازالة كلّ شكّ ورَيْب ونهاية اليقين
الاستبشار وحلاوة المناجاة وصفاء النظر الى الله تعالى بمشاهدة القلوب بحقايق
اليقين بازالة العِلَل ومعارضة التُهَم، قال الله (١٣)تعالى (١٣)إنَّ فِى ذٰلِكَ لَآيَاتٍ
(١٥)لِلْمُتَوَسِّمِينَ (١٦)وَفِى الْاَرْضِ آيَاتٌ لِلْمُوقِنِينَ، وقال الواسطى (٣)رحمه
الله (١٧)اذا ايقن بالمعنى وقع له مشاهدة (١٨)الاحوال واذا انكشف له حقايق

A f.31a

---

(١) احمد B.   (٢) B المعارضة.   (٣) B om.   (٤) B فدخل.   (٥) B احمد.

(١) بن B.   (٦) عن كل B.   (٧) A صار but يكون written above as a variant.

(٨) Altered in A to غيره which seems to be the reading of B.   (٩) فيوثر B.

(١٠) وباطن جميع الاحوال to واليه from B om.   (١١) تفقهوا فى الدين وتفهموا B.

(١٢) In marg. A اجلّ.   (١٣) تبارك وتعالى B.   (١٤) Kor. 15, 75.

(١٥) B om. from للمتوسمين to آيات.   (١٦) Kor. 51, 20.   (١٧) B يا.

(١٨) A الاحوال with الاضداد as variant.

المعنى خرج من (١) أشجان الخَلْقى، خاطَبهم بالتقريب وهو الكشف من
الصدِّيقيّة، وخاطبهم (٢) تعالى بالمشاهدة فقال (٣) الصدّيقين وَالشُّهَدَآء وَالصَّالِحِينَ،
الشهدآء باعوه نفوسهم (٤) والصالحون الذين هم لأماناتهم وعَهْدهم راعون،

<hr>

(٥) كتاب أهل الصفوة فى الفهم والاتّباع لكتاب الله عزّ وجلّ،

باب الموافقة لكتاب الله تعالى،

قال الشيخ رحمه الله قال الله عزّ وجلّ (٦) هُوَ ٱلَّذِى أَنْزَلَ عَلَيْكَ ٱلْكِتَابَ
مِنْهُ آيَاتٌ مُحْكَمَاتٌ هُنَّ أُمُّ ٱلْكِتَابِ وَأُخَرُ مُتَشَابِهَاتٌ، وقال (٧) وَنُنَزِّلُ مِنَ
ٱلْقُرآنِ مَا هُوَ شِفَآءٌ وَرَحْمَةٌ لِلْمُؤْمِنِينَ، وقال (٨) يسَ وَٱلْقُرآنِ ٱلْحَكِيمِ، وقال
(٩) حِكْمَةٌ بَالِغَةٌ، وقال (٢) النبى صلعم القران حَبْلُ الله المتينُ لا (١٠) تنقضى
عجائبُهُ ولا (١١) يَخْلَقُ عن كثرة الردّ من قال به صدق ومن عمل به رشد
ومن حكم به عدل ومن اعتصم به هُدِىَ، ورُوى عن عبد الله بن مسعود
(٢) رضى الله عنه انّه قال من اراد العلم فلْيُثَوِّر القران فانّ فيه علم الأوّلين
(١٢) والآخرين، وقد قال الله (١٣) تعالى (١٤) آلم ذَلِكَ ٱلْكِتَابُ لاَ رَيْبَ فِيهِ هُدًى
لِلْمُتَّقِينَ ٱلَّذِينَ يُؤْمِنُونَ (١٥) بِٱلْغَيْبِ، فعلم أَهْلُ العلم بهذا الخطاب انّ فى
كتاب الله الذى أُنزل على رسوله (٢) صلعم وهو القران الذى لا شكّ فيه

<hr>

(١) اسجان AB.   (٢) B om.   (٣) Kor. 4, 71. B has الصادقين for الصدّيقين.

(٤) A والصالحين.   (٥) B باب هذهب عز وجل لكتاب الله والاتّباع الفهم كتاب

اهل الصفوة فى الفهم والاتّباع والموافقة لكتاب الله عزوجل قال الله تبارك وتعلى هو الذى

انزل الخ.   (٦) Kor. 3, 5.   (٧) Kor. 17, 84.   (٨) Kor. 36, 1.

(٩) Kor. 54, 5.   (١٠) ينقضى B.   (١١) محلق AB.   (١٢) B الاخرين وعلم.

(١٣) B فى كتابه عزوجل.   (١٤) Kor. 2, 1.   (١٥) B adds ويؤمنون الصلاة.

لأحدٍ من المؤمنين أنّه من عند الله انّ فيه هُدًى (١)وبيانًا لهم فى جميع ما
أشكل عليهم من احكام الدين بعد ايمانهم بالغيب وهو التصديق بما اخبرهم
الله به عمّا غاب عن (٢)أعْيُنِهم، ثمّ قال فى آية أخرى (٣)وَنَزَّلْنَا عَلَيْكَ ٱلْكِتَابَ
تِبْيَانًا لِكُلِّ شَىْءٍ وَهُدًى وَرَحْمَةً وَبُشْرَى لِلْمُسْلِمِينَ، (٤)فأفادت هذه الآيـة
لأهل الفهم من اهل العلم بعد ايمانهم بالغيب ايضًا أنّ تحت كلّ حرف من   A f.31b
كتاب الله (٥)تعالى (٦)كثيرًا من الفهم مذخورًا لأهله على مقدار ما قُسم لهم من
ذلك واستدلّوا على ذلك بآياتٍ من القران مثل قوله عزّ وجلّ (٧)مَا فَرَّطْنَا
فِى ٱلْكِتَابِ مِنْ شَىْءٍ وقوله (٨)وَكُلَّ شَىْءٍ أَحْصَيْنَاهُ فِى إِمَامٍ مُبِينٍ وقوله
(٩)وَإِنْ مِنْ شَىْءٍ إِلَّا عِنْدَنَا خَزَائِنُهُ وَمَا نُنَزِّلُهُ إِلَّا بِقَدَرٍ مَعْلُومٍ، (١٠)وقالوا فى
١٠ معنى قوله (١١)عزّ وجلّ (١٢)مِنْ شَىْءٍ (١٢)انّ معناه من شىءٍ من عِلْم الدين
وعِلْم الاحوال التى بين الخلق وبين الله (١٢)تعالى وغير ذلك، (١٤)وقال
(١١)عزّ وجلّ فى آية أخرى (١٥)إِنَّ هَذَا ٱلْقُرْآنَ يَهْدِى لِلَّتِى هِىَ أَقْوَمُ بعنى
يدُلّ الى الذى هو أَصْوَبُ، فعلم اهل الفهم من اهل العلم ان لا سبيل الى
التعلّق بالأصْوب ممّا يهدى اليه القران الّا بالتدبّر والتفكّر والتيقّظ (١٦)والتذكّر
١٥ وحضور القلب عند تلاونه وعلموا ذلك ايضًا (١٧)بقوله (١٨)كِتَابٌ أَنْزَلْنَاهُ
إِلَيْكَ مُبَارَكٌ لِيَدَّبَّرُوا آيَاتِهِ وَلِيَتَذَكَّرَ أُولُوا ٱلْأَلْبَابِ، ثم استفاد اهل الفهم
من هذه الآية ايضًا ان التدبّر والتفكّر (١١)والتذكّر لا وصول اليه إلّا بحضور
(١٩)القلب (٢٠)لقول الله عزّ وجلّ (٢١)إِنَّ فِى ذَلِكَ لَذِكْرَى لِمَنْ كَانَ لَهُ قَلْبٌ
أَوْ أَلْقَى ٱلسَّمْعَ وَهُوَ شَهِيدٌ يعنى حاضر القلب، ثمّ لم يترك على ذلك حتى

---

(١) ‏وافاد B‏. (٢) In marg. A اعين روسهم‏. (٣) Kor. 16, 91. (٤) ‏وبيان A‏.

(٥) ‏جل ذكره B‏. (٦) ‏كبير B‏. In A the final *alif* has been supplied.

(٧) Kor. 6, 38. (٨) Kor. 36, 11. (٩) Kor. 15, 21. (١٠) ‏قالوا B‏.

(١١) B om. (١٢) ‏فى هذه الايات من علم الدين الخ B‏. (١٢) ‏عز وجل B‏.

(١٤) ‏ثم قال B‏. (١٥) Kor. 17, 9. (١٦) ‏والتفكر فى اياته B‏. (١٧) ‏بقوله B‏.

(١٨) Kor. 38, 28. (١٩) ‏القلوب B‏. (٢٠) ‏لقوله ان فى ذلك الخ B‏. ‏تعلى‏.

(٢١) Kor. 50, 36.

‏ذكر القلب فى آية أخرى فقال (١) يَوْمَ لَا يَنْفَعُ مَالٌ وَلَا بَنُونَ إِلَّا مَنْ أَتَى اللّٰهَ‏
‏بِقَلْبٍ سَلِيمٍ، (٢) ثُمَّ لم يترك على ذلك حتى اقام إِمامًا للخلاق فى القلب السليم‏
‏فقال عز وجل (٣) وَإِنَّ مِنْ شِيعَتِهِ لَإِبْرَاهِيمَ إِذْ جَاءَ رَبَّهُ بِقَلْبٍ سَلِيمٍ، قال‏
‏اهل الفهم القلب السليم الذى ليس فيه غير الله عز وجل، وقال سهل بن‏
٥ ‏عبد الله (٤) رحمه الله لو أُعطِيَ العبدُ لكل حرف من القران ألفَ فَهْمٍ ما بلغ‏
‏نهاية ما جعل الله (٤) تعالى فى آية من (٥) كتاب الله تعالى من الفهم (٦) لأنّه‏
‏كلام الله تعالى وكلامه صفته وكما أنّه ليس (٧) لله نهاية فكذلك لا نهاية لفَهْم‏
‏كلامه وإنّما يفهمون على مقدار ما يفتح الله (٤) تعالى على قلوب اوليآيه من فَهْمِ‏
‏كلامه وكلام الله غير مخلوق فلا تبلغ الى نهاية الفهم فيه (٨) فهوم الخلق (٩) لأنّها‏
١٠ ‏مُحْدَثَة مخلوقة، وقد ذكر الله تعالى الهداية فى القران (١٠) يقوله (١١) هُدًى لِلْمُتَّقِينَ،‏

A f. 32a

‏باب فى تخصيص الدعوة (١٢) ووجه الاصطفآء،‏

‏قال سهل بن عبد الله (٤) رحمه الله الدعوة عامّةٌ والهداية خاصّةٌ (١٣) وأشار‏
‏الى قوله تعالى (١٤) وَاللّٰهُ يَدْعُو إِلَى دَارِ السَّلَامِ وَيَهْدِي مَنْ يَشَاءُ (١٥) إِلَى صِرَاطٍ‏
‏مُسْتَقِيمٍ لأنّ الدعوة عامّة والهداية (١٦) مختصّة على تفاضلها لأنّه ردّ المشيّة فى‏
١٥ ‏باب الهداية اليه فكان (١٧) الذين اختارهم واحبّهم واصطفاهم (١٨) دون من‏
‏دعاهم، وقد ذكر الله تعالى الاصطفآء ايضًا فى (١٩) مواضع من كتابه فقال فى‏

(١) Kor. 26, 88—89.‏ ‏(٢) B om. from ثم to بقلب سليم جاء ربّه.‏ ‏(٣) Kor.
37, 81—82.‏ ‏(٤) B om.‏ ‏(٥) B كتابه من الفهم الخ.‏ ‏(٦) B app. انه.‏ ‏(٧) B
لله عز وجل.‏ ‏(٨) Suppl. in marg. A. B الخلق فيه من.‏ ‏(٩) A proceeds:
لأنّ فهوم الخلق محدثة مخلوقة فلا يجوز ان يفهم. In marg. A وقد ذكر الله تعالى الخ.
‏(١٠) B لقوله.‏ ‏(١١) Kor. 2, 1.‏ ‏المحدَث جميع احكام كلام المحدث. Text as in B.
‏(١٢) B وجوه.‏ ‏(١٣) B فأشار.‏ ‏(١٤) Kor. 10, 26.‏ ‏(١٥) B om. الى.
‏(١٦) B خاصة.‏ ‏(١٧) AB الذى.‏ ‏(١٨) B روى.‏ ‏صراط مستقيم.
‏(١٩) فى is the last word in B, fol. 43a. Fol. 43b begins وفرغ عن الاشغال وخرج

موضع (١)قُلِ ٱلْحَمْدُ لِلَّهِ وَسَلَامٌ عَلَى عِبَادِهِ ٱلَّذِينَ ٱصْطَفَى ٱللَّهُ خَيْرٌ أَمَّا يُشْرِكُونَ
فأشار بالسلّم الى عباد قد اصطفاهم واجتباهم ولم يبيّن من هم وكيف هم، ثمّ
لم يترك على ذلك (٢)وقال فى آية أخرى (٣)ٱللَّهُ يَصْطَفِي مِنَ ٱلْمَلَائِكَةِ رُسُلًا
وَمِنَ ٱلنَّاسِ، (٤)قال المفسّرون وَمِنَ ٱلنَّاسِ يعنى (٥)به الأنبيآء فلو ترك على
هذا ايضًا (٦)لكان للقايل ان يقول انّ الاصطفآء لا يجوز (٧)الّا للأنبيآء
فقال (٨)ثُمَّ أَوْرَثْنَا ٱلْكِتَابَ ٱلَّذِينَ ٱصْطَفَيْنَا مِنْ عِبَادِنَا (٩)فَمِنْهُمْ ظَالِمٌ لِنَفْسِهِ
وَمِنْهُمْ مُقْتَصِدٌ وَمِنْهُمْ سَابِقٌ بِٱلْخَيْرَاتِ، (١٠)ففرق بين الاصطفآء الذى ذكر
للرسل عليهم السلام (١١)والاصطفآء الذى ذكر لعباده الذين اورثهم الكتاب
وهم المؤمنون، ثم بيّن انّهم متفاوتون ايضًا فى احوالهم (١٢)التى بينهم وبين
الله (١٣)تعالى (١٤)فَمِنْهُمْ ظَالِمٌ لِنَفْسِهِ (١٥)ٱلْآيَةَ (١٦)فوقع الاصطفآء على وجهين
اصطفآء الأنبيآء (٥)عليهم السلم (١٧)بالعصمة والتأبيد والوحى وتبليغ الرسالة
ولسايرهم من المؤمنين الاصطفآء بصفآء المعاملة وحسن المجاهدة والتعلّق
بالحقايق والمنازلة، ثمّ قال عزّ وجلّ (١٨)لِكُلٍّ جَعَلْنَا مِنكُمْ شِرْعَةً وَمِنْهَاجًا،
وقال تعالى (١٩)وَلَوْ شَآءَ ٱللَّهُ لَجَعَلَكُمْ أُمَّةً وَاحِدَةً وَلَكِنْ لِيَبْلُوَكُمْ فِيمَا آتَاكُمْ
A f.32b فَٱسْتَبِقُوا ٱلْخَيْرَاتِ، فأمرهم الله تعالى بالاستباق والمسارعة (٥)والمبادرة الى
الخيرات مُجْمَلًا ولم يبيّن أيْشَ الخيرات التى أمرهم بالاستباق اليها، ثمّ (٢٠)فصّل
وبيّن فى مواضع (٢١)كثيرة (٢٢)كقوله (٢٣)هُدًى لِلْمُتَّقِينَ، (٢٤)وَمَوْعِظَةٌ لِلْمُتَّقِينَ،

باب آدابهم فى الوضوء والطهارات which occur in the chapter entitled نفسه للعبادة
(A fol. 63b, last line). The text of B resumes, without any lacuna, on fol. 69b, l. 1.

(١) Kor. 27, 60.　(٢) B فقال.　(٣) Kor. 22, 74.　(٤) B وقال.　(٥) B om.
(٦) B كان.　(٧) B الّا يكون.　(٨) Kor. 35, 29.　(٩) B om. the rest
of the verse.　(١٠) B فرق.　(١١) A الاصطفا. B الاصطفآ.　(١٢) B الذى.
(١٣) عزّ وجلّ.　(١٤) B فمنهم قال.　(١٥) B سابق ومنهم مقتصد ومنهم.
(١٦) B وقعت. ثمّ.　(١٧) B العظم.　(١٨) Kor. 5, 52.　العظيم.
B ولكل, and و has been suppl. in A.　(١٩) Kor. 5, 53.　(٢٠) B om.
فصّل و.　(٢١) Here A inserts in marg. العام التى يتعلق بها الايات ذكر باب.
وهى مثل كثيرة الابواب هذه والعام الخاص يستعملها التى الايات استعمال بعد والخاص.

^(١) وَإِيَّايَ فَاتَّقُونِ، ^(٢) وَإِيَّايَ فَارْهَبُونِ، ^(٣) فَلَا تَخَافُوهُمْ وَخَافُونِ، ^(٤) فَلَا تَخْشَوْهُمْ
وَاخْشَوْنِ، ^(٥) فَاذْكُرُونِى أَذْكُرْكُمْ، ^(٦) وَعَلَى اللّٰهِ فَتَوَكَّلُوا، ^(٧) أَطِيعُوا اللّٰهَ وَأَطِيعُوا
الرَّسُولَ، ^(٨) وَالَّذِينَ جَاهَدُوا ^(٩) فِينَا، ^(١٠) وَمَنْ شَكَرَ فَإِنَّمَا يَشْكُرُ ^(١١) لِنَفْسِهِ،
^(١٢) إِنَّ اللّٰهَ يُحِبُّ الصَّابِرِينَ، ^(١٣) وَمَا أُمِرُوا إِلَّا لِيَعْبُدُوا اللّٰهَ مُخْلِصِينَ لَهُ الدِّينَ،
^(١٤) وقال ^(١٥) رِجَالٌ صَدَقُوا مَا عَاهَدُوا اللّٰهَ ^(١٦) عَلَيْهِ، ثم ذكر القانتين والقانتات
والصادقين والصادقات والصابرين والصابرات والخاشعين والخاشعات وذكر
فى آيات من القرآن ^(١٧) ذَكَرَ ^(١٨) التوبة والانابة والتفويض والرضا والتسليم
والقناعة وترك الاختيار ثم قال ^(١٩) قُلْ مَتَاعُ الدُّنْيَا قَلِيلٌ وَالْآخِرَةُ ^(١٤) خَيْرٌ
لِمَنِ اتَّقَى، وقال ^(٢٠) ذَلِكَ مَتَاعُ الْحَيَاةِ الدُّنْيَا وَاللّٰهُ عِنْدَهُ حُسْنُ ^(٢١) الْمَآبِ،
^(٢٢) وَمَا الْحَيَاةُ الدُّنْيَا إِلَّا لَعِبٌ وَلَهْوٌ ^(٢٣) وَمَا حَيَاةُ الدُّنْيَا إِلَّا مَتَاعُ الْغُرُورِ، ثم
قال ^(٢٤) مَنْ كَانَ يُرِيدُ حَرْثَ الْآخِرَةِ نَزِدْ لَهُ فِى حَرْثِهِ وَمَنْ كَانَ يُرِيدُ حَرْثَ
الدُّنْيَا نُؤْتِهِ مِنْهَا وَمَا لَهُ فِى الْآخِرَةِ مِنْ نَصِيبٍ، ثم ذكر الشيطان فقال
^(٢٥) إِنَّ الشَّيْطَانَ لَكُمْ عَدُوٌّ فَاتَّخِذُوهُ عَدُوًّا، وقال ^(٢٦) أَفَرَأَيْتَ مَنِ اتَّخَذَ إِلَهَهُ
هَوَاهُ وَأَضَلَّهُ اللّٰهُ عَلَى عِلْمٍ ^(٢٧) وَخَتَمَ عَلَى سَمْعِهِ وَقَلْبِهِ وَجَعَلَ عَلَى بَصَرِهِ
غِشَاوَةً، وقال ^(٢٨) فَأَمَّا مَنْ طَغَى وَآثَرَ الْحَيَاةَ الدُّنْيَا ^(٢٩) الآية، وما يُشبه ذلك

---

^(٢٢) A قوله.   ^(٢٣) Kor. 2, 1.   ^(٢٤) Kor. 2, 62.

^(١) Kor. 2, 38.   ^(٢) Kor. 2, 38.   ^(٣) Kor. 3, 169.   ^(٤) Kor. 2, 145.

^(٥) Kor. 2, 147. B واذكرونى.   ^(٦) Kor. 5, 26.   ^(٧) Kor. 5, 93.   ^(٨) Kor.
29, 69.   ^(٩) B adds الآية.   ^(١٠) Kor. 27, 40.   ^(١١) A adds in marg.
أن الذين امنوا وهاجروا وجاهدوا باموالهم وانفسهم فى سبيل اله (Kor. 8, 73).
^(١٢) Kor. 3, 140. Kor. has وَاللّٰهُ.   ^(١٣) Kor. 98, 4.   ^(١٤) B om.
وقوله يايُّها الذين امنوا استجيبوا لله A adds in marg. ^(١٦)   ^(١٥) Kor. 33, 23.
وللرسول اذا دعاكم لما يحييكم الآية (Kor. 8, 24).   ^(١٧) B ايضًا.   ^(١٨) B adds
والاياب.   ^(١٩) Kor. 4, 79. B om. قل.   ^(٢٠) Kor. 3, 12. B om. ذلك.
^(٢١) B المأب.   ^(٢٢) Kor. 6, 32.   ^(٢٣) Kor. 3, 182.   ^(٢٤) Kor. 42, 19.
^(٢٥) Kor. 35, 6.   ^(٢٦) Kor. 45, 22.   ^(٢٧) B om. the rest of the verse.
^(٢٨) Kor. 79, 37—38.   ^(٢٩) B فان الجحيم هى الماوى واما من خاف مقام ربه ونهى
النفس عن الهوا فان الجنة هى الماوا (Kor. 79, 39—41).

من الآيات التى ندب الله (١)تعالى الخلق (٢)الى المسارعة والاستباق الى
(٣)التعلّق والتخلّق بها والصدق والاخلاص فيها كثيرةٌ والمؤمنون فى قبول
ذلك متساوون (٢)وفى منازلتها وركوب حقايقها متفاوتون، والجميع مخاطبون
وهم على ثلث درجات،

باب ذكر تفاوت المستمعين خطاب الله (٤)تعالى (٥)ودرجاتهم
فى قبول الخطاب،

(٦)قال الشيخ رحمه الله فمنهم من (٧)سمع الخطاب (٨)وقبله وأقرّ به
(٩)وتعرّض (١٠)لما خوطب (٩)به من هذه الآيات البيّنات التى (١١)ذكرناها
والتى لم (١٣)نذكرها (١٢)فيما يُشبه ذلك، وحالَ (١٤)بيّنه وبيّن العمل (٩)بها
والانتفاع بما وعدم الله (١٥)تعالى من الثواب (٩)عليها (١٦)الاشتغالُ بالدنيا
والغفلة ومتابعة (١٧)النفس واختيار (١٨)الحظوظ على الحقوق والاجابة لدواعى
العدوّ (١٩)والمَيْل الى أمّارات الهوى والشهوات، وهم الذين وصفهم الله
(٢٠)تعالى فى كتابه وزجرهم ووبّخهم حيث يقول (٢١)أَفَرَأَيْتَ مَنِ ٱتَّخَذَ إِلَهَهُ
هَوَاهُ وَأَضَلَّهُ ٱللَّهُ عَلَى عِلْمٍ، (٢٢)وقال (٢٢)وَلَا تُطِعْ مَنْ أَغْفَلْنَا قَلْبَهُ عَنْ ذِكْرِنَا
وَٱتَّبَعَ (٢٤)هَوَاهُ، وقال (٢٥)خُذِ ٱلْعَفْوَ وَأْمُرْ (٢٦)بِٱلْعُرْفِ، وقال (٢٧)زُيِّنَ لِلنَّاسِ
حُبُّ ٱلشَّهَوَاتِ مِنَ ٱلنِّسَاءِ وَٱلْبَنِينَ (٢٨)الى قوله حُسْنُ ٱلْمَآبِ، ثم قال

A f. 33a

---

(١) عز وجل B.   (٢) فى B.   (٣) السبق B.   (٤) تعالى ذكره B.

(٥) درجاتهم B.   (٦) B om. قال الشيخ رحمه الله.   (٧) يسمع B.   (٨) وقبلها B.

وأقر بها B.   (٩) B om.   (١٠) بما B.   (١١) ذكرها B.   (١٢) اذكرها B.

(١٧) النفوس B.   (١٤) بينهم B.   (١٥) عليها B.   (١٦) بالاشتغال B.   (١٣) ما.

(١٨) المحضوض B.   (١٩) والسير B.   (٢٠) عز وجل B.   (٢١) Kor. 45, 22.

(٢٢) وفيها قال B.   (٢٤) B adds وكان امره فرطا.   (٢٣) Kor. 18, 27.

(٢٥) Kor. 7, 198.   (٢٦) B adds واعرض عن الجاهلين.   (٢٧) Kor. 3, 12.

(٢٨) B الاية ثم قال الخ.

(١) عزَّ وجلَّ (٢) قُلْ أُؤنَبِّئُكُم بِخَيْرٍ مِّن ذَٰلِكُمْ لِلَّذِينَ ٱتَّقَوْا (٣) الى قولــه بَصِيرٌ
بِٱلْعِبَادِ، ومنهم من سمع الخطاب (٤) فأجاب وتاب وأناب وعمل فى الطاعات
وتحقَّق فى الاحوال والمنازلات وصدق فى المعاملات وأخلص فى المقامات
وهم الذين ذكرهم الله (١) تعالى فى كتابه وذكر ما أعدَّ (١) الله لهم فقال (٥) ٱلَّذِينَ
يُقِيمُونَ ٱلصَّلَاةَ وَيُؤْتُونَ ٱلزَّكَاةَ (٦) وَهُم بِٱلْآخِرَةِ هُمْ يُوقِنُونَ أُولَٰئِكَ عَلَىٰ
هُدًى مِّن رَّبِّهِمْ، وقال (٧) إِنَّ ٱلَّذِينَ آمَنُوا وَعَمِلُوا ٱلصَّالِحَاتِ كَانَتْ لَهُمْ
جَنَّاتُ ٱلْفِرْدَوْسِ نُزُلاً، وقال (٨) مَنْ عَمِلَ صَالِحًا مِّن ذَكَرٍ أَوْ أُنثَىٰ وَهُوَ مُؤْمِنٌ
فَلَنُحْيِيَنَّهُۥ حَيَاةً طَيِّبَةً (٩) وَلَنَجْزِيَنَّهُمْ، قالوا الحياة الطيبة هى الرضا والقناعـة
(١٠) بالله عزَّ وجلَّ، ثم قال (١١) قَدْ أَفْلَحَ ٱلْمُؤْمِنُونَ (١٢) ٱلَّذِينَ هُمْ فِى صَلَاتِهِمْ
خَاشِعُونَ وَٱلَّذِينَ هُمْ عَنِ ٱللَّغْوِ مُعْرِضُونَ (١) الآية، وقال عمرو المكّى (١) رحمه
الله فكلّ شىء غير الله ممّا (١٣) وقع فى القلوب فهو لغوٌ فأخبَرَ انَّ الموحِّدين
(١٤) عن كلِّ شىء غير الله مُعرِضون، ثم قال (١٥) أُولَٰئِكَ هُمُ ٱلْوَارِثُونَ ٱلَّذِينَ
يَرِثُونَ ٱلْفِرْدَوْسَ هُمْ فِيهَا خَالِدُونَ، (١٦) وذِكرُهم فى القران كثير وقد (١٧) فضَّلهم
(١٨) على غيرهم بذكره لهم ووعَده ايّام بالثواب الجزيل، والطبقة (١٩) الثالثة من
المخاطبين هم الذين ذكرهم الله (٢٠) تعالى وشرَّفهم بذكره لهم ونسبهم الى العلم
والخشية فقال (٢١) إِنَّمَا يَخْشَى ٱللَّهَ مِنْ عِبَادِهِ ٱلْعُلَمَاءُ، وقال (٢٢) وَأُولُوا ٱلْعِلْمِ
قَائِمًا بِٱلْقِسْطِ، وقال (٢٣) هَلْ يَسْتَوِى ٱلَّذِينَ يَعْلَمُونَ وَٱلَّذِينَ لَا يَعْلَمُونَ، ثمَّ
خصَّ من هؤلاء (٢٤) قومًا (٢٠) ايضاً فقال (٢٥) وَٱلرَّاسِخُونَ فِى ٱلْعِلْمِ زاد فى

A f. 33b

١٥

---

(١) B om.   (٢) Kor. 3, 13.   (٣) B الاية جنات ربهم عند.   (٤) B وأجاب.

(٥) Kor. 31, 3—4.   (٦) A has وهم راكعون (in which case the citation is
from Kor. 5, 60) but راكعون has been stroked out by a later hand and the
words الخ بالاخرة added in marg. Text as in B.   (٧) Kor. 18, 107.

(٨) Kor. 16, 99.   (٩) الاية.   (١٠) B om. بالله عز وجل.   (١١) Kor. 23, 1—3.

(١٢) B الخ هم الذين فقال ووصفهم.   (١٣) B وقعت.   (١٤) B om. شىء كل عن.

(١٥) Kor. 23, 10—11.   (١٦) B هولا نحو.   (١٧) B فضلهم الله.   (١٨) A عن.

(١٩) A الثانية.   (٢٠) B om.   (٢١) Kor. 35, 25.   (٢٢) Kor. 3, 16.

(٢٣) Kor. 39, 12.   (٢٤) B اقواما.   (٢٥) Kor. 3, 5. B الراسخون.

وصفهم (١)الذى شرّفهم به، معنى آخر (٢)قال ابو بكر الواسطى (٢)رحمه الله الراسخون فى العلم هم الذين رسخوا بأرواحهم فى غيب الغيب وفى سرّ السرّ فعرّفهم ما عرّفهم وأراد منهم من مُقْتَضَى الآيات ما لم يُردْ من غيرهم (٤)وخاضوا (٥)بحر العلم بالفهم لطلب الزيادات فانكشف لهم من مذخور الخزاين والمخزون

٥ تحت كلّ حَرْف وآية من الفهم وعجايب (٦)النصّ فاستخرجوا الدُّر والجواهــر ونطقوا بالحِكَم ومنهم من كانت البحار عنده (٧)كَنُفْلقٍ فيا شاهَدَ من المستأثَرات بعنى مستأثَرات العلم الذى استأثر الله (٢)تعالى بـه انبيآءه وخصّ بذلك اولياءه واصفياءه فغاص (٨)بسرّه عند صفاء ذكره وحضور قلبه فى بحار الفهم فوقع على الجوهر العظيم وهو الذى (٩)عَلِمَ مصادر الكلام من أَيْنَ

١٠ (١٠)فوقع على العَيْن فأغنامهم عن البحث والطلب والتفتيش، وهذا (١١)شرحٌ من كلام الواسطى فيا (١٢)ذُكر، وبيان مــا قال الواسطى فى كلام ذُكر (١٣)ذلك عن ابى سعيد الخرّاز فى معنى ذلك، (١٤)قال ابو سعيد (٢)رحمه الله اوّل الفهم (١٥)لكتاب الله (٢)عزّ وجلّ العمل به لانّ فيه العلم والفهم والاستنباط واوّل الفهم إلقآء السمع والمشاهدة لقول الله عزّ وجلّ (١٦)إِنَّ فِى

١٥ ذَٰلِكَ لَذِكْرَىٰ لِمَنْ كَانَ لَهُ قَلْبٌ أَوْ أَلْقَى ٱلسَّمْعَ وَهُوَ شَهِيدٌ، وقال (١٧)تعالى (١٨)ٱلَّذِينَ يَسْتَمِعُونَ ٱلْقَوْلَ فَيَتَّبِعُونَ أَحْسَنَهُ، والقران كلّه حَسَنٌ ومعنى اتّباع الاحسن ما يُكْشَفُ (١٩)للقلوب من العجايب عند الاستماع وإلقآء السمع من طريق الفهم (٢)والاستنباط،

---

(١) B الذين.   (٢) B وقال.   (٣) B om.   (٤) A وخاظوا.

(٥) Altered in A to البحر.   (٦) B الدهر.   (٧) AB كنفقله.   (٨) B سره.

(٩) B علمهم.   (١٠) B بوقع.   (١١) Altered in A to مستخرج.   (١٢) B قد

(١٣) A corrector of A has drawn his pen through ذلك. اختصرته.

(١٤) B فقال.   (١٥) B لكلام.   (١٦) Kor. 50, 36.   (١٧) B جل ذكره.

(١٨) Kor. 39, 19.   (١٩) A القلوب.

باب [٢] فى شرح استنباط إلقآء [١] السمع والحضور بالتدبّر عند التلاوة وفهم الخطاب بما خوطب به العبد، A f.34a

قال الشيخ رحمه الله [٤] واعلم انّ [٥] القآء السمع والحضور عند الاستماع [٣] على [٦] ثلثة اوجه، قال ابو سعيد الخزّاز [٧] رحمه الله فيما بلغنى عنـه اوّلُ إلقآء السمع لاستماع القران هو أن تسمعه كانّ النبي صلعم يقرأ [٨] عليك ثمّ تَرَقَّى [٩] عن ذلك فكانّك تسمعه من جبريل عليه السلم وقرآءته على النبي صلعم لقول الله عزّ وجلّ [١٠] وَإِنَّهُ لَتَنْزِيلُ رَبِّ ٱلْعَالَمِينَ نَزَلَ بِهِ ٱلرُّوحُ [١١] ٱلْأَمِينُ عَلَى قَلْبِكَ الآية [١٢]، ثم [١٣] تَرَقَّى عن ذلك [١٤] فكانّك تسمعه من الحقّ وذلك [١٥] قول الله عزّ وجلّ [١٦] وَنُنَزِّلُ مِنَ ٱلْقُرْآنِ مَا هُوَ شِفَآءٌ وَرَحْمَةٌ لِلْمُؤْمِنِينَ وقوله [١٧] تَنْزِيلُ ٱلْكِتَابِ مِنَ ٱللَّهِ ٱلْعَزِيزِ ٱلْحَكِيمِ [١٨]، فكانّك تسمعه من الله تعالى وكذلك [١٩] حم تَنْزِيلُ ٱلْكِتَابِ مِنَ ٱللَّهِ ٱلْعَزِيزِ ٱلْعَلِيمِ، [٢٠] ومخرجُ الفهم فى استماعك من الله [٧] تعالى عند حضور قلبك وغيبتك عن أشغال الدنيا وعن نفسك بقوّة [٢١] المشاهدة وصفآء الذكر وجمعُ الهمّ وحُسْن الأدب وطهارة السرّ وصدق التحقيق وقوّة [٧] دعائم التصديق والخروج الى السعة من الضيق وحضور المشاهدة [٢٢] لنفاذ الغيب بالغيب

---

(١) B om. from فى شرح to واعلم ان. The words (٢) باب الاستنباط B. (٣) B om قال. بما خوطب به العبد to فى شرح are suppl. in marg. A. (٤) Suppl. in marg. A. (٥) والقآ B. (٦) اوجه ثلث B. الشيخ رحمه الله. (٧) B om. (٨) عليه B. (٩) ترقا AB. (١٠) A جل وعز. (١١) Kor. 26, 192—194. (١٢) لتكون من المنذرين بلسان عربي مبين B. (١٣) ترقا B. (١٤) فكانه يسمعه B. (١٥) قوله عز وجل B. (١٦) Kor. (١٧) Kor. 39, 1. (١٨) B proceeds: وقوله حم تنزيل الكتاب من الله 17, 84, العزيز فكانك تسمعه من الله عز وجل. So A in marg. (١٩) Kor. 40, 1. (٢٠) A ومخرج من الفهم. (٢١) A app. لقوة. (٢٢) B لمال.

وسرعة الوصول الى المذكور بالغيب بكلام اللطيف الخبير، وشرحُ هذا كلِّهِ
مفهوم ومستنبَط [1] من قوله [2] تعالى [3]ٱلَّذِينَ يُؤْمِنُونَ بِٱلْغَيْبِ، قال ابو سعيد
[4]ابن الأعرابى هم فى غيبه مغيَّبون فبالغيب آمنوا بالغيب وهو [5]وان كان
[6]غيبًا فانّه لا [7]يلحقهم فى ذلك شكٌّ ولا رَيْبٌ، وقال [8]تعالى [9]قُلِ ٱللَّهُ
٥ يَهْدِى لِلْحَقِّ أَقَمَن يَهْدِى إِلَى ٱلْحَقِّ أَحَقُّ أَنْ يُتَّبَعَ أَمَّنْ لَا يَهِدِّى إِلَّا أَنْ يُهْدَى،
وقال [10]فَمَا ذَا بَعْدَ ٱلْحَقِّ إِلَّا ٱلضَّلَالُ فَأَنَّى تُصْرَفُونَ، وقال ابو سعيد
الخَرَّاز [11]رحمه الله كلَّما ادرك الخَلْقُ من [12]الله فانّها [12]ادركوا غيبًا
خارجًا عن نعوت الحقايق وهو قوله [14]ٱلَّذِينَ يُؤْمِنُونَ بِٱلْغَيْبِ والغيب هو
ما أَشْهَدَ اللهُ [11]تعالى القلوبَ من اثبات صفات الله وأسمآيه وما وصف به
١٠ نفسه وما [15]أَدَّى [16]اليم [17]الخَبَر فأثبتوا الصفات ولم يدَّعوا إدراكها على
نهاية ألا تسمع الى قوله [2] تعالى [18]وَلَوْ أَنَّ مَا فِى ٱلْأَرْضِ مِنْ شَجَرَةٍ أَقْلَامٌ
وَٱلْبَحْرُ يَمُدُّهُ مِنْ بَعْدِهِ سَبْعَةُ أَبْحُرٍ مَا نَفِدَتْ كَلِمَاتُ ٱللَّهِ، فاذا كان وصف
كلامه لا يُدْرَك ولا يُوصَل الى نهاية فهمه فكيف يُدْرَك حقيقة وصفه وهويّته
وكُنْهُه فلذلك قُرّر عند اهل الفهم من اهل العلم انّ كلّ شيء اشار اليـه
١٥ المحقّقون والواجدون والعارفون والموحّدون وما عبّروا عنه وما لم تسعه
العبارة ولا بُوِّى [19]اليه بالدلالة ولا يشار اليه بالاثارة من اختلاف
المعارف وتباين الاحوال والمقامات والاماكن وغير ذلك ممّا شاهدوه ظاهرًا
وباطنًا هو الغيب الذى [20] وصفه الله [2]تعالى بقوله [14]ٱلَّذِينَ يُؤْمِنُونَ بِٱلْغَيْبِ،

---

[1] B فى.   [2] B عز وجل.   [3] Kor. 2, 2.   [4] B بن.   [5] B ان.

[6] B الغيب.   [7] B بلهم.   [8] B الله جل ذكره.   [9] Kor. 10, 36.

[10] Kor. 10, 33.   [11] B om.   [12] B الله عزوجل.   [13] B ادركوه.

[14] Kor. 2, 2.   [15] B أدى الله.   [16] Obliterated in B.   [17] A الخبر.

The word is partly obliterated in B.   [18] Kor. 31, 26.   [19] AB اليها.

[20] B وصف.

باب (١) وصف ارباب القلوب فى فهم القرآن،

(٢) قال الشيخ رحمه الله وقد ذكر الله تعالى ووصف جميع ارباب القلوب
وأهل الحقايق من المريدين والعارفين والمحققين والواجدين وأهل المجاهدات
والرياضات والمتقرّبين اليه بانواع الطاعات ظاهرًا (٣) وباطنًا (٤) كما فى كتابه
٥ وهو قوله (٤) عزّ وجلّ فيما (٥) يصف به ملآيكته (٦) أُولَٰئِكَ ٱلَّذِينَ يَدْعُونَ
يَبْتَغُونَ إِلَىٰ رَبِّهِمُ ٱلْوَسِيلَةَ أَيُّهُمْ أَقْرَبُ، وقال للمؤمنين (٧) يَٰأَيُّهَا ٱلَّذِينَ آمَنُوا
ٱتَّقُوا ٱللَّهَ وَٱبْتَغُوا إِلَيْهِ ٱلْوَسِيلَةَ، (٨) فكان فى هذه الآية (٥) شرح وبيان فى صفة
الذين يؤمنون بالغيب بابتغآء الوسيلة، ثم زاد فى البيان والتفصيل فى آية
أُخرى يحثّ به المؤمنين على المسارعة الى الخيرات فقال عزّ وجلّ (٩) أَيَحْسَبُونَ
١٠ (١٠) A f. 35a أَنَّمَا نُمِدُّهُمْ بِهِ مِن مَّالٍ وَبَنِينَ نُسَارِعُ لَهُمْ فِى ٱلْخَيْرَاتِ بَلْ لَّا يَشْعُرُونَ،
(١٠) واستفاد اهل (١١) الفهم من هذه الآية انّ اوّل المسارعة الى الخيرات هو
التقلّل من الدنيا وترك الاهتمام للرزق والتباعد والفرار من الجمع والمنع
باختيار القلّة على الكثرة والزهد فى الدنيا على الرغبة فيها، ثم ذكر الذين
يسارع لهم فى الخيرات ووصفهم (١٢) فقال (١٣) ٱلَّذِينَ هُم مِّنْ خَشْيَةِ رَبِّهِم
١٥ مُّشْفِقُونَ فوصفهم بالاشفاق من الخشية، والخشية والاشفاق اسمان باطنان وها
عملان من اعمال القلب (١٤) فالخشية سرّ فى القلب خفىّ والاشفاق من الخشية
أَخْفَى من الخشية وهو الذى ذكر الله (١٥) تعالى فقال (١٦) يَعْلَمُ ٱلسِّرَّ وَأَخْفَى،
وقد قيل انّ الخشية انكسار القلب من دوام الانتصاب بين يدى الله
(١٧) تعالى، ثم (٤) من بعد هذه المرتبة الشريفة والحال (١٨) الرفيعة (١٩) التى

---

(١) فى وصف B.   (٢) B om. قال الشيخ رحمه الله.   (٣) B om.   (٤) B app. وفى.

(٥) وصف B.   (٦) Kor. 17, 59.   (٧) Kor. 5, 39.   (٨) B وكان.

(٩) Kor. 23, 57—58.   (١٠) B فاستفاد.   (١١) B الفهوم.   (١٢) B om.
from to فقال.

(١٣) B جل جلاله.   (١٤) Kor. 23, 59.   (١٥) B والخشية.   (١٦) فوصفهم to فقال.

(١٦) Kor. 20, 6.   (١٧) B عز وجل.   (١٨) B الرفيع.   (١٩) B الذى.

وصفهم الله (١) تعالى (٢) بها من الخشية والاشفاق وغير ذلك فقال (٤) وَالَّذِينَ
هُمْ بِآيَاتِ رَبِّهِمْ يُؤْمِنُونَ، وكانوا قَبْلَ الخشية والاشفاق مؤمنين بآيات الله
(٤) بعلم أنّه اراد بذلك زيادة الايمان الا ترى انّه يصف (٥) رسوله صلعم
بالايمان به بعد الرسالة والنبوّة وذلك قوله (٦) عزّ وجلّ (٧) فَآمِنُوا بِاللهِ
ه وَرَسُولِهِ النَّبِيِّ الأُمِّيِّ الَّذِي يُؤْمِنُ بِاللهِ وَكَلِمَاتِهِ، (٨) فاستنبط اهل الفهم واستفادوا
من هذه الآية انّ زيادة الايمان لا نهاية له وان جميع ما وصل اليه اهل
الحقايق من بدايتهم الى نهايتهم انّ ذلك من حقايق الايمان وزيادته وبراهينه
وانواره (٩) وأنْ لا نهاية لذلك، ثم قال (١٠) عزّ وجلّ (١١) وَالَّذِينَ هُمْ بِرَبِّهِمْ
لاَ يُشْرِكُونَ (١٢) فذكر أنّهم لا يشركون بربّهم بعد ما وصفهم بالخشية والاشفاق
١٠ والايمان، (١٣) فاستفاد اهل الفهم ايضًا من ذلك وعَلِمَ انّ مستنبط هذه الآية
وذكر الشرك هاهنا انّه من الشرك الخفيّ الذى يعارض القلوب من رؤية
الطاعات وطلب الأَعْوَاض بعد ما شهد (١٤) شاهدٌ صريح الايمان ان لا ضارّ
ولا نافع ولا مُعْطِى ولا مانع الاّ (١٥) الله فعند ذلك شمّروا وجدّوا وتضرّعوا
الى الله (١٦) تعالى وطلبوا منه الخلاص لقلوبهم بصدق الاخلاص فى الاخلاص A f.35b
١٥ وعلموا انّهم على قدر اخلاصهم فى ايمانهم ينظرون الى دفايق شِرْككم ورياءهم
الذى هو أَخْفَى من دبيب النَّمْل على الحَجَر الأَسْوَد فى (١٧) الليلة الظلماء،
وقد ذكر عن سهل بن عبد الله (١) رحمه الله انّه كان يقول أَهْلُ لا إِلَهَ
إلاّ اللهُ كثير والمُخْلِصُونَ (١٩) منهم قليل، وقال سهل ايضًا الدنيا كلّها
جَهْلٌ الاّ ما كان منه العلم والعلم كلّه حُجّةٌ الاّ ما كان العمل به والعمل كلّه
٢٠ هباءٌ الاّ موضع الاخلاص فيه وأهلُ الاخلاص على خطر عظيم، ثم قال

---

(١) B om.   (٢) AB به.   (٤) Kor. 23, 60.   (٤) B فعلم.   (٥) B رسول الله.

(٦) B تعالى.   (٧) Kor. 7, 158. B وآمنوا.   (٨) B واستيقظ.   (٩) B وانه.

(١٠) B جل ذكره   (١١) Kor. 23, 61.   (١٢) B فذكروا.   (١٣) B واستفاد.

(١٤) B هم.   (١٥) B adds عز وجل.   (١٦) B عز وجل.   (١٧) B ليلة ظلما.

(١٨) B والمخلص.   (١٩) B منه.

(١) عزَّ وجلَّ (٢) وَٱلَّذِينَ يُؤْتُونَ مَا آتَوْا وَقُلُوبُهُمْ وَجِلَةٌ أَنَّهُمْ إِلَى رَبِّهِمْ رَاجِعُونَ،
(٣) فاستنبط اهل الفهم (٤) من هذه الآية ايضًا ان وَجَلَ قلوبهم مع ما (٥) آتوا
من المسارعة والاستباق الى هذه الاحوال (٦) التى ذكرنا ان ذلك الوجل
هو الوجل الذى لا سبيل (٧) الى الكشف عن (٨) علم ذلك ولا وقوف عليه
٥ لأحدٍ من خَلْفه وهو علم الخاتمة وما سبق لهم من الله (٧) تعالى فى علم الغيب
من (٩) الشقاوة والسعادة فعند ذلك تنقطّع رباط قلوبهم وذهلت (١٠) عقولهم
وذهبت علومهم وغابت فهومهم واقبلوا (١١) على الله (٧) تعالى بصدق اللجأ واظهار
الفاقة ودوام الافتقار، وتصديق ذلك ما قد رُوى فى ذلك عن عائشة
رضى الله عنها انّها سألت رسول الله صلعم (١٢) فقالت يرسول الله ٱلَّذِينَ
١٠ يُؤْتُونَ مَا آتَوْا وَقُلُوبُهُمْ وَجِلَةٌ هو الذى يزنى ويسرق ويشرب فقال النبى
صلعم لا ولكن هو الذى يصلّى ويصوم ويتصدّق ويخاف ان لا يُقْبَل منه
ثم (١٣) قال (١٤) أُولَٰئِكَ يُسَارِعُونَ فِي ٱلْخَيْرَاتِ وَهُمْ لَهَا سَابِقُونَ، فدلَّ ذلك
على أن بالمسارعة الى هذه الخيرات ينال درجة السابقين ويبتغى منزلتهم،

باب ذكر السابقين والمقرَّبين والأبرار من طريق الفهم والاستنباط، A f. 36a

١٥ (١٥) قال الشيخ رحمه الله (١٦) قال الله تعالى (١٧) وَٱلسَّابِقُونَ
أُولَٰئِكَ ٱلْمُقَرَّبُونَ، ثم بيّن فضل المقرّبين على من دونهم من الابرار والسابقين
بعد ذلك فقال (١٨) كَلَّا إِنَّ كِتَابَ ٱلْأَبْرَارِ لَفِي عِلِّيِّينَ وَمَا أَدْرَاكَ مَا عِلِّيُّونَ،
ثم قال (١٩) إِنَّ ٱلْأَبْرَارَ لَفِي (٢٠) نَعِيمٍ عَلَى ٱلْأَرَائِكِ يَنْظُرُونَ، ووصف الكرامات

(١) وأستنبط B ذكره B.   (٢) Kor. 23, 62.   (٣) واستنبط B.   (٤) B om.
من هذه الاية (٥) أوتوا B.   (٦) الذى ذكرناه B.   (٧) B om.   (٨) B تكلّم.
(٩) السعادة والشقاوة B.   (١٠) قلوبهم B.   (١١) الى B.   (١٢) Instead of
قول الله عزوجل B has فقالت يرسول الله.   (١٣) B adds الله جل جلاله.   (١٤) Kor.
23, 63.   (١٥) B om.   (١٦) قول B.   (١٧) Kor. 56, 10—11.
(١٨) Kor. 83, 18—19،   (١٩) Kor. 83, 22—23.   (٢٠) عليين B but corr. above.

التى [١]أَكْرَمَ بها الابرار وما خصّهم به من النعيم والدرجات فى علّيين
فقال [٢]تَعْرِفُ فى وُجُوهِهِمْ [٣]نَضْرَةَ ٱلنَّعِيمِ يعنى ان اهل الجنّة يُعْرَفون
بالنضارة [٤]التى [٥]فى وجوههم بعنى فى وجوه الابرار من النعيم الذى [٦]خُصّوا
به من [٥]بين اهل الجنّة، ثم قال [٧]يُسْقَوْنَ مِنْ [٨]رَحِيقٍ [٩]ولم يصف
٥ لأهل الجنّة انّهم يسقون من الرحيق المختوم الى قوله [١٠]وَمِزَاجُهُ مِنْ تَسْنِيمٍ
عَيْنًا يَشْرَبُ بِهَا ٱلْمُقَرَّبُونَ [٦]فخصّ الابرار فى الجنّة من بين اهل الجنّة
بالرحيق المختوم، ثم فضّل شراب الابرار وهو الرحيق المختوم على شراب
اهل الجنّة بمزاج لانّ مزاجه من التسنيم والتسنيم هو العين [١١]التى يشرب
بها المقرّبون [١٢]فصار شراب الابرار الذى فُضّلوا به [١٣]على اهل الجنّة
١٠ معلولاً بمزاجه عند شراب المقرّبين الذى ليس بممزوج، [١٤]فانظرْ الى هذه
الاشارة ما أَلْطَفَها فى معنى المقرّبين لانّ الابرار الذين خُصّوا من اهل
[١٥]علّيين بالرحيق المختوم [١٦]ونضرة النعيم والاراك يُمْزَج لهم فى شرابهم
[١٧]مزاجًا من شراب المقرّبين الذى يشرب [١٨]به المقرّبون على الدوام،
[١٩]واستنبط اهل الفهم فيها [٢٠]معنيّين [٢١]احدها انّ شراب الابرار ممزوج
١٥ وشراب المقرّبين صِرْف غير ممزوج كما قال الله [٥]عزّ وجلّ فى آية أُخرى،
[٢٢]إِنَّ ٱلْأَبْرَارَ يَشْرَبُونَ مِنْ كَأْسٍ كَانَ مِزَاجُهَا كَافُورًا، ثم وصف ما أَعَدَّ
[٥]الله لهم ثم قال [٢٣]وَيُسْقَوْنَ فِيهَا كَأْسًا كَانَ مِزَاجُهَا زَنْجَبِيلاً عَيْنًا فِيهَا
تُسَمَّى سَلْسَبِيلاً، ثم اخذ فى صفة أُخرى من نعيم اهل الجنّة فقال [٢٤]وَإِذَا

---

[١] B adds اسل.   [٢] Kor. 83, 24.   [٣] B نظره.   [٤] B الى.

[٥] B om.   [٦] B خص.   [٧] Kor. 83, 25.   [٨] B adds
ختامه مختوم   [٩] B om. from ولم يصف to المختوم الرحيق من.   [١٠] Kor. 83,
27—28.   [١١] B الذى.   [١٢] B فكان   [١٣] B على شراب اهل الجنّة.
[١٤] B وانظر.   [١٥] B العليين.   [١٦] B ونظره.   [١٧] B مزاج.
[١٨] A بها and so app. B.   [١٩] B فاستنبط.   [٢٠] B app. تفسيرا.
[٢١] B احدهم.   [٢٢] Kor. 76, 5. B فقال ان.   [٢٣] Kor. 76, 17—18.
[٢٤] Kor. 76, 20.

رَأَيْتَ ثُمَّ رَأَيْتَ نَعِيمًا [١] وَمُلْكًا كَبِيرًا اشار الى نعيم لا صفة له بقوله ثُمَّ
رَأَيْتَ نَعِيمًا [٣] ولم يصف النعيم، فلمّا بلغ الى آخر القصّة قال [٤] وَسَقَاهُمْ رَبُّهُمْ
شَرَابًا طَهُورًا، فكلّما ذكر شُرْبَهم [٤] ووصف فى ذلك فعلم [٥] بقوله يَشْرَبُونَ
يذكر المزاج فى شربهم فلمّا قال وَسَقَاهُمْ رَبُّهُمْ [٧] شَرَابًا طَهُورًا لم يذكر المزاج
فى شربهم، والمعنى الآخر ان العين [٨] التى هى شراب المقرّبين يُمْزَج منه
بالعين [٨] التى هى شراب الابرار ففُضّلوا على اهل الجنّة بزاج مُزجتْ شرابهم
من التسنيم وهو العين التى يشرب بها المقرّبون، فهذا فرّقٌ بين الابرار
والمقرّبين والله اعلم، ثم قال [٩] جلّ ذكره [١٠] وَلَا نُكَلِّفُ نَفْسًا إِلَّا وُسْعَهَا
[١١] فبيّن [١٢] انّ المؤمنين [١٢] انّما أُعطوا الاستطاعة على قدر الطاقة فى
ركوب هذه الحقايق ومنازلة هذه الاحوال لانّ جميع ما أُوتوا بـه الانبياء
عليهم السلم فمَن دونهم من الحقايق هو داخلٌ فى قوله [١٤] عزّ وجلّ [١٥] اتَّقُوا
اللَّهَ مَا اسْتَطَعْتُمْ لم يخرج أحدٌ [١٦] من ذلك،

باب بيان التشديد فى القرآن ووجوه ذلك،

[١٧] قال الشيخ رحمه الله اعلم ان الله تعالى قد اوجب على عباده [١٨] بقوله
[١٩] فَاتَّقُوا اللَّهَ مَا اسْتَطَعْتُمْ فرضًا لو انّهم أتوا بجميع اعمال الملائكة والانبياء
والصدّيقين ثم يطالبهم بحقيقة ذلك كان الذى عليم فى ذلك من اثبات
الحُجّة أكثَرَ من الذى لهم، ألا ترى ان الملائكة مع ما جبلهم الله [٢٠] تعالى
عليه من انواع العبادات يقولون سُبْحَانَكَ رَبَّنَا مَا عَبَدْنَاكَ حَقَّ عِبَادَتِكَ

---

[١] AB om. from ملكًا to نعيمًا. The words are suppl. in marg. A.   [٣] A om.
ولم يصف النعيم.   [٥] B بقول.   [٤] فوصف B.   [٦] B om.   Kor. 76, 21.
شرابًا طهورًا.   [٧] B om. فى شربهم.   [٨] B الذى هو.   [٩] B تعالى for جل ذكره.
أن المؤمنين.   [١٠] Kor. 23, 64.   [١١] B وبن.   [١٢] B om.
عن.   [١٤] A أيضًا.   [١٥] Kor. 64, 16.   [١٣] تبارك وتعلى.   [١٦] B
قال الشيخ رحمه الله.   [١٨] B لقوله.   [١٩] اتقوا.   [٢٠] B om.   [١٧] B om.

ويقولون [١] سُبْحَانَكَ لَا عِلْمَ لَنَا إِلَّا مَا عَلَّمْتَنَا، فقد تبرّءوا من علمهم وعبادتهم عند مشاهدة الحقيقة، ومعنى قوله عزّ وجلّ [٢]اتَّقُوا اللَّهَ حَقَّ تُقَاتِهِ [۳] راجعٌ الى قوله [٤]فَاتَّقُوا اللَّهَ مَا اسْتَطَعْتُمْ لأن التقوى اصل جميع الاحوال فى البداية والنهاية وليس للتقوى غاية لأن المتَّقَى ليس له نهاية، لأجْل ذلك ه قلنا ان معنى قوله [٥]اتَّقُوا اللَّهَ حَقَّ تُقَاتِهِ راجعٌ الى قوله [٤]فَاتَّقُوا اللَّهَ مَا اسْتَطَعْتُمْ والتشديد فى قوله اتَّقُوا اللَّهَ مَا اسْتَطَعْتُمْ لأنّك لو صلّيتَ أَلْفَ A f. 37a ركعة واستطعت ان نصلّي ركعة أُخرى فأخّرت ذلك الى وقت آخر فقد تركتَ استطاعتك ولو ذكرتَ الله [٦]تعالى ألْف مرّة واستطعتَ ان تذكره مرّة أُخرى فتؤخّر ذلك الى وقت [٧]ثان فقد تركتَ استطاعتك وكذلك ١٠ لو تصدّقتَ على سائل بدرهم واستطعتَ ان نُعطيه درهمًا آخر او حبّةً أخرى [٨]فلم تفعل ذلك فقد تركتَ استطاعتك، فمن اجل ذلك قُلْنا التشديد فى [٩]قوله مَا اسْتَطَعْتُمْ، ومن الآيات [١٠]التى فيها التشديد ايضًا قولـه [١١]تعالى [١٢]فَلَا وَرَبِّكَ لَا يُؤْمِنُونَ حَتَّى يُحَكِّمُوكَ فِيمَا شَجَرَ بَيْنَهُمْ ثُمَّ لَا يَجِدُوا فِي [١٣]أنْفُسِهِمْ حَرَجًا مِمَّا قَضَيْتَ وَيُسَلِّمُوا تَسْلِيمًا، وموضع التشديد ١٥ فى هذه الآية ان الله [١٤]تعالى ذكر القَسَم أنَّهم لا يؤمنون حتى يحكمُوا رسول الله صلعم فيما شجر [١٥]بينهم ثم [١٦]إن وجدوا [١٧]فى انفسهم حرجًا يعنى فى قلوبهم واسرارهم [١٨]وباطنهم ضيقًا او كراهةً فى حُكْمه [١٩]لو انه حكم عليهم بالقتْل فقد خرجوا من الايمان [٢٠]وقد ذكر الله القسم على خروجهم من الايمان، فلو قِسْنا على ذلك ما أَمَرَنا الله [٢]تعالى به من الصبر على احكام

---

(١) Kor. 2, 30.   (٢) Kor. 3, 97.   (٣) B رجعوا.   (٤) B اتقوا.   (٥) B om. from اتقوا to قوله.   (٦) B om.   (٧) AB ثانى.   (٨) B فا.   (٩) B adds عز وجل.   (١٠) B الذى.   (١١) B تبارك وتعالى.   (١٢) Kor. 4, 68.   (١٣) B صدورهم.   (١٤) B عز وجل.   (١٥) B adds ثم لا يجدوا فى انفسهم حرجًا.   (١٦) B انهم ان.   (١٧) B فى انفسهم حرجًا مما قضا ويسلموا تسليمًا.   (١٨) B يعنى وباطنهم.   (١٩) A او. The reading of B is doubtful.   (٢٠) A om. from وقد to من الايمان.

الله [١] عزَّ وجلَّ والرضا بما قسم الله لنا من الاخلاق والارزاق [٢] والآجال
والاعمال [٣] لم نَجِدْ معنا ومع كثير من الناس ذرَّةً من الايمان ولولا رجاءَ
الخلق فى سعة رحمة الله تعالى لهلكوا بذلك ،

باب ما قيل فى فهم الحروف والاسماء ،

[٤] قال الشيخ رحمه الله يقال ان جميع ما [٥] ادركتْه العلوم [٦] ولحقتْه
الفهوم [٧] ما عبَّر عنه وما أشيرَ اليه فهو مستنبَطٌ من حرفين من اوّل كتاب
الله [٨] تعالى وهو قوله بِسمِ ٱللهِ وَٱلْحَمْدُ لِلّهِ لان معناه بالله ولله والاشارة
فى ذلك ان جميع ما أحاط به علوم الخلق وادركتْه فهومهم فليست هى قائمةً
بذواتِها انّما هى بالله ولله ، وقيل للشبلى [٨] رحمه الله كما بلغنى أيشَ الاشارةُ
فى البآءِ من بِسْمِ ٱللهِ فقال اى بالله قامت الارواح والاجساد والحركات
لا بذواتِها ، وقيل لأبى العبَّاس بن عطآءَ [٨] رحمه الله الى ما ذا سكتْ
قلوب العارفين فقال الى اوّل حرف من كتابه وهو البآء من بِسْمِ ٱللهِ
ٱلرَّحمٰنِ ٱلرَّحيمِ [٩] فانّ معناه [١٠] أن بالله ظهرت الاشياء وبه فنيتْ وبجَليه
حسنتْ وباستتاره قبحتْ وسمجتْ لأن فى اسمه الله هيبته [١١] وكبرياءه وفى
اسمه الرحمن محبّته ومودّته وفى اسمه الرحيم عَوْنه ونصرته فسبحان من [٨] فرق
بين هذه المعانى فى لطائفها بهذه الاسماءِ فى غوامضها، [٤] قال الشيخ رحمه
الله [١٢] معنى قوله بتجَليه حسنتْ يعنى بقبوله لها وبذا سُمّيت الحسنة حسنةً
لانّه قبلها ولو لم يقبلها ما سُمّيت الحسنة [٨] حسنةً ومعنى قوله باستتاره قبحتْ
وسمجتْ يعنى برده لها وإعراضه عنها [١٤] وبذلك سُمّيت السيّئة سيّئةً ولولا
ذلك لما سُمّيت السيّئة سيّئةً، وقال ابو بكر الواسطى [٨] رحمه الله كلّ اسم

ٱ ٨ف.٣٧ب

من اسمآء الله (١)تعالى يَتخلّق (٢)به الّا اسمه الله الرحمن لانّهما للتعلّق دون
التخلّق وكذلك الصَمَدية ممتنعة عن الادراك والاحاطة، قال الله تعالى (٤)ولَا
يُحِيطُونَ بِهِ عِلْمًا، وقد قيل ايضًا (٤)انّ اسم الله الأعظم هو الله لانه اذا
ذهب عنه الأَلِفُ يبقى له (٥)وان ذهب عنه اللام يبقى له فلم تذهب الاشارة
وان ذهب عنه اللام الآخر فيبقى (٦)هاَء (٧)وجميع الاسرار فى الهآء لانّ معناه
هو وجميع (٨)اسمآء (٤)الله تعالى اذا ذهب عنه حرفٌ واحدٌ يذهب المعنى
ولم يبق فيه موضع الاشارة (٩)ولا تُحْتَمَل العبارةُ فمن اجل ذلك لا يُسَمَّى
به غيرُ الله تعالى، وعن سهل بن عبد الله (٤)رحمه الله (٤)انّه قال الألفُ
اوّل الحروف واعظم الحروف وهو الاشارة فى الأَلِف (٤)اى الله الذى ألَّفَ
بين الاشيآء وانفرد عن الاشيآء، وقال ابو سعيد الخَرّاز (٤)رحمه الله اذا
كان العبد مجموعًا على الله (٤)تعالى لا يتصرّف منه جارحةٌ الى غير الله عزّ
وجلّ فعندها تقع له حقايق الفهم عند تلاوة كتاب الله (٤)عزّ وجلّ الذى
ليس مع الخَلْق، وقال ابو سعيد (٤)رحمه الله كلّما بدا حرفٌ من الأَحْرُف
من كتاب الله (٤)عزّ وجلّ على قدر قُرْبك وحضورك (١٠)عنه (١١)فله
مَشْربٌ وفهمٌ غير مُخْرِج الفهم الآخر، اذا سمعتَ بقوله (١٢)آلَم ذَلِكَ (١٢)فلِلْأَلِفِ
عِلْمٌ يُظْهِر فى الفهم غيرَ ما يُظْهِر اللام وعلى قدر المحبّة وصفآء الذِكر ووجود
القُرْب يقع التفاوت فى الفهم، قال ابو سليمان الدارانى ربّما أَبْقَى فى الآيـة
خمس (١٤)ليال فلو لا أَنّى أَتْرُكُ الفكر فيها ما جُزْتُها ابدًا وربّما جاءت الآية
من القران فيطير معها العقل فسبحان الذى يردّه بعد ذلك، وقال وُهَيْب
(١٥)بن الوَرْد (٤)رحمه الله نظرنا فى هذه الاحاديث والآداب فلم نجدْ شيئًا
ارقّ لهذه القلوب ولا اشدّ استجلابًا للحزن من تلاوة القران وتدبّره،

---

(١) جلّ وعلا B.   (٢) B بها.   (٣) Kor. 20, 100.   (٤) B om.

(٥) B فان.   (٦) In A هو is written above as a variant. B وهو.   (٧) B جميع.

(٨) AB اسم. A in marg. اسما.   (٩) B ولم.   (١٠) B عندها.   (١١) B له.

(١٢) Kor. 2, 1.   (١٣) A فالالف.   (١٤) B ولو.   (١٥) B om. بن الورد.

باب فى وصف من اصاب فى الاستنباطِ والاشارةِ والفِهم فى
القرآن ووصفُ من غلط وأخطأ فى ذلك،

(١)قال الشيخ رحمه اله (٢)وإمّا ما قال الناس من طريق الاستنباط والفِهم
فالصحيح من ذلك أن (٣)لا تُقدّم (٣)ما أَخَّرَ اللهُ (٣)تعالى ولا نُؤخّر ما قدّم
اله ولا تُنازع الربوبيةَ ولا تخرج عن العبودية ولا يكون فيه تحريف (٤)الكلِم،
وهذا كما حُكى عن بعضهم انّه سُئِل عن قوله (٥)عزّ وجلّ (٦)وَأَيُّوبَ إِذْ نَادَى
رَبَّهُ أَنِّى مَسَّنِىَ ٱلضُّرُّ فقال (٧)معناه ما (٧)سَاءَنِى الضُّرُّ، وبلغنى عن بعضهم
ايضًا انّه سُئِل عن قوله (٨)أَلَمْ يَجِدْكَ يَتِيمًا فَآوَى فقال معنى اليتيم مأخوذ
من (٩)الدُّرّة اليتيمة التى لا يُوجد مثلها، وكا سُئِل (٣)آخر عن معنى قوله
(٣)عزّ وجلّ (١٠)قُلْ إِنَّمَا أَنَا بَشَرٌ مِثْلُكُمْ فقال معناه انا بشر مثلكم (١١)عندكم،
فهذا وأشباه ذلك خطأ وبهتان وخسارة على اله (١٢)تعالى وجهلٌ وقلّة المبالاة
وهو تحريف الكلِم عن مواضعه فهذا هو (١٣)السقيم، وإمّا الصحيح (١٤)من ذلك
(١٥)فكما سُئِل ابو بكر (١٦)الكتّانى (٣)رحمه اله عن قوله (٣)تعالى (١٧)إِلَّا مَنْ
أَتَى ٱللهَ بِقَلْبٍ سَلِيمٍ فقال القلب السليم على ثلثة اوجه من طريق الفِهم أحدها
هو الذى يلقى اله (٣)عزّ وجلّ وليس فى قلبه مع اله شريك، والثانى هو
الذى (١٨)يلقى اله (٣)تعالى وليس فى قلبه شغل مع اله (٣)عزّ وجلّ ولا يريد
غير اله (٣)تعالى، والثالث الذى يلقى اله عزّ وجلّ ولا يقوم بـه غير اله

---

(١) قال الشيخ رحمه الله B om. (٢) B ٧٧٧. (٣) B om. (٤) AB الكلِم.

(٥) B تعلى. (٦) Kor. 21, 83. (٧) B اسانى. (٨) Kor. 93, 6. (٩) B دره.

(١٠) Kor. 18, 110. (١١) B وعندكُم. (١٢) B عز وجل. (١٤) In A

التغيير is written above as a variant. (١٤) B om. من ذلك. (١٥) B كَا.

(١٦) B بن الكتانى. (١٧) Kor. 26, 89. (١٨) The words from يلقى to

والثالث are written in marg. B.

(١)عزّ وجلّ فَنِىَ عن الاشياء باله ثم فنى عن الله باله، ومعنى قوله فنى عن
الله باله يعنى يذهب عن رؤية طاعة الله (١)عزّ وجلّ ورؤية ذِكر الله وروية
محبّة الله بذكر الله له ومحبّته قَبْلَ الخَلْق لان الخَلْق بذكره لم ذكروه ومحبّته
لهم احبّوه وبقديم عنايته بهم اطاعوه، وكما سُيل شاه الكرْمانى (١)رحمه الله
٥ عن معنى قوله (١)عزّ وجلّ (٢)اَلَّذِى خَلَقَنِى فَهُوَ (٣)يَهْدِينِ وَاَلَّذِى هُوَ (٤) يُطْعِمُنِى
وَيَسْقِينِ وَاِذَا مَرِضْتُ فَهُوَ يَشْفِينِ فقال الذى خلقنى فهو يهدينى اليه لا
غيره وهو الذى يُطعمنى الرضا ويسقينى المحبّة (٥)واذا مرضت بمشاهدة نفسى
فهو يشفينى بمشاهدته والذى يُميتنى (٦)عن نفسى ويُحيينى به فأقوم بـه لا
بنفسى والذى لا أطمَع ان لا يُحجلنى يوم ألقاه بنظرے الى طاعتى وأعمالى ثم
١٠ أفتقر اليه (٧)بكلّيّتى، لمّا علم انّه لم يَنَلْ ما نال الاّ به (٨) ولا ينال ما يأمل
الا به فقال (٩)رَبِّ هَبْ لِى (١٠) حُكْمًا وَأَلْحِقْنِى بِالصَّالِحِينَ، وكما سُيل ابو
بكر الواسطى (١)رحمه الله عن قوله (١١)تعالى (١٢)اَلَّذِينَ آمَنُوا وَتَطْمَئِنُّ قُلُوبُهُمْ
بِذِكْرِ (١٣)اَللّهِ فقال قَلْبُ المؤمن (١٤)قلبٌ يطمئنّ بذكر الله (١)تعالى وقَلْبُ
العارف لا يطمئنّ بسواه، وكما سُبل الشبْلى (١)رحمه الله عن قوله (١٥)قُلْ
١٥ لِلْمُؤْمِنِينَ يَغُضُّوا مِنْ أَبْصَارِهِمْ فقال أَبْصار (١٦)الرُّءوس عن محارم الله (١)تعالى
وأبْصار القلوب عمّا سوى الله تعالى، وكما سُيل (١٧)الشبلى رحمه الله عن
(١٨)قوله (١٩)إِنَّ فِى ذَلِكَ لَذِكْرَى لِمَنْ كَانَ لَهُ قَلْبٌ (٢٠)أَوْ أَلْقَى السَّمْعَ وَهُوَ
شَهِيدٌ فقال لِمَن كان الله تعالى قَلْبَهُ ثم انشد،

لَيْسَ مِنِّى إِلَيْكَ قَلْبٌ مَعَنَّى ٭ كُلُّ عُضْوٍ مِنِّى إِلَيْكَ قُلُوبُ،

٢٠ فهذا من طريق الفهم، وامّا طريق الاشارة فعلى ما قال ابو العبّاس بن

A f. 39a

---

(١) B om.   (٢) Kor. 26, 78—80.   (٣) B يهدينى.   (٤) B om. from

عن نفسى .to يطعمنى   (٥) B وان.   (٦) A om. اليه لا غيره وهو الذى.

عزّ وجل B (١١)   بكلّيته B (٧)   وما A (٨)   (٩) Kor. 26, 83.   (١٠) A ملكا.

(١٢) Kor. 13, 28.   (١٣) B adds الا بذكر الله تطمئن القلوب.   (١٤) A om.

(١٥) Kor. 24, 30.   (١٦) B الرووس.   (١٧) B om. الشبلى رحمه الله.

(١٨) B قوله تعلى.   (١٩) Kor. 50, 36.   (٢٠) B om. from او القى to شهيد.

عطاء رحمه الله الحقّ لا يوجد مع (١)الزلل وأشار الى (٢)قوله (٣)فَإِنْ زَلَلْتُمْ
مِنْ بَعْدِ مَا جَآءَتْكُمُ ٱلْبَيِّنَاتُ فَٱعْلَمُوٓا أَنَّ ٱللَّهَ عَزِيزٌ حَكِيمٌ، (٤)وكما كان يقول
المحبّ يسقط عنه التعذيب ووجود الألم بصفات البشرية، وكان يستدلّ
بقوله (٥)تعالى (٦)وَقَالَتِ ٱلْيَهُودُ وَٱلنَّصَارَىٰ نَحْنُ أَبْنَاءُ ٱللَّهِ وَأَحِبَّاؤُهُ قُلْ فَلِمَ
يُعَذِّبُكُمْ بِذُنُوبِكُمْ بَلْ أَنْتُمْ بَشَرٌ مِمَّنْ (٧)خَلَقَ، وكما اشار ابو يزيد البسطامى
(٨)رحمه الله حين سُئِل عن المعرفة فقال (٩)إِنَّ ٱلْمُلُوكَ إِذَا دَخَلُوا قَرْيَةً
أَفْسَدُوهَا وَجَعَلُوٓا أَعِزَّةَ أَهْلِهَآ أَذِلَّةً وكذلك يفعلون، اراد بذلك ان عادة
الملوك اذا نزلوا قرية ان يستعبدوا اهلها ويجعلوهم اذلّة لهم ولا (١٠)يقدرون
ان يعملوا شيئًا الّا بأمر المَلِك وكذلك المعرفة اذا دخلت القلب لا تترك
فيه شيئًا الّا اخرجته ولا يتحرّك (١١)فيه شىء الّا احرقته، وكما كان يشير
الجنيد (٨)رحمه الله اذا سُئِل عن (١٢)سكونه وقلّة اضطراب جوارحه عند
السماع الى قوله (١٤)وَتَرَى ٱلْجِبَالَ تَحْسَبُهَا جَامِدَةً وَهِيَ تَمُرُّ مَرَّ ٱلسَّحَابِ صُنْعَ
ٱللَّهِ ٱلَّذِيٓ أَتْقَنَ كُلَّ شَىْءٍ، وكما كان يشير ابو على الروذبارى (٨)رحمه الله
اذا رأى اصحابه مجتمعين فيقرأ (١٤)وَهُوَ عَلَىٰ جَمْعِهِمْ إِذَا يَشَاءُ قَدِيرٌ، واحتجّ
ابو بكر الزقّاق (٨)رحمه الله على ما قيل للزُّهرى فى تعريف الانسان فقال
إنّ (١٠)تَكَلَّمَ فى ساعة وإن سكت فى يوم (١٦)بقول الله (٥)تعالى (١٧)وَلَوْ
نَشَآءُ لَأَرَيْنَاكَهُمْ فَلَعَرَفْتَهُمْ بِسِيمَاهُمْ وَلَتَعْرِفَنَّهُمْ فِى لَحْنِ ٱلْقَوْلِ، فهذا وأشباه
(١٨)ذلك صحيح والله اعلم، فقِسْ على ما بيّنتُ لك ما تسمع من اشارات القوم
ومستنبطاتهم حتى تُميِّز بين الصحيح والسقيم والعاقل يستغنى بالقليل عن A f. 39b
الكثير ويستدلّ بالشاهد على الغايب، وبالله التوفيق،

---

(١) زلل B.   (٢) قوله تعلى B.   (٣) Kor. 2, 205.   (٤) B يقول وكان.

(٥) عز وجل B.   (٦) Kor. 5, 21.   (٧) B adds يشا لمن يغفر.   (٨) B om.

(٩) Kor. 27, 34.   (١٠) A يقدروا corr. by later hand.   (١١) B فيها.

(١٢) سكوته B.   (١٣) Kor. 27, 90.   (١٤) Kor. 42, 28.   (١٥) B الانسان تكلم.

(١٦) لقول AB.   (١٧) Kor. 47, 32.   (١٨) B هذا.

كتاب الأسوة والاقتداء برسول اللـه صلعم ،

باب ^(١) وصف اهل الصفوة فى الفهم ^(٢) والموافقة والاتّباع ^(٣) للنبى صلعم ،

^(٤)قال الشيخ رحمه الله قال الله ^(٥)تعالى ^(٢)لنبيّه صلعم ^(٦)قُلْ يَٰأَيُّهَا ٱلنَّاسُ
إِنِّى رَسُولُ ٱللَّهِ إِلَيْكُمْ جَمِيعًا فأعْلمَنا بذلك انّه بُعِث ^(٧)للخلق كافّةً ، ثمّ
^(٨)قال ^(٩)وَإِنَّكَ لَتَهْدِى إِلَىٰ صِرَاطٍ مُسْتَقِيمٍ صِرَاطِ ٱللَّهِ ٱلَّذِى لَهُ مَا فِى
ٱلسَّمَٰوَاتِ وَمَا فِى ٱلْأَرْضِ ، فقد شهد الله ^(٢)تعالى له بانّه يَهْدى الى صراط
مستقيم ثم اوجب علينا نفى الهوى عن نُطقه لقوله عزّ وجلّ ^(١٠)وَمَا يَنْطِقُ
عَنِ ٱلْهَوَىٰ ثم وصفه الله تعالى فقال ^(١١)هُوَ ٱلَّذِى بَعَثَ فِى ٱلْأُمِّيِّنَ رَسُولًا
مِنْهُمْ يَتْلُوا عَلَيْهِمْ آيَاتِهِ وَيُزَكِّيهِمْ وَيُعَلِّمُهُمُ ٱلْكِتَابَ وَٱلْحِكْمَةَ ، فأعلمنا انّه يتلو
علينا آياته ويعلّمنا ^(١٢)الكتاب وهو القرآن والحكمة ^(١٢)وهى الاصابة والاصابة
سُنّته وآدابه وأخلاقه وأفعاله ^(١٤)وأحواله وحقايقه ، ثم بلّغ رسولُ الله صلعم
ما أنزل اليه من ربّه وما أُمر بإبلاغه لقوله عزّ وجلّ ^(١٥)يٰأَيُّهَا ٱلرَّسُولُ
بَلِّغْ مَا أُنْزِلَ إِلَيْكَ مِنْ رَبِّكَ ، ثم أمر ^(١٦)اللهُ عزّ وجلّ الخلقَ كافّةً بطاعة
^(١٧)رسولِ الله صلعم كما أمرهم بطاعته لقوله ^(١٨)عزّ وجلّ ^(١٩)أَطِيعُوا ٱللَّهَ

---

(١) فى وصف B.   (٢) B om.   (٣) B لرسول الله.   (٤) B om. قال.
(٥) B جل ذكره.   (٦) Kor. 7, 157.   (٧) In A للخلق
has been altered to الخلق and الى suppl. in marg. before it. B om. الى but
has الخلق.   (٨) B قال تعالى.   (٩) Kor. 42, 52—53.   (١٠) Kor. 53, 3.
(١١) Kor. 62, 2.   (١٢) B الكتاب والحكمه.   (١٣) B om. from وهى to وأفعاله.
(١٤) B احواله.   (١٥) Kor. 5, 71.   (١٦) B om. الله عز وجل.   (١٧) B رسوله
for رسول الله.   (١٨) B تعلى.   (١٩) Kor. 24, 53.

وَأَطِيعُوا (١)الرَّسُولَ وقوله (٢)وَمَنْ يُطِعِ الرَّسُولَ فَقَدْ أَطَاعَ اللّٰهَ وأمرهم
بالقبول منه بقوله (٣)عزّ وجلّ (٤)مَا آتَاكُمُ الرَّسُولُ (٤)فَخُذُوهُ، وأمرهم بالانتهاء
(٥)عمّا نهى عنه بقوله (٦)جلّ وعلا (٧)وَمَا نَهَاكُمْ عَنْهُ فَانْتَهُوا ودلّهم على
الاهتداء باتّباعه (٦)بقوله (٣)تعالى (٨)وَاتَّبِعُوهُ لَعَلَّكُمْ تَهْتَدُونَ، ووعدهم الهداية
٥ بطاعته بقوله (٣)عزّ وجلّ (٩)وَإِنْ تُطِيعُوهُ تَهْتَدُوا، وحذّرهم الفتنة والعذاب
الاليم إن خالفوا أمره فقال (١٠)فَلْيَحْذَرِ الَّذِينَ يُخَالِفُونَ عَنْ أَمْرِهِ أَنْ تُصِيبَهُمْ
فِتْنَةٌ أَوْ يُصِيبَهُمْ عَذَابٌ أَلِيمٌ، ثم عرّفنا الله (١١)تعالى ان محبّة الله (١٢)للمؤمنين
ومحبّة المؤمنين (١٢)لله فى اتّباع (١٤)رسوله (٦)بقوله (٣)عزّ وجلّ (١٥)قُلْ إِنْ
كُنْتُمْ تُحِبُّونَ اللّٰهَ (١٦)فَاتَّبِعُونِي يُحْبِبْكُمُ اللّٰهُ، ثم ندب الله المؤمنين الى الأسوة
١٠ الحسنة (١٧)برسوله صلعم (٦)فقال (١٨)لَقَدْ كَانَ لَكُمْ فِى رَسُولِ اللّٰهِ أُسْوَةٌ حَسَنَةٌ،
ثم رُوى عن رسول الله صلعم أخبار فكلّ خبر ورد عن رسول الله صلعم
بنقل الثقة عن الثقة حتى انتهى الينا فالأخذ به لازم لجميع المسلمين (١٩)لقوله
عزّ وجلّ (٢٠)أَقِيمُوا الصَّلَاةَ وَآتُوا الزَّكَاةَ وَأَطِيعُوا الرَّسُولَ وقوله (٢١)إِنَّكَ
عَلَى صِرَاطٍ مُسْتَقِيمٍ، فصار الاسوة به والاتّباع له والطاعة لأمره (٢٢)واجبًا
١٥ على جميع خلقه ممّن شهد او غاب الى يوم القيمه غير الثلثة (٢٣)الذين رُفع
القلم عنهم، فمن وافق القرآن ولم يتّبع سُنَن رسول الله (٢٤)صلعم فهو مخالف
للقرآن غير متّبع له والمتابعة والاقتداء (٢٥)هى الاسوة الحسنة برسول الله صلعم
فى جميع ما صحّ عنه من اخلاقه وافعاله واحواله (٢٦)وأوامره ونواهيه وندب به

---

(١) B adds صلى الله عليه.   (٢) Kor. 59, 7. B من.   (٣) B om.   (٤) B adds

(٥) B نهاكم عنه فانتهوا.   (٦) B لقوله.   (٧) Kor 59, 7.

(٨) Kor. 7, 158.   (٩) Kor. 24, 53.   (١٠) Kor. 24, 63. A وليحذر.   (١١) B ذكره تعالى.

(١٢) B المؤمنين.   (١٣) B أله.   (١٤) B رسول الله صلى الله عليه وسلم.

(١٥) Kor. 3, 29.   (١٦) B فاتبعون.   (١٧) B برسول الله.   (١٨) Kor. 33, 21.

(١٩) B بقوله.   (٢٠) Kor. 24, 55.   (٢١) Kor. 43, 42.   (٢٢) B واجب.

(٢٣) B الذى.   (٢٤) B عليه السلام.   (٢٥) B هو.   (٢٦) B وأمره.

وترغيبه وترهيبه الّا ما قام الدليل [١] على خلافه كقوله [٢] عزّ وجلّ [٣] خَالِصَةً
لَّكَ مِن دُونِ الْمُؤْمِنِينَ [٤] وقول النبى صلّعم [٥] فى الوصال لستُ كَاَحَدِكم
وقوله صلّعم فى حديث [٦] الاضحية [٧] لأبى بُردة ينار اَذبَحْ ولا [٨] تَجزى عن
اَحَدٍ بَعدَكَ وما [٩] يُشبه ذلك ممّا [١٠] يقوم الدليل من نصّ الكتاب والآثار،
٥ فامّا ما رُوى عن رسول الله صلّعم فى الحدود والاحكام والعبادات من
[١١] الفرايض والسُّنن والامر والنهى والاستحباب والرُّخص والتوسيع فذلك من
اصول الدين وهو مدوّن عند العلماء والفقهاء ومستعمل فيا بينهم [١٢] ومشهور
عندهم لانّهم الايمّة الحافظون لحدود الله المتمسّكون بسُنن رسول الله صلّعم
A f.40b الناصرون لدين الله [١٣] عزّ وجلّ [١٤] يحفظون على الخلق دينهم ويبيّنون لهم
١٠ الحلال من الحرام والحقّ والباطل فهم حُجج الله [١٥] تعالى على خلقه والدُّعاة
[١٥] له فى دينه فهؤلاء هم الخاصّة من العامّة، فامّا الخاصّة من هؤلاء الخاصّة
لمّا [١٦] احكموا الاصول وحفظوا الحدود وتمسّكوا بهذه السُّنن ولم يبق عليهم
من ذلك بقيّة استبحثوا اخبار رسول الله صلّعم [١٧] التى وردت فى انواع
الطاعات والآداب والعبادات والاخلاق الشريفة والاحوال الرضيّة [١٨] وطالبوا
١٥ انفسهم بمتابعة رسول الله صلّعم والاسوة به [١٩] واقتفاء أثره بما بلغهم من آدابه
واخلاقه وافعاله واحواله فعظّموا ما عظّم وصغّروا ما صغّر وقلّلوا ما قلّل
وكثّروا ما كثّر وكرهوا ما كره واختاروا ما اختار وتركوا ما ترك وصبروا
على ما صبر وعادَوا من عادى ووالَوا من والى وفضّلوا من فضّل ورغبوا
فيا رغب وحذروا ما حذر [٢٠] لانّ عايشة رضى الله عنها سُيلت عن خُلق
٢٠ رسول الله صلّعم فقالت كان خُلقه القرآن تعنى موافقة القرآن، [٢١] ورُوى
عن النبى صلّعم انه قال بُعثتُ [٢٢] بمكارم الاخلاق ،

---

[١] B om. وكذلك.   [٢] B جلّ ذكره.   [٣] Kor. 33, 49.   [٤] B على خلافه.
[٥] B فى الوصال.   [٦] B الحجّ.   [٧] B om. لأبى بردة ينار.   [٨] B om.
لأبى بردة ينار.   [٩] B أشبه.   [١٠] In A به is suppl. after يقوم.   [١١] B السنن.
[١٢] B app. ومشهود.   [١٣] B om.   [١٤] B الحافظون.   [١٥] B الى.
[١٦] B والفرايض.

باب ما رُوى عن رسول الله صلّعم [١] فى اخلاقه
وافعاله واحواله [٢] التى [٣] اختارها الله تعالى له،

[٤] قال الشيخ رحمه الله [٥] رُوى عن النبى صلعم انه قال انّ الله تعالى
أدّبنى فأحسنَ أَدَبى، [٥] وقد رُوى عنه صلعم انّه قال أنا أعلَمُكم باللّه وأخشاكم
لله [٦]، وصحّ عن رسول الله صلعم انه قال خُيّرتُ بين أن أكون نبيًّا مَلِكًا
او [٧] أكون نبيًّا عبدًا فاشار الىّ جبريل عليه السلم ان تواضَعْ فقلتُ [٨] بل
أكون نبيًّا عبدًا أشبعُ يومًا وأجوعُ [٩] يومًا، [١٠] ورُوى عنه [١١] صلعم انه قال
عُرض علىّ الدنيا فأَبيتُها، وقال صلعم لو كان لى أُحُدٌ ذهبًا لأنفقْتُه فى سبيل
الله الّا شىء أرْصِدُه [١٢] للدَين، ورُوى عنه صلعم انه لم [١٣] يدَّخر شيئًا لغدٍ
وانّه انّما ادّخر مرّةً قُوتَ سَنةٍ لعياله ولِن يَرِدْ عليه من الوفود، وقد رُوى
عنه صلعم انّه لم يكن له قميصان ولم يُنخَل له طعام وانّه خرج صلعم من
الدنيا ولم يشبع [١٤] من خُبْزِ بُرّ قطّ اختيارًا لا اضطرارًا لانّه لو سأل الله
عزّ وجلّ ان يجعل له الجبال ذهبًا ولم يحاسَب عليه لَفَعَلَ ذلك وقد رُوى
شبهًا [١٥] بذلك [١٦] فى الاخبار والروايات، ورُوى عنه صلعم انه قال لبلال
[٧] رضى الله عنه أنْفِقْ بلال ولا تَخْشَ من ذى العرش إقْلالاً، ووضعت
بَريرة بين يديه صلعم طعامًا فأكل منه فردّته اليه [١٧] الليلة الثانية فقال

[١٩] B واقفا.   [١٨] A طالبوا.   [١٧] B الذى ورد.   [١٦] B حكموا.   دينه.
[٢٠] A أن with لا ترى suppl. in marg.   [٢١] B روى.   [٢٢] B لمكارم.
دينه.   [١] B من.   [٢] B الذى اختاره له عز وجل.   [٣] ها suppl. in A.   [٤] B om.
بل عبدًا B [٨].   [٧] B om.   [٦] B له.   [٥] B وروى.   [٥] قال الشيخ رحمه الله.
[٩] B ثلثنا.   [١٠] The words from وروى to لدين أرصه are suppl. in marg. A.
من for برًّا A [١١].   [١٢] A للدين على.   [١٣] B يذخر.   [١٤] B برًّا.   [١١] A om.
من ذلك B [١٥].   The words بُرّ قط are suppl. in marg. A.   خبز بُرّ قط
[١٦] B والاخبار.   [١٧] B ليلة.

لها (١)أما (٢)خَشِيتِ ان يكون (٣)له (٤)بُخارُ يوم القيمة لا تدَّخرى شيئًا لغدٍ
فانّ الله (٥)تعالى يأتى برزق كلّ (٦)غدٍ او قال (٧)يوم، ورُوى عنه صلّعم انّه
لم يَعِبْ طعامًا قطّ ان اشتهاه أكله وان (٨)لم يشتهه تركه ولا خيَّر بين امرَين
الّا اختار أيْسَرَها، ولم يكن رسول الله صلّعم زرّاعًا ولا تاجرًا ولا حرّاثًا وكان
٥ من تواضعه صلّعم يلبس الصوف وينتعل المخصوف ويركب الحمار ويحلب الشاة
ويخصف نعله ويرقع ثوبه وكان لا يأنف ان يركب الحمار ويُرِدِف خلفه، وقد
رُوى فى الخبر (٩)انّه صلّعم كان يكره الغنا ولا يخشى (٩)من الفقر وكان برّ
به وبأزواجه الشهر والشهران فلا يُوقَد فى بيته نارٌ للخُبْز وانّه كان طعامُهم
الأسودَين التمر والماء، ورُوسَ عنه صلّعم انّه (١٠)خُيِّر نساؤه فأخْترْنَ الله
١٠ ورسوله وفيهنّ نزل (١١)يَأَيُّهَا ٱلنَّبِيُّ قُل لِّأَزْوَاجِكَ إِن كُنتُنَّ تُرِدْنَ ٱلْحَيَاةَ ٱلدُّنْيَا
(٢)وَزِينَتَهَا الايتَين جميعًا، وكان من دعآيه (١٢)عليه السلّم اللهمّ (١٣)أَحْيِنِى
مسكينًا (١٤)وأمِتْنى مسكينًا واحشرْنى فى زمرة المساكين، ومن دعآيه (٢)صلّعم
ايضًا اللهمّ ارزقْ آل محمّد قوت يوم بيوم، وكان ابو سعيد الخُدْرى (٢)رضى
الله عنه يصف رسول الله صلّعم كما رُوى عنه (١٥)كان رسول الله صلّعم
A f.41b يعقل البعير ويعلف الناضح ويقمّ البيت ويخصف النعل ويرقع الثوب ويحلب
الشاة ويأكل مع الخادم ويطحن معها اذا هى (١٦)أعْيَتْ وكان لا يمنعه الحيآء
ان يحمل (١٧)بضاعته من السوق الى اهله وكان يصافح (١٨)الغنىّ والفقير
ويسلّم مبتديًا وكان لا يردّ من دعاه ولا يحقر ما دُعى اليه ولو الى حَشَفِ
التمر وكان ليّن الخُلُق كريم الطبع جميل المعاشرة طلْق الوجه بسّامًا من غير
٢٠ ضحك محزونًا من غير (١٩)عبوس متواضعًا من غير (٢٠)ذلّة جوادًا من غير

---

(١) B ما.   (٢) B حسب.   (٣) B om.   (٤) B محاه. A adds من جهنم

in marg.   (٥) B عز وجل.   (٦) B يوم.   (٧) B غد.   (٨) B يشتهيه

(٩) A عنه.   (١٠) So pointed in A.   (١١) Kor. 33, 28.   (١٢) B صلى

(١٦) B عيت.   (١٥) B وكان.   (١٤) B واميتى.   (١٣) B احيينى.   (١٢) الله عليه وسلم

(١٧) A بضاءه   (١٨) B الفقير والغنى.   (١٩) B عبوسه.   (٢٠) B مذلة

سَرَف رقيق القلب (١)دايم الإطراق رحيمًا بكل مُسْلِم لم يَحْشَأ قطُّ من (٢)شَبَع
ولا (٣)مدَّ يدَه الى (٤)طَمَع، وقالت عايشة رضى الله عنها كان رسول الله صلعم
أَجْوَدَ من الريح المُرْسَلَة، ووهب رسول الله صلعم ما بين جبلَيْن من الغنم
لرجل واحد فرجع ذلك الرجل الى (٥)قبيلته وقال انّ محمّدًا (٦)صلعم يُعطى
٥ عطاءَ (٧)من لا (٨)يَخشى الفقر، ولم يكن رسول الله صلعم سخّابًا ولا فحّاشًا
ولا متفحّشًا، وكان رسول الله صلعم يأكل على الارض ويجلس على الارض
ويلبس العباءَ ويجالس المساكين ويمشى فى الاسواق ويتوسّد يدَه ويقتص من
نفسه ولم يُرَ ضاحكًا (٩)مِلءَ فيه ولم يأكل وَحْدَه قطُّ ولا ضرب عبدَه قطُّ
ولا ضرب احدًا بين الاّ فى سبيل الله عزّ وجلّ (١٠)وكان لا يجلس متربّعًا
١٠ ولا يأكل مُتّكئًا ويقول آكُلُ كما يأكل العبد وأجلسُ كما يجلس العبد،
ورُوى عنه صلعم انه شدّ الحجر على بطنه من الجوع ولو سأل ربَّه ان يجعل
له (١١)ابا قُبَيْس ذهبًا لأجابه، وحمل رسولُ الله صلعم اصحابه الى بيت ابى
الهَيْثَم بن التَيّهان من غير أن دعاه وأكل فى بيته من طعامه وشرب من
شرابه وقال هذا من النعيم الذى نسألون عنه، ودعاه صلعم رجل آخر الى
A.f.42a بيته مع خمسة من اصحابه فلم يدخل معه السادس الاّ بإذنه، ويُرْوَى فى
الحديث انّ رسول الله صلعم لبس منديلاً له عَلَمٌ ثم رءى به وقال كاد ان
تُلهِينى أَعْلامه وقال ايتونى بأَنْبَجانيّة ابى جهم، وسُئل عن الصلاة فى ثوب
واحد فقال أوَكُلُّكم يجِدُ ثوبين، وقال انا ابن امرأة كانت تأكل القديد،
وقال لا تفضّلونى على يونس بن مَتّى عليه السلم، وقال (١٢)[مرّةً] انا سيّدُ

---

(۱) B دايب.   (۲) AB سبع.   (۳) B من.   (٤) B الطعم.   (٥) B اهله.

(٦) B om.   (۷) AB om. Suppl. in A.   (۸) B app. يامن.   (۹) B ملو.

(۱۰) Here ends in B the كتاب الاسوة والاقتداء برسول الله (B fol. 87b, l. 7).
The words عز وجل are followed immediately by the title of the next book,
viz., كتاب آداب الصوفية. The omitted portion extends from A fol. 41b, l. 15
to A fol. 62a, last line.   (۱۱) ابو corr. in marg.   (۱۲) Suppl. in marg.

وَلَد آدم ولا فَخْر، وقال صلعم انّى أُعطى اقوامًا وأمنع آخرين وليس الذى
أُعطيه باحبّ الىّ من الذى أمنعه، وقال اوّل من يدخل الجنّة فقراء
الأنصار الشعثة رءوسهم الدنسة ثيابهم الذين لا يَنكحون المتنعّمات ولا تُفتَح
لهم السُّدَد، وقال صلعم ما لى وللدنيا، وقال لِيَكُنْ بُلغة أحدكم كزاد الرّاكب،
٥ وقال يدخل فقراء أمّتى الجنّة قبل اغنيآيهم بنصف يوم وهو خمسمائة عام،
وقال نحن معاشر الانبياء اشدّ الناس بلآءً ثم الأَمْثَل فالأَمْثَل فيُبْتَلى الرجل
على (١) قدر دينه فان كان فى دينه صلابة فهو اشدّ بلآءً، وقال رجل للنبى
صلعم انّى أُحِبّك قال اسْتَعِدَّ للبلآء جِلْبابًا، ورُوِى عن النبى صلعم قال
حُبّب الىّ من دنياكم ثلثٌ، وقال انتم أَعْلَمُ بدنياكم فأضاف الدنيا اليهم
١٠ وأخرج نفسه منها، ولم يَضَعْ رسول الله صلعم لبنةً على لبنة الى أن خرج من
الدنيا، وخرج عليه السلم من الدنيا ودِرْعُه مرهونة عند يهودىّ على (٣) صاع
من شعير ولم يترك دينارًا ولا درهمًا ولم يُقسم له ميراثٌ ولم يوجد فى بيته
أثاثٌ، وقال نحن معاشر الانبيآء لا نورث ما تركنا صدقةٌ، وكان يقبل
الهديّة والكرامة والعطيّة وكان لا يأكل من الصدقة ويأخذها منهم، ورُوِى
١٥ عنه صلعم أنّه قال ما اوحى الله تعالى ان اجمع المال وإكون تاجرًا ولكن
اوحى الىّ أن (٤) سَبِّحْ بِحَمْدِ رَبِّكَ وَكُنْ مِنَ ٱلسَّاجِدِينَ وَٱعْبُدْ رَبَّكَ حَتَّى
يَأْتِيَكَ ٱلْيَقِينُ، ورُوِى عن عايشة رضى الله عنها (٥) انّها قالت ذبحْنا شاةً
فتصدّقنا بها حتى لم يبق الّا كتفها (٦) [قالت] فقلتُ يرسول الله ذهب كلّها
الّا كتفها فقال النبىّ صلعم بقيت كلّها الّا كتفها، قال الله عزّ وجلّ (٧) نَ
٢٠ وَٱلْقَلَمِ وَمَا يَسْطُرُونَ مَا أَنْتَ بِنِعْمَةِ رَبِّكَ بِمَجْنُونٍ وَإِنَّ لَكَ لَأَجْرًا غَيْرَ
مَمْنُونٍ وَإِنَّكَ لَعَلَى خُلُقٍ عَظِيمٍ، وقال النبى صلعم انّ الله يُحِبّ مكارم الاخلاق
ويَكْرَهُ سَفْسافها، وقال صلعم بُعثتُ لِأَتَمِّمَ بمكارم الاخلاق، وكان من خُلقه

---

(١) In marg. حسب.   (٣) After صلعم in marg. ....دل الله   (٤) أصُع.
(٤) Kor. 15, 98—99.   (٥) انه.   (٦) Suppl. above.   (٧) Kor. 68, 1—4.

صَلعم الحياءَ والسخاءَ والتوكّل والرضا والذِكر والشُكر والحِلم والصبر والعفو
والصفح والرأفة والرحمة والمداراة والنصيحة والسكينة والوقار والتواضع والافتقار
والجود والسماحة والخضوع والقوّة والشجاعة والرفق والاخلاص والصدق
والزهد والقناعة والخشوع والخشية والتعظيم والهيبة والدعاءَ والبكاءَ والخوف
والرجاءَ واللياذة واللجأ والتهجّد والعبادة والجهاد والمجاهدة، (١) وكما رُوى عنه
صَلعم أنّه كان متواصِل الاحزان دائم الفكرة وكان لصدرِه أزيزٌ كأزيزِ
المِرجَل وأنّه صَلعم صلّى حتى تورّمتْ قَدَماه فقيل له يُرسول الله أليس قد
غفر لك ما تقدّم من ذنبك وما تأخّر قال أفلا أكون عبدًا شكورًا، وكان
صَلعم يُعطى من حرمَه ويَصِلُ من قطَعَه ويعفو عمّن ظلَمه وما انتقم رسول
الله صَلعم لنفسه قطّ ولا غضبِ لنفسه قطّ الّا ان تُنتهك محارم الله (٢) فيغضب
(٢)[لله] وكان للأرملة كالزوج الشفيق ولليتيم كالأب الرحيم، وقال (٣)[صَلعم]
من ترك مالاً فلوَرَثتِه ومن ترك كلًّا او ضياعًا فالىَّ، وقال اللهمّ انّى بشرٌ
اغضب كما يغضب البشر فأيّما أمرىٍ سببتُهُ او لعنتُهُ فاجعلْ ذلك كفّارةً
(٤)له او كما قال، وقال أنَس بن مالك خدمتُ رسول الله صَلعم عشر سنين
فما ضربنى ولا كهرنى ولا قال لى لشىٍ فعلته لِمَ (٥) فعلتَ ولا لشىءٍ لم افعلْه
لِمَ لم (٥) تفعلْه، ولو لم يكن من كرمه وعفوه وحلمه الّا ما كان منه يوم فتح
مكّة لكان من كمال الكمال وذلك انّه دخل مكّة صُلحًا وقد قتلوا أعْمامه
واولياءَه بعد ان حصروه فى الشِعاب وعذّبوا اصحابه بانواع العذاب واخرجوه
وأدمَوه وطرحوا عليه الرَّوْث وأذَوْهُ فى نفسه وفى اصحابه وسفهوا عليه واجتمعوا
على كَيْدِه، فلمّا دخلها بغير حمدهم وظهر عليهم على صُغْر منهم قام خطيبًا محمد
الله وأَثْنى عليه ثم قال اقول كما قال اخى يوسف عليه السلم لا تثريب

---

(١) In marg. وكان كما.   (٢) Orig. فذلك الذى غضب. The words فذلك الذى
have been stroked through and فغضب has been altered to فيغضب.
(٣) Suppl. above.   (٤) Here is a marginal variant, which has been
partially destroyed by worms: it appears to be دونه.   (٥) كذا written above.

عليكم اليوم فغفر الله لكم وقال من دخل دار ابى سُفيْن فهو آمنٌ، وما يُشبه
ذلك ممّا يرِدُ من الاخبار الصحيحة فى هذا المعنى اكثر ممّا يتهيّاً ذِكْرُه وانّما
ذكرْنا طرقًا ليُستدلّ به على ما لم نذكره، والله اعلم بالصواب،

باب بيان ما رُوى عن النبىّ صلعم فى الرُّخَص

والتوسيع على الأُمّة فيا اباح الله تعالى لهم ووجْهُ ذلك فى حال
الخصوص والعموم فى الاقتداءً برسول الله صلعم،

فامّا ما رُوى عن رسول الله صلعم ممّا جمع الله عليه من اموال بنى
قُرَيْظة والنضير وفَدَك [١] وخيَبَر واشباه ذلك والحُلّة التى اُهديت اليه
والمَجَمع والسيف الذى فى قرابه فِضّة والستور التى كانت فى البيت والرأية
التى كانت له [والفرس] [٢] والبغل والناقة والحمار والبُردة والعمامة والخُفّ
الذى اهدى اليه النجاشى وغير ذلك ممّا يكثر [٣] ذكره وانّه كان يُحبّ
الحُلْوَ البارد وانّه اكل الخبيص والذى قال لاصحابه كُلوا واشبعوا وما
جانس ذلك من الاخبار المرويّة عنه صلعم فانّ جميع ذلك فى الرخصة [٤]
والتوسيع على الأُمّة والاباحة لها لانّه [كان صلعم] [٥] امام الخلق الى يوم
القيمة وانّه قال صلعم بُعثتُ بالحنيفيّة السَّمْحة وقال صلعم انّما انا لأُسَنّ
ولو لم يوسّع الله تعالى على الخلق التعلّق بالرُّخَص والأخْذ بما اباح الله تعالى
لهم فى الطلب والجَمع والامساك والمكاسب بشرْط العلم لَهلكوا لأنّ الله تعالى
لم يَدْعُ الخلق الى جمع الاموال والصنايع والتجارات ولكن اباح لهم ذلك
لعلّه بضعفهم وقد دعاهم الله تعالى الى طاعته وعبادته وندب كافّة المؤمنين
الى ذكْره وشكْره والتوكّل عليه والانقطاع اليه بقوله تعالى [٥] أيُّهَا الَّذِينَ

آمَنُوا اذْكُرُوا اللَّهَ ذِكْرًا كَثِيرًا وقوله تعالى (١) وَعَلَى اللَّهِ فَتَوَكَّلُوا إِنْ كُنْتُمْ
مُؤْمِنِينَ وقال تعالى (٢) وَأَنَا رَبُّكُمْ فَاعْبُدُونِ (٣) وَإِيَّايَ فَارْهَبُونِ (٤) وَإِيَّايَ
فَاتَّقُونِ وأشباهه، وليس حال الناس في هذه المباحات والرُّخَص كحال الانبياء
عليهم السلم لانّ تعلّق الناس اكثرِهِم بالرخص والمباحات من ضعف ايمانهم
٥ وميل نفوسهم الى الحظوظ وعجزهم عن حمل اثقال مرارة الصبر والقناعة بما
لا بدّ لهم منها وربّما يؤدّيهم ذلك الى اتّباع الشهوات واكتساب السيّئات
ان تخلّفوا عن اداء حقوقها ولم يقوموا بشرايط العلم في تناولها، فامّا الانبياء
عليهم السلم قد هُذّبوا بتأييد النبوّة وقوّة الرسالة وانوار الوحى حتى لا تأخذ
منهم الاشياء ويكون كونهم فيها لغيرهم وقيامهم فيها لحقوقهم لا لحظوظهم، ألا
١٠ ترى الى قوله تعالى (٤) مَا أَفَاءَ اللَّهُ عَلَى رَسُولِهِ مِنْ أَهْلِ الْقُرَى فَلِلَّهِ وَلِلرَّسُولِ
وَلِذِى الْقُرْبَى وَالْيَتَامَى وَالْمَسَاكِينِ وَابْنِ السَّبِيلِ، فقد أخبر بانّ ما افاء الله
عليه فهو لله وللرسول (٥) [ولذى القربى واليتامى، قالوا ومعنى فهو لله وللرسول]
يعنى وللرسول أن يضعه في مواضعه والذى قال خُمْس الخُمْس فانّ ذلك
كان يضعه حيث يشاء، والناس في موافقة كتاب الله تعالى واتّباع رسول
١٥ الله صلّعم على ثلثة اقسام فمنهم من تعلّق بالرُّخَص والمباحات والتأويل والسعة،
ومنهم من تعلّق بعلم الفرايض والسُّنَن والحُدود والاحكام، ومنهم من أَحْكَم A f.44a
ذلك وعلم من احكام الدين ما لا يسعه الجهل بـه ثمّ تعلّق بالاحوال
السنيّة والاعمال الرضيّة ومكارم الاخلاق ومعالى الامور وحقايق الحقوق
والتحقّق والصدق كما رُوى في الحديث انّ النبيّ صلّعم قال لحارثة لكلّ
٢٠ حقٍّ حقيقةٌ فما حقيقةُ إيمانك قال عزفتُ نفسى عن الدنيا فأسهرتُ ليلى
وأظمأتُ نهارى وكأنّى كما جاء في الحديث فقال النبيّ صلّعم عرفت فالزمْ
او قال عبدٌ نوّر الله قلبُه، ويقال انّ اصل جميع ما تكلّموا فيه من علم
الباطن اربعة احاديث حديث جبريل عليه السلم حيث سأل رسول الله

(١) Kor. 5, 26.   (٢) Kor. 21, 92.   (٣) Kor. 2, 38.   (٤) Kor. 59, 7.

(٥) Suppl. in marg.

صلعم عن الايمان والاحسان فقال الاحسان أن تعبد الله كأنّك تـراه
الحديث، وحديث عبد الله بن عبّاس رضى الله عنه انّه قال أخذ رسول الله
صلعم يدى وقال لى يا غلام احفَظ اللهَ يحفظْك، [١] وحديث وابصة الإثم
ما حاك فى صدرك والبرّ ما اطمأنّ اليه نفسك، وحديث النُّعمان بن بشير

٥ عن النبيّ صلعم الحلال بيّن والحرام بيّن، وقول النبيّ صلعم [٢] لا ضَرَرَ ولا
ضِرارَ فى الاسلام،

باب [٣] [ما] ذكر [٣] [عن] المشايخ فى اتّباعهم رسول
الله صلعم [٤] وتخصيصهم فى ذلك،

قال الشيخ رحمه الله سمعتُ [٣] [أبا عمرو] عبد الواحد بن علوان رحمه
١٠ الله قال سمعتُ الجُنَيْد رحمه الله يقول عِلْمُنا هذا مشتبكٌ بحديث رسول الله
صلعم، وسمعتُ أبا عمرو اسمعيل بن نُجَيْد يقول سمعتُ أبا عثمٰن سعيد بن
عثمٰن الحيرى يقول من أمّر السنّة على نفسه قولاً وفعلاً نطق بالحكمة ومن
أمّر الهوى على نفسه قولاً وفعلاً نطق بالبدعة قال الله تعالى [٥] وَإِنْ تُطِيعُوهُ
تَهتَدُوا، وسمعتُ [٦] طَيْفور البسطاى يقول [٣] [سمعتُ موسى بن عيسى المعروف

١٥ بعُمَىّ يقول] سمعتُ أبى يقول سمعتُ أبا يزيد البسطاى رحمه الله يقول قُمْ
بنا حتى ننظر الى هذا الرجل الذى قد شهر نفسه بالولاية وكان الرجل فى
ناحيته مقصوداً مشهوراً بالزهد والعبادة وقد سمّاه لنا طيفور ونسبته قال
فمضينا قال فلمّا خرج من بيته ودخل المسجد رمى ببزاقه تُجاة القِبْلة فقال
ابو يزيد قُمْ بنا ننصرف قال فانصرف ولم يسلّم عليه وقال هذا رجل ليس

٢٠ بمأمون على أَدَب من آداب رسول الله صلعم فكيف يكون مأموناً على مـا

---

[١] In marg. ‏وحديث جاء به وقرأ.‏   [٢] In marg. ‏لا ضرورة ولا اضرار فى الاسلام.‏
[٣] Suppl. in marg.   [٤] ‏وتحضيضهم.‏   [٥] Kor. 24, 53.   [٦] Suppl. above.

يدّعيه من مقامات الاولياء والصدّيقين، وسمعتُ طيفور يقول سمعتُ موسى
ابن عيسى يقول سمعتُ أبى يقول سمعتُ أبا يزيد رحمه الله يقول لقد همتُ
ان اسأل الله تعالى ان يكفينى مؤنة الأكل ومؤنة النساء ثم قلتُ كيف
يجوز لى ان اسأل الله عزّ وجلّ هذا ولم يسأله رسول الله صلعم فلم اسأله
٥ وكفانى الله تعالى مؤونة النساء حتى لا أبالى استقبلتُنى امرأةٌ او حائطٌ او
كما قال، وسمعتُ ابا الطيّب احمد بن مُقاتل العكّى البغدادى يقول كنت
عند جعفر الخُلْدى رحمه الله (١)[يوم مات الشبلى] فدخل عليه بُندار الدينورى
وكان خادم الشبلى رحمه (٢)الله وكان قد حضر موتَهُ فسأله جعفر أيْشَ رأَبتَ
منه فى وقت موته فقال لمّا أُمسك لسانُه وعرق جبينه اشار الىّ وَضِّئْنى
١٠ للصلاة فوضَّتُهُ فنسبت تخليل لِحْيته فقبض على يدى وأُدخل اصابعى فى
لحيته مخلّلها قال فبكى جعفر وقال أَيْشَ يهيّأ ان يقال فى رجل لم يذهب
عليه تخليل لحيته فى الوضوء عند نزع روحه وامساك لسانه وعَرَق جبينه او
كما قال، وسمعتُ احمد بن علىّ الوجيهى يقول سمعتُ ابا علىّ الروذبارى
يقول كان أُستاذى فى علم التصوّف الجُنَيْد وكان استاذى فى الفقه ابو
العبّاس بن سُرَيْج وكان استاذى فى النحو واللغة ثَعْلَب وكان استاذى فى
حديث رسول الله صلعم ابرهيم الحَرْبى، وسُئِل (٣)ذو النون رحمه الله بِما ذا
عرفتَ الله تعالى فقال عرفتُ الله بالله وعرفتُ ما سوى (٤)الله برسول الله
صلعم، وقال سهل بن عبد الله رحمه الله كلّ وَجْد لا يشهد لـه الكتاب
والسنّة (٥)فباطلٌ، وقال ابو سليمْن الدارانى رحمه الله ربّما (٦)تَنكُتُ الحقيقة
٢٠ قلبى اربعين يومًا فلا آذن (٧)لها أن تدخل قلبى الاّ بشاهدَيْن من الكتاب
والسُنّة، فهذا ما حضرنى فى الوقت ممّا ذهب اليه الصوفية فى اتّباعِهم رسول
الله صلعم وكرهتُ (٨)التثقيل واقتصرتُ على ما ذكرتُ للتخفيف، وبالله التوفيق،

---

(١) Suppl. in marg.   (٢) After الله the words مات الشبلى have been
stroked out.   (٣) ذا.   (٤) ذلك written above as variant.   (٥) In marg.
التطويل.   (٦) In marg. طرق.   (٧) له.   (٨) In marg. فهو باطل.

‪(١)‬[كتاب المستنبطـات]،

باب مذهب اهل الصفوة فى المستنبطات الصحيحة فى فهم
القرآن والحديث وغير ذلك وشرحها،

قال الشيخ رحمه الله ‪(١)‬[اذا] قالوا ما معنى المستنبطات ‪(٢)‬فيقال
المستنبطات ما استنبط اهلُ الفهم من المحقّقين بالموافقة لكتاب الله عزّ وجلّ
ظاهرًا وباطنًا والمتابعة لرسول الله صلعم ظاهرًا وباطنًا والعمل بها بظواهرهم
وبواطنهم، فلمّا ‪(١)‬[عملوا بما] علموا من ذلك ورّثهم الله تعالى علم ما لم يعلموا
وهو علم الاشارة وعلم مواريث الاعمال التى يكشف الله تعالى لقلوب اصفيآيه
من المعانى المذخورة واللطايف والاسرار المخزونة وغرايب العلوم وطرايف
الحِكَم فى معانى القرآن ومعانى ‪(٣)‬اخبار رسول الله صلعم من حيث احوالهم
واوقاتهم وصفآء اذكارهم قال الله تعالى ‪(٤)‬أَفَلَا يَتَدَبَّرُونَ الْقُرْآنَ أَمْ عَلَى قُلُوبٍ
أَقْفَالُهَا، وقال النبىّ صلعم من عمل بما علم ورّثه الله تعالى علم ما لم يعلم،
وهو العلم الذى ليس لغيرهم ذلك من اهل العلم وأقفال القلوب ما ‪(٥)‬يقع
على القلوب من ‪(٦)‬الصدأ لكثرة الذنوب وإتّباع الهوى ومحبّة الدنيا وطول
الغفلة وشدّة الحرص وحبّ الراحة وحبّ الثنآء والحمدة وغير ذلك من
الغفلات والزلّات والمخالفة والخيانات، فاذا كشف الله تعالى ‪(١)‬[ذلك عن]
القلوب ‪(٧)‬بصدق التوبة والندم على الحوبة فقد فتح الاقفال عن القلوب
وأتّه الزوايد والفوايد من الغيوب فيعبّر عن زوايه وفوايه بترجمانه وهو

‪(١)‬ Suppl. in marg.   ‪(٢)‬ Orig. فقال but corr. by later hand.   ‪(٣)‬ In marg.

‪(٧)‬ تصدق.   ‪(٦)‬ الصدى.   ‪(٥)‬ تقع.   ‪(٤)‬ Kor. 47, 26.   حديث.

اللسان الذى ينطق بغرايب الحِكَم وغرايب العلم، فاذا شرحوا هذه [1]النقط
المريدون والقاصدون والطالبون من تلك الجواهر بآذان واعية وقلوب
حاضرة فعاشوا وانتفعوا بذلك وأنعشوا، وقد قال الله عزّ وجلّ [2]أَفَلَا
يَتَدَبَّرُونَ ٱلْقُرْآنَ وَلَوْ كَانَ مِنْ عِنْدِ غَيْرِ ٱللَّهِ لَوَجَدُوا فِيهِ ٱخْتِلَافًا كَثِيرًا،
٥ فدلّ على ان [3]بتدبّرهم فى القرآن يستنبطون اذ لو كان القرآن من عند غير
الله لوجدوا فيه اختلافًا كثيرًا، ثم قال [4]وَإِذَا جَآءَهُمْ أَمْرٌ مِنَ ٱلْأَمْنِ أَوِ
ٱلْخَوْفِ أَذَاعُوا بِهِ وَلَوْ رَدُّوهُ إِلَى ٱلرَّسُولِ وَإِلَى أُولِي ٱلْأَمْرِ مِنْهُمْ لَعَلِمَهُ ٱلَّذِينَ
يَسْتَنْبِطُونَهُ مِنْهُمْ يعنى من اهل [5]العلم وقالوا أُولُوا ٱلْأَمْرِ هاهنا اهل العلم
فقد بيّن هاهنا خصوصيةً لأهل العلم وخصوصيةً لأهل الاستنباط من اهل
١٠ العلم، وقد رُوى فى الخبر ان رجلًا جاءَ الى رسول الله صلعم فقال يرسول
الله علّمنى من غرايب العلم فقال وما علمتَ فى اوّل العلم أَحكِمتَ اوّل العلم
ثم تَعالَ حتى أُعَلِّمَك غرايب العلم او كما قال، ولفقهاءَ الامصار وعلماَيها فى
كلّ وقت مستنبطات مشهورة فى آيات القرآن والاخبار الظاهرة مستعدّة
للاحتجاج بها بعضهم على بعض فى المساَيل الخلافية بينهم، وقد قال بعضهم
١٥ ان فى هذا الحديث الذى قال رسول الله صلعم الأعمال بالنيّات ولكلّ امرئ
ما نوى فمن كانت هِجْرته الى الله ورسوله على ما جاءَ فى الحديث إنّه يدخل
فى ثلثين بابًا من ابواب العلم، وهذا لا يكون الّا من طريق الاستنباط
وكذلك اهل الكلام والنظر احتجاجاتهم العقلية كلّها مستنبطات وكلّ ذلك
حسن عند اهله ومقبول اذ المقصود من ذلك النصرة للحقّ والردّ للباطل،
٢٠ وأحسنُ من ذلك مستنبطات اهل العلم بالعلم والتحقيق والاخلاص فى
العمل من المجاهدات والرياضات والمعاملات [6]والمتقرّبين الى الله تعالى
بأنواع الطاعات وأهلِ الحقايق،

---

(1) فالنقط.   (٢) Kor. 4, 84.   (٣) تدبرهم.   (٤) Kor. 4, 85.

(٥) In marg. الصفوة.   (٦) والمتقربون.

باب فى كيفيّة الاختلاف فى مستنبطات اهل الحقيقة

فى معانى علومهم واحوالهم ،

قال الشيخ رحمه الله اعلمْ أيّدك الله (١) بالفهم وأزال عنك الوهم ان
ابناء الاحوال وأرباب (٢)القلوب فانّ لهم ايضًا مستنبطات فى معانى احوالهم
٥ وعلومهم وحقايقهم وقد استنبطوا من ظاهر القرآن وظاهر الاخبار معانى
لطيفةً باطنةً وحِكمًا مستطرفةً (٣)وأسرارًا مذخورةً ونحن نذكر طرفًا من
ذلك ان شآء الله تعالى، وهم ايضًا فى مستنبطاتهم مختلفون كاختلاف اهل
الظاهر غير انّ اختلاف اهل الظاهر يوّدّى الى (٤)حُكمٌ الغلط والخطأ
والاختلاف فى علم الباطن لا يوّدّى الى ذلك لأنّها فضايل ومحاسن ومكارم
١٠ واحوال واخلاق ومقامات ودرجات، وقد قيل ان اختلاف العلمآء
(٤)[رحمة وهذا له معنّى امّا الاختلاف بين العلمآء] فى علم الظاهر رحمةٌ من
الله تعالى لانّ المصيب يردّ على المخطئ ويبيّن للناس غلط المخالف وخلافَهُ
للمصيب فى الدين حتى تجنّبوا منه ولو لا ذلك لهلك الناس بذهاب دينهم،
وإمّا الاختلاف بين اهل الحقايق (٥)ايضًا (٦)رحمة (٧)[من] الله لأنّ كلّ
١٥ واحد يتكلّم من حيث وقته ويجيب من حيث حاله ويشير من حيث وجْه
فتكون فيهم لكلّ واحد من اهل الطاعات وأرباب القلوب والمريدين
والمحقّقين فايدةٌ من كلامهم وذلك ايضًا على قدر تفاوتهم واختصاصهم
ودرجاتهم وبيان ما قلْنا فى (٨)اختلافهم ما حُكى عن (٩)ذى النون رحمه الله
انّه سُيِل عن الفقير الصادق فقال (٤)[هو الذى لا يسكن الى شىء وإليه

---

(١) Orig. الفهم, but corr. by later hand.   (٢) In marg. العلوم.   (٣) وأسرار.

(٤) Suppl. in marg.   (٥) Suppl. above.   (٦) The words رحمة الله have

been altered to رحمه الله and رحمة has been added in marg. after الله.

(٧) Text om.   (٨) منه suppl. above after اختلافهم.   (٩) ذا.

يسكن كلُّ شىء، وسُئل ابو عبد الله المغربى عن الفقير الصادق [١] فقال
النقير الصادق الذى يملك كلّ شىء ولا يملكه شىء، وسُئل ابو الحُرث
الأوْلاسى عن الفقير الصادق فقال هو الذى لا يأنس بشىء ويأنس به كل
شىء، وسُئل يوسف بن الحسين عن الفقير الصادق فقال من آثَرَ وقته
فان كان فيه نطلّع الى وقت ثانٍ لم يستحقّ اسم الفقر، وسُئل الحسين بن
منصور رحمه الله عن الفقير الصادق فقال الفقير الصادق الذى لا يختار
بصحّة الرضا ما بَرِدُ عليه من الاسباب، وسُئل النورى رحمه الله عن الفقير
الصادق فقال الفقير الصادق الذى لا يتّهم الله تعالى فى الاسباب ويسكن
اليه فى كلّ حال، وسُئل سُمْنون رحمه الله عن الفقير الصادق فقال الذى
يأنس [٢] بالمفقود كما يأنس الجاهل بالموجود ويستوحش بالموجود كما يستوحش
الجاهل بالفقد، وسُئل ابو حفص النيسابورى رحمه الله عن الفقير الصادق
[٣] فقال الذى يكون مع كل وقت بحكمه فاذا ورد عليه واردٌ يُخرجه عن
حكم وقته ويستوحش منه، وسُئل الجُنَيْد رحمه الله عن الفقير الصادق فقال
هو ان [١] لا يستغنى بشىء ويستغنى به كلّ شىء، وكما سُئل الرُرْنعش
النيسابورى رحمه الله عن الفقير فقال الذى يأكله القَمْل ولا يكون له ظُفْر
يحكُّ به نفسه، وقد اختلف هؤلاء فى اجوبتهم كاختلافهم فى اوقاتهم واحوالهم
وكلُّ ذلك حسن ولكلِّ جواب من اجوبتهم اهلٌ يليق بهم ما اجابوا وهى
فايدة ونعمة وزيادة لهم ورحمة،

باب فى مستنبطات اهل الصفوة (١) فى تخصيص النبىّ صلعم وشرفه
وفضله على اخوانه عليه السلام من كتاب الله عزّ
وجلّ من طريق الفهم،

قال الشيخ رحمه الله فامّا المستنبطات التى فى كتاب الله عزّ وجلّ فقد
٥ ذكرنا طرفًا من ذلك فى باب مذهب اهل الصفوة فى موافقة كتاب الله
عزّ وجلّ وهذا (٢) [الذى نذكره] انّما نذكره فى (٣) [معنى] خصوصية رسول
الله صلعم، (٤) وفيا استنبطوا فيا نطق القرآن بشرفه وما خُصّ به (٥) من
سائر الرُّسُل عليهم السلم قوله عزّ وجلّ (٦) قُلْ هَٰذِهِ سَبِيلِي أَدْعُوا إِلَى اللَّهِ عَلَى A f. 47a
بَصِيرَةٍ أَنَا وَمَنِ اتَّبَعَنِي وَسُبْحَانَ اللَّهِ وَمَا أَنَا مِنَ الْمُشْرِكِينَ، قال ابو بكر
١٠ الواسطى رحمه الله أَدْعُوا إِلَى اللَّهِ عَلَى بَصِيرَةٍ يعنى ان لا اشهد لنفسى يعنى
ان لا أَرَى نفسى فأُستقطعَهم بشواهدى، ومعنى آخر عَلَى بَصِيرَةٍ (٢) [ايقُن
انّه ليس (٧) الَىّ شىء فيكون الى نفسى من الهداية شىء، ومعنى آخر عَلَى بَصِيرَةٍ
انّه] لا نملك ضرًّا ولا نفعًا الّا أن يتولّى اللهُ تعالى (٨) تقريبها، ومعنى قوله أَنَا
وَمَنِ اتَّبَعَنِي على ذلك دعوتهم سبحان الله (٢) [أن يكون] احدٌ يلحق ما بهمّه
١٥ ويقصده الّا بـه، وَمَا أَنَا مِنَ الْمُشْرِكِينَ أن ارى الهداية من نفسى او منـه
بدعْوتى، قوله (٢) [تعالى] (٩) قُلْ أَمَرَ رَبِّي بِالْقِسْطِ وَأَقِيمُوا وُجُوهَكُمْ عِنْدَ كُلِّ
مَسْجِدٍ وَادْعُوهُ مُخْلِصِينَ لَهُ الدِّينَ كَمَا بَدَأَكُمْ تَعُودُونَ، قالوا معناه من طريق
الفهم والاستنباط قُلْ أَمَرَ رَبِّي بِالْقِسْطِ فيا بينى وبين الخلق وبينى وبين الله
تعالى وَأَقِيبُوا وُجُوهَكُمْ عِنْدَ كُلِّ مَسْجِدٍ يعنى عند كلّ قصد تقصدونـه

---

(١) و, but corr. in marg.   (٢) Suppl. in marg.   (٣) Suppl. above.

(٤) In marg. وما.   (٥) بين written above as variant.   (٦) Kor. 12, 108.

قُلْ suppl. above.   (٧) اليه.   (٨) تقريبهم.   (٩) Kor. 7, 28.

وَٱدْعُوهُ مُخْلِصِينَ لَهُ ٱلدِّينَ يعنى ادعوه بلا رياء ولا عُجْب ثم لا تعتمدوا على
هذا لانّه كما بَدَأَكُمْ تَعُودُونَ عند العواقب، وفى معنى قوله تعالى (١) سَنُرِيهِمْ
آيَاتِنَا فِى ٱلْآفَاقِ وَفِى أَنْفُسِهِمْ حَتَّى يَتَبَيَّنَ لَهُمْ أَنَّهُ ٱلْحَقُّ معناه سنريهم
نعوتنا وصفاتنا فى الملكوت حتى نبيّن لمن نبيّن لهم انه الحقّ وما سواه
٥ باطل لا جَرَمَ، فلذلك قال النبىّ صلعم أَصْدَقُ كلمة قالت العرب (٢)[ما
قال لَبِيدٌ]،

أَلَا كُلُّ شَىْءٍ ما خلا ٱللَّه باطلٌ،

ومِمَّا استنبطوا من خصوصية النبىّ صلعم انّ موسى عليه السلم سأل ربّه عزّ
وجلّ فقال (٣) رَبِّ ٱشْرَحْ لِى صَدْرِى وَيَسِّرْ لِى أَمْرِى [ونودى محمّد صلعم
١٠ بلا سؤال (٤) أَلَمْ نَشْرَحْ لَكَ صَدْرَكَ الى آخر (٥) السورة]، وكذلك سؤال
ابرهيم عليه السلم (٦) وَلَا تُخْزِنِى يَوْمَ يُبْعَثُونَ [فضّل الحبيب على الخليل]
وقال لنبيّنا صلعم من غير سؤال (٧) يَوْمَ لَا يُخْزِى ٱللَّهُ ٱلنَّبِىَّ وَٱلَّذِينَ آمَنُوا
مَعَهُ، وقيل له صلعم أَلَمْ نَشْرَحْ لَكَ صَدْرَكَ وَوَضَعْنَا عَنْكَ وِزْرَكَ الى قوله
(٨) إِنَّ مَعَ ٱلْعُسْرِ يُسْرًا، ومِمَّا قيل فى هذا المعنى ايضًا انّ الله عزّ وجلّ
١٥ خاطب جميع الخلق ودعاهم اليه ودلّهم عليه بذكر المُلْك والملكوت فقال
Af.47b (٩) وَكَذَلِكَ نُرِى إِبْرَهِيمَ مَلَكُوتَ ٱلسَّمَوَاتِ وَٱلْأَرْضِ وقوله (١٠) أَفَلَمْ يَنْظُرُوا
إِلَى مَا خَلَقَ ٱللَّهُ وقوله تعالى (١١) أَفَلَمْ يَتَفَكَّرُوا فِى أَنْفُسِهِمْ، وقوله (١٢) أَفَلَا
يَنْظُرُونَ إِلَى ٱلْإِبِلِ كَيْفَ خُلِقَتْ الى آخر الاية، فلمّا خاطب رسول الله صلعم
قال (١٣) أَلَمْ تَرَ إِلَى رَبِّكَ يا محمّد كَيْفَ مَدَّ ٱلظِّلَّ، فلمّا كان الخطاب مع
٢٠ الحبيب بدأ بذكره فقال أَلَمْ تَرَ إِلَى رَبِّكَ، وفى [معنى] قوله (٢)(١٤) وَٱتَّخَذَ ٱللَّهُ

---

(١) Kor. 41, 53.   (٢) Suppl. in marg.   (٣) Kor. 20, 26—27.   (٤) Kor. 94, 1.

(٥) The marginal note ends with two words which appear to be ونظر هذا.

(٦) Kor. 26, 87.   (٧) Kor. 66, 8.   (٨) Kor. 94, 6.   (٩) Kor. 6, 75.

(١٠) Kor. 7, 184 (quoted incorrectly).   (١١) Kor. 30, 7. Kor. has أَوَلَمْ

(١٢) Kor. 88, 17.   (١٣) Kor. 25, 47.   (١٤) Kor. 4, 124.

إِبْرَاهِيمَ خَلِيلًا قالوا انّ الخُلَّة ما يتخلّل القلب والمحبّة ما يكون فى حبّة القلب
يعنى سُوَيْدَاء القلب وسُمِّىَ المحبّة محبّة لانّها تحبو بها (١)ما سواها من القلب
فلذلك فضّل الحبيب على الخليل (٢)[وقال (٣)اَفْعَلَ مَا تُؤْمَرُ وقال لنبيّنا
صلّعم (٤)وَلَسَوْفَ يُعْطِيكَ رَبُّكَ فَتَرْضَى فدلّ بذلك فضّل الحبيب على الخليل]،
٥ وما قالوا فى هذا المعنى ايضًا انّ آدم صلوات الله عليه لمّا ذكر الله تعالى
توبته فقال (٥)وَعَصَى آدَمُ رَبَّهُ فَغَوَى فذكر جنايته قَبْلَ توبته (٦)ثُمَّ اجْتَبَاهُ
رَبُّهُ فَتَابَ عَلَيْهِ وَهَدَى، وذكر ايضًا خطيئة داود عليه السلم ثم قال (٧)فَغَفَرْنَا
لَهُ، وكذلك خبّر عن سليمن عليه السلم بقوله (٨)وَلَقَدْ فَتَنَّا سُلَيْمَنَ وَأَلْقَيْنَا
عَلَى كُرْسِيِّهِ جَسَدًا ثُمَّ أَنَابَ قَالَ رَبِّ اغْفِرْلِى، وقال للنبيّ صلّعم (٩)عَفَا اللّهُ
١٠ عَنْكَ لِمَ أَذِنْتَ لَهُمْ، قال بعضهم أنسه بذكر العفو حتى لا يوحشه ذكر
العتاب، وقال ايضًا (١٠)لِيَغْفِرَ لَكَ اللّهُ مَا تَقَدَّمَ مِنْ ذَنْبِكَ وَمَا تَأَخَّرَ، فابتدأ
بذكر الغفران قبل الذنب وغفر له الذنب قبل ان يُذْنب (٢)[وقبل العَتْبِ]،
(١١)وقالوا ايضًا معنى آخر انّ جميع ما أعطى الانبياء عليهم السلم من الكرامات
قد اعطى مثلَه محمّدًا صلّعم وزاد له (١٢)[عليهم] مثل انشقاق القمر ونبع الماء
١٥ من الاصابع والمعراج وغير ذلك، ثم ذكر الانبياء وذكر ما استخصّهم (١٢)[به]
وأضاف الى ابرهيم عليه السلم الخُلّة والى موسى عليه السلم الكلام والى سليمن
عليه السلم المُلْك والى ايوب عليه السلم الصبر ولم يضف الى محمّد صلّعم
شيئًا ممّا أعطاه من الكرامات فقال (١٣)لَعَمْرُكَ يا محمّد (١٣)فَلَا وَرَبِّكَ لَا يُؤْمِنُونَ
حتى يُحَكِّمُوكَ فِيمَا شَجَرَ بَيْنَهُمْ الآية، ثم قال (١٤)إِنَّ الَّذِينَ يُبَايِعُونَكَ إِنَّمَا
A f. 48a   يُبَايِعُونَ اللّهَ الآية، وقال (١٥)فَلَمْ تَقْتُلُوهُمْ وَلَكِنَّ اللّهَ قَتَلَهُمْ وَمَا رَمَيْتَ إِذْ رَمَيْتَ
وَلَكِنَّ اللّهَ رَمَى، ولم يذكر (١٦)لنبيّه صلّعم شيئًا غيره، فلمّا ادّبه بذلك قال

---

(١) من, but corr. above.   (٢) Suppl. in marg.   (٣) Kor. 37, 102.

(٤) Kor. 93, 5.   (٥) Kor. 20, 119.   (٦) Kor. 20, 120.   (٧) Kor. 38, 24.

Text has فغفر.   (٨) Kor. 38, 33.   (٩) Kor. 9, 43.   (١٠) Kor. 48, 2.

(١١) وقال, but corr. by later hand.   (١٢) Suppl. above.   (١٣) Kor. 4, 68.

(١٤) Kor. 48, 10.   (١٥) Kor. 8, 17.   (١٦) محمد suppl. in marg. after لنبيّه.

اللهمّ بك أَصولُ وبك أَجولُ وبك أُقاتلُ وبك أُحاولُ، وسبل الشبلى رحمه
الله عن معنى قوله (١)[تعالى] (٢)لَوِ ٱطَّلَعْتَ عَلَيْهِمْ لَوَلَّيْتَ مِنْهُمْ فِرَارًا وَلَمُلِئْتَ
مِنْهُمْ رُعْبًا، قال لَو ٱطَّلَعْتَ على ٱلكلّ ممّا (٣)سوانا لَوَلَّيْتَ مِنْهُمْ فِرَارًا البنا
يا محمّد، وقالوا فى معنى قوله (٤)سُبْحَانَ ٱلَّذِى أَسْرَى بِعَبْدِهِ لَيْلًا مِنَ
٥ ٱلْمَسْجِدِ ٱلْحَرَامِ إِلَى ٱلْمَسْجِدِ ٱلْأَقْصَى ٱلَّذِى بَارَكْنَا حَوْلَهُ انّه لو أَسرى بروحه
كما قال المخالفون لم يَقُلْ أَسْرَى بِعَبْدِهِ لانّ اسم العبد لا يقع الا على الروح
والجسد، وقيل ايضًا فى معنى قوله (٥)وَكَانَ فَضْلُ ٱللَّهِ عَلَيْكَ عَظِيمًا يعنى
باجتبايك واصطفايك لانّ النبوّة والرسالة لم تقسم على الجزاء والاستحقاق
ولو كانت من جهة الجزاء والاستحقاق لما فضّل (٦)نبيّنا صلعم على سايـر
١٠ الانبياء عليهم السلم لانّهم أَكثرُ أَعمالًا وأَطولُ أَعمارًا، وقالوا فى معنى قوله
عزّ وجلّ (٧)وَٱصْبِرْ لِحُكْمِ رَبِّكَ فَإِنَّكَ بِأَعْيُنِنَا انّه خاطبه باتمّ الخطاب وأخصّ
الفضيلة اذ قال وَٱصْبِرْ لِحُكْمِ رَبِّكَ فَإِنَّكَ بِأَعْيُنِنَا وقال لغيره (٨)ٱصْبِرُوا
وَصَابِرُوا وقال (٩)إِنَّمَا يُوَفَّى ٱلصَّابِرُونَ أَجْرَهُمْ بِغَيْرِ حِسَابٍ، طالبهم بالصبر
على المعاوضة (١٠)وطالب المصطفى صلعم بالصبر مع المراقبة، وقال فى موضع
١٥ آخر (١١)وَٱصْبِرْ وَمَا صَبْرُكَ إِلَّا بِٱللَّهِ لانّه صلعم اجلّ عنده من ان يطالبه
بمعاملة يُقْتَضى عليها معاوضة لانّ محلّه صلعم محلّ الاختصاص، فهذا (١٢)طَرَفٌ
من المستنبطات التى للقوم من القرآن (١٣)فى معنى خصوصية النبىّ صلعم،

(١) Suppl. above.   (٢) Kor. 18, 17.   (٣) Orig. سواه but corr. by later
hand.   (٤) Kor. 17, 1.   (٥) Kor. 4, 113.   (٦) محمدا suppl. above
after نبيّنا.   (٧) Kor. 52, 48.   (٨) Kor. 3, 200.   (٩) Kor. 39, 13.
(١٠) وطلب corr. in marg.   (11) Kor. 16, 128.   (١٢) طرق.   (١٣) ومعنى.

باب فى مستنبطاتهم فى خصوصية النبىّ صلعم وفضله على اخوانه

عليهم المسلم من الاخبار المرويّة عن رسول الله صلعم،

A f. 48b

قال الشيخ رحمه الله فامّا مستنبطاتهم فى اخبار رسول الله صلعم فكما قيل فى معنى قول النبىّ صلعم انّه كان يقول فى سجوده اعوذ برضاك من سُخْطك واعوذُ بمعافاتك من عقوبتك واعوذُ بك منك لا أُحصى ثناءً عليك انت كما أَثنيتَ على نفسك ، قالوا يقول الله (١) وَاسْجُدْ وَاقْتَرِبْ فوجد رسول الله صلعم فى سجوده معنّى من القُرب فقال اعوذ برضاك من سخطك واعوذ بمعافاتك من عقوبتك فاستعاذ بصفاته (٢) من صفاته ، ثم شاهد معنًى آخَرَ من القرب ما اندرج فيه القرب الذى شاهد (٣) [به] الصفات والنعوت فقال اعوذ بك منك (٤) وكان قد استعاذ بصفاته من صفاته فلمّا استعاذ به لم يكن المستعاذ به الّا منه ثم (٥) زيد فى قُرْبه ووجد من المشاهدة معنًى افناه عن الاستعاذة به فقال لا احصى ثناءً عليك فاحتشم من الاستعاذة به فى محلّ القرب فالتجأ الى الثناء عليه ومن لم يُطق الاستعاذة التى هى (٦) حدُّ العبودية فكيف يطيق الثناء، وهو صفة الربوبية فلذلك قال لا أحصى ثناءً عليك ثم احتشم ايضًا من الثناء عليه فى محلّ القرب فأخرج نفسه من الثناء عليه بما أثنى الله تعالى (٧) [به] على نفسه قبل الخلق وحمد نفسه قبل حمْدهم له وشهد لنفسه بالوحدانية قبل شهادتهم له فقال انت كما أثنيتَ على نفسك ، وهذا حقيقة نهاية التقريب وحقيقة التجريد ان (٧) بتلاشى العبد كما لم يكن ويكون الله تعالى كما لم يزل ، فلو جمع جميع (٨) [اشارات] الواجدين والعارفين والمحقّقين فى التوحيد لم يبلغ عُشر معشار ما اشار اليه رسول الله

---

(١) Kor. 96, 19.   (٢) عن corr. in marg.   (٣) Suppl. in marg.

(٤) لانّه written above instead of و.   (٥) In marg. زاد.   (٦) In marg.

محلّ. In marg. يذهب. (٧)

صلعم فى هذا المعنى، وقيل ايضًا فى معنى قول النبىّ صلعم لو تعلمون مـا
أعْلَمُ لَضحكتم قليلًا ولبكيتم كثيرًا وخرجتم الى الصُّعدات ولما تقاررتم على
الفُرُش، قالوا لو انّ الذى علم رسول الله صلعم (١) كان من العلوم التى
انزل الله تعالى عليه وأمر بابلاغه لبلّغهم ذلك، ولو علموا (٢) ذلك لم يقل
لو تعلمون ما اعلمُ، ولو علم انّهم يطيقون ذلك لعلّمهم كساير العلوم، ولو
كان من العلوم المتعارفة بين الخلق ايضًا لقالوا عَلِمْنا بعد ما قال لو تعلمون
ما اعلمُ لانّ حقايق رسالته وما خصّه الله تعالى به من العلم لو وُضعت على
الجبال لذابت الّا انّه كان يُظهرها لهم على مقاديرهم لانّ الله تعالى قال
(٣) فَاعْلَمْ أنَّهُ لَا إِلهَ إلّا اللهُ وقال (٤) وَقُلْ رَبِّ زِدْنِى عِلْمًا، وقال صلعم أنا
أعْلَمُكم بالله ولو تعلمون ما اعلَمُ وقد اشار رسول الله صلعم الى معنًى من
معانى تخصيصه اشارةً لا تُدْركها العقول ولا تَصِلُ اليها الفهوم وتعجز عنها علوم
جميع الخلق وهو قول النبىّ صلعم لستُ كأحدكم إنّى اظلُّ عند ربّى يُطْعمنى
ويسقينى، فلا يتهيّأ لاحد أن يُخبر عن الذى اطعمه وسقاه لانّ النبىّ صلعم
فى علوّ مرتبته وما خُصّ به من العلم بالله لم يُخبر عنه ولم يصفه، وقيل فى
معنى قول النبىّ صلعم فى دعوائه اللهمّ اكْفِنى كفالة الوليد لا تَكِلْنِى الى نفسى
طُرْفةَ عين وجّهتُ وجهى اليك وألجأتُ ظَهْرى اليك لا مَلْجأَ ولا مَنْجَى
منك الّا اليك وما يُشبه ذلك من دعوائه انّه صلعم اظهر من نفسه صدق
اللجأ واظهر الفاقة اليه والاستكانة بين يديه بلا مشاهدة حركة من حركاتــه
ولا اضافة فعلٍ الى نفسه، قال ابو بكر الواسطى رحمه الله وبصدق اللجأ
واظهار الفقر وصدق الفاقة تزيّنت السراير، وقيل فى معنى قول النبىّ صلعم
عند موته وا كَرْباه قالوا يسرت المنيّة عليه لمبادرته الى ما لاحظ عند الموت
من المراتب الرفيعة فقال وا كَرْبى من البقآء فيا بينكم شوقًا منّى الى اللقآء،

---

(١) كانت corr. in marg.   (٢) اصحابه suppl. in marg. after ذلك.

(٣) Kor. 47, 21.   (٤) Kor. 20, 113.

وسمعتُ محمّد بن داود الدينورى المعروف بالدُّقّى يقول سمعتُ الجريرى يقول
قيل للجُنيْد رحمه اله ما معنى قول النبىّ صلعم انا سيّدُ ولد آدم ولا فَخْر
فقال لى هاتِ أَيْشَ وقع لك فى ذلك فقلتُ معنى قوله انا سيّد ولد آدم
ولا فخر وهذا عطاؤه وأنا لا أفتخر بالعطآء لانّ فخرى بالمُعْطى فقال لى
٥ احسنتَ يأيا محمّد او كما قال، وسُئل [الجنيد] عن معنى قول النبىّ صلعم
فى زينب امرأة زيْد زوجه الحكمة فى ذلك فقال الجنيد رحمه اله كان
زيْد يُدْعَى ابن النبىّ صلعم وكان ابن الدعاية لا ابن الولادة فأراد اله عزّ
وجلّ ان يتزوّج بحليله حتّى يكون فرقًا بين ابناء الولادة وإبناء الدعاية،
وقال الجُنيْد رحمه اله فى معنى قول النبىّ صلعم استغفروا اله وتوبوا اليه
١٠ فانّى استغفر اله وأتوب اليه فى اليوم مأية مرّةٍ او كا قال، قالوا كان حال
النبىّ صلعم مع اله تعالى [زيادةً] فى كلّ نفَس وطرفة عين فكان اذا رُقى
به الى زيادة حال أَشْرَفَ من زيادته على حالته فى النَّفَس الماضى استغفر اله
من ذلك وتاب اليه، وسُئل الجُنيْد رحمه اله ايضًا كا بلغنى عن معنى قول
النبىّ صلعم رحم اله اخى عيسى عليه السلم لو ازداد يقينًا لمشى فى الهوَآء،
١٥ فقال معناه وإله اعلم انّ عيسى عليه السلم مشى على المآء بيقينه والنبىّ صلعم
مشى فى الهوآء ليلة المعراج بزيادة يقينه على يقين عيسى عليه السلم فقال لو
ازداد يقينًا يعنى لو أُعطى من زيادة اليقين مثلَ ما أُعطيتُ لمشى فى الهوآء،
يُخبر رسولُ اله صلعم عن حالته، وسمعتُ الحُصْرى رحمه اله يقول فى معنى
قول النبىّ صلعم لى مع اله وقتُ لا يَسَعُنى فيه معه شىءٌ غير اله عزّ وجلّ
٢٠ فقال ان صحّ ذلك عن النبىّ صلعم أنّه قال ذلك او لم يصحّ فانّ جميع
اوقات رسول اله صلعم كانت وقتًا لا يسعه فيه [معه] غير اله بسره A f. 50a
وقلبه ولكن كان يرُدّ بصفاته الى الخلق حتى يؤدّبهم ويعلّمهم ويُجرَّى على
صفاته تلوين الاحكام لينتفع به الخلق فاذا بدا على صفاته من انوار سرّه

---

(١) Suppl. in marg.   (٢) In marg. لزينب.   (٣) Suppl. above.

(٤) In marg. تكوين.

أخذه عن الخُلق كما قالت عايشة رضى الله عنها انتهبتُ ليلة فلم أجِدْ رسول
الله صلعم فى فراشه فقمتُ أطْلُبُهُ فوقعتْ يدى على قدميه وها منتصبتان
(١) ساجدًا لله عزّ وجلّ (٢) [وسمعتُهُ] وهو يقول اعوذ برضاك من سخطك
الحديث، فهذا هو الوقت الذى كان يبدو على سرّه والانوار على صفاته واذا
٥ رُدّت الانوار (٣) الى سرّه رُدَّ بصفاته الى الخُلق لينتفعوا به ويقتدوا به، معنى
صفاته اى ظاهره ومعنى سرّه اى باطنه،

باب فى مستنبطاتهم فى معانى اخبار مروية عن رسول الله
صلعم من طريق الاستنباط والفهم،

قال الشيخ رحمه الله سمعتُ ابا الحسن احمد بن محمّد بن سالم بالبصرة
١٠ وقد سُيل عن معنى قول النبىّ صلعم أطْيَبُ ما أكل الرجل من كسْب يدِه
فقال له السايل نحن مستعبَّدون بالاكتساب اذًا فقال (٤) الشيخ رحمه الله
الكسب سُنّة الرسول صلعم والتوكّل حال الرسول صلعم وانّما استنّ لهم الكسب
لعلْمه بضعفهم حتى اذا عجزوا عن التوكّل الذى هو حاله وسقطوا عن مرتبته
فى التوكّل ودرجته وقعوا فى الاكتساب التى هى سنته ولو لا ذلك لهلكوا،
١٥ (٢) [وقيل فى معنى ذلك إن رفع العبد يدَه الى الله تعالى فيدعو الله تعالى
فيجيبه فيكون ذلك كسْب يدِه] وسُيل الشِبْلى رحمه الله عن معنى قول النبىّ
صلعم جعل رزقى تحت ظلّ سيفى فقال كان سيفه (٢) [التوكّل على] الله تعالى
وامّا ذو الفقار فهو قطعة من حديد، ومثل ذلك فى مستنبطاتهم كثير إن
(٥) ذكرنا يطول الكتاب، وامّا ما كان من مستنبطاتهم فى غير هذا المعنى
من الحديث فهو كما سمعتُ ابا عمرو عبد (٦) الواحد بن علوان برَحْبة مُلك   A.f.50b

<hr>

(١) يذكر suppl. in marg. after ساجدًا.   (٢) Suppl. in marg.   (٢) In
marg. عن.   (٤) ابن سالم added in marg.   (٥) In marg. حكينا.
(٦) ابن written above as variant.

ابن طَوْق قال سأل رجل الجُنَيْد رحمه الله وأنا عنه جالسٌ عن معنى قول
النبىّ صلّعم لو توكّلتم على الله حقَّ توكّلِه لغذاكم كما يغذو الطير تغدو خِماصًا
وتروح بِطانًا وهو ذا نرى ان الطير يطير فى طلب الرزق من موضع الى
موضع ويتحرّك ويطلب (١)وينبعث، فقال الجُنَيْد رحمه الله قال الله تعالى
٥ (٢)إِنَّا جَعَلْنَا مَا عَلَى ٱلْأَرْضِ زِينَةً لَّهَا وإنّما طيران الطير وحركته من موضع
الى موضع ونقْلته من مكان الى مكان من اجْل الزينة التى ذكر الله تعالى
فقد جعل الله تعالى طيرانهم للزينة التى ذكر الله تعالى لا لطلب الرزق،
ووجدتُ فى كتاب عمرو بن عثمن المكّى رحمه الله فى معنى قول النبىّ صلّعم
لعبد الله بن عمر رضى الله عنه يا عبد الله بن عمر أعبد الله كأنّك تراه
١٠ فان لم تكن تراه فانّه يراك، وكذلك اجابة جبريل عليه السلم حين سأله
عن الاحسان فقال أن نعبد الله كأنّك تراه فان لم تكن تراه فانّه يراك،
فقال عمرو بن عثمن رحمه الله (٣)[معنى قوله] كأنّك تراه شىء بين شيئَيْن
بين رؤية ويقين فلم يُخرجها صلّعم الى رؤية عيان ولم يردّها الى صفة يقين
وإنّما مُثّل له (٤)مَثَلٌ يدلّ على نهاية من نهايات حقايق الايمان وبذلك
١٥ طالَبَ (٥)حارثةَ إن صحّ الخبر، وما كان كأنّ بمعنى أنَّ وليس هو أن ولكنّه
قد قرب من معنى الرؤية (٦)فى تغليب المشاهدة عند حضور القلب ومداناتها
الى ما وارته (٧)الغيوب فهذا أصْلُ الحُجّة على مشاهدة القلوب، وسُئل ابو
بكر الواسطى رحمه الله عن معنى قول النبىّ (٨)صلّعم (٨)جُبِلَ ولىُّ الله تعالى
على السخاء وحُسْن الخُلق فقال امّا السخاوة من ولىّ الله تعالى أن يهَبَ نفسه
٢٠ وقلبه لله عزّ وجلّ وحُسْنُ خُلقه أن يوافق خُلقُه (٩)اختلاف تدبير الله عزّ
A f.51a وجلّ، وسُئل الشبْلى رحمه الله عن معنى ما رُوى فى الحديث ان النفس اذا

---

(١) The original reading seems to have been وينبعث.   (٢) Kor. 18, 6.

(٣) Suppl. in marg.   (٤) In marg. مثالا.   (٥) الحديث added in marg.

(٦) وفى.   (٧) In marg. العيوب.   (٨) Orig. ما جُبِل, but ما has been
stroked through.   (٩) اخلاق corr. in marg.

أُحْرِزَتْ قوّتها اطمأنّت فقال اذا عرفت من يقوتها اطمأنّت ثم قرأ قوله
عزّ وجلّ (١) وَكَانَ ٱللّٰهُ عَلَىٰ كُلّ شَىْءٍ مُّقِيتًا، وسُئِل الجُنيْد رحمه الله عن
معنى قول النبيّ صلعم حُبّك (٢) للشئ يُعمى ويُصمّ فقال حُبّك للدنيا يُعمى
ويُصمّ عن الآخرة، وسُئِل الشبْلى رحمه الله عن معنى ما رُوِىَ عن النبيّ
٥ صلعم انّه قال اذا رأيتم اهل البلاء فسلوا الله ربّكم العافية فقال اهل البلاء
اهل الغفلة عن الله تعالى، وسُئِل ايضًا عن معنى حديث النبيّ صلعم الذى
رُوِىَ عنه انّه قال حرام على قلب عليه (٤) [زبانية (٤)] من الدنيا ان يجد
حلاوة الآخرة فقال صدق صلعم أن قال ذلك وأنا ذا اقول حرام على قلب
عليه (٥) زبانية] من الآخرة ان يجد حلاوة التوحيد، وسُئِل محمّد بن موسى
١٠ الفَرغانى رحمه الله عن معنى قول النبيّ صلعم لأبى حُجيْفة يأبا حُجيْفة سائِل
العلماء (٤) [وخائِل الحكماء وجالِس الكبراء] فقال سائِل العلماء بالحلال
والحرام وخالِل الحكماء الذين يسلكون بها على طريق الصدق والصفاء
(٤) [والاخلاص] وجالِس الكبراء الذين عن الله ينطقون وإلى ربوبيته يشيرون
وبنور (٦) قُرْبه ينظرون، وسُئِل سهل بن عبد الله رحمه الله عن (٧) [معنى]
١٥ قول النبيّ صلعم المؤمن من نَسْرُه حسنته ونَسوُّه سيّئته قال حسنته نِعَمُ الله
وفضله وسيّئته نَفْسُه إن وُكِلَ اليها، وسُئِل سهل ايضًا عن معنى قوله
(٧) [صلعم] الدنيا ملعونة ملعون ما فيها الّا ذِكْر الله نعالى، قال ذِكْر الله فى
هذا الموضع الزُّهْد (٨) فى الحرام وهو ان يكون اذا استقبله حرام يذكر الله
نعالى ويعلم انّ الله مطّلع عليه فيجتنب ذلك الحرام، ومثل هذا كثير من
٢٠ مستنبطاتهم فى معنى حديث رسول الله صلعم وذكرنا طرفًا منه وفيه كفاية
إن شاء الله نعالى، فان قال قائلٌ هل تجد للاستنباط فى القرآن والحديث
وغير ذلك أصْلاً فى العلم فيقال نَعَمْ قول النبيّ صلعم لأصحابه وهم (٤) [عنه]
مجتمعون وفيهم عبد الله بن عمر رضى الله عنه وهو أحدثُهم سنًّا فقال النبيّ

٨ f.51b

صلعم أيّما شجرة تشبه ابن آدم قال فوقع الناس فى اشجار البادية ووقع فى
قلبى انّها النخلة واستحييّتُ ان أجيب رسول الله صلعم فسكتُّ حتى قال
رسول الله صلعم هى النخلة قال ابن عمر رضى الله عنه فقلتُ لعمر رضى الله
عنه لقد كدتُ ان اقول انّها النخلة فقال عمر رضى الله عنه لئن قلت ذلك
كان أَحَبَّ الَىّ من حُمرِ النَّعَمِ او كما فى الخبر، والحُجَّة فى ذلك أنّ احدًا
لم يستنبط من اصحاب رسول الله صلعم معنى ما سألهم عنه رسول الله صلعم
الّا عبد الله بن عمر رضى الله عنه وهو أَصغرُهم سنًّا وكذلك الاستنباط فى
هذه المعانى على مقدار ما يفتح الله تعالى للقلوب من غيبه، وبالله التوفيق،

[كتاب الصحابة رضوان الله عليهم][1]،

١٠ باب فى ذكر اصحاب رسول الله صلعم ومعانيهم رضى الله عنهم،

قال الله تعالى [٢]﴿وَٱلسَّابِقُونَ ٱلْأَوَّلُونَ مِنَ ٱلْمُهَاجِرِينَ وَٱلْأَنصَارِ ٱلَّذِينَ
ٱتَّبَعُوهُم بِإِحْسَانٍ رَّضِىَ ٱللَّهُ عَنْهُمْ وَرَضُوا عَنْهُ﴾، فقد وقع اسم السابقين على
الجميع[٣] بظاهر الآية مع رضا الله تعالى عنهم وشهد لهم بأنّهم[٤] راضون عنه،
والسابقون هم المقرّبون بنصّ [٥]الآية، وقد ذكرنا تخصيص المقرّبين من
الأبرار وتخصيص الابرار من اهل الجنّة فى باب الموافقة لكتاب الله عزّ
وجلّ، فأمّا قوله تعالى رَضِىَ ٱللَّهُ عَنْهُمْ وَرَضُوا عَنْهُ فقد قال الله تعالى فى
آية أخرى [٦]﴿وَرِضْوَانٌ مِّنَ ٱللَّهِ أَكْبَرُ﴾، قال [٧]ذو النون رحمه الله [٨][يعنى]
أكبَرُ[٩] واقدم حين قال رَضِىَ ٱللَّهُ عَنْهُمْ وَرَضُوا عَنْهُ فى سابق علمه فلذلك

---

(١) Suppl. in marg.   (٢) الجمع corr. by later hand.   (٤) راضين.

(٥) Kor. 56, 10—11.   (٦) Kor. 9, 73.   (٧) اذ.   (٨) Suppl. above.

(٩) The penultimate letter of أكبر is pointed in the text both as ب and ث.

استرضاهم له وأرضاهم حتى رضوا عنه، وقال النبىّ صلعم أصحابى كالنُّجوم بأيّهم
اقتديتم اهتديتم، وقد ذكر الله تعالى القَسَم بالنجوم من الكواكب والنجوم ما
يُهتَدى به فى البرّ والبحر لكِبَره وكثرة ضَوْءه ونوره فلذلك شبَّههم بالنجوم
ولم يشبّههم بالكواكب لانّ الكواكب هى الصغار الذى لا يهتدى به ثم دل
على الاهتداء بالاقتداء بهم ولم يخصّ الاقتداء يعنى دون الآخر فعلَّمنا ان
الاهتداء بهم فى الاقتداء [بهم] فى جميع معانيهم الظاهرة والباطنة، فامّا
الظاهر فمشهور عند العلماء والفقهاء فى علم الحدود والاحكام والحلال
والحرام، وقد رُوى عن النبىّ صلعم انّه قال أَرحَمُ أمّتى بأمّتى ابو بكر
الصدّيق رضى الله عنه وأقواهم فى دين الله عُمَرُ رضى الله عنه وأصدقُهم
حياءً عثمن رضى الله عنه وأفرضُهم زَيد رضى الله عنه وأعلمهم بالحلال
والحرام معاذ بن جَبَل رضى الله عنه وأقرأُهم أُبَىّ بن كعب رضى الله عنه
وأقضاهم علىّ رضى الله عنه، وما اظلّت الخضراء ولا اقلّت الغبراء على
ذى لَهْجة أَصْدَقَ من ابى ذَرّ رضى الله عنه، وإمّا الباطن فنبدأ بما بدأ به
رسول الله صلعم بقوله أقتدُوا بالذين من بعدى ابى بكر وعمر رضى الله
عنهما، فنبدأ بأبى بكر ثم من بعد ابى بكر بعمر، وبلغنى عن ابى عُتبة
الحلوانى رحمه الله انّه قال ألا أُخبركم عن حال كان عليها اصحاب رسول
الله صلعم اوّلها لقاء الله تعالى كان احبّ [اليهم] من الحياة والثانية كانوا
لا يخافون عدوًّا قلّوا او كثروا والثالثة لم يكونوا يخافون عوزًا من الدنيا
وكانوا واثقين برزق الله تعالى والرابعة إن بدأ بهم الطاعون لم يبرحوا حتى
يقضى الله فيهم وكانوا أخوَفَ ما يكونون من الموت أصَحَّ ما يكونون، ويُحكَى
عن محمّد بن على الكتّانى رحمه الله انّه قال كان الناس فى ابتداء الاسلام

---

(١) Suppl. in marg.   (٢) Altered to الظاهره by a later hand.

(٣) حیا.   (٤) I cannot ascertain the correct form of this *nisba*: it
might be either حُلْوانى or حَلْوائى.

يتعاملون بالدين حتى رقّ الدين ثم تعامل القرن الثانى بالوفآء حتى ذهب
الوفآء ثم تعامل القرن الثالث بالمروّة حتى ذهبت المروّة ثم تعامل القرن A f.52b
الرابع بالحيآء حتى ذهب الحيآء ثم صار الناس يتعاملون بالرغبة والرهبة،

باب ذكر ابى بكر الصدّيق رضى الله عنه وتخصيصه من بين
رسول الله صلعم بالاحوال التى تعلّق بها اهل الصفوة ٥
من هذه الأمّة وتخلّق بذلك واقتدى به،

رُوى عن مطرّف بن عبد الله رحمه الله انّه قال قال ابو بكر الصدّيق
رضى الله عنه لو نادى (١)منادٍ من السمآء انّه لن يَلِجَ الجنّة الّا رجلٌ واحد
ارجوتُ ان اكون انا (٢)[هو] ولو نادى منادٍ من السمآء انّه لا يدخل النار
الّا رجلٌ واحد (٣)لخفتُ ان اكون انا هو، قال مطرّف رحمه الله هذا والله ١٠
(٤)أعظمُ الخوف (٤)واعظمُ الرجآء، وحكى عن ابى العبّاس بن عطآء رحمه
الله انّه سُيِل عن قوله تعالى (٥)كُونُوا رَبّانِيّينَ الآية قال معناه كونوا كأبى
بكر الصدّيق رضى الله عنه فانّه لمّا مات رسول الله صلعم اضطربت اسرار
المؤمنين كلّها لموته ولم يؤثّر ذلك فى سرّ ابى بكر رضى الله عنه شيئًا وخرج
وقال للناس (٦)[يا ايّها الناس] من كان يعبد محمّدًا صلعم فانّ محمّدًا صلعم ١٥
قد مات ومن كان يعبد الله تعالى فانّ الله حىٌّ لا يموت، فحُكم الربّانى ان
يكون بهنه (٦)الصفة لا تؤثّر الحوادث فى سرّه شيئًا ولو كان فيه انقلابُ
الخافقَين، وقال ابو بكر الواسطى رحمه الله اوّل لسان (٧)الصوفيّة ظهرت فى
هذه الأمّة على لسان ابى بكر رضى الله عنه اشارةً (٨)فاستخرج منها اهلُ الفهم

(١) منادى. عظم Orig. (٤) .لخشيت In marg. (٣) Suppl. in marg. (٢)
but corrected. (٥) Kor. 3, 73. (٦) التى added in marg. (٧) التصوف
corr. in marg. (٨) فاستخرجوا Orig. but corrected.

لطايف نَوَسْوَسَ (١)فيها العقلاء، قال الشيخ رحمه الله وهذا الذى اشار اليه
الواسطى فى قوله اوّل لسان الصوفيّة ظهرت على لسان ابى بكر رضى الله
A f.53a عنه فذلك قول ابى بكر رضى الله عنه لانّه حين خرج من جميع مُلْكه قال
له النبيّ صلعم أَيْشَ خَلَّفتَ لعيالك قال اللهَ ورسولَك قال اللهَ ثم قال ورسولَه
٥ ولَعَمرى انّها اشارة جليلة لأهل التوحيد فى حقايق التفريد غير ان لأبى بكر
الصدِّيق رضى الله عنه (٢)اشارات غيرها مستخرجة (٣)منها لطايف غير
ذلك وهى معلومة عند اهل الحقايق ومفهومة للتعلّق والتخلّق بها (٤)منها قوله
حين صعد المِنْبَر بعد ما مات رسول الله صلعم واضطرب قلوب اصحاب
رسول الله صلعم وخشوا على ذهاب الاسلام بموته صلعم وخروجه من بين
١٠ ظهرانَيْهم فقال من كان منكم يعبد محمّدًا صلعم فانّ محمّدًا صلعم قد مات
ومن كان يعبد الله فانّ الله حيٌّ لا يموت، واللطيفة فى ذلك ثباته فى التوحيد
وما ثبّت به قلوبَ الجماعة من الصحابة رضى الله عنهم، ومنها قوله يوم بَدْر
للنبيّ صلعم حيث (٥)[كان] يقول اللهمّ إن تهلك هذه العصابة لم تُعْبَدْ فى
الارض (٦)[من بعد ذلك]، فقال ابو بكر رضى الله عنه (٧)دَعْ مناشدتك
١٥ ربّك فانّه والله مُنْجزٌ لك ما وعدك او كما قال، وهو قول الله تعالى (٨)إذْ
بُوحى رَبُّكَ إلَى الْمَلاَئِكَةِ أَنِّى مَعَكُمْ فَثَبِّتوا الَّذِينَ آمَنُوا سَأُلْقِى فى قُلُوبِ الَّذِينَ
كَفَرُوا الرُّعْبَ، فخُصَّ بحقيقة التصديق لما وعدهم الله تعالى من النصر من
جميع الصحابة (٦)[عند اضطراب قلوبهم] فدلَّ على حقيقة ايمانه وخصوصيته،
فان قال قايلٌ فما معنى تغيّر النبيّ صلعم وثبات ابى بكر رضى الله عنه وهو
٢٠ اتمُّ من ابى بكر رضى الله عنه فى جميع الاحوال فيقال لأنّ النبيّ صلعم اعلمُ
بالله من ابى بكر رضى الله عنه وأبو بكر رضى الله عنه اقوى ايمانًا من اصحاب

(١) In marg. منها ذلك ولطايف.   (٢) اخرى added in marg.   (٣) منها. In marg.
A corrector has stroked out the words ذلك منها and has written عنه above.
(٤) Altered to فيها by later hand.   (٥) Suppl. above.   (٦) Suppl. in
marg.   (٧) بعض in marg.   (٨) Kor. 8, 12.

رسول الله صلعم فثبات ابى بكر رضى الله عنه من حقيقة ايمانه بما وعد الله

A f.53b تعالى وتغيُّر النبىّ صلعم من زيادة عِلْمه بالله تعالى لانّه يعلم من الله ما لا يعلم

ابو بكر رضى الله عنه ولا غيره ألا ترى انّه صلعم [١][كان] اذا اشتدّ هبوب

الريح تغيّر لَوْنُهُ [١][ولم ينغيّر لون واحد من اصحابه]، وقال لو تعلمون ما

٥ أَعْلَمُ لَضِحكتم قليلاً ولَبِكيتم كثيرًا ولخرجتم الى الصُعُدات تجْأرون الى الله

تعالى ولَّما تقارَرتم على قُرُشكم، ولأبى بكر الصدّيق رضى الله عنه [٢][ايضًا]

خصوصية فى الإلهام والفِراسة [١][من بين اصحاب رسول الله صلعم] فى ثلثة

مواضع احدها حين اتّفق رأىُ الجميع من اصحاب رسول الله صلعم على ترْك

مقاتلة اهل الرِدّة على منع الزكاة وثبت ابو بكر رضى الله عنه على قتالهم

١٠ وقال والله لو منعونى عِقالاً ممّا كانوا يُؤَدّون الى رسول الله صلعم لقاتلتُهم

عليه [١][بالسيف] فأصاب رأيه [٢][وقالوا انّ الاصابة فى رأيه مع خلافه لهم

فيما اشاروا عليه] ورجع الجميع الى رأيه حيث رأوا الصواب معه، والثانى

عند [٢]خلافه رأى جمهور الصحابة فيما رأوا من ردّ جيش أُسامة وقوله

والله لا أَحُلُّ عِقدًا عقفه رسول الله صلعم، والثالث قول ابى بكر رضى الله

١٥ عنه لعايشة رضى الله عنها انّى كنتُ نحلتُك نُحْلاً وانّما هو أَخواك وأُختُاك

وما عرفت [١][عايشة] الاّ أخَوَيْن وأُختًا، وكانت لأبى بكر رضى الله عنه

جارية حُبْلى فقال لقد أُلقِيَ فى رَوْعِى انّها أُنْثَى فولدت أُنْثَى فهذا انمّا ما كان

فى الفراسة والإلهام، وقال النبىّ صلعم اتّقوا فِراسة المؤمن فانّه ينظر بنور

الله تعالى، ولأبى بكر رضى الله عنه [٤]معان أُخَر ممّا تعلّق بها اهل الحقايق

٢٠ وأرباب القلوب وان ذكرنا جميع ذلك طَال الكتاب، وقد حُكى عن بكر

ابن عبد الله المُزَنى انّه قال ما فاق ابو بكر رضى الله عنه جميع اصحاب

رسول الله صلعم بكثرة الصوم والصلاة ولكن بشىءٍ [٥]كان فى قلبه قال بعضهم

---

(١) Suppl. in marg.   (٢) Suppl. above.   (٢) خلافته.   (٤) معانى.

(٥) In marg. وقر.

الذى كان فى قلبه الحُبّ لله عزّ وجلّ والنصيحة له، ويقال انّ ابا بكر رضى
الله عنه كان اذا دخل وقت الصلاة يقول يا بنى آدم قوموا الى ناركم التى A f. 54a
اوقدتموها فأطفِئُوها، ورُوى (١)[عنه] انه أكل طعامًا من شبهة فلمّا علم به
تقيّأً وقال والله لو لم تخرج الّا مع روحى لأخرجتُها سمعتُ رسول الله صلعم
يقول بَدَنٌ غُذِى بحرام فالنار أَوْلَى به، (١)[وكان يقول وددتُ ان أكون ٥
خضراءَ تأكلنى الدوابّ ولم أُخلَقْ مخافة العذاب وهَوْلَ يوم الحساب، ورُوى
عن ابى بكر الصدّيق انّه قال تلك آيات من كتاب الله عزّ وجلّ اشتغلتُ
بها عمّا سواها (٢)احداها قوله (٣)وَإِنْ يَمْسَسْكَ اللّٰهُ بِضُرٍّ فَلَا كَاشِفَ لَهُ
إِلَّا هُوَ وَإِنْ يُرِدْكَ بِخَيْرٍ فَلَا رَادَّ لِفَضْلِهِ فعلمتُ انّه اذا ارادنى بخير لم يقدر
احد ان يرفع عنّى غيره وان ارادنى بشرّ لم يقدر احد ان يصرف غيره، ١٠
والثانية قوله (٤)اذْكُرُونِى أَذْكُرْكُمْ فاشتغلتُ بذكر الله تعالى عن كلّ مذكور
سوى الله، والثالثة قوله (٥)وَمَا مِنْ دَابَّةٍ فِى ٱلْأَرْضِ إِلَّا عَلَى ٱللّٰهِ رِزْقُهَا فوله
ما هممتُ برزق منذ قرأتُ هذه الآية، ويقال ان هذه الابيات] (٦)لأبى بكر
الصدّيق رضى الله عنه،

(٧)يا مَنْ تَرَفَّعَ بالدُّنيـا وزينتِهـا * لَيسَ (٨)التَّرَفُّعُ (٩)رَفْعُ الطِّين بالطِّين ١٥
إِذا أَرَدْتَ شَرِيفَ الناسِ كُلِّهِم * فانْظُرْ إلى مَلِكٍ فى زِىِّ مِسْكِين
ذاكَ الَّذى عَظُمَتْ فى الناسِ (١٠)رِفْعَتُهُ * وذاكَ يَصْلُحُ للدُّنيـا وللدِّينِ،

(١)[وحُكى عن الجُنَيْد انّه قال اشرفُ كلمةٍ فى التوحيد قول ابى بكر سبحان
من لم يجعل للخلق طريقًا الى معرفته الّا العجز عن معرفته]،

---

(١) Suppl. in marg.   (٢) احداها.   (٣) Kor. 10, 107.   (٤) Kor. 2, 147.

(٥) Kor. 11, 8.   (٦) ولابى but و has been erased.   (٧) These verses

occur in the *Dîwân* of Abu 'l-'Atâhiya (Beyrout, 1886), p. 274, 9—11.

(٨) الرفيع.   (٩) رفيع.   (١٠) *Dîwân,* حُرْمَتُهُ.

باب فى ذكر عمر بن الخطّاب رضى الله عنه،

قال الشيخ رحمه الله وامّا عمر بن الخطّاب رضى الله عنه فانّه قد رُوى
عن النبىّ صلعم انّه قال قد كان فى الأمَم محدَّثون ومكلَّمون فان يك فى
هذه الأمّة فعمر رضى الله عنه، سُئِل بعض اهل الفهم عن المحدَّث فقال أَعْلَى
درجةٍ من درجات الصدّيقين، ودلايل ذلك ظهرت عليه وهو ما ذُكر عنه
انّه كان يخطب فصاح فقال فى وسط خُطْبته يا ساريةُ الجَبَلَ وسارية فى
عسكر على باب نهاوَند فسمع صوت عمر رضى الله عنه وأخذ نحو الجبل
وظفر بالعدوّ، وقيل لسارية كيف علِمتَ ذلك فقال سمِعتُ صوت عمر رضى
الله عنه يقول يا سارية الجَبَلَ الجَبَلَ، ورُوى عن ابى عثمان النهدىّ انّه
قال رأيتُ على عمر رضى الله عنه قميصا فيه اثنا عشر رُقْعةً وهو يخطب،
ورُوى عن عمر رضى الله عنه انّه قال رحم الله امرءًا أَهْدَى الىّ عيوبى، وقد
رُوى عن النبىّ صلعم انّه قال الشيطان يَفْرَقُ من ظِلّ عمر رضى الله عنه،
وقال عمر رضى الله عنه من خاف الله تعالى لم يَشْفِ غَيْظَهُ ومن اتّقى الله
لم يفعل كلّما يريد ولو لا القيمة لكان غير ما تَرَوْنَ، ويقال انّه أخذ رِتْبةً
من الارض فقال يا ليتنى لم تَلِدْنى أُمّى يا ليتنى كنت هذه التبنة يا ليتنى لم
أكُ شيئًا، وقد رُوى عن عمر رضى الله عنه انّه قال ما ابْتُليتُ ببليّة الّا
كان لله [(١)[علىّ فيها] اربع نِعَم اذ لم تكن فى دينى واذ لم تكن اعظم منها
واذ [(٢)]لم أُحرَم الرضا فيها وأن ارجو الثواب عليها، وقال عمر رضى الله
عنه لو كان الصبر والشكر بعيرَيْن لم أبالِ أيَّهِما ركبتُ، وجاء رجل الى
عمر رضى الله عنه فشكا اليه الفقر فقال عندك عشاء ليلتك قال نعم قال
لستَ بفقير، ورُوى عن علىّ رضى الله عنه انّه قال ما على وجه الارض

---

(١) Suppl. in marg.   (٢) لم يكن أحرم, but يكن has been stroked through
by a later hand.

احدٌ أَحبَّ الىَّ ان أَلْقَى اله نعالى بمثل صحيفته الاَّ هذا [١]المسجَّى عمر رضى
اله عنه، قال ورأى علىّ رضى اله عنه يومًا عمر رضى اله عنه وهو يعدو
فى وقت الهاجرة فسأله عن عدْوه فقال [٢][قد] أُغيرَ على إبل الصدقة
فرُحْتُ أَعدو فى طلبها قال فقال علىّ رضى اله عنه لقد أَتْعبتَ الخُلفاَء
٥ بعدك يا امير المؤمنين، قال الشيخ رحمه اله ولأهل الحقايق أُسوة وتعلُّق
بعمر رضى اله عنه بمعانى خُصَّ بذلك عمر رضى اله عنه من اختياره لبْس
المرقعة والخشونة وترْك الشبوات واجتناب [٣]الشبهات واظهار الكرامات
وقلّة المبالاة من لاية الخلق عند انتصاب الحقّ [٤]ومحْق الباطل ومساواة
الأقارب والأباعد فى الحقوق والتمسّك بالأشدّ من الطاعات واجتناب
١٠ ذلك ممّا رُوى عنه وبيانُه بطول، وإمّا ما رُوى عن عمر رضى اله عنه
انه رأى جماعةً جلوسًا فى المسجد فأمرهم بطلب الكسب والذى كتب به الى
سَلْمانَ فلعلّه عرف منهم عَجزًا فى جلوسهم [٥]وطمَعِهم فى الناس او غير ذلك
[٦][فلذلك أمرهم بطلب الكسب] [٧]وأبا بكر وعمر رضى اله
عنهما قد رأوا اصحاب الصُّفّة وهم نيف وثلثاية ولم يكرهوا ذلك ولم يؤمروا
بالخروج من المسجد وطلب المعاش، ورُوى عن عمر رضى اله عنه انه قال
لأخيه زَيْد بن الخطّاب يوم أُحُد ان شئْتَ نزعتُ دِرْعى هذه حتى تلْبسها
فقال له زَيْد أَنا ايضًا أُحبُّ الشهادة كما أَنّك تُحبُّ الشهادة، وهذه اشارة
عظيمة منهما تدلّ على حقيقة التوكّل، وأشباه ذلك كثيرة وفى القليل كفاية،
وقد رُوى عن عمر رضى اله عنه انه قال وجدتُ العبادة فى اربعة اشياَء
٢٠ اوّلها أداَء فرايض اله نعالى والثانى اجتناب محارم اله نعالى والثالث الأمْر
بالمعروف ابتغاَء ثواب اله نعالى والرابع النهى عن المُنكْر انقاَء غضبِ اله نعالى،

A f.55a

---

(١) After المسجَّى in marg. فقال على بثوب سُجى لما طُعن عمر ان وذلك الثوب بهذا
In (٤)   .الملاذ In marg. (٣)   .Suppl. above (٢)   .القول هذا ذلك عند
.وأبو (٧)   .Suppl. in marg (٦)   .وطمعًا Altered to (٥)   .وقع marg.

باب فى ذكر عثمْن رضى الله عنه،

قال الشيخ رحمه الله (١)[امّا عثمْن بن عفّان رضى الله عنه فقد خصّ
بالتمكين والتمكين من أعلى مراتب المحقّقين، وممّا يتعلّق به اهل الحقايق
من اهل التصوّف بعثمْن بن عفّان رضى الله عنه ما رُوى عن بعض
المتقدّمين (٢)[انّه سُئل] عن الدخول فى السعات فقال لا يصحّ الّا للانبيَاء
والصدّيقين، والدخول فى السعة التى هى من احوال الصدّيقين أن يكون
داخلاً فى الاشيآء (٢)[خارجًا منها وان يكون مع الاشيآء] باينًا عنها كما سُئل
يحيى بن مُعاذ رضى الله عنه عن صفة العارف فقال رجل (٣)كاينٌ (٢)[معهم] باينٌ
(٤)عنهم، وسُئل ابن الجلّآء رحمه الله عن الفقير الصادق فقال يكون دخوله
فى الاشيآء لغيره لا لنفسه، وهذا وَصْفُ حال عثمْن رضى الله عنه لانّه قد
رُوى عنه انّه قال لو لا أنّى خشيتُ ان يكون فى الاسلام ثلمة أَسُدُّها بهذا
المال ما جمعتُهُ، وعلامة من يكون هذا حاله أن يكون الإنفاق أَحَبَّ اليه
من الإمساك والخَرْج (٥)عنه آثَرُ من الدَّخْل كعثمْن رضى الله عنه فى تجهيز
جيش العُسْرة (٦)وشِرَى بئر رُومة حتى قال رسول الله صلعم ما ضَرَّ عثمْن
رضى الله عنه ما فعل بعد هذا، ورُوى عنه انّه بعث الى ابى ذرّ رضى الله
عنه بكيس فيها الف درهم ودفعها الى عبد له وقال ان قبِلَها فأنت حُرّ
لوجه الله تعالى، فدلّ ذلك على أنّ امواله كانت (٧)مستعدّة لمثل هذه الجهات
ولا يصحّ هذا الحال الّا لعبد كامل المعرفة، سمعتُ ابن سالم رحمه الله يقول
قال سهل بن عبد الله رحمه الله لا يصحّ الدخول فى السعة الّا لعبد يعرف
الإِذْن اذا أَذِنَ الله له أن يُنْفق أنفق على مقدار ما يأذن الله تعالى له وإن

A f.55b

(١) Altered to فاما.   (٢) Suppl. in marg.   (٣) Text om. but cf. Qushayrí,
169, 8.   (٤) منهم written above.   (٥) A corrector has indicated that the reading
should be عنه آثَر.   (٦) See Ṭabarí I, 3006, 1 foll.   (٧) In marg. معدّة.

امسكها امسك على حسب ما يأذن الله تعالى له ويكون قيامه فيا يجمع الله
عليه من الاموال للحُقوق ولا للمحظوظ فيكون مثله كمثل الوكيل يتصرّف فى
مال صاحبه نصرُّفَ المالكين بإذن ربّ المال وهو مكانٌ صعبٌ وقد غلط فى
ذلك خلق كثير بدَعْواهم هذا الحال وهم عَبيدُ الدنيا وعندهم أنّهم من
هؤلآء، وقد حُكِى عن سهل بن عبد الله رحمه الله أنّه قال ربّما يملك العبد
الدنيا ويكون أَزْهَدَ الخلق فى زمانه فقيل له مِثْل مَنْ فقال مثل عمر بن
عبد العزيز وكان (١)[رضى الله عنه أَعْنى عمر بن عبد العزيز] فى خلافته
يُميّزبين الزيت الذى يُسْرج لنفسه والزيت الذى يسرج للعامّة وكان يضع
سراجه على ثلث قَصَبات وفى يد خزاين الارض، فمن هاهنا غلط من غلط
فى تشريف الغنا على الفقر وذهب عليه أنّ هؤلآء لم يكونوا اغنيآء بأعراض
الدنيا ولا فقرآء بما يعدمون من الدنيا لانّ غناهم بالله وفقرهم (٢)اليه، وممّا
يتعلّق به اهل الحقايق بعثمن رضى الله عنه ما رُوى عنه أنّه حمل حزمة
حطب من بعض بساتينه وكان له عِدّة مماليك فقيل له لو دفعتها الى
بعض عبيدك فقال إنّى قد استطعتُ ان افعل ذلك ولكن أردتُ ان
اجرّب نفسى هل تعجز عن ذلك او هل تكره ذلك او كما قال، فدلّ ذلك
ايضًا (١)[على] أنّه كان لا يدع افتقاد نفسه وكان يفتقد رياضة نفسه لئلّا
يسكن الى ما جُمع اليه من الاموال لانّه ليس فى ذلك كغيره، ورُوى عنه
انّه كان يقرأ بالسَّبع الطُّول فى ركعة واحدة خَلْفَ المقام وهو مقنّعٌ رأسَه
بالليل، ورُوى عنه أنّه قال ما تَغنَّيْتُ ولا تَعنَّيْتُ ولا مسستُ ذكرى بيمينى
منذ بايعتُ رسول الله صلم، و(٢)[ممّا] (١)[يدلّ على] تخصيصه بالتمكين
والثبات والاستقامة ما رُوى عنه انّه يوم قُتِلَ لم يبرح من موضعه ولم يأذن
لأحد بالقتال ولا وضع المصحف من حَجْره الى أن قُتِل رضى الله عنه وسال
الدم على المصحف وتلطّخ بالدم ووقع الدم على موضع هذه الآية (٤)فَسَيَكْفِيكَهُمُ

(١) Suppl. in marg.   (٢) In marg. بأبه.   (٣) Suppl. above.

(٤) Kor. 2, 131.

اللهُ وَهُوَ السَّمِيعُ (١) الْعَلِيمُ، والتكين حال رفيع، سمعتُ ابا عمرو بن علوان يقول سمعت الجُنيَد رحمه الله ليلة من الليالى وهو (٢) [يقول] فى مناجاته الهوى أَتُريد أن تخدعنى (٣) [عنك] بقُربك أَم تريد أن تقطعنى بوَصلك هيهات هيهات، قلتُ لأبى عمرو ما معنى قوله هيهات هيهات قال التكين، ٥ ورُوى عن عثمٰن رضى الله عنه انّه قال وجدتُ الخير مجموعًا فى اربعـة اوّلها التحبّب الى الله تعالى (٤) [بالنوافل] والثانى الصبر على احكام الله تعالى والثالث الرضا بتقدير الله عزّ وجلّ والرابع الحيآء من نظر الله عزّ وجلّ،

باب فى ذكر علىّ بن ابى طالب رضى الله عنه،

قال الشيخ رحمه الله وامّا علىّ رضى الله عنه فانى سمعتُ احمد بن على ١٠ الوجيهى يقول سمعتُ ابا على الروذبارى يقول سمعت جُنيدًا رحمه الله يقول رضوان الله على امير المؤمنين علىّ رضى الله عنه لولا انّه اشتغل بالحروب لأفادنا من عِلْمنا هذا (٤) معانى كثيرة ذاك امروٌ أُعطىَ عِلْمَ اللَّدُنى، والعلم اللدنى هو العلم الذى خُصّ به الخَضِرُ عليه السلم قال الله تعالى (٥) وَعَلَّمْنَاهُ مِنْ لَدُنَّا عِلْمًا، وقد سمعتُ بقصّة الخَضِر وموسى عليهما السلم وقوله (٦) إِنَّكَ ١٥ لَنْ تَسْتَطِيعَ مَعِىَ صَبْرًا، فمن هاهنا غلط من غلط فى تفضيل الولاية على النبوّة وسنذكر ذلك فى باب الردّ على من قال ذلك إن شآء الله، ولأمير المؤمنين (٧) [علىّ] رضى الله عنه خصوصيةٌ من بين جميع اصحاب رسول الله صلعم بمعانى جليلة واشارات لطيفة وألفاظ مُفرَدة وعبارة وبيان للتوحيد والمعرفة والايمان (٨) [والعلم] وغير ذلك وخصال شريفة تعلّق وتخلّق به اهل الحقايق من

(١) Marginal note: ان قلت ما مشار هذه الاية ووقوع الدم عليها قلت مشارها الوعد
(٤) معانيا   (٣) Suppl. above.   (٢) Suppl. in marg.   بكفايته.
(٥) Kor. 18, 64.   (٦) Kor. 18, 66.   (٧) Suppl. above.   (٨) Suppl. in marg.

9

الصوفية وإن ذكرْنا ذلك كلّه (١)طال به الكتاب ولكن نذكر من ذلك طرفًا نكتفى به عن التطويل إن شَاء الله، فمنها ما سُئل امير المؤمنين رضى الله عنه وقيل له بما عرفتَ ربّك فقال بما عرّفنى نَفْسَه لا تُشبهه صورةٌ ولا يُدْرَك بالحواسّ ولا يقاس بالناس قريب فى بُعْده بعيد فى قُرْبـه فوق كل شىء، ولا يقال شىء تحته وتحت كلّ شىء، ولا يقال شىء فوقه أمامَ كلّ شىء، ولا يقال شىء أمامَه داخلٌ فى الاشيآء لا كثىء، (٢) ولا من شىء، ولا فى شىء، ولا بشىء، سبحان من هو هٰكذى ولا هٰكذى غيره، وكان أمير المؤمنين رضى الله عنه يقول فى خطبته خلق الاشيآء لا من شىء كان معه ولا عن شىء، احتذاه ولا عن شىء، امتثله فكلّ صانع ممن شىء صَنَعَ وكلّ عالم ممن بعد جهْل عَلِمَ والله تعالى عالم لا من بعد جهْل، وقوله فى الايمان كما ذكر عنه عمرو بن هِنْد قال سمعتُ عليًّا رضى الله عنه يقول الايمان يبدو (٣) لُمْظَةً بيضآء فى القلب فكلّما ازداد الايمان ازداد القلب بياضًا فاذا استكمل الايمان ابيضّ القلب وإنّ النفاق يبدو (٣) لُمْظَةً سودآء فى القلب فكلّما ازداد النفاق ازداد القلب سوادًا فاذا استكمل النفاق اسودّ القلب، وقام رجل الى علىّ بن ابى طالب رضى الله عنه فسأله عن الايمان فقال A f. 57a الايمان على اربع دعائم على الصبر واليقين والعدل والجهاد ثم وصف الصبر على عشر مقامات وكذلك اليقين والعدل والجهاد فوصف كلّ واحد منها على عشر مقامات، فان صحّ ذلك عنه فهو اوّل من تكلّم فى الاحوال والمقامات، وقيل لأمير المؤمنين رضى الله عنه من أسْلَمَ الناس من ساير العيوب قال من جعل عقله أميرَهُ وحَذَره وزيرَهُ والموعظة زمامَهُ والصبر قايدَهُ والاعتصام بالتقوى ظهيرَهُ وخوف الله تعالى جليسَهُ وذِكْر الموت واليِلَى أنيسَهُ، وقال علىّ رضى الله عنه فى حديث كُمَيْل بن زياد هـا إنّ هاهنا عِلْمٌ لو وجدتُ له حَمَلَةً وأشار الى قلْبه، فكان تخصيصه من بين

الصحابة بالبيان والعبارة عن التوحيد والمعرفة، والبيان من أتمّ المعانى (١) وأعلى
الاحوال قال الله تعالى (٢) وَإِذْ أَخَذَ ٱللَّهُ مِيثَاقَ ٱلَّذِينَ أُوتُوا ٱلْكِتَابَ لَتُبَيِّنُنَّهُ
لِلنَّاسِ، وقال تعالى (٣) هَذَا بَيَانٌ لِلنَّاسِ، ولا يبلغ العبدُ كمال الشرف الّا
بالبيان لانّه ليس كلّ من عقل (٤) يعلم ولا كلّ من علم يُحْسِن أن يُبَيّن فاذا
٥ أُعطِىَ العبدُ العقل والعلم والبيان فقد بلغ الى الكمال، والمشهور عن اصحاب
رسول الله صلم انّهم كانوا اذا أَشْكَل عليهم شىء من أمور الدّين سألوا
علِيًّا رضى الله عنه فكان يبيّن لهم الذى يُشْكِل (٥) عليهم، ورُوى عن علىّ
رضى الله عنه انّه كان يقول أَحْبِبْ حبيبك هَوْنًا ما كيا يكون بغيضك يومًا
ما وأَبْغِضْ بغيضك هونًا ما كيا يكون حبيبك يومًا ما، وذُكر عنه ايضًا انّه
١٠ وقف على باب الخزانة خزانة الاموال وقال يا صفرآء ويا بيضآء غُرِّى
غيرى، وذُكر عنه ايضًا انّه لبس قبيصًا شراء ثلثةُ دراهم (٦) فقطعه من رأس
أصابعه، وذُكر عنه انّه عمل بأُجْرَة فأخذ أجرته مُدًّا من تَمر وحمل ذلك
الى رسول الله صلم حتى تقوّت به، ورُوى عنه انّه قال لعمر بن الخطّاب
A f. 57b
رضى الله عنه إن أردتَ أن تلقى صاحبك فرَقِّع قميصك وأخصِفْ نعلك
١٥ وقصِّرْ أمَلك وكلْ دون الشبع، ورُوى عن عمر رضى الله عنه انّه قال لولا
علىّ رضى الله عنه لهلك عمر، ويقال انّه لمّا قُتل رضى الله عنه صعد الحسَن
رضى الله عنه منبر الكوفة وقال يا اهل الكوفة لقد قُتل بين ظهرانيكم امير
المؤمنين رضى الله عنه واللهِ إنّه ما خلّف من الدنيا شيئًا الّا اربعمأية درهم
وكان قد عزلها ليشترى بها خادمًا يخدمه، ويقال انّ عليًّا رضى الله عنه
٢٠ كان اذا جآء وقت الصلاة يتزلزل ويتغيّر لونه فيقال له ما لك يا امير
المؤمنين فيقول جآء وقت أمانة عرضها الله تعالى (٧) عَلَى ٱلسَّمَوَاتِ وَٱلْأَرْضِ
وَٱلْجِبَالِ فَأَبَيْنَ أَنْ يَحْمِلْنَهَا وَأَشْفَقْنَ مِنْهَا وَحَمَلَهَا ٱلْإِنْسَانُ فلا أدرى أحسِنُ

---

(١) In marg. وأرفع.   (٢) Kor. 3, 184.   (٣) Kor. 3, 132.   (٤)
علم.   (٥) In marg. حتى روى عن عمر رضى الله عنه انه كان يقول لولا على لهلك عمر.
(٦) فقطعها.   (٧) Kor. 33, 72.

ادآءَ ما احتملتُ ام لا، وقال علىّ رضى اله عنه ما أنا ونفسى الأكراعى
غَنَمٍ كلَّها ضمّها من جانب انتشرت من جانب، ولعلىّ رضى اله عنه اشباه
ذلك كثير من الاحوال والاخلاق والافعال (١)التى ينعلّق بهـا ارباب
القلوب وأهل الاشارات وأهل المواجيد من الصوفية، فمن تَرَكَ الدنيـا
كلّها وخرج من جميع ما يملك وجلس على بساط الفقر والتجريد بلا علاقة
فإمامُهُ فيه ابو بكر الصدّيق رضى اله عنه، ومن اخرج بعضها وترك البعض
لعياله ولصلة الرحم وأدآءَ الحقوق فإمامُهُ (٢)[فيها] عمر بن الخطّاب رضى
اله عنه، ومن جمع لله ومنع لله وأعْطَى لله وأنفق لله فإمامُهُ (٢)[فيها] عثمٰن
ابن عفّان رضى اله عنه، ومن لا يحوم حول الدنيا وان جُمعتْ عليه مِنْ
غير طلبِهِ رفضها وهرب منها فإمامُهُ فى ذلك علىّ بن ابى طالب رضى اله
عنه، وروى عن علىّ رضى اله عنه انّه قال الخير كلّه مجموع فى اربعـة
الصَّمْت والنُّطق والنظر والحركة فكلُّ نُطق لا يكون فى ذِكْر اله تعالى فهو
لغوٌ وكلّ صَمْت لا يكون فى ذِكْر فهو سهوٌ وكلّ نظر لا يكون فى عِبْرة فهو   A f. 58a
غفلة وكلّ حركة لا تكون فى تعبّد اله فهى فترة فرحم اله عبدًا جعل نطقه
ذكرًا وصمته فكرًا ونظره عبرةً وحركته تعبّدًا ويَسْلَمُ الناس من لسانه ويـهٖ،

باب (٣)صفة اهل الصّفّة رضوان الله عليهم اجمعين،

قال الشيخ رحمه اله ثم انّ اهل الصّفّة كانوا كما جآءَ فى الخبر نيف
وثلثاية لا يرجعون الى زَرْع ولا الى ضَرْع ولا الى تجارة وكان اكلهم فى
المسجد ونومهم فى المسجد وكان رسول اله صلعم يؤانسهم ويجلس معهم ويأكل
معهم ويحثّ الناس على إكرامهم (٤)و[معرفة] فضلهم، وقد ذكرهم اله تعالى فى

---

(١) الذى.   (٣) Suppl. above.   (٢) فى ذكر اصحاب written above.

(٤) Suppl. in marg.

مواضع من القرآن منها قوله عزّ وجلّ (١) لِلْفُقَرَآءِ ٱلَّذِينَ أُحْصِرُوا فِى سَبِيلِ
ٱللَّهِ ٱلآية وقوله (٢) وَلاَ تَطْرُدِ ٱلَّذِينَ يَدْعُونَ (٣) رَبَّهُمْ ٱلآية وقوله (٤) وَٱصْبِرْ
نَفْسَكَ مَعَ ٱلَّذِينَ يَدْعُونَ رَبَّهُمْ ٱلآية، وقد عاتب الله تعالى نبيّه صلعم فيهم قال
الله عزّ وجلّ (٥) عَبَسَ وَتَوَلَّى أَنْ جَآءَهُ ٱلأَعْمَى، قيل نزلتْ فى شأن ابن أمّ
٥ مكتوم رضى الله عنه وكان من اهل الصفّة فكان اذا رآه رسول الله صلعم
بعد ذلك يقول (٦) يا من عاتبنى فيه ربّى عزّ وجلّ، ويقال انّ رسول الله
صلعم كان لا يقوم من مجلسه اذا (٧) جلس اهل الصفّة حوله حتى يقومون
وكان اذا صافحهم لم ينزع يَدَ من ايديهم قَبْلَهم وربّما كان يفرّقهم على اهل
الجدات والسعة على كلّ واحد على مقداره يبعث بهم مع واحد ثلثة ومع
١٠ الآخر الاربعة والخمسة، قال فربّما كان ينقلب سعد بن مُعَاذ رضى الله
عنه بثمانين منهم الى بيته فيُطْعِمُهم، وقال ابو هُرَيْرَة رضى الله عنه رأيتُ
A f. 58b سبعين من اهل الصفّة يصلّون فى ثوب منهم من لا يبلغ ركبتيَّه فاذا ركع
احدهم قبض بيديه مخافة أن تبدو عورته، وقال ابو موسى الأشعرى رضى
الله عنه كان يُشبه رائحتنا رائحة الشاة من لبْس العَبَاءَ، وقال عبد الله بن
١٥ طلحة (٨) صحبنا جماعة اهل الصفّة يومًا فقلنا برسول الله (٩) أَحْرَقَ بُطُونُنا التَّمْر
وحرّمت علينا الجيفة فسمع ذلك رسول الله صلعم فصعد المنبر ثم قال ما
بالُ أقوام يُضحّون ويقولون أَحْرَقَتْ بطونَا (١٠) التَّمْر أما علمتم انّ هذا التمر
(١١) [انّما] هو طعام اهل المدينة فقد واسَوْنا به فواسيناكم ممّا واسونا به
والذى نفْسُ محمّد بيه أن منذ شهر او شهرَيْن لم ترتفع من (١٢) [بيت] رسول
٢٠ الله دُخان للخُبْز وليس لهم غير الأَسْوَدَين التمر والمَآء، والمعنى فى ذلك انّ
رسول الله صلعم اعتذر (١١) [فى ذلك] اليهم ولم (١٤) يردّ عليهم شكايتهم ولم

---

(١) Kor. 2, 274.   (٢) Kor. 6, 52.   (٣) After رَبَّهُمْ in marg.
بالغداة   (٤) Kor. 18, 27.   (٥) Kor. 80, 1—2.   (٦) In
marg. والعشى الى قوله الظالمين.   (٧) Orig. جلسوا.   (٨) Orig. طيفه
but corr. by later hand.   (٩) Altered to أحرقت.   (١٠) التمر.   (١١) Suppl.
in marg.   (١٢) Written above.   (١٣) ينكر written above.

يأمرهم بطلب المعاش (١)[من الاكتساب والتجارات]، وقد رُوِى فى الخبر
انّ النبىّ صلعم وقف على جماعة من اهل الصُفّة وقد استتر بعضهم ببعض
من العُرْى وقارِىٰٔ يقرأ عليهم القرآن وهم يبكون، فامّا غير اهل الصُفّة
فقد رُوِى عن كلّ واحد منهم ما انفردوا به وخُصّوا به من الاحوال
الرضيّة والاعمال الزكيّة ومكارم الاخلاق ما تعلّق بها اهل الحقايق من
المتصوّفة وطلب الاهتداء فى الاقتداء بهم، ويكثر ذكر ذلك ولكن نذكر
طرقًا لِيُستدلّ بذلك على ما لم نذكره إن شاء الله تعالى،

باب فى ذكر سائر الصحابة فى هذا المعنى،

قال الشيخ رحمه الله وامّا طلحة بن عُبَيْد الله رضى الله عنه فقد رُوِى
عن زياد بن حُدَيْر انّه قال رأيتُ طلحة بن عبيد الله رضى الله عنه فوق
ماية الف فى مجلس وانّه لَيخِيط طرف إزاره (٢)بيه، وامّا مُعاذ بن جَبَل رضى
الله عنه فقد روى عنه الحُارث بن عُمَيْرَة قال انّى لَجالسٌ عند معاذ بن جبل
رضى الله عنه وهو يجود بنفسه ويقول اخْنُقْ خَنْقَك فوعِدتُك انّى لَأُحبّك، وامّا
عِمْران بن حُصَيْن رضى الله عنه قال وددتُ انّى كنت تُرابًا تذرونى الرياح
ولم اخْلَقْ مخافةَ العذاب، وقال ثابت البُنانى رحمه الله انه يعنى عمران بن
حصين رضى الله عنه اشتكى بطنَه ثلثة وثلثين سنة فدخل عليه اصحابه
يعودونه فقالوا يمنعنا من الدخول عليك طول شكايتك فقال لا تفعلوا
(١)[ذلك] فانّ احَبَّه الى ربّى احَبُّه الّى، وامّا سلمان الفارسى رضى الله عنه
فقد قيل انه لمّا نزلت هذه الآية (٣)وَإِنَّ جَهَنَّمَ لَمَوْعِدُهُمْ أَجْمَعِينَ صاح
صيحةً ووضع (٤)[يده] على رأسه ثم خرج هاربًا ثلثة ايام، وفى الخبر ان سلمان

رضى الله عنه زار ابا الدرداء رضى الله عنه من العراق الى الشأم راجلاً
(١)وعليه كساء غليظ مضموم الرأس شاحبًا فقيل له شهرتَ نفسَك فقال الخَيْرُ
خيرُ الآخرة وإنّما أنا (٢)عبدٌ ألبسُ كما يلبس العبيد فاذا أُعتِقتُ لبستُ جبّةً
لابتلاء (٣)محاسنها، وإمّا ابو الدرداء رضى الله عنه فانّه قال كنتُ امرءًا تاجرًا
٥ فى الجاهلية فلمّا أسلمتُ (٤)أردتُ ان أجمع بين التجارة والعبادة فلم تجتمعا
لى فآثرتُ العبادة على التجارة، قال وسُيلتْ أمّ الدرداء رضى الله عنها عن
أفضل عبادة ابى الدرداء رضى الله عنه فقالت التفكّر والاعتبار، وإمّا ابو
ذرّ رضى الله عنه فانّه رُوى عنه انّه قال انّ قيامى بالحقّ لله تعالى لم يترك
لى صديقًا وإنّ خوفى من يوم الحساب ما ترك على بدنى لحمًا وإنّ (٥)يقينى
١٠ بثواب الله تعالى ما ترك فى بيتى شيئًا، ويُرْوَى عنه انّه قال قتلنى همُّ يوم
لم أُدركه فقيل له وما ذاك قال انّ أمَلى جاوز (٦)أجَلى وددتُ انّ الله تعالى
خلقنى شجرةً تُعضَد، ودُعى ابو ذرّ رضى الله عنه الى وليمة فسمع صوتًا فانصرف
وهو يقول من أكْثَرَ سوادَ قوم فهو منهم ومن رضى عَمَلَ قوم فهو شريكهم،
وحمل حبيب بن مسلمة الى ابى ذرّ رضى الله عنه الف درهم فردّ عليه وقال
١٥ عندنا عنزٌ نحلبها ومركوب يُسارعُ (٧)على ظَهْرها (٨)فلا حاجة لنا فى غير
ذلك، وإمّا ابو عُبيدة بن الجرّاح رضى الله عنه فانّه رُوى عنه انّه خرجت
فى كفّه طَعْنةٌ فى ايّام الطاعون فعظم ذلك على اصحاب رسول الله صلعم
(٩)وفرقوا منها فأقسم لهم ابو عبيدة رضى الله عنه ما (١٠)يحبّ ان له مكانَها
حُمْر النَّعَم، وجاءه رجل الى ابى عبيدة رضى الله عنه فسألـه فردّه ثم جاءه
٢٠ فسأله فأعطاه فقال الذى اعطاك والذى ردّك الله عزّ وجلّ، (١١)[وقال ابو
عبيدة وددتُ أن أكون كَبْشًا (١٢)لأُهْدَى فيُعَرّق لحمى (١٢)ويُجنّى فَرْقى ولم

A f.59b

(١) و suppl. below.　(٢) الله added in marg.　(٣) حواشيها corr. in marg.

(٤) راولت altered to راودت.　(٥) نفسى. In marg. ثقتى.　(٦) So above. The

orig. reading seems to have been اعلى.　(٧) وصل. Ibn Sa'd, IV (1), 173, 20

has وأحميرة تحمل عليها.　(٨) بلا.　(٩) Altered to وتفرقوا.　(١٠) يحب,

corr. to يحب.　(١١) Suppl. in marg.　(١٢) لاهلى.　(١٢) نقبى.

أُخْلَق]، وإمّا عبد الله بن مسعود رضى الله عنه فإنّه رُوى عنه انّه كان
يقول يا حبّذا المكروهان الموت والفقر فما أُبالى بايّهما ابتُدِئتُ، ورُوى عنه
ان فى بيته كانت (١)عشاش الخطاطيف وكان له (٢)بنون فقيل له لو نقضتَ
هذه (١)العشاش فقال والله لَئِن نقضتْ يدى من تراب قُبورهم يعنى اولاده
٥ أَحَبُّ الىَّ من ان أُكَسِّر من (١)عشاش هذه الخطاطيف بَيضةً واحدةً، وإمّا
البَرَاء بن مُلك فقد رُوى عن أنس بن مُلك رضى الله عنهما انّه قال
دخلتُ على البَرَاء بن مُلك رضى الله عنه وقد مال برجلَيْه (٣)على الحايط
وهو يترنَّم بالشعر فقلتُ يا اخى أَبْعَدَ الاسلام والقرآن فقال يا اخى ديوانُ
العرب ثم قال أترانى أموتُ على فراشى وقد قتلتُ تسعةً وتسعين مبارزًا
١٠ بين يدى رسول الله صلعم سوى ما أُشرِكتُ (٤)[فيه]، فلمّا كان يوم (٥)شهرك
مَلك نُسْتَر قال ابو موسى الأشعرى رضى الله عنه سمعتُ رسول الله صلعم
يقول كم من ذى (٦)طِمْرَيْن لا بُوّبَة له لو أَقْسَمَ على الله لَأَبَرَّه منهم البَرَاء
ابن مُلك رضى الله عنه، فقال البَرَاء اللهمّ فانّى أُقسِمُ عليك لمّا رزقتَنى
الشهادة ورزقتَ اصحابى الفتح، قال فاستُشهِد البَرَاء وفتح الله عليهم، وإمّا
١٥ عبد الله بن العبّاس رضى الله عنه فإنّه رُوى عنه انّه كان يقول أَفضَلُ
المجالس (٧)مجلسٌ فى قعر بيتك حتى لا تَرى ولا تُرى، ورُوى عنه انّه كان
يقول انّ الله تعالى لَيبتلى العبد بالفقر شوقًا الى دعآيه، ويقال ان هذا
الموضعA f.60a (٨)يعنى (٩)حُذْه (٤)[كان] مثل شِراك النَّعل من كثرة الدمع يعنى
ابن عبّاس رضى الله عنه، (١٠)وأرُوى] عنه انّه قال لَأَنْ أرقع ثوبًا فأُلبسه
٢٠ فيرفعنى عند الخالق أَحَبُّ الىَّ من أن ألبس ثيابًا نضعنى عند الخالق
وترفعنى عند المخلوقين، وإمّا كعب الأحْبار رضى الله عنه فقد رُوى عنه

---

(١) عشش.   (٢) بنين.   (٣) In marg. الى.   (٤) Suppl. in marg.

(٥) The last letter has been erased.   (٦) In marg. يُقتَلُ به   (٧) مجلسا.

(٨) Suppl. above.   (٩) حذه.   (١٠) روى suppl. above.

انّه قال لن ينالوا شرف الآخرة حتى يكرهوا المدحة والثناء وان ينالوا
الملامة فى الله تعالى، وقال كعب رضى الله عنه لن يستكمل العبد أجر الحجّ
والجهاد حتى يصبر على الأذى، وامّا حارثة رضى الله عنه فقد رُوِى عن
النبى صلعم انّه قال من اراد ان ينظر الى عبد نوّر الله تعالى الايمان فى
٥ قلبه فلينظر الى حارثة رضى الله عنه، وامّا ابو هُرَيْرة رضى الله عنه فانّ ثعلبة
ابن ابى مُلك قال رأيتُ ابا هريرة رضى الله عنه وهو يحمل حزمة حطب
وهو يومئذ خليفة مروان بن الحَكَم فقال أوْسِع الطريق للأمير يابن ابى
مالك فقلت اصلحك الله تُكْفَى هذا فقال اوسع الطريق للامير يابن ابى
مُلك، ورُوِى عنه انّه بكى لمّا حضرته الوفاة فقيل له ما يُبكيك قال بُعد
١٠ المفازة وقلّة الزاد وضعف اليقين وعقبة كَوُود والمهبط منها الى الجنّة او الى
النار، وقال ابو هريرة رضى الله عنه جزّأتُ الليل ثلثة اجزآء ثُلْثًا أُصلّى
وثُلْثًا أنامُ وثُلْثًا أستذكرُ [فيه] (١) حديث رسول الله صلعم، وامّا أَنس بن
مُلك رضى الله عنه فرُوِى عنه انّه قال انّ اوّل من يَرِدُ الحوض يوم القيمة
الذابلون (٢) الناحلون الذين اذا جنّهم الليل استقبلوه بحزن، وامّا عبد الله
١٥ ابن عمر رضى الله عنه فرُوِى عنه انّه كان يقول ما كنّا نام ونحن عُزّاب فى
ايّام رسول الله صلعم الّا فى المسجد ولم يكن لنا مسكن ولا مأوى، ورُوِى
عنه انّه قال لا تُحِبّ (٤) ابدًا الّا من تثق بدينه، وكان يقول لا تُطْعِموا
طعامكم الّا كلّ نقّى [نقّى] (١) ولا تأكلوا الّا من طعام نقّى نقّى، وعن ابن عمر
رضى الله عنه انّه قال انّما سُلّط على ابن آدم من يخافه ولو لم يَخَف ابن
٢٠ آدم الّا الله لم يُسَلّط الله تعالى عليه شيئًا، وامّا حُذَيْفة بن اليمان رضى الله
عنه فرُوِى عنه انّه قال انّ أقَرَّ يوم لعَيْنى ليوم اذا رجعتُ الى اهلى
فيشكون الىّ الحاجة، وقال حُذَيْفة رضى الله عنه كم من شهوة ساعة اورثت
صاحبها حزنًا طويلًا، ودُعِى حُذَيْفة الى مايدة فرأى عليها زِىّ العَجَم فانصرف

<hr>

(١) Suppl. above.   (٢) In marg. السايحون.   (٣) يحيب.   (٤) In
marg. احدا.

وهو يقول من نشبّه بقومٍ فهو منهم، وامّا عبد الله بن جحْش رضى الله عنه
فروى سعيد بن المسيّب رحمه الله قال قال عبد الله بن جحش رضى الله
عنه يوم أُحُد اللهمّ انّى أُقسم عليك ان ألْقَى العدوّ واذا لقيت العدوّ ان
يقتلونى ثم يبقروا بطنى ثم يمثّلوا بى فاذا لقيتك قلتَ (١)فيمَ قُتِلتَ فأقول فيك
٥ قال فلقى العدوّ فقُتِل وفُعِل به ذلك، وامّا صفوان بن مُحرز المازنى فانّه
كان يقول اذا أوِيتُ الى اهلى وأصبت رغيفًا أكلتُه فجزَى (٢)[الله] الدنيا
عن اهلها شرًّا وما زاد على ذلك الى ان خرج من الدنيا، وامّا ابو فَرْوة
فانّه رجل من اصحاب رسول الله صلعم كان مولًى لبنى سُلَيم سار ميلًا لم
يذكر الله تعالى فيه فرجع حتى (٢)[سار فيه] ذاكرًا لله تعالى فلمّا بلغ منتهاه
١٠ قال اللهمّ لا تَنْسَ ابا فَرْوة (٢)[فانّ ابا فروة] (٤)ليس ينساك، وامّا ابو بكرة
رضى الله عنه فانّه أُغْمِىَ عليه عند (٤)قبرٍ فصرخوا عليه فلمّا أفاق قال ما
من نفسٍ تخرج ولا نفسٍ (٥)دابّةٍ (٦)[الّا وهى] أَحَبُّ الىّ من نفسى (٧)قيل
له ولِمَ قال انّى أخاف ان أبقى الى زمانٍ لا آمُر فيه بالمعروف ولا أَنْهَى
عن المُنْكَر، وامّا عبد الله بن رواحة رضى الله عنه فذُكِر عنه انّه بكى فبكت
١٥ امرأته فقال لها ما يُبكيك قالت انّك بكيتَ فبكيتُ قال انّى أُنبِثتُ أنّى
وارد النار ولم أُنبَأ أنّى صادِر، وامّا تميم الدارى فذُكِر عنه انّه قام ليلةً الى
الصباح يبكى ويقرأ هذه الآية (٨)أَمْ حَسِبَ ٱلَّذِينَ ٱجْتَرَحُوا ٱلسَّيِّئَاتِ الآية،
٨٤f. 61a وامّا عدىّ بن حاتم رضى الله عنه فروى عنه انّه ربّما كان يفتّ الخُبْزَ للنَّمْل
ترحّمًا عليهم، وامّا ابو رافع مولى رسول الله صلعم رضى الله عنه فقد رُوِى
٢٠ عن ابن عمر رضى الله عنه انّه قال قال رجل يُرسول الله اىّ الناس افضلُ
قال كلُّ مخموم القلب صدوق اللسان قيل يُرسول الله وما مخموم القلب

---

(١) م corr. in marg.   (٢) Suppl. in marg.   (٣) In marg. لم.

(٤) In marg. موته.   (٥) Apparently altered to دبابة.   (٦) I have
supplied these words which the sense of the passage seems to require.
(٧) Orig. وقيل, but و has been stroked through.   (٨) Kor. 45, 20.

قال التقى النقى الذى لا كدر فيه (١)[ولا بغى] ولا حسد الذى (٢) يشنأ
الدنيا ويحبّ الآخرة قالوا فا نعرف فينا (٢)[مثل] ذلك غير ابى رافع مولى
رسول الله صلعم ورضى الله عنه، وامّا محمّد بن كعب رضى الله عنه فانّه
ذُكر عنه انّه قال اذا اراد الله بعبد خيرًا (١)[جعل فيه ثلث خلال] فقّهه
٥ فى الدّين وزهّده فى الدنيا وبصّره عيوب نفسه، وامّا زرارة بن أوفى رضى
الله عنه فانّه رُوى عنه انّه أمّ فى مسجد بنى قُشير فقرأ (٤)[فَإِذَا نُقِرَ فِى
ٱلنَّاقُورِ فَذَلِكَ يَوْمَئِذٍ يَوْمٌ عَسِيرٌ] فخرّ ميتًا، وامّا حنظلة الكاتب رضى الله عنه
فانّه رُوى عنه انّه قال كنّا عند رسول الله صلعم فذكّرنا الجنّة والنار حتى
كانّها رأىُ العين فعُدْتُ الى اهلى فضحكتُ ولقيتُ الناس فقلتُ نافَقَ حنظلةُ
١٠ فقال ابو بكر رضى الله عنه ما لك فأخبرتُه فقال انّا لنفعله ايضًا فذهب
حنظلة الى النبىّ صلعم فذكر له ذلك فقال يا حنظلة لو كنتم فى بيوتكم كما
تكونون عندى لصافحتكم الملآئكة على فُرشكم او كما قال يا حنظلة ساعــة
وساعة، وامّا الجلاج قال الشيخ وكُنيته ابو كثير هكذى فى كتاب ابى داود
السجستانى صاحبُ رسول الله صلعم فانّه رُوى عنه انّه قال أسلمتُ مع النبىّ
١٥ صلعم وأنا ابن خمسين سنة ومات الجلاج وهو ابن عشرين وماية سنة وقال
ما ملأتُ بطنى من طعام منذ أسلمتُ مع رسول الله صلعم آكُلُ حسبى وأشرَبُ
حسبى، وامّا ابو جُحَيْفة رضى الله عنه فانّه رُوى عنه انّ امرأته استخبأت ٨ f.61b
ثلثين درهمًا فنَسيَتها حتى مضت لها سنة ثم ذكرِها فقال لها يا أخت
هُذَيل أعْتَدّى بيس حشوة البيت أنتِ لو متّ لعُددتُ عنّد الله من
٢٠ الكنّازين انّ نبىّ الله صلعم مات وعَهْدُه بين أعيُنا جديدٌ لم يترك دينارًا
ولا درهمًا ولا فلسًا ولا برًّا ولا شعيرًا، وامّا حكيم بن حزام رضى الله عنه
فانّه رُوى عنه انّه قال ما أصبَحْتُ ذا صباحٍ قطٍّ لم أرَ عندى طالب حاجة

---

(١) Suppl. in marg.   (٢) يشنى (probably a misreading of ينسى).

(٢) Suppl. above.   (٤) Kor. 74, 8—9.

ولا مستعينًا على أمرٍ الّا عددتُه من المصايب التى أسألُ الله تعالى الأجْر
عليها، وإمّا أُسامة رضى الله عنه فانّه رُوى عنه انّه اشترى فرسًا الى شهرَيْن
فقال النبىّ صلعم لمّا بلغه ذلك انّ اسامة لَطويلُ الأَمَل، وإمّا بِلال وصهَيْب
رضى الله عنهما فانّه رُوى عنهما انّهما أيا قبيلةٍ من العرب فخاطبا اليم
ه فقيل لهما من أنتما فقالا بِلال وصُهَيْب كُنّا ضالّين فهدانا الله تعالى وكنّا
مملوكين فأَعْتَقَنا الله تعالى وكنّا عايلين فأغنانا الله تعالى فان تُزوِّجونا فنَحمد
الله وان تُردّونا فسبحان الله فقالوا تُزوَّجون والحمد لله فقال صهيب لِبلال
هلّا ذكرتَ مشاهدنا وسوابقنا مع رسول الله صلعم فقال بِلال اسكُتْ فقـد
صدقتَ فأَنكَحَك الصدق، وإمّا عبد الله بن ربيعة ومُصعَب بن عمر رضى
١٠ الله عنهما فكانا متواخيَيْن قال عبد الله كنتُ أنظرُ الى مصعب فتدمعُ عينى
رقّةً عليه وكنت رأيتُه بمكّة فى الرفاهية وكان على رأسه ثَلّةٌ من الشَّعْر قال
فكنت أمُرُّ الى بعض حيطان المدينة فأعْمَلُ فى السوّانى الى الأَدْلى على مُدّ
من التمر فأحْمِلُه الى مصعب بن عمر ومرّ مصعب يومًا الى رسول الله صلعم
فلم يجدْ عند رسول الله صلعم الّا قطعة حَيْسٍ فأكل بعضها وحمل النصف
الأخر الى عبد الله بن ربيعة، ورُوى انّ رسول الله صلعم آخَى بين عبـد A f.62a
الرحمن بن عَوْف وبين سعد بن الربيع رضى الله عنهما وكان لسعد
(١)امرأتان فقال سعد أُقاسِمُك مالى وأنزل عن إحْدَى امرأتَىّ حتى تَروج
بها فلم يفعل ذلك عبد الرحمن وقال دُلّونى على السوق فدخل السوق
وكسب حتى جمع شيئًا من التمر(٢)والسمن والأقط، ورُوى عنه انّه نزل
٢٠ برسول الله صلعم ضَيفٌ فلم يجد عند اهله شيئًا فدخل عليه رجل من
الأنصار فذهب الى اهله ووضع بين يديـه الطعام وقال لامرأتـه أطْفِى
السراج وجعل يمُدّ يَده كأنه يأكل حتى أكل الضيف الطعام فلمّا اصبح قال
له رسول الله صلعم لقد عجب الله تعالى من صنعتكم الى ضيفكم ونزلت هـذه

الآية (١) وَيُؤْثِرُونَ عَلَى أَنْفُسِهِمْ وَلَوْ كَانَ بِهِمْ خَصَاصَةٌ، وَرُوِى عن (٢)[ابن] عمر رضى الله عنه انه (٣)[قال] أُهْدِىَ لرجل من اصحاب رسول الله صلعم رأسُ شاة قال انّ أخى كان أَحْوَجَ اليه منّى فبعث اليــه فلم يزل يبعث الواحد الى الآخر حتى تناوله سبعةُ أبيات فرجعت الى الاوّل، قال ونزلت فيهم هذه الآية وَيُؤْثِرُونَ عَلَى أَنْفُسِهِمْ وَلَوْ كَانَ بِهِمْ خَصَاصَةٌ، قال الشيخ رحمه الله ومثل هذا كثير فى الأخبار عن الصحابة وما منهم احد الّا وله تخصيص فى معانى من هذا النوع الذى ذكرنا والمؤمنون مندوبون الى التعلّق بمثل هذه الافعال والتخلّى بأخلاقهم فيما أتوا به من انواع الطاعات ونطقوا بــه من (٤)[انواع] الحِكَم، وقد ذكرنا القليل من الكثير والمُراد من ذلك وقوف المسترشدين على المقصود والمُراد، وفى كلّ خبَر من هذه الأخبار التى ذكرناها عن هؤلاء الصحابة اشارةٌ ولطافةٌ (٤)تخصيصًا لأهله وله بيان وشرح كشرح مَن تقدّم ذِكْرُهُ فى اوّل الباب (٥)باب الايمّة الاربعة (٦)ابى بكر وعمر وعثمن وعلىّ رضى الله عنهم اجمعين، ولا يخفى على المتأمّل والمتدبّر بالنظر فيه بيان ذلك إن شآء الله تعالى،

(٧)كتاب آداب (٨)المتصوّفة،

A f. 62b

(٩)باب فى ذكر الآداب،

قال الشيخ رحمه الله قال الله (١٠)تعالى (١١)يَا أَيُّهَا الَّذِينَ آمَنُوا قُوا أَنْفُسَكُمْ وَأَهْلِيكُمْ نَارًا، ورُوِى عن (١٢)ابن عبّاس (١٣)رضى الله عنه قال فى تفسيره

(١) Kor. 59, 9.   (٢) Suppl. above.   (٣) Suppl. in marg.   (٤) وتخصيصا.
(٥) من with باب written above.   (٦) ابو.   (٧) Here B resumes on fol. 87b, l. 8.   (٨) الصوفة B.   (٩) B om. from باب to قال الشيخ رحمه الله.   (١٠) B عز وجل.   (١١) Kor. 66, 6.   (١٢) B بن.   (١٣) B om.

يعنى أَدِّبوهم وعَلِّموهم تَقوم بذلك من النار، ورُوى عن النبىّ صلعم انّه قال
ما نَحَلَ والدٌ ولدًا أفضَلَ من أدب حَسَن، ورُوى عن النبىّ صلعم انّه قال
انّ [١]اله أدّبنى فأحسَنَ أدبى، قال [٢]الشيخ رحمه اله موضع تخصيصه بالأدب
من جملة الأنبيآء [٤]عليهم السلم بقوله فاحسن ادبى والّا فجميع الانبيآ
٥ عليهم السلم كانوا ممّن [٥]أدّبهم اله [٦]تعالى، ورُوى عن محمّد بن سيرين
انّه سُئِل اىّ [٦]الآداب أقرَبُ الى اله تعالى وأزلَفُ للعبد عنه قال معرفةٌ
بربوبيته وعملٌ بطاعته والحمد لله على السرّاء [٧]والصبر على الضرّاء، وقيل
للحسن بن ابى الحسن البصرى [٢]رحمه اله قد اكثر الناس نعلُّم [٦]الآداب
فما أنفعُها عاجلاً وأوصَلُها آجلاً قال التفقّه فى الدّين فانّه يصرف اليه قلوب
١٠ المتعلّمين والزُّهدُ فى الدنيا فانّه يقرّبك من ربّ العالمين والمعرفة بما لله
عليك بجوبها كمال الايمان، وقال سعيد بن المسيّب [٢]رحمة اله عليه من
لم يعرف ما لله [٨]تعالى عليه [٩]فى نفسه ولم يتأدّب بأمره ونهيه كان من
الادب فى عُزلة، وقال كُلْثوم [٢]الغسّانى الأدب أدبان ادب قَوْل وأدب
فِعْل فمن [١٠]رفق لنفسه فى ادبه بقوله عدم ثواب العمل ومن تقرّب الى اله
١٥ تعالى بأدب فِعله منه محبّة القلوب [١١]وصرف عنه العيوب [٢]وجعله شريكًا
فى ثواب المتعلّمين، ورُوى عن [١٢]ابن المبارك [٢]رحمه اله انّه قال
نحن الى قليل من الادب أحوَجُ [٢]منّا الى كثير من العلم، وقال [١٢]ابن
المبارك [٢]رحمه اله ايضًا الادب للعارف بمنزلة التوبة للمستأنف، [١٣]قال الشيخ
رحمه اله والادب [١٤]سَنَد [١٥]للفقراء وزَيْن [١٦]للاغنياء، والناس فى الادب
٢٠ متفاوتون وهم على ثلث طبقات اهل الدنيا وأهل الدّين وأهل الخصوصية
من اهل الدّين، فأمّا اهل الدنيا فانّ أكثر آدابهم فى الفصاحة والبلاغة

---

(١) B عز وجل اله.   (٢) بعضهم B for الشيخ رحمه اله.   (٣) B om.   (٤) B قوله.

(٥) B قد ادبهم.   (٦) الادب B.   (٧) B om. الصبر على.   (٨) B عزوجل.

(٩) B من.   (١٠) B وفق.   (١١) B وضرب.   (١٢) B بن.   (١٣) B om.

(١٥) قال الشيخ رحمه اله.   (١٤) A سنة with سند in marg. as variant.   (١٥) B الفقرا.

(١٦) B الاغنيا.

A f.63a

وحفظ العلوم وأسمار الملوك وأشعار العرب ومعرفة الصنايع، وإمّا اهل
الدِّين فانّ اكثر آدابهم فى رياضة النفوس وتأديب الجوارح وطهارة الأسرار
وحفظ الحدود وترك الشهوات واجتناب الشبهات وتجريد الطاعات والمسارعة
الى الخيرات، وقد حُكى عن سهل بن عبد الله [١] رحمه الله انّه قال من
٥ قهر نفسه بالادب فهو يعبد الله [١] تعالى بالاخلاص، وقال سهل ايضًا [١] رحمه
الله [٢] استعانوا بالله على أمر الله فصبروا على ادب الله [١] تعالى، ويقال انّ
افضل [٣] الآداب التوبة ومنع النفوس عن الشهوات، وسُئِل بعضهم عن
ادب [٤] النفس فقال أن نُعرّفها الخير فتحبّها عليه ونُعرّفها الشرّ فتَزجُرها عنه،
ويقال انّ الادب كسائر الاشياء لا يصفو الاّ للانبياء والصدّيقين، [٥] قال
١٠ الشيخ رحمه الله فامّا ادب اهل الخصوصية من اهل الدِّين فانّ اكثر آدابهم
فى طهارة القلوب ومراعاة الأسرار والوفاء بالعقود بعد العهود وحفظ الوقت
وقلّة الالتفات الى الخواطر والعوارض والبوادى والطوارق [٦] واستواء السرّ
مع الإعلان وحسن الادب فى مواقف الطلب ومقامات القُرب واوقات
الحضور والقُربة والدنوّ والوصلة، سمعتُ احمد بن محمّد البصرى [١] رحمه الله
١٥ يقول سمعتُ الجلاجلى البصرى يقول التوحيد موجب [١] يوجب الايمان فمن
لا ايمان له لا توحيد له والايمان موجب يوجب الشريعة فمن لا شريعة له
لا ايمان [١] له ولا توحيد له والشريعة موجب يوجب الادب فمن لا ادب
له لا شريعة له ولا ايمان ولا توحيد، وسُئل ابو العبّاس بن عطاء [١] رحمه A f.63b
الله ما الادب فى ذاته فقال الوقوف مع المستحسَنات [٧] قيل [٨] وما الوقوف
٢٠ مع المستحسنات فقال أن تُعامل الله [١] تعالى بالادب سرًّا وإعلانًا فاذا كنت
كذلك كنت أديبًا وإن كنت أعجميًّا، ثم [٩] انشد [١٠] ابن عطاء فى هذا المعنى،
   اذا نَطَقَتْ جاءَتْ بكلّ مَلاحةٍ * وإن سكَتَتْ جاءَتْ بكلّ جَميلِ،

---

(١) B om.   (٢) B استعانوا.   (٣) In A orig. الأدب. The word is partially
obliterated in B.   (٤) B النفوس.   (٥) B om. قال الشيخ رحمه الله.
(٦) B فاستوى.   (٧) B فقيل.   (٨) B ما.   (٩) B انشا.   (١٠) B بن.

(١)قال الشيخ رحمه الله فالصوفية لهم آداب فى سفرهم وحضرهم وآداب فى
اوقاتهم واخلاقهم وآداب فى سكونهم وحركاتهم وهم مختصّون بها من غيرهم
ومعروفون بها عند أشكالهم وعند ابناء جنسهم يُعْرَفُ بذلك تفاضُلُ بعضهم
على بعض وبهذه الآداب (٢)تميّز بين الصادقين والكاذبين والمدّعين
(٣)والمحقّقين، وقد بيّنَّا طرقًا من آدابهم فى كلّ باب من هذه الابواب التى
(٤)ذكرنا على الاختصار لينظر الناظر فيه ويقف على ذلك إن شاء
الله (٥)تعالى،

باب آدابهم فى الوضوء والطهارات،

(١)قال الشيخ رحمه الله فاوّلُ ادب يُحتاج اليه فى باب الوضوء والطهارات
طَلَبُ العلم (٦)وتعلُّمُه ومعرفة الفرائض والسُّنن وما (٧)يُستحبّ وما يكره من
ذلك وما أُمِرَ به وما نُدِبَ اليه وما رُغِبَ فيه للفضيلة، وتفصيل ذلك لا
يُوقَف عليه الاّ (٨)بالتعلّم والسؤال والبحث (٩)عليه والاهتمام له حتى نأتى به
على موافقة الكتاب والسنّة بالاحتياط واتّباع الأحْسَن والأتَمّ ورفْع الملامة
وترْك الإنكار بالقلب على من لم يأخذ بالاحتياط والأشَدِّ لانّ الله (١٠)تعالى
(١١)يُحِبّ أن يؤخذ برُخَصه كما يُحِبّ أن (١٢)يؤخذ بعزائمه، وساير الناس لهم
أشغال وإسباب (١٣)لا بُدّ لهم من السعى فيها والاهتمام بهـا فان اخذوا
بالرُّخَص وما فيه السعة (١٤)فهم معذورون، وامّا المتصوّفة (١٥)ومن ترك
(١٦)الاسباب (١٧)وخرج عن (١٨)الاشتغال وفرّغ نفسه للعبادة والزهد فلا

---

(١) B om. .قال الشيخ رحمه الله ‏   (٢) A تميّز, B app. .تبيز   (٣) B والمحقّقين.

(٤) B ذكرنها.   (٥) B om.   (٦) B ومعرفته وتعلمه.   (٧) A adds به.

(٨) B بالتعليم.   (٩) B عنه.   (١٠) B عز وجل.   (١١) B مختار.   (١٢) B يوتا.

(١٣) B ولا.   (١٤) After فهم B has a word which looks like معك.   (١٥) B من.

(١٦) Here B breaks off on the last line of fol. 90a. The next words فدخل

كتاب آداب المتصوّفة (fol. 90b, l. 1) occur near the end of the الماء مرة الخ

A f.64a عُذرٌ له فى ترك التوقى والتنقى والاهتمام بإسباغ الوضوء والتمسُّك بالاحتياط والأتمّ فى ابواب الطهارة والنظافة فمن ليس له شُغلٌ غير ذلك فعليه أن يبذلَ مجهوده على قدر استطاعته (١) فى ذلك لقول الله (٢) تعالى (٣) فَاتَّقُوا اللَّهَ مَا اسْتَطَعْتُمْ ، وقد رأيتُ جماعةً كانوا يجدّدون الوضوء لكلّ صلاة

٥ فيقومون الى الوضوء قبلَ دخول وقت الصلاة حتى اذا فرغوا من وضوء هم يكون قيامهم الى الصلاة متّصلاً بفراغهم من الوضوء ، ومن آدابهم فى ذلك ايضًا أن يكونوا (٤) دهرَهم على الطهارة فى سفرهم وحضرهم ، وأصلهم فى ذلك انّهم لا يدرون متى تأتيهم المنيّة لقول الله (٥) تعالى (٦) فَإِذَا جَاءَ أَجَلُهُمْ (٧) لَا يَسْتَأْخِرُونَ سَاعَةً وَلَا يَسْتَقْدِمُونَ يريدون بذلك إن جاءهم الموت بغتةً

١٠ يخرجون من الدنيا على الطهارة ، سمعتُ الحُصرى (٨) رحمه الله يقول ربّما أنتبه (٩) بالليل فلا يحملنى النوم الّا بعد ما اقوم وأجدّد الوضوء ، (١٠) قال الشيخ رحمه الله تعالى (١١) وذلك أنّه كان ينام على الطهارة فاذا انتبه وقد نُقضتْ طهارته جدّد فقد أدّب نفسه بذلك أن لا يحمله النوم وهو على غير طهارة ، وكان شيخٌ من المشايخ الاجلّة به وسوسةٌ فى الوضوء وكان يُكثر صبّ

١٥ الماء ، فسمعته يقول كنتُ ليلةً من الليالى أجدّد الوضوء لصلاة العشاء وكنت أصبُّ الماء على نفسى حتى مضى شطرٌ من الليل فلم يطب قلبى ولم يذهب عنّى الوسوسة فبكيتُ (١٢) فقلتُ يا ربّ العفوَ فسمعتُ هاتفًا يقول يا فلان العفو فى العلم يعنى فى استعمال العلم ، وقال ابو نصر (١٣) وهو ابو عبد الله الروذبارى (٨) رحمه الله ، ويقال ان الشيطان يجتهد فى أن يأخذ (١٤) نصيبه

٢٠ من جميع اعمال بنى آدم فلا يُبالى أن يأخذ (١٤) نصيبه بأن يزدادوا فيما أُمروا

(A fol. 95b, l. 8). (١٧) The following text begins in B on fol. 43b, l.1.

(١٨) الاشغال B.

(١) وذلك B. (٢) عز وجل B. (٣) Kor. 64, 16. (٤) دهرهم ايضا A.

(٥) تبارك وتعلى B. (٦) Kor. 7, 32. (٧) فلا B. (٨) B om.

(٩) الليل B. (١٠) B om. (١١) قال الشيخ رحمه الله تعالى B والمعنى فى ذلك.

(١٢) وقلت B. (١٣) هو B. (١٤) نفسه B.

10

به او وينفصوا منه ، وذُكر عن ابن الكَرِينى وكان استاد الجُنَيْد رحمه الله
أنّه أصابته الجنابة ليلة من الليالى (١) وكانت عليه مرقّعة ثخينة (٢) غليظة
(٣) A f.64b كانت فرد كُمّه (٤) وتخاريزه عند جعفر الخُلْدى وكان فيه أرطال قال
فجاء الى (٥) الشطّ (٦) ليلة وكان بردٌ شديد (٧) فحرنت نفسه عن الدخول فى
٥ الماء لشدّة البرد قال فطرح نفسه فى الماء مع المرقّعة ولم يزل (٨) يغوص فى
الماء مع مرقّعته (٩) ثم خرج من الماء وقال اعتقدتُ ان لا أنزعها من بدنى
حتى تجفّ علىّ قال فلم تجنّ عليه شهراً كاملاً وأراد بذلك تأديباً لنفسه
لأنّها (١٠) حرنت عند الابتدار لما أمره الله (١١) تعالى به من غسل الجنابة،
وكان سهل بن عبد الله (١١) رحمه الله يحثّ اصحابه على كثرة شرب الماء
١٠ وقلّة صبّ الماء على الارض وكان يقول (١١) انّ الماء له حياة وموته أن
نصبّه على الارض وكان يرى انّ فى (١١) كثرة شرب الماء ضعف النفس
وإماتة الشهوات (١٢) وكسر القوّة، وأقام (١٤) أبو عمرو الزجّاجى (١١) رحمه الله
بمكّة سنين كثيرةً وهو مُجاور بها (١٤) وكان اذا اراد أن يقضى حاجته يخرج
من الحرم وهو مقدار فرسخ وكان لا يتغوّط فى الحرم كما بلغنى ثلثين سنة،
١٥ وكان ابرهم الخوّاص (١١) رحمه الله اذا دخل البادية لا يحمل معه الّا ركوةً
من الماء وربّما كان لا يشرب منها الّا القليل وكان يحتفظ بذلك للوضوء
ويؤثر وضوءه بالماء على الشرب عند العطش، (١٥) قال الشيخ رحمه الله تعالى
ورأيتُ جماعةً يمشون على (١١) شطوط الأنهار ولا يفارقهم الماء فى (١٦) ركوتهم
او فى كوز وذلك أنّه ربّما كان يشتدّ بهم البول ولا يُمكنهم الجلوسُ على
٢٠ شطّ النهر وكشفُ العورة من أجل الناس (١٧) فاذا كان معهم ركوة (١٨) او كوز

---

(١) B وكان. (٢) B عظيمة. (٣) This passage (which I must leave as it
stands) occurs again in A fol. 84b, l. 6, where the text runs: فكان فرد كُمّه وتخاريزه
B وتخاريزه, A وتخاريره. (٥) A in عند جعفر الخلدى فيه ثلثه عشر رطلا كما بلغنى
marg. فجينت, B شط الدجلة. (٧) A in marg. يعنى شط الدجلة. B adds.
(٨) B بقوم. (٩) B حتى. (١٠) A in marg. جينت, B جزعت. فجزعت.
قال B (١٥) كان B (١٤) عمرو ابو عمرو B (١٣) وكسره. (١٢) (١١) B om.

عدلوا الى خلوة فيكون أصوَنَ لأنفسهم، وكانوا يكرهون (١)كثرة الدَّلْك عند
(٢)البول لانّه ربّما يسترخى (٣)العروق فلا يُمسك البول ويتولّد منه التقطير
المُفْرِط، وكذلك تُكرَهُ الشدّة الّا عند عوز الماء والاضطرار، ولبس السراويل
(١)أَحبّ (٤)[الىّ] من الإزار بعد الطهارة والازار أَخفّ لنزعه عند النهى،

ويُجتنب لبسُ جميع ما (٥)يخرّز بشَعْر الخنزير قلّ او كثر رطبًا كان او يابسًا،
ولذلك اختاروا لبْس النعال ويقال (١)انّ الصوفى اذا رأيتَهُ وليس معه ركوة
او كوز فاعلَم انّه قد عزم على ترْك الصلاة وكشْف العورة شاء او أَبَى،
(٦)ورأيتُ من (٧)أقام بين ظهرانَيْ جماعة من النُّسّاك وهم مجتمعون فى دار
فما (٨)رآه (٩)احد منهم انّه دخل الخلاَء او خرج من الخلاَء وذلك انّه كان

١٠ قد أدّب نفسه وعوّدها القيام الى الحاجة فى وقتٍ واحد اذا خلا الموضع
حتى لا يراه احد اذا دخل الخلاَء او خرج منه، ورأيتُ ايضًا من كان قد
(١٠)عوّد نفسه (١١)وأدّبها حتى كان لا يخرج منه ريح الّا فى وقت (١٢)البراز
(١٣)وهو فى البادية وفى مواضع الخلوة، وكان ابرهيم الخوّاص (١)رحمه الله
تعالى يخرج من مكّة وَحْدَهُ فيجئ الى الكوفة (١٤)فلا يحتاج (١٥)ان يتيمّم

١٥ بالتُّراب وكان يحفظ الماء الذى يحمل لشُربه حتى يتوضّأ (١٦)به، وكان
جماعة من الشيوخ يكرهون دخول الحمّام الّا فى اوقات الضرورة فاذا
اضطرّوا الى ذلك لم يدخلوا الّا فى (١٧)حمّام (١٨)خال فاذا (١٩)دخلوها لم
يحلّوا ازارهم الى ان (٢٠)يخرجوا ولم يتركوا ان يسمّ القوّام ويعطوهم (٢١)طَعَمَهم

او كوز.   (١٨) B om.   (١٧) واذا B.   ركاهم.   (١٦) ابو نصر ورأيت الخ.

(١) B om.   (٣) A adds in marg. للإستبراء.   (٣) B العرق.   (٤) AB
om. Suppl. in marg. A.   (٥) Written in A with *tashdīd*.   (٦) B رأيت.

(٧) A in marg. adds سنين.   (٨) B رأى.   (٩) A واحد.   (١٠) B تعود.
ولا B.   (١٤) وهى B.   (١٣) البرارى.   (١١) A ادبه.   (١١) وادب نفسه.

(١٥) B تيمّم الى.   (١٦) A وكانوا.   (١٧) B الحمام الخالى.   (١٨) A خالى.
(١٩) B دخلوا.   (٢٠) A in marg. فان كانوا يعرفونهم اصحاب الحمام ويكرمونهم.

وبوقرونهم, but there is no indication of the place where these words should
be inserted. Probably they are intended to follow يخرجوا, in which case we

من غير ان يدنوا منهم حتى يوسّعوا عليهم المآء، (١)فان كانوا جماعة
(٢)دلكوا بعضهم بعضًا فان كان فى الحمام غيرهم استقبلوا بوجوههم (٣)الحائط
حتى لا تقع أعينُهم على عورات الناس، (٤)وكان جماعة من المنصوّفة اذا
دخلوا الحمّام لا يتركون (٥)احدًا يدخل معهم (٦)الاّ بازار، والاستحباب نَتْف
الإبْط وحَلْق العانة فمن لم يُحسن (٧)الحلق (٨)فليتنوّر بيه فى الخلوة، (٩)وكان
اصحاب سهل بن عبد الله (٩)رحمه الله تعالى يحلقون (١٠)رُءوسهم بعضهم
(١١)لبعض (١٢)كما بلغنى عنهم، وسمعتُ عيسى القصّار الدينورى (٩)رحمه الله
تعالى يقول (١٣)اوّل من فصّ (١٤)شاربى بيه الشبلى (٩)رحمه الله تعالى
وكنت أَخْدمه، (١٥)قال الشيخ رحمه الله تعالى وفرْق الرأس (١٦)اختاروا
جماعة من السنّة ويكْرَه ذلك للشباب ويحسن بالمشايخ ان ارادوا بذلك استعمال   A f. 65b
السنّة، وكان يقول بعض المشايخ هَبْ أنّ الفقر من الله (٩)تعالى فا بال
الوَسَخ، وأَحَبُّ الاشيآء الى المنصوّفة النظافة والطهارة وغسل الثوب والمداومة
على السِّواك والنزول عند المياه (٩)الجارية (١٧)والفضآء الواسعة والمساجد
التى فى الأطْراف والخلوة والاغتسال فى كلّ (٩)يوم جُمْعة فى الشتآء والصيف
والرائحة الطيّبة وأطْيَبُ الطيب المآء الجارى والمداومة على الاغتسال وتجديد
الوضوء (١٨)وإسباغ (١٩)الوضوء، وليس من الوسوسة (٢٠)ما يستفصى الانسان
فى (٢١)طهارته من التباعد وطلب المآء الجارى وترْك المياه المتغيّرة والتفتيش
على المواضع الطاهرة (٢٢)والاستفصاء على ذَلِك (٢٣)اعضآء الظاهرة وافتقاد

must read لم يتركوا instead of ولم يتركوا.   (٢١) B أطعمهم.

(١) B فاذا.   (٢) A دلكوا, B يدلكوا.   (٣) A الحائط.   (٤) A وكانوا.

(٥) B لاحد ان.   (٦) A adds in marg. من يتزر.   (٧) A in marg. استعمال.

السنة (٨) B تنور.   (٩) B om.   (١٠) B رءوس.   (١١) B بعضا.

(١٢) B om. كما بلغنى عنهم.   (١٣) B اقل.   (١٤) B شاربه,   (١٥) B om.
قال الشيخ رحمه الله تعالى.   (١٦) Altered in A to اختاره by a later hand.

(١٧) A الغضاه, B الفضا.   (١٨) B om. وإسباغ الوضوء.   (١٩) In marg. A

الطهارة.   (٢٠) B فيما.   (٢١) B الطهارة,   (٢٢) B والاستقصى.

(٢٣) B أعظاء الطهارة.

(١)اعضاء الباطنة ومواضع التشنيع (٢) والانضام وإبلاغ الماء (٣)الخياشيم وإمرار
الماء على الاعضاء (٤) وجميع (٥)البشر فى الغسل والوضوء وغير (٦) ذلك ،
وليس التوقّى والتنقّى من الوسواس المنهىّ عنه (٧)ايضًا لانّ جميع ذلك
داخل فى قوله (٨)اتَّقُوا اللّٰهَ مَا اسْتَطَعْتُمْ، وإنّما الوسوسة المنهيّة عنه ما
٥ (٩)يُخرجك عن حدّ العلم وهو أن تشغلك الفضايل عن الفرايض وأن
تُخالف العلم (١٠) وتُبطّل صلاةَ من يتوضّأ بالمُدّ ويغتسل بالصاع، والصواب
فى ذلك ان يكون العبد فى كلّ وقت بما هو أوْلَى بالوقت اذا وجد (١١)
الماء فيُسبغ وضوءه على الاحتياط حتى يطيب قلبه واذا لم يجد الماء الواسع
فيَحسُن ان يجدّد الوضوء او ينطّر بقليل من الماء كما رُوى فى الخبر انّ
١٠ اصحاب رسول الله صلعم كانوا يتوضّون وضوءًا لا (١٣) يُلَثّ منـه التُّراب ،
قال (١٢)الشيخ رحمه الله ورأيتُ من كان على وجهه (١٤) قَرْحةً لم تندمل
(١٥)اثنَىْ عشر سنةً وذلك أنّ الماء كان يضرّه (١٦) وكان لا يدع تجديد
الوضوء عند كل صلاة، ورأيتُ من نزل الماء فى عينَيْه (١٧)فحملوا اليـه
المُداوى وبذلوا له دنانير كثيرةً على أن يداويه فقال المداوى يحتاج أن لا
١٥ يمسّ الماء ايّامًا ويكون مستلقيًا على قفاه فلم يفعل ذلك وإختار ذهاب بصره
على ترك الوضوء والطهارة (١٨) وكان هذا ابو عبد الله (١٩)الرازى (٢٠)المُقْرى،

---

(١) B الاعضا.　　(٢) B الانطام.　　(٣) B الخياشيم على.　　(٤) In marg. A
والاستظهار بكثرة صبّ.　　(٥) B البشرة.　　(٦) A adds in marg. جميع ادخال
الماء من غير اسراف وتكلّف حضور النية والمداومة عليها فى الغسل والوضوء وغير ذلك
وتبطيل.　　(٧) B om.　　(٨) Kor. 64, 16.　　(٩) B يخرج.　　(١) B تبطيل
الشيخ (١٢) B om.　　(١١) B om. فى ذلك.　　(١٢) Altered in A to يبتلّ.
رحمه الله (١٤) B وقر.　　(١٥) AB اثنا.　　(١٦) صاحبها added in marg. A.
المقرى الرازى B (١٩)　　(١٨) B ابو عبد الله قيل هو.　　(١٧) B فحمل.
(٢٠) A adds in marg. وحكى عن الشبلى لما احذ فى النزع اشار الى خادمه ان يجدّد
وضوءه فنسى تخليل لحيته وكان قد أمسك لسان الشبلى فقبض على يد الخادم وإدخلها
فى لحيته.

وحُكِى عن ابرهيم (١) بن أَدْهَمَ (٢) رحمه الله انّه كان به قيامٌ فقام فى ليلة واحدة نيّف وسبعين مرّة كلّ مرّة (٢) يجدّد وضوءه ويصلّى ركعتيْن، ومات ابرهيم الخوّاص (٢) رحمه الله فى جامع الرّىّ (٢) فى وسط المَاء وذلك أنّه كان به علّة البطن فكان اذا قام (٢) مُجلِّسًا يدخل المَاء ويغسل نفسه فدخل مرّةً فى المَاء (٢) ليغسل نفسه فخرجت نفسه وهو فى وسط المَاء، فهذا ما حضرنى فى الوقت من آداب اهل الصفوة من الصوفية فى الوضوء والطهارة، وبالله التوفيق (٤)،

باب فى ذكر آدابهم فى الصلاة،

(٥) قال الشيخ رحمه الله وامّا آدابهم فى الصلاة فأوّلُ ذلك (٦) تعلُّم علم الصلاة ومعرفة (٧) فرائضها وسُنَنِها وآدابها وفضائلها ونوافلها وكثرة مسائلة العلماء، والبحث عمّا يُحتاج اليه فى ذلك ممّا لا يَسَعُ الجهل (٢) به لانّ الصلاة عماد الدين وقُرّة عيْن العارفين وزينة الصدّيقين وتاج المقرّبين ومقام الصلاة مقام الوصلة والدنوّ والهيبة والخشوع والخشية والتعظيم والوقار والمشاهدة والمراقبة والأسرار والمناجاة مع الله (٨) تعالى والوقوف بين يدى الله (٢) تعالى والاقبال على الله تعالى والاعراض عمّا سوى الله (٢) تعالى، فامّا العامة فلم أن يقلّدوا علماءهم ويسألوا فقهاءهم ويعتمدوا على اقاويلهم من الرُّخَص والسَّعات والفتوى والتأويلات التى أوْسَعَ الله (٢) تعالى للخلق، فامّا المتصوّفة وأهل الخصوص الذين باينوا الناس وانحازوا عن جملة الناس بتَرْك المكاسب (٩) وقطْع العلائق وانقطعوا الى الله (١٠) عزّ وجلّ وعَرفوا

---

(١) A corrector has stroked out the words أدهَم بن in A and has written الخوّاص above. (٢) B om. (٣) A جدد. (٤) B واله أعلم. (٥) B om.
(٧) B فرائضه وسنه وآدابه وفضايله ونوافله. (٦) B تعليم. قال الشيخ رحمه الله.
(٨) B عز وجل. (٩) A وترك. (١٠) B تعلى.

باله ونُسبوا الى الله فلا يَسَعُهم التخلّف عن استعمال الآداب والاهتمام
والتكلّف لأحكام الصلاة (١) وتجويزها وأحكام فرايضها وسُنَنها وفضايلها ونوافلها
(٢) وآدابها (٣) لأنهم ليس لهم شُغُل غير ذلك ولا ينبغى أن يَهُمّهم (٤) أمرٌ أكثرَ
من اهتمامهم بأمر الصلاة، (٥) فأوّل أدبهم (٦) من ذلك أن يكون تأهُّبهم للصلاة
٥ قَبلَ دخول (٧) وقت الصلاة حتى لا يفوتهم الوقت الاوّل الذى هو المختار
ولا يُمكِّنهم ذلك الاّ بمعرفة (٨) الوقت الاوّل لكلّ صلاة ولا يَقدِرُ على ذلك
الاّ بمعرفة وعلْم مع الوقوف على علْم الزوال ومقدار ظلِّ الزوال فى كلّ وقت
وأوان فى كلّ أقطار وأن يعلم على كم تزول الشمس من قَدَم فى كلّ وقت
وكم يزداد (٩) وينقص ويعتبر ذلك بمقدار قامته اذا لم يكن معــه مِقياس
١٠ لذلك ويعلم ذلك فى أىّ (١٠) موضع كان بظلِّ شخصه (١١) ويعتبره بقدمه
وكذلك يحتاج الى معرفة شىء من النجوم ومنازل القمر وطلوعها وغروبها
ونَوْبة طلوع كلّ نجم من منازل القمر حتى اذا نظر (١٢) بالليل الى النجوم لا
يخفى علية ما مضى من الليل وما بقى الى الصُبح، ويحتاج ايضًا الى معرفة
القُطب والكواكب (١٣) التى يُستدلّ (١٤) بها على القِبْلة ولا يصحّ له ذلك الاّ
١٥ (١٥) بالاجتهاد ومعرفة (١٦) سَمْت كلّ بلدة حتى اين تقع من الكعبة ولا يقف
على صحّة ذلك الاّ بعد افتقاده ذلك بمكّة ورجوعه الى البلدة التى قد عرف
اين يقع سَمْتُها من الكعبة وأين كان ذلك فى وقت معلوم من محاذاة
القطب والجدى والفرقدَين، (١٧) وأمّا النجوم (١٨) السيّارات فينبغى ايضًا ان
يعلم ذلك (١٩) للاستدلال والاهتداء بالليل فأنّه ربّما يقع فى المفاوز ويركب

---

(١) A وتجويدها with وتحديدها written above.   (٢) B adds وأحكامها and
قال وآدابهم من ذلك الخ B so A in marg.   (٤) B امرًا.   (٥) B لأنه.
(٧) B لان الوقت for وقت الصلاة حتى.   (٦) In A فى is given as a variant.
(٨) B om. from مع الوقوف على علم الوقت to الوقت.   (٩) B app. فينقص.   (١٠) B مواضع.
(١١) B ويعتبر.   (١٢) B الذى.   (١٣) B om.   (١٤) B بذلك.   (١٥) B باجتهاد.
(١٦) AB سمه.   (١٧) B فاما.   (١٨) B السيارات.   (١٩) AB للاستهلال
but A in marg. gives للاستدلال as a variant.

البُجُور فيحتاج الى معرفة ذلك، وكان سهل بن عبد الله (١) رحمه الله يقول
علامة الصادق ان يكون له (٢) تابع من الجنّ اذا دخل وقت الصلاة يحثّه
على ذلك وان كان نائمًا ينبّهه، ومنهم من يكون له اوراد بالليل والنهار
من العبادة والذكر وتلاوة القرآن على ممرّ ايّامه ونصير عادتهُ حتى لا يغلط
فى ذلك ليلَه ونهارَه حيث ما كان، وامّا (٣) آداب الدخول فى الصلاة ٥
بعد ما تأهّب اذا دخل اوّل الوقت وأراد الدخول فى الصلاة (٤) فتحريمها
بالتكبيرة المقرونة بتكبيرة الاحرام مع النيّة من حيث لا تسبق النيّة (٥) التكبيرة
ولا (٦) التكبيرة النيّة ويكونا معًا، وقد حُكى عن الجُنَيْد (١) رحمه الله انه قال
لكل شىء صفوة وصفوة الصلاة تكبيرة الاولى والمعنى فى ذلك ان التكبيرة
الاولى هى مقرونة بالنيّة التى لا تجوز الصلاة الاّ بها وهو عَقْدُك بانّ صلاتك ١٠
لله عزّ وجلّ فاذا صحّ العقد فا دخل بعد ذلك فى صلاتك من الآفات
الباطنة لم يُفسد الصلاة بل ينقص من فضايلها ويبقى للمصلّى عقدها ونيّتها،
سمعتُ (٦) ابن سالم (١) رحمه الله تعالى يقول النيّة باله (٧) ولله ومن الله
(٨) والآفات التى تدخل فى صلاة العبد بعد النيّة (٩) من العدوّ وهو نصيب
العدوّ (١٠) وانّ نصيب العدوّ وان كثر لا يوازن بالنيّة التى هى باله وله ١٥
ومن الله وان قلّ، وسُئل ابو سعيد الخرّاز (١) رحمه الله كيف الدخول
فى الصلاة (١٢) فقال هو ان تُقبل على الله (١) تعالى كاقبالك عليه يوم القيمة
ووقوفك بين يدى الله (١) تعالى ليس بينك وبينه نرجمان وهو مُقبل عليك
وأنت تُناجيه وتعلم بين يدَىْ من انت واقف فانّه الملك العظيم، وقيل
لبعض العارفين كيف نُكبّر تكبيرة الاولى (١٢) فقال (١٣) ينبغى اذا قلتَ الله ٢٠

---

(١) B om.   (٢) A تابعى B نابعى.   (٣) B ادب.   (٤) In B this
passage runs thus: فتحريها التكبير ومع النية بكونان معًا والمعرفة بتكبيرة الاحرام مع
والاوقات B (٨)   الله A (٧)   بن B (٦)   التكبير B (٥)   النية من حيث الخ.
قال B (١٢)   ومن الله A om. (١١)   ونصيب B (١٠)   من العدو B om. (٩)
(١٣) لك added in marg. A.

أكبُر ان يكون مصحوب قولك التعظيم مع الأَلِف والهيبـة مع اللام
والمراقبة والقرب مع الهَآء، وقال آخر اذا كبَّرتَ [١]التكبيرة الاولى فاعلمْ
انَّه ناظرٌ الى شخصك وعالمٌ بما فى ضميرك ومثِّل فى صلاتك الجنّة عن A f. 67b
يمينك والنار عن [٢]شمالك، ومن [٣]ادب الصلاة ان العبد اذا دخل فى
٥ الصلاة فلا يكون فى قلبه شىء غير الله الذى هو بين يديه حتى يعرف
كلامه ويأخذ من كلّ آية ذوقها وفهْمها لانّه ليس له من صلاته الاّ مـا
عقل، [٤]وقال ابو سعيد الخرّاز [٥]رحمه الله فى كتاب له يصف ادب
الصلاة فقال اذا رفعتَ [٦]يديك فى التكبير فلا يكن فى قلبك الاّ الكبرياَء
ولا [٧]يكن عندك فى وقت التكبير شىء أكبر من الله [٨]تعالى حتى تنسى
١٠ الدنيا والآخرة فى كبريآئه، [٩]قال الشيخ رحمه الله والمعنى [١٠]فى ما قال
ابو سعيد [١١]الخرّاز رحمه الله ان العبد اذا قال الله أكبر [١٢]ويكون فى
قلبه شىء غير الله فلا يكون صادقًا فى قوله الله أكبر ثم انه اذا أخذ فى
التلاوة فالادبُ فى ذلك ان يشاهد بسمع قلبه كأنه يسمع من الله [٥]تعالى
او كأنه يقرأ على الله [٥]تعالى، قال ابو سعيد [١١]الخرّاز رحمه الله وفيه
١٥ العلم الجليل لأهل الفهم، [١٣]واذا ركع فالادبُ فى ركوعه ان [١٤]يَنْصَبَ
ويدنو [١٥]ويتدلَّى حتى لا يبقى [١٦]فيه مَفْصِل الاّ وهو منتصب نحو العرش
ثم يعظِّم الله تعالى [١٧]حتى لا يكون فى قلبه شىء اعظم من الله عزّ وجلّ
ويصغِّر [١٨]نفسه حتى يكون اقلّ من الهَبآء فاذا رفع رأسه وحمد الله يعلم
انَّه هو [١٩]لَدَى يسمع ذلك، وإذا سجد فالادبُ فى سجوده ان لا يكون فى
٢٠ قلبه عند السجود شىء اقرب اليه من الله [٥]تعالى لأن اقرب ما يكون

---

[١] تكبيرة B.   [٢] بسارك B.   [٣] اداب B.   [٤] قال B.   [٥] B om.

[٦] يدك B.   [٧] يكون A.   [٨] عز وجل B.   [٩] B om. قال الشيخ

[١٠] Suppl. in A by a later hand. B كا for فى ما.   [١١] B om. رحمه الله

[١٢] B om. from ويكون to الله أكبر.   [١٣] فاذا B.   [١٤] الخراز رحمه الله

[١٥] In marg. A.   [١٤] A orig. نصت, altered to نصب. B بصب.   ويتذلل.

[١٦] B منه.   [١٧] B om. from حتى to عز وجل.   [١٨] فى نفسه A   [١٩] B ربى.

العبد من ربّه عند السجود فيجب ان ينزهه عن الاضداد بلسانه ولا يكون
فى قلبه اجلُّ منه ولا اعزُّ منه ويُتمّ صلاته على هذا ويكون معه من الخشية
والهيبة ما يكاد ان (١)يذوب ولا يكون له فى صلاته شُغْلٌ اكثر من شُغْلِه
بصلاته حتى لا (٢)يشتغل بشىء غير الذى هو (٣)واقف بين يديه فى صلاته
وكذلك اذا تشهّد ودعا وسلّم كلّ ذلك يعقل ما يقول وما يخاطب (٤)ولان A f. 68a
(٥)يخاطب حتى يخرج من الصلاة بالعقد الذى قد دخل (٦)فى الصلاة،
(٧)فهذا ما وجدتُ فى كتاب ابى سعيد الخرّاز (٨)رحمه الله ورأيت جماعةً
كانوا يكرهون تطويل الصلاة ويحبّون التخفيف لمبادرة الوسواس حتى يخرج
من (٩)صلاته (١٠)على النيّة والعقد الذى دخل (١١)به فيها،

فصل آخر فى (١٢)آداب (١٣)الصلاة،

(١٤)قال الشيخ رحمه الله تعالى وذلك ان العبد اذا كان متأدّبًا بأدب
الصلاة قبل دخول (٨)وقت الصلاة فكأنّه فى الصلاة ويكون قيامه الى
الصلاة من حال لا يُستغنى عنه فى الصلاة وذلك ان من آدابهم قَبْلَ
الصلاة المراقبة ومراعاة القلب من الخواطر والعوارض وذكْرُ كلِّ شىء غير
ذكر الله (١٥)تعالى فاذا قاموا الى الصلاة بحضور القلب فكأنّهم قاموا من ١٠
الصلاة الى الصلاة فيبقون مع النيّة والعقد الذى دخلوا فى الصلاة واذا
خرجوا من الصلاة رجعوا الى حالهم من حضور القلب والمراعاة والمراقبة

(١) B app. يكروب or بكروب but the middle letters are almost obliterated.
(٢) سرّه added in marg. A. (٣) B وأقف بين يديه. (٤) B ولم. (٥) A adds
بخاطب يخاطب من ذى هو ومع in marg. (٦) B بالصلاة. (٧) B هذا. (٨) B om.
(١١) Suppl. above. بالعقد الذى قد دخل فى الصلاة B (١٠) الصلاة B (٩)
قال الشيخ B om. (١٤) B adds قبل دخول الصلاة. (١٢) B أدب (١٣)
عزّ وجلّ B (١٥) رحمه الله تعالى.

فكانّهم فى الصلاة وان كانوا خارجين من الصلاة، (١) فهذا هو ادب الصلاة
وقد رُوى عن النبىّ صلعم انه قال العبد فى الصلاة ما دام ينتظر الصلاة،
فهذا هو الادب الذى يحتاج اليه المصلّى فى (٢) صلاته وفى انتظار الصلاة
قبْل الصلاة كما وصنتُ (٣) لك ان فهمتَ ذلك (٤) ان شآء الله تعالى، وقد
رأيتُ من اذا قام الى الصلاة كان يحمرّ ويصفرّ وجهه عند (٥) تكبيرة الاولى
من هيبة الله (٦) تعالى ورأيت من كان لا يتهيّأ له ان يحفظ العدد فكان
يجلس واحدًا من اصحابه ويعدّ عليه كم ركعة صلّى لانّه كان يراى قلبه على
(٧) ثبات العقد الذى دخل به فى الصلاة (٨) فكان يخاف الغلط على نفسه
(٩) لانّه (١٠) كان لا يدرى كم ركعة صلّاها فلذلك كان يستعين بمن يعدّ عليه
حتى يتيقّن كم ركعة صلّاها، وذُكر عن سهل بن عبد الله انه كان يضعف
حتى لا يكاد يقوم من موضعه حتى اذا دخل وقت الصلاة تُردّ اليه قوّته
فيقوم فى المحراب مثل الوتد فاذا فرغ من صلاته يرجع الى حالة ضعفه ولا
يقدر ان يقوم من موضعه، ورأيتُ من كان يسافر فى البادية على الوحدة
ولا بترك ورْده من التطوّع وصلاة الليل والفضائل والسنن والآداب (١١) التى
كان يستعمل فى الحضر (٨) فكان يقول احوال هذه الطائفة ينبغى ان تكون
فى السفر والحضر واحدةً، وكان اخ من اخوانى يصطحب فى مكان واحد
فكانت عادته انّه اذا اكل شيئًا يقوم (١٣) ويصلّى ركعتين (١٤) واذا شربَ المآء
يقوم ويصلّى ركعتين واذا لبس ثوبًا يقوم ويصلّى ركعتين واذا دخل المسجد
يصلّى ركعتين واذا اراد الخروج من المسجد يصلّى ركعتين وكذلك اذا
فرح او اغتمّ او (١٥) غضب يقوم (١٤) ويصلّى ركعتين، (١٦) وكان جماعة من

٨ f. 68b

(١) هذا B.   (٢) الصلاة B.   (٣) B om.   (٤) B om. ان شآء الله تعالى.
(٥) التكبيرة B.   (٦) عز وجل B.   (٧) A اثبات but ثبات in marg. as variant.
(٨) وكان B.   (٩) انه A.   (١٠) A om. كان لا يدرى.   (١١) A الذى.
(١٢) كانت تستعمل B.   (١٣) يصلى B.   (١٤) واذا لبس ثوبًا يقوم يصلى ركعتين B.
(١٥) Here the text of واذا شرب المآء يقوم يصلى ركعتين واذا دخل المسجد الخ.
B breaks off on the last line of fol. 52a＝A fol. 68b, l. 10. Fol. 52b begins

(۱)اصحابنا يسافرون مع ابى عبد الله بن جابان (۲)رحمه الله تعالى (۳)فحدّثونى
عنه انّه كان اذا بلغ (۳)الى الميل فى البادية وأراد (٤)التعقّب لا يجلس
حتى يصلّى ركعتين، ومن آدابهم ايضًا انّهم يكرهون الامامة والصلاة فى
(٥)الصفّ الاوّل بمكّة وغيرها ويكرهون (٦)التطويل، (۷)وإمّا الامامة فلو ان
احدهم يحفظ القرآن فانّهم يختارون الصلاة خلف من يُحسن ان يقرأ الحمد
وسورة أُخرى لانّ النبىّ صلعم قال الامام ضامن، وإمّا ترك الصلاة فى الصفّ
الاوّل فانّهم يريدون بذلك ان لا يزاحموا الناس (۸)ويضيّقوا عليهم لانّ
الناس يزدحمون (۹)ويطلبون الصفّ الاوّل لما جاء فى الخبر من الفضيلة
فيه يريدون بذلك ايثارهم (۱۰)وإذا كان الموضع خاليًا يغتنمون ذلك الفضل
الذى جاء فى الصفّ الاوّل، وإمّا التطويل فى الصلاة فكلّما طالت الصلاة
كثرت (۱۱)الهفوات (۱۲)والوسواس والاشتغال بتصحيح الاعمال أَوْلَى من الاشتغال A f.69a
(۱۳)بكثرته وتطويله، ورُوى عن رسول الله صلعم انّه اخفّ الناس صلاةً
فى تمام، سمعتُ (۱٤)ابن علوان (۲)رحمه الله يقول كان الجُنَيْد (۱٥)رحمه الله
لا يترك اوراده من الصلاة على كِبَر سِنّه وضعفه فقيل له فى ذلك فقال
حال وصلتُ به الى الله تعالى فى بدايتى كيف بهيّاً لى أن اتركه فى نهايتى،
ومن آدابهم فى الصلاة ايضًا انّ (۱٦)للصلاة اربع شُعَب حضور القلب فى
المحراب وشهود العقل عند الوهّاب وخشوع القلب بلا ارتياب وخضوع
الاركان بلا ارتقاب لانّ عند حضور القلب رفع الحجاب وعند شهود العقل

---

with the verse اموت بداً لا يصاب دوايها الخ which occurs in A on fol. 114a,
l. 8. The text of B ending on fol. 52a, last line, is continued without any
lacuna on fol. 68b, l. 1.   (۱٦) A وكانوا corr. above.

(۱) B اصحابه.   (۲) B om.   (۳) B حدثونى.   (٤) A adds in marg.
اصحابه.   (٥) B الصف.   (٦) A adds in marg. فى الصلاة.   (۷) B إما.
ان يعقب باصحابه   (۸) B ولا يضيقوا.   (۹) B يطلبون.   (۱۰) B فاذا.   (۱۱) A in marg.
(۱٥) B رحمهما   (۱٤) B بن   (۱۳) B بكثره.   (۱۲) B الوساوس.   (۱۳) الهفظات.
(۱٦) B الصلاة.

رفْع العتاب وعند (١)خشوع القلب فتْح الابواب وعند خضوع الاركان وجود الثواب ، فمن اتى بالصلاة بلا حضور القلب فهو (٢)مصلٍّ لاهٍ ومن اتاها بلا شهود العقل (٤) فهو مصلٍّ ساهٍ (٣) ومن اتاها بلا خشوع القلب فهو (٥)مصلٍّ خاطئ ومن اتاها بلا خضوع الاركان فهو (٦)مصلٍّ جافٍ ومن

٥ اتمّها فهو (٧)مصلٍّ وافٍ ، فهذا ما حضرنى فى الوقت من آدابهم فى الصلاة وبالله (٨)التوفيق ،

باب ذكر آدابهم فى الزكوات والصدقات ،

قال الشيخ رحمه الله تعالى امّا آدابهم فى الزكاة فان الله تعالى جدُّه لم يفرض عليهم الزكاة لأنه (٩) سبحانه قد زوى عنهم من اموال الدنيا ما يجب

١٠ عليهم فيه الزكاة والصدقة ، وقد حُكى عن مطرّف بن عبد الله بن الشخيّر رحمه الله انّه قال نعمة الله تعالى (١٠)[علىّ] فيما زوى عنّى من الدنيا اعظم من نعمة الله تعالى علىّ فيما اعطانى ، وكذلك اهل التصوّف نعمة الله تعالى عليهم فيما زوى عنهم من الدنيا (١٠)[اعظم من نعمته عليهم] فيما اعطاهم إن لو اعطاهم من الدنيا شيئًا كثيرًا ، وقد قال فى ذلك بعضهم وهو من

١٥ اهل الدنيا ،

وَمَا وَجَبَتْ عَلَىَّ زَكَاةُ مَالٍ * وَهَلْ تَجِبُ الزَّكَاةُ عَلَى كَرِيمِ ،

---

(١) B حضور النفس. ‫‬ (٢) مصلى لاهى AB. (٣) AB مصلى ساهى. (٤) B om. (٦) AB مصلى جافى. (٥) A مصلى. ‫‬ (٥) مصلٍّ خاطئ to ومن اتاها from (٧) AB مصلى. Here the text of B breaks off (fol. 69a, last line). The following words (fol. 69b, l. 1) مواضع من كتابه فقال occur in A fol. 32a, l. 7, near the beginning of the chapter entitled باب فى تخصيص الدعوة ووجه الاصطفآء. The portion of B corresponding to A fol. 69a, l. 12—fol. 95b, l. 8 is wanting. (٨) In marg. وهذا فصل بين كلام بعض المتقدمين. (٩) Suppl. above. (١٠) Suppl. in marg.

A f.69b يفتخر بذلك ويقول لم تجب علىّ زكاة قطّ يريد انه لم يترك حتى يجتمع عنده
مال يجب عليه فيه الزكاة، ويبلغنى عن ابرهيم بن شَيْبَان رحمه الله انه لقى
الشبلى رحمه الله وكان ابرهيم ينهى عن الذهاب اليه والوقوف عليه واستماع
كلامه فقال للشبلى رحمه الله وأراد (١)[بذلك] ان يمتحنه كم فى خَمْس من
٥ الابل قال شاةٌ فى واجب الامر وفيما يلزمنا نحن كلّها يعنى فيما ندّعيه من
مذهبنا فقال له ابرهيم ألَك فى هذا إمام قال نَعَمْ ابو بكر الصدّيق رضى
الله عنه حيث خرج من ماله كلّه فقال له النبّى صلع ما خلّفتَ لعيالك فقال
اللهَ ورسولَه فقام ولم ينه الناسَ بعد ذلك عنه، فأمّا آداب جماعة من
المتصوّفة فى الزكاة انّهم لا يأكلون منها ولا يطلبونها ولا يأخذونها وقد اباح
١٠ الله تعالى لهم أخذها وان أكلوا منها أكلوا حلالاً طيّبًا الاّ أنّهم يريدون بترك
ذلك ايثار الفقراء وترك المزاحمة للضعفاء وأهل الحاجات، ويقال ان
محمّد بن منصور صاحب ابى يعقوب السوسى رحمة الله عليهما كان اذا
اعطَوه شيئًا او حُمل اليه شىء من الزكاة والصدقة وكفّارة اليمين وعلم
انّها من هذه الجهات لم يأخذها ولم يفرّقها على اصحابه من الفقراء (٢) ويقول
١٥ (٣)شىء لا ارضاه لنفسى لا ارضاه لأصحابى واذا حُمل اليه ولم يعلم انّه من
الزكاة والصدقة اخذها وأكل منها، وإمّا الباقون فكانوا لا يرون الانبساط
فى مثل ذلك ولا يمدّون ايديهم الى الطمع وإلى السؤال وإلى ما يرون فيه
المنّة وان جاءَهم من غير مسئلة فكانوا يتعفّفون عن ذلك، ولقد بلغنى عن
بعض اخوانِنا من الصوفيّة انّه كان يُنفق على اخوانِه من الفقراء فقراء
٢٠ الصوفيّة فى كلّ سنة كما زعموا الف دينار وكان يحلف انّه ما انفق عليهم
ولا دفع اليهم درهمًا قطّ من زكاته وقد رأيتُه، وحكى عن ابى علىّ (٤)المُشتُولى
A f.70a انّه كان يُنفق على الصوفيّة ما يتعجّبون منه تُجّار مصر ويقولون (٥)مالنا لا
يفى بنفقته ويقال انّه لم تجب عليه زكاة قطّ، وسمعتُ بعض الاجلّة من مشايخ

---

(١) Suppl. in marg.   (٢) ويقال.   (٣) شيا.   (٤) المستولى.

(٥) In marg. اموالنا.

الصوفيّة وهو يقول [١][كان] يكون بينى وبين رجل من الاغنياء مودّة
مؤكّدة ويكون له فى قلبى محبّة وحرمة فيذكرنى عند إخراج زكاته وتفرقـة
صدقـته فيُذهب [٢][ذلك] جميع ما يكون له فى قلبى من المودّة، ورأيتُ
فى رقعة امام من الائمّة من المعروفين كَتَبَها الى رجل فقير من الصوفيّة
وكان فيها يا اخى قد انفذتُ اليك شيئًا ليس من الزكاة ولا من الصدقة
ولا لأحد غير الله تعالى عليك فيه منّةٌ فأسألك ان تُدخِل علىَّ السرور
بقبوله، فامّا ما جاءَهم من غير مسئلة [٣][ولا طمع] ولا استشراف نفس من
اقوام لا يعرفون [٤]الصوفيّة ولا يدّعون احوالهم ولا يداخلونهم بالمجانسة ولا
يعرفون اصولهم فلا ينبغى ان يُرَدّ ذلك للخبر الذى قال النبّى صلعم لعمر بن
الخطّاب رضى الله عنه ما آتاك الله من هذا المال من غير مسئلة ولا
استشراف نفس فخُذْه ولا تردّه فانّك هو ذا تردّه على الله عزّ وجلّ فاذا لم
يردّه وأخذه فهو بالخيار إن أكل منه أكل حلالاً طيّبًا وإن دفعه الى من
يعلم انّه احقّ بذلك منه فهو جميل، سمعتُ ابا بكر محمّد بن داود الدينورى
الدُّقّى رحمه الله يقول كان ابو بكر الفَرَغانى يُكتَب اسمه فى جملة من يأخذ
[٤]الجراية فى شهر رمضان من المساكين كان يأخذ كلّ ليلة الوظيفة ويحملها
الى امرأة عجوز فى جواره لم يكتبوا اسمها فى جملة من كان يأخذ الوظيفة
[١][من الجراية] التى [٢][كانت] تفرّق فى رمضان، وقال بعضهم من اخذ
من الله تعالى اخذ بعزّ ومن اخذ لغير الله تعالى اخذ بذلّ ومن ترك لله
عزّ وجلّ ترك بعزّ ومن ترك لغير الله تعالى ترك بذلّ فمن بنى [٥]أمرُه على
غير هذا فى الاخذ والاعطاء فهو على خطر عظيم والله تعالى يعلم المخطئ من
المصيب ولا يخفى على الله شىء، وتصديق من يأخذ لله ويعطى لله ويترك
لله هو ان يستوى عنده المنع والعطاء والشدّة [٦]والنعماء، وطبقـة اخرى A f.70b
[٧]اختاروا الزكوات والصدقات على الهدايا والهبات والايثار والمواساة فقالوا

(١) Suppl. in marg.   (٢) Suppl. above.   (٣) التصوف written above.   (٤) الجرايه.
(٥) اصله written above.   (٦) والرخا written above.   (٧) اخذوا but corr. above.

قد جعل الله تعالى للفقرآء حقًّا فى اموال الاغنيآء فاذا اخذْنا حقوقنا
التى جعل الله تعالى لنا فلا معنى لتركه وقالوا لا نختار على ما اختار الله
تعالى لنا ورسوله وقالوا الامتناع من اخذ الزكاة والصدقة ضربٌ من تعزُّز
النفوس وكراهية الفقر، وقد حُكى فى معنى ذلك عن ابى محمّد المُرْتَعِش

٥ انّه كان فى محفل من اصحابه من الاغنيآء والتُّجّار فنظر الى رجلٍ ومعه
خبزٌ يتصدّق به على المساكين والسوّال وقد ازدحموا عليه قال فقام المرتعش
من بين اصحابه وقصد هناك وأخذ من ذلك الخبز رغيفًا وجاءَ وجلس
فسُئِل عن فعله فقال خشيتُ ان لم أقُم وآخذ معهم من ذلك الخبز
أن يُمْحَى اسمى من ديوان الفقرآء، وقد رُوى عن النبىّ صلعم انّه قال لا

١٠ تحلّ الصدقة لغنىّ ولا لذى مِرّةٍ سوىّ، فالذى كره للمتصوّفة اخذ الزكاة
والصدقة (١)[كره] لذلك لان النبىّ صلعم قال ليس (٢)الغِنَى عن كثرة العَرَض
انّما الغنى غنى النفس او القلب، فهؤلآء وان كانوا فقرآء من أعراض
الدنيا فانّهم أغْنَى من الاغنيآء لانّ غِناهم بالله عزّ وجلّ، وقد حُكى فى
معنى ما قلنا ان علىّ بن سهل الاصبهانى قال حرام على من يدفع الى اصحابنا

١٥ شيئًا من اجل أنّهم فقرآء لانّهم اغنى خَلْقِ الله تعالى يعنى ان غناهم بالله
عزّ وجلّ، وقالوا يُحتمل ايضًا ان معنى قول النبىّ صلعم لا تحلّ الصدقة لغنىّ
ولا لذى مِرّة سوىّ أنّها كانت صدقةً (٣) بعينها مجعولة للزّمْنَى والمَرْضَى ومن
به عاهة لان قول الله تعالى (٤)إِنَّمَا الصَّدَقَاتُ لِلْفُقَرَآءِ وَالْمَسَاكِينِ لم يعلّق
عليها شرطَ غير النفير والفقير هو المُعْدِم فى الاصل به ثم بعد ذلك لـه

٨٤ف.٧١a اخلاق واحوال وتفاضل واسرار، ويقال ان اشتقاق (٥)الفقر من فَقار الظهر
مأخوذ والفِقار هو العظم الذى به قِوام الظهر فاذا انكسر وضعف واحتاج
الى غيره ممّا يقيمه سُمّى فقيرًا للضعف والحاجة الى ما يقيمه والله اعلم، ومن

---

(١) Suppl. in marg.   (٢) الغِنا.   (٣) معنيها. In marg.

(٤) Kor. 9, 60.   (٥) مأخوذ is suppl. in marg. after الفقر and مكرر is

written above it.

كره الصدقة من جهة ما قيل انها من اوساخ الناس فانما قيل ذلك على
معنى ان الصدقة تحطّ من اوزار الناس وخطاياهم للذين يتصدّقون (١)
بها ولو كان نقصًا للفقراء أخذُهم الصدقات والزكوات او وضعًا منهم من جهة أنها
اوساخ الناس لَزِمّ ذلك ايضًا (٢) للعاملين عليها (٢) [والمُؤَلَّفةِ قلوبُهم] والغارمين
وفى سبيل اله وابن السبيل، ومن ليس له شىء فى الدنيا وقد فاته فضل ٥
الصدقات التى ينصدّق بها من الاموال (٤) [فقد جعل اله له صدقات من
الاقوال] والافعال ممّا ليس فضلها بأقلّ من ذلك وهو ما رُوى عن النبىّ
صلعم انه قال مداراة الناس صدقةٌ (٢) [ومعاونتك لأخيك صدقةٌ]، ومن
الصدقة ان تَأتى اخاك بوجه طلق وأن تُفرغ من انآيك فى انآء اخيك
صدقةٌ، وقد حُكى عن بِشر بن الحُرث انه كان يقول يا اصحاب الحديث ١٠
أدّوا زكاة الحديث قيل وما زكاة الحديث قال اعملوا من كلّ مايتَى
(٤) [حديث] بخمسة احاديث يعنى من كلّ مايتى حديث تكتبونها وتحفظونها،
ومن وجب عليه الزكاة يحتاج الى اربعة اشياء حتى يكون مؤدّيًا للزكاة
اوّله ان يكون أخَذَ المال من حلال والثانى لا يكون جمعه للافتخار والتكثّر
والترفّع على من يكون دونه فى المال والثالث ان يبدأ بحسن الخُلق والسخاوة ١٥
مع الاهل والعيال والرابع مجانبة المنّ والاذى الى من يدفع اليه الزكاة،
والزكاة حقّ الفقراء قد جعله اله عزّ وجلّ فى مال الاغنياء فمن دفعها
اليهم فكأنّه قد ردّ اليهم مالهم وقد جمع بذلك رضا اله عزّ وجلّ والخلاص
من مناقشة الحساب والنجاة من اليم العذاب،

باب فى ذكر الصوم وآدابهم فيه،   ٢٠

A f.71b قال الشيخ رحمه اله رُوى عن النبىّ صلعم انه قال يقول اله تبارك
وتعالى الصوم لى وأنا أَجزى به فان قال قايلٌ ما معنى تخصيص الصوم

---

(١) به.   (٢) Cf. Kor. 9, 60.   (٣) Suppl. in marg.   (٤) Suppl. above.

11

من بين ساير العبادات وقد علمنا ان جميع الاعمال له وهو يجزى به فا
معنى قوله الصوم لى وانا اجزى به فيقال له معنيان احدهما ان (١)للصوم
تخصيص من بين ساير العبادات المفترضات لأن جميع المفترضات حركات
جوارح يتهيّاً للخلق ان ينظروا اليه الّا الصوم (٢)[فانّه عبادة بغير حركة
الجوارح فمن اجل ذلك قال تعالى الصوم] لى، والمعنى الآخر فى قوله لى
بعنى ان الصَّمَديّة لى لأن الصمد هو الذى لا جَوف له ولا يحتاج الى
الطعام والشراب (٢)[فمن تخلّق بأخلاق اجزبه ما لا يخطر على قلب بشر]،
وامّا معنى قوله وأنا اجزى به (٤)فانّ الله تعالى وعد على (٢)[جميع] فعل
الحسنات الثواب المعدود من الواحدة الى عشر أمثالها (٢)[من العشرة] الى
السبعماية الّا الصابين و(٢)[الصابون] هم الصابرون (٤)[وقد] قال الله عز
وجلّ (٥)إِنَّمَا يُوَفَّى ٱلصَّابِرُونَ أَجْرَهُمْ بِغَيْرِ حِسَابٍ، (٦)فخرج الصومُ من
الحسنات المعدودة وثوابها لان الصوم هو صبر النفس عن مألوفاتها وإمساك
الجوارح عن جميع (٧)شهواتها والصابون هم الصابرون، وقد رُوى فى معنى
ذلك عن النبىّ صلعم انه قال اذا صمتَ فلْيَصُمْ سمعك وبصرك ولسانك
وبدك، وقد رُوى عنه صلعم انه قال اذا صام احدكم فلا يرفث ولا يفسق
فان شتمه انسان فليقُلْ إنّى صائمٌ، وصحّة الصوم وحسن ادب الصائم فى
صومه صحّةُ مقاصد ومباينةُ شهوانه وحفظُ جوارحه وصفاء مطعمه ورعايةُ قلبه
ودوامُ ذكره وقلّةُ اهتمامه بالمضمون من رزقه وقلّةُ ملاحظته لصومه ووجله
من تقصيره والاستعانةُ باله (٤)[تعالى] على تأديته فذلك ادب الصائم فى
صومه، وحكى عن سهل بن عبد الله التُّستَرى رحمه الله انه انه كان يأكل فى
(٢)[كلّ] خمسة عشر يومًا مرّةً فاذا دخل رمضان لم يأكل فيها الّا آكلةً
واحدةً، فسألتُ بعض المشايخ عن ذلك فقال كان (٨)يُفطر على المآء القراح

---

(١) الصوم.   (٢) Suppl. in marg.   (٣) لان.   (٤) Suppl. above.

(٥) Kor. 39, 13.   (٦) In marg. وليس as a variant.   (٧) مألوفاتها corr.

in marg.   (٨) كل ليلة added in marg.

A f. 72a وَحْدَهُ كُلَّ ليلة ، وحكى عن ابى عُبَيد البُسْرى رحمه الله انه كان اذا دخل
رمضان دخل البيت وسدّ عليه الباب ويقول لامرأته اطرحى كلّ ليلة رغيفًا
من كوّة (١)[فى] البيت ولا يخرج منه حتى يخرج رمضان فتدخل امرأتـه
البيت فاذا (٢)الثلثون (٢) رغيفًا موضوع فى ناحية البيت، وامّا صوم التطوع

٥ فانّ جماعةً من المشايخ كانوا يصومون فى السفر والحضر على الدوام الى ان
لحقوا باللـه عزّ وجلّ وكان ادبهم فى صومهم ما رُوى عن النبى صلعم انـه
قال الصوم جُنّة ولم يقل جُنّة من اىّ شىء فقالوا معناه ان الصوم جُنّة فى
الآخرة من النار لأن الصوم (١)[للصائم] فى الدنيا جُنّة من سهام الاعداءٔ
الذين يدعونهم الى النار (٤) وهم الشيطان والنفس والهوى (١)[والدنيا]

١٠ والشهوات، ومن اختار المداومة على الصيام اختار ذلك للاحتراز بالجُنّة
من مكايد الاعداءٔ لكيلا يجدوا فرصةً فيظفروا (٥) به (٦)[ويطرحوه فى النار]،
سمعتُ احمد بن محمّد بن سُنَيد قاضى الدينور يقول سمعت (٧)رُوَيمًا يقول
اجتزتُ فى الهاجرة ببعض سِكك بغداد فعطشت فتقدّمت الى بـاب دار
فاستسقيت فاذا بجارية وقد (١)[فتحت باب الدار وخرجت] ومعها كوز جديد

١٥ ملآن من الماءٔ المبرَّد فلمّا اردت ان اتناول من يدها قالت (١)[الى وَيْحُك]
صوفىٌّ يشرب بالنهار وضربتْ بالكوز على الارض وانصرفتْ قال رُوَيم فلقد
استحييت منها ونذرت ان لا أُفطر ابدًا، (١)[قال صاحب الكتاب] وجماعة
اخرى كانوا يختارون صوم داود عليه السلم لِما رُوى عن ذلك عن النبى
صلعم انه قال افضل الصيام صيام اخى داود عليه السلم كان يصوم يومًا

٢٠ ويُفطر يومًا، وقد قالوا فى معنى قوله افضل الصيام لأنّه اشدّ الصيام وزعموا
ان هذا الصوم اشدّ على النفس من صوم الدهر (١)[لأن النفس اذا الفت
الصوم مع الدوام وتعوّدت عليها الافطار واذا الفت الافطار وتعوّدت
اشتدّ عليها الصوم] وهذا الصوم صوم يوم وافطار يوم لا تتعوّد فيه النفس

الافطار ولا الصوم فلذلك قال من قال انه اشدّ الصيام، وقد حُكى فى
[معنى] ذلك عن سهل بن عبد الله رحمه الله انه كان يقول اذا شبعتم A f. 72b
فاطلبوا الجوع ممّن ابلاكم بالشبع واذا جُعتم فاطلبوا الشبع ممّن ابلاكم
بالجوع ولاّ تماديم وطغيتم، وكان ابو عبد الله احمد بن جابان رحمه الله
قد صام نيف وخمسين سنةً لا يُفطر فى النفر ولا فى الحضر وجَهِدَ بـ ٥
اصحابه يومًا ان يُفطر فأفطر فاعتلّ من ذلك ايّامًا [من الايّام] حتى كاد
ان يفوته الفرض، ومن كره المداومة على الصيام كره ذلك لانّ النفس
معتادة [فاذا] الفت شيئًا واعتادته يكون قيامها فيه بحظوظها لا بحقوقها
فالادب فى ذلك ان لا يُجْمَعَ بينها وبين مألوفاتها وإن كانت عبادةً او طاعةً
لانّ النفس مايلة الى الحظوظ عاجزة عن الحقوق مجبولة على المنافرة من ١٠
الطاعات فاذا الفت بابًا من ابواب العبادات اتهمها اهل المعرفة بها وأهل
الخبرة والبصيرة بها وبكايدها وخَدَعها، وحُكى عن ابرهيم بن ادم رحمه
اله انه قال كان بصحبتى رجلٌ كثيرُ الصوم والصلاة فعجبتُ من ذلك ثم
نظرت فى مأكوله فكان من موضع غير طيّب قال فأمرته بالخروج من مِلْكه
وأخرجته معى فى سفر فكنت أطعمه الحلال من موضع اعرفه وأرضاه قال ١٥
فلمّا صحبنى مدّةً كبت احتاج ان اضربه بالدرّة حتى يقوم فيؤدّى الفرض،
فامّا الصوفية والفقرآء المجرّدون الذين قطعوا العلايق وتركوا المعلومات
وقنعوا بما قسم اله تعالى لهم من الارزاق ولا يدرون ايّ وقت يسوق اله
تعالى اليهم ارزاقهم من الغيب وعلى يد من يبعث اله تعالى لهم ذلك
فأوقات هؤلاء اتمّ من اوقات الصائم الذى يرجع الى معلوم ومعهود من ٢٠
الطعام المستعدّ لإفطاره فان صاموا فلا يلحقهم احد من الصايمين فى الفضل،
وهؤلاء الفقرآء الذين [قد] ذكرتهم ايضًا آداب فى صومهم ان صاموا
فمن آدابهم أن لا يصوم واحد من بين الجماعة الّا بإذن اصحابه لانّه اذا   A f. 73a

---

(١) Suppl. in marg.   (٢) و تعودت شيئًا added in marg.   (٣) مواضع.

(٤) المجردين.   (٥) القوم added in marg.   (٦) Suppl. above.

صام شغل قلوبَ اصحابه بإفطاره وهم على غير معلوم وان صام واحد من
دون الجماعة برضا اصحابه وحضر المفطرين شىءٌ من الطعام فليس يلزمهم
ان ينتظروا وقت افطار الصائم لانّه ربّما يكون فى الجماعة من يكون به
حاجة الى الطعام وربّما يُقبّح به فى وقت افطار الصائم منهم شىءٌ آخر
٥ بتَرْكه صومَهُ الّا أن يكون ضعيفًا (١) فينتظرون وقت افطاره لضعفه او يكون
شيئًا فلحرمته وليس للصائم ايضًا ان يأخذ نصيبًا لنفسه ويدّخرها لوقت
افطاره لانّ ذلك ضعف فى حاله الّا أن يكون ضعيفًا فيفعل ذلك لضعفه ،
وإذا كانوا جماعةً عادتُهم الصوم وفيهم جماعةٌ عادتُهم الافطار فليس للصُوّام
ان يدعوا هؤلّاء المفطرين الى احوالهم الّا أن احبّوا هؤلّاء مساعدتهم على
١٠ الصوم ومساعدةُ الصائم للمفطر على الافطار احسنُ من مساعدة المفطر للصائم
بالصوم الى ان تقع الصحبة فاذا وقعت الصحبة فمساعدة المفطر للصائم بالصيام
معهم احسن ، حُكى عن الجُنيد رحمه الله انه كان يصوم على الدوام فاذا
دخل عليه اخوانه افطر معهم ويقول ليس فضل المساعدة مع الاخوان بأقلّ
من فضل الصوم للصائم (٢)[اذا كان متطوّعًا] او كلامًا نحو هذا ، ويقال
١٥ اذا رأيتَ الصوفى يصوم صوم التطوّع فاتّهمهُ فانه قد اجتمع معه شىءٌ من
الدنيا، وإن كانوا جماعةً مترافقين متواخين (٤)اشكالًا وبينهم مُريدٌ يجنّوه
على الصيام فان لم يساعدوه يهتمّوا لافطاره ويتكلّفوا له رفقًا ولا يحملون
حاله على احوالهم وإن كانوا جماعةً ومعهم شيخٌ يصومون بصومه ويفطرون
بإفطاره الّا أن يأمرهم الشيخ بغير ذلك فانّهم لا يخالفون امره لانّ الشيخ يعلم
٢٠ ما يصلح لهم، وحُكى عن بعض المشايخ الاجلّة انه قال صمت كذى وكذى
سنةً لغير الله وذلك ان شابًّا كان يصحبه يصوم فكان يصوم حتى ينظر اليه ذلك
الشابّ فيتأدّب به ويصوم بصيامه، ورأيتُ ابا الحسن المكّى بالبصرة رحمه
الله فكان يصوم الدَّهْرَ ولا يأكل الخُبْزَ الّا كلّ ليلة جُمْعة وكان قوته كما ‏A f. 73b

(١) The last two letters are suppl. above.   (٢) Suppl. in marg.

(٤) اشكال.

قبل فى كلّ شهر اربعة دوانيق يعمل بيده يفتل حبال الليف ويبيعها وكان
قد هجره ابن سالم وكان يقول لا اسلّم عليه الّا ان يُفطر ويأكل [الخبز] [١]
لانّه كان قد اشتهر بترك الأكل، ويبلغنى عن بعضهم من اهل واسط انه
صام سنين كثيرةً فكان يفطر كلّ يوم قبل غروب الشمس الّا فى رمضان
وقومٌ انكروا [عليه] [٢] هذا لمخالفته العلم وان كان الصوم نطوّعًا وقومٌ كانوا
يستحسنون ذلك لانّ صاحبه كان يريد بذلك ان يؤدّب نفسه بالجوع ولا
يتمتّع برؤية الصوم ورؤية الثواب الذى قد وعد الله تعالى للصائمين ولا
يسكن الى ذلك وعندى ان الذى انكر فقد اصاب لانّه اعتقد الصوم فقد
لزمه الوفاَّء به وان لم يعتقد الصوم فسبيله سبيل المتفلّين [٣] فلا يقال له
صائمٌ وبالله التوفيق، وحُكى عن الشبلى رحمه الله انه قال لرجل تُحسنُ
[ان] [٢] نصوم الأَبَد قال فكيف الابد قال تجعل ما بقى من عُمُرك يومًا
ونصومه، فهذا ما حضرنى فى الوقت من آداب صوم المتصوّفة [واله [١]
الموقّق للصواب]،

باب ذكر آدابهم فى الحجِّ،

قال الشيخ رحمه الله فاوّل آدابهم فى الحجّ الاهتمام لحجّة الاسلام والتوجه
اليه باىّ وجه يجد اليه السبيل والاستطاعة ويبذل فى ذلك مُهجته ولا
يركن الى سعة العلم وطلب الرخصة فى الجلوس عن حجّة الاسلام بإعدام
الزاد والراحلة الّا ان يُقعده عن ذلك فرضٌ لازم لانّ الله عزّ وجلّ يقول
وَلله عَلَى ٱلنَّاسِ حَجُّ ٱلْبَيْتِ مَنِ ٱسْتَطَاعَ إِلَيْهِ سَبِيلاً [٤] وقال وَأَذِّن فِى [٥]
ٱلنَّاسِ بِٱلْحَجِّ يَأْتُوكَ رِجَالاً وقال فى التفسير [٦] رِجَالاً وَعَلَى كُلِّ ضَامِرٍ
يَأْتِينَ مِنْ كُلِّ فَجٍّ عَمِيقٍ فبدأ بذكر الرجال الذين يمشون، ورُوى عن

---

(١) Suppl. in marg.   (٢) Suppl. above.   (٣) In marg. المتعللين as

variant.   (٤) Kor. 3, 91.   (٥) Kor. 22, 28.   (٦) ثم قال added in marg.

النبىّ صلعم انه قال من مات ولم يحجّ حجّة الاسلام مات ان شآء يهوديًّا او
نصرانيًّا، فمن اجل ذلك لم يسقط عنهم مطالبة الحجّ وان عدموا الزاد
والراحلة لانّ من آدابهم أن يتمسّكوا بالأحْوَط فى الفرايض ويأخذوا بالاتّمّ
من علم الشريعة لانّ التعلّق بالرُّخَص سبيل العامّة والأخْذ بالسعة والتأويلات
حال الضعفآء، وذلك رحمة من الله تعالى لهم، فامّا العامّة فقصْدُهم الى الحجّ
وشَرْطِ العلم الذى يعلمه الفقهآء، والعلمآء والخاصّة والعامّة فى ذلك سوآء
وهو عِلْمُ المناسك فرايضه وسُنَنه وأحكامه وحُدوده، وإنّما قصدُنا ان نذكر
آداب من لبس سبيلهم فى الحجّ سبيل العامّة وهم على ثلثة اصناف، فصِنفٌ
منهم اذا حجّوا حجّة الاسلام جلسوا وإشتغلوا بحفظ اوقاتهم ومراعاة احوالهم
فطلبوا السلامة ولم يتعرّضوا للبلآء (١)ممّا يلحقهم من المشقّة فى ذلك ولصعوبة
اداء فرض الحجّ وقضاء مناسكهِ وحفظ حدودها، سمعتُ ابن سالم يقول
لم يحجّ سهل بن عبد الله الّا حجّة الاسلام حجّ وله ستّة عشر سنةً وكان
زادُه شيًا من الكبد المشوىّ المدقوق فكان يستفّ منه اذا جاع قليلاً،
وكذلك ابو يزيد البسطاىّ رحمه الله لم يحجّ الّا حجّة الاسلام وكذلك الجُنَيْد
رحمه الله وجماعة من المشايخ الاجلّة رحمهم الله لم يحجّوا الّا حجّة الاسلام
وحجّتهم فى اختيارهم فى ذلك ان النبىّ صلعم لم يحجّ الّا حجّةً واحدةً، وطبقة
اخرى من مشايخ الصوفية فانهم لما قطعوا العلايق وفارقوا الاوطان وهجروا
الاخوان قصدوا بيت الله الحرام وزيارة قبر رسوله عليهـ السلّم فقطعوا
(٢)البوادى والبرارى والقفار بغير حمْل نفقةٍ ولا زاد ولا (٣)سلكوا على الطريق
ولا تعلّقوا بمصاحبة الرفيق ولا (٤)عدّوا الأميال ولا البُرُدَ ولا طلبوا المنازل
ولا المناهل ولا تعرّجوا على سبب ولا التجوا الى طلب ولا انقضى من الحجّ
وَطَرُهم ولا انقطع عن تلك المَشاهد أثَرُهم وذلك لانّ الله عزّ وجلّ يقول

---

(١) The orig. reading seems to have been فى.   (٢) ودخلوا added in
marg.   (٣) سلكوا على erased, and سلكوا عن suppl. in marg.   (٤)
يعدوا.

وقولهُ الحقّ (١) وَإِذْ جَعَلْنَا ٱلْبَيْتَ مَثَابَةً لِلنَّاسِ وَأَمْنًا قال ابن عبّاس رضى
الله عنه يعنى لا يقضون منه وطرًا، ولا (٢) يُمكن ذكر آداب هؤلاء فى
معانيهم الّا بحكايات بلغنا عنهم يدلّ ذلك على آدابهم وصحّة مقاصدهم وعلوّ
مراتبهم وصفائهم، سمعتُ احمد بن علىّ الوجيهى يقول سمعت بعض
المشايخ يقول حجّ حسن القزّاز الدينورى رحم الله (٢) اثنى عشر حجّةً (٤) حافيًا
مكشوف الرأس فكان اذا دخل فى رجله شوك يمسح رجله بالارض ويمشى
ولا يطأطئ رأسه الى الارض من صحّة توكّله، وحكى عن ابى تُراب النخشبى
رحمه الله انه كان يأكل آكلةً بالبصرة وأكلةً (٥) بِنباج وأكلةً بالمدينة وكان
يدخل مكّة وعلى بطنه عُكَنٌ من السمن، وحكى عن ابرهيم بن شَيْبان انه
قال كان ابو عبد الله المغربى رحمه الله يدخل البادية وعليه ازار ورداء
ابيض وفى رجله نعلٌ طاقٌ كأنّه يمشى فى السوق فاذا دخل مكّة وفرغ من
الحجّ احرم من تحت الميزاب ويخرج من مكّة وهو مُحْرِمٌ ويقيم على إحرامه
الى ان يرجع الى مكّة، وسمعتُ جعفر الخُلْدى رحمه الله يقول سلكتُ البادية
وعلىّ قميص ابيض وبيدى كوز ورأيت فى (٦) البطانية التى فى وسط الرمل
دكاكين (٧) وتُجّارًا (٨) [كانت] تَرِدُ عليهم القوافل من البصرة، وحكى عن
ابرهيم الخوّاص رحمه الله انه قال اعرفُ فى البادية تسعة عشر طريقًا غير
الطريق الذى يسلكه الناس والقوافل (٩) طريقان (٨) [منها] (١٠) فيهما ينبت
الذهب والفضّة، وحكى جعفر عن ابرهيم الخوّاص رحمهما الله انه قال كنت
فى البادية فى موضع منها (١١) جالسًا مستجمع الهمّ وقد مضت علىّ اوقات لم
اتناول فيها الطعام فيما انا كذلك اذا (١٢) [انا] بالخَضِر عليه السلم مارًّا
فى الهواء فلمّا رأيته طأطأتُ رأسى وغمضتُ بصرى ولم انظر اليه فلمّا رآنى
(١٢) جاء فجلس الى جنبى فرفعتُ رأسى فقال لى يا ابرهيم لو (١٤) اعرنى الطرف

(١) Kor. 2, 119.   (٢) In marg. بهما as variant.   (٢) اثنا.   (٤) حافى.

(٥) بيُناج.   (٦) البطانيه.   (٧) وتجار,   (٨) Suppl. in marg.   (٩) طريقين.

(١٠) فيها.   (١١) جالس.   (١٢) Suppl. above.   (١٢) added عليه السلام.

ما جئتُ اليك، وحُكِىَ عن ابرهيم رحمه الله ايضًا انه قال خرجت فى بعض
السنين من مكّة واعتقدت ان لا اتناول شيئًا الى ان ادخل القادسيّة فلمّا
وافيت (١)الرَّبَذة وخرجتُ منها فاذا انا بأعرابىّ (٢)[يصيح] من ورائى فلم
اعطف عليه فلحقنى واذا بيده سيف مسلول وبيده الآخر قعبٌ فيه لبن فقال ٨ f. 75a
لى اشربْ هذا والّا ضربتُ رقبتك قال فبقيت (٢)[متحيّرًا] فتناولت منه ٥
وشربت وانصرف عنّى وما رأيت شيئًا آخر حتى دخلتُ (٤)القادسيّة،
وحكايات هؤلآء اكثرُ من ان يتهيّأ ذكرها (٢)[هاهنا] وفيما ذكرنا كفاية لمن
علم المراد من ذلك ان شآء الله تعالى، و(٤)[امّا] الطبقة الثالثة من المشايخ
الصوفية فانهم اختاروا الـمُقام بمكّة والمجاورة بها وحبسوا انفسهم هناك لِما
خصّ الله تعالى به (٥)تلك البقاع والمشاهد (٦)من الفضيلة والشرف ولِما ١٠
وجدوا فى انفسهم من التنافر والعجز عن المقام بها لانها (٧)وادٍ غير ذى زرع
كما قال الله جلّ وعزّ وهو الحجاز (٨)يعجز عن الشهوات واللذّات ولا سيّما
لمن كان قوته فى الغيب ورزقه مقسوم ورفقه معدوم والنفس مجبولة على
الاضطراب عند عدم الوفآء بها والعبد مُطالَبٌ بالسكون تحت الأحكام فعند
ذلك تُبين مقامات الرجال، ولهم فى المجاورة آداب يُذكر بعضها فى حكاياتهم ١٥
فيما بلغنى، سمعتُ ابا بكر محمّد بن داود (٢)[الدينورى] الدُّقّى يقول اقام ابو
عبد الله بن الجلّآء بمكّة ثمانية عشر سنة لم يأكل من طعام يُحمل اليها من
مصر لانّ مصر (٩)صَوافٍ (١٠)كان المتقدّمون يتورّعون عن أكْل طعامِها

---

in marg.   (١٤) The text has لو أَعَرَّتْنى الطَّرَفَ (vocalised by a later hand).
The story is told in the *Tadh. al-Awliyá*, II, 149, 9 foll., where the Persian
rendering is اگر در من نكرستى, «if you had looked at me».

(١) الربذه.   (٢) Suppl. in marg.   (٢) Suppl. above.   (٤) Here is
added in marg. a passage beginning قال الخوّاص رأيتُ شيخًا من اهل المعرفة and
ending والوقت كلّه حقيقة او كما قال قرب لهم شربة من مآء ولم آكل which occurs
in the text on p. ١٧٢, l. ١٢ (A fol. 77a, l. 8).   (٥) في erased before تلك.
(٦) Orig. بالفضيلة but corr.   (٧) وادى.   (٨) ميحر.   (٩) صوافى.
(١٠) corr. in marg. فانها يتورعون المتقدمون

وما يُحمل منها وكان لا يشرب الّا ماءَ زمزم يستقى بركوته وحبله من اجْل
أن الدلو والحبل المعلّق على زمزم (١) يكون من اموال السلاطين، وحُكى
عن ابى بكر الكتّانى رحمه الله انه ختم (٢) اثنى عشر الف ختمة فى الطواف،
وأقام ابو عمرو الزجّاجى رحمه الله بمكّة على ما بلغنى ثلثين سنة فاذا اراد
٥ ان يقضى حاجته خرج عن الحرم ويعتمر فى كلّ يوم ثلث عُمَر ويأكل فى
كلّ ثلثة ايّام اكْلة ومات عن نيف وسبعين وقفةً، وسمعت الدُّقّى يقول
اقمتُ بمكّة تسع سنين وكنت اعتقدت ان لا اصلّى صلاتَين فى موضع واحد
فكان (٤) يَمُرّ بى من الجوع ما اذا رأيت جنازةً اقول ليتنى كنت مكان هذا
الميّت قال وكان يقع فى قلبى فى الوقت يا هذا الست هذه الفاقة التى بك
١٠ لا يعلم بها احد غير الله (٤) فكنت اشتغل بذلك ويذهب عنّى ما أجدُ من
الجوع، ويقال ان كلّ من يقدر ان يصبر بمكّة على الجوع (٥) يومًا وليلةً فهو
يقدر ان يصبر فى ساير الدنيا ثلثة ايّام، وكانوا يقولون ان المُقام بمكّة
يغيّر الاخلاق ويكشف الاسرار ولا يصبر على المُقام بها على الصحّة الّا
الرجال، سمعت احمد الطَّرَسوسى يقول سمعت ابرهيم بن شَيبان بقول سمعت
١٥ ابرهيم الخوّاص رحمه الله يقول اقام هاهنا بمكّة فتى من الفقراءِ سنين فكنّا
نتعجّب من حسن جلسته وكثرة طوافه وعُمَره وصيانة فقره قال فجعلت فى
نفسى ان احمل اليه شيئًا من الدراهم حتى اداخله بذلك قال فحملت اليه
دراهم كثيرة وصببت على طرف خِرْقته قال فنظر الىّ ثم اخذ الخرقة وصبّ
الدراهم على الارض وخرج من المسجد فما رأيت قطّ اعزّ منه حين صبّها
٢٠ وأعرض عنها ولا اذلّ منّى حين جلستُ اجمعُها وألتقطُها من بين الحصا،
فأمّا الطبقة الذين سافروا اليها وألفوا ما يلحقهم من البلاَءِ فى القصد اليها
فلمعنيَين احدها ان النبىّ صلعم قال لا تشدّ الرحال الّا الى ثلثة مساجد
مسجد الحرام ومسجدى هذا ومسجد ايلياءَ، والمعنى الآخر هو ان النفس تدّعى

احوالاً فى الوطن وفى وسط المعارف والمألوفات من التوكّل والرضا والسكون
والتسليم والتفويض فاذا (١)فارقت الوطن والمعارف تغيّر اخلاقها ويبطل
دعواها، ويقال سُمّى السفر سفرًا لانّه يُسفر عن اخلاق الرجال، فاذا
عرفوها وعلموا عجزها وضعفها وشرها وعاينوا المكمنات التى فى انفسهم عملوا
فى تبديل هذه الاخلاق ومخالفتها ولم يغترّوا بدعاويها ولم يأمنوا خُدَعها
وشرها، وبلغنى ان جماعةً اقاموا بمكّة (٢)فكانوا اذا قام احدهم الى الطواف
بالنهار يعيبون عليه ذلك ويقولون هو ذى تمرّ وتستعدى وذلك انه ربّما

A f. 76a

يتّفق فى الطواف من يكون يُرفق الفقراء ويعطيهم شيئًا فكانوا ينتقدون
بعضهم على بعض هذه الاحوال، ومن آدابهم ايضًا انهم اذا اعتقدوا ان
يحجّوا ان يوفوا بعهودهم وإن احرموا من دون الميقات فى غير اشهر الحجّ
ان يوفوا بذلك وإن تلفت فى ذلك نفوسهم، وإذا قصدوا نحو الكعبة لم
يعدلوا عن الطريق بعد ما توجّهوا اليها ولا يقطعهم عن التوجّه اليها قلّة
النفقة ولا شدّة الحرّ والبرد، سمعتُ احمد بن دلويه يقول كنت قد اوجبت
على نفسى الرجوع الى مكّة من الشأم وكان البرد شديدًا فتأوّلتُ نفسى
فسألتُ ابا عمران الطبرستانى عن الرخصة فى ذلك وإستعمال العلم فقال
لى اذا خفتَ عليه (٣)فألقِه فى (٤)البحر (٥)فوقفتُ على اشارته فخرجتُ فما رأيت
الاّ كلّ خير وحججت، ومن آدابهم ايضًا انهم اذا دخلوا البادية ان يُموّا
الفرائض ولا يقصرون الصلاة (٦)[ولا ينيّمون] ولا يتركون شيئًا ممّا كانوا
يعملون فى اوطانهم ما اطاقوا ذلك وإن اباح لهم العلم تَرْكَ ذلك لانّ السفر
والحضر عندهم سواءٌ وليس لأسفارهم مدّة معلومة ولا يمشون بالأميال والبُرُد
والمنازل فاذا (٧)اقاموا الحقّ (٨)قاموا وإذا سار بهم ساروا وإذا نزل بهم نزلوا
فاذا بلغوا الميقات غسلوا ابدانهم بالماء وغسلوا قلوبهم بالتوبة وإذا نزعوا

---

(١) فارق. (٢) فكان. (٣) فالقيه. (٤) البحر erased and suppl.
in marg. (٥) In marg. فهمت as variant. (٦) Suppl. in marg.
(٧) اقامتهم الحقيقة corr. in marg. (٨) اقاموا.

ثيابهم للإحرام وتجرّدوا وحلّوا العُقَد [واتّزروا] وارتدَوْا فكذلك نزعوا
عن اسرارهم الغلّ والحسد وحلّوا عن قلوبهم عُقَد الهوى ومحبّة الدنيا ولم
يعودوا الى ما خرجوا منه من ذلك، ومن آدابهم ايضًا انهم اذا قالوا
لبّيك اللهمّ لبّيك لبّيك لا شريك لك أن لا يجيبوا بعد ذلك دواعى
النفس والشيطان والهوى بعد ما اجابوا الحقّ بالتلبية واقرّوا انه لا شريك
له فى مُلكه فاذا نظروا الى البيت بأعْيُن رُؤسهم نظروا بأعْيُن قلوبهم الى
من دعاهم الى البيت فاذا طافوا حول البيت بأبدانهم فمن آدابهم ان
يذكروا قول الله عزّ وجلّ وَتَرَى ٱلْمَلَآئِكَةَ حَآفِّينَ مِنْ حَوْلِ ٱلْعَرْشِ فكأنّهم
ينظرون الى طوافهم فاذا صلّوا خَلْفَ المَقام يعلمون انه مقام عبدٍ قد وفى لله
تعالى بعهده فندب الله الاوّلين والآخرين الى متابعة قدمه واتّخاذ صلوتهم
خَلْفَ مقامه فاذا استلموا الحَجَر وقبّلوه علموا انهم هو ذا يبايعون الله تعالى
بأيْمانهم فمن الادب ان لا يمُدّوا بعد ذلك أيمانهم الى مراد وشهوة فاذا
جآءوا الى الصفا فمن الادب ان لا يعترض بعد ذلك كدورة لصفآء
قلوبهم فاذا هرْوَلوا بين الصفا والمروة وأسرعوا فى مشيهم فمن الادب ان
يسرعوا بالفرار من عدوّهم ويهربوا من متابعة نفوسهم وهوامّ وشيطانهم
واذا وافوا الى مِنّى فمن آدابهم ان يتأهّبوا للقآء فلعلّهم يصلوا
الى مُناهم فاذا وافوا الى عَرَفات فأدبهم ان يتعرّفوا الى معروفهم ويذكروا
نشرهم وحشْرهم وبعْثهم من قبورهم فاذا وقفوا فأدبُ الوقوف ان يكون وقوفهم
بين يدى سيّدهم فاذا وقفوا لا يعرضوا عنه بعد وقوفهم فاذا دفعوا مع
الإمام الى المُزْدَلفة فأدبهم ان يكون فى قلوبهم العظمة والإجلال لله تعالى
فاذا دفعوا مع إمامهم جعلوا الدنيا والآخرة ورآء ظهورهم فاذا كسروا
الحجارة للرَّمْى كسروا مع الحجارة ارادات بواطنهم وشهوات اسرارهم ومكنات

(١) Suppl. in marg.　(٢) In marg. فمن الادب ان ينظروا.
written above.　(٤) الادب written above.　(٥) Kor. 39, 75.　(٦) Orig.
ومن but corr.　(٧) صعدوا in marg.　(٨) وهربوا.　(٩) منا.　(٢) الكعبة.

هوآيهم فاذا ذكروا الله تعالى عند المشعر الحرام فالادب عند ذلك ان
يكون مصحوبهم تعظيم مشاعرهم وتشريف مشاهدهم وإعظام حرماتهـا فاذا
رموا الجمر رموا بحسن الادب بملاحظة اعلامهم ومشاهدة افعالهم فاذا حلقوا
رءوسهم فأدبُهم ان يحلقوا عن بواطنهم حُبّ الثناءِ والحمنة مع حلق رءوسهم
فاذا ذبحوا فأدبُهم فى الذبح ان يبدءوا بذبح نفوسهم فى نفوسهم قبل ذبح
ذبيحتهم فاذا رجعوا الى طواف الزيارة وتعلّقوا بأستار الكعبة فمن الادب
ان لا يتعلّقوا بغيره ولا يلوذوا بأحد من خلفه بعد اللياذة والتعلّق به فاذا
رجعوا الى ^(١) مِنّى وإقاموا بها ايّام النشريق وحلّ لهم كلّ شىءٍ فمن الادب
ان لا يحلّلوا ما حرّموا على نفوسهم من مخالفة سيّدهم ومتابعة حظوظهم ولا
يكدّروا ما صفا من اوقاتهم ولا يتّكلوا الّا على سعة رحمة الله تعالى بعد
قضاءِ مناسكه لانّهم ^(٢) لم يتيقنوا بقبول حجّتهم ويستعينوا بالله على امورهم
ويستغيثوا الى الله بأسرارهم وعلانيتهم فانه قادر على كشف ضرّهم وخلاصهم،
^(٣) وحكى عن ابرهيم الخوّاص رحمه الله انه قال رأيتُ شيخًا من اهل المعرفة
فى البادية ممّن كان يشير الى التوكّل عرّج على سبب بعد سبعة عشر يومًا
فنهاه شيخ آخر فلم يقبل فهجروه ولم يعدّوه منهم، وسمعتُ الدُّقّى يقول دخلتُ
مصر فقصدت الزقّاق فسلّمت عليه فقال لى من اين اقبلتَ فقلت من
الحجاز فقال لى خُذْ حكايةً فى الحجاز رِهْتُ فى تيه بنى اسرآئيل سبعة عشر
يومًا لم آكل ولم اشرب فرأيت من بعيد ^(٤) خيالاً فطمعتْ نفسى فلمّا دنوت
فاذا انا بعسكر مع امير لهم مارّين الى قلزم فلمّا رأيت ^(٥)[انهم] من الجُند
آيستُ نفسى منهم فعرضوا علىّ الطعام فلم آكل والماءَ فلم اشرب فقال لى
اميرهم انت فى حالٍ تحلّ لك الميّتة فلمَ تمتنع من طعامنا فقلت نحن اذا
كنّا بين الناس بشرط العلم لا نرضى لأنفسنا ان ننبسط اليكم فكيف ننبسط

---

^(١) مِنا.   ^(٢) In marg. ما وثقوا.   ^(٣) The passage beginning حكى and ending
والوقت كلّه حقيقة او كما قال also occurs on the marg. of A fol. 75a. See note
٤ on p. ١٦٩.   ^(٤) The marginal version has خيال الناس.   ^(٥) Om. in text.

اليكم فى (١)[مثل] هذا الوقت والوقت كلّه حقيقة او كما (٢)قال، وحُكى انه
سُئل عن عينه (٣)وكانت احدى عينيه قد (٤)ذهبت فقال كنت تهت فى
التيه كذى وكذى يومًا فكان علىّ مِسْحٌ فهاجت عينى فكنت امسحه بالمسح
فسالتْ، وهو ان شاء الله فى هذه السَّفْرَة التى حكاها من امير الجند، (٥)وهاتان
الحكايتان وحكاية ابرهيم الخوّاص وحكاية الدُّقّى عن ابى بكر الزقّاق،   A f.77b

باب فى ذكر (١)[آداب] القرآء بعضهم مع بعض وأحكامهم
فى الحضر والسفر،

قال الشيخ رحمه الله تعالى (١)[قال الجُنَيْد رحمه الله] الفقر بحر البلاء
وبلاؤه كلّه (٢)عزّ، وقال الجُنَيْد رحمه الله تعالى علم الفقير اذا قوى (٧)ضعفت
محبّته واذا ضعف قوبت قوبتْ محبّته وحُكْم الفقير (٨)أن يكون فوق محبّته، سمعت
الدُّقّى رحمه الله تعالى بدمشق قال سمعت ابا بكر الزقّاق رحمه الله بمصر
يقول منذ اربعين سنةً اصحبُ هؤلاء الفقراء وأعاشرهم فما رأيت قط رفقًا
لأصحابنا الّا (٩)لبعضهم من بعض او ممّن يحجّهم ومن لم يصحبه التقيّة والورع
فى هذا الامر آكل الحرام (١٠)النصّ، وحُكى عن ابى عبد الله بن الجلّاء رحمه
الله تعالى انه قال من لم يصحبه الورع فى فقره آكل الحرام النصّ وهو لا
يدرى، وحُكى عن سهل بن عبد الله رحمه الله تعالى انه قال ادبُ الفقير
الصادق (١)[فى فقره] ثلثة اشياء لا يسأل اذا احتاج ولا يردّ اذا أُعطى ولا
يحبس لوقت (١١)ثانٍ اذا اخذ، وقال غيره ادبُ الفقير (١)[الصادق] فى فقره

---

(١) Suppl. in marg.   (٢) The marginal version adds:
قربت (فشربت) لم شربة.   (٥) وهاتين الحكايتين.   (٤) ذهب.   (٣) وكان.   من ماء ولم آكل شيئًا اخر
(٦) علم, but see my translation of the *Kashf al-Mahjûb*, p. 27, where this
saying is attributed to Shiblî.   (٧) صغرت.   (٨) Probably we should
read ان لا يكون عِلْمُهُ فوق محبّته.   (٩) بعضهم.   (١٠) المحض in marg.   (١١) ثانى.

ثلثة لا يسأل ولا يعارض وان عورض سكت، وحُكى عن سهل بن عبد

الله رحمه الله تعالى انه قال الفقير يلزمه ثلثة اشياء حِنْظ سرّه وأدآء فرضه

وصيانة فقره، وقال الجُنَيْد رحمه الله تعالى كلّ شىء يقدر الفقير ان [١] بعمله

الّا صَبْرَهُ على وقته الى انقضآء مدّته، وحُكى عن ابرهيم الخوّاص رحمه الله

٥ تعالى انه قال اثنا عشر خصلةً من خصال الفقرآء يعنى الصوفية فى حضرهم

وسفرهم اوّلها ان يكونوا بما وعدهم الله تعالى مطمئنّين والثانية ان يكونوا من

الخلق آيسين والثالثة ان ينصبوا العداوة مع الشياطين والرابعة ان يكونوا

لأمر الله [٢] مستمعين والخامسة ان يكونوا على جميع الخلق مُشْفقين والسادسة ٨ f. 78a

ان يكونوا لأذى الخلق محتملين والسابعة ان لا يَدَعوا النصيحة لجميع المسلمين

١٠ والثامنة ان يكونوا فى [٣] مواطن الحقّ متواضعين والتاسعة ان يكونوا بمعرفة

الله تعالى [٤] مشتغلين والعاشرة ان يكونوا الدَّهْرَ على الطهارة والحادى عشر

ان يكون الفقر رأس مالهم والثانى عشر ان يكونوا راضين فيما قلّ او كثر

وفيما احبّوا او كرهوا عن الله تعالى شيئًا واحدًا [٥] [راضين عنه] شاكرين له

وائقين به، وقال بعضهم من طلب الفقر لثواب الفقر مات فقيرًا، وقال

١٥ بعض [٦] المتصوّفة الفقير اذا كثر عقله ذهبت طيبته، قال الشيخ رحمه الله

من آداب الفقرآء الصوفية ان لا يقولوا فيما يسوق الله اليهم من غير سؤال

ولا طمع هذا لى وهذا لك ولا يجرى فى حديثهم كنت لك ولم تكن لى

وأفعلُ كذى عسى ان يكون كذى ولا افعلُ كذى لعلّ يكون كذى، وحُكى

عن ابرهيم بن شَيْبان رحمه الله تعالى انه قال كنّا لا نصحب من يقول نعلى

٢٠ وركْوتى، وقال ابو [٥] [عبد الله] احمد القلانسى رحمه الله [٥] [وكان استاد

الجُنَيْد] دخلتُ على قوم من الفقرآء بالبصرة فأكرمونى ويجِّلونى فقلت لبعضهم

[٥] [مرّةً] اين إزارى فسقطتُ عن أعينِهم، وقال ابرهيم بن المولّد الرّقّى دخلتُ

---

(١) In marg. بعمله.   (٢) مستمعلين corr. in marg.   (٣) مواضع corr.

in marg.   (٤) مستقلّين corr. in marg.   (٥) Suppl. in marg.   (٦) كذا

written above.

طَرَسوس فقيل لى انّ هاهنا جماعة من اخوانك وهم (١)مجتمعون فى دار
فدخلتُ عليهم فرأيت سبعة عشر من الفقراء كلّهم على قلب واحد، وقيل
لأبى عبد الله احمد القلانسى رحمه الله على اىّ شىء بنيتَ اصل مذهبك
فقال على ثلث خصال لا نطالب احدًا [(٢)من الناس] بواجب حقًّا
ونطالب انفسنا بحقوق الناس ونُلزم انفسنا التقصير فى جميع ما نأتى به،
وقال غيره بنَيّنا اصل مذهبنا على ثلث متابعة الامر والنهى ومعانقة الفقر
والشفقة على الخلق، وقال بعضهم اذا رأيتَ الفقير قد انحطّ من الحقيقة الى
العلم فاعلم انه قد فسخ عزمه وحلّ عقْدَه، وقال ابرهيم الخوّاص رحمه الله
ليس من آداب الفقراء يعنى الصوفية ان يكون له سبب يرجع اليه متى
احتاج او (٤)يدان يعمل بهما اذا اراد او لسان يطلب به اذا (٥)جاع
او همّة يطرق بها عند الشدايد الى الناس فهؤلاء أسباب وذخيرة
لشدايدهم (٦)وأرباب، وقال الجُنَيّد رحمه الله تعالى اذا لقيتَ الفقير فألْقَهْ
بالرفق ولا نلقه بالعلم فانّ الرفق يؤنسه والعلم يوحشه،

باب ذكر آدابهم فى الصحبة،

قال الشيخ (٧)[ابو نصر] رحمه الله حكى عن جماعة من المشايخ عن
ابرهيم بن شَيّبان رحمه الله تعالى انه كان يقول كنّا لا نصحب من بقول
نعلى [(٧)وركوتى]، وقال رجل لسهل بن عبد الله رحمه الله انى اريد ان
اصحبك فقال له سهل اذا مات احدنا فمن يصحب الآخَر فليصحبْه الآن،
وقال رجل لذى النون المصرى رحمه الله تعالى من اصحبُ فقال من اذا
(٨)مرضتَ عادك وإذا اذنبتَ تاب عليك، وقال بعضهم كلّ صاحب تقول

(١) مجتمعين. (٢) Suppl. in marg. (٣) يحتاج. (٤) يدين. (٥) احتاج corr.
(٦) وأرباب. (٧) Suppl. above. (٨) مرض عادك وإن اذنبت in marg.
تاب عنك corr. in marg.

قُمْ بنا يقول الى اين فليس ذاك بصاحب، وعن [١]ذى النون رحمه الله انه
قال لا نصحب مع الله الّا بالموافقة ولا مع الخلق الّا بالمناصحة ولا مع
النفس الّا بالمخالفة ولا مع الشيطان الّا بالعداوة [٢][والمحاربة]، وقال احمد
ابن يوسف الزجّاجى رحمه الله مثل المصطحبيّن مثل النورين اذا اجتمعا
٥ ابصرا باجتماعها ما لم يكونا [٣]يبصرانه قبْل ذلك، والخلاف اصل كلّ
فِرْقة وهى لطيفة الشيطان فى افتراق المتخالفيّن [٤]فى الله تعالى، وقال
ابو سعيد الخرّاز رحمه الله صحبتُ الصوفية خمسين سنة ما وقع بينى وبينهم
خلاف فقيل له وكيف ذاك قال لانّى كنت معهم على نفسى، وقال الجُنيْد
رحمه الله تعالى [٥]لانْ يصحبنى رجل فاسق حسن الخُلق احبُّ الىّ من أن
١٠ يصحبنى قارئ سيّئ الخُلق، وقال الجُنيْد رحمه الله رأيت مع ابى حفص النيسابورى
رحمه الله تعالى انسانًا اصلع كثير الصمت لا يتكلّم لأصحابه من هذا
فقيل لى هذا انسان يصحب ابا حفص ويخدمنا وقد انفق عليه ماية الف
درهم كانت له واستدان ماية الف اخرى انفقها عليه ما يسوّغه ابو حفص
ان يتكلّم بكلمة واحدة، وقال ابو يزيد البسطامى رحمه الله تعالى صحبت ابا
١٥ علىّ السّندى فكنت القّنه ما يقيم به فرْضَهُ وكان يعلّمنى التوحيد والحقايق
صرْفًا، وقال ابو عثمن صحبتُ ابا حفص رحمه الله تعالى وأنا غلام حدث
فطردنى وقال لا تجلس عندى فلم اجعل مكافأتى له على كلامه ان اولّى
ظهرى اليه فانصرفتُ امشى الى خلْف ووجهى مقابل له حتى غبتُ عنـه
واعتقدت ان احفر لنفسى بئرًا على بابه وأنزل وأقعد فيه ولا أخرج منه
٢٠ الّا باذنه فلما رأى ذلك منّى قرّبنى وقبلّى وصيّرنى من خواصّ اصحابه الى
ان مات، وسمعتُ ابن سالم يقول صحبتُ سهل بن عبد الله رحمه الله ستّين
سنة قال فقلت له يومًا قد خدمتك ستّين سنة ولم تُرِنى يومًا واحدًا من
هؤلاء الذين يقصدونك يعنى البُدلاء والاولياء فقال [٦][الى] الستَ هو

---

(١) ذا.   (٢) Suppl. in marg.   (٣) يبصراه.   (٤) بابه corr. in marg.
(٥) لن.

١٢

A f. 79a

ذى تُدخلهم علىَّ كلَّ يوم أما رأيتَ صاحب الفوطة والسواك الذى كان
يكلّمك بالامس كان منهم، وقال ابرهيم بن شَيْبان رحمه الله تعالى كنّا نصحب
ابا عبد الله المغربى رحمه الله ونحن شباب ويسافر بنا فى البرارى والفلوات
وكان معه شيخ اسمه حسنٌ و[كان](١) قد صحبه سبعين سنة فكان اذا جرى
٥ من احدنا خطأٌ وتغيّر عليه الشيخ نتشفّع اليه بهذا الشيخ [الذى يسمّى(٢)
حسنًا] حتى يرجع [لنا](١) الى ما كان، وذُكر عن سهل بن عبد الله رحمه
الله تعالى انه كان يقول لبعض اصحابه يومًا ان كنتَ ممّن يخاف السباع فلا
نصحبْنى، وقال يوسف بن الحسين [الرازى](٣) قلت [لذى(٣) النون رحمه الله
تعالى من اصحبُ فقال من لا تكتمه شيئًا يعلمه الله منك، وكان ابرهيم بن
ادهم رحمه الله تعالى اذا صحبه انسان يشارطه على ثلثة اشيآء ان يكون
الخدمة والاذان له وأن يكون يده فى جميع ما يفتح الله (٤)عليهما من الدنيا
كَيْدِه فقال له رجل من اصحابه انا لا اقدر على ذلك فقال اعجبنى صِدْقُك،
وكان ابرهيم بن ادم رحمه الله تعالى ربّما ينظر البساتين ويعمل فى الحصاد
ويُنفق على اصحابه، وقال ابو بكر الكتّانى رحمه الله صحبنى رجل وكان على
١٠ قلبى (٥)ثقيلاً فوهبت له يومًا شيئًا كسآءً او ثوبًا على ان يزول ما (٦)فى قلبى
فلم يزل فأخذت به يومًا الى البيت او الى مكان فقلت له ضع رِجْلك على
خدّى فأَبَى فقلت له لا بُدّ من ذلك ففعل فزال ما كنت اجدُه فى قلبى
عليه او كما قال، قال ابو نصر حكى لى هذه الحكاية الدُّقّ وقال قصدت
من الشأم الى الحجاز حتى سألتُ [ابا بكر](٧) الكتّانى عن هذه الحكاية،
٢٠ قال ابو على الرِّباطى رحمه الله تعالى صحبت عبد الله المَرْوزِىّ رحمه الله
وكان يدخل البادية قبل ان اصحبه بلا زادٍ فلمّا صحبته قال لى أيّما احبُّ
اليك تكون انت الامير او انا فقلت لا بل انت الامير فقال وعليك
الطاعة فقلت نعم فأخذ مِخْلاةً ووضع فيها الزاد وجعل على ظهره فاذا قلت

(١) Suppl. above. (٢) Suppl. in marg. (٣) لذا. (٤) عليهم.

(٥) ثقيل. (٦) Om.

له أَعْطِنى حتى احمله يقول السنُ انا الامير فعليك بالطاعة قال فأخذنا
المطرُ ليلةً فوقف على رأسى [‏لَيلَه] الى الصباح وعليه كساءٌ وأنا جالسٌ
يمنع عنّى المطر فكنت اقول مع نفسى ليتنى متُّ ولم أقُلْ له انت الامير ثم
قال لى اذا صحبك انسان فاصحبْه كما رأيتنى صحبتُك او كما قال ، وقال
سهل بن عبد الله رحمه الله تعالى اجتنب صحبة ثلثة اصناف من الناس
الجبابرة الغافلين والقرّاء المداهنين والمتصوّفة الجاهلين ، فهذا صحبة بعضهم
مع بعض يكون على هذا المعنى الذى ذكرت فى الحكايات وفى القليل كفاية
للعاقل وباله التوفيق ،

باب ذكر آدابهم عند مجاراة العلم ،

قال الشيخ رحمه الله سمعتُ احمد بن علىّ الوجيهى يقول سمعت ابا   A f. 80a
محمّد الجَريرى رحمه الله يقول الجلوس للمذاكرة غلق باب الفايدة والجلوس
للمناصحة فتح باب الفايدة ، وقال ابو يزيد رحمه الله من لم ينتفع بسكوت
المتكلّم لم ينتفع بكلامه ، وقال الجُنيَد رحمه الله كانوا يكرهون ان يتجاوز
اللسان معتقَدَ القلب ، وحُكى عن ابى محمّد الجَريرى انه قال الانصاف
والادب ان لا يتكلّم الرفيع فى هذا العلم حتى يُسأل ، وقال ابو جعفر بن
الفَرَجى صاحب ابى تُراب النخشبى رحمه الله مكثتُ عشرين سنة لا اسأل
عن مسئلة الّا كانت منازلتى فيها قَبْلَ قولى ، وقال ابو حفص رحمه الله
تعالى لا يصحّ الكلام الّا لرجل اذا سَتّ خاف العقوبة بسكوته ، وقال جاء
رجل الى ابى عبد الله احمد بن يحيى الجلّاء رحمه الله تعالى وسأله عن
مسئلة فى التوكّل وعنده جماعة فلم يُجِبه ودخل البيت وأخرج اليهم صرّةً فيها
اربع دوانيق وقال اشتروا بها شيئًا ثم اجاب الرجلَ عن سؤاله فقيل له فى

(١) Suppl. in marg.   (٢) مِن added above.   (٣) Erased by a later
hand.   (٤) والغافلين.   (٥) الدمشقى added in marg.

ذلك فقال اسخييتُ من الله تعالى ان انكلّم فى التوكّل (١) وعندى اربعة
دوانيق، وحُكى عن ابى عبد الله الحُصْرى انه قال لابن يزدانيار عند
مجاراة العلم ما ارى مع الخلق كلّهم الّا خبرًا عن (٢)الغيب فيُمكلك ان
تكون ذلك الغيب قال فقال لى أَعِدْ ما قلتَ قلتُ لا افعل، وقال ابرهيم
٥ الخوّاص رحمه الله تعالى لا يحسن هذا العلم الّا لمن يعبّر عن وجه وينطق
به عن فعله، وقال ابو جعفر الصيّدلانى سأل رجل ابا سعيد الخرّاز رحمه
الله مسئلةً وكان يشير فى سؤاله فقال له ابو سعيد نحن نبلغ (٣)مكانك
وموافقتك فيما تريد بلا هذه الاشارة فانّ اكثرَ الناس اشارةً الى الله سبحانه
ابعدُهم من الله تعالى، وقال الجُنيْد رحمه الله تعالى لو علمتُ ان علمًا
١٠ (٤)[تحت اديم السمآء] اشرفُ من علمنا هذا لسعيتُ اليه وإلى اهله حتى
A f. ٨٠٢ اسمع منهم ذلك ولو علمتُ ان وقتًا اشرفُ من وقتنا مع اصحابنا ومشايخنا
ومسايلنا ومجاراتنا هذا العلم لنهضتُ اليه، وقال الجُنيْد رحمه الله ما عندى
عصابةٌ ولا قومٌ اجتمعوا على علم من العلوم اشرف من هذه العصابـة ولا
اشرف من علم ولولا ذلك ما جالستهم ولكنّهم كذى عندى (٥)[وابيـن
١٥ الصورة، وقال ابو علىّ الروذبارى رحمه الله تعالى علمُنا هذا اشارةٌ فاذا
صار عبارةً (٦)[صار] خفًا، وقال ابو سعيد الخرّاز رحمه الله تعالى ذُكر لى
ابو حاتم العطّار وفضْلُه وكان بالبصرة فرحلتُ اليه من مصر حتى وافيت
البصرة فدخلت جامع البصرة فاذا به (٧)جالسًا وحوله جماعة من اصحابـه
وهو يتكلّم عليهم فاوّل شىء سمعته منه يقول بعد ما نظر الىّ انه قال انّها
٢٠ جلست لواحد وأيْنَ ذلك الواحد ومن لى بذلك الواحد ثم اشار (٨)الىّ
(٩)انه انت ثم قال أظهَرَهم الى (٦)[ما] (١٠)أهّلهم واعانهم على ما ألزمَهم وغيْرِهم
عمّا احضرهم فهُمْ به له عاملون ومنه اليه راجعون، وحُكى عن الجُنيْد رحمه

---

(١) In marg. ويكون فى يبقى.   (٢) فيه added above.   (٣) محاكك.   (٤) Suppl.
in marg.   (٥) Suppl. below.   (٦) Suppl. above.   (٧) جالس.   (٨) هو
added above.   (٩) انهم.   (١٠) اهلهم, vocalised by a later hand.

الله تعالى انه قال [لو كان علمُنا هذا مطروحًا على مزبلة لم يأخذ كلُّ [1]
واحد منه الاّ حظَّه على مقداره، وفيا حُكى عن الشبلى انه قال] لأهل مجلسه
يومًا انتم عَيْنُ القلادة يُنصَبُ لكم منابر من نور تغبطكم الملائكة فقال [2]
رجل على اى شىء تغبطهم الملائكة قال يتحدّثون بهذا العلم، سمعتُ جعفرَ
الخُلْدى يقول سمعت الجُنيْد رحمه الله يقول قال لى سَرِىّ السَّقَطى رحمه الله ٥
تعالى بلغنى ان جماعةً يجلسون حولك فى الجامع قلت نَعَمْ هم اخوانى نتذاكر
العلم ونستفيد بعضنا من بعض فقال هيهات يأبا القسم صرتَ مُناخًا للبطَّالين،
وعن الجُنيْد رحمه الله انه قال كان سَرِىّ رحمه الله تعالى اذا اراد ان
يفيدنى شيئًا سألنى [مسئلةً] فقال لى يومًا ما الشكر [يا غلام] فقلت أن [3] [3]
لا نعصى الله بنعَمِ انعم [الله] بها عليك فاستحسن ذلك منّى وكان يستعيد ١٠ [4]
منّى ويقول كيف قلتَ فى الشكر أعِدْها علىّ [فأعيدها عليه]، قال ابو [4]
نصر ووجدتُ هذه الحكاية بخطّ ابى علىّ الروذبارى عن الجُنيْد، وذُكر عن Af.81a
سهل بن عبد الله رحمه الله تعالى انه كان يُسأل عن مسائل من العلم فلا
يتكلّم فيها فلمّا كان بعد مدّة تكلّم فيها وأحْسَنَ الكلام فسُئل عن امتناعه
قبل ذلك فقال كان ذو النون فى الأحياء ما احببتُ ان اتكلّم فى العلم ١٥ [5]
وهو فى الاحياء إجلالاً له [وحرمةً]، وقال ابو سليمن الدارانى رحمه الله [4]
تعالى لو اعلمُ ان بمكّة رجل يفيدنى فى هذا العلم كلمة يعنى فى علم المعرفة
لحضرنى فيه أن امشى على رجلى ولو الف فرسخ حتى اسمعها منه، وقال ابو
بكر الزقّاق سمعت من الجُنيْد رحمه الله تعالى كلمةً فى الفناء منذ اربعين
سنة هيّجتنى وأنا بعدُ فى غمارها، سمعت الدُّقّى يقول سمعت الزقّاق ٢٠ [6] [7]
يقول هذه الحكاية، سمعت الدُّقّى يقول قيل لأبى عبد الله بن الجلّاء رحمه
الله تعالى لِمَ سُمّى ابوك الجلّاء فقال ما كان بجلّاءَ يجلو الحديد ولكن

---

(١) The passage beginning لو كان انه قال عن الشبلى and ending is suppl.
in marg. (٢) عين. (٣) Suppl. in marg. (٤) Suppl. above. (٥) ذا.
(٦) هيجتنى ذلك. (٧) خُمار in marg.

كان اذا تكلَّم على القلوب جلاها من (١)صدأ الذنوب، وكان حارث المحاسبى
رحمه الله يقول اعزُّ الاشيآء فى دار الدنيا عالم يعمل بعلمه وعارف ينطق عن
حقيقته، وسمعت ابن علوان يقول كان السايل اذا وقف على الجُنَيْد رحمه
الله تعالى (٢)وسأله عن المسئلة فلم يكن من حاله ذلك يقول الجنيد لا حول

٥ ولا قوّة الّا بالله فاذا كرّر عليه السؤال (٣)يقول حَسْبُنَا ٱللّٰهُ وَنِعْمَ ٱلْوَكِيلُ،
وحكى عن ابى عمرو الزجاجى رحمه الله انه قال اذا جالستَ شيخًا وهو يتكلَّم
فى علم من العلوم واشتدّ بك البول فلو بلتَ (٤)[فى] مكانك (٥)خيرٌ لك
من ان تقوم من موضعك لانّ البول يُغسل بالمآء وما يفوتك من فايدتك
فى كلامه عند قيامك لا تُدركه ابدًا، وقال الجُنَيْد رحمه الله تعالى قلت

١٠ لابن الكُرّينى رحمه الله الرجل يتكلَّم فى العلم الذى لا يبلغ استعارُه عِلْمَـهُ
(٦)فأحَبُّ اليك اذا كان هذا وصفه أن يسكت او يتكلَّم فأطرق ثم رفع
رأسه فقال (٤)[الى] ان كنتَ هو فتكلَّمْ، وكان الشبلى رحمه الله يقول مـا
ظنُّك بعلمٍ علمُ العلمآء فيه تهمةٌ، وقال سَرىّ السَقَطى رحمه الله تعالى من
تزيَّن بعلمه كانت حسناته سيِّئاتٍ، قال الشيخ رحمه الله لكلّ حكاية من هذه

١٥ الحكايات شرح واستنباط وبيان لا يخفى على اهل الفهم ان شآء الله تعالى،

     A f. 81 b

باب ما ذُكر من آدابهم فى وقت الطعام والاجتماعات والضيافات،

قال الشيخ رحمه الله تعالى حُكى عن ابى القسم الجُنَيْد رحمه الله انه قال
تنزل الرحمةُ (٧)[من الله عزّ ذكره] (٨)على الفقرآء يعنى الصوفية فى ثلثة

---

(١) صدى.   (٢) ويسأله.   (٣) Kor. 3, 167. حسبى written above.
(٤) Suppl. above.   (٥) كان in marg. before خير.   (٦) Corr. to فايّها.
(٧) Suppl. in marg.   (٨) هذه الطايفة added in marg. أحبّ.

(١)مواطن عند (٢)آكلِهم الطعام فانّهم لا يأكلون الّا عن فاقة وعند مجاراة العلم
فانهم لا يتكلّمون الّا فى احوال الصدّيقين (٣)والاولياء، (٤)وعند السماع فانهم
لا يسمعون الّا من (٥)حقّ ولا يقومون الّا بوجد ، وقال ابو العبّاس احمد
ابن محمّد بن مسروق الطوسى قال لى محمّد بن منصور الطوسى وقد نزل
٥ علينا ابا العباس أقِمْ عندنا ثلثًا فان زدتَ على ثلثة فهو صدقةٌ منك علينا ،
وذُكِر عن سَرىّ السَّقطى رحمه الله انه كان يقول (٦)آه على لقمة ليس علىّ
فيها تبعةٌ ولا لمخلوق علىّ فيها منّةٌ ، وقال ابو علىّ النّوريباطى اذا دخل عليكم
فقير فقدِّموا اليه شيئًا يأكل واذا دخل عليكم الفقهاء فسلوهم عن مسئلة واذا
دخل عليكم القرّاء فدُلّوهم على المحراب ، قال ابو بكر الكنّانى قال ابو حمزة
١٠ دخلتُ على سَرىّ رحمه الله فجأءَنى (٧)بفتيت فأخذ يجعل نصفه فى قدح
فقلت له أَيْشَ هو ذا تعملُ أنا اشرب هذا كلّه فى مرّة فضحك وقال هذا
افضلُ لك من حَجّةٍ ، وكان ابو علىّ الروذبارى رحمه الله اذا رأى الفقراء
مجتمعين فى مكان واحد يستشهد بهذه الاية (٨)وَهُوَ عَلَى جَمْعِهِمْ إِذَا يَشَاءُ
A f. 82a قَدِيرٌ وكان ابو علىّ يقول اذا اجتمع الفقراء فى مكان واحد يكون ارفقَ بهم
١٥ ويُفْتَحُ عليهم ويستشهد بهذه الاية (٩)قُل اللّه يَجْمَعُ بَيْنَنَا ثُمَّ يَفْتَحُ الاية ، وقال
جعفر الخُلْدى رحمه الله هذا الاكل بعد الاكل الذى (١٠)ترون أصحابَنا يقال
له الجوع (١١)المُفْرط ، وقال جعفر رحمه الله اذا رأيتَ الفقير يأكل كثيرًا
فاعلمْ انه لا يخلو من احدى ثلث إمّا لوقت قد مضى (١٢)[عليه] او لوقت
(١٣)[يريد ان] يستقبله او لوقت هو فيه ، وقال الشبلى رحمه الله تعالى لو
٢٠ ان الدنيا لقمةٌ فى فم طفل لرحمتُ ذلك الطفل ، وقال (١٤)ايضًا لو ان الدنيا

---

(١) In marg. اوقات.   (٢) وقت above.   (٣) In marg. والمقربين.

(٤) وقت added above.   (٥) حيث ينالهم added in marg.   (٦) آه.

(٧) In marg. بسويق   (٨) Kor. 42, 28.   (٩) Kor. 34, 25. Kor. has

يَجْمَعُ بَيْنَنَا رَبُّنَا.   (١٠) ررق corr. in marg.   (١١) المقرمط corr. in marg.

(١٢) Suppl. above.   (١٣) Suppl. in marg.   (١٤) اود added in marg.

بما فيها لقمة واحدة أكلتها وأُودِعُ الخلق بلا واسطـة مع الله تعالى، وقال

(١) بعضهم أَكلُ الطعام على ثلاثةٍ مع الاخوان بالانبساط ومع ابناء الدنيا

بالادب ومع الفقراء بالايثار، قال الشيخ رحمه الله ليس هذا من آداب

الفقراء لان من آداب الفقراء الصوفية ان لا يكونوا عند أَكلِ الطعام

٥ مغتمّين ولا مستوحشين ولا متكلّفين ولا يختارون الكثير الردئ على القليل

النظيف الجيّد ولا يكون لأَكلِهم وقت معلوم وإذا حضر الطعام فلا يلقمون

بعضهم بعضًا وان لقوم فلا يردّون ويكرهون الطعام الكثير الجافى وكلّما

كانوا أشدَّ جوعًا فيكون أدبهم فى الأكل أحسَنَ، سمعت شيئًا من الاجلّة

رحمه الله تعالى يقول جُعتُ عشرة ايام لم آكل شيئًا ثم قُدّم الىّ الطعام

١٠ فكنت آكل باصبعين فقال لى صاحب الطعام استعمل السنّة (٢) [و]كُلْ بثلثة

اصابع، وحُكى عن ابرهيم بن شَيْبان رحمه الله تعالى انه قال منذ ثمانين

سنة ما أكلت شيئًا بشهوتى، وكان ابو بكر الكتّانى الدينورى ببغداد ولم

يكن يأكل شيئًا يكون سببَ اظهاره السؤالَ والمعارضةَ، وعن (٣) الجُنَيْد رحمه

الله تعالى انه قال من النذالة ان يأكل الرجل بدينه، وقال ابو تُراب

عُرِض علىّ طعام فامتنعتُ من أكله فعوقبتُ بالجوع اربعة عشر يومًا فعلمت   A f.82b

انّى عوقبت فاستغثتُ الى الله تعالى وتبتُ، وكان الجُنَيْد رحمه الله تعالى

يقول بصفاء المطعم والملبس والمسكن يصلح الامر كلّه، وحُكى عن سَرى

السَّقَطى رحمه الله انه كان يقول أَكلُهم أكل المرضى ونومهم نوم الغرقى، وقال

ابو عبد الله الحُصرى رحمه الله تعالى مكثتُ سنين لا يصلح لى ان اقول

٢٠ لا أشتهى ولا يصلح لى ان آكل، وحُكى عن فتح الوَصِلى رحمه الله تعالى

انه دخل على بِشْر الحافى رحمه الله وجاءه زائرًا من الوَصِل فأخرج بِشْرٌ

درهمًا وأعطاه لأحمد الجلّاء، وكان يخدمه فقال مُرَّ الى السوق اشتر طعامًا

جيّدًا وأُدمًا طيّبًا قال فخرجت فاشتريت خبزًا نظيفًا وقلت لم يقل النبىّ صلعم

لثئ من الطعام اللهمّ بارك لنا فيه وزِدْنا منه الاّ اللبن فاشتريت اللبن
واشتريت تمرًا جيّدًا وجئت وقدّمت اليه فأكل ما أكل وأخذ الباقى وخرج
فلمّا خرج قال بشّر لمن كان عنك من هذا فتح الموصلى جاءنى يزورنى تدرون
لِمَ لم يقل لى كُلْ قال لانّه ليس للضيف ان يقول لصاحب الدار كُلْ
٥ تدرون لِمَ قلتُ [١]اشتر طعامًا طيّبًا لانّ الطعام الطيّب يستخرج خالص الشكر
تدرون لِمَ حمل ما بقى لانّه اذا صحّ التوكّل لم يضرّ الحَمْلُ، وقيل لمعروف
الكَرْخى رحمه الله تعالى كلّ من دعاك تَمُرُّ اليه فقال انّما انا ضيف أُنزِل
حيث أنزلونى، وحُكِى عن ابى بكر الكتّانى رحمه الله تعالى انه اجتمع
سنةٌ من السنين هاهنا يعنى بمكّة مقدار ثلاثمائة نفس من [٢]الفقراء والمشايخ
١٠ فكانوا كلّهم فى موضع واحد وكان لا يجرى فيما بينهم العلم والمذاكرة ويكون
[٣]اخلاق بينهم ومكارم [٤]وإيثار بعضهم مع بعض، وكان ابو سليمن الدارانى
رحمه الله تعالى يقول اذا اردتَّ حاجةً من حوايج الدنيا والاخرة فلا تأكل
حتى تقضيها فان الأكل يُميت القلب، وحُكِى عن رُوَيْم رحمه الله تعالى
انه قال منذ عشرين سنة لم يخطر بقلبى ذكرُ الطعام حتى يحضر، وسمعت
١٥ احمد بن عطاء [٥]ابا عبد الله الروذبارى يقول كان ابو علىّ الروذبارى
رحمه الله تعالى اشترى احمالًا من السُكَّر الابيض ودعا جماعةً من الحلاويّين
فاتّخذوا من ذلك السكر جدارًا عليه شُرُفات وفى الجدار محاريب على
أعمدة منقوشة كلّها من السكر ثم دعا الصوفية حتى هدموها وكسروها وانهبوها،
وسمعت ابا عبد الله الروذبارى انه كان يقول اتّخذ رجل ضيافةً فأوقد
٢٠ ألف سراج فقال له رجل قد اسرفتَ فقال له أدخل الدار فكلّ سراج
اوقدتُه لغير الله تعالى فأطفِها فدخل الدار ليُطفيها فما قدر ان يُطفى منهـا
سراجًا واحدًا وانقطع، وحُكى عن ابى عبد الله الحُصرى رحمه الله انه قال
سمعت احمد بن محمّد السُلَمى يقول كنت بمكّة وكان لى ثلثة ايام لم آكل

A f.83a

شيئًا فوقع فى نفسى ان اجمع النُّسّاك ومن بالحرم من الفقراء وأهل الفضل
قال فاكتريتُ احد عشر مِضْرِبًا وأَقْبَلَت الفتوح من كل جانب فلم يزل على
ذلك احد عشر يومًا وهو فى طول (١)تلك الايّام لم يأكل شيئًا،

باب فى ذكر آدابهم فى وقت السماع والوجود،

قال الشيخ رحمه الله حُكِيَ عن الجُنَيْد رحمه الله تعالى انه كان يقول
السماع يحتاج الى ثلثة اشياء والاّ فَتَرَكُهُ اولى الاخوان والزمان والمكان،
وحكى عن حارث المحاسبى رحمه الله تعالى انه كان يقول ثلث اذا وُجدتْ
(٢)مُتِعَ بهِنَّ وقد فقدناهنَّ حُسْن القول مع الديانة وحُسْن الوجه مع الصبانة
وحُسْن الإخاء مع الوفاء، وقال احمد بن مُقاتل رحمه الله تعالى (٣)[لمّا]
دخل ذو النون رحمه الله تعالى بغداد اجتمع اليه جماعة من الصوفية ومعهم ٨ f. 83b
قوّالٌ يقول فاستأذنوه بأن يقول شيئًا بين يديه فأذن لهم فابتدأ يقول،

صَغِيرٌ هَوَاكَ عَذَّبَنى ٭ فَكَيفَ بِهِ إذا احْتَنَكا
وَأَنْتَ جَمَعْتَ مِنْ قَلْبى ٭ هَوًى قَدْ كَانَ مُشْتَرَكا
أَما تَرَى لِمُكْتَئِبٍ ٭ إذا ضَحِكَ الخَلِىُّ بَكَى،

فقام ذو النون وسقط على وجهه والدم يقطر من جبينه ولا يسقط على ١٥
الارض قال ثم قام رجل من القوم يعنى يتواجد فقال له ذو النون رحمه
الله تعالى (٤)الَّذِى يَرَاكَ حِينَ تَقُومُ فجلس ذلك الرجل، قال وسُئِل ابرهيم
المارستانى رحمه الله عن الحركة عند السماع وتخريق الثياب فقال بلغنى ان
موسى عليه السلم قصّ فى بنى اسرائيل فمزّق واحدٌ قميصه فأوحى الله تعالى
الى موسى عليه السلم قُلْ له مزّق لى قلبك ولا تمزّق ثيابك، قال الشيخ رحمه ٢٠
الله تعالى ويُذكر فى باب (٥)وصف السماع وبيان الوجد تمام هذا الباب ان

(١) ذلك.   (٢) متعن به.   (٣) Suppl. in marg.   (٤) Kor. 26, 218.

(٥) نصره.

شآء الله تعالى، وقد حُكى عن الجُنَيْد انه قال لا يضرّ نقصان الوجد مع
فضل العلم وإنّما يضرّ فضل الوجد مع نقصان العلم، والمعنى فى ذلك
والله اعلم ان فضل العلم يوجب ضَبْط الجوارح عن الحركات عند السماع
على قدر طاقة المستمع حتى يقبض على جوارحه بعد جهدٍ وليس من الادب
استدعآء الحال والتكلّف للقيام، والفقرآء المجرّدون يليق بهم القيام والمطايبة ٥
من غير تذاهب ولا تساكن الى (١)ذلك وتَرْكُهُ اولى بهم وليس من الادب
المداخلة والمزاحمة فى السماع مع اهل السماع والسكون مع حضور القلب
والوقوف على مرأى المستمعين ومعانيهم اولى من المداخلة معهم بالتكلّف وربّما
A f. 84a   يصير التكلّف عادةً فيكون ذلك (٢)اغلظَها على القلوب وأظلمَها للوقت وكلّ
قلب ملوّث بحبّ الدنيا فسماعه لهوٌ وإن (٣)تلفت نفسه فيه وذهب روحه، ١٠

باب فى ذكر آدابهم فى اللباس،

قال الشيخ رحمه الله حُكى عن ابى سليمٰن الدارانى رحمه الله تعالى انه
لبس قميصًا ابيض يعنى غسيلاً فقال له احمد لو لبستَ قميصًا أجْوَدَ من هذا
او كما قال له يا احمد ليت قلبى فى القلوب مثل قميصى فى الثياب،
وحُكى عن ابى سليمٰن الدارانى رحمه الله تعالى انه قال يلبس احدكم عبآءة ١٥
بثلثة دراهم وشهوته فى قلبه خمسة دراهم فا يستحى ان تُجاوز شهوتُه لباسه،
وبلغنى عنه انه كان يقول فى قِصَر الثوب ثلث خصال محمودة استعمال
السُنّة والنظافة وزيادة رِخَرَقه، قال ودخل جماعةٌ على بِشْر بن الحُرْث رحمه
الله تعالى وعليهم المرقّعات فقال لم يا بشر يا قوم اتّقوا الله ولا نُظهروا هذا
الزىّ فانكم تُعَرّفون به وتُكَرّمون له فسكتوا كلّهم فقام شابٌ من بينهم فقال ٢٠
الحمد لله الذى جعلنا ممّن يعرف به ويكرم له والله لنُظهرنّ هذا الزىّ حتى

يكون الدين كلّه لله فقال له بشر احسنتَ يا غلام مثلك من يلبس المُرقّعة،
وسمعت الوجيهى يقول سمعت الجُريرى يقول كان فى جامع بغداد فقير لا
تكاد تجده الّا فى ثوب واحد فى الشتآء والصيف فسُئل عن ذلك فقال قد
كنت ولعتُ بكثرة لبس الثياب فرأيت ليلة فيا يرى النائم كأنّى دخلتُ
٥ الجنّة فرأيت جماعةً من اصحابنا من الفقرآء على مائدة فأردت ان اجلس
معهم فاذا بجماعة من الملآئكة اخذوا بيدى وأقامونى وقالوا لى هؤلآء اصحاب
ثوب واحد وأنت فلك قيصان فلا تجلس معهم فانتبهتُ فنذرت ان لا
ألبس الّا ثوبًا واحدًا الى ان ألقَى الله عزّ وجلّ، وقال ابو حفص الحدّاد
رحمه الله تعالى اذا رأيتَ ضَوْءَ الفقير فى ثوبه فلا [١] نرجُ خيره، وحكى عن A f. 84b
١٠ يحيى بن مُعاذ الرازى انه كان يلبس الصوف والخُلْقان فى ابتدآء امره ثم
كان فى آخر عمره يلبس الخَزّ واللّين فقيل ذلك لأبى يزيد رحمه الله تعالى
فقال مسكين يحيى لم يصبر على الدون فكيف يصبر على [٢] البُخْت، وسمعت
طَيْفور يقول مات ابو يزيد ولم يترك الّا قميصه الذى مات فيه وكانت
عاريّةً عليه [٣] فردّوه الى صاحبها، ومات ابن الكُرَينى وكان استاد الجُنَيْد
١٥ رحمه الله وعليه مرقّعته [٤] فكان فرد كُمّه وتخاريزه عند جعفر الخُلْدى فيه
ثلثة عشر رطلاً كما بلغنى، ويقال ان ابا حفص النيسابورى رحمه الله كان
يلبس قميصًا خزًّا وثيابًا فاخرةً وكان له بيت فُرش فيه الرمل، قال الشيخ
رحمه الله تعالى وآداب الفقرآء فى اللباس ان يكونوا مع الوقت اذا وجدوا
الصوف او اللّبَد او المرقّعة لبسوا واذا وجدوا غير ذلك لبسوا والفقير
٢٠ الصادق أَيْشَ ما لبس يحسن عليه ويكون عليه فى جميع ما يلبس الجلالة
والمهابة ولا يتكلّف ولا يختار واذا كان عليه فضلٌ يؤاسى من ليس معه
ويؤثر على نفسه اخوانه بإسقاط رؤية الايثار ويكون الخُلْقان احبّ اليه من
الجديد ويتبرّم بالثياب [٥] الكثيرة الجيّدة ويضنّ بالخُرَيْقات الخَلَق القليلة

---

(١) ترجوا.   (٢) البحت.   (٣) فردوها الى صاحبه.   (٤) Cf. p. ١٤٦, l. ٣.

(٥) الكثير الجيد.   supra.

ويتكلّف للنظافة والطهارة وإن اخذتُ فى ذكر ما يجب فى هذا الباب يطول وفيما ذكرته كفاية،

باب فى ذكر آدابهم فى اسفارهم،

قال الشيخ رحمه الله تعالى حُكى عن ابى علىّ الروذبارى رحمه الله تعالى

٥ انه جاءه رجل وكان عزمُهُ ان يسافر فقال يا أبا علىّ تقول شيئًا فقال يا فتى كانوا لا يجتمعون عن مَوْعد ولا يفترقون عن مشورة، (١) قيل وسُئل رُوَيْم رحمه الله تعالى عن ادب المسافر فى سفره اذا اراد ان يسافر فقال لا يجاوز همّهُ قدَمَهُ وحيث ما وقف قلبه يكون منزله، سمعت هذه الحكاية عن عيسى القصّار الدينورى قال سألتُ رُوَيْمًا، وحُكى عن محمّد بن اسمعيل

١٠ انه قال كنّا نسافر منذ عشرين سنة انا وأبو بكر الزقّاق وأبو بكر الكتّانى رحمة الله عليهم لا نختلط بأحد من الناس ولا نعاشر احدًا فاذا قدمنا (٢) [الى] البلد ان كان فيه شيخ سلّمنا عليه وجالسناه الى الليل فاذا جاء الليل رجعنا الى مسجد فيقدم الكتّانى فيصلّى من اوّل الليل الى ان يُصبح ويُختم القرآن ويجلس الزقّاق مستقبل القبلة وأنا متفكّر الى ان نُصبح ثم يصلّى كلّنا

١٥ صلاة الغداة بوضوء العتمة فاذا وقع معنا انسان (٣) ينام كنّا نرى انه افضلنا، وقال أبو (٤) الحسن المزيّن رحمه الله تعالى حكمُ الفقير ان يكون كلّ يوم فى منزل ولا يبوت الّا بين منزلين، وفيما حُكى عن المزيّن الكبير رحمه الله انه قال كنت يومًا مع ابرهيم الخوّاص رحمه الله فى بعض اسفاره فاذا عقربٌ يسعى على فخذه فقمتُ لأقتلها فمنعنى من ذلك وقال لى دعها كلّ شئ مفتقر

٢٠ الينا ولسنا مفتقرين الى شئ، وكان الشبلى رحمه الله تعالى اذا نظر الى من يسافر من اصحابه ويرى تقطّعهم فى اسفارهم يقول وَيْلكم أبدًا مِمّا ليس منه

---

(١) فِل.   (٢) Suppl. above.   (٣) نام.   (٤) الحسين.

بُدّ، وحكى عن ابى عبد الله النصيبى رحمه الله تعالى قال سافرتُ ثلثين سنة
ما خِطْتُ قطّ خرقةً على مرقّعتى ولا عدلت الى موضع علمت ان فيها رِفقًا
ولا تركت احدًا يحمل معى شيئًا، قال الشيخ رحمه الله تعالى ليس من آدابهم
ان يسافروا للدَّوَران والنظر الى البلدان وطلب الأرزاق ولكن يسافرون
٥ الى الحجّ والجهاد ولقاءَ الشيوخ وصلة الرحم وردِّ المظالم وطلب العلم ولقاء
من يفيدون منهم شيئًا فى علوم احوالهم او الى مكان له فضلٌ وشرفٌ ولا [١]
يتركون فى اسفارهم شيئًا من اخلاقهم واورادهم التى كانوا يعملونها فى الحضر [٢]
ولا يغتنمون قصر الصلاة وإفطار شهر رمضان وإذا كانوا جماعةً يمشون ٨ ف. ٨٥ب
يمشى اضعفهم ويخدمهم الاشفقُ عليهم وإذا جلس واحد لقضاء حاجة وقفوا
١٠ لفراغه وإن يخلّف واحدٌ انتظروه وإن عجز احدهم عن المشى او اعتلّ [٤]
اقاموا عليه واذا دخل وقت الصلاة لم يبرحوا من موضعهم حتى يصلّوا
الّا أن يكون معهم ماءٌ او بقُرب منهم الماء وهذا حال الضعفاء، وامّا حال
الاقوياء فكما قال ابرهيم الخوّاص رحمه الله تعالى ما هابنى شىء قطّ الّا
رَكِبْتُهُ وكما سُئل ابو عمران رحمه الله عن الجزع والعجز الذى يلحق المسافر
١٥ فى سفره فقال اذا خِفتَ عليه فأَلْقِهِ فى اليمّ بمعنى لا تُبال أَيشَ ما لحقك [٤]
بعد ما تكون متوجّهًا الى الله تعالى وهو ابو عمران الطبرستانى، وقال ابو
يعقوب السوسى رحمه الله تعالى يحتاج المسافر فى سفره الى اربعة اشياء والّا
فلا يسافر عِلْمٌ بسوسه وورعٌ يحجزه ووجدٌ يحمله وخُلُقٌ يصونه، وقال ابو [٥]
بكر الكتّانى رحمه الله اذا سافر الفقير الى اليمَن ثم رجع البه مرّةً اخرى
٢٠ هجروه وتآمروا بهجرانه، ويقال انّما سُمّى السفر سفرًا لانّه يُسفِر عن اخلاق
الرجال، فهذا ما حضرنى من آدابهم فى اسفارهم وبالله التوفيق،

باب فى ذكر آدابهم فى بذل الجاه والسؤال والحركة
من أجْل الاصحاب،

قال الشيخ رحمه الله تعالى سمعت جماعةً من اصحاب الشيخ ابى عبد الله الصُّبَيْحى يقولون لا يصحّ الفقر للفقير حتى يخرج من الاملاك فاذا خرج من الاملاك يتولّد له جاهٌ من ذلك فينبغى ان يبذل جاهه حتى لا يبقى له جاه فاذا بذل جاهه بقى عليه قوّة نفسه فيبذل ذلك يعنى نفسه لأصحابه بالخدمة لهم والحركة فى اسبابهم فعند ذلك يصحّ له الفقر، سمعتُ ابا عبد الله الروذبارى يقول دخل المظفّر القِرميسينى الرَّمْلة ومعه السيّد وكان لهما جاه عظيم عند اغنياءِ البلد فا زالوا يبذلون جاههم ويُنفقون على الفقراءِ حتى لم يبقى لهم جاه عند احد وكان لا يعطيهم احد شيئا بسؤال ولا بدَيْن ولا برهْن فعند ذلك كان يطيب وقتهم، وقيل لابرهيم بن شَيْبان رحمه الله أيْشَ حالُ مظفّر القرميسينى (١)الخِرْقتان والسؤال والخدمة لأصحابه فقال قد رفع قدمًا فى الفتوّة لله فلا يريد ان يتأخّر عن قدم رفعها لله تعالى، وكان بعض الصوفية ببغداد لا يكاد ان يأكل شيئًا الّا بذلّ السؤال فسُئل عن ذلك فقال اخترتُ ذلك لشدّة كراهية نفسى ذلك، ودخل شيخ من اجلّة الشيوخ بلدًا فرأى فيها مريدًا قد اجابته نفسه لكل شىءٍ من الطاعات والعبادات والفقر والتقلّل وكان قد تولّد له من ذلك قبول عند العامّة فقال له هذا الشيخ جميع ما انت فيه يصحّ لك الّا أن تُكدّى الكِسَر من الابواب ولا تاكل شيئًا غيرها فصعب ذلك على المريد وعجز عن ذلك فلمّا كبر سنّه اضطُرّ الى السؤال والحاجة فكان يرى ان ذلك عفوبة لمخالفته لذلك الشيخ فى ايّام ارادته، قال ابو نصر رحمه الله تعالى كان هذا الشيخ ابو عبد الله بن المُقْرى والشيخ الذى امره بالسؤال ابو عبد الله السِجزى

---

(١) الخرقتان. See Dozy, *Supplément aux dictionnaires arabes* under خِرْقة.

A f. 86a

رحمه الله، وبلغنى عن شيخ من الايمّة انه كان يصوم ويطلب لإفطاره كِسَرًا من الابواب ولا يأكل غيرها شيئًا الى وقت إفطاره من الليلة الثانية ففطن به رجل فوضع بين يديه طعامًا فلم يأكل منه وفارق ذلك الموضع الذى عُرف به ولم يرجع اليه بعد ذلك، وحُكى عن مِمْشاذ الدينورى انه كان ربّما يقدم عليه جماعة من اخوانه من الفقراء فكان يدخل السوق ويجمع فى حجره كِسَرًا من الدكاكين ويحمل اليهم، وحُكى عن بنان الحمّال انه قال ما علمتُ قطّ بأنّى صَنْعان الّا مرّةً واحدةً رأيت فقيرًا يصوم النهار ويخرج بعد المغرب الى السوق ويأخذ من كلّ دكّان لقمةً فاذا سدّ رمقه رجع الى موضعه فأخذتها معى ليلة وكنت آخذ من الناس الخبز الكثير واللحم والحلواء والفواكه وأدفع اليه حتى اجتمع معه من ذلك (١) شىء كثير فلمّا اراد ان ينصرف قال لى يا شيخ انت صاحب شُرْطة فقلت لا انا بُنان الحمّال فرى الجميع ما كان معه فى وجهى وقال لى يا صَنْعان هذا الذى تفعله انت انّما يفعله عندنا صاحب الشرطة لا المشايخ كلّ من تقول له هاتِ فيعطيك ما تريد، وحُكى عن بعض المريدين (٢) وطلب شيئًا لأصحابه وأكل معهم فأنكر عليه جماعةٌ من المشايخ اكله معهم وقالوا خدعتَك نفسك وطلبت لنفسك ولو كنت طلبت لأصحابك وبذلت جاهك لهم لم نأكل معهم، قال الشيخ رحمه الله تعالى وحُكْمُ من يفعل ذلك أن يترك ذلك اذا صارت عادته وسكتت الى ذلك نفسه ومن سأل الضرورة ولم يأخذ الّا ما لا بدّ له من ذلك فان اعطوه الكثير فيأخذ منه حاجته ويُخرج الباقى، والاكل بالسؤال اجمل من الاكل بالتقوى والفقير اذا اضطرّ الى السؤال فكفّارته صِدْقُه، ومرّ على بعض المشايخ ايّامٌ ولم يأكل شيئًا وكان فى بلد (٣) غُرْبة حتى كاد يتلف ولم يسأل فقيل له فى ذلك فقال معنى عن السؤال قول النبىّ صلعم لو صدق السايلُ ما افلح من ردّه وكرهتُ ان يردّنى مسلمٌ فلا يُفلح لقول النبىّ صلعم،

(١) شيا كثيرا.   (٢) Some words seem to have been omitted here.

(٣) So pointed in MS.

باب فى ذكر آدابهم اذا فُتح عليهم شىء من الدنيا،

قال الشيخ رحمه الله قال ابو يعقوب النَّهْرجورى رحمه الله تعالى سمعت
ابا يعقوب السوسى رحمه الله تعالى يقول جاءَنا فقير ونحن بأُرّجان وسهل
ابن عبد الله رحمه الله تعالى يومئذٍ بها فقال انّكم اهل العناية فقد نزلت
بى مِحْنَةٌ قال سهل بن عبد الله رحمه الله فى ديوان المِحَن وقعتَ منذ Af.87a
تعرّضتَ لهذا الامر فما هى قال فُتح لى شىء من الدنيا فاستأثرت بها فى غير
ذى مَحْرَم فنقدتُ ايمانى وحالى فقال سهل لأبى يعقوب رحمهما الله تعالى
أُيْشَ تقول فى هذا قال فقلت مِحْنتُهُ بحاله اعظمُ من محنته بايمانه فقال سهل
مثلك يقول هذا، وحُكى عن خَيْر النَّسّاج رحمه الله تعالى قال دخلتُ بعض
١٠ المساجد واذا فيه فقير من الفقراءَ وكنت اعرفه فلمّا رآنى تعلّق بى وبكى
وقال لى ايّها الشيخ تعطّف علىَّ فان محنتى عظيمة فقلت يا هذا وما محنتك
قال لى فقدتُ البلاءَ وقورنتُ بالعافية وأنت تعلم ان هذه مِحنة عظيمة قال
وكان قد فُتح عليه شىء من الدنيا، وقال ابو تُراب النَّخْشَبِى رحمه الله
تعالى اذا توافرت النِّعَم على احدكم (١) فليَبْكِ على نفسه فانه سُلك به غير
١٥ طريق الصالحين، وسمعت الوجيهى رحمه الله تعالى يقول حُمل الى بُنان
الحَمّال الف دينار وصبّوها بين يديه فقال للذى صبّه ارجع وخُذْهُ واللهِ
لولا ما عليه من كتابة اسم الله تعالى لبُلْتُ عليها هو ذى يغرّر بى ببريقه،
قال وفُتح لابن بُنان رحمه الله تعالى اربعاية درهم وهو نائمٌ فوضعوها عند
رأسه فرأى فى المنام كأنّ قايلاً يقول من اخذ من الدنيا فوق ما يكفيه
٢٠ اعمى الله تعالى قلبه فانتبه فأخذ منها دانقَيْن وترك الباقى، وسمعت ابن علوان
رحمه الله تعالى يقول حُمِل الى ابى الحسين النورى رحمه الله ثلثماية دينار قد
باعوا عقارًا له بمجلس على قنطرة الصَّراة وهو يحذف بواحد واحد منها الى

الماء ويقول سيّدى تريد ان تخدعنى عنك بهذا، وحكى جعفر الخُلْدى رحمه
الله تعالى قال كان ابن زيرى من اصحاب الجُنيْد رحمهما الله تعالى وكان
قد فُتح عليه شىء من الدنيا فانقطع من الفقراء فاستقبلنا يوماً وفى كُمّه
منديل فيه دراهم كثيرة فلمّا رآنا من بعيد قال يا اصحابنا اذا كنتم انتم
متعزّزين بالفقر ونحن (١)متعزّزون بالغنى فتى نلتقى قال ثم رمى الينا بجميع ما   ٨ f.87b
كان فى كُمّه، وقال ابو سعيد بن الأعرابى كان فتى يصحب ابا احمد القلانسى
رحمه الله ثم غاب عنه مدّةً ثم رجع من سفره وقد فُتح عليه شىء من الدنيا
واجتمع عنده مال فقلنا لأبى احمد تأذن لنا ان نزوره فقال لا فانّه كان
يصحبنا على الفقر ولو بقى على حاله كان ينبغى لنا ان نزوره فاذا رجع من
سفره على هذه الحالة فيجب عليه ان يزورنا، وحكى ابو عبد الله الحُصْرى   ١٠
رحمه الله تعالى قال مكث ابو حفص الحدّاد رحمه الله بالرَّمْلة وعليه (٢)خِرْقتان
وفى وَسَطه الف دينار وهو يمكث اليومين والثلثة والاربعة وأبى ان يأكل
منها وهو يؤاسى الفقراء منها الى ان فنى عن آخرها، وقال الحُصرى رحمه
الله تعالى خرجتُ مع الشبلى فى ايّام القحط نطلب شيئاً لصبيانه فدخل على
انسان فأعطاه دراهم كثيرةً قال فخرجنا من عنده وكُمّى مَلآ من الدراهم فكلّما   ١٥
لقينا انساناً من الفقراء اعطاه منه حتى لم يبق الّا القليل فقلت له يا سيّدى
الصبيان فى البيت جياعٌ فقال لى أيْشَ اعلُ (٣)فبَعْدَ الجهد حتى اشتريت
شيئاً من (٤)الكسب والجزر بما بقى من الدراهم وحملته الى صبيانه، وحكى عن
ابى جعفر الدرّاج رحمه الله تعالى قال خرج استاذى يوماً يتطهّر فاخذت
كِنّه ففتّشته فوجدت فيه شيئاً من الفضة مقدار دراهم اربعة فتغيّرتُ فى امره   ٢٠
وكان لنا اوقات لم نأكل شيئاً فلمّا رجع قلت له كان فى كنفك كذا
ونحن جياعٌ قال هاه اخذتَها رُدّه ثم قال لى بعد ذلك خذْه واشتر به شيئاً
فقلت بحقّ معبودك ما أمْرُ هذه الفضّة فقال لم يرزقنى الله تعالى شيئاً من

الدنيا (١) [لا] صفراء ولا بيضاء غيرها فأردت ان اوصى ان تدفن معى فاذا كان
يوم القيمة اردّها الى الله تعالى اقول هذه الذى اعطيتَنى من الدنيا او كما
قال، قال ودفع وزير المُعْتَضِد مالاً الى ابى الحسين النورى رحمه الله تعالى
حتى يفرّقه على المتصوّفة فنصبه فى بيت وجمع صوفية بغداد فقال لهم كلّ

A f. 88 a

من يحتاج منكم الى شىء فليدخل البيت ولياخذ حاجته منه فكان يأخذ
الرجُل ماية درهم والآخر اكثر والآخر اقلّ ومنهم من لا يأخذ شيئًا فلمّا فنيت
الدَراهم ولم يبق شىء قال لهم بُعْدَكم من الله تعالى على مقدار أخْذكم من
الدراهم وقُرْبكم من الله تعالى على مقدار تركّكم لها،

باب فى ذكر آداب من اشتغل بالمكاسب والتصرّف
فى الاسباب،

١٠

قال الشيخ رحمه الله تعالى قال سهل بن عبد الله رحمه الله من طعن
على الاكساب فقد طعن على السنّة ومن طعن على التوكّل فقد طعن على
الايمان، وسُئل الجُنَيْد رحمه الله عن الكسب فقال يستقى الماء ويلقط النوى،
وكتب اسحق المغازلى رحمه الله تعالى وكان من احد المشايخ الى بِشْر بن

١٥ الحُرث رحمه الله تعالى وكان بشر يعمل المغازل فكان فى كتابه بلغنى عنك
انك استغنيت عن امر معاشك بعمل هذه المغازل ارأيت إن اخذ الله تعالى
سمعك وبصرك الملتجأ الى من قال فترك بشرّ ذلك العمل وإشتغل بالعبادة،
وسأل رجل ابن سالم بالبصرة رحمه الله تعالى وأنا حاضر فى مجلسه وكان
يتكلّم فى فضل المكاسب فقال له ايّها الشيخ نحن (٢) مستعبدون بالكسب (٣) ام

٢٠ بالتوكّل فقال ابن سالم التوكّل حال الرسول والكسب سنّة الرسول صلعم
وإنّما (٤) استنّ لهم الكسب لعلمه بضعفهم حتى اذا سقطوا عن درجة التوكّل

---

(١) Text om.   (٣) مستعبدين app. altered into مستعبدين.   (٢) او.

(٤) استنزلهم.

التى هى حاله لا يسقطوا عن درجة طلب المعاش التى هى سنّته ولولا ذلك
هلكوا ، وحُكى عن عبد الله بن (١)المبارك انه كان يقول لا خير فيمن لا
يذوق ذلّ المكاسب ، وكان عبد الله بن (٢)المبارك يقول مكاسبك لا
تمنعك عن التفويض والتوكّل اذا لم (٣)تضيّعهما فى كسبك ، ويقال ان ابا
سعيد الخرّاز رحمه الله خرج سنةً من السنين من الشأم الى مكّة مع القافلة
فجلس ليلةً الى الصباح يخرز نعال اصحابه من الفقراء والصوفية ، وقال ابو
حفص رحمه الله تعالى تركتُ الكسب مرّةً ثم عاودتُه ثم تركنى الكسب فلم
اعاود اليه بعد ذلك ، وحُكى عن بعض الفقراء انه كان بدمشق رجل
اسود ويصحب الصوفية وكان يرّ كلّ يوم يدقّ الجصّ بثلثة دراهم ولا يأكلها
الّا فى ثلثة ايّام فاذا اخذ الاجرة يشترى به طعامًا (٤)[ما] ويجىء الى اصحابه
ويأكل معهم آكلةً ويرجع الى عمله ، وحُكى عن ابى القسم المنادى رحمه الله
تعالى انه كان يخرج من منزله فاذا كان وقع فى يده مقدار دانقَيْن يرجع
من الطريق الى منزله ايّ وقت كان ، وحُكى عن ابرهيم الخوّاص رحمه الله
تعالى (٥)[انه كان يقول اذا عرّج المريد على الاسباب بعد ثلثة ايّام] فالعمل
فى المكاسب ودخول السوق اولى به ، وحُكى عن ابرهيم بن ادهم] انه كان
يقول عليك بعمل الأبطال الكسب من الحلال والنفقة على العيال ، قال
ابو نصر رحمه الله تعالى ومن اشتغل بالمكاسب فأدبُه ان لا يشتغل عن
اداء الفرايض فى اوقاتها ولا يرى رزقه من ذلك وينوى بذلك معاونة
المسلمين ويُنصفهم فاذا فضل شىء من كسبه ونفقة عياله لا يجمع ولا يمنع
ويُنفق على اخوانه من الفقراء الذين ليس لهم معاش ولا معلوم ولا سؤال
لانّه وإن امتُحن بذلك فهو واحدٌ منهم وكذلك هؤلاء الذين ليس لهم
علاقة اذا فُتح عليهم شىء ساعدوه ويهتمّون بأسبابه أكثرَ من اهتمامهم

---

(١) المُبرك.   (٢) المُبرك.   (٣) تضعيها.   (٤) Suppl. above.   (٥) The
passage beginning وحكى عن ابرهيم بن ادهم and ending انه كان يقول is suppl.
in marg.   (٦) والعمل.

بأنفسهم، وحُكى عن ابى حفص الحدّاد رحمه الله تعالى انه كان أكثرَ من
عشرين سنةً يعمل فى كلّ يوم بدينار ويُنفقه عليهم يعنى الصوفية ولا يسأل
عن مسئلة ويصوم ثم يخرج بين العشاءَيْن فيتصدّق من الابواب، وقال
الشِبلى رحمه الله لرجل أَيْشَ حِرْفتُك فقال (١)خرّازٌ فقال له نسيتَ الله تعالى
بين (٢)الخرز والخرز، وقال (٣)ذو النون رحمه الله تعالى اذا طلب العارف
المعاش فهو فى لا شىء، والله تعالى اعلم،

باب فى آداب الأخذ والعطاء وإدخال الرفق على الفقراء،

قال الشيخ رحمه الله تعالى اخبرنى جعفر الخُلْدى رحمه الله قال سمعت
الجُنيْد رحمه الله تعالى يقول سمعت سَرىّ السَّقَطى رحمه الله تعالى يقول
اعرفُ طريقًا مختصرًا الى الجنّة لا تسأل احدًا شيئًا ولا تأخذ من احد شيئًا
ولا يكون معك شىء تعطى احدًا، حُكى عن الجُنيْد رحمه الله تعالى انه قال
لا يصحّ لأحد الأخذ حتى يكون الإخراج احبّ اليه من الاخذ، وقال ابو
بكر (٤)[احمد] بن حمويه صاحب الصُّبيّحى رحمه الله تعالى من أَخَذَ له اخذ
بعزّ ومن تَرَكَ له ترك بعزّ ومن اخذ لغير الله اخذ بذلّ ومن ترك لغير
الله ترك بذلّ، سمعت احمد بن علىّ الوجيهى يقول سمعت الرقاق يقول
استقبلنى يوسف (٥)الصايغ بمصر ومعه كيسٌ فيه دراهم فأراد ان يناولنى
فرددتُ يه الى صدره فقال خذها منّى ولا تردّها علىّ فلو علمتُ انّى املك
شيئًا او انّى أُعطيك شيئًا ما اعطيتُك هذا، سمعت احمد بن علىّ يقول
سمعت ابا علىّ الروذبارى رحمه الله تعالى يقول ما رأيت احسن ادبًا من
ابن رفيع الدمشقى فى إدخال الرفق على الفقراء وذلك أنّى بتّ عنه ليلةً
فحكيت عن سهل بن عبد الله رحمه الله تعالى انه قال علامة الفقير الصادق

ان لا يسأل ولا يردّ ولا يحبس فلمّا اردتُ ان افارقه حمل معه شيئًا من
الدراهم ووقف على الجانب الذى حملتُ ركوتى وقال لى كيف حكيتَ عن
سهل الحكاية فلمّا حكيت له الحكاية وقلت لـه لا نسأل ولا تردّ فطرحها
فى ركوتى وانصرف، وقال ابو بكر الزقّاق رحمه الله تعالى ليس السخآء ان
يعطى الواجدُ المُعْدِمَ انّما السخآء ان يعطى المعدم الواجد، وحكى عن ابى ٥
محمّد المُرتَعِش رحمه الله تعالى انه قال لا يصحّ الاخذ عندى حتى تقصد
من تأخذ منه فتأخذ له لا لك، وحُكى عن جعفر الخُلْدى عن الجُنَيْد رحمه
الله تعالى انه قال ذهبت يومًا الى ابن الكَرِّينى ومعى دراهم [اريدُ](١) ان
ادفعها اليه وكان عندى انه لا يعرفنى وسألتُ ان يأخذ ذلك فقال انا A f.89b.
عنه(٢) مستغنٍ وأبَى ان يأخذ منّى(٣) فقلت له ان كنت(٤) [انت] عنها(٢) مستغنيًا ١٠
فأنا رجل من المسلمين أسَرُّ بأخذك لها فتأخذها لإدخال السرور علىّ فأخذها
منّى، وذُكر عن ابى القسم المنادى رحمه الله تعالى انه كان اذا رأى دخانًا
يخرج من (٥)[بيت] بعض جيرانه فيقول لبعض من يكون عنده مُرَّ الى هؤلآء
فقل لهم أعْطُونا من هذا الذى تطبخون فقال له قايل فعسى يسخّنون المآء
وقال مُرَّ اليهم لأىّ شىء (٦) يصلح هؤلآء الاغنيآء غير أن يعطونا شيئًا ويشفعوا ١٥
لنا فى الآخرة، وقال الجُنَيْد رحمه الله تعالى حملت دراهم الى حسين بن البصرى
وكانت امرأته قد ولدت وهم فى الصحرآء وليس لهم جارٌ فأبِى أن يقبلها منّى
فأخذتُ الدراهم ورميت فى الحجرة التى كانت فيها المرأة وقلت ايّتها المرأة
هذه لك فلم يكن له حيلةٌ فيما فعلتُ، وسُئل يوسف بن الحسين رحمه الله
تعالى اذا واخيتُ رجلاً فى الله فخرجتُ اليه بكلّ مالى هل أكون قايمًا بحقّه ٢٠
فيما ملّكنى الله تعالى قال أنّى لك بما ألزمتَهُ من ذُلّ الأخذ وإستدركتَ من
عِزّ الإعطآء اذا كان فى العطآء رفعة وفى الاخذ مذلّة،

---

(١) Suppl. in marg. (٢) مستغنى. (٣) فقال. (٤) Suppl. above.

(٥) Text om. (٦) يصلحون.

باب فى آداب المتأهّلين ومن له ولد،

قال الشيخ رحمه الله تعالى قال ابو سعيد بن الأعرابى كان سبب
تزويج ابى احمد القلانسى واسمهُ مُصعَب بن احمد ان شابًّا من اصحابه
خطب ابنةً لصديق لأبى احمد فلمّا حضر وقت عقد النكاح امتنع الشابّ
٥ واستحيا من ذلك الرجل الذى كان يزوّجه بابنته فلمّا رأى ذلك ابو احمد
قال يا سجان الله يزوّج رجل بكريمته فتمتنع عليه فأعقدوا النكاح على ابى
احمد وقبّل رأس ابى احمد قال ما علمتُ ان لى عند الله تعالى من المقدار
ان يكون لى مثلك خَتنٌ وما علمتُ ان لابنتى عند الله تعالى من المقدار
ان يكون لها مثلك زوجٌ قال ابو سعيد بقيت عنده ثلاثين سنة وهى (١)بكرٌ
او كما قال، وحُكى عن محمّد بن علىّ الفصّار رحمه الله تعالى انه كان له A f.90a
اهل وولدٌ وكانت له بُنَيّةٌ (٢)وكان جماعة من اصدقآبه عنده يومًا فصاحت
الصبيّة يا ربّ السمآء نريد العِنَب فضحك محمّد بن علىّ وقال قد ادّبنهُم
بذلك حتى اذا احتاجوا الى شىء يطلبون من الله تعالى ولا يطلبون منّى،
وسمعت الوجيهى يقول كان لبنان الحمّال رحمه الله تعالى اولاد فربّما كان
١٥ يجىء ابنه ويقول يا ابى اريد خبزًا وكان يصنعه ويقول مُرّ كذا مثل ابيك
وقال وجآء يومًا فقال يا ابى انّى اريد (٣)مِشْمِشًا قال فأخذ بيه وجآء به
الى من يبيع المشمش وقال له ادفع اليه (٣)مشمشًا بقيراط حتى اصبح على
مشمشك الى ان تبيعه فدفع اليه الرجل ووقف بنان يصبح يأيّها الناس
اشتروا من هذا الصغير (٤)الغذآء الذى يفنى ولا يبقى فما لبث طويلاً حتى
٢٠ باع الرجل مشمشه كلّه، وحُكى عن ابرهيم بن ادم رحمه الله تعالى انه قال
اذا تزوّج الفقير فمَثَلُه مثل رجلٍ قد ركب السفينة فاذا وُلد له قد غرق،

_____

(١) بكرا.   (٢) وكانوا.   (٣) مشمش.   (٤) العرا.

وهذه الحكاية تُعرف لسفين النَّورى رحمه الله تعالى، وحُكى عن بِشْر بن
الحُرْث رحمه الله تعالى انه قال لو دفعتُ الى الاهتمام بمؤنة وحاجة ما أمنْتُ
على نفسى أن أُصبح شُرْطيًّا، وكان لأبى شُعَيب البرائى (١)كوخٌ فرّت به امرأة
من ابناء الدنيا فقالت له انّى اريد ان اتزوّج بك وأخدمك فخرجت من
جميع ما كانت تملكه وتزوّج بها ابو شعيب فلمّا ارادت ان تدخل الكوخ
نظرت الى قطعة خَصّاف فقالت ما انا بداخلة حتى تُخرجها اليس سمعتُك
تقول تقول الارض لابن آدم تجعل (٢)[اليوم] بينى وبينك شيئًا وأنت غدًا
فى بطنى فا كنتُ لأجعل بينى وبينك (٣)حجابًا فأخذ الخَصّاف وأخرجها
فرى بها ثم قال ادخلى فدخلتْ فمكثا يتعبّدان فى ذلك المكان سنين كثيرة
حتى توفّيا وهما على تلك الهيئة، قال الشيخ رحمه الله وليس من آداب من
تزوّج او كان له ولدٌ ان يُكِّل أَمْرَ عياله الى الله تعالى ويجب عليه ان يقوم
بفرضهم الّا أن يكونوا مثله فى الحال، وليس من آدابهم ان يتزوّجوا ذوات
اليسار ويدخلوا فى رِفْق نسائهم ومن ادبِ الفقير ان يتزوّج بفقيرة مُقْلَّة
وأن يُنصفها وإن رغبت فيه امرأة غنيّة أن لا يرتفق منها، وحُكى عن فتح
المَوْصِلى رحمه الله تعالى انه اخذ يومًا صبيًّا له فقبّله قال فتح سمعت هانئًا
يقول يا فتح ألا تستحى ان تحبّ معنا غيرنا قال فا قبّلتُ ولدًا لى بعد ذلك،
فان قال قايل قد كان لرسول الله صلعم اولاد وكان يقبّلهم ويعانقهم ويضمّهم
الى صدره وقال الأَقْرَع بن حابس لرسول الله صلعم يا رسول الله لى عشرة
من الولد ما قبّلتُ واحدًا منهم فقال عليه السلم من لا يَرْحَم لا يُرْحَم يقال
لقايل هذا القول قد ابعدتَ القياس لانّ النبّى صلعم امام الخلق الى يوم
القيمة ومصحوبُه العصمة وقوّة النبوّة وأنوار الرسالة فى جميع الاشياء لا تأخذ
منه الاشياء ولا يكون فى الاشياء بحظّه لانّ جميع حركاته (٤)تأديبٌ للغَيْر
من أمّته وهؤلاء ليس لهم (٥)تلك القوّة ولا ذلك التخصيص واذا لاحظهم
بعنايته يغار عليهم ان يَدَعهم ان يلتفتوا بخواطرهم الى من سواه،

(١) كوخا.   (٢) Suppl. in marg.   (٣) حجاب.   (٤) تأديبا.   (٥) ذلك.

باب فى ذكر آدابهم فى الجلوس والمجالسة ،

قال الشيخ رحمه الله تعالى حُكى عن سَرِىّ السَّقَطى رحمه الله تعالى انه
كان يقول الجلوس فى المساجد حوانيت ليس لها ابواب ، وسُئل سَرِىّ عن
المروّة فقال صيانة النفس عن الأدناس وإنصاف الناس فى المجالسة فان
زاد كان متنضّلاً ، وقال بعض المشايخ الفقير ينبغى له ان تكون عبادته على
ألهيّته يعنى من كثرة الجلوس ، وحُكى عن ابى يزيد رحمه الله انه قال قمت
ليلةً اصلّى فعييتُ فجلست ومددت رجلى فسمعت هاتفًا يقول من مجالس الملوك
ينبغى له ان يُحسن الادب ، وعن ابراهيم بن ادهم رحمه الله تعالى انه قال
تربّعتُ مرّةً فهتف بى هاتفٌ هكذى تجالس الملوك فما تربّعت بعد ذلك
ابدًا ، A f. 91a وقال ابراهيم الخَوّاص رحمه الله تعالى رأيت فقيرًا له جلسةً حسنةً
فتقدّمتُ اليه ومعى دراهم فصببتُها فى حجْره فقال اشتريت هذه الجلسة بماية
الف درهم تريد ان (١)أبيعها بهذا ، وقال يحيى بن مُعاذ رحمه الله تعالى مجالسة
المخالفين (٢)تُعمى الروح ورؤية الأضداد تمنع (٣)الذوق ، وسمعت الوجيهى يقول
رأيت ابن ملولة العطّار الدينورى وقد تبرّم بجليس له فقلتُ تجالس مثل
هذا فقال (٤)ابن ملولة لا تُمكن مفارقته ، ويقال اذا أشْكل عليك امرُ أخيك
فاعتبره بجليسه ، قال وكان حسن القزّاز رحمه الله تعالى له (٥)أخَذٌ (٦)فكان
يُكثر الجلوس بالليل فسُئل عن ذلك فقال بُنى هذا الامر على ثلثة اشياء
أن لا نأكل الّا عن فاقه ولا نتكلّم الّا عن ضرورة ولا ننام الّا عن غلبة ،
وقال جعفر كان الجُنَيْد رحمه الله تعالى يقول لو علمتُ ان صلاة ركعتيْن
٢٠ افضلُ من جلوسى عندكم ما جالستُكم ،

باب فى ذكر آدابهم فى الجوع،

قال الشيخ رحمه الله تعالى قال يحيى بن مُعاذ رحمه الله تعالى لو عَلِمتَ
ان الجوع يباع فى السوق ما كان ينبغى لطلّاب الآخرة اذا دخلوا السوق
اى يشتروا غيره، وقال الجوع على اربعة أوْجُه للمريدين رياضةٌ وللتائبين
تجربةٌ وللزهّاد سياسةٌ وللعارفين مكرمةٌ، قال وكان سهل بن عبد الله رحمه
٥ الله تعالى كلَّما جاع قوى واذا أكل شيئًا ضعف، وقال سهل رحمه الله تعالى
اذا شبعتم فاطلبوا الجوع مِمَّن ابتلاكم بالشبع واذا جعتم فاطلبوا الشبع مِمَّن
ابتلاكم بالجوع والّا تماديتم وطغيتم، وقال ابو سليمان رحمه الله الجوع عند
فى خزاين مدّخرة لا يعطيه الّا لمن يحبّه خاصّةً، وسمعت ابن سالم يقول كلامًا
١٠ فى معنى ادب الجوع ان لا تنقص من عادته الّا مثل أُذَنَى السِّنَّوْر فقلت له
قد حكيتَ بالامس، وقيل ذلك عن سهل بن عبد الله رحمه الله تعالى انه
كان لا يأكل الطعام نيف وعشرين يومًا فقال كان سهل رحمه الله تعالى لا
يترك الطعام ولكن كان الطعام يتركه انه كان يَرِدُ على قلبه ما يأخذه ويشغله
عن أكْل الطعام، وسمعت عيسى القصّار رحمه الله يقول من ادبِ الجوع
١٥ أن يكون الفقير معانقًا للجوع فى وقت الشبع حتى اذا جاع يكون الجوع
انيسه، وسمع شيخٌ من المشايخ رجلاً من الصوفية يقول انا جايع فقال له
كذبتَ فقيل له لِمَ قلت ذلك فقال لان الجوع سِرٌّ من سِرّ الله تعالى موضوع
فى خزاين من خزاين الله تعالى لا يضعه عند من يُفْشيه، قال ودخل
[رجلٌ](١) من الصوفية على شيخ فقدّم اليه طعامًا فأكله فقال له مذ كم لم
٢٠ تأكل الطعام قال مذ خمْس فقال ليس بك جوع الفقر جوعك جوع بُخْل
عليك ثيابٌ وأنت تجوع او كما قال،

٨٢.٩١٥

---

(١) Text om.

باب فى ذكر آداب المَرْضَى فى مرضهم،

قال الشيخ رحمه الله تعالى سمعت بعض اصحاب بمشاذ الدينورى يحكى
عن مشاذ رحمه الله تعالى انه اعتلّ علّةً شديدةً [١] فدخل عليه اصحابه عايدين
له فقالوا كيف تَجِدُك قال لا ادرى ولكن سَلُوا العلّة كيف تَجِدُنى فقالوا
له كيف تجد قلبك فقال قد فقدتُ قلبى منذ ثلثين سنة، وسمعت محمّد
٥ ابن معبد البانياسى يقول رأيت الكُرْدى الصوفى رحمه الله تعالى وقد اعتلّ
فعيدَ ستّة اشهر وكان قد وقع الدود فى موضع من بدنه فاذا وقع منها
دودةٌ ردّها الى موضعها، ودخل [٣] ذو النون على مريض من اصحابه يعوده
فقال [له] [٤] ليس بصادق فى حبّه من لم يصبر على ضرّه فقال المريض
١٠ ليس بصادق فى حبّه من لم يتلذّذ بضربه، وكان سهل بن عبد الله رحمه
الله تعالى اذا مرض احد من اصحابه يقول له اذا اردتَ ان تشتكى فقُل
اوه فانّه اسم من اسمآء الله تعالى يستَروح اليه المريضُ ولا تقلّ لـه اوخ
فانه اسم من اسمآء الشيطان، وسمعت ابا بكر احمد بن جعفر الطوسى
بدمشق يقول كان بأبى يعقوب النَّهرجورى رحمه الله تعالى وجعٌ فى بطنه
A f.92a سنين وكانت [٤] حَسه فى جوفه وكان يقول اعرف دوآءه بقيراط فضّة
يذهب بهذه العلّة ولكن لا يداويه الى ان خرج من الدنيا فسألتُ عن
ذلك بعض المشايخ فقال كان الكىّ فكان لا يداويه من اجل النُّهى، ومرض
الثَّورى رحمه الله تعالى مرضه فتخلّف عن عيادته رجل من اصحابه ثم اتاه
فجعل يعتذر اليه فقال له لا تعتذر فقل من اعتذر الاّ كذب، وكان بسهل
٢٠ ابن عبد الله رحمه الله تعالى البواسير [٥] الظاهرة فكان يحتاج ان يتوضّأ
لكلّ صلاة وكان يقول اعرف له دوآءً بقيراط ولم يداوه الى ان خرج من

---

(١) فدخلوا.   (٢) ذا.   (٣) Suppl. above.   (٤) So the MS. Perhaps

(٥) الظاهر،.   بُجرة.

الدنيا [١] فسألتُ عن ذلك فقالوا كان لا يداويها حتى لا تنكشف عورته
ولا ينظر الى عورته احد، ويقال ان [٢] بِشْرًا الحافى رحمه الله تعالى مرض
مرضه فدخل عليه الطبيب فأخذ بشر يصف للطبيب ما به فقيل له يا أبا
نصر أما تخشى ان تكون هذه شكايةً فقال لا انّما أخبره بقدرة القادر
[٣] [على]، ووجدتُ فى كتاب اظنّه بخطّ جعفر الخُلْدى رحمه الله قال اعتلّ
الجُنَيْد رحمه الله تعالى علّةً شديدةً فكان يقول ليس الّا ما قال [٤] ذو النون
رحمه الله تعالى يا من يشكر ما يَهَبُ هبْ لنا ما نشكر، وربّما كان يقول هذا
[٥] غذاؤهم من كلّ شىء يَحضره،

باب فى آداب المشايخ ورِفْقِهم بالاصحاب وعطْفهم عليهم،

١٠   قال الشيخ رحمه الله تعالى حُكى عن الجُنَيْد رحمه الله تعالى انه كان
يقول لأصحابه لو علمتُ ان صلاة ركعتين افضلُ من جلوسى معكم ما جلست
عندكم، وحُكى عن بِشْر الحافى رحمه الله تعالى انه قد كان تعرّى فى يوم
شديد البرد وهو ينتفض فقلنا له يا أبا نصر ما هذا فقال ذكرتُ الفقرآء
وأن ليس لهم شىء ولم يكن لى ما اؤاسيهم به فأحببتُ ان اؤاسيهم بنفسى،
١٥ وسمعت الدُّقّى يقول كنت بمصر وكنّا فى المسجد جماعة من الفقرآء جُلوس
فدخل الزقّاق فقام عند اسطوانة يركع فقلنا يفرغ الشيخ من صلاته ونقوم
ونسلّم عليه فقام وجآء الينا وسلّم علينا فقلنا نحن كنّا اولى بهذا من الشيخ
فقال ما عذّب الله تعالى قلبى بهذا قطّ، وسمعت الوجيهى يقول سمعت
الجريرى يقول وأفيتُ من الحجّ فابتدأتُ بالجُنَيْد رحمه الله تعالى وسلّمت
٢٠ عليه وقلت حتى لا ينعتّ ثم اتيت منزلى فلمّا صلّيت الغداة التفتُ فاذا
بالجُنَيْد رحمه الله تعالى خَلفى فقلت يا سيّدى انّما ابتدأت بالسلم عليك

A f.92b

لكى لا تتعنّى الى هاهنا فقال لى يأبا محمّد هذا حظُّك وذاك فضلٌ لك ،
وقال ابو سعيد بن الأعرابى كان شابٌّ يعرف بابرهيم الصايغ وكان لأبيه
نعمة فانقطع الى الصوفية وصحب ابا احمد القلانسى فربّما كان يقع بيد ابى
احمد شىء من الدراهم فكان يشترى له الدُقاق والشواءَ والحلواءَ ويؤثره
عليه ، وعن جعفر الخُلْدى قال [دخل](١) رجل الى الجُنَيْد رحمه الله تعالى
فأراد ان يخرج من مِلْكه كلّه ويجلس معهم على الفقر قال فسمعت الجنيد
رحمه الله تعالى يقول له لا تُخرِج كل ما معك احبس مقدار ما يكفيك
وأُخْرِج الفضل وتقوّتْ بما حبستَ واجتهدْ فى طلب الحلال لا تُخرِج كلّما
عندك فلستُ (٢)آمَنُ عليك أن نطالبك نفسك والنبىّ صلعم كان اذا اراد
ان يعمل عملاً أثبته، سمعت الوجيهى يقول سمعت ابا على الروذبارى رحمه الله
تعالى يقول كنّا فى البادية جماعة ومعنا ابو الحسن العطوفى فربّما (٣)كانت
تلحقنا الفاقة وتُظْلِم علينا الطريق فكان ابو الحسن يصعد بصعد تلًّا ويصيح صياح
الذئاب حتى يُسمع كلاب الحىّ فينبحون فيبرّ على صوتهم ويحمل البنا من
عندهم معونةً، وقال ابو سعيد الخرّاز رحمه الله تعالى دخلتُ الرُّمْلة فذهبت
الى ابى جعفر القصّاب فبثُّ عنه ثم خرجت من الرملة الى بيت المقدس
فجاءَ الى بيت المقدس خانى وقد حمل معه كُسَيَراتٍ وقال اجعلنى فى حِلّ
A f.93a كانت هذه فى البيت ولم أَدْرِ،

باب فى ذكر آداب المريدين والمبتديّن،

قال الشيخ رحمه الله تعالى وجدت فى كتاب ابى تُراب النَّخْشَبى رحمه
الله الحكمة جندٌ من جنود الله تعالى يُقوى بها آداب المريدين، وحُكى عن
الجُنَيْد رحمه الله تعالى انه قد سأله بعض الفقراء او بعض الشيوخ فقال

(١) Text om.   (٢) نامن.   (٣) كان.

له يا سيّدى ما للمريدين فى (١)مجاراة الحكايات فقال الحكايات جندٌ من
جنود الله تعالى يُقوِّى بها قلوب المريدين قال فقلت هل فى ذلك شاهدٌ
من كتاب الله تعالى فقال نَعَمْ قال (٢)وَكُلًّا نَقُصُّ عَلَيْكَ مِنْ أَنْبَاءِ ٱلرُّسُلِ
مَا نُثَبِّتُ بِهِ فُؤَادَكَ، وقال يحيى الحكمة مِرْوَحَةُ قلوب المريدين تروّحُ عنها
٥ وهج الدنيا، وحُكى عن مِمْشاذ الدينورى رحمه الله تعالى انه كان يقول ان
عينى لتقرّ بالفقير (٣)[الصادق] وانّ قلبى ليفرح بالمريد المختفِّق، وقال ابو
تُراب رحمه الله تعالى رياء العارفين إخلاص المريدين، وقال ابو علىّ بن
الكاتب رحمه الله تعالى اذا انقطع المريد الى الله تعالى بكلِّيّته اوّل ما يُفيث
الله تعالى الاستغناء به عمّن سواه، وسُئِل الشبلى رحمه الله عن المريد اذا
١٠ وقعت به الحَيرة فقال الحيرة من وجهين حيرةٌ تقع من شدّة خوف اقتراف
الذنوب وحيرةٌ (٤)[تقع من] كشْف التعظيم للقلوب، وقال الشبلى رحمه الله
تعالى كنتُ فى اوّل بدايتى اذا غلبنى النوم آكحَلُ بالمِلْح فاذا زاد علىّ الامرُ
أَحْمَيْتُ الميل فأكحَلُ به، وقال ابو سعيد الخرّاز رحمه الله تعالى من ادب
المريد وعلامة صِدق ارادته أن يكون الغالب عليه الرّقّة والشفقة والتلطّف
١٥ والبذل واحتمال المكاره كلّها عن عيبه وعن خلْقه حتى يكون لعبيه ارضًا
يسْعون عليها ويكون للشيخ كالابن البارّ وللصبىّ كالأب الشفيق ويكون مع
جميع الخلق على هذا يتشكّى بشكواهم ويغتمّ لمصايبهم ويصبر على أذاهم فان
هذا مراد الله تعالى من المريدين الصادقين أن يعطِفوا على الخلق من A.f.93b
حيث عطف الله تعالى عليهم (٥)ويتأدّبوا بآداب الانبياء والصدّيقين وآداب
٢٠ اوليائه وأحبابه حتى تُرْفَع الحُجُب التى بينه وبين الله تعالى فما دام هو
متمسِّكًا بهذه الآداب ومتخلِّقًا بهذه الاخلاق ويكون مستعينًا فى ذلك باله
متوكِّلًا على الله عزّ وجلّ راضيًا عنه، وقال سهل بن عبد الله رحمـه الله
تعالى شُغْلُ المريد فى قلبه اقامة الفرض والاستغفار من الذنب وطلب

---

(١) مجارات.   (٢) Kor. 11, 121.   (٣) Suppl. in marg.   (٤) Text om.
(٥) وتأدبوا.

السلامة من الخلق، وسُيل يوسف بن الحسين رحمه الله تعالى ما علامة
المريد فقال تركُ كلّ خليط لا يريد مثل ما يريد وأن يَسْلَم [١] منه
عدوّه كا يسلم [١] منه صديقه وعلامة المريد وجدانُه فى القرآن كلّ ما
يريد واستعمال ما يعلم وتعلُّم ما لا يعلم وترك الخوض فيا لا يعنيه وشدّة
٥ الحرص على ارادة النجاة من الوعيد مع الرغبة فى الوعد والنشاغل بنفسه
عن غيره، وقال ابو بكر [٢] البارزى رحمه الله تعالى اذا سلك المريد الهَوَلَ
فى اوّل قدم فلا يبالى فانّه لن يلقاه بعد ذلك الّا راحة،

باب فى ذكر آداب من يتفرّد ويختار الخلوة،

قال الشيخ رحمه الله تعالى حُكى عن بِشر الخافى رحمه الله تعالى انه كان
١٠ يقول [٣] ليبتقِ الله تعالى عند [٥] خلواته [٥] وليَلزَم بيته وليكُن انيسَه الله عزّ
وجلّ وكلامُه، سمعت الدُّقّى يقول سمعت الدرّاج يقول كان ابو المسيّب
[٦] رجلاً كبيرًا وكان يتنزّد فى المساجد الشعثة فصادفتُه ليلة فى مسجد فقلت
له من اين فقال لى انا من كلّ مكان فقلت من كان من كلّ مكان
فأيشَ علامته قال لا يستوحش من شىء ولا يستوحش منه شىء قال فحملتُ
١٥ اليه الشبْلى رحمه الله تعالى فنظر اليه وقال ليس هذا من دوابّ الاصطبل
والّا فأينَ سِمتُه قال فصاح الشبْلى رحمه الله تعالى ولطم وجهه وهام وهو
يقول صدق والله ان كان من دوابّ الاصطبل فاين سمته، وسُيل الجُنَيْد
رحمه الله تعالى عن الخلوة فقال ان السلامه مصاحبة لمن طلب السلامة
فترَكَ المخالفة وترك النطلّع الى ما اوجب العلم مفارقته، وحُكى عن ابى
٢٠ يعقوب السوسى رحمه الله تعالى انه قال الانفراد لا يقوى عليه الّا الاقوياء
من الرجال ولأمثالنا الاجتماع انفع يعلمون بعضهم برؤية بعض، وسمعت ابا

---

(١) عنه.   (٢) البارزى.   (٣) ينبغى للمريد ان added in marg.   (٤) ليبتق.

(٥) Suppl. in marg.   (٦) رجل كبير.

حفص عمر الخيّاط رحمه الله تعالى يقول رأيت ابا بكر بن المعلّم رحمه الله
تعالى بأنطاكية [يقول] طولبتُ شهادة أن لا اله الّا الله بعد ستّين سنة
فسُئل عن ذلك فقال كنت ستين سنة ادعو الخلق الى الله تعالى فلمّا
انفردتُ ودخلتُ اللُّكام اذا اردتُ ان اقوم الى أورادى التى كانت عادتى
بين الناس لم يتهيّأ لى فوقع فى قلبى انّى ما آمنت بالله تعالى بعدُ فجدّدت
ايمانى وأقمتُ هناك عشر سنين حتى صفا لى فى الخلوة اورادى كما كانت
تصفو لى فى الاوقات التى كنت بين المعارف، وحُكى عن ابرهيم الخوّاص
رحمه الله تعالى انه رأى رجلاً فى البادية حسن الادب حاضر القلب فسأله
فقال كنت اعمل بين الناس والمعارف فى التوكّل والرضا والتفويض فلمّا
فارقتُ المعارف لم يبق معى من ذلك ذرّة فبقيتُ حتى اطالب نفسى ماهنا
بدعاويها اذا انفردتُ عن المعلومات والمعارف،

باب فى ذكر آدابهم فى الصداقة والمودّة،

قال الشيخ رحمه الله تعالى قال ذو النون رحمه الله تعالى ما بَعُدَ
الطريق الى صديق ولا ضاق مكان من حبيب، وسمعت ابا عمرو اسمعيل
ابن نُجَيْد يقول سمعت ابا عثمن يقول لا تثق بودّة من لا يحبّك الّا معصوماً،
وفيما حكى جعفر الخُلْدى عن ابن السمّاك رحمه الله تعالى انه قال له
صديق الميعاد بينى وبينك غدًا نتعاتب فقال له ابن السمّاك رحمه الله
تعالى [بل] بينى وبينك غدًا نتغافر، ويقال ان كلّ مودّة يُزداد فيها
باللقاء فهى مدخولة فى المودّات، وسُئل عن حقيقة المودّة فقال هى التى لا
تزداد بالبرّ ولا تنقص بالجفاء، وهذه الحكاية عن يحيى بن مُعاذ الرازى
رحمه الله تعالى، وقال بعضهم الاعراض عن الصديق إبْقَاءً على المودّة، قال

---

(١) Suppl. above.   (٢) كان.   (٣) ذا.   (٤) اللقا.

ابو العبّاس بن مسروق رحمه الله تعالى فيما بلغنى وفى هذا سُنّة عن الرسول
صلعم قوله لأبى هُرَيْرَة رضى الله عنه زُرْ غِبّاً تزدد حُبّاً، وقيل ليحيى بن
مُعاذ رحمه الله تعالى كيف حالك فقال (١)كيف حالُ من يكون عدوّه داؤه
وصديقه بلاؤه، وقال الجنيّد رحمه الله تعالى لقد كنت أرى اقواماً تجزينى منهم
النظرةُ فهى زادى من الجُمعة الى الجُمعة، وقال بعض المشايخ اذا صحّ لى
مودّة اخٍ فلا أبالى متى لقيتُه، وعن النورى رحمه الله تعالى انه قال
الصديق لا يحاسَبُ بشىء والعدوّ لا يُحْسَب له شىء، وقال الجنيّد رحمه الله
تعالى اذا كان لك صديق فلا نسوْهُ فيك بما يكرهه، وعن جعفر الخُلْدى
قال سمعت ابا محمّد المغازلى رحمه الله تعالى يقول من اراد ان تدوم له
المودّة فليحفظ مودّة اخوانه القدماء ،

باب فى ذكر آدابهم عند الموت ،

قال الشيخ رحمه الله تعالى بلغنى عن ابى محمّد الهروى رحمه الله تعالى
انه قال مكثتُ عند الشِبْلى رحمه الله تعالى ليلة غداة التى مات (٢)فيها
فكان يقول طول الليل هاتين البيتين،

كُلُّ بَيْتٍ أَنْتَ سَاكِنُه ٭ غَيْرُ مُحْتَاجٍ إِلَى السُّرُجِ
وَجْهُكَ المَأْمُولُ حُجَّتُنا ٭ يَوْمَ يَأتى الناسُ بالحُجَجِ ،

وحكى عن ابن (٣)الفَرَجى رحمه الله تعالى انه قال رأيت حول ابى تُراب
النخشبى رحمه الله تعالى اصحاب ماية وعشرين ركوة فما مات منهم على النقر
الّا نفْسَيْن، قال بعضهم احدها ابن الجلَّاء والآخر ابو عُبَيْد البُسْرى، وورد
على قلب ابن بُنان المصرى رحمه الله تعالى شىء فهام على وجهه فلحقوه فى وسط
متاهة بنى اسرائيل فى الرمل ففتح عينيه ونظر الى اصحابه وقال ارجْ فهذا

---

(١) يكون added in marg.   (٢) فيه.   (٣) الفرجى.

مَرْتَعُ الأحباب وخرجتْ روحه، هذه الحكاية عن الوجيهى، وسمعت الوجيهى
رحمه الله تعالى يقول سمعت ابا علىّ الروذبارى رحمه الله تعالى يقول دخلتُ
مصر فرأيت الناس مجتمعين فقالوا كنّا فى جنازة فتى سمع قائلاً يقول،

كَبُرَتْ هِمَّةُ عَبِدٍ * طَمِعَتْ فى أَنْ يَرَاكا،[١]

٥ فشهق شهقةً فمات، وسمعت بعض اصحابنا يقول قال ابو يزيد رحمه الله
عند موته ما ذكرتُك الّا عن غفلة ولا قبضتَنى الّا عن فترة، وحكى عن
الجُنيد رحمه الله تعالى انه قال جلست عند استاذى ابن الكَرِّينى رحمه الله
تعالى عند موته فنظر الى السماء فقال بَعُدَ فطأطأتُ رأسى الى الارض فقال
بَعُدَ يعنى انه اقربُ الِيك من أن تنظر الى السماء او الى الارض وتشير
١٠ اليه بذلك، وقال الجَريرى رحمه الله تعالى حضرتُ وفاة ابى القسم الجُنيد
رحمه الله تعالى فلم يزل ساجدًا فقلت له يا أبا القسم اليس بلغتَ هذا المكان
وبلغ منك ما أرى من الجهد لو استرحتَ فقال لى يا أبا محمّد أحْوَجُ ما
كنتُ اليه هذه الساعة فلم يزل ساجدًا حتى فارق الدنيا وأنا حاضر، وقال
بكران الدينورى رحمه الله تعالى حضرتُ وفاة الشبلى رحمه الله تعالى فقال
١٥ لى على قلبى درهمٌ مظْلِمةً تصدّقتُ عن صاحبه بالسوق فما علىّ شغلٌ اعظمُ
من ذلك ثم قال وَضِّنى للصلاة ففعلتُ ذلك فنسيت تخليل لحيته وقد
أمْسَكَ لسانُه فقبض على يدى فأدخلتها فى لحيته ومات، وكان سبب وفاة
ابى الحسين النورى انّه سمع بهذا البيت،

لا زِلْتُ أَنْزِلُ مِنْ وِدَادِكَ مَنْزِلاً * تَتَحَيَّرُ الأَلْبَابُ عِنْدَ نُزُولِهِ،

٢٠ فتواجد وهام فى الصحراء فوقع فى أجمة قَصَب قد قُطعت وبقيت أصولها
مثل السيوف فكان يمشى عليها ويعيد البيت الى الغداة والدم يسيل من
رجلَيْه ثم وقع مثل السكران فورمت قدماه ومات رحمه الله تعالى، سمعت
الدُّقِّى يقول كنّا عند ابى بكر الزقّاق رحمه الله تعالى غداةً فكان يقول اللهمّ

٨ f.95b

كم تُبقينى هاهنا فا بلغ الأولى حتى مات، وكان سبب موت ابن عطاء رحمه
الله تعالى انه أُدخل على الوزير فكلّمه الوزير بكلام غليظ فقال ابن عطاء
ارفقْ يا رجل فأَمر بضرب خُفّه على رأسه فات فيه، ومات ابرهيم الخوّاص
رحمه الله تعالى فى جامع الرىّ وكانت به علّة الجوف فكان اذا قام مجلسًا
يدخل الماء ويغسل نفسه (١)فدخل الماء مرّةً (٢)فخرج روحه وهو فى وسط
الماء، وقال ابو عمران الإصطَخْرى (٣) رحمه الله تعالى رأيت ابا تُراب النخشَبى
(٣)رحمه الله تعالى فى البادية (٤)قائمًا ميتًا لا يمسكه شىء، وسمعت ابا عبد
الله احمد بن عطاء يقول سمعت بعض الفقراء يقول لمّا مات الإصطَخْرى
(٣)رحمه الله تعالى جلسنا حوله فقال (٣)له رجل منّا (٣)قل اشهدُ ان لا اله
الّا الله فجلس جالسًا ثم اخذ يد واحدٍ فقال قل اشهد ان لا اله الّا الله
(٥)وخلّى يده وأَخذ (٦)بيد (٧)الآخر الذى بجنبه (٨)وقال قل اشهد ان لا اله
الّا (٩)الله (١٠)وخلّى يده وأَخذ (٦)بيد (٧)الآخر الذى بجنبه حتّى عرض الشهادة
على كلّ واحد منّا ثم استلقى على قفاه (١١)وخرج روحه، وقيل للجُنَيْد كان
ابو سعيد الخَرّاز (٣) رحمهما الله تعالى كثيرًا ما كان يتواجد عند الموت
فقال الجُنيد (٣) رحمه الله لم يكن بعجب ان تكون تطير روحه اليه اشتياقًا،
(١٢)فهذا ما (١٣)حضرنى فى الوقت من آدابهم والذى لم (١٤)نذكره أكثر،
وبالله التوفيق،

(١٥)كتاب المسائل واختلاف اقاويلهم فى الأجوِبة،

(١٥)قال الشيخ رحمه الله تعالى (١٦)أذكُرُ طرقًا من اختلافهم فى مسائل

(١) Here B resumes (fol. 90b, l. 1). (٢) B خرجت. (٣) B om. (٤) A
فقال B (٨). واحد اخر A (٧) . بد B (٦) . فقال فخلا يده B (٥). قائم ميت
وخرجت B (١١) . ثم خلا B (١٠) . فقال اشهد ان لا اله الا الله B adds (٩)
قال الشيخ B om. (١٥) . نذكر B (١٤) . حضر B (١٣) . هذا B (١٢)
. وازكر B (١٦) . رحمه الله تعالى

A f.96a تفرّدوا بها بأجوبة شتّى بيان ما يُشكل من ذلك على العلمآء والنقهآء وساير

الناس من اهل الظاهر (١)الذين ليس هذا من شأنهم، مسئلة فى الجمع والتفرقة،

(٢)قال الشيخ رحمه الله تعالى الجمع والتفرقة اسمان فالجمعُ جَمعُ المتفرّقات

والتفرقة تفرقة المجموعات فاذا جمعتَ قلتَ الله ولا سواه واذا فرّقتَ قلتَ

٥ الدنيا والآخرة والكون وهو قوله (٣)شَهِدَ اللّٰهُ أَنّهُ لَا إِلٰهَ إِلّا هُوَ فقد جَمَعَ

ثم فرّق فقال (٤)وَالْمَلَائِكَةُ وَأُولُوا الْعِلْمِ قَايِمًا (٤)بِالْقِسْطِ، كذلك (٥)قوله

(٦)قُولُوا آمَنَّا بِاللّٰهِ وقد جمع ثم فرّق فقال وَمَا أُنْزِلَ إِلَيْنَا وَمَا أُنْزِلَ إِلَى

إِبْرَاهِيمَ الآية، فالجمع اصلٌ والتفرقة فرعٌ فلا تُعرَف الاصول الّا بالفروع

ولا (٧)تثبت الفروع الّا بالاصول وكلّ جمع بلا تفرقة فهو زندقة وكلّ تفرقة

١٠ بلا جمع فهو تعطيل، وقد (٨)نكلّم فى معنى الجمع والتفرقة المشايخ المتقدمون

فقال ابو بكر عبد الله بن طاهر الأبهرى (٩)رحمه الله تعالى وسُيل عن ذلك

(١٠)فقيل له الى ما ذا اشار القوم الى معنى الجمع والتفرقة فقال اشار قوم

الى (١١)ان جمعهم فى آدم (٩)عليه السلم وفرّقهم فى ذرّيّته (١٢)وأشار قوم الى

ان جمعهم فى المعرفة وفرّقهم فى الاحوال، وللجُنَيد (١٣)فى معرفة الجمع والتفرقة،

١٥ (١٤)فَتحقّقتُكَ فى سرّى (١٥)فناجاكَ لسانى * فأجتمعنا (١٦)لِمعان وأفترقنا لِمعانى

إِنْ يكُنْ غِيبُكَ التّعظِيم عَنْ لَحظِ عِيانى * فلقد صيّركَ الوَجدُ مِنَ الأحشآء دانى،

وقال اظنّه النورى الجمع بالحقّ تفرقةٌ عن غيره والتفرقة عن غيره (١٧)جمعٌ

به، وقال غيره الجمع اتّصال لا يشهد الانابة متى (١٨)يشهد الانابة فا وصلٌ

والتفرقة شهود لمن (١٩)شاهد (٢٠)المباينة، وقال قوم لا مجموع بحقّ (٢١)الّا

(١) AB الذى.   (٢) B om. قال الشيخ رحمه الله تعالى.   (٣) Kor. 3, 16.   (٤) B adds

the remainder of the verse: قوله عز وجل.   (٥) B لا اله [الّا] هو العزيز الحكيم.

(٦) Kor. 2, 130.   (٧) A يثبت. In B the word is partly obliterated.

(٨) AB نكلّموا.   (٩) B om.   (١٠) B اشار الخ فقال ما ذى.   (١١) B انه.

(١٢) B om. from وأشار to فى الاحوال.   (١٣) B الجمع والتفرقة فى شعر فى معنى.

(١٤) A تحقّقتك.   (١٥) B فخاطبك.   (١٦) AB لمعانى.   (١٧) B جمعاً.

(١٨) B شاهد or شاهد.   (١٩) Obliterated in B.   (٢٠) B بالمباينه.   (٢١) A ولا.

مفرّق عن نعت ولا مجموع بنعت الّا مفرّق عن حقّ وها (١)متنافيان لانّ
الجمع (٢)بالحقّ خروج عن حجّته (٢) وتفرّقها والجمع (٤)بالحقّ حَجْب بالحقّ
وتفرقة عنه، وقال قوم الجمع ما جمع البشرية فى شهود البشرية والتفرقة ما
(٥)فرّقها عن تقسيم الرسوم، وقد ذهب الجُنَيْد (٢)رحمه الله تعالى الى ان قُرْبه
بالوجد جمعٌ وغيبته فى البشرية تفرقةٌ (٦) وقال ابو بكر الواسطى (٢) رحمه الله
اذا نظرتَ الى نفسك قرّقتَ واذا نظرت الى ربّك جمعتَ واذاكنت قايمًا
بغيرك فأنت ميّت (٧)وهذه أحْرُف مختصرة فى معنى الجمع والتفرقة ولمن
يتدبّر فى فهمه ان شآء الله تعالى، مسئلة فى الفنآء والبقآء (٨)قال الشيخ
رحمه الله تعالى سُيِل ابو يعقوب النهرجورى عن صحّة الفنآء والبقآء (٩)فقال
هو فنآء رؤية قيام العبد لله (٢)عزّ وجلّ وبقآء رؤية قيام الله (٢)تعالى فى
احكام العبودية، وسُيِل ابو يعقوب (٢)رحمه الله تعالى عن صحّة علم الفنآء
والبقآء (١٠)قال (١١)يصحبه العبودية فى الفنآء والبقآء واستعمال علم الرضا
ومن لم يصحبه العبودية فى الفنآء والبقآء فهو (١٢)مدّع، قال (٨)الشيخ رحمه
الله تعالى الفنآء والبقآء اسمان وها نعتان لعبدٍ (١٢)موحّد يتعرّض الارتقآء فى
توحيد من درجة العموم الى درجة الخصوص، ومعنى الفنآء والبقآء فى
اوايله فنآء الجهل ببقآء العلم وفنآء المعصية ببقآء الطاعة وفنآء الغفلة ببقآء
الذكر وفنآء رؤيا حركات العبد لبقآء رؤيا عناية الله (١٤)تعالى فى سابق
العلم، وقد (١٥)تكلّم فى ذلك المشايخ المتقدّمون فقال سُمنون (٢)رحمه الله
تعالى العبد فى حال الفنآء محمول وفى حال (١٦)الحَمْل مورود (١٧) وهى نعوت
(١٨)تؤدّى الى نعوت، وقال اوّل مقامات الفنآء الوجود والمشاهدات

---

(١) يتنافيان B.   (٢) B om.   (٣) A وتفرّقها.   (٤) B الحقّ.

(٥) B فرّقهما.   (٦) B قال.   (٧) B om. from هذه to ان شآء الله تعالى.

(٨) B om. قال الشيخ رحمه الله تعالى.   (٩) B قال.   (١٠) B om. from قال

به.   (١١) A يصحب.   (١٢) AB مدّعى.   (١٤) A موجود.   to والبقآء

(١٥) A تكلّمو.   (١٦) B الجهل.   (١٧) B وهو.   (١٨) B يؤدى.

(١)للبقاء، وقال ابو سعيد الخزّاز (٢)رحمه الله تعالى فى معنى قوله (٣)وَمَا بِكُمْ
مِنْ نِعْمَةٍ فَمِنَ اللهِ قال أَخْلامم فى افعالهم من افعالهم وهو اوّل حال الفناء،
وعن جعفر الخُلْدى قال سمعت الجُنَيْد (٢)رحمه الله تعالى يقول وسُيِل عن
الفناء. فقال اذا فنى الفناء (٤)عن اوصافه ادرك البقاء بتمامه، قال وسمعت
٥ الجنيد (٢)رحمه الله تعالى (٢)يقول وقد سُيِل عن الفناء فقال (٥)استعجام كُلّك
عن اوصافك واستعمال الكلّ منك بكلّيّتك، وقال (٦)ابن عطآء من لم
(٧)يفن عن شاهد نفسه بشاهد الحقّ ولم (٧)يفن عن الحقّ بالحقّ ولم يغبْ
فى حضوره عن حضوره لم يقع بشاهد الحقّ، وقال الشبْلى (٢)رحمه الله تعالى
من فنى عن الحقّ بالحقّ لقيام الحقّ فنى عن الربوبية فضلاً عن
١٠ العبودية، (٨)وقال اظنّه رُوَيْم (٢)رحمه الله تعالى وقد سُيِل عن الفناء والبقاء
فقال اوّل علم الفناء هو النزول فى حقائق البقاء وهو الأثرة لله (٢)تعالى
على جميع ما دونه (٩)وتفقُّد كلّ حال معه حتّى يكون هو الحظّ وسقوط ما
سواه حتّى تفنى عبادتهم لله (٢)تعالى (١٠)بأنفسهم ببقاء عبادتهم لله باله وما
بعد ذلك لا يُدركه (١١)المعقول بالعقول ولا تنطق به الألسُن، وقد قال
١٥ الله (١٢)تعالى (١٣)كُلُّ مَنْ عَلَيْهَا فَانٍ فاوّل علامة الفانى ذهاب حظّه من
الدنيا والآخرة بورود ذكر الله (٢)تعالى ثم ذهاب حظّه من ذكر الله (٢)تعالى
عند حظّه بذكر الله (٢)تعالى له ثم تفنى (٢)رؤية ذكر الله تعالى له حتى يبقى
حظّه باله ثم ذهاب حظّه من الله (٢)تعالى برؤية حظّه (١٤)ثمّ ذهاب حظّه
برؤية حظّه بفناء الفناء (١٥)وبقاء البقاء، والكلام فى هذا (١٦)طويل وفيا

---

(١) B البقا.   (٢) B om.   (٣) Kor. 16, 55.   (٤) B فى.   (٥) A اذا
وقال رويم اظنه B (٨)   يفنا AB (٧)   بن B (٦)   استعجام for فى الفنا.
(٩) B ويفقد.   (١٠) A om. بانفسهم ببقاء عبادتهم bnt the words are suppl.
in marg.   (١١) B العقول.   (١٢) B اسه تعالى for جل ثناوه.   (١٣) Kor.
55, 26.   (١٤) A om. from ثم to حظّه. B has بروية حظّه الح but
رؤية ذهاب روية حظّه has been stroked out.   (١٥) A وفنا.   (١٦) B يطول.

ذكرناه كناية ان شاء الله [١] نعالى، مسئلة فى الحقايق، [٢]قال الشيخ رحمه الله
نعالى اخبرنى [٣]جعفر قال سمعت الجُنيْد [١] رحمه الله نعالى قال سمعت
[٤]سَريًّا يقول وقد وصف اهل [٥]الحقايق فقال أكلُهم أكلُ المَرْضَى ونَوْمهم
نوم الغَرْقَى، وسُيّل الجُنيْد [١] رحمه الله نعالى عن الحقيقة فقال [٦]أذْكُرُ ثم
أدَعُ هذا وهذا، وقال ابو تُراب [١] رحمه الله نعالى علامة الحقيقة [٧]البلوى،
وقال غيره علامة الحقيقة رفع [٨]البلوى، وحُكى عن رُوَيْم [١] رحمه الله نعالى
انّه قال انّ الحقايق ما [٩]قارن العلم، سمعت الوجيهى يقول سمعت ابا جعفر
[١٠]الصَّيْدلانى [١] رحمه الله نعالى يقول الحقايق ثلث حقيقة [١١]مع العلم   A f.97b
[١٢]وحقيقة [١٣]معها [١]العلم وحقيقة نشطح عن العلم، وقال ابو بكر الزقّاق
١٠ [١] رحمه الله نعالى كنت فى تيه بنى اسرائيل فوقع فى قلبى ان علم الحقيقة
يخالف علم الشريعة فاذا [١٤]بشخص تحت شجرة أُمّ غيلان [١٥]صاح يأبا بكر
كلّ حقيقة تخالف الشريعة [١٦]فهو كُفر، وقيل لبعضهم وأظنّه رُوَيْم [١] رحمه
الله نعالى واله [١] نعالى اعلم متى يتحقق العبد بالعبودية قال اذا سلّم [١٧]القياد
من نفسه الى ربّه وتبرّأ من حوله وقوّته وعلم انّ الكلّ [١٨]له وبه، وقال
١٥ رُوَيْم [١] رحمه الله نعالى اصحّ الحقايق ما قارن العلم، وقال الجُنيْد [١] رحمه
الله أبَت الحقايق ان تدع فى القلوب مقالةً للتأويلات، وقال المزيّن الكبير
[١] رحمه الله نعالى الذى حصل عليه اهل الحقايق فى حقايهم أنّ الله
[١٩]نعالى غير منفود فيُطْلَب ولا ذو غاية فيُدْرَكَ فمن ادرك موجودًا فهو
بالموجود [٢٠]مغرور وإنّما الموجود [٢١]عندنا معرفة حال وكشف علم بلا
٢٠ حال، وسمعت الحسين بن عبد الله الرازى [١] رحمه الله نعالى يقول سُبُل

---

[١] B om.   [٢] B om. قال الشيخ رحمه اسه نعالى.   [٣] B بن جعفر.

[٤] AB سرى.   [٥] B adds من العباد.   [٦] B adds ثم اجئ.   [٧] B التلوين.

[١٠]B الصيدلانى.   [٩] A فارق but corr. in marg.   [٨] B التلوين.   التلوين.

[١٤] B تشخص.   [١٣] B تبعها.   [١٢] B وحقيقتها.   [١١] B تبع.   المصرى.

[١٥] B وقال لى صاح.   [١٧] B الفؤاد.   [١٦] B فهى.   [١٨] B وله به.

[١٩] جل وعز.   [٢٠] A معروف.   [٢١] B عند.

عبد الله بن طاهر الأَبْهَرى [١] رحمه الله تعالى عن الحقيقة فقال الحقيقة كلّها
علم فسُئل عن العلم فقال العلم كلّه حقيقة، وعن الشِّبْلى [١] رحمه الله تعالى
انّه قال الأَلْسِنة ثلث لسان عِلْم ولسان حقيقة ولسان حقّ فلسان العلم مـا
تأدّى الينا بالوسائط ولسان الحقيقة ما اوصل الله [١] تعالى الى الاسرار بلا
واسطة ولسان الحقّ فليس [٢] له طريق، وحُكى عن ابى جعفر [٢] القَروىّ
[١] رحمه الله تعالى انّه قال حقيقة الانسانية ان لا يتأذّى منك انسان لأنّ
حقيقة الاسم فى نفسه أن [٤] يكون كلّ شىء بك [٥] مستأنِسًا، وسُئل بعض
الصوفية عن حقيقة الوصول فقال ذهاب العقول، وقال الجُنَيْد [١] رحمه الله
تعالى انّ الحقايق اللازمة [٦] والمقصود القوّية المُحْكَمة لم تُبْقِ على اهلها [٧] سببًا
الّا قطعتْه ولا معترَضًا الّا منعتْه ولا تأويلا [٨] مُوهِمًا لصحّة المراد الّا كشفتْه
فالحقّ عندم لصحّةِ الحال مجرّدًا والجِدّ فى دوام السَّيْرِ محدّدًا على براهين من
العلم واضحة ودلايل من [٩] الحقّ بيّنة، وقال الواسطى [١] رحمه الله تعالى
الحقايق المختزنة اذا بدت تحجبت الحقايق [١٠] المستترة، مسئلة فى الصدق،
[١١] قال الشيخ رحمه الله تعالى اخبرنى جعفر الخُلْدى [١] رحمه الله تعالى قال
سمعت الجُنَيْد [١] رحمه الله تعالى يقول ما من احدٍ طلب أمرًا بصدق وجدّ
الّا ادركه وان لم يدرك الكلّ ادرك البعض، [١٢] قال ابو سعيد الخرَّاز
[١] رحمه الله تعالى رأيتُ كأنّ مَلَكَيْن نزلا [١] علىَّ من السمآء فقالا لى مـا
الصدق قلتُ الوفآء بالعهد فقالا [١] لى صدقتَ فعرجا الى السمآء وأنا انظُرُ
اليهما يعنى فى النوم، وقال يوسف بن [١٣] الحسين [١] رحمه الله تعالى الصدق
عندى حُبُّ الانفراد ومناجاة الرب [١] جلّ وعلا وموافقة السرّ والعلانية مع
[١٤] صدق اللهجة والتشاغل بالنفس دون رؤية الخلق بعد هِمّة النفس ونعلّم

---

[١] B om.   [٢] B اليه.   [٣] A app. القروى.   [٤] B لا يكون لك

[٧] B app.   [٦] B والمقصود والعقود.   [٥] A مسنانس. شربك مستأنسًا.

[١١] B om.   [١٠] B السنيرة.   [٩] B الجد.   [٨] B منوهمًا. شيئًا

.قال الشيخ رحمه الله تعالى [١٢] B وقال.   [١٣] B adds الرازى.   [١٤] B الصدق.

العلم والاتباع مع تصحيح المطعم والملبس وأخْذ القوت، وسيل حكيمٌ ما علامة

الصادق قال كتمان الطاعة قيل ما أرْوَحُ الاشياء على قلوب الصادقين قال

(١) استنشاق عفو الله (٢) تعالى وحُسْن الظنّ باه (٢) تعالى، وقال (٢) تعالى، وقال (٢) ذو (٤) النون

(٢) رحمه الله تعالى الصدق سيف الله (٢) تعالى فى ارضه ما (٥) وُضع على شىء

٥ الّا قطعه، وسيل حارث (٢) رحمه الله تعالى عن الصدق (٦) فقال (٧) مصحوب

على جميع الاحوال، وقال الجُنَيْد رحمه الله تعالى حقيقة الصدق تجرى بموافقة

الله تعالى فى كلّ حال، وقال ابو يعقوب رحمه الله الصدق موافقة الحقّ

فى السرّ والعلانية وحقيقة صدق القول بالحقّ فى مواطن الهلكة، وسُيل آخر

عن الصدق فقال صحّة (٨) التوجّه فى القصد، مسئلة فى (٩) الاصول، يعنى

١٠ اصول مذهب القوم، حُكِى عن (١٠) الجُنَيْد (٢) رحمه الله تعالى انّه قال اتّفق

اهل العلم على ان اصولهم خمس خلال صيام النهار وقيام الليل واخلاص

العمل والإشراف على الأعمال بطول الرعاية (١١) والتوكّل على الله فى كلّ حال،

(٢) وحكُى عن ابى عثمٰن (٢) رحمه الله تعالى انّه قال اصلُنا (١٢) السكوت

والاكتفاء بعلم الله (١٣) عزّ وجلّ، وقال الجُنَيْد (٢) رحمه الله تعالى النقصان

١٥ فى الاحوال هى فروعٌ لا تضرّ وإنّما يضر التخلّف مثقال ذرّة فى حال الاصول

فاذا احكمت الاصول لم يضرّ (١٤) نقصٌ (٢) فى الفروع، وقال ابو احمـد

القلانسى (٢) رحمه الله تعالى بُنيت مذهبنا اصلُ على ثلث خصال لا نطالب

احدًا من الناس بواجب حقّا ونطالب أنفُسَنا بحقوق الناس ونُلزم أنفسنا

التقصير فى جميع ما نأتيه، وقال سهل بن عبد الله (٢) رحمه الله اصولنـا

٢٠ سبعة اشياء التمسّك بكتاب الله (٢) تعالى والاقتداء برسول الله (٢) صلعم

---

(١) A ذا.   (٢) B om.   (٣) A اشتياق with استنشاق in marg. as variant.   (٢) B om.

(٤) B adds المصرى.   (٥) A وضعها.   (٦) B قال.   (٧) B om. from مصحوب

to الصدق رحمه الله ابو يعقوب.   (٨) B seems to have التوحيد. The word is partially

obliterated.   (٩) B الاصول وهى مسئلة القوم مذهب اصول.   (١٠) A جنيد.

(١١) AB om. والتوكل الخ. The words are suppl. in marg. A.   (١٢) B السكون, but cf.

'Aṭṭár, Tadhkiratu'l-Awliyá, II, 60, 5.   (١٣) B تعلى.   (١٤) B يضر.

وأكلُ الحلال وكفُّ الأذى واجتناب الآثام والتوبة وإدآء الحقوق، وسمعت الحُصْرى (١) رحمه الله تعالى يقول اصولنا ستة اشياء رفْع الحدث وإفراد القدَم وهجر الاخوان ومفارقة الاوطان ونسيان ما عُلم وما جُهل، وقال بعض الفقرآء اصولنا سبعة اشياء ادآء الفرايض واجتناب المحارم وقطع العلايق ومعانقة الفقر وترك الطلب وترك الادّخار لوقتٍ (٢)ثانٍ والانقطاع الى الله تعالى (٣) فى جميع الاوقات، مسئلة فى الاخلاص، سُئِل الجُنَيْد (١) رحمه الله عن الاخلاص فقال ارتفاع رؤيتِك (٤) وفناؤك (٥)عن الفعل، وقال (٦)ابن عطآء الاخلاص ما (٧)تخلّص من (٨)الآفات، وقال حارث المحاسبى (١) رحمه الله تعالى الاخلاص إخراج الخَلْق من معاملة الله تعالى والنفسُ اوّل الخَلْق، وقال (٩)ذو النون (١) رحمه الله تعالى الاخلاص ما خلص من (١٠)العدوّ أن يُفْسِدَهُ، وقال ابو يعقوب السوسى (١) رحمه الله الاخلاص ما لم يعلم به مَلَكٌ فيكتبَهُ ولا عدوّ فيُفسِدَهُ ولا تُعْجَب النفس به، وحكى عن سهل بن عبد الله (١) رحمه الله تعالى انّه قال (١١)اهلُ لا اله الّا الله كثير والمخلصون (١٢)منهم قليل، وقال سهل (١٣)بن عبد الله (١) رحمه الله تعالى لا يعرف الرياءَ الّا المخلَص، وسُئل الجُنَيْد (١) رحمه الله تعالى مرّةً أُخْرَى عن الاخلاص فقال إخراج الخَلق من معاملة الله (١)تعالى والنفس اوّلُ الخَلق، وعن بعض المشايخ قال اذا قال لك قايلٌ ما الاخلاص (١٤)فقُل إفراد القصد الى الله (١)تعالى وإخراج الخَلق من معاملة الله (١٥)عزّ وجلّ بترك الحَوْل والقوّة مع الله (١) عزّ وجلّ، وعلامة المخلَص (١٦)محبّة الخلوات لمناجاة الله تعالى وقلّة التعرّف الى الخَلق بعبودية الله (١)عزّ وجلّ وكراهية علم الخَلق فى معاملة الله تعالى (١٧)، وسُئل اظنُّهُ (١٨)ابا الحسين النورى (١) رحمه الله تعالى عن الاخلاص

A f.٩٩a

(١) B om.   (٢) A باقى B .ثانٍ   (٣) B عزوجل.   (٤) B وفناك.

(٥) A ذا.   (٦) B بن.   (٧) A خلّص.   (٨) B الاوقات.   (٩) A من.

(١٠) B الاعدا.   (١١) A om. but قائل suppl. in marg.   (١٢) A منه.

(١٣) B om. بن عبد الله.   (١٤) A فقال.   (١٥) B تعلى.   (١٦) A محبة.

(١٧) B عزوجل.   (١٨) B om. ابا الحسين.

فقال تَرْك الموافقة للخلق، مسئلة فى الذِّكْرِ، [١]قال الشيخ رحمه الله تعالى
سمعت [٢]ابن سالم يقول وسُئِل عن الذكر فقال الذكر على ثلث [٣]فذِكرٌ
باللسان فذاك الحسنة بعشرة وذكرٌ بالقلب [٤]فذاك [٥]الحسنة [٦]بسبعمايـة
وذكر لا يوزن ثوابه ولا يُعَدُّ وهو الامتلاء من المحبّة والحياء من قُرْبه،
قيل لابن [٤]عطاء [٤]رحمه الله تعالى ما يفعل الذكر بالسراير فقال ذكرُ الله
[٤]تعالى اذا ورد على السراير [٧]بإشراقه [٨]ازال البشريةَ [٩]فى الحقيقـة
برعوناتها، وقال سهل بن عبد الله [٤]رحمه الله تعالى ليس كلّ من ادّعى
الذكر [١٠]فهو ذاكرٌ، وسُئِل سهل [١١]بن عبد الله رحمه الله تعالى عن الذكر
فقال تحقيق العلم بأنّ الله [٤]تعالى مُشاهدك فتراه بقلبك قريبًا منك ونستحى
منه ثم تؤثره على نفسك [١٢]وعلى احوالك كلّها، قال [١٣]الشيخ [٤]رحمه الله
تعالى قال الله [١٤]عزّ وجلّ [١٥]اذْكُرُوا اللهَ كَذِكْرِكُمْ آبَاءَكُمْ أَوْ أَشَدَّ ذِكْرًا
ثم قال فى آية اخرى [١٦]اذْكُرُوا اللهَ ذِكْرًا كَثِيرًا فهو [١٧]أخصَر من الاوّل
ثم قال فى آية أُخرى [١٨]اذْكُرُونِى أَذْكُرْكُمْ، [١٩]فصار [٢٠]الذاكرون [٢١]لله
متفاوتين فى ذكرهم [٢٢]كتفاوتهم [٤]فى المخاطبة لهم [٢٣]فى الذكر، [٢٤]قال
وسُئِل بعض المشايخ عن الذكر فقال المذكور واحدٌ والذكر مختلف ومحلّ
قلوب الذاكرين [٢٥]متفاوت، وأصلُ الذكر اجابة الحقّ من حيث اللوازم
والذكر على وجهيْن فوجهٌ منها التهليل والتسبيح وتلاوة القرآن ووجهٌ [٤]منها
تنبيه القلوب على شرايط [٢٦]التذكير على إفراد الله [٤]تعالى وأسمآئه وصفاته

[١] B om. قال الشيخ رحمه الله تعالى.   [٢] بن B.   [٣] ذكر B.   [٤] B om.
[٥] ازالت A.   [٦] سبع مايه B.   [٧] باشراقها A.   [٨] فالحسنة B.
[٩] عن A.   [١٠] هو B.   [١١] B om. from بن to تعالى.   [١٢] على A.
[١٣] ابو نصر B.   [١٤] تعالى فى موضع من كتابه B.   [١٥] Kor. 2, 196.
[١٦] Kor. 33, 41. A om. from اذكروا to فى آية اخرى.   [١٧] احصر B.
[١٨] Kor. 2, 147.   [١٩] فصاروا A.   [٢٠] الناكرين AB.   [٢١] لله تعالى B.
[٢٢] كتفاوت B.   [٢٣] بالذكر B.   [٢٤] كما سيل B.   [٢٥] متفاوتة AB.
[٢٦] التيقض B.

ونشر إحسانه ونفاذ تقديره على جميع خلقه فذكّر الراجين على وعْنه وذكّر
الخائفين على وعنه وذكّر المتوكّلين على ما كشف لهم من كفايته وذكّر المراقبين
على مقدار ما (١)طلع عليهم باطّلاع الله (٢)تعالى عليهم وذكّر (٣)المحبّين على
قدر تصفّح النَّعْماء، وسُئل الشِّبْلى (٢) رحمه الله تعالى عن حقيقة الذكر فقال
٥ نسيان (٤)الذكر يعنى نسيان ذكرك (٥)له (٢)تعالى ونسيان (٦)كلّ شىء سوى
الله عزّ وجلّ، مسئلة فى الغنا، سُئل الجُنَيْد (٢) رحمه الله تعالى ايّـها اتمّ
الاستغناء بالله (٢)تعالى ام الافتقار الى الله عزّ وجلّ فقال الافتقار (٧)الى الله
عزّ وجلّ مُوجِبة للغنا بالله (٢)عزّ وجلّ فاذا صحّ الافتقار الى الله (٢)عزّ وجلّ
كمل الغنا بالله (٢)تعالى فلا يقال (٨)أيّـهما اتمّ لانّهما حالان لا يتمّ احدها
١٠ الاّ بتمام الآخَر ومن صحّ الافتقار صحّ الغنا، (٢)قال وسُئل يوسف بن
الحسين (٢) رحمه الله تعالى ما علامة الغنا قال الذى يكون غِناه للدين لا
للدنيا (٢)قيل ومتى يكون الغنىّ محمودًا فى غِناه غير مذموم قال اذا كان
هذا الغنىّ آخِذَ الشىء من (٩)جهته غير مانع (٢)عن حقّه (١٠)متعاونًا فى كسبه
على البرّ والتقوى لا متعاونًا فى تجارته على الإثم والعدوان (١١)ولم يتعلّق قلبه
Af.100a ماله دون الله (٢)عزّ وجلّ ولا استوحش لفقْده ولا استأنس بمُلْكه وكان فى
(١٢)غِناه مفتقرًا الى الله عزّ وجلّ وفى فقره مستغنيًا بالله (٢)تعالى ويكون خازنًا
من خُزّان الله (٢)تعالى (١٣)فكان غِناه له لا عليه فاذا كان بهذه الصفة
كان من اهل النَّوز والنجاة ودخل الجنّة بعد الفقراء بخمسماية عام بخبر رسول
الله صلعم تدخل فقراء امّتى (٢)الجنّة قبل اغنيايها بخمسماية عام، وسُئل (١٤)عمرو
٢٠ ابن عثمن المكّى (٢) رحمه الله عن (١٥)الغنا الذى (٢)هو جامعٌ للغنا (١٦)فقال

---

(١) B اطلع.   (٢) B om.   (٣) A المحبّين with المحسن in marg. as variant.

(٤) B om. الذكر يعنى نسيان.   (٥) B له.   (٦) B ذكر كل.   (٧) A بالله.

(٨) A باهما.   (٩) B جهة.   (١٠) AB متعاون.   (١١) A ولا.

(١٢) B غنايه.   (١٣) B وكان.   (١٤) B عمر.   (١٥) B الغنى.   (١٦) A om.

B proceeds: الغنى الذى هو الغنى الذى للغنا الغنا عن الغنا.

الغنا عن الغنا لانّك اذا استغنيتَ بالغنا كنتَ محتاجًا اليها من اجْل [١]استغنآيك واذا كنت [٢]غنيًّا بالله [٣]عزّ وجلّ لا بالغنا تكون مستغنيًا عن الغنا وغير الغنا، وقال الجُنيْد [٤]رحمه الله تعالى النفس التى قد اعزّها الحقّ بحقيقة الغنا يزول عنها موافقات الفاقات، مسئلة فى الفقر، قال الجُنيْد [٤]رحمه الله تعالى [٤]الفقر بحر [٥]البلاء وبلاؤه كلّه عزّ، وسُئل عن الفقير الصادق متى يكون مستوجبًا لدخول الجنّة قبل الاغنيآء بخمسمائة عام [٦]فقال اذا كان هذا الفقير معاملًا لله [٣]عزّ وجلّ بقلبه موافقًا لله فيا مُنع حتى يعُدّ [٧]الفقر من الله نعمةً عليه يخاف على زوالها كما يخاف الغنّى على زوال غناه وكان صابرًا محتسبًا مسرورًا باختيار الله له الفقر صائنًا لدينه كاتمًا للفقر [٨]مظهرًا للايأس من الناس مستغنيًا بربّه فى فقره كما قال الله عزّ وجلّ [٩]لِلفُقَرَآءِ الَّذِينَ أُحْصِرُوا فِى سَبِيلِ [١٠]اللهِ الآية، فاذا كان الفقير بهذه الصفة يدخل الجنّة قبل الاغنيآء بخمسمائة عام ويُكْفَى يوم القيمة مؤنة الوقوف والحساب ان شآء الله [٣]تعالى، وقال [١١]ابن الجلّاء [٤]رحمه الله تعالى من لم يصحبه الورع فى فقره أكل الحرام [١٢]النّصّ [١٢]وهو لا يدرى، وسُئل الجُنيْد [٤]رحمه الله تعالى عن اعزّ [١٤]الناس فقال الفقير الراضى، [١٥]وقال المزيّن رحمه الله حدّ الفقر ان لا ينفكّ الفقير من الحاجة، وقال المزيّن [٤]رحمه الله تعالى اذا رجع الفقير الى الله [١٦]عزّ وجلّ كان موصوفًا مع العلوم فيخيّر فى وجوده، وقال الجُنيْد [٤]رحمه الله تعالى لا يحقّق الانسان بالفقر حتى يتقرّر عنه انّه لا يرِدُ القيمة أفقَر منه، مسئلة فى الروح وما [١٧]قالوا فيه، قال [١٨]الشِبلى رحمه الله [٣]تعالى [١٩]باله قامت الارواح والاجساد والخطرات

---

(١) استعائتك A.   (٢) B مستغنيا.   (٣) B om.   (٤) B الفقير.   (٥) B بلاوه.

(٦) B قال.   (٧) B الفقير bis.   (٨) B مظهر الايأس.   (٩) Kor. 2, 274.

(١٠) B adds لا يستطيعون ضربًا فى الارض.   (١١) B بن.   (١٢) B البض.

(١٣) B الاشيا.   (١٤) B ولا يدرى.   (١٥) B om. from وقال to الحاجة من.

(١٦) B وجل.   (١٧) B قالوه.   (١٨) ابو بكر الشبلى.   (١٩) باله جل وعلا.

لا بذواتها، وقال (١)الشبلى رحمه الله تعالى الارواح تلطَّفت فتعلَّقت عند
(٢)الدغات الحقيقة فلم (٣)تر معبودًا (٤)يستحقّ العبادة (٥)عن ان تتقرَّب الى
ذلك الشاهد بغير ذلك المُشاهد وأيقنتْ ان الحدث لا يدرك القديم
بصفته المعلولة، قال (٦)الشيخ رحمه الله تعالى ورأيتُ (٧)فى كلام الواسطى
٥ رحمه الله تعالى فى الروح روحان روح به حياة الخلق وروح
به ضياء (٨)القلب وهو الروح الذى قال الله (٩)عزَّ وجلَّ (١٠)وَكَذَلِكَ
اوْحَيْنَا إِلَيْكَ رُوحًا مِنْ أَمْرِنَا، (١١)وسمّى الروح روحًا للطاقته واذا اسَاءَت
الجوارح فى اوقاتها الأَدَبَ حُجِبَ الروح عن (١٢)ملادغات السَّبَب، (١٢)قال
(١٤)وكلَّما وقع للروح من الملاحظات (١٥)ذَنْبٌ على الايّام والاوقات عرفت
١٠ المخاطبات واشارت الى (١٦)المعاملات، وقال (١٧)الواسطى (١٨)رحمه الله تعالى
انّها ها شيئان الروح والعقل (١٨)فالروح لا (١٩)تُسْدى الى الروح محبوبًا ولا
العقل ينهّأ له ان يدفع عن العقل مكروهًا، وحُكى عن ابى عبد الله
النِباجى (١٨)رحمه الله تعالى انّه قال ان العارف اذا (٢٠)وصل فكان فيه
روح روحان روح لا يجرى عليه التغيير (٢١)والاختلاف وروح يجرى عليه التغيير
١٥ والتلوين، (١٨)وقال بعضهم روحان الروح القديمة والروح البشرية
(٢٣)واحتجَّ بقول النبىّ صلعم تنام عيناےَ ولا ينام قلبى، قال فظاهره ينام
بروح البشرية وباطنه يقظان لا يجرى عليه التغيير، وكذلك قوله انّما
Af.101a أنَّسى لأَسُنَّ (٢٤)وقد اخبر انّه لا يُنْسَى وانّما (٢٥)هو خبرٌ عمّا هو فيه من
الروح القديمة، وكذلك قوله لستُ كأحدكم إنّى أَظَلُّ عند ربّى، وهو صفة

---

(١) B ايضًا instead of الشبلى رحمه الله تعالى. (٢) B لذغات. (٢) B ترد.
(٤) B استحق. (٥) B app. ثم. (٦) B om. الشيخ رحمه الله تعالى. (٧) B لابى.
(١٠) Kor. (٩) B تعلى. (٨) B الخلق. بكر الواسطى فى كلامه فى الروح الخ.
42, 52. (١١) B وسمى. (١٢) A ملادعات. (١٢) B ملاوعات. (١٢) B وقال..
(١٤) B كلما. (١٥) A رفت. B app. دنب. (١٦) B المعايات. (١٧) B ابو.
(٢١) B om. (١٨) B om. (١٩) A سوى. (٢٠) B رحل. بكر الواسطى.
from اخبرعها B (٢٥). والاختلاف to التغيير. (٢٢) A والتكوين. (٢٣) B adds فى ذلك. (٢٤) B فقد.
.اخبرعها B (٢٥)

الروح القديمة لانّه اخبر عنها بما ليس من (١) وصْف الارواح، (٢) قال الشيخ
رحمه الله تعالى (٣) وهذا الذى قال (٤) القايل فى الروح لا يصحّ لانّ القديم
لا ينفصل من القديم والمخلوق غير متّصل بالقديم (٥) وبالله التوفيق، سمعت
(٦) ابن سالم وقد سُئل عن الثواب والعقاب يكون للروح وللجسد او للجسد
٥ وحْده فقال الطاعة والمعصية لم تظهر من الجسد دون الروح ولا من الروح
دون الجسد حتى يكون الثواب والعقاب على (٧) الجسد دون الروح او على
الروح دون الجسد، ومن قال فى الارواح بالتناسخ والتنقّل والقِدَم فقد ضلّ
ضلالاً بعيدًا وخسر خسرانًا مبينًا، مسئلة فى الاشارة، (٢) قال الشيخ رحمه الله
تعالى ان سأل سايلٌ ما معنى الاشارة (٨) فيقال لـه قول الله عزّ وجلّ
١٠ (٩) تَبَارَكَ (١٠) الَّذِى (١١) والذى كالكناية (١١) والكناية كالاشارة فى لطافتها
والاشارة لا يدركها الاّ الاكابر من اهل العلم، (١٢) وقال الشِبْلى (١١)
رحمه الله تعالى كلّ اشارة اشار (١٣) الخلق بها الى الحقّ فهى مردودة عليهم حتى
يشيروا الى الحقّ بالحقّ ليس لهم الى ذلك طريق، (١٢) وقال ابو (١٤) يزيد
(١١) رحمه الله تعالى أبْعَدُهم من الله (١١) تعالى أكْثَرُهم اشارة اليه، قال ودخل
١٥ رجل (١٥) الى الجُنَيْد (١١) رحمه الله تعالى (١٦) فسأله عن مسئلة فأشار الجنيد
بعينه الى السماء، فقال له الرجل يأبا القسم لا تشير اليه فانّه أقْرَب (١١) اليك
من ذلك فقال الجنيد (١١) رحمه الله صدقتَ وضحك، (١١) حُكى (١٧) عن عمرو
ابن عثمُن المكّى (١١) رحمه الله تعالى انّه قال اصحابنا حقيقتهم توحيد واشارتهم
شِرْك، وقال بعضهم كلّ يريد ان (١٨) يشير اليه (١٩) ولكن لم يجعل لأحد
٢٠ اليه سبيلاً، وحُكى عن الجُنَيْد (١١) رحمه الله تعالى انّه قال لرجل (٢٠) هو ذا

---

(١) صفْ B.   (٢) B om. قال الشيخ رحمه الله تعالى.   (٣) وهو A.   (٤) B هذا.
(٥) B om. وبالله التوفيق.   (٦) B بن.   (٧) B الجسد دون الروح
او الجسد دون الروح.   (٨) A فقال لقول الله.   (٩) Kor. 25, 1; 67, 1.
(١٠) B adds بيد الملك (Kor. 67, 1).   (١١) B om.   (١٢) B قال.   (١٤) B بها.
(١٥) B على.   (١٦) B بساله.   (١٧) B وعن.   (١٤) B adds البسطامى.   الخلق
(١٨) A يشيروا.   (١٩) B ولكنه.   (٢٠) B om. هو ذا نشير.

است

A.f.101b تُشير يا هذا فكم (١)تُشير اليه دَعْهُ يشير اليك، وقال ابو يزيد (٢)رحمه الله
تعالى من اشار اليه بعلم فقد كفَر لأنّ الاشارة بعلم لا تقع الا على معلوم ومن
اشار اليه بمعرفة فقد أَلْحَدَ (٣)لأنّ الاشارة بالمعرفة لا تقع الا على محدود،
سمعت الدُقّى يقول سُبُل (٤)الزّقّاق (٢)رحمه الله عن المريد فقال حقيقة المريد
ان يشير الى الله (٢)تعالى فيَجِدَ الله مع نفس الاشارة (٥)وقيل له فالذى
يَسْتَوعِبُ حالَهُ قال هو أن يجد الله (٢)تعالى بإسقاط الاشارة، وهذه المسئلة
تُعرّف لِلجُنَيْد رحمه الله (٢)تعالى وقال (٢)النّورى (٧)رحمه الله تعالى قُرْب
القُرْب (٨)فيا أَشَرْنا اليه بُعْد البُعْد، وقال يحيى بن (٩)مُعاذ (٢)رحمه الله
تعالى اذا رأيتَ الرجل يشير الى العمل فطريقه طريق الورع واذا رأيته
يشير الى العلم فطريقه طريق العبادة واذا رأيته يشير الى الأمْن فى الرزق
فطريقه طريق الزهد واذا رأيته يشير الى الآيات فطريقه طريق الأبْدال
واذا رأيته يشير الى الآلاءَ فطريقه طريق العارفين، وقال ابو علىّ الروذبارى
(٢)رحمه الله تعالى عِلْمُنا هذا اشارة فاذا صار عبارةً (١٠)خَفِىَ، وسأل رجل
ابا يعقوب السوسى (٢)رحمه الله تعالى مسئلةً وكان يشير فى سؤاله فقال له
يا هذا نحن نَبْلُغُ (١١)مجابك من غير هذه الاشارة (١٢)كأنّه يكره ذلك منه،
مسائل شتّى، مسئلة فى (١٤)الظرف، سُئِل الجُنَيْد (٢)رحمه الله تعالى عن
(١٤)الظرف ما هو فقال اجتناب كلّ خُلق دنِىّ واستعمال كلّ خُلق سنِىّ وأن
تعمل (١٥)لله ثمّ لا ترى انّك عملت، مسئلة فى المروّة، سُئِل احمد بن عطآء
(٢)رحمه الله تعالى عن المروّة فقال ان لا تستكثر لله عملاً علّتَهُ وكلّما عملتَ
عملاً كأنّك لم تعمل شيئًا وتريد أكثر من ذلك، مسئلة لِمَ سُمِّيت هذه الطائفة

(١) A سير. (٢) B om. (٣) B ٢٨. (٤) B الدقى altered to الدقّاق.
(٥) B قيل. (٦) AB سنوعب. (٧) B ابو الحسين النورى. (٨) B فيا معنى.
(٩) B adds الرازى. (١٠) A جفا. B خفا. (١١) A محابك.B محابك.
Cf. p. ١٨٠, l. ٧ supra, where read مجابك instead of مكانك. (١٢) B om. الخ كأنّه.
(١٣) A الطرق.B الطرو. (١٤) A الطرق.B الطرف. (١٥) B لله عز وجل.

Af.102a بهذا الاسم، يعنى الصوفية، قال (١)ابن عطآء (٢)رحمه الله تعالى لصفآيها من كدر الاغيار وخروجها من مراتب الاشرار، وقال النورى (٢)رحمه الله تعالى سمّيت بهذا الاسم (٣)لاشتمالها عن الخلق بظاهر العابدين وانقطاعها الى الحقّ بمراتب الواجدين، وقال الشبلى (٢)رحمه الله تعالى سمّيت بهذا الاسم لبقيّة (٤)بقيت عليهم من نفوسهم ولولا ذلك لما لاقت بهم الاسمآء، وقال بعضهم (٥)سمّيت بهذا الاسم لتنسّمها بروح الكناية وتظاهرها بوصف الانابة، مسئلة فى الرزق، قال يحيى بن معاذ (٢)رحمه الله تعالى فى وجود العبد الرزقَ من غير طلب دلالةً على أنّ الرزق مأمور بطلب صاحبه، وقال بعضهم ان طلبتُ الرزق قبل وقته لم أجدْه وإن (٦)طلبتُ الرزق بعد وقته لم اجدْه وإن (٧)طلبته فى وقته كفيته، وحُكى عن ابى يعقوب (٢)رحمه الله تعالى انّه قال اختلف (٢)الناس فى (٨)سبب الرزق فقال قوم سبب الرزق التكلّف والعناية وهو قول القَدَريّة وقال قوم سبب الرزق التقوى (٩)وذهبوا الى ظاهر القرآن (١٠)وَمَنْ يَتَّقِ اللَّهَ يَجْعَلْ لَهُ مَخْرَجًا وَيَرْزُقْهُ مِنْ حَيْثُ لاَ يَحْتَسِبُ، وغلطوا فى ذلك (١١)والعلمُ عند الله (٢)تعالى ان سبب الرزق الخِلْقة (١٢)لقوله عزّ وجلّ (١٣)خَلَقَكُمْ ثُمَّ رَزَقَكُمْ فلم يخصّ مؤمنًا دون كافر، وقال ابو (١٤)يزيد (٢)رحمه الله انثيتُ على (٢)رجل من المريدين عند بعض العلمآء خيرًا فقال العالم مِن اين معاشهُ فقلت لم اشكّ فى خالقه حتى اسأله عن رازقه فخجل العالم وانقطع، مسئلة، سُئِل الجُنَيْد (٢)رحمه الله تعالى اذا ذهب اسم العبد وثبت حُكْم الله (٢)تعالى قال أعلم رحمك الله (٢)تعالى انه اذا عظمت المعرفة بالله ذهبت آثار العبد (١٥)وامّحت رسومه فعند ذلك Af.102b يبدو علم الحقّ وثبت اسم حُكْم الله (٢)تعالى، مسئلة، سُئِل الجُنَيْد (٢)رحمه

---

(١) B بن‍. (٢) B om. (٣) A لاشتمالها. B appears to read لاشتمالها, but the word is indistinct. (٤) B بقيه. (٥) B الصوفية سميت. (٦) B طلبته. (٧) B طلبت. (٨) B سبيل. (٩) B ذهبوا. (١٠) Kor. 65, 2. (١١) A وللعلم. (١٢) B والخلقه. (١٣) Kor. 30, 39. (١٤) B adds البسطامى. (١٥) B وامّحت.

الله تعالى متى يستوى عند العبد حامدُه وذامُّه (١) فقال اذا علم انّه مخلوق
ويكون (٢) نِعمًّا، مسئلة، سُئِل (٤) ابن عطاء (٥) رحمه الله تعالى متى يُنال
سلامة الصدر او (٦) بما ينال سلامة (٥) الصدر قال بالوقوف على حقّ اليقين،
وهو القرآن ثم يُعطَى عِلمُ اليقين ثم يطالع بعد عَيْنَ اليقين فيَسْلَم صدرُه عند
ذلك وعلامة ذلك أن يرضى بقضايه وقدره هيبةً ومحبّةً ويراه حَفيظًا ووكيلاً
من غير تهمة (٧) اعترضت، مسئلة، سُئِل ابو عثمٰن (٥) رحمه الله تعالى عن
الغمّ الذى يجىء (٥) الانسان ولا يدرى من (٨) أيش هو فقال ابو (٩) عثمٰن
رحمه الله تعالى ان (١٠) الروح تحفّظ (١١) الذنوب واجنايات على النفس
وتنساها النفس فاذا وجدت الروح صحوًا من النفس عُرض عليها جناياتها
(١٢) فيغشاها الانكسار والذوبان وهو الغمّ الذى يجىء ولا يدرى من اين
دخل عليه، مسئلة فى الفراسة، سُئل (١٣) يوسف بن الحسين (٥) رحمه الله
تعالى عن حديث النبىّ صلعم اتّقوا فراسة المؤمن فانّه ينظر بنور الله (٥) تعالى
فقال هذا من رسول الله صلعم حقٌّ وخصوصية لأهل الايمان وزيادة
(١٤) وكرامة لمن نوّر الله (٥) تعالى قلبه وشرح صدرُه وليس لأحد ان يحكم
لنفسه بذلك وإن كثر صوابُه (١٥) وقلّ خطاؤه ومن لم يحكم لنفسه بحقيقة
الايمان والولاية والسعادة فكيف يحكم لنفسه بفضل الكرامة وإنّما ذلك
فضله لأهل الايمان من غير اشارة الى احد بعينه، مسئلة لابرهيم الخوّاص
(٥) رحمه الله تعالى فى الوهم، (١٦) سُئِل (١٧) ابرهيم الخوّاص رحمه الله تعالى عن
الوهم فقال الوهم هو قيام بين العقل والفهم لا منسوب الى العقل فيكون شيئًا
من صناته ولا منسوب الى الفهم فيكون شيئًا من صفاته وهو قيام وهو

---

(١) قال B.   (٢) يكون B.   (٣) A غا with كما written above. B م.
(٤) بن B.   (٥) B om.   (٦) م B.   (٧) عرضت B.   (٨) اى شى B.
(٩) B adds الحيرى.   (١٠) الروح الذى A.   (١١) بالذنوب B.   (١٢) A فغشاها.
(١٣) B موسك.   (١٤) كرامة B.   (١٥) كل A.   (١٦) وسيل B.   (١٧) B om.
تعالى to ابرهيم from.

Af.103a [١]شبيه [٢]بضوء بين شمس وماء فلا يُنسَب الى الشمس ولا ينسب الى المآء
وشبيه بوَسَن بين النوم واليقظة فلا نايم ولا يقظان فين [٣]صَحوٌ وهو [٤]نفاذ
العقل الى الفهم او الفهم الى العقل حتى [١]لا يكون بينهما قيام والفهم صفوة
العقل كما أنّ خالص الشىء لُبُّه، مسئلة، سُيل ابو [٥]يزيد [١]رحمه الله تعالى
عن معنى [٦]قوله [٧]ثُمَّ أَوْرَثْنَا ٱلْكِتَابَ ٱلَّذِينَ ٱصْطَفَيْنَا مِنْ عِبَادِنَا [٨]الآية،
قال ابو [٥]يزيد [١]رحمه الله تعالى السابق مضروب بسوط المحبّة مقتول
بسيف الشوق مضطجع على باب الهيبة والمقتصد مضروب بسوط الحسرة
مقتول بسيف الندامة مضطجع على باب الكرم والظالم مضروب بسوط الامل
مقتول بسيف الحرص مضطجع على باب العقوبة، [٩]وقال غيره الظالم لنفسه
معاقَب بالحجاب والمقتصد والج داخل الباب والسابق بالخيرات [١٠]ساجد
على البساط للملك الوهّاب، وقال غيره الظالم معاقب بالندامة على الافراط
والمقتصد مشتمل بالكلاية والاحتياط والسابق بالخيرات [١٠]ساجد بقلبه
للحقّ على البساط، الظالم لنفسه بتلويح [١١]الاشارة محجوب والمقتصد بتصريح
الاشارة مكنوف والسابق بالخيرات بتصحيح الاشارة محبوب، وقال غيره
الظالم لنفسه د والمقتصد ب والسابق بالخيرات م، مسئلة فى التمنّى، سُيل
رُوَيم بن احمد [١]رحمه الله تعالى هل للمريد ان يتمنّى فقال ليس له [١٢]ان
يتمنّى وله ان يأمل لأن فى التمنّى رؤية النفس وفى الآمال رؤيـة السبق
والتمنّى من صفات النفس والتأمّل صنعة القلب [١٢]واله اعلم، مسئلة فى سرّ
النفس، قال سهل بن عبد الله [١]رحمه الله وسُيل عن سرّ النفس فقال
للنفس سرٌّ ما ظهر ذلك السرّ على احد من خلقه الّا على فرعون فقال أنا

---

(١) B om.   (٢) B ضو.   (٣) B محوه.   (٤) AB نفاذ.   (٥) B adds
البسطامى.   (٦) B قوله عز وجل.   (٧) Kor. 35, 29.   (٨) Instead of
الآية   (٩) A om. فمنهم ظالم لنفسه ومنهم مقتصد ومنهم سابق بالخيرات باذن الله B has
الاضاره.   (١٠) B ساجى.   (١١) B الاشاره from والسابق بالخيرات m to وقال غيره
(١٢) B om. والله اعلم.   (١٢) ان يتمنى for ذلك B.

رَبُّكُم الأَعْلَى ولها سبع حُجُب سماوية وسبع حُجُب أرْضية فكما يدفن العبد
نفسَه أرْضًا أرضًا سما قلبــه سماءً سماءً فاذا دفنتَ النفسَ تحت الثرى
[١] وصلتَ بالقلب الى العرش، مسئلة، سُئِل الشبْلى [٢] رحمه الله تعالى عن
الغيرة فقال الغيرة غيرتان غيرة البشرية وغيرة [٣] الالهية فغيرة البشرية على
٥ الأشخاص وغيرة [٤] الالاهيه على الوقت أن يضيع فيا سوى الله [٤] تعالى،
مسئلة، قال فَتْح بن شَخْرَف [٢] رحمه الله تعالى [٥] سألتُ اسرافيل استاذ
[٦] ذى [٧] النون [٨] رحمهما الله تعالى فقلت له ايها الشيخ هل نُعَذَّبُ الأَسرار
قَبْلَ الزلل فلم [٩] يُجِبْنى [١٠] ايامًا ثم قال يا فتح [١١] إن نويتَ قبل العمل فتعذّب
الأَسرار قبل الزلل قال ثم صرخ صرخةً عاش ثلثة ايام ثم مات، مسئلة،

Af.103b

١٠ سبيل ابو بكر [١٢] محمّد بن موسى الفَرْغانى المعروف بالواسطى [٢] رحمه الله
تعالى عن صفة القلوب فقال القلوب على ثلثة احوال قلوب ممتحنة وأخرى
[١٣] مصطلَمة وأخرى [١٤] منتسفة وأوّايل احوالها الانتساف وهو المختفّ بأوّاّيله
انّه [١٥] لم يكن قَبْل شيئًا مذكورًا فاذا حضرتَ وقعتَ الى الاصطلام وهو
الموت ثم الطَّمْس وهو ذهابٌ فهذا [١٦] أوّلُكَ وآخِرُكَ كى لا تقول أنا اقبلتُ
١٥ وأدبرتُ وهذه الثلثة أَخْرَسَت الأَلسُنَ عن النطق، مسئلة، سبيل [١٧] الجُريرى
[٢] رحمه الله تعالى عن البلاَء فقال البلاَء على ثلثة اوجه على المُخلصين نِقَم
وعقوبات وعلى السابقين تمحيص [١٨] وكفّارات وعلى الانبياَء والصدّيقين من
صِدق [١٩] الاختيارات، مسئلة فى الفرق بين [٢٠] الحُبّ والوَدّ، الحُبّ فيه بُعْد
وفيه قُرْب والوَدّ لا فيه قطْع ولا بُعْد ولا قُرْب انّ شاهدَ الحُبّ حقُّ اليقين

---

(١) B العرش الى القلب وصل.   (٢) B om.   (٣) A الاهيه.   (٤) B عزوجل.

(٥) B وسالت.   (٦) B ذا. A ذو.   (٧) B adds المصوى.   (٨) B om.

(٩) A يخبر.   A orig. رحمه but corr. by later hand.   (١٠) B ايام.

(١١) A نودت اذ.   (١٢) A om.   (١٣) AB مظلمه.   (١٤) B منطسة.

(١٥) Cf. Kor. 76, 1.   (١٦) B لذاك.   (١٧) B الجريرى.   (١٨) وحامات.

(١٩) A الاختيارات. B الاحتارات.   (٢٠) B الود والحب.

وشاهد الودّ عَيْنَ اليقين وشاهد الصيانة عِلْمُ اليقين والودّ وَصْلٌ بلا مواصلة
لانّ الوصل ثابت والمواصلة تصرُّفُ الاوقات، مسئلة فى البُكَاء، سُئل ابو
سعيد الخرّاز (١) رحمه الله تعالى عن البُكَاء فقال البُكَاء من الله والى الله
وعلى الله، فالبُكَاء من الله لطول تعذيبه (٢)بالحنين عنه اذا ذكر طول المدّة
٥ الى لقائه والبُكَاء من خوف الانقطاع والبُكَاء من الفَرَق لما (٣)تواعده من
المكافأة (٤)لمن قصّر والبُكَاء من الفزع اذا قام الإشفاق من الحادثات التى
تحرم الوصول اليه، والبُكَاء اليه وهو أن يتكلّف سرُّه (٥)الهِيجان اليه والبُكَاء
من طيران الأرواح بالحنين (٦)اليه والبُكَاء من ولَّه العقل اليه والبُكَاء من
التأوّه والبُكَاء من الوقوف بين يديه والبُكَاء برقّة الشكوى اليه والبُكَاء
(٧)بالتضرّع على بساط الذلّ طَلَبَ الزُلْفَى لديه والبُكَاء عند المنافسة اذا توهّم
أنّه (٨)بُطِّئَ به عنه والبُكَاء خوفًا أن (٩)ينقطع الطريق فلا يصل اليه والبُكَاء
خوفًا أن لا يَصلح (١٠)للقائه والبُكَاء من الحياء منه بأيّ عين ينظر اليه، ثم
البُكَاء عليه اذا (٨)بُطِّئَ به عنه فى بعض الاوقات ممّا عوّده والبُكَاء من
الفرح فى نفس وصوله اليه اذا اكنفه بِبِرّه كالصبيّ (١١)الرضيع (١٢)يرتضع
١٥ ثدى أمّه وهو يبكى (١٣)فهذا ثمانية عشر وجهًا، مسئلة فى الشاهد، سُئل
الجُنَيد (١) رحمه الله تعالى لِمَ سُمّى الشاهد شاهدًا فقال الشاهد (١٤)الحقُّ شاهدٌ
فى ضميرك وأسرارك مطّلعًا (١٥)عليها وشاهدًا لجلاله فى خلقه وعباده فاذا نظر
الناظر اليه شهد عِلْمَة بنظره اليه، وشاهدُ الصوفيّة هو أنْ يقطع مَنْزِلَ
المُريدين فيشهد (١٦)عُمومَ العارفين (١٧)وحَمَلَةِ اسم الشاهد الحاضر فى الغَيْب
٢٠ لا يحرج ولا (١٨)يفتر ولا يتغافل فان غفل غفلة مريد فليس بشاهد، وكلّما
يجرى فيه غير هذا فى ظاهر الخليقة فهو باطل فليس هو طريق الصوفية،

(١) B om.   (٢) A بالحشر.   (٣) B تواعد.   (٤) A لما.   (٥) B الهيجان.

(٦) B عنه.   (٧) A بالتمرع B بالتصرع.   (٨) B نظر.   (٩) B om. from ينقطع

to ان خوفًا.   (١٠) B ...لدعا. The word is partly obliterated.   (١١) B المرضع.

(١٢) B يرضع.   (١٣) B فهذه.   (١٤) B شاهد الحق.   (١٥) B فى خلقه وشاهد الحال.

(١٦) B هوم.   (١٧) AB وحمله.   (١٨) A يفتر. B يعسر.

مسئلة فى صفآء المعاملة والعبادة، قال اجتمع مشايخ حرم الله [1] تعالى على
ابى [2] الحسين على بن هند [3] القرشى الفارسى [4] رحمه الله تعالى [5] فسألوه
عن صفآء العبادة والمعاملة فقال [4] ان للعقل دلالة وللحكمة اشارة وللمعرفة
شهادة فالعقل يدلّ [6] والحكمة تُشير والمعرفة تشهد ان صفآء العبادات لا
يُنال الّا بصفآء معرفة اربعةٍ فاوّل ذلك معرفة [7] الله تعالى والثانى معرفة
النفس والثالث معرفة الموت والرابع معرفة ما بعد الموت من وَعْد الله
ووعيد فمن عرف الله [4] تعالى قام بحقّه ومن عرف النفس استعدّ لمخالفتها
ومجاهدتها ومن عرف الموت استعدّ لوروده ومن شهد وعيد الله [4] تعالى
ينزجر عن نهيه وينتدب لأمره فراعاة حقّ الله [4] تعالى على ثلثة اوجهٍ على
الوفآء والادب والمروّة فامّا الوفآء فانفراد القلب بفردانيته والثبات على
مشاهدة وحدانيته بنور ازليته والعيش معه، وامّا الادب فمراعاة الاسرار من
الخطرات وحفظ الاوقات والانقطاع عن الحسد والعداوات، وامّا المروّة
فالثبات على الذِكر نطقًا وفعلاً وصيانة اللسان وحفظ النظر وحفظ المطعم
والملبس وينال ذلك بالادب لانّ اصل كلّ خير فى الدنيا والاخرة الادب
وبالله [8] التوفيق، مسئلة ما [9] الكريم، قال حارث [4] رحمه الله تعالى الكريم
[10] الذى [11] لا يبالى لمن أعْطَى، وقال الجُنَيْد [4] رحمه الله الكريم [12] من لا
يحوِّجك الى وسيلة، مسئلة فى الكرامة، قال قوم الكرامة أن يُبلغ المراد قبْلَ
ظهور الارادة، وقال قوم الإعطآء [14] قوق المأمول، مسئلة فى الفكر، سُيل
حارث المحاسبى [4] رحمه الله تعالى عن الفكر فقال [14] الفكر فى قيام الاشيآء
بالحقّ، وقال قوم التفكر صحّة الاعتبار، وقال آخرون الفكر ما ملأ القلوب
من حال التعظيم [15] لله عزّ وجلّ، والفرق بين الفكر والتفكّر أن التفكّر جولان

(١) B عزّ وجلّ. (٢) B الحسن. (٣) B القرشى. (٤) B om. (٥) B وسألوه.
(٦) B والمعرفة تشهد والحكمة تشير. (٧) B الرب. (٨) B بالتوفيق. (٩) B الكريم.
(١٠) B الذى الكريم وقال الحارث الكريم الذى الخ. (١١) B لم. (١٢) من لا يحوجك الى وسيلة.
(١٣) B الذى. (١٤) B التفكّر. (١٥) B لله تعالى. (١٣) A قول.

(١)القلب والفكر وقوف (١)القلب على ما عرف، مسئلة فى الاعتبار، (٢)قال
حارث المحاسبى ابو عبد الله بن أسَد رحمه الله تعالى الاعتبار استدلال
الشىء على الشىء، وقال قوم الاعتبار ما وضح فيه الايمان واستوفته العقول،
وقال قوم الاعتبار ما (٣)نفذ فى الغيب ولم يردّه مانع، مسئلة ما النيّة، قال
٥ قوم النيّة العزم على الفعل، وقال قوم النيّة معرفة اسم العلّ، وقال الجُنَيْد
(٤)رحمه الله تعالى (٤)النيّة تصوير الافعال، وقال آخر نيّة (٥)المؤمن الله
(٤)عزّ وعلا، مسئلة ما الصواب، قال قوم الصواب التوحيد فقط، وقال
الجُنَيْد (٤)رحمه الله تعالى كلّ الصواب كلّ نُطْق عن إذْنٍ، مسئلة، سِيل الجُنَيْد
Af.105a عن الشفقة على الخلق ما هو قال نُعطيهم من نفسك ما يطلبون ولا تُحمّلهم
١٠ ما لا يطيقون ولا تخاطبهم بما لا يعلمون، مسئلة فى التقيّة، قال قوم استعمال
الأمر والنهى وقال قوم ترك الشبهات، وقال قوم التقيّة حَرَّم المؤمن كما انّ
الكعبة حَرَمُ مكّة، وقال قوم التقيّة نور فى القلب يفرق بهـا بين الحقّ
والباطل، وقال سهْل والجُنَيْد (٦)والحرث وأبو سعيد (٤)رحمة الله تعالى عليهم
اجمعين التقيّة استوآء السرّ (٧)والعلانية، مسئلة فى السِرّ، قال بعضهم (٨)السر
١٥ ما لا يحسّ به هاجسُ النفس السرّ ما (٩)غيّبه (١٠)الحقّ وأشرف عليه بـه،
وقال قوم السرّ سرّان سرّ (١١)للحقّ وهو ما أشرف عليه بلا واسطة وسرّ
للخلق وهو ما أشرف عليه (٤)الحقّ بواسطة، (١٢)ويقال سرّ من السرّ للسرّ
وهو حقّ لا يظهر الّا بحقّ وما ظهر بخلق فليس بسرّ، وحكى عن الحسين بن
منصور الحلّاج (٤)رحمه الله تعالى انه قال أسرارنا بِكْرٌ لا يفتضّها وَهْمُ واهم،

---

(١) A القلوب.   (٢) B الح الاعتبار حارث قال.   (٣) B نقد.   (٤) B om.
(٥) B للمؤمن.   (٦) B app. وحارث.   (٧) Here B inserts the concluding
words of this chapter from نصف سؤال ونصف to فهذا ما حضرني فى الوقت الخ
السر ما عينه (?)الحق واسرف عليه به وقال بعضهم السر ما لا يحس B   (٨) جواب
الخلق.   (٩) A عنه. The reading of B is doubtful.   (١٠) A به هاجس النفس
(١١) A الحق.   (١٢) A وقال.

وقال يوسف بن الحسين (١) رحمه الله تعالى قلوب الرجال قُبور الاسرار، وعنه ايضًا انه قال لو اطّلع زرّى على سرّى قلعتُه، (٢) شعر،

حَاسٌ بِسِرٍّ قَدْ أَسَرَّ جَميعَها * (٤) وكِلاهُما فى سِرّها مَسْرُورُ

ما (٥) سِرُّ مَسْرُورٍ (٧) يُثيرُ (٦) بِسرّهِ * مِنْهُ إِلَيْهِ (٨) مُسَاوِيًا مَغْرُورُ

وقال آخر،

يَـا سِرَّ سِرٍّ يَـدِقُّ حَتَّى * يَخْفَى عَلَى وَهْمِ كُلِّ حَيِّ

وظَاهِرٌ بَـاطِنٌ تَجَلَّى * (٩) مِنْ كُلِّ شَيْءٍ لِكُلِّ شَيْءٍ،

وقال النورى (١) رحمه الله تعالى،

لَعَمْرِى ما اسْتَوْدَعْتُ سِرّى (١٠) وسِرَّها * سِوَانا حِذارًا أَنْ تَشيعَ السَّرَائِرُ

ولا لاحَظَتْهُ (١١) مُقْلَتَاكَ بِلَحْظَةٍ * فَتَشْهَدَ نَجْوَانَا العُيُونُ النَّواظِرُ

ولَكِنْ جَعَلْتُ الوَهْمَ بَيْنى وبَيْنَهُ * رَسُولًا فَأَدَّى ما تَكُنُّ الضَّمَائِرُ،

(١٣) Af.105b فهذا ما حضرنى فى الوقت من مسائلهم ومسائل هؤلاء اكثر من أن يتهيّأ (١٣) ذِكْرُها، (١٤) وقد حكى عن عمرو بن عثمٰن المكّى (١) رحمه الله تعالى انّه قال العلم كلّه (١٥) نصفان (١٦) نصفُه (١٧) سؤال (١٧) ونصفُه جواب، (١) وباله التوفيق،

---

(١٨) كتاب المكاتبات (١٩) والصدور والاشعار والدعوات والرسائل،

باب فى مكاتبات بعضهم الى بعض،

سمعت احمد بن علىّ (٢٠) الكَرَجى (١) رحمه الله تعالى يقول كتب الجُنَيْد

---

(١) B om. (٢) وقال بعضهم B. (٣) حاسر A. (٤) وكلاهما A.
(٥) سِرّ B. (٦) بِسرّ A. (٧) يَسْرُ B. (٨) مساوى A. مسارى B.
(٩) عن B. (١٠) وسره B. (١١) مقلتى AB. (١٢) This passage occurs
in B supra. See p. ٢٢١, note ٢. (١٣) ذكره B. (١٤) وحكى B.
(١٥) نصفين B. (١٦) نصف B. (١٧) ونصف B. (١٨) A om. from
الكرجى. (١٩) الصدور B. (٢٠) والرسائل to كتاب

الى ميمشاذ الدينورى [١] رحمه الله [٢] نعالى كتابًا فلمّا وصل الكتاب اليه [٣] فقلبه
وكتب على ظهره ما كتب صبح الى صبح قطّ ولا افترقا فى الحقيقة، وكتب
ابو سعيد الخرّاز الى ابى العبّاس [٤] احمد بن عطاء رحمهما الله يأبا العبّاس
نعرفُ لى رجلاً قد كملت طهارته وبرىء من آثار نفسه عنه به له موقوف
٥ مع الحقّ بالحقّ [٥] للحقّ من حيث أوقَفَه الحقّ حيث لا له ولا عليه فالحقّ
يعلّله امتحانًا له وامتحانًا للخلق به فان عرفتَ لى هذا فدُلّنى عليه حتى إن
قبلى كنت له خادمًا، وكتب عمرو بن عثمن المكّى [٢] رحمه الله كتابًا الى
بغداد الى جماعة الصوفية بها فكان [٦] فى كتابه وإنّكم [٧] لن تصلوا الى
حقيقة الحقّ حتى تجاوزوا تلك الطُّرُقات المنطمسة وتسلكوا تلك المفاوز
١٠ المُهْلِكة، فحضر عند قرآءته الجنيد والشبلى وأبو محمّد الجريرى [٢] رحمهم
الله فقال الجنيد [٢] رحمه الله ليت شعرى من الداخل فيها وقال الجريرى
ليت شعرى من الخارج منها وقال الشبلى يا ليتنى [٨] لم يكن لى منها مشامُّ
الريح، وفيا ذُكر عن الشبلى [٢] رحمه الله انه [٩] كتب الى الجنيد [٢] رحمه الله
كتابًا [١٠] فكتب فيه يأبا القسم ما تقول فى حال علا فظهر وظهر فقهر وقهر
١٥ فبهر [١١] فاستناخ واستقرّ فالشواهد منطمسة والاوهام خنسة والألسُن [١٢] خَرسة
والعلوم مندرسة ولو [١٢] تكاشفت الخليقة على من هذا حاله لم يزده ذلك الّا
[١٤] توحّشًا [١٥] ولو اقبلت الخليقة اليه تعطّفًا لم يزده ذلك الّا تبعُّدًا فالحاصل
فى [١٦] هذا الحال قد صُفد بالأغلال والأنكال [١٧] وغلبه على عقله مخال وحاد
الحقّ بالحقّ وصار الخلق [١٨] عقالًا [١٩] وكتب تحتها هذين البيتين،

---

(١) B رحمهما الله. (٢) B om. (٣) B أقلبه. (٤) A om. (٥) B للحق.
(٦) Here B (fol. 109b, l. 2) has احسن معانيا وألطف من الكرامات الخ. These words
occur near the end of the كتاب اثبات الآيات والكرامات (A fol. 147b, l. 2). The
continuation of the present passage occurs in B on fol. 232a, l. 6. (٧) B ان.
(٨) B لو كان for لم يكن. (٩) B كتبت. (١٠) B فكتبت. (١١) B واستناح.
(١٢) A in marg. تكاشفت as a variant. (١٤) A بعدًا written (١٢) B مخرسة.
above توحّشًا. (١٥) A om. from ولو to تبعُّدًا. (١٦) B هذه. (١٧) B وغلب.
(١٨) A عقال B عيالًا. (١٩) B وكتبت.

يا هلالَ السّما (١) إطَرْفٍ كَليل ۰ فَإذا ما بَدا أضاءَ طَرْفَيْهِ

كنتُ أبكى على بِنْهِ قَلَماً ۰ أن تَوَلّى بَكَيْتُ مِنْهُ عَلَيْهِ،

قال فترك الرقعة عنده من الاربعاء الى الاربعاء (٢) وكتب تحتها يابا بكر
اله اله فى الخلق كما نأخذ الكلمة (٣) فنستقها (٤) ونقرظها ونتحكّم بها فى
السراديب (٥) وقد جئتَ انت فخلعت العذار بينك وبين (٧) اكابر الخلق (٦)
ألفُ طبقة فى اوّل طبقة بذهب ما وصفتَ، (٨) قال الشيخ رحمه اله وكنتُ
بالرّملة وكان بها انسان هاشميّ وله جارية مشهورة بحسن الصوت والحذاقة
فى القول فسألَنا ابا على (٦) الروذبارى ان يكتب اليه (١٠) رقعةً (١١) يستأذن
لنا بالدخول عليها (١٢) حتى نسمع منها شيئاً فكتب اليه على البديهة بحضرتى
بسم اله الرحمن الرحيم (١٣) بلّغنى بلّغك اله سؤلك، وأعطاك مأمولك، ان
عندك من مناهل (١٤) الوُرود، منهلاً (١٥) بَرُدُ (١٦) عليه قلوب اهل الوجود،
فيشربون منه بعقد الوفاء، شراباً يُورثهم حقائق الصفاء، فان أذن لنا
بالدخول (١٧) عليه فلنا على رَبّ المهل أن يزيّن المجلس بفقد الأغيار، ويحجبه
(١٨) عن نواظر الأبصار، (١٩) ومجيئُنا (٢٠) مقرون بإذنك والسلم، وسمعت ابا
على بن ابى (٢١) خلد الصورى بصورَ يقول (٢٢) كتبتُ الى ابى على الروذبارى
(٢٤) رحمه اله كتاباً (٢٣) وكتبت فيه هذين البيتين،

إنَّ تَمنى أبا عَلـىّ (٢٥) لِحُبّيـكَ (٢٧) وِرارًا من (٢٦) النّشارِكُ فيه
حَيّداً رُوذَبارُ ما ذَى عَلَيْنا ۰ لَكَ حَقّاً (٢٨) وَذاكَ مِنْهُ (٢٩) بَتِيهِ،

---

(١) B يكرف.   (٢) B ثم كتب الى.   (٣) A منسفها.   (٤) A ونقرظها،

(٥) السر B.   (٦) A om.   (٧) B اكابر.   (٨) B om قال الشيخ رحمه الله.

(٩) B عطاء بن احمد اله عبد الله.   (١٠) B كتاباً.   (١١) B يستأذنه.   (١٢) B لسمع.

(١٣) B بلّغنا.   (١٤) A الورد.   (١٥) B نرد.   (١٦) B عليها.   (١٧) A عليها.

(١٨) B لم.   (١٩) AB ومحيونا.   (٢٠) A مقرونا.   (٢١) B جلّد.   (٢٢) A كتب.

(٢٣) A وكتب.   (٢٤) B app.   (٢٥) لحى B.   (٢٦) B فرارا.

(٢٧) A الشارك.   (٢٨) B منك for منه وذاك.   (٢٩) A بتيه B نبيه،

قال ثم استقبلنى بعد ذلك بأيّام وكان فى يدى (١)جُزءٌ (٢)وأخذ من
يدى وكتب على (٣)ظهره،

أغراكَ بالحُبّ (٤) حُبٌّ (٥) فى (٦)تُغْريهِ . لَطُفَتُ الجِنانُ (٧) وَعَطَفْتُ فى (٨)تعْنِيدِهِ
بابنِ الصَّباباتِ عَن ورْدٍ بِلا صَدرٍ . (٩)نَجَّعْتَ صَفْوَ الهَوَى فى غَيرِ مَطْلَبِهِ
٥ قِفْ تحتَ (١٠)صَِنْتِهِ بالورْدِ مِنْكَ (١١)لَهُ . مُسْتَنْهَرًا بِتَبارِيح الشُّجُونِ بِهِ،

١٢،١٠٠b قال ومرِض رجل من اصحاب (١٢)ذى النون فكتب اليه أن (١٣)ادْع الله
لى فكتب (١٤)اليه (١٥)ذو النون (١٦)رحمه الله (١٦) يا اخى سألتنى ان ادعو الله
لك أن يزيل عنك النِّعَمَ (١٥)واعلم (١٧) يا اخى ان المرِضَ والعِلّة يأنس (١٩)بها
اهل الصَّفاءِ، وإصحاب الهِمَمِ (١٢)والفَضاءِ، لانّها فى حياتهم (٢٠)درَكٌ (٢١)للشّفاءِ،

١٠ ومن (٢٢)لم يعُدّ البلاءَ نعمةً فليس من الحكماءِ ومن لم يأمن الشفيقَ على
نفسه فقد أمِن اهلَ التُّهمةِ على أمرِه فليكُنْ معك يا اخى من الله حياءٌ
يمنعك من الشكوى والسلم، وكتب رجل الى (١٢)ذى النون (١٥)رحمه الله
انسك الله (١٥)تعالى بقربه فكتب اليه (١٤)ذو النون (١٥)رحمه الله اوحشك
الله من قُربه فانّه (٢٣)اذا آنسك بقربه فهو قَدَرُك (٢٤)واذا اوحشك من
١٥ قربه فهو قَدَرُه ولا نهاية لقدره حتى (٢٥)بتركك مالهوئًا اليه، وسمعت جعفر
الخُلْدى (١٥)رحمه الله يقول سمعت الجُنَيْد (١٥)رحمه الله تعالى يقول دفع الىّ
سرىّ (١٥)السَّقَطى رقعةً (٢٦)قال هذا مكان قضائك لحاجتى ففتحتُ الرقعة
فاذا فيها مكتوب سمعتُ حادبًا فى البادية يحدو ويقول،

(١) جزا A .جزو B (٢) واخذ B (٣) ظاهرها هذه الآيات B (٤) حبا B.
(٥) من A (٦) تحبيه A تحسه B .عطف B (٧) .عطف B (٨) تعيبه B
(٩) نجعت B .فلته B app (١٠) A om (١١) ذا A (١٢) ادعوا AB
(١٣) الى B (١٤) B om (١٥) كتبت الى B يا اخى سألتى (١٦) .باخى B (١٧)
.للشفاء B (١٨) .والفضا A والفضا B (١٩) دركا A (٢٠) .الى B (٢١)
.بنزلك B بتركا A (٢٥) .ان B (٢٤) .وان B (٢٥) .ليس B (٢٢)
.وقال B (٢٦)

أَبْكِى [١] وَهَلْ تَدْرِينَ ما يُبْكِينِى

أَبْكِى حِذارًا أَنْ تُفارِقِينِى

وتَقْطَعَى وَصْلِى وتَهْجُرِينِى،

وقال الروذبارى [٢] رحمه الله كتب الىَّ بعض اصدقائى كتابى اليك [٣] كمودّتى
لك نورٌ منك دلّ عينى عليك وحجبها عن النظر الّا اليك والسلم، وكتب
ابو عبد الله ايضًا فى كتاب [٣] الى بعض اصدقائَه ما الذى أدّاك الى
الصبوة، [٣] بعد تمكّنك من الحظوة، وما الذى حداك على قطع حبل
الوصال، بعد المحافظة على [٤]الاتّصال، أَوَما علمتَ ان لورود الكتب فرحة
تعدل فرحة القُرب، وكتب شيخ من الاجلّة الى بعض المشايخ وجدى بك
١٠ حمانى عن الاشارة اليك وما بدا من قُربك غيّب عنّى مؤنة الذِكر لك
فحقيقتك ظاهرة، وأعلامك زاهرة، وسطوتك قاهرة، ظهرتْ سطوتك فخنست
معرفتى عند ظهورها، وذهل عقلى عند ورودها، وقصّر على عند شرح
بيان ظهورها وقصرت عبارتى [٥]عند استيلاء حقيقتك والسلم، [٦]سمعت ابا
الطيّب احمد بن مُقاتل العكّى يقول كتب ابو الخَير النيتانى الى جعفر الخُلْدى
١٥ رحمه الله كتابًا فكان فيه وِزرُ جهلِ الفقراء عليكم لأنكم ركنتم الى ابناء
الدنيا واشتغلتم بأموركم فبقوا جَهَلةً، وقال يوسف بن الحسين [٧] رحمه الله
[٨]كتبت الى بعض الحكماء وشكوتُ ركونى الى [٩]الدنيا وما أجدُ فى طبعى من
الاخلاق التى لستُ ارضاها من نفسى فكتب الىَّ بسم الله الرحمن
الرحيم وصل كتابك وفهمتُ ما ذكرتَ [١٠] ومُخاطبتك [١١]اكرمك الله شريكك
٢٠ فى شكواك، ونظيرك فى بلواك، إن رأيتَ ان تقدم الدعاء [١٢]وقَرَعَ الباب
[١٣]فانه من قرع الباب ولم يعجز عن القرع دخل وإن تهيّأ لك ما [١٤]تريد

---

(١) B ولا.   (٢) B om.   (٣) كودى B   (٤) A الاتصال B الاصال.

(٥) B عن.   (٦) B وسمعت.   (٧) B الرازى for رحمه الله.   (٨) A كتب.

(٩) B هذه الدنيا.   (١٠) A ومخاطبتك.   (١١) B ايدك.   (١٢) A وتقرع.

(١٣) B فان قروع الباب ولم بعجز الخ.   (١٤) B تريه.

من الصفاَء والطهارة فدَع ما [١]انت فيه من البلاَء من اقتراف مَساوى لا
[٢]تجدى عليك منفعةً فى دينك ولا دنياك وتجنّبْ قُرْبَ من لا تأمن على
نفسك فى [٣]مواصلته الغفلة والبطالة واستعنْ على ذلك كلّه بالقناعة والتجزّى
وسَلْه ان يمنّ عليك بتوبة [٤]طهرى لا عملى والسلم، [٥]وقال يوسف بن
الحسين [٦] رحمه الله كتب حكيم الى حكيم يسأله عمّا يؤدّيه الى صلاح نفسه
فكتب اليه ان فساد نفسى [٧]قد [٧]شغلنى عن صلاحك ولست أجدُ فى
نفسى فضلةً لغيرها والسلم، [٨]وقال كتب ابو العبّاس احمد بن عطاَء [٦]رحمه
الله الى ابى سعيد الخرّاز [٦]رحمه الله [٩]كتابًا فقال فيه وأُعْلمك ان الفقراَء
وأصحابنا بعدك صاروا يناقرون بعضهم لبعض، فكتب اليه ابو سعيد [٦]رحمه
الله وإمّا ما ذكرتَ [١٠]ان اصحابنا بعدى صاروا يناقرون بعضهم لبعض
فاعلمْ ان ذلك غيرةً من الحقّ عليهم حتى لا يسكن بعضهم الى بعض، وقال
الروذبارى كتب بعض المحبّين الى حبيبه يعاتبه ان المودّة لم تزل موصولةً
قزُرْ بلادى وأكْثر ودادى وإحذرْ عُداة الحيّ أن يلفوك ولْيَظُنَّ العُداة انك
[١١]جافٍ، وكتب بعض المشايخ كتابًا فكان فيه هذا النصل [١٢]وأنا وجدته
٨Af.107b بخطّ جعفر الخُلْدى، تفكّرى فى مرارة البين بمعنى [١٣]من التمتّع بحلاوة الوصل
ونكره عينى ان تقرّ بقُربك، مخافةَ أن تسخن ببعُدك، فلى عند الاجتماع كبد
ترجف، وعند التناَءى مقلةٌ تكفُ، وأقول كما قال الشاعر،

وَمَا فى الدَهْرِ أَشْقَى مِنْ مُحِبٍّ * وَإِنْ وَجَدَ الهَوَى حُلْوَ المَذَاقِ
تَرَاهُ بَاكِيًا فى كُلِّ حِينٍ * مَخَافَةَ فُرْقَةٍ أَوْ [١٤]لَاشْتِياقِ
فَيَبْكى إِنْ نَأوْا شَوْقًا إِلَيْهِمْ * وَيَبْكى إِنْ دَنَوْا خَوْفَ الفِرَاقِ
فَتَسخُنُ عَيْنُهُ عِنْدَ التَناَءى * وَتَسْخُنُ عَيْنُهُ عِنْدَ [١٥]التَلَّاقى،

---

(١) كتب. B (٤) طهر لى لا على B (٣) تجزّى B (٣) مواصله A
(٥) قال. B (٦) B om. (٧) شغلنى. B (٨) B om. قال. (٩) B om.
وأنا (١٢) B om. from (١١) جافى AB (١٠) من ان B كتابًا فقال.
الخُلدى. to الثلاق AB (١٥) عن. B (١٣) اشتياق B (١٤)

وحكى عن حسين بن جبريل (١)المَرَندى (٢)رحمه الله (٢) وكان من المشايخ
الاجلّة انه قال ورد علىّ كتاب من مكّة فقرأت على جماعة من اصحابنا
وكان (٢)من بعض تلامذته فكان فى الكتاب (٤)أُعْلمك يا شيخى ان اصحابك
كلّهم (٤)ترافقوا بعضهم مع بعض فبقيتُ بلا رفيق فرأيتُ يومًا فى الطواف
غزالاً يطوف فأعجبنى ذلك فرافقته وكان لى (٥)قرصان (٦) شعيرٌ (٦) فى كلّ ليلة
قرصٌ لى وقرصٌ له فبقى معى اشهرًا ليلها ونهارها فليلةً من الليالى لم اتفرّغ
للافطار وتأخّر ذلك فلمّا اردتُ ان افطر فاذا به قد أكل القرصين فقلت
وَيْحَك قد ظهر منك الخيانة فرأيت دموعه تسيل على خدّه فذهب حياءً
منّى فاسئَلُك ان تدعو الله (٢)تعالى انت وأصحابك ان يردّه علىّ، قال
وكتب شاه الكِرْمانى (٢)رحمه الله الى ابى حفص (٢)رحمه الله اذا رأيت أمرى
كلّه مصيبةً فكيف أكون فى مصايبى، فكتب اليه ابو حفص (٢)رحمه الله
آلِفْ مصايبك ولا تكن مع إلْفك لمصايبك، وفيما حُكى (٢) عن (٨)ابن
مسروق عن سَرىّ السَّقَطى (٢)رحمه الله انه قال كتب الىّ بعض اخوانى
فكتبت اليه يا اخى أوصيك بتقوى الله الذى يُسعد بطاعته من أطاعه
وينتقم بمعصيته من عصاه فلا تدعونّك طاعته الى الأمْن من عذابـه ولا
تدعونّك معصيته الى الاياس من رحمته جعلنا الله وايّاكم حَذِرين (٩)من
غير قنوط وله راجين (٩)من غير اغترار والسلم، وكتب الجُنَيْد (٢)رحمه
الله كتابًا الى علىّ بن سهل الإصْبهانى وكان فيه (١٠)واعلم يا اخى ان الحقايق
اللازمة (١١)والقصود القويّة المُحْكمة والعزايم الصحيحة المؤكّدة لم نُبق على
اهلها سببًا الّا قطعنْه ولا معترَضًا الّا منعنْه ولا أثرًا فى خفىّ السرايـر الّا
اخرجنْه ولا تأويلاً مُوهمًا لصحّة المراد الّا كشفنْه فالحقّ عندهم بصحّة الحال
(١٢)مجرّدًا (١٢)والجدّ فى دوام السَّير (١٤)محدّدًا على براهين من العلم واضحة

ودلائل من الحقّ بيّنة ، (١)قال الشيخ رحمه الله فامّا مكاتباتهم (٢)ومراسلاتهم
أكثر من ان يتهيّأ جمعُها (٣)فى الاجزآء الكثيرة وانّما ذكرنا (٤)هذا طرفًا
على حسب ما امكن فى الوقت لانّ المراسلات الطوال نحوَ رسالة (٥)النورى
الى الجنيّد (٤)رحمهما الله فى مسئلة البلآء ورسالة (٦)ابى سعيد الخزّاز الى
النورى ورسالة الجنيد الى يحيى بن (٧)مُعاذ وإلى يوسف بن الحسين
(٨)ومجاوبتيهما ورسالة عمرو المكّى الى (٩)ابن عطآء وغير ذلك لم يتهيّأ لنـا
ذكرُه ولكن نذكر رسالةً واحدةً للجنيّد الى ابى بكر (١٠)الكسائّى الدينورىّ
(٤)رحمهما الله وهى مختصرة (١١)إن شآء الله تعالى ، رسالة الجنيد الى ابى بكر
(١٠)الكسائّى (٤)رحمهما الله تعالى ، اخى اين مَحَلّك عند (١٢)تعطيل العشار ،
وأين دارُك وقد خربت الديار ، وأين مَنْزلك والمنازل فاغٌ صنصفٌ قِفار ،
وأين مكانك والاماكن (١٣)عوافٍ دوارسُ الآثار ، وما ذا خَبّرُك عند ذهاب
جوامع الأخبار ، وفيا نَظَرُك عند اصطلام مَحاضر النُظّار ، وفيا فكْرُك وليس
يحين نظار ولا افتكار ، وكيف هُدوّك على مرّ (١٤)الليل والنهار ، وكيف
حَذَرُك عند وقوع فواجع (١٥)الأقدار وكيف صَبْرُك ولا سبيل الى عزآء
ولا اصطبار ، فأبكِ الآن إن وجدتَ سبيلاً الى البكآء ، بكاء الوالهة الحزينة
الموجعة الثُّكْلى ، بفقد اعزّة الالاف ، وفنآء (١٦)اجلّة الأخلاف ، وإبادة ما
مضى من (١٧)الاكناف ، (١٨)وذهاب (١٩)مشايخ الاعتطاف ، وورُود بدّابه
الاختطاف ، (٢٠)وروادف عواصف الارتجاف ، وتتابع قواصف الانتساف ،
Af.108b وبواهر قواهر قواهر الاعتكاف ، وثواقب ملامح الاعتراف ، فإلى اين (٢١)مَوْئِلُك ،

(١) فى الاجزآء B om.　　　　(٢) ومراسلتهم A　　　(٣) B om.　　(٤) .قال الشيخ رحمه الله B om.
الكثيرة.　　(٤) B om.　　(٥) A .النورى　　(٦) B om. ابى سعيد.　　(٧) B adds
.الكسائى A (١٠)　　بن B (٩)　　.واجوبتهما B ومجاوبتاتهما A (٨)　　.الرازى
.عوافى A (١٣)　　ان شآء الله تعالى. A. Cf. Kor. 81, 4.　(١٢) A .تعطل　　(١١) B om.
.الليالى B (١٤)　　.الاخدار A (١٥)　　.خله A (١٦)　　.أكياب A (١٧)
(١٨) B om. ذهاب.　　　　　(١٩) Partly obliterated in B.　　　(٢٠) A .ووارد
(٢١) B .موئلك

وإلى ما يبلغ مَصْدرك، والأحلام متجزّقة، والقلوب متصدّعة، والعقول مخلعة،
(١) والأنباء كلّها (٢) مرتفعة، وأنت فى أوابد (٣) مندمسة، ونجوم منطمسة، وسُبُل
ملتبسة، قد (٤) أضلّك فى (٥) اختلاف (٦) مناهِجها ظلمآءها، وانطبقت (٧) عليك
ارضها (٨) وسمآءها، ثم افضى بك ذلك الى لَجّة اللُّجج، والبحر الزاخِر
٥ الغامر المختلَج، الذى كلّ بحر دونه او لُجّة، فهو فيه كَتُفْلَة او مُجّة، فقد
قذف بك فى كثيف امواجه، وتلاطم عليك (١٠) بعظيم هوله وارتجاجه،
(١١) فمن مستنقذك من مُتلفات المهالك، (١٢) او مُخْرِجك ممّا هنالك، كتابى
اليك ابا بكر وأنا احمد الله حمدًا كثيرًا وأسأله العفو والعافية فى الدنيـا
والآخرة، وصل الىّ منك كُتُبٌ فهمتُ ما ذكرتَ فيها ولم يمنعنى من اجابتك
١٠ عليها ما وقع فى وهمك، وشقّ (١٣) علىّ ما ذكرتَ من غمّك وليس حالك
عندى حال (١٤) معتوب عليه بل حالك عندى حال معطوف عليه، وبحَسْبك
من بلآئك ان اكون سببًا للزيادة فى البلآء عليك وإنّى عليك لمُشْفِق
وإنّما منعنى من مكاتبتك لأنّى حذرت ان يخرج ما فى كتابى اليك الى غيرك
بغير علمك وذلك أنّى كتبت منذ مدّة كتابًا الى (١٥) أقوام من اهل إصبهان
١٥ فتُفتح (١٦) كتابى وأُخذت نسختُهُ استعجم بعض ما فيه على قوم فأتعبنى تخلّصهم
(١٧) ولزمنى من ذلك (١٨) مؤنة عليهم وبالخُلق حاجة الى (١٩) الرفق وليس من
الرفق بالخُلق ملافأتهم بما لا يعرفون ولا مخاطبتهم بما لا يفهمون وربّما وقع
(٢٠) ذلك من غير قصد اليه ولا نعمُد له، جعل الله عليك واقيةً وجنّةً

---

(١) B لا ابا.   (٢) Here B proceeds (fol. 238b, 1): حقيقة (حق بك) موتك
الاخصاص عن لوائح الانتقاص الح. These words occur in the following chapter
(A fol. 109a, 16). The present passage is continued on فى صدور الكتب والرسائل
fol. 239b, 1.   (٣) A مندسه.   (٤) A أطلك.   (٥) B om.   (٦) B مناهج ملتبسها.
(٧) B عليها.   (٨) B وسمّاوها.   (٩) B الغابر.   (١٠) B بعظم.   (١١) A فهو.
(١٢) B و.   (١٣) B عليك.   (١٤) AB معنب. فمن as a variant. with
(١٥) B قوم.   (١٦) B كتابى وأخذت for كتاب واحد.   (١٧) B ولزمنى.
(١٨) B مووة.   (١٩) A الذن.   (٢٠) B لك.

وسلّمنا وإيّاك ، فعليك (١) رحمك الله بضبط لسانك ، ومعرفة اهل زمانك ،
وخاطِبِ الناسَ بما يعرفون ، ودَعْهم (٢) ممّا لا يعرفون ، فقلّ من جهل شيئًا
الّا عاداه وإنّما الناس كالإبل المائة ليس فيها راحلة وقد جعل الله (٣) تعالى
العلماءَ والحكماءَ رحمةً من رحمته (٤) وبسطها على عباده فاعمل على ان تكون
٥ رحمةً على غيرك إن كان الله قد جعلك بلاءً على نفسك وأخرِجْ الى الخلق
(٥) من حالك بأحوالهم وخاطبهم من قلبك على حسب مواضعهم فذلك البلغ Af.109a
لك ولهم والسلام (٦) عليكم ورحمة الله (٦) وبركاته ، قال (٧) الشيخ (٧) رحمه الله
وإنّما وضعتُ فى هذا الكتاب هذه (٢) الحكاية (٨) والرسالة حتى يتأمّل من ينظر
فيه ويستفيدَ منها بما فيها من الاشارات الصحيحة والعبارات الفصيحة ويقف
١٠ على مقاصد القوم فى مكاتباتهم لانّ بين كلّ طائفة من الناس مكاتبات
ومراسلات على حسب ما يليق بهم (٩) وبالله التوفيق ،

باب فى (١٠) صُدور الكُتب والرسايل ،

صدرٌ (١١) للجُنَيْد رحمه الله ، آثرك الله يا اخى بالاصطفاء ، وجمعك
بالاحتواء وخصّك بعلم اهل النُّهَى ، وأطْلعك (١٢) من المعرفة على ما هو أوْلَى ،
١٥ وتنّم لك ما تريد منك له ثم أخلاك منك له ومنه له به ليُفردك فى تقلّبه
لك بما يشهدك من حيث لا يلحقك شاهدٌ من الشواهد يُخرجك ، فذلك
اوّل الاوّل الذى (١٣) محا به (١٣) رسوم ما ترادف ممّا غيّبه به عنك بعلوّ
ما استأثر به منه لك ثم افردك منك له فى اوّل تفريد التجريد وحقيقـة
كاين التفريد (١٥) فكذلك (١٦) إذا انفرد (١٧) بذلك (١٨) اباد (١٩) وأفْنَى الابادة

٠ (١) رحمك A.   (٢) بها B.   (٣) B om.   (٤) بسطها B.   (٥) B عن.
(٦) عليك B.   (٧) ابو نصر B.   (٨) B om. و.   (٩) B والسلام.
(١٠) صدر A.   (١١) B لابى القسم الجنيد بن محمد.   (١٢) B om. المعرفة.
(١٦) B ان.   (١٥) A فذلك. B فكذلك.   (١٤) A الرسوم.   (١٣) A نحا.
(١٧) B كذلك.   (١٨) A إياك.   (١٩) A وافنا وفنا. B وافنا.

16

ما سلف من الحقّ من الشاهد بعد إفناء محاضر الخلق فعند ذلك يقع
حقيقه الحقيقة من الحقّ للحقّ ومن ذلك ما جرى بحقيقة علم الانتهاء الى
علم التوحيد على علم تفريد (١)التجريد فقد عزره الله وحجبه عن كثير ممّن
ينتحله ويدّعيه ويتحقّقه ويصطفيه، صدر (٢)آخر، (٣)موتّك حقيقة الاختصاص
٥ عن لوايح الانتقاص وآواك الحقّ فى خفىّ من الملاحظة لحظّك شغلاً بالإجلال
له عن ذِكر نفسك وحالك فى اوان ذِكره ثم أذكَرَك انه (٤)ذكَرَك فى قديم
الازل قبْل حين البلوى وقبْل حال البلوى إنه فعّالٌ لِما يشاء وهو قدير،
صدر (٥)آخر، (٦)أكرمك بطاعته وخصّك بولايته وجلّلك بستره ووفّقك
لسنّة نبيّه صلعم وأطلعك على فهم كتابه وأنطقك بالحكمة وآنسك بالقرب
وخصّك بالفوايد ومنحك الزيادات وألزمك بابه وكلّفك خدمته حتى تكون
له موافقًا ولكأس محبّته ذايقًا فيتّصل العيش بالعيش والحياة بالحياة والروح
بالروح فتتمّ النعمة ونسلم من (٧)المعنبة فتصحّ العافية وتكمل السلامة، صدر
(٥)آخر، بدت لك عجايب ما فى الغيوب من أنبآيها، وكشفت لك (٨)عن
حقايق ما نكنّ من أكانها، وأوضحت لك عن (٩)سرّ غرايب (١٠)إخفايها،
١٠ وخاطبتك بكلّ ما (١١)كنن من عطآيها، بلسانه الذى ينطق به عن خفىّ
مكانه، فأوضحُ منطقٍ يوضّح عن حُكم بيانه، ليس بما (١٢)صرّح به (١٢)من
النُصح من لسانه، لكن بما اوقفه الحقّ من مراد إعلانه، وذلك غير كاين
قبْل حينه وأوانه، والمراد بفهم ذلك هو المُفرّد الموجود من اهل دهره
وزمانه، صدر آخر، حاطك الله بحياطنه التى يحوط بها المستخلَصين من

(١) B التحديد.   (٢) This is the last word on B fol. 241a. Fol. 241b begins with the verse فيا حبّها زدنى جوّى كُلّ ليلة which occurs in A at fol. 113b, 5.
(٣) Here begins B fol. 238b. A حقّ بك.   (٤) A أذا ذكرَك.   (٥) B adds له.
(٦) B adds الله.   (٧) B الفتنة.   (٨) B om. from وأوضحت لك to عن حقايق.
(٩) B سراير.   (١٠) A اخفاها.   (١١) A لم نكن.   (١٢) B app. مزج.
(١٢) B om.

أحبابه وثبّتك وإيّانا على (١)سُبُل مرضاته وأولج بك قِباب أُنسه وأرقاك فى
رياض فنون كرامته وكلأك فى الاحوال كلّها كلاية الجنين فى بطن أمّه ثم
ادام لك الحياة المستخلصة من (٢)قيوميّة الحياة على دوام (٣)ديوميّة ابديته
وأفردك عمّا لك به وعمّا له (٤)بك حتى تكون فردًا به فى دوامها لا انت
٥ ولا ما لك ولا العلم به ويكون الله وَحْدَهُ، هذه الصدور كلّها للجُنَيْد (٥)رحمه
الله وفيها (٦)اشارات لطيفة ورموز خنيّة تعبّر عن الحقايق المشكلة (٧)وتُنبئ
عن السراير والخصوصية التى (٨)تنفرد بها هذه العصابة فى تجريد التوحيد
وحقيقة التفريد فمن نظر فيه فليتأمّل فانّ فيه لأهل (٩)الفهم فوايد ولأهل
العناية بهذا العلم زوايد (١٠)وعلى القلوب من المعرفة بذلك جميل عوايد ،
١٠ والله الموفّق (٥)للصواب ، (١١)ولغير الجنيد صدور حسنة اذكر من ذلك
طرفًا ان شاء (١٢)الله، (١٣)صدر لأبى علىّ الروذبارى رحمه الله، آنسك الله
فى كمال الاحوال وتمامها، وبلوغ الغايات ونظامها، وآنس بك قلوب اهل
Af.110a مصافاتك (١٤)وموالاتك فى دوام فضلك ومعافاتك، وجعل (٥)لك مـا
(١٥)اتّضح لك موصولًا بك فى حياتك، وبعد وفاتك، ومنّ علينا بما يقصر
١٥ عنه بلوغ الآمال، ونهاية الاحوال، وزادك من فضله الذى عوّدك من برّه
وألطافه وإحسانه والله يمنّ علينا فى ذلك (١٦)بما (١٧)نرجوه، صدر لأبى
سعيد (٥)ابن الاعرابى، كلاكم الله كلاية الوليد ، (١٨)وألحقنا وإيّاكم بصالح

(١) B سبيل.   (٢) B قيومية.   (٣) B ديّوميه. Here the text of B
breaks off (fol. 239a, last line). The following words (B fol. 239b, 1) are
مرتفعة وأنت فى اوايد مندمسة, which occur in A on fol. 108b, 2. The present
passage is continued in B on fol. 62b, 1.   (٤) B به.   (٥) B om.
(٦) B اشارة.   (٧) B وينبى.   (٨) B تنفرد.   (٩) A العلم.   (١٠) A على.
(١١) The words from ولغير to الله are suppl. in marg. A. A وإيضًا لغيره
with ومواداتك B وموّداتك.   (١٣) A صدور.   (١٤) A ومودّاتك B وموّداتك
the first alif stroked through.   (١٥) B انهج.   (١٦) B ما.   (١٧) B adds
ان شاء الله.   (١٨) B app. وألحقنا.

العبيد، الذين كشف عن قناع قلوبهم فشاهدوا الوَعْد والوعيد، فمن كان
منهم خائنًا فالرجاءُ منهم غير بعيد، ومن كان منهم راجيًا فالخوف فى قلبه
عتيد، فهم [1]بمحبّته [2]صايلون، ولهيبته خاضعون، بسطتهم المحبة والرجاءُ ان
يكونوا [3]قانطين، وقبضهم الخوف ان يكونوا مخدوعين او آمنين، فهم بين
٥ الخوف والرجاءِ واقفون، [4]فقد اقلقهم الشوق، وازعجهم الذوق، فحُسْنُ الظنّ
قايدُهم، وخوف النَوْت سايقُهم، والتوفيق رايدُهم، والحبّ مطيّتهم، طالبين
مطلوبين، منوَّرة لهم أعْلامُ الطريق، معمورة لهم المناهل [5]تَلَوّحُ لهم بالعوايد،
[6]منقلبين بالطُرَف والفوايد، صدر [7]آخر له، اماتك اله عنك وأحياك
به وأيّدك بالفهم، وفرّغ قلبك من كل وهم، وأفناك بالقُرب عن المسافة
١٠ وبالأُنس عن الوحشة، صدر آخر [8]له، كلأك اله كلاية الوليد المرحوم،
وحنظك حِنْظَ الوليّ المعصوم، ووهب لك معرفة ما انعم به عليك واستخرج
منك ما جبلك عليه وحجبك عن نفسك القاطعة دونه وكفانك عوايقها
وبوايقها [9] ورؤية عملك وآثار سعيك وتزكية نفسك، وأعتقك من رِقّها
وكفاك عوارض تحيّرها وفضول تكلّفها، [10]واستخصّك لنفسه منها [11]ليتحقّق
١٥ فيك العبودية فيزكو عملك وإن خفّ وينمو سعيك وإن قلّ وتطيب حياتك
وإن متّ حتى يوصلك بالحياة التى [13]لا [14]موت فيها والبقاءِ الذى لا
فناءَ بعده وتولّى أمرك بالحُسْنَى فى عزايقها كما كفاك التحيّر فى اوايلها، انّه
ولىُّ التمام لها [14]ابتداَه، [15]صدر لأبى سعيد [16]الخرّاز، عصمك اله بذِكْره
عن نفسك، وكاشفك بشُكْره عن [17]وصفك، وقسم لك من العلم به فى
٢٠ فعلك حتى تكون ممّن جمع له حبل الرشاد وأعلى فى ذلك مكانك

Af.110a

2011.1a

(1) B لمحبته.   (2) B صايلون.   (3) B قايين.   (4) B قد.   (5) A مُلَوِّح.

(8) A om.   (7) A om. اخره له.   (6) A منقلبون. B منقلون.   B تلوح.

(11) B لتحقّق.   (10) B واستخلصك.   (9) A gives ووقّاك رؤية as variant.

(13) B نموت.   (12) B om.   (14) B adds ان شاء اله.   (15) B صدر آخر.

(16) B احمد بن عيسى الخرّاز.   (17) B وضعك.

وكوشفتَ فى ذلك بالبيان ، وأنا اسأل الله [١] تعالى ان يجمع لك من نفسك
ما فرق [٢] ويُبين عنك [٣] منها ما جمع انّه الولىّ لذلك والقادر عليه ، صدر
آخر [٣] له ، حماك الله عن نفسك بذكره [٤] وصرّفك [١] فى ذلك بشكُره ، ولا
اخلاك فى ذلك باقباله ، وقسم لك من جزيل [٥] نواله ، وأعاذك من شديد
مِحاله ، انّه ولىّ ذلك والقادر عليه ، صدر آخر [٦] وأظنّه [٧] للخرّاز ، قسم الله
لك من العلم الرفيع ، وأفردك فى الذكر المنيع ، ولا اخلاك من رعايته ،
وأفردك بولايته ، وتولّاك فيما استرعاك ، وكان لك فى ذلك وكفاك ، وأقبل
عليك وشفاك ، وقسم الك من ذكُره [٨] وولاك ، وآنسك بطاعته وأعلاك ،
ولا وكلك الى نفسك وهواك ، صدر للكُردى الصوفى الأُرموى ، مخّك الله
بما به مخّك وحماك عن طويّات الصفات بالانابة [٩] لمن رتّب الرويّات ،
وحماك [١٠] عنك بشاهد ما فيه بدأك ، وعظيم ما به ابتدأك ، وأحلّك فى
محلّ [١١] التجلية لما اراد ولما به أربدَ [١٢] وأظلّم واقع [١٣] براه النسليم [١٤] نحوى
اسرارهم لمن [١٥] يُفانى ، [١٦] فتسرى همومهم لمن يعانى ، قد باشروا منه ما له
استبشروا ، [١٧] وفى [١٨] ميادين محبّته انتشروا ، [١٩] ألَمَأ بهم سواطع انوار
التوحيد ، ولوامع التجريد ، باينين عمّا [٢٠] له وبه بانوا ، فهُم كالذى كانوا ،
صدر كتاب [٢١] للدُقّى [١] رحمه الله [١] هنّأك الله كرامته فأنت [٢٢] غيثٌ لأهل
مودّته وكيفٌ لأهل موافقته ودالٌّ على معرفته [٢٣] ومنتسبٌ [٢٤] الى وحدانيته
ومُخّبِرٌ عنه به [٢٥] ومن اصطنعه لنفسه فى قديم ازليّته وأطّلعه على مكنون
سرّه وأشهه مجارى قدرته وأنطق لسانك بحكمته وأقامك لدلالته [٢٦] وجعلك

A.f.111a

---

(١) B om.   (٢) A om، وبين B.   (٣) A om.   (٤) B وصرك.

(٥) B نوابه.   (٦) B اظنه.   (٧) B للخراز لابى سعيد.   (٨) B ولاك.

(٩) B عن.   (١٠) B عنه.   (١١) A التخلية.   (١٢) B واطلم.   (١٣) So both MSS.

(١٤) A نحوى، B يحوى.   (١٥) A يعاين، B نفانى.   (١٦) B وسوى.   (١٧) A فى.

(١٨) B مدان.   (١٩) B واما هم for ألمأ.   (٢٠) B كالذى بهم بانوا لو بها.

(٢١) B للدقى لابى بكر.   (٢٢) B app. سيب.   (٢٣) B كانوا.

(٢٤) B على.   (٢٥) B ومن.   (٢٦) B وحطه.

معيارًا على المريدين (١) والمحقّقين البالغين المتأهّبين بحسن استبانته، انّه ولىُّ
ذلك ولا سبيل اليه الّا به والسلم، صدر آخر (٢) للدُّقّى، اكرمك الله وأعلاك،
وقرّبك بعطاياه وأدناك، وقسم لك من نواله وأرضاك، وأعاذك من بلآيه
وشفاك، وتولّاك فيا الزمك وكذاك، انّه ولىٌّ قديرٌ ذو رأفة لمن (٣) التجأ
اليه ومُهَيْمن على من استند اليه، نعوذ بالله لنا ولك من كلّ بليّة (٤) ونستعينه
ونستغفره من كلّ خطيّة، صدر آخر، تودّد الله اليك بعطفه، ولا اخلاك
من نايله ولطفه، وأعاذك من بلآيه وعنفه، ولا حجبك بفعلك عن ذِكْره،
ولا سترك بعملك عن شُكْره، انّه ولىٌّ قديرٌ (٥) صدر آخر، عصمك الله بما
عصم به المتّقين وأودعك من (٦) العشق السليم وكاشفك بذكره الرفيع
وأنسك بدوام اقباله عليك انّه ولىٌّ قدير، (٧) قال الشيخ رحمه الله والذى
حمّلنا على جمع هذه الرسايل والصدور والمكاتبات فى هذا الكتاب ما أودِعَ
فيها من المعانى والاشارات لينظر الناظر (٨) فيه ويستدلّ بذلك على مراتب
القوم ولطايف (٩) اشارتهم وطهارة اسرارهم وخصوصيّتهم بالفهم والعلم والعقل
والادب (١٠) لانّ من عادة اهل المعرفة والادب ان يعرفوا أشكالهم بمخاطباتهم
واشعارهم ومكاتباتهم اذا (١١) فاتهم المجالسة والمخالطة وبالله التوفيق،

باب فى اشعارهم فى معانى احوالهم وأشاراتهم،

حكى عن يوسف بن (١٢) الحسين انه قال سمعت بعض الثقات يحكى
عن (١٣) ذى النون (١٤) المصرى رحمه الله انه (١٥) قال،

---

(١) B المحقّين.   (٢) A om.   (٣) B لجا.   (٤) B om.   (٥) The
passage beginning انه ولىّ قدير and ending صدر آخر occurs in A at the end
of the chapter after the words وبالله التوفيق.   (٦) B العيش (العس).   (٧) B om.
لانّ (١٠) B om. from اشاراتهم.   (٩) B اشاراتهم.   (٨) B فيها.   قال الشيخ رحمه الله
to والادب،   (١١) B فاتهم.   (١٢) B adds الرازى.   (١٣) A ذا.   (١٤) B om.
هذه الابيات.   (١٥) B adds المصرى رحمه الله

إِذَا ٱرْتَحَلَ الكِرَامُ (١) إِلَيْكَ يَوْمًا * لِيَلْتَمِسُوكَ حَالًا بَعْدَ حَالِ

فَإِنَّ رِحَالَنَا حُطَّتْ رِضَاءً * بِحُكْمِكَ عَنْ حُلُولٍ وَٱرْتِحَالِ

أَنَخْنَا فِى فِنَاءَكَ يَا إِلَهِى * إِلَيْكَ مُفَوِّضِينَ بِلَا ٱعْتِلَالِ

Af.111b

(٢) قَسَمْنَا كَيْفَ شِئْتَ وَلَا نَكْنَا * إِلَى تَدْبِيرِنَا يَا ذَا (٣) الْمَعَالِى ،

٥ وَلذى النون (٥) رحمه الله ايضًا ،

مَنِ (٦) لَاذَ بِاللهِ نَجَا بِاللهِ * وَسَرُّهُ مَرَّ قَضَاءُ اللهِ

إِنْ لَمْ تَكُنْ نَفْسِى بِكَفِّ اللهِ * فَكَيْفَ أَنْقَادُ (٧) لِحُكْمِ اللهِ

(٨) لِلّهِ أَنْفَاسٌ جَرَتْ للّهِ * لَا حَوْلَ لِى فِيهَا بِغَيْرِ اللهِ ،

انشدنى ابو عمرو بن علوان (٩) للجنيد رحمه الله هذه الابيات ،

١٠ تَغَرَّبَ أَمْرِى عِنْدَ كُلٍّ غَرِيبِ * فَصِرْتُ عَجِيبًا عِنْدَ كُلٍّ عَجِيبِ

(١٠) وَذَاكَ لِأَنَّ الْعَارِفِينَ رَأَيْتُهُمْ * عَلَى طَبَقَاتٍ فِى (١١) الْهَوَاءِ (١٢) رُتُوبِ

فَأَصْبَحَ أَمْرِى لَيْسَ يُدْرَكُ غَوْرُهُ * سِوَى أَنَّى لِلْعَارِفِينَ خَطِيبُ ،

وللجنيد (٥) رحمه الله فى الاحتراق والتعذيب ،

يَا مُوقِدَ النَّارِ فِى قَلْبِى بِقُدْرَتِهِ * لَوْ شِئْتَ أَطْفَيْتَ عَنْ قَلْبِى بِكَ (١٣) النَّارَا

١٥ لَا عَارَ إِنْ مِتُّ مِنْ خَوْفٍ وَمِنْ حَذَرٍ * عَلَى فَعَالِكَ بِى لَا عَارَ لَا (١٤) عَارَا ،

(١٥) وله ايضًا ،

يَا (١٦) مَسْعَرِى أَسَفًا يَا مَثْلِى شَغَفًا * لَوْ شِئْتَ أَنْزَلْتَ تَعْذِيبِى بِمِقْدَارِ

حَاشَاكَ مِنْ إِسْتِغَاثَاتِى فَكَيْفَ وَقَدْ * أَوْلَيْتَنِى نِعَمًا (١٧) طَاحَتْ بِأَذْكَارِ ،

سمعت احمد بن علىّ الوجيهى (٥) بالرَّمْلة يقول كتب ابو الحسين النورى كتابًا

٢٠ الى ابى سعيد الخَرّاز (١٨) رحمه الله فكتب فيه هذه الابيات ،

(٤) B وله .   (٣) B الجلال .   (٢) A app. فشينا .   (١) A اليك يوما .

(٨) In A   (٧) A بحكم .   (٦) B لا .   (٥) B om. ولذى النون for

هذه الابيات للجنيد B (٩)   الله انقاد بوجه الله :the first hemistich runs

(١٠) A وذلك .   (١١) B الهوى .   (١٢) A ربوب .   (١٣) A النار .   (١٤) A عار .

(١٥) A وله ايضًا اخر for .   (١٦) B app. مسغدى .   (١٧) A حاطت .

(١٨) B رحمهما .

لَعَمْرِىَ ما اسْتَوْدَعْتُ سِرِّى وَسِرَّهُ * سِوانا حِذارًا أَنْ تَشِيعَ السَّرايِرُ

وَلا لاحَظَتْهُ (١) مُقْلَتاىَ بِنَظْرَةٍ * فَتَشْهَدَ نَجْوانا (٢) الْقُلُوبُ النَّواظِرُ

وَلٰكِنْ جَعَلْتُ الْوَهْمَ بَيْنِى وَبَيْنَهُ * رَسُولًا فَأَدَّى ما (٣) تَكُنَّ الضَّمايِرُ،

(٤) وأنشد (٥) القَنَّاد لأبى الحسين النورى (٦) رحمه الله يصف (٧) فَقَدَ حاله وينعاه

أَنْعَى إِلَيْكَ إِشاراتِ الْقُلُوبِ مَعًا * لَمْ يَبْقَ مِنْهُنَّ إِلّا دارِسُ الْعَلَمِ

أَنْعَى إِلَيْكَ قُلُوبًا طالَ ما هَطَلَتْ * سَحائِبُ الْجُودِ (٨) مِنْها أَبْحُرُ الْحِكَمِ

أَنْعَى إِلَيْكَ نُفُوسًا طاحَ شاهِدُها * فِيما وَرا (٩) الْحَيثِ (١٠) بَلْ فى شاهِدِ الْقِدَمِ

أَنْعَى إِلَيْكَ لِسانَ الْحَقِّ (١١) مُذْ زَمَنٍ * أَوْدَى (١٢) وَأَذْكارُهُ فى (١٣) الْوَهْمِ كالْعَدَمِ

أَنْعَى إِلَيْكَ بَيانًا (١٤) تَسْكِينُ لَـهُ * أَسْماعُ كُلِّ فَصِيحٍ مِقْوَلٍ فَهِمِ

١٠ (١٥) أَنْعَى وَحَقَّكَ أَخْلاقًا لَطائِفَةً * كانَتْ مَطاياهُمْ فى (١٦) مَكْنِنِ الْكَظَمِ،

(١٧) قال الشيخ رحمه الله (٤) انشدنى جعفر الخُلْدى (١٨) لِلجُنَيْد (١٩) رحمهما الله هذين البيتين،

(٢٠) فَلَمّا جُفِيتُ وَكُنْتُ لا أُجْفَى * وَدَلائِلُ الْهِجْرانِ لا تَخْفَى

(٢١) وَأَراكَ تَسْقِينِى وَتَمْزُجُنِى * وَلَقَدْ عَهِدْتُكَ (٢٢) شارِبِى صِرْفًا،

١٥ (٢٣) وفيا ذكر عبد الله بن الحسين قال سمعت احمد بن الحسين البصرى يقول حضرتُ مجلسَ الجُنَيْد رحمه الله فسأله رجل مسئلةً فأنشد،

نَمَّ عَلَى سِرِّ وَجْدِهِ النَّفَسُ * والدَّمْعُ مِنْ مُقْلَتَيْـهِ يَنْبَجِسُ

مُدَلَّـهٌ هايِمٌ لَـهُ حَرَقٌ * أَنْفاسُهُ بِالْحَنِينِ تَخْتَلِسُ

مُهَذَّبٌ عارِفٌ لَهُ فَطَنٌ * مِنْ نُورِ أُنْسِ الْحَبِيبِ يَقْتَبِسُ

---

(١) مقلتى AB. (٢) العيون B. (٣) لم تكن A. (٤) B وانشدنى. (٥) B أبو.
الحسين القناد. (٦) B om. (٧) A om. (٨) فيا B. (٩) A الحث.
الحب B. (١٠) بل فى (يَلْقَى) يلى A. (١١) منذ A. (١٢) B وافكاره.
مكمد B. (١٦) تسكن A. (١٤) B om. this verse. (١٥) الفهم A. (١٣)
الكظم. (١٨) B om. قال الشيخ رحمه الله (١٧) لابى الحسين النورى B.
وأراك A. (٢١) ما لى B. (٢٠) B ايضا and om. from رحمهما to البيتين. (١٩)
سارى B. (٢٢) B om. from وفيا to دنس خليق. (٢٣)

يا بِأَبِى الأَشْعَثُ الغَرِيبُ فَتًى ٭ أَبْسَ لَهُ دُونَ سُوْءِهِ أَرَسُ

يا بِأَبِى رِجْسُهُ الزَّكِىّ وَإِنْ ٭ كانَ عَلَيْهِ خُلَيْقٌ دَنِسُ،

(١)قال (٢)وأنشدنى (٣)ابو بكر الدُّقِّى (١)بدمشق قال انشدنى (٤)ابو علىّ احمد
ابن محمّد الروذبارى (١)رحمه الله لنفسه،

حَدُّ القَنَاعةِ مَحْوُ الكُلِّ مِنْكَ إذا ٭ لاحَ المَزِيدُ بِجَدٍّ (٥)عَنْهُ مُطَّلِعُ

فَإِنْ تَحَقَّقَ وَصْفُ الوَجْدِ مُشْتَمِلاً ٭ عَلَى الإشاراتِ أَمْ (٦)بَلْوى عَلَى الطَّمَعِ،

قال وأنشدنى الوجيهِ (٧)قال انشدنى ابو علىّ الروذبارى لنفسه،

كَتَبْتُ إِلَيْكُمْ بِمَاءِ الجُفُونِ ٭ وَقَلْبِى بِمَاءِ الهَوَى مُشْرَبُ

وَكَفِّى تَخُطُّ وَقَلْبِى يَمَلُّ ٭ وَعَيْناىَ تَمْحُو الَّذِى تَكْتُبُ،

Af.112b

١٠ (١)قال وأنشدنى (٨)ابو عبد الله احمد بن عطاءٍ الروذبارى لخاله ابى علىّ
(١)رحمه الله،

تَأَمَّلَ مِنْ بَعْدِ تَأْمِيلِهِ ٭ حَاوَلَ فِنَاءَكَ صَفْوُ الوِصَالِ

مَوَانِعُ عَنْ إِحْتِوَاءِ الوِصَالِ ٭ إِلَيْكَ عَنِ الوَصْلِ فى كُلِّ حَالِ

عَلَى أَنْ يَرُدَّ عَلَيْكَ الصِّفَاتِ ٭ بِنَعْتِ التَّمَكُّنِ عِنْدَ الكَمَالِ

(٩)فاقنع (١٠)بقنعته (١١)أَنْ تراهُ ٭ (١٢)فَفُتَّ (١٣)مَدَى لَحْظِهِ فى (١٤)النَّوالِ ١٥

(١٥)وله،

إِنِّى أُجِلُّكَ عَنْ رُوحِى (١٦)وَأَبْذُلُها ٭ (١٧)فِدَاءٍ (١٨)عَبِيدِكَ (١٩)رُوحٌ أَنْتَ واهِبُها

(٢٠)وَكَيْفَ تَفْدِيكَ (٢١)رُوحٌ أَنْتَ واهِبُها ٭ وَقَدْ مَنَنْتَ عَلَى مَنْ يَفْتَدِيكَ بِها

(١) B om. ‏‎(٢) B ‏‎‏انشدنى‎. ‏‎(٣) B om. ‏‎‏ابو بكر‎. ‏‎(٤) B om. ‏‎‏ابو علىّ‎.
‏‎‏قال انشدنى ابو على‎ B om. ‏‎(٧) ‏‎‏يلق‎ B. ‏‎(٦) ‏‎منه‎ B. ‏‎(٥) ‏‎‏احمد بن محمّد‎.
‏‎‏ابو على الروذبارى‎ A ‏‎(٨) ‏‎(٩) Both the text and the meaning of this verse
are uncertain. ‏‎(١٠) B ‏‎‏بقنعه‎. ‏‎(١١) B ‏‎‏اين‎. ‏‎(١٢) B ‏‎‏ففت‎. ‏‎(١٣) AB ‏‎‏مدا‎.
‏‎(١٤) The original reading in A seems to have been ‏‎‏السوال‎. ‏‎(١٥) B adds ‏‎‏ايضًا‎.
‏‎(١٦) B ‏‎‏وانزلها‎. ‏‎(١٧) B ‏‎‏وقد‎. ‏‎(١٨) A ‏‎‏عندك‎. B ‏‎‏اعيذك‎. ‏‎(١٩)B ‏‎‏روحًا‎. ‏‎(٢٠)Here
the text of B breaks off and proceeds ‏‎‏بقوم يصلّى ركعتين‎ (B fol. 68b, 1 = A fol.
68b, 10). The present verse occurs in B on fol. 54b, 1. ‏‎(٢١) A ‏‎‏روحًا‎.

(١)قال وإنشدنى ابو بكر احمد بن ابرهيم المؤدّب البيروتى بمصر (٢)للخوّاص (١)رحمه الله ،

صَبَرْتُ عَلَى بَعْضِ الأَذَى خَوْفَ كُلِّهِ * وَدَافَعْتُ عَنْ نَفْسِى لِنَفْسِى فَعَزَّتِ

وجَرَّعْتُها المَكْرُوهَ حَتَّى تَدَرَّبَتْ * وَلَوْ (٣)جَرَعْتُهُ جُمْلَةً لَاشْمَأَزَّتِ

أَلَا رُبَّ ذُلٍّ سَاقَ للنَّفْسِ عِزَّةً * وبا رُبَّ نَفْسٍ بالتَّعَزُّزِ ذَلَّتِ

إذا ما مَدَدْتُ الكَفَّ ألتَمِسُ الغِنَى * إلَى غَيْرِ مَنْ قَالَ ٱسْتَلُونى فَشِلَتْ

سَأَصْبِرُ نَفْسِى إِنَّ فى الصَّبْرِ عِزَّةً * وأَرْضَى بِدُنْيَائِى وإِنْ هِىَ قَلَّتِ

(٤)وإنشدنى ابو حفص عُمَر الشَّمشَاطى بالرَّمْلَة للخوّاص رحمه الله ،

لَقَدْ وَضَحَ الطَّرِيقُ إِلَيْكَ قَصْدًا * فَما (٥)أَحَدٌ أَرَادَكَ يَسْتَدِلُّ

فإِنْ وَرَدَ الشِّتَاء (٧)فَنِيكَ صَيْفٌ * وإِن وَرَدَ المَصِيفُ فأَنْتَ ظِلُّ

قال (١)عُمر معناه من كتاب الله تعالى قال (٧)كَلَّا مَعِىَ رَبِّى (٨)سَيَهْدِينِ ، ولِسُمْنون وكان يقال له سمنون المُحِبّ بِصفْ (٩)الوجد،

هَبنِى وَجَدْتُكَ بالعُلُومِ (١٠)ووجَدِها * مَنْ ذا يَجِدُكَ بِلا وُجُودٍ يَظْهَرُ

أَيْقَظْتَنِى بالعِلْمِ ثُمَّ تَرَكْتَنِى * حَيْرَانَ فِيكَ (١١)مُلَدَدًا لا أَبْصَرُ

يَا غَايِبًا والدَّهْرُ يَبْرُزُ عِزَّهُ * ما لَاحَ مِنْكَ صَغِيرَةً قَدْ يَبْهَرُ

قَدْ كُنْتُ أَطْرَبُ للوُجُودِ مَرُوَّعًا * طَوْرًا يَغِيبُنى وطَوْرًا أَخْضَرُ

أَفْنَى الوُجُودَ بِشَاهِدٍ مَشْهُودُهُ * يُفْنِى الوُجُودَ وكُلُّ مَعْنًى (١٢)يَحْضُرُ

(١٤)وطَارَحَتْنى فى بَحْرِ قُدْسِكَ سَابِحًا * أَبْغِيكَ مِنْكَ بِلا وُجُودٍ يَظْهَرُ

(١٤)وله ،

شَغَلْتُ قَلْبِى عَنِ الدُّنْيَا ولَذَّتِهَا * فأَنْتَ(١٥) فى القَلْبِ شَيْءٌ (١٦)غَيْرُ مُفْتَرِقِ

---

(١) B om. (٢) B om. (٣) جَرعتها A. (٤) ولابرهيم B. (٢) لابرهيم الخوّاص.

ولابرهيم B (١) B om. (٢) جَرعتها A. (٣) الخوّاص ايضًا رحمه الله (٤)

(٥) احدا B. (٦) فأنت B. (٧) Kor. 26, 62. (٨) سيهدين B.

(٩) التوحيد A. (١٠) وجدتها B. (١١) ملذذا لا A. (٨) B

(١٢) B يحضر. (١٢) B but in marg. ابصر and مبلذا as variants. يبصر

طوحتنى .(١٤) B adds ايضًا. (١٥) والقلب شيا B. (١٦) ليس يفترق A.

Af.113a

وَمَا تَطَابَقَتِ الْأَجْفَانُ عَنْ سِنَةٍ ۞ إِلَّا وَجَدْتُكَ بَيْنَ الْجَفْنِ وَالْحَدَقِ

(١) اخبرنى جعفر الخُلْدى رحمه الله فيا قرأتُ عليه قال سمعت الجُنيد رحمه
الله يقول كان ابو الحسن سَرىّ السَّقَطِى رحمه الله كثيرًا يُنشد هذه الابيات،

وَلَمَّا ادَّعَيْتُ الْحُبَّ قَالَتْ كَذَبْتَنِى ۞ فَا لِى أَرَى الْأَعْضَاءَ مِنْكَ كَوَاسِيَا

فَا الْحُبُّ حَتَّى يَلْصَقَ الْجِلْدُ بِالْحَشَا ۞ وَتَذْبُلَ حَتَّى لَا تُجِيبَ الْمُنَادِيَا

وَتَنْحَلَ حَتَّى لَا يُبْقِى لَكَ الْهَوَى ۞ سِوَى مُقْلَةٍ تَبْكِى (٣)بِهَا او تُنَاجِيَا

قال الجُنيد رحمه الله (٣)دخلتُ (٤)غُرْفَته (٥)وهو (٦)يكنس بيته بخرقة ويقول،

وَمَا رُمْتُ الدُّخُولَ عَلَيْهِ حَتَّى ۞ حَلَلْتُ مَحَلَّةَ الْعَبْدِ الذَّلِيلِ

وَأَغْضَيْتُ الْجُفُونَ عَلَى قَذَاهَا ۞ وَصُنْتُ النَّفْسَ عَنْ قَالٍ وَقِيلِ

قال وكان (٧)يقول كثيرًا هذا البيت،

مَا فِى النَّهَارِ وَلَا فِى اللَّيْلِ لِى (٨)فَرَجٌ ۞ فَمَا أُبَالِى أَطَالَ اللَّيْلُ أَمْ قَصُرَا

انشدنى ابو (٩)عمرو الزَّنْجَانِى (١٠)بتبريز قال كان الشِّبْلِى (١٠)رحمه الله يقول
عند (١١)موته،

قَالَ سُلْطَانُ حُبِّهِ ۞ أَنَا لَا أَقْبَلُ الرِّشَا

فَسَلُوهُ قَدَيْتُهُ ۞ لِمَ (١٢)قَتْلِى تَحَرَّشَا

(١٣)وله،

أَظَلَّتْ عَلَيْنَا مِنْكَ يَوْمًا غَمَامَةٌ

(١٤)أَضَاءَتْ (١٥)لَنَا بَرْقًا (١٦)وَأَبْطَى (١٧)رِشَاشُهَا

(١) B انشدنا الخلدى عن الجنيد عن سرى السقطى قال كان كثيرًا ما ينشد الخ.
(٢) B ودخلت. (٣) A بها with به written above as a variant. (٤) The
reading of B is doubtful as the beginning of the word is obliterated: the
last three letters seem to be رفه. (٥) B وهو ينشد هذين البيتين يعرفه ويقول.
(٦) A يكش. (٧) B ينشد. (٨) B فرح. (٩) B عمر. (١٠) B om.
(١١) A in marg. الحرش اصطياد. (١٢) B تقتلى. A نقتلى. هذين البيتين
أضاءت B. (١٤) B adds انشدنى فى مجلسه يومًا. الضبّ وأيضا يعنى الخمش
(١٥) A لها. (١٦) AB ابطا. (١٧) A رشيشها.

Af.113b

فلا غيْمُها (١)يَجْلُو فيأيَسَ (٢)طامِعٌ ۞ ولا غيْمُها يأتى فيَرْوَى عِطاشُها

ثم قال للنسّاج اين موضعك من هذا قال (٣)بحيث الذلّ فقال (٤)آه تذكر الذلّ بحضرتى غيرةً منه على المكان (٥)ثم انشأ يقول،

لَقَدْ فُضّلَتْ ليْلَى على النّاسِ كالّتى ۞ على ألْفِ شَهْرٍ فُضّلَتْ ليْلَةُ القَدْرِ

٥ (٦)فيا حبّها زِدْنى جَوىً كُلَّ ليْلَةٍ ۞ ويا سَلْوَةَ الأيّامِ مَوْعِدُكِ الحَشْرُ،

(٧)وقال الشبلى رحمه الله فى مجلسه يوماً،

وعيْنانِ قالَ اللهُ (٨)كُونا فكانَتا ۞ فعُولانِ بالألْبابِ ما (٩)فعَلَ الخَمْرُ،

ثم قال لستُ أعنى (١٠)العيونَ النُّجْلَ ولكنّى اعنى عيون القلوب ذوات الصُّدور فطُوبَى لمن كان له عيْنٌ فى قلبه وأُذنٌ واعبةٌ وألفاظٌ مرضيّةٌ، فقال

١٠ ابو الفرج (١١)العُكْبَرىُّ (١٢)سألتُهُ عن الغَيْرة فقال غيرة البشريّة للأختصاص وغيرة الالهية على الوقت أن يضيع فيما سوى الله ثم (١٣)انشأ (١٤)وهو يقول،

ذابَ ممّا فى فُؤادى بَدَنى ۞ وفُؤادى ذابَ ممّا فى البَدَنْ

فأقْطَعُوا حَبْلى وإنْ شِئْتُمْ صِلُوا ۞ كُلُّ شَىْءٍ مِنْكُمُ عِنْدى حَسَنْ

صحّ عِنْدَ النّاسِ أنّى عاشِقٌ ۞ غَيْرَ أنْ (١٥)لَمْ يَعْلَمُوا عشْقى لمَنْ

١٥ وجرى شىء من العلم فأنشأ يقول،

وشَغَلْتُ عَنْ فَهْمِ الحديثِ سِوَى ۞ ما كانَ مِنْكَ (١٦)وحُكْمُكُمْ شُغْلى

وأُديمُ نَحْوَ مُحَدّثى (١٧)نَظَرى ۞ أنْ قَدْ فَهِمْتُ وعِنْدَكُمْ عَقْلى

وكان يُنشد هذيْن البيتيْن كثيراً (١٨)فى مجلسه،

رآنى فأورانى عَجائبَ لُطْفِهِ ۞ فهِمْتُ وقَلْبى بالفِراقِ يَذُوبُ

---

(١) A يحكى B يصحوا. (٢) B طامعا. (٣) B حب. (٤) B له.
(٥) B وانشا. (٦) Here B proceeds (fol. 56b, 1): اهابك ان اقول هلكت وجدّا (A fol. 115b, 5). The present passage is continued in B on fol. 241b, 1.
(٧) B وانشدنى for وقال الشبلى رحمه الله. (٨) B كونى. (٩) B يفعل. (١٠) B عيون. (١١) B البكرى. (١٢) A يساله. (١٣) B أنثى. (١٤) B om. (١٥) B الناس (١٦) A وحبهم. (١٧) AB كما ارى قد فهمت (١٨) B om. فى مجلسه.
لم يعلموا عشقى for لا يدروا الخ, but corr. in marg. A.

فَلَا (١) غَائِبٌ عَنّى فَأَسْلُو بِذِكْرِهِ * وَلَا هُوَ عَنّى (٢) مُعْرِضٌ فَأَغِيبُ

وله، (٣)

جَرَى السَّيْلُ فَاسْتَبْكَانِى السَّيْلُ (٤) إِذْ جَرَى * وَفَاضَتْ لَهُ مِنْ مُقْلَتَىَّ غُرُوبُ

Af.114a يَكُونُ أُجَاجًا دُونَكُمْ فَإِذَا انْتَهَى * إِلَيْكُمْ تَلَقَّى طِيبَكُمْ فَيَطِيبُ ،

٥ ويقال ان هذه الابيات لسهل بن عبد الله (٥) رحمه الله فى الصبر (٦) على المكاره،

أَتَذَكَّرُ سَاعَةً أَلِفْتَ فِيهَا * وَأَنْتَ (٧) وَلِيدُهَا عَسَلًا وَصَبْرَا

لِتَعْلَمَ أَنَّ هذَا الدَّهْرَ (٨) بُؤْسَى * وَيُصْبِحُ طَعْمُهُ حُلْوًا وَمُرَّا

فَلَا يَمْلَأَكَ مَحْبُوبٌ سُرُورًا * وَإِنْ وَافَاكَ مَكْرُوهٌ فَصَبْرَا

وَإِنْ فَارَقْتَ فى دُنْيَاكَ ذَنْبًا * فَقُلْ فى إِثْرِهِ يَا رَبِّ غَفْرَا،

١٠ وليحيى بن مُعَاذ الرَّازِى (٥) رحمة الله عليه،

أَمُوتُ بِدَاءٍ لَا يُصَابُ دَوَائِيَا (٩) * وَلَا فَرَجٌ مِمَّا أَرَى (١٠) فى بَلَائِيَا

يَقُولُونَ يَحْيَى جُنَّ مِنْ بَعْدِ صَحَّةٍ * وَلَا يَعْلَمُ العُذَّالُ مَا فى حَشَائِيَا

إِذَا كَانَ (١١) دَاءُ المَرْءِ حُبَّ مَلِيكِهِ * فَمَنْ (١٢) غَيْرُهُ يَرْجُو طَبِيبًا مُدَاوِيَا

مَعَ اللهِ (١٣) يَقْضِى دَهْرَهُ (١٥) مُتَلَذِّذًا * (١٤) تَرَاهُ مُطِيعًا كَانَ (١٥) أوْكَانَ عَاصِيَا

١٥ ذَرُونِى وَشَأْنِى لَا تَزِيدُونَ كُرْبَتِى * وَخَلُّوا عِنَانِى نَحْوَ مَوْلَى الدَّوَالِيَا

أَلَا فَاهْجُرُونِى وَارْغَبُوا فى قَطِيعَتِى * وَلَا (١٦) تَكْشِفُوا عَمَّا يَجُنُّ فُؤَادِيَا

رِكُونِى إِلَى المَوْلَى وَكُفُّوا مَلَامَتِى * لَآنَسَ بِالمَوْلَى عَلَى كُلِّ مَا بِيَا،

لأبى العباس بن عطاء فى الشكر،

وَكَمْ بَيْدَلَكَ عِنْدِى (١٧) مَا شَكَرْتُ لَهَا * حَمَلْتَهَا أَنْتَ عَنِّى مَعْ (١٨) بَوَادِيكَا

٢٠ ضَعُفْتُ عَنْ حَمْلِهَا عَجْزًا لِتَحْمِلَهَا * لَكِنْ أَبَادِيكَ تَحْمِلُهَا (١٩) أَيَا دِيكَا،

(١) B ان.   (٤) AB غايبا.   (٢) AB معرضا.   (٣) B وللشبلى رحمه الله.

(٥) B om.   (٦) A فى.   (٧) A وليها.   (٨) B يبسا.   (٩) This verse

is the beginning of B fol. 52b.   (١٠) B من.   (١١) A ذا.   (١٢) B دونه.

(١٣) B يضى.   (١٤) B يراه.   (١٥) B ام.   (١٦) A لتفتوا.   (١٧) A وما.

(١٨) A بوادك.   (١٩) A اياديك.

(١)وله،

(٢)كَيفَ شُكرى لِمَنْ بِهِ يَحسُنُ الشُّكرُ ۞ ومِنهُ شُكرـــهُ لَـهُ في الوِدادِ

إنّما يَشكُرُ المُحبّونَ وَجـدًا ۞ وصَفاءً مِنْ خاصّةِ الإنفرادِ،

(٣)وله،

٥ حقًّا أَقولُ لَقَد كَلَّفَتني شَطَطًا ۞ حَملَ هَواكَ وصَبرى إنَّ ذا (٤)لَعَجيبُ

جَمَعتَ شَيئَين في قَلبى (٥)لَهُ خَطَرٌ ۞ نَوعَين ضِدّين تَبريدٌ وتَلهيبُ

(٦)نارٌ (٧)تَلَقّني والشَوقُ يُضرِمُها ۞ فكَيفَ يَجتَمِعا روحٌ وتَعذيبُ   Af.114b

لاكُنتُ إن كُنتُ أَدرى كَيفَ يُسلِمُني ۞ صَبرى عَلَيكَ وصَبرى صَبرٌ (٨)أَيّوبا

لَمّا تَحَقَّقَ بِالبَلوى اقشَعَرَّ لَها ۞ فَظَلَّ مِن ثِقلِها عُريانَ (٩)مَكروبا

١٠ قَد مَسَّنى الضُّرُّ والشَيطانُ يَنصُبُ لى ۞ وأَنتَ ذو قُوَّةٍ والعَبدُ مَنكوبُ

فلا تَكِلْني إلى نَفسى فيَظفَرَ بى ۞ مَن كانَ يَقرُنِى (١٠)إذ كُنتُ (١١)مَحجوبا،

ولأبى حمزة الصوفى (رحمه الله)، (١٢)يقال انه وقع في بئرٍ فطمّوا رأسها فجأةً

سبعٌ ففتح رأس البئر، ونزل فتعلّق ابو حمزة برجله فأخرجه من البئر

فسمع هاتفًا يقول هذا حَسنٌ يأبا حمزة نجّيناك من التلف بالتلف من البئر

١٥ بالسبع فقال (١٢)عند ذلك،

نَهانى حَيائى مِنكَ أَن أَكتُمَ الهَوى ۞ (١٤)وأَغنَيتَنى بِالنَهمِ عَنكَ مِنَ الكَشفِ

تَلَطَّفتُ في أَمرى فأَبدَأتُ شاهِدى ۞ إلى (١٥)غائبى واللُّطفُ يُدرَكُ بِاللُّطفِ

تَرَأَيتَ لى بِالغَيبِ حَتّى كَأَنَّما ۞ (١٦)تُبَشِّرُنى بِالغَيبِ أَنَّكَ في الكَفِّ

أَراكَ وبى مِن هَيبَتى لَكَ وَحشَةٌ ۞ (١٧)فتُؤنِسُنى بِاللُّطفِ مِنكَ (١٨)وبِالعَطفِ

٢٠ (١٩)وتُحيى مُحِبًّا أَنتَ في الحُبِّ حَتفُهُ ۞ (٢٠)وذى عَجبٌ كَونُ الحَياةِ مَعَ الحَتفِ،

---

(١) B وله أيضًا.   (٢) B om. this and the following verse.   (٣) B om.

(٤) So both MSS.   (٥) B لها.   (٦) Partly obliterated in B.   (٧) B يقلبها.

(٨) AB أيوب.   (٩) AB مكروب.   (١٠) B ان.   (١١) AB محجوب.

(١٢) A تعالى.   (١٣) B om. عند ذلك.   (١٤) B وأعنيتنى.   (١٥) B غائبى.

(١٦) A وبالقطف   (١٧) A فيؤنسنى, vocalised by a later hand.   (١٨) B بسر.

(١٩) B ويحيا محبّ.   (٢٠) B وذا.

ولأبى نصر بِشْرِ بن الحُرث (١) رحمة الله عليه،

لا تَعجبَنَّ لِوَحْدَتى وتَفَرُّدِى ٭ ومِنَ التَّفَرُّدِ فى زَمانِكَ فازْدَدِ

ذَهَبَ الإخاءُ فَليسَ ثَمَّ أُخُوَّةٌ ٭ إلّا التَّمَلُّقُ باللِّسانِ وباليَدِ

فإذا تَكَشَّفَ لى بِها فى قَلْبِهِ ٭ عايَنْتُ (٢) ثَمَّ نَقيعَ سَمِّ الأسْوَدِ،

٥ وليوسف بن الحسين (٣) الرازى رحمة الله عليه،

أُحبُّ مِنَ الإخوانِ كُلَّ مُوَاتى ٭ (٤) غَبِيًّا عَمِىَ الطَّرْفِ عَنْ عَثَراتى

يوافِقُنى فى كُلِّ أمْرٍ أُحبُّهُ ٭ ويَحفَظُنى حَيًّا وبَعْدَ وَفاتى

فَمَنْ لى بِهذا لَيتَنى قَدْ وَجَدْتُهُ ٭ فَقاسَمتُهُ مالى ومِنْ حَسَناتى،

ولأبى عبد الله القُرَشى (٥) رحمة الله عليه، Af.115a

١٠ وأنتَ خَليطُ النَّفْسِ فى كُلِّ شأنِها ٭ ولكِنَّ نَفْسَ الذَّاتِ مِنْكَ مُبايِنَه

تُخامِرُها حَتَّى كأنَّكَ (٦) أنَّها ٭ وتَفْنَى قُواها فالقُوَى بِكَ فانِيَه

(٧) يُعارِضُها الواشُونَ فيكَ بِكُلِّ ما ٭ (٨) يُقَلِّقُها فى سِرِّها والعَلانِيَه

وبَلَّغَتْها (٩) ما كُنْتَ أنتَ لَها بِهِ ٭ (١٠) فتَعذِرُهُم فى كُلِّ ما كانَ كائِنَه

لَقَدْ فَرِحَتْ (١١) آماقُها فيكَ مَرَّةً ٭ وقَدْ (١٢) قَرِحَتْ مِنْها السُّوَيْداءُ ثانِيَه،

١٥ (١٣) وكتب ابو عبد الله (١٤) الهيكلى الى ابى عبد الله القُرَشى رحمه الله تعالى،

ذاتٌ هُوِيّةٌ تَكونُ مُذَكَّرَه ٭ مَعْروفةٌ تَحْتَ الخَواطِرِ مُنكَرَه

لا تَجْتَلى عَينُ العُقولِ (١٥) ضِياءَها ٭ فَلَها بِها الأبصارُ عَنها مُبْصِرَه

وأعَزُّ مُمتَنِعٍ مَكانُ تَناوُلٍ ٭ مِنها عَلى مَنْ لا يَراها مُخبِرَه

سُبُلُ المَعارِفِ كُلُّها إلّا بِها ٭ (١٦) مَسْدودةٌ عَنها المَذاهِبُ مُقفِرَه

٢٠ فإذا عَلِقْتَ بِها ورَغِبْتَ بِعَينِها ٭ عَنها تَجَلَّتْ لِلْعُقولِ مُخبِرَه،

---

(١) B الحافى instead of رحمة الله عليه. (٢) B om. فيه. (٣) B om. رحمة اله. (١) الرازى رحمة اله

(٤) B غبيا. A in marg. وكل غضيض الطرف as a variant. (٥) B om. عليه.

(٦) A أنها. B إنها. Cf. Massignon, Ṭawāsīn, 162. إنّها A, or أنّها, or إنّيتها stands for أتّيتها or

(٧) A تعارضها. B يعاتيها. (٨) B نطرها. (٩) A وبلغتها. B فلمها. إنّيتها.

وكتب (١) B om. from أماها. (١١) B فرحت. (١٢) AB فتعذرهم. (١٣) B om. from

عنها مسدودة. (١٦) ضياورها A (١٥) الهيكلى A (١٤) to للعقول مخبّره.

٢٠

ولأبي سعيد الخَزّاز (١) رحمة الله عليه ،

قَلْبٌ يُحِبُّكَ لا يُوِى إلَى (٢) أَحَدِ ٭ نَكادُ هِمَّتُهُ (٣) تَنْقالُكَ بالخَبَرِ

فُؤادُهُ بِكَ مَشْغُوفٌ ومُهْجَتُهُ ٭ تَذُوبُ مِن قَلَقِ (٤) التَّقْرِيبِ والنَّظَرِ

قَلْبٌ بِها تَجْنِي الأَذْهانُ فِطْنَتُهُ ٭ إذا سَمَتْ بِكَ يا عِزّى ومُفْتَخَرِى

٥ (٥) مُرَبَّغاتٌ مِن الشَّجْوِ (٦) الدَّفِينِ (٧) لَها ٭ كَوامِنٌ جُمِّعَتْ فى السَّمْعِ والبَصَرِ

سُبْحانَ مَنْ (٨) لَوْ يَشا أَبْدَى عَجائِبَها ٭ حَتَّى تَرَى سِرَّها فى الوَجْهِ كالقَمَرِ ،

(٩) جواب ابى عبد الله القُرَشِى لِلذَّبَكِى وهو فيما قيل قول ابى سعيد الخَزّاز ،

إذا أَلْبَسَ الحَقُّ المُحِقُّ حَقِيقَةً ٭ مِن الوَجْدِ بانَتْ عَنْ نُعُوتِ السَّرائِرِ

ولَيْسَ لِأَنَّ السِّرَّ سُمِّى (١٠) بِما يَلِى ٭ عَلَيْهِ بِهِ لكِنْ أَوْصافُ قادِرِ

ولا تَأْبَ عَنْ مَكنُونِها لَفْظَ عارِفٍ ٭ ولكِنْ بِتَمْثِيلِ اللَّطِيفِ المُآثِرِ

إذا طَلَعَتْ شَمْسٌ عَلَيْها بِنُورِها ٭ فَأَنْتَ خَلِيطٌ للشُّعاعِ (١١) المُباشِرِ

بَعِيدٌ مِنْ الذَّاتِ العَزِيزِ مَكانُها ٭ ولَمْ تَعَرَ مِنْ نَعْتٍ لِنَعْتِكَ قاهِرِ ،

ولأبي الحُدَيد (١٢) كتبها الى القُرَشِى ،

(١٣) أهابُكَ أَنْ أَقُولَ هَلَكْتُ وَجْدًا ٭ عَلَيْكَ وَقَدْ هَلَكْتُ عَلَيْكَ وَجْدا

(١٤) وأَوْ أَنَّ الرُّقادَ (١٥) دَنا (١٦) لِطَرْفِى ٭ جَلَدْتُ جُفُونَها بالدَّمْعِ (١٧) جَلْدا ،

١٥ جواب ابى عبد (١٨) الله ،

ولكِنّى أَقُولُ حَيْثُ حَقًّا ٭ (١٩) إذا الوَجْدُ المُبَرِّحُ مِنْكَ يَهْدا

---

(١) B om.   (٢) B app. بشر.   (٣) A يلقاك B يلقا.   (٤) A التقرب.

(٥) A مرتخات B مزيحات Perhaps مُرَتَّغات.   (٦) B الدقيق.   التعزب A app. B

(٧) A بها.   (٨) A شا لو.   (٩) B om. from جواب to لنعتك قاهر.   (١٠) A

بها لبن.   (١١) A المآشر.   (١٢) B كتبه الى ابى عبد الله القرشى.   (١٣) These words,

وكيف which occur in B on fol. 54a, last line, are followed by the verse

تفذيك روح أنت واهبها الخ (p. ٢٤٩, l. ١٨ supra). The remainder of B's text to

the end of fol. 56a corresponds with the text of this edition from p. ٢٥٠,

l. 1 to p. ٢٥٢, l. 4.   (١٤) This is the beginning of fol. 56b in B.

(١٤) B فلو.   (١٥) A زنا.   (١٦) AB بطرف.   (١٧) A جَدا.   (١٨) B

adds اليه.   (١٩) B ان.

وإنْ حَلَّ الرُّقادُ بِجَفْنِ عَيْنِى ٭ رَقَدْتُ إجابَةً لَكَ لا لأَهْدا،

(١)قال الشيخ رحمه الله وهذه الاشعار فيها ما هى مشكلة وفيها ما هى جليّة ولهم

فيها اثارات لطيفة (٢)ومعانٍ دقيقة فمن نظر (٣)فيها فليتدبّرها حتى يقف

على مقاصدهم ورموزهم حتى لا ينسب قائلها الى ما (٤)لا يليق بهم واذا اشكل

عليه ولم يفهم (٥)فليستبحث بالسؤال عن من يفهم لان لكلّ مقام (٦)مقالاً ولكلّ

علم (٧)اهلاً ولو اشتغلنا بشرحه لطال (٨)الكتاب،

باب الدعوات التى كان يدعو بها المشايخ المتقدّمون
من اهل الصفوة،

دعاءٌ كان يدعو به (٩)ذو النون رحمه الله، (١٠)اللهمَّ الحَوْلُ حَوْلُكَ

والطَّوْل طَوْلُك ولك فى كلّ خلقك مدد قوّةٍ وحولٍ وأنت الفعّال لما

يشاء لا العجز ولا الجهل يعارضانك ولا النقصان ولا الزيادة يُحيلانك وأنّى

يعارضانك وها ما أحدثتَ او برومان إحالتك وها ما خلقتَ وكيف لا

يكونان ممّا احدثتَ وما خلقتَ وأنت الموجود بالدلايل عليك فلن يخلق Af.116a

خلقك غيرك أنت فتباركتَ يا من كلُّ مدروك فمن خلفِهِ وكلُّ محدود

المدروكات فمن صنعِهِ أنت الذى لا يُدركك فى الدنيا العيان ولا يستغنى

عنك مكان ولا يعرفك غيرك الاّ باقراره لك بالوحدانية ولا يجهلك من

خلقك الاّ ناقصُ المعرفة ولا (١١)يُسهّيك شىءٌ عن شىء ولا يحُدُّ قدرتك احدٌ

ولا يخلو منك مكانٌ ولا يشغلك شأنٌ عن شأن دعاءٌ آخر (١٢)لذى النون

رحمه الله اللهمَّ اجعل العيون منّا فوّارات بالعَبَرات، والصدور منّا محشوّةً

(١) قال ابو نصر هذه الاشعار الخ B.   (٢) ومعانى AB.   (٣) فيه B.   (٤) B om.

(٥) The original reading of A seems to have been فلتستبحّث السؤال.   (٦) مقال B.

(٧) اهل B.   (٨) B adds وبالله التوفيق.   (٩) ذا A.   (١٠) B om. from

لذا A.   (١٢) يُسهيك.   (١١) دعاء آخر لذى النون رحمه الله to اللهمّ.

بالعبر والحرقات، واجعل قلوبنا غوّاصةً فى (١)موج (٢)قَرْعِ ابواب السموات،
تابهةً من خوفك فى (٣)البوادى والفلوات، افتح لأبصارنا بابًا الى معرفتك
ولمعرفتنا أفهامًا الى النظر فى نور حكمتك يا حبيب قلوب الواهين ومنتهى
رغبة الراغبين، (٤)ولذى النون رحمه الله اللهمّ انت آنَسَ المؤنسين لأوليآيك
٥ (٥)وأقْرَبُهم بالكفاية من المتوكّلين عليك لِمَشاهدهم فضمآيرُهُمْ تَطَّلِع على أسرارهم،
الهى سرّى اليك مكشوف وأنا اليك ملهوف اذا اوحشنى الذنْبُ آنَسنى
ذِكْرُكَ عالمًا بأنّ أَزِمّة الأمور بيدك وإنّ (٦)مصدرها عن قضآيك الهى مَنْ
أوْلَى بالذلّ والتقصير منّى وقد خلقتنى ضعيفًا ومن أوْلَى بالعفو منك وعِلمُك
(٧)بى سابقٌ (٧)وأمْرُك (٨)بى مُحيطٌ أطَعْتُك بإذْنك والمِنّةُ لك علىَّ وعصيتُك
١٠ بعِلمُك والحُجّةُ لك علىَّ، أسْئَلُك بوجوب رحْمتك وانقطاع حُجّتى وتفقّرى
اليك وغناك عنّى أن تغفر لى (٩)خطِيّتى الظاهرة والباطنة، (١٠)دعآء ليوسف
ابن الحسين (٢)رحمه الله، اللهمّ أنا نباتُ نِعَمك فلا تجعلنا حصآيَد نِقَمك،
(٢)اللهمّ أعْطِنا ما تريد منّا يا من أعطانا الايمان به من غير سؤال لا تمنعْنا
عفوُك مع السؤال فاِنّا اليك آيبون (١١)ومن الاصرار على معصيتك (١٢)تايبون،
(١٣)فاِنّا اليك ذاعنون تايبون، اللهمّ تقبّلْ ما (١٤)مننتَ به علينا من الاسلام
والايمان الذى به هدَيتنا وأعْفُ عنّا، الهى (١٥)نِعَمُك محيطة بنا وأنتَ
المذخور لشُكُرها وعِزّتك وشكرك ما شكرك (١٦)احدٌ الّا بك، وقال يوسف (٢)رحمه
الله سمعت حكيمًا يقول فى دعآيه الحمد لله الذى شكر على ما به أنْعَمَ وذمّ
على ما لو شآء (١٧)منه عَصَمَ، شكَرَ نفْسَهُ بنفسه عن خَلْقه لانّه الله الذى لا
٢٠ اله الّا هو، قال سمعت بعض المشايخ يقول فى مناجاته،

(١) موج B.   (٢) B om.   (٣) B البرارى.   (٤) A ولذا. دعا اخر B.

فى B.   (٥) A وأقربهم. B وأورهم.   (٦) B مصدرك.   (٧) B فى. اللهم الخ له.

(٨) A أمرك.   (٩) B الظاهر والباطن برحمتك.   (١٠) B دعا اخر.   (١١) B ومن أصرّ.

(١٢) A om.   (١٣) B om. فانا اليك ذاعنون تايبون.   (١٤) A ثبت به منا.

(١٥) B نعمتك.   (١٦) B عبد.   (١٧) B عصم منه.   مننت به علينا but written above.

أَ يا جُودَ رَبِّى ناجِ رَبِّى بِحاجَتى ٭ فَما لى إلَى رَبِّى سِواكَ شَفِيعُ،

دعاءٌ للجُنَيْد (١) رحمة الله عليه (٢)مستخرج من كتاب المناجاة، اللهمّ إنِّى اسئلك

يا خير السامعين وبِجُودك (١) وبِمَجْدك يا أَكْرَمَ الاكرمين (٣) وبكرمك وفضلك

يا أَسْمَحَ السامحين وإحسانك ورأفتك يا خير (٤)المُعْطِين اسئلك سؤالَ

٥ خاضع خاشع متذلّل متواضع ضارع اشتدّت اليك فاقتُهُ وأَنْزَلَ بك على

قدر الضرورة حاجتُهُ (٥) وعَظُمتْ فيما عندك رغبتُهُ وعَلِمَ ان لا يكون شىءٌ

الّا بمشيئتك ولا يشفع شافع اليك الّا من بعد إذْنِك، فكم من قبيح قد سترتَهُ

وكم من بلاَء قد صرفتَهُ وكم من عثرة قد أَقَلْتَها وكم من زلّة قد (٦)سهلتَ

(٧)بها وكم من مكروه (٨)قد رفعتَه وكَم (٩)من ثناَء قد نشرتَهُ، اسئلك يا

١٠ سامع اصوات (١٠)المستغيثين، وعالم خفِّى إضمار الصامتين، ومطّلع فى الخلوات

على أفعال المتحرّكين، وناظر الى ما دقّ وجلّ (١١)من آثار الساعِين،

اسئلك أن لا تحجب بسوُء فعلى عنك صوتى، ولا تفضحنى بخفِّى ما اطَّلعتَ

عليه من سرِّى، ولا تعاجلنى العقوبة على ما علمتَه من خلواتى وكن (١٢)بى

فى (١)كلّ الاحوال (١٣)رافقًا، وعلىَّ فى كلّ (١٤)الاحوال عاطفًا، الهى وسبّدى

١٥ وسَنَدى أنا بك عايذ لايذ مستغيث مستجير من (١٥)تكائف (١٦)مَخاوِفِ عِلَلِ

سرِّى، ومن لزوم ذلك ضيرى وقلبى، حتى يكاد ذلك أن يملأَ صدرى،

ويُوقِف على الانبساط الى ذِكْرك عقلى ولسانى ويمنع من الحركة فى الخدمـة

جسمى، فأنا فى حبس ما يعارضنى من ذلك من النقص والتقصير، (١)اسئلك

ان تُخرج ذلك عن (١٧)ذكرى وتمنعه من (١٨)قلبى وأجعل اوفانى من الليل

---

(١) B om.   (٢) A مستخرجه كذا with written above.   (٢) B وبفضلك   (٤) A المطاعين with معطين as variant. B المطيعين.   (٥) A وعظم   وكرمك.   (٦) A gives سمحت as a variant.   (٧) B به.   فيها but corr. above.   (٨) B om. وكم   (٩) B ومن.   (١٠) It is doubtful whether B reads المستعيين or المستغيثين.   (١١) B فى.   (١٢) B لى.   (١٣) B رافعًا.   (١٤) B الامور.   (١٥) B بك انف.   (١٦) A مخاوف. B عارف.   (١٧) B قلبى.   (١٨) B ذكرى.

والنهار بذكرك معمورةٌ وبخدمتك وعبادتك موصولةً حتى يكون الورود ورودًا
واحدًا والحال حالاً واحدًا لا سآمة فيه ولا فتور ولا مَلَل ولا تقصير حتى
أُسرع به إليك فى حين المبادرة وأسرح بذلك إليك فى ميادين المسابقة
وارزقنى من طعم ذلك اللذاذَ السايغة يا أكرمَ الاكرمين، سمعتُ ابا سعيد
الدينورى بأطرابُلُس يدعو [1] هذا الدعاءَ فى مجلسه، اللهمّ انى اسئلك بحقّك
عليك فلا حقٌّ احقُّ من حقّك عليك بحقّك على اهل الحقّ [2] وبحقّ اهل
الحقّ عليك وبحقّ كلّ ذى حقٍّ بان لك بقدَمك بعلمك بكلّ شىءٍ، ومُلكِك
لكلّ شىءٍ، وقدرتك على كلّ شى [3] صلّ على محمّد وعلى [4] آله وأن تفعل
بى كذا [5] وكذا، وحُكى عن [6] عمر بن بَحر قال هذا دعاءَ. حفظتُه عن
الشبلى انّه كان يدعو [7] به، اللهمّ لك الحمد يا ضياءَ السموات والارض
ويا بهاءَ السموات والارض ويا قيّوم السموات والارض ويا نور السموات
والارض بحقّ أسمآيك عليك [8] وبحقّك عليك فلا حقّ اجلّ منك عليك
[9] وبحقّ ما انزلتَ وبحقّ من جعلتَ له فهمًا فيما انزلتَ يا الله ويا من لا
سِواكَ الله ويا من [10] أنت الله صلّ على محمّد وعلى آل محمّد [11] واجمعهم
ولا تُشتّهم وأرحم ظواهرهم وأعمُر بواطنهم [12] وقُم لهم بالكلآبة والكفاية وكن
لهم عِوَضًا من كلّ عِوَض وأرحمهم ولا تردّهم اليوم طُرفةَ عَين ولا أقلّ من
ذلك بحقّ كلّ حقٍّ أنت ذلك الحقّ واجعلهم أتقياءَ [13] وأجلّاءَ فى معانيك
[14] اللَّدُنيّة واجعلهم مِمّن اذا قال [15] قال على التحقيق واذا سكت فلا سِواك،
ومن دعوات يحيى بن مُعاذ الرازى [16] رحمة الله عليه الهى وسيّدى وأَمَلى
ومن به يتمّ عملى وكان يقول الهى ادعوك بلسان املى حين كلّ لسان عملى

---

(١) .بهذا B   (٢) .وبحقّ اهل الحقّ B om.   (٣) B .صلّى   (٤) B .ال محمّد.

(٥) B adds .كما قال   (٦) B adds .دايمًا   (٧) B .عمرو بن يحيى.

(٨) A om. .وبحقّك عليك   (٩) A .بحقّ   (١٠) B .هو   (١١) B app.

(١٢) .وارحمهم   (١٣) B .واخلا   (١٤) B .اللدن   (١٥) B .فالك

(١٦) B om.

(1)Af.117b والهى ما أطيَبَ واقعات الإلهام منك على خطرات القلوب وما الذ
مناجاة الإسرار اليك فى وطنات الغيوب الهى اذا قلت لى فى القيمة عَبْدى
ما غرَّك بى فأقول سيّدى برُّك بى وإن ادخلتنى النار بين اعدآيك (2)لأخبرتُهم
بانّى كنت فى الدنيا احبّك لانّك مولاى ومن جميع الاشيآء مغناى، وكان
٥ يقول اللهمّ إن نجّيتنى نجّيتنى بعفوك وإن عذّبتنى عذّبتنى بعدلك رضيتُ
بى لانّك ربّى وأنا عبدُك الهى أنت تعلم انّى لا اقوى على النار (3)وأنا اعلم
انّى لا اصلح للجنّة فا الحيلة الا عفوك، وقال الهى (4)وسيّدى وسرورى تكرُّمك
شغلنى عن قبيح عملى وإن كان فيه (5)شقاى وسرورى بنعتك شغلنى عن
حسن عملى وإن كان فيه نجاتى وسرورى بك أنسانى السرور (6)بنفسى،
١٠ وكان يقول اللهمّ انّى اتقرّب اليك وبك أَدَلّ عليك وحُجَّتى نِعَمُك لا على
وما (7)اظنّك تحاسب غدًا بعدلك من غشيته اليوم بفضلك وعفوُك (8)يستغرق
الذنوب ورضوانك يستغرق الآمال (9)ولولا انّك بالعفو تجود ما كان عبدك
(10)بالذنب يعود، وكان يقول الهى وسيّدى ومولاى ومن جميع الاشيآء
مغناى ضيّعتُ نفسى بالذنوب فردُّها علىّ بالتوبة (11)أنت تعلم انّ الكريم
١٥ من عبادك يعفو عمّن ظلمه وقد ظلمتُ نفسى وأنت أكرم الاكرمين فأعفُ
عنّى (12)الهى أنت تعلم انّ إبليس عدوّ لك ولى وليس شىء (13)أنّكَ
(14)لكنه وأقطعُ لكيه من غفرانك لى فأغفر لى يا ارحم الراحمين، سمعتُ
(15)عمر المَلطِى (16)بأنْطاكية يقول قلتُ لبعض المشايخ ينبغى أن تدعو لى
(17)فقال يا فتى انا ادعو لك ولكن ينبغى (18)لك ايضًا ان تكون بالحضرة
٢٠ فاذا (19)دعوت لك ولم تكن بالحضرة لم ينفع دعاى، وحُكى عن ابرهيم بن

<hr>

(١) B الهى. (٢) A لاخبرهم. (٣) B om. from وأنا to وقال. (٤) B om.
وتجب عن الحلفه (الخليقة) انى بذلك B adds (٦) سمانى B (٥). وسيّدى وسرورى
B (١٠). ولو B (٩). تستغرق B (٨). ظنّك B (٧). يا مولاى نفسى
لكنه B (١٤). انكا AB (١٣). اللهم انك تعلم B (١٢). ان B (١١). بالذنوب.
لك انت B (١٨). فقال لى B (١٧). يقول بانطاكية B (١٦). B om. (١٥).
دعوتك B (١٩).

ادم [١] رحمه الله انّه كان فى سفينة [٢]فهاج البحر وأمروا الناس ان يرموا
بأمتعتهم الى البحر فقيل له يا أبا اسحق ادع الله لنا فقال ليس هذا وقت
الدعآء [٣]هذا وقت التسليم، [٤]وقال بعضهم صِدق الاجابة من ربّك فى
صدق الدعآء من قلبك، قال وسمعتُ جعفرًا قال سمعت الجُنَيْد رحمه الله
قال كان سَرِىّ السَّقَطى رحمه الله اذا دعا يقول اللهم مهما عذّبتنى بشىء،
فلا تعذّبنى بذلّ الحجاب، وعن ابى حمزة [١] رحمه الله قال قلت لسرى
السقطى [١] رحمه الله ادع لى فقال جمع الله بينى وبينك تحت شجرة طُوبى
فانّه بلغنى انّه اوّل ما يدخل الاولياء الجنّة يستريحون تحت [٥]شجرة طوبى،
[١]وفيا حُكى عن ابى محمّد الجَريرى [٦]قال سمعت ابرهيم المارستانى [١]رحمه
الله تعالى يقول رأيت الخضر [١] رحمه الله فى المنام فعلّمنى عشر كلمات
وأحصاها علىّ بيه إنّى اسألك حُسن الاقبال عليك والاصغآء اليك
والفهم عنك والبصيرة فى أمرك والنفاذ فى طاعتك والمواظبة على ارادتك
والمبادرة فى خدمتك وحُسن الأدب فى معاملتك وبرد التسليم اليك
[٧]والنظر الى وجهك، وحُكى عن ابى عُبَيْد البُسرى [١] رحمه الله تعالى قال
رأيت عائشة [١] رضى الله عنها فى [٨]المنام فقلت لها يا امّى علّمينى دعآءً
[١]قال قالت يأبا عبيد قل اللهم اقلل مؤنتى وأحْسِن معونتى وأعنّى على
أمر دنياى وآخرى قال قلت يا امّى زيدينى [٩]قالت يكفيك يأبا عبيد،
وكان بعض المشايخ اذا دعا يقول [١٠]فى دعآيه الهى ادعوك فى الملأ كما
[١١]تُدْعَى الارباب وأدعوك فى الخلآء كما [١١]تُدْعَى الاحباب، [١٢]قال [١٢]الشيخ
رحمه الله وسألتُ بعض المشايخ عن الدعآء ما وَجْهُهُ لأهل التسليم والتفويض
فقال يدعو الله [١٤]عزّ وجلّ على وجهين احدها يزيد [١٥] بذلك [١٦]تربين

(١) B om.   (٢) فهاج B.   (٣) هذا B.   (٤) B om. from وقال to
والنظر B om.   (٥) شطره B.   (٦) انه قال B.   (٧) B om.   الجنيد رحمه الله قال
فى دعايه.   (١٠) B om.   (٩) فقالت B.   (٨) النوم B.   الى وجهك
(١١) يدعوا B.   (١٢) وقال B.   (١٣) الشيخ رحمه الله.   (١٤) B om.
عز وجل.   (١٥) لك B.   (١٦) تربن.

الجوارح الظاهرة بالدعاء (١)لأنّ الدعاء ضربٌ من الخدمة (٢)يريد ان
(٢)يزيّن جوارحه بهذه الخدمة والوجه الثانى (٤)ان يدعو ايثارًا لما امره الله
(٤)تعالى بالدعاء، (٥)دعاء للجنيد رحمه الله (٤)تعالى الهى وسيّدى ومولاى
من احسنُ منك حكمًا لمن ايقن بك ومن اوسعُ منك رحمةً لمن انقالك
وقصدك ومن اسرعُ منك عطفًا ورأفةً لمن ارادك واقبل على طاعتك A f.118b
فكمّهم فى نعمآيك يتقلّبون ولك بفضلك عليهم يعبدون (٦)سرت همومهم بك
اليك وانفردت اراداتهم لديك واقبلت قلوبهم بك عليك وفنيت حظوظهم
من (٧)دونك واجتمعت لك وَحْدَك فهم اليك فى الليل والنهار (٨)متوجّهون
وعليك فى كلّ الاحوال (٩)مقبلون ولك على (١٠)الاحوال (١١)مؤثرون فأنا
اسئلك الهى وسيّدى ومولاى ان تكون لى بفضلك كاليًا كافيًا عاصمًا راحمًا ١٠
فانّى (١٢)اليك (١٣)لاجٍ وبك مستغيث واليك راغب ومنك راهب وعليك
فى امور الدنيا والآخرة متوكّل لا اله الاّ انت سبحانك انّى كنت من الظالمين،
فهذه طرفٌ من (١٤)دعواتهم فى معانى مقاصدهم واحوالهم (١٥)مختصرٌ لمن اراد
ان ينظر (١٦)فيها ويتبرّك بذلك (١٧)وبالله التوفيق،

باب فى (١٨)وصاياهم التى اوصى بها بعض لبعض، ١٥

قال بعض المشايخ قلتُ لرُوَيم (٤)رحمه الله أوْصِنى بوصيّة فقال (٤)لى
يا بُنَىّ ليس غير بذْل الروح فان قدرتَ على ذلك والاّ فلا تشتغل بتُرّهات
الصوفيّة، واجتمع اصحاب يوسف بن الحسين، عند يوسف (١٩)رحمه الله فقالوا

(١) B ان. (٢) A ترين. (٣) A نورك. (٤) B om. (٥) B وللجنيد.
(٦) B app. نشرت. (٧) B دونهم. (٨) A متوجهين. (٩) A مقبلين.
(١٠) B الارواح which is also given by A as a variant. (١١) A مؤثرين.
(١٢) AB اسلك وانا اليك. (١٣) B لاجى. (١٤) B دعواهم. (١٥) A محصّة.
(١٦) B فيه. (١٧) B وبالله الموفق. (١٨) B وصاهم الذى اوصوا بها بعضهم الى.
(١٩) B الرازى instead of رحمه الله بعض.

(١) له أوصِنا فقال اقتدوا بجميع ما رأيتم منّى الّا شيئَيْن (٢) فلا تستدينوا على
الله (١) تعالى ولا تصحبوا المردان، وقيل لسَرىّ السَّقَطى (١) رحمه الله اوصِنا
بشىء فقال لا تستدينوا على الله (١) تعالى ولا تنظروا فى وجوه المُرْد،
(٢) وقال رجل لأبى بكر البارزى اوصِنى فقال أحذر ألفتك وعادتك والسكون
٥ الى راحتك، وقال ابو العبّاس بن عطآء (١) رحمه الله فى (٤) بعض وصاياه
لإخوانه احذروا ان يكون غُمومكم من اجْل ما يظهر لكم وعليكم بما (٥) شآءَ
(٦) الله دون ما تشآءُون، (٧) وعن جعفر الخُلْدى (١) رحمه الله انّه قال كان
الجنيد (١) رحمه الله يوصى لرجل ويقول قدِّمْ نفْسك وأخِّرْ عزمك (٨) ولا Af.119a
تقدّم عزمك ونؤخّر نفسك فيكون (١) فيها إنطآء كثير، ووجدتُ فى كتاب
١٠ لأبى سعيد الخزّاز (١) رحمه الله يوصى مريدًا او صديقًا له فيقول يا اخى
(٩) خالصْ اصحابك (١٠) مخالصةً وخالطْ اهل الدنيا مخالطةً شاهدْهم بظاهرك
وخالفْهم بفعلك ودينك لا (١١) تتلبْ ان (١٢) ضحِكوا فأبكِ وان فرحوا فأحزنْ
وان استراحوا فجِدّ وان شبعوا فتجوّعْ وان ذكروا الدنيا فأذكر الآخرة واصبر
على قلّة الكلام والنظر والحركة والطعام والشراب واللباس حتى يُسكنك الله
١٥ من الفردوس حيث يشآءُ برحمته، وقال ابو سعيد الخزّاز (١٣) يوصى بوصيّة
لبعض اصحابه أحفظ وصيّتى ايّها المريد وأرغب فى ثواب الله (١) تعالى
وإنما هو ان ترجع الى نفسك الخبيثة (١٤) فتُذبيها بالطاعة وتُفارقها وتُهينها
بالخالفة وتذبحها بالاياس فيما سوى الله وتقتلها بالحيآء من الله (١) عزّ وجلّ
ويكون الله حسبك وتُسارع فى جميع الخيرات وتعمل فى جميع المقامات
٢٠ وقلبُك وَجِلٌ (١) أن لا يقبل منك (١٥) فهذا حقايق القبول والاخلاص

(١) B om.   (٢) B لا.   (٣) B قال.   (٤) A معنى.   (٥) B يشا.

(٦) A adds وعليكم.   (٧) B عن.   (٨) B om. ولا تقدم عزمك.   (٩) B خالظ (sic).

(١٠) B مخالظة.   (١١) A تتل. B app. تبلههم.   (١٢) B ضحوا.   (١٣) B om.

(١٤) A فمدلها with فتدسها written above as a variant.   يوصى بوصية

(١٥) B app. فهذه but the latter half of the word is almost illegible.

والصدق حتى (١)تتخلّص وتصير الى الله (٢)تعالى والله يفعل ما يشآء ويحكم
ما يريد ، وصيّة اوصى بها (٣)ذو النون لبعض اخوانه فقال يا اخى اعلم انّه
لا شرف اعلى من الاسلام ولا كرم اعزّ من التُّقى ولا عقل احرز من الورع
ولا شفيع انجحُ من التوبة ولا لباس اجلّ من العافية ولا وقاية(٤) امنعُ من
٥ السلامة ولا كنز اغنى من القنوع ولا مال اذهب للفاقة من الرضا بالقوت
ومن اقتصر على بلغة الكفاف فقد انتظم الراحة والرغبةُ مفتاح التعَب ومطيّة
النصَب والحرصُ داع الى التهجّم فى الذنوب والشره جامع لمساوى العيوب
وربّ (٥)كاذب وأمل خايب ورجآء يؤدّى الى الحرمان وإرْباح يئول
الى الخسران ، (٦)وقال الجُنَيْد (٧)رحمه الله فى كلام له لبعض أصحابه
Af.119b(٨)أوصيك بقلّة الالتفات الى الحال الماضية عند ورود (٩)الحال الكاينة،
(٧)قال وقلت لأبى عبد الله الخيّاط الدينورى (٧)رحمه الله أوصنى بشىء
فقال أوصيك بخصلةٍ ما أَعْلَمُ أن يكون خصلةٌ (١٠)لم تصحبْه آفةٌ غيرها قلت
وما هى (١١)قال ذِكْرُك لأخيك (١٢)بالجميل فى ظهر الغيب ودعاؤَك لـه ،
وحُكى عن ابى بكر الورّاق (٧)رحمه الله انه قال بعْتُ العزَّ من شهوة العزّ
١٥ وإشتريتُ الذُلّ من خوف الذُلّ (١٣)هذا جزآء من خالف (١٤)وصيّة الله
(٧)تعالى، وأتى رجلٌ ذا النون المصرى (٧)رحمه الله فقال له اوصى فقال
له بما أوصيك إن كنتَ أُيِّدْتَ فى علم الغيب بصدق التوحيد فقد سبق
لك قبْلَ أن نُخْلَقَ من لَدُنْ آدم (٧)عليه السلام الى يومك هذا دعوةُ النبيّين

---

(١) B om. و تخلّص. ‏(٢) B عز وجل. ‏(٣) A ذا. ‏(٤) A افنع. ‏(٥) B om.
from كاذب to الخسران. The words وربّ طمع which are the last words in B
fol. 62a are followed on fol. 62b by the words ابديه وأفردك عما لك به which occur
in A on fol. 109b, l. 13 = p. ٢٤٢, l. ٢ supra. ‏(٦) The sentence وقال الجنيد
الخ begins in B on the last line of fol. 131a. The passage beginning وأمل كاذب
خايب and ending عند ورود حال الكاينة is repeated in B on fol. 242b, ll. 1—3
‏(٧) B om. ‏(٨) B app. الى أوصيك. ‏(٩) B حال الكافية. ‏(١٠) A لمن.
‏(١١) B فقال. ‏(١٢) B بالجميد. ‏(١٣) B وهذا. ‏(١٤) B ربه او وصية.

والمُرْسَلِين فذلك خير لك وإن (١)تكن غير ذلك فأنّى يُنفذ النداءَ الغَرْقَى،
سمعتُ ابا محمّد المهلب بن احمد بن مرزوق المصرى يقول لمّا (٢)حضرتْ
ابا محمّد المُرْتَعِش (٣)رحمه الله الوفاةَ أوصى الىّ بأن اقضى دَيْنه وكان عليه
ثمانية عشر درهمًا فلمّا دفنّاه قُوِّمتْ ثيابُ بَدَنِه بثمانية عشر درهمًا (٤)فبعتُها
ه بثمانية عشر درهمًا فخَرَج رأسًا برأس وقضيّنا دَيْنه واجتمع المشايخ فأخذوا
كِرْفنه وكان فيه قُماشٌ مثل ما يكون فى الكفن فأخذ كلّ واحد منهم شيئًا
وتفرّقوا، ودخل رجل على ابرهيم بن شَيْبان (٣)رحمه الله فقال له اوصى
بشىء. فقال له ابرهيم اذكر الله ولا (ه)تَنْسَهُ فان لم تستطع ذلك فلا (٦)تَنْسَ
الموت، وقيل لبعض المشايخ اوصى فقال (٧)اخّ اسمك من ديوان القُرّاء،
١٠ وقيل لأبى بكر الواسطى رحمه الله اوصنا فقال (٨)عُدّوا انفاسكم واوقاتكم
والسلم، وقيل لآخَرَ اوصى فقال (٩)القِلّة والذِّلّة واللحوق بالله عـزّ وجـلّ،
وقال (١٠)ذو النون (٣)رحمه الله بينا أنا (١١)اسير فى جبل (١٢)المُقَطَّم اذا
أنا برجل على باب كهف فسمعتُه يقول سُبْحانَ من عطّل قلبى (١٣)من
الإياس وعمّرَه بالآمال فاليأسُ منه قد فارقنى والأمل فيه قد (١٤)أوصلنى
١٥ فتأمّلتُه فاذا هو رجل قد أكمدته العبادة وأقرحته الزهادة فدنوتُ منــه
فتركنى وولّى فقلت له (١٥)اوصنى (١٦)قال (١٧)أنظُرْ أن لا تقطع أمَلَك عن
الله Af.120a (٣)تعالى طُرْفةَ عين وأجمع بين السَّرّاء والضّرّاء (١٨)وصِلْ بينك وبين
الله (٣)تعالى ترى السرور فى يوم (١٩)يخْسَرُ (٣)فيه المُبْطِلون قلت زِدْنى قال
حَسْبك حَسْبك، (٢٠)وقال رجل لذى (٢١)النون (٣)رحمه الله زوِّدْنى كلمةً
٢٠ فقال لا تُؤْثِرنّ الشكّ على اليقين ولا (٢٢)تَرْضَ من نفسك بغير التسكين

(١) تكون A. (٢) B om. حضر. (٣) B om. (٤) فبعت B. (ه) AB تنسه.
(٦) تنسا A. (٧) B om. from احّ to اوصنا فقال. (٨) قيدوا B. (٩) الذلّة B.
(١٠) ذا A. (١١) ساير B. (١٢) المقطب AB. (١٣) A بالإياس.
(١٤) أوطنى B. (١٥) B adds رحمك الله. (١٦) فقال B. (١٧) B om.
(١٨) ودخل B. (١٩) A يخشر. Cf. Kor. 45, 26. (٢٠) قال B.
(٢١) B adds المصرى. (٢٢) ترضى B.

وإن [١] تأتك نايبة [٢] الدهر فتحمّلها بحُسن الصبر وارْمِ بآمالك نحو الدايم الخبير تجده بآمالك قايمًا واغتنم مواصلة الله [٣] تعالى فان لله عبادًا ألفوه فاستأنسوا به وعرفوه فأمّلوه على معرفته وواصلوه على عَيْن يقين فسمَت أبصارهم نحو عظيمٍ جليلٍ [٤] قُدرتُه فسقاهم من [٥] حلاوة [٤] مواصلته وألعقهم من [٦] لذاذة [٤] مخالصته فلبِكايهم حَوْلَ العرش دوىٌّ ولدُعايهم حنينٌ تتفعفع أبوابُ السماء لسرعة تفتحها لإجابة دعايهم، [٧] وللجُنَيْد فى بعض وصاياه يقول يا أخى فاعمل ثم اعمل قَبْلَ أَن يعجل الموت بك وبادرْ ثم بادر قبل ان يُبادَرَ اليك [٨] وقد وعظك الله [٩] تعالى فى الماضين من اخوانك والمنقولين من الدنيا من أقرانك [١٠] وأخدانك فذاك حظُّك الباقى عليك والنافع لك وكلّ ما سوى ذلك فعليك لا لك وهذه موعظتى [٣] لك ووصيّتى ايّاك فاقبَلْها تَحمَد الأمر بقبولها وتفوز باستماعها [١١] والسلام، فهذا طرفٌ من وصاياهم وتخصيص مقاصدهم فى ذلك وبالله التوفيق،

[١٢] كتاب السماع،

باب فى حُسن الصوت [٢] والسماع وتفاوت المستمعين،

[١٤] قال الشيخ رحمه الله قال الله عزّ وجلّ [١٤] يَزِيدُ فِى الْخَلْقِ مَا يَشَآء قالوا فى التفسير الخُلُق الطيّب والصوت الحَسَن، ورُوى [١٥] فى الحديث عن النبىّ صلعم انه قال ما بعث الله نبيًّا الّا حَسَنَ الصوت، [١٦] وعن النبىّ

(١) تأتيك AB. (٢) B om. (٣) عز وجل B. (٤) A om. (٥) حلاوته A.
(١٠) احوانك B. (٩) جل ثناوه B. (٨) فقد B. (٧) وللجنيد B. (٦) لذاذته A.
(١١) A om. from وبالله التوفيق to والسلام. (١٢) A om. كتاب السماع.
(١٣) قال الشيخ رحمه الله B om. (١٤) Kor. 35, 1. (١٥) B om. فى الحديث.
(١٦) وعنه B for وعن النبى.

صلعم انه قال ما أذِنَ اللهُ (١) تعالى لشىءٍ كأَذَنِه لنبىٍّ حَسَنِ الصوت الحديث، وقال (١) النبىّ صلعم (٢) اللهُ أَشَدُّ أَذَنًا (٣) بالرجل الحَسَنِ الصوت بالقرآن من صاحب القَيْنة بقينته، وفى الحديث ان داود عليه السلم (٤) قد أُعطِىَ من حُسن الصوت حتى كان يستمع لقراءَته اذا قرأ الزَّبور الجِنّ والإِنس والوحش والطير وكان بنو اسرائيل يجتمعون فيستمعون (٥) وكان يُحمَل من مجلسه اربعاية جنازة ممّن قد مات كما رُوى فى الحديث، (٦) ورُوى عن النبىّ صلعم انه قال (٧) لقد أُعطِىَ ابو موسى مِزمارًا من مزامير (١) آل داود لِما أُعطى من حُسن الصوت، وفى الحديث ان النبىّ صلعم قرأ يوم الفتح (٨) فمدَّ مدًّا وأَنه كان يرجِّع، وعن مُعاذ بن جَبَل انه قال لرسول الله صلعم لو علمتُ انّك هو ذى تَسمع لحبَّرتُه (٩) تحبيرًا، وقد رُوى عن النبىّ صلعم انه قال زيِّنوا القرآن بأصواتِكم، (١٠) قال الشيخ رحمه الله (١١) يحتمل هذا معنيَيْن (١٢) والله اعلم احدهما انه اراد (١) بذلك ان يزيِّن قراءَته للقرآن وهو رفعُ صوته (١٣) بقراءَة القرآن فيحسِّن الصوت عند قراءَته ويطيِّب النغة لانَّ القرآن كلام الله غير مخلوق فلا يزيِّن ذلك بصوت مخلوق ونغمٍ مكتسَبٍ، والمعنى الآخر يحتمل (١٤) انه اراد بذلك (١٤) اى زيِّنوا اصواتكم بالقرآن فيكون (١٥) مقدَّمًا ومؤخَّرًا (١٦) فى المعنى (١٧) كقوله (١٨) الحَمْدُ لِلّهِ الَّذِى أَنزَلَ عَلَى عَبْدِهِ الْكِتَابَ وَلَمْ يَجْعَل لَّهُ عِوَجًا قَيِّمًا معناه مقدَّم ومؤخَّر (١٩) على معنى أنزل الكتاب على عبد قيِّمًا ولم يجعل له عوجًا ومثل ذلك فى القرآن كثير، وقد ذمّ الله (١) تعالى الاصوات المُنْكَرة بقوله (١) عزّ وجلّ (٢٠) إِنَّ أَنْكَرَ الْأَصْوَاتِ

(١) B om.   (٢) A لله. B لا اله لا with لا اله لا suppl. in marg. after لا.

(٣) B للرجل.   (٤) B كان قد.   (٥) B فكان.   (٦) A روى.   (٧) A om.

(٨) B فهم.   (٩) B تحبيرا لك.   (١٠) B قالوا for الله رحمه الشيخ قال.

(١١) B ويحتمل.   (١٢) B om. والله اعلم.   (١٣) A نقراء. B يقرا.   (١٤) B ان.

(١٥) A ومؤخر ومقدم.   (١٦) A والمعنى.   (١٧) B adds تعلى.   (١٨) Kor. 18, 1—2.

(١٩) B om. from معنى على to عوجا.   (٢٠) Kor. 31, 18.

أَصَوتُ ٱلْحَبِيرِ [١] وفى ذمّ الاصوات المنكرة محمدةٌ [٢]للاصوات الطيّبة،
وقد تكلّم ٱلْحكماء فى معنى الاصوات الحسنة والنغات الطيّبة وأكثروا فى
ذلك فقال [٣]ذو [٤]النون [٥] رحمه الله وقد سُئل عن الصوت الحسن فقال
مخاطبات وإشارات الى الحقّ أَوْدَعَها كلَّ طيّب وطيّبة، وعن يحيى بن مُعاذ
الرازى [٥] رحمه الله انه قال الصوت الحسن [٦] رَوْحة من الله [٥] تعالى لقلب
فيه حبُّ الله [٥] تعالى، وقال آخر النغمة الطيّبة رَوْحٌ من الله [٥] تعالى يروّح
بها قلوبًا محترقةً بنار الله [٥] تعالى، وسمعتُ احمد بن علىّ الوجيهى يقول
سمعت ابا علىّ الروذبارى [٥] رحمه الله [٥] يقول ان ابا عبد الله الحُرث بن
أسد المحاسبى [٥] رحمه الله كان [٧] يقول ثلثٌ اذا وُجِدْنَ [٨]مُنعَ بهنّ وقد
فقدناهن أجمع حُسْنُ [٩] الصوت مع الديانة وحسن الوجه مع الصيانة وحسن   Af.121a
الاخاء مع الوفاء، وعن بُنْدار بن الحسين [٥] رحمه الله انه كان يقول
الصوت الطيّب حكمةٌ مجيبةٌ وآلةٌ سليمة بصوتٍ رخيمٍ ولسانٍ لطيفٍ [١٠]ذٰلِكَ
تَقْدِيرُ ٱلْعَزِيزِ ٱلْعَلِيمِ، ومن اللطيفة التى جعل الله فى الاصوات [٥]الطيّبة
ان الطفل فى المهد يبكى لوجود ألمٍ فيُسْمَعُ الصوتَ الطيّبَ فيسكت وينام،
ومشهور [١١]ان الأوايل كانوا يعالجون من به العلّة من السَّوْدَاء بالصوت
الطيّب فيرجع الى حال صحّته، [١٢]قال الشيخ رحمه الله ومن السرّ الذى
جعل الله فى الاصوات الطيّبة التى فيها إنداءً ترى فى البوادى اذا عَيِيَت
الجِمال وقصّرت عن السيّر يحدو لها الحادى فتستمع وتمدّ أعناقها
وتُصْغى بآذانها نحو الحادى وتجود [١٣]فى السير حتى تتزعزع محاملُها من
شدّة سيرها وربّما تُلف انفسها اذا انقطع عنها حدْو الحادى من ثِقَل

---

(١) The words from وفى to للاصوات الطيّبة are suppl. in marg. A.   (٢) A
لحنة.   (٣) A ذا.   (٤) B adds المصرى.   (٥) B om.   (٦) B لحنة.

(٧) B بله.   (٨) AB متعن به. A gives منع بهن as a variant.   (٩) A القول.

(١٠) Kor. 6, 96.   (١١) B فى.   (١٢) B om. from قال to ترى فى.

(١٣) AB om.

حنيْنُها (١) وسرعة (٢) سيرها بعد ما (٣) كانت لا تُحِسّ بذلك من إصغائها الى
حدْوِ حاديها واستماعها الى حُسْن (٤) نغمته وطيب صوت حاديها، (٥) قال الشيخ
رحمه الله وقد حكى (١) لى فى هذا المعنى (٦) الدُّقِّى بدمشق (٧) وقد كان سئل
عن ذلك فقال كنتُ فى البادية فوافيت قبيلةً من قبائل العرب فأضافنى
رجل منهم وأدخلنى خِباءَه فرأيت فى الخباء عبدًا اسود (٨) مقيّدًا بقَيْد
ورأيت جملاً قد مانت بين يدى البيت ورأيت جملاً قد نحل وهو
(٩) ذابلٌ كأنّه (١٠) هو ذا ينزع روحه قال فقال لى الغلام المقيّد انت الليلةَ
ضيفٌ (١١) لمولاى وأنت عنه كريم (١٢) فتشفع فىّ حتى يَحُلّ عنّى هذا القيد
فانّه لا يردّك قال فلمّا قدّموا (١٣) لى الطعام أبيْتُ ان آكل فاشتدّ ذلك
على صاحبى فقال لى ما لك فقلت لا آكل طعامًا الاّ بعد ان تَهَبَ لى
جنابة هذا الغلام وتحلّ عنه قيد فقال يا هذا انّ هذا الغلام قد افقرنى
وأهلك جميع مالى وأضرّ بى وبعيالى فقلت له ما فعل قال ان هذا الغلام
له صوت طيّب وكنت اعيش من ظهر هذه الجمال (١٤) فحمّلهم أحمالاً (١٥) ثقيلة
وحدا لهم حتى قطعوا مسيرة (١٧) ثلثة (١) أيّام فى ليلة (١) وأحدة من
طيب نغمته فى (١٨) حدْوه لهم فلمّا (١٩) وافوْنا وحطّوا أحمالهم (٢٠) ماتوا
كلّهم الاّ هذا الجمل الواحد (٢١) وأنت ضيفى ولكرامتك قد (٢٢) وهبتُه لك
قال فحلّ عنه قيد وأكلنا الطعام فلمّا اصبحنا احببْنا ان اسمع صوته قال
فسألته ان يُسْمعنى صوتَه قال فأمره ان يحدو على جمل كان (٢٣) يُسْنَى
(٢٤) عليه الماء من بير ثَمّ هناك قال فتقدّم هذا الغلام وجعل يسوق ذلك
الجمل ويحدو قال فلمّا رفع صوته هام ذلك الجمل وقطع حباله ووقعتُ

(١) B om.   (٢) B وسيره.   (٣) AB كان.   (٤) B نغمها.   (٥) B om.
(٧) وكان قد.   (٦) B الدق الديبورى بن داود محمد بكر ابو.   (٥) قال الشيخ رحمه الله
(٨) B مقيد.   (٩) B داخل.   (١٠) B om.   (١١) B مولاى.
(١٦) B ويحدوا.   (١٥) B ثقالا.   (١٤) B فيحملهم.   (١٣) A الى.   (١٢) B فاشفع.
(١٧) B ثلث.   (١٨) A حدوته.   (١٩) B وافوا.   (٢٠) B فماتوا.   (٢١) B ولكن.
(٢٢) B اوهبته.   (٢٤) A على.   (٢٣) B يستقى.   انت B (٢٢)

Af.121b

انا على وجهى وما اظنّ انى (١) قطّ سمعتُ صوتًا أطيبَ (٢) من (٣) صوته وكان
مولاه يصيح ويقول يا رجل أيّشَ تريد منّى قد افسدتَ علىّ جَمَلى اذهبْ
عنّى، حكاه الدُّقّى على هذا المعنى او كما قال والله اعلم، سمعت احمد بن
محمّد (٤) الطلّى بأنطاكية يقول سمعت ابى يقول سمعت (٥) بشرًا يقول سألت
٥ اسحق بن ابرهيم المَوْصِلى من الحاذقُ فى القول يعنى فى الغِناء فقال من
تمكّن من أنفاسه وتنزّع فى إحباسه ولطف فى اختلاسه،

باب (٦) فى السماع وإختلاف اقاويلهم فى معناه،

(٦) قال الشيخ رحمه الله بلغنى انه سئل (٧) ذو (٨) النون (٣) رحمه الله عن
السماع فقال وارِدُ حقٍّ يُزعج القلوب الى الحقّ فمن أصغَى اليه بحقٍّ تَحقّق
١٠ ومن اصغى اليه بنفْسٍ تزندق، وعن احمد بن ابى الحوارى (٣) رحمه الله
انه قال سألت ابـا سليمٰن الدارانى (٣) رحمه الله عن السماع (٣) واستماع
(١٠) القصائد التى تُنْشَد بالالحان فقال من اثنَين أحَبُّ الىَّ (٣) منه من واحدٍ،
وسئل ابو يعقوب النهْرجورى (٣) رحمه الله عن السماع فقال حالٌ يُبْدى
الرجوع الى الأسرار من حيث الاحتراق، (١١) وقال بعضهم (٣) السماع لُطْف
١٥ غذاءِ الارواح لأهل المعرفة لأنّه وصفٌ يدقّ ويرقّ عن سايِر الاعمال
ويُدركُ برقّة الطبع لرقّته ويدرك بصفاء السرّ اصفاءِ ولُطفه عند اهله، وعن
ابى الحسين الدرّاج انه كان يقول جال بى السماع فى ميدان من ميادين
البهَاء فأوجدنى (٣) فى وجود الحقّ عند العطاءِ فأسقانى بكأس الصفاءِ
فأدركتُ به منازل الرضا وأخرجنى الى (١٢) رياض النزهة (١٣) والفضاء، وسبّل

Af.122a

(١) B سمعت فقط.   (٢) B منه.   (٣) B om.   (٤) B om. A الطلى with الطلحى as variant.   (٥) B عيسى.   (٦) B om. قال الشيخ رحمه الله.   (٧) A ذا.   (٨) B adds المصرى.   (٩) A واستماعه.   (١٠) B هذه القصائد.   (١١) A om. وقال بعضهم.   (١٢) B الرضا.   (١٣) B والصفا.

الشِّبْلى (١) رحمه الله كما بلغنى عن السماع فقال السماع ظاهره فِتْنَةٌ وباطنـه عِبْرَةٌ فمن عرف الاشارة حَلَّ له استماع (٢) العبرة والّا فقد استدعى الفتنة ونعرّض للبليّة، وحُكى عن الجُنَيْد (١) رحمه الله انه (٤) كان يقول من سمع السماع يحتاج الى ثلثة اشيآء والّا فلا يسمع قيل (١) له وما (٤) تلك الثلثة قال الزمان والمكان والإخْوان، ويقال ان كلَّ من (٥) لا يُحبّ السماع الطيّب من الآدميين فلنقْصٍ فيه وإشتغال قد ورد على خاطره فأذهله، وحُكى عن جعفر عن الجُنَيْد (١) رحمه الله انه قال تنزل الرحمة على الفقرآء فى ثلثة مواطن عند السماع فانّهم لا يسمعون الّا عن حقّ ولا يقومون الّا عن وَجْد (٧) وعند مجاراة العلم فانّهم لا يتكلّمون الّا فى احوال الصدّيقين والاولياء وعند أكلهم الطعام فانّهم لا يأكلون الّا عن فاقة، قال وسبِّل ابو على الروذبارى (١) رحمه الله عن السماع فقال ليتنا (٨) خلصنا منه رأسًا برأس، وسبِّل ابو الحسين النورى (١) رحمه الله عن الصوفى فقال الصوفى (٩) الذى سمع السماع وآثر (١) على الاسباب، وسمعت ابا الطيّب احمد بن (١٠) مُقاتل العكّى يقول قال جعفر كان ابو الحسين بن (١١) زيرى من اصحاب الجُنَيْد وكان (١٢) شيخًا فاضلاً ربّما كان يحضر (١٢) فى موضع يكون فيه السماع فان استطابه فرش إزاره وجلس وقال الفقير مع قلبه اين ما وجد (١) قلبه جلس وإن لم يستطب قال السماع لأرباب القلوب وأخذ نعله وإنصرف، وسمعت الحُصرى (١) رحمه الله يقول فى بعض كلامه أيْشَ اعملُ بالسماع ينقطع اذا انقطع من يسمع منه ينبغى ان يكون سماعك (١٤) متّصلاً غير منقطع، وسبِّل عن السماع فقال ينبغى ان يكون ظمأٌ دائمٌ وشرابٌ دائمٌ فكلّما ازداد شُرْبُهُ ازداد ظمأُهُ،

---

(١) B om.   (٢) A الغيرة. B الغنا.   (٣) B قال for كان يقول.   (٤) B ذلك.

(٥) B لم.   (٦) A بوجد.   (٧) A om. from مجاراة وعند to فاقة عن الّا.

(٨) B تخلص.   (٩) B من.   (١٠) AB مقابل.   (١١) B ريرى.   (١٢) A شيخ

فاضل.   (١٢) B فى موضع فى مكان.   (١٤) B متّصل. A منصل B سماعا منصلا.

باب فى وصف سماع العامّة وإباحة ذلك لهم اذا سمعوا ذِكرَ A f.122b
الترغيب والترهيب بالاصوات الطيبة ويحثّهم [1] ذلك
على طلب الآخرة ،

قال بُنْدار بن الحسين [2] رحمه الله كلّ من لم يحبّ السماع الطيّب من
الآدميين فلنقصٍ فى حاسّته لانّ كلّ نقصٍ يتمتّع به الانسان فيه تكلّفٌ وان
كانت من المباحات الّا السماع [3] فانّه اذا [4] خلص من المقاصد الفاسدة
إباحةٌ لا تحتاج الى التكلّف وكل من سمع السماع من طريق [4] الطيبة والتلذّذ
بالنغمة واستحسان الصوت فليس ذلك [5] محرّمًا عليهم ولا محظورًا ان لم يكن
قصدهم فى ذلك الفساد والمخالفة واللهو وترك الحُدود ان شاَء الله [6] تعالى ،

فصل ، [6] قال الشيخ رحمه الله وممّا يُستدلّ بذلك على اباحة السماع قوله
تعالى [7] وَفِى أَنْفُسِكُمْ أَفَلاَ تُبْصِرُونَ وقوله تعالى [8] سَنُرِيهِمْ آيَاتِنَا فِى الآفَاقِ
وَفِى أَنْفُسِهِمْ ، [9] وما أرانا [10] الله فى انفسنا [11] وأبْصرنا ذلك فى الحواسّ
الخمسة التى [12] قد يُميّز بها بين الشىء وضدّه [13] كالعين تُميّز بالنظر بين
الحسن والقبيح والأنف يميّز بين [15] الرائحة الطيّبة والمُنتنة [16] والفم يميّز
بالذوق [17] بين الحلاوة والمرارة [18] واليد تميّز باللمس بين اللّين والخشن
[19] وكذلك الأذن تميّز بين الاصوات الطيّبة وغير الطيّبة والمُنكرة ، قال
الله تعالى [20] إِنَّ أَنْكَرَ الأَصْوَاتِ لَصَوْتُ الحَمِيرِ فى مذمّته [21] للاصوات

---

(١) على ذلك A. (٢) B om. (٣) فإنّها B. (٤) الطبع B. (٥) A محرم.
(٦) B om. قال الشيخ رحمه الله. (٧) Kor. 51, 21. (٨) Kor. 41, 53. (٩) B وما.
(١٠) جل ذكره B. (١١) وإبصارنا B. (١٢) تميز B. ميز for قد يميّز A. (١٣) العين B.
(١٤) والشم B. (١٥) الشجرتين الرائحة A. (١٦) والذوق B. (١٧) الذوق B.
(١٨) واللمس يميز بين الخشونة واللينة B. (١٩) A om. (١٩) وهكذا السماع B.
(٢٠) Kor. 31, 18. (٢١) الاصوات B. قال الله تعلى الخ.

المنكرة محمّةٌ للاصوات (١) الحسنة ولا يميّز بينهما الّا بالسماع (٢) وهو الإصغاء
(٣) والاستماع بحضور القلب وإدراك الفهم وإزالة الوهم ، فصل آخر ، (٤) قال
الشيخ رحمه الله وذلك ان الله تعالى وصف ما أعدّ لأهل الجنّة من النعيم
فذكر ما ذكر فى كتابه من السدْر المخضود والطَّلْح المنضود والفاكهة الكثيرة
٥ (٥) وذكر لحْم الطير والحُور (٦) العين والسُّنْدُس والإسْتَبْرَق والرَّحيق (٧) المختوم
والأرايك (٧) والقصور والغُرَف (٨) والأشجار والأنهار وغير ذلك وذكر انهم
(٩) فى (١٠) رَوْضَةٍ يُحْبَرُونَ ، قال مُجاهد وهو السماع الذى يسمعون فى الجنّة
بأصوات شجيّة ونغمات شهيّة من (١١) الجوارى الحسان والحور العين يقلُن
بأصواتهنّ نحن الخالدات فلا نموت (١٢) أبدًا ونحن الناعمات فلا نبوس أبدًا
١٠ كما جاءَ فى الحديث، وقد ذكر الله (٧) تعالى تحريم الخمر من جميع ذلك
فقال النبى صلعم من شَرِبَها فى الدنيا لم يشربها فى الآخرة الّا ان يتوب فقد
دخل السماع فى جملة ما اباح الله (٧) تعالى للمؤمنين فى الدنيا من جميع ما
ذكر من نعيم اهل الجنّة وصار الخمر مخصوصًا من جميع ذلك بالتحريم بنصّ
الكتاب والأثر وظاهر (١٣) الخَبَر، فصل آخر، وهو ان النبّى صلعم دخل بيت
١٥ عايشة رضى الله عنها فوجد فيه جاريتين تغنّيان وتضربان بالدُفّ فلم يَنْهَهما
عن ذلك وقال لعمر (١٤) بن الخطّاب رضى الله عنه حين (١٥) غضب وقال
أمزمار الشيطان فى بيت رسول الله صعلم (١٦) فقال (١٧) دَعْهما يا عمر فان
لكلّ قوم عيدٌ، ولو كان محظورًا لكان سواءً فى العيد وغير العيد، والأخبار
فى مثل ذلك تكثر ومثل ما رُوى عن ابى بكر الصدّيق رضى الله عنـه
٢٠ حين (١٨) دخل على عايشة رضى الله عنها وقد وعكت وكان يقول،

(١) الطيبة B.   (٢) والاصغا B.   (٣) B om. from الوهم to والاستماع.
(٤) قال الشيخ رحمه الله B om.   (٥) وكحوم الطير B.   (٦) والعين A.   (٧) B om.
(٨) B om.   (٩) Kor. 30, 14.   (١٠) روض B.   (١١) الجوار B.   والاشجار والانهار.
(١٢) A om.   (١٣) B adds وبالله التوفيق.   (١٤) B om. from بن to عنه.
(١٥) غضب عليهم B.   (١٦) فقال النبى صلى الله عليه B.   (١٧) دعها B.
(١٨) B دخلت عايشة رضى الله عنها وقد وعكت فكانت تقول.

Af.123a

كُلُّ ٱمْرِىءٍ مُصَبَّحٌ فى أَهْلِهِ ٭ وَالمَوْتُ أَدْنَى مِنْ شِرَاكِ نَعْلِهِ،

ومثل بلال كان يرفع حنجرته اذا اشتدّ به الوعك ويقول،

(١)أَلَا لَيْتَ شِعْرِى هَلْ أَبِيتَنَّ لَيْلَةً ٭ (٢)بِوَادٍ وَحَوْلِى (٤)إِذْخِرٌ وَجَلِيلُ

(٤)وَهَلْ أَرِدَنْ يَوْمًا مِياهَ مَجَنَّةٍ ٭ وَهَلْ يَبْدُوَنْ لِى (٥)شَامَةٌ وَطَفِيلُ،

وكذلك عايشة رضى الله عنها كانت تقول شعر لبيد،

٥

ذَهَبَ الَّذِينَ يُعاشُ فى أَكْنافِهِمْ ٭ وَبَقِيتُ فى خَلْفٍ كَجِلْدِ الأَجْرَبِ،

ثم قالت (٦)رحمة الله على لبيد كيف لو أدرك زمانَنا هذا، وقد انشد

Af.123b الشِّعْرَ جماعة اصحاب رسول الله صلع (٧)وذِكْرِه (٨)يطول، انشدنى ابو عبد

الله الحسين بن خالوَيه النَّحْوى قال انشدنى (٩)ابن الأَنبارى بإنشاد رفعه

١٠ قال (١٠)انشد كعب بن زُهَير بين يدى رسول الله صلع (١١)هذه الابيات،

بانَتْ سُعادُ فَقَلْبِى اليَوْمَ مَتْبُولُ ٭ مُتَيَّمٌ إِثْرَها لَمْ (١٢)يُفْدَ مَكْبُولُ

وَما سُعادُ غَداةَ البَيْنِ إِذْ ظَعَنُوا ٭ إِلَّا (١٣)أَغَنُّ غَضِيضُ الطَّرْفِ مَكْحُولُ

(١٤)شُجَّتْ بِذِى شَبَمٍ مِنْ ماءٍ (١٥)مَحْنِيَةٍ ٭ (١٦)صافٍ بِأَبْطَحَ أَضْحَى وَهْوَ مَشْمُولُ

تَنْفِى الرِّياحُ القَذَى عَنْهُ وَأَفْرَطَهُ ٭ مِنْ صَوْبِ سارِيةٍ بِيضٌ (١٧)يَعالِيلُ

أَكْرِمْ بِها خُلَّةً لَوْ أَنَّها صَدَقَتْ ٭ مَوْعُودَها أَوْ لَوْ أَنَّ النُّصْحَ مَقْبُولُ

١٥

لَكِنَّها خُلَّةٌ قَدْ (١٨)سِيطَ مِنْ دَمِها ٭ فَجْعٌ وَوَلْعٌ وَإِعْراضٌ وَتَبْدِيلُ

كانَتْ مَواعِيدُ عُرْقُوبٍ لَها مَثَلًا ٭ وَما مَواعِيدُهُ إِلَّا الأَباطِيلُ

(١٩)أَرْجُو وَآمُلُ أَنْ (٢٠)يَعْجَلْنَ فى أَبَدٍ ٭ وَما لَهُنَّ (٢١)إِخالُ الدَّهْرَ تَعْجِيلُ

<hr>

(١) Both verses are cited in *Lisân* 13, 127 penult., and the second verse
ibid., 429, 16.   (٢) *Lisân* has بفجّ.   (٣) B ادحر وخليل.   (٤) This
hemistich is partly obliterated in B.   (٥) B سامت.   (٦) B رحم الله لبيدا.
(٧) B وذكرم.   (٨) A يطوّله.   (٩) B بن.   (١٠) B انشدنى.   (١١) B هذه وسمع.
(١٢) B نحن يُجْزَ.   (١٣) B أغر,   (١٤) This verse is the seventh in A.
(١٥) A محنيه with محنيه written above.   (١٦) A صافى B سجت.
corr. in marg. بابح.   (١٧) A تعاليل.   (١٨) A شط.   (١٩) In B this and the
following verse are transposed.   (٢٠) A يعجلنى فى امد.   (٢١) A طوال B طوال.

وَلَا نَمْسِكُ بِالوَصْلِ الَّذِى زَعَمَتْ * إِلَّا كَمَا يُمْسِكُ المَاءَ الغَرَابِيلُ

(١)فَلَا يَغُرَّنْكَ مَا مَنَّتْ وَمَا وَعَدَتْ * إِنَّ الأَمَانِى وَالأَحْلَامَ تَضْلِيلُ

أَمْسَتْ سُعَادُ بِأَرْضٍ لَنْ يُبَلِّغَهَا * إِلَّا العِنَاقُ النَّجِيبَاتُ المَرَاسِيلُ

وَأَنْ يُبَلِّغَهَا إِلَّا (٢)عُذَافِرَةٌ * فِيهَا (٣)عَلَى الأَيْنِ (٤)إِرْقَالٌ وَتَبْغِيلُ

ضَخْمٌ مُقَلَّدُهَا فَعْمٌ مُقَيَّدُهَا * فِى خَلْقِهَا عَنْ بَنَاتِ الفَحْلِ تَفْضِيلُ

حَرْفٌ أَخُوهَا أَبُوهَا مِنْ مُهَجَّنَةٍ * وَعَمُّهَا خَالُهَا قَوْدَاءَ شِمْلِيلُ،

وَقَدْ رُوِى عَنِ النَّبِىّ صلعم انه قال ان من الشعر (٥)حِكْمَةً وقد قيل ان الحِكْمَة ضالّة المؤمن، ولمّا صحّ جواز (٦)الإنشاد للشعر فسواءٌ (٧)كان انشاده باللغة الطيّبة والصوت الحسن او يكون انشاده (٨)بالحَدْو (٩)والحَدْرِ والنَّصْبِ (١٠)والرَّمَل والرَّجَزِ اذا لم يكن لذلك مَقَاصِدُ فاسدةٌ وإرادة باطلة ومجاوزة الحدّ ومخالفة ومعانَدة، (١١)والله اعلم، فصل آخر، (١٢)قال الشيخ رحمه الله وقد رخّص فى السماع (١٣)وإستجازه جماعةٌ من ايمة العلماء والفقهاء منهم مالك بن أَنَس (١٤)ذُكر عنه انه سمع رجلاً فى وقت الهاجرة مجتازًا بباب داره وهو يغنّى (١٥)ويقول،

مَا بَالُ قَوْمِكِ يَا رَبَابْ * (١٦)خُزْرًا كَأَنَّهُمُ غِضَابْ،

قال فقال له مالك لقد أَسَأْتَ (١٧)التأدية ومَنَعْتَ القايلَة قال فسأله (١٨)ذلك الرجل عن تأديته فقال له تريد ان تقول أَخَذْتُها من مالك بن انس، والمشهور عنه وعن اهل المدينة انهم كانوا لا يكرهون ذلك وفى تجويز ذلك أخبار عن عبد الله بن (١٩)جعفر (٢٠)رضى الله عنه وعن عبد الله بن

(١) B om. this and the next four verses.   (٢) A عُذَنفرة.   (٣) A من.

(٤) A والارقال تبغيل.   (٥) B الحكمة.   (٦) B الاتِّجاد.   (٧) B انشاد.   (٨) B بالحد.

(٩) B والحذر.   (١) B والوجل.   (١١) B om. والله اعلم.   (١٢) B om.

(١٣) B إستجارها.   (١٤) A om. from ذكر عنه to أخذتها but the passage has been suppl. in marg. Cf. Aghánì, IV 21 foll.   (١٥) A بهذا البيت.   (١٦) B حدرا A حدر فانهم.   (١٧) A البادية.

(١٨) A om.   (١٩) B adds بن أبى طالب.   (٢٠) B om.

عمر (١) الله عنه (٢) وعن غيرها من الصحابة والتابعين، وقد اجاز الشافعى
(٣) رحمه الله عليه ايضًا السماع والترنّم بالشعر ما لم يكن فيه إسقاط المروّة،
وقد ذكر عن (٤) ابن جُرَيج مع جلالته انه قال ما كان سبب قُدوّى من
اليمن ومقامى بمكّة الّا بيتيْن من الشعر سمعتهما يومًا وها،

٥ بِاللَّهِ قَوْلَى لَـهُ مِنْ غَيْرِ مُعْتَبِـقٍ ۞ ما ذا أَرَدْتَ بِطُولِ المَكْثِ بِاليَمَنِ
إنْ كُنْتَ أَلْمَمْتَ ذَنْبًا أَوْ هَمَمْتَ بِـهِ ۞ فَما وَجَدْتَ بِتَرْكِكَ الحَجَّ مِنْ ثَمَنِ،
وقد ذكر عن (٤) ابن جُرَيج ايضًا انه كان يرخص فى السماع فقيل له اذا
(٥) أُتِىَ بك يوم القيْمة (٦) وتُوُفِّىَ بحسناتك وسيّئاتك ففى اىّ الجِنْبَيْنِ (١) يكون
سماعك قال (٤) ابن جريج لا يكون فى الحسنات ولا فى السيّئات لانّه شبيهٌ
١٠ باللغو لا يدخل فى الحسنات ولا فى السيّئات قال الله تعالى (٧) لاَ يُؤاخِذُكُمُ
اللّهُ بِاللَّغْوِ فِى أَيْمَانِكُمْ، (٨) قال الشيخ رحمه الله فيْه فصول مختصرة فى
اباحة السماع للعامّة اذا لم يصحبهم فى ذلك مقاصدُ فاسدةٌ ودخولٌ فى نهى
رسول الله صلعم سماعَ الأوْتار (٩) والمزامير والمعازف والكُوبة والطبل لان ذلك
سماعُ اهل الباطل وهو المحظور المنهى عنه بالأخبار الصحاح المرويّة عن
١٥ رسول الله صلعم،

باب فى وصف سماع الخاصّة وتفاضلهم فى ذلك ،

سمعت ابا عمرو اسمعيل بن نُجَيْد قال سمعت ابا عثمن سعيد بن
Af.124b عثمن الرازى (١) الواعظ يقول السماع على ثلثة أوجُهٍ فوجهٌ منها للمريدين
والمبتديين يستدعون بذلك الاحوال الشريفة (١٠) ويُخْشَى عليهم فى ذلك
٢٠ الفتنة والمُراياة، والوجه الثانى (١١) للصدّيقين (١٢) يطلبون الزيادة فى احوالهم

---

(١) B om.   (٢) B من.   (٣) B رحمه الله.   (٤) B بن.   (٥) B أوتى.

(٦) A وتوفى B وبوتا.   (٧) Kor. 2, 225.   (٨) B om. قال الشيخ رحمه الله.

(٩) B والمعازف والمزامير.   (١٠) B ويحى.   (١١) B للصادفين.   (١٢) B يطلبون بذلك.

ويسمعون من ذلك ما يوافق احوالهم وأوقاتهم، والوجه الثالث لأهل
الاستقامة من العارفين فهم لا يعترضون ولا يتأبّون على الله فيما يَرِدُ على
قلوبهم فى حين السماع من الحركة والسكون او كما (١)قال، وحكى عن ابى
يعقوب اسحق بن محمّد (٢)بن ايّوب النهرجورى انه قال اهل السماع على
٥ ثلث طبقات فطبقة منهم (٣)مُطَّرَحٌ بحكم الوقت فى سكونه وحركته وطبقة منهم
(٤)صامت (٥)ساكن الصفة وطبقة منهم (٦)متخبّط عند ذوقه فهو الضعيف منهم،
وعن بُنْدار بن (٧)الحسين انه قال السماع على ثلثة اوجه فمنهم من يسمع بالطبع
ومنهم من يسمع بالحال ومنهم من يسمع بالحقّ، (٨)قال الشيخ رحمه الله فمن
يسمع بطبعه اشترك فيه الخاصّ والعامّ وكلّ ذى رُوح يستطيب الصوت
١٠ (٩)الطيّب لانّه من جنس الروح روحانىٌّ وقد تقدّم ذكر ذلك ومن يسمع بحاله
فانّه يتأمّل اذا سمع حتى يَرِدَ عليه معنًى من ذِكْرِ عتاب او خطاب او ذِكْر
وَصْل او هَجْر او قُرْب او بُعْد او تأسُّفٍ على فائت او نعطُّشٍ الى ما هو
آتٍ او ذِكْرِ طَمَعٍ او بأس او بسط او استئناس (١٠)او خوف الافتراق او
وفاء بالعهد او تصديق بالوعد او نقض للعهد او ذِكْر قلقٍ (١١)واشتياق او
١٥ فَرَح الاتصال او تَرَح الانفصال او التحسّر على ما لم ينل (١٢)او القنوط على
الذى أمِل او ذِكْر صفاء المحبّة او التمكّن من المودّة او ذِكْر اعتراض الصبوة
بعد تمكّنه من الحظوة او ذِكْر محافظة الرقيب عند ملاحظة الحبيب او
(١٤)تباريح الشجون (١٥)وفنون الفنون وإهمال الجُفون وسُكوب العَبَرات
وتردّد الزَّفَرات وتجدّد الحَسَرات فاذا طرق سَمْعَهُ من ذلك (١٦)حالٌ مِمّا
يوافق حاله فيكون (١٧)كالقادح يقدح فى سرّه على قدر صفاء وقتِهِ وقوّة

Af.125a

---

(١) B adds والله اعلم. (٢) B om. (٣) A نَطرح. مطَّرحة يعنى B.
(٤) صامتة B. (٥) B ساكنة. (٦) متخبطة عند ذوقها فهى الضعيفة B. (٧) B adds
الرجاى. (٨) B om. قال الشيخ رحمه الله. (٩) B om. (١٠) B om.
(١١) B adds او خوف الافتراق. (١٢) A والقنوط. او خوف الافتراق
العيون B. (١٥) A الفنون. وفنون B. وفتور B. (١٤) B تبارع.
(١٦) A حالا. (١٧) B ذلك كالقادح.

قادحهِ فتشتعل نارٌ [١] ترى بشَرَرها فيبِين ذلك على الجوارح ويظهر على ظاهر صفاته التغيير والحركة والاضطراب والتهيج فعلى قدر طاقته يضبط وعلى قدر قوّة وارِدهِ يعجز عن الضبط فسبحان من يتولّى سياستهم وحفظهم ولولا فضلُ الله [٢] عليهم ورحمته [٣] ورفْقه بِهم لطارت عُقولهم وتلفت نفوسهم وذهبت ارواحهم ، ومن [٤] يسمع بالحقّ ومن الحقّ فانّه لا [٥] يترسّم بِهذ الرسوم ولا يلتفت الى هذه الاحوال ولا يشهد هذه الافعال لانّها وإن كانت شريفةً فهى ممزوجة بحظوظ البشرية مرتبطة بحدود الانسانية وهى مُنَفّاة مع العِلَل ولا يُؤْمَنُ عليها الزِلَلَ حتى يكون سماعُهُ باسه ولله ومن الله والى الله وهُمُ الذين وصلوا الى الحقايق وعبروا الاحوال وفَنُوا عن الافعال والاقوال ووصلوا الى محض الإخلاص وصفاء التوحيـد فخمدت بشريتهم وفنيت حُظوظهم وبقيت حُقوقهم فشهدوا مَوارِدَ الحقّ بالحقّ بلا علّة ولا حظّ للبشرية ولا تنعُّم الروح بالنعمة فشهدوا من موارد السماع على أسرارهم إظهار حكمته وآثار قُدرته وعجايب [٦] لُطْفه وغرايب عِلْمه، [٧] ذلِكَ فضْلُ اللّهِ يُؤْتِيهِ مَنْ يَشَاءُ وَاللّهُ ذُو الْفَضْلِ الْعَظِيمِ، وقال [٨] بعضهم اهل السماع فى السماع على ثلثة ضروب فضربٌ [١٠] منهم ابناء الحقايق وهم الذين يرجعون [١١] فى [٩] سماعهم الى مخاطبة [١٢] الحقّ لهم فيا يسمعون وضربٌ منهم [١٣] يرجعون فيا يسمعون الى مخاطبات احوالهم واوقاتهم ومقاماتهم وهم مرتبطون بالعلم [١٣] ومطالَبون بالصدق فيا يشيرون اليه من ذلك والضرب الثالث هم الفقرآء [١٤] المجرّدون الذين قطعوا العلايق ولم تتلوّث قلوبهم بمحبّة الدنيا والاشتغال بالجمع والمنع فهم يسمعون بطيبة قلوبهم ويليق بِهم السماع وهم أقربُ الناس الى السلامة وأسلمُهم من الفتنه والله اعلم،

---

[١] ترفى B برسم. [٥] B لا يترسّم. [٣] وراقته B. [٤] يستمع B. [٥] B om.

[١١] فيا B. [١٠] منها B. [٩] ثلث B. [٨] بعض B. [٧] Kor. 57, 21. [٦] لفظه A.

[١٤] المجردين A. [١٣] ومطالبين A. [١٢] يرجعون الحقّ B.

باب فى ذكر طبقات المستمعين،

(١)قال الشيخ رحمه الله اختلف المستمعون فى السماع على طبقات فطبقة
منهم اختاروا (٢)سماع القُرآن ولم يَرَوْا غير ذلك واحتجّوا بقوله تعالى (٤)وَرَتِّلِ
الْقُرْآنَ تَرْتِيلاً (٤) وقوله (٥)أَلاَ بِذِكْرِ اللهِ تَطْمَئِنُّ الْقُلُوبُ وقوله (٦)مَثَانِيَ تَقْشَعِرُّ
مِنْهُ جُلُودُ الَّذِينَ يَخْشَوْنَ رَبَّهُمْ ثُمَّ تَلِينُ جُلُودُهُمْ وَقُلُوبُهُمْ إِلَى ذِكْرِ اللهِ وقوله
(٧)الَّذِينَ إِذَا ذُكِرَ اللهُ وَجِلَتْ قُلُوبُهُمْ (٨) وقوله (٩)لَوْ أَنْزَلْنَا هَذَا الْقُرْآنَ عَلَى
جَبَلٍ (١٠)الآية وقوله (١١)وَنُنَزِّلُ مِنَ الْقُرْآنِ مَا هُوَ (١٢)شِفَاءٌ وقوله (١٣)الَّذِينَ
يَسْتَمِعُونَ الْقَوْلَ فَيَتَّبِعُونَ أَحْسَنَهُ، (١٤) والآيات فى ذلك (١٥)تَكثُر، واحتجّوا
بقول النبىّ صلعم زيّنوا القرآن بأصواتكم وقول النبىّ صلعم لابن مسعود
(١٦)رضى الله عنه اقرأ فقال انا اقرأ وعليك أُنْزِلَ قال انا أُحِبُّ ان اسمع
من غيرى، وقول البَرَاء (١٧)سمعت رسول الله صلعم يقرأ بالتين والزَّيتون
فما رأيت احسن من قراءَته، وقوله عليه السلم شيّبَنِى هُودٌ وأخَواتِها، وقوله
لأبى موسى (١٨)لقد أُوتى مزمارًا من مزامير آل (١٩)داود، (٢٠) وقوله حين
سئل مَنْ احسنُ قراءَةً قال من اذا قرأ رأيت انه يخشى الله (١٦)تعالى،
وأن النبىّ صلعم مرّ على عصابة من اهل الصُّفَّة يستر بعضهم بعضًا من
العُرْى (٢١)وقارىءُ يقرأ لهم، وأن النبىّ (٢٢)صلعم قرأ (٢٢)فَكَيْفَ إِذَا جِئْنَا مِنْ

---

(١) B om. قال الشيخ رحمه الله.   (٢) B لسماع.   (٣) Kor. 73, 4.   (٤) B وقوله تعالى.
(٥) Kor. 13, 28.   (٦) Kor. 39, 24.   (٧) Kor. 22, 36.   (٨) A وقال.
(٩) Kor. 59, 21.   (١٠) B لرأيته خاشعا متصدعا من خشية الله.   (١١) Kor. 17, 84.
(١٢) B adds ورحمة للمومنين.   (١٣) Kor. 39, 19.   (١٤) B والاى.   (١٥) B كثير.
(١٦) B om.   (١٧) Kor. 95, 1. B التين.   (١٨) B om. لقد اوتى.   (١٩) B داوود.
(٢٠) B وقوله عليه السلام.   (٢١) B وقار.   (٢٢) Here A proceeds: مر على
عصابة من اهل الصفة يستر بعضهم بعضا وانه عليه السلم وان النبى صلعم قرأ فكيف الخ.
(٢٣) Kor. 4, 45.

كُلِّ أُمّةٍ بِشَهِيدٍ فَصَعِقَ، (١) وأنه قرأ (٢) إِنْ تُعَذِّبْهُمْ فَإِنَّهُمْ عِبَادُكَ فبكى ،
وأنه عليه السلّم كان اذا مرّ بآية (٣) رحمة دعا واستبشر واذا مرّ بآية عذاب
دعا واستعاذ، والأخبار فى (٤) ذلك (٥) كثيرة فمن اختار استماع القرآن فقد
روى عن النبىّ صلعم انه قال لا خير فى قراءة ليس فيها (٦) تدبّر، وقد ذكر ٥
الله تعالى المستمعين القرآن فى مواضع من كتابه على وجهَيْن فوجهٌ (٧) منها
قوله (٨) عزّ وجلّ (٩) وَمِنْهُمْ مَنْ يَسْتَمِعُ إِلَيْكَ حَتَّى إِذَا خَرَجُوا مِنْ عِنْدِكَ
(١٠) الى قوله عَلَى قُلُوبِهِمْ، فيؤلاء كانوا يستمعون القرآن بآذانهم ولم يحضروا
بقلوبهم فذمّهم الله (١١) عزّ وجلّ بذلك وطبع على قلوبهم (١٢) وهم الذين قال
الله (١٣) عزّ وجلّ (١٤) وَلَا تَكُونُوا كَالَّذِينَ قَالُوا سَمِعْنَا وَهُمْ لَا يَسْمَعُونَ، والوجه
الثانى هم الذين وصفهم الله (٨) عزّ وجلّ فقال (١٥) وَإِذَا سَمِعُوا مَا أُنْزِلَ إِلَى ١٠
الرَّسُولِ (١٦) الآية فهؤلاء (١٧) هم (١٨) الذين سمعوا القرآن لانهم حضروا بقلوبهم
عند استماعهم القرآن فمدحهم (١٩) الله (١١) تعالى بذلك ومثل ذلك فى القرآن
كثير، ولو ذكرتُ ما يدخل فى هذا الباب ممّن سمع القرآن فصعق وبكى
ومن مات ومن انفصل بعض اعضابه ومن غُشى عليه من الصحابة والتابعين
وبعد التابعين الى وقتنا هذا لطال به الكتاب وخرج عن حدّ الاختصار ١٥
إن لو ذكرنا مثل زُرارة بن أُوْفَى من الصحابة قرأ بالناس فقرأ آيةً من
كتاب الله (١١) تعالى فصعق ومات، (٢٠) ومثل (٢١) ابى جهير من التابعين قرأ
عليه صالح المرّى فشهق ومات، (٢٢) وقد حكى عن الشبلى (١١) رحمه الله أنه
(٢٣) سأله (٢٤) ابو علىّ المغازلى (١١) رحمه الله (٢٥) فقال ربّما تطرق سمعى آيةً من

---

(١) B adds من ايات الرحمة.   (٢) Kor. 5, 118.   (٣) B adds صلى الله عليه.

(٤) مثل ذلك B.   (٥) كثير B.   (٦) تدبير A.   (٧) منه B.   (٨) تعالى B.

(٩) Kor. 47, 18.   (١٠) Instead of الى قوله B has ما ذا.   قالوا الذين اوتوا العلم

(١١) B om. تعالى.   (١٢) B om. هم.   (١٣) قال انفا اوليك الذين طبع الله

(١٤) Kor. 8, 21.   (١٥) Kor. 5, 86.   (١٦) عرفوا B ما الدمع من فيض اعينهم ترى.

(١٧) A om.   (١٨) B adds اذا.   (١٩) Illegible in B.   (٢٠) B om. من الحق

(٢١) The name is doubtful. See *JRAS.* for 1901,   ومثل to ومات from.

كتاب الله [١] تعالى فتُحذّرنى على ترك الاشياء والاعراض عن الدنيا ثم
ارجعُ الى احوالى والى الناس ثمّ لا أبقَى على هذا [٢] وأُدفَعُ الى [٣] الوطن
الأولَى [٤] فقال ما طرق [٥] مَسامعَك من القرآن فاجْتَذَبَك [١] به اليه فذاك
عطفٌ منه عليك ولطفٌ منه بك وما رُدِدتَ الى نفسك فهو شفقةً منه عليك
لانّه لم يصحّ لك التبرّئ من الحول والقوّة فى التوجّه اليه، وقد حُكى عن
احمد بن ابى الحوارى عن ابى سليمن الدارانى [١] رحمهما الله انه قال ربّما
ابقى فى الآية خمس ليالٍ ولولا أنى اترك الفكر فيها ما جُزْتُها ابدًا وربّما
جاءَت الآية من القرآن فيطير فيها العقل فسبحان الذى يرُدّه بعد ذلك،
وقد حُكى عن الجُنَيْد [١] رحمه الله انه قال دخلتُ على سَرِى السَّقَطى [١] رحمه
الله انه فرأيتُ بين يديه رجلاً قد غُشى عليه فقال [١] لى هذا رجل سمع آيةً
من كتاب الله [١] عزّ وجلّ فغُشى عليه [٦] فقلت اقْرُؤ عليه [١] هذه الآية التى
قُرئَتْ عليه فقرأ فأفاق فقال لى من اين لك هذا فقلت رأيتُ يعقوب عليه
السَّلم كان عماه من اجْل مخلوق فبمخلوق أبْصَرَ ولوكان عماه من اجْل
الحقّ [٧] ما ابصر بمخلوق فاستحسن منّى ذلك، [٨] وحُكى عن بعض الصوفية
انه قال كنت اقرأ ليلة هذه الآية [٩] كُلُّ نَفْسٍ ذائقَةُ الْمَوْتِ فجعلتُ أردّدُها
وإذا انا بهاتف يهتف الَيّ كم تُردّد هذه الآية [١٠] وقد قتلتَ اربعةً من الجنّ
لم يرفعوا رُؤوسهم الى السماء منذ خُلقوا، سمعت ابا الطيّب احمد بن مُقاتل
العكّى يقول كنت مع الشبلى [١] رحمه الله فى مسجد ليلةً [١١] فى شهر رمضان
وهو يصلّى خَلْفَ إمام له وأنا بجنبه فقرأ الامام هذه الآية [١٢] وَلَئِنْ شِئْنَا
لَنَذْهَبَنَّ بِالَّذِى أَوْحَيْنَا إِلَيْكَ الآية فزعق زعقة [١٣] فقلت [١] قد طارت روحه
[١٤] ورأيته قد اخضرَّ وهو برتعد وكان يقول بمثل هذا تُخاطب الأحباب

p. 735, note 1.   [٢٣] B وحكى.   [٢٤] A سأل.   [٢٥] A ابا.   [٢٦] B قال له.
[١] B om.   [٢] B وارجع.   [٣] A gives الوقت as a variant for الوطن.
[٤] A فطال.   [٥] B سمعك.   [٦] B فقال.   [٧] A om.   [٨] B وقد حكى.
[٩] Kor. 3, 182.   [١٠] B قد.   [١١] B من.   [١٢] Kor. 17, 88.
[١٣] B فقلت.   [١٤] B ورأيت وجهه.

(١) يردّد ذلك مرارًا، فمن اختار سماع القرآن اختاره لما ذكرنا من هذه الآيات (٢) والأخبار (٣) والمعوّل عند استماع القرآن حضور القلب (٤) والتدبّر والتفكّر والتذكّر وعلى ما يصادف (٤) قلْبَهُ (٥) عليه من قراءته (٦) فيكون الغالب على وقته فى وقت استماعه القرآن فاذا لم يكن له حالٌ ولم يكن فى قلبه وجدٌ يطرقه (٧) ما سَمِعَهُ من القرآن ويوافقه ويُزْعِجه فمثَله (٨) كمَثَلِ ٱلَّذِى يَنْعِقُ بِمَا لَا يَسْمَعُ (٩) ٱلآية،

باب (١٠) ذِكْرُ من اختار سماع القصايد والابيات من الشعر،

(١١) قال الشيخ رحمه الله فاما الطبقة التى اختارت السماع سماع القصايد وهذه الابيات من الشعر فحُجّتهم من الظاهر فى ذلك قول النبىّ صلعم ان الشعر (١٢) حِكْمَة وقوله الحِكْمَة ضالّة المؤمن، وزعمت هذه الطائفة ان القرآن كلام الله (١٣) وكلامه صفته وهو حقّ لا (١٤) يُطيقه البَشَر اذا بدا (١٥) لانّه غير مخلوق لا تطيقه الصفات المخلوقة ولا يجوز ان يكون بعضه احسن من بعض ولا يزيّن بالنغات المخلوقة بل به تزيّنُ الاشياء وهو احسنُ الاشياء ومع حُسنه لا تُستَحسَن المستحسنات، قال الله (١٦) تعالى (١٧) وَلَقَدْ يَسَّرْنَا ٱلْقُرْآنَ لِلذِّكْرِ (١٨) فَهَلْ مِنْ مُذَّكِّرٍ وقال (١٩) لَوْ أَنْزَلْنَا هَذَا ٱلْقُرْآنَ عَلَى جَبَلٍ (٢٠) ٱلآية، (٢١) فكذلك لو (٢٢) أنزاه (٢٣) الله تعالى على القلوب بحقايقه (٢٤) وكُشفت للقلوب

(١) B om. يردد ذلك. (٢) A adds والقرآن. (٣) والتدبير B. (٤) A om.
(٥) B om. (٦) ويكون B. (٧) B om. ما سمعه. (٨) Kor. 2, 166.
(٩) B om. (١٠) فى ذكر B. (١١) لا. دعا وندا صم بكم عمى فهم لا يعقلون B.
(١٢) حكمة B. (١٣) وكلام الله B. (١٤) تطيقه البشرية B. (١١) قال الشيخ رحمه الله.
(١٥) ولانه A. (١٦) جل ذكره B. (١٧) Kor. 54, 17. (١٨) B om.
(١٩) Kor. 59, 21. (٢٠) B لرايته خاشعًا متصدعًا من خشية الله. (٢٠) فهل من مذكر.
(٢١) فلذلك A. (٢٢) انزل A. (٢٣) B om. الله تعالى. (٢٤) وكشف القلوب B.

ذرّة من التعظيم والهيبة عند تلاوته لتصدّعت وذهلت [١] ودهشت وتحيّرت
ولمّا رأوا أولى فى المتعارف [٢] بين الخلق ان احدهم ربّما يختم القرآن ختمات
[٤] ولا يجد رقّةٌ فى قلبه عند التلاوة فاذا كان مع القراءة صوتٌ حسنٌ او
نغمة [٤] طيّبة شجيّة وجد الرقّة وتلذّذ بالاستماع ثمّ انه اذا كان ذلك الصوت
٥ الحسن والنغمة الطيّبة على شىء غير القرآن ايضا فوجد تلك الرقّة [٥] وذاك
التلذّذ [٦] والتنعّم علموا ان الذى هو ذا يظنّون من الرقّة والصفاء والتلذّذ
والوجود انه من القرآن لو كان كذلك [٧] لكان فى حين التلاوة ووقت
القراءة غير منقطع منهم على الدوام، والنغات الطيّبة موافقة للطبايع [٨] ونسبته
نسبة الحظوظ لا نسبة الحقوق والقرآن كلام الله ونسبته نسبة الحقوق لا
١٠ نسبة الحظوظ وهذه الابيات [٩] والقصايد [٤] نسبتها نسبة الحظوظ لا
نسبة الحقوق وهذا السماع وان كان اهله [١٠] متفاوتين فى درجاتهم وتخصيصهم
فان فيه موافقةً للطبع [١١] وحظًّا للنفس [١٢] وتنعّما للروح لتشاكُلِه بتلك
اللطيفة التى جُعلت فى الاصوات الحسنة والنغات الطيّبة وكذلك الاشعار
فيها [١٣] معانٍ دقيقة ورقّة [١٤] وفصاحة ولطافة واشارات فاذا [١٥] عُلّقت
١٥ هذه الاصوات والنغات على هذه القصايد والابيات بشاكل بعضها بعضًا
بموافقتها ومجانستها ويكون اقرب الى الحظوظ واخفّ محملاً على السراير
والقلوب واقلّ خطرًا [١٦] لتشاكُل المخلوق بالمخلوق، فمن اختار استماع القصايد
على استماع القرآن اختار لحُرمة القرآن وتعظيم ما فيه من الخطر لانّه حقٌّ
[١٧] والنفوس تخنس عندها وتموت عن حركاتها وتفنى عن حظوظها وتنعّمها
A.f.127b اذا [١٨] اشرقت عليها انوار [١٩] الحقوق [٢٠] بتشعشعها وأبدت بها عن معانيها،

---

(١) A وذهبت،   (٢) A من.   (٣) B لا.   (٤) B om.   (٥) B وذلك.
(٦) AB والتنعم   (٧) B كان كذلك.   (٨) The passage beginning
ونسبته
and ending فان فيه موافقة للطبع is suppl. in marg. A.   (٩) A والقصايد.
(١٣) A معانى AB.   (١١) B متفاوتون.   (١١) A وحظ.   (١٢) A وتنعم.   (١٠) والاشعار
B النفس.   (١٧) B لتشابك.   (١٦) B لتشابك.   (١٥) A غلبت.   (١٤) B فصاحة.
(١٨) A اشرفت.   (١٩) B الحقيقة.   (٢٠) B وتشعشعها.

فقالوا ما دامت البشرية باقيةً ونحن بصفاتنا وحظوظنا وأرواحنا متنعمّة
بالنغمات الشهيّة والاصوات الطيّبة فانبساطنا بمشاهدة بقاء هذه الحظوظ الى
القصايد أوْلَى من انبساطنا بذلك الى كلام الله [1] عزّ وجلّ الذى هو صفته
وكلامه الذى منه بدا واليه يعود، وقد كره جماعةٌ من العلمآء القرآءة
بالتطريب ووضْع الألحان الموضوعة على القرآن غيرُ جايز عندهم قال الله
تعالى [2] رَتِّلِ الْقُرْآنَ تَرْتِيلاً وإنّما فعل من فعل ذلك لانّ الطبايع البشرية
متنافرةٌ [3] عن سماع القرآن وتلاوته لانّه حقٌّ [4] فعلّقوا على تلاوتهم هذه
الاصوات المصوغة ليجتذبوا بذلك [5] طبايع العامّة الى الاستماع ولو كانت
القلوب حاضرةً والاوقات معمورة والاسرار طاهرة والنفوس مؤدّبةً وطبايع
البشرية [6] مختنسةٌ لما احتيج الى ذلك وبالله التوفيق،

باب فى وصف سماع المريدين والمبتدئين،

[7] قال الشيخ رحمه الله سمعت ابا عمرو عبد الواحد بن علوان بالرَّحْبة
[8] رَحْبة مالك بن طَوْق قال كان شابٌ يصحب الجُنَيْد [9] رحمه الله فكان
اذا سمع شيئًا من الذكر يزعق فقال له الجنيد يومًا ان فعلتَ ذلك مرّةً
أخرى لم تصحبنى قال فربّما كان يتكلّم الجنيد [9] رحمه الله فى شيء من
العلم فينغيّر ويضبط عند ذلك نفسه حتى يفطر عن كلّ شعرة من بدنه
قطرةٌ من المآء، وحكى [9] لى [10] ابو عمرو انه صاح يومًا من الايّام صيحةً
فانشقّ وتلفت نفسه، ورأيتُ ابا الحسين السيروانى صاحب الخوّاص [9] بدمياط
وكان يحكى عن الجنيد [9] رحمه الله انه قال رأيت رجلاً [11] قد سمع السماع
حتى تفسّخ ورأيت رجلاً سمع الذكر حتى مات او كما قال، وسمعت الدّقّى

---

[1] B تعلى.   [2] Kor. 73, 4.   [3] B عند.   [4] A فعللوا.   [5] B الطبايع.

[6] B محسبه.   [7] B om. قال الشيخ رحمه الله.   [8] A om. رحبة مالك بن.

[9] B om.   [10] B غيرابى.   [11] B om. from قد to رجلاً.   طوق.

Af.128a يقول (١)سمعت الدرّاج يقول كنت أنا (٢)وإبن النوطى مارّين على الدجلة
بين البصرة والأُبلّة وإذا بقصر حسن له مَنْظَر وعليه رجل بين يديه جارية
تغنّى وتقول،

(٣)كُلَّ يَوْمٍ نَتَلَوَّنْ غَيْرُ هَـذا بِكَ أَجْمَلْ

فى سَبِيلِ اللهِ (٤)وُدٌّ كانَ (٥)مِنّى لك (٦)يُبْذَلْ،

قال وإذا شابّ تحت المنظر بيه ركوة وعليه مرقّعة (٧)يتسمّع فقال (٨)يـا
جارية بالله وبحياة مولاك إلّا أَعَدْتِ علىّ هذا البيت (٩)قال فأقبلت الجارية
عليه وهى تقول هذا البيت،

كُلَّ يَوْمٍ نَتَلَوَّنْ غَيْرُ هذا بِكَ أَجْمَلْ،

وكان الشابّ يقول هذا وإله تناوّلى مع (١٠)الحقّ فى حالى، (١١)قال (١٢)فشهق
شهقةً وحمّد فتأمّلناه فاذا هو ميّت قال (١٣)فقلنا قد استقبلنا فرضٌ فوقفنا
فقال صاحب القصر للجارية انتِ حُرّة لوجه الله (١١)تعالى قال ثمّ خرج
اهل البصرة وصلّوا عليه فلمّا فرغوا من دفنه قام صاحب القصر وقال
اليس تعرفونى انا فلان بن فلان أُشْهِدكم ان كلّ شىء لى فى سبيل الله
(١١)تعالى وكلّ جوارى أحرارٌ وهذا القصر للسبيل، قال ثمّ رمى بثيابه وأتّزر
بإزار وإرتدى (١٤)بالآخر ومرّ على وجهه والناس ينظرون إليه حتى غـاب
عن أَعْيُنهم وهم يبكون فما رآه بعد ذلك ولا سُمع له خَبَرٌ وما رأيت
يوماً احسن من ذلك اليوم او كلامًا هذا (١٥)معناه وإله اعلم، (١١)قال
وسمعت الوجيهى يقول سمعت (١١)ابا علىّ الروذبارى يقول دخلت مِصْر
٢٠ فرأيت الناس (١٦)مجتمعين او منصرفين من الصحراء فسألتهم فقالوا كنّا فى
جنازة فتى سمع قائلاً يقول،

---

(١) B om. سمعت الدرّاج يقول.   (٢) B وإبن الغوطى.   (٣) In B these verses
are transposed.   (٤) B ودا.   (٥) A gives لى منك as a variant. A مثلى
in marg.   (٦) A تبدل.   (٧) B يسمع.   (٨) B- بالله يا جارية.
(٩) B فقالت كل يوم تتلون الخ.   (١٠) A الحال.   (١١) B om.   (١٢) B وشهق.
(١٣) B فقمنا فوقفنا الخ.   (١٤) B باخر.   (١٥) B adds او نحوه.   (١٦) B مجتمعون.

كَبُرَتْ هِمّةُ عَبْدٍ طَمَعَتْ فى أَنْ نُرَاكا،

(١) وزعق زعقةً ومات، ومِمّا حكى الدُّقّى قال سمعت ابا عبد الله بن الجَلّاء
يقول رأيت بالمغرب شيئَيْن عجيبين رأيت فى جامع قَيَرَوان رجلاً يتخطّى
الصُّفوف ويسأل الناس ويقول ايّها الناس تصدّقوا عَلَىّ فانّى كنت رجلاً
٥ صوفيًّا فضعفتُ، والآخَر أنّى رأيت شيخَين (٢) اسم احدها جَبَلة (٣) والآخر
زُرَيْق ولكلّ واحد منهما تلامذة ومريدون فزار يوماً من الايّام جبلة (٤) زريقٌ
مع اصحابه فقرأ رجل من اصحاب زريق شيئًا من القرآن فصاح من اصحاب
جبلة رجل صيحةً فات فلمّا كان غداة يوميذٍ قال جبلة لزريق اين صاحبك
الذى قرأ بالامس فدعاه وقال له اقرأ فقرأ شيئًا فصاح جبلة صيحة فات
١٠ القارئ فى مكانه فقال واحدٌ بواحدٍ والبادى (٥) أظْلَمُ او كلامًا هذا معناه،
(٦) وحكى محمّد بن يعقوب (٧) عن جعفر (٨) المبرقع وكان من الأجلّة انه حضر
فى موضع فيه سماع فقام وتواجد وقال فى قيامه (٩) ختم بنا (١٠) المريدين،
قال (١١) الشيخ رحمه الله ولا يصحّ السماع للمريد حتى يعرف اسماء الله تعالى
وصفاته حتى يضيف الى الله ما هو أولى به ولا يكون قلبه ملوّثًا بحُبّ الدنيا
١٥ وحبّ الثناء والمحمدة ولا يكون فى قلبه طمَع فى الناس ولا (١٢) نشوّفٌ الى
المخلوقين مراعيًا لقلبه حافظًا لحدوده متعاهدًا لوقته فاذا كان كذلك يسمع
ما يكون داخلاً فى صفة (١٣) التابيين والقاصدين والطالبين والمنيبين (١٤) والخاشعين
والخائفين ويسمع ما يحثّه على المعاملة والمجاهدة ولا يسمع على الجُمْلة ولا يتكلّف
ولا يسمع للاستطابة والتلذّذ لكيلا يصير عادتَهُ فيشغله عن عبادته ورعايـة

---

(١) B om. وزعق زعقة ومات.   (٢) B أحدها اسمه.   (٣) B واسم الآخر.
(٤) B لزريق.   (٥) A و، B om.   (٦) The passage beginning وحكى and
ending المريدين is suppl. in marg. A but several words have been cut off
in binding.   (٧) A بن.   (٨) B app. المترفع.   (٩) A ختم. The following
word is almost entirely obliterated in A, and is written in B without diacritical points.   (١٠) A المريدون.   (١١) B om. الشيخ رحمه الله.   (١٢) A نشرف
and so app. B.   (١٣) A التامين.   (١٤) B والخائفين والخاشعين.

قلبه، فان لم يكن كذلك يجب عليه ترْكُ ذلك والاجتناب والتباعد عن
(١)المواضع التى يحضر (٢)فيها ذلك ولا يحضر السماع الاّ فى مواضع يجرى
ذِكْر ما يحثّه على المعاملة ويجدّد عليه ذِكْرَ الله (٣)تعالى والثناء على الله وما
فيه رضا (٤)الله وان كان مبتديًا لا يعلم شرايط السماع فينصِد من يعلم
ذلك من المشايخ حتى يتعلّم منه ذلك حتى لا يكون سماعه لهوًا ولعبًا ولا
يضيف الى الله (٤)تعالى ما هو منزّه عنه فيكفر ولا يدرى ولا تدعوه نفسه
وهواه الى اتّباع الحظوظ ويخيّل اليه (٤)الهوى والشيطان انه من الحقوق
فيهلك عند ذلك والله (٥)ولىُّ التوفيق،

باب فى وصف المشايخ فى السماع وهم (٦)المتوسّطون العارفون،

(٧)قال الشيخ رحمه الله سمعت الوجيهى يقول سمعت (٨)الطيالسى الرازى
يقول دخلت على إسرافيل استاد (٩)ذى النون (٤)رحمهما الله وهو جالس   ٨A.f.129a
ينكت بإصبعه على الارض ويترنّم مع نفسه بشىء، فلمّا رآنى قال احسن
(١٠)تقول شيئًا قلت لا قال انت بلا قلب، سمعت ابا الحسن علىّ بن محمّد
الصيرفى قال سمعت رُوَيْمًا وقد سيل عن المشايخ الذين لقيهم كيف كان
يجدهم فى وقت السماع فقال مثل قطيع الغنم اذا وقع فى وسطه (١١)الذياب،
(٤)قال وسمعت قيس بن عمر الحِمّصى يقول ورد علينا ابو القسم بن (١٢)مروان
(٤)النهاوندى وكان قد صحب ابا سعيد الخرّاز (٤)رحمه الله وكان قد ترك
الحضور عند السماع سنين كثيرة فحضر معنا فى دعوة فيها انسان يقول ابياتًا
فيها هذا البيت،

---

(١) اللهو B .الموضع الذى B (٢) B فيه.   (٣) B om.   (٤) A الهوا B .الموضع الذى
(٥) B الموفى للصواب .قال الشيخ رحمه الله   (٦) B المنطوسون   (٧) B om.
(٨) A الملاس B .الطلاسى Cf. Ansáb, 375, 17.   (٩) A ذا.   (١٠) B ان تقول
(١١) B الذباب.   (١٢) B مردان and so A as a variant.

واقِفٌ فى المَاءِ عَطْشانَ وَلٰكِنْ لَيْسَ يُسْقٰى،

(١)قال فكان اصحابنا يقومون ويتواجدون فلمَّا سكنوا سأل كلُّ واحد منهم
عن معنى ما وقع له فى هذا البيت فكان اكثرُهم (٢)يقولون على معنى التعطُّش
الى الاحوال وأن يكون العبد ممنوعًا عن الحال (٣)الذى يتعطَّش (٤)اليه
فكان لا يُقنعه منهم ذلك فسألناه (٥)وقلنا هاتِ ما عندك فقال فيكون فى
وسط الاحوال ويُكرَم بجميع الكرامات ولا (٦)يعطيهم الله منه ذرَّةً او كا
قال كلامًا هذا معناه والله اعلم، وسمعت يحيى بن الرضا العلوىَ ببغداد
يقول وكتب لى هذه الحكاية بخطِّه قال سمع ابو حُلْمان الصوفى رجلاً يطوف
وينادى (٧)يا سَعْتَرًا بَرّى فسقط وغُشِى عليه فلمَّا افاق (٨)سُئِل عن ذلك
(٩)وقال سمعته يقول (١٠)اسْعَ تَرَى بَرّى، (١١)قال الشيخ رحمه الله (١٢)فكذلك
(١٣)قال المشايخ الذين هم العلَماء بهذا (١٤)الشأن وأهل الفهم بهذه القصَّة ان
السماع على حسب ما (١٥)يقرُّ فى القلوب من حيث شُغْله ووقته وحضوره
ألا ترى ان صوت الصايت حيث (١٦)أدّىَ الى ابى حلمان سمعَه من حيث
وقته وشغْله، (١٧)وما يُسندلُّ بذلك على ما (١٨)قلناه والله اعلم حكايةٌ حُكِيت
عن عُتْبة الغلام (١)رحمه الله انه سمع رجلاً يقول،

سُبْحانَ جبَّارِ السَّما ۞ إِنَّ المُحِبَّ لَفى عَنا،

A.f.129b فقال عتبة (١)رحمه الله صدقتَ (١٩)وسمعه رجل آخر فقال كذبتَ فقال
بعض من هو عارفٌ بهذا الشأن كلاها اصابا امّا عتبة (١)رحمه الله صدَّقه
لوجود تعبه فى محبَّته وإمّا الآخر فكذَّبه لوجود راحته وأُنسه فى محبَّته، وعن
احمد بن مُقاتل ان ذا النون المصرى (١)رحمه الله دخل بغداد فاجتمع اليه قوم

(١) B om.‬   (٢) B يقول.‬   (٣) B انى.‬   (٤) B اليها.‬   (٥) B وقلنا له.
(٦) A يعطيه اله as variant.   (٧) يا سعتر in Iḥyā, II, 250 penult. A in marg.
اسع.   (٨) B وسبل.   (٩) B فقال.   (١٠) B and A in marg. من يشترى زعترًا برى.
(١١) B om. قال الشيخ رحمه اله.   (١٢) A فلذلك.   (١٣) B وكذلك.   (١٤) B قالوا.
(١٥) A يضرم فى القلوب with عدم فيه as a variant for يضرم القلوب.   (١٥) B اللسان.   (١٤) B بقر
يضرم.   (١٦) من القلوب.   (١٧) B وما.   (١٨) B فلنا.(١٩) B وسمع.

من الصوفية ومعهم قوّال فاستأذنوه فى ان يقول شيئًا فأذن له فى ذلك فأنشأ يقول،

صَغيرٌ هَواكَ عَذَّبَنى * فَكَيفَ بِهِ إذا (١)احْتَنَكا

وَأَنتَ جَمَعْتَ (٢) فى قَلْبى * هَوًى قَدْ كانَ مُشْتَرَكا

أَما تَرْثِى لِبُكْتِيبٍ * إذا ضَحِكَ الخَلِيُّ (٤)بَكَى،

٥ قال فقام (٤)ذو النون (٥)رحمه الله ثمّ سقط على وجهه ثمّ قام رجل آخر فقال ذو النون (٥)رحمه الله (٦)الَّذى يَراكَ حِينَ تَقُومُ قال فجلس ذلك الرجل، (٧)قال الشيخ رحمه الله والمعنى فى قوله الَّذى يَراكَ حِينَ تَقُومُ اشار الى قيامه ومزاحمته لغيره بالتكلّف فعرّفه بانّ الخصم فى دعواك بقيامك ليس (٨)غير الله (٩)ولو كان الرجل صادقًا فى قيامه لم فى مجلس، وذلك ان المشايخ

١٠ منهم مُشْرِفون على احوال من هو دونهم بفضل معرفتهم ولا يجوز لهم ان يسامحوهم اذا (١٠)جاوزوا حدودهم وادّعوا حال غيرهم، وعن ابى الحسين النورى (٥)رحمه الله انه حضر مجلسًا فيه سماع فسمع هذا البيت،

ما زِلْتُ أَنْزِلُ مِنْ وِدادِكَ مَنْزِلاً * (١١)تَتَحَيَّرُ الأَلْبابُ عِنْدَ نُزُولِهِ،

قال فقام وتواجد وهام على وجهه فوقع فى أجَمَة قَصَبٍ قَدْ (١٢)كُسِحت

١٥ وبقى (١٣)أُصولُها مثل السيوف فأقبل يمشى (١٤)عليها ويعيد البيت الى الغداة والدم يخرج من رجليه ثمّ (١٥)ورمت قدماه وساقاه وعاش بعد ذلك ايّامًا قلايل (١٦)ومات، وحُكى عن ابى سعيد الخَرَّاز (٥)رحمه الله انه قال رأيت

Ａ f.130a   علىّ بن الموفّق وكان من اجلّة المشايخ وقد حضر (٥)فى وقت السماع وقد سمع شيئًا فقال اقيونى فاقاموه وتواجد ثمّ قال فى تواجده انا الشيخ (١٧)الزَّقّان،

٢٠ قال (١٨)ابو نصر رحمه الله والمعنى فى ذلك (١٩)والله اعلم انـه يريد ان يغطّى بذلك حاله على جلسآيه وقرنآيه يقول انا الشيخ (٢٠)الزقّان ومن حُسْنِ

ادبه (١)انه يتكلّم حتى يجتنب بذلك عن التساكن والذهاب لانّه من احوال
المريدين والمبتديّين، حكى لى بعض اخوانى عن ابى الحسين الدرّاج انه
قال قصدت يوسف بن (٢)الحسين من بغداد للزيارة والسلام عليه قال فلمّا
دخلت الرّىّ سألت عن منزله فكلّ من (٣)اسألُ عنه يقول أَيْشَ تعملُ بذلك
الزنديق فضِبقُوا صدرى حتى عزمت على الانصراف فبتُ تلك الليلة فى
بعض المساجد فلمّا اصبحت قلت فى نفسى قد جئتُ (٤)هذا الطريق كلّه لا
أقَلُّ من ان أراه فلم ازل (٥)اسأل عنه حتى دفعت الى مسجِدِه فدخلت
عليه وهو قاعد فى المحراب وبين يديه (٦)رجل وفى حِجْرِه مصحف (٧)وهو
يقرأ وإذا شيخ بهىّ حسن الوجه واللحية فدنوت (٨)اليه وسلّمت عليه (٩)فردّ
علىّ السلم وقعدت بين يديه فأقبل علىّ وقال (١)لى من اين انت قلت من
بغداد فقال وما الذى جاءَ بك فقلت قصدت الشيخ للسلام عليه فقال لى
لو أن فى بعض هذه البلدان قال لك انسان نقيم عندنا حتى اشترى لك
دارًا وجاريةً او كما كان يُقعدك عن هذا المجىءَ قال فقلت ما امْحنى
اله بشىءٍ من ذلك ولو امتحنى ما كنت ادرى كيف اكون ثمّ قال تُحسن
ان تقول شيئًا (١٠)فقلت نعم (١١)قال لى هاتِ فابتدأت اقول،
(١٢)رَأَيْتُكَ تَبْنِى دايِبًا فى قَطِيعَتى * وَلَوْ كُنْتَ ذا (١٣)حَزْم لَهَدَّمْتَ ما تَبْنِى
كَأَنى بِكُم واللَّيْثُ أفضَلُ قَوْلِكُمْ * ألا لَيْتَنا كُنّا إذِ اللَّيْثُ (١٤)لا (١٥)نُغْنِى،
قال فأطبق المصحف ولم يزل يبكى حتى ابتل لحيته وثوبه حتى رحِمْتُه مِمّا
بكى ثم قال (١)لى يا بنّى تلوم اهل الرّىّ يقولون يوسف زنديق من صلاة
الغداة هو (١٧)ذا اقرأُ فى المصحف لم تقطر من عينى قطرة وقد قامت علىّ

(١) B om.   (٢) B adds الرازى.   (٣) B سالته.   (٤) هذه B.   (٥) اسل B.
(٦) A om. رجل وفى حِجْرِه.   (٧) A om.   (٨) منه B.   (٩) B om. فردّ.
(١٠) قلت B.   (١١) فقال B.   (١٢) Aghâni, VI, 111, 1. Other
references in J.R.A.S. for 1901, p. 746, note 3.   (١٣) جرم A.   (١٤) ما B.
(١٥) يغنى B.   (١٦) من كثرة ما B.   (١٧) ذى B.   على السلم.

القيامة بهذين البيتين، قال وكان الشِّبْلى (١) رحمه الله (٢) يتواجد كثيرًا اذا A.f.130b
سمع هذا البيت،

ودادُكُمُ هَجْرٌ وَحُبُّكُمُ قِلًى * وَوَصْلُكُمُ صَرْمٌ وَسِلْمُكُمُ حَرْبُ،

وقام الدُّقّى ليلةً الى شطر الليل وهو يتخبّط ويسقط على رأسه ويقوم والخلق
يبكون (٤) والقوّالون يقولون هذا البيت،

بِاللهِ فَأَرْدُدْ فُؤَادَ مُكْتَئِبٍ * لَيْسَ لَهُ مِنْ حَبِيبِهِ خَلَفُ،

وأشباه (٤) ذلك كثير ولا يخفى على العاقل اذا تأمّل فى مقاصدهم واختلاف
شربِهم وأماكنهم فى السماع اذا تأمّل فى هذا القليل الذى ذكرت ويقفُ على
مُرادى من ذلك ان شاء الله (٥) وباله التوفيق،

١٠ باب فى وصف خصوص الخصوص واهل الكمال فى السماع،

(٦) قال الشيخ رحمه الله سمعت ابا الحسن محمّد بن احمد بالبصرة قال
سمعت ابى يقول خدمتُ سهل بن عبد الله ستّين سنةً فما رأيته تغيّر عند
شىء كان (٧) يسمعه من الذِّكر والقرآن او غير ذلك فلمّا كان فى آخر عمره
قرأ رجل بين يديه هذه الآية (٨) فَأَلْيَوْمَ لَا يُؤْخَذُ مِنْكُمْ فِدْيَةٌ الآية فرأيته
قد ارتعد وكاد ان يسقط (٩) فلمّا رجع الى (١٠) حال صحوه سألته عن ذلك
(١١) فقال نَعَمْ يا حبيبى قد ضعفْنا، وحكى (١٢) ابن سالم ايضًا (١٣) عن ابيه
انه قال (١٤) رأيت سهلاً مرّةً اخرى وكنت (١٥) أصطلى بين يديه (١٦) بالنار
فقرأ رجل من تلامذته سورة النُّرقان قال فلمّا بلغ الى قوله تعالى (١٧) الْمُلْكُ

---

(١) والقوّال B. (٢) والقوّالين A. (٣) كثيرا ما يتواجد B. (٤) هذا B.
(٥) وباله التوفيق B om. (٦) قال الشيخ رحمه الله B om. (٧) سمعه B.
(٨) Kor. 57, 14. (٩) The passage beginning فلمّا and
ending وكاد ان يسقط (p. ٢٩٣, 1. 1) is suppl. in marg. A. (١٠) A om.
(١١) فقال لى A. (١٢) عن بن سالم B. (١٣) عن ابيه B om. (١٤) A om.
(١٥) أصلى A. (١٦) بالنهار A. (١٧) Kor. 25, 28. (١٥) رأيت سهلا.

يَوْمَئِذٍ الْحُقُّ لِلرَّحْمٰنِ اضطرب وكاد ان يسقط قال فسألته (١)عن ذلك
لانّه لم يكن عهدى به ذلك فقال قد ضعفتُ، وسمعت (٢)ابن سالم يقول
قلتُ لسهل بن عبد الله (٣)رحمه الله كلامًا (٤)هذا معناه واللهُ اعلم ان
الذى ذكرتَ انه ضعفتُ حالك (٥)تعنى تغيُّرك واضطرابك فا الذى يوجب
٥ قوّة الحال فقال لا يَرِدُ عليه واردٌ الّا وهو يبتلعه بقوّة حاله فن اجْل ذلك
لا تغيّره الواردات وإن كانت قويّةً، قال (٦)الشيخ رحمه الله (٧)وكذلك
اصلٌ فى العلم وهو قول ابى بكر الصدّيق رضى الله عنه حين سمع رجلاً وهو
يبكى عند قراءة القرآن فقال هٰكذا كنّا حتى قَسَت (٨)القلوب يعنى اشتدّت
وثبتت، فلا يتغيّر اذا (٩)طرقه ضربٌ من السماع لانّ حاله قبل السماع
١٠ وبعده سواآء، ومعنًى آخر وذلك ان سهل بن عبد الله (٣)رحمه الله قد   Af.131a
حُكى عنه انه قال حالى فى الصلاة وقبل الدخول فى الصلاة شىء واحد
وذلك انه (١١)يراعى قلبه ويراقب الله (٣)تعالى بسرّه قبل دخوله فى الصلاة
ثمّ يقوم الى الصلاة بحضور قلبه وجمْع همّه فيدخل فى الصلاة بالمعنى الذى
كان به قبل الصلاة فيكون حاله فى الصلاة وقبل الصلاة (١٢)واحدًا وكذلك
١٥ حاله قبل السماع وبعده بمعنًى واحد فيكون سماعه متّصلاً ووجْده متّصلاً وشرْبه
دايمًا وعطشه دايمًا وكلّما ازداد (١٣)شرْبه ازداد (١٤)عطشه وكلّما ازداد
(١٤)عطشه ازداد (١٣)شرْبه فلا ينقطع (١٥)ابدًا، وسمعت احمد بن علّى
(١٦)الكرجى المعروف بالوجيهى يقول كان جماعة من الصوفية مستجمعين فى
بيت حسن القزّاز (١٧)وعندهم قوّالون يقولون وهم يتواجدون فأشرف عليهم
٢٠ (١٨)ممشاذ فلمّا نظروا اليه (١٩)سكتوا جميعًا فقال لهم ممشاذ (٢٠)ما لكم قد سكتم

---

(١) A om. عن ذلك.   (٢) B بن.   (٣) B om.   (٤) B معناه هذا.
(٥) A يعنى. B يعنى.   (٦) B om. الشيخ رحمه الله.   (٧) A ولذلك.   (٨) B قلوبنا.
(٩) B طرقها.   (١٠) B وبعد السماع.   (١١) B راعى.   (١٢) A وأحد.
(١٣) B شربه.   (١٤) B عطشه.   (١٥) B adds على سيدنا وصلى الله والحمد لله.
(١٦) B الكرخى.   (١٧) B ومعم.   محمد سهل للى (سيّد البشر) وسلم تسليما.
(١٨) B adds الدينورى.   (١٩) So both MSS.   (٢٠) B om. ما لكم قد سكتم.

ارجعوا الى ما كنتم فيه فلو (١)جُمِعَتْ ملاهى الدنيا فى أُذنى ما (٢)شغلت
همّى ولا (٣)شفت بعض ما بى، قال (٤)الشيخ رحمه الله وهذا (٥)ايضًا من
صفات اهل الكمال (٦)لا يكون فيهم فضلة لطارق يطرقهم ولوارد يَرِدُ عليهم
ولم يبق من طباعهم ونفوسهم وبشريتهم حاسّة الاّ وهى مبدلة ومهذّبة لا
٥ (٧)تأخذ (٥)من النغمات حظوظها ولا تتلذّذ بالاصوات الطيّبة ولا (٨)تتنعّم
بها لانّ همومهم مفردة وأسرارهم (٩)طاهرة وصفاتهم لا يعارضها كدورة الحسوس
وظلمات النفوس وتغيير البشرية ومقارنة الانسانية (١٠)ذٰلِكَ فَضْلُ اللّٰهِ يُؤْتِيهِ
مَنْ يَشَآءُ، وبلغنى عن (١١)ابى القسم الجُنَيْد (٥)رحمه الله انه قيل له كنتَ
تسمع هذه القصايد وتحضر مع اصحابك فى اوقات السماع وكنت تتحرّك
١٠ والان فأنت هٰكذى ساكن الصفة فقرأ عليهم (٥)الجنيد هذه الآية (١٢)وَتَرَى
الْجِبَالَ تَحْسَبُهَا جَامِدَةً وَهِىَ تَمُرُّ مَرَّ السَّحَابِ صُنْعَ اللّٰهِ الَّذِى أَتْقَنَ كُلَّ شَىْءٍ
فكأنه يشير بذلك والله اعلم يعنى انكم تنظرون الى سكون جوارحى وهُدُوّ
ظاهرى ولا تدرون اين انا بقلبى، وهذه ايضًا صفة من صفات اهل الكمال
فى السماع، قال (٤)الشيخ رحمه الله وهٰؤلآءِ ربّما يحضرون فى هذه المواضع
١٥ التى فيها السماع لأحوالٍ شتّى وجهاتٍ مختلفة فربّما يجتمعون معهم من جهة
مساعدة (١٣)اخٍ من إخوانهم وربّما يحضرون لعِلْمهم (١٤)وثباتهم وكِبَر عقولهم
حتى يعرّفوهم ما لهم وما عليهم من شرايط السماع وآدابه وربما يجتمعون مع
(٥)غير ابنآء جنسهم من سعة اخلاقهم وتحمّلهم فيكونون معهم (١٥)باينين منهم
(١٦)ومنفردين عنهم ببواطنهم وإن كانوا مع جلسايهم (١٧)بظواهرهم،

---

(١) جمع B. (٢) B اشغل. (٣) B اشفا. (٤) B om. الشيخ رحمه الله.
(٦) A ظاهرة. (٧) B يأخذ. (٨) B يتنعّم. (٦) B لا ان. (٥) B om.
(١٢) Kor. (١١) B om. ابى القسم. (١٠) Kor. 57, 21. طاهر طاهره B.
27, 90. (١٣) B الاخ. (١٤) A ونيانهم. (١٥) B باينون. (١٦) ومتفردون B.
(١٧) B adds وبالله التوفيق.

باب فى سماع الذِكر والمواعظ والحكمة وغير ذلك ،

(١)قال سمعت ابا بكر محمّد بن داود الدينورى الدُقى يقول (٢)سمعت
ابا بكر الزقّاق يقول سمعت من الجُنيّد (١) رحمه الله تعالى كلمة فى التوحيد
(٣)هيّمتنى اربعين سنة وأنا بعدُ فى غِمار ذلك ، وقال جعفر الخُلْدى (١) رحمه
٥ اله دخل رجل من اهل خراسان على الجنيد (١) رحمه الله وعنه جماعة من
المشايخ (٤)فقال يأبا القسم متى يستوى على العبد حامدُه وذامه فقال بعض
اولئك المشايخ اذا (٥)أدخل المارستان وقُيّد بقيدَين فقال (١)له الجنيد (١) رحمه
الله ليس هذا من شأنك ثمّ اقبل على الرجل فقال يا حبيبى اذا علم وتيقّن
انه مخلوق (٦)فشهق الرجل شهقة وخرج، وقال يحيى بن (٧) مُعاذ (١) رحمه
١٠ الله الحكمة جُندٌ من جنود الله (١)تعالى يقوّى بها قلوب اوليآبه، ويقال ان
الكلام اذا خرج من القلب يقع على القلب واذا خرج من اللسان لم (٨) يجاوز
الأذنين، قال (٩)الشيخ (١) رحمه الله ومثل هذا (١٠)فى الاخبار كثير (١١)من
ذكر من سمع كلمة او ذكرًا او موعظة او حكمة حسنة (١٢)راقه ذلك ونار
(١٣)من ذلك فى سرّه وجدًا او فى قلبه احتراقًا، ويقال كلّ من (١٤)لا يزهّدك
Af.132a لَحْظُه (١٥)عن لَفْظِه لم (١٦)يُغْنِك وَعْظُه (١٥)عن لَفْظِه، وقال ابو عثمن فعلُ
من حكم فى ألف رجل انفع من (١٧)موعظة الف رجل فى (١٨) رجل، وأنّما
هى مصادفات (١٩)للقلوب من حيث صفآء القلوب عند ما (٢٠)يطرّقها من
واردات الغيوب من المسموعات والمنظورات فاذا اتّفقت قويت واذا اختلفت

---

(١) B om.   (٢) B om. from سمعت to يقول.   (٣) A همتنى.   (٤) B فقالوا.

(٥) A دخل.   (٦) B قال فشهق.   (٧) B adds الرازى.   (٨) A تجاوزه.

(٩) B ابو نصر.   (١٠) B كبير فى الاخبار والاثار.   (١١) B فى.

(١٢) B رقه.   (١٣) B om. من ذلك.   (١٤) B لم.   (١٥) AB من.

(١٦) B يغنيك.   (١٧) B مواعظه.   (١٨) رجل واحد.   (١٩) B القلوب.

(٢٠) B يطرقه.

وتضادّت ضعفت الّا لأهل الاستقامة والصدق والكمال فانهم قد جاوزوا
ذلك (١) وسقطت عنهم روئة التبييز فلا يتغيّرون ولكن ربّما (٢) تُجَدَّدُ لم
أذكارهم بما يسمعون وتصفو لهم المشاهدات وقتًا بعد وقت (٣) وذلك زيادات
الصفاء (٤) تَجَدَّدُ لهم عند سماع الحكمة والإصغاء الى (٤) طرايف (٥) الحكمة،
والمراد فيا ذكرتُ ان مقصود القوم فى السَّماع (٦) الذى يسمعون من القرآن
والقصايد والذكر (٧) وغير ذلك من انواع الحِكَم ليس كلّه لحُسن النغـة
(٨) ولطيب الصوت والتنعّم والتلذّذ بذلك لانّ الرقة والهيجان والوجد كامنْ
(٩) فيهم ايضًا عند فقْدان الاصوات والنغمات والسكون والهُدوَء (١٠) كامن
(٩) فيهم عند وجْدان الاصوات والنغات، فعلمْنا ان المقصود فى جميع ما
يسمعون ما تصادف قلوبهم من جنس ما فى قلوبهم من المواجيد والأذكار
فيقوى الوجد بما تصادفه (١١) بمشاكلته،

باب آخر فى السَّماع،

(١٢) قال الشيخ رحمه الله قد ذكرنا ان المعوّل والمقصود فى ذلك على
مقاصد المستمعين فيا يسمعون وعلى حسب مصادفات اسرارهم من ذلك ومن
حيث اوقاتهم وما يكون الغالب على قلوبهم فاذا سمعوا شيئًا يوافق ما هم به
فى الوقت تَقْوَى (١٣) بذلك مُكْمَنَات سرايرهم وما (١٤) انضمّت عليه ضمايرهم
فينطقون من حيث وجْدهم ويشبرون من حيث قصدهم وصدقهم وإلى مـا
يليق بحالهم ولا يخطر بهالهم قصدُ الشاعر (١٥) فى شعره ومراد القايل بقوله
وكذلك لا (١٦) تصطلهم غفلة القارئ عند قراءته اذا كانوا منتبهين ولا

(١) وسقط B. (٢) بحدد B. (٣) وذلك B. (٤) طوارقه B. (٥) B om.
(٦) منهم B. (٧) الذين A. (٧) وبالحكم وغير ذلك ليس الخ B. (٨) ولطية B. (٩) منهم B.
(١٠) كان B. كاين B. (١١) B adds وبالله التوفيق. (١٢) B om. قال الشيخ.
(١٣) رحمه الله. (١٤) ذلك B. (١٤) انظمت A. انطوت B. (١٥) وشعره B.
(١٦) نستطهم A.

يُوحِشهم نشئَت الذاكر عند ذكره اذا كانوا مستجمعين وربّما تتّفق الحالان
(١) ونتشاكل الوقتان وتجانس الارادتان فيكون (٢)القادح أقوى والوقت أَصْفى
والعلَل أَخْفَى (٣)واذا شملتهم العناية وصحبهم التوفيق فهم محفوظون عن الزلَل
ومبرّءون من العلَل فى جميع احوالهم، وبيان ما ذكرتُ فى هذه (٤)الحكايات
التى اذكرها ان شآء الله، ذكر عن محمّد بن مسروق البغدادى انه قال
خرجتُ ليلةً فى ايّام جاهليّتى وأنا نشوان وكنتُ أُغنّى (٥)بهذا البيت،

بطيزنابادَ كَرْمٌ ما مَرَرتُ بِهِ ۞ إِلّا تَعَجَّبْتُ مِمَّنْ يَشْرَبُ المآءَا،

قال (٧)فسمعت قايلاً (٨)يقول،

وَفى جهَنَّمَ (٩)مآءٌ ما تَجَرَّعَهُ ۞ حَلْقٌ فأَبْقى لَهُ فى الجَوفِ أَمعآءَا،

(١٠)قال فكان ذلك سبب توبتى وإشتغالى بالعلم والعبادة او كما قال، أَلا
ترى انه حين ادركه العناية (١١)امتحق (١٢)الباطل الذى كان فيه (١٣)بمصادفة
الحقّ له وكان باطله سببًا لنجاته حين صحبه التوفيق وشملته الرعاية، وقد
حُكى ايضًا عن ابى الحسن بن رزءان انه قال كنت امشى مع رجل من
اصحابنا بين بساتين (١٤)بالبصرة اذ سمعنا ضاربًا بالطنبور وهو يقول،

يا صِباحَ الوُجوه ما (١٥)تُنْصِفونا ۞ طُولَ ذا الدَّهر كُلَّكُمْ تَظلِمونا
كانَ فى واجبِ الحُقوقِ عَلَيْكُمْ ۞ إِذْ (١٦)بُلينا بِحُكْمِ تُنْصِفونا،

قال فشهق صاحبى شهقةً ثمّ قال (١٧)وما ذا عليك لو قلتَ،

يا صِباحَ الوُجوه سوفَ تَموتُو ۞ نَ وَتَبْلى خُدودُكُمْ والعُيونا
وَتَصيرونَ بَعدَ ذلكَ رَسْمًا ۞ فَاعلَموا ذاكَ إِنَّ ذاكَ يَقينا،

أَلا ترى انه (١٨)اجابه من حيث وقته (١٩)وأبان عمّا فى ضيره ولم يحشه

(١) ونتشاكل B. ‏ ‏ (٢) A الفلاح. ‏ ‏ (٣) A اذا. ‏ ‏ (٤) A الحكاية with الحكايات as variant. ‏ ‏ (٥) B هذا. ‏ ‏ (٦) واست بطنناباز B. See Yáqút under طيزناباد. Other readings in J.R.A.S. for 1901, p. 724, note 3. ‏ ‏ (٧) B سمعت. ‏ ‏ (٨) B يقول لى. ‏ ‏ (٩) B نهر. ‏ ‏ (١٠) B om. ‏ ‏ (١١) A امتحق with امتخق as variant. ‏ ‏ (١٢) A بالباطل. ‏ ‏ (١٣) A بمصادفه. ‏ ‏ (١٤) B البصرة. ‏ ‏ (١٥) B تظلمونا. ‏ ‏ (١٦) B سقينا. ‏ ‏ (١٧) B ما. ‏ ‏ (١٨) B قد اجابه. ‏ ‏ (١٩) B فأتانه.

A f.133a قُبّحَ مقصد القائل فى قوله لاستيلاء الحقايق عليه وامتلائه بوجهٍ، وقد حُكى

فى هذا المعنى ايضًا عن الشبلى (١) رحمه الله انه سئل عن معنى قوله (٢) وَمَكَرُوا

وَمَكَرَ ٱللّٰهُ (٣) وَٱللّٰهُ خَيْرُ ٱلْمَاكِرِينَ فقيل له قد علمتُ موضع مكرهم فا موضع

مكر الله بهم فقال ترکهم على ما هم فيه ولو شآء ان يغيّر لغيّر قال فشهد

٥ الشبلى (١) رحمه الله فى السايل انه لم (٤) يُغْنِه جوابُه فقال (٥) أما سمعتَ بفلانة

(٦) الطُّنبُرانية فى ذلك الجانب (٧) تقول،

وَيَقْبُحُ مِنْ سِوَاكَ الفِعْلُ عِنْدى ٭ (٨) وَتَفْعَلُهُ فَيَحْسُنُ مِنْكَ (٩) ذَاكَا

(١٠) قال الشيخ رحمه الله فانظرْ (١١) اين نفع اشارته من قصدها، وجميع ذلك

داخلٌ فى الذى قيل ان الحكمة ضالّة المؤمن وصاحب المسئلة (١) والسؤال

١٠ ابو (١٢) عبد الله بن (١٣) خفيف (١٤) رحمه الله كما بلغنى والله علم،

باب فيمن كره السماع والذى كره الحضور فى المواضع (١٥)التى

يقرؤون (١٦) فيها القرآن بالالحان ويقولون القصايد

ويتواجدون ويرقصون،

فقد كُره ذلك من جهات شتّى (١٧)فقوم كرهوا ذلك لأخبار رُويت

١٥ عن بعض الايمّة المتقدمين والعلماء والتابعين انهم كرهوا ذلك، فكره من

كره من ذلك اقتداءً بهم ومتابعةً لهم اذ كانوا هم الايمّة فى احكام الدين

(١٨) والمقدَّمين فى عصرهم على جماعة المسلمين، وقوم كرهوا ذلك للمريدين

والقاصدين والتابيين لعِظَم ما فيه من الخطر إن استلذّوا ذلك وتابعوا

---

(١) B om.   (٢) Kor. 3, 47.   (٣) A وهو.   (٤) AB يغنيه.   (٥) A ما.

(٦) الطبرانية B.   (٧) B تغنى ونقول.   (٨) B فنفعله.   (٩) B ذاك.

(١٠) B om. قال الشيخ رحمه أنه.   (١١) A ان.   (١٢) A بكر for عبد الله.

(١٣) B حفينة.   (١٤) B om. from رحمه to وإنه أعلم.   (١٥) B الذى.   (١٦) A om.

(١٧) B وقوم.   (١٨) AB والمقدمون.

حظوظهم فتنحلّ عند ذلك عقودهم [1] وتنفسخ عزيمتهم [2] ويركنوا الى [3] شهواتهم
[4] ويتعرّضوا للفتنة ويقعوا فى البليّة، وطائفة اخرى كرهت ذلك وزعمت ان
الذى يتعرّض لاستماع هذه الرباعيات لا يخلو من احد وجهين إمّا هم قوم
[5] متلهّون من اهل [6] الدُّعابة والفتنة او هم قوم [7] وصلوا الى الاحوال
٥ الشريفة [8] وعانقوا المقامات الرضية وأمانوا نفوسهم بالرياضات والمجاهدات
وطرحوا الدنيا وراء ظهورهم وانقطعوا الى الله [9] عزّ وجلّ فى جميع معانيهم A f.133b
قالوا ولسنا نحن من هؤلاء ولا من هؤلاء فلا معنى لاشتغالنا بذلك وترْكُ
ذلك اولى بنا والاشتغال بالطاعات وإداء المفترضات واجتناب المحرّمات
يشغلنا عن ذلك، [10] قال سمعت [11] احمد بن علىّ الوجيهى يقول سمعت
١٠ ابا علىّ الروذبارى [10] رحمه الله يقول [10] قد بلغنا فى هذا الأمر الى مكان
مثل حدّ السيف فان [12] مِلنا [13] كذى ففى النار، [14] قال وأخبرنى جعفر
الخُلْدى فيما قرأت عليه قال سمعت الجُنَيْد [10] رحمه الله يقول جيْتُ الى سَرىّ
السَّقَطى [10] رحمه الله يومًا فقال لى أيْشَ [15] خبّرَ اصحابك يقولون [16] قصايد
قلت نعم قال يقولون عاشقٌ دَنِفٌ لو شيّت ان اقول هذا الذى [17] بى من
١٥ هذا اللون لقلتُ قال الجنيد [10] رحمه الله وكان معه هذا [18] كثيرًا كان
يستره وكان معوَّلُه الخوف، وكرهت طائفة اخرى ذلك من جهة ان العامّة
لا تعرف مقاصد القوم فيما يسمعون فربّما غلطوا فى مقاصدهم وزلفوا فكرهوا
ذلك شفقةً على العامّة وصيانةً للخاصّة وغبرةً على الوقت الذى اذا فات لا
يُدْرَك، وطائفة اخرى كرهت ذلك لِما قد فقد من اخوانه وعدم من
٢٠ أشكاله وقرنآيه ومن كان يصلح لذلك ولما قد بُلى من [19] الاختلاط بغير
ابناء جنسه ولما قد دُفع الى مجالسة الاضداد ومخالطة اهل العناد فقد ترك

[1] وتنسخ B.   [2] ويركون B.   [3] هوايهم B.   [4] وينعرضون B.
[5] متلهين AB.   [6] الدعاية A.   [7] قد وصلوا B.   [8] A gives السنية
as a variant.   [9] عز وجل تعلى for B.   [10] B om.   [11] A على
[12] خير A.   [13] قال و B om.   [14] كذا B.   [15] فلنا AB.   [12] ابن احمد
B.   [16] فصايدا B.   [17] فى B.   [18] كثير AB.   [19] الاختلاف B.   حبر B.

ذلك طلبًا للسلامة لاقباله على شأنه ومعرفته بأهل زمانه، وطايفة اخرى كرهت ذلك لقول النبى صلعم فيما رُوى عنه انه قال من حُسن اسلام المرء تَرْكُهُ ما لا يعنيه فقالوا هذا ما لا يعنينا لانّا ما أُمرنا بذلك وليس هو من زاد [١] القبر ولا ممّا يُطلب به النجاة فى الآخرة فكرهوا ذلك لهذا المعنى، ٥ وطايفة اخرى [٢] من اهل المعرفة والكمال كرهوا ذلك لانّ احوالهم مستقيمة وأوقاتهم معمورة وأذكارهم صافية وأسرارهم طاهرة وقلوبهم حاضرة وهمومهم مجتمعة لم يخطر ببالهم خاطرٌ ولا يجرى فى أفكارهم عارضٌ الّا وهم مُشرِفون [٤] عليه يعلمون من ابن [٤] مَوْرده وإلى ابن [٥] مَصْدره ليس فيهم فضلـة لطوارق سمع الظاهر من معارضة طوارق سمع الباطن من دوام المناجاة ١٠ ولطايف الاشارات وخفّ المعانبات والمخاطبات [٦] والمجاوبات [٧] فينكره جليسه [٨] ولا يعرفه انيسه فهم مع الله [٩] تعالى ببواطنهم وإن كانوا مع الخلق بظواهرهم [١٠] ذَٰلِكَ فَضْلُ ٱللَّهِ يُؤْتِيهِ مَنْ يَشَآءُ، [١١] فهذا ممّا [١٢] حضرنى فى هذا الوقت وباله التوفيق،

الأف.134a

<h1 style="text-align:center">كتاب الوجد،</h1>

<h2 style="text-align:center">باب فى ذكر اختلافهم فى ماهية الوجد،   ١٥</h2>

[١٤] قال الشيخ رحمه اه اختلف اهل التصوّف فى الوجد ما [١٤] هو فقال عمرو بن عثمن المكّى [٩] رحمه الله لا يقع على كيفية الوجد عبارة لانّها سِرُّ

---

(١) العبد B.   (٢) B om.   (٣) من اهل المعرفة والكمال B.   (٤) عليها B.   (٤) موردها B.

(٥) مصدرها B.   (٦) والمجاوبات A.   (٧) فيذكره B.   (٨) ويعرفه B.

(٩) B om.   (١٠) Kor. 57, 21.   (١١) وهذا B.   (١٢) حضرنا B.

(١٤) قال الشيخ رحمه الله B om.   (١٤) B هى.

الله [١] تعالى عند المؤمنين الموقنين، وذُكر عن الجُنَيْد [١] رحمه الله انه قال
[٢] كما اظنّ ان الوجد هو المصادفة بقوله عزّ وجلّ [٣] وَوَجَدُوا مَا عَمِلُوا
حَاضِرًا يعنى صادفوا، وقال [٤] وَمَا [٥] تُقَدِّمُوا لِأَنْفُسِكُم مِنْ خَيْرٍ تَجِدُوهُ عِنْدَ
اللهِ اى تُصادفوا، وقال [٦] حَتَّى إِذَا جَاءَهُ لَمْ يَجِدْهُ [٧] شَيْئًا يعنى لم يصادفه،

وكلّ ما صادف القلب من غم او فرح فهو وجدٌ [٨] وقد اخبر الله [١] تعالى
عن القلوب انها تنظر وتبصر وهو وجدٌ لها قال الله تعالى [٩] فَإِنَّهَا لَا تَعْمَى
الْأَبْصَارُ وَلَكِنْ تَعْمَى الْقُلُوبُ الَّتِي فِي الصُّدُورِ اى عن وجدها ففرّق بين
التى تجد [١٠] وبين التى لا تجد، وقد قيل ايضًا ان الوجد مكاشفات من
الحقّ ألا ترى ان احدهم يكون ساكنًا فيتحرّك ويظهر منه الزفير والشهيق

١٠ وقد يكون من هو [١١] أقْوَى منه [١٢] ساكنًا فى وجد لا يظهر منه شىءٌ من
ذلك قال الله تعالى [١٣] الَّذِينَ إِذَا ذُكِرَ اللهُ وَجِلَتْ قُلُوبُهُمْ، قال بعض
المشايخ من المتقدّمين الوجد وجدان وجد مُلْكٍ ووجد لقاءٍ لقول الله [١٥] عزّ
وجلّ [١٥] فَمَنْ لَمْ يَجِدْ يعنى [١٦] من لم يملك وقوله تعالى [١٧] وَوَجَدُوا مَا عَمِلُوا
حَاضِرًا [١٨] يعنى [١٩] لقوا، وقال بعضهم كلّ وجدٍ يجدك فيملكك فذاك وجدُ
A f. 134b

١٥ مُلْكٍ وكلّ وجدٍ تجده فذاك وجدُ اللقاءِ [٢٠] تلقى بقلبك [٢١] شيئًا ولا يثبت،
وسمعت [١] ابا الحسن [٢٢] الحُصرى [١] رحمه الله يقول الناس اربعة [٢٣] مُدّعٍ
مكشوف ومعترضٌ تارةً [٢٤] له وتارةً عليه ومحقّقٌ قد اكتفى بحقيقته وواجدٌ
قد فنى بما [٢٥] يجد، وحُكى عن سهل بن عبد الله [١] رحمه الله انه قال كلّ
وجدٍ لا يشهد [٢٦] له الكتاب والسنّة فهو باطل، وقال ابو سعيد احمد بن

---

(١) B om. (٢) B الوجد الخ كل طران. (٣) Kor. 18, 47. (٤) Kor. 2, 104.

(٥) A ووجد الله عنده تفعلوا من خير الخ. (٦) Kor. 24, 39. (٧) B adds

(٨) B قد. (٩) Kor. 22, 45. (١٠) B om. بين. (١١) B أقدر.

(١٢) A ساكن. (١٣) Kor. 22, 36. (١٤) B جل ذكره. (١٥) Kor. 2, 192.

(١٦) B فمن. (١٧) Kor. 18, 47. (١٨) B اى. (١٩) B ولقوا. (٢٠) B لقا.

(٢١) B شى. (٢٢) B البصرى. (٢٣) AB مدعى. (٢٤) A om. (٢٥) B وجد.

(٢٦) B لك.

بشر بن زياد بن الاعرابى (١) رحمه الله اوّل الوجد رفع الحِجاب ومشاهدة
الرقيب وحضور الفهم وملاحظة الغيب ومحادثة السرّ وإيناس المفقود وهو
فناؤك انت من حيث انت، (٢) قال ابو سعيد (١) رحمه الله الوجد اوّل
درجات الخصوص وهو ميراث التصديق بالغيب فلمّا ذاقوها وسطع فى
قلوبهم نورها زال عنهم كلّ شكّ ورَيْب، وقال ايضًا الذى يحجب عن
الوجد رؤيةُ آثار النفس والتعلّق بالعلائق والاسباب لانّ النفس محجوبـة
باسبابها فاذا انقطعت الاسباب وخلص الذكر وصحا القلب ورقّ وصفا
(٣) ونجعت فيه الموعظة والذكر وحلّ من المناجاة فى محل (٤) غريب وخوطب
وسمع الخطاب بأذن واعية وقلبٍ شاهد وسِرّ (٥) طاهر (٦) فشاهَدَ ما كان منه
خالِيًا فذلك هو (٧) الوجد لانّه وجد ما كان عنه (٨) عدمًا معدومًا،

باب فى صفات الواجدين،

(٩) قال الشيخ رحمه الله قال الله (١٠) عزّ وجلّ (١١) مَثَانِىَ تَقْشَعِرُّ مِنْهُ جُلُودُ
ٱلَّذِينَ يَخْشَوْنَ رَبَّهُمْ ثُمَّ تَلِينُ جُلُودُهُمْ وَقُلُوبُهُمْ إِلَى ذِكْرِ اللهِ هذه صفة من
صفات الواجدين، وقوله (١٢) تعالى (١٣) وَجِلَتْ قُلُوبُهُمْ فالوجل صفة من صفات
الواجدين، وفى الحديث ان النبى صلعم قرأ (١٤) فَكَيْفَ إِذَا جِئْنَا مِنْ كُلِّ أُمَّةٍ
بِشَهِيدٍ وَجِئْنَا بِكَ عَلَى هَؤُلَاءِ شَهِيدًا فصعق فالصعقة صفة من صفات
الواجدين، والاخبار تكثر من مثل الزفير والشهيق والبكاء والغشية والأنين
والصعقة (١٥) والصراخ والصيحة فكلّ ذلك من صفات الواجدين، وهم على
طبقتين واجدٌ ومتواجدٌ فامّا الواجدون فهم على ثلثة اصناف فصنفٌ منهم

---

(١) B om.   (٢) B وقال.   (٣) A ونجعت with وقعت written above. B
فشاهده.   (٤) Iḥyá, II, 269, 22, has قريب.   (٥) Iḥyá ظاهر.   (٦) B ونجحت
تعلى.   (١٠) B قال الشيخ رحمه الله.   (٩) B om.   (٨) AB عدم معدوم.   (٧) B الوجود.
(١١) Kor. 39, 24.   (١٢) B وجله.   (١٣) Kor. 22, 36. B جل ذكره.
(١٤) Kor. 4, 45.   (١٥) B والصوارخ.

وَجْدُهم مصحوبهم الّا انّه يعارضهم فى الاحايين دواعى النفوس والاخلاق
البشريّة ومزاج [١]الطبع [٢]فيكدر عليهم الوقت ويتغيّر عليهم الحال، والصنف
الثانى وَجْدُهم مصحوبهم الّا انه اذا [٣]طرى عليهم ما يشاكل وجدهم من
طوارق السمع تنعّموا بذلك وعاشوا وانتعشوا ثم يتغيّر عليهم الوجد، والصنف
٥ الثالث وَجْدُهم مصحوبهم على الدوام وقد افناهم ذلك الوجد لانّ كلّ واجد
قد فنى بما وجد [٤]فليست [٥]فيهم فضلة عن موجودهم لانّ كلّ شىء عندهم
كالمفقود عند وجدهم بوجودهم بذهاب رؤية وجدهم، [٦]فامّا المتواجدون
فهم ايضًا على ثلثة اصناف فى تواجدهم فصنفٌ منهم المتكلّفون والمتشبّهون
وأهل الدعابة ومن لا وزن له، وصنفٌ منهم الذين يستدعون الاحوال
١٠ الشريفة [٧]بالتعرّض بعد قطع العلايق المشغلة والاسباب القاطعة فذلك
التواجد يجمل منهم وان كان غيرُ ذلك أوْلَى بهم لانّهم نبذوا الدنيا وراَء
ظهورهم فتواجدهم مطايبةً [٨]وتسليًا وفرحًا وسرورًا بما قـد عانقوا من خَلْع
الراحات وتَرْك المعلومات، قال [٩]الشيخ رحمه الله فمن انكر ذلك ويقول
[١٠]ليس هذا فى العلم فيقال له قد [١١]رُوى عن رسول الله صلعم انه قال
١٥ اذا دخلتم على هؤلاَء المعذّبين فابكوا فان لم تبكوا فتباكوا، فالتواجد من
الوجد بمنزلة التباكى من البكاَء والله اعلم، [١٢]وصنفٌ ثالثٌ [١٣]اهل الضعف
من ابناَء الاحوال وأرباب القلوب والمحقّقين بالارادات فاذا عجزوا عن
ضبط جوارحهم وكتمان ما بهم تواجدوا ونقضوا ما لا طاقة لهم بحمله ولا
سبيل لهم الى دفعه عنهم وردّه فيكون تواجدهم طلبًا [١٤]للتفرّج والتسلّى فهم
٢٠ اهل الضعف من اهل الحقايق، [١٥]قال سمعت عيسى [١٦]القصار يقول
رأيت الحسين بن منصور حين أُخرج من الحبس ليقتل فكان آخر [١٧]كلامه

(١) A طبع. (٢) B فيتكدر. (٣) A طرق. (٤) B وليست. (٥) B لهم.
(٦) B واما. (٧) B بالتفرص. (٨) A وتسلى. (٩) B ابو نصر for الشيخ.
(١٠) B ليس هذا. (١١) B ورد. (١٢) B والصنف الثالث. (١٣) A اهل الضعف.
(١٤) A للتفرج. (١٥) B om. (١٦) B ابن
B om. (١٤) (١٥) A للتفرج. اهل الضعف. (١٣) B om. (١٢) ورد B. (١١) B هذا ليس. (١٠) رحمه الله
ابن B. (١٦) (١٧) A كلمه. القصار.

ان قال حَسبُ (١)الواجد إفراد الواحد قال وما سمع احـد من المشايخ
(٢)الذين كانوا ببغداد هذا الّا استحسنوا منه (٣)هذه الكلمة، وسيل ابو يعقوب
(٤)النهرجورى (٥)رحمه الله عن صحّة وجد (٦)الواجد وسقمه فقال صحّته قبول
قلوب الواجدين له وكذلك سقمه انكار قلوب الواجدين له وتبرّم جلساً به
(٧)اذ كانوا (٨)أشكالاً غير أضداد وليس ذلك لغير ابناء جنسهم،

باب (٩) فى ذكر تواجد المشايخ الصادقين،

(١٠)قال الشيخ رحمه الله حُكى عن الشبلى (٥)رحمه الله انه تواجد يومًا
فى مجلسه فقال (١١)آه ليس يدرى ما بقلبى سِواهُ فقيل له (١١)آه من اىّ شىء
فقال (١٢)من كلّ شىء، وذُكر عنه ايضًا انه تواجد يومًا فضرب يد على
الحايط (١٣)حتى عَمِلت عليه يده قال فعمدوا الى بعض الاطبّاء فلمّا اتاه
(١٤)قال للطبيب وَيْلك باىّ شاهد جيتنى قال جيتُ حتى اعالِج يدك
(١٥)فلطمه الشبلى (١٦)رحمه الله وطرده قال فعمدوا الى طبيب آخر ألطَفَ منه
فلمّا اتاه قال (٥)له ويلك باىّ شاهد جيتنى قال (١٧)بشاهك قال فأعطاه
يدَ (١٨)فبطّها وهو ساكت فلمّا اخرج الدواء يجعله عليها صاح وتواجد وترك
إصبعه على موضع الداء (١٩)وهو يقول،

أَنبَتَتْ صَبابَتُكُمْ ٭ قَرحةً عَلَى كَبِدى
بثٌّ مِن تَفَجُّعِكُمْ ٭ كالأَسيرِ فى الصَّفَدِ،

وذُكر عن ابى الحسين النورى (٥)رحمه الله انه اجتمع مع جماعة من المشايخ

---

(١) المتواجد B.   (٢) الذى B.   (٣) ذلك الكلام B.   (٤) اسحق بن B.
(٥) B om.   (٦) الواجدين B.   (٧) اذا B.   محمد بن ابوب النهرجورى
(٨) أشكال A.   (٩) A om.   (١٠) B om.   قال الشيخ رحمه الله.   (١١) آه B.
(١٢) أه من B.   (١٣) فعملت B.   (١٤) فقال B.   (١٥) قال فلطمه B.
(١٦) رحمه الله B for لعطة.   (١٧) بشاهدك B.   (١٨) فبسطها B.   (١٩) وانشا وهو B.

فى دعوة فجرى بينهم مسئلة فى العلم وأبو الحسين النورى (١)رحمه الله ساكت
قال ثم رفع رأسه فأنشدهم هذه الابيات ،

رُبَّ وَرْقَآءَ هَتُوفٍ فى الضُّحَى • ذاتِ شَجْوٍ (٢)صَدَحَتْ فى فَنَنِ

فَبُكَائى رُبَّما أَرْقَها • وبُكَاها رُبَّما أَرَّقَنِى

(٤)هِىَ إِنْ تَشْكُو فَلا أَفْهَمُها • وإذا أَشْكُو فَلا تَفْهَمُنِى

غَيْرَ أَنِّى بالجَوَى أَعْرِفُها • وَهْىَ أَيْضًا بالجَوَى تَعْرِفُنى ،

قال فا بقى فى القوم احد الّا قام وتواجد لمّا انشد النورى (٤)هذه الابيات ،
(٥)وقال بعض الصوفية هو ذى (٦)اشتهى منذ سنين ان اسمع كلمةً فى المحبّة
من رجل واجد يتكلّم بها عن وجه، ويقال ان ابا سعيد الخرّاز (١)رحمه
الله كان كثير التواجد عند ذكر الموت فسئل عن ذلك الجُنيد (١)رحمه الله
فقال (٧)العارف قد ايقن ان (٨)الله لم يفعل به شيئًا من المكاره بغضًا له
ولا عقوبةً ويشاهد فى صنائع الله (١)تعالى الحالة به من المكاره صفو المحبّة
بينه وبين الله (١)عزّ وجلّ وإنّما يُنزل به هذه النوازل (٩)ليردّ روحَهُ اليه
اصطفآءً له واصطناعًا (١٠)له فاذا كوشف العارف بهذا وما اشبهه لم يكن
بعجب ان تطير روحه اليه اشتياقًا وتنقلب من وطنها (١)اشتياقًا فلذلك ما
رأيت من التواجد عند ذكر الموت وربّما اتى ذلك على قرب (١١)مُنيّته
وإله يفعل بوليّه ما يشآء وما يُحبّ، وسئل بعض المشايخ عن الفرق بين
الوجود والتواجد فقال الوجود بوادى (١٢)الغيبة وإرسالات الحقيقة والتواجد
داخلٌ فى الاكتساب راجعٌ الى اوصاف العبد من حيث العبد والذى كره
(١٣)الوجد (١٤)لمشاهدة (١٥)علّةٍ فى الذى يتواجد عن ابى عثمٰن الحيرى الواعظ،

---

(١) B om.   (٢) B صدقت with لعله حت written above.   (٣) A هو.

(٤) A om. هذه الابيات.   (٥) The words from وقال to كلمةً are suppl. in
marg. A. The copyist states that they were omitted in the original MS.

A فال.   (٦) A om.   (٧) B العارف ان.   (٨) B adds ذكره جل.
(٩) A لترد.   (١٠) B اليه.   (١١) A منيّه.   (١٢) B الفتنه.   (١٣) B الوجده.

(١٤) A مشاهده.   (١٥) A علمه.

20

حُكى عنه انه رأى رجلاً قد تواجد فقال [١]له ان كنت صادقًا فقد اظهرتَ
كتمانه وان كنت كاذبًا فقد اشركتَ، والله اعلم بمقصه من [٢]ذاك ويُشَبَّهُ انه
اراد بذلك شفقةً عليه وحذرًا من الفتنة والآفة والله اعلم،

باب فى قوّة سلطان الوجد وهيجانه [٣]وغلباته،

[١]قال اخبرنى جعفر بن محمّد الخُلْدى [١]رحمه الله [٤]فيما قرأت عليه
قال سمعت الجُنَيْد [١]رحمه الله يقول [١]قال ذكر يومًا عند سَرِىّ السَّقَطى
[١]رحمه الله تعالى المواجيد [٥]الحادّة فى الأذكار القويّة وما جانس هذا ممّا
[٦]يقوى [١]على العبد فقال سرىّ [١]رحمه الله وقد سألتُه فيه فقال نَعَمْ
يُضرَب وجهه بالسيف وهو لا يحسّه قال ابو القسم [١]رحمه الله كان عندى
فى ذلك الوقت ان هذا لا يكون فراجعته انا فى ذلك الوقت فقلت [١]له
يضرب بالسيف ولا يحسّ انكارًا منّى لذلك فقال نعم يضرب بالسيف
[٧]ولا يحسّ وأقام على ذلك، وعن الجُنيد [١]رحمه الله انه كان يقول اذا
قوى [٨]الوجد يكون اتمّ ممّن يستأثر العلم، وذُكر عنه ايضًا انّه قال لا
[٩]يضرّ نقصان [١]الوجد مع [١٠]فضل العلم وفضل العلم اتمّ من فضل
الوجد، وقد ذكر [١١]عنه جعفر الخُلْدى [١٢]رحمه الله انه قال الحُمْلان فى
الوجد بعد الغلبة اتمّ من حال الغلبة فى الوجد والغلبة فى الوجد اتمّ من
المحمول قَبْلَ الغلبة فقيل له كيف نَزَّلْتَ هذا التنزيل فقال المحمول عن
حال غلبته بالحمل بعد القهر اتمّ [١٣]والمغلوب بعد حُمْلانه عن نفسـه
وشاهده اتمّ، [١٤]قال الشيخ رحمه الله وبيان ما قال والله اعلم ان من يكون

A.f.136b

---

(١) B om.   (٣) ذلك B.   (٣) وغلباته B.   (٤) مما B.   (٥) ايجاده B.

(٦) B app. يقول.   (٧) وهو لا B.   (٨) بوجد B.   (٩) يضرب B.

(١٠) الوحيد A. B om.   (١١) عن A.   (١٢) رحمه الله for ايضًا B.

(١٣) والمغلوبات B   (١٤) قال الشيخ رحمه الله B om.

محمولاً يعنى ساكنًا بعد غلبات الوجود وقوّة الوارد يكون اتمّ فى معناه ممّن
يغلبه حتى يظهر على ظاهر صفاته والغلبة لسلطان الوجد من قوّة الوارد
عليه والمصادفة لقلبه تكون اتمّ من حال الساكن الذى لا يقدح فيه القادح
ولا [١]يبجع [٢]فيه الوارد، سمعت [٣]ابن سالم يقول عن ابيه ان سهل بن
٥ عبد الله كان يقوى [٤]عليه الوجد حتى يبقى خمسة وعشرين يومًا [٥]او
اربعة وعشرين يومًا لا يأكل فيه طعامًا وكان يعرق عند البرد الشديد
فى الشتاء وعليه قميص واحد وكانوا اذا سألوه عن شىء من العلم يقول لا
تسألونى فانكم لا [٦]تنتفعون فى هذا الوقت بكلامى، [٧]سمعت ابا عمرو بن
علوان يقول سمعت الجُنيد [٨]رحمه الله يقول الشِّبلى [٨]رحمه الله سكران ولو
١٠ افاق من سُكره لجاء منه [٩]امام يُنتَفع به، وحُكى عن الجنيد [٨]رحمه الله
انه كان يقول ذكرتُ المحبّة بين بدى سَرِىّ السَّقَطى [٨]رحمه الله فضرب
يده على جِلْد ذراعه فمدّها ثم قال لو قلتُ انّما جفّ هذا على هذا من المحبّة
لصدقتُ قال ثم أُغمى عليه حتى غاب ثم تورّد وجهه حتى صار مثل دارة
القمر فما استطعنا ان ننظر اليه من حُسنه حتى غطّينا وجهه، وقال عمرو بن
١٥ عثمن المكّى [٨]رحمه الله الذى يجلّ بالقلوب من الامتلاء والوجد حتى لم
[١٠]يبق فيه فضلٌ لوجود حال كان [١١]يعرفها قبل ذلك انّما هى [١٢]زيادة
[١٣]للنفوس فى معرفتها [١٤]لعظم قدر الحقّ وقدر ما يستحقّ حتى [١٥]يتبيّن لها
عن الحال [١٦]التى يكون هو [١٧]منفردًا بها عن كلّ شىء حتى لا تجد غيره
فعند ذلك انقطع عنها [١٨]حسّ كلّ محسوس وانّما أُدركت انقطاعه [١٩]عن
٢٠ المحسوسات بما أوقعه الحقّ عليه منه فلم يكن فيه فضلٌ لغيره، وعن ابى

---

(١) AB يبجع but A gives يبخع as a variant.   (٢) A om. فيه الوارد.

(٣) ابا الحسين بن B.   (٤) A على.   (٥) و B.   (٦) AB تنتفعوا.

(٧) وسمعت B.   (٨) B om.   (٩) امامًا B.   (١٠) يكن B.   (١١) يعرفها B.

(١٢) زيادات B.   (١٣) النفوس B.   (١٤) لعظيم B.   (١٥) تبين B.

(١٦) الذى B.   (١٧) منفرد B.   (١٨) حسر ' B.   (١٩) من A.

عثمُن (١)المزيّن رحمه الله انه كان يقول،

فَسُكْرُ الوَجْدِ فى مَعْنَاهُ صَحْوٌ * وَصَحْوُ الوَجْدِ سُكْرٌ فى الوِصالِ،

باب فى الواجد الساكن والواجد المتحرّك (٤)ايُّهما اتمّ،

(٤)قال الشيخ رحمه الله قال ابو سعيد بن الأعرابى (٥)رحمه الله فى
كتابه فى الوجد ان (٦)سائلاً سأل (٧)فقال ايُّما افضلُ واتمُّ الحركة فى الوجد
ام السكون فيه وقد قال قوم ان السكون والتمكّن (٨)افضلُ وأعلى من الحركة
والانزعاج، قال (٩)ابو سعيد فالجواب فى ذلك والله اعلم ان الواردات
من الأذكار منها ما يوجب السكون فالسكون فيها افضل من الحركة ومنها
ما يوجب الحركة فالحركة (٥)فيها اتمّ اذ حكمُها القهر لأهلها فاذا لم (١٠)يقُمْ
بهذا القهر كان الوارد ضعيفًا فى وروده ولو ورد (١١)بحقيقته لأوجب ضرورةَ A.f.137b
الحركة والواردات من العلوم والأذكار الكاين عنها الوجد والاستبشار على
القلوب (١٢)فيشاهدها، ورأيت جماعةً يفضّلون اهل السكون لكِبَر عقولهم
وقوّتها وإشرافها على ما ورد عليها وتمكّنها (١٣)فيه وهذا لَعَمْرى كذلك ولكن
ربما (١٤)ورد ما لا (١٥)يلاوم العقول المخلوقة فيكون نوره اقوى وبرهانه
اقوى فيقوم شاهد منه ويعجز العقل عن إدراكه فيكون الوارد اقوى من
العقل فحُكْمُ هذه الحركة (٥)اتمُّ، قال ابو سعيد ومن الواردات ما يكون
(١٧)للعقل (١٨)ملاومًا فيُدْرِكه ويساكنه فلا يظهر مع ذلك حركةٌ لتمكّن العقل

---

(١) B om. (٢)المزيّن رحمه الله. B سُكر (٣). B ايُّم (٤). B om.

(٥) B om. (٦) A سال سايلا. (٧) B قال. قال الشيخ رحمه الله

(٨) B وأفضل. أعلا (٩) A الشيخ رحمه الله. B يقهر. (١٠) A بحقيقته (١١).

(١٢) A فشاهدها. B فيشاهدها. (١٣) A فيها. (١٤) In A عليها is suppl.

after ورد. (١٥) A يلازم. (١٦) B om. فحُكم هذه. (١٧) B العقل.

(١٨) A ملازما. B ملاومه.

لانّه [١] يشير اليه [٢] بما قد عرفه فمن شرّف اهلَ السكون انّما شرّفوهم بفضل
عقولهم وشدّة تمكّنهم [٣] ومن فضّل المتحرّكين فضّلهم بقوّة الوارد من الذكر
الذى يجَنّس دون فهم العقل فكان افضل [٤] لفضل الوارد واذا كان
العقلان [٥] مستويّن ليس احدها افضل فالساكن اتمّ وهذا ما لا احسبُه
يكون ان يستوى رجلان او عقلان او واردان وقد أبَى ذلك [٦] اهل العلم
واذا بطل التساوى رجعنا الى ما [٧] قلنا فى اوّل المسئلة [٨] ان لا معنى
لتفضيل الساكن على المتحرّك ولا المتحرّك على الساكن لاختلاف الحال الواردة
التى توجب [٩] الحركة والحال التى توجب السكون [١٠] لأنّ الواجدين لا
يستوون فيما كوشفوا به ولا ما شاهدوه من حالة الذكر الموجبة احدى
الحالَيْن من الحركة والسكون [١١] وفى الواردات التى توجب السكون ما هو
اعلى من الواردات التى توجب الحركة [١٢] وفى الواردات التى توجب الحركة
ما هو افضل من الواردات التى توجب السكون فليس الفضل هاهنا بالحركة
ولا بالسكون حتى نعلم الحال [١٣] الواردة على المتحرّكين وعلى الساكين [١٤] فان
كانت الحال توجب سكونًا فلم تُسكن صاحبها فهو ناقصٌ عن غيره وان
كانت توجب حركةً فلم تُحرّكه دلّ [٤] ذلك على نقص واردِه والمشاهدات
الواردات على قدر [١٥] صفاء القلوب وتخلّيها عن الحجُب المانعة لإدراك
الواردات فهذه صفة الأذكار لأهل الاحوال وقيامهم بها من حيث ما يوجبه
العلم فامّا اهل الغلبات والشُكر فلا يجوز عليهم [١٦] شىء من هذا [١٧] الكلام،

---

(١) بشير به B.   (٢) B بما.   (٣) B من.   (٤) B om.   (٥) B مستوين.

(٦) أكثر suppl. in A before اهل.   (٧) B قلناه.   (٨) B لان.   (٩) B om.

(١٠) A ولان.   (١١) B فى.   (١٢) B وكذلك فى.   توجب الحركة to from.

(١٣) B الوارد.   (١٤) B فاذا.   (١٥) B الصفا.   (١٦) B شيما.

(١٧) B adds وﷲ اعلم.

باب جامع مختصر من كتاب الوَجد الذى (١)أَلَّفه ابو
سعيد بن (٢)الأَعرابى،

قال ابو سعيد (٣)بن الاعرابى الوجد ما يكون عند ذِكرٍ مُزعِجٍ او
خوفٍ (٤)مُقْلِقٍ او توبيخ على زلّة او محادثة بلطيفة او اثارة الى فايدة او شوق
الى غايب او اسف على فايت او ندم على ماضٍ او استجلاب الى حال او
داعٍ (٥)الى واجب او مناجاة بسرّ وهى مقابلة الظاهر بالظاهر والباطن
بالباطن والغيب بالغيب والسرّ بالسرّ واستخراج ما لك بما عليك ممّا سبق
لك (٦)لتسعى فيه فيُكْتَبَ لك بعد (٧)(٨)كونه منك فيثبت لك قَدَمٌ بلا قدم
وذِكرٌ بلا ذكر (٦)اذ كان هو المبتدئ بالنِّعَم والمتولّى لها (٩) ومُلهِم الشُّكر عليها
والمُضيف اليك كسبها فيثبت لك بها درجة عاجلة وإليه يرجع الأمر كلّه
فهذا (١٠) جُملةٌ ظاهرُ علم الوجود، (١١)قال ابو سعيد (٣)رحمه الله الوجد
مباشرة رَوحٍ ومطالعة مزيد لا يَصبِرُ عن قليله ولا يُقْدَرُ على كثيره (١٢)التخييل
منه متدارك والاستخاثث منه اليه متواتر فلذلك يقع (١٣)اللهف وربّما كان
دونه التلف فامّا البكاء والشهيق فلقُربه ما يزداد (٦)اذ كان لم يُعرَف قبل
وروده ولا أُنسَ به مع سرعة (١٤)تقضّيه مع وقوعه حتى (١٥)كأنهما جميعًا
(٦)معًا فلم يتمّ الاستبشار بوروده حتى لحق الأسف على نقضيه، والرعدةُ
والغشيه وزوال الاعضاء والغلبة على العقل فبِعِظَم قدر الوارد وقوّة سطوته
وكذلك كلّ وارد مستغرب او مُفزِع مهوّل فنى سرعة وروده مع سرعـة
تقضّيه حكمةٌ بالغة (١٦)ونعمةٌ ظاهرة ولولا انه امسك اولياءَه وألقى على كلّ

---

(١) B الفها. (٣) B adds رحمه الله. (٣) B om. بن الاعرابى. (٤) B مقلقل.

(٥) A داعى. (٦) B om. (٧) Iḥyâ, II, 269, 28, has السعى. (٨) A كونك.

B app. كونه, but the last letter is obliterated. (٩) B om. ملهم. (١٠) AB جمله.

(١١) B وقال. (١٢) A التخييل. (١٤) B التلهف. (١٤) A مضيه. (١٥) B كانهما.

(١٦) B وحكمة.

قلب من ذلك ما اطاقه لطاشت عقولهم وذهلت نفوسهم ولكن لا حال
معلومة ومناهل مورودة وذلك لا يدوم لحظةً او طرفةً [١]عين رفقًا منه
باولياّيه حتى [٢]ينّسيّهم فيا اراد كما يريد ، وقال الوجد فى الدنيـا فليس
بكشفٍ ولكن مشاهدة قلبٍ وتوهّم حقٍّ وظنّ يقينٍ فيشاهد من رَوْح اليقين
وصفاّء الذكر لانّه منتبّه فاذا افاق من غَمْرته فقَدَ ما [٣]وجد وبقى عليه
عِلمُه فتتّع بذلك رُوحه مع ما زيد من اليقين بالمكاشفة وهذا من العبد
على حسب قرّبه وبُعْده وعلى ما يُشهد من ذلك خالئةً ، ومنهم من [٤]ثبت
فى وجهٍ وشاهد من ذلك بتمكينه فوصف بعضَ ما شاهد فيكون ذلك
حجّةً على غيرهم ولولا ذلك ما [٥]خبّروا به توقيًّا عليه وصيانةً [١]له واشفاقًا
ان يضعوه [٦]غير موضعه [٧]فيُسلبوه وربّما وقع بهم الوجد من المسموع قَبْلَ
تدبّره ومن المنظور اليه قبل الفكر فيه ولا يأمنون ان يكون ذلك من الطبع
واستحسان النفس مع ما يجدون فيه من الرقّة ويشهدون بعثه من الزيادة
فيلتبس عليهم تمييز الحقّ من الباطل [٨]ولا يجب لمن يدّعى معرفة خالقه ان
يسكن الى سواه [٩]او يشغل خاطره بناقص او يقع وهمه على زايلٍ وهذا
وإن كان مشكلاً عليه لتشابهه فانـه عند اهل النظر والتحصيل [١٠]ميّز
بالتفضيل اذ ليس ما تلقّته القلوب بمشاهدتها كما توهّمته بظنونها ولا من
كان متروكًا مُهْمَلاً كمن كان محفوظًا ولا [١]ما استُجلب كونه كما فاض عن
معدنه ولا ما نتج عن الفكر كما [١١]رشح عن الذكر وربّما يختلط ذلك على
اهل التمييز لعلّةٍ وينكشف لهم بعد زوال العلّة لانّ المتميّز بالفكر ليس كالمستهتَر
بالذكر ولا المتخيّر المختار كمن غلب عليه الوجد والاستهتار وليس هذا صفة
كلّ واجد لاختلاف احوالهم فمنهم من وجهٍ عن العلم ومنهم من وجهٍ بالعلم
ومنهم من وجهٍ علمٌ، فأمّا الوجد الذى يكون لأهل الثبات [١٢]من السكون

Af.139a

---

(١) A om.   (٢) B سسيم.   (٣) B وجه.   (٤) B سب.   (٥) B حروا.

(٦) B om.   (٧) B فيسلبه.   (٨) B لا اذ.   (٩) B و.   (١٠) B ميزا.

(١١) B رسح.   (١٢) B فى.

عن الحركة [١] والمَنَعَة بالخلوة لانّ الأُنس افنام عن الوحشة والقُرْب عن
رؤية المسافة قريبًا بما لم [٢] بادٍ [٣] فيتعالون فى وجودهم وربّما ردّهم الى
صفاتهم [٤] بُقيا عليهم لما [٥] افتطروا عليه من الحاجـة الى الغذاءِ، والنساء
فيغشهم ذلك [٦] فينزعجون من رؤيتهم ذلك [٧] انزعاجًا يظنّونها لعلّةٍ وقـد
خافوا زمانًا فيلحقهم عند ذلك الوله لطلب ما فقدوه فيحملهم على الاقتحام على
كلّ ما توهّموه انه يوصلهم، غلبت [٨] رؤيتهم التمييز فبادروا مسرعين كلّما رأوا
سرابًا ظنّوه ماءً وكلّما رأوا ماءً ظنّوه سرابًا لغلبة الطع فهم على وجوههم
[٩] ذاهبون فى كلّ وادٍ يهيمون ولكلّ بارق يتبعون، سبق سَيْلُهم مَطَرَهم
وذِكْرُهم فِكْرَهم، الى كلّ سبب [١٠] يُسْلِمون وعليه لا يعوّلون والطع يطمح
ابصارهم واليأس يزجرهم فلا يأسم يدوم [١١] فينصرفوا ولا طعم يصحّ [١٢] فيأتلفوا
أشْبَهَ شئٍ بالمجانين قد سمحت أنْفُسهم بتلف مُهَجتهم عند ما يطلبون لو
توهّموه فى تيه سلكوه او [١٣] وراءَ [١٤] بحر سجوه او [١٥] وراءَ [١٥] نار تأجّج
اقتحموها اذا [١٦] رأى ضوءَ النار لا يفصر عن تقحمها أوَما رأيتهم
مشرّدين مهيمين بالمفاوز والمهالك والقفار لا يأوون ولا [١٧] يؤوون الّا انهم
فى ذلك محفوظون [١٨] من الزلل بصدقهم فى قصدهم فهم من العلم على سَنَن،
وامّا [١٩] من فارق العلوم الظاهرة فغير مأمون عليه الزلل ومن سلك غير
المحجّة كان من السلامة على خَطَر، وكلّما [٢٠] ذكرنا من علوم الوجد ظاهرًا
وما لحقته العبارة [٢١] او أوّمَيْنا اليه بالاشارة او بدليل قام عليه او مثال
[٢٢] قاربه، فامّا ما كان غير ذلك فانه عِلْمُهُ منه وشاهدُهُ فيه وحقيقته كونه
ووصفُهُ ذَوْقه لانّ حُجج الله [٢١] تعالى على عباده [٢١] باهرةٌ [٢١] وأهلُهُ غير محتاجين

---

(١) والمنعة بالخلوة B om.   (٢) بادى AB   (٣) فيتعالون A   (٤) لقيام B.

(٥) فطروا B   (٦) فيزعجون B   (٧) ازعاجًا B   (٨) رعهم B.   (٩) ذاهين B.

(١٠) بسمون A   (١١) فينصرفون AB   (١٢) فيأتلفون AB.   (١٤) رأوا A.

(١٤) بجرًا A   (١٥) نارًا AB   (١٦) رأ B   (١٧) يؤون A   (١٧) يوون B.

(١٨) ومن A   (١٩) ما A   (٢٠) ذكرناه B.   (٢١) B om.   (٢٢) قاربه B.

الى (١) عليها لقيام الشاهد (٢) فيها وإنتفاء كلّ وصف (٣) عنها (٤) لانّها ممّا تولّى

الله (٥) كونها وإنفرد بعلم (٦) كنهها ومتّع اهل الايمان (٧) بها لما كاشفهم (٨) فيها

فلم يجتثوا عمّا وراء ذلك (٨) لغناهم (٩) بها عن غيرها لانّ ما ابدى لهم منه

فهم له مشاهدون ظاهرًا وفيه مقيمون باطنًا وهو الغيب الذى وصف الله

٥ (١٠) المؤمنين (١١) فقال (١٢) اَلَّذِينَ يُؤْمِنُونَ بِالْغَيْبِ فهم فى غيبه مغيّبون وهو

وإن (١٣) كان (١٤) غيبًا لا يلحقهم فى ذلك شكّ ولا رَيْب، فان سأل سَائِل

عن الزيادة فى وصف الوجد فيهيهات دون ذلك فكيف يوصف من ليس

له صفة غيره ولا يقام عليه شاهد غيره فهو شاهدُ نفسه وحقيقته كونه يعرفه

من وجه وينكره من لم يعرفه ويعجز الجميع (١٥) من عرفه ومن لم يعرفه

١٠ (١٦) فهو بالذوق (١٧) محسوس وصاحبُه (١٨) بالمراد مكاشَف وهو (١٩) عزيـز

موجود منيع مفقود محتجب بأنواره عن نوره وبصفاته عن إدراكه وباسمآئه

عن ذاته اعنى ذات الوجد واليقين والايمان والحقايق وكذلك المحبّة والشوق

والقرب كلّ ذلك يدقّ وصفه ولا يُدْرِكُ كنهَهُ الّا من ذاقه وتفضّل عليه

باريه (١٨) به (٢٠) فيخيّلون فيه ولا يصفونه ولا يدركونه يُلبسهم إلباسًا (٢١) ويُذهب

١٥ عنهم الوحشة ايناسًا فكلّما ازدادوا من صفته وصفًا (٢٢) كانوا من حقيقته اشدّ

بُعدًا فخرسهم فيه ابلغُ من النطق فلن يعرف منه اهله الّا ما عرّفوه واعترافهم

بالتقصير فيها نهاية العلم بها فنطقهم عىٌّ وعيّهم بلاغة ولُكَّتهم فصاحةٌ فالسايل

عن طعمه وذوقه يسأل عن محال لانّ الطعم والذوق لا يُدْرك بالوصف

دون النطعّم والتذوّق والسايل عن كنهه دليل على جهله بـه ولا

٢٠ سبيل للعالم الى جواب كلّ سايل اذ كان بعضهم يسأل عمّا لـه وبعضهم

---

(١) B عله.   (٢) B فيه.   (٣) B عنه.   (٤) B لانه.   (٥) B كونه.

(٦) B كنهه.   (٧) B به.   (٨) A لقيامهم with لغناهم in marg. as variant.

(٩) B به عن غيره and so A in marg.   (١٠) B للمؤمنين.   (١١) B adds تعلى.

من لم يعرفه B (١٥)   غيب B (١٤)   كانوا B (١٣)   Kor. 2, 2. (١٢)

ومن عرفه B (١٦)   فهم B (١٧) منسوبون.   (١٨) B om.   غريق B (١٩)

ذ حلون B (٢٠)   ويذهب B (٢١)   كان B (٢٢)

يسأل عمّا عليه فقد اخذ [١]اله على العلمآء [٢]ان لا يكتموا العلم اهله كما
اخذ [٢]اله على العلمآء ان يصونوه عن غير اهله وقد قلنا ان اهله غير
مرتابين [٤]فيسألوا ولا شاكّين [٥]فيتعرّفوا وباله التوفيق ، ولِما كانت هذه
الاحوال [٦]ليس لها نهاية كان الكلام فيها [٦]ليس لـه نهاية فقطعناه فلو
وصلناه لاتّصل الى ما لا نهاية [٨]له لانّها [٧]ازديادات فى المعارف [٨]وليست
من كسب الآدميين بل هى داخلة فى قوله [٩]عزّ وجلّ [١٠]وَلَدَيْنَا مَزِيدٌ فهذا
بعض عطاياه [١١]المعمومة لا نهاية لها ولا يُبْلَغُ وصفُها فكيف باختصاصه
اوليآءَه [١٢]بما يُورد عليهم فى كلّ وقت وزمان وطرفة عين [١٣]وأَقَلَّ من
ذلك من الاحوال التى هى مذكورة عندنا [٩]عالماً [١٤]بفضله معلومةٌ [١٥]لَا
يَعْزُبُ عَنْهُ مِثْقَالُ ذَرَّةٍ ، وهذه وان كانت ليست باكساب الآدميين وإنّما
هى خصوص وبعضها مواريث الأعمال فالطالب مـن عنـد اله المزيد قد
[١٦]احكم الأصل الذى يوجب المزيد فمن فرّط فيه فليس بمأمون عليه ان
يُسْلَبَ الاصل الذى معه [١٧]اذ لم [١٨]يَرْعَهُ حقّ رعايتـه لانّ التوقّف مع
النفوس يقطع الهجوم والهجوم مع مفارقة العلوم خطأٌ بيّنٌ فاذا قويت الرغبة
عن التوقّف فالهجوم ربّما أوصل ، فأمّا [١٩]من كان مطالبًا [٢٠]بأصل فخطأً
[٢١]يخطّيه الى الفرع قَبْلَ إحكام الاصل [٢٢]لا يؤمن عليه الزلل وباله
التوفيق ، فهذا ما [٢٣]اختصرته من كتاب الوجد لابن الاعرابى [٢٤]وباله
التوفيق ،

[١] B adds وجلّ عزّ.   [٢] The words from ان to العلماء are suppl. in
marg. A.   [٣] A om.   [٤] فيسألون A فيشكّون B.   [٥] فيتعرفون AB.
[٦] ليست B.   [٧] ارادات A اردبات B.   [٨] وليس B.   [٩] B om.
[١٠] Kor. 50, 34.   [١١] المعموضة B.   [١٢] لها B.   [١٣] اقل B.
[١٤] معضله B.   [١٥] Kor. 34, 3.   [١٦] علم B.   [١٧] اذا A.   [١٨] يرعاه AB.
[١٩] ما A.   [٢٠] B om.   [٢١] يخطّيه خطأً بأصل.   [٢١] محطه A.   [٢٢] A om.
[٢٣] اختصر A.   [٢٤] رحمه اله B.   لا يومن عليه الزلل.

كتاب (١)اثبات الآيات والكرامات،

باب فى معانى الآيات والكرامات (٢)وذكر من كان له شىءٌ من ذلك،

(٣)قال الشيخ رحمه الله حُكى عن سهل بن عبد الله (٤)رحمه الله انه قال الآيات (٥)لله والمُعجزات للانبياء والكرامات للاولياء ولخيار المسلمين، وحُكى عن سهل بن عبد الله (٤)رحمه الله انه كان يقول من زهد فى الدنيا اربعين يومًا (٦)صادقًا مُخلصا فى ذلك تظهر له الكرامات من الله عزّ وجلّ ومن لم يظهر له ذلك فلما عدم فى زهده من الصدق والاخلاص او كلامًا نحو ذلك، وعن الجُنيْد (٤)رحمه الله انه قال من (٧)يتكلّم فى الكرامات ولا يكون له من ذلك شىء مَثَله مثلُ من يضع التبن، قيل لسهل (٤)رحمه الله فى الحكاية التى قبل هذه فمن زهد فى الدنيا اربعين يومًا (٨)كيف يكون ذلك فقال يأخذ (٩)ما يشآء كما يشآء من حيث يشآء، وسمعت (١٠)ابن سالم يقول الايمان اربعة اركان ركنٌ منه الايمان بالقدر وركنٌ منه الايمان بالقدرة وركنٌ منه التبرّئ من الحول والقوة وركنٌ منه الاستعانة بالله عزّ وجلّ فى جميع الاشياء، وسمعت (١٠)ابن سالم (٤)رحمه الله وقيل له ما معنى قولك الايمان بالقدرة فقال هو ان تؤمن ولا ينكر قلبك بأن يكون لـه عبدٌ (١١)بالمشرق (١٢)ويكون من كرامة الله (١٣)تعالى (٤)له ان يعطيه من القدرة

A f.140b

---

(١) الاثبات B.   (٢) B وذكر من كان for ومن ذكر.   (٣) B om. قال

(١) الشيخ رحمه الله.   (٥) B adds عز وجل.   (٤) B om.   (٦) B adds من قلبه.

(٧) نكلم B.   (٨) وكيف B.   (٩) من A.   (١٠) بن B.   (١١) كالمشرق B.

(١٢) يكون B.   (١٣) عز وجل B.

وما يتقلّب (١) من بينه على يساره فيكون بالمغرب بعنى تؤمن بجواز ذلك
وكونه، والصحيح عن سهل بن عبد الله انه كان يقول لشابّ كان يصحبه
ان (٢) كنتَ تخاف من السَّبُع بعد ذلك فلا تصحبنى، (٣) ودخلتُ (٤) مع جماعة
(٥) بتُسْتَرَ (٦) قصر سهل بن عبد الله (٤) رحمه الله (٧) فدخلنا فى القصر بيتًا
كان الناس (٨) يسمّونه بيت السَّبُع فسألناهم عن ذلك فقالوا كان تجىء السباع
الى سهل بن عبد الله (٤) رحمه الله فكان (٩) يُدخِلها هذا البيت (١٠) ويضيفها
ويطعمها اللحم ثمّ (١١) يخلّيها وإنه اعلم بذلك وما رأيتُ احدًا من صالحى اهل
نُستَر ينكر ذلك، وسمعت ابا (١٢) الحسين البصرى (١٣) رحمه الله يقول كان
بعبّادان رجل اسود فقير يأوى الخرابات فحملتُ معى (١٤) شيئًا وطلبته فلما
وقعت عينه علىّ نبسّم وأشار بيده الى الارض فرأيت بعنى الارض (١٤) كلّها
ذهبًا (١٥) تلمع ثمّ قال لى هاتِ ما معك فناولته ما كان معى وهربت منـه
وهالنى امرُه، وسمعت الحسين بن احمد الرازى (٤) رحمه الله يقول سمعت ابا
سليمان الخوّاص (٤) رحمه الله يقول كنت راكبًا حمارًا (٤) لى بومًا وكان
يؤذيه الذباب فيطأطئ رأسَه (١٦) فكنت اضرب رأسه بخشبة كانت فى
(١٧) يدى فرفع الحمار رأسه (١٨) الىّ وقال اضربْ فانّك هو (١٩) ذا تضرب
(٢٠) على رأسك (٢١) فقال ابو عبد الله فقلت لأبى سليمان يأبا سليمان وقع لك
ذلك او سمعتَه فقال سمعتُه يقول كما تسمعنى، وسمعت احمد بن عطاء
الروذبارى يقول كان لى مذهبٌ فى امر الطهارة (٢٢) فكنت ليلةً من الليالى
استنجى او قال كنت (٢٣) اتوضّأ الى ان مضى من الليل رُبعه ولم يطب قلبى
فتفجّرت وبكيت وقلت يا ربّ العفوَ صونًا فسمعت صونًا ولم (٢٤) ار احدًا يقول

A.f.141a

---

(١) B عن.   (٢) B عدت.   (٣) B ودخلنا.   (٤) B om.   (٥) B يعرف بتستر.

(٦) B فى قصر.   (٧) B فرايت.   (٨) B بسموه.   (٩) B يدخلهم.   (١٠) B ويضيفهم.

(١١) B يخلّيهم.   (١٢) B app.   (١٣) B الخير.   (١٤) B شى.   (١٤) B كله.

(١٥) B بلع.   (١٦) B فكان تضرب.   (١٧) B بيد.   (١٨) B اليه.   (١٩) B ذى.

(٢٠) A om.   (٢١) B قال.   (٢٢) B وكت.   (٢٣) B اتوضى.   (٢٤) B ارا.

يأبا عبد الله العفو فى العلم، وكان عند جعفر الخُلْدِىّ [١] رحمه الله نصٌّ
وكان يومًا من الايّام راكبًا فى سارية فى الدجلة فأراد ان يعطى الملّاح
[٢] قطعته فحلّ [٣] الشُّسْتَكه وكان النصّ فيها فوقع النصّ فى الدجلة وكان
عنه دعاء للضالّة مجرَّبٌ فكان به يدعو [١] فوجد النصّ فى وسط اوراق
كان يَصْفحها والدعاء اللهمّ يا جامع الناس لِيَوْمٍ لا رَيْبَ فيه اجمعْ علىّ
ضالّتى، قال ثم أورانى ابو الطيّب العكّى [٤] جُزْءٌ قد جمع فيه ذِكْرَ كلِّ ضالّة
ردّ الله الى من دعا بهذا الدعاء فى مدّة قليلة فنظرتُ فيه [٥] وكان اوراقًا
كثيرةً، وسمعت حمزة بن عبد الله العَلَوى يقول دخلت على ابى الخَيْرِ
التيناتى وكنت قد اعتقدت فى سرّى فيما بينى وبين الله [١] تعالى ان اسلّم
عليه وأخرج ولا اتناول عنــه طعامًا ثمّ دخلت فسلّمت عليه وودّعتــه
وخرجت من عنه فلمّا تباعدت من القرية فاذا به وقد حمل [١] معه طعامًا
فقال لى يا فتى كُلْ هذا فقد خرجتَ الساعةَ من اعتقادك او [٦] كلامًا هذا
معناه، وهؤلاء القوم مشهورون بالصدق والديانة وكلّ واحد منهم امام مُشار
اليه فى [٧] ناحيته ومقتدًى [٨] به فى أحكام الدين [٩] فقد صدّقهم المسلمون فى
احكام دينهم وقبلوا [١٠] شهادتهم على رسول الله صلعم فيما رووا عنه وأسندوا
اليه من الاخبار والآثار [١١] ولا يجوز ان يكذّبهم احدٌ [١٢] ويتهّمهم فى هــذه
الحكايات وما يُشبه ذلك واذا كانوا صادقين فى واحد ففى الجميع كذلك
وبالله التوفيق،

---

(١) B om.   (٢) قطعه B.   (٣) السمسكه B.   (٤) جزوا B.

(٥) وكان فيه B.   (٦) كلام A.   (٧) ناحيه A.   (٨) فى احكامهم فى B.

(٩) الدين B.   (١٠) شهادانهم B.   (١١) فلا B.   (١٢) او B.

ويتهمهم.

باب فى حُجّة من انكر (١)كون ذلك من اهل الظاهر والحُجّة عليهم
فى جواز ذلك للاولياء والفرق بينهم وبين الانبياء
(٢)عليهم السلم فى ذلك،

(٣)قال الشيخ رحمه الله قال اهل الظاهر لا يجوز كون هذه الكرامات
لغير الانبياء عليهم السلم لانّ الانبياء مخصوصون بذلك والآيات (٤)والمعجزات
والكرامات (٤)واحدة وانّما (٥)سُمّيت معجزات لإعجاز الخلق عن الاتيان بمثلها
فمن اثبت من ذلك شيئًا لغير الانبياء (٦)عليهم السلم فقد ساوى بينهم ولم
يفرّق بين الانبياء وبينهم، (٢)قال الشيخ رحمه الله (٦)من انكر ذلك فانّما
انكرها احترازًا من ان يقع وهنٌ (٧)فى معجزات الانبياء عليهم السلم وقد
غلط قائل هذا القول لان بينهم وبين الانبياء عليهم السلم فى ذلك (٨)فرقًا
من جهات شتّى فوجهٌ منها ان الانبياء (١)عليهم السلم مستعبدون باظهار
ذلك للخلق والاحتجاج بها على (٩)من يدعوهم الى الله (١٠)تعالى فمتى ما كتموا
ذلك فقد خالفوا الله (١)تعالى فى كتمانها والاولياء (١١)مستعبدون بكتمان
ذلك عن الخلق واذا اظهروا من ذلك شيئًا للخلق لاتّخاذ (١٢)الجاه عندهم
فقد خالفوا الله (١)تعالى وعصَوْه باظهار ذلك، والوجه الآخر فى الفرق بينهم
وبين الانبياء عليهم السلم ان (١٣)الانبياء (١)عليهم السلم يحتجّون بمعجزاتهم على
المشركين لانّ قلوبهم قاسية لا يؤمنون بالله (١)عزّ وجلّ والاولياء يحتجّون
بذلك على نفوسهم حتى تطمئنّ وتُوقن ولا تضطرب ولا (١٤)تجزع عند فوت

(١) B om.   (٢) B om.   (٣) B om.   عليهم السلم.
(٤) واحد B   (٥) A سمى.   (٦) ومن B.   (٧) من A.   (٨) AB فرق.
(٩) ما B.   (١٠) عز وجل B.   (١١) مستعبدين A.   (١٢) فى الجاه B.
(١٣) والانبيا B   (١٤) A تجرع.

الرزق لأنها أمّارةٌ بالسوٰء جاحدة مشركة مجبولة على الشكّ ليس عندها يقين
بما ضمن لها خالقها من الرزق وذكر القَسم عليها، وقد سألتُ (١)ابن سالم عن
ذلك فقلت له ما معنى الكرامات وهم قد أُكرموا حتى تركوا الدنيا اختيارًا
فكيف أُكرموا بأن يجعل لهم الحجارة ذهبًا فما وجه ذلك فقال لا يعطيهم
ذلك لقدرها ولكن يعطيهم ذلك حتى يحتجّوا بكون ذلك على انفسهم عند
اضطرابها وجزعها من فوت الرزق الذى قسم الله لهم (٢)فيقولوا الذى يقدر
على ان يصير (٣)تلك الحجارة ذهبًا كما هو (٤)ذا تنظر اليه أليس بقادر ان
يسوق (٥)رزقك اليك من حيث لا (٦)تحسبه فيحتجّوا بذلك على (٧)ضجيج
نفوسهم عند فوت الرزق ويقطعوا (٨)بذلك حُجَج انفسهم فيكون ذلك سببًا
لرياضة نفوسهم وتأديبًا لها، وقد حكى لنا (٩)ابن سالم فى معنى ذلك حكايةً
عن سهل بن عبد الله (١٠)رحمه الله انه قال كان رجل بالبصرة يقال له
اسحق بن احمد وكان من ابناء الدنيا فخرج من الدنيا اعنى من جميع ما
كان له وتاب وصحب سهلاً (١٠)رحمه الله فقال يومًا لسهل (١٠)رحمه الله يا أبا
محمّد انّ نفسى هذه (١١)ليس تترك الضجيج والصراخ من خوف فوت القوت
والقِوام فقال (١٠)له سهل (١٠)رحمه الله خُذْ ذلك الحجر وسلْ ربّك ان
(١٢)يصيّره لك طعامًا تأكله فقال له ومن إماى فى ذلك حتى (١٣)افعل
(١٠)ذلك فقال سهل إمامك ابرهيم عليه السلٰم (١٠)حيث قال (١٤)رَبِّ أَرِنِى
كَيْفَ نُحْيِى ٱلْمَوْتَىٰ قَالَ أَوَلَمْ تُؤْمِنْ قَالَ بَلَىٰ وَلَٰكِنْ لِيَطْمَئِنَّ قَلْبِى، فالمعنى فى
ذلك ان النفس لا تطمئنّ الّا بروٰية العين لان من جبلّتها الشكّ فقال
ابرهيم عليه السلٰم أرِنِى كَيْفَ تطمئنّ نفسى فانّى مؤمن بذلك والنفس لا تطمئنّ
الّا بروٰية العين، فكذٰلك الاولياٰء يُظهر الله (١٠)تعالى لهم الكرامات تأديبًا

Af.142a

لنفوسهم وتهذيبًا لها وزيادةً [1] لها ويكون فى ذلك [2] فرقٌ بينهم وبين الانبيآء [3] عليهم السلم [4] لأنّهم يُعطَوْن المعجزة للاحتجاج بها [5] فى الدعوة والدلالة على الله [6] تعالى والاقرار [7] بوحدانيته تعالى، والوجه الثالث فى الفرق بينهم وبين الانبيآء عليهم السلم [7] لان الانبيآء كلّما زيدت معجزاتهم وكثرت يكون اتمَّ لمعانيهم وأَثبَتَ لقلوبهم كما كان نبيّنا صلعم قد أُعطى جميع ما أُعطى الانبيآء [8] عليهم السلم من المعجزات ثم [8] زيادةَ اشيآء لم [9] يُعطَ [10] احدٌ غيره مثل المعراج وانشقاق القمر ونبع المآء من بين اصابعه، وشرح ذلك يطول ومقصودنا من ذلك ان الانبيآء عليهم السلم كلّما زيدت لهم من المعجزات يكون اتمَّ لمعانيهم وفضلهم وهؤلآء الذين لهم الكرامات من الاولياء كلّما زيدت فى كراماتهم يكون وَجَلهم أكثرَ وخوفهم [11] أكثرَ [12] حذرًا ان يكون ذلك من المكر الخفىّ [3] لهم والاستدراج وأن يكون ذلك نصيبهم من الله عزّ وجلّ وسببًا لسقوط منزلتهم عند الله عزّ وجلّ،

باب فى الادلة على اثبات الكرامات للاوليآء وعلّة قول من قال

لا يكون ذلك الّا للانبيآء عليهم السلم،

[14] قال الشيخ رحمه الله والدليل على جواز ذلك الكتاب والأثر قال الله [14] تعالى [15] وَهُزِّى إِلَيْكِ بِجِذْعِ ٱلنَّخْلَةِ تُسَاقِطْ عَلَيْكِ رُطَبًا جَنِيًّا ومَرْيَم لم تكن نبيّةً، وحديث النبىّ صلعم فى قصّة جُرَيْج الراهب وكلام الصبىّ وجريج لم يكن نبيًّا، وقال النبىّ صلعم فى قصّة الغار بينا ثلثة [16] يمشون اذ

---

(١) A لها.   (٢) AB فرقًا.   (٣) B om.   (٤) A ثم أنهم. The passage beginning لأنهم and ending وبين الانبيآء عليهم السلم is suppl. in marg. A.
(٥) B على.   (٦) B بوحدانية الله.   (٧) A om. لان الانبيآء.   (٨) B زاده.
(٩) B تعط.   (١٠) B لاحد.   (١١) B أزيد.   (١٢) B حذارًا.   (١٣) B om.
(١٤) B adds ذكره.   (١٥) Kor. 19, 25.   (١٦) B يسون.   قال الشيخ رحمه الله

أوام الليل الى غار الحديث، وما رُوِى [1] عنه صلعم بينا رجل يمشى ومعه
بقرة فركبها فقالت [3] يا عبد الله ما خُلقنا لهذا انّما خُلقنا للحرث فقال القوم
سبحان الله فقال النبيّ صلعم آمنت به [2] أنا وأبو بكر وعمر [4] رضى الله عنهما
وليس ها فى القوم ولم يُذكر ان [5] الراكب [6] للبقرة كان نبيًّا، وكذلك
٥ حديث الذيب الذى كلّم الراعى ولم يُذكر انه كان نبيًّا، وقد رُوِى عن
النبيّ صلعم انه قال ان فى أُمّتى مكلَّمون ومحدَّثون وانّ عمر بن الخطّاب
رضى الله عنه منهم والمكلَّم والمحدَّث اتمّ [7] فى معناه من جميع الكرامات التى
ذكر [7] الله [8] عزّ وجلّ [9] على البُدلاء والاولياء والصالحين، وحديث عمر
رضى الله عنه انه قال [10] فى خطبته يا ساريةُ الجَبَلَ فسَمع صوتُه [11] بالعسكر
١٠ على باب نهاوند، وقد رُوِى فى الحديث لعلىّ بن ابى طالب ولفاطمة رضى
الله عنهما كرامات [12] وإجابات كثيرة، وقد رُوِى عن جماعة من اصحاب
رسول الله صلعم فى مثل ذلك اشياء مثل حديث أُسَيد بن [13] حُضَيْر
[14] وعتّاب بن بشير انهما خرجا من عند رسول الله صلعم فى ليلة مظلمة
فاضاء لهما رأس عصا احدها كالسراج على حسب ما رُوِى فى الخبر،
١٥ وحديث ابى الدّرداء وسلمان الفارسى [4] رضى الله عنهما انه كان بينهما قصعة
فسبّحت حتى سمعا تسبيحها، وقصّة [15] العلاء بن الحضرى حيث بعثه رسول
الله صلعم فى غزاة فحال بينهم وبين الموضع قطعة من البحر فدعا الله [4] تعالى
باسمه الاعظم ومشوا على الماء كما جاء [16] فى الخبر، وكذلك [16] دعاؤه لَمّا
استقبله السبع، وحديث عبد الله بن عمر [4] رضى الله عنه حين لقى الجماعة
٢٠ الذين وقفوا على الطريق [17] من خوف السبع فطرد السبع من طريقهم ثمّ

---

(١) B عن النبى. (٢) B يا ابا. (٣) B وانا. (٤) B om. (٥) B الرجل.
(٦) B البقرة. (٧) B ذكرت. (٨) B. om. (٩) B عن. الله عز وجل.الراكب
(١٠) B om. فى خطبته. (١١) B فى العسكر. (١٢) B وإجابات. (١٣) B حصين. العلى.
(١٤) A gives as عباد a variant. (١٥) B الحصين.
(١٦) AB دعاه. (١٧) B om. من خوف السبع.

21

قال انّما يُسَلَّطُ على (١) ابن آدم من يَخافه ولو ان ابن آدم لم يَخف شيئًا
غير الله لم يُسلّط (٢) الله عليه شيئًا يُخافه غيره، ومثله فى الاخبار (٣) كثير، Af.143a
والصحيح عن رسول الله صلعم ما قال رُبُّ أَشْعَثَ أَغْبَرَ (٤) ذى طِمْرَيْن لو
أَقْسَمَ على الله لأَبَرَّ قَسَمَهُ وان مُلِك منهم، ولا يكون فى الكرامات
٥ شىء اتمّ من ان يُقسم (٢) العبد على الله (٢) تعالى فيُبِرَّ قسمه وقد قال الله (٥) عزّ
وجلّ (٦) اَدْعُونِى أَسْتَجِبْ لَكُمْ ولم يقل فى شىء دون شىء، وقد رُوى ايضًا
لجماعة من التابعين بالاسانيد (٧) الصحيحة كرامات (٨) وإجابات يطول ذكرها
(٩) إن ذكرْنا بعضها فكيف كلّها، وقد صنّف العلماء (١٠) فى ذكرها (١٠) ورواياتها
عنهم مصنّفات، وقد (١١) رُوى اشياء فى الحديث من الكرامات (١٢) كثيرة
١٠ من ذلك لعامر بن عبد (١٣) القيس وللحسن بن ابى الحسن البصرى ولمُسلم
ابن يسار ولثابت (١٤) البُنانى ولصالح المُرّى ولبكر بن عبد الله المُزَنى
ولأُوَيْس القَرَنى ولهَرِم بن حيّان ولأبى مُسلم الخَوْلانى ولصلة بن أَشْيَم وللربيع
ابن خُثْيم ولداود الطائى ولمُطَرّف بن عبد الله بن الشِّخِّير ولسعيد بن
المسيّب ولعطاء (١٥) السُّلَمى ولغيرهم من التابعين قد (١٦) رووا عن كلّ واحد
١٥ من هؤلاء وغير هؤلاء كرامات كثيرة (١٧) وإجابات وأشياء قد (١٨) ظهرت
لهم لا يتهيّأ لأحد ان يدفع ذلك (١٩) لصحّتها عند اهل الرواية، وكذلك لطبقة
أخرى بعدهم مثل مُلِك بن دينار وفَرْقَد السَّنجى وعُتْبة الغلام وحبيب العجمى
ومحمّد بن واسع ورابعة العدويّة وعبد الواحد بن زَيد وأيّوب (٢٠) السّختيانى
وغير ذلك مِمّن كان فى عصرهم فاذا (٢١) روى عنهم العلماء (٢٢) والرواية
٢٠ (٢٣) الذين كانوا فى عصرهم وقد صحّ عنهم ذلك عندهم وقد حدّثوا بها مثل

(١) AB بنى. (٢) B om. (٣) B كثيره. (٤) A om. ذى طمرين.

(٥) B ثناوه جلّ. (٦) Kor. 40, 62. (٧) B الصحاح. (٨) B اجبات.

(٩) وان B. (١٠) ورواياتها. (١١) B رووا. (١٢) B كبيرا. قيس.

(١٤) B النانى بن. (١٥) A السليمى. (١٦) B روى. (١٧) B اجبات.

(١٨) B ظهر. (١٩) B لصحته. (٢٠) B الشختيانى. (٢١) A رووا B روا.

(٢٢) B om. و. (٢٣) B الذى.

ايّوب (١)السختيانى وحمّاد بن زيد وسُفْيَن الثَّورى وغيرهم من الايمّة والثقات
ولم (٢)ينكر ذلك واحد منهم وهم ايمّتنا فى الدين وبرواياتهم صحّ عندنا علم
الحدود والأحكام وعلمُ الحلال والحرام فكيف يجوز ان نصدّقهم فى بعض ما
يروون ولا نصدّقهم فى بعض ذلك ، وقد رأيتُ جماعة من اهل (٣)العلم
٥ جمعوا ما يشاكل هذا الذى ذكرنا من كرامات الاولياء والاجابات والذى
ظهر لهم فى الوقت فى هذا المعنى فذكروا انهم قد جمعوا فى ذلك اكثر من
الف حكاية والف خبر فكيف يجوز ان يقال (٤)ذلك كلّه كذبٌ موضوع
وان صحّ من الجميع واحد فقد صحّ الكلّ فانّ القليل والكثير فى ذلك سواء،
والذى يحتجّ بانّ الذى كان قبل النبيّ صلعم من ذلك كان إكرامًا لنبيّ
١٠ ذلك الزمان الذى كان (٥)ذلك فى وقته والذى كان لأصحاب رسول الله
صلعم كان ذلك إكرامًا للنبيّ صلعم فيقال له فالذى كان ايضًا للتابعين
ولمن بعدهم وما يكون من مثل ذلك الى يوم القيمة (٦)من الكرامات فكلّ
ذلك إكرامًا للنبيّ صلعم لأنه افضلُ الانبياء (٧)عليه السلم وأمّته خير الأمم
وكما استحال ان يكون لنبيّ من الانبياء (٨)عليهم السلم شىء من المعجزات الّا
١٥ وقد كان للنبيّ صلعم (٨)من مثل ذلك (٩)او اتمّ من ذلك وأكثر(١٠)فكذلك
يستحيل ان يكون فى الأمم السالفة لقوم منهم شىء من الكرامات إكرامًا
(١١)لأنبيائهم الّا ويكون فى أمّة محمّد صلعم ايضًا لطايفة منهم اكثر من ذلك
إكرامًا لمحمّد صلعم مَعَمّا ان فى أمّة محمّد صلعم من لا يرى ذلك حالاً ولا
مرتبةً ولا كرامةً ويرى ذلك اختبارًا(١٢) ومحنة موضوعةً على طُرُق اصفياءه
٢٠ والمحصوصين من اوليآيه فهم يحشون من ذلك اذا ظهر لهم سُقوطَ منزلتهم
عند الله (١٣)تعالى ونكوصهم على عقبيهم ونزولهم عن درجتهم ولا يعدّون (١٤)مَنْ

(١) الشختيانى B.   (٢) النقل B.   (٣) ان ذلك B.   (٤) يذكر B.   (٥) فى A.

الشختيانى for ذلك فى وقته B.   (٦) من الكرامات B om.   (٧) B om. In A

صح is written over عليه.   (٨) B om.   (٩) و B.   (١٠) A فذلك.

لمن B (١٤)   عزّوجل B (١٣)   او محنة A (١٢)   لنبيهم B (١١).

ركن الى ذلك ورضى به حالاً أنه من اهل الخصوص، ونحن نذكر فى ذلك
بابًا نبيّن فيه ذلك ان شَاءَ الله وإنّما اردنا بذكر ذلك جواز كونه وبطلان
قول من زعم ان كون ذلك غير جائزٍ فى الأُمّة،

باب فى ذكر (١) مقامات اهل الخصوص فى الكرامات وذِكْرِ من
ظهر له شئ من (٢) الكرامات (٣) فكره ذلك
وخشى من الفتنة،

(٤) قال الشيخ رحمه الله ذُكر عند سهل بن عبد الله (٥) رحمه الله الكرامات
فقال (٦) وما الآيات (٧) وما الكرامات شئ (٨) تنقضى لوقتها ولكن اكبر
الكرامات أن تبدل خُلُقًا مذمومًا من اخلاق نفسك بخُلُق محمود، وعن Af.144a
ابى يزيد البسطامى (٥) رحمه الله انه قال كان فى (٩) بدايتى (١٠) يُربنى الحقّ
الآيات والكرامات فلا ألتفتُ اليها فلمّا رآنى كذلك جعل لى الى معرفته
سبيلاً، وقيل لأبى (١١) يزيد (٥) رحمه الله فلان يقال (٥) انه يبرّ فى ليلة الى
مكّة فقال الشيطان يبرّ فى لحظة (٥) من المشرق الى المغرب وهو فى لعنة الله،
وقيل له (١٢) انّ فلانًا (١٣) يمشى على المَاء فقال الحيتان فى المَاء والطير فى
الهوَاء اعجبُ من ذلك، سمعت طيفُور بن عيسى يقول قال موسى بن عيسى
قال ابى قال ابو يزيد (٥) رحمه الله لو ان رجلاً بسط مصلاه على المَاء
وتربّع فى (١٤) الهوَاء فلا تغترّوا به حتى تنظروا كيف (١٥) تجدونه فى الامر
والنهى، (١٦) قال الجنيد (٥) رحمه الله حجاب قلوب الخاصة المختصّة (١٧) برؤية

---

(١) مقالات B. (٢) ذلك B. (٣) فكره وخشى B. (٤) B om. قال
.الشيخ رحمه الله (٥) B om. (٦) ما B. (٧) والكرامات B. (٨) ينقص B
.مشا B (٩) .بداى B (١٠) .يوربنى B (١١) زيد B. (١٢) .يقال ان B
.الهوى B (١٤) .تجدوه B (١٥) .وقال B (١٦) .لروية B (١٧)

التّنعّم والتلذّذ بالعطآء والسكون الى الكرامات، سمعت [١]ابن سالم يقول
سمعت ابى يقول كان رجل يصحب سهل بن عبد الله [٢]رحمه الله يقال له
عبد الرحمن بن احمد فقال يومًا لسهل يأبا محمّد ربّما اتوضّأ للصلاة
فيسيل المآء من يدى فيصير قُضبان ذهب وفضّة فقال له سهل يا حبيبى
٥ أما علمتَ ان الصبيان اذا بكوا يُناوَلون خشخاشةً حتى [٣]يشتغلوا بها فانظرْ
أيشَ هو [٤]ذا تعمل، [٥]وفيا حكاه جعفر الخُلْدى [٢]رحمه الله قال حدّثنى
ابو بكر الكتّانى قال لى ابو الأزهر وغير واحد من إخواننا حكى عن
ابى حمزة قال اجتمعوا على باب يفتحونه فلم ينفتح لهم [٣]قال ابو حمزة تعوّذوا
فأخذ [٦]الغلق [٧]بيده فحرّكه فقال بكدى إلّا فتحتَهُ فانفتح الغلق، [٨]وذُكر
١٠ عن النورى [٢]رحمه الله انه وافى ليلةً الى الدجلة قال فوجدتها وقد [٩]التزق
الشطّ بالشطّ فقلت قال وعزّتك لا [١٠]عبرتها إلّا فى زَوْرق، [٨]وحكى
عن ابى يزيد البسطامى [٢]رحمه الله انه قال دخل علىَّ ابو علىّ السِّنْدى
[٢]رحمه الله وكان أُستاذه وكان معه جرابٌ [١١]فصبّه بين يدىَّ فاذا هو
الوان الجواهر فقلت له من اين الك هذا قال وإفيتُ واديًا هاهنا فاذا
١٥ [١٢]هى نُصىء كالسراج فحملتُ هذا منها قال [١٣]فقلت له كيف كان وقتُك
وقتَ ورودك الوادىَ قال كان وقتى وقت فترة عن الحال الذى كنت
فيه قبل ذلك وذكر الحكاية، والمعنى فى ذلك ان فى وقت فترته [١٤]شغلوه
بالجواهر، [٢]قال أَملَى علينا احمد بن علىّ الوجيهى بالرَّملة حكايةً عن
[١٥]محمّد بن يوسف البنّاء قال كان ابو تُراب النَخْشَبى [٢]رحمه الله صاحب
٢٠ كرامات فسافرتُ معه سنةً فاجتمع معنا اربعون رجلاً وكان يظهر لهم من
الإرفاق ما [١٦]شآء الله قال ثمّ دلّهم ابو تُراب [٢]رحمه الله على الطريق

(١) B بن. (٢) B om. (٣) A يشغلوا. (٤) B ذى. (٥) B فى،
(٦) A المغلق. (٧) In A فحرّكه is suppl. in marg. before بين. (٨) B حكى
(٩) B النصق. (١٠) B اعبرها. (١١) B فصبها. (١٢) B هو يضى،
(١٣) B قلت، (١٤) B أشغلوه، (١٥) A احمد. (١٦) B يشا،

وعدلْنا فلم يبق معنا الَّا شابٌ نحيل فقال ابو تراب ليس فيهم اقوى ايمانًا
من هذا قال فسِرْنا ايّامًا واحتجْنا الى طعام نأكله قال فعدل ابو تراب عن
الطريق ساعةً ثمّ جاء ومعه عِذْقٌ من المَوْز فوضع بين ايدينا ونحن فى
وسط الرمال قال فجهد ابو تراب بهذا الفتى ان يأكل من ذلك (١)الموز
فلم يأكل فقلنا له لِمَ لا تأكل فقال الحال الذى اعتقِدُه فيما بينى وبين
الله (٢)تعالى تَرْكُ المعلومات وأنت قد صرتَ معلوى فلا أصحبك من بعد
ذلك، قال محمّد بن يوسف قلتُ لأبى تراب (٣)رحمه الله ان شِيئتَ أَعزِمْ
عليه وان شِيئتَ أَتْركُه فقال له ابو تراب كُنْ مع ما وقع لك (٤)من ذلك
او كما قال والله اعلم، سمعتُ (٥)ابن سالم يقول لمّا مات اسحق بن احمد
دخل سهل بن عبد الله صومعته فوجد فيها سَفَطًا فيه (٧)قارورتان فى
(٧)واحدة منها شىء احمر وفى (٨)الأخرى شىء (٩)اصفر ووجد (١٠)شوشقة
ذهب (١١)وشوشقة فضّة قال فأمر (١٢)أبى حتى رمى (١٣)بالشوشقتين فى الدجلة
وخلط ما فى القارورتين (١٤)بالتراب وكان على اسحق بن احمد دَيْنٌ قال
(٥)ابن سالم قال ابى قلتُ لسهل (٣)رحمه الله أَيْشَ كان الذى فى القارورتين
قال امّا الاحمر فلو طُرح وزن درهم منه على مثاقيل من النحاس لصار ذهبًا
وامّا (١٥)الاصفر فلو طُرح وزن درهم منه على مثاقيل من النحاس لصار فضّةً
Af.145a (١٦)والشوشقتان كانت تجربةً، قال فقلت له ايش منعه من ان بعل ذلك
ويؤدّى دَيْنه قال يا دوست خاف على ايمانه قلت انا لابن سالم فلو أدّى من
ذلك دَيْنه سهلُ بن عبد الله (٣)رحمه الله (١٧)أَلم يكن أَوْلَى من إفساده فقال
(٥)ابن سالم كان سهلُ (٣)رحمه الله أخْوَفَ على ايمان نفسه منه ثم قال منعه

(١) A om. from الموز to لا تأكل.   (٢) B عزوجل.   (٣) B om.

(٤) B om. من ذلك.   (٥) B بن.   (٦) B قارورتين.   (٧) B واحد.

(٨) B الاخر.   (٩) B ايضا.   (١٠) A سوسقة.   (١١) A وسوسقة.   (١٢) B لابى.

(١٣) A بالسوسقتين.   (١٤) A فى التراب.   (١٥) B الايض.   (١٦) A والسوسقتين

B والشوسقتين.   (١٧) A لم.

من ذلك الوَرَع لأن ذلك يتغيّر بعد سبعين سنة، وذُكر عن ابى حفص او عن غيره انه كان جالسًا وحَوْلَهُ اصحابه قال فنزل ظبىٌ من الجبل وبرك عندهم قال فبكى ابو حفص (١)او الشيخ وسيّب ذلك الظبى فسُئل عن بكآيه فقال كنتم حولى فوقع فى قلبى ان لو كان لى شاة لذبحتُ لكم فلمّا برك هذا ٥ الظبى عندنا (٢)شبّهتُ نفسى بفِرْعَوْن حين سأل الله (٣)تعالى ان يُجرى معه النيل (٤)فأجراه فبكيتُ وسألتُهُ الإقالة ممّا تمنّيتُ وسيّبتُ الظبى، وقال بعض المشايخ لا تعجّبوا ممّن (٥)لم يضع فى جيبه شيئًا فيُدخل يد فيُخرج من جيبه ما يريد ولكن تعجّبوا ممّن وضع فى جيبه شيئًا فيُدخل يد فى جيبه فلا (٦)يجِد فلا يتغيّر، (٧)قال (٨)ابن عطآء سمعت ابا الحسين النورى يقول كان ١٠ فى (٩)نفسى من هذه الكرامات شىء فأخذتُ قَصَبةً من الصبيان وقمت بين زَوْرقين ثم قلت وعزّتك لَئِن لم تخرج لى سمكة فيها ثلثة أرطال (٩)فلأُغرقنّ نفسى قال (١٠)فخرج لى سمكة فيها ثلثة أرطال قال فبلغ ذلك الجُنَيْد (٣)رحمه الله فقال (٩)كان حكمُهُ ان يخرج له أَفْعَى تلدغه يعنى انه لو (١١)لدغته حيّةٌ كان انفعَ له فى دينه من ذلك لأن فى ذلك فتنةٌ وفى لدغ الحيّة تطهير ١٥ وكفّارة، (٧)قال يحيى بن مُعاذ (٩)رحمه الله اذا رأيتَ الرجل يشير الى الآيات والكرامات فطريقه طريق الأبدال واذا رأيته يشير الى الآلآء والنّعمآء فطريقه طريق (١٢)اهل المحبّة وهو أعْلَى من الذى قَبْلَ واذا رأيته يشير الى الذِّكر ويكون معلّقًا بالذكر الذى (١٣)ذكَرَهُ فطريقه طريق العارفين وهو أعْلَى درجة من جميع الاحوال،

---

(١)باب فى ذكر من كان له شىء من هذه الكرامات فأظهرها
لأصحابه لصدقه وطهارته وسلامة قلبه وصحّته،

(٢)قال الشيخ رحمه الله اخبرنى جعفر (٤)الخُلْدى (٤)رحمه الله فيما قرأتُ
عليه قال حدّثنى الجُنَيْد (٤)رحمه الله قال دخلتُ على سرىّ (٤)السَّقَطى (٤)رحمه
الله يوماً فقال لى أُعْجِبُك من عصفور يجىء فيسقط على هذا الرواق فآخذُ
(٥)لقّةً فأقُفُها فى كفّى فيسقط على أطراف اناملى فيأكل فلمّا كان (٦)فى وقت
من الاوقات سقط على الرواق ففتتُ الخُبْزَ فى يدى فلم يسقط على يدى
كما كان قبل ذلك ففكرتُ فى سبب العلّة فى وحشته (٧)عنّى فذكرتُ أنّى
أكلتُ مِلْحاً بأبْزار فقلتُ (٨)بسرّى انا نايبٌ من الملح (٩)المطيَّب فسقط على
يدى فأكل وانصرف، وعن ابى محمّد المُرْتَعش قال سمعت ابرهيم الخوّاص
(٤)رحمه الله يقول تِهْتُ فى البادية (٤)أيّاماً فاذا (١٠)بشخص وافانى فقال لى
السلم عليك فقلت وعليك السلم فقال تِهتَ (١١)فقلتُ نعم فقال لى أَلا أدُلُّك
على الطريق (١١)فقلت نعم (٤)قال فمشى بين يدىّ خطواتٍ وغاب عن عينى
(١٢)فاذا انا على الجادّة ومنذ فارقتُ الشخص ما تِهتُ ولا اصابنى الجوع ولا
العطش، وفى حكاية جعفر الخُلْدى عن الجُنَيْد (٤)رحمه الله قال جاءنى ابو
حفص النيسابورى (٤)رحمه الله مرّةً ومعه عبد الله الرّباطى (٤)رحمه الله
وجماعة وكان فيهم رجلٌ اصلح قليل الكلام فقال يوماً لأبى حفص (٤)رحمه
الله قد كان فيهن مضى لهم الآيات الظاهرة يعنى به (١٣)الكرامات (١٤)وليس

---

(١) B adds لصدقه. (٢) B om. قال الشيخ رحمه الله. (٣) B بن محمد.

(٤) B om. (٥) B لقمه. (٦) A om. (٧) B منى. (٨) B لنفسى.

(٩) B الطيب. (١٠) B شخص. (١١) B قلت. (١٢) B وإذا.

(١٣) B هذه الكرامات. (١٤) A وليست.

لك شىء من ذلك فقال له ابو حفص [١] رحمه الله تعالى فجآءَ به الى السوق
الحدّادين الى كور عظيم مُحمّى فيه حديدة عظيمة فأدخل يده فى الكور فأخذ
الحديدة المُحماة فأخرجها فبردت فى يده فقال له يجزيك هذا، فسُئل بعضهم
عن معنى إظهار ذلك من نفسه فقال كان مُشْرِفًا على [٢] حاله مختثى على حاله
ه ان يتغيّر عليه ان لم يُظهر ذلك له فمحّصه بذلك شفقةً عليه وصيانةً لحاله
وزيادةً لايمانه، وحُكى عن ابرهيم بن شَيْبان انه كان فى حداثته يصحب ابا
عبد الله المغربى قال فبعثنى يومًا الى موضع احمل له الماء قال فوافيت
الماء وإذا انا بالسبع قد قصد الماء قال فالتقينا جميعًا فى مضيق بيننا وبين
الماء قال فكنت مرّةً ازاحمه ومرّةً يزاحمنى حتى سبقتُه ووصلتُ الى الماء
١٠ قبله، وعن احمد بن محمّد السُّلَمى قال دخلتُ على [٣] ذى النون المصرى
[١] رحمه الله فرأيت بين يديه [٤] طشتًا من ذهب وحوله الندّ والعنبر [٥] يُسْجَرُ
فقال لى انت ممّن يدخل على الملوك فى اوقات بسطهم ثم اعطانى درهمًا
فأنفقتُ منه الى بَلْخ، وحُكى عن [٢] ذى النون [١] رحمه الله انه [١] كان ربّما
يقضم الشعير قضمًا مثل الدوابّ، وعن ابى سعيد الخرّاز [١] رحمه الله انّه
١٥ قال كان حالى مع الله عزّ وجلّ ان يُطعمنى فى كلّ ثلثة ايّام قال فدخلتُ
البادية فمضى علىّ [٧] ثلثٌ ما طَعمتُ شيئًا فلمّا كان [٨] اليوم الرابع وجدت
ضعفًا فجلستُ مكانى فاذا انا بهاتف [٩] يقول يأبا سعيد أيّما احبّ اليك
سببٌ او قُوّى قال فصحتُ وقلتُ لا [١] إلّا القُوى فقمتُ من وقتى وقد
استقللت فمشيت بعد ذلك اثنا عشر يومًا ما طعمت شيئًا ولا وجدت ألمًا
٢٠ لذلك، وعن ابى عمر الأنْماطى قال كنت مع استاذى فى البادية فأخذنـا
المطر فدخلنا [١٠] مسجدًا نُكِنّ فيه من المطر وكان فيه خَسْفٌ فى سقفه فصعدت
انا والشيخ لنُصلحه وكانت معنا خشبة فذهبنا لنجعلها على الحايط فقصرتْ فقال

[١] B om.   [٢] B حال.   [٣] A ذا.   [٤] B طشتًا.   [٥] The
commentator on Qushayrí, 194, 18 gives بتغيّر به as a variant.   [٦] A قال.
[٧] B لله.   [٨] B يوم.   [٩] يقول لى.   [١٠] B مسجد الى.

لى الشيخ مُدّ فبدّدتُها فركبّت الحائط من هاهنا ومن هاهنا، قال عمر وكنت
عند خيّر النسّاج (١) رحمه الله فجاءه رجلٌ فقال أيها (٢) الشيخ (٣) رأيتك يوم
أمس وقد بعتَ الغَزل بدرهميّن فجبتُ خلفك (٤) فجعلتَهما من طَرَف إزارك
وقد صارت يدى منقبضةً على كفّى قال فضحك وأوّى بيه الى (٥) يـه
ففتحها ثم قال أمضِ واشتر به شيئًا لعيالك ولا تَعُدْ لمثل ذلك،

باب فى ذكر الخصوص وأحوالهم التى لا تُعَدُّ من الكرامات وهى
فى معانيها أتمُّ وألطفُ من الكرامات،

(١) قال سمعت طلحة العصايّدى البصرى بالبصرة يقول سمعت (٦) المقصى
صاحب سهل بن عبد الله (١) رحمه الله يقول كان سهل بن عبد الله يصبر
عن الطعام سبعين يومًا وكان اذا أكل ضعف وإذا جاع قوى، وعن (١) أبى
الحُرث الأوّلاسى (١) رحمه الله انه قال مكثتُ ثلثين سنة (٧) ما (٨) سمع (٩) لسانى
الّا من سرّى (١٠) ثم حالت الحال فمكثت بعد ذلك ثلثين سنة لا يسمع سرّى
الّا من لسانى، وعن (١) أبى الحسن (١١) المزيّن قال كان ابو عُبَيد البُسْرِيّ
(١) رحمه الله اذا كان أوّل يوم من (١٢) رمضان يدخل البيت ويقول لامرأته
طينى علىّ الباب وألقى (١٣) الى كلّ ليلة رغيفًا فى الكوّة فاذا كان يوم العيد
(١٤) رفس الباب ودخلت امرأته البيت فاذا بالثلثين رغيفًا (١٥) موضوعة فى
زاوية البيت فلا أكل ولا شرب ولا تهيّأ للصلاة ولا (١٦) فاته ركعة من
(١٧) صلاة، (١٨) وحُكى عن ابى بكر محمّد بن علىّ الكتّانى (١) رحمه الله قال ما

---

(١) B om. (٢) B ايش. (٣) B رأيت. (٤) B فجعلتها. (٥) AB يدى.

(٦) A المعمى. B المقعى. Perhaps المقنعى. (٧) B لا. (٨) اسمع. (٩) B سرى.

(١٠) B om. from ثم to لسانى. (١١) B المرقى. (١٢) B شهر رمضان.

(١٣) B الى. (١٤) B فتح. (١٥) B موضوع. (١٦) B فاته. (١٧) B صلاته.

(١٨) B om. حكى.

استودعتُ قطَّ قلبى شيئًا فخانى، وعن ابى حمزة الصوفى قال دخل علىَّ رجل
من اهل خراسان فسألنى عن الأمْن قال فقلت له اعرفُ من لو كان على
يمينه سَبُعٌ وعلى يساره مِسْورةٌ ما ميّز على ايّهما (١) يتكئ قال فقال الرجل هذا
عِلمُ هاتِ حقيقةً لجواب مسألتى قال فسكتُّ قال فخذها يا (٢) بَذْبَخت اعرفُ
٥ من لو خرج من المغرب يريد المشرق ما تغيّر عليه سرُّه بين ذلك قال
ابو حمزة فبقيتُ اربعين يومًا وليلة لم آكل ولم اشرب ولم أَنَم حتى تبيّن
لى علمُ ما قال، وسمعت ابا عمرو بن علوان يقول كان شابٌّ يصحب الجُنيد
(٣) رحمه الله وكان له قلبٌ (٤) فطِنٌ وربّما يتكلّم بخواطر الناس وما يعتقدون
فى سرايرهم فقيل للجنيد ذلك فدعاه وقال أيْشَ هذا الذى يبلغنى عنك
١٠ فقال لا ادرى ولكن اعتقدُ فى قلبك ما شيتَ قال الجنيد (٣) رحمه الله
اعتقدتُ فقال الفتى اعتقدتَ (٥) كذا وكذا فقال الجنيد (٣) رحمه الله لا فقال
اعتقد مرّةً اخرى فقال الجنيد (٣) رحمه الله اعتقدتُ فقال (٦) الشابُّ (٧) هو
كذى وكذى فقال الجنيد (٣) رحمه الله لا قال (٨) فاعتقدْ ثالثًا فقال الجنيد
(٣) رحمه الله اعتقدتُ فقال الشابُّ هو كذى (٩) وكذى فقال الجنيد (٣) رحمه
١٥ الله لا فقال الشاب (٣) هذا والله (١٠) عجيب انت عندى صادق وأنا اعرف
قلبى وأنت تقول لا قال فتبسّم الجنيد (٣) رحمه الله ثم قال صدقتَ يا اخى
فى الاوّل وفى الثانى (١١) وفى الثالث وإنّما كنت امتحنُك هل تتغيّر عمّا انت
عليه، وعن جعفر الخُلْدى (٣) رحمه الله قال سمعت جنيدًا (٣) رحمه الله يقول
دخل حارث المحاسبى (٣) رحمه الله دارى فلم يكن عندى شىء طيّب أُطعمه
٢٠ قال فمضيت الى دار عمّى فاخرجت منها (١٢) شيئًا (١٣) وحملت لقمةً ففتح فه
فجعلت فى فه فكان يحوّله من جانب الى جانب ولا (١٤) يبتلعه ثم قام وخرج

فألقاه فى الدهليز (١)فذهبت خلفه وقلت يا (٢)عمّى رأيتك لم (٣)تبلع ثم
قمتَ وألقيتَه فى الدهليز قال نعم بُنَّى وذلك (٤)ان يبنى وبين الله تعالى انه
اذا كان شىء من غير وجهه لا يتهيّأ لى بلْعه (٥)وكنت فتحت فى لإدخال
السرور عليك ولم يتهيّأ لى ان ابلعه فقمتُ فألقيته فى الدهليز، وعن ابى
جعفر الحدّاد انه قال (٦)اشرف علَىّ (٧)ابو تراب (٤)رحمه الله فى الباديـة
وأنا جالس على بركة ولى ستّة عشر يومًا لم آكل ولم اشرب من البركة المَاء
(٨)وأنا جالس فقال لى (٩)ما جلوسك هاهنا فقلت انا بين العلم واليقين
انتظرُ من يغلب فأكون معه قال سيكون لك شأن، قال ابو عبـد الله
الحُصْرى (٤)رحمه الله رأيت انسانًا يعنى من الصوفيّة مكث سبع سنين لم
يأكل الخبز ورأيت رجلاً مكث سبع سنين لم يشرب المَاء ورأيت رجلاً
اذا مدّ يده الى (١٠)طعام فيه شبهة جفّت، وعن جعفر (١١)البَرْقَعِى انه قال
منذ ثلثين سنة ما عقدتُ مع الله عقدًا مخافة ان يفسخ ذلك فيكذّبنى على
لسانى، وقال ابو بكر (١٢)الزقّاق (٤)رحمه الله سافرنا مع اسمعيل السُّلَمِى
A f.147b فوقع من رأس جبل (١٣)فكُسِرت (١٤)قَصَبة ساقه فبكينا فقال (١٥)ما لكم لا
تغتمّوا انّما هو ساق من قطعة طين فاذا جفّت فركناه، ومثل ذلك (١٦)فى
الحكايات كثير وما لم نذكره أكثر وجميع ذلك (١٧)احسنُ معانيَ وألطفُ
من الكرامات التى ذكرناها وفى ذلك كفاية لمن عقل وأنصف (١٨)وفهم،

---

(١) قال فذهبت B.   (٢) B عم.   (٣) B تبلع.   (٤) B om.

(٥) A om. from وكنت to ابلعه.   (٦) B اشرفت.   (٧) B ابى.   (٨) B om.

(٩) وانا جالس.   (١٠) B الطعام.   (١١) B المترفع.   (١٢) B الدقاق.

(١٣) B فكسر.   (١٤) B عظمه.   (١٥) B om. ما لكم.   (١٦) B من.

(١٧) Here the text of B breaks off (f. 191a l. 4) and proceeds قال ابو محمّد
الجريرى الخ (A f. 153a, 1. 18). The words احسن معانى الخ occur in B on
f. 109b, 1. 2.   (١٨) B adds وانه اعلم.

كتاب البيان عن المُشْكِلات،

باب فى شرح الالفاظ المشكلة الجارية فى كلام الصوفية،

مثل قول القابل الحقّ بالحقّ للحقّ، ومنه به له، (١) والحال والمقام
والمكان والوقت والبادے والبادئُ والوارد (٢) والخاطر والواقع (٣) والقادح
٥ والعارض والقَبْض والبَسْط والغَيْبة (٣) والحضور (٤) والصحو والسُّكر (٥) وصَفْوُ
الوَجْد والهجوم والغلبات والفنآء والبقآء والمبتدئ والمريد والمُراد والوجد
والتواجد والتساكن والمأخوذ والمستلَب والدهشة والحيرة والتحيّر والطوالع
والطوارق والكشف والمشاهدة واللوايح واللوامع واللحّق والحقوق والتحقيق
والتحقّق والحقيقة والحقايق والخصوص والخصوص وخصوص الخصوص والاشارة والايمآء
١٠ والرمز والصفآء وصفآء الصفآء والزوايد والفوايد والشاهد والمشهود والموجود
والمفقود والمعدوم والجمع والتفرقة والشَّطْح والصَّوْل والذهاب وذهاب
الذهاب والنَّفْس والحسّ وتوحيد العامّة وتوحيد الخاصّ والتجريد والتفريد
(٥) وهمّ مفرّد وسِرّ مجرّد والاسم والرَّسْم والوَسْم والمحادثة والمناجاة والمسامرة
Af.148a   ورؤية القلوب والروح والتروّح والنعت والصفة والذات والحجاب والدعوى
١٥ (٦) والاختيار والبلآء واللسان (٧) والسرّ (٨) والعَقْد (٩) والهمّ واللَّحْظ (١٠) والمحو
والمحّق والاثَر (١١) والكَوْن والبَوْن والوَصْل (١٢) والفَصْل والاصْل والفَرْع
والطَّمْس والرَّمْس (٩) والدَّمْس والسبب والنِّسْبة وصاحب قَلْبٍ وربَّ حال
وصاحب مقامٍ وفلان بلا نَفْسٍ وفلان صاحب إشارة وأنا بلا أَنا ونَحْنُ

---

(١) والحال والمقام B om.   (٢) الحاضر B.   (٣) B om.   (٤) A om.
(٥) AB مجرّدًا وسرّا مفردًا وهمّا،   (٦) والاختيار B.   (٧) والسعر B.
(٨) A om. اللعة   The word is illegible in B.   (٩) والهجر B والهم،
(١٠) والصحو A.   (١١) الصحو والكون B.   (١٢) A om. والفصل والاصل،

بلا نَحْن (١) وأَنْتَ أَنْتَ وأَنا أَنا وأَنْتَ أَنا وأَنا أَنْتَ وأَنا أَنْتَ وهو بـلا هو وقطع العلائق وبادى بلا بادى والتَجلِّى (٢) والتَخلِّى والتَحلِّى والعِلّة والأزل والأبـد والأمد ووقتى مُسَرْمَد وبَحرى بلا (٣) شاطئ ونَحْن (٤) مُسِبّرون والتلوين وبَذْل المُهَج والتلَف واللَجأ والانزعاج وجَذْب الأرواح والوَطَر (٣) والوطن والشرود (٥) والقصود والاصطناع والاصطفاء (٣) والسَخْط واللطيفة والامتنان والحدث والكلّية والتلبيس والشَرَب والذَّوْق والعَيْن والاصطلام والحُرِّيـة والرَّيْن (٧) والغَيْن والوسايط وما (٨) يشاكل (٣) هذه من الالفاظ،

باب بيان هذه (٩) الالفاظ،

(١٠) قال الشيخ رحمه الله (١١) وأمّا معنى قولهم الحقّ بالحقّ فالحقّ هو الله (١٢) عزّ وجلّ وفى التفسير (١٣) عن أبى صالح فى قوله (١٤) عزّ وجلّ (١٥) وَلَوِ اتَّبَعَ الْحَقُّ أَهْوَاءَهُمْ قال الحقّ هو الله (١٦) تعالى، قال ابو سعيد الخَزّاز (٢) رحمه الله فى بعض كلامه عبدٌ موقوف مع الحقّ بالحقّ يعنى موقوف مع الله بالله (١٧) وكذلك منه به له يعنى من الله بالله لله، وربّما يكون فى مواضع يُعْنَى به ما يكون من آكتساب العبد بالعبد للعبد كما قال ابو يزيد (٢) رحمه الله (١٨) قال لى ابو علّى السِّنْدى كنتُ فى حال مِنّى بى لى ثمّ صرتُ فى حال منه به له، والمعنى فى ذلك انّ العبد يكون ناظرًا

Af.148b

الى أفعاله ويُضيف الى نفسه أفعاله فاذا غلب على قلبه انوار المعرفة يرى جميع الاشياء من (٢٠) الله قائمةً بالله معلومةً لله مردودةً الى الله، والحال

(١) وأنت أنت وأنا أنا B om. ‏   (٢) B om. ‏   (٣) A شط corr. in marg. ‏   (٤) مُسبّرين AB. والمسح B سرط. ‏   (٤) سرط B. ‏   (٥) والمقصود AB. ‏   (٦) والمسح AB. ‏   (٧) والضن A. ‏   (٨) شاكل B. ‏   (٩) وشرحها B adds. ‏   (١٠) B om. ‏   (١١) فاما B. ‏   (١٢) قال الشيخ رحمه الله B. ‏   (١٣) جل ذكره B. ‏   (١٣) على B. ‏   (١٤) تعالى B. ‏   (١٤) Kor. 23, 73. B om. ولو. ‏   (١٦) عزّ وجلّ B. ‏   (١٧) B om. ‏   (١٨) قال قال B. ‏   (١٩) A om. ‏   (٢٠) الله تعالى B. وكذلك from الله to الله.

نازلةٌ ‏(١)‏ تتنزل بالعبد فى ‏(٣)‏الحين ‏(٢)‏فيحلّ بالقلب من وجود الرضا والتفويض
وغير ذلك فيصفو له فى الوقت ووقته حاله ويزول، وهذا كما قال
الجُنَيْد ‏(٤)‏ رحمه الله وعند غيره الحال ما ‏(٥)‏يحلّ بالاسرار من صفاء الاذكار
ولا يزول فاذا زال فلا يكون ذلك ‏(٦)‏حالاً، والمقام هو الذى يقوم ‏(٧)‏بالعبد
٥ فى الاوقات مثل مقام الصابرين والمتوكّلين وهو مقام العبد بظاهره وباطنه
فى هذه المعاملات والمجاهدات والارادات فتى ‏(٨)‏اقام العبد فى شىء منه على
التمام فهو مقامه حتى ينتقل منها الى مقام ‏(٩)‏آخر كما ‏(١٠)‏ذكرته فى باب
المقامات والاحوال، والمكان ‏(١١)‏ هو ‏(١٢)‏لأهل الكمال والتمكين والنهاية فاذا
كمل العبد فى معانيه تمكّن له المكان لأنّه قد عبر المقامات والاحوال فيكون
١٠ صاحب مكان، قال بعضهم،

مَكانُكَ مِنْ قَلْبى هُوَ القَلْبُ كُلُّه ٭ فليسَ لِشَىْءٍ فيه غَيْرِكَ مَوْضِعُ،

والمشاهدة ‏(١٣)‏بمعنى المداناة والمحاضرة، والمكاشفة والمشاهدة ‏(١٤)‏تتقاربان فى
المعنى الاّ ان الكشف اتمّ فى المعنى، قال عمرو بن عثمان المكّى ‏(٤)‏ رحمه الله
اوّل المشاهدة زوائد اليقين سطعت بكواشف الحضور غير ‏(١٥)‏خارجة عن
١٥ تغطية الغيب وهو التماس القلب دوامَ المحاضرة لما وارثه الغبوب، قال الله
‏(١٦)‏تعالى ‏(١٧)‏إِنَّ فى ذَلِكَ لَذِكْرَى لِمَنْ كَانَ لَهُ قَلْبٌ أَوْ أَلْقَى السَّمْعَ وَهُوَ شَهِيدٌ
‏(١٨)‏يعنى حاضر، واللوائح ما يلوح ‏(١٩)‏للاسرار ‏(١٩)‏الظاهرة لزيادة السموّ والانتقال
من حال الى حال أَعْلَى من ذلك، قال الجُنَيْد ‏(٤)‏ رحمه الله لقد فاز قوم
دَلَّهم ‏(٢٠)‏ ولَّهم على مختصر الطريق فأوقفهم على ‏(٢١)‏ محجّة ‏(٢٢)‏المناجاة ولوّح لهم

‏(١)‏ B ‏ينزل‏. ‏(٢)‏ B app. ‏الخير‏. ‏(٣)‏ A ‏فتحلى من القلب‏. ‏(٤)‏ B om.
‏(٥)‏ A ‏يحلى‏. The word is partly obliterated in B. ‏(٦)‏ AB ‏حال‏. ‏(٧)‏ B ‏العبد‏.
‏(٨)‏ B ‏اقم‏. ‏(٩)‏ B ‏اخرى‏. ‏(١٠)‏ B ‏ذكرنا‏. ‏(١١)‏ B ‏فهو‏. ‏(١٢)‏ B ‏لا رهن‏.
‏(١٣)‏ A ‏جاحدة‏. ‏(١٤)‏ A ‏يتقاربان‏. B app. ‏يتقاربين‏. ‏(١٥)‏ B ‏معنى‏. ‏(١٦)‏ B ‏للكمال‏.
‏(١٦)‏ B ‏تبارك وتعلى‏. ‏(١٧)‏ Kor. 50, 36. ‏(١٨)‏ B ‏الاسرار‏. ‏(١٩)‏ So both MSS.
Cf. p. ٣٣١, l. ١٦ seq. ‏(٢٠)‏ Perhaps ‏دليلهم‏, but the MSS read as above.
‏(٢١)‏ The last two letters are obliterated in B. ‏(٢٢)‏ B ‏النجاة‏.

(١) على فِم الدعوة (٢) الى المسارعة بالمناسبة الى فِم الخطاب اذ يقول (٣) جلّ
وعزّ (٤) وَسَارِعُوا إِلَى مَغْفِرَةٍ مِنْ رَبِّكُمْ فنهضت العقول مستجيبة بحُسْن (٥) التوجّه
لاقامة ما به يحظَوْن عنه، واللوامع معناه قريب من اللوايج وهو مأخوذ من
لوامع البَرق اذا لمعت فى السحاب طمع (٦) الصادى والعطشان فى المطر،
قال عمرو بن عثمن المكّى (٧) رحمه الله انّ الله (٨) تعالى يُورِدُ فى صفاء الاوهام
كمثل لوامع البرق بعضها فى إثر بعض ويبدى ذلك لقلوب اوليآيه بلا نوم
بأصل ما عقدت عليه القلوب من التصديق والايمان بالغيب وما بدا للقلوب
لوامعُه من زيادة النور حتى لا يُمكن (٩) النفوسَ نومُ ذلك النور فى صفاء
الاوهام ولو (١٠) توهّمت انقطع ذلك، وقال القايل،

وَاغْتَرَّ ذو طَمَعٍ يَلْمَعِ (١١) سَراب،

والحقّ هو الله (٧) عزّ وجلّ قال الله عزّ وجلّ (١٢) وَإِنَّ ٱللَّهَ هُوَ ٱلْحَقُّ ٱلْمُبِينُ،
والحقوق معناه الاحوال والمقامات والمعارف والارادات (١٣) والقصود
والمعاملات والعبادات قال (١٤) الطَّيالسى الرازى (٧) رحمه الله اذا ظهرت
الحقوق غابت الحظوظ واذا ظهرت الحظوظ غابت الحقوق ومعنى الحظوظ
حظوظ النفس والبشرية لا تجتمع مع الحقوق لأنّهما ضدّان لا يجتمعان،
والتحقيق تكلّف العبد لاستدعآء الحقيقة جَهْدَهُ وطاقته، قال (١٥) ذو (١٦) النون
(٧) رحمه الله قلتُ لبعض الحكمآء الذين لقيتُهم لِمَ وقف سالكُ الطريق
فى كيد فِجاج المضيق فقال من ضعفِ دعايم التصديق وأخْذِ القلوب بالتحقيق،
والتحقّق معناه معنى التحقيق وهو مثل (١٧) التعلّم والتعليم، والحقيقة اسم والحقايق
(١٨) جمعُ الحقيقة ومعناه وقوف القلب بدوام الانتصاب بين يدى من آمن

(١) B على. (٢) B om. الى المسارعة. (٣) B ثناوه جل. (٤) Kor. 3, 127.

(٥) A التوحيد. (٦) B للصادى. (٧) B om. (٨) B تبارك وتعلى.

(٩) B للنفوس. (١٠) B توهمته. (١١) B السراب. (١٢) Kor. 24, 25.

(١٣) B والفصول. (١٤) A الطلاس B الطالسى. انّ الله Kor. has

(١٥) A ذا. (١٦) B adds المصرى. (١٧) B التعليم والتعلم. (١٨) B جميع.

به فلو داخل (١)القلوبَ شكٌّ او مخيلة فيما آمنتْ به حتى لا نكون به واقفةً
وبين يديه منتصبةً لبطل الايمان وهو قول النبيّ صلعم لحارثة لِكلّ حقٍّ حقيقةٌ
فما حقيقة ايمانك فقال عَزَفْتُ نفسى عن الدنيا فأسهرتُ ليلى وأظمأتُ نهارى
وكأنِّى انظرُ الى عرش ربّى بارزًا (٢)وكأنِّى وكأنِّى يعبّر عن مشاهدة قلبه ودوام
وقوفه وإنتصابه بين يدى الله (٣)تعالى (٤)لما آمن به حتى كأنّه رأى العَين، Af.140b
قال الجُنَيْد (٥) رحمه الله أَبَت الحقايق أن تدع للقلوب (٦) مقالةً للتأويل،
والخصوص اهل الخصوص هم الذين خصّهم الله (٥) تعالى من عامّة المؤمنين
بالحقايق والاحوال والمقامات، (٧) وخصوص الخصوص هم اهل التفريد
وتجريد التوحيد ومن عَبَرَ الاحوال والمقامات وسَلَكَها وقطع مفاوزها،
١٠ قال الله (٨) عزّ وجلّ (٩) وَمِنْهُمْ مُقْتَصِدٌ وَمِنْهُمْ سَابِقٌ بِالْخَيْرَاتِ، فالمقتصد
خصوص (١٠)والسابق خصوص الخصوص، حُكى عن الشبلى (٥) رحمه الله
انّه قال قال (١١)لى الجُنَيْد (٥) رحمه الله يأبا بكر ما ظنُّك بمعنى خصوص
الخصوص فيما (١٢)تجرى اليه (٥)من القول عمومٌ ثمّ قال خصوص الخصوص
فى نعت الايماء اليه عموم، والاشارة ما يخفى عن المتكلّم كَشْفُه بالعبارة
١٥ (١٣)اللطافة معناه، قال ابو علىّ الروذبارى (٥) رحمه الله عِلْمُنا هذا اشارةٌ فاذا
(١٤)صار (١٥) عبارةٌ (١٦) خفى، والايماء اشارة بحركة جارحة، قال الجُنَيْد
(٥) رحمه الله جلستُ عند رأس (١٧) ابن الكُرّينى فأوميتُ برأسى الى الارض
فقال (١٨) بُعْدٌ ثمّ اوميتُ برأسى الى السماء فقال (١٩) بُعْدٌ، وقال الشبلى (٥) رحمه
الله ومن أَوْمَى اليه فهو كعابد وَثَنٍ لأنّ الايماء وَثَنٌ لا يصلح الّا الى الاوثان،
٢٠ وقال القايل،

---

(١) AB القلب. (٢)B فقد أخبر عن مشاهدة الحجّ. (٣)B عزّ وجل. (٤)B لما حقيقة.
(٥) B om. (٦) B مقال. (٧) B om. from والمقامات to وخصوص الخصوص.
(٨) B تعلى. (٩) Kor. 35, 29. (١٠) B والسابق بالخيرات. (١١) A om.
(١٢) AB تجرى. (١٣) B العبارة. (١٤) B صارت. (١٥) B للكافه. (١٦) A جفا.
Cf. B بعد. A بعد. B بعد. (١٨) A بعد. B بعد. (١٩) B بين. (١٧) B حفا. B

Nafaḥāt al-Uns, p. 93, l. 2 foll.

وَلَّى عِنْدَ اللِّقَآءِ وفيهِ عَتَبْ ٭ بِايمَآءِ الجُفُونِ إلَى الجُفُونِ

(١)فَأَبْهَتُ خِيفَةً وأَذُوبُ خَوْفًا ٭ وأَفْنَى عَنْ حَرَاكٍ أَوْ سُكُونِ،

والرَّمْزُ معنًى (٢)باطنٌ مخزونٌ تحت كلامٍ ظاهرٍ لا يظفر به الاّ أهلُهُ، قال القَنَّاد،

إذا نَطَقُوا أَعْجَزَكَ (٣)مَرْمَى رُمُوزِهمْ ٭ وإنْ سَكَتُوا هَيْهَاتَ مِنْكَ (٤)اتّصالُهُ،

٥ وقال بعضُهم من ارادَ أن يقفَ على رموزِ مشايخِنا فلينظرْ فى مكاتباتِهم

ومراسلاتِهم فانّ رموزَهم فيها لا فى مصنّفاتِهم،

والصفآءُ ما خلَص من مازجةِ الطبعِ ورؤيةِ الفعلِ من الحقايقِ فى (٥)الحِين،

قال الجُرَيْرِى (٦)رحمه اللهُ ملاحظةُ ما صفا بالصفآءِ (٧)جفآءٌ لأنَّ معـه

مازجةَ الطبعِ ورؤيةَ الفعلِ، (٨)قال (٩)ابنُ عطآءٍ (٦)رحمه اللهُ لا تغترّوا

١٠ بصفآءِ العبوديةِ فان فيها نسيانَ الربوبيةِ لأنَّها مازجةٌ بالطبعِ ورؤيةِ الفعلِ

A f.150a واللهُ اعلمُ، وسُئِلَ الكَتَّانِى (٦)رحمه اللهُ عن الصفآءِ فقال مزايلةُ المذمومات،

وسُئِلَ عن صفآءِ الصفآءِ فقال مزايلةَ الاحوالِ والمقاماتِ والدخولَ الى

النهاياتِ، وصفآءُ الصفآءِ ابانةُ الاسرارِ عن المُحْدَثاتِ (١٠)لمشاهدةِ الحقِّ بالحقِّ

على الاتّصالِ بلا علّةٍ، قال القايل،

١٥ صَفْوُ الصَّفَا فى صَنْوِهِ إذْعَانُ ٭ وصَفَآؤُهُ فى كَوْنِهِ (١١)إيقَانُ

مَنْ بَانَ بَيَّنَ ما أَبَانَ بِهِ لَهُ ٭ حَقَّ البَيَانِ بِواضِحٍ (١٢)التِّبْيَانُ

هٰذا حَقيقةُ وَجْدِهِ مِنْ وَجْدِهِ ٭ ولوُجُودِهِ هَلْ فَوْقَ ذاكَ يَانُ،

والزوايدُ زياداتُ الايمانِ بالغيبِ (١٣)واليقينِ كلَّما (١٤)ازدادت (١٥)الايمانُ

واليقينُ زاد (١٦)الصدقُ والاخلاصُ فى الاحوالِ والمقاماتِ والاراداتِ

٢٠ والمعاملاتِ، قال عمرو بنُ عثمنَ المكّى (٦)رحمه اللهُ زوايدُ اليقينِ اذا

(1) A om. this verse. It occurs in B after the words فان رموزهم فيها لا فى
انقصانه A (٤) .ما فى B (٣) .مرما A (٣) .باطن خفى B (٢) .(l. ٦) مصنّفاتهم
with اتصاله in marg. (٥) A الحيز B .الحين (٦) B om. (٧) A حقا.
البيان A (١٢) .اتقان B (١١) .شاهد A (١٠) .بن B (٩) .وقال B (٨)
.اليقين B (١٣) .ازدادوا A (١٤) .A om. و الايمان (١٥) .B app التصديق (١٦)

سطعت بكواشف الحضور عن تغطية القلوب لما وارثه الغيوب، والفوايد

تُحَف الحقّ لاهل معاملته فى وقت الخدمة بزيادة الفهم (١)للتنعّم بها، قال

ابو سليمان الدارانى (٢)رحمه الله رأيت الفوايد (٢)تَرِدُ فى ظُلَمِ الليل، والشاهد

ما يُشهدك (٣)بما غاب عنك يعنى يُحضر قلبك لوجوده، قال القايل،

(٤)   وفى كُلِّ شَىْءٍ لَهُ شاهدٌ   (٥)يَدُلُّ عَلَى أَنَّهُ واحِدُ،

والشاهد ايضا بمعنى الحاضر، وسيل الجُنَيْد (٢)رحمه الله عن الشاهد فقال

الشاهد الحقّ (٦)شاهد فى ضميرك واسرارك مطّلع عليها، والمشهود ما يشهده

الشاهد، قال ابو بكر الواسطى الشاهد الحقّ والمشهود الكون، قال (٧)عزّ

وجلّ (٨)وَشَاهِدٍ وَمَشْهُودٍ، والموجود والمفقود اسمان منضادّان فالموجود ما

خرج عن (٩)حيّز العدم الى حيّز الوجود والمفقود ما خرج من حيّز الوجود

الى حيّز العدم، قال (١٠)ذو (١١)النون (٢)رحمه الله لا (١٢)تحزن على منفقود

ويكون ذِكْرًا (١٣)لعبدٍ موجودٍ، والمعدوم الذى لا يوجَدُ ولا يُمْكن وجودُه

فاذا عدمتَ شيئًا ويمكن وجوده فذاك (١٤)مفقود وليس بمعدوم، قال بعض

اهل المعرفة العالَم (١٥)وجودٌ (٢)من بين طَرَفَىْ (١٦)عدم لأنّه (١٧)موجود كان

عدمًا معدومًا ويصير عدمًا معدومًا ولا يشهد (١٨)العارف الاّ بعدم معدوم

فيجعل له عند رؤية عدمه معرفة وحدانية خالقه، والجمع لفظ (١٩)مُجْمَل

(٢٠)يعبَّر عن اشارة من اثار الى الحقّ بلا خلقٍ (٢١)قَبْلُ ولا كَوْنٍ كان اذ

الكون والخلق (٢٢)مكوَّنان لا قوام (٢٣)لهما بنفسهما لأنّهما وجود بين طرَفَىْ

عدم، والتفرقة ايضًا لفظ مُجْمَل (٢)يعبَّر عن اشارة من اثار الى الكون

---

(١) B للتنعّم.   (٢) B om.   (٢) B بما.   (٤) B in marg.

(٦) A شاهدا.   (٥) B دليلى.   وفى كل شى له ايةٌ تدل على أنه واحد.

(٧) B جلّ ذكره.   (٨) Kor. 85, 3.   (٩) A حين and so throughout this

definition.   (١٠) A اذا.   (١١) B adds المصرى.   (١٢) B بحزى.

(١٣) B لمعبود.   (١٤) B منفقودا.   (١٥) B وجوده.   (١٦) B عدم معدوم.

(١٧) A معدوم corr. in marg. B om.   (١٨) A المعارف.   (١٩) B مجمع.

(٢٠) B app. يعنى.   (٢١) A قبل. B قبل.   (٢٢) A تكون.   (٢٣) A لها بنفسها لانها.

والخلق وهما اصلان لا يستغنى احدها عن الاخر فمن اشار الى نفرقة بلا

جمع فقد جحد البارئ ومن اشار الى الجمع بلا تفرقة فقد انكر قدرة القادر

فاذا جمع بينهما فقد وحّد، وقال القايل،

جَمَعتُ وفَرَّقتُ عَنّى بِهِ * وفَرْدُ التَواصُلِ مثَنّى العَدَدْ،

٥ يعنى جمعت به وفرّقت عنّى وفرد التواصل فى الجمع مثنى العدد فى التفرقة،

والغيبة غيبة القلب عن مشاهدة الخلق بحضوره ومشاهدته للحقّ بلا تغيير ظاهر

العبد، والغَشْية [١] هى غيبة القلب بما بَرَدُ عليه ويظهر ذلك [٢] على ظاهر

العبد، والحضور حضور القلب لما غاب عن عيانه بصفاَ اليقين فهو كالحاضر

عنه وإن كان غايبًا عنه، قال القايل،

١٠   أنتَ وإِن غُيِّبتَ عَنّى سَيِّدى [٣] كالحاضِرِ،

وقال النورى [٤]،

إذا [٥] تَغَيَّبتُ بَدا * وإِن بَدا غَيَّبْنى،

وكذلك الصحو والسُّكر معناها قريب من معنى الغيبة والحضور غير ان

الصحو والسكر اقوى وأتمّ واقهر من الغيبة والحضور، [٦] وقد قال [٧] فى

١٥ ذلك بعضهم،

فحالان لى حالان صَحْوٌ وسُكرةٌ [٨] * فلا زِلتُ فى حاَىٍّ [٩] أصحو وأسكَرُ

كفاكَ بِأنّ الصَحْوَ [١٠] أوجَدَ كأَّبى * فكَيفَ بِحالِ السُّكرِ والسُّكرُ أجدَرُ [١١]

جَحَدتُ الهَوَى إِن كُنتُ مُذ جَعَل الهَوَى * عيونُكَ [١٢] لى عَينًا نَغُضُّ [١٣] وتُبصِرُ

نَظَرتُ إِلى شَىٍّ سِواكَ وإِنَّما [١٤] * أرَى [١٥] غَيَّرنا [١٦] أحلامَ نَومٍ [١٧] يُقدِّرُ [١٧]

والفرق بين [١٨] السكر والغشية ان [١٨] السكر [١٩] ليس [١٩] نشئتَهُ [٢٠] من الطبع   Af.151a

(١) B om.   (٢) عن B.   (٣) كالحاضر الصحو B.   (٤) ذو النون المصرى B.

(٥) تغيب A.   (٦) فقد B.   (٧) فى ذلك B om.   (٨) فحالاك B.

(٩) حاليك B.   (١٠) اوجدك انى A. اوجدك انى B. وحدك انى.   (١١) احدر AB.

(١٢) عونك A. عيونك B.   (١٣) نطق A.   (١٤) سوانا B.   (١٥) ارتى B.

(١٦) عيون B.   (١٧) نقدر A. نقدر B.   (١٨) السكرة A.   (١٩) ليست B.

(٢٠) ششه A. انشيت من الطبع.

لا يتغيّر عند وروده الطبع والحواسّ والغشية [١] نشئتُها ممزوجةٌ بالطبع تتغيّر
عند [٢] ورودها الطبع والحواسّ [٣] وتنتقض [٤] منها الطهارة والغشية لا تدوم
والسكر يدوم، والفرق بين [٥] الحضور والصحو انّ الصحو حادث والحضور
على الدوام، ومعنى صفو الوجد ان لا يعارضه فى وجهٍ غيرُ [٦] وجوده
كما قال القائل،

تَحَقَّقَ صَفْوُ الوَجْدِ مِنّا فَما لَنا * عَلَيْنا سِوانا مِنْ رَقيبٍ يُخَبِّرُ ،

والهجوم والغلبات [٧] متقاربا المعنى الّا انّ الهجوم فِعْلُ صاحب الغلبات وذلك
عند قوّة الرغبة [٨] والانفلات من دواعى الهوى والنفوس عند قوّة رغبـة
الطالب اذا لاح له أَعلام المزيد فى حال طلب [٩] المطلوبَ [١٠] فلو ظنّ انّ
مطلوبه وراءَ بحرٍ سَبَحَه او فى تِيه سَلَكَه بالهجوم عند غلبات الارادة وقوّة
سلطان المطالبة عليه لو رأى نارًا اقتحمها بالهجوم بتلَف الروح وبَذْل المُهْجة
سواءٌ اوصله ذلك الى مطلوبه او لم [١١] يُوصله، فذلك معنى الهجوم والغلبات،
والبقاءَ قد [١٢] ذكرته فى بابه ومعنى الفناءَ فناءَ صفة النفس وفناءَ
المنع والاسترواح الى حال وقع، والبقاءَ بقاءَ العبد على ذلك، وايضًا
[١٣] فناءَ هو فناءَ رؤيا العبد [١٤] فى أفعاله لأفعاله [١٥] بقيام الله له [١٦] فى
ذلك، والبقاءَ بقاءَ رؤية العبد بقيام الله له فى قيامه [١٧] لله قَبْلَ قيامه لله
باله، والمبتدئ هو الذى يبتدئ بقوّة العزم فى سلوك طرقات المنقطعين
الى الله [١٩] تعالى ويتكفّف لآداب ذلك ويتأهّب [١٨] للتأدّب بالخدمة والقبول
من الذى يعرف الحال الذى ابتدأ به وأشرف عليه من بدايته الى نهايته،
والمُريد [١٩] الذى صحّ له الابتداءَ [٢٠] وقد دخل فى جملة المنقطعين الى الله

(١) A تشبه. B أنشيت.   (٣) AB وروده.   (٣) B وبعض.   (٤) AB منه.
(٥) B الصحو والحضور.   (٦) B وجه.   (٧) A متقاربى. B متقاربين.   (٨) A
والانقلاب.   (٩) B المطلوب.   (١٠) B فان.   (١١) B يواصله.   (١٢) B ذكر.
(١٦) B om.   (١٥) B قيام.   (١٤) B om لأفعاله فى افعاله.   (١٥) فى افعاله لأفعاله B om.   (١٤) B om.
from فى ذلك to له الله بقيام.   (١٧) B عز وجل له.   (١٨) A المخادب.
(١٩) A اذا.   (٢٠) B om, from وقد to بالاسم.

نعالى بالاسم وشَهِدَ له قلوبُ الصادقين (١)بصحّة ارادته ولم (٢)ينرسّم بَعْدُ بجال
A.f.151b ولا مقام فهو فى السيْر مع ارادته، والمُراد العارف الذى لم يبق له ارادةٌ
وقد وصل الى النهايات وعبر الاحوال والمقامات والمقاصد والارادات فهو
مراد (٤)أُريدَ به ما أُريدَ ولا يُريد الاّ ما بُريدُ، والوجد مصادفة القلوب
لصفآء ذِكْرٍ كان عنه (٤)مفقودًا، والتواجد (٥)والتساكر (٦)قريبا المعنى وهو ما
يتزج من اكساب العبد بالاستدعاء للوجد والسكر وتكلّفه للتشبّه بالصادقين
من اهل الوجد والسكر، والوقت ما بين الماضى والمستقبل، قال الجُنَيْد
(٧)رحمه الله الوقت عزيز اذا فات لا يُدْرَك يعنى (٨)نَفَسك ووقتك الذى
بين النَّفَس الماضى والنَّفَس المستقبل (٩)اذا فاتك بالغفلة عن ذكر الله (٧)نعالى
(١٠)فلا تلحقه ابدًا، والبادى هو الذى يبدو على القلب فى (١١)الحين من
حيث حال العبد فاذا (٧)بدا بادى الحقّ يُبيد (١٢)كلّ (١٢)بادٍ غير الحقّ،
قال ابرهيم الخوّاص (٧)رحمه الله اذا بدا بادى الحقّ أفنَى كلّ (١٤)بادٍ،
والوارد (١٥)ما بَرِدُ على القلوب بعد البادى فيستغرقها والوارد له فِعْلٌ وليس
للبادى فعل لأنّ البوادى بدايات الواردات، قال (١٦)ذو (١٧)النون (٧)رحمه
الله واردُ حقٍّ جاءَ يزعج القلوب، والخاطر تحريك السرّ لا بداية له واذا
خطر بالقلب فلا (١٨)ثبت فيزول بخاطر (١٩)آخَر مثله، والواقع ما (٢٠)ثبت
ولا يزول بواقع آخر، سمعتُ بعض المشايخ وهو ابو الطيّب الشيرازى رحمه
الله قال سألتُ شيخًا من مشايخى مسئلةً فقال لى أرجو ان يقع جوابُه، قال
الجُنَيْد (٧)رحمه الله لخَيْر النسّاج رحمه الله حين خرج اليه هلّا خرجتَ مع
اوّل خاطرك وذلك انّه خطر بقلبه بانّ الجنيد (٧)رحمه الله على باب داره

١.اريد بما اراد ولا يريد الا ما يراد B (٣) .يتوسم A (٢) .بصحو B (١)
وقتك B (٨) .B om. (٧) .قريبى AB (٦) .والتساكى A (٥) .مفقود A (٤)
ونفسك are suppl. in marg. من حيث حال العبد اذا The words from (٩)
A. A in marg. فاذا (١٠) A in marg. لا. (١١) الحين B. (١٢) A لكل
بادى AB (١٣) .بادى A (١٤) .الذى B (١٥) .ذا A (١٦) .B adds (١٧)
المصرى A. (١٨) .يلبث A (١٩) .خاطر A (٢٠) .ثبت A

فَلَا تَلُمْنِى عَلَى مَا كَانَ مِنْ قَلَقِى ۞ إِنِّى بِحُبِّكَ مَأْخُوذٌ وَمُسْتَلَبُ ،
والدهشة سطوة تَصدِمُ عقل المحبّ من هيبة محبوبه اذا لقيه عند الايّاس لم
يجد لها عاهةً اذا انقضت ، وقد (١) رُوى عن بعضهم انه قال اللهمّ انك لا
تُرَى فى الدنيا فهبَّ لى من عندك ما يسكن اليه قلبى قال فغُشى عليه فلمّا
افاق قال سُبْحنَ الله فقيل له مِمَّ سبحت قال أَلْقَى الىَّ (٢) سكينتَهُ بدلاً من
النظر اليه وهل من بدل لذلك فقلت يا ربّ (٣) دهشتُ من حُبّك فلم
أمالك أن قلتُ ما قلتُ ، ولبعضهم يقول ،

إِنَّ مَنْ أَهْوَاهُ قَدْ أَدْهَشَنِى ۞ لَا خَلَوْتُ الدَّهْرَ مِنْ ذَاكَ الدَّهَشْ ،
وكان الشبلى (٤) رحمه الله يقول يا دَهشًا معناه كلّ شىء مع الخَلْق منك
دَهِشْ كُهّ ، والحَيْرة بديهةً تَرِدُ على قلوب العارفين عند تأمّلهم وحضورهم
وتفكّرهم (٧) تُحجِبهم عن التأمّل والفكرة ، قال الواسطى (٤) رحمه الله حيرة البديهة
اجلُّ من سكون التولّى عن الحيرة ، (٧) والتحيّر منازلة (٨) تتولّى (٩) قلوب العارفين
بين (١٠) اليأس والطمع فى الوصول الى مطلوبه ومقصوده لا تُطمِعهم فى الوصول
(١١) فيَرْتَجوا ولا نُويسِّهم عن الطلب (١٢) فيستريحوا فعند ذلك يتحيّرون ، وقد
سُئِل بعضهم (١٣) عن المعرفة ما هى فقال التحيّر ثمّ الاتّصال ثمّ الافتقار ثمّ
الحيرة ، قال (١٤) قايل ،

قَدْ تَحَيَّرْتُ فِيكَ خُذْ بِيَدِى ۞ يَا دَلِيلاً لِمَنْ تَحَيَّرَ فِيكْ ،
والطوالع انوار التوحيد تطلع على قلوب اهل المعرفة بتشعشعها فيُطمينّ ما
فى القلوب من الانوار (١٥) بسلطان نورها كالشمس (١٦) الطالعة اذا طلعت يَخْفَى
على (١٧) الناظر من سطوة نورها انوارُ الكواكب وهى فى اماكنها ، قال الحسين
ابن منصور فى هذا المعنى ،

---

(١) B ذكر.   (٢) A تسله B تسله.   (٣) A ذهمت.   (٤) B om.

(٥) AB دهشًا.   (٦) A تحجبهم.   (٧) B والحيرة.   (٨) B تنزل.   (٩) B بقلوب.

(١٠) B الناس.   (١١) AB فيرتجون.   (١٢) AB فيستريحون.   (١٣) B om عن المعرفة.

(١٤) B القايل.   (١٥) B سلطان.   (١٦) B الطالع.   (١٧) B الناظرين.

قَدْ تَجَلَّتْ طَوَالِعُ زَاهِرَاتٌ ۞ يَتَشَعْشَعْنَ فِى لَوَامِعِ بَرْقِ
خَصَّنى وَاحِدى بِتَوْحِيدِ (١)صِدْقٍ ۞ مَا إِلَيْهَا مِنَ الْمَسَالِكِ طُرْقُ،

والطوارق ما (٢) يطرق قلوب اهل الحقايق من طريق السمع فيجدّد لهم
حقايقَهم، حُكى عن بعض المشايخ انه قال يطرق سمعى علمٌ من علوم اهل
٥ الحقايق فلا أدَعُ ان يدخل قلبى الاّ بعد أن أَعْرِضُها على الكتاب والسنّة،
والطوارق فى اللُّغة ما يطرق بالليل، (٣) ورُوى عن النبىّ صلعم انه كان
(٤) يدعو وأعوذُ بك من شَرِّ طوارق الليل والنهار الاّ (٥)طارقًا يطرق بخَيْر،
والكشف بيان ما يستتر على الفهم فيُكْشَفُ عنه للعبد كأنّه رأىُ (٦)عَيْنٍ،
(٧)قال ابو محمّد الجُريرى من لم يعملْ فيما بينه وبين الله (٨)تعالى بالتقوى
١٠ والمراقبة لم يَصِلْ الى الكشف والمشاهدة، وقال النورى (٨)رحمه الله مكاشفات
العبون بالإبصار (٩)ومكاشفات القلوب بالاتّصال، والشطح كلام يترجمـه
اللسان عن وَجْدٍ (١٠)يفيض عن مَعْدِنه مقرونٌ بالدعوى الاّ ان يكون
صاحبه (١١)مستلبًا ومحفوظًا، قال ابو حمزة سألنى رجل خراسانى عن الأمْن
فقلتُ اعرفُ من لو كان على بينه سَبُعٌ وعلى يساره مِسْوَرَةً ما مَيَّزَ على ايّهما
١٥ (١٢)أتّكى فقال لى هذا شطحٌ فهاتِ (١٣)العلم، وكان بعضهم اذا سأله انسان
مسئلةً فيها دعوًى يقول أعوذُ بالله من شطْح اللسان، وقد فسّر الجُنَيْد
(٨)رحمه الله شطحات ابى (١٤)يزيد (٨)رحمه الله ولو كان ابو يزيد (٨)رحمه
الله فى ذلك عنه معلولاً ما فسّرها، وقد قال القنّاد،

شَطْحُ الْحَقِيقَةِ (١٥)وَالْأَحْوَالِ بَيْنَهُمَـا ۞ شَطْحٌ (١٦)لِذَا الْبَيْنِ يَزْهُو بَيْنَ هَاتَيْنِ

(١) A صرفى. B صرف. This verse is cited (unmetrically) in Massignon's edition
of the Kitâb al-Ṭawâsîn, p. 138. (٢) A تطرق. (٣) B فقد روى. (٤) B
يقول. (٥) B طارق. (٦) B العين. (٧) Here B proceeds (fol. 122a,
1. 10 اذا دعا. These words occur in A on fol. 173a,
last line. The text of the present passage is resumed in B on fol. 191a, l. 4.
(٨) B om. (٩) A مكاشفة. (١٠) A قبض. (١١) B ومحفوظ(?) مسلب.
(١٢) B يتكى. (١٣) B علم. (١٤) B adds البسطامى. (١٥) A والحوال. (١٦) B لذا.

فكان يدفع خاطره مرارًا فلما خرج قال له الجنيد ذلك ، ويقال ان الخاطر

الصحيح اوّلُ الخاطر اى اوّل ما يخطر ، [1] ومعنى الخاطر ايضًا ما لا يكون

للعبد نسبةٌ فى ظهوره فى الاسرار [2] والخاطر ايضًا [3] قهرٌ يستوعب الاسرار،

والقادح قريب من الخاطر الّا انّ الخاطر لقلوب اهل اليقظة والقادح لأهل

٨ل١٥٢a الغفلة فاذا [4] تقشّع [5] عن قلوبهم غيوم الغفلة قدح فيها قادحُ الذِّكْرِ وهى

لفظة مأخوذة من قَدَحَ النارَ بالزِّناد [6] والقادح الذى يستوقد النار،

قال القايل ،

يا قادحَ النار بالزِّنادِ ،

وقال بعضهم ليس ما قدحتْه الحقيقة كما ساكنته البشريّة ، [7] والعارض ما

١٠ [8] يعرض للقلوب والاسرار من إلقآء العدوّ والنفس والهوى فكلّ ما يكون

من القآء النفس والعدوّ والهوى فهو العارض لانّ الله [9] تعالى لم يجعل

لهؤلآء الاعدآء طريقًا الى قلوب اوليآيه الّا بالعارض دون الخاطر والقادح

والبادى والوارد ، قال [10] انشد ،

يُعارِضُنى الواشونَ قلْبى بِكِيْلُما ٭ يُقَلِّقُلُهُ فى سِرِّهِ والعَلانِيَهْ ،

١٥ والقبض والبسط حالان شريفان لأهل المعرفة [11] اذا قبضهم الحقّ احشهم

عن تناول القِوام والمُباحات والأكل والشرب والكلام واذا بسطهم ردّهم الى

هذه الاشيآء [12] وتولّى حِفْظَهم فى ذلك ، فالقبض حالُ رجل عارف ليس فيه

فضْلٌ لشىءٍ غير معرفته والبسط حالُ رجل عارف بَسَطَه الحقّ وتولّى حفْظه

حتى يتأدَّب بالحلق به ، قال الله تعالى [13] وَاللّٰهُ يَقْبِضُ وَيَبْسُطُ وَإِلَيْهِ تُرْجَعُونَ ،

٢٠ [14] وقال الجُنَيْد [15] رحمه الله فى معنى القبض والبسط يعنى الخوف والرجآء

[1] ويقال ايضًا فى معنى الخاطر ما لا يكون الخ B.   [2] ويقال ايضا انه قهر B.

[3] فهو A.   [4] انقشع B.   [5] على B.   [6] واذا قدحه القادح A   B om.

والقادح to بالزناد from   [7] والمعارض A.   [8] يعارض القلوب A.

[9] تبرك وتعلى B.   [10] وانشد B.   [11] فاذا B.   [12] تولى B.

[13] Kor. 2, 246.   [14] قال B.   [15] B om.

فالرجاءُ يبسط الى الطاعة والخوف يقبض عن المعصية، وقد قال القائل فى صفة حال العارف المنقبض وصفة حال العارف المبسط فقال،

مَعارِفُ الحَقِّ نَحْوِيها إذا نُشِرَتْ • ثَالِثَةٌ بَعْـدَهـا الأَرْواحُ نُخْتَلَسُ
فَعارِفٌ بِحُظُوظِ الحَقِّ آبِسَ لَـهُ • عَنـهُ سِواهُ ولا مِنـهُ لَـهُ نَفَسُ
وعارِفٌ (١) بِوَلا (٢) المَلِيكِ (٣) مُعْترِفٌ • (٤) يَحُثُّهُ الوَجْدُ (٥)ما وَلَّى لَهُ الغَلَسُ
وعارِفٌ غابَ عَنْهُ العُرْفُ(٦)فاعْنَسَفَتْ • مِنْهُ السَرايِرُ مَطْوِىٌّ (٧)الذَّرَى شَرَسُ
(٨) حَتَّى اسْتَكانَ وغابَ الوَعْثُ فى مَهَلٍ • (٩) فطارَ شَيْئانِ عَنْهُ النُّطْقُ والحَرَسُ
أغاثَهُ الحَقُّ عَمَّا دُونَهُ فَلَـهُ • مِنْهُ(١٠)إلَيْهِ سِرارُ(١١)وَحْيُها (١٢)خَنَسُ،

يذكر ان العارفين على ثلثة أصناف صنفٌ منهم ليس هم (١٣) منهم نَفَسٌ وصنفٌ منهم (١٤) يَحِثُّهم الوجد الى الحال الذى يتولاَّهم الحقُّ بالكلاية فيها وصنفٌ منهم غاب عنهم العُرْف والعادة واستوى عندهم النطق والصمت وغير ذلك بعناية الحقّ لهم فان سكنوا فله يسكنون وان نطقوا فعن الله ينطقون، والغيبة والحضور والصحو والسكر والوجد والهجوم والغلبات والفناء والبقاء فاعلم ان ذلك من احوال القلوب المحققة بالذكر والتعظيم لله عزَّ وجلَّ، والمأخوذ (١٥) والمسلَب بمعنى واحد الاَّ ان المأخوذ اتمُّ فى المعنى (١٦) وهم العبيد الذين وصفُهم فى الحديث المروىّ عن النبىّ صلعم الذى قال يظنّ الناس انّهم قد خولطوا وما خولطوا ولكن خالط قلوبهم من عظمة الله (١٧) تعالى ما أَذْهَبَ بعقولهم، وفى الحديث رُوِى ايضًا عن النبىّ صلعم انه قال لا يبلغ العبد حقيقة الايمان حتى يظنّ الناس انه مجنون، وقد رُوِى (١٨) عن الحسن فى الخبر كنت اذا رأيتُ مجاهدًا كأنه خَرْبَنْدَجٌ قد ضلّ حمارُهُ لِما كان فيه من الوله، والاخبار تكثر فى وصف المأخوذ والمسلَب وقال القائل،

(١) لولا B. (٢) التمليك A. (٣) معترفا B. (٤) يحثه B. (٥) B app.
(٦) فاعنسقت A. (٧) الذرى A. (٨) B om. this verse. (مادو له الغلس)
(٩) فصار A. (١٠) A om. (١١) وجيها A. (١٢) خُلَسُ B. (١٣) منه B.
(١٤) يحثم B. (١٥) والمسلوب A. (١٦) وهو العبد الذى وصفه B. (١٧) B om.
(١٨) B om. عن الحسن.

فَالْحَالُ كَالْحَالِ فِى التَّلْوِينِ شاطِحُها * وَالْعَيْنُ (١)تُدْنَى إِلَى شَطْحِ اللِّقَاءَيْنِ،
وَالصَّوْلُ (٢)الاستطالة باللسان من المريدين والمتوسّطين على ابناء جنسِهم
بأحوالِهم وهو مذموم، قال ابو عليّ الروذبارى (٣)رحمه الله (٤)أنّ من أعظم
الكبائر أن تَخوّن الله فى نفسك وتتوهّم أنّ الذى انالك لم يُبِلّ غَيْرَك فتجعل
٥ دعواك صَوْلَكَ على (٤)من يستحى من الله (٣)تعالى (٥)أن يُخبرك بحاله، (٦) وتأنّفُ
من الصَّوْلِ لانه حِجَّةٌ اذا كان على من فوقك وقلّة معرفة اذا كان على
من (٣)هو دونك وسوء ادب اذاكان على من هو مثلك، فأمّا (٧)الصادقون
وأهل النهايات يصولون بالله (٨)لقلّة المساكنة الى ما سوى (٤)الله، وروى
عن النبيّ صلعم انه كان يقول فى دعآيه اللهمّ (١٠)بك أصولُ وبك أحولُ، وقال
١٠ ابرهيم الخوّاص (٣)رحمه الله فى كتاب لـه ثمّ إنّى أقولُ وبالله أصولُ،
(١١)وقال القائل،

وَكَيْفَ يَطِيبُ العَيْشُ مِنْ بَعْدِ مَنْ بِهِ * عَلَى نائِباتِ الدَّهْـرِ كُنْتُ أَصُولُ،
والذهاب بمعنى الغَيْبة الّا ان الذهاب اتمّ من الغيبة وهو ذهاب القلب عن
حسّ المحسوسات بمشاهدة ما شاهَدَ ثمّ يذهب عن ذهابه والذهاب عن
١٥ الذهاب هذا (١٢)ما لا نهاية له، قال الجُنَيْد (٣)رحمه الله فى تفسير قول ابى
يزيد (٣)رحمه الله فى كلامه لَيْسَ بِلَيْسَ قال هو ذهاب ذلك كلّه عنه وذهابه   A f. 154 a
عن ذهابه وهو معنى قوله لَيْسَ فى لَيْسَ يعنى قد غابت (١٣)المَحاضِرُ وتلفت
الاشيآء فليس يُوجَدُ شىء ولا يُحَسّ وهو الذى بسمّيه قوم الفنآء والفنآء عن
الفنآء وفَقْدُ الفَقْدِ فى الفَقْدِ فهو الذهاب عن الذهاب، والنَّفْسُ (١٤)رُوحُ
٢٠ (١٥)القلب عند الاحتراق، (١٦)قال بعض الشيوخ النَّفْس رُوحٌ من ريح الله

---

(١) A تدرى but تدنى in marg.   (٢) B والاستطالة.   (٣) B om.

(٤) B الصادقين A (٧)   .ويألف B (٦)   .أيخبرك B (٥)   .من هو دونك اما تستحى الخ B
بك اصاول (١٠) Lisan xiii, 200, 22 has   (٩) B بقلة.   (٨) B بقلة.
.يروح B (١٤)   .المحاضرة A (١٣)   .حال B (١٢)   .قال B (١١)   .وبك احاول
.وقال B (١٦)   .للقلب B (١٥)

المسلَّطة على نار اله [١] تعالى وكذلك التنفّس، قال [٢] ذو النون رحمه اله ،

مَنْ لاذَ بِاللهِ نَجا بِاللهِ * وَسَرُّهُ مَرُّ قَضَاءَ اللهِ

لِلّٰهِ أَنْفاسٌ جَرَتْ لِلّٰهِ * لا حَوْلَ لى فيها بِغَيْرِ اللهِ،

والنَّفَس ايضًا نَفَسُ العبد، قال الجُنَيْد [١] رحمه اله أخَذَ على العبد حِفْظَ

٥ أنفاسه على ممرّ اوقاته، قال القايل ،

وَما تَنَفَّسْتُ إلّا كُنْتَ مَعْ نَفَسى * تَجرى بِكَ الرُّوحُ مِنّى فى مَجاريها،

والحِسّ رَسْمُ ما يبدو من صفة النفس، وقال عمرو المكّى [١] رحمه اله من

قال انّى لم أَجِدْ حسًّا عند غلبات الوجد فقد غلط لأنّه لم يُدْرِك فقْد الحُسوس

الّا بِحسّ والوجد [٢] والفقد يُدْرَكان بحاسّة وها محسوسان، وتوحيد العامّة

١٠ معناه توحيد الإقرار باللسان والتحقيق بالقلب [٤] لِما يقرّ به اللسان باثبات

الموحّد بجميع [٥] أسمآيه وصفاته باثبات ما أثبت [٦] ونَفى ما نَفى باثبات ما

اثبت اله لِنفْسه ونَفْى ما نفى اله عن نفسه، وتوحيد الخاصّة قد ذكرْنا فى

باب التوحيد وهو وجودُ عظمة وحدانية اله [١] تعالى وحقيقة قُرْبه بذهاب

حسّ العبد وحركتِهِ لقيام اله [١] تعالى له فيا اراد منه، وقد حكى عن الشِّبْلى

١٥ [١] رحمه اله انه قال لرجل وقد جرى ذِكْرُ التوحيد فقال هذا [٧] توحيدك

أَنْتَ قال فأَيْشَ [١] عندى غَيرُ [٨] ذا فقال الشبلى [١] رحمه اله توحيد الموحّد

وهو أن يوحِّدك اللهُ به ويُفردك له ويُشْهِدك ذلك [٩] ويغيّبك به عمّا

يشْهَدك، وهذا صفة توحيد [١٠] الخاصّ، والتفريد إِفْراد المُفْرَد برَفع الحدث Af.154b

[١١] وإِفراد القِدَم بوجود حقايق الفردانية، قال بعضهم الموحّدون له من

٢٠ المؤمنين كثير والمتفرّدون من الموحّدين قليل، قال الحسين بن منصور

[١] رحمه اله فى بعض ما تكلّم به عند قتْلِه حَسْبُ الواجد إِفراد الواحِد،

والتجريد ما تجرّد للقلوب من شواهد الالوهية اذا صفا من كدورة البشرية،

(١) B om.   (٢) A ذا.   (٣) B به   (٤) A بها. The reading

of B is doubtful.   (٥) A اسبايه.   (٦) B ابقا ما.   (٧) A توحدك.

(٨) B ذى.   (٩) B ويعينك.   (١٠) B الخاصة.   (١١) B والافراد.

وقال بعض الشيوخ وقد سُئِل عن التجريد فقال إفراد الحقّ (١)من كلّ ما
يُجرى وإسقاط العبد فى كلّ ما بُبدى ، والتجريد (٢)والتفريد والتوحيد ألفاظ
مختلفة (٤)لمعانٍ متّفقة وتفصيلها على مقدار حقايق الواجدين وإشاراتهم ،
قال القايل ،

حَقيقَةُ الحَقِّ حَقٌّ لَيْسَ يَعْرِفُهُ ٭ إلّا المُجَرَّدُ فيهِ حَقَّ تَجْريدِ ،

والهَمّ المفرَد والسِرّ المجرَّد بمعنى واحد (٤)وهو همّ العبد وسرّه اذا تجرّد من
جميع الأشغال وتفرّد بمراقبة ذى الجلال فلا تُعارضه خواطر قاطعة ولا
عوارض مانعة عن (٥)التوجّه والإقبال والقُرْب والاتّصال ، قال الجُنَيْد
(٦)رحمه الله قال (٦)الى (٧)إبرهيم الأجُرّى يا غلام لَأَن تردَ بهمّك الى الله
طرفة عينٍ خيرٌ لك ممّا طلعت عليه الشمس ، وقال الشبْلى (٦)رحمه الله
(٦)لرجل هيمانُ الهِمَم فى فضاءِ العدم همّك همّ (٨)هايج وهمّى همّ هايم ،
والمحادثة وصفُ لنهاية الصدّيقين ، سُئِل ابو بكر الواسطى عن أَعْلى حال
(٩)لنهاية الصدّيقين فقال هو الطالع (١٠)والمحدَّث ، وقال النبى صلعم فيما رُوى
عنه إنّ فى أُمَّتى مكلَّمون ومحدَّثون وإنّ عُمَرَ (٦)رضى الله عنه لمنهم ، وقال
سهل بن عبد الله (٦)رحمه الله خلق الله الخلق لِيُسارَّهم ويسارّوه (١١)قال
الله عزّ وجلّ خلقتُكُم لتسارّونى فان لم تفعلوا فكلّمونى وحدَّثونى فان لم تفعلوا
(١٢)فناجونى فان لم تفعلوا فاسمعوا منّى ، والمناجاة (١٣)مخاطبة الأسرار عند صفاء
الأذكار للملك الجبّار ، (١٤)قال ابو عمرو (٦)بن علوان سمعت الجُنَيْد (٦)رحمه
A.f.155aالله ليلةً الى الصباح بقول فى مناجاته الهى وسيّدى تريد أن تقطعنى عنك

<hr/>

(١) B فى.   (٢) B والتوحيد والتفريد.   (٣) AB لمعانى.   (٤) A وهى with
  (٥) B التوحيد.   وها B written above.   (٦) B om.   (٧) AB ابرهيم وهو
الاجرى بن, but cf. p. ٥٥, l. ٩ *supra* and the *Nafaḥát al-Uns* of Jámí, N° 22.
  (٨) A جائح.   (٩) B النهاية.   (١٠) B المحدث.   (١١) AB om. from قال
فاحرونى B لتسارّنى. The words are suppl. in marg. A.   (١٢) B to
  (١٣) B مخاطبات.   (١٤) B وقال.

بوصلك او نريد أن تخدعنى عنك بترك هيهات قلت لأبى عمرو ما معنى
هيهات قال التمكين، والمسامرة عتاب الأسرار عند خفىّ التذكار، قال
الروذبارى،

سامَرتُ صَفوَ صَبابتى أتشجانها ٭ حَرقُ الهَوَى وعَليها نيرانها،

٥ وسُئل بعض [١]المشايخ عن المسامرة فقال استدامة طول العتاب مع صحّة
الكتمان، ورؤية القلوب هو نظرُ القلوب الى [٢]ما توارت [٣]فى الغيوب
بأنوار اليقين عند حقائق الايمان، وهو على معنى ما قال أمير المؤمنين علىّ
ابن ابى طالب [٤] رضى الله عنه حين سُئل هل ترى ربّنا فقال وكيف نعبد
من لم نَرَهُ ثم قال لم تَرَهُ العيون يعنى فى الدنيا بكشف العيان ولكن رأته
١٠ القلوب بحقائق الايمان قال الله [٥]تعالى [٦]ما كَذَبَ الْفُؤَادُ مَا رَأَى فأثبت
الرؤية [٧]بالقلب فى الدنيا، وقال النبىّ صلعم أعبُد الله كأنّك تراه فان لم
[٢]تكن تراه فانّه يراك، والاسم حُروف جُعلت لاستدلال المسمّى بالتسمية
على [٨]إثبات المسمّى فاذا سقطت الحروف معناه لا ينفصل عن المسمّى،
حكى عن [٩]الشبلى [٢]رحمه الله انه كان يقول ليس مع الخلق منه الّا اسمه،
١٥ وكان يقول هاتِ من يقول الاسم باشتقاقه قولاً، وكان ابو الحسين النورى
[٢]رحمه الله يستشهد فى اشارته [١٠]بهذا البيت،

إذا أمرُ طِفلٍ مَسّها جُوعُ طِفلِها
غَذَتهُ بِاسمٍ [١١]الطِفلِ [١٢]فاسْتَعصَمَ الطِفلُ،

وكان الشبلى [٢]رحمه الله يقول أُريدُ من قال الاسم [١٣]وهو يتحقّق [١٤]ما
٢٠ يقول، وكان يقول تاهت الخليقة [١٥]فى العلم وتاه العلم فى الاسم وتاه الاسم
فى الذات، والرّسم ما رُسِمَ به ظاهر الخلق برسم العلم [١٦]ورسم الخلق

---

(١) الشيوخ B.   (٢) B om.   (٣) ٨ om.   (٤) عليه السلام B.

(٥) عز وجل B.   (٦) Kor. 53, 11.   (٧) للقلب B.   (٨) أفات A.

(٩) ابى بكر الشبلى دلف بن جحدر B.   (١٠) الى هذا AB.   (١١) النصل A.

(١٢) واستعصم B.   (١٣) فهو B.   (١٤) يا B.   (١٥) بالعلم B.   (١٦) ورسوم B.

(١)فيمتحى باظهار سلطان الحق عليه، سيّل الجنيد عن رجل غاب اسمه وذهب وصْنه (٢)وامتحى رسومه فلا رسْم له قال نَعَمْ عند (٣)مشاهدته قيام الحق (٤)له بنفسه لنفسه فى مُلْكه، (٥)فيكون ذلك معنى قوله امتحى رسومه يعنى عِلْمُه وفِعْلُه المضاف اليه امتحى بنظره الى قيام الله له فى قيامه، قال القايل،

بِرُسُومٍ دَارِساتٍ وطَلَلْ،

والوَسْم ما وسم الله به الخلوقين فى سابق عِلْمه بما شآء كيف شآء فلا يتغيّر عن ذلك ابدًا ولا يطّلع على علم ذلك احدٌ، قال (٧)احمد بن عطآء (٧)رحمه الله يظهر (٨)الوسمان على المقبولين والمطرودين لانّهما نعتان يجريان على الابد بما جريا فى الازل، والروح والتروّح نسيم تُنَسَّم به قلوب اهل الحقايق فيتروّح من تَعَبٍ ثِقَل ما حُمِّل من الرعاية بحُسْن العناية، قال يحيى ابن (٩)معاذ (٧)رحمه (٧)الله الحكمة جندٌ من جنود الله (١٠)يُرسلها الى قلوب العارفين حتى نُرَوّح عنها وَهَجَ الدنيا، وقال رُوحُ ولىّ الله (٧)فى القُدْس (١١)نشغله بمولاه، وقال (٧)سُفْيٰن (١٢)مجال قلوب العارفين بروضة سماوية من دونها حُجُبُ الربّ مَعَسْكُرُها فيها ومُجْنَى ثمارها بنعيم رَوْح الأُنْس بالله من القُرْب، والنعت إخبار (١٤)الناعتين عن افعال المنعوت واحكامه واخلاقه ويُحتمل ان يكون النعت والوصف بمعنى واحد الّا ان الوصف يكون مُجْمَلاً والنعت يكون مبسوطاً فاذا وصف جَمَعَ واذا نعت فَرَّقَ، والصفة ما لا (١٤)ينفصل عن الموصوف ولا يقال هو الموصوف ولا غير الموصوف، والذات (١٥)هى الشىء القايم بنفسه والاسم والنعت والصفة مَعالِمٌ (١٦)للذات فلا يكون الاسم والنعت والصفة الّا لذى ذات ولا يكون ذو ذات الّا مسمّى

(١) AB فيبقى. A in marg. فيمتحى. (٢) B فامتحى. (٣) A مشاهدة.
(٤) A om. (٥) AB app. سكون. (٦) B بن عطا احمد. (٧) B om.
(٨) A الوسمين. (٩) B adds الرازى. (١٠) B يرسلها الله. (١١) B شغله.
(١٢) B محال. (١٣) B الناعت. (١٤) A تنفصل. (١٥) AB هه.
(١٦) B الذات.

(١)منعوتًا (٢)موصوفًا وذلك أن القادر اسمٌ من اسمآء الله (٣)تعالى والقدرة
صفة من صفات الله (٤)تعالى والتقدير نعتٌ من نعوت الله (٣)تعالى والمتكلّم
اسم من اسمآء الله (٤)عزّ وجلّ والكلام صفة من صفات الله (٣)تعالى والغفران
نعت من نعوت الله (٤)تعالى، قال (٥)الواسطى ليس مع الخلق منه الّا اسم
او نعت او صفة والخلق محجوبون باسمآيه عن نعوته (٦)وينعوته عن صفاته
وبصفاته عن ذاته فتى ما ذكر العبد تدبيره وتصويره وفضله وطَوْله ذَكَرَ   A f.156a
نعوته ونعته بنعوته واذا ذكر عِلْمه وقدرته وكلامه ومشيّته ذكر صفاته ووَصَفَه
بصفاته وقال،

إذا طَلَعَتْ شَمْسٌ عَلَيْكَ بِنُورِها ٭ وَأَنْتَ خَلِيطٌ لِلشُّعَاعِ المُبَاشِرِ
بَعِيدٌ مِنَ الذّاتِ العَزِيزِ مَكانُها ٭ وَلَمْ تَعْرَ مِنْ نَعْتٍ لِنَفْسِكَ قَاهِرِ

والحجاب (٧)حائلٌ يحول بين الشىء المطلوب المقصود وبين طالبه وقاصه،
كان سرىّ السَّقَطى (٣)رحمه الله يقول اللهمّ مهما عذّبتَنى بشىء٭ فلا تعذّبْنى
بذُلّ الحجاب، وقال محمّد بن علىّ الكتّانى (٣)رحمه الله رؤية الثواب حجاب
(٨)عن الحجاب ورؤية الحجاب حجاب عن الإعجاب، معناه والله اعلم ان
رؤية العبد الثواب لعبادته وذكره حجاب له عن الحجاب المَنْهِىّ عنه ورؤيته
للحجاب حجاب له عن إعجابه بعله، والدعوى إضافة النفس اليها ما ليس
لها، قال سهل بن عبد الله اغلظُ حجاب بين العبد وبين الله الدعوى وقال،
وَلَمّا ادَّعَيْتُ الحُبَّ (٩)قَالَتْ كَذَبْتَنى ٭ فَما لى أَرَى الأَعْضآءَ مِنْكَ كَوَاسِيا،
وكان ابو عمرو الزجّاجى (٣)رحمه الله يقول من لبس له دعوّ فليس
(١٠)فيه معنّى وكان يعنى بذلك أن تُضيف النفس اليها من الطاعات التى
ليست من اخلاقها وتكون (١١)معها (١٢)بيّنةً لما تدّعى، والاختيار اشارة الى

ما يختار الله للعبد ويختار العبد ذلك بعناية الله له حتى يختار باختيار الله

له لا باختيار نفسه ، قال يحيى بن [١] مُعاذ [٢] رحمه الله ما دام العبد يتعرّف

بقال له لا تَخْتَرْ فانّك لستَ بأمين فى اختيارك حتى تعرف فاذا عرف يقال

له [٣] إن شئتَ اخْتَرْ وان شئت لا تختر فانّك إن اخترتَ فبنا اخترتَ وان

٥ تركتَ اختيارك فباختيارنا تركتَ فأنتَ بنا فيما [٤] تختار وفيما لا تختار ، والاختبار

امتحان الحقّ للصادقين ليعبر بذلك منازل المخصوصين [٤] ويستخرج بامتحانه

لهم [٥] منهم صِدقهم إثباتًا لحجّته على المؤمنين ليتأدّب بهم [٧] المريدون ،

[٧] وروى عن النبى صلعم انه قال [٨] اخْبُرْ تَقْلَهُ بعنى [٩] اخبر من شئت

وامتحنه حتى [١٠] تقلاه عند استخراجك [١١] بالامتحان صدقَهُ عن الحال الذى

١٠ هو فيه ، والبلاء ظهور امتحان الحقّ لعبده فى حقيقة حاله بالابتلاء وهو ما

ينزل به من التعذيب ، قال ابو محمّد الجريرى [٢] رحمه الله الإنسان حيث

ما كان بلاءه ، وروى عن النبى صلعم انه قال نحن معاشرَ الأنبياء اشدُّ الناس

بلاءً الحديث ، وقال بعضهم فى البلاء ،

دايراتُ [١٢] البَلا عَلَىَّ تَدُورُ * وَإِلَى [١٣] ما [١٤] تَرَى عَلَىَّ [١٥] تَثُورُ

ما أرَى لِلْبَلا بَلاءً سِواءَ * [١٦] وَبَلائِى عَلَى [١٣] البَلاءَ كُدُورُ

فَأَنا مِحْنَةُ البَلا وَبَلائِى * [١٧] حاصِنٌ لِلْبَلا عَلَيهِ غَيُورُ

يا بَلائِى عَلَى البَلا لا [١٨] تَعَدَّى * كُنْ بِهِ مالِكًا [١٩] رَحِيمًا غَفُورُ

[٢٠] يا مُعِينَ البَلا عَلَىَّ أَعِنّى * فى البَلا فالبَلا عَلَىَّ سَعِيرٌ ،

واللسان معناه البيان عن علم الحقايق ، كتب ابو الحسين النورى [٢] رحمه

---

(١) B adds الرازى. (٢) B om. (٣) B محاح. (٤) B وبخرج. (٥) B من.

(٦) B المريدين. (٧) B وى. (٨) B اختبر. This saying is explained in

Lisân 5, 308, penult. Cf. Lane under خبر. (٩) B اختبر. (١٠) B تلقاه.

(١١) A استخراجك بالامتحان يظهر لك صدقه. (١٢) B اللى. (١٣) B كم. In

A ما has been written above the line by a later hand. (١٤) A منى.

(١٥) A نشور. The reading of B is doubtful. (١٦) A وبادى. (١٧) A حاصل.

(١٨) A تعدنى. B تنعدا. (١٩) B رحيم. (٢٠) A om. this verse.

B خاصل.

23

الى الجُنَيْد كتابًا فقال فيه يا سيِّدى لك فى علم البَلَاء لسان [1] وفى علم
بلَاء البَلَاء سنان يعنى بيان عن علمه، وسُئِل الشِّبْلى [2] رحمه الله عن الفرق
بين لسان العلم ولسان الحقيقة فقال لسان العلم ما تأدَّى الينا بواسطة
ولسان الحقيقة ما تأدَّى الينا بلا واسطة، فقيل له ولسان الحقّ ما هو قال
٥ ما ليس [3]للخلق اليه طريق يريد به اذا قال اللسان يعنى بيان علمه
والكشف عنه بالعبارة، والسِّرّ خَفَآءٌ بين العدم والوجود موجود فى معناه،
وقد قيل السِّرّ ما غيَّبه الحقّ ولم يُشرِفْ عليه [4]الخلق، فسِّرُ [5]الخلق ما
اشرف عليه الحقّ بلا واسطة وسِرُّ [6]الحقّ ما لا يطَّلع عليه [7]الاّ الحقّ،
وسِرُّ السِّرّ ما لا يحسّ به السِّرّ فان [8]احسَّ به فلا يقال له سِرّ، قال سهل
١٠ ابن عبد الله [2]رحمه الله للنفس سِرٌّ ما اشاعها الحقّ الاّ على [9]لسان فِرعَوْن
فقال أنا رَبُّكُم الأَعْلَى، وقال القائل،

يا سِرَّ سِرٍّ يَدِقُّ حتَّى * يَخْفَى عَلَى وَهْمِ كُلِّ حَيِّ

وظاهِرٌ باطِنٌ [10]تَجَلَّى * [11]مِنْ كُلِّ شَئٍ لِكُلِّ شَئِّ

Af.157a

والعقد [12]عَقْدُ [13]السِّرّ وهو ما يعنقد [2]العبدُ بقلبه بينه وبين الله [14]تعالى
١٥ ان يفعل كذى او لا يفعل [15]كذى، قال الله تعالى [16]يَاَيُّهَا الَّذِينَ آمَنُوا
أَوْفُوا بِالْعُقُودِ، وقيل لحكيم [17]بِمَ عرفتَ الله [2]تعالى [18]فقال بجلِّ العُقود
وفَسْخِ العزائم، وقال محمَّد بن بعقوب [19]الفَرَجى فيما حُكِى عنه منذ ثلثين
سنة ما عقدت بينى وبين الله [2]عزّ وجلّ عقدًا مخافةَ أن يَفسَخَ علَّ ذلك
فيكذِّبنى على لسانى، ويقال ان الفرق بين الخاصّ والعامّ ان العامّة من
٢٠ المؤمنين قد اوجب الله عليهم الوفآء [20]اذا عهدوا بألسنتهم عهدًا والخاص

---

(١) B om. from وفى to سنان.   (٢) B om.   (٣) B الى الحقّ.   (٤) B خلق.

(٥) B الحقّ.   (٦) B الخلق.   (٧) B غير.   (٨) B حس.   (٩) A om.

(١٠) A حكى.   (١١) B عن.   (١٢) A عهد with عقد suppl. above.   (١٣) B الشى.

(١٤) B عز وجل.   (١٥) B كذا.   (١٦) Kor. 5, 1.   (١٧) B بما.   (١٨) B قال.

(١٩) A الفرخى. B بن الفرجى.   (٢٠) B om. from اذا to الوفآء.

قد اوجب الله عليهم الوفاء اذا عقدوا بقلوبهم عقدًا، والهمّ اشارة الى جمع
الهموم فيجعلها همّا واحدًا، قال ابو سعيد الخرّاز [١] رحمه الله اَجمعُ [٢] همّك
بين يدى الله [٣] تعالى، وذُكر عن بعضهم انه قال ينبغى [٤] للعبد ان يكون
همّهُ تحت قَدَمه بمعنى لا يهمّ بحال [٥] ماضٍ ولا بحال مستقبل ويكون مع
وقته فى وقته، واللحظ اشارة الى ملاحظة أبصار القلوب لما يلوح لها من
زوائد اليقين بما آمن به فى الغيوب، [٦] قال [٧] الروذبارى،

لاحَظْتُهُ فَرَآنِى فِى [٨] مُلاحَظَتِى * فَغِبْتُ عَنْ رُؤْيَتِى مِنِّى [٩] بِمَعْنَاهُ
[١٠] وَصَادَفَتْ هِمَّتِى لُطْفَ الخَفِىِّ بِمَا * تَمَكَّنتْ مِنْ [١١] تَكَنْ دُونَ مَنْشَاهُ
فَلَا إِلَى أَحَدٍ [١٢] هَمِّى وَلَا فَطَنِى * وَلَا إِلَى راحـةٍ أَسْلُو فَأَنْسَاهُ
اَللهُ يَعْلَمُ أَنِّى لَسْتُ أَذْكُرُهُ * وَكَيْفَ أَذْكُرُهُ [١٤] إِذْ لَسْتُ أَنْسَاهُ،

والمحو ذهاب الشىء اذا لم يبق له أثرٌ [١٤] واذا بقي له اثرٌ فيكون [١٥] طَمْسًا، قال
النورى [١] رحمه الله الخاصّ والعامّ فى قميص العبودية الاّ [١] أن من يكون
منهم أرْفَعَ جَذَبهم [١٦] الحقّ ومحاهم عن نفوسهم [١٧] فى حركاتهم وأثبتهم عنـد
نفسه، [١٨] قال [١] الله تعالى [١٩] يَمْحُوا اللهُ مَا يَشَآءُ وَيُثْبِتُ، معنى قوله جذبهم
الحقّ يعنى جمعهم بين يدَيْه ومحاهم عن نفوسهم يعنى عن رؤية نفوسهم فى
حركاتهم وأثبتهم عند نفسه بنظرهم الى قيام الله لهم فى أفعالهم وحركاتهم،
والمحق [٢٠] بمعنى المحو الاّ ان المحق اتمّ لانّه اسرعُ ذهابًا من المحو، قال رجل
للشبلى [١] رحمه الله ما لى أراك قَلِقًا فقال [٢١] أليس هو معك وأنت معه فقال
الشبلى [١] رحمه الله [٢٢] لو كنت أنا معه [٢٣] فأنَى ولكنّى [٢٤] محوٌ فيما هو يعنى

A f. 157 b

---

(١) B om.   (٢) عز وجل B.   (٣) B om.   (٤) A om.   (٥) ماضى A.
(٦) وقال B.   (٧) B adds هذه الابيات.   (٨) ملاحظته A.   (٩) بمعناه B.
(١٠) B om. this verse.   (١١) تكى كون منشاه A.   (١٢) همى B.   (١٣) من B.
(١٤) فاذا B.   (١٥) طمس AB.   (١٦) الى الحقّ B.   (١٧) B om. فى حركاتهم.
(١٨) The words from قال to عند نفسه are suppl. in marg. A.   (١٩) Kor.
13, 39.   (٢٠) معنى B.   (٢١) ليس B.   (٢٢) لكنت for لو كنت B.
(٢٣) فاتى B. فأنى A.   (٢٤) So both MSS.

ليس منّى شىءٌ ولا بى شىءٌ ولا عنّى شىءٌ والكلّ منه وبه وله كقول القائل،

كُلٌّ لَهُ وَبِهِ وَمِنْهُ فَأَيْنَ لِى ٭ شَىءٌ فَأُوثِرَهُ فَطاحَ لِسانُها،

والاَثَر علامةٌ لِباقٍ (١)شىءٍ قد زال، قال بعضهم من مُنِع من النَّظَرِ استأنَس بالاَثَر ومن عَدِمَ الاَثَرَ (٢)تعلّل بالذِّكْرِ، قال القائل،

فَما عِندى لَكُمْ أَثَرٌ ٭ وَلَمْ أَسْمَعْ لَكُمْ خَبَرٌ،

ويقال (٣)انّه وُجِدَ على قصر لبعض الملوك مكتوبٌ،

إنَّ آثارَنا تَدُلُّ عَلَينا ٭ فَانْظُرُوا بَعْدَنا إلَى الاثارِ،

وقال (٤)الخوّاص (٥)رحمه الله فى معنى الاَثَر وسُئِل عن توحيد الخاصّ فقال التفريد لله (٥)عزّ وجلّ فى كلّ الاشياء بالإعراض عمّا يلحق نفوسهم من آثار الاشياء (٦)وقال،

لَوْ أَنَّ دُونَكَ بَحْرَ الصِّينِ مُعْتَرِضًا ٭ لَخُلْتُ ذاكَ سَرابًا ذاهِبَ الاَثَرِ،

والكَوْن اسم مُجْمَل لجميع ما كوّنه المكوّن بين الكاف والنون، (٧)والبَوْن معناه البينونة والكَوْن والبَوْن معناها فى علم التوحيد (٥)ما قال الجُنَيْد (٥)رحمه اله فى (٨)جواب مسئلةٍ فى التوحيد يصف (٩)الموحّدين فقال كانوا بلا كَوْن وبانوا بلا بَوْن معناه انّ الموحّدين يكونون فى الاشياء كأنّهم لا يكونون ويبينون عن الاشياء كأنّهم لا (١٠)يبينون لانّ كَوْنَهم فى الاشياء بأشخاصهم وبَوْنهم عن الاشياء بأسرارهم، فهذا معنى الكون والبون قال،

أَقَدْ ناَهَ فى رَيبِهِ التَّوَحيدِ وَحْدَهُ ٭ وَغابَ (١١)بِعِزِّ مِنْكَ (١٢)حينَ طَلَبْتُهُ

ظَهَرَتْ لِمَنْ (١٣)أَنِّتَهُ بَعْدَ بَوْنِهِ ٭ فَكانَ بِلا كَوْنٍ كَأَنَّكَ كُنْتَهُ،

Af.158a والوصل معناه لحوق الغايب، قال يحيى بن مُعاذ (٥)رحمه الله من لم (١٤)يُعَمِّ (١٥)عينَيْه عن النظر الى ما تَحْت العرش لم يَصِلْ الى ما فوق العرش يعنى

---

(١) الشى الذى B. (٢)استأنَس B. (٣)أن B. (٤)B ابرهيم الخوّاص.

(٥)B om. (٦)قال القايل B. (٧)A om. (٨)كتاب A. (٩)التوحيد B.

(١٠)يثبنون A. (١١)بعزم B. (١٢)حتى B. (١٣)أنهته B.

(١٤)يعمى A. B om. (١٥)عمه B.

لم يلحق [١]ما فانه من مراقبة الذى خلق العرش، وقال الشبلى [٢]رحمه الله من زعم انه واصلٌ فليس له حاصلٌ، وقال بعضهم انّما [٣]حُرموا الوصول لتضييع الأصول، وقال،

[٤]وَوَصْلُكُمْ هَجْرٌ وَوُدُّكُمْ قِلاً ∗ وَقُرْبُكُمْ بُعْدٌ وَسِلْمُكُمْ [٥]حَرْبٌ،

والفصل فوت الثىء المرجوّ من المحبوب، ذكر عن بعض الشيوخ انه كان يقول من زعم او ظنّ انه [٢]قد وصل [٦]فليَتَقنْ انه قد انفصل، وقال آخر فَرَحُ اتّصالك ممزوج بتَرَح الانفصال، [٧]وقال القايل،

فَلا وَصْلٌ وَلا فَصْلٌ وَلا يَأْسٌ وَلا طَمَعْ

والأصل هو الثىء الذى يكون له تزايدٌ فأَصْل [٨]الأصول الهداية والأصول أصول الدين مثل التوحيد والمعرفة والايمان واليقين [٢]والصدق والاخلاص، والفرع ما تزايد من الأصل فاذا تزايد من الفرع [٩]زيادةٌ نسمّى باسم الأصل فالأصل حجّةٌ للزيادات التى هى الفروع [١٠]والزيادات التى هى الفروع مردودة الى الأصول [١١]والأصل الهداية والتوحيد والمعرفة والايمان والصدق والاخلاص زيادتها بزيادة الهداية والاحوال والمقامات والاعمال والطاعات زيادات هذه الأصول وفروعها وهى مسمّاة باسم [١٢]الأصول لتزايدها [١٣]وتزايد فروعها، قال عمرو بن عثمن المكّى [٢]رحمه الله إقرارنا [١٤]بالأصول لزوم الحُجّة علينا فى التقصير ولزوم الحجّة [١٥]بالانكار بعد الايمان [١٦]والاقرار بالاصول، وقال بعض العلمآء [١٧]ما دعا اليه الرسول صلعم فهو الأصل وما تزايد عن ذلك الأصل فهو فرعٌ مردود الى الأصل، والطمْس محو البيان عن الثىء البيّن، [٧]وقال الجُنيّد [٢]رحمه الله فى

(١) A الى ما.   (٢) B om.   (٣) B احرموا.   (٤) B فوصلكم.   (٥) A adds وعطفكم صرم.   (٦) B فليتيقن.   (٧) B قال.   (٨) A الوصول.   (٩) B زايد.   (١٠) B om. from الزيادات to الفروع هى   (١١) B om. from والاصل to وفروعها وهى مسمأة باسم الوصول A adds الوصول.   (١٢) A الوصول.   (١٣) A وتزايدها.   (١٤) A بالوصول.   (١٥) A الانكار.   (١٦) B فالاقرار.   (١٧) B دعى.

رسالته الى ابى بكر الكسائى وأنْتَ فى سُبُل ملتبسةٍ ونجوم منطمسةٍ قال Af.158b
الله تعالى وَإِذَا ٱلنُّجُومُ طُمِسَتْ يعنى ذهب ضَوْءُها، وقال عمرو المكّى
رحمه الله وإنك لا تَصِلُ الى حقيقة الحقّ حتى تسلك تلك الطُّرُقات
المنطمسة يعنى تُنازِل تلك الاحوال التى لم يُنازِلها احدٌ غيرك وقد ذهب
أثَرُها، والرَّمْس والدمْس بمعنى الدفن ويقال للمقبرة الدِّيماس، قال الجُنَيْد ٥
رحمه الله فى رسالته الى يحيى بن مُعاذ رحمه الله ثمّ أدمَسَ شاهدَهُ فى
دَمْس الاندماس وأرمَسَ مَرْمَسَهُ فى غَيْب غافِر الارتماس وأخْفى فى إخْفاء
عن اخفايه ثمّ قطع النسبة عن الاشارة اليه وعن الإيماء بما تفرّد له
منه به، وهذه اشارة الى حقيقة التوحيد بذهاب الخلق فيما كان كأنه
لم يكن، وقال سهل رحمه الله اذا دفنتَ نفْسك تحت الثَّرى وصل ١٠
قلبك فوق العرش يعنى اذا خالَنْتَها وفارقتْها، والقصم الكَسْر، حكى عن ابى
بكر الزقّاق رحمه الله انه قال لو أنّ المعاصى كانت شيئًا أختَرْتُهُ
لنفسى ما أحْزنى ذلك لانّ ذلك يُشِبهُني وانّما قُصِمَ ظَهْرى حينَ
سبق لى منه ذلك، وقال الواسطى ظهرت الأمور كلّها فى حقايقها على
الدُّهور فمن شاهدها بشاهد القِدَم انقصم مقابلته لذلك، والسبب الواسطة ١٥
والأسباب الوسايط التى بين الخلق وبين الله تعالى، قال احمد بن
عطاء رحمه الله من شهد صُنْعَ المُسَبِّب فى السبب أوْصَلَه مشاهدة صُنْعَ
المسبّب الى السبب لانّ من شهد السبب امتلأ قلبُهُ من زينة الأسباب ومن
عرف الاسباب الشاغلة عن الطاعات انقطع عنها واتّصل بالاسباب الداعية

---

(١) رساله B.   (٢) الكسائى A. Cf. p. ۳۲۹, l. ۸ supra. The following words occur
on p. ۲٤۰, l. ۳.   (٣) Kor. 77,8.   (٤) عمرو بن عثمان B.   (٥) B om.   (٦) فقد.
B.   (٧) رساله B.   (٨) B app. غاص.   (٩) اقطع B.   (١٠) تقرب A. بمرد with
written above as a variant.   (١١) Illegible in B.   (١٢) لَه B.   (١٣) كم B. لم. The reading
of B is doubtful.   (١٨) طهر B.   (١٩) بذلك B.   (٢٠) ما قابلته B.   (١٤) قال B.
   (١٥) الدقاق B.   (١٦) كان B.   (١٧) يشبهنى A.
(٢١) والوسايط A.   (٢٢) B om. from فى السبب to المسبّب.

الى صالح الاعمال، ولأبى على الروذبارى رحه الله،

مَنْ آمَ[١] يَكُنْ بِكَ فانِيًا عَنْ حُبِّهِ ۞ وَعَنِ الهَوَى والأُنْسِ بالأَحْباب

أَوْ بَيْتَهُ صَبابَةً جَمَعَتْ [٢]لَهُ ۞ ما كانَ مُفْتَرِقًا مِنَ الأَسْباب

فكأَنَّهُ بَيْنَ المَراتِبِ واقِفٌ ۞ لِمَنالِ حَظٍّ أَوْ لِحُسْنِ مَآبِ،

Af.159a

[٣]والنسبة الحال الذى [٤]يتعرّف به صاحبُ [١]بمعنى انتسابه اليه، قال جعفر

[٥]الطَّيالِسِى الرازى [١] رحه الله النسبة نسبتان نسبة الحُظوظ ونسبة الحُقوق

اذا غابت الخليقة ظهرت الحقيقة واذا ظهرت الخليقة غابت الحقيقة، وسُئِل

القنّاد عن الغريب فقال [٦]الذى ليس له فى العالم نسيب، وقال النورى

[١] رحه الله كلّما رأته العيون نُسِبَ الى العلم وكلّما علمته القلوب نُسِبَ الى

١٠ اليقين، فلذلك قُلْنا معنى [٧]النسبة الاعتراف، وقال عمرو بن [٨]عثمن

[١] رحه الله صفة الكُسوف للأسرار أن لا يكون قايمًا فى رؤية ولا مُتجلّيًا فى

نسبة يعنى فى الاعتراف، وفلان صاحبُ قلبٍ معناه [٩]أن ليس له عبارة

اللسان وفصاحة البيان عن العلم [١٠]الذى قد اجتمع فى قلبه، حُكى عن

الجُنَيْد [١] رحه الله انه كان يقول أهْلُ خُراسان اصحاب قلوب، ورَبُّ حالٍ

١٥ معناه انه مربوط بحال من الاحوال التى ذكرنا من المحبّة والخوف والرجاء

والشوق وغير ذلك فاذا كان الأغْلَبَ على العبد [١١]حالٌ من هذه الاحوال

يقال له رَبُّ حالٍ، وصاحبُ مقامٍ معناه أن يكون مقيمًا فى مقام من مقامات

القاصدين والطالبين مثل التوبة والورع والزهد والصبر وغير ذلك فاذا

عُرِف بالمقام فى شىء من ذلك يقال له صاحب مقام، حُكى عن الجُنَيْد

٢٠ [١] رحه الله انه قال لا يبلغ العبد الى حقيقة المعرفة وصفاء التوحيد حتى

يعبر الاحوال والمقامات، [١٢]وذُكر عن بعض المشايخ انه قال وقفتُ على

الشِّبْلى رحه الله غير مرّة فا رأيته تكلّم إلّا فى الاحوال والمقامات، وفلان

(١) B om.   (٢) B به.   (٣) والنسب B.   (٤) لم يتعرف B.   (٥) A الطلاش.

B المكّى.   (٦) الغريب الذى B.   (٧) النسب B.   (٨) B adds الظلامير B.

(٩) A اى.   (١٠) فاذا اجتمع B.   (١١) حاله B.   (١٢) B om. from

وذكر to المقامات.

بلا نَفْسٍ معناه انه لا نظهر عليه اخلاق النفس لانّ من اخلاق النفس
الغضبُ والحِدّة والتكبّر والشره والطمع والحسد فاذا كان عبدٌ قد سَلِمَ من
هذه الآفات وما شاكَلَ ذلك يقال له بلا نفس (١) يعنى (٢) كأنّه ليس لـه
نفْس، قال ابو سعيد الخَرّاز (١) رحمه الله عبْدٌ رجع الى الله (١) عزّ وجلّ
فتعلّق باله وركد فى قُرْب الله فقد نسى نفْسه وما سوى الله (١) تعالى فلو
قلتَ له من انت والى أيْنَ له جواب غير ان يقول له لانّه لا يعرف
سوى الله (١) تعالى لِما قد (٣) وجد فى قلبه من التعظيم لله عزّ وجلّ، وفُلان
صاحبُ إشارةٍ معناه ان يكون كلامه مشتمِلًا على (٤) اللطايف والاشارات
(٥) وعلم المعارف، قال الروذبارى،

فإِنْ تَحَقَّقَ صَفْوُ الوَجْدِ مُشْتَمِـلًا ٭ عَلَى الإِشَارَاتِ لَمْ (٦) يَلْوِى عَلَى أَحَدِ،
وإمّا قول القايل أنا بلا أنا ونَحْنُ بلا نَحْنُ يعنى بذلك تَخْلِيَةُ من أفعاله
فى أفعاله، سُيِل ابو سعيد الخَرّاز (١) رحمه الله عن معنى قوله (٧) وَمَا بِكُمْ
مِنْ نِعْمَةٍ فَمِنَ اللهِ قال أَخْلَاهم من افعالهم (٨) فى افعالهم، وامّا قول القايل
لصاحبه أنا أنت وأنت أنا (٩) فمعناه معنى الاشارة الى ما (١٠) اشار اليـه
الشبلى (١) رحمه الله حيث قال فى مجلسه يا قوم هذا مجنونُ (١١) بنى عامرٍ كان
اذا سُيِل عن لَيْلَى فكان يقول أنا لَيْلَى فكان يغيب بلَيْلَى عن لَيْلَى حتى يبقى
بمشْهَد لَيْلَى (١٢) وبغَيْبتُه عن كلّ معنى سوى لَيْلَى ويشْهَدُ الاشياء كُلَّها بلَيْلَى
فكيف يدّعى من يدّعى محبّته وهو صحيحٌ مُمَيِّزٌ يرجع الى معلوماته ومألوفاته
وحظوظه فيهمات أنَّى له ذلك ولم يزهد فى ذرّةٍ منه ولا زالت عنه صفةٌ
من أوصافه مَعَما أنّ بَذْلَ المجهود للمعبود أَدْنَى رُتْبةٍ عند القوم، قال الشبلى
(١) رحمه الله (١٢) إنّ مُتَحَابَّيْن ركبا بعض البِحار فسقط احدها فى البحر وغرق

فألقى (١) الآخر نفسه الى البحر فغاص الغوّاصون فأخرجوها سالمين فقال الاوّل
لصاحبه امّا أنا (٢) فقد سقطتُ فى البحر أنت لِم رميتَ نفسك فى البحر فقال

٨٤ف١٦٠ا له أنا غايب بك عن نفسى توهّمتُ أنّى أنت، وقال بعضهم وقف غلام
على حلقة الشبلى (١) رحمه الله فقال يا أبا بكر (٣) أخذَنى منّى وغيّبنى عنّى وردّنى
٥ الىّ كما أنا بلا أنا (٤) فقال له الشبلى (١) رحمه الله وَيْلك من أَيْن لك هذا
أَعْماك الله فقال (٥) الغلام يأبا بكر (٦) من اين لى أن أَعْمى فيه ثم هرب
من بين يديه، (٧) وقال بعضهم،

ذكَرْنا وما كُنّا (٨) نَسينا فنَذْكُر ٭ ولكنْ نَسيمُ القُرْبِ يَبْدُو فيَظْهَر
فأَفْنى بِهِ عنّى (٩) وأَبْقى بِهِ لهُ ٭ (١٠) إذِ الحَقُّ عنهُ (١١) مُخْبِرٌ ومُعبِّر،

١٠ وقال بعضهم،

أَنا مَنْ أَهْوى ومَنْ أَهْوى أَنا ٭ فاذا (١٢) أَبْصَرْتَنى أَبْصَرْتَنا
نَحنُ رُوحانِ معًا فى جَسَدٍ ٭ أَلْبَسَ اللهُ عَلينا البَدَنا،

(١٣) وقال غيره،

يا مُنْيةَ المُتَمنّى ٭ أفْنَيْتَنى بِكَ عنّى
أَدْنَيْتَنى مِنكَ حتّى ٭ ظَنَنْتُ أَنَّكَ أَنّى،

١٥ وهذه مخاطبة مخلوق لمخلوق فى هواه فكيف لمن (١٤) ادّعى محبة من هو اقربُ
اليه من حَبْلِ الوَريد، وامّا قول القايل هو بلا هو فهى اشارة الى تفريد
التوحيد كأنّه يقول هو (١٥) بلا قول القايل هو ولا كتابة الكاتب هو وهو
بلا ظهور هذَيْن الحرفَيْن يعنى الهآء والواو بمعنى هو، (١٦) قال الجُنَيْد (١) رحمه
٢٠ الله فى وصف التوحيد فقال حُكمُها على (١) ما جَرَتْ عليه (١٧) جار وسلطانها

(١) B om. ‏.‏ (٢) B فسقط. (٣) B خذَنى. (٤) B قال. (٥) B om. الغلام
واحيا B (٩) ‏.‏ ومن B (٦) ‏.‏ فقال B (٧) ‏.‏ لننسا B (٨) ‏.‏ يأبا بكر
وقيل فى B (١٠) A اذا. (١١) B يعبر الغيوب. (١٢) B ابصرته.
وهو بلا هذين الحرفين A (١٥) ‏.‏ ادّعى محبة B om. (١٤) ‏.‏ معنى هذا
The missing words have been supplied in marg. but only part of them is
legible. (١٦) B وقال، (١٧) A جارى.

على كلّ حقّ [١] عالٍ ظهرت فقهرت وخفيت فاستترت [٢] وصالت [٣] فغالت
هى هى بلا هى [٤] تُبْدَى [٥] فتبيدُ ما بَدَت عليه [٦] وتُفْنِى ما اشارت اليه قريبها
بعيدٌ وبعيدها قريبٌ [٧] وقريبها مُريبٌ، وقد اشار الجُنَيْد [٨] رحمه الله الى
[٨] معنى ما ذكرتُ [٩] وإله اعلم، وإمّا قطْعُ العلائق فمعنى العلائق الاسباب
[١٠] التى قد علّق على العبد [١١] وشغله بذلك حتى قطعه عن الله [١٢] تعالى،
قال ابو سعيد الخرّاز [٨] رحمه الله اهل التوحيد قطعوا [١٣] منه العلائق
وهجروا فيه الخلائق [١٤] وخلعوا الراحات [١٥] وتوحّشوا من كلّ [١٦] مأنوس
واستوحشوا من كلّ مألوف، وبادى بلا بادى [٨] يريد بذلك ما يبدو على
قلوب اهل المعرفة من الاحوال والانوار وصفآء الاذكار فاذا قال البادى
اثارى الى ذلك فاذا قال بلا بادى اشار الى أن البادى مُبْدئٌ هو [١٧] يُبدى
هذه البوادى على القلوب، قال الله تعالى [١٨] إنّهُ هُوَ يُبْدئُ وَيُعيد، فاذا شاهد
الحال الذى أبْدأَ به [٨] هو المبدئ فقال بادى وأثبته واذا شاهد المُبْدئ
الذى منه البوادى يقول بلا بادى، قال [١٩] الخوّاص [٨] رحمه الله فى
[٢٠] كتاب معرفة المعرفة الحقّ اذا بدا بدا بلا بادى ولا بادى من حيث
[٨] لا بادى لانّ البادى أَفْنَى كلّ بادى من حيث البادى فلا بادى وهو
بادى من حيث لا بادى وإنّما ذلك على [٢١] قُرْب مشاهدة الحقّ منهم،
والتخلّى التلبّس والتشبّه بالصادقين [٢٢] بالأقوال وإظهار الأعمال، رُوى عن
النبيّ صلعم انه قال ليس الايمان بالتخلّى ولا بالتمنّى ولكن [٢٣] ما وقر فى
[٢٤] القلب [٢٥] وصدّقته الأعمال، وقال بعضهم،

---

(١) عالى. A. (٢) وصالت B. (٣) فقالت A. فقالت B. (٤) وقريبها B om. (٥) يبدى B. (٦) ويفنى B. (٧) فيبيد B. فبيد A. (٨) B om. (٩) وإله اعلم B. (١٠) الذى B. (١١) واشغله B. (١٢) عزوجل B. (١٣) فيه B. (١٤) وجعلوها يعنى الراحات B. (١٥) توحّشوا A. (١٦) ما بونس AB. (١٧) مبدى A. (١٨) Kor. 85, 13. (١٩) B ابرهيم. (٢٠) A om. (٢١) قدر A with قرب in marg. as variant. الخوّاص. (٢٢) بلا قول A. (٢٣) بما B. (٢٤) القلوب B. (٢٥) وصدقه A.

مَنْ تَحَلَّى بِغَيْرِ ما هُوَ فِيهِ ٭ فَضَحَتْهُ شَواهِدُ الإِمْتِحانِ،
والتجلّى إشراق أنوار إقبال الحقّ على قلوب المُقْبِلِين عليه [١] وقال [٢] النورى
[٤] رحمه الله تجلّى [٤] لخلقه بخلقه واستتر عن خلقه بخلقه، وقال الواسطى [٥] رحمه
الله فى قوله [٤] تعالى [٥] ذلِكَ يَوْمُ التَّغابُنِ قال تغابن اهل الحقّ على مقادير
٥ الفنآء والرؤية والتجلّى، وقال النورى [٢] رحمه الله بتجلّيه حسنت المحاسن
[٢] وجملت وباستتاره قبحت وسمجت، [١] وقال بعضهم،

قَدْ [٧] تَجَلَّى لِقَلْبِهِ مِنْهُ نورٌ ٭ [٨] فاسْتَضاءَتْ بِهِ مِنَ الظُّلُماتِ،
والتخلّى هو الاعراض عن العوارض [٩] المشغّلة بالظاهر [٤] والباطن وهو
اختيار الخلوة وايثار العزلة وملازمة الوحدة، قال الجُنَيْد [٢] رحمه الله القلوب
١٠ المحفوظة لا يعرضها وليها [١٠] لمجانبة محادثة غيره [١١] ضنًّا منه بها ونظرًا منه
لها وإبقاء عليها لِيَخْلُصَ لهم ما أصفاهم به وما جمعهم له وما عاد به عليهم،
وهذه بعض صفات من اراده الله للخلوة وجمعه [١٢] للأنس وحال بينه
وبين ما يكرهه له، وعن يوسف بن الحسين [٢] رحمه الله فى معنى التخلّى قال
هو العزلة لانّه لم [١٤] يَقْوَ على نفسه وضعف فاعتزل من نفسه الى ربّه،
١٥ وقال بعضهم،

إِنَّ قَلْبَ الفَتَى وَلَوْ عاشَ دَهْرًا ٭ فى الهَوَى لا يَكادُ أَنْ يَتَخَلَّى،
[١٤] والعلّة كناية عن بعض ما لم يكن فكان، حكى عن الشبلى [٢] رحمه الله
انّه كان يقول فى صفة الخلق انّ الذُّلَّ كايِنُهُمْ والعلّة كَوْنُهُمْ، وقال [١٥] ذو
النون المصرى [٢] رحمه الله [٢] علّة كلّ شئ، صُنْعُه ولا علّة لصُنْعِه، معناه
٢٠ والله اعلم انّ وجود النقصان فى كلّ شئ مصنوع كايِن لانّه لم يكن فكان
وليس فى صُنْع الصانع [١٦] لمصنوعاته علّةٌ، وقال [٢] بعضهم،

[١] قال B.   [٢] ابو الحسين النورى B.   [٣] B om.   [٤] A بخلقه لخلقه.
[٥] Kor. 64, 9.   [٦] A الضنا altered to الضيا.   [٧] A تجلّت.   [٨] B فاستضا.
[٩] B المشغلة.   [١٠] B لمباينة.   [١١] B ظنا.   [١٢] قلبه من الظلمات.
[١٢] A الانس.   [١٤] B يقوا.   [١٥] A ذا.   [١٦] A لمضيق غاية.

يا شِفَائي مِنَ السَّقَامِ وإنْ كُنْتَ عِلَّتِي ،

والازل معناه معنى (١)القِدَم لأنّ القديم يسمّى به (٢)غير البارئ، ويقال
شىء أقْدَمُ من شىء، والازل والازلية لله تعالى لا (٣)ينسمّى بالازل شىء
غير الله (٤)جلّ جلاله والازل اسم من اسماء (٥)الأوّلية فهو الله (٦)الاوّل
القديم الذى لم يزل ولا يزال، والازلية صفة من صفاته، قال بعض المتقدّمين
الحقّ فيما لم يزل كهو فيما لا يزال فقوم استحسنوا هذه المقالة لِنَفْىِ التغيير
عن الحقّ لانّه بجميع أسمآئه (٧)وفعاله لم يزل وقوم قالوا يَلْزَمُ القايلَ لهذا
القولُ بقِدَم الاشيآء وفرّقوا بين اسمآء الفعل واسمآء الذات وصفات الفعل
وصفات الذات والله اعلم، والابد والابدية نعت من نعوت الله تعالى والفرق
بين الازلية والابدية انّ الازلية لا بداية لها (٨)ولا اوّلية والابدية لا نهاية
لها ولا آخرية، وسُئِل الواسطى عن الابد فقال اشارة الى ترك انقطاع فى
العدد ومحو الاوقات فى (٩)السَّرْمَد، وقال الوسم والرسم نعتان يجريان فى
الابد (١٠)بما جريا فى الازل، وقال آخر الازل والقِدَم والابد (١١)غير
مرتفعة فى حقيقة الاحدية لانّها عبارات واشارات تعرَّف بذلك الى خلقه
(١٢)لخلقه، وحكى عن الشبلى (٤)رحمه الله انّه قال سُبْحان من كان ولا مكان
ولا زمان ولا اوان ولا دهر ولا ابد ولا ازل ولا اوّل ولا آخر وهو فى
حال ما أحْدَثَ الاشيآء غير مشغول عنهم ولا مستعين بهم عدلٌ فى جميع
ما حكم عليهم، وقال عمرو بن عثمٰن (٤)المكّى (٤)رحمه الله سبحان الصَّمَد
القديم فى ازل لم يزل فى سَرْمَد الابد، (١٣)ووَقتى مُسَرْمَدٌ وأمّا قول القايل
وقتى مسرمد يعنى بذلك انّ الحال الذى بينه وبين الله لا يتغيّر فى جميع
اوقاته وهو كلام واجدٍ (١٤)خبّر عن سرّه لا عن نعت صفاته لانّ

---

(١) القديم B.   (٢) عن. B.   (٣) يسمى B.   (٤) B om.   (٥) الاولية الله
(٦) القديم الاول B.   (٧) B om. from وفعاله to واله اعلم.   (٨) والاولية B.
(٩) والسرمد A.   (١٠) لما A.   (١١) عنه A.   (١٢) It is uncertain
whether A has لخلقه or مخلقه.   (١٣) وفى B.   (١٤) B app. يخبر.

الصفات كاينة التغيير وهى متغيّرة [١]اذا لم تتغيّر لانّها اذا لم تتغير فقد تغيّر
عن الحال الذى جُبلتْ [٢]عليه ، قال بعضهم [٣]وهو الشبلى [٤]،

نَسَرمَدَ وَفْتى فيكَ [٤]وَهُوَ مُسَرمَدْ ٭ وَأَفْنَيتنى عَنّى فَصرتُ [٥]مُجَرَّدا ،

[٦]بَحْرى بلا شاطئ ، وقول القايل بجرى بلا شاطئ معناه ايضًا قريب
من المعنى [٧]الذى ذكرنا فى الوقت المسرمد [٨]وهذه لفظة [٩]قد حُكيت
عن الشبلى [١٠]رحمه الله تعالى انه قال يومًا فى مجلسه فى [١١]عقيب كلام
جرى له قال [١٢]أنتمْ اوفانكم مقطوعة ووقتى ليس له [١٣]طَرَفان وبحرى
بلا شاطئ يعنى بذلك ان الحال الذى خصّنى الله [١٥]تعالى به من التعظيم
له وخالص الذِكْر له والانقطاع اليه لا نهاية [١٤]لها ولا انقطاع والشىء اذا
لم تكن [١٥]له نهاية ولا غاية فلا يُعبَّر عنه [١٦]بأكْثَر من ذلك ، قال الله
[١٧]عزّ وجلّ [١٨]قُلْ لَوْ كَانَ ٱلْبَحْرُ مِدَادًا لِكَلِمَاتِ رَبّى لَنَفِدَ ٱلْبَحْرُ قَبْلَ أَنْ
تَنْفَدَ كَلِمَاتُ رَبّى وَلَوْ جِئْنَا بِمِثْلِهِ مَدَدًا لم يجعل لها غايةً لانّ الموصوف بها
[١٩]ليس له نهاية ، وقال بعضهم من عرف الله احبَّ ومن احبَّه غرق فى
[٢٠]بحر الهمّ ، وقال [٢١]آخر ،

لَوْ أَنَّ دُونَكَ بَحرَ الصّين مُعْتَرضًا ٭ لَخُلْتُ ذاكَ [٢٢]سَرَابًا [٢٣]ذاهِبَ الاَثَرِ ،

وقول [٢٤]القايل نَحْنُ [٢٥]مُسَيَّرون يريد بذلك [٢٦]تسيير القلوب وسَيْرها عند
انتقالها من حال الى [٢٧]حال ومن مقام الى مقام ، وقال بحيى بن [٢٨]معاذ
[١٠]رحمه الله الزاهد سيّار والعارف طيّار يعنى فى سرعة الانتقال فى المقامات
والاحوال عند [٢٩]الزوايد وطُرَف الفوايد ، قال بعضهم [٣]وهو الشبلى ،

(١) A om. اذا لم تتغير.   (٢) B عليها.   (٣) B om.   (٤) B فهو.

(٥) B مجرد.   (٦) B om. بجرى بلا شاطئ.   (٧) B اذا.   (٨) B فهذه.

(٩) B حكى عن.   (١٠) B om.   (١١) B عقب.   (١٢) A انم.   (١٣) AB طرفين.

(١٤) So AB.   (١٥) A om.   (١٦) A أكثر.   (١٧) B تعلى.   (١٨) Kor.

18, 109.   (١٩) B ليست.   (٢٠) B مجرى.   (٢١) B adds هذا البيت.

(٢٢) B شرابا.   (٢٣) B زايل.   (٢٤) B القايلين.   (٢٥) B مسيرين.   (٢٦) A سير.

(٢٧) B حال اخر.   (٢٨) B adds الرازى.   (٢٩) B التزايد.

Af.162a

(١)اَسْتُ مِنْ جُمْلةِ المُحِبِّينَ إِنْ لَمْ * أُجَمِّلِ القَلْبَ بَيْتَهُ والمَقَامَا

وَطَوَافِى (٢)إِخَالُهُ السَّيْرَ فِيهِ * وَهْوَ رُكْنِى إذا أَرَدْتُ اسْتِلَامَا

بريد بذلك سير القلوب، والتلوين معناه (٣)تلوُّنُ العبد فى احواله، (٤)قال
قومٌ علامة (٥)الحقيقة التلوين لانّ التلوين ظهور قدرة القادر ويُكْتَسَبُ منه
(٦)الغيرة، ومعنى التلوين (٧)معنى (٨)التغيير (٩)فمن اشار الى تلوين الصفات
وتغيّر الاحوال فقال علامة الحقيقة رَفْعُ التلوين، ومن اشار الى تلوين القلوب
والاسرار الخالصة لله (١٠)تعالى فى مشاهدتها وما يَرِدُ عليها من التعظيم والهيبة
وغير ذلك من تلوين الواردات (١١)فقال علامة الحقيقة التلوين لانّهم فى كلّ
(١٢)سَيْرٍ مع الله (١٣)تعالى فى زيادة (١٤)من تلوين الواردات على اسرارهم، وامّا
تلوين الصفات فهو كما قال القايل،

كُلَّ يَوْمٍ تَتَلَوَّنْ * غَيْرُ هذا بِكَ أَجْمَلْ،

قال الواسطى (١٣) رحمه الله من تخلَّق بخُلُقٍ لم تقع به طوارق التلوين فى
طبعه، ولبعضهم (١٥)هذان البيتان فى صفة (١٦)المسيرين،

زَجَرْتُ فُؤَادِى فَلَمْ يَنْزَجِرْ * وَيَطْلُبُ شَيْئًا وَمِنْهُ بَفَرْ

(١٧)بَسِيرُ إِلَى الحَقِّ مُسْتَظْهِرًا * وَإِنِّى عَلَيْهِ شَفِيقٌ حَذِرْ،

وبذلُ المُهَج معناه بذلُ مجهودٍ (١٨)استطاعة العبد على (١٩)قدر طاقته فى
توجّهه الى الله (١٣)تعالى (١٩)وإيثاره (٢٠)الله عز وجل على جميع محابّه، قال
(٢١)الخُوّاص (١٣) رحمه الله كل متوجّهٍ بتوجّه الى الله (١٣)عزّ وجلّ (٢٢)ومَواضِعُ
الاستراحة فيه قايمةٌ فلا ينفذ فى توجّهه، قال القايل،

A f.162b

١٥

---

(١) B ليس.   (٢) B حاله.   (٣) A تلوين.   (٤) B وقال.   (٥) Here A

has in marg. some words which have been partly cut away:

تلوين[ا]]بظهر
النفس A.   (٦) B الغيرة.   (٧) A يعنى.   (٨) A التغيير [منه الاس]نقامة وقال قوم [علام]ة الحقيقة.

(٩) B om. from فمن to رفع التلوين.   (١٠) B عز وجل.   (١١) A وقال.

هذين البيتين AB (١٥)   .B om (١٣)   فى تلوين من الواردات A (١٤)   نفس B (١٢).

(١٦) A adds لحق فى موضعه.   (١٧) A يشير.   (١٨) A واستطاعة.   (١٩) B وإيثار.

(٢٠) B ما لله.   (٢١) B الخوّاص ابرهيم.   (٢٢) A فمواضع.

يا مَلِيحَ (١)الدَّلِّ والغُنْجِ ٭ آلَكَ سُلْطَانٌ عَلَى الـمُهَجِ،
(٢)ومعنى المُهَج جميع المحبوبات اليك من النفس والمال والولد، والتَّلَف
معناه (٣)معنى الحَتْف والحَتْف (٤)والتلف ما يُنتظر منه الهلاك فى حينه، وقد
حكى عن ابى حَمزة الصوفى انه قال وقعتُ فى بئر فطرَّوا رأسها فأيستُ
من نفسى وسلَّمتُ الأمر الى الله (٦)تعالى واستسلمتُ فاذا (٥)بسبعٍ قد (٦)نزل
البئر فنعلَّقتُ (٧)برجله فأخرجنى من البئر فسمعتُ هاتفًا يقول يا أبا حمزة هذا
حَسَنٌ نجَّيناك من التلف بالتلف فقال ايانًا وفيها هذَين البيتَين،
أراكَ وَبى من هَيبتى لَكَ وَحْشةً ٭ فتُؤنِسُنِى باللُّطفِ مِنْكَ وبالعَطْفِ
ونُحْيِى مُحِبًّا أَنْتَ فى الحُبِّ حَتْفُهُ ٭ (٧)وَذَى عَجَبٌ كَوْنُ الحَياةِ مَعَ الحَتْفِ،
١٠ قال الجَريرى (٣)رحمه الله من لم يَقِفْ على علم التوحيد بشاهد من شواهد
زلَّ به قَدَمُ (٨)الغُرور فى مَهواةٍ (٩)من التلف، واللَجَأ توجَّه القلوب الى الله
(٩)تعالى بصدق الفاقة والرجاء، قال (١٠)الواسطى (٣)رحمه الله من لم يكن
فى صدق الفاقة واللجأ إلاّ عند الموت بقِيَت الذلّة عليه على دوام الاوقات،
وقال بعض اهل الفهم فى معنى (١١)قوله (١٢)أدخِلْنى مُدْخَلَ صِدْقٍ وَأَخرِجْنى
١٥ مُخْرَجَ صِدْقٍ قال أظْهَرَ محمّد صلم من نفسه صدق اللجأ بصدق الفاقة بين
يدى الله (٩)تعالى وبصدق اللجأ ترتّبت السراير، والانزعاج تحرُّكُ القلب للمُراد
باليقظة من سِنة الغفلة، ذُكر عن الجُنَيْد (٣)رحمه الله انه قال فى بعض كلامه
كيف لا تَسْمو اليه السراير وتنزع بما فيها اليه الضماير وكيف لا نسرع اليه
الأقدام بالطاعة وتنهض اليه بالجِدّ (١٣)والمبادرة أُنسًا منها (١٤)ببلاياه وسُرورًا
٢٠ بعظيم عطاياه، والانزعاج والازدعاج بمعنى (١٥)الانكساب والاكساب، وقد
قيل لبعض المشايخ اظنّه ابرهيم الخوّاص (٣)رحمه الله اصحابك يقولون نحن

(١) الذَل A.   (٢) معنى B.   (٣) B om.   (٤) والتكفف A.   (٥) سبع B.
(٦) حفرونزل B.   (٧) وذا B.   (٨) المغرور B.   (٩) عز وجل B.
(١٠) والمبالدة B.   (١١) قوله تعلى B.   (١٢) Kor. 17, 82.   (١٣) ابو بكر الواسطى B.
(١٤) ببلاياه AB app.   (١٥) الاكساب AB.   الاكساب والاكساب.

نأخذ من [١]الله اذا أخذنا ولا نراهم إلّا يأخذون من الناس فقال من [٢]ذا
الذى يُزعِج قلوب الناس حتى يُعظِّموهم من غير أن يطلبوا [٣]منهم شيئًا
ويسألوهم، وجذب الأرواح، فامّا جذب الارواح وسموُّ [٤]القلوب ومشاهدة
الأسرار والمناجاة والمخاطبة وما يشاكل ذلك فان أكثرَ [٢]ذلك عباراتٌ
[٥]نُعبِّر عن التوفيق والعناية وما يبدو على القلوب من انوار الهداية على
مقدار قُرب الرجل وبُعْده وصدقه وصفائه فى وجه، قال ابو سعيد [٦]الخرّاز
انّ الله [٧]تعالى جذب ارواح اوليائه اليه ولذّذها بِذِكْره والوصول الى قُرْبه
وعجّل لأبدانهم التلذّذ بكلّ شىء، فعيشُ أبدانهم عيش الحيوانيين وعيشُ ارواحهم
عيش الربّانيين، وقال [٨]الواسطى [٢]رحمه الله انّما أشهَدَهم ألطافَه [٩]التى
بها جذب سرايرهم الى [١٠]نفسه، وقال اذا [١١]جذب الارواح عن الأشباح
[١٢]ثبت الاشباح مع العقول والصفات [١٣]لانه حجبها بشرط العقول [١٤]وأيسِمهم
أن يكون لهم شىء من غير سرايرهم بقوله [٢]تعالى [١٥]قُلْ بِفَضْلِ اللّهِ،
[١٦]والوَطَر مُنية وتَمنَّع محمودة خارجة عن نعت البشرية وحظوظ النفسانية،
ويقال فلان هو [١٧]المتمكّن فى وطَنه والمُعلَّى فى وطَره، قال القايل،

تَرَحَّلْتُ يا لَيْلَى وَلَمْ أَقْضِ أَوْطارى * وما زِلْتُ مَحْزونًا أَحِنُّ إِلَى دارى،
وقال [١٨]ذو [١٩]النون رحمه الله،

أَموتُ وما ماتَتْ إِلَيْكَ صَبابَتى * ولا قُضِيَتْ عَنْ ورْدِ حُبّكَ أَوْطارى
[٢٠]مُناىَ المُنَى كُلُّ المُنَى أَنْتَ لى مِنّى * وَأَنْتَ الغِناكُلُّ الغِنا عِنْدَ إِقْتارى،
وقيل لحكيم اىُّ المواطن احبُّ للسكون [٢١]والتوطُّن فيه فقال احبّ المواطن

---

(١) B الله عز وجل.   (٣) B om.   (٢) B منه.   (٤) A القلب.

(٥) B om. A غير.   (٦) B الخرّاز احمد بن عيسى.   (٧) B تبارك وتعالى.

(٨) B ابو بكر الواسطى.   (٩) B الذى.   (١٠) B قربه.   (١١) B جذبت.

(١٢) B ثبتت.   (١٣) B لا.   (١٤) A يسمهم. B اسمهم.   (١٥) Kor. 10, 59.

(١٦) B والوطن.   (١٧) B الممكن.   (١٨) A ذا.   (١٩) B adds المصرى.

(٢٠) AB منا.   (٢١) B والتواطن.

الى (١)صاحبه (٢)مَوْطِنٌ اذا دعا (٣)فيه او طارَه أُجابَتْه، والاوَطَن وطن العبد
حيث انتهى به الحال واستقرّ به القرار، ويقال قد توطّن فى حال كذى
ومقام كذى، قال الجُنَيْد (٤)رحمه الله فى كلام له ان لله عبادًا على وطنات
مطىّ (٥)حُمْلانه يركبون وبالسرعة والبِدار اليه يستبقون، وقال النورى
(٤)رحمه الله،

أما تَرى هِيَمِى ٭ شَرَّدَنى عَنْ (٦)وَطَنى
إذا تَغَيَّبْتُ بَـدا ٭ وإنْ بَدا غَيَّبَنى
(٧)يَقُولُ لا تَشْهَدُ ما ٭ تَشْهَدُ أَوْ تَشْهَدَنى،

وقال ابو سليمان الدارانى (٤)رحمه الله الايمان افضل من اليقين لانّ الايمان
وطنات واليقين خطرات وإنّما وَصَفَ قدرَ ما شاهد من (٨)يقينه ووَصَفَ
نفسه بذلك وأراد بذلك غُرْبته عنه لانّ اليقين صفآء العلم فى القلب
واستقراره فيه والناس فيه متفاوتون، والشُرود (٩)نَفْرُ الصفات من منازلات
الحقائق وملازمة (١٠)الحقوق، قال (١١)ابن الأَعْرابى (٤)رحمه الله (١٢)أَوَما
تَرام مشرّدين فى كلّ (١٣)وادٍ يهيمون ولكلّ بارقٍ يتّبعون، (١٤)قال الواسطى
غذام بترية الاحوال ونعِّمهم بالملاحظة لهم فى الأعمال يَجِبُ على المرءِ أن
يكون فى صِدْق الفاقة واللجأ فى ايّام حياته لِيَلاً يَرِدَ عليه ذلك الشرود
(١٥)فيجيسُ بذُلّ الشرود (١٦)ويطلب من كلّ أحد (١٧)عَوْنًا بدعآء ويكلّمه ولو
كانت صحّة الوجد فى الاوقات مصعوبةً ما أصابه ذلك الشرود، والقُصود
معناه الارادات والنيّات الصادقة المقرونة بالنهوض اليه، حُكِى عن احمد
ابن عطآء (٤)رحمه الله انه قال من قصد فى قصوده غير الحقّ فقد (١٨)عظمت
استهانته بالحقّ، وقال الواسطى (٤)رحمه الله خواطر القصود جحود للمعبود

(١) B صاحبها. (٢) AB مواطن. (٣) B فيها. (٤) B om. (٥) B حملانه
(٦) A وطرى. (٧) A om. this verse. (٨) A نفسه. (٩) B نفى
(١٠) B الخوف. (١١) B بن. (١٢) A وما. (١٣) A وادى. (١٤) B وقال،
(١٥) B فيجيس. (١٦) B يطلب. (١٧) B غوثا. (١٨) A عظم.

24

وكيف يشهد المقصود من هو فى معانى المقصود، معناه أن من [1] يشاهد
المقصود فى قصده سقط عنه رؤية قصده فى قصده، والاصطناع مرتبة خصّ
بها الانبياء [2] صلوات الله عليهم اجمعين [3] والصدّيقون، وقال قوم الاصطناع
خصّ به [4] موسى من جميع الانبياء [5] عليهم السلام لقوله [6] وَٱصْطَنَعْتُكَ لِنَفْسِى، Af.164a
وقال قوم هى مرتبة الانبياء [5] عليهم السلام دون غيرهم، قال ابو سعيد الخَرّاز
[5] رحمه الله اوّل [7] بادٍ من الحقّ قد أخفاهم فى أنفسهم وأمات أنفسهم فى
أنفسهم واصطناعهم لنفسه [8] هذا اوّل دخول فى التوحيد من حيث ظهور
التوحيد بالدَّيمومية، وسُئل بعضهم عن قوله [9] جلّ جلاله وَٱصْطَنَعْتُكَ لِنَفْسِى
[10] وَلِتُصْنَعَ عَلَىٰ عَيْنِى فقال ما نجا نبىّ ولا ولىّ من [11] مِحنته ولا سلم احدٌ
فى مِنته من فِتنته، والاصطفاء معناه الاجتباء فى سابق العلم وهو اسمٌ
مشترك، قال الله [9] تعالى [12] وَٱجْتَبَيْنَاهُمْ وَهَدَيْنَاهُمْ، وقال الله [5] تعالى
[13] يَصْطَفِى مِنَ ٱلْمَلَٰئِكَةِ رُسُلًا وَمِنَ ٱلنَّاسِ، وقال [14] الواسطى [5] رحمه الله
ابتدأك بنفسه واصطفاك لنفسه فمن استعظم ذلك حَسُنَتْ إخطار نفسه فيا
بَذَلَتْ فان قابلتَهُ بنفس [15] العناية [16] تضمّنك ما منه من الهداية، والمَسْخ
معناه مسخُ القلوب وذلك للمطرودين من الباب كانت لهم قلوبٌ متوجهةٌ
فمُسِخَتْ بالإعراض عنها [17] وجعلت توجّهها الى الحظوظ دون الحقوق،
فاذا قال القائل فلانٌ قد مُسِخ به معناه [5] اى أعْرَضَ بقلبه، واللطيفة
اثارة [18] تلوحُ فى الفم وتلمع فى الذهن [19] ولا تسعُها العبارة لدقّة معناها،
قال ابو سعيد [5] بن الاعرابى [20] رحمه الله الحقّ [5] يُريدك بلطيفة من لدُنْه
تُدْرِكُ بها ما يريد بك إدراكَهُ، [21] وقال ابو حمزة [5] الصوفى [22] رحمه الله،

---

[1] B شاهد.   [3] والصدّيقون B.   [2] عليهم السلام B.   [4] موسى B.

وهذا B [8].   عليه السلام [5] B om.   [6] Kor. 20, 43.   [7] AB بادى.

فضمّتك A [11].   محبته A [11].   [10] Kor. 20, 40.   [9] عز وجل B.

حتى تسعها B [19].   ابو بكر الواسطى B [14].   السعاية B [15].   فضمّتك A [16].   [13] Kor. 22, 74.   [12] Kor. 6, 87.

يريدك B [20].   فى معنى ذلك B [21].   [22] B om. B adds app.   الى تلوح A [18].   وجعل B [17].   فضمّتك B.

تَلَطَّفْتَ فى أَمْرى فأبدأتَ شاهدى ٭ إلى (١)غابى واللُّطفُ يُدْرَكُ باللُّطْفِ،
والامتحان ابتلاَءٌ من الحقّ يحلّ بالقلوب المُقْبِلة على الله (٢)تعالى ومحنتُها
انقسامُها وتشتتُها، حُكِى عن خير النسّاج (٣)رحمه الله انه قال دخلتُ بعضَ
المساجد فتعلّق بى شابٌّ من اصحابنا فقال لى يا شيخ تعطّف علىّ فانّ محنتى
عظيمة فقلت وما محنتُكَ فقال افتقدتُ البلاَءَ وقورنتُ بالعافية وأنت تعلم
انّ هذه محنة عظيمة، والامتحان على (٤)ثلثة لقوم منهم عقوبة (٥)ولقوم منهم
تمحيص وكفّارة ولقوم استدعاءٌ الزيادة وارتفاع درجة، والحُدَث اسمٌ لما Af.164b
(٦)لم يكن فكان، قال (٦)بعضهم اذا اراد الله (٧)تعالى تنبيه العامّة أحْدَثَ
فى العالم آيةً من آياته واذا اراد تنبيه الخاصّة ازال عن قلوبهم ذِكْرَ حدثِ
الاشياءِ، والكلّية اسمٌ لجماع الشيء الذى لم يَبْقَ منه بقيّةٌ (٧)فاذا قال القايل
الكلّ يريد بذلك (٧)أنْ لم يبق منه بقيّة الاّ بمعناه، قال بعضهم لا يكون
العبد عبدًا بالكلّية (٨)ويكون (٩)منه لغير الله بقيّةٌ، وقال آخر إن أقبلتَ
(١٠)عليه (١١)بكليّتك أقْبَلَ عليك بكلّ الكلّ، (١٢)وقال،

(١٣)بل كل ما كل مِنْ كُلّى عَلَيْكَ كَما ٭ بِكُلِّ كُلّكَ كُلّى كانَ مَنْشَاءُ،

والتلبيس تحلّى الشيءِ بنعت ضدّه، حُكِى عن الواسطى (٣)رحمه الله انه قال
التلبيس (١٤)عين الربوبية معناه ان المؤمن يُظهره فى زىّ الكافر والكافر فى
زىّ المؤمن، قال الله تعالى (١٥)وَلَبَسْنَا عَلَيْهِمْ مَا يَلْبَسُونَ، وقال الجُنَيْد (٣)رحمه
الله امتزج بالالتباس (١٦)واختلط متلوّنًا فى الإحساس وما يتغيّر عنها فى
الالتباس يُؤْخَذُ عنه كأسْرَعِ مأخوذٍ (١٧)ومُختَلَسٍ، وللقنّاد (١٨)فى هذا المعنى،

---

(١) AB غابى. Cf. p. ٣٥٤, l. ١٧. ‏ (٢) B عز وجل. ‏ (٣) B om. ‏ (٤) B ثلث.

(٥) B ولقوم منهم آخر for فيكون. ‏ (٦) B واذا. ‏ (٧) A اى. ‏ (٨) B فيكون.

(٩) A has منه with فيه written above. ‏ (١٠) B على الله. ‏ (١١) B بكلك.

(١٢) B فقال القايل. ‏ (١٣) It is not clear how the following words should
be pointed. B has بكل بل كما من كلى عليك كا. ‏ (١٤) B عن. ‏ (١٥) Kor. 6, 7.

(١٦) B om. from واختلط to الالتباس. ‏ (١٧) A ومحلبس B مختلس. ‏ (١٨) B om.

فى هذا المعنى. In marg. B شعر.

بنا يُكْشَفُ التَّلْبِيسُ فى كُلِّ ماكِـرٍ ۞ إذا طاحَ فى الدَّعْوَى وطاحَ اَنْتِحالُهُ ،
والشِّرْب تلقى الارواحِ والاسرار [1] الطاهرة لِما يَرِدُ عليها من الكرامات وتنعُّمُها
بذلك [2] فشبّه ذلك بالشِّرْب لتهنِّيه وتنعُّمه بما يَرِدُ على قلبه من انوار
مشاهدة قُرْب سيّده، قال [3] ذو النون [4] رحمه الله وردتْ قلوبهم على بحر
المحبّة فاغترفتْ منه رِيًّا من الشراب فشربتْ منه بمخاطرة القلوب فسهل عليهم
كلُّ عارضٍ عرض لهم دون لقاء المحبوب، وقال القايل فى هذا المعنى،

شَرِبْتُ كأْسًا عَلَى ذِكْراكَ صافِيةً ۞ فَما [5] يُعَلِّلُ فيكَ القَلْبَ تَعْلِيلُ
فَما وَجَدْتُ لِشَىءٍ عَنْكَ لِى شُغْلاً ۞ لا عِشْتُ إِنْ قُلْتُ إِنِّى عَنْكَ مَشْغُولُ

والذَّوْقُ ابتداءُ الشِّرْب، قال [3] ذو النون [4] رحمه الله لمّا اراد ان يسقيهم
من كأس محبّته ذَوَّقهم من [6] لذاذته وأَعْقَمهم من حلاوته، قال القايل [7] فى
هذا المعنى،

يَقُولُونَ [8] تَكْلَى وَمَنْ لَمْ يَذُقْ ۞ فِراقَ الأَحِبّةِ لَمْ يَثْكَلِ ،

والعَيْن اشارة الى ذات الشىء الذى تبدو منه الاشياءُ ، قال [9] الواسطى
[4] رحمه الله [10] وقومٌ علموا مصادر الكلام من اين فوقعوا على العَيْن فأغْناهم
عن البحث والطلب، وقال الجُنَيْد [4] رحمه الله حكايات ابى يزيد البسطامى
[4] رحمه الله تدلُّ انه [4] كان قد بلغ الى عَيْن الجَمْع وعين الجمع اسم من
اسماء التوحيد له نعتٌ ووصفٌ يعرفه اهلُه ، [11] وقال النورى ،

[12] مَضَى الجَمِيعُ فَلا عَيْنَ ولا أَثَرْ ۞ [13] مُضِىَّ عادٍ وَفِقْدانَ [14] الأُلَى إِرَمْ ،
والاصطلام نعت غَلَبةٍ تَرِدُ على العقول [15] فيستلبها بقوّة سلطانه وقهره، قال
بعضهم [16] قلوب ممتحنة [16] وقلوب مصطلَمة وان وقع [17] الاصطلام فهو ذهابُهُ

(1) Perhaps الظاهرة. Cf. p. ٢٣٥, l. ١٧.   (٢) A فيشبه with فشبه written
above.   (٣) A ذا. B adds المصرى.   (٤) B om.   (٥) A أعلل B من على
بعلى من B.   (٦) A ارادته.   (٧) B om. فى هذا المعنى.   (٨) B ثكلا.
ذكراك تقليل.   (٩) B ابو بكر الواسطى.   (١٠) B وقوما.   (١١) B قال.   (١٢) A trans-
poses the two hemistichs of this verse.   (١٣) B مضا.   (١٤) AB الاولى.
(١٥) B فيسلبها.   (١٦) A وقلب.   (١٧) B الى الاصطلام.

وطَمْسَهُ، (١)قال،

(٢)إذا ما بَدَتْ لى تَعاظَمُتها ٭ فأَصْدُرُ فى حال مَنْ لَمْ يَرِدْ

فيَصْطَلِمُ الكُلَّ (٣)منّى بها ٭ ويَحْجُبُ عَنّى بها مـا أَجِدْ

والحُرّية اشارة الى نهاية (٤)التحقّق بالعبودية لله (٥)تعالى وهو أن لا (٦)يملكك

شىءٌ من المكوّنات (٧)وغيرها فتكون حُرًّا اذا كنتَ لله عبدًا كما قال (٨) بشّرَ

لسَرىّ (٩)رحمهما الله فيما حُكِى عنه انه قال انّ الله (٩)تعالى خلقك حُرًّا

فكن كما خلقك لا (١٠)تُرَآئى أهْلَك فى الحَضَر ولا (١١)رُفْقتك فى السَفَر اعملْ

لله ودع الناس عنك، (١٢)قال الجُنَيْد (٩)رحمه الله آخرُ مقام العارف الحُرّية،

وقال بعضهم لا يكون العبد عبدًا حقًّا ويكون لما سوى الله مُسْتَرَقًّا، والرَّيْن

هو (١٣)الصَّدأ الذى يقع على القلوب، قال الله (١٤)تعالى (١٥)كَلَّا بَلْ رَانَ

عَلَى قُلُوبِهِمْ مَا كَانُوا يَكْسِبُونَ، وقال بعض اهل العلم حُجِبَ القلوب على

اربعة (١٦)أوْجُه فمنها الخَتم والطبع وذلك لقلوب الكُفّار ومنها الرَّيْن والقَسْوة

وذلك لقلوب المنافقين ومنها (١٤)الصَدأ (١٧)والغِشاوة وذلك لقلوب المؤمنين،

سيِّل (١٨)ابن الجلَّاء لِمَ سُمّى (١٩)أبوك الجلَّاء (٢٠)فقال ما كان (٢١)بجَلَّاءِ

الحديد ولكن كان اذا تكلّم على القلوب جلّاها من (٢٢)صدأ الذُنوب،

والغَيْن قد اكثروا فى وصفه وهو خَبَرٌ ضعيفٌ (٢٣)قد رُوِى عن النبى صلعم

(٢٤)أنّه قال إنّه ليَغانُ على قلبى فأستغفرُ الله وأتوبُ اليه فى اليوم مائة مرّة،

فقالوا الغَيْن الذى كان يعارض قلبَ النبىّ صلعم وكان يتوب منه مثلهُ مثلُ

المرآة اذا تنفّس فيها الناظر فينقص من (٢٥)ضوءها ثمّ تعود الى (٢٦)حالـة

ضوءها، (٢٥) وقال قوم هذا مُحال لانّ قلْب النبىّ صلعم لا يلحقه قهرٌ (١٦)من

---

(١) B adds القايل.   (٢) B om. this verse.   (٣) B عنّى.   (٤) B التحقيق.

(٥) B عز وجل.   (٦) A يملك.   (٧) A وغيره.   (٨) B بشر بن السرى.

(٩) B om.   (١٠) B تراعى.   (١١) B رفيقك.   (١٢) B وقال.   (١٣) A الصدى.

(١٤) جل ذكره B.   (١٥) Kor. 83, 14.   (١٦) A om.   (١٧) A والقساوة.

(١٨) B بن.   (١٩) B أبو.   (٢٠) B قال.   (٢١) B يجلوا.   (٢٢) A صدى.

(٢٣) B فيا.   (٢٤) B om. أنه قال.   (٢٥) B ضوء.   (٢٦) B حال.

الخلق لانّه مخصوص بالرؤية، قال الله [1] تعالى [2] مَا كَذَّبَ الفُؤَادُ مَا رَأَى،
وليس لأحد ان يحكم على قلب النبى صلعم بوصْف او نعت او يشبّهه بشئ
او يضرب له [3] مثلًا او يعلّله بعلّة خفيّة او جليّة، وقال ابو علىّ الروذبارى
[4] رحمه الله فى معنى الاغانة،

الغَيْنُ يُحْبَسُ عَنْ تَحْصِيلِ لُبْسِنِهِ * لِقَلْبٍ لابِسٍ حَقٍّ بَانَ عَن عِلَّهْ
[5] فَانْ تَرَآءَتْ يَسْبِقُ الحَقُّ رُؤْيَتَها * [6] كَانَ التَّغَيُّنُ فِى التَّصْرِيفِ عَنْ [7] ثِقَلَهْ
[8] لَكِنَّى قُلْتُ ما لاحَتْ طَوالِعُهُ * مِنَ المُؤَمَّلِ تَنْبِيهٌ إِلَى أَمَلَهْ
[9] والثَّوْبُ مِنْهُ عَلَى مَعْنَى الوِفاقِ وَما * تُبْدِى سَرائِرُها [10] غَيْنًا لِمُحْتَمِلَهْ،

وهذه [11] الالفاظ قد [12] شرحناها على حسب ما فتح الله [4] به على قلبى فى
الوقت والذى بقى اكثرُ وان استقصيتُ فى [14] شرحها يطول بـه الكتاب
ويخرج عن الاختصار ونذكر بعد ذلك شرح [14] الشطحيات من كلامهم
الذى يكون ظاهره [15] مستشنعًا وباطنه [16] صحيحًا مستقيمًا والله الموفّق
للصواب، والوسايط الاسباب التى بين الله [4] تعالى وبين العبد من [4] اسباب
الدنيا والآخرة، سئل بعض المشايخ عن الوسايط فقال الوسايط على ثلثة
اوجُه وسايط مواصلات ووسايط متّصلات ووسايط منفصلات [17] فالمواصلات
بوادى الحقّ والمتّصلات [18] العبادات والمنفصلات حظوظ النفس، وقال
ابو علىّ الروذبارى [4] رحمه الله وهو الذى جعل الوسايط رحمةً للعارفين
لِيُؤْثِروه عليها،

[1] B عز وجل.   [2] Kor. 53, 11.   [3] AB مثل.   [4] B om.
[5] In B the third verse precedes the second.   [6] B كانه عنه فى التصريف.
[7] A عما.   [10] A والنور.   [9] B لكن قلبى ما لاحت.   [8] B app. نقله.
[14] B الشطحيات   [12] B شرحها.   [14] B شرحه   [11] B الفاظ.   [11] B غيبًا.
[17] B والمواصلات   [16] B صحيحة مستقيمة.   [15] B مستشنعة . A مستبنعة.
[18] A العادات . B العبودبات.

كتاب تفسير (١) الشَّطحيات والكلمات التى ظاهرها (٢) مستشنع وباطنها (٣) صحيح (٤) مستقيم،

باب فى معنى الشَّطْح والردّ على من انكر ذلك برأيه،

ان سأل سائلٌ فقال ما معنى الشطح فيقال معناه عبارةٌ (٥) مستغرَبةٌ فى
وصْف وَجْدٍ فاضَ بقوّته وهاجَ بشدّة غليانه وغلبته، وبيان ذلك ان الشطح
فى لغة العرب هو الحَرَكة يقال شَطَحَ يَشْطَحُ اذا تحرّك ويقال للبيت الذى
يجوزون فيه الدَّقيق المِشْطاحُ، قال الشاعر،

قِفْ بشَطِّ الفُراتِ مَشْرَعةِ الخَيْـــلِ (٦) قَبِيْلَ الطريقِ بالمِشْطاحِ
بالطَّواحِينِ مِنْ حجارةٍ بِطِرِيْـــقٍ بِدَيْرِ الغِزْلانِ دَيْـــرِ المِلاحِ
(٧) وإذا لاحَ بالمُسَنّاةِ ظَبْىٌ ∗ قَدْ كَساهُ الإشراقُ ضَوْءَ الصَّباحِ
فأقِرَّ ذاكَ الغزالَ مِنّى سَلامًا ∗ كلَّمـا صاحَ صائحٌ بِفَلاحِ،

وإنّما سُمّى (٨) ذلك البيت المِشْطاح من كثرة ما يحرّكون فيه الدقيق فوق
ذلك الموضع الذى (٩) يَحْلونه به وربّما يَفيضُ من جانبيه من كثرة مـا
(١٠) يحرّكونه فالشطح (١١) لفظة مأخوذة من الحَرَكة لانّها حَرَكةُ أسرار الواجدين
اذا قَويَ وَجْدُهم (١٢) فعبّروا عن وَجْدهم بعبارة (١٣) يَستغرب (١٤) سامعُها
فمفتونٌ هالكٌ (١٥) بالإنكار والطعن عليها اذا سمعها وسالمٌ ناجٍ برفع الانكار

---

(١) الشطيحات B.   (٢) مستشنعة A.   (٣) مستبشعة B.   (٤) AB صحيحة.

(٤) مستقيمة A.   (٥) B om.   (٥) مستعبرة B.   (٦) ومل B. فدا A.   (٧) B om.

this and the following verse.   (٨) لذلك A.   (٩) يخلوه A.   (١٠) يحركوه A.

(١١) لفظ A.   (١٢) فيعبروا B.   (١٣) تستغرب B.   (١٤) سامعه AB.

(١٥) بالانكار عنها B.

عنها والبَحْثِ عمّا (١) يُشكل عليه منها (٢) بالسؤال (٣) عمّن بعلم عِلْمَهـا، ويكون ذلك من شأنها ألا تَرى انّ الماء الكثير اذا جرَى فى نهرٍ ضيّقٍ فيفيض من (٤) حافَتِه (٥) يقال شَطَحَ الماءُ فى النهرِ، (٦) فكذلك المُريد الواجد اذا قوى وَجْدُهُ ولم يُطِقْ حَمْلَ ما بَرَدَ على قلبه من سَطوة انوار حقايقه سطع ٥ ذلك على لسانه فيترجم عنها بعبارةٍ مستغرَبةٍ مُشكِلةٍ على فُهوم سامِعيها إلّا من كان من أهْلها ويكون متجوّزًا فى علمها فسُمّى ذلك على لسان اهل (٧) الاصطلاح شَطْحًا، وبَعْدُ فانّ الله تعالى فتح قلوب اوليآئـه وأَذِنَ (٨) لهم بالإشراف على درجات متعالية وقد جاد الحقّ (٩) تعالى على إهل صَفْوته والمُتحقّقين بالتوجّه والانقطاع اليه بكشْف ما كان مستترًا عنهم قَبْلَ ذلك من ١٠ مراتب صفوته ودرجات اهل الخصوص من (١٠) عباده فكلّ واحد منهم ينطق بحقيقة ما وجد ويصدق (١١) عن حاله ويصف ما ورد على سرّه (١٢) بُنطْقه ومقاله لانّهم لا يرون حالًا أَعْلَى من حالهم حتى يُحْكِموها فاذا احكموها فعند ذلك يَسْمون (١٣) بهِمَّهم الى حالة أَعْلَى من ذلك حتى تنتهى (١٤) الطُّرق والاحوال والأماكن الى غاية ونهاية هى أَعْلَى النهايات وغاية الغايات، قال ١٥ الله تعالى (١٥) وَفَوْقَ كُلِّ ذِي عِلْمٍ عَلِيمٌ، (١٦) وقال (١٧) وَرَفَعْنَا بَعْضَهُمْ فَوْقَ بَعْضٍ دَرَجَاتٍ، وقال (١٨) انْظُرْ كَيْفَ فَضَّلْنَا بَعْضَهُمْ عَلَى بَعْضٍ، وليس لأحد أن يَبْسُطَ لسانَه بالوقيعة فى اوليآئه (١٩) ويَقِيسَ بفهمه ورأيه ما يسمع من الفاظهم وما يُشْكل على فهمه من كلامهم لانّهم فى اوقاتهم متفاوتون وفى احوالهم متفاضلون (٢٠) ومتشاكلون ومتجانسون بعضهم لبعض ولم أَشكالٌ ونُظَرَاؤه ٢٠ معروفون فمن بان شَرَفُهُ وفضْله على أشكاله بفضل عِلْمه وسِعة معرفته فله

(١) يشكل B. (٢) بالسؤال B. (٣) عن من B. (٤) حافته B.
(٥) فيقال B. (٦) وكذلك B. (٧) الصلاح B. (٨) لها B. (٩) جل ذكره B.
(١٠) عباده وخليقته B. (١١) من A. (١٢) لنطقه A. (١٣) بهمهم A.
(١٤) الظرف B. (١٥) Kor. 12, 76. (١٦) وقال جل ذكره B.
(١٧) Kor. 43, 31. (١٨) Kor. 17, 22. (١٩) ويفسر A. (٢٠) هم B ومتشاكلون.

أن يتكلّم في عِلْمِهم وإصابتهم ونقصانهم وزيادتهم ومن لم يسلك سُبُلهم ولم يَنْحَ
نَحْوَهم ولا يقصد مقاصدهم فالسلامةُ له في رفع الانكار عنهم وأن يَكِلَ أمورهم
الى الله تعالى ويتّهم نفسه بالغلط فيما ينسبهم اليه من الخطأ، وبالله التوفيق،

باب تفسير العلوم وبيان ما يُشْكِل على [١]فهم العلماء من
علوم الخاصّة وتصحيح ذلك بالحُجّة،

Af.167a   [٢]قال الشيخ رحمه الله، اعلمْ انّ العلم أكثر من ان يحيط به فهْمُ الفهماء
او يُدرِكه عقول العقلاء وكذاك بقصّة موسى والخضر عليهما السلم مع جلالة
موسى [١]عليه السلم وما خصّه الله به من الكلام والنبوّة والوحى والرسالة،
وقد ذكر الله [٢]تعالى في المُحْكَم الناطق على لسان [٤]نبيّه الصادق عَجْزَ
موسى [١]عليه السلم عن إدراك علم عبْدٍ من عباده [٥]اذ قال تعالى [٦]عَبْدًا
مِنْ عِبَادِنَا آتَيْنَاهُ رَحْمَةً مِنْ عِنْدِنَا [٧]الآيَة حتى [٨]سأله فقال [٩]هَلْ أَتَّبِعُكَ
الآية مع تأبيد موسى [١]عليه السلم [١٠]وشرفه وعصمته من الانكار [١]عليـه
على [١]أن الخضر [١]عليه السلم لم يلحق درجة موسى [١]عليه السلم في النبوّة
والرسالة والتكليم ابدًا، وقال النبيّ [١١]صلعم لو [١٢]تعلمون ما أَعْلَمُ لضحكتم
قليلاً ولبكيْتم كثيرًا [١٢]ولَما تلذّذتم [١]بالنساء [١٤]ولا تقاررتم على فُرُشكم
ولخرجتم الى الصُّعدات تجأرون الى الله [١]تعالى والله لوددتُ أنّى كنت شجرةً
[١٤]تُعْضَدُ، رواه اسرائيل عن ابرهيم بن مُهاجر عن [١٥]مُجاهد عن مورّق
عن ابى ذرّ عن النبيّ صلعم، وفى هذا الخبر دليل على ان [١٦]قوله [١٧]يَأَيُّهَا

(١) B om.   (٢) B om.   (٣) قال الشيخ رحمه الله. B   (٤) النبى. B

(٥) وقال جل ذكره. B   (٦) عبد. A Kor. 18, 65.   (٧) الرحمة. B   (٨) B adds

عليه. B   (٩) Kor. 18, 65.   (١٠) وعصمته وشرفه. B   (١١) موسى عليه السلام

السلام.   (١٢) علمتم. B   (١٣) وما.   (١٤) تحصد. B   (١٥) A om.

مجاهد عن.   (١٦) قوله تعالى. B   (١٧) Kor. 5, 71.

الرَّسُولُ بَلِّغْ مَا أُنْزِلَ إِلَيْكَ مِنْ رَبِّكَ وَلَمْ يَقُلْ ما نعرِّفُنا به اليك وقولُه
صلعم لو تعلمون ما (١)اعلم لو كان من العلوم (٢)الَّتى أُمِر بالبلاغ لبلَّغهم ولو
صلح لهم أن يعلموه لعلَّمهم لانّ الله (٣)تعالى خصَّ النبيَّ صلعم بعلومٍ ثلثٍ، عِلمٌ
بيِّنٌ للخاصّة والعامّة وهو علم الحُدود والأمر والنهى، وعِلم خُصَّ به (٤)قومٌ
من الصحابة دون غيرهم (٥)هو العلم الذى كان يعلم حُذَيْفَة بن اليَمان
(٦)رضى الله عنه حتى كان يسأله عمر بن الخطَّاب (٧)رضى الله عنه مع جلالته
وفضله ويقول يا حذيفة هل أنا من المنافقين، وكذلك رُوِى عن علىّ بن
ابى طالب (٧)رضى الله عنه انه قال علَّمنى رسول الله صلعم سبعين بابًا من
العلم لم يعلم ذلك (٨)احدٌ غيرى (٦)قال وكان اصحاب رسول الله صلعم اذا
أشكل على (٩)احدهم شىء يلتجون فى ذلك الى علىّ بن ابى طالب (٧)رضى
الله عنه، وعِلمٌ (١٠)خُصَّ به رسول الله صلعم لم يشاركه فيه احدٌ من (١١)اصحابه
وهو العلم الذى قال لو تعلمون ما اعلمُ، فمن اجل ذلك قُلْنا لاينبغى لأحد   Af.167b
ان يظنّ انه (١٢)يحوى جميع العلوم حتى يخطِّئ برأيه كلامَ المخصوصين
ويكفِّرهم ويزندقهم وهو (١٣)متعرٍّ من مارسة احوالهم ومنازلة حقايقهم واعمالهم،
(١٤)وعلوم الشريعة على اربعة اقسام (١٥)فالقسم الاوّل منها علم الرواية والآثار
والاخبار وهو العلم الذى (١٦)ينقله الثقات عن الثقات، والقسم الثانى علم
الدراية وهو علم الفقه والاحكام وهو العلم المتداول بين العلماء والفقهاء،
والقسم الثالث علم القياس والنظر والاحتجاج على المخالفين وهو علم الجدل
وإثبات الحُجّة على اهل البدع والضلالة نصرةً للدين، والقسم الرابع (٥)هو
أعلاها وأشرَفُها وهو علم الحقايق والمنازلات وعلم المعاملة والمجاهدات
والاخلاص فى الطاعات والتوجُّه الى الله (٦)عزَّ وجلَّ من جميع الجهات

---

(١) B adds قوما.   (٢) B الذى.   (٣) B عزوجل.   (٤) B adds لبيكيم.

(٥) B وهو.   (٦) B om.   (٧) B عليه السلام.   (٨) B لاحد.   (٩) B احد.

(١٠) A خبر. B خصّ الله.   (١١) B الصحابة.   (١٢) B يحنوى.   (١٣) AB منعرى.

(١٤) B وعلم.   (١٥) B فقسمه الاولى.   (١٦) B نقل.

والانقطاع البه فى جميع الاوقات وصحّة القصود والارادات وتصفية السراير
من الآفات والاكتفاء بخالق السموات وإمانة النفوس بالمخالفات والصدق
فى منازلة الاحوال والمقامات وحُسْن الادب بين يدى (١)الله فى السرّ
والعلانية فى الخلوات والاكتفاء بأخْذ البُلْغة عند غلبة الفاقات والإعراض
٥ عن الدنيا وترْك ما (٢)فيها طلبًا للرفعة فى الدرجات والوصول الى الكرامات،
فمن غلط فى علم الرواية غلطًا لم يسأل عن غلطه احدًا من اهل (٣)الدراية
ومن غلط فى علم الدراية شيئًا لايسأل عن غلطه احدًا من اهل علم الرواية
ومن غلط فى شىء من علم القياس والنظر فلا يسأل عن غلطه احدًا من
اهل (٤)علم الرواية والدراية (٥)وكذلك من غلط فى شىء من علم الحقايق
١٠ والاحوال فلا يسأل عن غلطه الا عالمًا منهم (٦)كاملًا فى معناه، ويُمْكن
ان توجد هذه العلوم كلّها فى اهل الحقايق ولا يمكن ان يوجد علم الحقايق
فى هؤلاء الا ما شاء الله لانّ علم الحقايق ثمرة العلوم كلّها (٧)ونهاية جميع
العلوم، (٨)وغاية جميع العلوم الى علم الحقايق فاذا انتهى اليها وقع فى بحر ‌Af.168a
لا غاية له وهو علمُ القلوب وعلم المعارف (٩)وعلم الاسرار وعلم الباطن وعلم
١٥ التصوّف وعلم الاحوال وعلم المعاملات (١٠)اىّ ذلك شيتَ معناه واحد،
قال الله (١١)تعالى (١٢)قُلْ لَوْ كَانَ ٱلْبَحْرُ مِدَادًا لِكَلِمَاتِ رَبِّى لَنَفِدَ ٱلْبَحْرُ قَبْلَ
أَن تَنفَدَ كَلِمَاتُ رَبِّى وَلَوْ جِئْنَا بِمِثْلِهِ مَدَدًا، (١٣)ألا ترى انّ هؤلاء لا يُنكرون
شيئًا من علومهم وهم ينكرون علوم هؤلاء الا (١٤)ما شاء الله وكل صنْف من
هؤلاء اذا تبحّر فى علمه فصار مُتْقِنًا فى فهمه فهو السيّد لأصحابه لا بدّ لهم من
٢٠ الرجوع اليه فيا يُشكل عليهم، فاذا اجتمعت هذه الاقسام الاربعة فى واحد

---

(١) B اله عز وجل.   (٢) B adds على من فيها.   (٣) B ومن فى الدراية
العلم.   (٤) B فى العلم.   (٥) B فكذلك.   (٦) B كلامًا.   غلط فى شى من علم القياس الخ
(٧) A om. ونهاية جميع العلوم but is suppl. in marg.   (٨) B وغايتها.
(٩) B om. from وعلم الاسرار to وعلم التصوف.   (١٠) B اى for وغاية جميع العلوم.
(١١) B جل ذكره.   (١٢) Kor. 18, 109.   (١٣) B الا ان ترى.   ذلك شى
(١٤) B من.

فهو الامام الكامل وهو القُطْب والحُجَّة والداعى الى المنهج [1] والحُجَّة كا [2]
رُوى عن علىّ بن ابى طالب [3] رضى الله عنه انّه قال فى [4] كلام له لكُمَيْل
ابن [5] زياد اللهمّ [6] بَلَى لا تَخْلُو الارض من قائم لله [7] بحُجَجه لِئَلّا تَبْطُلَ
آياتُهُ وَتَدْحَضَ حُجَّتُهُ اولئك الاقلّون عددًا الأعظمون عند الله [8] تعالى
قدرًا، وقد رجعتُ الى معنى الشطح وتفسير [9] الشطحيات [10] وأقلُّ ما يوجَدُ
لأهل الكمال الشطحُ لانّهم متمكّنون فى معانيهم وانّما وقع [11] فى الشطح من
كان فى بداية وكان مُرادًا بالوصول الى الكمال والغاية فتكون [12] بدايتُهُ
نهاية الارادات وهى [13] فى معناها بداية الغايات والكمال والنهايات ، والله
اعلم [8] بالصواب ،

[14] باب فى كلمات شطحيات تُحْكَى عن ابى يزيد [15] [قد فسّر الجنيد] طرفًا منــه ،

قال الشيخ رحمه الله قد فسّر الجنيد [8] رحمه الله شيئًا قليلًا من [16] شطحات
ابى يزيد [8] رحمه الله والعاقل يستدلّ بالقليل على الكثير ومن المحال أن
أجدَ للجُنَيْد [8] رحمه الله تفسيرًا لكلامه [17] فأَدَعَ ذلك وأتكلّم من عنده
[8] له جوابًا [18] غيرَهُ، قال الجنيد [8] رحمه الله الحكايات عن ابى يزيد مختلفة
والناقلون عنه فيما سمعوه [19] مفترقون وذلك والله اعلم لاختلاف الاوقات
الجارية عليه فيها ولاختلاف المواطن [20] المتداولة با خصّ منها فكلّ يحكى
عنه ما ضبط من قوله ويؤدّى ما سمع من [21] تفصيل مواطنه، وقال الجنيد

ٱٱ

(١) المنهاج B.   (٢) والحجة B.   (٣) عليه السلام B.   (٤) كلامه B.
(٥) زيد B.   (٦) ربى B.   (٧) بحجته B.   (٨) B om.   (٩) الشطحيات B.
(١٠) وقل B.   (١١) الى B.   (١٢) بدايه A.   (١٣) A om.   (١٤) باب B.
تفسير كلمات شطحيات حكى عن ابى يزيد البسطامى رضى الله عنه طرف منه قد فسر الجنيد الخ
(١٥) AB om.   (١٦) شطحيات B.   (١٧) ان ادع B.   (١٨) غيرها A.   (١٩) متفرقون B.
(٢٠) المتداولة AB. المبذولة In A is written above.   (٢١) تفصيل A.

(۱) رحمه الله وكان من كلام ابى (۲) يزيد (۱) رحمه الله لقوّته وغَوْره وانتهآء معانيه (۳) مُغْتَرَفٌ من بحر قد انفرد (٤) به وجُعل ذلك البحر له وَحْدَهُ، (٥) قال الجنيد (۱) رحمه الله ثمّ انى رأيت الغاية القُصْوَى من (٦) حاله يعنى من حال ابى يزيد رحمه الله حالًا قلّ من يفهمها عنه او يعبّر (٧) عنها عند استماعها لانّه لا يحتمله الّا من عرف معناه وأدرك مُسْتَنْقاهُ ومن لم تكن هذه هيئَتَهُ عند استماعه فذلك كلّه عنه مردود، وقال الجنيد (۱) رحمه الله رأيتُ حكايات ابى يزيد (۱) رحمه الله على ما نَعْتُهُ يُنبئُ عنه انّه قد غرق (۸) فيما وجد منها وذهب عن حقيقة الحقّ (۹) اذا لم (۱۰) يَرِدُ عليها وهى (۱۱) معان (۱۲) غرّقته على تارات من الغَرَق كلّ واحدٍ منها (۱۳) غيرُ صاحبتها، وقال الجنيد (۱) رحمه الله امّا ما وصف من بدايات حاله (۱٤) فهو قوىٌّ مُحْكَمٌ قد بلغ منه الغاية وقد وصف اشياءَ من علمِ التوحيد صحيحةً الّا انّها بدايات فيما يُطلب منها المُرادون لذلك، وهذه الكلمات التى أُريدُ ان أذكرها ليست (۱) هى ممّا (۱٥) يُكْتَبُ فى المصنّفات لانّها ليست من العلوم المبثوثة عند العلمآء ولكن رأيت الناس قد اكثروا الخَوْض فى معانيها فواحدٌ قد جعله حُجّةً لباطله وآخَرُ قد اعتقد فى قايلها الكُفْرَ والجميعُ قد غلطوا فيا ذهبوا اليه، والله (۱٦) الموفّق للصواب،

باب فى ذكر حكاية (۱۷) حُكيت عن ابى يزيد البسطامى (۱) رحمه الله تعالى ،

وقد (۱۸) شاع فى كلام الناس انّه قال (۱۹) ذلك ولا أدْرى يصحّ منه

---

(۱) B om.   (۲) B adds قوله.   (۳) B مغترق.   (٤) A بها.   (٥) B وقال.

(٦) B الح حالًا ابى يزيد حال.   (۷) A om.   (۸) B فيها.   (۹) A اذ.

(۱۰) B يزد.   (۱۱) AB معانى.   (۱۲) A عرفته B عرفته.   (۱۳) B عن.

(۱٤) AB هو.   (۱٥) A تكتب.   (۱٦) B الموفق للصواب for اعلم.   (۱۷) A حكى.

(۱۸) A اشاع.   (۱۹) B om. from انه قال to ذلك.   حكيت عن B om.

ذلك ام لا، ذُكِر عن ابى يزيد انّه قال (١)رفعنى مرّةً فأقامنى بين يديه
وقال لى يا با يزيد إنّ خلقى يحبّون ان يَرَوْك فقلت زَيّنى بوحدانيتك
وأَلْبِسْنى أَنانيتك وارْفعْنى الى أَحديتك حتى اذا رآى خَلْقُك قالوا رأيناك
فتكون أَنتَ ذاك ولا اكون انا هناك، فان صَحّ عنه (٢)ذلك فقد قال
٥ الجُنيْد (٣)رحمه الله فى كتاب تفسيره لكلام ابى يزيد (٣)رحمه الله هذا كلام
(٤)من لم يُلبِسه حقايقَ وجْد التفريد فى كمال حقّ التوحيد فيكون (٥)مستغنيًا
بما ألبسه عن كون ما (٦)سأله، وسؤالُه لذلك يدلّ على انّه مقارب لِما
هناك وليس المقارب للمكان بكاين فيه على الإمكان والاستكان، وقوله
أَلْبِسْنى وزَيّنى (٧)وارْفعْنى يدلّ على حقيقة ما وجده ممّا هذا مقدارُهُ ومكانُهُ
١٠ ولم يَنَل الحُظْوة الّا بقدر ما استبانه، قلتُ فهذا الذى (٨)فسّر الجُنيْد (٣)رحمه
الله فقد وصف حالَهُ فيما قال وبيّن مكانَهُ فيما اشار اليه ابو يزيد (٣)رحمه
الله، فامّا ما يَجِدُ المتعنّت والمعاند مقالًا بالطعن على من يقول مثل ذلك
فلم يبيّن، والى ذلك (٩)المعنى (١٠)والمَقصَد وبالله التوفيق قولُهُ رفعنى مرّةً
فأقامنى بين يديه يعنى أَشْهَدَنى ذلك وأَحضَرَ قلبى لذلك لانّ الخلق كلّم
١٥ بين يدى الله (١١)تعالى لا يذهب عليه منهم نَفَسٌ ولا خاطرٌ ولكن يتفاضلون
فى حضورهم لذلك ومشاهدتهم ويتفاوتون فى صفائهم من كدورة ما تَحْجُبُ
بينهم وبين ذلك من الأشغال القاطعة والخواطر المانعة، وقد رُوِىَ فى
الحديث ان النبىّ صلعم كان اذا اراد ان يدخل فى الصلاة يقول وقفتُ
بين يدى الملك الجبّار، وامّا قوله قال لى وقُلتُ له فانّه يشير بذلك الى
٢٠ مناجاة الأسرار وصفاء الذِّكر عند مشاهدة القلب لمراقبة الملك الجبّار فى آناء
الليل والنهار فقِسْ على ما (١٢)بيّنتُ لك فان الجميع يُشبه بعضُهُ بعضًا واعلمْ

(١) رفعنى اله B. (٢) ذاك A. (٣) B om. (٤) A om. (٥) B app.
المعزا A. (٦) شاله B. (٧) وافعل بى AB. (٨) فسره B. (٩) A
المعنى written above as a variant. (١٠) أو المقصد B. (١١) B عز وجل.
(١٢) B app. ينسب.

انّ العبد اذا تيقّن بقُرْب سيّده منه (١) ويكون حاضرًا (٢) بقلبه مراقبًا لخواطره
فكلّ خاطر يخطر بقلبه فكانّ الحقّ يخاطبه بذلك وكلّ شىء يتفكر (٣) بسِرّه
فكانّه يخاطب اله (٤) تعالى به اذ الخواطر وحركات الاسرار وما يقع فى
القلوب بَدْوُهُ من اله وانتهاؤهُ الى اله فهذا على (٥) هذا المعنى واله اعلم
بالصواب (٦)، وقد قال (٧)القايل،

مَثَّلْتُهُ (٩)المُنى فَظَلَّ نَديى ٭ فَتَنَعَّمْتُ فاقِدًا لِلنَّعيمِ

(١٠)مَثَّلْتُهُ حَتَّى كَأَنّى أُناجيهِ بِسِرّى وَسِرِّهِ المَكْتُومِ،

Af.169b

(١١)وقال آخر،

قالَ لى حينَ (١٢)رِمْتُهُ ٭ كُلُّ ذا قَدْ عَلِمْتُهُ

لَوْ بَكَى طُولَ (١٣)عُمْرِهِ ٭ بِدَمٍ ما رَحِمْتُهُ،

يريد مناجاة الاسرار ومثلُ ذلك كثير فى الشعر وغيره، وامّا قولـه زَيّنّى
بوحدانيتك والبِسْنى آنانيتك وارفعْنى الى احديتك يريد بذلك الزيادة
والانتقال من حاله الى نهاية (١٤)احوال المحقّقين بتجريد التوحيد (١٥)والمفرّدين
(١٦)له بحقيقة التفريد، وقد ذُكر عن رسول اله صلعم فيا رُوى عنه سَبَقَ
المفرّدون قيل يُرسول (١٧)اله (١٨) ومن المفرّدون قال الحامدون اله فى السرّآء
والضرّآء، وامّا قوله (١٩)البِسْنى انانيتك حتى اذا رآنى خَلْقُك قالوا رأيناك
فتكون أنْتَ ذاك ولا اكون أنا هناك فهذا وأشباه ذلك نصف فنآءه
وفنآءه عن فنآيه وقيام الحقّ عن نفسه بالوحدانية ولا خَلْقَ قَبْلُ ولا كون
كان وكلّ ذلك مستخرج من قوله صلعم يقول اله (٤)تعالى ما زال عَبْدى
يتقرّب الَىّ بالنوافل حتى أُحِبَّه فاذا أُحْبِبْتُه كنتُ عَيْنَه (٢٠)التى يبصر (٢١)بها

---

(١) B يكون. (٢) B قلبه. (٣) B بسر. (٤) B عز وجل. (٥) B وصف.
(٦) B om. (٧) B adds فى هذا المعنى. (٨) B تمثلته. (٩) B المنى.
(١٠) B مثله. (١١) A om. قال. (١٢) A رايته. (١٣) B دهره.
(١٤) B الاحوال. (١٥) AB والمفردون. (١٦) B فيه. (١٧) B adds صلى.
(١٨) B من. (١٩) B والبسنى. (٢٠) AB الذى but in A اله عليك.
(٢١) B به. التى is written above.

وسَمِعَه الذى يسمع به ولسانه الذى ينطق به ويدِه [١] التى يبطش [٢] بها كما
[٣] جاء فى الحديث، وقد قال القائل فى وجْدِه بمخلوق مِثْلُهُ [٤] وقد وصف
وجده بمحبوبه حتى [٥] قال،

أَنَا مَنْ أَهْوَى وَمَنْ أَهْوَى أَنَا ٭ فاذا [٦] أَبْصَرْتَنِى أَبْصَرْتَنَا
نَحْنُ رُوحَانِ مَعًا فِى جَسَدٍ ٭ أَلْبَسَ اللّٰهُ عَلَيْنَا البَدَنَا،

فاذا كان مخلوقٌ يَعِدُ [٧] بمخلوق حتى يقول مثل ذلك فا ظنُّك بما وراء
ذلك، وبلغنى عن بعض الحكماء انّه قال لا يبلغ [٨] المتحابّان حقيقة المحبّة
حتى يقول الواحد للآخَرِ يا أَنَا، وشرحُ ذلك يطولُ [٩] ان استقصيتُ وفيا
ذكرتُ كفايةٌ، وباللّٰه التوفيق،

باب [١٠] آخر فى [١١] تفسير حكاية [١٢] ذُكرت عن ابى
يزيد [١٠] [١٤] رحمه الله،

[١٤] قال الشيخ رحمه الله قلتُ وقد حُكِىَ [١٥] ايضًا عنه انّه قال اوّل ما
صِرتُ الى وحدانيته فصِرتُ طَيْرًا [١٦] جسمه من الأحدية وجناحاه من
الدَّيْمومية فلم أَزَلْ أطير فى هواء الكَيفية عشر سنين حتى صرتُ الى هواء
مثلِ ذلك مائة ألف ألف مرّة فلم ازل اطير الى أن صرتُ فى ميْدان الأزلية
فرأيت [١٠] فيها شجرة الأحدية، ثم وَصَفَ أَرْضَها وأَصْلَها وفَرْعها وأغصانها
وثِمارها ثمّ قال، فنظرتُ [١٧] فعلمتُ ان هذا كلّه خُدْعة، قال الجنيد [١] رحمه
الله امّا قوله اوّل ما صرتُ الى وحدانيته فذاك اوّلُ لحظِهِ الى التوحيد

---

(١) وقت A الذى with التى written above. (٣) B به. (٢) A om. (٤) B

مخلوق. (٥) B adds هذه الايبات ٠ (٦) B ابصرته. (٧) B يجب

وجده بمحبوبه.

ذكر B (١١) B om. (١٠) اذا. B (٩) اذا. المتحابين B المتحابون A (٨)

قال الشيخ رحمه الله. B om (١٤) البسطامى. B adds (١٤) ذكر ذلك B (١٢)

عنه ايضا B (١٥) حسنه. B (١٦) فقلت. B (١٧)

فقد وصف ما (١)لاحظ من ذلك ووَصَفَ النهاية فى حال بُلوغه والمستقرّ
فى تناهى رُسوخه، وهذا كلّه طريقٌ من (٢)طريق المطلوبين بالبُلوغ الى حقيقة
علم التوحيد بشواهد معانيها منظورًا اليها (٣)متوهًّا بأهلها فيها مُرْسَلين فى
حقّ ما لاحظوه ممّا (٤)شهدوه وليس لذلك اذا كان (٥)كذلك غاية (٦)كُنْهُ
٥ (٧)يَقوّى عليه المطلوبُ به ولا رُسوبٌ فى إرماس بصيرون اليه بل (٨)ذلك
على شاهد التأبيد فيه وإيثار التخليد فيه وجدوا مِنه، وقال الجُنيد (٩)رحمه
الله وإمّا قول ابى يزيد ألْفَ ألْف مرّة (١٠)فلا معنى له لانّ نعْنَهُ اجلّ
وأعظم ما وصفه وقاله وإنّما نَعَتَ من ذلك على حسب ما أمْكَنَهُ، ثمّ وصف
ما (١١)هناك وليس هذا بَعْدُ الحقيقةَ المطلوبة ولا الغاية المستوعبة وإنّما هذا
١٠ بعضُ الطريق، فهذا ما (١٢)فسّره الجُنيد (٩)رحمه الله وفيه بُلغة وكفاية لمن
يفهم وإنه والله الموفِّق (١٣)للصواب، قال الشيخ رحمه الله غير أن الجُنيد قد تكلّم
على حال ابى يزيد (٩)رحمه الله (١٤)فيما شَطَحَ به (١٥)وما نطق (٩)بذلك عن
وجْده فامّا ما يَجِدُ المتعنّت مطْعَنًا فيا (١٦)قال ابو يزيد فلم يذكره وهو
(١٧)قوله صِرْتُ طيرًا ولم ازل اطيرُ فكيف للمرء أن يصير طيرًا
١٥ (١٨)ويطير، والمعنى فيما أشار اليه سُمُوُّ الهمم وطَيَران القلوب وذلك موجود
فى لُغة العرب أن يقول القائل كِدْتُ أن اطيرَ من الفرح وقد طار قلبى
وكاد أن يطيرَ عقلى، وقال يحيى بن مُعاذ (٩)رحمه الله الزاهد سيّار والعارف
طيّار (١٩)يريد بذلك أن العارف فى قصده الى مطلوبه أسْرَعُ من الزاهد
وهذا جائزٌ وقد قال (١٩)الله (٢٠)تعالى (٢١)وكُلَّ إنْسَانٍ ألْزَمْنَاهُ طَائِرَهُ فِى A f.170b
٢٠ عُنُقِهِ، رُوِى عن سعيد بن جُبَير (٩)رحمة الله عليه فى معنى تفسيره أُلحَقْنا

---

(١) لاحظه B.   (٣) So AB.   (٣) A متراميا، B app. منوهًا.   (٤) B شاهدوه.

(٩) B om.   (٧) B يعر.   (٨) B ذلك.   (٦) B إنه.   (٥) B لذلك.

(١٤) B om. from   (١٣) B قسره قد.   (١١) B هنالك.   (١٠) A لا، B ولا.

رحمه الله to للصواب.   (١٤) A مما.   (١٥) B مما.   (١٦) B قال قد.

(١٧) B جل.   (١٨) B او يطاير.   (١٩) B ونبه.   (٢٠) جل ذكره.

(٢١) Kor. 17, 14.

به ما سبَقَ له من السعاده والشقاوة، وقال الشاعر،

رُبَّ يَوْمٍ كَأَنَّـهُ يَوْمَ بَانُوا ٭ مِنْ دُمُوعِ الفِرَاقِ يَوْمٌ مَطِيرٌ

لَوْ تَرَانِى (١)رَأَيْتَ يَوْمَ (٢)تَوَلَّوْا ٭ جَسَدًا وَاقِفًا (٤)وَقَلْبًا يَطِيرُ

وإمّا قوله وما (٤)يُضِيف (٥)جَناحَيْهِ وجِسْمَهُ الى الأحديَّة والدَّيمومية بريـد

٥ بذلك (٦)تَبَرِّيَهُ من حَوْله وقوّته فى طيرانه يعنى فى قصده الى مطلوبه وأن
يضيف فِعْله وحركته فى قصده الى الأحد الدَّائم بلفظة (٧)مستغرَبة، ومثل
ذلك موجود فى كلام الواجدين والمستهترين وإذا كان الغالبَ على سرّ الواجد
وقلبِه ذِكْرُ من يَجِدُ به يَصفُ جميع أحواله بصفات محبوبه مثل مجنون بنى
عامر كان اذا نظر الى الوحش يقول لَيْلَى وإن نظر الى الجبال يقول الى لَيْلَى

١٠ وإن نظر الى الناس يقول لَيْلَى (٨)حتى اذا قيل له ما اسمُكَ وما حالُكَ
يقول لَيْلَى وفى ذلك قال،

أَمُرُّ عَلَى الدِّيارِ دِيارِ لَيْلَى ٭ أُقَبِّلُ ذَا الجِدَارِ وَذَا الجِدَارا

وَمَا حُبُّ الدِّيَارِ شَغَفْنَ قَلْبِى ٭ وَلَكِنْ حُبُّ مَنْ سَكَنَ الدِّيَارا،

وقال غيره،

١٥ أُفَتِّشُ سِرِّى عَنْ هَوَاكُمْ فَلَا أَرَى ٭ سِوَاىَ (٩)وَأَنِّى (١٠)عَنْكَ وَالكُنْهُ أَكْبَرُ

فَإِنْ وَجَدَتْ أَنِّى فَفِى الوَجْدِ أَنَّها ٭ فَإِنْ عَبَّرَتْ عَنِّى فَعَنْها تُعَبِّرُ،

(١١)ومثل ذلك كثير ومستحسَن من القايلين فى معنى ما قالوا فى وصف
وجدهم بمخلوق وفى هوًى باطل والاشارة فى معنى المراد من ذِكْر ذلك تُغنى
عن العباره وبالله التوفيق، وإمّا (١٢)معنى قوله عشر سِنين وألف ألف مرّة

٢٠ وميدان الازليّة وهوَاء (١٣)الكيفية فذاك (١٣)قد قال الجنيد رحمه الله انّه وصفُ
بعض الطريق وفيا قال الجنيد رحمه الله كفايةٌ عن كلامنا (١٢)وتكرارنـا

---

(١) Suppl. in A. B om.   (٢) B adds وبانوا.   (٣) B قلب.   (٤) AB يصف.

(٥) A بجناحيه. B لجناحيه.   (٦) A تبرته. B تبرىه.   (٧) B app. مستعين به.

(٨) B om. from حتى to ليلى.   (٩) B دانى.   (١٠) A انت with عنك

written above.   (١١) A واشباه.   (١٢) B om.   (١٣) B om. from قد

فيا قال الجنيد رحمه اله to قال.

فى هذا، وامّا قوله فنظرتُ فعلمت ان ذلك كلّه خدعةٌ معناه وإله اعلم ان

الالتفات والاشتغال بالملاحظة الى الكون والمملكة خدعةٌ عنـد وجود ١٨٨f.171a

(١)حقايق التفريد وتجريد التوحيد فمن اجلِ ذلك قال الجنيد (٢) رحمه الله

(٢)لو ان ابا يزيد (٣) رحمه الله على عِظَم اشارته خرج من (٤)البداية والتوسّط

٥ ولم اسمع له نُطقًا يدلّ على المعنى الذى يُنبئ عن الغاية وذلك (٤)ذِكرِه للجسم

والجناح (٥)والهواء والميدان وقوله فعلمتُ ان ذلك كلّه خدعة (٦)لانّ عند

اهل النهاية أن الالتفات الى كلّ شىء سوى الله خدعة فمن انكر ذلك فقد

قال سيّد الاوّلين والآخرين صلعم أصدَقُ كلمةٍ (٧)قالتها العرب قَولُ لَبِيدٍ،

ألا كُلُّ شَىءٍ ما خَلا اللهَ باطِلُ،

١٠   باب ايضًا فى شرح كلام حُكى عن ابى (٨) يزيد

(٩)رحمه الله تعالى ،

(١٠)قال الشيخ رحمه الله وقد (١١)ذُكِر عن ابى يزيد ايضًا انّه قال أشرفتُ

على ميدان اللَيسية فا زلتُ اطيرُ فيه عشر سنين حتى صِرتُ مِنْ لَيسَ فى

أَيسَ بِلَيسَ ثمّ أشرفتُ على التضييع وهو ميدان التوحيد فلم أزَلْ اطيرُ بِأَيسَ

١٥ فى التضييع حتى (١٢)ضِعتُ فى الضياع ضياعًا وضِعتُ فضِعتُ عن التضييع

بِلَيس فى ليس (١٣)فى ضياعه التضييع ثمّ اشرفت على التوحيد (١٤)فى (١٥)غيبوبة

الخلق (١٦)عن العارف (١٧)وغيبوبة العارف عن الخلق، قال الجنيد (٢) رحمه

الله هذا كلّه وما (١٨) جانسه (١٩)داخلٌ فى علم الشواهد على الغيبة عن استدراك

---

(١) A دقايق corr. by later hand.   (٢) B om.   (٣) B البادية.   (٤) A ذكِر.

(٥) B والهوى.   (٦) B om. from لانّ to خدعة.   (٧) B قالته.   (٨) B adds

البسطامى.   (٩) B om. رحمه الله تعالى.   (١٠) B om. قال الشيخ رحمه الله.

(١١) A ذكرنا.   (١٢) B ضعفت.   (١٣) B من.   (١٤) AB عن.   (١٥) A شيبوبة.

(١٦) A om. عن العارف.   (١٧) B وشيبوبة.   (١٨) B جانسها.   (١٩) B داخله.

الشاهد وفيها [١] معانٍ من الفناء بتغيُّب الفناء عن الفناء ، ومعنى قوله
اشرفتُ على ميدان اللِّيسية حتى صرتُ مِنْ لَيْسَ فى أَيْسَ بلَيْسَ فذلك اوّل
النزول فى حقيقة الفناء والذهاب عن كل ما يُرى ولا يُرى وفى اوّل وقوع
الفناء انطماس آثارها وقوله ليس بليس [٢] هو ذهاب ذلك كلّه عنه وذهابه
عن ذهابه ومعنى [٣] ليس بليس اى ليس شىء يُحَسُّ ولا يوجَدُ قد طُمِسَ
على الرسوم وقُطِعت الاسماء وغابت [٤] المحاضر وبُعدت الاشياء عن المشاهدة
فليس شىء يوجَدُ ولا يُحَسُّ [٥] بشىء يُفقَد ولا اسم لشىء يُعهَد ذهب ذلك
كلّه بكلّ [٦] الذهاب عنه ، وهو الذى يسمّيه قوم الفناء [٧] ثمّ غاب الفناء
فى الفناء فضاع فى [٨] فناؤه فهو التضييع الذى كان فى لَيْسَ وبه فى لَيْسَ
وذلك حقيقة فَقْد كل شىء وفَقْد النفس بعد ذلك وفقْد النقْد [٩] فى النقْد
[١٠] والارتماس فى الانطماس والذهاب عن الذهاب وهذا شىء ليس له أمَد
ولا وقت يُعهَد ، وقال الجُنيد [١١] رحمه الله ذِكْرُهُ لعشر سنين [٣] هو [١٢] وَقْتُهُ
ولا معنى له لانّ الاوقات فى هذا الحال [١٣] غائبة واذا مضى الوقت وغاب
بمعناه [١٤] عمّن غِيِّبَ عنه فعشر سنين ومائة وأكثر من ذلك كلّه فى معنًى
واحدٍ ، قال الجُنيد [١١] رحمه الله [١٥] فيما بلغنى ثمّ قال ابو يزيد [١١] رحمه
الله اشرفتُ على التوحيد فى غيبوبة الخلق عن العارف وغيبوبة العارف عن
الخلق ، يقول عند إشرافى على التوحيد تحقّق عندى غيبوبة الخلق كلّهم عن
الله تعالى وانفراد الله [١١] عزّ وجلّ بكبريائه عن خليقته ، ثمّ قال الجُنيد
[١١] رحمه الله هذه الالفاظ التى قال ابو يزيد [١١] رحمه الله معروفة فى إدخال
المُراد فيما أُريدَ منها ، فهذا ما بلغنى عن الجُنيد [١١] رحمه الله فى تفسير هذه
الكلمات لابى يزيد [١١] رحمه الله والذى فسّر الجُنيد [١١] رحمه الله [١١] ايضًا

---

(١) .معانى AB.   (٢) .وهو B.   (٣) A om. from .شىء to لَيْسَ B.   (٤) B المخاطر.

(٥) .لثى A.   (٦) .ذهاب B.   (٧) A om. ثمّ غاب الفناء.   (٨) B فناه.

(٩) B om. فى النقد.   (١٠) Illegible in B.   (١١) B om.   (١٢) A نعته.

(١٣) A غابه.   (١٤) .عن من B.   (١٥) B om. فيما بلغنى.

(١)مشكل الاّ عند اهله فانّها يُشكل ذلك (٢)وأشباهه على من (٣)لم يتبحّر فى
العلم ولم ينظُرْ فى الروايات وما دُوِّنَ فى الكُتب عند العلمآء فى وصف عظمة
الله (٣)تعالى وكبريآيه حتى يستدلّ بذلك على ما لم يدوَّن فى الكتب ممّا
(٤)انفرد وخُصَّ به قلوبُ اوليآيه وخاصّتِه وخالصتِه على انّ الفهمآء من العلمآء
٥ باللّه يعلمون انّ كلّ من شاهد زيادته فى حاله الذى خُصَّ به من احوال
المنقطعين الى الله (٥)تعالى فهو فى زيادة الحال مع الله (٦)عزَّ وجلَّ فى كلّ
نَفَس وطَرْفة عين من المزيد كاينةٌ (٧)فى كلّ نَفَس فيا رُبط به من الحال
فهو (٨)فى الانتقال فى كلّ نَفَس من حال الى حال الى ما لا نهاية له حتى
يبلغ وطنُه فى مكانه الى محلّه الذى هو مُرادٌ بذلك فكلّ حال هو منقول اليه
١٠ فهو (٨)فان به عن الحال الذى (٩)انتقل منه، وهذا معنى (١٠)قوله النفآء
والفنآء عن الفنآء والذهاب والذهاب عن الذهاب وضعْتُ فصعْتُ عن   Af.172a
التضييع ضياعًا وان كانت عباراته مختلفة فانّ معانيه متّفقة وحقآيقه متّسقة،
وبيان ذلك فيا رُوى عن عبد الله بن عبّاس (٤)رضى الله عنه فى قوله
تعالى (١١)ثُمَّ ٱسْتَوَى إِلَى ٱلسَّمَآءِ وَهِيَ دُخَانٌ فَقَالَ لَهَا وَلِلْأَرْضِ ٱئْتِيَا طَوْعًا
١٥ أَوْ كَرْهًا قَالَتَا أَتَيْنَا طَآيِعِينَ، قال فقالت الملايكة يا ربّ فلو لم تأنك ما
كنتَ (١٢)صانعًا (١٣)بهما قال كنتُ (١٤)عليهما أُسلّط (١٤)عليهما دابّةً من دوابّى
(١٥)تبتلعهما فى لُقْمة قالت يا ربّ وأَيْنَ تلك الدابّة قال فى مَرْج من مروجى
قالت يا ربّ وأين ذلك المرج قال فى غامض علْمى، ألا ترى (٤)أنّ فى
الدابّة واللقمة (١٦)ذهاب السموات والارض وفى المرج ذهاب الذهاب، وفى
٢٠ الذهاب تنبيه (١٦)قلوب العارفين فا شاهد بقلبه ذلك فكيف يشهد (١٧)نفْسه

---

(١) B فِشكل.   (٢) B ذلك وإشباه   (٣) B om.   (٤) B انفرد قد.

(٥) B ذكره جل.   (٦) B ثناوه جل.   (٧) B من.   (٨) A فانى.

(٩) The words منه انتقل are obliterated in B.   (١٠) B قول   (١١) Kor.

41, 10.   (١٢) B تصنع.   (١٣) A بها.   (١٤) A عليها   (١٥) A تبتلعها.

(١٦) A om.   (١٧) Obliterated in B.

والمُلْك (١) وجميع ما خلق الله (٢) تعالى، ويقال إنّ فى (٣) بعض الكُتُب أن
الله أوحى الى جهنّم إن لم (٤) تأتمرى ما آمُرُك به لأحرقتُك بنيرانى الكُبْرى
فقيل لبعض العارفين ما معنى قوله لأحرقتُك بنيرانى الكُبْرى قال (٥) يطالع
بذرّة من حَبّة قَدَمَهُ فيكون مَثَلُ جهنّم فيها كنتّور خبّاز فى حريق الدنيا بل
اقلّ من ذلك، ومعنى قوله لَيْسَ بلَيْسَ فى لَيْسَ فانّه يشير الى ليسيته فيما
هو فيه اذ الاشياء كلّها فى معانيها ووجودها أشباح فيما لله تعالى فهى وإن
كانت (٦) بالايجاد مرسومةً فى حقائقها بالعدم والتلاشى مرسومة ولأهل الحقايق
فى مشاهدتها مرانب مقسومةٌ (٧) وَٱللّٰهُ يَقْبِضُ وَيَبْسُطُ وَإِلَيْهِ تُرْجَعُونَ،

باب آخر فى شرح ألفاظ حُكيت عن ابى يزيد
رحمه الله وكان يكفّره فى ذلك ابن سالم بالبصرة وذِكْرُ مناظرة
جرت بينى وبينه فى معنى ذلك،

قال الشيخ رحمه الله سمعتُ ابن سالم يقول فى مجلسه يوماً فِرْعَوْنُ لم يقل
ما قال ابو يزيد رحمه الله لانّ فرعون قال أنا ربُّكم الأَعْلَى والربّ يسمَّى
به المخلوق فيقال فلان رَبُّ دارٍ وربُّ مالٍ وربُّ بيتٍ وقال ابو يزيد رحمه
الله سُبْحانى سُبْحانى وسبُّوح وسُبْحان اسمٌ من اسمآء الله تعالى الذى لا يجوز
ان يسمَّى به غير الله تعالى، فقلتُ له هذا الكلام قد صحّ عندك عن ابى
يزيد رحمه الله وصحّ عندك أنّ اعتقاده فى ذلك كان كاعتقاد فرعون فى
قوله أنا ربُّكم الاعلى فقال ابن سالم قد قال ذلك حتى يصحّ عندى انّه
أيْشَ اراد بذلك يلزمه الكُفْر فقلتُ اذا لم يتبيّأ لك أن تشهد عليه بما

ويصفه بما to بعض الكُتُب B (١). جميع B. (٢) B om. (٣) B om. from
نفسه وإذا كان الامر هاكذا (p. ٢٩١, 1. ٦). The following words are the
beginning of B fol. 230b. (٤) تأمرى A. (٥) يطالعه A. (٦) بالاتحاد A,
(٧) Kor. 2, 246.

اعتقدَ عند قوله ذلك فبطل أن تُكَّره لانّه يُحْتَمَل ان يكون لهذا الكلام
مقدمّاتٌ فيقول (١) يعقّبه سُبْحانى سُبْحانى يحكى عن الله بقول سبحانى
سجانى لأنّا لو سمعنا رجلاً يقول (٢)لَا إِلَهَ إِلَّا أَنَا فَاعْبُدُونِ ما كان يختلج
فى قلوبنا شىءٌ غير أن نعلم انّه هو ذا يقرأ القرآن او هو ذا يصف الله
تعالى بما وصف به نفسه وكذلك لو سمعنا دايمًا ابا يزيد رحمه الله او غيره
وهو يقول سجانى سجانى لم نشكّ بأنّه يسبّح الله تعالى ويصفه بما وصف به
نفسه وإذا كان الامر (٣) هكذى وعلى ما قُلْناه فتكبيرك لرجل مشهور بالزهد
والعبادة والعلم والمعرفة من اعظم المُحالات وقد قصدتُ بسطام وسألت
جماعةً من اهل بيت ابى يزيد (٤) رحمه الله عن هذه (٥)الحكاية فأنكروا ذلك
وقالوا لا نعرف شيئًا من ذلك ولولا انّه شاع فى أفواه الناس (٦) ودوّنوه
فى الكتُب ما اشتغلتُ بذكر ذلك ، وسمعتُ ابن سالم ايضًا (٧) وهو يحكى فى
مجلسه عن ابى يزيد (٤) رحمه الله انّه قال ضربتُ خيمتى بإزآء العرش او
عند العرش (٨) وكان يقول هذه (٩)الكلمة كفرٌ ولا يقول مثل هذا الّا كافرٌ،
وكان يقول ايضًا انّ ابا يزيد (٤) رحمه الله اجتاز بمقبرة اليهود فقال
(١٠) معذورون ومرّ بمقبرة المُسلمين فقال (١١)مغرورون ، ومع جلالة (١٢)ابن
سالم كان يُسْرف فى الطعن على ابى يزيد (٤) رحمه الله وكان يكفّره من
اجل انّه قال ذلك فقلتُ له عافاك (١٣)الله ان علمآء (١٤) نواحينا يتبرّكون
بتُربة ابى يزيد (٤) رحمه الله الى يومنا هذا ويحكون عن المشايخ المتقدّمين
انّهم كانوا يزورونه (١٥) وكانوا يتبرّكون بدعآيه وهو عندهم من (١٦)أجلّة
العبّاد والزهّاد وأهل المعرفة بالله ويذكرون (١٧)انّه فاق اهل عصره بالورع

---

(١) A عقبه.   (٢) Kor. 21, 25.   (٣) B هاكذا.   (٤) B om.   (٥) B الحكايات.

(٦) B ودون.   (٧) B فى مجلسه وهو يحكى.   (٨) B ويقول.   (٩) B كلمة.

(١٠) AB معذورين.   (١١) AB مغرورين.   (١٢) B بن.   (١٣) The words

from رحمه to من اجل are obliterated in B.   (١٤) The words from ان to الله

are obliterated in B.   (١٥) B ويتبركون.   (١٦) B اجل.

(١٧) A بانه.

والاجتهاد ودوام (١)الذكر لله (٢)تعالى حتى (٣)حكى عنه جماعـة انهّم رأوه
(٤)قد ذكر اله (٢)تعالى حتى بال الدم من خشية اله تعالى ودوام تعظيمه له
(٢)عزّ وجلّ وكيف يجوز ان نعتقد فيه الكفر بحكاية (٥)تُحكَّى عنه (٦) ولم
نعرف ارادته فيما قال ولا نطّلع على حاله فى الوقت الذى قال وهل يجوز
٥ لنا أن نحكم عليه فيما يبلغنا عنه الاّ بعد أن يكون لنا مثل حال حاله ووقت
مثل وقته ووجد مثل وجه أوليس قد قال اله تعالى (٧)يَا أَيُّهَا الَّذِينَ آمَنُوا
اجْتَنِبُوا كَثِيرًا مِنَ الظَّنِّ إِنَّ بَعْضَ الظَّنِّ (٨)إِثْمٌ، فهذا كلام (٩)جرى بينى
وبين ابن سالم فى مجلسه فى الحكايات التى حكاها عن ابى يزيد (٢)رحمه اله
او كلام هذا معناه (١٠)او قريب من معناه، فامّا قوله ضربتُ خيمتى (١١)بازاء
١٠ العرش او عند العرش فان صحّ عنه انه قال ذلك فهذا غير مجهول ان
الخلق كلّهم والكون وجميع ما خلق اله (٢)تعالى تحتَ العرش وبازاء العرش
ومعنى قوله ضربتُ خيمتى بازاء العرش يعنى وجّهتُ (١٢)خيمتى نحو (٢)مُلْكِ
العرش (١٣) ولا يوجَدُ فى العالم موضع قَدَم الاّ وهو بازاء العرش فلا سبيل
للمتعنّت فى هذا بالطعن، وامّا قولـه عند اجتيازه بمقبرة اليهود وقولـه
١٥ (١٤)معذورون اى كأنهّم (١٥)معذورون (١٤)فكأنّه لمّا نظر الى ما سبق لهم
من اله بالشقاوة واليهودية من غير فعلٍ كان موجودًا فى الأزل وأن اله
(١٦)تعالى جعل نصيبهم منه السخط عليهم فكيف يجوز لهم أن يكونوا مستعمَلين
الاّ بعل اهل السخط فقال كأنهّم (١٤)معذورون وهم غير معذورين من
حيث ما رسم (١٧)القلم ونطق به الكتاب وما وصفهم اله (٢)تعالى بقولهم
٢٠ (١٨)عُزَيْرٌ ابْنُ اللَّهِ (١٩)وَنَحْنُ أَبْنَاءُ اللَّهِ وَأَحِبَّاؤُهُ، واله تعالى عَدْلٌ فى جميع

---

(١) B حكيت.   (٢) B om.   (٣) AB حكوا.   (٤) B وقد.   (٥) B حكيت.

(٦) B ولا يعلم ارادته.   (٧) Kor. 49, 12.   (٨) B adds الآية.   (٩) The

words جرى بينى وبين ابن are obliterated in B.   (١٠) B وقريب.   (١١) A ازاأ.

(١٢) B وجهى.   (١٣) A om. from ولا يوجد to العرش بازاء.   (١٤) AB

معذورين.   (١٥) B وكانه.   (١٦) B adds ذكره.   (١٧) B العلم.

(١٨) Kor. 9, 30.   (١٩) Kor. 5, 21.

ما حكم حكيم فى جميع ما رسم (١)لَا يُسْأَلُ عَمَّا يَفْعَلُ وَهُمْ يُسْأَلُونَ، وامّا
قوله لمّا مرّ بمقبرة المسلمين فقال (٢)مغرورون ان صحّ (٣)عنه ذلك كأنّه لمّا
نظر الى (٤)المتعارَف بين عامّة المسلمين فى نظرهم الى اعمالهم وطمعهم فى النجاة
باجتهادهم وقلّة من (٥)تخلّص من ذلك فسمّاهم مغرورين لانّ اعمال الخلق A.f.173b
كلّها لو (٦)جُعلت بازاء نِعَم مِمّا أنْعَمَ الله (٧)تعالى على الخلق بأن دلَّهم
عليه وزيّن قلوبهم بالايمان (٨)به والمعرفة بوحدانيته لَبطل واضمحلّ ذلك
وليس من جميع الخلق (٩)حركة ولا نَفَس الاّ (١٠)وبَدْؤُها من الله (٧)سبحانه
(١١)وانتهاؤها الى الله (٧)عزّ وجلّ فمن ظنّ ان احدًا ينجو الاّ بفضل الله
وسعة رحمته فهو مغرور هالك، ألا ترى سيّد الانبياء وامام الاتقياء صلعم
يقول ليس منّا احدٌ يُنجيه عملُه (١٢)قالوا ولا أنت يرسول الله (١٣)فقال ولا
أنا الاّ أن يتغمّدنى الله منه برحمة، (٧)فالتعنّت (١٤)والجسارة بالطعن
والوقيعة (١٥)من العلماء فيمن تكون جوارحه مضبوطةً مقيّدةً بالعلم والادب
بحكاية او بكلام لا يحيط به الفم فى الوقت زلّةٌ من العالم وهَفْوةٌ من الحكيم
وخطأً بيّن من العاقل لانّه ربّما تَصَحَّفَ على الحكيم لانّ الحكمة ربّما تجرى
ويُحضرها من لا يَقِفُ على معانيها ولا يلحق فَهْمُه مقاصدَ المتكلّم بها فعند
ذلك تجرى على الأسنة بضدّ معناها (١٦)فيلحق الحكيم عند ذلك نقصٌ عند
من لا يقف على مراميه ويُشكِل عليه معانيه ولم يُشرِف على مكانه ولا
(١٧)يَسأل عن بيانه لانّ الغامض من (١٨)العلوم لا يُدرَك الاّ بالغامض من

---

(١) Kor. 21, 23.   (٢) AB مغرورين.   (٣) B ذلك عنه.   (٤) Here B
(fol. 232a, 1. 6) proceeds: فى كتابه وإنكم ان تصلوا الى حقيقة الحق الح. These words
form part of the chapter entitled باب فى مكاتبات بعضهم الى بعض and occur
in A on fol. 105b, 1. 12. The continuation of the present passage بين عامة
المسلمين الح occurs in B on fol. 122a, 1. 10.   (٥) B تخلص.   (٦) B جعل.
(٧) B om.   (٨) A om.   (٩) B حركة.   (١٠) B بدوها.   (١١) A فأتهاؤها.
(١٢) B قيل.   (١٣) B قال.   (١٤) A والجسارة.   (١٥) A بين.
(١٦) B فلحق.   (١٧) B بسل.   (١٨) B العلم.

(١)الفهوم والتصحيف الذى يقع فى الحكمة يقع من وجهَيْن فوجهٌ منها تصحيف
الحروف وذلك أَيْسَرُهُ (٢)والوجه الثانى تصحيف المعنى وهو أن يتكلّم الحكيم
بكلمة من حيث وقته وحاله فلا (٤)يكون المستمع لذلك الحالُ والوقتُ
فيصحّف معناه (٤)فيعبّر عنها من حيث ما يليق بحاله ووقته ومقامه ووجْه
فيغلط فى ذلك ويهلك، سمعتُ ابا عمروَ بن علوان يقول سمعتُ الجنيد ٥
رحمه الله يقول كنتُ اصحبُ هذه الطائفة وأنا حَدَثٌ فكنت اسمعُ منهم
كلامًا (٦)لم (٧)أَفْهَم عنهم ما يقولون الاّ أن قلبى قد سلم من الانكار عليهم
فبذلك (٨)نلتُ ما (٨)نلتُ، وممّا يُقوى هذا الذى ذكرتُ أنّى كنت فى مجلس
(٩)ابن سالم بالبصرة بعد هذا الخَوْض الذى جرى بينى وبينه فى كلام ابى
يزيد (٥)رحمه الله فحكى يومًا (١٠)عن سهل بن عبد الله رحمه الله انه قال ١٠
ذِكرُ الله تعالى باللسان هَذَيان وذِكرُ الله تعالى بالقلب وسوسة فسُئل عن
ذلك فقال كأنه اراد بذلك أن يكون قايمًا بالمذكور لا بالذكر، ثم حكى فى
مجلس آخر عن سهل (١١)بن عبد الله رحمه الله ايضًا انه قال مَوْلاىَ لا
ينام وأنا (٥)لا أنام فقلتُ لبعض اصحابه مِمّن كان يخصّه لولا أن الشيخ أَمْيَلُ
الى سهل بن عبد الله (٥)رحمه الله منه الى ابى يزيد (٥)رحمه الله لكان يخطّيه ١٥
ايضًا فيا قد حكى عنه (١٢)كما خطّأً ابا يزيد (٥)رحمه الله وكثّره بين يديك
فى الكلام الذى حكى عنه لأن فى هذا الذى (٥)قد حكى عن سهل (٥)رحمه
الله وهو إمامه وأفضل الناس عنه يَجِدُ المتعنّت (١٣)مقالاً إن قصد الى ذلك
والذى يعلم ان لهذا الذى حكاه عن سهل بن عبد الله (٥)رحمه الله وجهًا
غير ما يجد المتعنّت فيه مطعنًا (١٤)فكذلك يجوز ان يكون لكلام ابى يزيد ٢٠
(٥)رحمه الله الذى حكاه عنه (١٥)وجهٌ غير الوجه الذى هو (١٦)ذا يكفّره به

(١) B الفهم.   (٢) B والثانى.   (٣) B يكن.   (٤) B فيغبر.   (٥) B om.

(٦) A om.   (٧) A لافهم.   (٨) B نبت.   (٩) B بن.   (١٠) B om.

(١١) B om. ثم حكى فى مجلس آخر to عن سهل from
بن عبد الله رحمه الله.

(١٢) B لما.   (١٣) B مقالا.   (١٤) B وكذلك.   (١٥) AB وجها.   (١٦) B ذى.

ويخطّبه فيا قال فلم يكن له جواب عند ذلك [١] او كلام [١] هذا قريب من
معناه وبالله التوفيق، ويقال لولا ما خصّ الله [٢] تعالى [٢] موسى [٣] عليه السلم
بالعصمة والتأييد وما [٤] شملته من انوار النبوّة والكلام والرسالة حتى وُفِّقَ
وسُدِّدَ من الانكار على [٥] الخَضِر ممّا كان منه من قتْل النفس التى
٥ حرم الله [١] تعالى وهى من أَعْظَمِ الكبائر فكان يرضى ان يقول له [٦] أَقَتَلْتَ
نَفْسًا زَكِيَّةً بِغَيْرِ نَفْسٍ لَقَدْ جِئْتَ شَيْئًا نُكْرًا حتى كان يردّ عليه [٧] أَلَمْ أَقُلْ
لَكَ إِنَّكَ لَنْ تَسْتَطِيعَ مَعِيَ صَبْرًا فيقول [٨] إِنْ سَأَلْتُكَ عَنْ شَيْءٍ بَعْدَهَا فَلَا
نُصَاحِبْنِي قَدْ بَلَغْتَ مِنْ لَدُنِّي عُذْرًا بعد ما [٩] عاين منه من قتْلَ النفس التى حرم
الله تعالى وأمر فيه بالقصاص فكان يَجِبُ على موسى [١] عليه السلم ان يطالبه
١٠ بالقَوَد [١٠] وبهجره ولا يستقلّ مجالسته ومصاحبته غير ان عناية الله [١] تعالى
وتخصيصه وتسديده وتوفيقه [١١] الذى [١٢] كان مصحوبَه حجز بينه وبين ذلك،
فكذلك دأبُ كلّ ولىّ وصدّيق الى يوم القيمة ولا يجوز لواحد منهم أن
يلحق درجةً من درجات النبوّة [١٣] واله الموفّق للصواب، وحُكى عن ابى A f.174b
[١٤] يزيد [١] رحمه الله انه لم يستند قطّ الى جدار الاّ ان يكون جدارَ مسجدٍ
١٥ او رباطٍ ويقال انه ما [١٥] رَأوْءُ مُفْطِرًا قطّ الاّ أيّامَ العبد حتى لحق بالله عزّ
وجلّ ويكثر فى مثل هذا عنه الأخبار،

[١٦] باب فى ذكر كلام حكى عن الشبلى رحمه الله وشرحه عن ذلك،

[١٧] قال الشيخ رحمه الله سمعتُ ابا عبد الله [١٨] ابن جابان يقول دخلتُ

---

(١) B om.   (٢) تبارك وتعلى B.   (٣) موسى بن عمران B.   (٤) B شمله.
(٥) B adds عليم السلام.   (٦) Kor. 18, 73.   (٧) Kor. 18, 74.   (٨) Kor.
18, 75.   (٩) بر B.   (١٠) A om.   (١١) التى B.   (١٢) كانت AB.
(١٣) واله علم B.   (١٤) البسطامى B adds.   (١٥) راى A.   (١٦) باب فى B.
(١٧) B om.   قال الشيخ رحمه الله.   ذكر الشبلى فى شرح كلام حكى عنه ذلك
(١٨) احمد بن محمّد الهمدانى B.

على الشبلى [1] رحمه الله فى [2] سنة القحط فسلّمت عليه فلمّا قمتُ على ان أُخرج
من عنه فكان يقول لى ولمن معى الى ان خرجنا من الدار مرُّوا أنا معكم
حيث ما كنتم أنتم فى رعايتى وفى كلايتى، قلتُ اراد بقوله ذلك [3] ان الله
[1] تعالى معكم حيث ما كنتم وهو يرعاكم ويكلأكم [4] وأنتم فى رعايته وكلايته
والمعنى فى ذلك [1] انه برى نَفْسَهُ حَقًّا فيا غلب على قلبه من تجريد التوحيد
وحقيقة التفريد والواجد اذا كان وَقتُهُ كذلك فاذا قال أنا يعبّر عن وَجْه
ويترجم [5] عن الحال الذى قد [6] استولى على سرّه فاذا قال انا يشير بذلك
الى ما غلب عليه من حقيقة صفة [7] مشاهدته قُرْبَ سيّده، وسمعت الحُصْرى
[1] رحمه الله [8] يَحكى عنه انه كان يقول لو عرضتُ ذُلّى على ذُلّ اليهود
والنصارى [9] لكان ذُلّى أَذَلَّ من ذُلّهم فان قال القايل [10] أَيْنَ تقع هــذه
الحكاية من ذلك فيقال [11] له [12] الحكايتان صحيحتان [13] والوقتان [14] مختلفان
[15] وقتًا [16] خُصَّ بصفاء المشاهة فنطق عن وجه وحقيقته بمحض الاخلاص
وخالص التوحيد [17] ووقتًا رُدَّ الى صفته وعَجَز بشريته وذُلّ آدميته فنطق
بما وجد من ذلك كما قال يحيى بن مُعاذ الرازى [1] رحمه الله العارف اذا
ذكر ربّه افتخر واذا ذكر نفسه افتقر واحتقر، وهذا المعنى موجود فى العلم،
روى عن النبىّ صلعم انه قال [18]لى وقتٌ لا يسعنى شىءٌ غير الله وأنا سيّدُ
وَلَدِ آدم ولا فَخْر، ورُوى عنه صلعم انه قال لا تفضلونى على يونس بن
مَتّى عليه السلم أنا ابن امرأة كانت تأكل القديد، فكم بين الخبرين   Af.175a
وتفاوت ما بين الوقتين وإله اعلم، [20] ومِمّا [21] يضاهى هذا الذى [22] قلنا

---

(١) B om.   (٢) A شدة and so app. B. سنة is a correction in A.

(٣) B اى.   (٤) B أنتم.   (٥) B على.   (٦) A استدل.   (٧) B مشاهة.

(٨) B يقول يحكى.   (٩) B وكان.   (١٠) A ان.   (١١) B هذه.

(١٢) AB الحكايتين صحيحتين.   (١٤) A والوقت.   (١٤) B والوقتين مختلفين.

(١٥) AB فوقت.   (١٦) A يخص.   (١٧) AB ووقت.   (١٨) A om from

(١٩) B منا.   (٢٠) A وما.   (٢١) B يطاهى.   وروى عنه صلعم انه قال to لى وقت

(٢٢) B قلناه.

ما حُكى [1]عنه بعنى عن الشبلى رحمه الله انه اخذ من يد انسان كسرة خُبْزٍ
فأكلها ثمّ قال ان نفسى هذه نطلب منّى كسرة خبز ولو التفت سرّى الى
العرش والكُرْسى لاحترق او كما قال يريد بذكر [2]الالتفات بسرّه الى العرش
والكُرْسى أن يَجِدُ له فى سرّه أَثَرًا فى [3]الوحدانية والقِدَم لانّ العرش والكُرْسى
مُحْدَثان مخلوقان ممّا لم يكن فكان، وحكى عن الشبلى [4]رحمه الله انه سُئِل
عن ابى يزيد البسطامى [4]رحمه الله وعُرض عليه ما حُكى عنه ممّا ذكرناه
وغير ذلك فقال الشبلى [4]رحمه الله لوكان ابو يزيد [4]رحمه الله هاهنا لأَسْلَمَ
على [5]يد [4]بعض صبيانا وقال لو ان احدًا يفهم ما اقول لشددتُ
الزنانير، قلتُ قد اشار الى ما قال الجنيد [4]رحمه الله ان ابا يزيد [4]رحمه
اله مع [6]عِظَم حاله وعلوّ اشارته لم يخرج من [7]حال البداية ولم اسمع [8]منه
كلمة تدلّ على الكمال والنهاية، والمعنى فى ذلك ان هؤلاء المخصوصين بهذا
العلم فكأنّه قد اخذ عليهم ان كلّ واحد منهم يُرى ان حاله أَعْلَى الاحوال
وذلك غيرةً من الحقّ عليهم حتى لا يسكن بعضهم الى بعض ألا ترى ان
ابا يزيد [4]رحمه الله [4]نكلّم بأشياءَ عجز عن فهم ذلك فهمآء زمانه وأهل
عصره، ثمّ قال الجنيد [4]رحمه الله انه لم يخرج من [4]حدّ البداية ولم اسمع
له لفظًا يدلّ على انه وصل الى النهاية، ثمّ يقول الشبلى [4]رحمه الله لوكان
ابو يزيد [4]رحمه الله عندنا لأسلم على [10]يد [4]بعض صبيانا بعنى لأستفادَ
من المُريدين [11]الذين [4]هم فى وقتنا، وحُكى عن بعض المشايخ انه قال
وقفتُ على الشبلى عشرين سنة ما سمعتُ منه كلمةً فى التوحيد كان كلامه كلّه
فى الاحوال والمقامات، وهذا كلّه قليل فى عِظَم ما اشاروا اليه من الحقيقة
لانّ حقيقة التوحيد لا غاية لها ولا نهاية وكلّ واحد منهم قد غرق فى بحر

---

(١) عن الشبلى انه اخذ الخ B.   (٢) التفات سره B.   (٣) التوحيد B.

(٤) B om.   (٥) يدى B.   (٦) A om.   (٧) حاله B.

(٨) له B.   (٩) قد نكلم B.   (١٠) يدى B.   (١١) الذى B.

A f. 175 b لا يوصَفُ حَدُّه ولا يُدْرَكُ [1] منتهاه [2] وَذَلِكَ فَضْلُ اللهِ يُؤْتِيهِ مَنْ يَشَآءُ وَاللهُ ذُو الْفَضْلِ [3] الْعَظِيمِ،

باب فى معنى حكاية حكيت عن الشبلى رحمه الله،

[4] قال الشيخ رحمه الله قال بعضهم وقفتُ على الشبلى [5] رحمه الله فسمعته
يقول أمَرَ الله [5] تعالى الارض ان تبتلعنى إن كان فىّ فضل منذ شهر [6] او
شهرَيْن لِذِكْر جبريل [7] وميكائيل [5] عليهما السلم، وسمعت الحُصْرى يقول كان
الشبلى [5] رحمه الله يقول لى إن مرّ بخاطرك ذِكْرُ جبريل وميكائيل [5] عليهما
السلم أشْرَكْتَ، فرأيتُ جماعةً قد انكروا هذا مع تخصيص جبريل وميكائيل
[5] عليهما السلم من الملائكة المقرَّبين، وفى [8] الخبر عن النبى صلعم انه قال
رأيتُ جبريل [5] عليه السلم مثل [9] الحِلْس البالى فعلمتُ [5] به فضْلَ عِلْمِه
وخشيتَهُ علىّ [10] او كما قال فقالوا اذا كان رسول الله صلعم يفضّله على نفسه
فكيف [5] يجوز لقائل [5] ان يقول مثل ذلك، فأقولُ وبالله التوفيق ان كلام
الواجدين والمستهترين بذِكْر الله تعالى يكون [11] مُجْمَلًا [12] وتفصيلًا وإنما يجد
المُتَعَنِّت فرصةً بالوقيعة [13] والطعن فى الكلام المُجْمَل دون المفصّل لانّ
المُجمل ربما يكون له مقدّمات لم [14] تبلغ المستمع والمفصّل يكون مشروحًا مُبيَّنًا
محترزًا والمُجْمَل لا يكون كذلك وهذا الكلام الذى حُكى عن الشبلى [5] رحمه
الله [15] كلام مجمل له مقدّمات فاذا سمع [16] العاقل مقدّمانه لم يتشنّع عليه
ما قال الشبلى [5] رحمه الله وإذا لم يسمع [17] بالمقدّمات التى قد [18] تقدّمت
قبل هذا الكلام أحْرَى ان يتشنّع عليه ويُنكر قلبه [19] ذلك، وبيان مــا

ذكرتُ فى حكاية حكاها ابو محمّد النسّاج وهو الذى ذكر مقدّمات هـٰذه
[١]الحكاية بتمامها حتى أوْضَحَ معناها وأزال الانكار عنها وذلك انه قال
وقف رجلٌ على الشبلى [٢]رحمه الله فسأله عن صورة جبريل [٢]عليه السلام
فقال الشبلى [٢]رحمه الله سمعتُ فى الرواية ان لجبريل [٢]عليه السلام سبعمائة
لُغة وسبعمائة جناح منها [٣]جناحان اذا [٤]نشر واحدًا غطّى به المشرق واذا
نشر الآخر غطّى به المغرب فأيشَ تسألُ عن مَلَكٍ تغيب الدنيا بين جناحَيْه
ثمّ قال الشبلى [٢]رحمه الله [٥]للرجل نَعَمْ وروى عن [٦]ابن عبّاس [٢]رضى
الله عنه ان صورة جبريل [٢]عليه السلام فى قائمة الكُرسى مَثَلُ الزَّرَدة فى
الجَوشَن والكرسى وجبريل والعرش كلّ [٧]ذا مع الملكوت الذى ظهر لأهل
العلم مَثَلُ الرملة فى أرضٍ فلاةٍ ثمّ قال ايّها السايل هٰذه علومٌ [٨]أظهَرَها
تحمِلها الأجساد [٩]او نطيقها [١٠]البنية او يحويها المعقول او تحدُّها الأبصار
او تخرق فى [١١]الأسماع [١٢]يدُلُّ بها منه وعليه [١٣]وإليـه استأثَرَ الحقُّ
بمُلكٍ هو له غَيبٍ لا يسع سِواه لوكُشف منه ذرّةٌ ما وقف على الارض
ديّار ولا حملت الأشجار ولا جرت البحار ولا أظلم [١٤]لَيْلٌ ولا [١٥]أشرق
نهار ولكنّه حكم [١٧]علم أنهم لا يطيقون هذا، ثمّ قال ايّها السايل انّك
سألتنى عن جبريل [٢]عليه السلام وأحواله فأمر الله [٢]تعالى الارض ان
تبتلعنى إن كان فى فضلٍ [١٨]منذ شهرٍ ولا شهرَيْن لذِكر جبريل ولا ميكائيل
[٢]عليهما السلام فاذا كان كلامًا يحتاج ان يكون له مثل هذه [١٩]المقدّمات
التى ذكرْنا حتى [٢٠]يتبيّن معناه [٢١]فيقصد المتعنّت الى آخر الكلام منهـا

---

(١) B الحكايات.   (٢) B om.   (٣) B جناحين.   (٤) B نشرها غطا.

(٥) B لرجل.   (٦) B بن.   (٧) B ذى.

(٨) B يجهل.   (٩) B وتطيقها.   (١٠) Unpointed in the MSS.   (١١) A السباع.

(١٢) A بدل. B بدل.   (١٣) B اليه.   (١٤) B الليل.   (١٥) B أضا.

(١٦) B النهار.   (١٧) B علم.   (١٨) AB من.   (١٩) A المقالات.

(٢٠) B بين.   (٢٢) A فقصد.

وينقلها الى من لا يفهم ذلك حتى يبسط لسانه بالوقيعة والطعن فى اولياء
الله [١] تعالى وأهل خاصّته فيكون ذلك من أكبر الكبائــر وأعظم الإثم
[٢] وبالله التوفيق،

باب آخر فى معنى احوال كانوا يُنكرون على الشبلى رحمه الله،

[٤] قال الشيخ رحمه الله وممّا يُنكرون على الشبلى [١] رحمه الله ايضًا انه
كان ربّما يلبس ثيابًا مُثمنةً ثمّ ينزعها ويضعها فوق النار، وذُكر عنه انه
أخذ قطعة عنبر فوضعها على النار فكان بغرّيها تحت ذَنَب حمار وإنه كان
يقول لو كانت الدنيا لقمةً فى فم طِفل لرحمنا ذلك الطفل، وقال بعضهم
دخلتُ عليه فرأيت بين يديه اللَّوز والسُّكَّر وهو يحرقهما بالنار، وحُكى عنه
ايضًا انه كان يقول وددتُ ان لو كانت الدنيا لقمةً والآخرة لقمةً أجعَلَهما
فى فمى أَترُكَ هذا الخلق بلا واسطة، وحكى عنه [١] ايضًا انه باع [٤] عقارًا
بمال كثير فا قام من موضعه حتى نثرها وفرّقها على الناس وكان له عيال
لم يدفع اليهم شيئًا من ذلك فقالوا هذا وأشباه [٥] هذا مخالفة للعلم وقد نهى
رسول الله صلعم عن إضاعة المال ومن إمامهُ فى الذى كان يدفع الى الناس
ولم يترك لعياله فيقال إمامه ابو بكر الصدّيق رضى الله عنه إنه خرج من
جميع ما كان يملك فلمّا قال الرسول صلعم ما خلّفتَ لعيالك قال الله
ورسولهُ فلم يُنكر عليه رسول الله صلعم ذلك، وإضاعة المال أن يُنفقها فى
معصية الله [١] تعالى فلو انفق رجلٌ [٦] دانقًا فى [٧] معصية يكون ذلك من
اضاعة المال ولو انفق ماية الف درهم فى غير المعصية لم يكن ذلك من
اضاعة المال، وأمّا الذى كان يحرقه بالنار فلأنّه كان يشغل قلبَهُ عن الله

---

(١) B om. ‏ (٢) B om. ‏ وبالله التوفيق. ‏ (٤) B om. قال الشيخ رحمه الله.

(٤) عقار له B. ‏ (٥) ذلك A. ‏ (٦) دانق A. ‏ (٧) B adds الله.

تعالى وقد ذكر الله تعالى فى قصّة سليمٰن بن داود عليه السلٰم فقال [١] وَوَهَبْنَا
لِدَاوُدَ سُلَيْمٰنَ نِعْمَ الْعَبْدُ إِنَّهُ أَوَّابٌ إِذْ عُرِضَ عَلَيْهِ بِالْعَشِىِّ الصَّافِنَاتُ الْجِيَادُ
فَقَالَ إِنِّى أَحْبَبْتُ حُبَّ الْخَيْرِ عَنْ ذِكْرِ رَبِّى حَتَّى تَوَارَتْ بِالْحِجَابِ رُدُّوهَا
عَلَىَّ فَطَفِقَ مَسْحًا بِالسُّوقِ وَالْأَعْنَاقِ، يقال انه [٢] كان له ثلٰثمائة فرس عربيّات
٥ لم يكن لأحد من الملوك مثلها قَبْلَهُ ولا بَعْده فكان يُعْرَضُ عليه [٢] ذلك
فاشتغل قلبه لذلك حتى فاتته صلاة العصر عن [٢] وقتها فعند ذلك قال
رُدُّوهَا عَلَىَّ فَطَفِقَ مَسْحًا بِالسُّوقِ وَالْأَعْنَاقِ [٤] فعرقب الجميع وضرب اعناقهم
Af.177a فشكر الله له ذلك وردّ له الشمس الى [٥] موضعها الذى تكون فيه وقْتَ
العصر حتى صلٰها كما جآء فى [٦] الخبر، وقد رُوى ايضًا عن رسول الله
١٠ صلعم فى هذا المعنى انه لمّا فاتته صلاة العصر يومَ الخَنْدَق وجد رسول الله
صلعم لذلك وجدًا شديدًا حتى قال شغَلونا عن [٧] الصلاة الوُسطَى صلاة
العصر ملأ الله [٨] قُلوبهم وبيوتهم نارًا وكانوا قد آذَوْهُ قبل ذلك أَذًى كثيرًا
وضربوه وطردوه وشتموه وطرحوا عليه [٩] الكِرْس والدم ولم [١٠] يَدْعُ صلعم
ولم يَزِدْ على ان قال [١١] اللهمّ اغفِر لقوى فانّهم لا يعلمون فلمّا اشتغل قلبه
١٥ بما فاته من الصلاة عن وقتها دعا عليهم من شدّة وجْه بذلك، وهذا اتمُّ
فى معناه ممّا [١٢] فعل سليمٰن عليه السلٰم، فان سأل سايلٌ فقال أيْشَ
[١٢] المعنى فى ردّ الشمس لسليمٰن الى موضعها ولم تُرَدّ للنبىّ صلعم فيقال لانّ
النبىّ صلعم بُعث بالحنيفية السَّمْحة فسومِح [٢] له بذلك لانّ فرضًا منعه عن
الفرض لانّ حفْر الخندق كان من [٢] أمْر الجهاد فى سبيل الله فلمّا حبسه
٢٠ فرض الجهاد عن فرض الصلاة سومِح له بذلك [١٤] وسليمٰن [٢] عليه السلٰم
لم يحبسه عن فرض الصلاة فرضٌ ولا تطوُّعٌ فمن اجل ذلك لم يسامَحْ له

---

(١) Kor. 38, 29—32.   (٢) B om.   (٢) وقته B.   (٤) فاعقب A.

(٥) الموضع B.   (٦) B adds واله اعلم.   (٧) صلاة A.   (٨) قبورهم B.

(٩) الكرش A.   (١٠) يدعوا B.   (١١) الله B.   (١٢) فضل B.

(١٢) B adds بن داود.   (١٤) معنى رد الشمس B.

26

وإكرامُ نبيِّنا صلعم بالمسامحة (١)له اتمّ من ردّ الشمس لسليمن (١) عليه السلم
ولو (٢)سامحه لم تُرَدّ عليه الشمس، وبعدُ فان عند اهل الحقايق ان كلّ شى.
شغلهم عن الله (١) تعالى من الدنيا والآخرة فذاك عدُوُّهم بطلبون الخلاص
منه بجميع ما يُمكنهم ولا ينبغى ان يكون فيهم (٣) فضلٌ (٤) لسواهُ فهذا على
٥ هذا المعنى (٥) وبالله التوفيق، والذى قال وددتُ ان الدنيا لقمةٌ أجعلها فى فم
يهوديّ (٦) فذاك من هوانها عنده، وقد رُوى فى هوان الدنيا عن النبى صلعم
أكثرُ من ذلك ورُوى عنه (١) صلعم انه قال الدنيا (٧) ملعونة ملعون ما فيها،
ورُوى عنه (١) صلعم انه قال لو ان الدنيا تزنُ عند الله جناحَ بعوضة ما
سقى كافرًا منها شربةً من ماء الحديث،

A f.177 b

باب آخر فى شرح كلام تكلّم به الشبلى (١) رحمه ١٠
الله وهو ممّا يشكُل فهمُه على قلوب العلماء والفقهاء وألفاظ
(٨) جرت بينه وبين الجُنيد (٩) رحمه الله،

(١٠) قال الشيخ رحمه الله حُكى عن الشبلى (١) رحمه الله انـه قال يومًا
لأصحابه يا قوم أُمرُ الى ما لا وراء (١١) فلا أَرَى الاّ وراء (١٢) وأُمرُ يمينًا
١٥ وشمالاً الى ما لا وراء (١٢) فلا ارى الاّ وراء (١٣) ثم أَرجعُ فأرى هذا كلّه فى
شعرة من خِنصرى، قال فأُشكِّل على جماعة من أصحابه اشارتُه فيما قال، (١٤) قال
الشيخ ابو نصر [اشارته] فيا قال وإله اعلم الى الكون لأن الك[رسى] والعرش

(١) B om.   (٢) B adds بذلك.   (٣) A فضلا.   (٤) A سواه.   (٥) B om.

(٩) رحمة الله عليهما B.   (٨) جرى A.   (٧) ملعون B.   (٦) فقال B.   وبالله التوفيق.

(١٠) B om. قال الشيخ رحمه الله.   (١١) B ولا.   (١٢) B om. from وأمرُ to

(١٣) The words فلا ارى الاّ وراء are suppl. in marg. A.   فلا ارى الاّ وراء.

(١٤) The passage beginning قال الشيخ and ending لا نهاية له is omitted in B
and suppl. in marg. A. Several words have been mutilated by the binder.

محدثاً...... حد وليس فى الدنيا وراءه وراءه ولا تحته تحتُ لا نهاية [1]له ولا
يقدر احدٌ [2]من الخلق ان يحدَّه او يصفه الّا بما وصفه الله [3]تعالى به ولا يحيط
بذلك عِلمُ الخلق قد انفرد بعلم ذلك خالقهُ وصانعهُ، ثمّ قال [4]أرجع فأرى
هذا كلّه فى شعرة من خنصرى يريد بذلك ان قُدرة القادر فى خلق هذا كلّه
وفى خلق شعرةٍ من خنصرى واحدٌ ويحتمل وجهًا آخر وهو ان يقول ان الكون
وجميع ما خلق وان كانت مسافته بعيدةً وطوله وعرضه عظيمًا [5]فى كبرياء
خالقه وعظمة صانعِه كشعرةٍ من خنصرى بل اقلُّ من ذلك، وحُكى عنه انه
قال ان قلتُ [6]كذى فاله [7]وان قلتُ كذى فاله [8]وانّما اتمنّى منه ذرّةً كانّه
يشير الى [9]قوله [10]وَهُوَ مَعَهُم أَينَ مَا كَانُوا وأنه حاضرٌ لا يغيب وهو بكلّ
مكان [11]لا يسعه مكان ولا يخلو منه مكان، وقوله انّما اتمنّى منه ذرّةً يعنى الخلق
[12]محجوبون عنه بأسمآيه وصفاته وما أعطاهم [13]منه غيرَ اسمه وذكرِه لانّهم لا
يطيقون [14]اكثر من ذلك، وفى ذلك كان يُنشد الشبلى [15]رحمه الله ويقول،

فَقُلتُ أَلَيسَ قَدْ نَضُّوا كِتابى   *   فَقالَ نَعَم فَقُلتُ فَذاكَ حَسبى،

[16]وله ايضًا،

أَلَيسَ مِنَ السَّعادَةِ أَنَّ دارى   *   مُجاوِرَةٌ لِدارِكَ فى [17]البِلادِ،

[18]وأنشد ،

أَظَلَّت عَلَينا مِنكَ يَومًا غَمامَةٌ

أَضاءَت [19]لَنا [20]بَرقًا [21]وأَبطَى رِشاشُها

فَلا غَيمُها يَجلُو [22]فيَأيَسَ طامِعٌ

وَلا غَيثُها يَأتى فَيَروَى عِطاشُها،

Af.178a

٣٠

---

(١) A in marg. adds فارجع .
(٢) B om. من الخلق .
(٣) B om.
(٤) A فلا يقدر .
(٥) B فامّا فى .
(٦) B كذا .
(٧) B om. وان قلت كذى فاله .
(٨) A فانا .
(٩) B adds تعلى ذكره .
(١٠) Kor. 58, 8. Kor. has اِلّا هُوَ .
(١١) B ولا يشغله .
(١٢) A محجوبين .
(١٣) B من غير .
(١٤) B اكبر .
(١٥) B om. رحمه الله ويقول .
(١٦) B وكان يقول ايضا .
(١٧) B بلادى .
(١٨) B adds فى هذا المعنى .
(١٩) A لها .
(٢٠) A فرما .
(٢١) AB وابطا .
(٢٢) A اقتباس .

(١) وقال الشبلى رحمه الله كتبتُ الحديث والفقه ثلثين سنة حتى اسفر الصبحُ فجِئتُ الى كلّ من كتبتُ (٢)عنه فقلت اريدُ فِقْهَ الله تعالى فما كلَّمنى احدٌ، ومعنى قوله حتى اسفر الصبح يعنى به (٣)[حتى بدا] انوار الحقيقة ومنازلة ما دعتْ اليه حقيقةُ الفقه والعلم والمعرفة، معنى قوله هاتِ فِقْهَ الله تعالى يعنى التفقّه فى علم الاحوال الذى بين العبد وبين الله تعالى فى كلّ لحظة وطَرْفة عَيْن، ٥ قال وقال الشبلى للجُنَيْد رحمه الله (٤)[يأبا القسم ما تقول فيمن كان الله حَسْبَهُ قولاً وحقيقةً فقال له الجنيد رحمه الله] يأبا بكر بينك وبين آكابر الناس فى سؤالك هذا عشرة الآف مقام اوّلُه محوُر ما بدأتَ به، والمعنى فى ذلك ان الجنيد رحمه الله كان متشرّفًا على حاله بفضل علمه وتمكينه فأوراه موضع ما يُخشى عليه من الدعوى فيما يقول لانّ من كان الله حسبه قولاً وحقيقةً ١٠ يستغنى عن السؤال فسؤاله للجنيد رحمه الله عن ذلك (٥)ينبئ عن انه مقارب لما هناك، وهكذى سمعت ابن علوان يقول كان الجُنَيْد رحمه الله يقول قد أوقف الشبلى رحمه الله فى مكانه فما (٦)بَعُدَ ولو (٦)بَعُدَ لجَآءَ منه إمامٌ، وقال ابو عمرو ربّما كان يجىء الشبلى رحمه الله الى الجُنَيْد رحمه الله فيسألـه ١٥ مسألة فلا يُجيبه ويقول يأبا بكر هو ذا أُشْفِقُ عليك وعلى ثبانك لانّ هذا الاضطراب والانزعاج والحِدّة والطيش والشطح ليست هى من احوال المتمكّنين وهى منسوبة الى احوال اهل البدايات والارادات، وكذلك حُكِى عن الشبلى رحمه الله انه قال قال الجُنَيْد (٧)[يومًا] يأبا بكر أبِشَ تقول فقلت انا اقول الله فقال مُرُ سلَّمك الله يعنى بذلك انك الله فى خطر عظيم فان لم يسلّمك ٢٠ الله فى قولك الله من الالتفات الى شىء سوى الله فما أَسْوَأَ حالَكَ، وكان الشبلى رحمه الله يقول الف عام ماضية فى الف عام واردة هو ذا الوقت   Af.178b

---

(١) Here B proceeds (fol. 131a, last line): وقال الجنيد فى كلام له الخ. This passage occurs in the chapter entitled باب فى وصاياهم التى أوصى بها بعض لبعض (fol. 119a, penult. in A).   (٢) Text om.   (٣) Suppl. in marg.   (٤) Suppl. in marg. The words يأ ابا and كان الله have been cut away in binding and are restored by conjecture.   (٥) سنى على.   (٦) بعد.   (٧) Suppl. above.

ولا تغرنّكم الأشباح، وكان يقول انتم اوقاتكم مقطوعة ووقتى ليس له [١]طَرَفان،
وربّما كان يشطح ويقول انا الوقت ووقتى عزيزٌ وليس فى الوقت غيرى
وأنا محقٌّ وكان يُنشد هذين البيتين،

مَكينٌ فى مُعامِلِهِ مَكينُ * أمينُ الحَقّ [٢]آمَنَهُ أمينُ

تَعازَزَ عِزُّهُ فَأَعْتَزَّ عِزًّا * فَقَدْ فاتَ اليَقينُ مِنَ اليَقينِ،   ٥

وربّما كان يقول نظرتُ [٣]فى كلّ عز فزاد عزّى عليهم ورأيت عزّهم ذلك
فى عزّى، ثمّ كان يتلو فى إثره [٤]مَنْ كانَ يُريدُ الْعِزّةَ فَلِلّهِ الْعِزّةُ جَميعًا
ثمّ يقول،

مَنِ أعْتَزَّ بِذى العِزّ * فَذُو العِزّ أَـهُ عِزُّ،

قال الشيخ رحمه الله امّا قوله الوقت فانّه يشير الى النَفَس [٥]الذى بين   ١٠
النَفَسين والخاطر الذى بين الخاطرين اذ كان باله وله وهو الوقت واذا
فات نَفَسٌ ولو فى الف سنة فقد فات ما لا يُلْحَقُ ولا يُدْرَكُ بالتأسّف عليه
يعنى ان الف عام ماضية وألف عام واردة وفيك نَفَسُك الذى بين نفسيك
يجب ان لا تفوتك والعزيز من اعزّه الله به فلا يلحقه احدٌ فى عزّه وكذلك
الذليل من شغله الله عنه بغيره لا يلحقه احدٌ فى ذُلّه، وقولـه لا تغرنّكم   ١٥
الأشباح فكلّ شىء سوى الله تعالى أشباح ان سكنتَ اليه فقد غرّك، وقوله
انا محقٌّ يعنى فى قولى انا الوقت انا المحق لانّ قوله انا لا يشير بذلك الى
إيّاه، وقوله وقتى ليس له طرفان لانّ فى كلّ [٦][شىء] مسامحة الاّ فى
الوقت فان الاشتغال بغير الله والسكون الى جميع ما خلق الله تعالى فى
الوقت ليس فيه مسامحة ولو نَفَسٌ فى الف سنة، وحُكى عن الشبلى انه قال   ٢٠
ايضًا اللهمّ ان كنت تعلم ان فىّ بقيةً لغيرك فأَحْرِقْنى بنارك لا اله الاّ انت،
فهذا وما يُشبه ذلك غلبات وجدٍ عبّر عنه على حسب ما وجد فى وقته ولا
يكون ذلك على الدوام لان ذلك حالٌ فيه الحال نازلةٌ تنزل بالعبد فى

الحين ولا تلبث به على الدوام وذلك رِفْقٌ من الله عزّ وجلّ بأوليائه Af.179a
وخاصّته ولو دام ذلك لبطلوا عن الحدود والحقوق وتعطّلوا عن الآداب
والاخلاق ومعاشرة الخلق، ألا ترى ان اصحاب رسول الله صلعم سألوا عن
ذلك رسول الله صلعم فقالوا يُرسول الله إنّا اذا كنّا عندك وسمعنا منك
ترقُّ قلوبنا فاذا خرجنا من عندك نرجع الى الاشتغال بالأهل والولد فقال ٥
رسول الله صلعم لو بقيتم على الحال الذى تكونون عندى لصافحتْكم الملايكة
كما جاء فى الحديث، وذُكر عن الشبلى رحمه الله انه كان يقول لو خطر
ببالى ان الجحيم بنيرانها وسعيرها تحرق منّى شعرةً لكنت مُشْرِكًا او كما قال،
فكذلك نقول نحن ايضًا ان جهنّم ليس اليها شىء من الاحراق لانها مأمورة
وإنّما يُوصَّل الم الاحتراق الى اهل النار بقدر ما قُسم لهم، فامّا ما حُكى عنه ١٠
ايضًا انه قال أَيْنَ اعملُ بلَظَى وسَقَرَ عندى أنْ لَظَى وسَقَرَ فيها تسكُنُ يعنى
فى القطيعة والإعراض لان من عرّفه الله بالقطيعة فهو اشدُّ عذابًا ممّن عذّبه
بلَظَى وسَقَرَ، وذُكر عنه انه سمع قاريًا يقرأ هـٰذه الآية (١) اخْسَأوا فيها ولاَ
تُكَلِّمُونِ فقال الشبلى ليتنى كنتُ واحدًا منهم كأنه اشار الى ردّ جوابه (٢) اليم
فقال ليتنى كنت مـمّن يُرَدُّ جوابى ولو فى النار من شدّة وجله لأنه لا يدرى ١٥
ما سبق له منه بالسعادة والشقاوة والاعراض عنه او بالاقبال عليه، وذُكر
عنه ايضًا انه قال فى مجلسه ان لله عبادًا لو بزقوا على جهنّم لأطْفَوهـا
فصعب ذلك على جماعة ممّن كان بسمع ذلك، وقد رُوى عن النبيّ صلعم
انه قال تقول جهنّم يوم القيمة للمؤمن جُزْ يا مؤمن فقد اطفأ نورك لَهَبى،
وفيما يُحكى عن الشبلى رحمه الله مثل هذا كثير لا يتهيّأ ذِكره لكراهة التطويل ٢٠
والعاقل يستدلّ بالقليل على الكثير وبالله التوفيق،

باب فى ذكر ابى الحسين النورى رحمه الله (١) وما ....

A.f.179b

.... صلعم وقالت بحمد الله لا بحمدك وكان شرفُها وفضلُها وفخرُها
برسول الله صلعم الّا انها لم تلاحظ رسول الله صلعم عند ملاحظة الحقّ فى
نزول القرآن (٢) ببراءَتها ولم يزدْها (٣) ذلك عند رسول الله صلعم الّا رفعةً
ه ومحبّةً ودرجةً وفضيلةً، فقسْ على هذا المعنى جميع ما تسمع من نحو ذلك فى
هذا الباب، وامّا قوله صَلِّ عليهم بالاوتار ولا تجعلْ لها فى قلبك (٤) مقدارًا ليس
كما ظنّ المتعنّت انه لا تجعلْ للانبيآء عليهم السلم فى قلبك (٤) مقدارًا ولكن
يريد بذلك اى لا تجعل لكثرة صلاتك عليهم عندك مقدارًا اى لا نستكثر
ذلك فانهم يستحقّون اكثر من ذلك لأن النبيّ صلعم قال من صلّى علىَّ مرّةً
١٠ واحدةً صلّى الله عليه عشرًا يقول وان كثرت الصلاة عليهم فلا تجعل لها فى
قلبك مقدارًا باستكثارك لها لأن صلوات الله عليك اذا صلّيتَ على رسوله
صلعم اكثر من صلاتك عليه، ومن قال انه اراد بقوله لا تجعل لها فى قلبك
(٤) مقدارًا يعنى الانبيآء عليهم السلم يعنى به عند مقدار عظمة الله تعالى

---

(١) At this point there is a considerable lacuna in the text (A), five whole
chapters and a portion of a sixth chapter having fallen out. Their titles are
given in the table of contents at the beginning of the MS. as follows:

(٢) ببرائها.   (٤) مقدار.   (٣) بذلك.

وكبريآئه لأنه لا يجوز ان يأخذ مقدار شىء من جميع ما خلق الله من
الملائكة والانبيآء والجنّة والنار والعرش والكرُسى موضعًا من قلوب المؤمنين
عند موضع مقدار عظمة الله تعالى وكبريآئه وقدرته وسلطانه ووحدانيته فهذا
فى معنى التوحيد وحقيقة التفريد، وإمّا من حيث العلم والشرع وما ندب
الله اليه الخلق ودعاهم الى تعظيم الرُسُل والايمان بما جآءوا به وبما خصّ الله
به نبيًّا صلعم من جميع الرُسُل فقد ذكرتُ فى هذا المعنى ابوابًا فى باب
مستنبطات اهل الصفوة فى تخصيص النبىّ صلعم من كتاب الله تعالى وأخبار
رسول الله صلعم وما فُتح من ذلك على قلوب اوليآء الله، وأقْرَبُ مـا
يقول اهل الصفوة فى الرسول صلعم انه عبدٌ اوحدٌ لا يجوز لأحـد أن [١]
يدركه فى جميع ما خُصّ به، سُئل ابو يزيد البسطاى رحمه الله هل يزيد ٨ ف.١٨٠a
احدٌ على النبىّ صلعم [فقال وهل بدركه احدٌ] ثمّ قال ابو يزيد رحمـه [٢]
الله جميع ما يفهم الخلق وأدركوه من شرف رسول الله صلعم فيما لم يفهمه ولم
يدركه مَثَلُ ذلك مثل بِقَرْبة [٣] زرقآء، [٤] ملآى من المآء فا رُثِح [٥] ادرك
الخلقُ وفهموه من شرفه وفضله وما سوى ذلك فلم يفهمه احدٌ ولم يدركه،
وأقْرَبُ ما يصف به اهل الصفوة رسولَ الله صلعم انهم قالوا لمّا [٦] وعد ١٥
الله تعالى رسوله صلعم بأن يعطيه جميع ما يسأله بقوله يا محمّد سَلْ نُعْطَهُ فلا
يجوز ان يسأله شيئًا الّا ان يعطيه، وكان من دعآيه صلعم اللهمّ اجعلْ من
فوقى نورًا ومن تحتى نورًا وعن يمينى نورًا وعن شمالى نورًا ومن ورآيى
نورًا [٢] [ومن قدّاى نورًا] ومن خلفى نورًا اللهمّ اجعلْ فى قلبى نورًا وفى
بصرى نورًا وفى سمعى نورًا وفى لحيى نورًا وفى عظمى نورًا كما جآء فى ٢٠
الحديث قالوا الدليل على ان الله تعالى اعطاه ذلك قوله صلعم والله انّى

---

(١) يقولون.   (٢) Suppl. in marg.   (٣) ازرق.   (٤) ملآن.

(٥) Text om. from ادرك to وفضله. The words suppl. in marg. have been
partially cut away in binding. In marg. وما ادرك الخلق.   (٦) اوعد.

لأراكم خلف ظهرى كما اراكم قدّامى ، وكلّ فضيلة وشرف خُصّ بذلك احد
من امّة محمّد صلعم فذلك شرف رسول اللّه صلعم وفضله فلا ينبغى لأحد
ان يقول ما لا يعلم قال بعض الحكماء اذا ألِفَ القلبُ الإعراض عن اللّه
تعالى اورثه الوقيعة فى اولياء اللّه تعالى ، والمستبحث عن هذا العلم يجد فى
كُتُب هؤلاء وفى كلامهم مثل ذلك (١) كثيرًا وإنّما بيّنتُ هاتين الكلمتين
وفسّرت على الاختصار حتى يقاس بذلك على ما لم نذكره وباللّه التوفيق ،

باب فى ذكر من غلط من المترسّمين بالتصوّف ومن اين يقع الغلط وكيف وجوه ذلك ،

قال الشيخ رحمه اللّه سمعت احمد بن علىّ الكرخى يقول سمعت ابا علىّ
الروذبارى رحمه اللّه يقول قد بلغنا فى هذا الامر الى مكان مثل حدّ السيف
فان قلنا كذى ففى النار وان قلنا كذى ففى النار يعنى ان غلطنا فيما نحن فيه
بدقيقة فنصير من اهل النار لأن الغلط فى كلّ شىء أهوَنُ من الغلط فى
التصوّف وفى علمه لأنها مقامات وأحوال وإرادات ومراتب وإشارات فمن
(٢) تخطّى فى ذلك الى ما ليس له فقد اجترى على اللّه فيكون اللّه خصمَهُ
فان شاء عفا عنه وان شاء عاقبه بما شاء كيف شاء وكلّ من ترسّم برسوم
هذه العصابة او اشار الى نفسه بأن له قَدَمٌ فى هذه القصّة او توهّم انه متمسّك
ببعض آداب هذه الطايفة ولم يُحكّم اساسه على ثلثة اشياء فهو مخدوع ولو
مشى فى الهواء ونطق بالحكمة او وقع له قبول عند الخاصّة او العامّة وهذه
الثلثة اشياء اوّلها اجتناب جميع المحارم كبيرها وصغيرها والثانى اداء جميع
الفرايض عسيرها ويسيرها والثالث ترك الدنيا على (٤)[اهل] الدنيا قليلها
وكثيرها الّا ما لا بدّ للمؤمن منها وهو ما رُوى عن النبىّ صلعم انه قال اربعة

فى الدنيا وليست هى من الدنيا كِسرةٌ تسدُّ بها جوعتك وثوب توارى
عورتك وبيت تُكَنُّ فيها وزوجة صالحة تسكن اليها، فامّا ما سوى ذلك من
الجمع والمنع والامساك وحبّ التكاثر والمباهاة لجميع ذلك حجاب قاطع يقطع
العبد عن الله عزّ وجلّ فكلّ من ادّعى حالاً من احوال اهل الخصوص او
توهّم انه سلك منزلاً من منازل اهل الصفوة ولم يبن اساسه على هذه الثلثة
فانه الى الغلط اقربُ منه الى الاصابة فى جميع ما يشير اليه او يدّعيه او
يترسّم برسمه والعالم مقرٌّ والجاهل [١]مدّعٍ،

باب فى ذكر الفرقة الذين غلطوا وطبقاتهم وتفاوتهم فى الغلط،

قال الشيخ رحمه الله ثمّ انّى نظرتُ الى الفرق الذين غلطوا فوجدتهم
على ثلث طبقات فطبقة منهم غلطوا فى الاصول من قلّة إحكامهم لأُصول
الشريعة وضعف دعائمهم فى الصدق والاخلاص وقلّة معرفتهم بذلك كما قال
بعض المشايخ حيث يقول انّهم حُرِموا الوصول لتضييع الاصول، وطبقة ثانية
منهم غلطوا فى الفروع وهى الآداب والاخلاق والمقامات والاحوال والافعال
والاقوال فكان ذلك من قلّة معرفتهم بالاصول ومتابعتهم [٢]لحظوظ النفوس
ومزاج الطبع لأنهم لم يدنوا ممّن يروضهم ويجرّعهم المرارات ويوقفهم على
المنهج الذى يؤدّيهم الى مطلوبهم فمثلهم فى ذلك كمثل من يدخل بيتاً مُظلماً
بلا سراج فالذى يُفسد أكثر ممّا يُصلحه وكلّما ظنّ انه قد ظفر بجوهر نفيس
فلم يجد معه الّا خزفًا خسيسًا لأنه لم يتّبع اهل البصيرة الذين يميّزون بين
الأشباه والأشكال والأضداد والأجناس فعند ذلك يقع لهم الغلط ويكثر منهم
الهفوة والشطط فهم [٣]متحيّرون [٤]ومتفرّقون بين منهزمٍ ومفتونٍ، ومتجبّر
ومحزونٍ، [٥]ومغترٍّ بالظنون، [٦]ومحترفٍ بالجنون، ومتلبّس بالجنون، ومكمّد

(١) مدّعى.   (٣) متحيّرين.   (٤) ومتفرّقين.   (٥) ومغترّ.   (٢) محظوظ.
(٦) ومحترف.

(١) بالشّجون، (٢) وملدّع ومفتون (٣) ومتمنّ للمنون، فسبحان من قسم لهم بذلك
وهو العالم بدائهم ودوائهم، وسقمهم وشفائهم، والطبقة الثالثة كان غلطهم فيا
غلطوا فيه زلّة وهفوة لا علّة وجفوة فاذا تبيّن ذلك عادوا الى مكارم
الاخلاق ومعالى الامور فسدّوا الخلل ولمّوا الشعث وتركوا العناد وأذعنوا
٥ للحقّ وأقرّوا بالعجز فعادوا الى الاحوال الرضيّة والافعال السنيّة والدرجات
الرفيعة فلم تنقص مراتبهم هفوتهم، ولم تُظلم الوقت عليهم جفوتهم، ولم تمتزج
بالكدورة صفوتهم، وكلّ طبقة من هذه الطبقات الثلثة على احوال شتّى من
التفاوت والارادات والمقاصد والنيّات، وقد قال القايل،

مَنْ تَحَلَّى بِغَيْرِ ما هُوَ فيهِ * فَضَحَتْهُ لِسانُ ما يَدَّعيهِ،

١٠ وقد ذهب عليه ما رُوى عن النبيّ صلعم انه قال ليس الايمان بالتحلّى ولا
بالتمنّى ولكن هو ما وقر فى القلب وصدّقته الأعمال كما رُوى فى الحديث،
فمن غلط فى الاصول فلا يسلم من الضلالة ولا يُرجَى لدائه دواً الّا ان
يشاء الله ذلك، والغلط فى الفروع اقلّ آفةً وان كانت بعيدةً من الاصابة،

A f.181b

باب فى ذكر من غلط فى الفروع التى لم (٤) تُؤدِّهم الى الضلالة
ونبتدىُ فى ذكر الطايفات الذين غلطوا فى الفقر والغنا،
١٥

قال الشيخ رحمه الله ثمّ انّ طايفةً من المترسّمين بالصوفية تكلّموا فى
تشريف الغنا على الفقر وكانت اشارتهم فى ذلك الى الغنا بالله لا الى الغنا
بالأعراض الدنية من الدنيا (٥)[فغلطت طايفة] فطلبت التأويلات وتعلّقت
بالاحتجاجات والاختراعات من الآيات والروايات أن تجعل الغنا بأعراض
٢٠ الدنيا حالاً محمودةً او مقامًا من مقامات طلّاب الآخرة فتاهت فى ذلك

وغلطت لانّ الذى تكلّم فى الفقر والغنا وعدّ الغنا حالاً من احوال المنقطعين
الى الله تعالى اشار الى الغنا باللّه لا الى الغنا بأعراض الدنيا التى لا تَزِنُ
عند الله جناحَ بعوضةٍ، وطبقة اخرى تكلّمت فى حقايق الفقر والافتقار الى
الله تعالى وما يقارنها من الصبر والشكر والرضا والتفويض والسكون
٥ والاطمأنينه عند العدم، فضلّت طايفة اخرى وتوهّمت ان الفقير المحتاج
الذى يعدم الصبر والرضا لا فضيلة له ولا ثواب لـه على فقره والفقير
المضطرّ المُعدم الرضا والصبر له فضلٌ على الغنىّ الذى يكون غناه بالدنيا،
وخُلقت النفس محتاجةً وليس من صفات البشرية الاطمأنينة والسكون عند
عدم القِوام والقِرى والفقر تكرهه النفس ولا يلاومه (١)الطبع والهوى لأنه
١٠ من (٢)[الحقوق والغنا تحبّه النفس ويلاومه الطبع والهوى لأنه من] الحظوظ،
وقد وعد الله تعالى الغنىّ على الحسنة الواحدة اذا عملها عشر أمثالها لقولـه
عزّ وجلّ (٣)مَنْ جَآءَ بِالْحَسَنَةِ فَلَهُ عَشْرُ أَمْثَالِهَا، والحسنة من الفقير كاينةٌ فى
كلّ نَفَس لصبره على مرارة الفقر وليس لثواب الصبر نهايةٌ معدودةٌ لقوله
عزّ وجلّ (٤)إِنَّمَا يُوَفَّى ٱلصَّابِرُونَ أَجْرَهُمْ بِغَيْرِ حِسَابٍ، والفقر فى ذاته محمود Af.182a
١٥ فان صحبته علّةٌ فالعلّة فيه مذمومة لقول النبى صلعم الفقر أزْيَنُ على المؤمن
من العذار الجيّد على خدّ الفرس، ولم يشترط مع الفقر غير الفقر شيئًا، والغنا
بالدنيا فى ذاته مذموم فان صحبته خصلة محمودة من أعمال البرّ فهى المحمودة
لا نَفْسُ الغنا لقول النبى صلعم ليس الغنا عن كثرة العَرَض، ولم يشترط مع
الغنا شيئًا غير الغنا فشتّان بين خصلةٍ محمودةٍ فى ذاتها لا يقع اسم المذمّة
٢٠ عليها الاّ بعلّةٍ نادرة من أعمال الشرّ وخصلةٍ مذمومةٍ فى ذاتها لا يقع اسم
المحمدة عليها الاّ بخصلة نادرة من اعمال الخير، وطبقة اخرى زعمت ان الفقر
والغنا حالان ليس للعبد ان يتبعهما بل يجب عليه ان يعبرها ولا يقف

---

(١) الطبع.   (٢) Suppl. in marg. The words تحبّه and لأنه have been cut
away in binding and are restored by conjecture.   (٣) Kor. 6, 161.
(٤) Kor. 39, 13.

معهما وهذا عند اهل الحقايق والمعارف وأحكام الحقيقة عند النهايات، فظنّت طايفة اخرى ان الذى قال ذلك فقد ساوى بين الفقر والغنى وقالوا لا فَرْقَ بين الفقر والغنى فى معنى الحال، فيقال لهم قد رأيناكم كارهين للفقر وما رأيناكم كارهين للغنى فان كانا [1] حالَين مستويَّن فأين استواۤءكم فى المساكنة البهما والاحتراز منهما والمعانقة لهما، فقد تبيّن غلطهم فى ذلك، وغلطت طايفة اخرى فى الفقر فتوهّمت ان المراد من حال الفقر العدم والفقر فقط فاشتغلت بذلك ولم [2] تَسِمْ بهِمّتها الى آداب الفقر وخَفِيَتْ عليها ان رؤية الفقر فى الفقر حجاب النفير عن حقيقة الفقر وليس للفقير الصادق فى حال الفقر خصلة اقلّ من الإعدام والفقر والصبر والرضا والتفويض فى معانيها اتمّ من الفقر الذى لم يكن مقرونًا بهذه الخصال ورؤية الفقر والمساكنة الى الفقر والإعجاب به عِلّةٌ فى الحال وحجاب فى المكان، والله اعلم بالصواب وباله التوفيق،

باب فى ذكر من غلط فى التوسّع وترك التوسّع من الدنيا بالتقشّف والتقلّل ومن غلط فى الاكتساب وترك الاكتساب،

قال الشيخ رحمه الله لا يصحّ الدخول فى السعات الا لنبىّ او صدّيق، معناه لأنهم يكونون فى الاشياۤء لغيرهم ويقومون فى الاسباب بحقوقها لا بحظوظها يعرفون الإذن اذا أَذِنَ الله لهم بالإنفاق انفقوا واذا اذن لهم بالإمساك امسكوا فمن لم يعرف الاذن ولم يكن من اهل الكمال والنهايات فغلط عند دخوله فى السعات بالغرور والتأويلات، ومن زعم انه لا يسكن الى ذلك فيقال له من لا يسكن الى ما فى يديه من اسباب الدنيا ينبغى ان لا يُمسك ولا يطلب ويكون القليل والكثير عنه سواۤء فمن لم يكن

القليل آثَرَ عنه من الكثير (١) ولا يكون الواحد آثَرَ عنه من الاثنين ولا يخلو
سرُّه من الطلب (٢) لمفقودٍ من اسباب الدنيا والإمساك لموجودها فهو من
طلّاب الدنيا والمرتبطين باكتسابها بحظّها لا بحقّها فمن توهّم بأن لـه حالٌ
غير ذلك فهو فى غلط، وطبقة اخرى تعلّقوا بالتقشّف والتقلّل واعتادوا
الدون من اللباس والقليل من القوت وظنّوا ان كلّ من رفق بنفسه او
ناول شيئًا من المباحات او اكل شيئًا من الطيّبات ان ذلك علّة وسقوط
من المنزلة وكلّ حال غير الحال الذى هم عليه عندهم زلّة وقد غلطوا فى
ذلك لأن العلّة كاينة فى التقلّل والتقشّف (٣) [كما ان العلّة كاينة فى الترفّع
والترفه والتقلّل والتقشّف] بالعادة والتكلّف معلول الّا ان يكون العبد مرادًا
بذلك وقتًا من الاوقات او يكون تأديبًا له او رياضةً لنفسه فاذا شاهد
آفاتها واستخلى ملاحظة الخلق له بذلك ولم يعمل فى الانقلاع عنها بجهـد
فيكون هالكًا ولا يُرْجَى خيرُهُ ابدًا، وطبقة اخرى من (٤) المتنسّكين تعلّقوا بأخذ
القوت من الكسب وركنوا الى اكتسابهم وأنكروا على من لم يكتسب مثلهم
وتوهّموا وظنّوا ان الحال لا يصحّ الّا بتصفية الغذاء وتصفية الغذاء والقوت *Af.183a*
عندهم لا تصحّ الّا بالاكتساب واحتجّوا بقول النبى صلعم أَحَلَّ ما يأكل المؤمن
كسبُ يده، وقد غلطوا فى ذلك لأن الكسب رخصة وإباحة لمن لم يُطِقْ
حالَ التوكّل لأن التوكّل حال الرسول صلعم وكان الرسول صلعم مأمورًا
بالتوكّل والثقة بالمضمون من الرزق وكذلك الخلق كلّهم مأمورون بالتوكّل
على اه عزّ وجلّ والثقة بما وعدها اه تعالى والسكون عند عدم الرزق حتى
يسوق اه عزّ وجلّ اليهم أرزاقهم فمن ضعف عن ذلك ولم يُطِقْ فقد سَنَّ
له رسول اه صلعم الكسبَ المباح بشروطه حتى لا يهلك، وشروط الكسب
ان لا يركن الى كسبه ولا يرى رزقه من كسبه (٥) ولا يكون فى كسبه (٦) مغتنمًا

---

(١) والواحد من عنه أثر الاثنين وبكون.   (٢) المفقود.   (٣) Suppl. in marg.
The last two letters of والترفه have been cut away in binding and are restored
by conjecture.   (٤) المنسكين.   (٥) يكن ولم.   (٦) مغتنما.

بل ينوى بذلك معاونة المسلمين ولا يشغله كسبٌ عن اوّل اوقات الصلاة المفروضة ويتعلّم العلم حتى لا يأكل الحرام فمتى ما ترك خصلةً من هـذه الخصال فقد صار كسبه معلولاً [1]بعاهة وان كان له اخوانٌ مـمّن لم يكتسبوا ويعلم انهم محتاجون فيجب عليه ان يتفقّدهم بما فضل من قُوته ، فمن لم يقُمْ
٥ بهنَّ الشروط فأُخْشَى عليه الغلط فى إعجابه ونعلّه باكتسابه ، وطبقة اخرى طعنوا على المكتسبين وجلسوا معتمدين على [2]حالهم متشرّفين الى من يتفقدهم وعندهم أن هذا هو الحال ، وقد غلطوا فى ذلك لأن الجلوس عن المكاسب ينبغى ان يكون من قوّة اليقين والصبر فمن ضعف يقينُه وغلب عليه طبعُه وطمعُه يؤُمَر بالدخول فى الطلب والطلبُ مباحٌ وترْك الطلب بقوّة الايمان
١٠ أتمُّ وأفضل ،

باب فى ذكر طبقات الذين فتروا فى الارادات وغلطوا فى المجاهدات وسكنوا الى الراحات ،

قال الشيخ رحمه الله ثمّ انّ طبقة من الصوفية غلطت فى العبادات
Af.183b والمجاهدات ورياضات النفوس والمكابدات فلم تُحْكِم فى ذلك اساسها ولم تضع
١٥ الاشيآء فى مواضعها فانهزمت ونكصت على أعقابها القَهْقَرَى وذلك انهم حين سمعوا بمجاهدات المتقدّمين وما نشر الله بذلك أعلامهم فى خلقه بالثنآء الجميل والقبول عند [3]الناس وإظهار الكرامات فطبعت نفوسهم وتمنّوا فتكلّفوا شيئًا من ذلك فلمّا طالت المدّة ولم يصالوا الى مرادهم [4]كسلوا فاذا دعاهم داعى العلم الى المجاهدة والعبادة ورياضة النفس لا يقُمْ ذلك عندهم وزنًا
٢٠ ولو جذبهم الحقّ جذبة الى خدمته وأرادهم بالمداومة على طاعتـه وأدركهم بلطفه وعنايته لازدادت رغباتهم وقويت نيّاتهم ودامت على ما كانوا عليه نيّاتهم فلمّا لم يكونوا مُرادين بذلك لضعف دعائهم وفساد قصدهم توهّموا

ان ذلك فتور، وقد غلطوا فى ذلك لأن الفتور ما يتروّح به قلوب المجتهدين
وقتًا دون وقت ثمّ تعود الى الحال، فامّا ما (١) وقع فيه هؤلاء فهو الكَسَل
والتوانى والامانى الكاذبة، قال وسمعت احمد بن علىّ الكرخى يقول سمعت
ابا علىّ الروذبارى رحمه الله يقول البداية هى كالنهاية والنهاية فهى كالبداية
٥ فمن ترك شيئًا فى نهايته ممّا كان يعمل فى بدايته فهو مخدوع، وطبقة اخرى
ساحت وسافرت ولقيت المشايخ وجلست وتصدّرت وتطاولت على ابناء
جنسها بأنها قد لقيت ما لم يلق قرناؤها ونظرت الى ما لم ينظر اليه
جلساؤها وعدّت نفسها من المستقلّين، وقد غلطت فى ذلك لأن السفر سُمّى
سفرًا لانه يُسفر عن اخلاق الرجال وانّما يسافرون حتى يشاهدوا من
١٠ انفسهم خُلُقًا مذمومًا (٢) فيعملون فى تبديلها ويعرفون ايضًا من انفسهم من
(٣) المخبيّات ما لم يعرفوا ذلك فى حضرهم ومعارفهم ولقاءَ المشايخ يحتاج الى
الادب والحرمة والرغبة والارادة وأن ينسى جميع ما يعلم ويقبل من الشيخ
ما يُوصيه به ويشير عليه ويطالب نفسه بحقّ الشيخ ولا يقتضى لنفسه من الشيخ
إقبالًا عليه ولا رفقًا ويحفظ قلبه ويغتنم نظره اليه ويخاف أن يكون صحبته
١٥ ولقْياه للشيخ حُجّةً عليه، فمن ساح او سافر او لقى شيخًا من المشايخ على غير
ما ذكرتُ وتوهّم انه من المسافرين او ممّن قد صحب المشايخ فهو فى غلط
عظيم، وطبقة اخرى انفقوا الاموال والأملاك وبذلوا وتوهّموا ان المراد
البذلُ والإنفاق والتخلّى بالسخاوة والبذل والسماحة، وقد غلطوا فى ذلك لأن
مراد القوم وقصودهم فيما انفقوا وبذلوا لم يكن إظهار السخاوة ولا الاشتهار
٢٠ بالسماحة ولكن رأوا ان التعلّق بالاسباب مع المسبّب علّةٌ فى المكان وحجابٌ
قاطعٌ عن الحقيقة فكان إنفاقهم وبذلهم وخروجهم من الأملاك فرارًا من العلّة
وقطعًا للعلاقة فمن بذل شيئًا من طريق السماحة والسخاوة وظنّ ان طريقه
طريق القوم فهو فى غلط، وقوم آخر انبسطوا فى المباحات ولم يتكلّفوا المراءاة
فى الاوقات وقالوا ليس لنا معلوم أيْثَ ما وجدْنا أكلْنا ونمْنا فذلك وقْتُنا،

---

(١) وقعوا .   (٢) يعلمون .   (٣) المخبيات .

وقد غلطوا فى ذلك لأن الوقت اذا فات لا يُدْرَكُ وليس الوقت ما يكون
معموراً بالإرفاق انّما الوقت ما يكون معموراً بدوام الذكر ومربوطاً بالاخلاص
والشكر والرضا والصبر والنُّنْس والهوى والشيطان أعداءً يطلبون فرصة الظفر
بالعبد فاذا غفل العبد عنهم طرفة عين فلا يُرْجَى خيرُهُ ولا يُؤمَنُ هلاكُهُ
٥ فمن توهّم انه وصل الى حال قد أَمِنَ مَن ذلك فهو فى غلط،

باب فى ذكر طبقات الذين غلطوا فى ترك الطعام والعزلة
والانفراد وغير ذلك،

قال الشيخ رحمه الله ثم انّ جماعةً من المريدين والمبتدئين سمعوا علم
مخالفة النفوس فتوهّموا ان النفس اذا انكسرت بترك الطعام يُؤمَنُ شرُّها
١٠ وبلوايها وعوايقها فتركوا عاداتهم من الطعام والشراب ولم يستعملوا الادب فى
A f.184b ترك الطعام ولم يستبحثوا عن الاستاذين آدابها فعمدوا الى ترك الطعام وواصلوا
الليالى والايّام وظنّوا ان ذلك حالٌ، وقد غلطوا فى ذلك لأن المريد ينبغى
ان يكون له مؤدّبٌ يوقفه على ما يحتاج اليه حتى لا يتولّد من ارادته بلاَءٌ
وفتنة لا يقدر ان يتلافاها ولا يتخلّص من فسادها والنفس لا يؤمن شرُّها
١٥ ولا يذهب عنها ما جُبِلَتْ عليه من الشر وهى الامّارة بالسوء فمن ظنّ ان
النفس اذا انكسرت بالجوع بقلّة المَطْعَم فقد زال عنها شرُّها وآفات بشريّتها
حتى يأمنها صاحبُها فقد غلط، وسمعت ابن سالم يقول كانوا اذا ارادوا ان
يتقلّلوا ينقصون من طعامهم فى كل جُمْعة مثلَ أُذن السِّنَّوْر، وسمعته يقول
كان سهل بن عبد الله رحمه الله يأمر اصحابه ان يأكلوا اللحم فى كلّ جُمعة
٢٠ مرّةً حتى لا يضعفوا عن العبادة، ولقد رأيتُ جماعةً حملوا على انفسهم فى
مثل هذه الاشياء من التقلّل وأكل الحشيش وترك شرب الماء حتى فاتتهم
الفريضة لأنهم لم يأتوا بها على سيّتها ولم يتأدّبوا بآداب من سلك هذا المسلك
من المتقدّمين، وطايفةٌ اعتزلت ودخلوا كهوف الجبال وظنّوا انهم هو ذا

يهربون من الخلق او يأمنون فى الجبال والفلوات من شرّ نفوسهم او يوصلهم
الله تعالى بالانفراد والخلوة الى ما اوصل اليه اولياءه من الاحوال الشريفة
ولا يوصلهم الى ذلك بين الناس، وقد غلطوا فى ذلك لأن الايمّة من المشايخ
الذين قلّ [١] طعمهم ودامت خلوتهم وانفرادهم واختاروا العزلة انّما [٢] حداهم
على ذلك ودعاهم اليه داعى العلم وقوّة الحال فورد على قلوبهم ما اذهلهم وشغلهم
عن المعارف والاوطان وأخذهم عن الطعام والشراب وجذبهم الحقّ اليه
جذبةً اغناهم بها عمّن سواه فمن لم يكن مصحوبه قوّة الحال وغلبة الوارد ثمّ
يتكلّف ويحمل على نفسه ما لا تطيقه يظلم نفسه فيدخل على نفسه الضرر
ولا يُدرك ما فاته ويفوته ما معه فمن فعل شيئًا من ذلك بتكلّفه ويتوّهم انه
قد وصل الى شىء من مراتب المخصوصين فهو فى غلط، قال ورأيتُ جماعةً
من الاحداث كانوا يُقلّون الطعام ويسهرون الليل ويذكرون الله تعالى على
الدوام حتى كان احدهم ربّما يُغشّى عليه وكان يحتاج بعد ذلك الى ان
يُدارَى ويُرفَق به ايّامًا حتى يقدر ان يصلّى الفريضة، وجماعةٌ جبّوا انفسهم
وظنّوا انهم اذا قطعوا ذلك سلموا من آفات الشهوة النفسانية، وقد غلطوا
فى ذلك لأن الآفات تبدو من الباطن فاذا قُطعت الآلة والعلّة موجودةٌ فى
الباطن لم ينفع ذلك بل يضرّ وتزداد الآفة فمن ظنّ ان الآفة فى الآلة
الظاهرة ويتخلّص بقطع ذلك من شرّها فهو فى غلط، وقومٌ هاموا على وجوههم
ودخلوا البرارى والبوادى بلا زاد ولا ماء ولا آلة الطريق وتوهّموا انهم
اذا فعلوا ذلك نالوا ما نال الصادقون من حقيقة التوكّل، وقد غلطوا فى
ذلك لأن القوم الذين كان هذا دأبهم كانت [٣] لهم بدايات وتأدّبوا بآداب
وراضوا انفسهم قبل ذلك بالمجاهدات وكانوا مستقلّين باحوالهم لم يبالوا بالقلّة
ولم يستوحشوا من الوحدة فكم من مَوْتةٍ ماتوا وكم من مرارة ذاقوا حتى استوتْ
احوالهم فى الخراب والعمران والسهل والجبل والجماعة والوحدة والعزّ والذلّ
والجوع والشبع والحياة والموت، فمن فعل شيئًا من ذلك وتوهّم انـه قد

نطق بشىء من احوال المتوكّلين فهو فى غلط، وجماعةٌ تكلّفوا لبس الصوف
واتّخذوا المرقّعات المعمولة وحملوا الركاء ولبسوا المصبوغات وتعلّموا الاشارات
وظنّوا انهم اذا فعلوا ذلك إنّهم من الصوفية، وقد غلطوا فى ذلك لأن
التّحلّى والتلبّس والتشبّه لا يورث لصاحبه غير الحسرة والندامة والعتب والملامة
والشنار والنار فى يوم القيمة، فمن ظنّ او توهّم انه يصل الى احوال اهل
الحقايق (١)بالتلبّس والتشبّه بهم فهو فى غلط، وجماعةٌ اخرى جمعوا علوم القوم
وعرفوا اشاراتهم وحفظوا حكاياتهم وتكلّفوا ألفاظًا صحيحة وعبارات فصيحة
وظنّوا انهم اذا فعلوا ذلك فقد صاروا منهم ووصلوا الى شىء من احوالهم
وقد غلطوا فى ذلك، وجماعةٌ اخرى احرزوا قوتهم وسكنت نفوسهم بنفقة
معلومة ودراهم موضوعة ثمّ عمدوا بعد ذلك الى اورادهم من الصوم والصلاة
وقيام الليل والورع ولباس الخشن والبكاء والخشية وظنّوا ان هذا هو الحال
المقصود الذى لا يكون بعد حالٌ، وقد غلطوا فى ذلك وما اظنّ ان احدًا
ممّن اشار الى علم التصوّف يُذكر عنه انه لم يخرج فى بدايته من المعلوم ولم
يأمر اصحابه فى اوّل الأمر بقطع العلايق وأن يجعلوا قوتهم فى الغيب فمن
كان منهم (٢)ورجع الى سبب معلوم او ادّخار قوت فانّ ذلك لم يكن من
اجْل نفسه ولكن لمن حَوْلَهُ من اصحابه وعياله. ولمن بَرِدَ عليه من إخوانه فمن
اشار الى التصوّف وادّعى حالهم وعدّ نفسه منهم ولم يكن اصله كذلك على
ما ذكرتُ فهو (٣)[فى] غلط، قال الشيخ رحمه الله وجماعةٌ ظنّوا ان التصوّف
هو السماع والرقص واتّخاذ الدعوات وطلب الإرفاق والتكلّف (٤)للاجتماعات
على الطعام وعند سماع القصايد والتواجد والرقص ومعرفة صياغة الألحان
بالأصوات الطيّبة واللغات الشّجيّة والاختراع من الأشعار الغزليّة بما يُشبه
احوال القوم على نحو ما (٥)رأوا من بعض الصادقين او بلغهم ذلك عن
المحقّقين، وقد غلطوا فى ذلك لأن كلّ قلب ملوّث بحُبّ الدنيا وكلّ نفس
معتادةٍ بالبطالة والغفلة فسماعه ووجوده معلولٌ وحركته وقيامه تكلّفٌ، فمن

---

(١) بالنفس.   (٢) رجع.   (٣) Text om.   (٤) الاجتماعات.   (٥) رأينا.

ظنّ انه بصير بتكلّفه وحِيَله وتمنِّيه من المتحقّقين فى وقت السماع والحركة
والوجود وغير ذلك فقد غلط فى ذلك،

باب ذكر من غلط فى الأُصول وأدّاه ذلك الى الضلالة ونبتدئ
بذكر القوم الذين غالطوا فى الحُرِّية والعبودية،

قال الشيخ رحمه الله تكلّم قوم من المتقدّمين فى معنى الحُرِّية والعبودية
على معنى ان العبد لا ينبغى له ان يكون فى الاحوال والمقامات التى بينه
وبين الله تعالى كالأحرار لأن من عادة الاحرار طلب الأُجرة وانتظار العِوَض
على ما يعملون من الأعمال وليس عادة العبيد كذلك لأن العبد لا ينتظر
من مولاه اجرةً ولا عِوَضًا على ما يأمره به مولاه فمتى طمع فى شىء من ذلك
١٠ فقد ترك سِمة العبيد لأن العبيد ان اعطاهم مولاهم (١)[عطيّةً] على ما امرهم
به واستعملهم فيه كان ذلك من تفضّل مولاهم عليهم لا باستحقاقهم وليس عادة
الاحرار كذلك، وقد صنّف شيخٌ من المشايخ كتابًا فى مقامات الاحرار
والعبيد فى هذا المعنى فظنّت الفِرقة الضالّة ان اسم الحُرِّية اتمّ من اسم
العبوديّة للمتعارف بين الخلق أن الاحرار أَعْلَى مرتبةً وأَسْنَى درجةً فى احوال
١٥ الدنيا من العبيد فقاست على ذلك فضلّت وتوهّمت ان العبد ما دام
بينه وبين الله تعالى تعبُّدٌ فهو مسمّى باسم العبودية فاذا وصل الى الله فقد
صار حُرًّا واذا صار حُرًّا سقطت عنه العبودية، وانّما ضلّت هذه الفرقة لقلّة
فهمها وعِلمها وتضييعها لأصول (٢)الدين، خَفِيَتْ على هذه الفرقة الضالّة ان
العبد لا يكون فى الحقيقة عبدًا حتى يكون قلبه حُرًّا من جميع ما سوى الله
٢٠ عزّ وجلّ فعند ذلك يكون فى الحقيقة عبدًا لله وما سمّى الله تعالى المؤمنين

Af.186a

---

(١) Suppl. above.   (٢) Here the text adds: فى احوال الدنيا من العبيد.

If these words are genuine, there must be a lacuna in the text.

باسم احسن من اسم العبد اذ يقول (١) وَعِبَادُ ٱلرَّحْمَٰن (٢) نَبِّى عبادى لأنه
اسم سمَّى به ملايكته فقال (٣) عِبَادٌ مُكْرَمُونَ ثمَّ سمَّى به انبياءه عليهم السلم
ورسُله فقال (٤) وَٱذْكُرْ عِبَادَنَا (٥) وَٱذْكُرْ عَبْدَنَا وقال (٦) نِعْمَ ٱلْعَبْدُ وقال
لحبيبه وصفيَّه صلعم (٧) وَٱعْبُدْ رَبَّكَ حَتَّى يَأْتِيَكَ ٱلْيَقِينُ، فكان صلعم يصلَّى
حتى ورمت قدماه فقيل له يرسول اله اليس قد غفر اله لك ما تقدّم من
ذنبك وما تأخَّر قال أفلا أكون عبدًا شكورًا، (٨) [وروى عن النبى صلعم
انه خيَّرتُ بين ان اكون نبيًّا مَلكًا ونبيًّا عبدًا] فأشار الىَّ جبريل عليه
السلم تواضع فقلت بل نبيًّا عبدًا، فلو كان بين الخلق وبين اله تعالى درجةٌ
أعْلَى من درجة العبودية لم (٩) يُبْثْ ذلك (١٠) رسولَ اله صلعم واله جلّ وعلا
كان يُعطيه ذلك، وباله التوفيق،

باب فى ذكر من غلط من اهل العراق فى الاخلاص،

قال الشيخ رحمه اله وزعمت الفرقةُ الضالّة من اهل العراق (٨) [وغيره]
ان الاخلاص لا يصحّ للعبد حتى يخرج عن روَية الخلق ولا بوافقهم فى
جميع ما يريد أن يعمله كان ذلك حقًّا او باطلاً وإنّما ضلّت هذه الفرقة ان
جماعةً من اهل الفهم والمعرفة تكلَّموا فى حقيقة الاخلاص ان لا يَصْفُو لهم
ذلك حتى لا يبقى على العبد بقيّةٌ من روَية الخلق والكون وكلّ شىء غير
اله تعالى فظنّت هذه الفرقة وطمعت ان ذلك يصحّ لهم بالدعوى والتقليد
والتكلُّف قَبَل سلوك مناهجها والتأدُّب بآدابها والابتداءَ ببدايتها حتى بوَدّيه
ذلك الى نهاياتها حالاً بعد حال ومقامًا بعد مقام فأدّام الدعوىَ والطمع
الكاذب الى قلَّة المبالات وترْك الادب ومجاوزة الحُدود فأسرهم الشيطان

(١) Kor. 25, 64.   (٢) Kor. 15, 49.   (٣) Kor. 21, 26.   (٤) Kor. 38, 45.
(٥) Kor. 38, 40.   (٦) Kor. 38, 44.   (٧) Kor. 15, 99.   (٨) Suppl. in
marg.   (٩) يبعث written above as a variant.   (١٠) لرسول.

وغلبتهم النفس والهوى بما خُيّل اليهم أنهم برسم المخلصين فى الاخلاص وهُم
فى عين الضلالة والانتقاص وأنّى لهم من ذلك الخلاص، وقد خفيت عليهم
لشقاوتهم أن العبد المطلوب بدرجة الاخلاص هو العبد المهذّب المؤدّب
الذى هجر السيّئات وجرّد الطاعات وعمل فى الارادات ونازل الاحوال
والمقامات حتى ادّاه ذلك الى صفاء الاخلاص، فامّا من هو اسيرُ هواه
ورهينُ نفسه وشيطانه وهو فى ظُلُماتٍ (١)بَعْضُهَا فَوْقَ بَعْضٍ إِذَا أَخْرَجَ يَدَهُ
لَمْ يَكَدْ يَرَاهَا فهو محجوب عن حال اهل البدايات فكيف يصِلُ الى ما بعد
ذلك، فمثل هؤلاء كمثل من سمع بالجوهرة النفيسة أنها تكون صافية مدوّرة
فوقع فى يه خرزةٌ من الزجاج فاعجبته تلك لأنها مدوّرة صافية فلمّا احتاج
اليها حملها الى من يعرف الجواهر فقال (٢)[له] هى زجاجة لا قيمة لها فلم
يَدَعْهُ الجهل والطمع (٤)[الكاذب] ان يرى بها من قلّة معرفته بالزجاج والجوهر،   ٨f.187a
فهؤلاء كلّ يوم فى ضلالتهم يخسرون وفى طغيانهم يعمهون اعاذنا الله وايّاكم،

باب فى ذكر من غلط فى النبوّة والولاية،

قال الشيخ رحمه الله ثمّ ضلّت فرقة اخرى فى تفضيل الولاية على النبوّة
(٤)ووقع غلطهم فى قصّة موسى والخضر عليهما السلم وتنكّرهم فى ذلك برأيهم   ١٥
اذ يقول جلّ وعزّ (٥)عَبْدًا مِنْ عِبَادِنَا آتَيْنَاهُ رَحْمَةً مِنْ عِنْدِنَا وَعَلَّمْنَاهُ مِنْ
لَدُنَّا عِلْمًا، ثمّ قال لموسى عليه السلم مع تخصيصه بالكلام والرسالة وما كتب
الله له (٦)فِى الْأَلْوَاحِ مِنْ كُلِّ شَيْءٍ مَوْعِظَةً وَتَفْصِيلًا لِكُلِّ شَيْءٍ يقول له
الخضر عليه السلم (٧)إِنَّكَ لَنْ تَسْتَطِيعَ مَعِيَ صَبْرًا فيقول له موسى عليه السلم
(٨)لَا تُؤَاخِذْنِي بِمَا نَسِيتُ وَلَا تُرْهِقْنِي مِنْ أَمْرِي عُسْرًا الى آخر القصّة،   ٢٠

---

(١) Kor. 24, 40.   (٢) Suppl. above.   (٣) Suppl. in marg.   (٤) ورفع.

(٥) Kor. 18, 64.   (٦) Kor. 7, 142.   (٧) Kor. 18, 66.   (٨) Kor. 18, 72.

(١)فظنّت هذه الطائفة الضالّة ان ذلك (٢)نصٌّ فى نبوّة موسى عليه السلم
وزيادةٌ للخضر عليه السلم على موسى فى الفضيلة فأدّام ذلك الى ان فضّلوا
الاولياء على الانبياء عليهم السلم وقد ذهب عنهم ان الله جلّ وعزّ يخصّ
من يشاء بما يشاء كيف يشاء كما خصّ آدَمَ عليه السلم بسجود الملايكة له
وخصّ نوحٌ عليه السلم بالسفينة وصالحٌ عليه السلم بالناقة وإبرهيم عليه السلم
بأن جُعل عليه النار بردًا وسلامًا وخصّ موسى عليه السلم بإحياء الموتى
وخُصّ نبيّنا صلعم بانشقاق القمر ونبع الماء بين اصابعه، فأمّا غير الانبياء
عليهم السلم فقد ذكر الله تعالى مَرْيَمَ حيث يقول (٣)وَهُزِّـــى إِلَيْكِ بِجِذعِ
ٱلنَّخْلَةِ تُسَاقِطْ عَلَيْكِ رُطَبًا جَنِيًّا ولم تكن مريم نبيةً ولم يكن ذلك لغيرها من
الانبياء عليهم السلم ولا يجوز لقايل (٤)[ان يقول] انها تزيد بالفضل على
الانبياء عليهم السلم، وآصَفُ بن بَرْخِيَاء كان عنه علمٌ من الكتاب حتى
بعرش بِلْقِيس قبل ان يرتدّ (٥)[اليه] طَرْفُهُ فكيف يجوز ان تقول انه
اتمّ من سليمٰن عليه السلم مع ما آتاه الله تعالى من النبوّة والفهم والملك ،
وقد سمعتَ بقصّة الهُدْهُد وكان قد خُصّ بمعرفة المياه لم يخصّ بذلك غيره
من الطيور وغيرها من الجنّ والإنس، وقد رُوى عن النبيّ صلعم انه قال
أَفْرَضُكم زَيْدٌ وَأَقْرَأُكم أُبَيٌّ وأعلمكم بالحلال والحرام مُعاذ بن جَبَل رضى الله
عنهم، وقد شهد رسول الله صلعم لعشرة من الصحابة بالجنّة ليس هؤلاۤء فيهم
ونحن نعلم ان ابا بكر الصدّيق رضى الله عنه افضلُ منهم، ومثل ذلك كثير
وكلّ ولىّ من الاولياۤء ينال ما ينال من الكرامة بحسن اتّباعه لنبيّه صلعم
فكيف يجوز ان يفضّل التابع على المتبوع والمقتدى على المقتدى به وإنّما
(٦)يُعطَى الاولياۤء رِشاشةً ممّا (٧)يعطى الانبياۤء عليهم السلم والذىۤ قال ان
الانبياۤء عليهم السلم يُوحَى اليهم بواسطة والاولياۤء يتلقّون من الله بلا واسطة
فيقال لهم غلطتم فى ذلك لأنّ الانبياۤء عليهم السلم هذا حالهم على الدوام

بعنى الإلهام [(١)] [والمناجاة] والتلقُّف من الله عزّ وجلّ بلا واسطة والاولياء
وقتًا دون وقت، وللانبياء عليهم السلم الرسالة والنبوّة ووحىٌ بنزول جبريل
عليه السلم وليس للاولياء ذلك، ولو بدَت ذرّة على الخضر عليه السلم من
انوار موسى عليه السلم وتخصيصه بالكلام لاتمحق الخضر عليه السلم ولكن
٥ حجبه الحقّ عن ذلك تهذيبًا وزيادةً لموسى عليه السلم فافهم ذلك ان شاء
الله تعالى، والولاية والصدّيقية منوّرة بأنوار النبوّة فلا تلحق النبوّة ابدًا فكيف
تتفضّل عليها،

باب فى ذكر الفرقة التى غلطت فى الإباحة والحظر والردّ عليهم،

قال الشيخ رحمه الله ثمّ زعمت الفرقة الضالّة فى الحظر والاباحة ان
١٠ الاشياء فى الاصل مُباحة [(٢)] وإنّما وقع الحظر للتعدّى فاذا لم يقع التعدّى
تكون الاشياء على اصلها من الاباحة وتأوّلوا قول الله عزّ وجلّ [(٣)] فَأَنْبَتْنَا ٨٤،188a
فِيهَا حَبًّا وَعِنَبًا وَقَضْبًا وَزَيْتُونًا وَنَخْلًا وَحَدَائِقَ غُلْبًا وَفَاكِهَةً وَأَبًّا مَتَاعًا لَكُمْ
وَلِأَنْعَامِكُمْ فقالوا هذا على الجملة غير مفصّل فأدّاهم ذلك بجهلهم الى ان
طمعت نفوسهم بأن المحظور الممنوع منه المسلمون مباحٌ لهم اذا لم يتعدّوا فى
١٥ تناوله، وإنّما غلطوا فى ذلك بدقيقة خفِيَت عليهم من جهلهم بالأصول وقلّة
حظّهم من علم الشريعة ومتابعتهم شهوات النفوس فى ذلك أنهم سمعوا بمكارم
الأخلاق وحُسن عشرة ومؤاخاة كانت بين جماعة من المشايخ المتقدّمين
تجرى بينهم احوال من رفْع الحشمة والبسط بعضهم مع بعض حتى كان
احدهم يمرّ الى دار اخيه ويمدّ يده فيأكل من طعامه ويأخذ من كسبه حاجته
٢٠ ويفتقد احوال اخيه وهو غايب كما يفتقد لنفسه، وهذا كما حُكى عن فتح
المَوْصِلى انه مرّ الى دار بعض اخوانه فقال لجاريته أخرجى لى كيس اخى
فأخرجته اليه فأخذ منه حاجته فلمّا رجع اخوه الى البيت أخبرته الجارية

(١) Suppl. in marg.   (٢) مباح.   (٣) Kor. 80, 27—32.

فقال ان كنتِ صادقةً فأنت حُرّة لوجه الله تعالى، وكما ذكر الحسن البصرى
رحمه الله انه كان يأكل من رؤوس زنابيل اخٍ من اخوانه وهو غايب
فسُئل عن ذلك قال يا لُكَع وهل كان الناس قَبْلَنا الّا مثل هذا كان احدهم
يمرّ الى بيت اخيه فيأخذ من طعامه ويأخذ من دراهه بذلك يريد بذلك إدخال
٥ السرور على اخيه ويعلم ان ذلك احبُّ اليه من حُمُر النَّعَم، وكذلك جماعة
كانوا يقولون ليس بين هذه الطايفة مراساة انّما استنَّ مذهبهم على المؤاساة
كما قال ابرهيم بن شَيْبان كنّا لا نصحب من يقول نَعْلى ومثلُ ذلك كثيرٌ،
فظنّت هذه الطايفة الضالّة بالاباحة ان ذلك كان منهم على حال جاز لهم
تركُ الحدود او [(١)][(٢)أن] [(٣)]يجاوزوا [(٣)]حدَّ متابعة الأمر والنهى فوقعوا من
١٠ جهلهم فى التيه وتاهوا وطلبوا ما مالت اليه نفوسهم من اتّباع الشهوات
وتناول المحظورات تأويلاً وحيَلاً وكذبًا وتمويهًا والذى زعم ان الاشياء فى ٨٨٦.A.E.1
الاصل [(٤)]مباحةٌ فهلّا قال ان الاشياء فى الاصل محظورة وإنّما وقعت
اباحتها بالأمر والنهى فى التوسعة والرُّخص حتى لا يقع فى الغلط معَما ان
الحلال ما حلّه الله تعالى والحرام ما حرّمه الله تعالى وليس احد من
١٥ المؤمنين مستعبَدًا باستعمال الشرايع المتقدّمة ولا باستعمال ما [(٥)]كان عليه الاوايل
بل المؤمنون مستعبدون بالايثار لما امرم الله تعالى به والانتهاء عمّا نهاهم
الله عنه واجتناب ما اشتبه عليهم لقول النبّى صلعم الحلال بيّن والحرام بيّن
وبينهما امورٌ مشتبهات، وحرامُ الله حِمّى فمن وقع حول الحِمّى يوشك أن
يقع فيه وليس قول من زعم ان الاشياء فى الاصل على الاباحة بأوْلى من
٢٠ قول من يقول ان الاشياء فى الاصل محظورة وإذا استملك لا يُبيح ذلك
لأحد الّا بحُجّة، وليس هذا من قياس النجاسة والطهارة لأنّ الاشياء عند
الفقهاء وجماعة من اهل العلم فى الاصل طاهرة حتى يقوم الدليل على
نجاستها والفرق بين هذا وبين ذلك ان النجاسات والطهارات تدخل فى

العبادات والحظر والاباحة تقع على الأملاك وما وقع عليه الملْك لا يبيح
ذلك لأحد الّا بدليل وحُجّة وبالله التوفيق ،

باب فى ذكر غلط الحُلوليّة وأقاويلهم على ما بلغنى فلم اعرف منهم
احدًا ولم يصحّ عندى شئٌ غير (١)البلاغ،

قال الشيخ رحمه اله بلغنى ان جماعة من الحلولية زعموا ان الحقّ تعالى
ذِكره اصطفى اجسامًا حلَّ فيها بمعانى الربوبية وأزال عنها معانى البشرية فان
صحَّ عن احد (٢)[انه] قال هذه المقالة وظنّ ان التوحيد أَبْدَى له صَفْحَتَهُ بما
اشار اليه فقد غلط فى ذلك وذهب عليه ان الثىءَ فى الثىءِ مجانس
للثىءِ الذى حلَّ فيه واله تعالى باينٌ من الاشياءِ والاشياءُ باينة منه بصفاتها
Af.189a والذى اظهر فى الاشياءِ . فذلك آثار صنعته ودليل ربوبيته لأن المصنوع يدلُّ
على صانعه والمؤلَّف يدلُّ على مؤلِّفه، وإنّما ضلَّت الحلولية ان صحّ عنهم ذلك
لأنهم لم يميّزوا بين القدرة التى هى صفة القادر وبين الشواهد التى تدلُّ على
قدرة القادر (٣)وصنعة الصانع فتاهت عند ذلك، فبلغنى ان منهم من قال
بالأنوار، ومنهم من قال بالنظر الى الشواهد المستحسنات نظرًا يُجْهَلُ، ومنهم
من قال حالٌ فى المستحسنات وغير المستحسنات، ومنهم من قال حالٌ فى
المستحسنات فقط، ومنهم من قال على الدوام، ومنهم من قال وقتًا دون
وقت فيا بلغنى، فمن صحّ عنه شىء من هذه المقالات فهو ضالٌّ بإجماع الأُمّة
كافر يلزمه الكفر فيا اشار اليه، والأجسام (٤)التى اصطفاها الله تعالى اجسام
اولياًيه وإصفياًيه اصطفاها بطاعته وخدمته وزينّها بهدايته وبيّن فضلَها على
خلقه واله تعالى موصوف بما وصف به نفسه كما وصف به نفسه ليس كمثله
شىءٌ هو السميع البصير، والذى غلط فى الحلول غلط لأنه لم يُحسن أن يميّز

<hr>

بين اوصاف الحقّ وبين اوصاف الخلق لأن اله تعالى لا يحلّ فى القلوب
وإنّما يحلّ فى القلوب الايمان به والتصديق له والتوحيد والمعرفة وهـذه
اوصاف مصنوعاته من جهة صنع اله بهم لا هو بذاته او بصفاته يحلّ فيهم،
تعالى اله عزّ وجلّ عن ذلك علوًّا كبيرًا،

باب فى ذكر من غلط فى فناء البشرية،

قال الشيخ رحمه اله امّا القوم الذين غلطوا فى فناء البشرية سمعوا كلام
المحقّقين فى الفناء فظنّوا انه فناء البشرية فوقعوا فى الوسوسة فمنهم من ترك
الطعام والشراب وتوهّم ان البشرية هى [١]القالب والجثّة اذا ضعفت زالت
بشريتها [٢]فيجوز ان يكون موصوفًا بصفات الالهية، ولم تُحسن هذه الفرقة
الجاهلة الضالّة أن تفرق بين البشرية وبين أخلاق البشرية لأن البشرية
لا تزول عن البشر كما ان لون السواد لا يزول عن الأسود ولا لون
البياض عن الابيض وأخلاق البشرية تُبَدَّل وتغيَّر بما بَرُد عليها من سلطان
انوار الحقايق وصفاتُ البشرية ليست هى [٣]عين البشرية والذى اشار الى
الفناء اراد به فناء رؤيا الأعمال والطاعات بـبقاء رؤيا العبد لقيام الحقّ
للعبد بذلك وكذلك فناء الجهل بالعلم وفناء الغفلة بالذكر [٤]والذى طبّع
فى فناء البشرية فناء البشرية طبّع فى ذلك وفناء البشرية بالبشرية صفة
من صفات البشرية والذى يتوهّم [٥]انه ذهاب النفس وزوال التلوين عن
العبد وقتًا دون وقت وذهاب البشرية فقد غلط وجهل عن وصف البشرية
لأن التغيير والتلوين من صفة البشرية فاذا زال عنها التغيير والتلوين فقد
تغيّر الآن عن صفتها [٦]وتلوَّن عن معناها لأنها اذا لم تتغيّر ولم تتلوّن فقد
تغيّر وتلوّن عن صفتها واله اعلم،

باب ذكر من غلط فى الرؤية بالقلوب،

قال الشيخ رحمه اله بلغنى عن جماعة من اهل الشأم انهم يدّعون الرؤية
بالقلوب فى دار الدنيا كالرؤية بالعيان فى دار الآخرة ولم أر احدًا منهم ولا
بلغنى عن انسان انه رأى منهم رجلاً له محصولٌ ولكن رأيتُ لأبى سعيد
الخرّاز رحمه اله كتابًا كتبه الى اهل دمشق يقول فيه بلغنى ان بناحيتكم
جماعة قالوا كذا وكذا وذكر قولاً قريبًا من هذا القول ويشبّه أن فى زمانه
قوم غلطوا فى ذلك وضلّوا وتاهوا، والذى قال اهل الحقّ والاصابة فى
هذا المعنى وأشاروا الى رؤية القلوب انّما [١]اشاروا الى التصديق والمشاهدة
بالايمان وحقيقة اليقين كما رُوى فى حديث حارثة حيث يقول كأنّى انظرُ الى
عرش ربّى بارزًا كما جاءَ فى الحديث بطوله حتى قال النبى صلم عبدٌ نوّر
اله تعالى قلبَهُ او كما قال كما جاءَ فى الرواية، والذى ناه وتوسوس فى هذا
المعنى قوم من اصحاب الضُّبيعى من اهل البصرة كما بلغنى وقد رأيتُ جماعةً
منهم وذلك أنهم حملوا على انفسهم فى المجاهدة والسهر وترك الطعام والشراب
والانفراد والخلوة وكثرة التوكّل وصحبهم الإعجاب مع ذلك بما هم فيه فاصطادهم
ابليس لعنه اله فخُيّل اليهم كأنه على عرش او سرير وله انوارٌ تتشعشع فمنهم
من ألقَى الى بعض الاستاذين الذين يعرفون مكايد العدوّ فعرّفوهم ذلك
ودلّوهم وردّوهم الى الاستقامة كما حُكِى عن سهل بن عبد اله رحمه اله ان
بعض تلامذته قال له يومًا يا استاذ أنا فى كلّ ليلة ارى اله بعين رأسى
فعلم سهلٌ رحمه اله ان ذلك من كيد العدوّ فقال له يا حبيبى اذا رأيتَه
الليلة فابزق عليه قال فلمّا رآه من لبلته بزق عليه قال فطار عرشه وأظلمت
انواره وتخلّص من ذلك ذاك الرجل ولم ير شيئًا بعد ذلك، ومن لم يقع

<hr>

(١) اثار.

_{٨٤.١٩٥a}

الى الاستاذين فيدفع ذلك ويتكلّم بالهوس وينسلخ عن دينه بالظنون الكاذبة الى آخر عمره، وبلغنى ايضًا ان جماعة هربوا من عبد الواحد بن زيد حيث كان يأمرهم بالمجاهدة والعبادة وأكْل الحلال والزهد فى الدنيا وبلغنى ان عبد الواحد رحمه الله رأى واحدًا منهم بعد مدّة فسأله عن خبره وخبر

٥ اصحابه فقال يا استاذ نحن كلّ ليلة ندخل الجنّة ونأكل من ثمارها قال فقال له خُذونى الليلة معكم قال فأخرجوه معهم الى الصحراء فلمّا جنّهم الليل فاذا بقوم عليهم ثياب خُضر واذا بساتين وفواكه قال فنظر عبد الواحد الى أرجُل هؤلاء الذين عليهم الثياب الخُضر فاذا هو مثل حوافر الدوابّ فعلم انهم شياطين فلمّا ارادوا ان يتفرّقوا قال لهم الى اين تذهبون ايس ادريس

١٠ النبىّ صلعم لمّا دخل الجنّة لم يخرج منها قال فلمّا اصبحوا فاذا هم على مزابل بين روث الدوابّ وبعر الحمار فتابوا ورجعوا الى صحبة عبد الواحد بن زيد رحمه الله، وينبغى ان يعلم العبد ان كلّ شىء رأته العيون فى دار الدنيا من الانوار ان ذلك مخلوق ليس بينه وبين الله تعالى شبه وليس ذلك

A.F.1906 صفةً من صفاته بل جميع ذلك خَلْقٌ مخلوقٌ، ورؤية القلوب بمشاهدة الايمان

١٥ وحقيقة اليقين والتصديق حقٌّ لقول النبىّ صلعم أعبُد الله كأنك تراه فان لم تكن تراه فانه يراك، والذى قال من التابعين لو كشف الغطاء ما ازددتُ يقينًا اشار الى حقيقة يقينه وصفاء وقته وتكلّم بذلك من غلبات وجه وليس الخبر كالمعاينة فى جميع المعانى فى الدنيا والآخرة، وقد قيل فى قول الله تعالى (١) مَا كَذَبَ ٱلْفُؤَادُ مَا رَأَى يعنى لم تكذب عينه ما رآه

٢٠ بقلبه ولم يكذب فؤاده ما رآه بعينه وهذا خصوصٌ للنبىّ صلعم ليس لأحد غيره،

باب ذكر من غلط فى الصفاء والطهارة،

قال الشيخ رحمه الله وطائفة ادّعت الصفاء والطهارة على الكمال والدوام

---

(١) Kor. 53, 11.

وأن ذلك لا يزول عنهم وزعموا ان العبد يصفو من جميع الكدورات
والعِلَل بمعنى البينونة منها، وقد غلطوا فى ذلك لأن العبد لا يصفو على
الدوام من جميع العلل وإن وقعت له الطهارة (١) وقتًا فلا يخلو من العلل
وإنّما نصفو له وقتًا دون وقت على مقدار أماكنهم فيذكر الله بنعت الصفآء
ثمّ يبقى عليه الذكر مع جريان اذكار الاشياء عليه، والطهارة تكون لقلب
العبد من الغِلّ والحسد والشرك والتُّهَم فامّا الصفآء الذى لا يحتمل العلّة
والطهارة من جميع اوصاف البشرية على الدوام بلا تلوين ولا تغيير ليس ذلك
من صفات الخلق لأن الله تعالى هو الذى لا تلحقه العلل ولا تقع عليه الأغيار
والخلقُ مُرادٌ بالابتلاَء أنَّى يخلون من العلل والأغيار، وحكمُ العبد اذا كان
ذلك كذلك ان يتوب الى الله تعالى ويستغفر الله تعالى فى كلّ وقت لقول
الله عزّ وجلّ (٢) وَتُوبُوا إِلَى ٱللَّهِ جَمِيعًا أَيُّهَا ٱلْمُؤْمِنُونَ لَعَلَّكُمْ تُفْلِحُونَ كَمَا رُوِى
عن النبيّ صلعم انه (٣) [قال] لَيُغَانُ على قلبى فاستغفر اللهَ فى اليوم ماية مرّة،

باب ذكر من غلط فى الانوار،

قال الشيخ رحمه الله وطايفة غلطت فى الانوار وزعمت انها ترى انوارًا
و(٤) [بعضهم] بصف قلْبُهُ بأن فيه انوارًا ويظانّ (٤) [ان] ذلك من الانوار التى
وصف الله تعالى بها نفسه، وهذه الطايفة تصف ذلك النور بصفة انوار الشمس
والقمر وتزعم ان ذلك من انوار المعرفة والتوحيد والعظمة وتزعم انها ليست
بمخلوقة، وقد (٥) غلط هؤلآء فى ذلك غلطًا عظيمًا لأن الانوار كلّها مخلوقةٌ
نور العرش ونور الكُرْسى ونور الشمس والقمر والكوآكب وليس لله نور موصوف
محدود والذى وصف الله تعالى به نفسه (٦) فليس ذلك بمُدْرَك ولا محدود
ولا يحيط به علم الخلق وكلّ نور تحيط به العلوم والفهوم فهو مخلوق وأنوار

(١) له وقتا.   (٢) Kor. 24, 31.   (٣) Suppl. above.   (٤) Text om.

(٥) غلطوا.   (٦) وليس.

الله تعالى كلّها هدايات الخلق وأنوار المصنوعات دلايل وعبرة ليستدلّوا بها
على معرفة التوحيد يُهتَدى بها فى ظلمات البرّ والبحر، ومعنى أنوار القلوب
معرفة الفرقان والبيان من الله عزّ وجلّ وذلك قوله (١) يَاۤ أَيُّهَا ٱلَّذِينَ آمَنُوۤا
إِن تَتَّقُوا ٱللَّهَ يَجْعَل لَّكُمْ فُرْقَانًا قالوا فى التفسير نورًا يوضع فى القلب حتى
يفرق به بين الحقّ والباطل، هذا معرفة الانوار كما ذكرتُه فى الوقت،

باب ذكر من غلط فى عين الجمع،

قال الشيخ رحمه الله وجماعة غلطوا فى عين الجمع فلم يضيفوا الى الخلق
ما اضاف الله تعالى اليهم ولم (٢) يصفوا انفسهم بالحركة فيما تحركوا فيه وظنّوا
ان ذلك منهم احترازًا حتى لا يكون مع الله شىء سوى الله عزّ وجلّ فأدّاهم
ذلك الى الخروج من الملّة وترك حدود الشريعة لقولهم انهم مجبرون على
حركاتهم حتى اسقطوا اللائمة عن انفسهم عند مجاوزة الحدود ومخالفة الاتّباع،
ومنهم من اخرجه ذلك الى (٣) الجسارة على التعدّى والبطالة وطمعتْه نفسه
على أنه معذور فيما هو عليه مجبور، وإنّما (٤) غلط هؤلاء لقلّة معرفتهم بالأصول
والفروع فلم يفرقوا بين الاصل والفرع ولم يعرفوا الجمع والتفرقة فأضافوا
الى الاصل ما هو مضاف الى الفرع وأضافوا الى الجمع ما هو مضاف الى
التفرقة فلم يُحسنوا وَضْع الاشياء فى مواضعها فهلكوا، وقد سُئل سهل بن
عبد الله رحمه الله عن ذلك كما بلغنى فقيل له ما تقول فى رجل يقول أنا
مثل الباب لا أتحرّكُ الّا أن يحرّكونى فقال سهل بن عبد الله هذا لا يقوله
الّا احد رَجُلين إمّا رجل صدّيق او رجل زنديق، والمعنى فيما قال سهل
رحمه الله الصدّيق يرى قوام الاشياء بالله ويرى كلّ شىء من الله تعالى
ويرجع فى كلّ شىء الى الله عزّ وجلّ مع معرفة ما يحتاج اليه من الاصول

---

(١) Kor. 8, 23.   (٢) يضيفوا.   (٣) الخسارة   (٤) غلطوا.

والفروع والحقوق والمحظوظ [(١)[والمعرفة بين الحقّ والباطل] ومتابعة الأمر
والنهى وحُسن الطاعات والقيام بشرط الادب وسلوك المنهج على حدّ الاستقامة،
وامّا معنى قول الزنديق بهذه المقالة فانّما يقول ذلك حتى لا يزجره شىء
من ركوب المعاصى انه أدّاه جهله الى (٢)الجسارة والاعتداء باضافة افعاله
٥ وجميع حركاته الى الله تعالى حتى ازال اللائمة عن نفسه فى ركوب المآثم
بغواية الشيطان (٣)وتسويله وتأويل الباطل، اعاذنا الله وايّاكم من ذلك،

باب فى ذكر من غلط فى الأُنس والبسط (٤)[وترك] الخشية،

قال الشيخ رحمه الله وطبقة اشاروا الى القُرب والأُنس وتوهّموا ان
بينهم وبين الله عزّ وجلّ حالٌ من القرب والدنوّ فأحشمهم عند ذلك التوهّم
١٠ (٥)الرجوعُ والالتفات الى الآداب التى كانوا يراعونها والحدود التى كانوا
يحفظونها قبل ذلك فانبسطوا الى ما كانوا محتشمين وأنسوا باشياء كانوا
عنها مستوحشين من قبل ذلك وتوهّموا ان ذلك قُربهم ودنوّهم، وقـد
غلطوا فى ذلك [(١)[وهلكوا] لأن الآداب والاحوال والمقامات خِلَعٌ من الله
تعالى على عباده وكرامةٌ لهم وهم (٢)مستوجبون الزيادة اذا صدقوا فى قصودهم
١٥ فمتى ما تركهم وخلّاهم عن توفيقه وعنايته بهم حتى جاوزوا الحدود وخالفوا
ما أُمروا به قد نكصوا على أَعْقابهم وسُلبوا الخِلَع التى أُكرموا بهـا من
الطاعات وقد طُردوا من الباب وصارت سِمَتهم سمة المطرودين وهُم عندهم
أنهم من المقبولين وكلّما توهّموا ان الذى هم عليـه هم قربٌ ودنوٌّ ازدادوا
بذلك من الله سُحقًا وبُعْدًا، وهذا كما حُكى (٤)[عن] (٧)ذى النون رحمه الله
٢٠ انه قال ينبغى للعارف ان لا يُطفئ نور معرفته نورَ ورعه ولا يعتقد باطنًا

---

(١) Suppl. in marg.   (٣) الجسارة.   (٣) وتسويل.   (٤) Text om.

(٥) والرجوع.   (٦) مستوجبين.   (٧) ذا.

من العلم ينقض عليه (١)ظاهرٌ من الحُكْمِ ولا تحمله كثرة الكرامة من الله تعالى على هتك أَسْتار محارم الله تعالى كما كان يقول بعض الحكماء اللهمّ لا تشغلْنى بك عنك واشغلْنى بطلبك بعد ما كنتَ لى من غير طلبى، فهذا على المعنى والله اعلم بالصواب،

باب فى ذكر من غلط فى فنآيهم عن اوصافهم،

قال الشيخ رحمه الله وقد غلطت جماعة من البغداديين فى قولهم انهم عند فنآيهم عن اوصافهم دخلوا فى اوصاف الحقّ وقد اضافوا انفسهم بجهلهم الى معنًى يؤدّيهم ذلك الى الحُلُول او الى مقالة النصارى فى المسيح عليه السلم، وقد زُعم انه سُمع (٢)[عن] بعض المتقدّمين او وُجد فى (٣)كلامه انه قال فى معنى الفنآء عن الاوصاف والدخول فى اوصاف الحقّ، فالمعنى الصحيح من ذلك ان الارادة للعبد وهى من عند الله عطيّة ومعنى خروج العبد من اوصافه والدخول فى اوصاف الحقّ خروجُهُ من ارادته ودخولُهُ فى ارادة الحقّ وبمعنى أن يعلم ان الارادات (٤)[هى عطيّة من الله تعالى وبمشيّته شآء وبفضله جعل له ما بعطيّة ذلك قطعه عن رؤية نفسه حتى ينقطع بكلّيّته] الى الله تعالى وذلك منزلٌ من منازل اهل التوحيد، وإمّا الذين غلطوا فى هذا المعنى انّما غلطوا بدقيقة خفيت عليهم حتى ظنّوا ان اوصاف الحقّ هو الحقّ وهذا كلّه كُفْرٌ لأن الله تعالى لا يحلّ فى القلوب ولكن يحلّ فى القلوب الايمان به والتوحيد له والتعظيم لذِكْره (٥)بمعانى التحقيق والتصديق ولا فَرْقَ فى ذلك بين الخاصّ والعامّ غير أن (٦)للخاصّة معنًى (٧)يتفرّدون به وهو مفارقتهم دواعى الهوى وإفنآء حظوظهم من الدار وما فيها وخلوص أسرارهم بمن آمنوا بـه وساير العوامّ (٨)محجوبون عن هذه الحقايق (٩)بانقيادهم للهوى ومطاوعتهم للنفوس، فهذا هو الفرق بين الخاصّ والعامّ فى هذا المعنى وبالله التوفيق،

---

(١) طاهرا.   (٢) Text om.   (٣) كلامهم.   (٤) Suppl. in marg. The
marginal passage reads وإرادة العبد هى عطية الخ.   (٥) وبمعانى.   (٦) الخاص.
(٧) تفردوا.   (٨) محجوبين.   (٩) من انقيادهم.

باب فى ذكر من غلط فى فقد الحسوس،

قال وزعمت طائفة من اهل العراق انهم يفقدون حِسّهم عند المواجيد
حتى لا يحسّون بشئ ويخرجوا عن اوصاف المحسوسين، وقد غلطوا فى ذلك
لأن فقد الحسّ لا يعلمه صاحبه الا بالحسّ لأن الحسّ صفة البشرية وإن
غلب عليه (١) بادٍ من الواردات التى تَرِدُ على الأسرار (٢) وتقهرها بسلطانها
(٣)فيطمسَّ (٤) ويتمحق ويكون مثل ذلك كمثل الكواكب اذا طلع عليها
سلطان انوار الشمس فتطمسُ انوارُ الكواكب وهى ممتحقة فى أماكنها فكذلك
الحسّ لا يزول ولا يُفقَد على (٥)البشر الحىّ ولكن ربّما يغيب العبد عن
حسّه بحسّه عند المواجيد الحادّة عن الأذكار القويّة كما حكى جعفر الخُلْدى
فيما قرأتُ عليه عن الجُنَيْد رحمه الله انه قال سألتُ سَرِىّ السَّقَطى رحمه الله
عن المواجيد الحادّة عند الأذكار القويّة ممّا يقوى على العبد فقال نَعَمْ يُضرَب
وجهه بالسيف ولا يحسّ وإنّما يعنى بقوله والله اعلم لا يحسّ يعنى لا يَجِدُ
ألَمًا وهو بالحسّ لا يجد الألَمَ كما أنه بالحسّ كان يجد الألَمَ وما دام فى العبد
روحٌ وهو حىٌّ لا يزول عنه الحسّ لأن الحسّ مقرون بالحياة والروح
وبالله التوفيق،

باب فى ذكر من غلط فى الروح،

قال الشيخ رحمه الله ثمّ جماعة غلطوا فى الارواح وهم طبقات شتّى
كلّهم تاهوا وغلطوا لأنهم تفكّروا فى كيفية ما رفع الله عنه الكيفيّة ونزّهه عن
إحاطة العلم فى ان يصفه احدٌ الاّ بما وصفه الله به، فقومٌ قالوا الروح نور

---

(١) بادى.   (٢) بقهرها.   (٣) فطبين.   (٤) ولا تمتحق.   (٥) النسر. The
word is almost obliterated.

[١][من نور] الله فتوهّموا انه نور ذاته فهلكوا، وقوم قالوا حياة من حياة
الله تعالى، وقوم قالوا الارواح مخلوقة وروح القُدْس من ذات الله تعالى،
وقوم قالوا ارواح العامّة مخلوقة وارواح الخاصّة ليست بمخلوقة، وقوم قالوا
الارواح قديمة إنها لا تموت ولا تعذّب ولا تُبْلَى، وقوم قالوا الارواح تتناسخ
٥ من جسم الى جسم، وقوم قالوا للكافر روح واحد وللمؤمن ثلثة ارواح
وللانبياء والصدّيقين خمسة ارواح، وقوم قالوا الروح خلقٌ من النور،
وقوم قالوا الروح روحانية خُلقت من الملكوت فاذا صَفَتْ رجعت الى
الملكوت، وقال قوم الروح روحان روح لاهوتية وروح ناسوتية، وهؤلاء
كلّهم قد غلطوا فيا ذهبوا اليه وضلّوا ضلالاً مُبِيناً وجهلوا ما يلزمهم فى ذلك
١٠ من الخطأ وذلك من تعمّقهم وتفكّرهم بآرآيهم فيا منع الله تعالى قلوبَ العباد
من التفكّر فيه بقوله تعالى [٢]وَيَسْأَلُونَكَ عَنِ الرُّوحِ قُلِ الرُّوحُ مِنْ أَمْرِ رَبِّى،
والذى عليه اهل الحقّ والاصابة عندى والله اعلمُ أن الارواح كلّها مخلوقة
وهى أمْرٌ من أمْر الله تعالى ليس بينها وبين الله تعالى سببٌ ولا نِسْبَةٌ غير
أنها من مُلْكه وطَوْعه وفى قبضته غير متناسخة ولا تخرج من جسم فتدخل
١٥ فى غيره وتذوق الموت كما يذوق البدن وتتنعّم بتنعّم البدن وتعذّب بعذاب
البدن وتُحشر فى البدن [٣]الذى تخرج منه، وخَلَقَ الله تعالى روح آدم عليه
السلم من الملكوت وجسمه من التُراب، ولكلّ فرقة من هؤلاء الذين ذكرتُ A.f.193b
لهم فى غلطهم احتجاجاتٌ ولأهل الحقّ والاصابة ردٌّ عليهم وبيان واضح لغلطهم،
وقد اختصرتُ ذِكْر ذلك لكراهية التطويل وفيا ذكرتُ كفاية وبُلْغةً لمن
عقل من المسترشدين والراغبين فى هذا العلم ان شآء الله تعالى،

تمّ الكتاب بحمد الله وعونه وتوفيقه وحسْبُنا الله ونِعْمَ الوكيل
وصلّى الله على سيّدنا محمّد وآله ما زهر كوكب، وما أظلم غيهب،

(١) Suppl. in marg.   (٢) Kor. 17, 87.   (٣) التى.

وما وضح فجْر، وما عبر دهْر، وما عرض فكْر، وما ذكر ذاكرٌ،
وما سار سايرٌ، وما هطل هاطلٌ، وما أفل آفلٌ، وما نطق
قايلٌ، وما امتدَّ الظلُّ، وما درّ (١)الوابلُ، وما عُرف الكلامُ، وما
بقى الانامُ، وما حسن الاسلامُ، وما عسعس الدَّيجورُ، وما اختلف
الظلامُ والنورُ، وما قُلى الأصباحُ، وما هبّت الرياحُ، وما (٢)سبحت
الأملاكُ، وما جرت الأفلاكُ، وما زال فَيْء، وما بقى حَيّ، وما
عُدّ عَدَد، وما بقى الأبد، وما نطق لسان، وصدق (٣)عِيان، وما
درّ القطر، وما امتدّ الدهر، وما اضطربت الامواج، وما اضآءَ
السراج، وما تلألأت (٤)الأنوآء، وما (٥)اعلنكست الظلمآء، صلاةً
دايمةً على الأبد، متّصلةً بلا نهاية ولا امد، فرغتهُ فى عاشر ربيع
الآخر سنة ثلث وثمانين وستّماية،

---

(١) الوبل.   (٢) سبحت. If الأملاك is the plural of المَلَك (see Dozy),
either سَبَحَت (cf. Kor. 79, 3) or سَبَّحَت would be possible.   (٣) عِيان.
(٤) الانوار.   (٥) اعلملست.

ح

ق

أبو القاسم بن مروان النهاوندى، ٢٨٨

أبو القاسم المنادى، ١٩٦، ١٩٨

القرشى، أبو الحسين على بن هند الفارسى، ٣٢٠

القرشى، أبو عبد الله، ٢٥٥، ٢٥٦

القرميسينى، المظفّر، ١٩١

القرنى، انظر اويس القرنى

القروى، أبو جعفر، ٢١٦

القصّاب، أبو جعفر، ٣٠٥

القصّاب، محمّد بن على، ٣٤

الصّار، محمّد بن على، ١٩٩

القلانسى، أبو احمد مصعب بن احمد، ١٩٤، ١٩٩، ٣٠٥، ٢١٧

القلانسى، أبو عبد الله احمد، ١٧٥، ١٧٦

القنّاد، أبو الحسن على بن عبد الرحيم، ٢٥–٢٧، ٥٠، ٥٢، ٦١، ٨٢٤، ٢٢٨، ٢٥٩، ٢٤٦، ٢٧١

قيس بن عمر الحمصى، ٢٨٨

ك

الكتّانى، انظر أبو بكر الكتّانى

الكرجى، احمد بن على، ٣٢٢، ٢٩٣، انظر الوجيهى، احمد بن على الكرجى

الكردى الصوفى الأرموى، ٣٠٢، ٢٤٥

الكرمانى، انظر شاه الكرمانى

كريمة ابنة عبد الوهّاب بن على بن الخضر القرشية، امّ الفضل، ١

ابن الكريفى، ١٤٦، ١٨٢، ١٨٨، ١٩٨، ٢١٠، ٢٢٧، والصحيح ابن الكَرنْبى

١٥٦، ١٥٩-١٦٢، ١٦٧، ١٧٠، ١٨٤، ١٩٢، ١٩٥، ٢٠٠، ٢٠٥،
٢٠٩-٢٧٢، ٢٦١، ٢٧٦، ٢٦٠، ٢٢٢، ٢٣٣، ٢٤٢، ٢٥٣، ٢٦٠، ٢١٧،
٢٧٧، ٢٨، ٢٨١، ٢٨٢، ٢٠٠، ٢٠٢، ٢١٢، ٢٠٠، ٢٢-٢٢٢،
٢٣٢، ٢٣٢، ٢٤٤، ٢٤٦، ٢٤٧، ٢٤٩، ٢٥٠، ٢٥٢، ٢٥٧، ٢٢٢، ٢٦٢،
٢٦٣، ٢٦٧، ٢٧٢، ٢٧٤، ٢٧٧، ٢٧٨، ٢٨٢، ٢٨٢، ٢٩٦، ٢٩٨،
٤٠٠، ٤٠٢-٤٠٦-٤٠٩، ١٤٣، ٢١١، ٢١٢، ٢١٤، ٢٥١، ٢٥٢، ٢٥٥،
٢٦٨-٤٢٠.

محمّد بن احمد ، ابو الحسن ، ٢٩٣

محمّد بن اسحق بن يسار، ٢٢

محمّد بن اسمعيل ، ١٨٩

محمّد بن داود الدينورى ، ابو بكر، ١١٥، ١٥٩، انظر الدُّقّى

محمّد بن سيرين ، ١٤٢

محمّد بن عبد الواحد بن احمد بن المتوكّل على اله ، ابو عبد اله ، ١

محمّد بن على القصّاب ، ٢٤

محمّد بن على القصّار، ١٩٩

محمّد بن على الكتّانى ، ١٢٠، انظر ابو بكر الكتّانى

محمّد بن الفضل السمرقندى، ٢٧

محمّد بن كعب ، ١٢٩

محمّد بن مسروق البغدادى ، ٢٩٧

محمّد بن معبد البانياسى، ٢٠٢

ابو محمّد المغازلى ، ٢٠٩

محمّد بن منصور الطوسى ، ١٥٨، ١٨٢

محمّد بن موسى الفرغانى ، ابو بكر، ١١٨، ٢٢٨، انظر ابو بكر الواسطى

ابو محمّد الهروى ، ٢٠٩

محمّد بن واسع ، ٤٢، ٢٢٢

فهرست الاماكن والقبائل والكتب وغير ذلك ،